CONTEMPORARY COMPANY LAW

CONTEMPORARY COMPANY LAW

by

Farouk HI Cassim (managing editor)
LLB (*cum laude*) LLM (mark of distinction) (London)
HDip Company Law (Witwatersrand)
Advocate of the High Court of South Africa
Professor of Law, University of Johannesburg

Maleka Femida Cassim
MBChB (*cum laude*) LLB (*cum laude*) LLM (*cum laude*) (Witwatersrand)
Attorney and Notary Public of the High Court of South Africa
Senior Lecturer, University of Pretoria

Rehana Cassim
BA (*cum laude*) LLB (*cum laude*) LLM (*cum laude*) (Witwatersrand)
Attorney and Notary Public of the High Court of South Africa

Richard Jooste
BA BCom (Hons) (Taxation) LLB (Cape Town) DCLS LLM (Cantab)
Attorney of the High Court of South Africa
Professor of Law, University of Cape Town

Joanne Shev
BBusSc MBusSc PGDip Tax Law (Cape Town) CA (SA)
Senior Lecturer, University of Cape Town

Jacqueline Yeats
BA LLB LLM (Stellenbosch)
Attorney of the High Court of South Africa
Lecturer, University of Cape Town

JUTA

First Published 2011

© JUTA & CO LTD
First Floor,
Sunclare Building,
21 Dreyer Street,
Claremont 7708
lawproduction@juta.co.za

This book is copyright under the Berne Convention. In terms of the Copyright Act, No 98 of 1978, no part of this book may be reproduced or transmitted in any form or by any means, electronic or mechanical, including photocopying, recording or by any information storage and retrieval system, without permission in writing from the publisher.

Although every care is taken to ensure the accuracy of this publication, supplements, updates and replacement material, the authors, editors, publishers and printers do not accept responsibility for any act, omission, loss, damage or the consequences thereof occasioned by a reliance by any person upon the contents hereof.

ISBN 978 0 7021 8544 1

SET IN 11 ON 12 POINT TIMES ROMAN BY HELANNA TYPESETTERS
PRINTED AND BOUND BY INTERPAK BOOKS, PIETERMARITZBURG

PREFACE

The Companies Act 71 of 2008 is an exciting and challenging but also a complex piece of legislation. It is the outcome of many years of discussion, debate and consultation. The Act introduces a large number of new legal concepts, underlying philosophies and rules that a wide range of persons — from legal practitioners, legal advisors and accounting practitioners to company directors and company secretaries, to name just a few — may find perplexing, and they will no doubt need guidance and direction. *Contemporary Company Law* is intended to fulfil this need.

The work strives to be a comprehensive and thorough, though not exhaustive, discussion and analysis of the most important and innovative provisions of the Companies Act of 2008. In writing this book, the authors, without exception, have been sailing uncharted waters. It has not by any means been an easy task to grapple with many of the esoteric provisions of the Act, especially since we have not had the benefit of authoritative judicial pronouncements on the meaning, interpretation and scope of the many strange and innovative concepts introduced by the Companies Act of 2008. We nevertheless hope that this work will provide useful direction on the likely interpretation and application of the new legal principles.

Contemporary Company Law is written with a view to providing guidance to legal practitioners and accounting practitioners, law students and commerce students at all levels (both undergraduate and postgraduate), legal advisors, company secretaries and company directors. It was necessary for the authors to strike a balance between the need to provide an in-depth investigation of the new company law and the (equally important) need to simplify some aspects of the new law for the benefit of a wider readership. While we have attempted to write this work in a clear and uncomplicated style and language, it must be remembered that the entire subject bristles with unavoidable and innate complexities and technicalities. This book is consequently not a basic book or an easy one, but we hope that it is a rewarding one.

This work states the law at a time when both the draft Companies Amendment Bill, 2010 (Bill 40 of 2010) and the draft Companies Regulations, 2010 have not been finalised. However, we have included, wherever relevant, a brief indication of the amendments proposed to the Companies Act by the Companies Amendment Bill.

All the dominant company law topics are discussed in *Contemporary Company Law*. In addition, insider trading and market manipulation receive detailed treatment even though they do not strictly form part of core company law. Common law precepts and principles which have been preserved by the new Act are also discussed wherever relevant. Comparative foreign law is taken into account as well.

The authors wish to acknowledge the support, co-operation and assistance received from the publishers, Juta Law. We acknowledge in particular the support received from Linda van de Vijver and her team. We also acknowledge the very positive and encouraging comments of the two corporate law experts who peer-reviewed this work prior to its publication. Their assessment of this work has been an important source of assurance and encouragement to the authors, who place great value on their comments.

Last, but certainly not least, all the authors of this work acknowledge with grateful thanks the infinite patience, unfailing faith and endless support of our families.

Farouk HI Cassim
Managing editor, on behalf of the authors
January 2011

CONTENTS

PREFACE v

TABLE OF CASES ix

CHAPTER 1
INTRODUCTION TO THE NEW COMPANIES ACT: GENERAL OVERVIEW OF THE ACT 1
Farouk HI Cassim

CHAPTER 2
THE LEGAL CONCEPT OF A COMPANY 26
Rehana Cassim

CHAPTER 3
TYPES OF COMPANIES 62
Maleka Femida Cassim

CHAPTER 4
FORMATION OF COMPANIES AND THE COMPANY CONSTITUTION 100
Maleka Femida Cassim

CHAPTER 5
CORPORATE CAPACITY, AGENCY AND THE TURQUAND RULE 153
Farouk HI Cassim

CHAPTER 6
GROUPS OF COMPANIES AND RELATED PERSONS 179
Richard Jooste

CHAPTER 7
SHARES, SECURITIES AND TRANSFER 197
Richard Jooste and Jacqueline Yeats

CHAPTER 8
CORPORATE FINANCE 240
Richard Jooste

CHAPTER 9
GOVERNANCE AND SHAREHOLDERS 327
Rehana Cassim

CHAPTER 10
GOVERNANCE AND THE BOARD OF DIRECTORS 372
Rehana Cassim

CHAPTER 11
CORPORATE GOVERNANCE 432
Rehana Cassim

CHAPTER 12
THE DUTIES AND THE LIABILITY OF DIRECTORS 459
Farouk HI Cassim

CHAPTER 13
THE AUDITOR, FINANCIAL RECORDS AND REPORTING 542
Joanne Shev and Richard Jooste

CHAPTER 14
PUBLIC OFFERINGS OF COMPANY SECURITIES 590
Jacqueline Yeats

CHAPTER 15
FUNDAMENTAL TRANSACTIONS, TAKEOVERS AND OFFERS 614
Maleka Femida Cassim and Jacqueline Yeats

CHAPTER 16
SHAREHOLDER REMEDIES AND MINORITY PROTECTION 678
Maleka Femida Cassim

CHAPTER 17
ENFORCEMENT AND REGULATORY AGENCIES 746
Maleka Femida Cassim

CHAPTER 18
BUSINESS RESCUE AND COMPROMISES 781
Farouk HI Cassim

CHAPTER 19
WINDING-UP 821
Jacqueline Yeats

CHAPTER 20
INSIDER TRADING AND MARKET MANIPULATION 833
Richard Jooste and Rehana Cassim

CHAPTER 21
TRANSITIONAL ARRANGEMENTS 908
Farouk HI Cassim and Maleka Femida Cassim

INDEX 923

TABLE OF CASES

A

3M Australia Pty Ltd v Kemish (1986) 10 ACLR 371 SC (NSW) 255
Aberdeen Railway Co v Blaikie Bros (1854) 1 Macq 461 .... 485, 486, 488, 495, 515, 516
Abro v Softex Mattress (Pty) Ltd 1973 (2) SA 346 (D) 117
Abromowitz v Pretoria District Rural Licensing Board 1938 TPD 478 342
A Company (No 00477 of 1986) [1986] BCLC 376, Re 693
A Company (No 8699 of 1985) [1986] BCLC 382, Re 693
A Company (No. 008699 of 1985) [1986] 2 BCC 99, Re 685
A Company [1983] 2 All ER 36 (Ch), Re 684
A Company: Ex parte Harries [1989] BCLC 383, Re 693
A Company: Ex parte Glossop [1988] 1 WLR 1068 (Ch), Re 695
Adams v Cape Industries plc [1990] 1 Ch 433, [1991] 1 All ER 929 (CA) 183
Adams v Cape Industries plc [1990] Ch 433 (CA) 45, 51, 501
Adams v Cape Industries plc [1991] 1 All ER 929 (CA) 50
Adcock-Ingram Laboratories Ltd v SA Druggists Ltd; Adcock-Ingram Laboratories Ltd v
 Lennon Ltd 1983 (2) SA 350 (T) 53, 182
Administrateur, Natal v Trust Bank van Afrika Bpk 1979 (3) SA 824 (A) 572, 574
Administrator, Natal v Bizo 1978 (2) SA 256 (N) 574
Advance Seed Co (Edms) Bpk v Marrok Plase (Edms) Bpk 1974 (4) SA 127 (NC) 336
African Organic Fertilizers and Associated Industries Ltd v Premier Fertilizers Ltd 1948 (3)
 SA 233 (N) 423
African Universal Stores Ltd v Dean 1926 CPD 390 151
Airport Cold Storage (Pty) Ltd v Ebrahim 2008 (2) SA 303 (C) 32, 39, 58
Aitchison v Dench 1964 (2) SA 515 (T) 394
Albert E Touchet Inc v Touchet 163 NE 184 (Mass. 1928) 345
Albert v Papenfus 1964 (2) SA 713 (E) 290, 296
Alexander v Standard Merchant Bank 1978 (4) SA 730 (W) 226
Alexander v Standard Merchant Bank Ltd [1978] 3 All SA 109 (W) 650
Alexander Ward & Co Ltd v Samyang Navigation Co Ltd [1975] 2 All ER 424 (HL) 699
Alldrew Holdings Ltd v Nibro Holdings (1993) 16 OR (3d) 718 (Gen Div), Re 694
Allen v Gold Reefs of West Africa Ltd [1900] 1 Ch 656 (CA) 125, 126, 140
Allen v Hyatt (1914) 30 TLR 444 (PC) 842
Allied Business & Financial Consultants Ltd Sub Nom O'Donnell v Shanahan [2009] 2
 BCLC 666 (CA), Re 486, 487
Allison v General Motors Corp 604 F Supp 1106 (D. Del. 1985) 705
Ally v Courtesy Wholesalers (Pty) Ltd 1996 (3) SA 134 (N) 650, 653, 654
Altim Pty Ltd [1968] 2 NSWLR 762, Re 402
American Cyanamid Co v Ethicon Ltd [1975] AC 396 710
Amlin (SA) Pty Ltd v Van Kooij 2008 (2) SA 558 (C) 38, 45, 46
Ammonia Soda Co Ltd v Chamberlain [1918] 1 Ch 266; [1916–17] All ER Rep 708 (CA) ... 265, 266
Amoils v Fuel Transport (Pty) Ltd 1978 (4) SA 343 (W) 409
Anderson v Dickson 1985 (1) SA 93 (N) 538
Anderson v James Sutherland (Peterhead) Ltd 1941 SC 203 388
Anglo Petroleum Ltd v TFB (Mortgages) Ltd [2008] 1 BCLC 185 (CA) 289
Anglo-Transvaal Collieries Ltd v SA Mutual Life Assurance Society 1977 (3) SA 631 (T) ... 200
Anns v London Borough of Merton [1977] 2 All ER 492 (HL) 580
Antigen Laboratories Ltd [1951] 1 All ER 110 (Ch), Re 697
ANZ Executors & Trustee Company Ltd v Qintex Australia Ltd (1990) 2 ACSR 676 SC (Qld) 190
AP Smith Manufacturing Co v Barlow 98 A2d 581 (NJ 1953) 470
Apco Africa (Pty) Ltd v Apco Worldwide Inc 2008 (5) SA 615 (SCA) 385, 824

Armour Hick Northern Ltd v Armour Trust Ltd [1980] 3 All ER 833 (Ch) 290, 291, 296, 297
Armstrong v Gardner (1978), 20 OR (2d) 648 (Ont. HC) 705
Aronson v Lewis, 473 A.2d 805 (Del. 1984) 713
Ashbury Railway Carriage and Iron Co v Riche (1875) LR 7 HL 653 .... 19, 154, 155, 162, 483
Ashton & Co Ltd v Honey (1907) 23 TLR 253 266
Asic v Citigroup (2007) 62 ACSR 427 855
Aspek Pipe Co (Pty) Ltd v Mauerberger 1968 (1) SA 517 (C) 684, 685
Astec (BSR) plc [1998] 2 BCLC 556, Re 688
Atlas Maritime Co SA v Avalon Maritime Ltd [1991] 4 All ER 769 .... 43, 53
Atlasview Ltd v Brightview Ltd [2004] 2 BCLC 191 682
Augusto v Socieda de Angolana de Commercio International Limitada (Sacilda) 1998 (4) SA
    124 (NM) 291
Austral Mining Construction Pty Ltd v NZI Capital Corporation Ltd (1991) 4 ACSR 57 SC
    (Qld) 213, 214
Australian National Industries Ltd v Greater Pacific Investments Pty Ltd (1992) 7 ACSR 176
    SC (NSW) 191
Australian Oil and Exploration Ltd v Lachberg (1958) 101 CLR 119 (HC of A) 265
Australian Securities & Investment Commission v Doyle [2001] WASC 187 377
Australian Securities Commission v Lucas (1992) 7 ACSR 676 689
Automatic Self-Cleansing Filter Syndicate Co Ltd v Cuninghame [1906] 2 Ch 34 ... 138, 345, 383, 385
Aveling Barford v Perion Ltd [1989] BCLC 626 (ChD) 155
Avondzon Trust (Edms) Bpk 1968 (1) SA 340 (T), Ex parte 696
Axiam Holdings Ltd v Deloitte & Touche 2006 (1) SA 237 (SCA) 582
Azisa (Pty) Ltd v Azisa Media CC 2002 (4) SA 377 (C) 110, 111

B

Bader v Weston 1967 (1) SA 134 (C) 698
Bagot Pneumatic Tyre Co v Clipper Pneumatic Tyre Co [1902] 1 Ch 146 (CA) 267
Bagradi v Cavendish Transport Co (Pty) Ltd 1957 (1) SA 663 (D) 150, 151
Ball v Metal Industries Ltd 1957 SC 315 347
Baltic Real Estate (No 2) [1993] BCLC 503, Re 683, 695
Baltic Real Estate Ltd (No 1) [1993] BCLC 499, Re 683
Bamford v Bamford (1969) 1 All ER 969 (CA) 479, 529
Bamford v Bamford [1970] Ch 212 345
Bank of Lisbon and South Africa Ltd v The Master 1987 (1) SA 276 (A) 226
Bank of Tokyo Ltd v Karoon [1987] AC 45, [1986] 3 All ER 486 (CA) 183
Barclays Bank Ltd v TOSG Trust Fund (1984) BCLC 1 166
Barings v Coopers & Lybrand (No 1) [2002] 1 BCLC 364 745
Barings plc (No 5) sub nom Baker v Secretary of State for Trade and Industry [1999] 1 BCLC
    433, Re 510, 511
Barlows Manufacturing Co Ltd v RN Barrie (Pty) Ltd 1990 (4) SA 608 (C) 418
Barnard v Carl Greaves Brokers (Pty) Ltd 2008 (3) SA 663 (C) 682, 685, 694
Barnett, Hoares & Co v South London Tramways Co (1887) 18 QBD 815 389
Barron v Potter [1914] 1 Ch 895 345
Barron 1977 (3) SA 1099 (C), Ex parte 403
Basic Inc v Levinson 485 US 224 (US SC, 1988) 899
Bates [1928] Ch 682, Re 265
Bauer Securities Ltd (1990) 4 ACSR 328 SC (Qld), Re 213, 214
Bay Loan Investment (Pty) Ltd v Bay View (Pty) Ltd 1972 (2) SA 313 (C) 291, 294
Bayly v Knowles 2010 (4) SA 548 (SCA) 694
BDC Investments Ltd (1987) 13 ACLR 201 SC (NSW), Re 217
Beattie v Beattie Ltd [1938] 3 All ER 214 (CA) 135
Beattie v E&F Beattie Ltd [1938] Ch 708 .... 395, 414
Beeton & Co Ltd [1913] 2 Ch 279, In re 416
Belfry Marine Ltd v Palm Base Maritime SDN BHD 1999 (3) SA 1083 (SCA) 864

Table of Cases

Bell Houses Ltd v City Wall Properties Ltd [1966] 2 All ER 674 (CA) 157
Bellador Silk Ltd [1965] 1 All ER 667 (Ch), Re 698
Bellairs v Hodnett 1978 (1) SA 1109 (A) 48, 224, 225, 494
Belmont Finance Corp Ltd v Williams Furniture Ltd (No 2) [1980] 1 All ER 393 (CA) ... 291, 296, 298
Ben-Tovim v Ben-Tovim 2001 (3) SA 1074 (C) 345, 354, 355, 684, 686, 695, 698
Benjamin v Elysium Investments (Pty) Ltd 1960 (3) SA 467 (E) 683
Bennett 1978 (2) SA 380 (W), Ex parte 401
Berman v Chairman, Cape Provincial Council 1961 (2) SA 412 (C) 355, 389
Betty: in re First Mutual Investment Trust Ltd 1974 (1) SA 127 (W), Ex parte 202
Bevray Investments (Edms) Bpk v Boland Bank Bpk 1993 (3) SA 597 (A) 428
Bhullar v Bhullar sub nom Re Bhullar Bros Ltd [2003] 2 BCLC 241 .... 486, 495
Bhullar v Bhullar [2003] 2 BCLC 241 (CA) 459, 494
Birch v Cropper, re Bridgewater Navigation Co Ltd (1889) 14 App Cas 525 (HL) 199, 202
Bishop v Smyrna & Cassaba Railway Co (No 2) [1895] 2 Ch 596 .... 265, 267
Bishop v Smyrna and Cassaba Railway Co [1895] 2 Ch 265 201
Bishopsgate Investment Management Ltd (In liquidation) v Maxwell (No 2) [1994] 1 All ER
  261 (CA) 480
Blackburn v Industrial Equity Ltd (1976) 2 ACLR 8 265
Blair v Consolidated Enfield Corp (1995) 128 DLR (4th) 73 355
Bloxam v Metropolitan Railway Co (1868) 3 Ch App Cas 337 266
Boardman v Phipps [1966] 3 All ER 721 486
Boardman v Phipps [1966] 3 All ER 721 (HL); [1967] 2 AC 46 .... 490, 504
Body Corporate of Greenwood Scheme v 75/2 Sandown (Pty) Ltd 1999 (3) SA 480 (W) 689
Bolton v Natal Land and Colonization Co [1892] 2 Ch 124 267
Bonanza Creek Goldmining Co v R [1916] AC 566 20
Bond v Barrow Haematite Steel Co [1902] 1 Ch 353; [1900–3] All ER Rep 484 .... 200, 267
Borg v International Silver Co 11 Fed (2d) 147 (1925) 281
Borland's Trustee v Steel Brothers & Co Ltd [1901] Ch 279 225
Botha v Fick 1995 (2) SA 750 (A) 223, 227, 237
Botha v Myburgh 1923 CPD 482 222
Botha v Van Niekerk 1983 (3) SA 513 (W) 45, 148
Boulting v Association of Cinematograph, Television and Allied Technicians [1963] 2 QB
  606 .... 378, 379, 425
Boulting v Association of Cinematograph, Television and Allied Technicians [1963] 1 All ER
  716 (CA) 482, 486
Bourke's Estate v Commissioner for Inland Revenue 1991 (1) SA 661 (A) 266
Bradbury v English Sewing Cotton Co Ltd [1923] AC 744 (HL) 198
Brady v Brady [1988] 2 All ER 617 (HL) 297
Brady v Brady [1988] BCLC 20 (CA) 468
Brady v Brady [1988] BCLC 579 (HL) 155
Brady v Brady [1989] AC 755 291
Bray v Ford [1896] AC 44 486
Braymist v Wise Finance Co Ltd [2002] Ch 273 149
Brazilian Rubber Plantations & Estates Ltd [1911] Ch 425 (CA), Re 505, 506, 521
Breetveldt v Van Zyl 1972 (1) SA 304 (T) 689, 697, 828
Brey v Ford [1896] AC 44 515
Bridgewater Navigation Co [1891] 2 Ch 317; [1891–94] All ER Rep 174, Re 264
Briess v Woolley [1954] AC 333; [1954] 1 All ER 909 (HL) 842
Briggs v James Hardie & Co Pty Ltd [1989] 16 NSWLR 549 CA (NSW) 182, 183
Bristol and West Building Society v Mothew [1998] Ch 1 465
British Commonwealth Holdings plc v Barclays Bank plc [1996] 1 All ER 381 290
British India Steam Navigation Co v Inland Revenue Commissioner (1881) 7 QBD 165 213
Brooks v Heritage Hotel Adelaide Pty Ltd (1996) 20 ACSR 61 SC (SA) 255
Broomberg v Hilewitz 1970 (3) SA 568 (W) 204
Brown v Nanco (Pty) Ltd 1976 (3) SA 832 (W) 416

Brunninghausen v Glavanics (1999) 32 ACSR 294 CA (NSW)......................... 842
Build-a-Brick BK v Eskom 1996 (1) SA 115 (O)...................................... 142
Bulfin v Bebarfald's Ltd (1932) 38 SR (NSW) 423 350
Burland v Earle [1902] AC 63 701
Burnstein v Yale 1958 (1) SA 768 (W) 422, 423
Burton v Palmer (1980) 5 ACLR 481 CA (NSW) 290
Burton v Palmer [1980] 2 NSWLR 878 (SC) 294, 296
Bushell v Faith [1970] AC 1099 ....412, 413
Byng v London Life Association Ltd [1990] Ch 170 ....343, 352

C

Calzaturificio Zenith Pty Ltd v New South Wales Leather & Trading Co Pty Ltd [1970] VR
    605 255
Camelot Resources Ltd v MacDonald (1994) 14 ACSR 437 519
Canada Safeway Ltd v Thompson (1952) 2 DLR 591 492
Canadian Aero Service Ltd v O'Malley (1973) 40 DLR (3d) 371 (SCC) 416, 459, 465,
    490, 493, 497, 498, 499
Canadian Land Reclaiming & Colonizing Co [1880] 14 ChD 660, In re 380
Candler v Crane, Christmas & Co [1951] 1 All ER 426 (CA) 579
Caparo Industries plc v Dickman [1989] 1 All ER 798 391
Caparo Industries plc v Dickman [1990] 1 All ER 568 391
Cape Explosives Works Ltd v South African Oil and Fat Industries Ltd 1921 CPD 244...... 222
Cape Pacific Ltd v Lubner Controlling Investments (Pty) Ltd 1995 (4) SA 790 (A)......38, 39, 42,
    44, 45, 46, 56, 59
Capel Finance (2005) 52 ACSR 601, Re 200
Capital Estate & General Agencies (Pty) Ltd v Holiday Inns Ltd 1977 (2) SA 916 (A) 110
Capitec Bank Ltd v Quorus Holdings Ltd 2003 (3) SA 302 (W) 10
Cargill v Hardin 452 F 2d 1154 (8th Cir 1971).. 898
Carl M Field v Bankers Trust Company and First National City Bank of New York 296 F 2d
    109 (1961).. 10
Carlen v Drury (1812) Ves & B54 476
Carr v British International Helicopters Ltd [1994] 2 BCLC 474.....................794, 795
Cashmere Pacific Ltd v NZ Dairy Board [1996] 1 NZLR 218 ....296, 298
Catalinas Warehouse & Mole Co Ltd [1947] 1 All ER 51, Re......................... 201
Caxton Ltd v Reeva Forman (Pty) Ltd 1990 (3) SA 547 (A) 29
Central Transportation Co v Pullman's Palace Car 139 US 24 60 (1890) 155
Chan v Zacharia (1984) 154 CLR 178 486
Charterbridge Corporation Ltd v Lloyds Bank Ltd [1969] 2 All ER 1185 469
Charterbridge Corporation Ltd v Lloyds Bank Ltd [1970] Ch 62....................181, 182, 476
Charterbridge Corporation Ltd v Lloyds Bank Ltd [1970] Ch 62; [1969] 2 All ER 1185...190, 191, 192
Charter Communications Inc. Securities Litigation v Scientific-Atlanta, Inc.; Motorola, Inc.
    443 F 3d 987 (8th Cir 2006), In re 891
Charterhouse Investments Trust Ltd v Tempest Diesel Ltd [1986] 1 BCLC 1 ....289, 291
Chaston v SWP Group plc [2002] EWCA Civ 1999, [2003] BCC 140 290
Chaston v SWP Group plc [2003] 1 BCLC 675 (CA)...........................287, 289, 291
Chew v R (1992) 173 CLR 626 502
Chez Nico (Restaurants) Ltd [1992] BCLC 192, Re................................841, 842
Chiarella v US 445 US 222 (1980)... 836
Chief Nchabeleng v Chief Phasha 1998 (3) SA 578 (LCC) 710
Christensen v Scott [1996] 1 NZLR 273 745
CIR v Collins 1992 (3) SA 698 (A) 798
Citybranch Group Ltd, Gross v Rackind [2004] 4 All ER 735......................... 691
City Equitable Fire Insurance Co Ltd [1925] 1 Ch 407 (ChD), In re........384, 506, 510, 521, 570
Cleveland Trust plc [1991] BCLC 424, Re.. 211
Clutchco (Pty) Ltd v Davis 2005 (3) SA 486 (SCA)...............................368, 369

Table of Cases

CMS Dolphin Ltd v Simonet [2001] 2 BCLC 704 .... 498, 416, 490, 497
Coetzee v Rand Sporting Club 1918 WLD 74 .... 213, 214
Cohen Brothers v Samuels 1906 TS 221 347
Cohen v Segal 1970 (3) SA 702 (W) 10, 386, 467
Coleman v Myers [1977] 2 NZLR 225 CA (NZ) 291, 740, 841, 842
Combrinck Chiropraktiese Kliniek (Edms) Bpk v Datsun Motor Vehicle Distributors (Pty)
    Ltd 1972 (4) SA 185 (T) 573
Commercial Grain Producers Association v Tobacco Sales Ltd 1983 (1) SA 826 (ZS) 224
Commission for Corporate Affairs (WA) v Ekamper (1987) 12 ACLR 519 SC (WA) 403
Commissioner for Inland Revenue v Collins 1923 AD 347 211
Commissioner for Inland Revenue v George Forest Timber Co Ltd 1924 AD 516 266
Commissioner for Inland Revenue v Legal & General Assurance Society Ltd 1963 (2) SA 876
    (A) 211
Commissioner for Inland Revenue v Pick 'n Pay Employee Share Purchase Trust 1992 (4) SA
    39 (A) 266
Commissioner for Inland Revenue v Richmond Estates (Pty) Ltd 1956 (1) SA 602 (A) 28
Commissioner of Taxation v B & G Plant Hire Pty Ltd (1994) 14 ACSR 283 (HC of A) 841
Commissioners of Inland Revenue v Blott [1921] 2 AC 171 (HL) 211
Companie de Electricidad de la Provincia de Buenos Aires Ltd [1980] Ch 146; [1978] 3 All
    ER 668, Re 217
Cook v Deeks [1916] 1 AC 554 (PC) 459, 491, 492, 502, 529
Coomber, Coomber v Coomber [1911] 1 Ch 723, Re 841
Cooper v A & G Fashions (Pty) Ltd; Ex parte Millman 1991 (4) SA 204 (C) 827
Cooper v Boyes 1994 (4) SA 521 (C) 198
Coronation Syndicate Ltd v Lilienfeld and New Fortuna Co Ltd 1903 TS 489 .... 354, 425
Corporate Affairs Commission v Drysdale (1978) 141 CLR 236 376
Cotman v Brougham [1918] AC 514 (HL) 520 .... 155, 157
County Marine Insurance Co (Rance's Case) (1870) LR 6 Ch App 104, Re 266
Cousins v International Brick Co Ltd [1931] 2 Ch 90 .... 341, 342
Couve v Reddot International (Pty) Ltd 2004 (6) SA 425 (W) 864
Cranleigh Precision Engineering (Pty) Ltd v Bryant [1965] 1 WLR 1293 491
Credit Corporation Australia Pty Ltd v Atkins (1999) 30 ACSR 727 (Fed C of A) 255
Crookes v Watson 1956 (1) SA 277 (A) 151
Cross v Imperial Continental Gas Association [1923] 2 Ch 553; [1923] All ER Rep 628 265
Cullerne v London and Suburban General Permanent Building Society (1890) 25 QBD 485
    .... 156, 484
Cumberland Holdings Ltd (1976) 1 ACLR 361 SC (NSW), Re 689
Cunninghame v First Ready Development 249 2010 (5) SA 325 (SCA) 83, 84
Customs and Excise Commissioners v Hedon Alpha Ltd [1981] 2 All ER 697 (CA) 528

D

Da Silva v CH Chemicals (Pty) Ltd 2008 (6) SA 620 (SCA) 459, 489, 495, 499, 497, 498, 476, 501
Da Silva v Coutinho 1971 (3) SA 123 (A) 572
Dadoo Ltd v Krugersdorp Municipal Council 1920 AD 530 ...... 31, 33, 39, 44, 187, 313, 384, 466
Daimler Co Ltd v Continental Tyre and Rubber Co [1916] 2 AC 307 .... 43, 44
Dairy Containers Ltd v NZI Bank Ltd [1995] 2 NZLR 30 570
Daniels t/as Deloitte Haskins & Sells v AWA Ltd (1995) 37 NSWLR 438 .... 384, 466, 508, 528
Daniels v Anderson (1995) 13 ACLC 614 (CA (NSW)) 506
Darvall v North Sydney Brick & Tile Co Ltd (1987) 12 ACLR 537 SC (NSW) 296, 297, 298
Darvall v North Sydney Brick & Tile Co Ltd [1989] 16 NSWLR 260; (1989) 15 ACLR 230
    CA (NSW) 294
Darvall v North Sydney Brick & Tile Co Ltd (1989) 15 ACLR 230 SC (NSW) 476, 478
Davis and Co Ltd v Brunswick (Australia) Ltd [1936] 1 All ER 299 (PC) 825
Davis v Buffelsfontein Gold Mining Co Ltd 1967 (4) SA 631 (W) 331
Day v Cook [2002] BCLC 1 CA 745

De Villiers v Jacobsdal Saltworks (Michaelis and De Villiers) (Pty) Ltd 1959 (3) SA 873
(O) 134, 135, 138, 140, 395, 414
De Villiers NNO: in re Carbon Developments (Pty) Ltd (in liquidation) 1993 (1) SA 493 (A),
Ex parte 248, 540
De Witt Truck Brokers Inc v W Ray Flemming Fruit Co 540 F 2d 681 (1976) 49
Dean v Prince [1954] Ch 409; [1954] 1 All ER 749 (CA) 225
Delavenne v Broadhurst [1931] 1 Ch 234 224
Dennill v Atkins & Co 1905 TS 282.. 573
Dent v London Tramways Co (1990) 16 ChD 334..................................... 268
Dernacourt Investments Pty Ltd (1990) 20 NSWLR 588, Re 684, 691
Dhlomo v Natal Newspapers (Pty) Ltd 1989 (1) SA 945 (A).......................... 29
DHN Food Distributors Ltd v London Borough of Tower Hamlets [1976] 3 All ER
462 .... 50, 51, 53, 182
DHN Food Distributors Ltd v London Borough of Tower Hamlets [1976] 3 All ER 462,
[1976] 1 WLR 852 (CA) 182, 183
Diamond v Oreamuno 24 NY 2d 494 (1969) 839
Dibowitz v Commissioner for Inland Revenue 1952 (1) SA 55 (A)...................... 211
Die Dros (Pty) Ltd v Telefon Beverages CC 2003 (4) SA 207 (C) 40, 45
Dimbleby & Sons Ltd v National Union of Journalists [1984] 1 All ER 751, [1984] 1 WLR
427 (HL).. 183
Dimbula Valley (Ceylon) Tea Co Ltd v Laurie [1961] Ch 353; [1961] 1 All ER 769 ..202, 211, 265, 266
Dimond Manufacturing Co Ltd v Hamilton [1969] NZLR 609 (CA)................... 579, 581
Diner v Dublin 1962 (4) SA 36 (N) 395
Dirks v SEC 436 US 646 (1983)... 836
Dithaba Platinum (Pty) Ltd v Econovaal Ltd 1985 (4) SA 615 (T).................... 50, 183
D'Jan of London Ltd [1994] 1 BCLC 561 (Ch), Re 509, 528
DML Resources Ltd (In Liquidation) [2004] 3 NZLR 490 (HC), Re................... 253
Dodge v Ford Motor Co 204 Mich 495; 170 NW 668 (1919) 472
Donaldson 1947 (3) SA 170 (T), Ex parte 28
Donaldson Investments (Pty) Ltd v Anglo-Transvaal Collieries Ltd 1979 (3) SA 713
(W)... 686, 687, 692, 698
Donaldson Investments (Pty) Ltd v Anglo-Transvaal Collieries Ltd 1980 (4) SA 204
(T).. 202, 686, 687, 692, 695, 698
Donaldson Investments (Pty) Ltd v Anglo-Transvaal Collieries Ltd 1983 (3) SA 96 (A)....202, 695
Donaldson Investments (Pty) Ltd v Anglo-Transvaal Collieries Ltd: SA Mutual Life Assurance Society Intervening 1979 (3) SA 713 (W)............................. 200, 202
Dorchester Finance Co Ltd v Stebbing [1989] BCLC 498 (Ch)...................... 509
Dorman Long & Co Ltd [1934] Ch 635, In re 340
Dovey v Cory [1901] AC 477, [1895–99] All ER Rep 724 (HL) 266, 267, 268
Dovey v Cory [1901] AC 477 (HL) 510
Duomatic Ltd [1969] 2 Ch 365, In re 336
Duomatic Ltd [1969] 1 All ER 161 (ChD), In Re 527, 528
Du Plessis NO v Phelps 1995 (4) SA 165 (C) 467, 505
Du Preez v Garber: In re Die Boerebank Bpk 1963 (1) SA 806 (W) 340
Dublin v Diner 1964 (1) SA 799 (D)... 336
Dunn v Shapowloff (1978) 3 ACLR 775 CA (NSW) 255
Dworsky 1970 (2) SA 293 (T), Ex parte... 402
Dyment v Boyden [2004] 2 BCLC 423 ChD; [2005] 1 BCLC 163 (CA) 296

E

EBBW Vale UDC v S Wales Traffic Area Licensing Authority [1951] 2 KB 366, [1951] 1 All
ER 806 (CA)... 183
East West Promotions Ltd (1986) 10 ACLR 222, Re............................... 689
Eastern and Australian SS Co [1893] WN 31, Re................................. 264
Ebrahim v Airports Cold Storage (Pty) Ltd [2009] 1 All SA 330 (SCA)............. 38, 45

Table of Cases	xv

Ebrahimi v Westbourne Galleries Ltd [1973] AC 360, [1972] 2 All ER 492   842
Ebrahimi v Westbourne Galleries Ltd [1972] 2 All ER 492 . . . . 47, 48
Edmonds v Blaina Furnaces Co (1887) 36 ChD 215. . . . . .213, 214
Edwards v Halliwell [1950] 2 All ER 1064 (C)   701
EG Electric Co (Pty) Ltd v Franklin 1979 (2) SA 702 (EC) 574, 579
EH Dey (Pty) Ltd v Dey 1966 VR 464 . . . . .296, 297
EIC Services Ltd v Phipps [2004] 2 BCLC 589 . . . . .336, 337
Elder v Elder & Watson [1952] SC 49. . . . . .684, 692
Eley v Positive Government Security Life Assurance Co (1876) 1 ExD 88 . . . . .135, 136
Emphy v Pacer Properties (Pty) Ltd [1979] 2 All SA 35 (D)   385
English v Dedham Vale Properties Ltd [1978] WLR 93 (ChD) 110.   465
Equitable Life Assurance Society v Human [2002] 1 AC 408, Re   507
Equiticorp Finance Ltd v Bank of New Zealand (1993) 11 ACSR 642 CA (NSW) 191, 192
Equiticorp Financial Services Ltd v Equiticorp Financial Services Ltd (1992) 9 ACSR 199 SC
    (NSW).   191
Erasmus v Pentamed Investments (Pty) Ltd 1982 (1) SA 178 (W)   842
Ernest v Nicholls (1857) 6 HL Cas 401   168
Ernst & Ernst v Hochfelder 425 US 185 (US SC, 1976). 890, 894, 895
Ess Kay Electronics PTE Ltd v First National Bank of Southern Africa Ltd 1998 (4) SA 1102
    (W)   879
Esselen v Argus Printing & Publishing Co Ltd 1992 (3) SA 764 (T).   875
Estate Milne v Donohoe Investments (Pty) Ltd 1967 (2) SA 359 (A). 73, 224, 225
Estate Salzmann v Van Rooyen 1944 OPD 1   35
Estmanco (Kilner House) v Greater London Council [1982] 1 WLR 2   698
Evans v Brunner Mond & Company Ltd [1921] ChD 359.   470
Evrard v Ross 1977 (2) SA 311 (D)   294
EW Savory Ltd [1951] 2 All ER 1036, Re.   201
Exchange Banking Co (Flitcroft's Case) (1882) LR 21 ChD 519, Re   383
Extrasure Travel Insurances Ltd v Scattergood [2003] 1 BCLC 598 . . . . 476, 478, 479

F

F & C Building Construction Co (Pty) Ltd v Macsheil Investments (Pty) Ltd 1959 (3) SA 841
    (D).   827
Farren v Sun Service SA Photo Trip Management (Pty) Ltd 2004 (2) SA 146 (C). 171, 653
Faure Electric Accumulator Co (1889) LR 40 ChD 141, Re. 383, 384, 385
Federal Commissioner of Taxation v Miller Anderson Ltd (1946) 73 CLR 341 (HC of A). . . .   264
Federal Commissioner of Taxation v St Helens Farm (ACT) Pty Ltd (1980) 146 CLR 336
    (HC of A)   222
Ferguson and Forrester Ltd v Buchanan [1920] SC 154 (Ct Sess).   201
Ferguson v Wilson (1866) 2 Ch App 77. . . . . .383, 384
Ferreira v Levin 1995 (2) SA 813 (W). 709, 710
Ferreira v Levin, Vryenhoek v Powell 1996 (1) SA 984 (CC)   749
Fexuto Pty Ltd v Bosnjak Holdings Pty Ltd (2001) 37 ACSR 672   692
Fiduciary Ltd v Morningstar Research Pty Ltd (2005) 53 ACSR 732   714
Financial Mail (Pty) Ltd v Sage Holdings Ltd 1993 (2) SA 451 (A)   29
Financial Services Board and The Directorate of Market Abuse v Timotheus Pretorius, case
    13 of 2009.   896
Fisheries Development Corporation of SA Ltd v Jorgensen; Fisheries Development Corpora-
    tion of SA Ltd v AWJ Investments (Pty) Ltd 1980 (4) SA 156 (W). 379, 437, 463, 482,
                                                                                            506, 507, 511, 538
Fomento (Sterling Area) Ltd v Selsdon Fountain Pen Co Ltd [1958] 1 All ER 11 (HL)   569
Forest of Dean Coal Mining Co (1878) LR 10 Ch 450, Re. 383, 385
Fose v Minister of Safety and Security 1997 (3) SA 786 (CC)   875
Foss v Harbottle (1843) 2 Hare 461, 67 ER 189 . . . . 11, 20, 136, 698, 699, 701, 702, 717, 741

Foster Bryant Surveying Ltd v Bryant and Savernake Property Consultants [2007] EWCA
 Civ 200; [2007] 2 BCLC 239 499
Foster v New Trinidad Lake Asphalt Co Ltd [1901] 1 Ch 208 265
Frame v Smith (1987) 42 DLR (4th) 466
Francis George Hill Family Trust v South African Reserve Bank 1992 (3) SA 91 (A) 33, 36
Freeman & Lockyer v Buckhurst Park Properties (Mangal) Ltd [1964] 1 All ER 630 (CA)
 171, 174, 175, 176
Fulham Football Club Ltd v Cabra Estates Plc [1994] 1 BCLC 363 (Ch and CA) 480, 481
Fundstrust (Pty) Ltd (In Liquidation) v Van Deventer 1997 (1) SA 710 (A) 79, 168

G

Gaiman v National Association for Mental Health [1970] 2 All ER 362 ....468, 479
Gamlestaden Fastigheter AB v Baltic Partners Ltd [2007] UKPC 26, [2007] Bus LR 1521 .....685, 686
Garden Province Investment v Aleph (Pty) Ltd 1979 (2) SA 525 (D) 692, 693
Gardner v Margo 2006 (6) SA 33 (SCA) 287, 291, 292, 297
Gardner v Richardt 1974 (3) SA 768 (C) 142, 149, 151
Gemma Ltd v Davies [2008] BCC 812 380
Genville Pastoral Co Pty Ltd v Commissioner of Taxation of Commonwealth of Australia
 (1963) 109 CLR 199 (HC of A) 264
George Newman & Co [1895] 1 Ch 674 (CA), In re 416, 417
George Raymond Pty Ltd; Salter v Gilbertson (2000) 18 ACLC 85, Re 692
Gerald Cooper Chemicals Ltd [1978] 2 All ER 49, In re 537
Gering v Gering 1974 (3) SA 358 (W) 49
Gething v Kilner [1972] 1 WLR 337, [1972] 1 All ER 1166 476
Giles v Rhind [2003] Ch 618 CA 745
Gilford Motor Co Ltd v Horne [1933] Ch 935 (CA) 40, 42
GJ Mannix Ltd [1984] 1 NZLR 309, Re 28
Glandon Pty Ltd v Strata Consolidated Pty Ltd (1993) 11 ACSR 543 CA (NSW) 841, 842
Glossop v Glossop [1907] 2 Ch 370 416
Gohlke & Schneider v Westies Minerale (Edms) Bpk 1970 (2) SA 685 (A) 132, 134, 336,
 337, 338, 393
Goldcorp Exchange Ltd [1994] 2 All ER 806 (PC), Re 841
Gold Fields Ltd v Harmony Gold Mining Co Ltd 2005 (2) SA 506 (SCA) 300, 595, 596
Gompels v Skodawerke of Prague 1942 TPD 167 142
Goode, Durrant & Murray Ltd v Hewitt & Cornell NNO 1961 (4) SA 286 (N) 181
Goozee v Graphic World Group Holdings Pty Ltd [2002] NSWSC 640 708
Gordon and Rennie v Standard Merchant Bank Ltd 1984 (2) SA 519 (C) 537
Goss v EC Goss & Co (Pty) Ltd 1970 (1) SA 602 (D) 296
Government Stocks Securities Investment Co Ltd v Christopher [1956] 1 All ER 490 (CH) .. 595
Gradwell (Pty) Ltd v Rostra Printers 1959 (4) SA 419 (A) 289, 291, 292, 294, 296
Gray v New Augarita Porcupine Mines Ltd (1952) 3 DLR 1 519
Gray v Thesing Vastgoed BV 1987 (1) SA 744 (A) 290, 296
Greenacre v Falkirk Iron Co Ltd 1953 (4) SA 289 (N) 224
Greenfield Engineering Works (Pty) Ltd v NKR Construction (Pty) Ltd 1978 (4) SA 901 (N) ..572, 574
Greenhalgh v Arderne Cinemas [1950] 2 All ER 1120 (CA) 476
Greenhalgh v Arderne Cinemas Ltd [1946] 1 All ER 512 (CA) 734, 736
Greenhalgh v Arderne Cinemas [1951] Ch 286; [1950] 2 All ER 1120 (CA) 71, 468
Greenhalgh v Mallard [1943] 2 All ER 234 (CA) 73, 224
Greymouth Point Elizabeth Railway & Coal Co Ltd [1904] 1 Ch 32, Re 424
Guinness plc v Saunders (1988) 2 All ER 940 (CA) 518, 520
Guinness plc v Saunders [1990] 2 AC 663 (HL) 416, 417
Gumede v Bandhla Vukani Bakithi Ltd 1950 (4) SA 560 (N) 33
Gundelfinger v African Textile Manufacturers Ltd 1939 AD 314 355
Guth v Loft Inc 5 A 2d 503 (1939) 490

H

Haig v Bamford 72 DLR (3d) 68 (1976)	579
Halt Garage (1964) Ltd [1982] 3 All ER 1016 (ChD), Re	417, 418, 161
Handevel Pty Ltd (1983) 8 ACLR 44 SC (Vic), Re	203
Handevel Pty Ltd v Comptroller of Stamps (1986) 10 ACLR 207 (HC of A)	213, 214
Hardie v Hanson (1960) 105 CLR 451 (HC of A)	689
Harding and Others NNO v Standard Bank of South Africa Ltd 2004 (6) SA 464 (C)	415
Harley Street Capital v Tchigirinsky (No 2) [2006] BCC 209	709
Harold Holdsworth & Co (Wakefield) Ltd v Caddies [1955] 1 All ER 725	181
Harold Holdsworth & Co (Wakefield) Ltd v Caddies [1955] 1 All ER 725, [1955] 1 WLR 352 HL (SC)	183
Harrison v Harrison 1952 (3) SA 417 (N)	300
Harrod 1954 (4) SA 28 (SR), Ex parte	402
Harrods Ltd v Lemon [1931] 2 KB (CA)	904
Hartley Baird Ltd [1955] Ch 143	357
Haygro Catering BK v Van der Merwe 1996 (4) SA 1063 (C)	57
Heckmair v Beton & Sandstein Industrieë (Pty) Ltd (1) 1980 (1) SA 350 (SWA)	697, 689
Hedley Byrne & Co Ltd v Heller & Partners Ltd [1963] 2 All ER 575 (HL)	573, 579
Heide Pty Ltd v Lester (1990) 3 ACSR 159 SC (Vic)	255
Hely-Hutchinson v Brayhead Ltd [1967] 2 All ER 14 (CA)	174, 177
Hely-Hutchinson v Brayhead Ltd [1967] 3 All ER 98 (CA)	171
Henderson v James Louttit & Co Ltd (1894) 21 Rettie 674	357, 356
Hendriks, NO v Swanepoel 1962 (4) SA 338 (A)	256
Henry v Great Northern Railway Co (1857) 1 De G & J 606; 44 ER 858	201
Herman & MacLean v Huddleston 459 US 375 (1983)	893
Heron International Ltd v Lord Grade [1983] BCLC 261	744
Herschel v Mrupe 1954 (3) SA 464 (A)	573, 574
Hickman v Kent or Romney Marsh Sheep Breeders' Association [1915] 1 Ch 881	134, 135, 139, 156
Hoare & Co Ltd [1904] 2 Ch 208; [1904–7] All ER Rep 635 (CA), Re	264
Hodge v James Howell & Co [1958] CLY 446, CA	736
Hogg v Cramphorn Ltd [1967] Ch 254	345, 476, 478, 479, 529
Holaway v Allighan 1950 (3) SA 542 (W)	204
Holzman v Knights Engineering & Precision Works (Pty) Ltd 1979 (2) SA 784 (W)	226, 254
Hooker Investments Pty Ltd v Baring Bros Halkerston & Partners Securities Ltd (1986) 4 ACLC 243	869
Hopkins v TL Dallas Group Ltd [2005] 1 BCLC 543 (Ch)	174
Horsley & Weight Ltd [1982] 3 All ER 1045 (CA), Re	154
Hospital Products Limited v United States Surgical Corporation (1984) 156 CLR 41 (HC of A)	465, 517, 841
Horbury Bridge Coal, Iron, and Waggon Company (1879) LR 11 ChD 109, In re	353
Houldsworth v City of Glasgow Bank (1880) 5 App Cas 317 (HL)	137
Howard Smith Ltd v Ampol Petroleum Ltd [1974] AC 821 (PC)	478, 479
Howard v Herrigel 1991 (2) SA 660 (A)	464, 536
Howard v Patent Ivory Manufacturing Co (1888) 38 ChD 156	170, 171
HR Harmer Ltd [1958] 3 All ER 689 (CA), Re	689, 697
HR Harmer Ltd [1959] 1 WLR 62, Re	394
Huckerby v Elliott [1970] 1 All ER 189	510
Hulett v Hulett 1992 (4) SA 291 (A)	47, 48, 842
Hull v Turf Mines 1906 TS 68	181
Hülse-Reutter v Gödde 2001 (4) SA 1336 (SCA)	44, 46, 54, 56
Hutton v West Cork Railway Co (1883) 23 ChD 654 (CA)	416, 417, 468, 469, 472, 473
Hydrodam (Corby) Ltd [1994] BCC 161, Re	378, 380, 381, 382

I

Imageview Management Ltd v Jack [2009] BCLC 725 (CA)	485

In the Matter of Merrill Lynch, Pierce, Fenner & Smith Inc 43 SEC 933 (1968) 856
Indac Electronics (Pty) Ltd v Volkskas Bank Ltd 1992 (1) SA 783 (A)................. 572
Independent Steels (Pty) Ltd v Ryan (1989) 15 ACLR 518 SC (Vic) 297
Indrieri v Du Preez 1989 (2) SA 721 (C) 142
Industrial Developments Consultants Ltd v Cooley [1972] 2 All ER 162 .... 459, 492, 493, 494,
                                                                          495, 497, 498, 499
Industrial Equity Ltd v Blackburn (1977) 2 ACLR 421 CA (NSW); (1977) 137 CLR 567;
   (1977) 3 ACLR 89 (HC of A)... 265
Industrial Equity Ltd v Blackburn (1977) 137 CLR 567; (1977) 3 ACLR 89 (HC of A)...... 264
Industrial Equity Ltd v Blackburn (1977) 137 CLR 567 (HC of A)..................... 183
Industrial Equity Ltd v Blackburn (1978) 52 ALJR 89............................... 181
Innes v Visser 1936 WLD 44 875
Institute for Democracy in South Africa v African National Congress 2005 (5) SA 39 (C).... 369
International Sales and Agencies Ltd v Marcus [1982] 3 All ER 551 .... 161, 166
International Shipping Co (Pty) Ltd v Bentley 1990 (1) SA 680 (A) 572, 574, 576, 577
Investigating Directorate: Serious Economic Offences v Hyundai Motor Distributors (Pty)
   Ltd; In re Hyundai Motor Distributors (Pty) Ltd v Smit NO 2001 (1) SA 545 (CC) 29
Investors Mutual Funds Ltd v Empisal (South Africa) Ltd 1979 (3) SA 170 (W).......... 695, 688
IPF Nominees (Pty) Ltd v Nedcor Bank Ltd (Basfour 130 (Pty) Ltd, Third Party) 2002 (5) SA
   101 (W)... 176
Island Export Finance Ltd v Umunna [1986] BCLC 460............................. 498

J

Jacobson v Liquidator of M Bulkin & Co Ltd 1976 (3) SA 781 (T)................... 296, 297
Jeffery v Pollak and Freemantle 1938 AD 1 331
Jenkins v Enterprise Gold Mines NL (1991) 6 ACSR 539 SC (WA).................... 191
JH Rayner (Mincing Lane) Ltd v Department of Trade and Industry 1990 2 AC 418 (HL) ... 36
John Shaw and Sons (Salford) Ltd v Shaw [1935] 2 KB 113 (CA).................. 329, 345
John Smith & Sons v Moore [1921] 2 AC 13 (HL) 266
John Smith's Tadcaster Brewery Co [1953] Ch 308 (CA), Re 736, 739
Johnson v Gore Wood & Co [2001] 1 BCLC 313 (HL); [2002] 2 AC 1 469
Johnson v Gore, Wood & Co [2001] 1 BCLC 313 (HL) 745
Johnson v Gore, Wood & Co [2002] 2 AC 1 (HL)............................... 744, 745
Johnson v Johnson 1983 (2) SA 324 (W)... 300
Jon Beauforte (London) Ltd (1953) Ch 131, Re................................... 157
Jones v Lipman [1962] 1 All ER 442 42
Jonker v Ackerman 1979 (3) SA 575 (O)...................................... 355, 389
Joosab v Ensor NO 1966 (1) SA 319 (A)... 256

K

K 1971 (4) SA 289 (D), Ex parte 402
Karnovsky v Hyams 1961 (2) SA 368 (W).. 291
Kaytech International plc; Portier v Secretary of State for Trade and Industry [1999] BCC
   390, Re... 380, 383
Keech v Sanford (1726) Sel. Cas. Ch 61 485
Kelner v Baxter [1866] LR 2 CP 174.. 142
Kergeulen Sealing and Whaling Co Ltd v Commissioner of Inland Revenue 1939 AD 487 ... 222
Kingston Cotton Mill Co (2) [1896] 2 Ch 279 (CA), In re 266, 267, 391, 466, 568, 569
Kirsten v Bankorp Ltd 1993 (4) SA 649 (C).................................. 324, 325, 429
Knightsbridge Estates Trust Ltd v Byrne [1940] AC 613; [1940] 2 All ER 401 (HL) 213, 214
Knop v Johannesburg City Council 1995 (2) SA 1 (A) 572
Koekemoer v Taylor & Steyn 1981 (1) SA 267 (W).............................. 826, 827
Kolback Group Ltd (1991) 4 ACSR 165 SC (NSW), Re 256
Konamaneni v Rolls-Royce Industrial Power (India) Ltd [2002] 1 WLR 1269............. 709
Konyn v Viedge Bros (Pty) Ltd 1961 (2) SA 816 (E)............................... 225

Kregor v Hollins (1913) 109 LT 225 (KB and CA)	480
Kregor v Hollins (1913) 109 LT 225 CA	379
Kuter v South African Pharmacy Board 1954 (2) SA 423 (T)	388
Kuwait Asia Bank EC v National Mutual Life Nominees Ltd [1991] 1 AC 187 (PC)	381, 383, 393, 394, 481
Kuwait Asia Bank EC v National Mutual Life Nominees Ltd [1990] 3 All ER 404 (PC)	36
Kuwait Asia Bank EC v National Mutual Life Nominees Ltd [1991] 1 AC 187; [1990] 3 All ER 404 (PC)	192, 839
Kyle v Maritz & Pieterse Inc [2002] 3 All SA 223 (T)	254

L

L Suzman (Rand) Ltd v Yamoyani (2) 1972 (1) SA 109 (W)	387
L Taylor & Kie (Edms) Bpk v Grabe 1976 (3) SA 75 (T)	338
Lagarde v Anniston Lime & Stone Company 28 So 199 (Ala.1899)	490
Lagunas Nitrate Co v Lagunas Syndicate [1899] 2 Ch 392	506
Lands Allotment Co Ltd (1894) Ch 616 (CA), Re	480, 484
Langeberg Koöperasie Bpk v Inverdoorn Farming & Trading Co Ltd 1965 (2) SA 597 (A)	181
Larsen v Hansen 1944 2 PH E8 (C)	225
Lascon Properties (Pty) Ltd v Wadeville Investment Co (Pty) Ltd 1997 (4) SA 578 (W)	572
Lawrence v Lawrich Motors (Pty) Ltd 1948 (2) SA 1029 (W)	825
Le Roux Hotel Management (Pty) Ltd v East Rand (Pty) Ltd (FBC Fidelity Bank Ltd (under curatorship) Intervening) 2001 (2) SA 727 (C)	17, 463
Le'Bergo Fashions CC v Lee 1998 (2) SA 608 (C)	40, 41, 42
Lebowa Development Corporation Ltd 1989 (3) SA 71 (T), Ex parte	505, 527, 528, 538, 540, 827
Lee, Behrens & Co Ltd [1932] 2 Ch 46, Re	395, 470
Lee v Chou Wen Hsien [1984] 1 WLR 1202	411
Lee v Lee's Air Farming Ltd 1961 AC 12	37, 38
Lee v Lee's Air Farming Ltd [1960] 3 All ER 420 (PC)	417
Lee v Neuchatel Asphalte Co (1889) 41 ChD 1; [1886–90] All ER Rep 947 (CA)	266, 267
Lees Import and Export (Pvt) Ltd v Zimbabwe Banking Corporation Ltd 1999 (4) SA 1119 (ZS)	159
Legal Costs Negotiators Ltd [1999] 2 BCLC 171 (ChD and CA), Re	683, 688, 689, 695
Lehman Bros v Schein 416 US 386 (1974)	839
Lemon v Austin Friars Investment Trust [1926] Ch 1; [1925] All ER Rep 255 (CA)	213
Lennard's Carrying Co Ltd v Asiatic Petroleum Co Ltd [1914–15] All ER Rep 280 (HL)	28
Letseng Diamonds Ltd v JCI Ltd; Trinity Asset Management (Pty) Ltd v Investec Bank Ltd 2007 (5) SA 564 (W)	329, 345
Levi v Guerlini (1997) 24 ACSR 159 SC (WA)	255, 256
Levy v Abercorris Slate & Slab Co (1887) 37 ChD 260	213, 214
Levy v Zalrut Investments (Pty) Ltd 1986 (4) SA 479 (W)	336, 653
Lewis v Oneanate (Pty) Ltd 1992 (4) SA 811 (A)	287, 290, 291, 292, 294, 295, 297
Lief v Dettmann 1964 (4) SA 252 (A)	227
Lief v Western Credit (Africa) (Pty) Ltd 1966 (3) SA 344 (W)	828
Linderen v L & P Estates Co Ltd [1968] All ER 917	469
Lindgren v L & P Estates Ltd [1968] Ch 572	192
Lindner v National Bakery (Pty) Ltd 1961 (1) SA 372 (O)	650, 654
Liniton v Telenet Pty Ltd (1998) 30 ACSR 465 CA (NSW)	192
Linter Group Ltd v Goldberg (1992) 7 ACSR 580 SC (Vic)	190
Lion Nathan Australia Pty Ltd v Coopers Brewery Ltd 2006 56 ACSR (FCA) 163	226
Lipschitz NO v UDC Bank 1979 (1) SA 789 (A)	291, 292, 293, 294, 295, 297, 298, 299
Lipschitz v Landmark Consolidated (Pty) Ltd 1979 (2) SA 482 (W)	190
Littlewoods Mail Order Stores Ltd v McGregor [1969] 3 All ER 855, [1969] 1 WLR 1241 (CA)	182
Livanos v Swartzberg 1962 (4) SA 395 (W)	683, 692
Lloyd v Casey [2002] 1 BCLC 454	682

Loch v John Blackwood [1924] AC 783 (PC) 825
Lo-Line Electric Motors Ltd [1988] Ch 477, Re 376, 401
Lombard v Suid-Afrikaanse Vroue-Federasie, Transvaal 1968 (3) SA 473 (A) 224, 225
Lomcord Agencies (Pty) Ltd v Amalgamated Construction Co (Pty) Ltd 1976 (3) SA 86 (D) . . . 291, 294
London and General Bank: Ex parte Theobald (No 2) [1895] 2 Ch 673, In re 391, 570
London Ranch (Pty) Ltd v Hyreb Estate (Pty) Ltd 1963 (2) SA 570 (E) 290
Lonrho Ltd v Shell Petroleum (CA) [1980] 2 WLR 367 181
Lord Advocate v Huron & Erie Loan and Savings Co 1911 SC 612 92
Lord Provost Magistrates of the City of Edinburgh v British Linen Bank [1913] AC 133 (HL) 203
Lourenco v Ferela (Pty) Ltd (No 1) 1998 (3) SA 281 (T) 682, 697
Lubbock v British Bank of South America [1892] 2 Ch 198 .... 265, 266
Lundie Bros [1965] 1 WLR 1051, Re 686
Lyle & Scott Ltd v Scott's Trustees [1959] AC 763; [1959] 2 All ER 661 (HL) 224, 225
Lynch v Agnew 1929 TPD 974 875

M

Maasdorp v Haddow 1959 (3) SA 861 (C) 32
Macadamia Finance Bpk v De Wet 1993 (2) SA 743 (A) 50, 51, 183
Macaura v Northern Assurance Co Ltd [1925] AC 619 (HL(Ir)) 33, 34, 384
MacDougall v Gardiner (1875) 1 Ch 13 (CA) 137, 742
Mackenzie & Co Ltd [1916] 2 Ch 450, Re 734
MacLaine Watson & Co Ltd v Department of Trade and Industry [1989] 3 All ER 523 (HL) 36
Madrassa Anjuman Islamia v Johannesburg Municipal Council 1919 AD 439 28
Magafas v Carantinos [2006] NSWSC 1459 .... 708, 714, 709
Magna Alloys & Research Pty Ltd (1975) 1 ACLR 203 SC (NSW) 205, Re 401, 403
Magnum Financial Holdings (Pty) Ltd v Summerly 1984 (1) SA 160 (W) 37
Maher v Honeysett & Maher Electrical Contractors Pty Ltd [2005] NSWSC 859 .... 708, 714
Maidstone Building Provisions Ltd [1971] 3 All ER 363 (Ch), Re 536
Majola Investments (Pty) Ltd v Uitzigt Properties (Pty) Ltd 1961 (4) SA 705 (T) 422, 423
Malleson v National Insurance and Guarantee Corp [1894] 1 Ch 200 134
Manitoba Investment Holdings v Lipchin 2010 (2) SA 612 (GNP) 95
Manong & Associates (Pty) Ltd v Minister of Public Works 2010 (2) SA 167 (SCA) 28, 159
Marais v Ruskin 1985 (4) SA 659 (A) 189
Maritz v Maritz & Pieterse Inc 2006 (3) SA 481 (SCA) 79
Markham v South African Finance & Industrial Co Ltd 1962 (3) SA 669 (A) 418
Markwell Bros Pty Ltd v CPN Diesels (Qld) Pty Ltd (1982) 7 ACLR 425 SC (Qld) 377
Marra Developments Ltd v BW Rofe Pty Ltd (1977) 3 ACLR 185 CA (NSW) . . 263, 264, 265, 266, 268
Marshall v Marshall (Pty) Ltd 1954 (3) SA 571 (N) 825
Martian Entertainments (Pty) Ltd v Berger 1949 (4) SA 583 (E) 152
McConnell v Newco Financial Corporation, (1979) 8 BLR 180 (BCSC) 734
McCullogh v Fernwood Estate 1920 AD 204 .... 142, 145, 150, 151, 152
McLaren v Thomson [1917] 2 Ch 261 (CA) 358
Mea Corporation Ltd [2007] BCC 288, Re 376
Mercato Holdings v Crown Corp Ltd [1989] 3 NZLR 704 .... 296, 297
Meskin v Anglo-American Corp of SA Ltd 1968 (4) SA 793 (W) 843
Meyer v Scottish Co-operative Wholesale Society [1954] SC 381 687
Mielie-Kip Ltd 1991 (3) SA 449 (W), Ex parte 661
Milburn v Pivot Ltd (1997) 149 ALR 439, 25 ACSR 237 .... 294, 296
Miller v Bain Sub Nom Pantone 485 Ltd [2002] BCLC 266 (ChD) 468
Miller v Muller 1965 (4) SA 458 (C) 294
Mills v Mills (1938) 60 CLR 150 (HC of A) 479
Minister of Police v Rabie 1986 (1) SA 117 (A) 879
Minister of Water Affairs and Forestry v Stilfontein Gold Mining Co Ltd 2006 (5) SA 333
  (W) 416, 433, 436
Minister van Polisie v Ewels 1975 (3) SA 590 (A) 572

Table of Cases xxi

Mistmorn Pty Ltd (in liq) v Yasseen (1996) 21 ACSR 173 388
Mitchell's Plain Town Centre Merchants Association v McLeod 1996 (4) SA 159 (A). 65
Mncube v District Seven Property Investments CC [2006] JOL 17381 (D). 57
Moodie v W & J Shepherd (Bookbinders) Ltd [1949] 2 All ER 1044 (HL). 224
Moosa v Lalloo 1956 (2) SA 237 (D) 71, 221
Moosa, NO v Mavjee Bhawan (Pty) Ltd 1967 (3) SA 131 (T) 47, 385, 825
Morgan v 45 Flers Avenue Pty Ltd (1986) 10 ACLR 692 . . . . 684, 691
Moriarty v Regent's Garage & Engineering Co Ltd [1921] 1 KB 423 395
Morphitis v Bernasconi [2003] 2 BCLC 53 537
Morris v Kanssen [1946] AC 459 . . . . 170, 171
Morrison v Standard Building Society 1932 AD 229. 65
Morseby White v Rangeland Ltd 1952 (4) SA 285 (SR) 388
Movitex Ltd v Bulfield [1988] BCLC 104. . . . . 518, 519
MT Realisations v Digital Equipment [2003] 2 BCLC 117 (CA) 291
Mukheiber v Raath 1999 (3) SA 1065 (SCA). 572
Mulkana Corp NL (in liq) v Bank of New South Wales (1983) 8 ACLR 278 SC (NSW). . . . 384, 385
Multinational Gas and Petrochemical Co v Multinational Gas and Petrochemical Services Ltd
  [1983] 2 All ER 653 (CA). 469
Myer Retail Investments Pty Ltd (1983) 8 ACLR 102 SC (ACT), Re 296, 297
Myers v Claudianos (1990) 2 ACSR 73 869

N

Natal Coal Exploration Co Ltd 1985 (4) SA 279 (W), Ex parte 661
National Bank of Wales Ltd [1899] 2 Ch 629; [1895–99] All ER Rep 715 (CA), Re 266, 267
National Dock Labour Board v Pinn & Wheeler Ltd [1989] BCLC 647. . . . . 182, 183
National Dwellings Society v Sykes [1894] 3 Ch 159. . . . . 355, 389
National Telephone Co [1914] 1 Ch 755, Re 200
NBS Bank Ltd v Cape Produce Co (Pty) Ltd 2002 (1) SA 396 (SCA) 176, 177
NBSA Centre Ltd 1987 (2) SA 783 (W), Ex parte 659
Neath Rugby Ltd (No 2); Hawkes v Cuddy (No 2) [2009] 2 BCLC 427, Re. 482
Nel v McArthur 2003 (4) SA 142 (T) 537
Nel v Metequity Ltd 2007 (3) SA 34 (SCA). 47
Neptune (Vehicle Washing Equipment) Ltd v Fitzgerald (No 2) [1995] 1 BCLC 352 (ChD) . . 477
Neptune (Vehicle Washing Equipment) Ltd v Fitzgerald (No 2) [1995] BCC 1000 519
New British Iron Co [1898] 1 Ch 324, Re 139
New Cedos Engineering Co Ltd [1994] 1 BCLC 797, Re. 337, 363
Newspaper Proprietary Syndicate Ltd [1900] 2 Ch 349, In re 388
New Theatre Co Ltd (1864) 33 LJ Ch 574, Re. 221
New World Alliance Pty Ltd; Syncotes Pty Ltd v Baseler (No 2) (1994) 51 FCR 425, Re 255
New Zealand Flock & Textiles [1976] 1 NZLR 192, Re 265
Nicholas v Soundcraft Electronics Ltd [1993] BCLC 360 193
Nine Hundred Umgeni Road (Pty) Ltd v Bali 1986 (1) SA 1 (A) 151
NLRB v Bildisco 465 US 513 (1983). 783
Nordis Construction Co (Pty) Ltd v Theron, Burke & Isaac 1972 (2) SA 535 (D) 142
North v Marra Developments Limited (1981) 148 CLR 42 (HC Aus) 887, 889
Northwest Forest Products Ltd [1975] 4 WWR 724 (BCSC), Re 705
North-West Transportation Co Ltd v Beatty (1887) 12 App Cas 589 (PC) 355, 516
Northern Counties Securities Ltd v Jackson & Steeple Ltd [1974] 2 All ER 625 . . . . 355, 687
Northern Homes Ltd v Steel-Space Industries Ltd (1976) 57 DLR (3d) 309 28
Northside Developments (Pty) Ltd v Registrar-General (1990) 170 CLR 146 172
Northside Developments (Pty) Ltd v Registrar-General (1990) 8 ACLC 611 . . . . 170, 171
Norvabron Pty Ltd (No 2) (1986) 11 ACLR 279, Re 684, 691
Novick v Benjamin 1972 (2) SA 842 (A) 573
Novick v Comair Holdings Ltd 1979 (2) SA 116 (W) 291, 425, 427
Nusca v Da Ponte 1994 (3) SA 251 (BG) 401, 402, 403

Nurcombe v Nurcombe [1985] 1 WLR 370 .... 708, 709
Nuwe Suid-Afrikaanse Prinsipale Beleggings (Edms) Bpk v Saambou Holdings Ltd 1992 (4)
  SA 387 (W) 339, 341

O

O'Neill v Phillips [1999] 2 All ER 961 .... 685, 693, 694
O'Neill v Phillips [1999] 2 BCLC 1 (HL) 685
Oakland Nominees (Pty) Ltd v Gelria Mining & Investment Co (Pty) Ltd 1976 (1) SA 441
  (A) 227, 331, 333
Oatorian Properties (Pty) Ltd v Maroun 1973 (3) SA 779 (A) 853
Ocean Coal Co Ltd v Powell Duffryn Steam Coal Co Ltd [1932] 1 Ch 654; [1932] All ER Rep
  845 .... 73, 225
OK Bazaars (1929) Ltd v Stern and Ekermans 1976 (2) SA 521 (C) 573
Olifants Tin 'B' Syndicate v De Jager 1912 TPD 301 490
Ooregum Gold Mining Co of India v Roper [1892] AC 125 (HL) 10, 207
Ord v Belhaven Pubs Ltd [1998] BCC 607 51
Otto v Klipvlei Diamond Areas (Pty) Ltd 1958 (2) SA 437 (T) 349

P

Pacific Acceptance Corporation Ltd v Forsyth (1970) 92 WN (NSW) 29 .... 391, 568, 569, 570
Panorama Developments (Guildford) Ltd v Fidelis Furnishing Fabrics Ltd [1971] 3 All ER 16
  (CA) 177
Panorama Developments (Guildford) Ltd v Fidelis Furnishing Fabrics Ltd [1971] 2 QB 711   389
Parke v Daily News Ltd [1962] 2 All ER 929 (ChD) 468, 469
Parker & Cooper Ltd v Reading [1926] 1 Ch 975 .... 336, 337
Parker v Mckenna (1874) LR 10 Ch App 96 .... 466, 485
Parlett v Guppys (Bridport) Ltd [1996] 2 BCLS 34 290
Pathescope (Union) of SA Ltd v Mallinick 1927 AD 292 137
Pavlides v Jensen (1956) Ch 565 529
Peak Lode Gold Mining Company v Union Government 1932 TPD 48 146
Pender v Lushington (1877) 6 ChD 70 .... 137, 354, 741
Percival v Wright [1902] 2 Ch 421 .... 468, 740, 839, 840, 841, 842, 843, 844
Peregrine Group (Pty) Ltd v Peregrine Holdings Ltd 2000 (1) SA 187 (W) 110
Pergamon Press Ltd v Maxwell [1970] 1 WLR 1167 344
Pergamon Press Ltd v Maxwell [1970] 2 All ER 809 .... 190, 839
Perlman v Zoutendyk 1934 CPD 151 579
Permanent Secretary, Department of Welfare, Eastern Cape Provincial Government v Ngxuza
  2001 (4) SA 1184 (SCA) 749
Perry v Day [2005] BCLC 405 745
Peskin v Anderson [2000] 2 BCLC 1 .... 842, 843
Peskin v Anderson [2001] 1 BCLC 372 740
Peters NNO v Schoeman 2001 (1) SA 872 (SCA) 287
Phillips v Base Metals Exploration Syndicate Ltd (in Liquidation) 1911 TPD 403 416
Phillips v Fieldstone Africa (Pty) Ltd 2004 (3) SA 465 (SCA) 465, 488, 489, 501
Phillips v Manufacturer's Securities Ltd (1917) 16 LT 290; (1917) 86 LJ Ch 305 (CA) 225
Philotex v Snyman 1998 (2) SA 138 (SCA) 536, 537, 538
Phosphate of Lime Co v Green (1871) LR 7 CP 43 529
Piercy v Mills [1920] 1 Ch 77 479
Pilkington Brothers (SA) (Pty) Ltd v Lillicrap, Wassenaar & Partners 1983 (2) SA 157 (W);
  1985 (1) SA 475 (A) 572
Pioneer Concrete (Vic) Ptd Ltd v Stule (1996) 20 ACSR 475 SC (Vic) 255, 256
Pioneer Concrete Services Ltd v Yelnah Pty Ltd (1986) 5 NSWLR 43
Pioneer Concrete Services Ltd v Yelnah Pty Ltd (1986) 11 ACLR 108 SC (NSW) 183
Pires v American Fruit Market (Pty) Ltd 1952 (2) SA 337 (T) 300
Platinum Asset Management (Pty) Ltd v Financial Services Board; Anglo Rand Capital
  House (Pty) Ltd v Financial Services Board 2006 (4) SA 73 (W) 29

Table of Cases

Platt v Platt [1999] 2 BCLC 745 841
PNC Telecom plc v Thomas [2008] 2 BCLC 95 (ChD) 527
Polaris Capital (Pty) Ltd v Registrar of Companies 2010 (2) SA 274 (SCA) 110
Polly Peck plc [1996] 2 All ER 433, Re 41, 51, 54
Polyresins Pty Ltd (1998) 28 ACSR 671, Re 683, 695
Porteus v Kelly 1975 (1) SA 219 (W) 355, 688
Portfolios of Distinction Ltd v Laird [2004] 2 BCLC 741 709
Powdrill v Watson [1995] 2 AC 394 782
Powertech Industries Ltd v Mayberry 1996 (2) SA 742 (W) 391, 537
Premier Paper Ltd 1981 (2) SA 612 (W), Ex parte 127
Pretorius v Natal South Sea Investment Trust Ltd 1965 (3) SA 410 (W) 222, 843, 844
Primlake Ltd v Matthews Associates [2007] EWHC 1227 (Ch) 381
Prince Jefri Bolkiah v KPMG [1999] 1 All ER 517 855
Produce Marketing Consortium Ltd (No 2) [1989] BCLC 520 (ChD), Re 528
Prudential Assurance Co Ltd v Newman Industries Ltd (No 2) [1982] 1 All ER 354 (CA) 469
Prudential Assurance Co Ltd v Newman Industries Ltd (No 2) [1981] Ch 257; 1982 [1] Ch 204 (CA) 744
Punt v Symons & Co Ltd [1903] 2 Ch 506 .... 479, 480
Purpoint Ltd [1991] BCLC 491, Re 541

Q

QBE Insurance Group Ltd v Australian Securities Commission (1992) 8 ACSR 631 (Fed C of A) 265, 266
Quadrangle Investments (Pty) Ltd v Witind Holdings Ltd 1975 (1) SA 572 (A) 122, 268, 336, 337, 338
Quin & Axtens Ltd v Salmon [1909] AC 442 (HL) 136
Quintex Australia Finance Ltd v Schroeders Australia Ltd (1990) 3 ACSR 267 SC (NSW) ... 183

R

R v Byrnes (1995) 183 CLR 501 485
R v Findlater [1939] 1 All ER 82 (CA) 213
R v Mall 1959 (4) SA 607 (N) 380, 387
R v McLachlan and Bernstein 1929 WLD 149 888
R v Milne and Erleigh (7) 1951 (1) SA 791 (A) 50, 181, 190
RA Hill v Permanent Trustee Co of New South Wales Ltd [1930] AC 720; [1930] All ER Rep 87 (PC) 211, 265
Railtrack Plc [2002] 1 WLR 3002, Re 795
Raines v Toney 313 SW2d 802 (1958) 416
Rakusens Ltd v Baser Ambalaj Plastik [2002] 1 BCLC 104 CA 92
Rakusen v Ellis, Munday & Clarke [1912] 1 Ch 831 855
Randfontein Estates Gold Mining Co Ltd v Custodian of Enemy Property 1923 AD 576 ... 213, 214
Rayfield v Hands [1960] 1 Ch 1; [1958] 2 All ER 194 138
Raymond v Cook (1998) 29 ACSR 252 (CA) 689
Reddy v Siemens Telecommunications (Pty) Ltd 2007 (2) SA 486 (SCA) 498
Regal (Hastings) Ltd v Gulliver [1942] 1 All ER 378 486
Regal (Hastings) Ltd v Gulliver [1942] 1 All ER 378 (HL); [1967] AC 134 .... 487, 488, 489, 492, 501, 503, 527, 529, 531, 839
Regal (Hastings) Ltd v Gulliver [1967] 2 AC 134 386
Regentcrest plc v Cohen [2001] 1 BCLC 80 476
Reid Murray Holdings v David Murray Holdings Pty Ltd (1972) 5 SASR 386 191
Reitzer Pharmaceuticals (Pty) Ltd v Registrar of Medicines 1998 (4) SA 660 (T) 709
Rentekor (Pty) Ltd v Rheeder and Berman 1988 (4) SA 469 (T) 48, 354, 424, 842
Revlon Inc v Cripps and Lee Ltd 1980 FSR 85 (CA) 53, 182
Rhode Island Hospital Trust National Bank v Swartz 455 F (2d) 847 (1972) 579
Richter v Riverside Estates (Pty) Ltd 1946 OPD 209 71

Ritz Hotel Ltd v Charles of The Ritz Ltd 1988 (3) SA 290 (A)....................50, 53, 182
Roberts & Cooper Ltd [1929] 2 Ch 383, Re....................................... 201
Robinson v Imroth 1917 WLD 159...425, 427
Robinson v Randfontein Estates Gold Mining Co 1921 AD 168...............40, 181, 193, 459,
467, 486, 487, 488, 489, 492, 501
Roderick v AB Jackson (Pty) Ltd; Roderick v Bremco (Pty) Ltd [2007] JOL 20079 (C)..... 385
Rolled Steel Products (Holdings) Ltd v British Steel Corporation [1985] 3 All ER 52.....154, 155, 161
Rookes v Barnard [1964] AC 1129 (HL)... 875
Rosebank Television & Appliance Co (Pty) Ltd v Orbit Sales Corp (Pty) Ltd 1969 (1) SA 300
(T).. 415
Rosenbach & Co (Pty) Ltd v Singh's Bazaar (Pty) Ltd 1962 (4) SA 593 (D)............... 540
Ross & Co v Coleman 1920 AD 408...139, 140
Rossfield Group Operations (Pty) Ltd v Austral Group Ltd 1981 QdR 279................ 291
Rosslare (Pty) Ltd v Registrar of Companies 1972 (2) SA 524 (D)....................... 135
Royal British Bank v Turquand (1855) 5 E and B 248; (1856) 6 E & B 327; [1843–60] All ER
Rep 435... 306
Royal British Bank v Turquand (1856) 6 E & B 327; 119 ER 886......................20, 169
RP Crees (Pvt) Ltd v Woodpecker Industries (Pvt) Ltd 1975 (2) SA 485 (R)............... 36
Ruben v Great Fingall Consolidated [1906] AC 439 (HL).............................. 170
Runciman v Walter Runciman plc [1992] BCLC 1084..............................517, 521
Russell v Northern Bank Development Corporation Ltd [1922] 1 WLR 589.............. 132
Ryan v Independent Steels Pty Ltd (1988) 13 ACLR 379 SC (Vic)....................296, 297

S

S v Arenstein 1964 (1) SA 361 (A).. 861
S v Coetzee 1997 (3) SA 527 (CC).. 856
S v de Blom 1977 (3) SA 513 (A)... 859
S v De Jager 1965 (2) SA 616 (A)..33, 34, 35, 181, 379, 382, 416
S v Heller (2) 1964 (1) SA 524 (W)... 181
S v Hepker 1973 (1) SA 472 (W)..296, 379
S v Marks 1965 (3) SA 834 (W)...888, 889
S v Pouroulis 1993 (4) SA 575 (W)...............................313, 314, 315, 317, 318, 429
S v Shaban 1965 (4) SA 646 (W)...378, 379, 464, 483
S v Weinberg 1979 (3) SA 89 (A)... 864
S v Western Areas Ltd (2006) 2 All SA 653 (W)..................................... 865
SEC v Chenery Corporation 318 US 80 (1943)...................................... 467
SA Securities Ltd v Nicholas 1911 TPD 450.. 177
SAA Distributors (Pty) Ltd v Sport & Spel (Edms) Bpk 1973 (3) SA 371 (C).............. 827
Safeguard Industrial Investments Ltd v National Westminster Bank [1980] 3 All ER 849 (C) 224
Sage Holdings Ltd v The Unisec Group Ltd 1982 (1) SA 337 (W).........185, 268, 379, 840, 842
Salomon v A Salomon & Co Ltd [1897] AC 22, [1895–9] All ER Rep 33................. 51
Salomon v Salomon & Co Ltd [1897] AC 22 (HL).......29, 30, 31, 32, 35, 36, 37, 39, 48, 70, 337
Saltergate Insurance Co Ltd v Knight [1982] 1 NSWLR 369........................... 298
Sammel v President Brand Gold Mining Co Ltd 1969 (3) SA 629 (A).........133, 332, 333, 350,
354, 355, 694
Sam Weller and Sons Ltd [1990] Ch 682, Re....................................... 693
Sandell v Porter (1966) 115 CLR 666.. 255
Sarflax Ltd [1979] 1 All ER 529 (Ch), In re.....................................537, 689
Saul D Harrison & Sons plc [1995] 1 BCLC 14 (CA), Re............................. 693
Schein v Chasen 313 So 2d 739 (1975).. 839
Schein v Chasen 478 F 2d 817 (2d Cir 1973)....................................... 839
Schiowitz v IOS Ltd (1971) 23 DLR (3d) 102...................................... 698
Schreuder 1965 (2) SA 174 (O), Ex parte.. 402
Schreuder 1974 (2) SA 358 (O), Ex parte.......................................402, 403
Scott Group Ltd v McFarlane [1978] 1 NZLR 553 (CA)...........................574, 579

Scott v Brown, Doering, McNab & Co, Slaughter & May v Brown, Doering, McNab & Co [1892] 2 QB 724 (CA)	889
Scott v Brown, Doering, McNab & Co, Slaughter & May v Brown, Doering, McNab & Co	889
Scott v Frank Scott (London) Ltd [1940] Ch 794 (CA)	127
Scottish Co-operative Wholesale Society Ltd v Meyer [1958] 2 All ER 66 (HL)	192, 481
Scottish Co-operative Wholesale Society Ltd v Meyer [1959] AC 324	379, 684, 688, 689, 691, 692, 695
Scottish Insurance Corporation Ltd v Wilsons and Clyde Coal Co Ltd [1949] AC 462; [1949] 1 All ER 1068 (HL)	201
SEC v Texas Gulf Sulphur Co 401 F 2d 833 (1968)	837, 838
Secretary of State for Business, Enterprise and Regulatory Reform v Neufeld [2009] BCC 687	37
Secretary of State for Trade and Industry v Deverell [2001] Ch 340	383
Secretary of State for Trade and Industry v Hollier [2007] BCC 11	380, 383
Secretary of State for Trade and Industry v Tjolle [1998] BCC 282	380
Sekretaris van Binnelandse Inkomste v Aveling 1978 (1) SA 862 (A)	266
Selangor United Rubber Estates Ltd v Cradock (No 3) [1968] 1 WLR 1555	383, 384
Selangor United Rubber Estates Ltd v Cradock (No 3) [1968] 2 All ER 1073 (ChD)	483
Semer v Retief and Berman 1948 (1) SA 182 (C)	151
Sentrale Kunsmis Korporasie (Edms) Bpk v NKP Kunsmisverspreiders (Edms) Bpk 1970 (3) SA 367 (A)	150, 152
SH & Co (Realisations) 1990 Ltd [1993] BCLC 1309, Re	213, 214
Shatterproof Glass Corporation v Ned James 466 SW2d 873, 46 ALR (3d) 968	579
Shaw v Digital Equipment Corp 82 F 3d 1194 (1st Cir, 1996)	853
Shearer (Inspector of Taxes) v Bercain Ltd [1980] 3 All ER 295	263
Shell and BP South African Petroleum Refineries v Osborne Panama SA 1980 (3) SA 653 (D)	572
Shepherds Investment Ltd v Walters [2007] 2 BCLC 207	381
Shuttleworth v Cox Bros & Co (Maidenhead) Ltd [1927] 2 KB 9; [1926] All ER Rep 498 (CA)	476
Shuttleworth v Cox Brothers & Co (Maidenhead) Ltd [1927] 2 KB 9 (CA)	134, 140, 513
Sibex Construction (SA) (Pty) Ltd v Injectaseal CC 1988 (2) SA 54 (T)	485, 490
Sindler NO v Gees 2006 (5) SA 501 (C)	73, 74, 225
Singer v Beckett, Sub Nom Continental Assurance Co of London plc (In Liquidation) [2007] 2 BCLC 287 (ChD)	541
Slade v Shearson, Hammil & Co Inc CCH Fed SEC L Rep 193 (SDNY 1974)	856
Smith v Croft (No 2) [1988] Ch 114	345
Smith & Fawcett Ltd [1942] Ch 304 (CA), Re	467, 476
Smith & Fawcett Ltd [1942] Ch 304; [1942] 1 All ER 542 (CA), Re	224, 226
Smith v Hennicker-Major & Co [2002] 2 BCLC 655	171
Smith, Knight & Co, Weston's Case (1868) 4 Ch App 20, Re	224
Smith v Sadler [1997] NSWSC 525	345
Smith v Van Gorkum 488 A 2d 858 (Del. Supr. 1985)	515
Smith, Stone & Knight Ltd v Lord Mayor, Aldermen Citizens of the City of Birmingham [1939] 4 All ER 116	52, 53
Smuts v Booyens; Markplaas (Edms) Bpk v Booyens 2001 (4) SA 15 (SCA)	72, 73, 224, 225
Software Toolworks, Inc. Securities Litigation 50 F 3d 615 (9th Cir 1994) 627, In re	893
Solaglass Finance Co (Pty) Ltd v Commissioner for Inland Revenue 1991 (2) SA 257 (A)	191
Sonnenberg McLoughlin Inc v Spiro 2004 (1) SA 90 (C)	80
South African Association of Personal Injury Lawyers v Heath 2000 (10) BCLR 1131 (T)	749
South African Broadcasting Corporation Ltd v Mpofu [2009] 4 All SA 169 (GSJ)	355, 389, 423, 425, 433, 439
South African Mutual Life Assurance Society v Anglo-Transvaal Collieries Ltd 1973 (3) SA 642 (A)	202
Southern Foundries (1926) Ltd v Shirlaw [1940] AC 701	388, 395, 414, 416
Southern Foundries (1926) Ltd v Shirlaw [1940] AC 701, [1940] 2 All ER 445 (HL)	140

Southern Witwatersrand Exploration Co Ltd v Bisichi Mining plc 1998 (4) SA 767 (W)...362, 426, 427
Sprawson: In re Hebron Diamond Mining Syndicate Ltd 1914 TPD 458, Ex parte.......... 832
Springbok Agricultural Estates Ltd [1920] 1 Ch 563, Re..................... 201
Standard Bank Group Ltd and Liberty Group Ltd, Ex parte [2007] 4 All SA 1298 (W)...... 659
Standard Bank of SA Ltd v Neugarten 1988 (1) SA 652 (W)................. 427
Standard Bank of South Africa Ltd v Hunkydory Investments 188 (Pty) Ltd (No. 2) 2010 (1)
 SA 634 (WCC)..650, 651
Standard Bank of South Africa Ltd v Ocean Commodities Inc 1983 (1) SA 276 (A).......227, 332
Standard Chartered Bank of Australia Ltd v Antico (Nos 1 and 2) (1995) 18 ACSR 1 SC
 (NSW).. 255
Standard Chartered Bank of Canada v Nedperm Bank Ltd 1994 (4) SA 747 (A)........... 574
Stapley v Read Bros Ltd [1924] 2 Ch 1; [1924] All ER Rep 421 ....264, 265
State Bank of Victoria v Parry (1990) 2 ACSR 15 SC (WA)......................... 183
Statek Corp v Alford [2008] BCC 266.. 381
Stech v Davies (1987) 53 Alta LR (2d) 373...................................... 694
Stein v Blake (No 2) [1998] 1 All ER 724......................................469, 745
Stellenbosch Farmers' Winery Ltd v Distillers Corporation (SA) Ltd 1962 (1) SA 458 (A)... 33
Sterileair (Pty) Ltd v Papallo (1998) 29 ACSR 461............................290, 296, 297
Stern v Vesta Industries (Pty) Ltd 1976 (1) SA 81 (W)............................... 32
Stewarts (Brixton) Ltd [1985] BCLC 4, Re..................................... 687
Stewart v Schwab 1956 (4) SA 791 (T).. 409
Straiton v Cleanwell Dry Cleaners (Pty) Ltd 1960 (1) SA 355 (SR)..................... 291
Strydom: In re Central Plumbing Works (Natal) (Pty) Ltd, Ex parte; Spendiff: In re Candida
 Footwear Manufacturers (Pty) Ltd, Ex parte; Spendiff: In re Jerseytex (Pty) Ltd 1988 (1)
 SA 616 (D), Ex parte... 827
Stubbs: In re Wit Extensions Ltd 1982 (1) SA 526 (W), Ex parte 831
Sugden v Beaconhurst Dairies (Pty) Ltd 1963 (2) SA 174 (E)......................336, 337
Suid-Afrikaanse Bantoetrust v Ross en Jacobz 1977 (3) SA 184 (T)..................... 574
Suiderland Development Corporation 1986 (2) SA 442 (C), Ex parte.................... 661
Sutton's Hospital (1612) 10 Co Rep 23a 158
Swaledale Cleaners Ltd [1968] 3 All ER 619 (CA), Re............................. 224
Swanee's Boerdery (Edms) Bpk (in Liquidation) v Trust Bank of Africa Ltd 1986 (2) SA 850
 (A)..191, 336
Swansson v R A Pratt Properties Pty Ltd (2002) 42 ACSR 313 ....708, 709, 710
Swart v Cilliers 1976 (2) PH E10... 224
Swerdlow v Cohen 1977 (1) SA 178 (W)....................................... 413
Swerdlow v Cohen 1977 (1) SA 178 (W); 1977 (3) SA 1050 (T)...................... 410
Swerdlow v Cohen 1977 (3) SA 1050 (T) 412
Sycotex Pty Ltd v Baseler (1994) 13 ACSR 766 (Fed C of A)......................... 255
Symington v Pretoria-Oos Privaat Hospitaal Bedryfs (Pty) Ltd 2005 (5) SA 550 (SCA)....415, 498

T

Tallglen Pty Ltd v Optus Communications Pty Ltd (1998) 28 ACSR 610 ....294, 296
Taylor v Australian and New Zealand Banking Group Ltd (1988) 13 ACLR 780 SC (Vic) ... 255
Taylor v Carrol (1991) 6 ACSR 255 SC (Qld)..................................255, 256
Taylors Industrial Flooring Ltd v M & H Plant Hire (Manchester) Ltd [1990] BCC 44...... 256
Tayob 1989 (2) SA 282 (T), Ex parte... 403
Tayob 1990 (3) SA 715 (T), Ex parte..402, 403
TC Newman (Pty) Ltd v DHA Rural (Qld) Pty Ltd (1987) 2 ACLR 257 SC (Qld).......... 225
TCN Channel Nine Pty Ltd v Scotney (1995) 18 ACSR 393 (Fed C of A)................ 255
Teck Corp Ltd v Millar (1972) 33 DLR (3d) 288 (BCSC)....................473, 476, 477, 479
Terblanche v Nothnagel 1975 (4) SA 405 (C) 142
The Albazero [1975] 3 All ER 21 (CA)..50, 181
The Albazero [1977] AC 774, [1975] 3 All ER 21 (CA).............................. 182
The Master: In re Niagara Ltd 1913 TPD 38, Ex parte............................... 222

Table of Cases   xxvii

The Mine Workers' Union v Prinsloo (1948) 3 SA 831 (A) 171
The Second Consolidated Trust Ltd v Ceylon Amalgamated Tea & Rubber Estates Ltd [1943]
  2 All ER 567 355
The Shipping Corporation of India Ltd v Evdomon Corporation 1994 (1) SA 550 (A) 33
The Unisec Group Ltd v Sage Holdings Ltd 1986 (3) SA 259 (T) 285
Thomas Gerrard & Son Ltd [1967] 2 All ER 525 (Ch), Re 568
Thomas v HW Thomas Ltd [1984] 1 NZLR 686 CA (NZ) 692
Thorby v Goldberg (1964) 112 CLR 597 481
Thoroughbred Breeders' Association of South Africa v Price Waterhouse 1999 (4) SA 968
  (W) 573
Thoroughbred Breeders' Association v Price Waterhouse 2001 (4) SA 551 (SCA) 570
TJ Jonck BK h/a Bothaville Vleismark v Du Plessis NO 1998 (1) SA 971 (O) 55, 57
Tjospomie Boerdery (Pty) Ltd v Drakensberg Botteliers (Pty) Ltd 1989 (4) SA 31 (T) 842
Tonkwane Sawmill Co Ltd v Filmalter 1975 (2) SA 453 (W) 391, 568, 569
Topham v Greenside Glazed Fire-Brick Co (1887) 37 ChD 281 213
Transcash SWD (Pty) Ltd v Smith 1994 (2) SA 295 (C) 336, 423, 425, 427
Treasurer-General v Lippert (1880) ISC 291 313
Trever Investments (Pty) Ltd v Friedhelm Investments (Pty) Ltd 1982 (1) SA 7 (A) 152
Trevor v Whitworth (1887) 12 App Cas 409 (HL) 268
Trinity Asset Management (Pty) Ltd v Investec Bank Ltd 2009 (4) SA 89 (SCA) 350
Triptomania Twee (Pty) Ltd v Connolly 2003 (3) SA 558 (C) 537
Trust Bank of Africa Ltd v Standard Bank of South Africa Ltd 1968 (3) SA 166 (A) 226
TSC Industries, Inc. v Northway, Inc. 426 US 438 (1976) 899, 900

U

Ultraframe (UK) Ltd v Fielding [2005] EWHC 1638 (Ch) 486, 491, 519
Ultramares Corporation v George A Touche 74 ALR 1139 574
Umfolozi Co-operative Sugar Planters Ltd v St Lucia Sugar Farms (Pty) Ltd 1983 (1) SA 792
  (N) 344
Underwood Ltd v Bank of Liverpool and Martins [1924] KB 775 (CA) 170
Underwood v London Music Hall Ltd [1901] 2 Ch 309 734
Union Government v Warneke 1911 AD 657 572
Unisec Group Ltd v Sage Holdings Ltd 1986 (3) SA 259 (T) 185, 186, 187, 188, 268
Unisoft Group Ltd (No 3) [1994] 1 BCLC 609, Re 687, 688
United States v Brown 79 F 2d 321 (2d Cir 1935) 894, 895
United Trust (Pty) Ltd v SA Milling Co 1959 (2) SA 426 (W) 224
Universal Non-Tariff Fire Insurance Co (Ritso's Case) (1877) 4 ChD 774 (CA), Re 221
Universal Stores Ltd v OK Bazaars (1929) Ltd 1973 (4) SA 747 (A) 582
US v Carpenter 791 F 2d 1024 (1986); 108 S CT 316 (1987) 836
US v Newman 664 F 2d 12 (1981); 722 F 2d 729 (1981) 836
Utopia Vakansie-Oorde Bpk v Du Plessis 1974 (3) SA 148 (A) 693, 733, 735, 736, 737

V

Van der Merwe Burger v Munisipaliteit van Warrenton 1987 (1) SA 899 (NC) 572
Van Eeden v Sasol Pensioenfonds 1975 (2) SA 167 (O) 142
Van Tonder v Pienaar 1982 (2) SA 336 (SE) 395, 422, 425, 427
Velkes 1963 (3) SA 584 (C), Ex parte 400
Vermeulen v CC Bauermeister (Edms) Bpk 1982 (4) SA 159 (T) 828
Verner v General & Commercial Investment Trust [1894] 2 Ch 239 (CA) 266, 267
Vickerman 1935 CPD 429, Ex parte 145, 152
Visser v Van Tonder 1986 (2) SA 500 (T) 152
Volvo (Southern Africa) (Pty) Ltd v Yssel 2009 (6) SA 531 (SCA) 465, 466, 494

W

Walker v Wimborne (1976) 50 ALJR 446 181
Walker v Wimborne (1976) 137 CLR 1 (HC of A) 190, 191

Wall v London & Provincial Trust Ltd [1920] 1 Ch 45; [1920] 2 Ch 582 (CA) 265, 268
Wallersteiner v Moir (No 2) [1975] 1 All ER 849 (CA). 699
Wallersteiner v Moir (No 2) [1975] QB 373 (CA). 715, 716
Wallersteiner v Moir [1974] 3 All ER 217 (CA) 49, 295
Wambach v Maizecor Industries (Edms) Bpk 1993 (2) SA 669 (A) 50, 51, 183
Wayde v NSW Rugby League Ltd (1985) 3 ACLC 799. 694
Webb v Earle (1857) LR 20 Eq 556 201
Wellington Publishing Co Ltd [1973] 1 NZLR 133, Re. 291
Welton v Saffery 1897 AC 297 (HL) 138
Westbourne Galleries [1970] 3 All ER 374, Re 686
Westburn Sugar Refineries Ltd v Inland Revenue Commissions 1960 SLT 297 265
Westminister Property Management Ltd, Official Receiver v Stern [2001] BCC 121, Re. 402
W Foster & Son Ltd [1942] 1 All ER 314, Re 201
Wharfedale Brewery Co Ltd [1952] Ch 913; [1952] 2 All ER 635, Re 201
White v Bristol Aeroplane Co Ltd [1953] 1 All ER 40 (CA). 736, 739
Whitwam v Watkin (1898) 78 LT 188 708
Will v United Lankat Plantations Co Ltd [1914] AC 11 (HL) 201
William Leitch Bros Ltd [1932] All ER 892, Re 537
Williamson v Durban City Council 1977 (3) SA 342 (D). 350
Wilmer v McNamara & Co Ltd [1895] 2 Ch 245 . . . . 266, 267
Wincham Shipbuilding, Boiler, and Salt Co (Poole, Jackson and Whyte's Case) (1878) 9 ChD
    322, Re 839
Winthrop Investments Ltd v Winns Ltd [1975] 2 NSWLR 666 (CA) (NSW). 345, 841
Wiseman v Ace Table Soccer (Pty) Ltd 1991 (4) SA 171 (W). 37, 254, 255, 256
W & M Roith Ltd [1967] 1 All ER 427, Re 477
Wolpert v Uitzigt Properties (Pty) Ltd 1961 (2) SA 257 (W) 177, 388
Wood v Odessa Waterworks Co (1889) 42 ChD 636. . . . . .138, 210
Woolfson v Strathclyde Regional Council 1978 SC 90 (HL) 96. .182, 183
Woolfson v Strathclyde Regional Council 1978 SLT 159 . . . . .51, 53

Y

Yates Investments (Pty) Ltd v Commissioner for Inland Revenue 1956 (1) SA 364 (A) 28, 159
Yende v Orlando Coal Distributors (Pty) Ltd 1961 (3) SA 314 (W) 348
Yenidje Tobacco Co Ltd [1916] 2 Ch 426 (CA), In re. 47, 385, 825
York Corporation v Henry Leetham & Sons Ltd [1924] 1 Ch 557. 155
Young v Ladies' Imperial Club Ltd [1920] 2 KB 523 (CA). 423

Z

Zentland Holdings (Pty) Ltd v Saambou Nasionale Bouvereniging 1979 (4) SA 574 (C). 297

CHAPTER 1

INTRODUCTION TO THE NEW COMPANIES ACT: GENERAL OVERVIEW OF THE ACT

Farouk HI Cassim

1.1	INTRODUCTION	2
1.2	THE REASONS FOR A NEW COMPANIES ACT	3
1.3	THE FRAMEWORK AND THE SCOPE OF THE COMPANIES ACT	5
1.4	SOME IMPORTANT INNOVATIVE FEATURES OF THE ACT	6
	1.4.1 Interpretation, anti-avoidance and substantial compliance	6
	1.4.2 Company formation	8
	1.4.3 Types of companies	9
	1.4.4 Archaic and obsolete concepts and doctrines jettisoned	10
	1.4.5 The constitution of a company and default provisions of the Act	11
	1.4.6 Disclosure, transparency and reporting standards	13
	1.4.7 Related persons	14
	1.4.8 Mergers and amalgamations	14
	1.4.9 Business rescue	15
	1.4.10 The directors of a company	17
	1.4.11 The enlightened shareholder value approach	18
	1.4.12 The capacity of a company	19
	1.4.13 Shareholder remedies	20
	(a) Derivative action	20
	(b) Order to have a director declared a delinquent director or place him or her under probation	21
	(c) Oppressive or unfairly prejudicial conduct	21
	(d) A declaratory order	22
	(e) Appraisal rights	22
	(f) Piercing the veil of corporate personality	23
	1.4.14 Alternative dispute resolution	23
	1.4.15 Enforcement	23
1.5	CONCLUSION	24

1.1 INTRODUCTION

The Companies Act 71 of 2008 (hereafter 'the Act') was signed into law on 8 April 2009.[1] The Act could not come into force before 8 April 2010, because a waiting period of one year is prescribed by s 225 of the Act. This was done to give corporate lawyers, directors, accountants, auditors, company secretaries and others time to understand and apply the new law. In addition to this waiting period of at least a year, a transitional period of two years is conferred[2] on all pre-existing companies, providing them with an opportunity to file free of charge an amended Memorandum of Incorporation to harmonise their constitutional documents with the new Act.

The Act is intended to be the modern corporate law for a modern commercial world. It consists of a mere 225 sections and five Schedules coupled with 191 regulations[3] and four annexures. It is a concise piece of legislation. To put this in perspective, the Australian Corporations Act 2001, despite a lengthy process of simplification of the company law legislation, consists of approximately 1463 sections and eight schedules, while the recently modernised United Kingdom Companies Act 2006, which is the longest statute ever passed by the UK Parliament, has 1297 sections and over 16 schedules. But there is much more to legislation than brevity. It is the clarity and comprehensiveness of the legislation that is of far greater importance. The guideline should be less complexity and more simplicity and clarity.

Two further preliminary observations may be made. First, the new Act attempts to rely on plain language, instead of the usual complex corporate law terminology and legal jargon. This is to be welcomed. However, the problem with this approach — which is not always consistently adhered to — is the risk that plain language drafting may sometimes lead to fuzzy law.

Despite the plain-language approach, the Act contains throughout many of its provisions, strange wording and unclear concepts imported from other jurisdictions, which our courts and corporate law practitioners, directors, auditors, company secretaries and others are simply not familiar with. In short, the Act is not entirely user-friendly, nor is it drafted in entirely clear and unambiguous language. Fortunately, regarding technical and grammatical errors, including incorrect cross-references, of which about 104 have been found, notice has been given[4] of the rectification of the Act before it has come into effect and a draft Companies Amendment Bill, 2010 has recently been prepared to remedy these errors.

The second preliminary point is that the new Act preserves much of our current company law rules and concepts, and some of what appears to have worked. This is borne out in the policy paper issued by the Department of Trade and Industry (DTI) entitled 'South African Company Law for the 21st Century: Guidelines for Corporate Law Reform'[5] where it is stated:

---

[1] GN 421 *GG* 32121.
[2] Item 4(2) of Schedule 5 to the Act. See further chapter 21: Transitional Arrangements.
[3] Currently, draft regulations. See GN 1664 *GG* 32832 of 22 December 2009.
[4] GN 1663 *GG* 32832 of 22 December 2009.
[5] GN 1183 *GG* 26493 of 23 June 2004 at 9.

Although the intention is to engage in a comprehensive review of company law, it is not the aim of the DTI simply to write a new Act by unreasonably jettisoning the body of jurisprudence built up over more than a century.

This approach is commendable, instead of a 'clean slate' approach. However, it is unavoidable that such an approach would cause some conflict between the old and the new rules unless the new rules are properly and carefully blended in and harmonised with the old. The task of restating, consolidating and harmonising the provisions of the Companies Act 61 of 1973 (hereafter 'the 1973 Act') is not an easy one. It requires meticulous care and diligence.[6]

1.2 THE REASONS FOR A NEW COMPANIES ACT

Company law has a significant impact on the economy in general and on commercial activity in particular. It can promote and facilitate commercial enterprise and economic growth or it can restrict and retard it.[7] Companies play a vital role in wealth creation and social renewal. It no longer needs to be emphasised that a good corporate law system lies at the very foundation of a prosperous economy. It is consequently imperative, almost a *sine qua non*, for corporate law to be clear, certain and accessible. But our current corporate law regime is bulky, complex and full of conflict in its underlying philosophy and policy. This is attributable to the fact that the 1973 Act has been amended about 42 times in the 37 years of its existence. This sort of patchwork and piecemeal reform has inevitably led to conflict in the policy and objectives underpinning South Africa's current company law system. Our current company law has become cumbersome, complex, archaic and excessively technical.

In addition to this, during the 37 years of the existence of the 1973 Act, both the domestic and the global environment have changed dramatically. Many of the traditional company law doctrines and concepts inherited from 19th century England have been abandoned or substantially modified. New corporate law concepts have been developed, such as solvency and liquidity, new and higher standards of corporate governance, new standards of accountability, disclosure and transparency, market manipulation, and new ideas and approaches to mergers and amalgamations, shareholder appraisal rights and corporate rescue. The underpinning principle is that legislation that has outlived its usefulness and that is stifling the development of the economy must be repealed.

The DTI policy paper[8] likewise states that we live in a world of greater globalisation, increased electronic communication, greater sensitivity to social and ethical concerns, greater competition for capital, goods and services, and increased mobility of international capital that emphasises the importance of investor-friendly domestic laws. Over and above all this, there has been dramatic socio-political and economic change in South Africa as well as a new constitutional dispensation.

Apart from an investor-friendly corporate law regime, the DTI policy paper emphasises, as major themes of the corporate law reform programme, the import-

---

[6] See FHI Cassim 'The Companies Act, 2008: An Overview of a Few of its Core Provisions' (2010) 22 *SA Merc LJ* 157–75.
[7] See Modern Company Law for a Competitive Economy: Final Report (July 2002) (CM 553–1) vol 1 at 11 (UK).
[8] Op cit n 5 at 13.

ance of a corporate law system that is flexible, simplified, modernised and transparent. The five pillars or main themes of the DTI policy paper outlining the objectives of a new company law regime are stated to be as follows:[9]

- to simplify the procedure for the formation of companies and to reduce the costs of forming and maintaining a company,
- to promote flexibility in the design and the organisation of companies and to ensure a predictable and effective regulatory environment,
- to promote the efficiency of companies and their management,
- to encourage transparency and high standards of corporate governance,
- to harmonise our company law[10] with best-practice jurisdictions internationally.

While these objectives are undeniably worthy and laudable goals and while they may be properly expounded in a policy document or in a preamble to an Act of Parliament, it is quite another matter for such broad objectives to be inserted in the Act itself. Section 7 of the Act read with s 158(1)(b) and 5(1), which require the Act to be interpreted and applied in a manner that gives effect to the purposes set out in s 7, gives rise to some concern. How exactly would a court or regulatory agency give effect to the 14 wide-ranging purposes of the Act as set out in s 7? How is a court (or regulatory agency) to decide which particular purpose should have priority? A closer examination of these purposes shows that they are prefatory in nature and ought to remain so.

Some of the purposes stated in s 7, apart from those mentioned above as the main themes of the corporate law reform programme, are:

- to reaffirm the concept of a company as a means of achieving economic and social benefits,
- to promote the development of companies within all sectors of the company,
- to provide for the promotion, operation and accountability of non-profit companies,
- to balance the rights and obligations of shareholders and directors within companies,
- to encourage the efficient and responsible management of companies,
- to provide a predictable and effective environment for the efficient regulation of companies,
- to provide for the efficient rescue and recovery of financially distressed companies in a manner that balances the rights and interests of all relevant stakeholders,
- to promote compliance with the Bill of Rights as provided for in the Constitution, in the application of company law,
- to promote innovation and investment in the South African markets.

---

[9] Op cit n 5 at 11.
[10] Harmonisation must extend further than harmonisation with other jurisdictions — it must extend also to harmonisation with other relevant local and domestic legislation that is affected by the new company law legislation. For instance, it is vital for the Act to be harmonised or made compatible with tax legislation generally and the Income Tax Act 58 of 1962 in particular, as well as the Securities Services Act 36 of 2004 and the Auditing Profession Act 26 of 2005.

1.3 THE FRAMEWORK AND THE SCOPE OF THE COMPANIES ACT

The new Companies Act comprises nine chapters and five Schedules. Chapter 1 deals with some of the new concepts introduced by the Act, such as 'related persons', the definition of a subsidiary, the solvency and liquidity test, the general interpretation of the Act and the types of companies that may be formed.

Chapter 2 deals with the name of a company, the formation of a company, the Memorandum of Incorporation and pre-incorporation contracts. The financial statements of a company, company records and transparency and accountability are also dealt with in this chapter, as are corporate finance, the governance of companies, the winding-up of solvent companies and the deregistration of companies. Chapter 3 contains the enhanced accountability and transparency provisions, particularly those concerning the company secretary, auditor and audit committee.

Chapter 4 regulates the public offerings of the securities of a company and Chapter 5 is concerned with fundamental transactions, including mergers and amalgamations, takeovers and offers. The provisions relating to business rescue and compromises are contained in Chapter 6. Chapter 7 deals with the protection of minority shareholders and the streamlined derivative action together with other remedies, and the enforcement of the Act, including alternative dispute resolution and the role of the Companies and Intellectual Property Commission ('the Companies Commission'). Chapter 8 is concerned with regulatory agencies and Chapter 9 with offences and miscellaneous matters.

The Schedules to the Act regulate inter alia non-profit companies, the conversion of a close corporation into a company and the fundamentally important transitional provisions of the Act.

Insider trading, market manipulation and the regulation of securities trading are contained in the Securities Services Act 36 of 2004. The (draft) regulations to the Companies Act[11] contain important supplementary provisions relating to accountability and transparency, the social and ethics committee, the matters to be included in a prospectus, the financial reporting standards and business rescue, among other matters.

The Act is clearly not a self-contained code and certainly does not consolidate the whole of corporate law. Apart from the Companies Act, there is also the Close Corporations Act 69 of 1984, which is to be amended mainly in order to reduce regulatory arbitrage. A new uniform Insolvency Act is also expected to be introduced to deal with the winding-up of companies. There are, in addition, the common-law principles developed by the courts over the past few centuries and, of course, the King Report on Governance for South Africa 2009 ('the King III Report') and the King Code of Governance for South Africa 2009 ('the Code').

This book is intended to deal principally with core company law concepts and principles. Insider trading and market manipulation traditionally fall outside the purview of core company law. These topics are nevertheless discussed in this book in order to provide a fuller and more comprehensive treatment of company law. At the time of writing, the Companies Amendment Bill, 2010 was still a draft Bill, as

---

[11] Hereafter 'the draft Companies Regulations'. At the time of writing the Regulations were not finalised; they are draft regulations (GN 1664 *GG* 32832 of 22 December 2009).

are the Companies Regulations. Consequently, important provisions of the draft regulations and the proposed amendments to the Act have been discussed mainly in the footnotes, where appropriate.

1.4 SOME IMPORTANT INNOVATIVE FEATURES OF THE ACT

A large number of novel and innovatory provisions are spread throughout the Act. Without in any way being exhaustive, some of the new features of the Act may be adumbrated as follows:

1.4.1 Interpretation, anti-avoidance and substantial compliance

Regarding the general interpretation of the Act, s 5(2) provides that, to the extent that it is appropriate, a court interpreting or applying the Act may consider foreign law. The section is permissive — not peremptory.

Section 5(4) states that, if there is an inconsistency between any provision of the Act or a provision of any other national legislation, the provisions of both Acts apply concurrently to the extent that it is possible to apply and comply with one of the inconsistent provisions without contravening the second. To the extent that this is not possible, then the applicable provisions of the following legislation will prevail:[12]

- Auditing Profession Act 26 of 2005
- Labour Relations Act 66 of 1995
- Promotion of Access to Information Act 2 of 2000
- Promotion of Administrative Justice Act 3 of 2000
- Public Finance Management Act 1 of 1999
- Securities Services Act 36 of 2004
- Banks Act 94 of 1990.[13]

Any conflict between Chapter 8 of the Companies Act, which establishes and deals with the Companies Commission, the Companies Tribunal, the Takeover Regulation Panel ('the Panel') and the Financial Reporting Standards Council, and a provision of the Public Service Act of 1994 (Proclamation 103 of 1994) must be resolved in favour of the latter.[14] In all other instances, the Companies Act will apply, subject to s 118(4), which deals with the Takeover Regulations.[15]

In respect of the general interpretation of the Act, see also the discussion of s 5(1) above, which requires the Act to be interpreted and applied in a manner that gives effect to its numerous purposes (set out in s 7).

---

[12] Except to the extent provided otherwise in s 49(4). It is notable that there is no reference to the Protected Disclosures Act 26 of 2000. See however, s 159 of the Act, which confers additional protection on whistle-blowers.

[13] See the draft Companies Amendment Bill, 2010 (cl 2(1)), which proposes to correct the erroneous definition of the Banks Act in s 1 of the Act.

[14] Section 5(5).

[15] This states that other public regulations will prevail over irreconcilable provisions of the Takeover Regulations or Chapter 5 Part B or C of the Act.

Equally unusual is s 6(1)*(a)* and *(b)*, which empowers a court on the application of the Companies Commission or the Panel[16] to declare 'any' agreement, transaction, arrangement, resolution or provision of a company's Memorandum of Incorporation or rules to be void on the grounds that it is primarily or substantially intended to defeat or *reduce* the effect of a prohibition or a requirement established in terms of an unalterable provision of the Act.

There are three elements to the anti-avoidance provision in s 6(1), namely:

- it must relate to an agreement, transaction, arrangement, resolution or a provision of a company's Memorandum of Incorporation or rules,
- it must be primarily or substantially intended either to defeat or to 'reduce' the effect of a prohibition or requirement,
- the prohibition or requirement must have been established by an unalterable provision of the Act.[17]

A court would have to examine the substance of a transaction, an agreement or arrangement, or a constitutional provision or resolution, as the case may be, to ascertain whether it is designed to circumvent an unalterable prohibition or mandatory requirement. This type of anti-avoidance provision may be common in tax legislation, but it is quite new in company regulation. The provision may also be unnecessarily wide because many shareholder agreements may innocuously 'reduce' the effect of a prohibition of the Act. The anti-avoidance provision is discussed further in later chapters of this book. It is noteworthy at the outset that, in the interest of flexibility, provision is made for the Companies Tribunal to exempt such transactions, constitutional provisions, rules, etc from any prohibition or requirement established by or in terms of an unalterable provision of the Act (s 6(2) and (3)).

A further unusual provision intended to promote flexibility is s 6(8)*(a)* and *(b)*, which introduces a doctrine (if one may call it that) of substantial compliance. According to this provision, if a form of document, record, statement or notice is prescribed by the Act for any purpose, it suffices that the document (or record, statement or notice) satisfies the 'substantive requirements of the prescribed form'. A deviation from the design or content of the prescribed form would not invalidate it unless it would materially and negatively affect the substance of the document, or is such that it may reasonably mislead a person reading it. A similar provision exists in respect of the prescribed manner of delivery of a document, record, statement or notice.[18]

Moreover, a notice or document in terms of the Act may validly be transmitted electronically, provided that this is done in a manner and form that permits the recipient to conveniently print it within a reasonable time and at reasonable cost.[19]

---

[16] Or an exchange in respect of a company listed on that exchange, in terms of cl 5 of the draft Companies Amendment Bill, 2010.

[17] The new approach of the Act in specifying certain of its provisions as alterable or unalterable is discussed further below in 1.4.5.

[18] See s 6(9).

[19] See further s 6(10) and (11).

1.4.2 Company formation

It has only recently been widely acknowledged that company formation is good for the economy. Company formation stimulates commercial activity and the development of the economy. It also facilitates access to capital.

The DTI policy paper[20] thus states:

> Corporations, in various forms, are central to a country's economy and its prosperity, for wealth creation and social renewal.

There is nothing new in this approach. Many decades ago it was stated in *Ballantine on Corporations*:[21]

> The primary purpose of corporation laws is not regulatory. They are enabling acts, to authorize businessmen to organize and operate their business, large or small with the advantages of the corporate mechanism. They are drawn with a view to facilitate efficient management of business and adjustment to the needs of change. They provide the legal frame and financial structure of the intricate corporate device. . . .

This approach is echoed in the DTI policy document[22] where it is stated that '[c]ompany law should be facilitative, enabling and flexible'. There is thus to be a paradigm shift in the underlying basis of our new corporate law system from a prohibitive and restrictive model to an enabling or facilitative one. The new underpinning approach is that the Companies Act should facilitate efficient investment and growth by making it easier to form companies.

Following this new approach, unnecessary hurdles and obstacles that obstruct company formation and make it a cumbersome process have been removed. Company formation has been made easier. Incorporation is no longer seen as the conferral of a state privilege, but rather the exercise by individuals of their constitutional right to freedom of association and freedom of contract.

Only minimal legal requirements for the formation of a company are prescribed by the new Act. Section 13(1) enables single-member profit companies to be formed whether they be private or public companies, although a non-profit company requires a minimum of three persons for its incorporation.

The formation of a company essentially requires the filing of a Notice of Incorporation, containing inter alia details of the directors of the company and a suitable name for the company, which could even be the registration number of the company followed by the expression '(South Africa)' together with the mandatory ending that describes the type of company it is. The Notice of Incorporation informs the Companies Commission of the intention of the incorporators or founder members to form a company for the purpose of having it registered (s 13(1)(*b*) read with s 1 of the Act). The Notice of Incorporation must be filed together with the constitution of the company, known as the Memorandum of Incorporation, and the payment of the prescribed fee.

Under the 1973 Act, the formation of a company required the lodgment of two documents, namely the memorandum of association and the articles of association. This was required for historical reasons related to the unalterability of the

---

[20] Op cit n 5. See the foreword to the document.
[21] Henry Winthrop Ballantine *Ballantine on Corporations* rev ed (1946) 41–2.
[22] Op cit n 5 at 27.

memorandum of association, which was regarded as sacrosanct. There is no longer any reason for two documents. Accordingly, under the new Act only one constitutive document, known as the Memorandum of Incorporation, is mandatory. This document merges into one the previous memorandum and articles of association. This follows modern trends in other jurisdictions. There is nothing to stop the shareholders from also entering into a shareholder agreement. The board of directors has also been given the power to make interim rules that are necessary or incidental to the governance of the company, although such rules would have to be ratified by the shareholders in order to be permanently binding.[23]

Company formation is further facilitated and made less cumbersome by a system of electronic lodgment of documents and electronic filing. There is no need for a trading certificate or a certificate to commence business, nor is there a minimum share capital requirement.[24]

1.4.3 Types of companies

After much controversial debate and discussion, the Act sweeps aside unnecessary complexities relating to the types of companies that may be formed. The Act provides for two broad categories of companies, namely profit companies and non-profit companies, the latter being formed for a public benefit object or a social, cultural, communal or group object. It replaces the current association incorporated under s 21, popularly known as a section 21 company. A non-profit company need not have any members, although it must have a board of directors consisting of at least three directors (s 66(2)*(b)*). A number of Chapters and provisions of the Act do not apply to non-profit companies.[25]

A profit company could be a state-owned company, a public company, a private company or a personal liability company, which is the modern substitute for the incorporated or professional company formed under s 53*(b)* of the 1973 Act. The company's Memorandum of Incorporation in this case must state that it is a personal liability company. A public company, whose shares may or may not be listed on a securities exchange, is defined by default as a profit company that is not a state-owned company, a private company or a personal liability company.

Foreign companies are brought within the purview of the new Act as external companies if they are conducting business or non-profit activities within South Africa.[26] The registration of such foreign companies as external companies serves a useful purpose, including the protection of persons, particularly employees, who have dealings with these companies.

The Close Corporations Act 69 of 1984 is to be preserved with necessary amendments to prevent regulatory arbitrage. No new close corporations may be registered nor will any new conversions to a close corporation be permitted when

---

[23] See s 15(3) and (4).
[24] In the UK, s 763 of the Companies Act 2006 prescribes a minimum share capital of £50 000 for public companies.
[25] See s 10(2).
[26] Section 23.

the new Act comes into force.[27] This dramatic change in policy, insofar as it preserves the close corporation instead of abolishing it, is to be welcomed, because the close corporation has proved to be a very popular type of legal entity and is worth preserving. It has catered for the needs of small (and not so small) businesses more effectively than the private company, and is expected to continue to do so in the case of pre-existing close corporations.

The basis for the approach of preserving existing close corporations while preventing the formation of new close corporations is twofold: First, it represents a compromise between on the one hand abolishing the close corporation entirely, as was originally planned, and on the other hand permitting the formation of close corporations without any restrictions; and secondly, it is expected that the new Act would cater for the needs of small owner-managed companies to an extent that would render the close corporation redundant and unnecessary. Perhaps — time will tell.

1.4.4 Archaic and obsolete concepts and doctrines jettisoned

Many archaic and obsolete concepts and doctrines have finally been abandoned. Most notable of these is the complete abandonment of the remnants of the capital maintenance concept that regards the issued share capital of a company as a permanent fund or a guarantee fund intended for the payment of the claims of the company's creditors.[28] Creditors required a measuring rod by which to assess the company's ability to pay its debts and the issued share capital of the company. In *Carl M Field v Bankers Trust Company and First National City Bank of New York*[29] it was said that the stated capital which a corporation is required to retain serves as a buffer to absorb losses without impairing assets necessary to satisfy all creditors.

Some but not all the offshoots of the capital maintenance concept, such as the rule that a company must pay dividends out of divisible profits or the rule that a company may not repurchase its own shares, were abandoned in 1999.[30] Instead of the capital maintenance concept, the modern twin tests of solvency and liquidity were adopted.

The new Act now completes this process by purging South African company law of all the remnants of the capital maintenance concept, and by adopting the test of solvency and liquidity as one of its core provisions.[31]

---

[27] Schedule 3, item 2. This will entail a repeal of s 27 of the Close Corporations Act to ensure that no company may be converted into a close corporation when the Act comes into force.
Segal
[28] *Ooregum Gold Mining Co of India v Roper* [1892] AC 125 (HL); *Cohen v Segal* 1970 (3) SA 702 (W).
[29] 296 F. 2d 109 (1961) 109.
[30] See the Companies Amendment Act 37 of 1999; FHI Cassim 'The new statutory provisions on company share repurchases: A critical analysis' (1999) 116 *SALJ* 760; FHI Cassim and Rehana Cassim 'The Capital Maintenance Concept and Share Repurchases in South African Law' (2004) 15 *International Company and Commercial Law Review* 188; FHI Cassim 'The Right of a Company to Purchase its own Shares' (1985) 48 *THRHR* 318; *Capitec Bank Ltd v Quorus Holdings Ltd* 2003 (3) SA 302 (W).
[31] For a full discussion see chapter 8: Corporate Finance.

Also jettisoned are the common-law derivative action and the rule in *Foss v Harbottle*,[32] which proclaimed that when a wrong is done to a company, it is the company as a separate legal person, and not its shareholders, that is the proper plaintiff in respect of that wrong. A legal action to redress the wrong must therefore be brought by the company. It was only in certain exceptional circumstances that a shareholder could, if the company failed to institute an action, bring an action on its behalf by way of the common-law derivative action. The Act now abolishes the common-law derivative action and substitutes a new statutory regime to govern derivative actions.

In terms of the new Act, par value shares are to be abandoned subject to a transitional period prescribed by Schedule 5 to the Act.[33] The Transitional Arrangements of the Act in Schedule 5 enable pre-existing par value shares issued by a company to continue in existence subject to regulations made for their conversion into no par value shares.[34] Special provision is also made for pre-existing par value shares issued by a bank.

Non-voting shares, which were prohibited under the 1973 Act, are permitted under the new Act in certain circumstances. Furthermore, the general provisions relating to share buy-backs, the giving of financial assistance by a company for the purchase of its shares and the making of distributions have all been streamlined and the restrictions to which they have thus far been subject have been relaxed.

1.4.5 The constitution of a company and default provisions of the Act

The Memorandum of Incorporation is the sole governing or constitutive document of a company under the new Act, as discussed above. The approach of the Act is to provide only for core company law rules that are mandatory or 'unalterable', and for certain default or 'alterable' rules that would apply unless varied or altered in the company's Memorandum of Incorporation. The default provisions of the Act are directly attributable to the modern approach that company law should be enabling and facilitative (as discussed above), rather than mandatory and restrictive.

The 'alterable' and 'unalterable' provisions of the Act are designed to promote flexibility. This approach enables a company to regulate more effectively the conduct of its affairs by adopting appropriate provisions in its Memorandum of Incorporation. The 'alterable' provisions of the Act may be regarded as default rules. Examples of such default provisions are the formalities for convening board and members' meetings, the period of notice required for meetings, the quorum, the manner in which meetings may be held, and even the threshold majority

---

[32] (1843) 2 Hare 461; 67 ER 189. See further chapter 16: Shareholder Remedies and Minority Protection.
[33] Item 6 of Schedule 5; discussed in chapter 21: Transitional Arrangements.
[34] The draft Companies Regulations op cit n 3 propose that a pre-existing company may not authorise any new par value shares after the Act comes into force. Within five years of the effective date of the Act (ie the date of its coming into force) existing companies must convert their par value shares into no par value shares.

required for company resolutions.[35] In the absence of explicit provisions in the company's Memorandum of Incorporation regulating these matters, the default rules laid down by the Act will apply to the company. This type of approach is a flexible control mechanism. It is the very essence of an enabling statute, which the Act purports to be. A similar approach is also adopted in the Close Corporations Act 69 of 1984. In short, if a company chooses not to alter an alterable provision of the Companies Act, the default provision of the Act will apply to the company.

The distinction between the alterable and unalterable provisions of the Act is nothing other than a distinction between the mandatory and the optional provisions of the Act. The core company law rules must be, and are, mandatory. In accordance with this distinction an 'unalterable provision' is defined in s 1 to mean a provision of the Act that does not expressly contemplate that its effects may be negated, restricted, limited, qualified, extended or otherwise altered in substance or effect by a company's Memorandum of Incorporation or rules. Conversely, an 'alterable provision' means a provision of the Act in which it is expressly contemplated that its effect on a particular company may be negated, restricted, limited, qualified, extended or otherwise altered in substance or effect by the company's Memorandum of Incorporation.

Another way of looking at it is that, apart from the mandatory or unalterable provisions of the Act, a company may 'opt out' of the default provisions if it so chooses. Occasionally in certain sections of the Act an 'opt-in' approach instead of an 'opt-out' approach is adopted. The 'opt-out' approach confers on companies the freedom and the flexibility to deviate from the standard form rules. This does, however, create uncertainty in the application of these rules. The intended effect of this sort of approach is to confer on companies some latitude in the regulation of their internal affairs. This is subject to the overriding principle that each provision of the company's Memorandum of Incorporation must be consistent with the Act and is void to the extent of its inconsistency (s 15(1)).[36]

Under the 'opt-out' approach, corporate law functions as a sort of standard form contract that the parties may freely alter and use for their convenience.[37] This is coupled with some core mandatory rules, such as the fiduciary duties of directors, which, in order to protect shareholders and creditors, no company may opt out of in its constitution and rules.

While default rules may reduce transaction costs for companies and investors, their distinct disadvantage is that they generally apply to all companies irrespective of whether these companies are public or private companies and whether they are listed or not.

This is nevertheless a definite step away from a mandatory structure of corporate law to one that is enabling and facilitative. The issue that has been left unsettled is whether this sort of standard form contract, or 'off the rack' set of terms that the parties may use and modify or alter for their convenience, is the

---

[35] See further chapter 9: Governance and Shareholders.
[36] See further chapter 4: Formation of Companies and the Company Constitution.
[37] Jeffrey N Gordon 'The Mandatory Structure of Corporate Law' (1989) 89 *Columbia Law Review* 1549; Ian Ayres and Robert Gertner 'Filling Gaps in Incomplete Contracts: An Economic Theory of Default Rules' (1989) 99 *Yale LJ* 87.

correct approach for a developing or emerging economy such as ours, or whether it is perhaps more suited to a more developed economy.[38]

1.4.6 Disclosure, transparency and reporting standards

An important aspect of the new Act relates to corporate reporting, disclosure and transparency. Disclosure and transparency remain crucial to a proper corporate law regime and to managerial and directorial accountability. They are still seen to be the best guarantee of fair dealing and the best deterrent to fraud, mistrust and suspicion. Transparency is thought to raise the standards of corporate behaviour. But there must be proper limits, because too much disclosure clogs up the system and is costly. More disclosure does not necessarily mean better disclosure. It is the quality rather than the quantity of corporate reporting that must be improved.[39] A proper balance must be found between adequate disclosure and overregulation.

As far as corporate reporting is concerned, while all companies must prepare annual financial statements, private or non-public companies need no longer have their annual financial statements audited (unless their Memorandums of Incorporation provide otherwise).[40] An independent review by a professional accountant suffices, unless it is a significant private company in terms of its turnover, the nature and extent of its activities, the number of employees and its economic or social impact. In this event, even though it is a private company, it may be required by regulations to have its annual financial statements audited.[41] An independent review is expected to be less rigorous, less onerous and less costly than an audit.[42]

Public companies (and state-owned companies), as part of their more arduous and demanding duty of transparency and disclosure, must have their annual financial statements audited. Additionally, their financial statements must be consistent with the International Financial Reporting Standards of the International Accounting Standards Board. This is commendable, because it promotes the general standardisation of the accounting methods used in financial reporting standards without which there would be no proper basis of comparability.[43] The financial information disclosed by a company is useful only if it is comparable. Hence the importance, among other reasons, of the adoption by public companies of International Financial Reporting Standards.

---

[38] See Bernard Black and Reiner Kraakman 'A Self-Enforcing Model of Corporate Law' (1996) 109 *Harvard LR* 1911 at 1920.

[39] See the UK White Paper 'Modernising Company Law' (July 2002), CMND 5555–1 at para 4.1 p 37.

[40] The 1973 Act required all companies to have their annual financial statements audited. Close corporations were never required to have their annual financial statements audited.

[41] See s 30(2)*(b)* and s 30(7). A non-profit company would in certain circumstances be required to have its annual financial statements audited. See Regulation 29 of the draft Companies Regulations (GN 1664 *GG* 32832 of 22 December 2009 — op cit n 3).

[42] The draft Companies Regulations in Regulation 30(2)*(b)* (op cit n 3) require a private company to have its financial statements independently reviewed if it has assets that in the immediately preceding three years averaged at least R100 million or it had a turnover that averaged at least R200 million in the immediately preceding three years.

[43] See Frank Iacobucci, Marilyn L Pilkington, J Robert, S Prichard *Canadian Business Corporations* (1977) at 368.

A Financial Reporting Standards Council is set up by the Act[44] to advise the Minister on matters relating to the financial reporting standards. It is expected that by giving statutory backing to International Financial Reporting Standards, dubious accounting practices would be minimised if not eliminated altogether.

The Act enhances flexibility by permitting differential reporting standards for different categories of companies.[45] But whatever accounting standard is adopted, the primary requirement is that the company's financial statements must fairly present the state of affairs and the business of the company and explain the financial position of the company.

1.4.7 Related persons

Numerous modern concepts have been introduced by the new Act. These are discussed throughout this book, but the concept of 'related' persons warrants a brief discussion, because it permeates the whole of the Act.

'Related parties' is defined in s 2 of the Act, according to which an 'individual' (ie a natural person) is related to another individual if they are married or live together in a relationship similar to a marriage, or are separated by no more than two[46] degrees of natural or adopted consanguinity or affinity.

An individual is related to a juristic person if that individual directly or indirectly controls the juristic person.[47] A juristic person is related to another juristic person if either of them directly or indirectly controls the other or the business of the other. A holding company and its subsidiary are related to one another and likewise, two companies are related if both companies are controlled by the same person. (The concept of control is defined in s 2(2) of the Act for these purposes.)

In the earlier draft versions of the Companies Bill, 2007 the concept of 'interrelated' persons was defined in s 2(1)*(d)*. Curiously, this provision no longer appears in the Act. Perhaps this unintended consequence would be rectified in amending legislation, because the absence of such definition leaves an unnecessary and easily avoidable lacuna in the law. (See in this regard the draft Companies Amendment Bill, 2010 (cl 2(1)*(p)*).

1.4.8 Mergers and amalgamations

Another entirely new feature of the Act is that it introduces into South African company law the concept of a merger[48] in its true sense, thereby making it possible for one company to be absorbed by another. Alternatively, two or more companies may merge into a new company. An amalgamation or merger is thus, in broad terms, the fusion of two or more companies into one company — which

---

[44] See ss 203 and 204 of the Act.

[45] See s 29(5)*(b)* and *(c)*.

[46] Reduced to two degrees from the proposed three degrees of consanguinity or affinity.

[47] A person 'controls' a company or its business if that company is its subsidiary; or it together with any related or interrelated person has control of a majority of the voting rights of the company; or has the right to appoint directors of the company who control a majority of votes at board meetings; or if that person has the ability to materially influence the policy of the company (s 2(2)). See further chapter 6: Groups of Companies and Related Persons.

[48] The merger provisions of the Act are modelled on the US and particularly on the Delaware General Corporation Law.

could result in either the dissolution or the disappearance of one or more of the companies and/or in the formation of a new company — that would hold all the assets and liabilities previously held by the merging companies. As a result of amendments to the draft Companies Bill, 2007, there is now no difference between a merger and an amalgamation.

Provided that all the merged companies involved would be solvent and liquid[49] upon the implementation of the merger, all that is required for a merger is a merger agreement, shareholder approval by special resolution, notice to creditors and, if required, compliance with the Competition Act 89 of 1998 and/or other relevant legislation. The approval of a court is not generally required, although there are exceptions. It is therefore not a court-driven process.

There are diverse reasons for a merger. The purpose could, for instance, be to build or diversify an existing business or it could simply be the combining of resources. Mergers, within limits, are good for the economy, for wealth creation and for corporate efficiency. For this reason, the merger provisions of the Act are to be welcomed, particularly in a developing economy such as ours.[50]

Shareholders who object to the merger are given new appraisal rights in terms of which they may require the company in which they hold shares to pay them out in cash the fair value of their shares. In this way, a proper balance is drawn between the interests of the merging companies, the shareholders concerned and the economy in general.[51]

1.4.9 Business rescue

The business rescue provisions are some of the most important and innovatory sections of the Act. They are modelled largely but not exclusively on Chapter 11 of the US Bankruptcy Code.[52] The US Bankruptcy Code initiated the modern corporate rescue trend that focuses on the rehabilitation of a business instead of its winding-up.

The business rescue provisions apply to companies and close corporations that are 'financially distressed', in contrast to companies that are insolvent. A company is 'financially distressed' when it appears to be reasonably unlikely that it will be able to pay all its debts as they fall due and payable over a period of six months, or when it appears to be reasonably likely that the company will become insolvent within the ensuing six months.[53] The company is not insolvent at this stage — it is merely experiencing problems of liquidity or cash flow. The six-month period gives the company an opportunity to place itself under business rescue proceedings in order to avoid insolvency or its winding-up.

---

[49] See chapter 8: Corporate Finance.
[50] See further Maleka Femida Cassim 'The Introduction of the Statutory Merger in South African Corporate Law: Majority Rule Offset by the Appraisal Right (Part 1)' (2008) 20 *SA Merc LJ* 1; and (2008) 20 *SA Merc LJ* 147 for Part 2.
[51] See further Maleka Femida Cassim op cit n 50 and Chapter 15: Fundamental Translators, Takeovers and Offers.
[52] Bankruptcy Reform Act 1978.
[53] Section 128(1)(*f*).

The winding-up or shut-down of a company has widespread repercussions for the incumbent management, shareholders and employees of the company, and also for creditors, suppliers and the economy. It is better to attempt to rescue the company than to shut it down. The underlying object of business rescue is to keep a company going as far as possible by reviving or resuscitating it instead of winding it up. When this happens, creditors and suppliers more often than not are left unpaid. The very concept of business rescue thus springs from the realisation that the continued existence of the company — instead of its winding-up — is more beneficial to the economy in general.

But perhaps the most startling aspect of the business rescue provisions is that, despite its far-reaching consequences, a company may without recourse to a court place itself under voluntary business rescue simply by a resolution of the board of directors. Admittedly, there are safeguards against the abuse of this procedure.[54] Business rescue may also be initiated by way of a court order.

When a company is placed under business rescue, it gets vital breathing space while a business rescue plan is implemented by a turnaround expert, called the business rescue practitioner. The practitioner is given full control of the company, even though the incumbent board of directors continues to hold office. The company placed under business rescue automatically obtains a far-reaching but temporary moratorium (with certain exceptions)[55] on legal proceedings instituted against the company. This obviously includes the claims of creditors, but even a guarantee or surety agreement signed by the company is subject to the moratorium. The business rescue practitioner has statutory power to suspend agreements or apply to court to cancel agreements,[56] except employment agreements, entered into by the company.[57] This leaves the plaintiff with a claim for damages only.

The effect of the moratorium is that even inept directors get the benefit of the moratorium, even if they had been the cause of the mismanagement of the company and its financial problems. When the company is placed under business rescue and the existing management and directors remain in office, they become subject to supervision by the business rescue practitioner. They are then required to assist and to co-operate with the business rescue practitioner.

Employees and trade unions are regarded as important stakeholders and are given a vital role in business rescue proceedings. During this time they have much more say than when the company is functioning normally. Employees generally continue to be employed on the same terms and conditions, and may not be retrenched unless applicable labour legislation is complied with.[58] Employees are treated as preferred unsecured creditors to the extent of unpaid remuneration that

---

[54] 'Affected persons', ie shareholders, creditors and employees or a trade union, are entitled to object to the business rescue resolution.

[55] That is, a freezing of claims, including a freeze on legal proceedings, except criminal proceedings as well as certain other exceptions.

[56] The right to cancel agreements is to be curtailed by the Companies Amendment Bill, 2010. For a discussion see chapter 18: Business Rescue and Compromises.

[57] Section 136(2).

[58] See further chapter 18: Business Rescue and Compromises.

had become due and payable before the commencement of business rescue. The claims of employees to unpaid remuneration that became due and payable during the business rescue must be paid before any other post-commencement finance (even if secured) and all unsecured claims.

The moratorium makes inroads into the fundamental precept of the sanctity of contracts, but this is essential in order to give a financially distressed company the opportunity to recover. If the entire process is not completed within a period of three months (although a longer period may be granted by the court when necessary), the practitioner must prepare a report on the progress of the business rescue and update it monthly. The temporary supervision of the company and the temporary moratorium coupled with a business rescue plan are all designed to rehabilitate the company.

It is also clear from the very nature of the process that the skill, experience and integrity of the business rescue practitioner are fundamental to its success. He or she has full management control of the company. A safeguard against abuse is that the business rescue practitioners' profession will be regulated.[59]

The prime function of the business rescue practitioner is to draw up a business rescue plan that is acceptable to and approved by the creditors.[60] If shareholder rights are altered by the business rescue plan, a majority of (the voting rights of) the holders of the affected classes of shares would also have to approve the business rescue plan. Employees of the company would have to be consulted and be taken into account in the business rescue plan. Once the requisite majority approves the business rescue plan, it becomes binding on all parties. The business rescue plan is of great importance because it is designed to lead the company out of its financial difficulties and place it on the path to recovery.

A new profession of business rescue practitioners or turnaround specialists would have to evolve in South Africa. The profession would have to be regulated by prescribed qualifications and licensing. New skills have to be developed to resuscitate financially distressed companies. These special skills would be quite different from those of the liquidator of a company, who dismantles rather than rescues a company.

The new business rescue provisions of the Act are undoubtedly a considerable improvement on the judicial management model that previously applied in our law.[61]

1.4.10 The directors of a company

For the first time in our corporate law regime, the common-law fiduciary duties of directors as developed by the courts over the past 200 years are to be set out in the Companies Act. This statutory statement of the duties of directors is by no means an original idea — it follows the approach adopted in Australia, New Zealand and

---

[59] There are other safeguards.
[60] Section 152(2).
[61] See *Le Roux Hotel Management (Pty) Ltd v East Rand (Pty) Ltd (FBC Fidelity Bank Ltd (under curatorship) Intervening)* 2001 (2) SA 727 (C) at para 37 where it was stated: 'The concept of judicial management was introduced into South African law in the Companies Act 46 of 1926 as a business rescue provision.'

the United Kingdom. The disadvantage of this approach is that it is a 'one size fits all' approach.

The object of this partial codification of the fiduciary duties of directors is to ensure that directors are made aware of their fiduciary duties instead of having to find these duties in the complex and inaccessible decisions of the courts. Regrettably, it is open to serious doubt whether this object will be achieved. On the contrary, there will be more, not less complexity. The common-law fiduciary duties of directors and the extensive body of case law relating to these duties have been preserved, so that the fiduciary duties of directors will now be derived from two sources instead of just one. Apart from this, the statutory statement of directors' duties is not only incomplete, it is poorly drafted.

The directors' fiduciary duties are fundamental to any developed corporate law system. Their object is to raise standards of corporate or directorial behaviour. The typical fiduciary duties of directors are the duty of good faith and loyalty, and the duty to act in the best interests of the company. Directors also have a duty to exercise reasonable care and skill. At the same time, the opportunity was taken to afford directors wider protection against liability for poor business decisions or errors of judgment by the adoption of a new US-style Business Judgment Rule and also by a very conservative enlargement of the scope for indemnification for directors.[62]

As a further example of the modernisation of our corporate law system, directors who fail to comply with their duties may be placed under probation by a court or be declared delinquent, both of which could have some dire consequences for the miscreant director.

1.4.11 The enlightened shareholder value approach[63]

One of the most fiercely debated issues in company law is the role of a company in society. In South African law, the Act has resolved the issue by requiring directors to perform their duties and exercise their powers in the best interests of the 'company'.[64] By 'company' is meant the interests of the collective body of the shareholders of the company. This implicitly rejects the pluralist approach.[65]

The interests of stakeholders, such as creditors, employees, customers, suppliers, the environment and the local community in which the company operates, are subordinate to shareholder interests. These interests may be taken into account only when it is in the interests of the company itself. In the event of a clash between the interests of shareholders and the interests of stakeholders, it is the interests of shareholders that must prevail. The interests of stakeholders have received no formal recognition (subject to some exceptions) under the Act even though modern responsible corporate behaviour requires that directors consider

---

[62] For a discussion of these new provisions, see further chapter 12: The Duties and the Liability of Directors.

[63] See Rehana Cassim and Femida Cassim 'The Reform of Corporate Law in South Africa' (2005) 16 *International Company and Commercial Law Review* 411 for a discussion of the enlightened shareholder value and pluralist approach.

[64] See s 76(3)(*b*).

[65] See further below. See also chapter 12: The Duties and the Liability of Directors.

and take into account the importance of fostering and nurturing a good, positive relationship with employees, customers, suppliers, creditors and the environment. The underlying basis of this view is that a good corporate reputation is a corporate asset and by taking into account the interests of stakeholders, the interests of the company are thereby enhanced. Companies can and do, in fact, create wealth while at the same time paying heed to the interests of society, the community in which they operate and the environment.

This in essence is the enlightened shareholder approach. The South African approach appears to be that stakeholders must look to separate and specific legislation, rather than to the Act, for the protection of their interests.[66]

The promotion of stakeholder interests has been left largely to the King III Report and the Code, which strongly recommend the 'triple bottom line' or 'intergrated' approach.[67] This is buttressed by s 72(4) of the Act, which empowers the Minister to prescribe that certain types of companies, including significant[68] private companies, must, if this is in the interests of the public, appoint a social and ethics committee. Regulation 50 of the draft Companies Regulations[69] requires all public and state-owned companies (unless exempted) to appoint a social and ethics committee. The function of this committee is to monitor the company's contribution to the development of the community in which it conducts most of its activities, including the company's environment, health, public safety and consumer relationships.

1.4.12 The capacity of a company

The 1973 Act required every company to state in its memorandum of association, the main object for which the company was formed.[70] This served the purpose of defining the capacity of the company. This capacity was automatically by operation of law, augmented by conferring on the company unlimited objects ancillary to its main object.[71]

Tied to this was the common-law *ultra vires* doctrine, according to which any business activity that fell outside the scope of the company's main object was absolutely null and void, and could not be ratified even by the unanimous assent of all the members of the company.[72]

---

[66] See Rehana Cassim and Femida Cassim op cit n 63 at 412.

[67] That is, companies must have regard for social, economic and environmental factors. This requires companies to take into consideration the interests of all stakeholders. It is certainly important for companies to be environmentally accountable.

[68] That is, having regard to its annual turnover, the number of employees, the nature and extent of its activities and the public interest.

[69] Op cit n 3.

[70] Section 52(1)(*b*) of the 1973 Act.

[71] See s 33(1) of the 1973 Act.

[72] *Ashbury Railway Carriage and Iron Co v Riche* (1875) L.R. 7 H.L 653. See FHI Cassim 'The Rise, Fall and Reform of the Ultra Vires Doctrine' (1998) 10 *SA Merc LJ* 293.

The Companies Act of 2008 modernises and streamlines the *ultra vires* doctrine, as well as the Turquand Rule[73] and abolishes the doctrine of constructive notice.[74]

The Act adopts the modern approach that it is archaic to restrict the company to a specific business activity. It accordingly confers on all companies the legal powers and the capacity of an individual,[75] except to the extent that the company's Memorandum of Incorporation provides otherwise. The *ultra vires* doctrine has been castigated as one of the most confused branches of corporate law,[76] and will fortunately no longer apply to a company unless its Memorandum of Incorporation restricts its capacity.

Likewise, the archaic and troublesome doctrine of constructive notice has been abolished.[77] According to the doctrine of constructive notice, persons dealing with a company were presumed to have knowledge of the public documents of the company, such as its constitution, because these documents were open to public inspection. Sadly, however, a muted version of this doctrine continues to apply to companies that specify any special or restrictive conditions in their Memorandums of Incorporation (prohibiting or restricting the amendment of certain provisions), and to the personal liability of the directors and former directors of a personal liability company.

1.4.13 Shareholder remedies

There are new and more effective remedies for minority shareholders. This section does not propose to discuss them in detail but merely to introduce the main remedies. Important remedies available to minority shareholders (and others) are as follows:

(a) Derivative action

Section 165 of the Act abolishes the common-law derivative action[78] and the rule in *Foss v Harbottle*[79] as well as s 266 of the 1973 Act. Instead, the new Act substitutes, for the previous s 266, a more modern and hopefully more effective statutory derivative action on which a shareholder, director, prescribed officer, a trade union or employee representative or any other person with the leave of the court may rely, in order to institute legal proceedings to protect the legal interests of the company.

---

[73] Derived from *Royal British Bank v Turquand* (1856) 6 E & B 327; 119 ER 886. The rule is preserved by s 20(7) and 20(8) of the Act. See chapter 5: Corporate Capacity, Agency and the Turquand Rule.

[74] Discussed in chapter 5: Corporate Capacity, Agency and the Turquand Rule.

[75] This finally puts to rest the dictum of the court in *Bonanza Creek Goldmining Co v R* [1916] AC 566 at 577 that the legislature did not intend to create a company with a capacity resembling that of a natural person.

[76] Ballantine 'Recent Legislative Developments' (1927) 15 *California LR* 422. 'The mischievous doctrine of ultra vires has long been in almost hopeless confusion' (Ballantine op cit n 21 at 241).

[77] See s 19(4).

[78] That is, the common-law right of a person other than the company to institute legal proceedings on behalf of the company.

[79] See n 33.

A director, who has for instance committed some wrong against the company or is otherwise in breach of his or her fiduciary duty to the company, could well face a derivative action instituted (in terms of s 165) against him or her by a minority shareholder to protect the interests of the company. In order to obtain the leave of the court for derivative proceedings, the minority shareholder must be in good faith, the derivative proceedings launched by him or her must be in the company's best interests, and it must relate to a serious question of material consequence to the company. This requirement, together with s 165(11) which empowers a court to require security for costs, would deter vexatious or frivolous actions against a director of the company.[80]

The Act thus attempts to draw a proper balance between the protection of minority shareholders and the harassment of the directors of a company. Section 165 offers ample scope for judicial control of the new derivative action.

(b) *Order to have a director declared a delinquent director or place him or her under probation*

The Act enables a company, shareholder, director, company secretary or prescribed officer,[81] a registered trade union or an employee representative, or even the Companies Commission, the Panel[82] or an organ of State to apply to court for an order declaring a director of a company[83] to be a delinquent director or to put the director under probation (s 162).

A director who has for instance grossly abused the position of director or who has intentionally or by gross negligence inflicted harm upon the company or a subsidiary (contrary to s 76(2)(*a*)) could be declared by the court to be a delinquent director, or could be placed under probation if he or she has, among other things, acted in a manner that is materially inconsistent with the duties of a director. The immediate effect of an order of delinquency is that the director becomes disqualified for a period of seven years or longer, and in some case even for his or her lifetime, to hold office as a director.[84] A delinquent director or one placed under probation could in terms of s 162(10) be ordered also to undertake a designated programme of remedial education or carry out a designated programme of community service, or even compensate a person who is adversely affected by his or her conduct as a director to the extent that such a person does not otherwise have a legal basis to claim compensation.

(c) *Oppressive or unfairly prejudicial conduct*

A shareholder or director, but not a creditor or an employee, of the company may apply to court for relief if any act or omission of the company or of a related

---

[80] See also s 165(3).
[81] 'Prescribed officers' are the holders of an office within a company that has been designated by the Minister in terms of s 66(10). Certain company officers perform functions that are of sufficient importance to be subjected to the accountability standards and the fiduciary duties of company directors.
[82] But not a creditor.
[83] And even a person who was a director within the 24 months preceding the application.
[84] Section 69(8)(*a*).

person[85] is oppressive or unfairly prejudicial to the applicant or unfairly disregards his or her interests (s 163). The same applies where the conduct of the business of the company or a related person (eg a subsidiary), or the exercise of the powers of a director or prescribed officer[86] of the company or a related person, is or has been oppressive or unfairly prejudicial to the minority shareholder (or applicant) or unfairly disregards his or her interests.

The court is given very wide powers to remedy the grievance, including an order to pay compensation to the aggrieved person.[87]

(d) A declaratory order

A shareholder or securities holder may apply to court for a declaratory order determining any rights of that shareholder or securities holder (s 161). This remedy may also be relied upon to protect any right of a shareholder or securities holder or to rectify harm done to him or her. This is a new remedy in South African companies legislation.

(e) Appraisal rights

Fundamental to the new philosophical approach to modern company law are the appraisal rights of dissenting shareholders, as provided for by s 164.

The appraisal rights of shareholders are an exit mechanism for disgruntled shareholders who do not wish to remain shareholders of the company.[88] Minority shareholders are no longer locked in a company in the event of fundamental transactions or alterations of class rights.

When a company enters into a merger or amalgamation or a scheme of arrangement, or disposes of all or the greater part of its assets or undertaking, or where the company amends its Memorandum of Incorporation in a manner that is materially adverse to the rights or interests of that class of shareholders, dissenting shareholders may exercise their appraisal rights by demanding that the company purchases their shares and compensates them in cash for the fair value of their shares, as determined initially by the company or, failing that, then by the court.

Shareholders would only exercise their appraisal rights if they do not wish to remain shareholders of the company. A number of requirements must be strictly complied with before a dissenting shareholder becomes entitled to demand the fair value of his or her shares in cash.[89] The procedure is unnecessarily complex and calls for strict compliance with the requisite procedural steps before a shareholder becomes entitled to exercise his or her appraisal rights.[90]

---

[85] See above 1.4.7.
[86] See above.
[87] Section 163(2)(*j*).
[88] See Maleka Femida Cassim Part 2 op cit n 50 at 157–174.
[89] See s 164(3)–(8).
[90] See Maleka Femida Cassim Part 2 op cit n 50 at 159–60 and chapter 15: Fundamental Transactions, Takeovers and Offers.

(f) Piercing the veil of corporate personality

The Act[91] adopts a similar provision to s 65 of the Close Corporations Act 69 of 1984, which entitles a court on application by an interested person or otherwise in any legal proceedings in which a company is involved, to disregard the separate legal personality of the company where there has been an 'unconscionable abuse of the juristic personality of the company as a separate entity . . .'.

The difficulty with this section is that it creates uncertainty, because one can never be sure whether a particular act constitutes an 'unconscionable abuse' of the juristic personality of a company.[92]

1.4.14 Alternative dispute resolution

There are now four alternative means for addressing contraventions of the Act or enforcing rights. The new Companies Commission, which replaces the present Companies and Intellectual Property Registration Office (CIPRO), will play a much more active role in ensuring that companies comply with the mandatory provisions of the Act.[93] In terms of the Act, the Companies Commission may initiate or receive complaints regarding alleged contraventions of the Act or infringements of rights. The Panel (ie the Takeover Regulation Panel) may also receive complaints on matters within its jurisdiction.

In addition to the Companies Commission, the Act sets up a new and independent Companies Tribunal which may resolve disputes with or within a company. The Companies Tribunal would thus serve as an alternative dispute resolution forum through mediation, conciliation or arbitration.

Apart from its role in alternative dispute resolution, the Companies Tribunal must also adjudicate disputes brought before it in terms of specific provisions of the Act.[94] It must also perform any other functions assigned to it by the Act or any other law.[95] Thus a shareholder may, instead of resorting to a court for relief, refer the matter to the Companies Tribunal for adjudication where the Act so provides.[96]

1.4.15 Enforcement

Enforcement is of pivotal importance. All legal rules are ineffective unless they are enforced. But enforcement is more about compliance than about force.

The new Act has been largely decriminalised. It does not rely as extensively on criminal sanctions and penalties as the 1973 Act. The 1973 Act created a large number of criminal offences, many of which were never prosecuted in practice. This was compounded by the fact that criminal offences also require a higher burden of proof. The result was that many of these technical criminal offences

---

[91] Section 163(4). See also the draft Companies Amendment Bill, 2010, which proposes to shift this provision to s 20 of the Act.
[92] See further chapter 2: The Legal Concept of a Company. The Companies Amendment Bill, 2010 proposes to re-insert this provision in s 20(9) of the Act.
[93] See further 1.4.15 on enforcement.
[94] Section 195(1)(*a*).
[95] See Schedule 4 to the Act.
[96] Section 156(*b*).

were simply not enforced. There is no point in having criminal sanctions if these are not applied.

The object of decriminalising company law is not to trivialise the importance of effective sanctions for non-compliance, but instead to ensure more effective enforcement.

However, the Act is not entirely devoid of criminal penalties. Some criminal sanctions have been preserved and new ones introduced on the underpinning basis that criminal penalties are indispensable deterrents to fraud and dishonesty. The criminal penalties also serve to underscore the gravity of the offence. But the difference in approach now is that the new Act makes much more effective use of non-criminal sanctions.

The Act does attempt to keep criminal penalties to a minimum. It relies on a combination of criminal penalties, civil remedies and administrative fines for enforcement. Many of the criminal offences relate to the falsification of accounting records, the publication of false or misleading information and, more importantly, the financial reporting standards that companies must comply with. Criminal liability has also been imposed on the 'preparers' of financial statements who know that these statements are materially false, misleading or incomplete in a material respect. If properly utilised, criminal sanctions would result in higher compliance levels.

Overall responsibility for monitoring compliance with the Act is placed on the Companies Commission. Any person, including stakeholders ranging from the company secretary, shareholders, directors, trade unions or employee representatives, may lodge complaints with the Companies Commission. The Companies Commission may also act on its own initiative. It may investigate alleged contraventions of the Act and may appoint an investigator or inspector to investigate the complaint.

After investigating an alleged contravention of the Act or an infringement of the rights of the complainant, the Companies Commission may inter alia decide to terminate the matter, refer the matter to the National Prosecuting Authority or other regulatory authority, or resolve to issue a compliance notice. Failure to comply with a compliance notice could result in an administrative fine levied by the court, which may not exceed the greater of 10 per cent of the company's turnover during the period that the company failed to comply with the compliance notice, and the maximum fine prescribed by regulations.[97] Failure to comply with a compliance notice could alternatively result in a referral for prosecution by the National Prosecuting Authority. This means that, despite the decriminalisation of the Act, a failure to comply with a compliance notice could result in a criminal sanction.

1.5 CONCLUSION

The Companies Act of 2008 is the outcome of over six years of deliberation, discussion and debate. While the Act will undoubtedly remove some of the complexities of the 1973 Act, inevitably new complexities will take their place.

---

[97] Section 175; draft Regulation 174 op cit n 3 lays down a maximum fine of R1 million.

The Act is still in need of more refinement. The draft Companies Amendment Bill, 2010 is a major step towards this. The Act introduces a fresh and modernised approach to corporate rescue, mergers and amalgamations and the new appraisal rights of dissenting shareholders.

It is widely acknowledged nowadays that the corporate law system of a country must take into account that country's economic organisations, its political and social structures as well as its history and cultural values.[98] We have had the advantage of following the example of other jurisdictions that have already modernised their corporate law systems. It remains to be seen whether we have successfully adopted the best of other modernised jurisdictions,[99] and to what extent the new Act has taken into account our specific economic and political structures, including our cultural values.[100]

---

[98] See Troy A Paredes 'A Systems Approach to Corporate Governance Reform: Why Importing U.S. Corporate Law isn't the Answer' (2003–4) 45 *William & Mary Law Review* 1055.

[99] Tshediso Matona, Director-General, Trade and Industry, in his keynote address at the Conference on 'South African Law for the 21st Century' Pretoria, 19 March 2007, said 'the [Companies] Bill has taken the best out of best practice jurisdictions . . .'.

[100] See FHI Cassim 'The Companies Act, 2008: An Overview of a Few of its Core Provisions' (2010) 22 *SA Merc LJ* 157–75.

CHAPTER 2

THE LEGAL CONCEPT OF A COMPANY

Rehana Cassim

2.1 INTRODUCTION 27
2.2 DEFINITION OF A 'COMPANY' 27
2.3 LEGAL PERSONALITY 28
    2.3.1 The concept of separate legal personality 28
    2.3.2 *Salomon v Salomon & Co Ltd* 30
    2.3.3 Legal consequences of separate legal personality 31
        (a) Limited liability 31
        (b) Perpetual succession 32
        (c) Property and assets of the company belong to the company 33
        (d) Profits of the company belong to the company 34
        (e) Debts and liabilities of the company belong to the company 35
        (f) A shareholder has no right to manage the company's business or to enter into transactions on its behalf 36
        (g) Company can sue or be sued in its own name 36
        (h) Company may contract with its shareholders 37
2.4 EXCEPTIONS TO THE PRINCIPLE OF SEPARATE LEGAL PERSONALITY 38
    2.4.1 Examples of the abuse of separate legal personality 39
        (a) Where separate legal personality was used as a device by a director to evade his or her fiduciary duty 40
        (b) Where separate legal personality was used to overcome a contractual duty 40
    2.4.2 The distinction between piercing the veil and lifting the veil . 42
    2.4.3 The approach adopted to piercing the veil in our common law .. 44
    2.4.4 Domestic companies 47
    2.4.5 Agency/Alter ego doctrine 48
    2.4.6 Company groups 50
    2.4.7 Piercing the corporate veil under the Act 54
        (a) 'Application' or 'proceedings' 55
        (b) 'Interested person' 55
        (c) Incorporation of the company, act by or on behalf of the company or the use of the company 56
        (d) 'Unconscionable abuse' 56
        (e) 'Deemed not to be a juristic person' 59

		(f)	Rights, obligations or liabilities.................	59
		(g)	Further orders..................................	59
	2.4.8		Imposing personal liability on the directors of a company....	60
		(a)	Acting without authority.........................	60
		(b)	Reckless trading................................	60
		(c)	Fraud	61
		(d)	False or misleading statements	61
		(e)	Unlawful distributions...........................	61
		(f)	Causing the company to act contrary to the Companies Act or the Memorandum of Incorporation............	61
		(g)	Contravening the Companies Act	61

2.1 INTRODUCTION

The foundation of company law rests on the concept that a company has a separate legal personality. Several consequences flow from this concept, such as the privilege of limited liability bestowed on shareholders; perpetual succession of a company; the fact that the property, profits, debts and liabilities of the company belong to it and not to the shareholders, and the fact that a company may sue and be sued in its own name, to name a few. But the separate legal personality of a company has often been abused. This has been recognised by both the courts and the legislature, which have made exceptions to this sacrosanct principle in order to curb extreme cases of abuse, in the form of the doctrine of piercing the corporate veil. These issues are explored in this chapter.

2.2 DEFINITION OF A 'COMPANY'

A 'company' is defined in s 1 of the Companies Act 71 of 2008 (hereafter 'the Act') as meaning:

> a juristic person incorporated in terms of this Act, or a juristic person that, immediately before the effective date —
> *(a)* was registered in terms of the —
>   (i) Companies Act, 1973 (Act No. 61 of 1973), other than as an external company as defined in that Act; or
>   (ii) Close Corporations Act, 1984 (Act No. 69 of 1984), if it has subsequently been converted in terms of Schedule 2;
> *(b)* was in existence and recognised as an 'existing company' in terms of the Companies Act, 1973 (Act No. 61 of 1973); or
> *(c)* was deregistered in terms of the Companies Act, 1973 (Act No. 61 of 1973), and has subsequently been re-registered in terms of this Act.[1]

This definition makes it clear that the Act applies both to companies formed under the Companies Act of 2008 and to companies formed under the Companies Act of

---

[1] The draft Companies Amendment Bill, 2010 proposes to include 'domesticated companies' in the definition of a 'company' (see cl 2(1) of the draft Companies Amendment Bill, 2010). A 'domesticated company' is a foreign company whose registration has been transferred to South Africa in terms of s 13(5)–(9). Under s 13(5) a foreign company may apply to transfer its registration to South Africa from the foreign jurisdiction in which it is registered, and thereafter exist as a company in terms of the Act as if it had been originally so incorporated and registered. See further chapter 3: Types of Companies.

1973 (hereafter 'the 1973 Act'). The Companies Act of 2008 would also apply to close corporations that have been converted into companies under Schedule 2 of the Act. On the registration of a company converted from a close corporation, the juristic person that existed as a close corporation before the conversion continues to exist as a juristic person, but in the form of a company.[2]

2.3 LEGAL PERSONALITY

2.3.1 The concept of separate legal personality

At the heart of company law is the concept of a company as a separate legal person. What is a legal person? All human beings are legal persons, which means they have the capacity to acquire legal rights and incur legal duties. But the essential difference between a legal person and a human person is that a legal person is merely a legal concept and as such has no physical existence. In the famous oft-quoted words attributed to Lord Chancellor Baron Thurlow in the late 18th century, a company has 'no soul to damn and no body to kick'.[3]

A legal or juristic person cannot perform acts that are inherently human in nature — such as entering into a marriage, occupying land,[4] appearing in court in person,[5] or being appointed the guardian of a minor, since the relationship between guardian and ward is a personal one that necessitates personal contact and a human relationship.[6] But even though a legal person is merely a legal concept and as such has no physical existence, it does possess its own legal personality to acquire rights and incur obligations that are distinct from those of the directors and shareholders of the company. This is known as the concept of separate legal personality.

The separate legal personality of a company is affirmed in s 19(1)(b) of the Act. This section states that, from the date and time that the incorporation of a company is registered, the company has all the legal powers and capacity of an individual, except to the extent that a juristic person is incapable of exercising any such power or having any such capacity, or except to the extent that the company's Memorandum of Incorporation provides otherwise.

The Constitution of the Republic of South Africa, 1996 provides in s 8(4) that a company is entitled to the same fundamental rights as natural persons insofar as these may be exercised by a juristic person. The section provides as follows:

---

[2] See s 2(2)(a) of Schedule 2 of the Act.

[3] This statement of Lord Chancellor Thurlow does not appear in any of his reported judgments and has not been tracked to a primary source. See also *Commissioner for Inland Revenue v Richmond Estates (Pty) Ltd* 1956 (1) SA 602 (A) 606; *Manong & Associates (Pty) Ltd v Minister of Public Works* 2010 (2) SA 167 (SCA) para 4; *Lennard's Carrying Co Ltd v Asiatic Petroleum Co Ltd* [1914–15] All ER Rep 280 (HL) 283; *Re GJ Mannix Ltd* [1984] 1 NZLR 309 at 311 and *Northern Homes Ltd v Steel-Space Industries Ltd* (1976) 57 DLR (3d) 309 para 22.

[4] *Madrassa Anjuman Islamia v Johannesburg Municipal Council* 1919 AD 439.

[5] *Yates Investments (Pty) Ltd v Commissioner for Inland Revenue* 1956 (1) SA 364 (A); *Manong & Associates (Pty) Ltd v Minister of Public Works* 2010 (2) SA 167 (SCA) para 4.

[6] *Ex parte Donaldson* 1947 (3) SA 170 (T) 173.

> A juristic person is entitled to the rights in the Bill of Rights to the extent required by the nature of the rights and the nature of that juristic person.[7]

Thus s 8(4) of the Constitution renders the Bill of Rights applicable to juristic persons. A juristic person accordingly has the right to be treated equally to other persons, and may sue for defamation if its reputation is injured,[8] or to protect its right to privacy.[9] But it doesn't have the right to human dignity[10] or the right to life. The Constitutional Court did however caution against equating the right to privacy of a juristic person with that of a natural person in *Investigating Directorate: Serious Economic Offences v Hyundai Motor Distributors (Pty) Ltd; In re Hyundai Motor Distributors (Pty) Ltd v Smit NO*[11] as follows:

> As we have seen, ... privacy is a right which becomes more intense the closer it moves to the intimate personal sphere of the life of human beings, and less intense as it moves away from that core. This understanding of the right flows ... from the value placed on human dignity by the Constitution. Juristic persons are not the bearers of human dignity. Their privacy rights, therefore, can never be as intense as those of human beings. However, this does not mean that juristic persons are not protected by the right to privacy ... Juristic persons ... do enjoy the right to privacy, although not to the same extent as natural persons.[12]

As a matter of general policy, the courts have, in the sphere of personality rights, tended to equate the respective positions of natural and legal persons where it is possible and appropriate for this to be done.[13]

An understanding of the concept of the separate legal existence of a company is crucial to the understanding of company law as a whole. The leading case on the separate legal personality of a company, which is probably the most famous case in and the cornerstone of company law, is that of *Salomon v Salomon & Co Ltd*,[14] which is discussed below. This was the first case to establish the principle that a

---

[7] See also s 8(2) of the Bill of Rights of the Constitution of the Republic of South Africa, 1996, which states that a provision in the Bill of Rights binds a natural or juristic person if, and to the extent that it is applicable, taking into account the nature of the right and the nature of any duty imposed by the right.

[8] *Dhlomo v Natal Newspapers (Pty) Ltd* 1989 (1) SA 945 (A); *Caxton Ltd v Reeva Forman (Pty) Ltd* 1990 (3) SA 547 (A); *Financial Mail (Pty) Ltd v Sage Holdings Ltd* 1993 (2) SA 451 (A) 461–2. In *Financial Mail (Pty) Ltd v Sage Holdings Ltd* 1993 (2) SA 451 (A) the Appellate Division stated that, although a corporation has no feelings to outrage or offend, it has a reputation in respect of business or other activities in which it is engaged that could be damaged by defamatory statements, and that it is only proper that a corporation should be afforded the usual legal processes for vindicating that reputation (at 462). In *Dhlomo v Natal Newspapers (Pty) Ltd* (supra) it was held that the remedy of a defamatory action may be available to a non-trading corporation as well (such as a benevolent society or a religious organisation) if the defamatory statement is calculated to cause financial prejudice to it.

[9] See for example *Financial Mail (Pty) Ltd v Sage Holdings Ltd* 1993 (supra) at 462; *Investigating Directorate: Serious Economic Offences v Hyundai Motor Distributors (Pty) Ltd; In re Hyundai Motor Distributors (Pty) Ltd v Smit NO* 2001 (1) SA 545 (CC) para 17 and *Platinum Asset Management (Pty) Ltd v Financial Services Board; Anglo Rand Capital House (Pty) Ltd v Financial Services Board* 2006 (4) SA 73 (W) 106–7.

[10] *Investigating Directorate: Serious Economic Offences v Hyundai Motor Distributors (Pty) Ltd: In re Hyundai Motor Distributors (Pty) Ltd v Smit NO* (supra) para 18.

[11] 2001 (1) SA 545 (CC).

[12] Para 18.

[13] *Financial Mail (Pty) Ltd v Sage Holdings Ltd* (supra) at 461.

[14] [1897] AC 22 (HL).

company is a separate legal person quite distinct from its shareholders and directors and that shareholders are in principle not liable for the debts and liabilities of the company.

2.3.2 *Salomon v Salomon & Co Ltd*

The facts of *Salomon* are that Mr Aron Salomon was a sole trader for many years and had carried on a prosperous business as a leather merchant and wholesale boot manufacturer. He wished to expand his business and wanted to enjoy the benefits of limited liability and perpetual succession.[15] Accordingly, he sold his business to a company with a nominal capital of 40 000 shares of £1 each. Salomon, his wife, daughter and four sons were shareholders in the company, with each of them subscribing for one £1 share in the company. Salomon and two of his sons were directors of the company. In payment of the purchase price of £39 000 the company issued 20 000 fully paid shares of £1 each to Salomon, £9 000 was paid in cash and for the balance of £10 000 the company issued debentures secured over its assets to Salomon.[16] The terms of the sale were approved by all the shareholders of the company. Salomon thus held 20 001 out of the 20 007 shares issued by the company. He was a secured creditor, a controlling shareholder, a director and an employee of the company. The company's business failed and a year later it went into liquidation. It was found that if the amount realised from the assets of the company were to be applied in payment of the debentures held by Salomon there would be no funds left for payment to the ordinary creditors.

The liquidator objected on behalf of the trade creditors and contended that the company was a mere alias or sham and a scheme designed to enable Salomon to conduct his business in the name of the company and thereby to limit his liability for the debts of the company. It was also contended that since Salomon owned all but six of the shares issued by the company, he and the company were one and the same person and that consequently the company's debts were his debts. The liquidator succeeded in the Court of Appeal, which held that the company was Salomon in another form who had employed the company as his agent. The Court of Appeal held further that the company was entitled to be indemnified by Salomon against the claims of the ordinary creditors and that no payment should be made on the debentures held by Salomon until the ordinary creditors had been paid in full.

The House of Lords reversed the decision of the Court of Appeal and unanimously found in favour of Salomon. The House of Lords found that the company had been validly formed and registered. It was therefore a legal person. The court stated that once the company was legally incorporated, it was a completely different person with its own rights and liabilities. The motives of those who took part in the formation of the company were irrelevant in discussing what those rights and liabilities were.[17] The court held further that there was no requirement in the Companies Act of 1862 that required the subscribers to the memorandum to

---

[15] These concepts are discussed below.
[16] A debenture is a written acknowledgment of indebtedness and may be a secured or unsecured debenture.
[17] At 30.

be independent or unconnected, or that required them to take a substantial interest in the company.[18] The court remarked that it was a common practice to have nominee shareholders in a company who did not intend to take part in the company.[19] Lord Macnaghten expressed the legal principle as follows:

> The company is at law a different person altogether from the subscribers to the memorandum; and, though it may be that after incorporation the business is precisely the same as it was before, and the same persons are managers, and the same hands receive the profits, the company is not in law the agent of the subscribers or a trustee for them.[20]

The House of Lords concluded that the secured debentures issued by the company to Salomon as part of the purchase price for his business were valid as against the company's creditors, and that the business belonged to the company and not to Salomon, who was not liable for the debts of the company. Of fundamental importance to the outcome of the case was that there was no fraud on the part of Salomon nor any fraud on the creditors of the company.

Salomon v Salomon & Co Ltd legitimated the one-man company. It showed that incorporation was as readily available to the small private partnership or sole trader as to a large public company.[21] The principles laid down in *Salomon's* case comprise the very gist of the concept of separate legal personality. As the Appellate Division in the leading South African case of *Dadoo Ltd v Krugersdorp Municipal Council*[22] asserted, the 'conception of the existence of a company as a separate entity distinct from its shareholders is no merely artificial and technical thing. It is a matter of substance . . . '.[23]

Section 14(4) of the Act provides that a registration certificate issued by the Companies and Intellectual Property Commission ('the Companies Commission') is conclusive evidence that: *(a)* all the requirements for incorporation have been complied with; and *(b)* the company is incorporated under the Act as from the date, and the time, if any, as stated in the registration certificate. Thus, once the registration certificate has been issued, the company acquires its own separate legal personality. This is confirmed in s 19(1)*(a)* of the Act, which provides that, from the date and time that the incorporation of a company is registered, as stated in its registration certificate, the company is a juristic person that exists continuously until its name is removed from the companies register, or unless, of course, the court decides to pierce the veil of corporate personality. Important legal consequences flow from the separate legal personality of a company, as discussed below.

2.3.3 Legal consequences of separate legal personality

(a) Limited liability

Limited liability means the liability of shareholders for the company's debts is limited to the amount they have paid to the company for its shares. The share-

---
[18] At 50–1.
[19] Ibid.
[20] At 51.
[21] Paul L Davies *Gower and Davies' Principles of Modern Company Law* 8 ed (2008) at 36.
[22] 1920 AD 530.
[23] At 550.

holders are as a general principle not liable for the debts of the company.[24] They are under no obligation to the company or its creditors beyond their obligations based on the value of their shares. The claims of creditors of the company are confined to the assets of the company — the creditors of the company cannot obtain satisfaction of their debts from the personal assets of the shareholders of the company because the debts and liabilities of the company are those of the company alone and not of its shareholders. Section 19(2) of the Act states that a person is not, solely by reason of being an incorporator, shareholder or director of a company, liable for any liabilities or obligations of the company, except to the extent that the Act or the company's Memorandum of Incorporation provides otherwise.

It is the shareholders that enjoy limited liability — not the company, which is fully liable for its debts. It is thus not correct to describe a company as a limited liability company. But note that, in a personal liability company, the directors and past directors are jointly and severally liable, together with the company, for any debts and liabilities of the company that were contracted during their respective periods of office.[25] This is because they expressly undertake personal liability.

The concept of limited liability is a characteristic at the core of company law. Because they enjoy the privilege of limited liability, business people are able to limit the risk of investing funds into a business venture. Thus the concept of limited liability encourages the growth and expansion of companies, which is of crucial importance to the economy because successful companies generate wealth and employment. In *Salomon v Salomon & Co Ltd*[26] Lord Macnaghten stated the following with regard to some of the reasons that induce persons to form companies:

> Among the principal reasons which induce persons to form private companies . . . are the desire to avoid the risk of bankruptcy, and the increased facility afforded for borrowing money. By means of a private company . . . a trade can be carried on with limited liability, and without exposing the persons interested in it in the event of failure to the harsh provisions of the bankruptcy law.[27]

But much potential exists for abusing the privilege of limited liability, as discussed below.

(b) Perpetual succession

A company enjoys a potentially perpetual existence, which means that, notwithstanding changes in its membership, through a transfer of shares, by death or any other cause, the company retains its legal identity and continues to survive.[28] In other words, the existence of a company is not affected by any changes in its membership.

---

[24] See *Airport Cold Storage (Pty) Ltd v Ebrahim* 2008 (2) SA 303 (C) para 6.
[25] See s 19(3) of the Act.
[26] [1897] AC 22 (HL).
[27] At 52.
[28] *Maasdorp v Haddow* 1959 (3) SA 861 (C) 866; *Stern v Vesta Industries (Pty) Ltd* 1976 (1) SA 81 (W) 85.

(c) Property and assets of the company belong to the company

The company's property and assets belong to the company and not to the shareholders.[29] Only once the company is liquidated do the shareholders have a right to share in a division of the company's assets.[30] But a shareholder does have a financial interest in the dividends paid by the company and is entitled to share in the division of the assets of the company that remain after its creditors have been paid, and thus has a financial interest in the success or failure of the company. The contrast between mere pecuniary interest on the one hand and actual legal right on the other is crisply stated in *Stellenbosch Farmers' Winery Ltd v Distillers Corporation (SA) Ltd*[31] as follows:

> The fact that the shareholder is entitled to an *aliquot* share in the distribution of the surplus assets when the company is wound up proves that he is financially interested in the success or failure of the company but not that he has any right or title to any assets of the company.[32]

A company does not hold its property as an agent or trustee of the shareholders — all the property purchased by the company belongs to the company itself and not to its shareholders. Even a shareholder holding all the shares in a private company does not have a proprietary interest in the company's assets.

The principle that property purchased by a company belongs to the company itself and not to its shareholders is clearly illustrated by the leading case of *Dadoo Ltd v Krugersdorp Municipal Council*.[33] Under certain legislation enacted in the then Transvaal province, Indians were prohibited from owning immovable property in the Transvaal. In 1915 a company called 'Dadoo Ltd' was formed with two Indian shareholders: Dadoo, who owned all the shares in the company save for one share, and Dindar, who owned the other share in the company. The company purchased property in Krugersdorp and subsequently let the property out to Dadoo in his personal capacity, where he carried on a general dealer's business. The Krugersdorp Municipal Council contended that the company had contravened the statute prohibiting Indian people from owning immovable property in the Transvaal. The then Appellate Division rejected this argument on the ground that the statute did not apply to companies, even if all the shares of the company were held by Indian people. The court held that ownership by Dadoo Ltd was not in substance ownership by its Indian shareholders, and that property vested in the company was not to be regarded as vested in its shareholders.[34] It followed that the statute in question had not been contravened by the company.[35]

---

[29] *Dadoo Ltd v Krugersdorp Municipal Council* 1920 AD 530 at 550–1; *Macaura v Northern Assurance Co Ltd* [1925] AC 619 (HL(Ir)); *Stellenbosch Farmers' Winery Ltd v Distillers Corporation (SA) Ltd* 1962 (1) SA 458 (A) 471–2; *Francis George Hill Family Trust v South African Reserve Bank* 1992 (3) SA 91 (A) 102; *The Shipping Corporation of India Ltd v Evdomon Corporation* 1994 (1) SA 550 (A) 565–6.
[30] See *Stellenbosch Farmers' Winery Ltd v Distillers Corporation (SA) Ltd* (supra) at 471–2; *S v De Jager* 1965 (2) SA 616 (A) 625.
[31] *Stellenbosch Farmers' Winery Ltd v Distillers Corporation (SA) Ltd* (supra).
[32] At 472.
[33] 1920 AD 530.
[34] At 550–1.
[35] See also *Gumede v Bandhla Vukani Bakithi Ltd* 1950 (4) SA 560 (N), where the court followed *Dadoo's* case in holding that a limited liability company could not be susceptible to a test of race

If the property or assets of a company belong to the company and not to its shareholders, it follows that a shareholder has no legal interest in the company's property and lacks an insurable interest in the company's property. This principle was illustrated in *Macaura v Northern Assurance Co Ltd*.[36]

The facts of this case are that Macaura was the owner of a timber estate. He had sold the timber estate to a company for the amount of £42 000. This amount was paid to him (and his nominees) in the form of 42 000 fully paid shares of £1 each in the company. The company did not issue any further shares to anyone else, which meant that Macaura and his nominees were the only shareholders of the company and that Macaura was the controlling shareholder of the company. Macaura had lent £19 000 to the company to finance the felling of the timber on the estate, and was accordingly also an ordinary unsecured creditor of the company. Macaura insured the timber against fire by means of insurance policies that were taken out in his own name. Most of the timber was subsequently destroyed by fire, but the insurance company refused to pay Macaura on the ground that the timber belonged to the company and not to Macaura, and contended that Macaura had no insurable interest in the timber. The House of Lords upheld the contention of the insurance company and stated as follows:

> He [Macaura] owned almost all the shares in the company, and the company owed him a good deal of money, but, neither as creditor not as shareholder, could he insure the company's assets. The debt was not exposed to fire nor were the shares, and the fact that he was virtually the company's only creditor, while the timber was its only asset, seems to me to make no difference. He stood in no 'legal or equitable relation to' the timber at all. He had no 'concern in' the subject insured. His relation was to the company, not to its goods, and after the fire he was directly prejudiced by the paucity of the company's assets, not by the fire.[37]

Macaura's case illustrates the principle that property owned by a company is not owned by its shareholders and accordingly not even a controlling shareholder or a creditor has a legal right to insure the company's property in his or her own name.[38]

(d) Profits of the company belong to the company

The company's profits belong to the company itself and not to the shareholders.[39] The shareholders have a right to profits only once the company declares a dividend. Not even a sole shareholder of a company may help him- or herself to

---

because a company possesses a legal personality apart from its members. It cannot possess any characteristics which belong to a race of people.

[36] [1925] AC 619 (HL(Ir)).

[37] At 630.

[38] Note that a person who has a lien or security over the company's assets, such as a secured debenture holder, may have a legal interest in the company's assets because his or her debenture would be secured over the company's assets. This would give him or her a commercial interest in the safety of the assets, with the result that he or she may have an insurable interest in the company's assets (see *Macaura v Northern Assurance Co Ltd* (supra) at 630).

[39] *S v De Jager* 1965 (2) SA 616 (A).

the profits of the company, and should he or she do so, he or she would be guilty of the criminal offence of theft.[40]

In *S v De Jager* the accused, who was a director and a shareholder of a public company, was charged with theft for abstracting the company's funds for his own purposes and not for the benefit of the company. His defence was that the crime of theft consists of depriving an owner of his ownership without his consent. He contended that his taking money from the company did not constitute theft because the shareholders of the company, he and Shaban, had agreed to the payments.

The then Appellate Division rejected this defence, and stated that it amounted to the proposition that De Jager, in his capacity as a shareholder, could be a party to the company's agreeing to be despoiled by him in his capacity as director.[41] The court said that this in effect gave a general right to the company to distribute its assets to the shareholders.[42] This, the court stated, offended certain principles of company law underpinning the concept of limited liability, namely that the company is a separate legal person and owns the funds of the company; the directors manage the affairs of the company in a fiduciary capacity to it, and the shareholders' general right of participation in the assets of the company is deferred until winding-up, subject to the claims of creditors.[43] The court declared that neither the shareholders, nor the directors, nor the company itself, may violate these principles, regardless of what is provided in the constitution of the company.[44]

The Appellate Division observed that De Jager was attempting to have it both ways. On the one hand he was attempting to retain the advantage of limited liability as a shareholder and on the other hand he was attempting to absolve himself from the fiduciary duty a director owes to the company, via the company's supposed consent to him that he may abstract the company's funds, to which consent he was a party.[45] On this issue the Appellate Division stated as follows:

> To allow this would be to avoid basic legal consequences of incorporation as a company. To combine in substance the common-law advantages of individual ownership with the statutory benefits of limited liability without regard to fiduciary duties as a director — this would not be company law at all.[46]

The Appellate Division accordingly held that De Jager was guilty of theft.

(e) Debts and liabilities of the company belong to the company

It follows that, if the profits of the company belong to the company itself, so do the debts and liabilities of the company.[47] Except in certain exceptional circumstances, the shareholders of a company cannot be compelled to pay the debts of

---

[40] *S v De Jager* 1965 (2) SA 616 (A).
[41] At 624.
[42] Ibid.
[43] At 625.
[44] Ibid.
[45] At 625.
[46] Ibid.
[47] *Salomon v Salomon* [1897] AC 22; *Estate Salzmann v Van Rooyen* 1944 OPD 1.

the company.[48] If the company is liquidated, this will not generally result in the shareholders' estates being sequestrated and, should the estates of the shareholders be sequestrated, this will not generally result in the liquidation of the company. As discussed, s 19(2) of the Act provides that a person, solely by reason of being an incorporator, shareholder or director of a company, is not liable for any liabilities or obligations of the company, except to the extent that the Act or the company's Memorandum of Incorporation provides otherwise.

Of course, the shareholders of a company may voluntarily assume personal liability for the company's debts. As the court in *JH Rayner (Mincing Lane) Ltd v Department of Trade and Industry*[49] stated, '[s]ince *Salomon's* case, traders and creditors have known that they do business with a corporation at their peril if they do not require guarantees from members of the corporation or adequate security.'[50] Should shareholders of a company agree to guarantee the obligations of the company, they effectively nullify the limited liability they enjoy.

Note that in a personal liability company the directors and past directors are jointly and severally liable, together with the company, for any debts and liabilities of the company that were contracted during their respective periods of office.[51]

(f) A shareholder has no right to manage the company's business or to enter into transactions on its behalf

Membership of a company does not qualify a shareholder to manage the company's business or to bind the company to a contract.[52] A shareholder is not an agent of the company. This position is not affected even if the shareholder holds all the shares in the company.[53] Only those persons who are authorised as representatives to bind the company may do so. Contracts entered into by a company are the company's contracts and not the contracts of its shareholders.[54]

(g) Company can sue or be sued in its own name

If a company sustains a loss for which it has a right of action, a shareholder of the company does not have a direct right of action for the loss. The company's loss is not in law the shareholder's loss, even though the company's loss could reduce the value of the shareholder's shares.[55] Thus a shareholder of a company cannot institute legal proceedings to obtain redress for injury done to the company, or

---

[48] *Salomon v Salomon* [1897] AC 22. These exceptional circumstances relate to a court piercing the corporate veil. This is discussed further in 2.4 below.

[49] 1990 2 AC 418 (HL); *sub nom MacLaine Watson & Co Ltd v Department of Trade and Industry* [1989] 3 All ER 523 (HL).

[50] At 531.

[51] See s 19(3) of the Act.

[52] *Francis George Hill Family Trust v South African Reserve Bank* 1992 (3) SA 91 (A) 97.

[53] *Salomon v Salomon* [1897] AC 22 at 42–3; *RP Crees (Pvt) Ltd v Woodpecker Industries (Pvt) Ltd* 1975 (2) SA 485 (R) 487.

[54] *JH Rayner (Mincing Lane) Ltd v Department of Trade and Industry*; *sub nom MacLaine Watson & Co Ltd v Department of Trade and Industry* (supra) at 531; *Kuwait Asia Bank EC v National Mutual Life Nominees Ltd* [1990] 3 All ER 404 (PC) 423.

[55] RP Austin and IM Ramsay *Ford's Principles of Corporations Law* 13 ed (2007) para 4.175 p 123.

institute an action to enforce a contract entered into by the company — the company itself must institute the action, as it is in law capable of suing or being sued in its own name.[56]

(h) Company may contract with its shareholders

A company may enter into transactions with its shareholders because it is a person separate from its shareholders. A company may also employ one of its shareholders as an employee under a contract of service. This is illustrated in *Lee v Lee's Air Farming Ltd*.[57]

The facts are that the appellant's husband, Lee, was a qualified pilot and had formed a company called 'Lee's Air Farming Ltd' for the purpose of engaging in the business of aerial top-dressing of crops. Lee was the controlling shareholder and sole managing director of the company. Lee was also employed by the company as its chief pilot. He was killed in an air crash that occurred in the course of performing his duties as chief pilot of the company. His widow then claimed compensation from the company under the Workmen's Compensation Act 1922 on the ground that Lee had been a 'worker' of the company within the meaning of the Act. The question before the court was whether Lee had indeed been a 'worker' for the purposes of workmen's compensation, or whether his position as the sole managing director of the company had precluded him from being a servant of the company. The insurers of the company argued that it had been impossible for Lee, as the director of the company, to have made, on its behalf, a contract with himself.

The Court of Appeal of New Zealand held that the appellant was not entitled to compensation since Lee could not be regarded as a 'worker' within the meaning of the Workmen's Compensation Act 1922, but the Privy Council reversed this decision. The Privy Council held that Lee and the company were entirely distinct and separate persons. It found that Lee had been contractually employed as an employee of the company and had been paid wages for the work done by him. The court held that the fact that Lee had also been the sole managing director of the company had not prevented him from being a servant of the company.[58] It stated that, assuming that the company was not a sham,[59] the capacity of the company to contract with Lee could not be impugned merely because he had been the agent of the company in its negotiation.[60] The court stated further that it is a logical consequence of *Salomon v Salomon & Co Ltd* that one person may function in dual capacities and that such a person could in one capacity give orders to himself

---

[56] See *Magnum Financial Holdings (Pty) Ltd v Summerly* 1984 (1) SA 160 (W) 163 and *Wiseman v Ace Table Soccer (Pty) Ltd* 1991 (4) SA 171 (W) 175.
[57] 1961 AC 12.
[58] Para 25.
[59] See *Secretary of State for Business, Enterprise and Regulatory Reform v Neufeld* [2009] BCC 687 where the English Court of Appeal commented that where a company is a sham and the courts have considered it appropriate for policy reasons to pierce the corporate veil (see also 2.4.2 and 2.4.3 below) and treat the company as the alter ego of the controlling shareholder, that is, to treat them as one, then any suggestion that an individual had a service contract with the company would not succeed (para 34). See further the discussion below in 2.4 on piercing the corporate veil.
[60] Para 26.

in another capacity.[61] In other words, Lee in his capacity as sole managing director could on behalf of the company have given orders to himself to do certain work for the company in his capacity as chief pilot.

It was accordingly held that the appellant was entitled to receive compensation under the Workmen's Compensation Act 1922 because her husband had been an employee of the company and a worker for the purposes of the Workmen's Compensation Act 1922. *Lee's* case illustrates the proposition that an individual who owns all the shares in a company and is the sole director of the company, and thus has total control over it, may also be employed by that company under a contract of service. Gower succinctly summarises this case by stating that '[i]n effect the magic of corporate personality enabled him to be master and servant at the same time and to get all the advantages of both (and of limited liability).'[62]

2.4 EXCEPTIONS TO THE PRINCIPLE OF SEPARATE LEGAL PERSONALITY

Metaphorically, once a company is formed, a veil or a curtain is drawn between the company and its shareholders and directors, which separates the company from its shareholders and directors and protects them from liability for the debts and wrongful acts of the company. When the corporate veil is pierced, the protection afforded to the shareholders and directors is removed and the substance of the company is examined, rather than the form in which it has been cast. As the court in *Amlin (SA) Pty Ltd v Van Kooij*[63] observed, piercing the veil necessitates that a court '"opens the curtains" of the corporate entity in order to see for itself what obtained inside'.[64] The focus then shifts from the company to the natural person behind it or in control of its activities as if there were no dichotomy between such a person and the company.[65] In this way personal liability is attributed to someone who misuses or abuses the principle of corporate personality.

Both the courts and the legislature have recognised that the corporate structure may be abused, and have made exceptions to the principle of separate legal personality. The Supreme Court of Appeal in *Ebrahim v Airports Cold Storage (Pty) Ltd*[66] stated:

> ... it is an apposite truism that close corporations and companies are imbued with identity only by virtue of statute. In this sense their separate existence remains a figment of law, liable to be curtailed or withdrawn when the objects of their creation are abused or thwarted.[67]

Examples of the manner in which the corporate structure has been abused are discussed in 2.4.1 below.

---

[61] Para 26.
[62] Paul L Davies op cit n 21 at 202.
[63] 2008 (2) SA 558 (C).
[64] Para 12.
[65] *Cape Pacific Ltd v Lubner Controlling Investments (Pty) Ltd* 1995 (4) SA 790 (A) 802.
[66] [2009] 1 All SA 330 (SCA).
[67] Para 15.

When will a court pierce the corporate veil? This has been a most controversial and undecided issue in our law. Piercing the veil is an exceptional procedure;[68] it is a drastic remedy, and in most instances the courts uphold the separate existence of a company despite arguments that they should not do so (see 2.4.2 and 2.4.3 below). There must be compelling reasons for a court to ignore the separate legal existence of a company. But the grounds on which courts will pierce the corporate veil have been difficult to state with certainty. Courts have grappled with the correct approach to adopt in determining whether or not to pierce the corporate veil, as discussed in 2.4.3 below.

Apart from piercing the corporate veil, other exceptions have been made in our law to the principle of separate legal personality. For instance, where there is an underlying partnership intention between parties, the courts may recognise this intention and take cognisance of the individuals behind the corporate veil even though the parties had formed a company to carry their intention into effect. Such companies are known as domestic companies or quasi-partnerships, as discussed in 2.4.4 below. As an alternative to piercing the corporate veil, courts sometimes rely on agency principles to impose liability on a director or controlling shareholder (see 2.4.5 below). Courts have also been willing to treat a subsidiary company as an agent of the holding company in certain instances. These issues are discussed in 2.4.6 below.

Apart from the common law, a broad general statutory provision to pierce the corporate veil is provided in s 163(4)[69] of the Act, which for the first time makes provision for the corporate veil to be pierced in instances of unconscionable abuse (see 2.4.7 below). There are also a number of statutory provisions in the Act that impose liability on the directors of the company, as discussed in 2.4.8 below.

2.4.1 Examples of the abuse of separate legal personality

As discussed, piercing the corporate veil entails making exceptions to the concept of the company as a separate legal person. But in light of leading decisions such as *Salomon v Salomon & Co Ltd*[70] and *Dadoo Ltd v Krugersdorp Municipal Council*,[71] piercing the corporate veil is not a remedy that courts resort to easily. It is useful to examine some common-law instances where the separate legal personality of a company was abused, and where the court thought it necessary to pierce the corporate veil. Note that there is no definite categorisation of the instances when a court would pierce the corporate veil. These are merely examples where the corporate veil has been pierced by the courts.

While many academics and commentators have attempted to categorise the instances when our courts will pierce the corporate veil, in *Cape Pacific Ltd v Lubner Controlling Investments (Pty) Ltd*[72] the Supreme Court of Appeal implied that we do not have a categorising approach to piercing the corporate veil in our law, and that there are no set categories of instances governing when a court will

---
[68] *Airport Cold Storage (Pty) Ltd v Ebrahim* 2008 (2) SA 303 (C) para 9.
[69] Under the draft Companies Amendment Bill, 2010 this provision has been moved to s 20(8).
[70] [1897] AC 22.
[71] 1920 AD 530.
[72] 1995 (4) SA 790 (A) 802.

pierce the corporate veil. The rejection of a categorising approach is commendable. This approach could lead to uncertainties in our law as the categories do not constitute an exhaustive list of instances when the corporate veil will be pierced and the authorities tend to differ on the applicable categories. Furthermore, some categories may overlap so that more than one category may be applicable. More significantly, a danger of a categorising approach is that a situation may arise where justice or equity calls for the court to pierce the veil, but a court may refuse to do so on the ground that the facts of the situation do not fit into any of the established categories. While a court may sometimes develop a new category in such a situation, this may not result in any meaningful principles being developed. It could hinder the development of the doctrine of piercing the veil.

(a) Where separate legal personality was used as a device by a director to evade his or her fiduciary duty

A director will not be permitted to evade the fiduciary duties he or she owes to the company by the device of interposing some other company between him- or herself and the company of which he or she is a director so as to make it appear that it is that other company and not him- or herself that is in fact entering into the transaction in question.[73] In *Robinson v Randfontein Estates Gold Mining Co Ltd*[74] the Appellate Division refused to recognise the separate legal personality of a subsidiary where Robinson had attempted to use the subsidiary as a device to evade the fiduciary duties he owed to the holding company as a director of that company. By disregarding the separate legal personality of the subsidiary company, the court prevented Robinson from evading his fiduciary duties to the holding company. The court held that the subsidiary company was no different from the holding company because it was a mere device or camouflage to allow Robinson to evade his fiduciary duties to the holding company.

(b) Where separate legal personality was used to overcome a contractual duty

Where a company has been used as a means to evade or overcome a contractual duty, courts have pierced the corporate veil. For instance, in *Die Dros (Pty) Ltd v Telefon Beverages CC*[75] the court stated that it would permit the separate corporate personality of a close corporation or a company to be disregarded where a natural person who is subject to a restraint of trade uses a close corporation or company as a front to engage in the activity that is prohibited by an agreement in restraint of trade. This occurred in *Gilford Motor Co Ltd v Horne*[76] and *Le'Bergo Fashions CC v Lee*.[77]

In *Gilford Motor Co Ltd v Horne*[78] the defendant, a former managing director of the plaintiff, had signed a restraint of trade agreement under which he had bound

---

[73] *Robinson v Randfontein Estates Gold Mining Co Ltd* 1921 AD 168.
[74] *Robinson v Randfontein Estates Gold Mining Co Ltd* (supra).
[75] 2003 (4) SA 207 (C) para 24.
[76] [1933] Ch 935 (CA).
[77] 1998 (2) SA 608 (C).
[78] *Gilford Motor Co Ltd v Horne* (supra).

himself not to be engaged directly or indirectly in any business similar to that of the plaintiff for a period of five years after his employment. Following the termination of that employment, the defendant formed a company that competed with the plaintiff's business. The plaintiff sought an interdict to restrain the defendant as well as the company from competing with the plaintiff's business.

The defendant contended that he was not contravening the restraint of trade agreement since it was the company that had been competing with the plaintiff and not himself personally. The court in rejecting this argument described the use of the company as 'a device and a stratagem, in order to mask the effective carrying on of a business'[79] by the defendant. The court held that the company's purpose was to attempt to enable the defendant, 'under what is a cloak or a sham'[80] to evade his contractual duties relating to the restraint of trade covenant. The court accordingly interdicted both the defendant and the company from competing with the plaintiff even though the company was not a party to the restraint of trade agreement. In extending the interdict to the company, the court held that the company was a mere channel used by the defendant for the purpose of enabling him for his own benefit to compete with the plaintiff company. Accordingly, an interdict could be granted against the company.[81]

On similar facts, in *Le'Bergo Fashions CC v Lee*[82] the first respondent had signed a restraint of trade agreement in her personal capacity not to compete with the applicant, but had then used her company, the second respondent, of which she was the sole shareholder and director, to compete with the applicant. The company was not a party to the restraint of trade agreement and the question before the court was whether the restraint of trade obligation could be imposed on the company. The court found that the first respondent had effectively carried on the business of the company. In their daily activities, the first respondent and the company had acted as one *persona*, and by her conduct and business activities she had not treated the company as a separate entity but as a mere instrumentality or conduit for promoting her business affairs.[83] The court held that this was sufficient to sustain the argument that the first respondent had been guilty of improper conduct in using the company as a façade behind which she had engaged in business in breach of the restraint of trade agreement.[84] Thus, even though the company had not been a party to the restraint of trade agreement, the court held that its competition with the applicant had amounted to intentionally assisting the first respondent to breach her undertaking in the restraint clause, which was wrongful in law and could thus be interdicted.[85] Accordingly, both the first respondent and the company were interdicted from competing with the applicant.

---

[79] At 956.
[80] At 956 and 961–2. In *Re Polly Peck plc* [1996] 2 All ER 433 at 445 the court said that the word 'façade' or 'cloak' or 'mask' is used most aptly where one person (individual or corporate) uses a company either in an unconscionable attempt to evade existing obligations or to practise some other deception (at 447).
[81] At 965.
[82] 1998 (2) SA 608 (C).
[83] At 613.
[84] At 613–14.
[85] At 614.

In *Gilford Motor Co Ltd v Horne* a new company had been formed with the specific intention of using it to evade the restraint of trade undertaking, while in *Le'Bergo Fashions CC v Lee* the company in question had already been established and had existed, quite innocently and honestly. But in both cases the court disregarded the separate legal personality of the respective companies in question. As the court in *Cape Pacific Ltd v Lubner Controlling Investments (Pty) Ltd*[86] stated, it is not necessary that a company should have been conceived and founded in deceit and never have been intended to function genuinely as a company, before its corporate personality may be disregarded.[87] Hence it matters not whether the company was formed with the specific intention of being used to evade a contractual obligation or whether the company was formed with a legitimate purpose but was later used for an improper purpose — its separate legal personality may be disregarded in either event.

Jones v Lipman[88] is a further example where the court disregarded the separate legal personality of the company in circumstances where the company was used to overcome a contractual obligation. Lipman had concluded a contract to sell land to Jones. Thereafter Lipman asked to be released from the contract, but Jones refused, intimating that, if necessary, he would sue for specific performance. Pending completion of the sale, Lipman formed a company of which he and a clerk of his solicitor were the sole shareholders and directors, and conveyed the land to the company in order to defeat Jones's right to specific performance. The court ordered specific performance against both Lipman and the company, since it was found that the company was merely a mask used by Lipman to attempt to evade his contractual obligations. The court held that such relief could not be resisted by a seller in Lipman's position who, by his absolute ownership and control over the company in which the property was vested, was in a position to cause the contract to be completed.[89] The court described the company as follows:

> The defendant company is the creature of the first defendant [Lipman], a device and a sham, a mask which he holds before his face in an attempt to avoid recognition by the eye of equity.[90]

2.4.2 The distinction between piercing the veil and lifting the veil

It is important to draw a distinction between the concepts of 'piercing the veil' and 'lifting the veil' or 'looking behind the veil'. Courts sometimes refer to the phrase 'piercing the veil' when the effect is lifting the veil, and conversely. When the court pierces the veil, it treats the liabilities of the company as those of its shareholders or directors, and disregards the corporate personality of the company. On the other hand, when the court lifts the veil it is merely taking into account who the company's shareholders or directors are. This does not necessarily entail ignoring the separate identity of the company or treating the liabilities of the

---
[86] 1995 (4) SA 790 (A).
[87] At 804.
[88] [1962] 1 All ER 442.
[89] At 444.
[90] At 445.

company as those of its shareholders or directors. In *Atlas Maritime Co SA v Avalon Maritime Ltd*[91] Staughton LJ expounded the distinction as follows:

> Like all metaphors, this phrase [piercing the corporate veil] can sometimes obscure reasoning rather than elucidate it. There are, I think, two senses in which it is used, which need to be distinguished. To *pierce* the corporate veil is an expression that I would reserve for treating the rights or liabilities or activities of a company as the rights or liabilities or activities of its shareholders. To *lift* the corporate veil or *look behind it*, on the other hand, should mean to have regard to the shareholding in a company for some legal purpose.[92]

In *Pioneer Concrete Services Ltd v Yelnah Pty Ltd*[93] the court also commented on the meaning of the phrase 'lifting the veil' and stated '[t]hat although whenever each individual company is formed a separate legal personality is created, courts will on occasions, look behind the legal personality to the real controllers.'[94]

An example of a case where the court lifted the veil is that of *Daimler Co Ltd v Continental Tyre and Rubber Co*,[95] where this was done to determine the residence of the shareholders of a company so as to decide whether the company was an enemy alien or not. The facts are that the plaintiff company had been incorporated in England for the purpose of selling in England tyres made in Germany by a German company that held the bulk of the shares in the English company. All the directors and shareholders (save for one) were German nationals resident in Germany. The one share was registered in the name of the secretary, who had been born in Germany but resided in England and had become a naturalised British subject. After the outbreak of war between England and Germany in 1914, the plaintiff company instituted an action against the defendant company for payment of a trade debt. The defendant raised the defence that the plaintiff was an alien enemy company and that payment of the debt would be tantamount to trading with the enemy.

The House of Lords accepted that the company was a legal person distinct from its shareholders, but stated that this did not necessarily mean that the character of its shareholders was irrelevant to the character of the company because the rule against trading with the enemy depended upon enemy character.[96] It stated that, for certain purposes a court must look behind the legal or artificial person and take account of the persons who control the company.[97] The court stated that a company may assume an enemy character if the persons in *de facto* control of its affairs are resident in an enemy country or, wherever resident, adhere to the enemy or take instructions from or act under the control of enemies.[98] On the facts, the House of Lords was of the opinion that the plaintiff company was an alien enemy on the grounds that the persons in *de facto* control of the affairs of the company were resident in an enemy country and the plaintiff company was taking instructions from enemies. Thus, although the plaintiff company was an English com-

---

[91] [1991] 4 All ER 769.
[92] At 779.
[93] (1986) 5 NSWLR.
[94] At 264.
[95] [1916] 2 AC 307.
[96] At 338.
[97] At 340.
[98] At 345.

pany, the controllers of the company were based in Germany. The company was taking instructions from persons resident in Germany, and accordingly the plaintiff company was regarded as an enemy company.

Daimler's case is an example of the court lifting the veil. A company cannot be a friend or an enemy, and in order to determine whether it is an enemy or a friend the court had to look at the identity of the shareholders. The court did not pierce the veil because it did not ignore the legal personality of the company, but simply took into account the identity of the shareholders to determine whether the company was an enemy or a friend.

In *Dadoo Ltd v Krugersdorp Municipal Council*[99] Innes CJ opined that the difference between the facts of *Dadoo* and those of *Daimler* was that in *Daimler's* case the enquiry related to attributes that could not attach to a mere legal person.[100] As the learned judge stated, a 'company cannot have an enemy character; ... it has neither body, parts not passions; it cannot be loyal or disloyal.'[101] Therefore, for policy reasons and reasons relating to national security, it was necessary for the court to look behind the veil to determine the residence of the company's shareholders so as to see who was in control of the company. Such a dilemma did not arise in *Dadoo's* case where the question before the court was whether the ownership of the company was in reality the ownership of the shareholders. As Innes CJ stated, a company may own land and its right to do so and the consequences of ownership are not merely matters of form, but are attributes a company could have.[102] It was thus not necessary in *Dadoo's* case for the court to pierce the veil or to look behind the veil.

2.4.3 The approach adopted to piercing the veil in our common law

The common-law instances of piercing the veil have tended to be problematic because the courts have not generally followed consistent principles in determining when they would depart from the principle that a company is a separate legal person. The position has not been reached in our law where it is possible to state with any degree of accuracy the circumstances in which the court will pierce the veil. On the contrary, the Appellate Division in *Cape Pacific Ltd v Lubner Controlling Investments (Pty) Ltd*[103] acknowledged that, in certain circumstances, a court would be justified to disregard the separate legal personality of a company, but remarked that the law is far from settled with regard to the circumstances in which it would be permissible to pierce the veil.[104] In *Hülse-Reutter v Gödde*[105] the Supreme Court of Appeal again commented that the circumstances in which a court would pierce the corporate veil are far from settled.[106]

---

[99] 1920 AD 530; see also 2.3.3(c) above.
[100] At 551–2.
[101] At 552.
[102] Ibid.
[103] 1995 (4) SA 790 (A).
[104] At 802.
[105] 2001 (4) SA 1336 (SCA).
[106] Para 20.

There is thus a need for a firm guiding principle in our law as to when a court will pierce the corporate veil. The approach of our courts to piercing the veil was laid down in the leading case of *Cape Pacific Ltd v Lubner Controlling Investments (Pty) Ltd*[107] where the then Appellate Division laid down a number of general principles relating to the common-law instances of piercing the veil. These are as follows:

- At the outset, the Appellate Division asserted that it is a salutary principle that our courts should not lightly disregard a company's separate personality, but should strive to give effect to and uphold it.[108] To do otherwise, the court said, would 'negate or undermine the policy and principles that underpin the concept of separate corporate personality and the legal consequences that attach to it.'[109]
- The Appellate Division made it clear that a court has no general discretion simply to disregard a company's separate legal personality whenever it considers it just to do so.[110]
- The court stressed that it was not formulating any general principles with regard to when the corporate veil would or would not be pierced, and that each case must be decided on its own facts which, once determined, are of decisive importance.[111] This implies that we do not have a categorising approach in our law. Many academics have attempted to categorise the instances when our courts will pierce the veil, but it is now clear that our law does not adopt a categorising approach and that there are no set categories of instances governing when a court will pierce the veil.
- The court stated that, where there is fraud or dishonesty or other improper conduct, the 'need to preserve the separate corporate identity would in such circumstances have to be balanced against policy considerations which arise in favour of piercing the corporate veil.'[112] In other words, the court adopted a balancing approach and laid down the principle that the concept of separate legal personality must be weighed against those principles in favour of piercing the veil. In the balancing approach, conflicting principles must be balanced or weighed against each other.[113] In such an approach a court would be entitled to look to substance rather than form to arrive at the facts.[114]
- In *Botha v Van Niekerk*[115] it was held that a court would pierce the corporate veil where the plaintiff has suffered unconscionable injustice as a result of improper conduct on the part of the defendant.[116] The Appellate Division in

---
[107] 1995 (4) SA 790 (A).
[108] At 803. See also *Ebrahim v Airports Cold Storage (Pty) Ltd* [2009] 1 All SA 330 (SCA) para 22.
[109] At 803.
[110] Ibid. See also *Amlin (SA) Pty Ltd v Van Kooij* 2008 (2) SA 558 (C) para 22; *Die Dros (Pty) Ltd v Telefon Beverages CC* 2003 (4) SA 207 (C) para 23, and *Adams v Cape Industries plc* [1991] 1 All ER 929 (CA) at 1019.
[111] *Cape Pacific Ltd v Lubner Controlling Investments (Pty) Ltd* (supra) at 802.
[112] At 803.
[113] See also *Die Dros (Pty) Ltd v Telefon Beverages CC* (supra) para 23.
[114] *Cape Pacific Ltd v Lubner Controlling Investments (Pty) Ltd* (supra) at 803–4.
[115] 1983 (3) SA 513 (W).
[116] At 525.

Cape Pacific Ltd v Lubner Controlling Investments (Pty) Ltd rejected this test on the basis that it was too rigid, and held that a more flexible approach ought to be adopted, which would allow the facts of each case ultimately to determine whether the piercing of the veil was called for or not.[117]

- As discussed earlier, the Appellate Division stressed that it is not necessary that a company should have been conceived and founded in deceit and never have been intended to function genuinely as a company, before its corporate personality would be disregarded.[118] The court made it clear that, if a company that has been legitimately established and operated is misused in a particular instance:

    ... there is no reason in principle or logic why its separate personality cannot be disregarded in relation to the transaction in question (in order to fix the individual or individuals responsible with personal liability) while giving full effect to it in other respects.[119]

- The court remarked that the fact that the plaintiff has an alternative remedy to piercing the veil did not bar the court from piercing the veil.[120] This statement seems to conflict with the court's earlier statement that the corporate veil should not be lightly disregarded. In *Hülse-Reutter v Gödde*[121] the Supreme Court of Appeal took a much stricter approach and adopted the view that piercing the veil ought to be used only as a last resort.[122] In *Amlin (SA) Pty Ltd v Van Kooij*[123] the court agreed with this approach and stated:

    I accept that 'opening the curtains' or piercing the veil is rather a drastic remedy. For that reason alone it must be resorted to rather sparingly and indeed as the very last resort in circumstances where justice will not otherwise be done between two litigants. It cannot, for example, be resorted to as an alternative remedy if another remedy on the same facts can successfully be employed in order to administer justice between the parties ... The guiding principle is that the veil is lifted only in exceptional circumstances.[124]

In *Hülse-Reutter v Gödde* the Supreme Court of Appeal asserted that the separate legal personality of a company must be recognised and upheld, except in the most unusual circumstances.[125] The court stated further that a court had no general discretion to disregard the existence of a separate corporate existence simply whenever it considered it just or convenient to do so.[126] The court acknowledged that the circumstances in which a court would pierce the veil were far from settled, and stated that much depended on a close analysis of the facts of each case, considerations of policy and judicial judgment.[127] But what is clear, the court emphasised, is that:

---

[117] At 805.
[118] At 804.
[119] Ibid.
[120] At 805.
[121] 2001 (4) SA 1336 (SCA).
[122] Para 23.
[123] 2008 (2) SA 558 (C).
[124] Para 23.
[125] Para 20.
[126] Ibid.
[127] Ibid.

as a matter of principle ... there must at least be some misuse or abuse of the distinction between the corporate entity and those who control it which results in an unfair advantage being afforded to the latter.[128]

The mere fact that a company has only one shareholder who is in full control of the company does not in itself constitute a basis for disregarding its separate legal personality.[129] Likewise, the mere fact that two companies have the same shareholders and directors does not constitute a basis for disregarding the separate legal personality of the company.[130]

To sum up, it is clear from these judgments that our courts uphold the independence of the corporate entity as an almost inviolable concept and that they will not easily or readily disregard the separate identity of the company. Separate legal personality is at the very core of a company's reason for existence and it is only in exceptional circumstances that the corporate veil will be disregarded. But as discussed, the law is not settled with regard to the circumstances in which the corporate veil will be pierced and much will depend on a close analysis of the facts of each case, policy considerations and, of course, judicial judgment.

2.4.4 Domestic companies

Where there is an underlying partnership intention between parties, the courts may recognise this intention and take cognisance of the individuals behind the corporate veil even though the parties had formed a company to carry their intention into effect. Such companies are known as domestic companies or quasi-partnerships.[131] In *Ebrahimi v Westbourne Galleries Ltd*[132] the House of Lords stated as follows:

> ... there is room in company law for recognition of the fact that behind it, or amongst it, there are individuals, with rights, expectations and obligations inter se which are not necessarily submerged in the company structure.[133]

The recognition of an underlying partnership intention applies predominantly to small private companies. But the mere fact that a company is a small private company is not sufficient reason for a court to recognise it as a domestic company; in some small private companies the association between the shareholders and the directors may be purely commercial.[134] Some indications that the parties had formed a domestic company are the fact that an association was formed or continued on the basis of a personal relationship involving mutual confidence,[135] an agreement or understanding that all or some of the shareholders will participate

---

[128] Ibid.
[129] *Nel v Metequity Ltd* 2007 (3) SA 34 (SCA) para 11.
[130] Ibid.
[131] See *Hulett v Hulett* 1992 (4) SA 291 (A) 307.
[132] [1972] 2 All ER 492.
[133] At 500. This statement was approved by the Appellate Division in *Hulett v Hulett* (supra) at 307.
[134] *Ebrahimi v Westbourne Galleries Ltd* [1972] 2 All ER 492 at 500; *Hulett v Hulett* (supra) at 307.
[135] *Ebrahimi v Westbourne Galleries Ltd* (supra) at 500. See also *In re Yenidje Tobacco Co Ltd* [1916] 2 Ch 426 (CA) and *Moosa, NO v Mavjee Bhawan (Pty) Ltd* 1967 (3) SA 131 (T) 137–8.

in the conduct of the business,[136] or an agreement that the profits of the company will be distributed in the form of salaries instead of by way of dividends.[137]

In *Bellairs v Hodnett*[138] the Appellate Division applied the concept of a domestic company in determining whether a *de facto* managing director of a company had a fiduciary duty to acquire certain property for the company or whether he was legitimately entitled to acquire the property for himself. The object of the company, as stated in its memorandum of association, was that of township development. The company comprised two directors, who were also its sole shareholders. Based on the facts, the court found that the parties had an underlying partnership intention and regarded the company as a domestic company. The court held that, since the company was in effect a partnership, in order to decide whether a shareholder and *de facto* managing director of such a company owed a fiduciary duty to the company to acquire certain property for the company and not for himself, the court was required to concern itself not with the cold print of the company's memorandum of association, but with the business that the company was actually carrying on or intended to carry on at the time, as determined and agreed upon by its shareholders and directors.[139] Taking into account the intention of the parties, the court held that the object of the entity was not township development. Instead, the court found, the parties had limited their joint venture to the development of the particular properties held by the company.[140] Accordingly, the court held that the director in question had not committed a breach of his fiduciary duty by acquiring the property in question for himself and not for the company.[141] The acquisition of the additional property by a director of the company fell outside the limits of the joint venture that the parties had embarked on.

2.4.5 Agency/Alter ego doctrine

In the normal relationship between a company and its directors or shareholders, the company is the principal and the directors and shareholders are agents of the company. In *Salomon v Salomon & Co Ltd*[142] the House of Lords rejected the conclusion of the lower courts that Salomon & Co Ltd was an agent of Mr Aron Salomon, and the court established that a company is not, as such, the agent of its shareholders. But in certain circumstances it may be that, on the particular facts, the normal relationship between a company and its directors or shareholders is in fact inverted, whether expressly or impliedly.

This may occur for instance where a director or controlling shareholders do not treat the company as a separate entity, but treat it as if it were merely a means of furthering their own private business affairs. In this instance the company may be regarded as the 'agent' or the 'alter ego' or 'instrumentality' of its directors or

---

[136] *Ebrahimi v Westbourne Galleries Ltd* (supra) at 500.
[137] See further on domestic companies *Rentekor (Pty) Ltd v Rheeder and Berman* 1988 (4) SA 469 (T) 500 and *Hulett v Hulett* (supra) at 307–8.
[138] 1978 (1) SA 1109 (A).
[139] At 1128.
[140] At 1133.
[141] Ibid.
[142] [1897] AC 22 at 42–3.

controlling shareholders. Since the directors or shareholders manage the company in such a way as not to separate their personal affairs from those of the company, the company does not carry on its own business or affairs, but acts merely to further the business or affairs of its directors or controlling shareholders. There is thus an abuse of the company's separate legal existence where the directors or shareholders strive to obtain the advantages of separate legal personality of the company without treating the company as a separate legal person.[143]

Note that, in treating the company as the agent of its directors or controlling shareholders, the separate legal personality of the company is still recognised. Hence the corporate veil is not pierced. But liability is imposed personally on the directors or shareholders in their capacity as the principal of the company. This is an example of lifting the veil. The practical effect of piercing the corporate veil is achieved by establishing an agency relationship, without having to pierce the veil.

In applying the agency or alter ego doctrine, the courts are concerned with reality and not with form, with the manner in which the company operated and with the individual's relationship to that operation.[144] In *Gering v Gering*,[145] the court stated in relation to a shareholder:

> ... those companies are his creatures and his instruments. He is conducting business through them, or holding assets through them, and, though they are separate juristic personalities, they are in substance merely part of the machinery by which he alone conducts his business affairs.[146]

There need not be an express agency agreement; an agency relationship may be implied. Some factors that are emphasised in applying the agency or alter ego doctrine are the following: the fact that the company is grossly undercapitalised for the purposes of the corporate undertaking; there is a failure to observe corporate formalities; non-payment of dividends while substantial sums are paid by way of salary or otherwise to the controlling shareholder; the profits of the company are treated as though they were the profits of the director or shareholder concerned; siphoning off the company's funds by the dominant shareholder; an absence of corporate records, and officers or directors that are non-functioning.[147] On its own no single factor is relevant, but all the factors together are to be regarded as a whole.[148]

For example, in *Wallersteiner v Moir*[149] Mr Wallersteiner was found to have used many companies as if they belonged to him. He was in complete control of the companies and had entered into large contracts on their behalf, without consulting anyone else. He had used money of the companies as if the money had belonged to him. For instance, when money was paid to him for shares of which he was the beneficial owner, he paid the money into the company's account, and

---

[143] MS Blackman et al *Commentary on the Companies Act* vol 1 (2002) (Revision Service 7, 2010) at 4–140–4–142.
[144] *De Witt Truck Brokers Inc v W Ray Flemming Fruit Co* 540 F 2d 681 (1976) 685.
[145] 1974 (3) SA 358 (W).
[146] At 361.
[147] See *De Witt Truck Brokers Inc v W Ray Flemming Fruit Co* (supra) at 685–7.
[148] Ibid at 687.
[149] [1974] 3 All ER 217 (CA).

when he paid out money or personal loans of his own he drew the cheques in the name of the company. Lord Denning MR was prepared to treat the companies through which Wallersteiner had operated as if they were 'just the puppets'[150] of Wallersteiner. The learned judge stated as follows:

> He controlled their every movement. Each danced to his bidding. He pulled the strings. No one else got within reach of them. Transformed into legal language, they were his agents to do as he commanded. He was the principal behind them. I am of the opinion that the court should pull aside the corporate veil and treat these concerns as being his creatures — for whose doings he should be, and is, responsible.[151]

2.4.6 Company groups

Each company in a group of companies is a separate legal entity with its own separate legal personality and rights, privileges, duties and liabilities separate from those of the other member companies.[152] The fact that a group of companies effectively forms one economic unit does not mean that the separate identity of each company is to be ignored and that the group is to be treated as one entity.[153] As the Appellate Division in *Ritz Hotel Ltd v Charles of The Ritz Ltd*[154] stated, the acts of a holding company are not per se the acts of its wholly owned subsidiary, or vice versa, since the holding company is a separate legal entity from its subsidiary.[155]

But, as acknowledged by the Appellate Division in *Ritz Hotel Ltd v Charles of The Ritz Ltd*,[156] in recent years there has been a more relaxed approach to the application of this basic principle that a holding company and its subsidiary are separate legal entities. When the corporate veil is pierced in a group of companies, the court treats the group as a single entity as opposed to a collection of different corporate entities. In *DHN Food Distributors Ltd v London Borough of Tower Hamlets*[157] the English Court of Appeal stated that there was evidence of a tendency by courts to ignore the separate legal entities of various companies within a group, and to look instead at the economic entity of the whole group.[158] The court continued as follows:

---

[150] At 238.
[151] Ibid. However, the other members of the court thought it was inappropriate to make such a finding on an interlocutory appeal and on affidavit evidence, where there had not been any cross-examination, and were of the view that such an issue was best to be decided at the forthcoming trial (see the judgments of Buckley LJ at 250 and Scarman LJ at 254).
[152] See *R v Milne and Erleigh (7)* 1951 (1) SA 791 (A) 827–8; *Dithaba Platinum (Pty) Ltd v Erconovaal Ltd* 1985 (4) SA 615 (T) 625; *The Albazero* [1975] 3 All ER 21 (CA) 28, and *Adams v Cape Industries plc* [1991] 1 All ER 929 (CA) 1016.
[153] See *Adams v Cape Industries plc* (supra) at 1016–22; *Wambach v Maizecor Industries (Edms) Bpk* 1993 (2) SA 669 (A) and *Macadamia Finance Bpk v De Wet* 1993 (2) SA 743 (A).
[154] 1988 (3) SA 290 (A).
[155] At 314.
[156] At 314–15.
[157] [1976] 3 All ER 462.
[158] At 467.

This is especially the case when a parent company owns all the shares of the subsidiaries, so much so that it can control every movement of the subsidiaries. These subsidiaries are bound hand and foot to the parent company and must do just what the parent company says.[159]

But in *Adams v Cape Industries plc*,[160] which dealt with the question of piercing the veil in the group context, the English Court of Appeal adopted a stricter approach and asserted that courts are not entitled to disregard the separate legal personality of a company in a group simply because it is just to do so. The court stated:

> ... save in cases which turn on the wording of particular statutes or contracts, the court is not free to disregard the principle of *Salomon v A Salomon and Co Ltd* [1897] AC 22, [1895–9] All ER Rep 33, merely because it considers that justice so requires. Our law, for better or worse, recognises the creation of subsidiary companies, which though in one sense the creatures of their parent companies, will nevertheless under the general law fall to be treated as separate legal entities with all the rights and liabilities which would normally attach to separate legal entities.[161]

The Appellate Division cases of *Wambach v Maizecor Industries (Edms) Bpk*[162] and *Macadamia Finance Bpk v De Wet*[163] approved the dicta in *Adams v Cape Industries plc*, and in both cases the courts refused to pierce the veil and to view the companies in the group as forming a single economic entity.

In *Wambach v Maizecor Industries (Edms) Bpk* the Appellate Division refused to pierce the corporate veil so as to hold that an asset registered in the name of a wholly owned subsidiary was owned by the holding company even though the board of directors of the holding company effectively operated as the board of directors of the wholly owned subsidiary. The court ruled that the fact that the board of directors of a controlling company could effectively take decisions concerning an asset of a subsidiary did not entail the asset thereby becoming an asset of the controlling company.[164]

In *Macadamia Finance Bpk v De Wet* certain assets of a subsidiary company had been destroyed. The subsidiary company attempted to hold the liquidators of the holding company, which had been placed in liquidation, liable for having failed to insure the assets of the subsidiary company. The court held that the liquidators

---

[159] At 467. While piercing of the corporate veil in a group context was supported by the English Court of Appeal in *DHN Food Distributors Ltd v London Borough of Tower Hamlets* [1976] 3 All ER 462, in *Woolfson v Strathclyde Regional Council* 1978 SLT 159 (at 161) the House of Lords cast doubt on whether the Court of Appeal had properly applied the principles relating to this doctrine. See further MP Larkin 'Regarding Judicial Disregarding of the Company's Separate Identity' (1989) *SA Merc LJ* 277 and chapter 6: Groups of Companies and Related Persons.
[160] [1991] 1 All ER 929 (CA).
[161] At 1019. See also *Ord v Belhaven Pubs Ltd* [1998] BCC 607 where the English Court of Appeal rejected the approach adopted by the trial judge of viewing a group as one economic entity. The court held that a group of companies could be regarded as a single entity only in very limited circumstances where there was some impropriety or the company was a façade concealing the true facts. The court stated further that companies are entitled to organise their affairs in group structures and to expect the courts to apply the principles of *Salomon v Salomon & Co Ltd* in the ordinary way (at 615).
[162] 1993 (2) SA 669 (A).
[163] Ibid.
[164] See also *Re Polly Peck plc* [1996] 2 All ER 433 at 445.

owed no legal duty to the subsidiary company in relation to its assets and proclaimed that the fact that, prior to the liquidation, the directors of the holding company had been the same persons as the directors of the subsidiary made no difference to this finding.

Hence the better view is that, save where the wording or purpose of a particular statute or contract justifies the treatment of a holding company and a subsidiary as one corporate entity, the mere fact that a group of companies constitutes a single economic unit does not in itself justify the treatment of the group as a single entity. The position may be different where the subsidiary is a façade or sham.

But rather than piercing the corporate veil in company groups, courts have been more willing to treat a subsidiary company as an agent of the holding company and as conducting the latter's business for it. If it can be shown that a subsidiary company acted as the agent of its holding company, then on ordinary agency principles, liability will attach to the holding company and not to the subsidiary. Whether or not such an agency relationship exists would depend on the facts pertaining to the relationship between the holding company and the subsidiary.

A classic example of an agency relationship between a holding company and a subsidiary is illustrated in *Smith, Stone & Knight Ltd v Lord Mayor, Aldermen Citizens of the City of Birmingham*.[165] The court was required to determine whether a subsidiary was carrying on the business as the agent of the holding company or whether it was carrying on its own business. The issue before the court related to the compensation payable by a local authority for a compulsory purchase when the property of the subsidiary company was acquired by the holding company. The holding company instituted the claim for the compensation in its own name when it became clear that, if the subsidiary had instituted the claim in its name, the local authority would have escaped having to pay any compensation in terms of the Land Clauses Consolidation Act 1845. The holding company contended that the subsidiary carried on business as its agent and that, accordingly, the holding company was entitled to institute the claim for compensation, while the local authority asserted that the proper claimant was the subsidiary company and not the holding company.

The holding company held all the shares in the subsidiary company save for five, which the directors of the subsidiary company, who were also directors of the holding company, held in their respective names in trust for the holding company. More importantly, the profits of the subsidiary company were regarded as the profits of the holding company, and all the books and accounts of the subsidiary company had been kept by the holding company.

The court held that the mere fact that a man holds all the shares in a company does not make the business carried on by that company his business, nor does it make the company his agents for the carrying on of the business.[166] The court asserted that this proposition is just as true if the shareholder is itself a limited company.[167] Whether there is an agency relationship between the holding com-

---

[165] [1939] 4 All ER 116.
[166] At 120.
[167] Ibid.

pany and the subsidiary is a question of fact in each case, but the court identified the following six factors as being relevant to determine this question:

- Were the profits treated as those of the holding company?
- Were the persons conducting the business appointed by the holding company?
- Was the holding company the head and brain of the trading venture?
- Did the holding company govern the venture and decide what should be done and what capital should be embarked on the venture?
- Were the profits made by the skill and direction of the holding company?
- Was the holding company in effectual and constant control?[168]

Based on the facts, the court answered all the above six questions in the affirmative and found that the arrangement between the holding company and the subsidiary company was such that the business belonged to the holding company, and that the subsidiary did not operate on its own behalf but on behalf of the holding company.[169] The court concluded that an agency relationship did indeed exist between the holding company and the subsidiary, and that the holding company was entitled to claim the compensation from the local authority.

Thus, to sum up, each company in a group of companies is a separate legal entity with its own separate legal personality. In certain instances, veil piercing may take place in a group of companies and the group may be treated as a single entity. But it is more common for the courts to invoke principles of agency law and to treat the subsidiary as the agent of its holding company, and in this way, attach liability to the holding company. But there is no presumption that a subsidiary is the holding company's agent.[170] In *Adcock-Ingram Laboratories Ltd v SA Druggists Ltd; Adcock-Ingram Laboratories Ltd v Lennon Ltd*[171] Nicholas J said control did not mean that there was a relationship of agency and principal between the holding company and the subsidiary.[172] The fact that most of the members of the board of directors of the subsidiary company were also members of the board of directors of the holding company would also not necessarily indicate that there was an agency relationship between the subsidiary and the

---

[168] At 121.
[169] Ibid.
[170] See *Smith, Stone & Knight Ltd v Lord Mayor, Aldermen Citizens of the City of Birmingham* [1939] 4 All ER 116 at 120–1 and *Atlas Maritime Co SA v Avalon Maritime Ltd* [1991] 4 All ER 769 at 779.
[171] 1983 (2) SA 350 (T) 353.
[172] But note that in an aside the same judge, Nicholas AJA, stated in *Ritz Hotel Ltd v Charles of The Ritz Ltd* 1988 (3) SA 290 (A) 316 that, in light of the judgment in the *Revlon* case it may become necessary to reconsider the decision that he had made in *Adcock-Ingram Laboratories Ltd v SA Druggists Ltd; Adcock-Ingram Laboratories Ltd v Lennon Ltd* 1983 (2) SA 350 (T). In *Revlon Inc v Cripps and Lee Ltd* 1980 FSR 85 (CA) the court supported the piercing of the veil in a group context, and relied on *DHN Food Distributors Ltd v London Borough of Tower Hamlets* [1976] 3 All ER 462 as support. But, as mentioned earlier, the House of Lords in *Woolfson v Strathclyde Regional Council* 1978 SLT 159 at 161 doubted whether the Court of Appeal's decision in *DHN Food Distributors Ltd v London Borough of Tower Hamlets* to pierce the corporate veil was properly justified. See further chapter 6: Groups of Companies and Related Persons.

holding company.[173] Whether or not the subsidiary was acting as the agent for the holding company would depend on an analysis of all the facts.

2.4.7 Piercing the corporate veil under the Act

Section 163(4) of the Act states as follows:

> Whenever a court, on application by an interested person, or in any proceedings in which a company is involved, finds that the incorporation of, or any act by or on behalf of, or any use of, that company constitutes an unconscionable abuse of the juristic personality of the company as a separate entity, the court may declare that the company is deemed not to be a juristic person in respect of such rights, obligations or liabilities of the company, or of such member or shareholder thereof, or of such other person as specified in the declaration, and the court may give such further order or orders as it may deem fit in order to give effect to such declaration.[174]

For the first time in our company law, a statutory provision has been enacted in the Companies Act that permits a court to disregard the separate juristic personality of a company. While previously there had been some legislative provisions in our company law that permitted a court to impose personal liability on directors and shareholders in certain instances, we have not had in our company law a statutory provision that gives a court general authority to pierce the corporate veil. Such a provision is not new in the Close Corporations Act 69 of 1984 (hereafter 'the Close Corporations Act'), where s 65 of that Act permits a court to deem a close corporation not to be a juristic person.[175] Section 163(4) of the Act encapsulates s 65 of the Close Corporations Act.

Does s 163(4) of the Act override the common-law instances of piercing the corporate veil? It is suggested that where the requirements of s 163(4) are not met and cannot be relied on, the common-law remedy of piercing the veil would probably still apply, because s 163(4) does not override the common-law instances of piercing the corporate veil. The principles developed at common law with regard to piercing the corporate veil would also serve as useful guidelines in interpreting s 163(4) of the Act and in deciding whether there had been an unconscionable abuse of the juristic personality of the company.

At common law the remedy of piercing the veil is to be used as a last resort.[176] But in light of s 163(4) of the Act it is questionable whether piercing the veil in terms of the Act is to be used as a last resort. It may well be that reliance may be placed on s 163(4) of the Act despite other remedies also being available. Courts

---

[173] *Re Polly Peck plc* [1996] 2 All ER 433 at 445.

[174] Clause 14 of the draft Companies Amendment Bill, 2010 has neatened the language of this provision.

[175] Section 65 of the Close Corporations Act states as follows: 'Whenever a Court on application by an interested person, or in any proceedings in which a corporation is involved, finds that the incorporation of, or any act by or on behalf of, or any use of, that corporation, constitutes a gross abuse of the juristic personality of the corporation as a separate entity, the Court may declare that the corporation is deemed not to be a juristic person in respect of such rights, obligations or liabilities of the corporation, or of such member or members thereof, or of such other person or persons, as are specified in the declaration, and the Court may give such further order or orders as it may deem fit in order to give effect to such declaration.'

[176] *Hülse-Reutter v Gödde* 2001 (4) SA 1336 (SCA) para 23.

may now also have a wider discretion to pierce the corporate veil under s 163(4) of the Act compared to their discretion under the common law. Nonetheless, consideration must be given to the fact that piercing the veil is an exceptional remedy that must be used sparingly.

The advantage of a statutory provision relating to piercing the corporate veil is that it gives more certainty and visibility to the doctrine of piercing the veil. But a danger is that it may result in the rigidity of the doctrine, particularly if the courts interpret the provision in a highly technical way.[177]

It is questionable why s 163(4) of the Act is contained in s 163 of the Act, which deals with remedies given to a shareholder or a director of a company for oppressive or prejudicial conduct. The section seems out of place here and might have been better placed in s 6 of the Act, which deals with anti-avoidance provisions.[178]

(a) 'Application' or 'proceedings'

The declaration by the court that a company is deemed not to be a juristic person may be sought by way of application or may occur in terms of action proceedings. This is made clear from the use of the word 'proceedings' in s 163(4). The court may also act on its own initiative in deeming a company not to be a juristic person if it finds in any proceedings in which a company is involved that there was an unconscionable abuse of the juristic personality of the company as a separate entity.

(b) 'Interested person'

Section 163(4) permits any interested person to bring an application to court requesting the court to deem a company not to be a juristic person. The section does not define the term 'interested person'.

In *TJ Jonck BK h/a Bothaville Vleismark v Du Plessis NO*[179] the court stated, with reference to the meaning of the term 'interested person' in s 65 of the Close Corporations Act, that the term is not to be interpreted too restrictively, but at the same time it is not to be interpreted too widely as to include an indirect interest.[180] The court stated further that the interest is limited to a mere financial or monetary interest.[181] A creditor of a corporation, for instance, would be an interested person and may bring an application in terms of s 65 of the Close Corporations Act.[182] It is submitted that this interpretation of the term 'interested person' under s 65 of the Close Corporations Act would offer some useful guidance in determining who an interested person would be for purposes of bringing an application in terms of s 163(4) of the Act.

---

[177] See MP Larkin op cit n 159 at 280 in the context of a discussion of s 65 of the Close Corporations Act.
[178] The draft Companies Amendment Bill, 2010 proposes to move this provision to s 20 of the Act (dealing with the validity of company actions), which may not be the most appropriate place for it either.
[179] 1998 (1) SA 971 (O).
[180] At 986.
[181] Ibid.
[182] Ibid.

(c) Incorporation of the company, act by or on behalf of the company or the use of the company

Unconscionable abuse of the juristic personality of a company may occur:

- on the incorporation of the company,
- as a result of any act by, or on behalf of, the company,
- as a result of the use of the company as a legal entity.

Section 163(4) may be invoked not only where a company is formed as a sham or a stratagem, but also where a company has initially been legitimately established but is subsequently misused. This accords with the position in the common law. In *Cape Pacific Ltd v Lubner Controlling Investments (Pty) Ltd*[183] the Appellate Division asserted that in the common law the corporate personality of a company may be disregarded even if the company had been legitimately established and operated but was misused in a particular instance, and that it is not necessary for the company to have been 'conceived and founded in deceit'[184] before its corporate personality may be disregarded.

There is much scope for the courts to interpret the words 'any use of' a company widely, should it choose to do so.

(d) 'Unconscionable abuse'

As discussed earlier, in *Cape Pacific Ltd v Lubner Controlling Investments (Pty) Ltd*[185] the Appellate Division adopted a balancing approach to piercing the corporate veil in terms of which the need to preserve the company's separate legal personality must be balanced or weighed against those conflicting principles in favour of piercing the corporate veil. In *Hülse-Reutter v Gödde*[186] the Supreme Court of Appeal declared that, in order for the corporate veil to be pierced, there must be some abuse of the distinction between the corporate entity and those who control it, which results in an unfair advantage being afforded to the latter. But the test for piercing the corporate veil envisaged in s 163(4) of the Act concentrates only on the abuse of the juristic personality of the company as a separate entity, and whether that abuse constitutes 'unconscionable abuse'. It is not a requirement under s 163(4) that the abuse should result in an unfair advantage being afforded to those who control the company, as was laid down in *Hülse-Reutter v Gödde*. The test for piercing the corporate veil is to this extent simplified under s 163(4) of the Act.

However, the term 'unconscionable abuse' is not defined in s 163(4) and the section does not provide any guidance as to the facts or circumstances that would constitute an 'unconscionable abuse' of the juristic personality of the company as a separate entity. This is probably the most troublesome aspect of s 163(4).

Section 163(4) of the Act is worded similarly to s 65 of the Close Corporations Act. However, a difference between the two sections is that s 65 of the Close Corporations Act deems a corporation not to be a juristic person in instances of a

---

[183] 1995 (4) SA 790 (A).
[184] At 804.
[185] Supra at 803.
[186] 2001 (4) SA 1336 (SCA) para 20.

'gross abuse' of the juristic personality of the corporation as a separate entity, whereas s 163(4) of the Act deems a company not to be a juristic person where there is an 'unconscionable abuse' of the juristic personality of the company as a separate entity.

In *Mncube v District Seven Property Investments CC*[187] the court stated that, in the context of s 65 of the Close Corporations Act, broadly put, abuse of corporate personality would occur where the fact that a corporation is a person separate from its members is used for some 'nefarious purpose'.[188] This is as vague and uncertain as 'unconscionable'. How nefarious would the abuse have to be to constitute 'unconscionable abuse'? This is an issue our courts will have to contend with in interpreting s 163(4) of the Act.

It may be useful to consider some examples in our common law where the courts had regarded the abuse of the juristic personality of a close corporation as a separate entity to be a 'gross abuse' under s 65 of the Close Corporations Act. For instance, in *Haygro Catering BK v Van der Merwe*[189] the court held the members of a close corporation, together with the close corporation, jointly and severally liable for the debts of the close corporation where the name of the close corporation had not been displayed anywhere on the corporation's business premises, documents or correspondence, in contravention to s 23 of the Close Corporations Act. The court found that the failure to display the name of the corporation constituted a gross abuse of the juristic personality of the corporation as a separate entity, and held that it was justified in making an order in terms of the discretion conferred on it by s 65 of the Close Corporations Act.[190] The court held that whether s 23 or s 65 of the Close Corporations Act was applicable depended on the particular circumstances of the case, but that s 65 made provision for a more all-embracing manner of conduct.[191]

In *TJ Jonck BK h/a Bothaville Vleismark v Du Plessis NO*[192] a member of a close corporation had made significant loans to a close corporation. Even though he was aware that the corporation was insolvent, he had given written authorisation for the registration of a notarial bond over the movable property of the corporation as security for his loans to the corporation. A few months later he obtained an order entitling him to take possession of all the movable assets of the corporation in terms of the notarial bond, and to dispose of those assets as he saw fit. In this way the member acquired ownership of the business in his name, without any creditors, and he continued to conduct business from the same premises under a new name, using the equipment and stock that had previously been that of the close corporation.

The court held that the member of the close corporation was personally liable for the debts of the corporation in terms of s 64 of the Close Corporations Act, which makes provision for a member of a close corporation to be personally liable

---

[187] [2006] JOL 17381 (D).
[188] At 14.
[189] 1996 (4) SA 1063 (C).
[190] At 1070.
[191] At 1068.
[192] 1998 (1) SA 971 (O).

for the debts of the corporation where the business of the corporation is carried on recklessly, with gross negligence or for any fraudulent purpose. But the court went further and held that the plaintiff could also have succeeded in terms of s 65 of the Close Corporations Act because the member's actions had constituted a gross abuse of the juristic personality of the close corporation. The court found that the member had protected his own loan to the corporation in such a way that if the corporation encountered any difficulties he would be able to take over the movable assets immediately and leave an empty shell for the creditors, which is in fact, exactly what he had done.[193] The court ruled that this constituted a gross abuse of the juristic personality of the close corporation.[194]

A further example of gross abuse of juristic personality arises from the case of *Airport Cold Storage (Pty) Ltd v Ebrahim*.[195] Some of the factors that the court considered relevant in coming to the conclusion that there had been a gross abuse of the juristic personality of the corporation include the following:

- the close corporation had formed part of a conglomerate of associated family businesses that had been conducted with scant regard for the separate legal personalities of the entities concerned,
- the close corporation had not kept proper books of account,
- the close corporation had operated without having appointed an accounting officer,
- the close corporation had voluntarily assumed a debt owing by the family business when it was incorporated and had acquired significant debts from the start of commencing business, which had amounted to reckless trading.

The court found that, when it suited the defendants, they chose to ignore the separate juristic identity of the corporation. They could not 'now choose to take refuge behind the corporate veil'[196] of the corporation in order to evade liability for its debts. Accordingly, the court granted a declaratory order in terms of s 65 of the Close Corporations Act to the effect that the corporation was deemed not to be a juristic person, and held the defendants liable jointly and severally to the plaintiff for the amounts owing to the plaintiff by the corporation.[197]

Is there a difference between 'gross abuse' and 'unconscionable abuse'? How far would the abuse have to go before it is considered to be 'unconscionable'? One might argue that any abuse of the juristic personality of a company would be unconscionable. These are issues that the courts will have to grapple with in giving content to the meaning of the phrase 'unconscionable abuse'. The principles developed with regard to piercing the corporate veil in the context of s 65 of

---

[193] At 986.
[194] Ibid.
[195] 2008 (2) SA 303 (C).
[196] Para 52.
[197] On appeal, the Supreme Court of Appeal found it unnecessary to consider the application of s 65 of the Close Corporations Act to the facts of this case because it found that the appellants had acted recklessly in the running of the corporation's business and had contravened s 64 of the Close Corporations Act. The decision of the court *a quo* would nevertheless provide guidance to the scope of s 163(4) of the Act.

the Close Corporations Act and at common law generally may serve as useful guidelines in this regard.

(e) 'Deemed not to be a juristic person'

The consequence of a court declaring a company not to be a juristic person is that the company will cease to have a separate legal personality in respect of certain rights, obligations or liabilities of the company, or of a certain member or shareholder of the company or of any other person specified in the declaration.

In *Cape Pacific Ltd v Lubner Controlling Investments (Pty) Ltd*,[198] as discussed earlier, the Appellate Division stressed that the corporate veil cannot be disregarded by a court whenever it considers it just to do so.[199] As the court asserted, it is a salutary principle that our courts should not lightly disregard a company's separate personality, but that they should strive to give effect to and uphold it.[200] It is submitted that courts should bear this underpinning guiding principle in mind when applying s 163(4) of the Act and should not lightly deem a company not to be a juristic person. Perhaps the balancing approach envisaged in *Cape Pacific Ltd v Lubner Controlling Investments (Pty) Ltd*, discussed earlier, ought to be applied to the interpretation of s 163(4), that is, the need to preserve the company's separate legal personality must be balanced against those policy considerations in favour of piercing the veil.[201]

(f) Rights, obligations or liabilities

A court may declare a company not to be a juristic person in respect of certain rights, obligations or liabilities of the company, or of a certain member or shareholder of the company, or of any other person specified in the declaration. The unconscionable abuse must be in respect of particular rights, obligations or liabilities of the company, or of its members (in the case of a non-profit company) or shareholders or of another person specified in the declaration. A court does not have the power to intervene under s 163(4) of the Act where the unconscionable abuse is not in respect of any such right, obligation or liability.[202] For example, where a court comes to the conclusion that a company was incorporated for an unlawful purpose, such as lending money above the permitted rate in terms of the provisions of the Usury Act 73 of 1968, the court may not intervene under s 163(4) of the Act where the company has never made a loan to anyone, whether at or above the permissible rate.[203]

(g) Further orders

In declaring that a company is deemed not to be a juristic person, a court is given a wide discretion to make any further order or orders which it deems fit in order to give effect to such declaration.

---

[198] 1995 (4) SA 790 (A).
[199] At 805.
[200] At 803.
[201] Ibid.
[202] See B Galgut & Jennifer A Kunst *Henochsberg on the Close Corporations Act* vol 3 (1997) (Service Issue 24, June 2010) at Com–191–2.
[203] Ibid at Com–192.

2.4.8 Imposing personal liability on the directors of a company

In certain instances, the Act imposes liability on the directors and prescribed officers of the company for the loss, damages or costs sustained by the company. Such instances have often been described as instances of piercing the corporate veil, but they are more accurately described as instances of lifting the veil.[204] Where the Act makes provision for the corporate veil to be lifted, the courts are not faced with the vexing question of whether in the circumstances the corporate veil ought to be pierced, and do not have a discretion whether or not to pierce the veil, as is the case in the common law. The justification for the statutory lifting of the veil is to be found in the policy of the statute; the legislature is free to decide that policy requires the corporate veil to be lifted in certain instances.[205] Some instances where the Act imposes personal liability on the directors of a company are mentioned below. See also chapter 12: The Duties and the Liability of Directors.

(a) Acting without authority

In terms of s 77(3)(a) of the Act, where a director acts in the name of the company, signs anything on behalf of the company, purports to bind the company or authorises the taking of any action by or on behalf of the company, despite knowing that he or she lacks the authority to do so, he or she will be personally liable for any loss, damages or costs sustained by the company as a direct or indirect consequence of his or her actions.

(b) Reckless trading

Section 77(3)(b) of the Act provides that a director of a company will be liable for any loss, damages or costs sustained by the company as a direct or indirect consequence of the director having acquiesced in the carrying on of the company's business, despite knowing that it was being conducted in a manner prohibited by s 22(1) of the Act. Section 22(1) of the Act provides as follows:

> A company must not —
> (a) carry on its business recklessly, with gross negligence, with intent to defraud any person or for any fraudulent purpose; or
> (b) trade under insolvent circumstances.

(c) Fraud

In terms of s 77(3)(c) of the Act, a director will be liable for any loss, damages or costs sustained by the company as a direct or indirect consequence of the director

---

[204] Blackman describes these so-called statutory instances of 'piercing the veil' as being instances of 'veil limitation'. Blackman reasons that a company has separate legal personality only in so far as it is recognised as having separate personality by the legislature, and therefore no harm is done to the theory of corporate personality when the law limits the extent of that personality. Thus it is argued that these statutory instances of piercing the veil are simply instances of veil limitation (see Blackman et al op cit n 143 at 4–144). Blackman argues further that these statutory instances of piercing the veil may also be viewed as being exceptions to the law of agency (Blackman et al op cit n 143 at 4–146). Directors are agents of the company and in terms of agency rules an agent is not liable on a contract that he or she enters into on behalf of his or her principal. Thus where legislation renders directors personally liable for the debts of the company Blackman argues that the corporate veil is not pierced but rather an exception is made to the rule that agents are not liable under contracts entered into on behalf of their principals (see Blackman et al op cit n 143 at 4–146).
[205] Paul L Davies op cit n 21 at 200.

having been a party to an act or omission by the company, despite knowing that the act or omission was calculated to defraud a creditor, employee or shareholder of the company, or had another fraudulent purpose.

(d) False or misleading statements

Under s 77(3)(d) of the Act, a director will be liable for any loss, damages or costs sustained by the company as a direct or indirect consequence of the director having signed, consented to or authorised the publication of *(a)* any financial statements that were false or misleading in a material respect, or *(b)* a prospectus or written statement required when secondary offers are made to the public (in terms of s 101 of the Act) that contains untrue statements, or a statement to the effect that a person had consented to be a director when no such consent had been given, despite knowing that the statements were false, misleading or untrue.[206]

(e) Unlawful distributions

Under s 77(3)(e) of the Act, a director of a company will be liable for any loss, damages or costs sustained by the company as a direct or indirect consequence of the director having been present at a meeting, or participated in the making of a decision by means of a round robin resolution, and knowingly failing to vote against various decisions, such as those relating to the issuing of shares, distributions, the provision of financial assistance for the acquisition of securities of a company, the provision of financial assistance to a director and the acquisition by a company of its shares.

(f) Causing the company to act contrary to the Companies Act or the Memorandum of Incorporation

Under s 20(6) of the Act each shareholder of a company has a claim for damages against any person who fraudulently or due to gross negligence causes the company to do anything inconsistent with the Act or with a provision in the company's Memorandum of Incorporation which limits, restricts or qualifies the purposes, powers or activities of the company, or limits the authority of the directors to perform an act on behalf of the company, unless that action is ratified by special resolution. Any act in contravention of the Act cannot be ratified by special resolution. See also chapter 5: Corporate Capacity, Agency and the Turquand Rule.

(g) Contravening the Companies Act

Section 218(2) of the Act provides that any person who contravenes any provision of the Act is liable to any other person for any loss or damage suffered by that person as a result of that contravention.

---

[206] The liability of a director relating to untrue statements is limited by the provisions of s 104(3) of the Act.

CHAPTER 3
TYPES OF COMPANIES

Maleka Femida Cassim

3.1	INTRODUCTION	63
	3.1.1 Policy and purposes	63
	3.1.2 Close corporations	64
	3.1.3 Partnerships	64
	3.1.4 Pre-existing companies	65
3.2	PROFIT AND NON-PROFIT COMPANIES	65
3.3	TYPES OF PROFIT COMPANIES	66
	3.3.1 Introduction	66
	3.3.2 General characteristics of profit companies	67
3.4	THE PRIVATE COMPANY	69
	3.4.1 Definition	69
	3.4.2 Other characteristics of private companies	69
	3.4.3 Restriction on transferability of securities of private companies	71
	(a) Manner or form of restriction	71
	(b) Effect of a restriction on transferability	72
	(c) Distinction between pre-emptive rights in terms of s 8(2)(b) and s 39	74
3.5	THE PUBLIC COMPANY	74
	3.5.1 Definition	74
	3.5.2 Other characteristics of public companies	75
	3.5.3 Listing the securities of public companies	76
	3.5.4 Differences between public and private companies	76
3.6	THE PERSONAL LIABILITY COMPANY	77
	3.6.1 Definition	77
	3.6.2 Other characteristics of personal liability companies	78
	3.6.3 Pre-existing section 53(b) companies	78
	3.6.4 The liability of the directors in a personal liability company	79
3.7	THE STATE-OWNED COMPANY	81
	3.7.1 Definition	81
	3.7.2 Other characteristics of state-owned companies	82
	3.7.3 Pre-existing ('state-owned') companies	83
3.8	NON-PROFIT COMPANIES (NPCs)	83
	3.8.1 Definition	83
	3.8.2 Other characteristics of NPCs	84
	3.8.3 Objects and policies of NPCs	86

		(a)	Assets and income	86
		(b)	Financial benefit or gain	86
		(c)	Winding-up or dissolution	87
		(d)	Tax	87
	3.8.4	Incorporators of NPCs		88
	3.8.5	Members of NPCs and voting rights		88
	3.8.6	Directors of NPCs		89
	3.8.7	Fundamental transactions of NPCs		89
	3.8.8	Pre-existing section 21 companies		90
3.9	EXTERNAL COMPANIES			90
	3.9.1	Definition		90
	3.9.2	Types of external companies		92
	3.9.3	Application of the Act to external companies		93
3.10	CLOSE CORPORATIONS			95
	3.10.1	A new approach		95
	3.10.2	Conversion of a close corporation to a company		97
3.11	CONVERSION OF COMPANIES			98

3.1 INTRODUCTION

3.1.1 Policy and purposes

It has long been recognised in company law that the entity of the company is not just limited to the alliance of a large body of persons for the conduct of business with the object of financial gain or profit making. On the contrary, the company structure is as available to large groups of members and the investing public in general as it is to small groups of members or even a single individual who wishes to conduct business under limited liability. Nor is the purpose of the company as an entity limited to profit making only — the company structure may likewise be used for conducting public benefit activities or communal, social, charitable or other non-profit activities. The company structure may also serve many other functions, including the holding of the legal title to assets, the holding of family assets, or serving as the corporate vehicle for a joint venture where several parties are involved in a particular project. In recognition of the many and varied functions of companies, the Companies Act 71 of 2008 (hereafter 'the Act') creates scope for a number of different types or categories of companies, which are examined in this chapter.

The recognition of various types of companies under the Act is aligned with the stated purposes of the Act. In this regard, the Act purports to create 'flexibility' and 'simplicity' in the formation and maintenance of companies to promote the development of the South African economy.[1] The availability of a diversity of corporate structures, together with the flexibility in the design and organisation of companies under the Act, is in line with one of the main themes of the corporate law reform programme. These features may also serve the stated purposes of the Act to 'promote innovation and investment in the South African markets', and to 'continue to provide for the creation and use of companies, in a manner that

---
[1] Section 7*(b)*(ii) of the Act.

enhances the economic welfare of South Africa as a partner within the global economy'.[2] In relation to non-profit companies, the Act sets forth an individual and specific purpose, in that it purports to 'provide for the formation, operation and accountability of non-profit companies in a manner designed to promote, support and enhance the capacity of such companies to perform their functions.'[3] The pertinent or underpinning purposes of the Act must be borne in mind when contemplating the detailed sections that relate to the types of companies that may be formed.

3.1.2 Close corporations

The Act thus serves as a single statute governing diverse types of companies, ranging from the very simple and basic single-shareholder company to the most complex listed public company and the non-profit company. In tandem with this, the Act makes a significant impact on close corporations and the Close Corporations Act 69 of 1984.[4] *Existing* close corporations are free to retain their current status indefinitely or until such time as their members decide that it is in their interest to convert the close corporation to a company. But no *new* close corporations may be formed after the effective date of the Act, nor may companies be converted into close corporations once the Act has come into force.

The underlying policy on close corporations is that the Companies Act is intended to provide the scope and simplicity to structure and maintain small companies in a way that resembles the characteristics of the close corporation. It is consequently anticipated that the formation of new close corporations would be rendered unnecessary[5] as small owner-managed companies will have absorbed most of the features of a close corporation. This policy is, however, debatable.

3.1.3 Partnerships

Partnerships are not addressed in the Act and continue to be governed largely by common law. In contrast with the Companies Act 61 of 1973 (hereafter 'the 1973 Act'),[6] the new Act no longer places any restriction on the number of partners or members of an association formed for carrying on business for the acquisition of gain. A partnership may now have an unlimited number of partners.

Section 8(3) of the Act states that an association of persons formed for the purpose of carrying on any business, that has for its object the acquisition of gain by the association or its individual members, may not be a company or other form of body corporate unless it is registered as a company under the Act (or is formed pursuant to another law; or was formed pursuant to Letters Patent or Royal Charter before 31 May 1962). This provision, which has its equivalent in the 1973

---

[2] Section 7*(c)* and *(e)*.
[3] Section 7*(h)*.
[4] Hereafter 'the Close Corporations Act'.
[5] *Memorandum on the Objects of the Companies Bill, 2008*, Companies Bill [B 61D–2008] at paras 1 and 2.
[6] Section 30 of the 1973 Act imposed a maximum limit of 20 partners. This was done to avoid the practical difficulties that arose in dealing with large unincorporated associations.

Act,[7] makes it clear that, where an association is formed for the acquisition of gain and wishes to enjoy corporate personality, it must be formally registered as a company.[8] Thus a 'company' formed for profit remains precluded from becoming a body corporate at common law by simply conducting itself as a legal person.[9]

3.1.4 Pre-existing companies

Turning to pre-existing companies, the Act applies equally to companies that were registered under the 1973 Act (save for external companies), as well as those that were recognised as 'existing companies' under the 1973 Act.[10] The Transitional Arrangements explicitly state that pre-existing companies continue to exist as companies as if they had been incorporated and registered in terms of the Act. They also continue to bear the same name and registration number previously assigned to them.[11]

Pre-existing companies are given two years in which to amend their constitutions without charge or fee, to bring them in harmony with the new Act. Their names may also be altered without charge or fee within this two-year period, to satisfy the requirements of the new Act.[12] Pre-existing companies are generally deemed to have changed the concluding words or concluding expressions of their names (as appropriate for the relevant type of company, eg Inc., NPC) as required in order to comply with the Act.[13]

3.2 PROFIT AND NON-PROFIT COMPANIES

There are now two broad categories of companies that may be formed and incorporated under the Act, namely:[14]

- profit companies (of which there are four types), and
- non-profit companies.

A non-profit company is formed for a public benefit object, or an object relating to a cultural or social activity or communal or group interest. It is part of the essence of a non-profit company that its income and property cannot be distributed to its members or directors.[15] Non-profit companies are subject to a modified application of the Act and to a distinct set of essential rules (set out in Schedule 1 to the Act) that govern matters unique to non-profit companies. The non-profit company is examined in detail below in 3.8.

---

[7] Section 31 of the 1973 Act.
[8] *Mitchell's Plain Town Centre Merchants Association v McLeod* 1996 (4) SA 159 (A).
[9] FHI Cassim 'The Companies Act 2008: An Overview of a Few of its Core Provisions' (2010) 22 *SA Merc LJ* 157 at 162. See for instance *Morrison v Standard Building Society* 1932 AD 229.
[10] See the definitions of 'company' and 'pre-existing company' in s 1 of the Act.
[11] Subject to Schedule 5 item 4 (Schedule 5 item 2).
[12] Schedule 5 item 4(2).
[13] Schedule 5 item 4(1) read with s 11(3) and cl 115 of the draft Companies Amendment Bill, 2010. See further chapter 4: Formation of Companies and the Company Constitution and chapter 21: Transitional Arrangements.
[14] Section 8(1).
[15] Or to its incorporators, officers or persons related to any of them, except to the extent permitted by Schedule 1 item 1(3) (s 1). See further below.

A profit company, on the other hand, is formed for the purpose of financial gain for its shareholders.[16] Profit companies are subdivided into four categories: the private company, the public company, the personal liability company and the state-owned company. Each type of profit company is dealt with in turn below.

The distinction between profit and non-profit companies may be compared and contrasted with the distinction in terms of the 1973 Act between companies having a share capital and companies not having a share capital, known as companies limited by guarantee.[17] Profit companies under the new Act are analogous to companies having a share capital under the 1973 Act — profit companies are in fact companies with shares.[18] Non-profit companies under the new Act are companies without a share capital, but they are not at all akin to companies limited by guarantee. The non-profit company is best regarded as the modern successor to the Section 21 company under the 1973 Act. Companies limited by guarantee have now been consigned to history.

The company limited by guarantee as classified by the 1973 Act has no real counterpart under the new Act.[19] An entity that was incorporated under the 1973 Act as a company limited by guarantee may elect to become a profit company under the Act. It does so by filing a notice electing to become a profit company and changing the concluding expression of its name to correctly reflect the type of company that it now is. The notice must be filed within 20 business days after the general effective date of the Act. If a company limited by guarantee fails to file such a notice, it is deemed to have amended its Memorandum of Incorporation to expressly state that it is a non-profit company, and to have changed its name as appropriate, with effect from the general effective date of the Act.[20]

3.3 TYPES OF PROFIT COMPANIES

3.3.1 Introduction

In terms of the Act, profit companies are categorised as follows:[21]

- the private company (which is the successor to the private company under the 1973 Act),
- the public company (which is comparable to the public company under the 1973 Act),

---

[16] Section 1.
[17] Section 19 of the 1973 Act.
[18] See also the definition of 'share' in s 1 as 'one of the units into which the proprietary interest in a *profit* company is divided' [emphasis added].
[19] Except for the Section 21 company which, in terms of the 1973 Act, was classified as a public company limited by guarantee.
[20] Schedule 5 item 4(1)(*d*). The erroneous reference in this item to s 11(3)(*b*) of the Act is to be corrected by the draft Companies Amendment Bill, 2010 (cl 115), so as to now refer to s 11(3). The reference in this item to the existing Memorandum of Incorporation is simply taken to mean the memorandum of association and articles of association of a pre-existing company (see chapter 21: Transitional Arrangements).
[21] Section 8(2).

- the personal liability company (which is the successor to the incorporated or professional company formed under s 53*(b)* company of the 1973 Act), and
- the state-owned company.

Each type of profit company is discussed under a separate heading below.

The preservation of the well-established and familiar distinction between public and private companies under the Act is welcome. The Act thankfully does away with the confusing and controversial concepts of a 'limited interest' company and a 'widely held' company that were introduced to the 1973 Act,[22] by the Corporate Laws Amendment Act 24 of 2006.

3.3.2 General characteristics of profit companies

There are a number of important characteristics common to all profit companies. First, the purpose of the incorporation of a profit company, as opposed to a non-profit company, is financial gain for its shareholders.[23] Secondly, a profit company is formed by one or more persons as incorporators, regardless of the type of profit company it is.[24] This may be distinguished from a non-profit company which requires a minimum of three incorporators. Thirdly, profit companies may have any number of shareholders. Unlike the 1973 Act, the new Act does not prescribe a mandatory minimum number of shareholders for public companies.[25] Nor does it place any limitations or restrictions on the maximum number of shareholders of any type of profit company.[26] Profit companies may consequently have an unlimited number of shareholders and, by the same token, single-shareholder public companies are now permissible.

Certain requirements of the Act are universally applicable to all types of companies, whereas other additional requirements apply to selected companies only. Significantly, companies that bear a greater responsibility to a wider public are subjected to a more demanding disclosure, accountability and transparency regime. This pertains mainly to public companies and state-owned companies. It applies also to certain private companies and personal liability companies that have a significant social or economic impact.[27] The extended accountability and transparency requirements include, among other things, the auditing of financial statements and the obligatory appointment of company secretaries, auditors and

---

[22] See the Corporate Laws Amendment Act 24 of 2006.

[23] Section 1.

[24] Sections 1 and 13(1). The draft Companies Amendment Bill, 2010 (cl 9) proposes that an organ of state may also incorporate a profit company, while a non-profit company may be incorporated by an organ of state, a juristic person, or three or more persons acting in common.

[25] Public companies under the 1973 Act required a minimum of seven members while for private companies two persons, or even one person, sufficed (ss 32 and 54(2) of the 1973 Act; see also s 66 of the 1973 Act). The term 'member', as used by the 1973 Act, is the equivalent of a shareholder in a profit company under the current Act.

[26] Under the previous company law regime, private companies were limited to a maximum of 50 members or shareholders (excluding employees and former employees who continued to be members) (s 20 of the 1973 Act).

[27] *Memorandum on the Objects of the Companies Bill, 2008* op cit n 5 para 6; see s 84(1); s 30(2) and (7); s 34(1) and (2).

audit committees, as dealt with further below.[28] Public and state-owned companies must also appoint a social and ethics committee that would monitor the extent to which the company takes stakeholder interests into account.[29] In this respect the Act[30] provides that the Minister may by regulation prescribe that a company or a category of companies must have a social and ethics committee, if this is desirable in the public interest, having regard to its annual turnover, the size of its workforce, or the nature and extent of its activities.

As an added measure to create flexibility in the Act, exceptions are created for owner-managed companies in which all the shareholders are also directors. This results in a diminished need to seek shareholder approval for certain board actions, since ownership and control are not split in such companies.[31] Exceptions are also created for companies in which all the shares are owned by 'related persons',[32] which results in a diminished need to protect minority shareholders.[33]

Further special provisions apply to single-shareholder and single-director companies. In a single-shareholder profit company (other than a state-owned company), the single shareholder may exercise any voting rights on any matter, at any time, without notice or compliance with any other internal formalities.[34] By the same token, in a single-director profit company (other than a state-owned company) the sole director may at any time, without notice or compliance with any other internal formalities, exercise any power or perform any function of the board.[35] Although it is not expressly stated in the Act, the latter provision cannot apply to public companies, because public companies in any case are obliged to have at least three directors.

These provisions enhance flexibility in the regulation of small, owner-managed companies and single-shareholder or single-director companies, which need not be regulated to the same extent as other companies.

---

[28] See also chapter 13: The Auditor, Financial Records and Reporting for further detail.

[29] See s 72(4) read with Regulation 50 of the draft Companies Regulations Pursuant to the Companies Act, 2008 (Act No. 71 of 2008) GN 1664 *GG* 32832 of 22 December 2009 (hereafter 'the draft Companies Regulations') and cl 45 of the draft Companies Amendment Bill, 2010. The requirement of a social and ethics committee is subject to some exceptions. See further chapter 10: Governance and the Board of Directors and chapter 12: The Duties and the Liability of Directors.

[30] Section 72(4).

[31] If every shareholder of a particular company (other than a state-owned company) is also a director of that company, any matter that is required to be referred by the board to the shareholders for decision may be decided by the shareholders at any time after being referred by the board, without notice or compliance with any other internal formalities, except to the extent that the Memorandum of Incorporation provides otherwise and subject to the conditions set out in s 57(4). When acting in their capacity as shareholders, those persons are not subject to the provisions of ss 73–8 relating to the duties, obligations, liabilities and indemnification of directors (see further s 57(4) and chapter 9: Governance and Shareholders).

[32] As defined in s 2.

[33] *Memorandum on the Objects of the Companies Bill, 2008* op cit n 5 para 4.

[34] Except to the extent that the company's Memorandum of Incorporation provides otherwise or if the company is a state-owned company; additionally ss 59–65 do not apply to the governance of that company (s 57(2)). See also s 57(1).

[35] Except to the extent that the company's Memorandum of Incorporation provides otherwise or if the company is a state-owned company; and ss 71(3)–(7), 73 and 74 do not apply to the governance of that company (s 57(3)).

3.4 THE PRIVATE COMPANY

3.4.1 Definition

A profit company is a private company if:
- it is not a state-owned company,[36] and
- its Memorandum of Incorporation *both*:
  - prohibits the offer of any of its securities to the public, *and*
  - restricts the transferability of its securities.[37]

The two core characteristics of a private company are that its securities may not be offered to the public and the transferability of its securities must be restricted. These features may consequently be considered to be the quintessence of a private company. (It is noteworthy that these two essential features apply also to a personal liability company, which may be regarded as a subcategory of a private company.)

Indeed, the essential distinctions between a private company and a public company are that, while a private company is proscribed from making any offer to the public of any of its securities, a public company is permitted to do so to raise capital from the public. Additionally, while the Memorandum of Incorporation of a private company must restrict the transferability of its securities, that of a public company need not do so.

The requirements for a private company under the Act closely approximate those in terms of the 1973 Act,[38] save for two major differences: First, the restriction of shareholders in a private company to a maximum number of 50 has now been abolished. This is in the interests of flexibility and modernisation and also because of the realisation that the number of shareholders bears no true correlation to the type of company that it is. As a result, the legislation now relies more on functional grounds of distinction between public and private companies.[39] Secondly, the restriction on the right to transfer 'shares' in terms of the 1973 Act has apparently been widened under the new Act to a restriction on the transferability of 'securities'. This is considered further below.

3.4.2 Other characteristics of private companies

An important attribute of a private company is that its name must end with the expression 'Proprietary Limited' or its abbreviation '(Pty) Ltd.'.[40]

A private company need only have one director at a minimum, but this is subject to the company's Memorandum of Incorporation which may specify a

---

[36] Section 1 of the Act states in contrast, and apparently erroneously, that a private company means a profit company that 'is not a company or a personal liability state-owned company' and that satisfies the criteria in s 8(2)(*b*). This presumably is intended to read 'is not a public, personal liability or state-owned company' (as now proposed by the draft Companies Amendment Bill, 2010 (cl 2(1)).

[37] Section 1 read with s 8(2)(*b*).

[38] Section 20(1) of the 1973 Act.

[39] FHI Cassim op cit n 9 at 162.

[40] Section 11(3)(*c*). The draft Companies Amendment Bill, 2010 (cl 7) proposes the expression 'Pty. Ltd.' instead.

higher minimum number of directors.[41] A private company, as stated above, is formed by one or more persons as incorporators.[42]

It is not mandatory for a private company to appoint a company secretary or an audit committee, unless it voluntarily elects to do so in terms of its Memorandum of Incorporation. Private companies are not required to appoint social and ethics committees either.[43] As a general principle, it is not mandatory for a private company to appoint an auditor — unless its Memorandum of Incorporation provides otherwise or it is a significant private company that is required by the Act or regulations to have its financial statements audited.[44]

Turning to financial statements, the default position is that the annual financial statements of (some) private companies need to be independently reviewed, but need not be audited. An audit is necessary only if the company voluntarily opts to do so, or if it is required to do so by regulations in terms of the Act.[45] The latter applies to those private companies that have a significant social or economic impact and consequently have a greater responsibility to a wider public, as indicated by their turnover, the size of their workforce and/or the nature and extent of their activities.[46]

Moreover, in order to create further flexibility under the Act, an exemption is granted from both the independent review and the audit of the annual financial statements of a private company where one person holds (or has all of the beneficial interest in) all the securities issued by the company; or alternatively, where every person who is a holder of (or has a beneficial interest in) any securities of the company is also a director of the company.[47] The draft Companies Regulations also impose certain thresholds and requirements for the independent review of the annual financial statements of a private company.[48]

---

[41] Section 66(2) and (3). Where a private company is required to appoint an audit committee (or a social and ethics committee), whether in terms of the Act or in terms of its Memorandum of Incorporation, more than one director would be required to be appointed (see s 94, which states that an audit committee must comprise at least three members, who must be directors and who must not be involved in the day-to-day management of the company's business; see also cl 42 of the draft Companies Amendment Bill, 2010).

[42] Section 13(1) (or it may be incorporated by an organ of state, in terms of the draft Companies Amendment Bill, 2010 (cl 9)).

[43] Section 72(4) read with Regulation 50 of the draft Companies Regulations. However, s 72(4) empowers the Minister to prescribe by regulation that a private company or any other company must have a social and ethics committee, if this is desirable in the public interest, having regard to its annual turnover, the size of its workforce, or the nature and extent of its activities.

[44] Section 84(1); s 34(2); cl 51 of the draft Companies Amendment Bill, 2010.

[45] Section 30(2); s 30(7); see also cl 20 of the draft Companies Amendment Bill, 2010.

[46] Section 30(2) read with s 30(7). See further Regulation 29 of the draft Companies Regulations.

[47] Section 30(2)(*b*)(ii). The first exemption (above) may be deleted, in terms of the draft Companies Amendment Bill, 2010 (cl 20).

[48] See further Regulation 30 of the draft Companies Regulations and chapter 13: The Auditor, Financial Records and Reporting.

Types of Companies

3.4.3 Restriction on transferability of securities of private companies

(a) Manner or form of restriction

The Act requires that the Memorandum of Incorporation of a private company restricts the free transferability of its securities. But the Act does not prescribe the manner or form of restriction.[49] In a similar vein, the 1973 Act merely required a restriction on the free right to transfer shares, without any further specification. Compliance with this core criterion under the previous regime was attained by restricting transferability in any of a number of different ways. It is to be expected that under the new Act, the restriction on the free transferability of securities would be interpreted and applied in a similar way as under the 1973 Act.

In this regard, the restriction on the right to transfer shares under the previous regime was frequently achieved by means of rights of pre-emption under the company's constitution. Such rights of pre-emption effectively prohibit an existing shareholder from selling his or her shares to a non-shareholder, unless the other shareholders of the company have first had an opportunity to purchase the shares. This could be, for instance, at a price agreed on by the shareholders or, failing agreement, at a price determined by the auditors.[50]

Another possibility is to state that the shares may be transferable to a non-shareholder only upon approval of the board of directors of the company.[51] Alternatively, the transfer of shares could be subject to the approval of the other shareholders.[52] Since shares are, in principle, freely transferable, any restriction on transferability would suffice for this purpose.

While the 1973 Act required a restriction on the right to transfer the 'shares' of a private company,[53] the new Act refers to 'securities' and not shares. The term 'securities' has a much wider meaning than 'shares'. According to its definition in the Act,[54] the term 'securities' bears the meaning set out in s 1 of the Securities Services Act 36 of 2004[55] and includes shares held in a private company. Thus

---

[49] Section 8(2)*(b)*(ii)*(bb)*.

[50] See eg articles 21–24 of Table B (Model Articles for a private company), Schedule 1 of the 1973 Act.

[51] See eg *Moosa v Lalloo* 1956 (2) SA 207 (D); *Richter v Riverside Estates (Pty) Ltd* 1946 OPD 209.

[52] See eg *Greenhalgh v Arderne Cinemas* [1951] Ch 286; [1950] 2 All ER 1120 (CA).

[53] Section 20(1) of the 1973 Act.

[54] Section 1. This definition is proposed to be amended by the substitution of the words 'shares held in a private company' with the words 'any share issued, or authorised to be issued by a profit company' (draft Companies Amendment Bill, 2010, cl 2(1)).

[55] This states that 'securities' *(a)* means: (i) shares, stocks and depository receipts in public companies and other equivalent equities, other than shares in a share block company as defined in the Share Blocks Control Act 1980; (ii) notes; (iii) derivative instruments; (iv) bonds; (v) debentures; (vi) participatory interests in a collective investment scheme as defined in the Collective Investment Schemes Control Act 2002, and units or any other form of participation in a foreign collective investment scheme approved by the Registrar of Collective Investment Schemes in terms of section 65 of that Act; (vii) units or any other form of participation in a collective investment scheme licensed or registered in a foreign country; (viii) instruments based on an index; (ix) the securities contemplated in subparagraphs (i) to (viii) that are listed on an external exchange; and (x) an instrument similar to one or more of the securities contemplated in subparagraphs (i) to (ix) declared

'debt instruments' are also 'securities', as defined.[56] The extension of the restricted transferability of 'shares' to also include other 'securities' could have far-reaching practical implications for private companies. One wonders whether the drafters actually intended this or whether this is an unintended consequence. (This is more so in view of the statement in the *Memorandum on the Objects of the Companies Bill, 2008*[57] that private companies under the Act are comparable to companies of the same status under the 1973 Act).

(b) Effect of a restriction on transferability

Turning to the effect of a restriction on transferability, the decision in *Smuts v Booysens; Markplaas (Edms) Bpk v Booysens*[58] must be considered. It was held in this case that the restricted transferability of shares (in the context of s 20(1) of the 1973 Act) is an essential attribute of a private company. As to the meaning of the term 'transfer', the court stated that transfer is restricted in the full, technical sense of the word, so that the entire series of steps comprising a transfer is restricted, comprising the agreement to transfer, the execution of the deed of transfer *and* the registration of the transfer.[59]

The court stated further that, if any restrictions on transferability in terms of the company's constitution are not complied with, then the shares are not transferable at all. To legally transfer his or her shares to a purchaser, a shareholder must comply with the procedure for transfer and/or the restrictions on transfer set out in the company's constitution. Failing compliance, no rights in respect of the shares may be transferred to the purchaser at all and the rights lack transmissibility *ab initio*. The court accordingly laid down that the restriction on transferability is an absolute prohibition in the form of a *pactum de non cedendo*. The court stated that, in terms of the 1973 Act, it was irrelevant that the purchaser had been unaware of the restrictions on the transfer of the company's shares.

It is consequently clear that, if any restriction on transferability in terms of the company's constitution is not observed, there can be no effective 'transfer' of the shares. However, the court's interpretation of the word 'transfer' in this context as embracing the agreement to transfer, the execution of the deed of transfer *and* the registration of the transfer (ie the entire series of steps comprising a transfer) has been the subject of some debate. The opposing view is that a shareholder who fails to comply with a restriction on 'transfer' is not prohibited from transferring the *beneficial ownership* of the shares (by way of cession, which requires no formalities), and that the Act merely prohibits and denies the right to have the transfer

---

by the registrar by notice in the *Government Gazette* to be a security for the purposes of this Act; (xi) rights in the securities referred to in subparagraphs (i) to (x); and 'securities' *(b)* excludes: (i) money market instruments (except for the purposes of Chapter IV); and (ii) any security contemplated in paragraph *(a)* specified by the registrar by notice in the *Government Gazette*. See further chapter 7: Shares, Securities and Transfer.

[56] See s 43.
[57] *Memorandum on the Objects of the Companies Bill, 2008* op cit n 5 para 4.
[58] 2001 (4) SA 15 (SCA).
[59] At 21–2.

registered (in terms of the formal process by which the new shareholder is recognised by the company and third parties).[60]

This counterargument has not been accepted by the courts and the current position at common law, as decided by the Supreme Court of Appeal in *Smuts v Booysens*, remains that non-compliance with the restrictions on transferability in terms of a private company's constitution has the effect that the transfer of the beneficial ownership (or beneficial interest) of the shares by cession is entirely void.

Smuts v Booysens was, as stated above, decided under the 1973 Act. It is noteworthy in this regard that while the 1973 Act (s 20(1)*(a)*) required a private company to restrict 'the *right* to *transfer* its shares', the current Act differs slightly in wording in that it requires a private company to restrict 'the *transferability*' of its securities. This change in wording could have an impact on this debate. The optimal course of action would, of course, be to clearly express this matter in terms of the company's constitution, particularly since the provisions restricting the transferability of shares tend to be strictly interpreted.[61] It remains to be seen whether a future court would strictly apply the *ratio decidendi* of *Smuts v Booysens* to s 8(2)*(b)*(ii)*(bb)* of the new Act.

Where an existing shareholder of a private company wishes to exercise a right of pre-emption in terms of s 8(2)*(b)*, the shareholder must agree to purchase the *total* number of the shares that are offered, and cannot purchase merely a *part* of them. This was laid down in *Sindler NO v Gees*[62] where the court was faced with a pre-emptive right restricting the transfer of the company's shares under the 1973 Act. In this case a shareholder, who had a pre-emptive right to purchase 50 per cent of the 300 shares in the company, wished to purchase only three shares and to pay for the shares on the basis of the proportionate price for the full 150 shares. The court held that the offer to the shareholder could not be construed as a separate offer for each share, and that the selling price of the shares could not be converted into a price for each share offered. Accordingly, a shareholder who holds a pre-emptive right in terms of s 8(2)*(b)* of the Act would probably have to be willing to purchase *all* the shares in question. Although *Sindler v Gees* is partly based on the wording of the Model articles in terms of the 1973 Act,[63] this principle may well continue to apply to the exercise of pre-emptive rights in terms of s 8(2)*(b)* of the new Act. This too remains to be seen.[64]

---

[60] MS Blackman et al *Commentary on the Companies Act* 1 (2010) 5–184–5–187; MP Larkin and FHI Cassim 'Company Law' in *Annual Survey of South African Law* (2001) 547–8.

[61] *Greenhalgh v Mallard* [1943] All ER 234 (CA) 237; *Estate Milne v Donohoe Investments (Pty) Ltd* 1967 (2) SA 359 (A).

[62] 2006 (5) SA 501 (C).

[63] Articles 21–24 of Table B of Schedule 1.

[64] This case is based on the English law case of *Ocean Coal Co Ltd v Powell Duffryn Steam Coal Co* [1932] 1 Ch 654; [1932] All ER 845. It might however be possible for a shareholder holding a pre-emptive right to purchase only a portion of the shares on offer where the company's constitution expressly so provides. The decision in *Sindler v Gees* (supra) was based on the construction of the particular clause in the company's constitution.

(c) Distinction between pre-emptive rights in terms of s 8(2)(b) and s 39

The rights of pre-emption that may be imposed to satisfy the requirement of s 8(2)(b) of the Act (namely that the securities of a private company must be restricted from free transferability) must not be confused with the pre-emptive rights that shareholders in a private company generally enjoy in terms of s 39 of the Act. In this regard, s 39 confers on each shareholder of a private company a pre-emptive right to be offered (and within a reasonable time to subscribe for) a percentage (that is equal to the shareholder's general voting power immediately before the offer is made) of any *new* shares[65] that the company proposes to issue, before those shares may be offered to a non-shareholder.[66]

The distinction between the s 39 pre-emptive rights and a pre-emptive right restricting the transferability of shares in terms of s 8(2)(b) is that the former is concerned with the *issue* of shares, while the latter is related to the *transfer* of shares. These are two different and distinct methods by which a person may acquire title to the shares of a company.

To elaborate, the pre-emptive right in terms of s 39 is concerned with the acquisition of new shares *directly from the company* (that is, a subscription for shares) and the company in this case 'issues' the shares to the subscriber. On the other hand, the pre-emptive right in satisfaction of s 8(2)(b) applies to the situation where one acquires shares in the company from an *existing shareholder* who wishes to dispose of them (usually by way of a purchase) and the shares are then 'transferred' into the name of the acquirer.[67]

A private company must both restrict the transferability of its shares and comply with the pre-emptive rights of existing shareholders to subscribe for new shares — although the latter (but not the former) may be excluded under the company's Memorandum of Incorporation.[68]

Unlike the decision in *Sindler v Gees,* which applies to s 8(2)(b) pre-emptive rights, a shareholder who exercises a s 39 pre-emptive right is permitted to subscribe for fewer shares than the total number offered to him or her.[69]

3.5 THE PUBLIC COMPANY

3.5.1 Definition

A public company is, for all intents and purposes, undefined in the Act. Section 1 simply states that a public company is a profit company that is not a state-owned company, nor a private company, nor a personal liability company.[70] In other words, a public company is defined by exclusion or by default in the sense that a

---

[65] The pre-emptive right in terms of s 39 applies to 'shares' and not to 'securities', unlike s 8(2)(b).
[66] See further s 39.
[67] See further chapter 7: Shares, Securities and Transfer.
[68] The s 39 pre-emptive right applies to a private company and a personal liability company, but may be excluded in terms of the company's Memorandum of Incorporation. It does not apply to a public company or a state-owned company unless the company's Memorandum of Incorporation provides otherwise (s 39(1) and (3)).
[69] Section 39(4).
[70] Section 1; s 8(2)(d).

Types of Companies

public company is one that is not a private company or any other type of profit company.

Unlike a private company, the securities of a public company may be freely offered to the public. This facilitates the raising of capital from the general public. Additionally, the shareholders in a public company may freely transfer their securities unless, of course, the company elects to impose restrictions on transferability in its Memorandum of Incorporation.

3.5.2 Other characteristics of public companies

Due to their public nature, public companies have a greater responsibility to a wider public. They raise their share capital from members of the public. In recognition of this, it is a matter of policy that there ought to be more safeguards for this type of company and, in particular, a more demanding disclosure and transparency regime.[71] Accordingly, the enhanced accountability and transparency requirements of chapter 3 of the Act apply to public companies.[72]

It is consequently mandatory for a public company to appoint a company secretary, an audit committee and an independent auditor,[73] and to have its annual financial statements audited.[74] The annual financial statements must generally be drawn up in accordance with International Financial Reporting Standards. The annual return that every company files with the Companies and Intellectual Property Commission ('the Companies Commission') must, in the case of a public company, include a copy of its annual financial statements.[75] Public companies must also appoint a social and ethics committee, as pointed out above.[76] Chapter 4 of the Act regulates the public offerings of company securities.

A significant characteristic of a public company is that its name must end with the word 'Limited' or its abbreviation 'Ltd.'.[77]

In terms of the Act the board of directors of a public company must consist of a minimum of three directors,[78] but to be more accurate, more than three directors are really required by and large, bearing in mind that the mandatory audit committee of a public company must consist of at least three non-executive directors.[79] There is no longer a mandatory minimum number of shareholders for a public

---

[71] *Memorandum on the Objects of the Companies Bill, 2008* (at n 5) para 6.

[72] Section 34(1).

[73] Section 84(4). The appointment of an audit committee is subject to certain exemptions in terms of s 94(2).

[74] Section 30(2)*(a)*.

[75] Section 33.

[76] Subject to certain exceptions — see s 72(4), Regulation 50 of the draft Companies Regulations, and the draft Companies Amendment Bill, 2010, cl 45.

[77] Section 11(3)*(c)*.

[78] Section 66(2).

[79] Section 66(2) of the Act fails to take account of the requirement that a public company must have an audit committee comprising at least three members, each of whom is a director of the company who is not involved in the day-to-day management of the company's business (s 94). It also fails to take into account that the mandatory *social and ethics committee* of a public company, according to the draft Companies Regulations, must comprise at least three directors, a majority of whom must be non-executive directors (see further Regulation 50). The draft Companies Amendment Bill, 2010 (cl 42) now proposes to amend s 66(2) to state that a public company must have at least three

company, in contrast with the 1973 Act which required at least seven members for public companies.[80] A public company (like all other types of profit companies) is incorporated by one or more incorporators.[81]

3.5.3 Listing the securities of public companies

The offer by a public company of shares to the public must be distinguished from listing the shares of a public company on a securities exchange, such as the JSE Limited. The shares (securities) of a public company may or may not be listed. The advantage of a listing is that listed securities are traded in an organised and accessible public securities market. The effect of a trading market is that members of the public are more willing to trade in the securities of the company. This facilitates access to finance for the listed public company.

Listing also makes it easier for shareholders to later sell their securities should they wish to do so. Listed companies are, however, subject to additional exchange rules such as the JSE Rules and JSE Listings Requirements, which prescribe stricter and more demanding requirements and often more extensive duties of disclosure of certain information than the Act. This provides additional safeguards for members of the public and for those who trade in securities on the exchange.

3.5.4 Differences between public and private companies

The Act thus preserves the traditional distinction in our law between public and private companies. The differences between these two types of profit companies include the following characteristics and requirements:

- The essence of a private company is that its Memorandum of Incorporation must both:
  - restrict the transferability of its securities, and
  - prohibit it from offering its securities to the public.[82]

  On the other hand, public companies may offer their securities to the public and may, but need not, restrict the transferability of their securities.
  - The name of a public company must end with the term 'Ltd.' or 'Limited', while that of a private company must end with the expression '(Pty) Ltd.' or 'Proprietary Limited'.
  - The minimum number of directors on the board of directors of a public company is at least three directors according to the Act, but taking into account the membership of the audit committee and the social and ethics committee, more than three directors would be required.[83] In contrast, the default position for a private company is a minimum of one director on the board.

---

directors, in addition to the minimum number of directors that the company must have to satisfy any requirement to appoint an audit committee or a social and ethics committee.

[80] See s 66 of the 1973 Act; also ss 32 and 54 of the 1973 Act.

[81] Section 13(1) (or an organ of state, in terms of cl 9 of the draft Companies Amendment Bill, 2010). This simplifies the position as contrasted with the 1973 Act, which required at least seven persons for the formation of a public company and at least two persons for a private company, save that where the private company was to have only a single member, one person sufficed (s 32, s 54).

[82] Section 8(2)(b).

[83] See now the draft Companies Amendment Bill, 2010 (cl 42).

- In view of the public nature of public companies, the Act imposes more onerous legal duties of disclosure, accountability and transparency on public companies. The more stringent disclosure and transparency regime set out in Chapter 3 of the Act requires a public company, although not a private company (subject to certain exceptions, as discussed above), to appoint:
  - a company secretary,
  - an auditor, and
  - an audit committee.

  A public company, but not a private company, is also required to appoint a social and ethics committee (subject to certain exceptions).
- Public companies are generally required to have their annual financial statements audited, and must also include copies of their annual financial statements in their annual returns. By contrast, the annual financial statements of a private company must be independently reviewed but not audited — unless an audit is required by regulations in terms of the Act or the company voluntarily audits its financial statements. Moreover, an exemption is granted from both an audit and an independent review for certain private companies (including single-shareholder private companies and owner-managed private companies where, in broad terms, every holder of securities is also a director, as explained above).[84]
- A public company is obliged to convene an annual general meeting of its shareholders. This provision no longer applies to private companies.[85]
- The existing shareholders in a private company, as a default rule, enjoy pre-emptive rights in respect of new shares to be issued by the company in terms of s 39, unless the company opts out of this provision in its Memorandum of Incorporation. These pre-emptive rights do not, however, apply to public companies as the default position; they only apply if the public company opts in to s 39 in terms of its Memorandum of Incorporation. Such pre-emptive rights protect the existing shareholders of a company by enabling them to preserve their voting power and prevent dilution of their voting power.[86]

3.6 THE PERSONAL LIABILITY COMPANY

3.6.1 Definition

A profit company is a personal liability company if:
- it satisfies the criteria for a *private* company, and
- its Memorandum of Incorporation states that it is a personal liability company.[87]

---

[84] See further Regulation 30 of the draft Companies Regulations; see also the draft Companies Amendment Bill, 2010 (cl 20) which proposes to delete the first exemption above.
[85] Section 61(7).
[86] D Davis et al *Companies and Other Business Structures in South Africa* (2009) at 50–1.
[87] Section 1 read with s 8(2)*(c)*.

Since a personal liability company must fulfil the criteria for a private company, it may be regarded as a special type of private company. As such, its Memorandum of Incorporation must both prohibit it from offering any of its securities to the public and restrict the transferability of its securities.

The distinguishing characteristic of the personal liability company is that its Memorandum of Incorporation must specifically state that it is a personal liability company. This has the effect that its directors, including its past directors, are jointly and severally liable, together with the company, for any debts and liabilities of the company that are or were contracted during their respective periods of office (s 19(3)). Based on the wording of the Act, it seems that the Memorandum of Incorporation need not include a statement to this effect; it need merely state that the company is a personal liability company. The Act specifically provides that a person must be regarded as having received notice and knowledge of the effect of s 19(3) on a personal liability company.[88]

3.6.2 Other characteristics of personal liability companies

A personal liability company must have the word 'Incorporated' or its abbreviation 'Inc.' suffixed as the last word of its name.[89] This type of company is the successor to the incorporated or professional company formed under s 53*(b)* of the 1973 Act.

The personal liability company is expected to be used primarily by associations of professional persons, such as attorneys, stockbrokers, public accountants, auditors and quantity surveyors, who wish to have the convenience and advantages of separate legal personality, especially perpetual succession, while still complying with their professional rules, which require personal liability. It may also be used by persons who are not members of professions yet wish for the directors of the company to bear personal liability.

Like the private company, the personal liability company need only have a minimum of one director on the board of directors (subject to the Memorandum of Incorporation, which may specify a higher minimum number in substitution).[90] As with all other profit companies, a personal liability company is formed by one or more persons as incorporators.[91]

A personal liability company is subject to similar accountability and transparency requirements as the private company. In this regard, it need not appoint a company secretary or an audit committee, unless its Memorandum of Incorporation provides otherwise. The appointment of an auditor is only necessary if its Memorandum of Incorporation so requires, or if the company is required to have its financial statements audited in terms of the Act or the regulations.[92]

3.6.3 Pre-existing section 53*(b)* companies

The position of pre-existing section 53*(b)* companies (that is, companies that were incorporated under the 1973 Act with constitutions that imposed personal liability

---

[88] Section 19(5) — see further below.
[89] Section 11(3)*(c)*.
[90] Section 66. See also cl 42 of the draft Companies Amendment Bill, 2010.
[91] Section 13(1) (or an organ of state in terms of cl 9 of the draft Companies Amendment Bill, 2010).
[92] Section 34 (2), s 84(1); cl 51 of the draft Companies Amendment Bill, 2010.

on the directors and past directors in terms of s 53*(b)* of that Act) requires consideration. In this regard, the Transitional Arrangements to the Act state that a pre-existing section 53*(b)* company is deemed to have amended its Memorandum of Incorporation as at the general effective date of the new Act to expressly state that it is a personal liability company, and to have changed the ending expression of its name to 'Inc.' or 'Incorporated'.[93]

3.6.4 The liability of the directors in a personal liability company

The effect of personal liability on the directors of a personal liability company is elucidated in s 19(3) of the Act. This section states that the directors and past directors of a personal liability company are jointly and severally liable, together with the company, for any debts and liabilities of the company that are or were 'contracted' during their respective periods of office.[94]

The Act states further that a person must be regarded as having received notice and knowledge of the effect of s 19(3) on a personal liability company.[95] This, in effect, constitutes an exception to the abolition of the doctrine of constructive notice under the Act.[96] However the rationale for this provision is open to question.

The effect of s 19(3) on a personal liability company is that it renders the directors and past directors co-debtors with the company.[97] The directors and the company are liable *singuli et in solidum* for the contractual debts and liabilities of the company.[98]

The liability of a director or a past director is limited to the debts and liabilities of the company that were contracted *during his or her period of office* as a director. It is further limited to the *contractual* debts and liabilities of the company, as opposed to debts and liabilities of some other nature.

The decision in *Fundstrust (Pty) Ltd (In Liquidation) v Van Deventer*,[99] which was decided under the 1973 Act, would no doubt continue to apply. There is no reason why it should not, since the wording of both the 1973 Act and the new Act are very similar. In this case it was laid down that the extent of the directors' liability is limited to the company's contractual debts and liabilities that were contracted during their periods of office, and that the directors' joint and several liability does not include any liability for delictual claims or unjustified enrichment claims against the company, because these liabilities are not 'contracted'. Nor does it extend to liability for tax and other statutory charges (including statutory liability in respect of voidable and undue preferences under the Insol-

---

[93] Schedule 5 item 4(1)*(b)*. The erroneous reference in this item to s 11(3)*(b)* of the Act is to be corrected by the draft Companies Amendment Bill, 2010 (cl 115), so as to now refer to s 11(3). See further chapter 21: Transitional Arrangements.
[94] Section 19(3).
[95] Section 19(5)*(b)*.
[96] See further chapter 4: Formation of Companies and the Company Constitution.
[97] *Maritz v Maritz & Pieterse Inc* 2006 (3) SA 481 (SCA).
[98] *Fundstrust (Pty) Ltd (In Liquidation) v Van Deventer* 1997 (1) SA 710 (A) 715.
[99] 1997 (1) SA 710 (A). This case was decided under the 1973 Act. It remains relevant, particularly in the light of the wording of s 53*(b)* of the 1973 Act which is substantially similar to the wording of s 19(3) of the new Act.

vency Act 24 of 1936 (which was in fact the issue in this matter), as none of these liabilities are of a *contractual* nature. The court found that the intention of the legislature was to relate the directors' liability to nothing other than the company's ordinary financial or commercial commitments.[100]

Sonnenberg McLoughlin Inc v Spiro[101] proclaimed that the intention of the legislature was not simply to impose on the directors a liability equivalent to the common-law liability of partners. It was rather to impose on the directors an entirely new statutory liability and to give creditors an entirely new remedy that would enable them to hold the directors liable *singuli et in solidum* for the company's debts and liabilities before its liquidation.[102] There is accordingly a twofold effect:

- first, creditors are entitled to hold the directors jointly and severally liable for the company's contractual liabilities contracted during their periods of office,
- secondly, if a director pays any such debt of the company, he or she would have a right of recourse against his or her fellow directors for their proportional shares of the debt.

Importantly, however, the company itself does not have a right of recourse against its directors, where the company has paid any of its debts.[103] The reasoning underlying this decision would presumably continue to apply to personal liability companies under the new Act.

Under the previous company-law regime, an additional safeguard for creditors was that the consent of the court was required for a special resolution to remove the personal liability provision from the company's constitution. The court had to be satisfied that the removal or alteration would be just and equitable.[104] The new Act has dispensed with this protective measure for creditors of the company. One expects that the removal of the personal liability provision from a company's constitution in terms of the Act would be interpreted to provide no scope at all for the retrospective termination of the personal liability of any director or past director of the company, so that all liabilities that were already contracted or had already accrued to the directors would remain unaffected.[105]

---

[100] At 734.
[101] 2004 (1) SA 90 (C).
[102] At 97.
[103] Ibid.
[104] Section 56(3) of the 1973 Act.
[105] The draft Companies Amendment Bill, 2010 (cl 12) now proposes to insert a new provision relating to the conversion of a personal liability company (as s 6(10) and (11) of the Act). It states that if an amendment to the Memorandum of Incorporation of a personal liability company has the effect of transforming that company into any other category of company, the company must give at least ten business days advance notice of the filing of the notice of amendment to: any professional or industry regulatory authority that has jurisdiction over the business activities carried on by the company; any persons who, in their dealings with the company, may reasonably be considered to have acted in reliance upon the joint and several liability of any of the directors for the debts and liabilities of the company; or any persons who may be adversely affected if the joint and several liability of any of the directors for the debts and liabilities of the company is terminated as a consequence of the amendment to the Memorandum of Incorporation. A person who receives, or is

3.7 THE STATE-OWNED COMPANY

3.7.1 Definition

Although state-owned companies were indeed incorporated under the 1973 Act, they were not recognised as a distinct type of company under that Act. State-owned companies are now recognised as a separate type of company. A state-owned company is defined[106] as an enterprise that is registered as a company in terms of the Act and either:

- falls within the meaning of 'state-owned enterprise' in terms of the Public Finance Management Act 1 of 1999,[107] or
- is owned by a municipality[108] and is otherwise similar to a 'state-owned enterprise'.

Oddly, the term 'state-owned enterprise' is not defined in the Public Finance Management Act at all. It appears that state-owned enterprises may be regarded as enterprises that are directly or indirectly controlled by the state, and which are referred to in the Public Finance Management Act as 'public entities'.[109] The Public Finance Management Act draws a distinction between national and provincial public entities,[110] which include national and provincial government business enterprises respectively.[111]

(It is fortunately now proposed, in terms of the draft Companies Amendment Bill, 2010, to amend the first part of the above definition of a state-owned company so as to refer to a company that 'is listed as a public entity in Schedule 2

---

entitled to receive, such a notice may apply to a court in the prescribed manner and form for an order sufficient to protect the interests of that person.

[106] Section 1 read with s 8(2)(*a*).

[107] It is proposed to amend this part of the definition to refer to a company that 'is listed as a public entity in Schedule 2 or 3 of the Public Finance Management Act, 1999' (in terms of the draft Companies Amendment Bill, 2010, cl 2(1)). Although this amendment would clarify the first part of the definition of a state-owned company, it still leaves the term 'state-owned enterprise' unclear and undefined under the second part of the above definition.

[108] In terms of the Local Government: Municipal Systems Act 2000.

[109] Phoebe Bolton 'The regulation of preferential procurement in state-owned enterprises' 2010 *TSAR* 101 at 101.

[110] 'National public entity' as defined in s 1 of the Public Finance Management Act includes a 'board, commission, company, corporation, fund or other entity (other than a national government business enterprise) which is established in terms of national legislation; fully or substantially funded either from the National Revenue Fund, or by way of a tax, levy or other money imposed in terms of national legislation; and accountable to Parliament'. A 'provincial public entity' means substantially the same except that it involves the provincial sphere.

[111] 'National government business enterprise' according to s 1 of the Public Finance Management Act means (*a*) a juristic person under the ownership control of the national executive; (*b*) that has been assigned financial and operational authority to carry on a business activity; (*c*) that as its principal business, provides goods or services in accordance with ordinary business principles; and (*d*) that is financed fully or substantially from sources other than the National Revenue Fund or by way of a tax, levy or other statutory money. A 'provincial government business enterprise' means substantially the same except that it involves the provincial sphere.

or 3 of the Public Finance Management Act, 1999'. This will, to some extent, clarify the definition of a state-owned company.)[112]

3.7.2 Other characteristics of state-owned companies

Since state-owned companies were not formerly recognised as a distinct type of company, they did not previously receive separate legislative treatment with regard to certain matters so as to avoid conflict or overlap with other legislation that applied specifically to state-owned companies but not to other companies in general.[113] The new Act now revolutionises this position.

In this regard, all provisions of the Act that apply to *public* companies generally also apply to state-owned companies (subject to some exceptions).[114] But the Minister has the power to grant exemptions to state-owned companies, exempting them from having to comply with one or more provisions of the Act.[115] The application of the Act to state-owned companies is also subject to s 5(4) and 5(5) of the Act, dealing with inconsistencies between the Act and other national legislation. It is noteworthy that the Public Finance Management Act 1999 prevails in the case of an irreconcilable inconsistency with the Companies Act.

In respect of exemptions from the Act, the Minister[116] may grant a total, partial or even conditional exemption from one or more provisions of the Act, on the grounds that those provisions overlap with or duplicate an applicable regulatory scheme established in terms of other national legislation. The Minister may grant such exemptions in respect of all state-owned companies or any class of them, or even just one or more specific state-owned companies. The Minister grants exemptions by way of notice in the *Government Gazette*, after taking the advice of the Companies Commission. An exemption may be granted only to the extent that the relevant alternative regulatory scheme ensures that the purposes of the Act are achieved at least as well as the provisions of the Act. Any exemption must be subject to any limits or conditions that are necessary to ensure the achievement of the purposes of the Act.[117]

Like the public company, the state-owned company is subject to the extended accountability and transparency requirements in terms of Chapter 3 of the Act.[118] A state-owned company must consequently appoint a company secretary, an audit committee and an auditor (subject to any exemptions granted in terms of s 9).[119] A

---

[112] See cl 2(1) of the draft Companies Amendment Bill, 2010. Although this amendment would clarify the first part of the above definition of a state-owned company, it still leaves the term 'state-owned enterprise' in the second part of the definition unclear and undefined.
[113] *Memorandum on the Objects of the Companies Bill, 2008* op cit n 5 para 4.
[114] See eg s 57(2), (3) and (4), s 66(4)(*b*), s 84(3).
[115] Section 9.
[116] Being the member of Cabinet responsible for companies (s 1).
[117] Section 9.
[118] Section 34(1).
[119] Section 84(1) and 84(4). This is subject to any exemptions granted in terms of s 9 and subject also to s 84(3) dealing with requirements under the Public Audit Act 2004. See also s 94(2).

state-owned company must also appoint a social and ethics committee (subject to certain exceptions).[120]

The name of a state-owned company ends with the expression 'SOC Ltd.'.[121]

3.7.3 Pre-existing ('state-owned') companies

Pre-existing companies that were registered under the 1973 Act and yet fall within the definition of a state-owned company under the new Act, are deemed to have amended their constitutions to have changed the ending expressions of their names to 'SOC Ltd.' as at the general effective date of the Act.[122]

3.8 NON-PROFIT COMPANIES (NPCs)

3.8.1 Definition

As explained above, there are two broad categories of companies that may be incorporated under the Act: First, profit companies (which may be private companies, public companies, personal liability companies or state-owned companies) and secondly, non-profit companies.[123]

According to the definition of a 'non-profit' company:[124]

- a non-profit company is a company that is incorporated for:
  ○ a public benefit object,[125] or
  ○ an object relating to one or more cultural or social activities, or communal or group interests,[126] *and*
- it is of the essence that the income and property of a non-profit company must not be distributable to its incorporators, members, directors, officers or persons related to any of them, subject to certain exceptions permitted by the Act.

It must be emphasised that both of these essential requirements must be satisfied for a company to constitute a non-profit company.

The main object of a Section 21 company under the 1973 Act (which was the predecessor of the non-profit company under the new Act) was more specifically defined as 'the main object of promoting religion, arts, sciences, education, charity, recreation, or any other cultural or social activity or communal or group interests'.[127]

The question recently arose as to the meaning of 'communal or group interests' in *Cunninghame v First Ready Development 249 (association incorporated under section 21)*,[128] in the context of s 21 of the 1973 Act. The Supreme Court of Appeal rejected the contention that 'group interests' could be viewed as a stand-

---

[120] Section 72(4) read with Regulation 50 of the draft Companies Regulations; see further cl 45 of the draft Companies Amendment Bill, 2010.
[121] Section 11(3)*(c)*.
[122] Schedule 5 item 4(1)*(c)*. The erroneous reference in this item to s 11(3)*(b)* of the Act is to be corrected by the draft Companies Amendment Bill, 2010 (cl 115), so as to now refer to s 11(3).
[123] Section 8(1).
[124] Section 1 read with item 1(1) of Schedule 1. See further below.
[125] Item 1(1)*(a)*(i) of Schedule 1.
[126] Item 1(1)*(a)*(ii) of Schedule 1.
[127] Section 21(1)*(b)* of the 1973 Act.
[128] 2010 (5) SA 325 (SCA).

alone object, in itself, and held instead that the expression 'communal or group interests' had to be interpreted *eiusdem generis* with the preceding words in the section. The phrase 'communal or group interests' consequently relates to cultural or social activities, and excludes those of a purely commercial nature. Purely commercial enterprises are thus excluded from the ambit of non-profit companies.

The court in *Cuninghame's* case stated further that the reason for the inclusion in the section of 'communal or group interests', is to avoid restricting the section solely to associations that pursue the relevant activities in the wider interests of the general public. To do this would be unduly restrictive and would unduly exclude certain relevant organisations, e g local sports organisations, from the ambit of the section. The pursuit of 'group' interests requires at least a group with common interests.

On the facts of *Cuninghame's* case where the main object of the respondent company had changed from managing a rental pool on a non-profit basis to the management of the hotel business as a whole, the court ruled that, since purely commercial enterprises were excluded from the ambit of the expression 'communal or group interests', the result was that the company's commercial hotel business fell outside the ambit of the section and was not a permissible object for a Section 21 company.

In view of the similarity between the wording of s 21(1)*(b)* of the 1973 Act and that of the new Act, the decision in *Cuninghame's* case may be expected to apply also to the expression 'communal or group interests' under the Act (in terms of item 1(1)*(a)*(ii) of Schedule 1 to the Act). The phrase 'communal or group interests' in terms of the Act may be similarly interpreted *eiusdem generis* so as to relate to cultural or social activities, and to exclude purely commercial activities. These would, furthermore, tend to be cultural or social activities that advance a 'communal or group' interest, and that are not necessarily for the wider benefit of the general public. (Where the object of a company is for the benefit of the general public this would, of course, constitute a 'public benefit object' in terms of item 1(1)*(a)*(i) of Schedule 1.) It is notable, as discussed below, that a non-profit company does have the scope to carry on a business, trade or undertaking in terms of item 1(2)*(b)*(ii) of Schedule 1. But this must be consistent with or 'ancillary' to its stated objects. This implies that it cannot be some activity that is unrelated to the stated objects of the company. Any profits derived from such activity may not of course be distributed to its members, directors, officers or related persons, but must instead be applied to advance the stated objects of the non-profit company.

3.8.2 Other characteristics of NPCs

The company name of a non-profit company ends with the expression 'NPC'.[129]

A non-profit company must be formed by at least three persons as incorporators (in contrast with a profit company, which requires only one incorporator).[130]

---

[129] Section 11(3)*(c)*.

[130] Section 1 and s 13(1). The draft Companies Amendment Bill, 2010 (cl 9) proposes to permit the incorporation of a non-profit company by an organ of state, a juristic person or three or more persons acting in common.

An important innovation is that a non-profit company may be formed with or without members. Where such a company has members, the members need not necessarily be voting members.[131] The concept of a 'member' of a non-profit company refers to a person who holds membership in, and specified rights in respect of, the non-profit company.[132]

The Act establishes a detailed regime for non-profit companies. It sets out a special set of fundamental rules for non-profit companies in Schedule 1. This is in line with the stated purpose of the Act to 'provide for the formation, operation and accountability of non-profit companies in a manner designed to promote, support and enhance the capacity of such companies to perform their functions.'[133]

The Act also applies with modified effect to non-profit companies. It contains a useful list of specific sections that have no direct relevance to non-profit companies and do not apply to them, namely:[134]

- Part D of Chapter 2 — Capitalisation of profit companies,
- Part E of Chapter 2 — Securities registration and transfer,
- Parts B and D of Chapter 3 — Company secretaries and audit committees, except to the extent contemplated in s 34(2),
- Chapter 4 — Public offerings of company securities,
- Chapter 5 — Takeovers, offers and fundamental transactions (except as contemplated in Schedule 1),
- sections 146*(d)* and 152(3)*(c)* — Rights of shareholders to approve a business rescue plan (except to the extent that the non-profit company is itself a shareholder of a profit company engaged in business rescue proceedings),
- section 164 — Dissenting shareholders' appraisal rights (except to the extent that the non-profit company is itself a shareholder of a profit company),
- sections 58 to 65 (dealing with shareholders and governance of companies), which do not apply to a non-profit company unless it has voting members.

A non-profit company is not generally subject to the extended disclosure, transparency and audit requirements of the Act. It accordingly need not appoint an auditor, a company secretary or an audit committee, except if its Memorandum of Incorporation calls for it to do so. An independent auditor must also be appointed in the event that a non-profit company is obliged to have its financial statements audited in terms of the Act or regulations.[135]

As a general principle, the annual financial statements of a non-profit company require only an independent review. An audit is unnecessary, unless the company voluntarily opts for an audit or if regulations in terms of the Act call for an audit.[136] (The draft Companies Regulations require a non-profit company to have

---

[131] Schedule 1 items 4(1) and 4(2)*(d)*.
[132] Section 1.
[133] Section 7*(h)*.
[134] Section 10. It has been proposed that s 66(8) and (9) (regarding the election of directors) be added to this list in terms of the draft Companies Amendment Bill, 2010 (cl 6). Other minor changes are also proposed.
[135] Section 84(1) read with s 34(2); cl 51 of the draft Companies Amendment Bill, 2010.
[136] See s 30(2) and (7). See further Regulation 29 of the draft Companies Regulations. See also the draft Companies Amendment Bill, 2010, cl 20.

its annual financial statements audited if, for instance, it holds assets in a fiduciary capacity for a broad group of persons who are not related to the company.)[137]

The special set of fundamental rules for non-profit companies contained in Schedule 1 to the Act is dealt with in detail below. Suffice it to say, Schedule 1 substantially retains the principles of the 1973 Act relating to the objects of non-profit companies, as well as the restrictions on the distribution of residual assets on dissolution of the company, while also dealing with other matters unique to non-profit companies.[138]

3.8.3 Objects and policies of NPCs

The Memorandum of Incorporation of a non-profit company must set out at least one object of the company. Each object must be either:
- a public benefit object, or
- an object relating to one or more cultural or social activities, or communal or group interests.[139]

See further the discussion above on the definition of a non-profit company (at 3.8.1), for the meaning of the expression 'communal or group interests'.

The Memorandum of Incorporation of a non-profit company must also be consistent with all the other requirements of item 1 of Schedule 1, which deals with the objects and policies of non-profit companies, particularly the application of their assets and income, the distribution of their residual assets on dissolution and the voting rights of voting members, as examined below.[140]

(a) Assets and income

It is of fundamental importance that all the assets and income of a non-profit company, however derived, are applied to advance its stated objects.[141]

Subject to this prerequisite, it is permissible for a non-profit company to:[142]
- acquire and hold securities issued by a profit company, or
- carry on any business, trade or undertaking, whether it does so directly or indirectly and whether it does so alone or with any other person, provided that this is consistent with or 'ancillary' to its stated objects.

(b) Financial benefit or gain

It is crucial that a non-profit company does not pay or distribute any portion of its income or transfer any of its assets, whether directly or indirectly, to an incorporator, member, director or any person appointing a director of the company. This is subject to a number of reasonable exceptions, namely:

---

[137] See further Regulation 29 of the draft Companies Regulations and chapter 13: The Auditor, Financial Records and Reporting.
[138] *Memorandum on the Objects of the Companies Bill, 2008* op cit n 5 para 4.
[139] Item 1(1)*(a)* of Schedule 1.
[140] Item 1(1)*(b)* of Schedule 1.
[141] Item 1(2)*(a)* of Schedule 1. This is consistent with the 1973 Act (s 21(1)*(c)* of the 1973 Act).
[142] Item 1(2)*(b)* of Schedule 1.

- reasonable remuneration for goods delivered to the company or for services rendered to the company (or at the direction of the company),
- reasonable payment or reimbursement for expenses incurred in advancing a stated object of the company,
- payment of an amount due and payable by the company in terms of a *bona fide* agreement (between the company and that person or another),
- payment in respect of any rights of that person, to the extent that those rights are administered by the company in order to advance one of its stated objects, or
- payment in respect of any legal obligation that is binding on the company.[143]

(c) Winding-up or dissolution

Despite any provision in any law or agreement to the contrary, upon the winding-up or dissolution of a non-profit company, no past or present member, director or person appointing a director of the company is entitled to any part of the net value of the company after its obligations and liabilities have been met.

The entire net value of the company must instead be distributed to one or more non-profit companies that have objects similar to its main object, or alternatively to any external non-profit company[144] carrying on activities within South Africa, or a voluntary association or non-profit trust with objects similar to the non-profit company's main object.

This matter is determined either in terms of the company's Memorandum of Incorporation, or by its members (if any) or its directors, at or immediately before the time of its dissolution. Failing either of these, the issue will be determined by the court.[145]

Where the non-profit company has no remaining members or directors, and had failed to make a determination on this matter or to apply to the court for a determination, then the Companies Commission may apply to the court on behalf of the non-profit company for a determination by the court.[146]

(d) Tax

A non-profit company that complies with the Act does not necessarily or automatically qualify for any tax advantages.

It specifically does not qualify for any particular status, category, classification, treatment or advantage in terms of the Income Tax Act 58 of 1962 or any other legislation, except to the extent that the legislation provides otherwise.[147] This position also applies to a registered external non-profit company. To obtain any tax exemption or tax advantage it must satisfy the requirements of the Income Tax Act.

---

[143] Item 1(3) of Schedule 1.
[144] This provision ought preferably to have referred to a registered external non-profit company.
[145] Item 1(4) of Schedule 1.
[146] Item 1(5) of Schedule 1.
[147] Item 1(6) of Schedule 1.

3.8.4 Incorporators of NPCs

A non-profit company is incorporated by three or more persons (as opposed to a profit company which may be incorporated by even one person).[148] The incorporators of a non-profit company are its first directors and its first members (if any).[149]

3.8.5 Members of NPCs and voting rights

A non-profit company, as discussed above, may be incorporated with or without members. A non-profit company is not required to have members unless its Memorandum of Incorporation so provides.[150] The term 'member', when used in relation to a non-profit company, means a person who holds membership in, and specified rights in respect of, that non-profit company.[151]

A non-profit company with members may have voting members or non-voting members. No more than two classes of members may be provided for in the Memorandum of Incorporation, ie voting and non-voting members.[152]

Where there are voting members, each voting member has at least one vote.[153] Generally, the votes of voting members carry equal value or weight on any matter, but the company's Memorandum of Incorporation may provide otherwise.[154] In other words, the voting rights in a non-profit company may be loaded disproportionately in terms of its Memorandum of Incorporation. Sections 58 to 65 of the Act (dealing with shareholders and the governance of companies) apply to a non-profit company only if it has voting members.[155]

A non-profit company with members must maintain a membership register.[156] Where the Memorandum of Incorporation provides for a non-profit company to have members, it must also set out the qualifications for membership, as well as the grounds for suspension or loss of membership. It may allow for membership to be held by juristic persons, including profit companies. The Memorandum of Incorporation must not restrict or regulate membership in any manner that amounts to unfair discrimination in terms of s 9 of the Constitution.[157] Nor may it presume the membership of any person, regard a person to be a member, or provide for the automatic or *ex officio* membership of any person, on any basis

---

[148] Section 13(1). As stated above, the draft Companies Amendment Bill, 2010 (cl 9) proposes to permit an organ of state, a juristic person or three or more persons acting in common, to incorporate a non-profit company.
[149] Item 3 of Schedule 1.
[150] Item 4(1) of Schedule 1.
[151] As contemplated in item 4 of Schedule 1; see s 1.
[152] Item 4(2)(*d*) of Schedule 1.
[153] Item 1(7) of Schedule 1.
[154] Item 1(8) of Schedule 1.
[155] See further chapter 9: Governance and Shareholders. In this case, ss 58–65 are subject also to the provisions of Schedule 1 item 4 (s 10(3)). In respect of a non-profit company with voting members, a reference in the Act to 'a shareholder', 'the holders of a company's securities', 'holders of issued securities of that company' or 'a holder of voting rights entitled to be voted' is a reference to the voting members of the non-profit company (s 10(4)).
[156] Item 1(9) of Schedule 1 read with s 24(4).
[157] Constitution of the Republic of South Africa, 1996.

other than life-time membership awarded to a person for service to the company or to its stated public benefit objects, and with that person's consent.[158]

The Memorandum of Incorporation may provide for a membership cost. The membership cost may be initial and/or periodic and may apply to any class of membership. The Memorandum of Incorporation must also deal with the process for applying for membership, as well as any rights and obligations of membership in any class.[159]

3.8.6 Directors of NPCs

A non-profit company must have at least three directors.[160]

In a non-profit company without members, the directors are appointed by the board or by other persons on the basis set out in the Memorandum of Incorporation. On the other hand, in a non-profit company with members, the members choose the directors on the basis set out in the Memorandum of Incorporation. If the voting members are to elect any directors, then the Memorandum of Incorporation must provide for the election of at least a third of those elected directors each year.[161]

A non-profit company is prohibited from giving loans to its directors, securing the debts or obligations of directors, or otherwise giving direct or indirect financial assistance to directors. This prohibition extends also to the directors of related or interrelated companies and/or to persons related to any such directors. But there are certain exceptions to the general prohibition, in that it does not prevent transactions that:[162]

- are in the ordinary course of the company's business and for fair value,
- constitute an accountable advance to meet legal expenses in relation to a matter concerning the company,
- constitute an accountable advance to meet anticipated expenses to be incurred by the person on behalf of the company,
- are to defray the person's expenses for removal at the company's request, or
- are in terms of an employee benefit scheme generally available to all employees or a specific class of employees.

3.8.7 Fundamental transactions of NPCs

Importantly, a non-profit company is prohibited from *converting* to a profit company.[163] This fundamental rule, which applied also to the 1973 Act,[164] continues to apply to the new Act.

---

[158] Schedule 1 item 4.
[159] Schedule 1 item 4.
[160] Section 66(2)*(b)*. This is subject to the minimum number of directors that the company must have to satisfy any requirement to appoint an audit committee or a social and ethics committee (cl 42 of the draft Companies Amendment Bill, 2010).
[161] Item 5(1) and (2) of Schedule 1.
[162] Item 5(3) and (4) of Schedule 1.
[163] Item 2(1) of Schedule 1.
[164] Secton 24 of the 1973 Act.

Moreover, a non-profit company may not amalgamate or merge with a *profit* company. Nor may it dispose of any part of its assets, undertaking or business to a profit company, other than for fair value, except to the extent that such disposals of assets occur in the ordinary course of the activities of the non-profit company.

Where a non-profit company with voting members proposes to dispose of all or the greater part of its assets or undertaking to another *non-profit* company, or proposes to amalgamate or merge with another non-profit company, such proposal must be submitted to the voting members for approval in a manner comparable to that required of profit companies.[165]

3.8.8 Pre-existing section 21 companies

The non-profit company is the successor to the section 21 company under the 1973 Act, which was also known as the incorporated association not for gain. While section 21 companies under the 1973 Act were deemed to be public companies,[166] under the new Act the non-profit company is an entirely separate type of company. The distinction between public and private companies is wholly inapplicable to non-profit companies.

The Transitional Arrangements of the Act provide that pre-existing companies that were incorporated under s 21 of the 1973 Act, are recognised as non-profit companies under the new Act. Such companies are deemed to have amended their Memorandums of Incorporation as at the general effective date of the Act to state that they are non-profit companies, and to have changed the ending expressions of their company names to 'NPC'.[167]

3.9 EXTERNAL COMPANIES

3.9.1 Definition

It is essential to distinguish a 'foreign company' from an 'external company'. A 'foreign company' simply means an entity incorporated in some other jurisdiction outside the Republic of South Africa. This is irrespective of whether it is a profit or a non-profit entity, and irrespective of whether it carries on its business or non-profit activities within South Africa.[168] But where a foreign company carries on business or non-profit activities (as the case may be) within South Africa, it then qualifies as an 'external company'[169] that must be registered as such under the Act.

An external company is a subcategory of a foreign company. The importance of the distinction is that it is only external companies (but not other foreign compa-

---

[165] In accordance with ss 112 and 113 respectively. Sections 115 and 116, read with the changes required by the context, apply to the approval of the proposal (Item 2 of Schedule 1). See further chapter 15: Fundamental Transactions, Takeovers and Offers.
[166] Section 19(3) of the 1973 Act. A section 21 company was classified as a company limited by guarantee under the 1973 Act, and companies limited by guarantee were deemed to be public companies for the purposes of that Act.
[167] Schedule 5 item 4(1)*(a)*. The erroneous reference in this item to s 11(3)*(b)* of the Act is to be corrected by the draft Companies Amendment Bill, 2010 (cl 115), so as to now refer to s 11(3).
[168] Section 1.
[169] Section 1.

nies) that are specifically required to register with the Companies Commission, and to observe those provisions of the Act that apply to external companies.[170]

The question arises when is a foreign company 'conducting business or non-profit activities (as the case may be) within the Republic'[171] of South Africa? This crucial criterion qualifies a foreign company for registration as an 'external company' under the Act. A foreign company is to be regarded as conducting business or non-profit activities in South Africa if it is engaged in or has engaged in any *one* or more of the following activities in South Africa:[172]

- the holding of a shareholders' meeting or board meeting, or otherwise conducting its internal affairs in South Africa,
- the establishment or maintenance of any bank accounts or other financial accounts,
- the establishment or maintenance of offices or agencies for the transfer, exchange or registration of the foreign company's own securities,
- the creation or acquisition of any debts, mortgages or security interests in any property,
- the securing or collection of any debt, or the enforcement of any mortgage or security interest,
- the acquisition of any interest in any property,
- the entering into of contracts of employment.

This extremely wide definition of 'conducting business or non-profit activities' in South Africa is striking. It is clear from the wording of the Act that engaging in any one of these activities in South Africa would oblige the foreign company to register as an external company under the Act. Moreover, either being currently engaged in an activity or *having engaged* in one of the listed activities would suffice. This is more far-reaching than is necessary. It may well be expected to net a greater number of foreign companies within the ambit of the Companies Act.[173]

---

[170] Section 23(1).

[171] The Act appears to equate the term 'conducting' business or non-profit activities (in terms of s 23(2)) with the term 'carrying on' business or non-profit activities (in terms of the definition of an external company in s 1).

[172] Section 23(2). Substantial changes are proposed to this crucial criterion in terms of the draft Companies Amendment Bill, 2010. If implemented, these amendments would narrow the scope of activities that would compel a foreign company to register as an external company. The draft Companies Amendment Bill, 2010 (cl 15) provides that a foreign company must be regarded as 'conducting business, or non-profit activities, as the case may be, within the Republic if that foreign company —
   (a)   is a party to one or more employment contracts within the Republic; or
   (b)   subject to subclause (2A), is engaging in a course of conduct, or has engaged in a course or pattern of activities within the Republic over a period of at least six months, such as would lead a person to reasonably conclude that the company intended to continually engage in business or non-profit activities within the Republic.'
Subclause (2A) significantly states that a foreign company must *not* be regarded as 'conducting business activities, or non-profit activities, as the case may be, within the Republic' solely on the ground that the foreign company is or has engaged in one or more of the activities set out in s 23(2)(a)–(f) (as set out above).

[173] As discussed above (n 172), this may be significantly narrowed down in terms of the draft Companies Amendment Bill, 2010.

By contrast, under the 1973 Act, an entity incorporated outside South Africa was required to register as an external company if it had established a 'place of business' within South Africa. A 'place of business' was defined as any place the company transacted or held itself out as transacting business, including a share transfer or share registration office, as well as the acquisition of immovable property.[174] 'Establishing a place of business' (as in the 1973 Act) is quite different from 'carrying on business' or 'conducting business' (as in the new Act) — the latter phrase is much wider in scope than the former.[175] The Act thus significantly extends the definition of an 'external company' and it would certainly result in many more foreign companies having to comply with the formalities of registration as external companies in South Africa.

The protection of third parties who deal with external companies, including employees,[176] is in turn catered for by the widening of the definition of 'external company', with the effect that more 'external companies' will have to register and consequently disclose specified information to the Companies Commission both upon registration and as part of their annual returns.[177] As discussed in chapter 4: Formation of Companies and the Company Constitution, an external company must register its registered office in South Africa with the Companies Commission.[178] It must also provide the names of its directors at the time, the address of its principal office outside South Africa and, very importantly, the name and address of the person in South Africa who has undertaken to accept service of documents on its behalf.[179] Such information will to a certain extent protect employees of external companies and third parties who deal with external companies. The requirements on the use of the name and registration number of an external company will also ensure the provision and disclosure of basic information to third parties who deal with such a company.

3.9.2 Types of external companies

An external company that registers with the Companies Commission in terms of the Act, must register either as an *'external profit company'* or as an *'external non-profit company'*.[180]

This depends on whether, if within the jurisdiction in which it was incorporated, the external company meets legislative or definitional requirements that are com-

---

[174] Section 1 and s 322 of the 1973 Act.

[175] See eg *Lord Advocate v Huron & Erie Loan and Savings Co* 1911 SC 612 at 616 cited in *Rakusens Ltd v Baser Ambalaj Plastik* [2002] 1 BCLC 104 CA 115. These judicial decisions may still have persuasive force.

[176] Even if cl 15 of the draft Companies Amendment Bill, 2010 (see above at n 172) is implemented, employees would nonetheless be protected. This is in view of cl 15(2)*(a)*, which proposes that a foreign company must be regarded as 'conducting business, or non-profit activities, as the case may be, within the Republic of South Africa' if that foreign company is a party to one or more employment contracts within South Africa, with the result that such foreign companies would have to register as external companies in South Africa.

[177] Section 33. There is presently no prescribed form but the information required in the terms of the form may perhaps be quite significant.

[178] Section 23(3).

[179] Regulation 22 of the draft Companies Regulations.

[180] Section 23(1).

parable with those of a profit company or a non-profit company (as the case may be) that is incorporated under the Act.[181] The Act leaves unanswered the question of whether registration is necessary and, if so, what the registration requirements are, for an external company that does not meet such comparable legislative or definitional requirements — an issue that must inevitably arise.[182]

Once an external company has registered its office and has been assigned a registration number, it is by definition a *'registered external company'*.[183] The registration of external companies and company names for external companies are discussed in chapter 4: Formation of Companies and the Company Constitution.

3.9.3 Application of the Act to external companies

Since foreign companies are incorporated in another jurisdiction outside South Africa, the Act does not apply to foreign companies, save for those that qualify as external companies. There is one important exception: Chapter 4 of the Act, which deals with public offerings of company securities, does apply to the securities of foreign companies that are offered to the public in South Africa, irrespective of whether the foreign company carries on business in South Africa and irrespective of whether it qualifies as an external company.[184]

The approach of our company law to external companies has undergone a remarkable change. The 1973 Act applied generally to external companies by virtue of a catch-all phrase[185] which stated that the 1973 Act would apply to every company as well as every external company. But under the new company law regime there is no such section. Consequently only certain specified sections of the Act extend to external companies.

These include:

- the obligation of an external company to register as such[186] and to provide certain information upon registration (discussed in chapter 4: Formation of Companies and the Company Constitution),
- the obligation to continuously maintain at least one office in South Africa and register the address of its office (or principal office),[187]
- the duty to file an annual return in the prescribed form,[188]
- obligations relating to the use of the company name and registration number (also discussed in the aforementioned chapter 4),

---

[181] Section 23(1).
[182] It is now proposed by the draft Companies Amendment Bill, 2010 (cl 16), that such companies would have to be registered as external *profit* companies.
[183] Section 1.
[184] Chapter 4 of the Act; see also the definition of 'company' in s 95(1) which includes a foreign company for the purposes of Chapter 4 of the Act.
[185] Section 2(2) of the Companies Act 61 of 1973 which stated, 'This Act shall apply to every company incorporated under this Act, every external company and, save as is otherwise provided herein, to every existing company'. See also s 323(1) of the 1973 Act which stated that an external company upon registration under that Act was subject to the applicable provisions of the 1973 Act.
[186] Section 23.
[187] Section 23(3).
[188] Section 33.

- various sections protecting the names of registered external companies (see also the aforementioned chapter 4),
- certain provisions on fundamental transactions and, in particular, requirements for a special resolution by external holding companies,[189]
- protection for whistle-blowers who disclose information about external companies.[190]

Among the advantages of registration for external companies are various provisions that protect the names of registered external companies (discussed in chapter 4: Formation of Companies and the Company Constitution).[191] Also, upon the dissolution or winding-up of South African non-profit companies, that have similar main objects to those of an external non-profit company, the external company qualifies to receive the net value and assets of the South African company.[192]

The underlying policy approach to external companies requires consideration. It appears that the legislative policy to widen the scope of the activities that compel a foreign company to register as an 'external company',[193] has been counterbalanced or offset by a second policy to reduce the regulation of external companies under the Act. Even though more foreign companies may now be obliged to register as external companies in South Africa, the extent of their regulation in terms of the Act has been diminished.

The former rationale for subjecting external companies by and large to most of the 1973 Act was motivated by the mindset that external companies ought to be placed on the same footing as South African companies, and should neither receive preferential treatment nor be subjected to disadvantages that were not also applicable to South African companies.[194] The converse approach in the new Act, ie to reduce the extent of the regulation of external companies, consequently reflects a significant change in the underlying policy. It may be expected to promote investment in the South African markets, in line with the stated purposes of the Act,[195] while concurrently providing some degree of protection for employees and third parties who deal with external companies.

If a foreign company ought to register as an external company but fails to do so, it could be subject to a compliance notice issued by the Companies Commission,

---

[189] A special resolution by an external holding company is required in the case of a proposed disposal of all or the greater part of the assets or undertaking of its subsidiary, if the disposal by the subsidiary company will (having regard to the holding company's consolidated financial statements) constitute a disposal of all or the greater part of the assets or undertaking of the holding company (s 115(2)(b)). A 'special resolution', in the case of an external company, means a decision by its owners or another authorised person, that requires the highest level of support to be adopted, in terms of the relevant law under which the external company was incorporated (cl 2(1)(cc) of the draft Companies Amendment Bill, 2010).
[190] Section 159(3)(b).
[191] Section 11(2)(a) and s 12(2)(b).
[192] Schedule 1 item 1(4).
[193] This may however be substantially changed and narrowed down, as proposed by the draft Companies Amendment Bill, 2010 (see above at n 172).
[194] Supplementary Report of the Van Wyk De Vries Commission at para 62.01.
[195] Section 7(c).

requiring the company to register or to otherwise cease carrying on business or activities in South Africa.[196]

However, a mere failure to register as an external company in South Africa would probably not affect the validity of a contract or other transaction entered into with a third party. This would, of course, depend on the circumstances of the case. In *Manitoba Investment Holdings v Lipchin*[197] the court held, in relation to the 1973 Act, that where an external company has been deregistered, this will not render the agreements that it enters into null and void. The same principle would arguably apply to an external company that has not registered locally.

Significantly, the draft Companies Amendment Bill, 2010, proposes to make provision also for 'domesticated companies'. A domesticated company is a foreign company whose registration has been transferred *to* the Republic of South Africa.[198]

3.10 CLOSE CORPORATIONS

3.10.1 A new approach

The Companies Act 71 of 2008 adopts a momentous stance on close corporations. While *existing* close corporations are permitted to continue indefinitely, no *new* close corporations may be formed after the effective date of the Act.[199]

The driving policy behind this is that the Act is intended to implement an effective and simplified regime for forming and maintaining small companies, based on the characteristics of the close corporation, which renders it unnecessary to retain the application of the Close Corporations Act 69 of 1984 for the forma-

---

[196] Section 23(6). While the Act states that a compliance notice may be issued upon a failure to register within 12 months of commencing activities in South Africa, the draft Companies Amendment Bill, 2010 (cl 15) proposes to shorten this period to six months.

[197] 2010 (2) SA 612 (GNP).

[198] Clause 2(1) of the draft Companies Amendment Bill, 2010. In terms of cl 9 of the Amendment Bill, it is proposed that a foreign company may apply to transfer its registration to South Africa from the foreign jurisdiction in which it is registered, and thereafter exist as a company in terms of the Companies Act of 2008 as if it had been originally so incorporated and registered.

A foreign company may transfer its registration (in terms of the Amendment Bill) if: *(a)* the law of the jurisdiction in which it is initially registered permits such a transfer, and the company has complied with the requirements of that law in relation to the transfer; *(b)* the transfer has been approved by the company's shareholders in the specified manner; *(c)* the whole or greater part of its assets and undertaking are within the Republic, other than the assets and undertaking of any subsidiary that is incorporated outside the Republic; *(d)* the majority of its shareholders are resident in the Republic; *(e)* the majority of its directors are or will be South African citizens; and *(f)* immediately following the transfer of registration, the company will satisfy the solvency and liquidity test; and will no longer be registered in another jurisdiction.

However, a foreign company may not transfer its registration to the Republic if, inter alia: *(a)* it is permitted to issue bearer shares, or has any bearer shares that remain issued; *(b)* it is in liquidation; *(c)* a receiver or manager has been appointed in relation to its property; *(d)* it is engaged in business rescue or a comparable procedure, or has entered into a compromise or arrangement with a creditor, that is in force; or if it is in some other specified type of financial distress.

The registration of a domesticated company does not inter alia affect its continuity as a juristic person; or affect its property, rights, liabilities or obligations; or render ineffective any legal proceedings by or against it (see further cl 9 of the Amendment Bill).

[199] Schedule 3 item 2(1).

tion of new close corporations.[200] However, this policy is debatable, particularly in view of the resounding success of the close corporation as a form of business entity, the large numbers of active close corporations in South Africa and the relative simplicity, clarity and brevity of the legislation governing close corporations as contrasted with the Companies Act.

Since existing close corporations are permitted to continue to exist under the new regime, the Act provides for the co-existence of the Close Corporations Act alongside the Companies Act. In an attempt to harmonise the law as far as practicable to avoid regulatory arbitrage,[201] various amendments are made to the Close Corporations Act (in terms of Schedule 3 to the Companies Act).

Included among these are amendments to ss 2 and 13 of the Close Corporations Act, to the effect that a close corporation may only be formed, and a founding statement of a close corporation may only be lodged, until such time as s 13 of the Companies Act (dealing with the right to incorporate a company) comes into operation.[202] After the coming into operation of s 13 of the Companies Act, no new close corporations may be formed.

In tandem with this, no companies may convert to close corporations after the effective date of Schedule 2 to the Companies Act (although pending conversions that were already filed by then must be concluded).[203] Schedule 2 facilitates the conversion of close corporations into companies, as discussed further below.

Other amendments to the Close Corporations Act include changes to the definition section in order to align that Act with the Companies Act, and provisions that render various sections on names under the Companies Act equally applicable to the names of close corporations. There are also amendments to the transparency and accountability of close corporations, dealing with, inter alia, financial statements and the voluntary opting-in by close corporations to the enhanced accountability and transparency provisions of Chapter 3 of the Companies Act. Further matters dealt with in Schedule 3 are the disqualifications of a person from participation in the management of close corporations; the rescue of financially distressed close corporations, which renders Chapter 6 of the Companies Act on business rescue applicable to close corporations; the dissolution and deregistration of close corporations; as well as enforcement, offences and penalties. A detailed discussion of the Close Corporations Act is beyond the scope of this chapter.

Thus, existing close corporations that were formed under the Close Corporations Act continue to retain their status as close corporations, subject to the amendments to the Close Corporations Act, until and unless their members determine that it is in their interests to convert to a company.[204] Schedule 2 to the Act specifically deals with the conversion of close corporations to companies.

---

[200] *Memorandum on the Objects of the Companies Bill, 2008* op cit n 5 para 2.
[201] Ibid.
[202] Schedule 3 item 2(1) and (2).
[203] Schedule 3 item 2(3) which repeals s 27 of the Close Corporations Act; Schedule 5 item 3(2).
[204] *Memorandum on the Objects of the Companies Bill, 2008* op cit n 5 para 2.

3.10.2 Conversion of a close corporation to a company

An existing close corporation may convert to a company at any time under the Companies Act. It does so by filing a notice of conversion in the prescribed manner and form, accompanied by the following:[205]

- First, a certified copy of the special resolution approving the conversion of the close corporation. This provision is curious, because close corporations do not pass special resolutions. The draft Companies Amendment Bill, 2010[206] now provides that this requirement would be satisfied by a written statement of consent signed by members of the close corporation holding in aggregate at least 75 per cent of the members' interests in the corporation. The 75 per cent requirement facilitates the conversion of close corporations to companies, in comparison with the 1973 Act[207] which required the unanimous written consent of all the members.
- Secondly, a new or amended Memorandum of Incorporation that is consistent with the Act. This provision is also strange, because a close corporation does not have a Memorandum of Incorporation to amend, but is instead governed by its founding statement. It would thus either have to adopt a standard-form Memorandum of Incorporation or draft one. The draft Companies Amendment Bill, 2010[208] in contrast, states simply that a Memorandum of Incorporation (consistent with the Act) is required.
- Thirdly, the prescribed fee.

The Companies Commission then registers the converted close corporation in a similar way to the registration of new companies. Upon the conversion of a close corporation to a company, the Companies Commission cancels its registration under the Close Corporations Act, gives notice in the *Government Gazette* of the conversion and enables the Registrar of Deeds to effect the necessary changes resulting from conversions and name changes.[209]

The effects of a conversion of a close corporation to a company may be summarised as follows:

- Every member of the converted close corporation is entitled to become a shareholder of the resulting company, although the shares to be held in the company by each shareholder need not necessarily be proportionate to his or her member's interest in the close corporation.[210] (This provision may be contrasted with s 29C of the 1973 Act, which obliged — as opposed to entitled — every member of the close corporation to become a member of the company.)
- The juristic person that existed as a close corporation prior to the conversion continues to exist as a juristic person in the form of a company.

---

[205] Schedule 2 item 1.
[206] Clause 112.
[207] Section 29C of the 1973 Act.
[208] Clause 112.
[209] Schedule 2 item 1.
[210] Schedule 2 item 2(1).

- All the assets, liabilities, rights and obligations of the close corporation vest in the company.
- Any legal proceedings instituted by or against the close corporation, before the registration, may be continued by or against the company (and any other thing done by or in respect of the close corporation, is deemed to have been done by or in respect of the company).
- Any enforcement measures that could have been commenced in respect of the close corporation under the Close Corporation Act, for conduct occurring before the date of registration, may be brought against the company on the same basis.
- Any liability of a member of a corporation for the debts of the corporation under the Close Corporations Act, survives the conversion and continues as a liability of that person as if the conversion had not occurred.[211]

3.11 CONVERSION OF COMPANIES

A company of a certain type or category may for various reasons wish to convert into another type of company. The 1973 Act contained a number of explicit and detailed provisions on the conversion of companies, including provisions dealing with notice of an intended conversion and the effect of conversion on such matters as the corporate existence of the company, its debts and liabilities, rights and obligations, contracts and legal proceedings. The new Act, by contrast, is almost silent on the matter.

However, the Act does specifically preclude the conversion of a non-profit company to a profit company, as discussed above.[212] This is an indispensable provision.

As for profit companies, the Act states that where a profit company amends its Memorandum of Incorporation in such a manner that it no longer meets the criteria for its particular category of profit company, the company must at the same time also amend its name by altering the ending expression, as appropriate, to reflect the category of profit company into which it thereafter falls.[213] This suggests that a conversion of one type of profit company to another type of company is effected by amending the company's Memorandum of Incorporation, generally by way of special resolution, to effect the necessary changes to the criteria for the relevant category of company. The Act does not specify any further requirements for and the effects of conversions of companies.

This applies to a personal liability company as well. It is particularly important that the requirement of the 1973 Act[214] — for a special resolution confirmed by the court in order to remove the provision imposing joint and several liability on the directors of a Section 53*(b)* company (ie the equivalent of the personal liability company) — is not duplicated in the new Act.[215] This leaves creditors of a

---
[211] Schedule 2 item 2(2). This is comparable to s 29D of the 1973 Act.
[212] Schedule 1 item 2(1).
[213] Section 16(6).
[214] Section 56(3) of the 1973 Act.
[215] Fortunately it is now proposed by the draft Companies Amendment Bill, 2010 (cl 12) to insert a provision in s 16 to the effect that, if an amendment to the Memorandum of Incorporation of a personal liability company has the effect of transforming that company into any other category of

personal liability company without a right of recourse to the directors and former directors of the company once this provision is removed by special resolution. One expects that the removal of personal liability by way of special resolution would be interpreted to have no retrospective effect on the liability of the directors and former directors of the company.

Although the Act is silent on the effects and consequences of conversions of companies, s 19, which deals with the legal status of companies in general, states the general proposition that a company is a juristic person from the time of its incorporation and exists continuously until its name is removed from the companies register. The section states further that, after a company has changed its name, any legal proceedings that might have been commenced or continued by or against the company under its former name may be commenced or continued under its new name.[216]

---

company, the company must give at least ten business days advance notice of the filing of the notice of amendment to: any professional or industry regulatory authority that has jurisdiction over the business activities carried on by the company; any persons who, in their dealings with the company, may reasonably be considered to have acted in reliance upon the joint and several liability of any of the directors for the debts and liabilities of the company; or any persons who may be adversely affected if the joint and several liability of any of the directors for the debts and liabilities of the company is terminated as a consequence of the amendment to the Memorandum of Incorporation. A person who receives, or is entitled to receive, such a notice may apply to a court in the prescribed manner and form for an order sufficient to protect the interests of that person.

[216] Section 19(1)(*a*) and s 19(7).

CHAPTER 4

FORMATION OF COMPANIES AND THE COMPANY CONSTITUTION

Maleka Femida Cassim

4.1	INCORPORATION AND REGISTRATION OF COMPANIES	101
	4.1.1 Underlying philosophy and principles	101
	4.1.2 Incorporation of the company	102
	(a) The incorporators	102
	(b) The procedure for incorporation	102
	4.1.3 Registration of the company	103
	(a) The registration certificate	104
	(b) Rejection of the Notice of Incorporation by the Companies Commission	104
	(c) Registration of external companies	105
	4.1.4 The registered office	107
4.2	COMPANY NAMES	108
	4.2.1 Introduction	108
	4.2.2 Criteria for company names	108
	4.2.3 Registration of company names and disputes concerning names	111
	4.2.4 Changing the company name	113
	4.2.5 Name reservation and defensive names	114
	4.2.6 Use of the company name and registration number	116
4.3	THE MEMORANDUM OF INCORPORATION	117
	4.3.1 Underlying philosophy	117
	4.3.2 Contents of the Memorandum of Incorporation	119
	4.3.3 Restrictions and prohibitions on the amendment of provisions of the Memorandum of Incorporation	121
	4.3.4 Amending the Memorandum of Incorporation	124
	(a) Correction of patent errors in the Memorandum of Incorporation or rules	127
	(b) Translations of the Memorandum of Incorporation	128
	(c) Consolidations of the Memorandum of Incorporation	128
	(d) Authenticity of versions of the Memorandum of Incorporation	128
4.4	RULES OF THE COMPANY	129
4.5	SHAREHOLDER AGREEMENTS	131
4.6	THE LEGAL STATUS OF THE MEMORANDUM OF INCORPORATION AND RULES	133

	4.6.1	Introduction	133
	4.6.2	The relationship between the company and each shareholder . . .	135
		(a) Are shareholders bound only in their capacity as shareholders?	135
		(b) Enforcement by shareholders against the company	137
	4.6.3	The relationship between or among the shareholders *inter se* . . .	137
	4.6.4	The relationship between the company and each director, prescribed officer, member of the audit committee or member of a board committee, in the exercise of their respective functions within the company	138
4.7	PRE-INCORPORATION CONTRACTS	141
	4.7.1	Introduction	141
		(a) Significance of pre-incorporation contracts and the common-law hurdles.	141
		(b) The main methods of contracting on behalf of a company to be formed	142
	4.7.2	Section 21 pre-incorporation contracts	143
		(a) General	143
		(b) Ratification of a section 21 contract	145
		(c) Liability of the promoter for a section 21 contract	146
		(d) Other important issues	149
	4.7.3	The *stipulatio alteri* or contract for the benefit of a third party . .	150

4.1 INCORPORATION AND REGISTRATION OF COMPANIES

4.1.1 Underlying philosophy and principles

The Companies Act 71 of 2008 (hereafter 'the Act') adopts a new core principle relating to the formation of companies, namely that the formation of a company is a right and not a privilege.[1] This is buttressed by the constitutional right to freedom of association coupled with the common-law right to freedom of contract.[2] The recognition by the Act of the right to form a company is laudable. It stems from the underlying philosophy that the formation of companies promotes commercial enterprise and the growth and development of the economy.[3] The principle that incorporation is a right, rather than a privilege bestowed by the state, is reflected in the general approach of the Act to company formation and in many of its provisions and procedures regulating the formation of a company.

A fundamental object of the Act is 'to promote the development of the South African economy by creating flexibility and simplicity in the formation and maintenance of companies'.[4] Arising from these underlying themes of 'simplicity' and 'flexibility' is an innovative and simplified procedure comprising minimal

---

[1] This is made clear from the heading of s 13 of the Act; see also the *Memorandum on the Objects of the Companies Bill, 2008*, Companies Bill [B 61D–2008] at para 5.

[2] *Memorandum on the Objects of the Companies Bill, 2008* op cit n 1 at para 5; Constitution of the Republic of South Africa, 1996.

[3] FHI Cassim 'The Companies Act 2008: An Overview of a Few of its Core Provisions' (2010) 22 *SA Merc LJ* 157 at 159.

[4] Section 7(b)(ii).

requirements and formalities for the incorporation of companies. This new approach may be expected to eliminate the delay in the formation of companies and its associated costs. There is also considerable flexibility in corporate structure and organisation. Together with this enhanced simplicity and flexibility, the regulatory oversight of the formation and structure of companies has been reduced.[5] These themes are evident in the detailed provisions of the Act, which are discussed and elucidated below.

4.1.2 Incorporation of the company

(a) The incorporators

The 'incorporators' (ie the founders of the company) are responsible for the incorporation of the company.[6] One or more incorporators may incorporate a profit company, regardless of whether it is a public or a private company, while at least three persons are required for the incorporation of a non-profit company.[7] This simplifies the position compared to the Companies Act 61 of 1973 (hereafter 'the 1973 Act'). The 1973 Act required at least seven persons for the formation of a public company and at least two for a private company, or one person in the case of a private company that was to have only a single member.[8]

The Act, seemingly, no longer requires the incorporator to subscribe for shares in the company.[9] The responsibilities of an incorporator include the requirements that each incorporator of a company must sign the Memorandum of Incorporation, whether in person or by proxy, and that each incorporator is automatically a first director of the company who serves as director until such time as sufficient directors (as required by the Act or the company's Memorandum of Incorporation) have been appointed or elected.[10]

(b) The procedure for incorporation

The procedure to incorporate a company under the Act has been simplified and pruned down to a bare minimum of formal requirements. Under the previous company law regime, for instance, the name of the company had to first be approved and reserved before the incorporation of the company could commence, so that the company could be incorporated in the reserved name.[11] This is no longer necessary under the new regime.

In order to incorporate a company now, in terms of the Act, the incorporators must first complete and sign a Memorandum of Incorporation, either in person or

---

[5] *Memorandum on the Objects of the Companies Bill, 2008* op cit n 1 at para 5.
[6] Section 1.
[7] Sections 1 and 13(1). The draft Companies Amendment Bill, 2010 (cl 9) proposes to amend s 13 to provide that one or more persons, or an organ of state, may incorporate a profit company, and an organ of state, a juristic person, or three or more persons acting in common, may incorporate a non-profit company.
[8] Section 32 of the 1973 Act.
[9] Parallels may be drawn with the US Revised Model Business Corporation Act 1984, as amended, which no longer requires an incorporator to be a subscriber of shares.
[10] Section 67(1).
[11] Section 42(1) of the 1973 Act.

Formation of Companies and the Company Constitution

by proxy.[12] The Memorandum of Incorporation is the sole founding or governing document of the company, setting out the rights, duties and responsibilities of shareholders, directors and others within and in relation to the company, together with various other matters.[13]

The next step is for the incorporators to file with the Companies and Intellectual Property Commission ('the Companies Commission') the following:[14]

- A Notice of Incorporation, the purpose of which is to inform the Companies Commission of the incorporation of the company for the purpose of having it registered.[15] The prescribed form of the Notice of Incorporation is to be dealt with by regulations in terms of the Act.[16] The Act itself requires certain information to be stated in the Notice of Incorporation, such as the name of the company, its initial directors, its registered office and the date of its financial year-end. A notice of the appointment of the first company secretary, auditor or audit committee (where appointed) may be filed as part of the Notice of Incorporation.[17]
- A copy of the Memorandum of Incorporation, which may be either in the prescribed form or in a form unique to the company.[18]
- Payment of the prescribed fee.

If the Memorandum of Incorporation contains: *(a)* any restrictive or procedural requirements impeding the amendment of any provision of the Memorandum of Incorporation, or *(b)* any prohibitions on the amendment of any provision of the Memorandum of Incorporation, then the Notice of Incorporation must contain a prominent statement drawing attention to each such provision together with its location in the Memorandum of Incorporation.[19] (Furthermore, the company name must be immediately followed by the expression '(RF)', which presumably means ring-fenced, as discussed in 4.2 on company names below.)

4.1.3 Registration of the company

After accepting the filed Notice of Incorporation from the incorporators, the Companies Commission must as soon as practicable register the company.

To do so, it must: *(a)* assign a unique registration number to the company, *(b)* enter certain prescribed information concerning the company, including the company name, in the companies register, *(c)* endorse the Notice of Incorporation and

---

[12] Section 13(1)*(a)*.
[13] Section 1.
[14] Section 13(1)*(b)*.
[15] Section 1.
[16] See Form CoR 15.1 in Annexure 1 of the draft Companies Regulations Pursuant to the Companies Act, 2008 (Act No. 71 of 2008) GN 1664 *GG* 32832 of 22 December 2009 (hereafter 'the draft Companies Regulations').
[17] Section 85(4).
[18] Section 13(1)*(a)*. The Act does not contain a prescribed form or model of the Memorandum of Incorporation. This is to be contained in the Companies Regulations (see Annexure 4 of the draft Companies Regulations).
[19] Section 13(3) read with the amendments proposed by the draft Companies Amendment Bill, 2010 (cl 11) to s 15(2)*(b)* of the Act (discussed below).

the copy of the Memorandum of Incorporation, and *(d)* issue and deliver a registration certificate to the company.[20]

(a) The registration certificate

The registration certificate is issued by the Companies Commission as evidence of the incorporation and registration of the company.[21] The registration certificate serves as conclusive evidence that all the requirements for incorporation have been complied with.[22] It is regrettable that this presumption does not explicitly exclude fraud — the 1973 Act specifically provided that the registration certificate was conclusive proof of due compliance only in the absence of fraud.[23]

Once the registration certificate has been issued, the company is incorporated and comes into existence as a separate legal person or juristic person, with effect from the date and time, if any, stated on the registration certificate.[24] In this regard, the Companies Commission dates the registration certificate either as at the date and time it issued the certificate, or as at the specific date (if any) requested by the incorporators in terms of the Notice of Incorporation, whichever of these two dates happens to be the later one.[25]

Consequent to the policy of simplification and decreased regulatory oversight of company formation, the requirement of a certificate to commence business has been abolished. The certificate to commence business was crucial under the 1973 Act, where no company having a share capital could commence business or exercise borrowing powers until it had received such a certificate.[26] A company may now generally commence business once it is registered.

(b) Rejection of the Notice of Incorporation by the Companies Commission

In certain circumstances the Companies Commission has the power to reject the Notice of Incorporation filed by the incorporators and to refuse to register the company. There are two grounds for a mandatory rejection and one for a discretionary rejection.

Where the number of initial directors of the company is less than the prescribed statutory minimum, the Companies Commission must reject the Notice of Incorporation.[27] In the case of a private company or a personal liability company at least one director is required, whereas for a public company or a non-profit company at least three directors are required.[28] Their names must be stated in the Notice of Incorporation.

---

[20] Section 14(1).
[21] Section 1.
[22] Section 14(4).
[23] Section 64(2) of the 1973 Act. FHI Cassim op cit n 3 at 161.
[24] Section 14(4) and s 19(1)*(a)*.
[25] Section 14(1)*(b)*(iii).
[26] Section 172 of the 1973 Act.
[27] Section 13(4)*(b)*(i).
[28] Section 66(2). See further the draft Companies Amendment Bill, 2010 (cl 42), which proposes to make this subject to the minimum number of directors that the company must have to satisfy any requirement to appoint an audit committee or a social and ethics committee.

Formation of Companies and the Company Constitution

The second ground for a mandatory rejection of the Notice of Incorporation is where the Companies Commission reasonably believes that any of the initial directors are disqualified from being appointed a director of a company,[29] with the result that the *remaining* initial directors are fewer than the prescribed statutory minimum.[30] Evidently the Companies Commission could accept a Notice of Incorporation, regardless of the disqualification of any initial director(s), if the remaining initial directors still make up the requisite minimum number.

Turning to the discretionary rejection of the Notice of Incorporation, the Companies Commission *'may'* reject the Notice of Incorporation where it (or anything required to be filed with it) is either incomplete or improperly completed.[31] The discretion of the Companies Commission is subject to the substantial compliance provision of the Act. This provides that a prescribed notice, document, record or statement will suffice if it is completed in a form that satisfies all the substantive requirements of the prescribed form, and that a deviation from the prescribed design or content will not invalidate it unless the deviation negatively and materially affects its substance, or is such that it would reasonably mislead a person reading the notice, document, record or statement.[32]

Finally, it is noteworthy that, where the proposed name of the company turns out to be unsuitable in terms of the Act, this of itself does not constitute grounds for the rejection of the Notice of Incorporation. This innovation is to be welcomed. As a matter of policy, the process of incorporation should not be unduly delayed pending the registration of a suitable company name, as this would stifle the use of commercial opportunities by the company to be formed. (See further 4.2 on company names below.)

(c) Registration of external companies

An external company must register with the Companies Commission within 20 business days of conducting business or non-profit activities (as the case may be) within the Republic of South Africa.[33] (The meaning and definition of an 'external company' as well as the circumstances in which a foreign company is regarded as 'conducting business' within South Africa are dealt with in chapter 3: Types of Companies.)

An external company registers either as an external non-profit company or as an external profit company. This depends on whether, within the jurisdiction in which it was incorporated, it satisfies legislative or definitional requirements that are comparable to those for a non-profit company or a profit company incorporated under the Act. The Act leaves open the question whether registration is

---

[29] On any of the grounds of disqualification set out in s 69(8), see further chapter 10: Governance and the Board of Directors.

[30] Section 13(4)*(b)*(ii).

[31] Section 13(4)*(a)*.

[32] Section 6(8). The Act does not set out a prescribed form for the Notice of Incorporation, although it does require certain details to be addressed in the Notice of Incorporation. The prescribed Notice of Incorporation will form part of the Companies Regulations (see Form CoR 15.1 of Annexure 1 of the draft Companies Regulations).

[33] Section 23(1).

necessary and, if so, what the registration requirements are, for an external company that does not meet such comparable legislative or definitional requirements — an issue that is bound to arise.[34]

On registration, the Companies Commission assigns a unique registration number to the external company.[35] The Companies Commission must maintain a register of external companies containing certain prescribed information.[36] An external company must continuously maintain at least one office in South Africa. It registers the address of its office by providing the required information when filing its registration.[37] In terms of the draft Companies Regulations, an external company, when registering as such, must provide a certified copy of its certificate of registration (or equivalent document) in its jurisdiction of incorporation. It is also required to provide the name and address of any person within South Africa who has undertaken to accept service of documents on its behalf, the names of its directors at the time and the address of its principal office outside South Africa.[38]

Although the Act does not provide explicitly for the issue of registration certificates to external companies, it appears from the definition of 'registration certificate' (in s 1) that the Companies Commission will indeed issue a registration certificate to a registered external company.[39] Once an external company has been assigned a registration number and has registered its office, it satisfies the definition of a 'registered external company'.[40]

If an external company fails to register within 12 months of commencing its activities in South Africa, the Companies Commission may issue a compliance notice requiring it to register within 20 business days after receiving the notice or, if it fails to register within this time, to cease carrying on its business or activities in South Africa.[41]

There has been a remarkable change in the approach to external companies. While the 1973 Act applied generally to external companies by virtue of a catch-all phrase,[42] under the new company law regime only certain specified sections of the Act apply to external companies. Included among these are the requirements that external companies must provide certain information upon registration and must file annual returns;[43] sections on the use of the company

---

[34] It is now proposed by the draft Companies Amendment Bill, 2010 (cl 16), that such companies would have to be registered as external *profit* companies.
[35] Section 23(5).
[36] Section 23(5). Where the name of an external company consists of its foreign registration number, without any indication of the foreign jurisdiction in which it was incorporated, the Companies Commission must append the name of that jurisdiction to the name of the company on the registry (s 23(5)).
[37] Section 23(3).
[38] Regulation 22 of the draft Companies Regulations.
[39] See also Regulation 22(2) of the draft Companies Regulations.
[40] Section 1. See further 4.1.4 on the registered office below.
[41] Section 23(6).
[42] Section 2(2) of the 1973 Act, which stated, 'This Act shall apply to every company incorporated under this Act, every external company and, save as is otherwise provided herein, to every existing company'. See also s 323(1) of the 1973 Act.
[43] Section 33.

name and registration number (discussed in 4.2 below);[44] various provisions protecting the names of registered external companies (discussed in 4.2 below),[45] and certain sections on fundamental transactions.[46]

4.1.4 The registered office

Each company and every external company must continuously maintain at least one office in South Africa and register the address of its office.[47] Where the company has more than one office, the address of the principal office is registered.[48] As explained above, a company incorporated in South Africa registers its office by providing the requisite information on its Notice of Incorporation, while an external company does so at the time of filing its registration as an external company.

A company that wishes to amend its registered office may do so by filing a notice of change of registered office.[49] A change of registered office takes effect five business days after the filing of the notice or, if a later date is stated in the notice, it takes effect on such later date.[50]

The registered office serves a vital purpose, since a company lacks a physical existence. Service of process of court is effected at the registered office of a company, or at its principal place of business within the court's jurisdiction.[51] In addition, a company's accounting records must be kept at or must be accessible from its registered office.[52]

Other records of the company[53] (whether in written or electronic form) may also be kept at the registered office or may alternatively be kept at another South African location, in which case a Notice of Location of records must be filed.[54] Some of these records must be kept for a period of seven years.[55] The relevant records include a copy of the Memorandum of Incorporation and the rules of the company; the record of directors; copies of reports presented at annual general meetings; copies of annual financial statements and accounting records; notices and minutes of shareholders' meetings, including shareholders' resolutions and documents made available to the holders of securities in relation to shareholders' resolutions; written communications sent to the holders of any class of securities; minutes of directors' meetings and directors' resolutions; minutes of directors' committee meetings, including those of the audit committee; the securities register

---

[44] Section 32(1) and (5).
[45] Section 11(2)*(a)* and s 12(2)*(b)*.
[46] See further chapter 3: Types of Companies and chapter 15: Fundamental Transactions, Takeovers and Offers.
[47] Section 23(3).
[48] Section 23(3)*(b)*.
[49] Together with the prescribed fee (s 23(3)*(b)*(ii)).
[50] Section 23(4). In this regard, s 23(4) erroneously refers to s 23(2)*(b)*(ii) — the reference is intended to be to s 23(3)*(b)*(ii), as proposed by the draft Companies Amendment Bill, 2010 (cl 15).
[51] Rule 4(1)*(a)*(v) of the Supreme Court Rules and Rule 9(3)*(e)* of the Magistrate's Court Rules.
[52] Section 28(2).
[53] These records are referred to in s 24.
[54] Section 25(1). Refer further to chapter 9: Governance and Shareholders.
[55] Section 24(1)*(b)*. The draft Companies Regulations require a company's Memorandum of Incorporation (as amended from time to time), registration certificate, register of directors and securities register to be kept indefinitely.

(for profit companies) and the record of company secretaries and auditors, if applicable.[56]

4.2 COMPANY NAMES

4.2.1 Introduction

Often the first step in forming a company is the selection of a suitable company name. In selecting a name for the company, the incorporators must bear in mind the criteria for company names laid down by the Act. The principal legal objectives are to protect the goodwill associated with names and to prevent public deception by the use of names that are misleading and imply a non-existent association. It also remains a crucial objective to prevent hateful or unconstitutional names. The Act stipulates numerous requirements and restrictions on company names. In doing so, the intention of the legislature is also to give maximum effect, within limits, to the constitutional right of freedom of expression.[57]

The Act simultaneously removes the wide administrative discretion that existed under the 1973 Act, in terms of which the Registrar of Companies could reject a proposed name if, in his subjective opinion, it was 'undesirable'.[58]

The Act preserves the general practice of registration of company names, but implements some significant reforms and improvements. Unlike the previous system under the 1973 Act,[59] it is no longer mandatory to first make an application to approve and reserve the name of the company prior to initiating the registration of the company. The proposed name of the company may now be submitted in the Notice of Incorporation, which is filed with the Companies Commission. The abolition of name reservation as a mandatory first step in the process simplifies the incorporation and registration process under the new Act. Name reservation does, however, remain available under the Act as an optional facility, in acknowledgement of its useful practical purpose.

4.2.2 Criteria for company names

A company name may consist of words in any language. This is irrespective of whether the words are commonly used or are contrived for the purpose. Together with these words, the name of the company may include any letters, numbers or punctuation marks, and/or round brackets if used in pairs to isolate any part of the name.[60] Symbols are now also permitted in company names. The permissible symbols are the symbols +, &, #, % and = and any others that may be permitted in terms of regulations.[61] The symbols @ and — are also proposed to be included.[62] The more intricate details, such as which alphabet is permissible or whether

---

[56] Also to be included are the members' register (for non-profit companies) and the company's registration certificate (in terms of cl 16 of the draft Companies Amendment Bill, 2010).
[57] *Memorandum on the Objects of the Companies Bill, 2008* op cit n 1 at para 5.
[58] See ss 41, 43 and 44 of the 1973 Act.
[59] See s 42(1) of the 1973 Act.
[60] Section 11(1).
[61] Section 11(1) read with s 11(4).
[62] Regulation 9(6) of the draft Companies Regulations. The draft Companies Amendment Bill, 2010 now proposes to insert '@' in s 11(1)(*a*)(ii) of the Act (cl 7(*a*)).

Formation of Companies and the Company Constitution

Arabic or Roman numerals may be used or the circumstances when translations of names are required, are proposed to be dealt with in terms of regulations.[63]

In the case of a profit company, but not a non-profit company, the company's registration number may now be used as its name, provided that it is immediately followed by the expression '(South Africa)'.[64] This innovatory provision is to be welcomed. It will prevent delays in incorporation and registration where incorporators experience difficulty in finding a suitable name. Moreover, some companies, due to the nature of their business, may not have any real need for a name and the simple use of their registration numbers would now suffice.

The expression '(RF)', which is taken to mean 'ring-fenced', must immediately follow the name of the company if its Memorandum of Incorporation prohibits the amendment of any provisions or if it contains provisions with restrictions on their amendment.[65] The purpose of inserting the expression '(RF)' is to alert third parties to the restrictions or prohibitions on the amendment of certain provisions of the Memorandum of Incorporation, so that they may exercise appropriate caution.

The concluding words or concluding expression in the name of the company continue to depend on the category or type of company it is. The appropriate expression for each category of company is as follows:[66]

- in the case of a private company, the company name must end with the expression 'Proprietary Limited' or its abbreviation '(Pty) Ltd.',[67]
- the name of a personal liability company must end with the word 'Incorporated' or the abbreviation 'Inc.',
- the word 'Limited' or its abbreviation 'Ltd.' must appear at the end of the name of a public company,
- in the case of a state-owned company the expression 'SOC Ltd.' is required,
- in the case of a non-profit company the expression 'NPC' is prescribed.

Turning to the statutory restrictions on company names, since the Act seeks to give effect to the constitutional right to freedom of expression, company names are restricted as far as necessary:[68]

- first, to protect the owners of names and other forms of intellectual property from those passing themselves off or 'coat-tailing' on their reputations and goodwill,

---

[63] See eg Regulations 9(2) and 9(3) of the draft Companies Regulations. See also the draft Companies Amendment Bill, 2010.

[64] Section 11(1)(b) read with s 11(3)(a).

[65] Section 11(3)(b) read with s 15(2)(b) and (c); see further cl 7 of the draft Companies Amendment Bill, 2010, which proposes to delete the reference to special conditions in terms of s 15(2)(b), and to instead require the expression '(RF)' where a company's Memorandum of Incorporation contains any restrictive or procedural requirements impeding the amendment of any of its provisions. The significance of the expression '(RF)' is further discussed in 4.3.3 below.

[66] Section 11(3)(c). Pre-existing companies are *deemed* to have changed their names insofar as required to comply with these provisions — see the Transitional Arrangements in Schedule 5, item 4(1) and chapter 21: Transitional Arrangements.

[67] The draft Companies Amendment Bill, 2010 (cl 7) proposes the expression 'Pty. Ltd.' instead.

[68] *Memorandum on the Objects of the Companies Bill, 2008* op cit n 1 at para 5.

- secondly, to protect the public from misleading names that falsely imply a non-existent association, and
- thirdly, to prohibit hateful names or names that fall outside the scope of the constitutional protection of freedom of expression.

These policy issues are fleshed out in the Act as follows: Regarding the first group of statutory restrictions, the Act provides[69] that the name of a company must not be the same as or confusingly similar to the name of another company, external company, close corporation or co-operative, unless the company forms part of a group of companies using similar names. (The exemption of company groups may be criticised — while it is understandable why companies in a group may have names that are 'confusingly similar', it is undesirable, misleading and indeed unnecessary to permit their names to be the 'same'.[70]) Additionally, the name of the company may neither be the same as nor confusingly similar to a name registered as a business name under the Business Names Act;[71] or to a trade mark that has been registered or filed for registration or a well-known trade mark;[72] or to a mark, word or expression the use of which is protected in terms of the Merchandise Marks Act.[73] In interpreting the phrase 'confusingly similar', the common-law principle of reasonable likelihood of confusion as laid down in case law, may still be relevant.[74] It is notable that the Act does not specifically proscribe the use of a company name that is the same as that of a dissolved company. It would be advisable to do so, as it might otherwise result in confusion between the business of a company and the business of a dissolved company.

Superadded to the statutory criteria on company names, the common-law rules must also be borne in mind, particularly the delict of 'passing off'. The delict of passing off is linked to the first group of restrictions (above) on company names. 'Passing off' occurs where the use of a name could result in a reasonable likelihood of members of the public being confused into believing that the business of the company is, or is connected with, that of another. There are two significant elements of passing off: that confusion or deception is reasonably likely to ensue and, if confusion or deception does ensue, it will probably cause damage to the applicant.[75]

---

[69] Section 11(2)(a).

[70] The draft Companies Amendment Bill, 2010 (cl 7) proposes a number of amendments to s 11(2)(a). One such amendment is that the above exemption of company groups will now sensibly be restricted to 'confusingly similar' names. The Amendment Bill proposes furthermore to proscribe company names that are the same as or confusingly similar to the names of domesticated companies, or to names that have been registered as defensive names. The Amendment Bill also proposes certain exceptions in terms of which a company's name may be the same as or confusingly similar to a name, trade mark, mark, word or expression contemplated in s 11(2)(a).

[71] Act 27 of 1960.

[72] As defined in s 35 of the Trade Marks Act 194 of 1993.

[73] Act 17 of 1941, except to the extent permitted by that Act.

[74] See eg *Polaris Capital (Pty) Ltd v Registrar of Companies* 2010 (2) SA 274 (SCA).

[75] *Peregrine Group (Pty) Ltd v Peregrine Holdings Ltd* 2000 (1) SA 187 (W) 198 and the appeal case 2001 (3) SA 1268 (SCA); *Polaris Capital (Pty) Ltd v Registrar of Companies* (supra); see also *Azisa (Pty) Ltd v Azisa Media CC* 2002 (4) SA 377 (C) and the commentary by FHI Cassim 'Company Law' in *Annual Survey of South African Law* (2002) 636–8; *Capital Estate & General*

Formation of Companies and the Company Constitution

Turning to the second group of restrictions on company names, ie names that falsely imply a non-existent association, a proposed company name must not falsely imply or suggest, or be such as would reasonably mislead a person to believe incorrectly, that the company: (i) is part of or associated with another person or entity, or (ii) is owned, managed or conducted by a person having any particular educational designation or by a person who is a regulated person or entity,[76] or (iii) is an organ of state or a court, or is operated, sponsored, supported or endorsed by the state or any organ of state or court, or that it (iv) is owned, operated, sponsored, supported or endorsed by, or enjoys the patronage of, any international organisation or any foreign state (or head of state, head of government, government or administration or any department thereof).[77]

The third group of statutory restrictions, ie names that are offensive or unconstitutional forms of expression,[78] proscribes company names that include any word, expression or symbol that (whether in isolation or in its context within the rest of the name) may reasonably be considered to constitute either: (i) propaganda for war, or (ii) incitement of imminent violence, or (iii) advocacy of hatred based on race, ethnicity, gender or religion or incitement to cause harm.[79]

4.2.3 Registration of company names and disputes concerning names

It must be emphasised at the outset that a proposed company name that is unsuitable, inappropriate or incomplete, does not prevent or delay the process of incorporation and registration of the company. This is a laudable change in approach that would ensure that the commencement of business by the company is not stifled.

In this regard, where the name of a company, as entered on the Notice of Incorporation, lacks the appropriate expression indicative of the type of company (eg Ltd., Inc.,), the Companies Commission itself may insert or substitute the requisite expression when attending to the registration of the company.[80] The same principle applies where the name of a company does not have the expression '(RF)' or '(South Africa)', where this is required.

Agencies (Pty) Ltd v Holiday Inns Inc 1977 (2) SA 916 (A). In *Azisa* the court stated that there is no hard-and-fast rule, and that much depends on the degree of similarity of the names, the likelihood of confusion and the business activities of the parties.

[76] A regulated person or entity means one who has been granted authority to conduct business by a regulatory authority (s 1 of the Act). 'Regulatory authority' means an entity established in terms of national or provincial legislation responsible for regulating an industry, or sector of an industry (s 1).

[77] Section 11(2)*(b)*. (The draft Companies Amendment Bill, 2010 proposes to change this to s 11(2)*(c)*.)

[78] Section 11(2)*(c)*. (The draft Companies Amendment Bill, 2010 proposes to change this to s 11(2)*(d)*.)

[79] The Transitional Arrangements in Schedule 5 item 4(2) provide that a pre-existing company (which was incorporated prior to the effective date of the Act) may file, without charge, within two years of the general effective date of the Act, a notice of name change together with a copy of the relevant special resolution to alter its name in order to meet the requirements of the Act. See further chapter 21: Transitional Arrangements.

[80] Section 14(2)*(a)*.

In the event that the proposed name of the company is the same as that of another company, close corporation or co-operative or has been reserved for another, the Companies Commission will nonetheless register the company by using an interim name instead of the proposed company name. The interim name is used in the companies register and on the registration certificate.[81] The interim name consists merely of the company's registration number followed by the appropriate expression indicating the type of company it is.[82] Once the company has been registered in the interim name, the Companies Commission invites the company to file an amended Notice of Incorporation using another, satisfactory name. When the company does so, the Companies Commission enters the amended company name in the companies register and issues an amended registration certificate reflecting the amended company name.[83]

This new procedure is in harmony with the policy of simplicity and the removal of unnecessary and burdensome formalities. It also promotes the efficiency of enterprises by enabling the company to nevertheless commence with its business and other activities in the interim. However, the Act is silent on the consequences of a failure by such a company to file an amended Notice of Incorporation in an amended name. In the case of a profit company, the company's registration number (followed by the appropriate expression, as discussed above) may perhaps continue to be used as its name. This solution cannot apply to a non-profit company, because a non-profit company may not use its registration number as a name.[84] The failure by a company to file an amended Notice of Incorporation in an amended name could possibly result in a compliance notice being issued by the Companies Commission. Failure to comply with such a compliance notice could have far-reaching consequences.[85]

Where the Companies Commission, in attending to the registration of a company name, has reasonable grounds for considering that the name of the company may fall within the first or second groups of restricted names discussed above (ie proposed names that infringe existing legal rights in the name or intellectual property, and misleading names that falsely imply a non-existent association), the Companies Commission may by way of written notice order the applicant to serve a copy of the application on any particular person or class of persons on the grounds that they may have an interest in the applicant's use of the name.[86] A

---

[81] The draft Companies Amendment Bill, 2010 (cl 10) proposes to widen the scope of this provision to include all names that fall within the first group of restrictions on company names (discussed above) and that are the *same* as a name, trade mark, mark, word or expression contemplated in s 11(2)*(a)* of the Act (including registered defensive names and names of domesticated companies). This is a welcome development.

[82] Section 14(2)*(b)*(i).

[83] Section 14(2)*(b)*.

[84] Section 11(3)*(a)*.

[85] See s 171; see further chapter 17: Enforcement and Regulatory Agencies.

[86] Section 14(3)*(a)* read with s 11(2)*(a)* and *(b)*. The draft Companies Amendment Bill, 2010 (cl 10) proposes that this provision will apply to the first group of restricted names only where the relevant name is '*confusingly similar*' to a name, trade mark, mark, word or expression contemplated in s 11(2)*(a)*; where the relevant name is the '*same*' as one of these, then the Companies Commission would instead register the company by using an interim name (as discussed above).

Formation of Companies and the Company Constitution

person to whom a notice is delivered, or any other person with an interest in the name, may then apply to the Companies Tribunal for a determination and an order on whether the name satisfies the requirements of the Act.[87] If, on the other hand, the Companies Commission on reasonable grounds considers that the name of the company is inconsistent with the third group of restricted names discussed above (ie names that are offensive or unconstitutional forms of expression), it may refer the application to the South African Human Rights Commission, which could then apply to the Companies Tribunal.[88] Disputes concerning company names are dealt with by the Companies Tribunal in terms of s 160.[89]

An application to the Companies Tribunal in terms of s 160 must be made within three months after the date of the notice (if any). In any other case, it may be made on good cause shown at any time after the date of registration of the relevant name.[90] The Companies Tribunal, in turn, considers the application together with the submissions made by the applicant and any other person with an interest in the name, and determines whether the company name satisfies the requirements of the Act. The Companies Tribunal may make a number of administrative orders in this context. It may direct the Companies Commission to register the contested name as the name of the company, or it may order the company to choose a new name and register it by way of filing a notice of amendment to its Memorandum of Incorporation.[91] The Act also makes provision for applications to a court to review the notice or the decision of the Companies Tribunal.[92]

It is noteworthy that all the above provisions apply equally to the registration of a *change* of company name, which is discussed in the section below.

4.2.4 Changing the company name

A change of the name of a company is generally effected in the same way as any other alteration to the Memorandum of Incorporation, ie usually by a special resolution in terms of s 16.[93] After changing its name, the company must file with the Companies Commission a Notice of Amendment, including a copy of the amendment.[94] The Companies Commission thereafter issues an amended registration certificate and alters the company's name on the companies register, provided

---

[87] Section 14(3)*(a)* and s 160(1). (The drafting of s 14(3) may be criticised, in that it states that the 'application and name reservation' must be served (s 14(3)*(a)*(i) and s 14(3)*(b)*(i)). The reference to 'name reservation' in the context of s 14 is unclear and appears to be erroneous. Section 14(3)*(a)*(i) (and its equivalent s 14(3)*(b)*(i)) also refers to persons having an interest in the applicant's use of the 'reserved name'. The reference to 'reserved name' is unclear and appears also to be erroneous.)

[88] Section 14(3)*(b)* read with s 11(2)*(c)*.

[89] Section 160 regulates disputes concerning the registration or reservation of company names.

[90] Section 160(2).

[91] The notice of amendment must be filed within a period and on any condition that the Companies Tribunal considers just, equitable and expedient in the circumstances, including a condition exempting the company from paying the prescribed filing fee for the ordered name change (s 160(3)).

[92] Within 20 business days after receiving a notice or decision issued by the Companies Tribunal, an incorporator, a company, a person who received a notice, an applicant under s 160 or any other person with an interest in the name, may apply to a court to review the notice or decision of the Companies Tribunal (s 160(4)).

[93] Section 16(5)*(b)*. See further 4.3.4 below on amending the Memorandum of Incorporation.

[94] Together with payment of the prescribed fee (s 16(7)).

that the relevant name is not the registered name of another company, registered external company, close corporation or co-operative, nor reserved for another.[95]

The criteria for company names, the registration of company names and disputes concerning company names, as discussed in 4.2.2 and 4.2.3 above, apply equally to an amended company name.[96]

Where a profit company amends its Memorandum of Incorporation such that it falls into a different category of profit company, the concluding expression in the name of the company must simultaneously be amended to reflect the new type of profit company it is.[97]

A change in the name of a company will have no effect on any legal proceedings by or against the company. Legal proceedings may be commenced or continued by or against the company under its new name.[98] This is a useful, practical provision.

4.2.5 Name reservation and defensive names

Company names may be reserved for use at a later stage. Under the new Act, the reservation of company names is available on an optional or voluntary basis. This may serve a useful purpose in certain circumstances, for instance where the incorporators have an interest in ensuring that a particular name is reserved for the company prior to proceeding with the formalities for incorporating and registering the company.

A name may be reserved for later use either for a newly incorporated company or for an amendment to the name of an existing company.[99] The Companies Commission will reserve a name for an applicant provided that the name requested to be reserved has not already been reserved nor is the registered name of another company, close corporation, co-operative or registered external company.[100] A proposed reserved name must also comply with the prescribed criteria for company names and must not fall within any of the groups of restricted names, as discussed above.[101] Should the Companies Commission have reasonable grounds to consider the name in question to be inconsistent with these criteria, a similar notification procedure applies as in the case of the registration of company

---

[95] Section 16(8)(*b*).
[96] Section 16(8). It is proposed that the amendment of the company name will take effect on the date set out in the amended registration certification (cl 12 of the draft Companies Amendment Bill, 2010).
[97] Section 16(6).
[98] Section 19(7).
[99] Section 12(1).
[100] Section 12(2). The draft Companies Amendment Bill, 2010 (cl 8) proposes to widen the grounds of refusal to encompass a name that falls within the first group of restrictions on company names (see 4.2.2 above) and that is the *same* as a name, trade mark, mark, word or expression contemplated in s 11(2)(*a*) (including registered defensive names and names of domesticated companies).
[101] In terms of s 11(2)(*a*), (*b*) and (*c*) of the Act (in its present form), as discussed above in 4.2.2 on the criteria for company names.

Formation of Companies and the Company Constitution

names,[102] and the Companies Tribunal may similarly deal with disputes concerning the reservation of company names (see paragraph 4.2.3 above).[103]

A name reservation endures for a period of six months from the date of the application. On good cause shown, the Companies Commission may extend the six-month reservation period for a period of 60 business days at a time.[104] The Act also permits reserved names to be transferred. Name reservations may be transferred to another simply by filing a signed notice of transfer,[105] without any reason or cause for the transfer ordinarily being required.

However, no person may attempt to abuse the name reservation system for the purpose of selling access to names or trading in or marketing names (or for 'name squatting'). The Act gives the Companies Commission the power to issue a notice to a person suspected of attempting to abuse the name reservation system, requiring that person to show cause why the name should be transferred to or reserved for it, or the Companies Commission may simply refuse to grant the transfer or extension of the name reservation, or even cancel the name reservation.[106] Furthermore where, as a result of a pattern of conduct by a person (or related or inter-related persons),[107] the Companies Commission has reasonable grounds to believe that the person has abused the name reservation system,[108] it may apply to court for an order prohibiting that person from reserving any names for a period that the court considers just and reasonable.[109] It is submitted that this power ought also to be coupled with the imposition of a fine in order to enhance the deterrent effect.

Turning to defensive names, a person may register any name as a defensive name if he or she is able to prove to the satisfaction of the Companies Commission that he or she has a *direct and material* interest in respect of the name. The registration of a defensive name subsists for a period of two years and is renew-

---

[102] See s 12(3); see also the draft Companies Amendment Bill, 2010 (cl 8).

[103] See s 160 and 4.2.3 above on the registration of company names and disputes concerning names. The Companies Tribunal may, in this context, make an administrative order directing the Companies Commission to reserve a contested name for the applicant, or to cancel a name reservation (s 160(3)*(b)*).

[104] Section 12(4). This requires an application by the person for whom the name is registered, accompanied by the prescribed fee.

[105] Together with payment of the prescribed fee (s 12(5)).

[106] Section 12(6). Section 160, dealing with disputes concerning company names (see 4.2.3 above), is proposed to apply also to applications to transfer name reservations (see the draft Companies Amendment Bill, 2010 (cl 92).

[107] In considering whether a person has either abused or may be attempting to abuse the name reservation system, the Commission may consider any relevant conduct by that person or any related or interrelated persons (s 12(8)). Events that may indicate abuse include the reservation of more than one name in a single application or a series of applications; a pattern of repetitious applications to reserve a particular name or a number of substantially similar names, or to extend the reservation of a particular name; a failure to show good cause for a reservation period to be extended; or a pattern of unusually frequent transfers of reserved names without apparent legitimate cause having regard to the nature of the person's profession or business (s 12(8)).

[108] Whether by selling access to names or trading in or marketing reserved names, or by repeatedly attempting to reserve names for these purposes.

[109] Section 12(7).

able for a further two-year period.[110] The term 'defensive name' is undefined in both the new Act and in the 1973 Act.[111] Notwithstanding the lack of such definition, it may be said that the purpose of registering a defensive name is essentially to protect the name from use by another company. The phrase 'direct and material interest' in the context of defensive names has been said to mean a significant or important pecuniary or proprietary interest, which is directly connected with the name,[112] for instance, a trade mark to which the applicant owns the rights; a description of a product to which the applicant has exclusive rights; or it is associated with the applicant's business in the mind of the public.[113] The word 'material' is defined in s 1 of the Act as 'significant in the circumstances of a particular matter, to a degree that is of consequence in determining the matter; or might reasonably affect a person's judgment or decision making in the matter'.

The Transitional Arrangements generally enable names that were reserved or that were registered as defensive names under the 1973 Act, to continue to be so reserved or registered under the new Act.[114]

4.2.6 Use of the company name and registration number

All companies and all external companies are required to provide on demand to any person their full registered names and registration numbers. Companies and external companies are, moreover, proscribed from misstating their names or registration numbers in a manner that would be likely to mislead or deceive.[115] Failure to comply with these provisions constitutes an offence.[116]

A company must have its name and registration number stated in legible characters in all notices and other official publications of the company, including those in electronic format,[117] and in all letters, negotiable instruments, orders for money or goods, and business documents, such as delivery notes, invoices, receipts, and letters of credit of the company.[118] Failure to do so is an offence.

The new Act abandons the need for companies to post their registered names outside each place of business. This aligns and harmonises the legal position in South Africa with that in many other jurisdictions.

---

[110] Section 12(9). The draft Companies Amendment Bill, 2010 (cl 8) proposes to make provision for the transfer of the registration of defensive names. The registration and the transfer of registration of defensive names are also proposed to be subject to s 160, which deals with disputes concerning company names (see clause 92 of the Bill).
[111] See s 42 of the 1973 Act.
[112] In the context of s 43 of the 1973 Act (Jennifer A Kunst, P Delport and Q Vorster *Henochsberg on the Companies Act* vol 1 (2008) 87).
[113] Ibid.
[114] See Schedule 5 item 8 and the draft Companies Amendment Bill, 2010 (cl 115); see further chapter 21: Transitional Arrangements.
[115] Section 32(1).
[116] Section 32(5). If the company has been issued with an interim name, as reflected on its registration certificate (s 14(2)*(b)* as discussed above), the company must use its interim name until its amended name has been registered (s 32(2)).
[117] As contemplated in the Electronic Communications and Transactions Act 25 of 2002.
[118] Section 32(4) read with s 32(5). See also s 79(2) of the Consumer Protection Act 68 of 2008 regarding business names.

The Act has made some important changes to this area of company law as contrasted with the 1973 Act. Unlike the 1973 Act, personal liability is not explicitly imposed on the signatory for failure to properly describe the name of the company.[119] Personal liability may, however, be imposed on the signatory in accordance with the principles of the law of negotiable instruments.[120]

The Act makes it an offence for any person to use the name or registration number of a company in a manner likely to convey the impression that he or she is acting on behalf of that company when he or she is in fact unauthorised to do so, or to use a form of name that is likely to convey a false impression in the circumstances that the name is the name of a company.[121]

The practice under which a company using its trading name must use it in conjunction with its registered name,[122] will now be affected by the Consumer Protection Act 68 of 2008. Section 79 of the Consumer Protection Act prohibits a juristic person from carrying on business (within the meaning of that Act) under any name except its registered name (as registered under the Companies Act) or a business name that has been registered to it under the Consumer Protection Act (or another public regulation). The term 'business name' refers to a name other than its registered name under which a juristic person carries on business.[123] A company may consequently trade only under its registered company name or under any business name that has been registered for the use of that company in terms of the Consumer Protection Act or another public regulation.[124]

4.3 THE MEMORANDUM OF INCORPORATION

4.3.1 Underlying philosophy

The Memorandum of Incorporation is the founding document of the company. It sets out the rights, duties and responsibilities of shareholders, directors and others within and in relation to the company, together with various other matters.[125] The Memorandum of Incorporation is the sole governing document of the company.

Previously under the 1973 Act, the constitution of a company, by contrast, consisted of two documents. These were the memorandum of association, which was the dominant document dealing with the external characteristics of the company, and the articles of association, which largely governed the internal affairs of the company. The abandonment of the 'two-document constitution' under the new Act is welcome. The two-document constitution served no real purpose because

---

[119] Section 50(3)(b) of the 1973 Act.
[120] See s 24 of the Bills of Exchange Act 34 of 1964. Section 32(6) and (7) of the Companies Act provides that personal liability may be imposed on any shareholder, director or incorporator of the company who misrepresents the true legal status of the company, whether by act or omission, and whether in any way or to any degree. However, the draft Companies Amendment Bill, 2010 (cl 21) proposes to repeal s 32(6).
[121] Section 32(3) read with s 32(5).
[122] See for instance *Abro v Softex Mattress (Pty) Ltd* 1973 (2) SA 346 (D).
[123] Section 1 of the Consumer Protection Act.
[124] The provisions of the Consumer Protection Act regarding business names are not yet in force.
[125] Section 1. The draft Companies Amendment Bill, 2010 (cl 2(1)) proposes to use the term 'Memorandum' interchangeably with the term 'Memorandum of Incorporation'.

its original rationale was long-abandoned. Originally, the underlying principle was that the memorandum of association should contain provisions that were sacrosanct, inflexible and unalterable by the company, while the provisions of the articles of association were subject to alteration by special resolution.[126] But with the gradual erosion of this principle, it made little sense to sustain a two-document constitution.

In line with the stated purpose of the Act to create 'flexibility and simplicity in the formation and maintenance of companies',[127] the content of the Memorandum of Incorporation is quite flexible. This creates some leeway for companies to regulate their affairs, especially their internal affairs. As a result, a diversity of company structures is possible under the Act, ranging from simple to more complex companies.

As its basic nucleus or foundation, the Memorandum of Incorporation must contain certain mandatory, core provisions ('unalterable provisions'). These are generally designed to protect the interests of shareholders[128] as well as creditors and others dealing with the company. Crucially, each provision of the Memorandum of Incorporation must be consistent with the Act.[129] Over and above this basic nucleus, various company structures may be fashioned by altering any of the 'alterable provisions' of the Act or even by creating new provisions on matters on which the Act is silent. The 'alterable provisions' of the Act may be regarded as default rules that would apply to a company unless it specifically opts out of these in its Memorandum of Incorporation. A company may, furthermore, insert restrictive or procedural requirements that impede the amendment of any provision of its Memorandum of Incorporation.[130] The Memorandum of Incorporation may even prohibit the amendment of any of its provisions. These aspects are fleshed out in more detail below.

There has been a remarkable change in the underlying philosophy and approach to the company constitution. The regulation of the internal affairs of the company under the 1973 Act followed the English approach, while under the new Act the approach has swung towards the US style. In this regard, in English company law, the company itself regulates its internal affairs by way of rules laid down in the company's constitution.[131] By contrast, the US style is that the allocation of power between the organs of the company is done by legislation. The US approach nevertheless retains flexibility in respect of the constitution by means of default rules that may be changed by the company's constitution.[132] Accordingly, despite

---

[126] Paul L Davies *Gower and Davies' Principles of Modern Company Law* 7 ed (2003) at 57.
[127] Section 7*(b)*.
[128] *Memorandum on the Objects of the Companies Bill, 2008* op cit n 1 at para 5.
[129] Section 15(1).
[130] It is proposed to delete the present reference to 'special conditions' on s 15(2)*(b)* of the Act and to substitute it with 'restrictive or procedural requirements impeding the amendment of any particular provisions of the Memorandum of Incorporation', in terms of the draft Companies Amendment Bill, 2010 (cl 11).
[131] See Paul L Davies op cit n 126 at 63.
[132] Section 8.01 of the US Revised Model Business Corporation Act, 1984, states that the board of directors has management powers but allows shareholders to limit this in the constitution of the company or in a shareholder agreement.

Formation of Companies and the Company Constitution

the difference in the underlying philosophies, the end result and the flexibility in the division of powers between the shareholders and the board of directors may be the same whether one relies on the English or the US approach. The new Companies Act has seemingly adopted the US style: The new underlying approach evidently is that the allocation of powers between the organs of the company is the result of a legislative act. In this regard, s 66(1) of the Act confers management powers on the board of directors, except to the extent that the Act or the company's Memorandum of Incorporation provides otherwise. The new Act imposes on the board of directors both the power and the responsibility to manage the business of the company subject to the Act and the company's constitution (or Memorandum of Incorporation).

The Transitional Arrangements of the Act provide that a pre-existing company (that was incorporated prior to the new Act) may file, without charge, an amendment to its Memorandum of Incorporation to bring it in harmony with the Act, at any time within two years of the general effective date of the Act.[133] During this period, if there is a conflict between a provision of the Act and a provision of the constitution of the pre-existing company, the latter provision prevails (except to the extent that Schedule 5 of the Act provides otherwise) and a compliance notice may not be issued to the company in respect of the inconsistency.[134]

4.3.2 Contents of the Memorandum of Incorporation

The Memorandum of Incorporation, broadly and generally, would deal with matters such as the powers of the company; the amendment of the Memorandum of Incorporation; the ability to create rules of the company; securities of the company and debt instruments; shareholders, shareholders' meetings and procedures; the composition of the board of directors; the authority and powers of directors; board meetings and committees of the board; indemnification of directors and, in the case of non-profit companies, the disposal of the company's assets upon dissolution of the company. These will, of course, vary depending on each company, the type of company it is and the envisaged needs and structure of the company.

The Act introduces a novel and vitally important approach to the contents of the Memorandum of Incorporation by providing for 'unalterable provisions' and 'alterable provisions'.

In this regard, the Act imposes certain mandatory requirements or core requirements that must form part of the Memorandum of Incorporation of every company. As mentioned above, the purpose of these requirements is to protect the interests of shareholders, as well as creditors and others dealing with the company. This basic nucleus or core of the Memorandum of Incorporation consists of the so-called '*unalterable provisions*' of the Act.

By definition, an 'unalterable provision' means a provision of the Act that does not *expressly* contemplate that its effect on any particular company may be altered,

---

[133] Schedule 5 item 4(2). The reference to the Memorandum of Incorporation of a pre-existing company (ie one incorporated prior to the Act) is taken to mean its memorandum of association and articles of association (see chapter 21: Transitional Arrangements).
[134] Schedule 5 item 4(4); see further chapter 21: Transitional Arrangements.

whether by a company's Memorandum of Incorporation or its rules. In this context, an alteration has a wide meaning and includes a negation, restriction, limitation, qualification, extension or alteration in any other manner, whether in substance or in effect.[135] Accordingly, every company's Memorandum of Incorporation must comply with the unalterable provisions or core requirements of the Act.

A company is prevented from 'contracting out' of the Companies Act.[136] In this regard, the Act lays down that each provision of a company's Memorandum of Incorporation must be consistent with the Act. In circumstances where a provision in a company's Memorandum of Incorporation is inconsistent with or contravenes the Act, it is *void* to the extent of its inconsistency or contravention of the Act.[137]

This is bolstered further by the anti-avoidance provisions of the Act, which empower a court to declare any provision of a company's Memorandum of Incorporation or rules (or any agreement, transaction, arrangement or resolution) to be primarily or substantially intended to defeat or *reduce* the effect of a prohibition or requirement established by an unalterable provision, and to declare it void to that extent.[138]

Apart from the mandatory nucleus of unalterable provisions, there are certain default rules that a company may choose to accept or alter in its Memorandum of Incorporation.[139] These default provisions are termed '*alterable provisions*'. The alterable provisions of the Act allow for flexibility in respect of the contents of the Memorandum of Incorporation. An 'alterable provision' means a provision of the Act in which it is *expressly* contemplated that its effect on a particular company may be altered by that company's Memorandum of Incorporation, whether by negation, restriction, limitation, qualification, extension or other alteration in substance or effect.[140]

If a company wishes to alter an 'alterable provision' of the Act, this must be 'noted in' (or done in terms of) its Memorandum of Incorporation,[141] failing which the alteration will be ineffective. Most of the alterable provisions of the Act are 'opt-out' provisions, ie they will apply to the company unless it opts out of them by explicitly stipulating so in its Memorandum of Incorporation. (This may be contrasted with the 'opt-in' provisions, which do not apply to a company unless it specifically so provides in its Memorandum of Incorporation.) The alterable provisions of the Act enable a company to tailor the contents of its constitution to fit its needs.

Apart from the unalterable and alterable provisions, another type of provision that the company may include in its Memorandum of Incorporation is any other provision dealing with a matter that the Act has left silent or unaddressed.[142] This

---

[135] Section 1.
[136] *Memorandum on the Objects of the Companies Bill, 2008* op cit n 1 at para 5.
[137] Section 15(1).
[138] Section 6(1). See further chapter 1: Introduction to the New Companies Act.
[139] Section 15(2)(*a*)(ii) and *Memorandum on the Objects of the Companies Bill, 2008* op cit n 1 at para 5.
[140] Section 1.
[141] Section 19(1)(*c*)(ii) read with s 15(2)(*a*)(ii).
[142] Section 15(2)(*a*)(i).

Formation of Companies and the Company Constitution

further enhances the latitude and flexibility in respect of the contents of the Memorandum of Incorporation.

The Memorandum of Incorporation of a company may be either in a form unique to the company or in the prescribed form. The prescribed or standard (or model) form constitutes the simplest possible form of company, as the incorporators simply adopt the mandatory provisions of the Act and accept the default provisions with or without alterations.[143]

Finally, it is notable that in certain circumstances, in the interests of flexibility, a person may apply to the Companies Tribunal to exempt a company's Memorandum of Incorporation or rules (or any agreement, transaction, arrangement or resolution) from an unalterable provision of the Act. The Companies Tribunal may grant an administrative order of exemption if it is satisfied that the relevant provision in the company's Memorandum of Incorporation serves a reasonable purpose other than to defeat or reduce the effect of the unalterable provision in question, and that it is reasonable and justifiable to grant the exemption.[144] While this provision no doubt promotes flexibility, it does confer a wide discretionary power on the Companies Tribunal.

The company's Memorandum of Incorporation may also contain restrictions and prohibitions on the amendment of its provisions,[145] which add further to the flexibility of the contents of the Memorandum of Incorporation in terms of the Act. These are dealt with below.

4.3.3 Restrictions and prohibitions on the amendment of provisions of the Memorandum of Incorporation

Although a special resolution generally suffices for the amendment of the Memorandum of Incorporation (in terms of s 16), it is permissible for the Memorandum of Incorporation to prohibit the amendment of any of its particular provisions.[146] The Memorandum of Incorporation may also contain restrictive or procedural requirements (in addition to the requirements set out in s 16) that impede the amendment of any of its particular provisions.[147] This accordingly provides scope for the incorporators (or shareholders, by special resolution, as the case may be) to couple any key provision of the company's constitution with a particular restrict-

---

[143] *Memorandum on the Objects of the Companies Bill, 2008* op cit n 1 at para 5.
[144] Section 6(2) and (3).
[145] Section 15(2)*(b)* and *(c)* respectively.
[146] Section 15(2)*(c)*.
[147] Section 15(2)*(b)* as proposed to be amended by the draft Companies Amendment Bill, 2010 (cl 11). Section 15(2)*(b)*, in its present form, refers to a 'special condition' without defining it and provides that '[t]he Memorandum of Incorporation of any company may contain any special conditions applicable to the company, and any requirement for the amendment of any such condition in addition to the requirements set out in section 16'. The Amendment Bill now proposes to delete the reference to 'special conditions' in s 15(2)*(b)*, and to instead state that a company's Memorandum of Incorporation may 'contain any restrictive or procedural requirement in addition to the requirements set out in section 16 impeding the amendment of any particular provision of the Memorandum of Incorporation'. The above discussion proceeds on the assumption that the proposed amendment in terms of the Amendment Bill is very likely to be implemented.

ive method of alteration or even to entrench it in the constitution by an absolute prohibition on its amendment.[148]

Where a company's Memorandum of Incorporation includes any of these types of provisions, this must be indicated both in the company's Notice of Incorporation, and by the expression '(RF)' (which means 'ring-fenced') suffixed to the company name. To elaborate, the company's Notice of Incorporation (or Notice of Amendment, as the case may be) must include a prominent statement drawing attention to each such provision and its location in the Memorandum of Incorporation.[149] Additionally, the name of the company must immediately be followed by the expression '(RF)' (ie ring-fenced).[150] The purpose of these two features is to draw the attention of third parties to the presence of restrictions or prohibitions on the amendment of certain provisions of the Memorandum of Incorporation. This provides the new statutory basis for the limited application of the doctrine of constructive notice.

In this regard, the Act provides that third parties are 'regarded as having received notice and knowledge' of any restriction or prohibition on the amendment of any particular provision of the company's constitution, provided that the company's Notice of Incorporation has drawn attention to it.[151] The expression '(RF)' that must be suffixed to the company's name is fortunately now expected to be a second prerequisite for the application of constructive notice of the restrictions or prohibitions.[152] Since the expression '(RF)' forms part of the name of the company, it may be expected to be more effective in alerting third parties to the presence of restrictions or prohibitions on the amendment of certain provisions of the company's Memorandum of Incorporation.

The creation of deemed notice and knowledge is tantamount to the preservation of the doctrine of constructive notice in respect of the prohibitions and restrictions on the amendment of particular provisions of the Memorandum of Incorporation. This is remarkable, as the doctrine of constructive notice has by and large been abolished by the Act. Unlike the 1973 Act, third parties dealing with a company are no longer regarded as having received notice or deemed to have knowledge of the contents of the company's constitution or other company documents merely because they are public documents. In this regard, the new Act expressly states that a person must not be regarded as having received notice or knowledge of the

---

[148] In respect of such conditions (or special conditions) under the 1973 Act, see ss 53(*a*) and 56 of the 1973 Act. See also *Quadrangle Investments (Pty) Ltd v Witind Holdings Ltd* 1975 (1) SA 572 (A); MS Blackman et al *Commentary on the Companies Act* vol 1 (2010) 4–92.
[149] Section 13(3).
[150] Section 11(3)(*b*). The Transitional Arrangements (Schedule 5 of the Act) provide that, in respect of a pre-existing company (ie one incorporated prior to the Act), a special condition or a prohibition on the amendment of any provision of the constitution will continue to have the same validity as it had under the 1973 Act, despite a failure by the company to draw attention to the provision as contemplated by s 13(3) (item 7(9); see also 7(8)(*b*)). When the company files a notice of the relevant provision, s 19(4) of the Act (dealing with the limited application of the doctrine of constructive notice, as discussed below) will apply to the company (item 7(10) of Schedule 5). See further chapter 21: Transitional Arrangements.
[151] Section 19(5)(*a*).
[152] See the draft Companies Amendment Bill, 2010 (cl 13).

contents of any document relating to a company merely because it has been filed or is accessible for inspection at an office of the company.[153]

The abolition of the doctrine of constructive notice is, however, subject to three notable exceptions under the new Act. The first exception is that persons are 'regarded as having received notice and knowledge' of any restrictive or procedural requirement (in addition to the requirements of s 16) that impedes the amendment of any particular provision of the Memorandum of Incorporation.[154] The second exception relates to prohibitions on the amendment of any particular provision of the Memorandum of Incorporation. (Oddly, in terms of the Act itself, persons are not regarded as having had constructive notice of such prohibitions on amendment. This apparent oversight is fortunately now proposed to be remedied by the draft Companies Amendment Bill, 2010.)[155] Thirdly, the doctrine of constructive notice applies to the effect of the personal liability of directors and former directors of a personal liability company (discussed in chapter 3: Types of Companies).[156]

The third party's constructive notice of restrictive methods of amendment and prohibitions on the amendment of particular provisions of a company's constitution may in certain circumstances have important and far-reaching implications. If, for instance, a limitation of the authority of the directors of a company is coupled with a restrictive method of alteration, then any third party who deals with the company would be deemed to have notice and knowledge of the directors' lack of authority (depending on the nature of the limitation). As such, this could destroy the third party's prospects of relying on the ostensible authority of the directors. For example, if the Memorandum of Incorporation of a company contains an entrenched provision (that may not be amended) to the effect that no contract of loan in excess of R1 million shall be valid unless approved in writing by two directors, and a third party purports to enter into such a contract with the company that is signed by only one director, the effect could be that the third party cannot hold the company bound to the contract, whether on the basis of actual authority (which was absent) or ostensible authority (which is destroyed by the third party's constructive knowledge of the director's lack of authority to contract on his or her own, in terms of the entrenched constitutional provision).[157]

A second example is where a provision that limits the capacity of a company is entrenched in the Memorandum of Incorporation. If, for instance, the Memorandum of Incorporation contains an entrenched provision (that may not be amended) stating that the company may not enter into any transactions related to the motor industry and the company nevertheless enters into such a transaction with a third party, then the third party could be 'regarded as having received notice and

---

[153] Section 19(4).
[154] To which the Notice of Incorporation has drawn attention — s 19(5)(a) read with s 15(2)(b) and the draft Companies Amendment Bill, 2010 (cl 11) (which proposes to delete the term 'special' condition' in s 15(2)(b), as discussed above). See also D Davis et al *Companies and Other Business Structures in South Africa* (2009) 41.
[155] Clause 13.
[156] Section 19(5)(b).
[157] However, the third party, as well as the company, may have a remedy against the director.

knowledge' of the limited capacity of the company under the entrenched constitutional provision.[158] Although the contract will not be void,[159] the company may be restrained from performing the contract, for instance by its shareholders. In this event, the third party will have rights to damages only if he or she was in good faith and lacked 'actual knowledge' of the company's limited capacity (s 20(5)). In this regard, the suffix '(RF)' to the company name (in view of the entrenched provision in the constitution) may have led the third party to examine the company's constitution, in which event the third party would then have had 'actual knowledge' and would be precluded from obtaining damages. If not, then in terms of s 19(5), the third party 'must be regarded as having received notice and knowledge' of the entrenched provision limiting the company's capacity. Although this is not entirely clear, 'knowledge' in this context is constructive knowledge and does not amount to 'actual knowledge', with the effect that the third party may retain the rights to damages in terms of s 20(5) (provided that the third party's good faith has not been destroyed).[160]

4.3.4 Amending the Memorandum of Incorporation

The Memorandum of Incorporation of a company may be amended at any time by means of a special resolution.[161]

The amendment may be proposed either by the board of directors or by shareholders holding at least 10 per cent of the voting rights that may be exercised on the matter. This provision is, however, subject to the company's Memorandum of Incorporation, which may stipulate different requirements in respect of proposals for amendment.[162]

A special resolution to amend the Memorandum of Incorporation may be adopted at a formal meeting of shareholders or, alternatively, may be submitted for consideration to shareholders to be voted on in writing in accordance with s 60.[163] A written resolution in terms of s 60 is a useful mechanism as it avoids the costs and inconvenience associated with convening a meeting of shareholders and, furthermore, encourages voting by apathetic or passive shareholders who do not usually attend meetings. Shareholders must exercise their votes in writing, in terms of s 60, within 20 business days after receiving the resolution, and the resolution will be adopted if it is supported by the requisite number of voting rights for a special resolution.[164] A special resolution to amend the Memorandum of Incorporation must be supported by at least 75 per cent of the voting rights

---

[158] Section 19(5).
[159] Section 20(1). See further chapter 5: Corporate Capacity, Agency and the Turquand Rule; see also specifically the discussion of the *ultra vires* doctrine in that chapter.
[160] See further the discussion of good faith and actual knowledge in the context of s 20(5) in chapter 5: Corporate Capacity, Agency and Turquand Rule.
[161] Section 16(1)(*c*); s 65(11)(*a*).
[162] Section 16(1)(*c*); s 16(2). In the case of a non-profit company with no voting members, s 16(3) provides that the board of the company may amend the Memorandum of Incorporation, in terms of s 16(1)(*c*)(i)(*aa*).
[163] Section 16(1)(*c*)(ii).
[164] Section 60(1) and s 60(2). See further chapter 9: Governance and Shareholders.

exercised on the resolution,[165] but a company's Memorandum of Incorporation may validly decrease the threshold requirement for a special resolution (provided that there is a minimum margin of at least 10 per cent between the requirements for approval of an ordinary resolution and a special resolution, on any matter).[166]

It must be borne in mind that some provisions of the Memorandum of Incorporation may be subject to additional restrictive or procedural requirements for their amendment (over and above the requirements for the amendment of the Memorandum of Incorporation in terms of s 16),[167] while others may be prohibited from amendment.[168] Under the previous company law regime, a provision in the articles of association that purported to deprive the company of the statutory power to alter its articles was held to be invalid.[169] A company could not contract out of its power to alter its articles. Section 15(2)(c) of the new Act now overrides this, to the extent that the Memorandum of Incorporation may validly prohibit the amendment of any of its provisions. Entrenched status may evidently be conferred on provisions in the Memorandum of Incorporation either on the formation of the company or at a subsequent stage, by way of amending the Memorandum of Incorporation.[170] The question inevitably arises whether in South African law one may prohibit the alteration of the entire Memorandum of Incorporation. From a practical point of view, this clearly would be unwise for any company to adopt.[171]

An amendment of a company's Memorandum of Incorporation may either take the form of a new Memorandum of Incorporation that will substitute the existing one or, alternatively, alterations could be made to the existing Memorandum of Incorporation (whether by changing the name of the company, deleting, altering or replacing any of its provisions, or inserting any new provisions).[172] It is noteworthy that, where a profit company amends its Memorandum of Incorporation in

---

[165] Section 65(9).
[166] Section 65(10). See also s 65(8). An important amendment is proposed by the draft Companies Amendment Bill, 2010, which states that a company's Memorandum of Incorporation may permit a 'different' (as opposed to a 'lower') percentage of voting rights to approve a special resolution, provided that there must at all times be a margin of at least 10 percentage points between the highest established requirement for approval of an ordinary resolution on any matter and the lowest established requirement for approval of a special resolution on any matter (cl 2(1)(cc), cl 41). This would mean that a company's Memorandum of Incorporation may require a higher or a lower percentage (than 75 per cent) of voting rights for the approval of a special resolution. See further chapter 9: Governance and Shareholders.
[167] Section 15(2)(b) read with cl 11 of the draft Companies Amendment Bill, 2010. See n 147 above regarding special conditions.
[168] Section 15(2)(c). See 4.3.3 above on restrictions and prohibitions on the amendment of provisions of the Memorandum of Incorporation.
[169] See e g *Allen v Gold Reefs of West Africa Ltd* [1900] 1 Ch 656 (CA) 671.
[170] In either case, s 13(3) of the Act must be complied with. The Notice of Amendment or Notice of Incorporation (as the case may be,) filed by the company must include a prominent statement drawing attention to each such provision and its location in the Memorandum of Incorporation.
[171] Section 15(2)(c) may be compared with the UK Companies Act 2006, which introduces a new provision permitting companies to entrench elements of their constitutions in their articles (s 22); but entrenchment cannot make the articles completely unalterable (see s 22(3)(a) which expressly provides that entrenchment cannot prevent amendment of the articles by agreement of all the members of the company).
[172] Section 16(5).

such a manner that it no longer meets the criteria for the relevant type of profit company, the concluding expression in the name of the company must simultaneously be amended to reflect the new type of profit company it is.[173]

After amending its Memorandum of Incorporation, the company must file a Notice of Amendment with the Companies Commission, together with payment of the prescribed fee.[174] This must be accompanied by a copy of the new, substituted Memorandum of Incorporation (if any) or a copy of the amendment (where the amendment has altered the existing Memorandum of Incorporation).[175] Where there is a change in the name of the company, the discussion at 4.2.4 above applies.[176]

The amendment of the company's Memorandum of Incorporation takes effect from the date on and time at which the Companies Commission accepts the filing of the Notice of Amendment,[177] or the later date (if any) set out in the Notice of Amendment.[178] The company's previous Memorandum of Incorporation, in the form prior to the amendment, has no force or effect with respect to any right, cause of action or matter occurring or arising after the date on which the amendment took effect.[179]

At common law under the previous company law regime, the power to alter the constitution of a company had to be exercised *bona fide* for the benefit of the company as a whole, and in a manner that did not constitute a fraud on the minority.[180] This principle may well continue to apply. An alteration of the company's constitution could be contested by a shareholder under the previous Act on the grounds that it involved the conduct of the affairs of the company in a manner unfairly prejudicial, unjust or inequitable to the shareholder.[181] The same principle would probably apply to the oppression remedy under s 163 of the Act.

Apart from the alteration of a company's Memorandum of Incorporation by special resolution as described above, there are also two other methods of amendment. First, the Memorandum of Incorporation may be amended in compliance with a court order.[182] In this case, a special resolution of the shareholders is not needed and the amendment is instead effected simply by a resolution of the board

---

[173] Section 16(6). See further chapter 3: Types of Companies.
[174] Section 16(7). Section 13(3) and (4) (on rejection of the Notice of Amendment by the Companies Commission) and s 14 (on registration and company names) apply to the filing of the Notice of Amendment, read with the changes required by the context.
[175] Section 16(7)*(b)*. In the latter event the Companies Commission may require the company to file a full copy of its amended Memorandum of Incorporation within a reasonable time.
[176] Section 16(8).
[177] This is proposed to be changed to the date and time at which the Notice of Amendment is filed. In the case of an amendment of the name of a company, the amendment is proposed to take effect on the date set out in the amended registration certification (cl 12 of the draft Companies Amendment Bill, 2010).
[178] Section 16(9).
[179] Section 19(6).
[180] See eg *Allen v Gold Reefs of West Africa Ltd* [1900] 1 Ch 656 (CA); Blackman et al op cit n 148 at 4–104.
[181] In terms of s 252 of the 1973 Act.
[182] Section 16(1)*(a)*.

Formation of Companies and the Company Constitution

of directors of the company.[183] A court may, for instance, order an amendment of the Memorandum of Incorporation in terms of s 163 where, on considering an application for relief from oppressive or prejudicial conduct, the court has the discretion to make an order directing the company to amend its Memorandum of Incorporation. In this event, the directors must promptly file a Notice of Amendment to give effect to that order.[184]

The second method of an amendment to the Memorandum of Incorporation is provided by s 36(3) and (4) relating to authorisation and classification of shares, in which case no special resolution of shareholders is required either.[185] Where the board of a company acts pursuant to its authority in terms of s 36(3), the company must file a Notice of Amendment of its Memorandum of Incorporation setting out the changes effected by the board of directors.[186]

(a) Correction of patent errors in the Memorandum of Incorporation or rules

This is an innovative and commendable section of the Act, which allows for the correction of patent errors, such as grammatical or typographical errors, in the Memorandum of Incorporation. It overcomes, to some extent, the decision in *Ex parte Premier Paper Ltd*,[187] where the court refused to grant rectification of a company's constitution on the ground that it had no power to do so, and stated that to vary the constitution, a special resolution of the company was required.[188]

In this regard, where there is a patent error in spelling, punctuation, reference, grammar or a similar defect on the face of the document, the Act permits the board of directors of a company or an individual authorised by the board to alter the company's Memorandum of Incorporation or rules in any manner necessary to correct the error. This is done by publishing a Notice of Alteration (in the manner set out in the Memorandum of Incorporation or the rules) and filing the Notice of Alteration with the Companies Commission.[189]

This new procedure promotes greater efficiency and avoids the need to seek shareholder approval by special resolution or to comply with all the other formalities for an amendment of the Memorandum of Incorporation.

This provision may, however, be open to misuse. In order to counter potential abuse, the Act provides, as a safeguard, that where an alteration exceeds the authority to correct a patent error or defect, an application may be made to the Companies Tribunal, by either the Companies Commission or a director or a

---

[183] Section 16(4).
[184] Section 163(3). Moreover, no further amendment altering, limiting or negating the effect of the court order may be made to the Memorandum of Incorporation, until a court orders otherwise.
[185] Section 16(1)*(b)*.
[186] Section 36(4).
[187] 1981 (2) SA 612 (W). See also the similar decision in *Scott v Frank Scott (London) Ltd* [1940] Ch 794 (CA).
[188] See FHI Cassim op cit n 3 at 166.
[189] Section 17(1).

shareholder of the company, for an administrative order setting aside the published Notice of the Alteration.[190]

(b) Translations of the Memorandum of Incorporation

A company may, at any time, file one or more translations of its Memorandum of Incorporation in any of the official languages of South Africa.[191] Such a translation must be accompanied by a sworn statement by the person who made the translation, stating that it is a true, accurate and complete translation of the Memorandum of Incorporation.[192]

In the event of a conflict between the Memorandum of Incorporation of a company and a filed translation, the Memorandum of Incorporation (as altered or amended) will prevail.[193]

(c) Consolidations of the Memorandum of Incorporation

After a company has filed its Memorandum of Incorporation, and has subsequently filed one or more alterations or amendments to it, the company may at any time file a consolidated revision of its Memorandum of Incorporation, as so altered or amended. The Companies Commission may also require the company to file a consolidated revision of its Memorandum of Incorporation, as altered or amended.[194]

A consolidated revision must be accompanied by a sworn statement by a director of the company or a statement by an attorney or notary public to the effect that it is a true, accurate and complete representation of the Memorandum of Incorporation, as altered and amended up to the date of the statement.[195]

(d) Authenticity of versions of the Memorandum of Incorporation

If there is a conflict between the Memorandum of Incorporation of a company and a filed translation, the Memorandum of Incorporation (as altered or amended) will prevail. Similarly, in the event of a conflict between the company's Memorandum of Incorporation and a filed consolidated revision, the Memorandum of Incorporation, as altered or amended, will prevail, unless the consolidated revision has subsequently been ratified by a special resolution at a general shareholders' meeting of the company.[196]

The latest version of a company's Memorandum of Incorporation that has been endorsed by the Companies Commission prevails in the case of any conflict between that version and any other purported version of the company's Memorandum of Incorporation.[197]

---

[190] Section 17(2).
[191] Section 17(3).
[192] Section 17(4).
[193] Section 18(1)(a).
[194] Section 17(5).
[195] Section 17(6).
[196] Section 18(1).
[197] Section 18(2).

4.4 RULES OF THE COMPANY

The regulation of company rules is a new concept introduced by the Act. It seems to have been modelled on US and Canadian law. It appears that the reach of company rules under the Act embraces binding rules made by the board of directors that govern the internal affairs of the company or apply to intra-corporate matters.[198] The Act provides that,[199] subject to the Memorandum of Incorporation, the board of directors of a company may make, amend or repeal any 'necessary or incidental'[200] rules, relating specifically to the governance of the company, and dealing with matters that are not addressed in either the Act or the Memorandum of Incorporation. The binding status of such rules is now regulated by the Act, as discussed further below.

The Act does not provide a prescribed or model set of rules. This would have served as a useful guideline for the types of matters that should be contained in the rules. The benefit of addressing important aspects of a company's governance in the rules, is that the rules are binding. Moreover, from the perspective of the board of directors, there are certain governance matters that could conceivably be addressed in the company's rules instead of its Memorandum of Incorporation, with the result that these provisions would be more conveniently and easily alterable than the Memorandum of Incorporation (see further below).

Significantly, the Memorandum of Incorporation of a company takes precedence over its rules. Company rules must be consistent both with the Act and with the Memorandum of Incorporation, and any inconsistent rules are void to the extent of their inconsistency.[201] Rules are also subject to the anti-avoidance provisions of the Act.[202] Company rules may not be used to alter any 'alterable provisions' of the Act — this may only be done in the company's Memorandum of Incorporation.[203]

The board of directors has the power to make rules, unless the Memorandum of Incorporation provides otherwise. The board of directors may make, amend or repeal rules by 'publishing' a copy of the relevant rules in the manner specified in the Memorandum of Incorporation or in the rules themselves. The board must thereafter file a copy of the rules with the Companies Commission.[204] A rule takes effect 20 business days after it has been 'published'[205] or on a later date if so stated in the rules.[206]

---

[198] Parallels may perhaps be drawn between company rules in terms of the Act and by-laws in terms of both the US Revised Model Business Corporation Act 1984, as amended (s 2.06) as well as the Canada Business Corporations Act, R.S.C. 1985 (s 103). By-laws under the Model Business Corporation Act may provide for the management of the business of the company and regulating the affairs of the company. Under the Canada Business Corporation Act, by-laws may 'regulate the business or affairs of the corporation'.
[199] Section 15(3).
[200] The phrase 'necessary or incidental' is undefined in the Act.
[201] Section 15(4)(a).
[202] Section 6(1) (discussed under 4.3.2. above; see also chapter 1: Introduction to the New Companies Act).
[203] See the definition of 'alterable provision' in s 1; see also s 19(1)(c)(ii) read with s 15(2)(a)(ii); see further 4.3.2 above.
[204] Section 15(3).
[205] The draft Companies Amendment Bill, 2010 (cl 11) proposes to change this to ten days after the rule is *filed* with the Companies Commission.
[206] Section 15(4)(b).

The status of company rules is a fundamentally important issue. Although a rule is binding from its effective date, it is initially binding on an interim basis only. The interim effect of the rule endures until the rule is put to a vote at the next general shareholders' meeting.[207] If the rule is ratified by an ordinary resolution at the meeting, the rule then becomes binding on a permanent basis.[208] If, on the other hand, the rule is not ratified, it is no longer binding on the company and it simply lapses. Where a 'published' rule is not ratified, the board of directors may not thereafter make a substantially similar rule within the ensuing 12 months[209] unless the new rule has been approved in advance by an ordinary resolution.[210] This would deter the board from taking inappropriate advantage of the interim enforceability of unratified rules.

The question arises as to the legal status of a *non-ratified* or rejected rule during the *interim* period. It appears that a non-ratified rule will nonetheless be binding during the interim period, despite its subsequent rejection by the shareholders. Accordingly, a failure to ratify the rule would not affect the validity of anything done in terms of that rule during the interim period. (This is proposed by the draft Companies Amendment Bill, 2010.) This is the preferable outcome, as much confusion would otherwise result. It is nonetheless odd, given the general principle that ratification (and non-ratification) operates retrospectively. The jurisprudential basis of this state of affairs is rather mysterious. Perhaps the intention of the drafters of the Act was to give the shareholders in general meeting the power to '*reject*' or '*confirm*' rules as opposed to the power to 'ratify' rules.

Once rules are in force, their legal status is the same as that of the Memorandum of Incorporation. See further 4.6 below on the legal status of the Memorandum of Incorporation and rules.

It is obvious from the above analysis that company rules are generally amended more easily than the Memorandum of Incorporation. While an amendment of the Memorandum of Incorporation usually requires a special resolution,[211] company rules are made, amended or repealed by the board of directors subject to confirmation by an ordinary resolution of shareholders. This factor is of practical significance. In this regard, there may be certain provisions that could justifiably be placed *either* in a company's Memorandum of Incorporation *or* in its rules. Relevant considerations in deciding its placement include the ease with which it may be inserted as well as the ease with which it may be later amended. This applies to matters that are unaddressed in the Act and that relate to the internal governance of the company, for instance, the maximum number of directors, the venue of directors' meetings and the notice of directors' meetings.

---

[207] Section 15(4)*(c)*(i).

[208] Section 15(4)*(c)*(ii).

[209] It is unclear whether the 12-month period is calculated from the time of 'publication' of the rule or from the time of rejection of the rule by the general shareholders' meeting. It is submitted that the relevant date is the latter one.

[210] Section 15(5). The draft Companies Amendment Bill, 2010 (cl 11) fortunately proposes to substitute 'published' with 'filed'. The Amendment Bill also requires the company to file a notice of ratification or non-ratification (as the case may be) within five business days after the ratification vote.

[211] Section 16.

The Transitional Arrangements specifically recognise and regulate the company 'rules' of pre-existing companies, that is, any binding provisions that were adopted before the Act came into force and that are comparable in purpose and effect to the rules of a company, regardless of the style or title of those provisions.[212]

4.5 SHAREHOLDER AGREEMENTS

The new Act explicitly recognises shareholder agreements. Section 15(7) of the Act expressly provides that the shareholders[213] of a company may enter into any agreement with one another concerning 'any matter relating to the company'. Although a shareholder agreement may only cover matters 'relating to the company', the precise ambit of this phrase is uncertain. The company is, notably, not a party to a shareholder agreement in terms of s 15(7).

Shareholder agreements have a number of advantages. First, a shareholder agreement is a private document. It is not filed with the Companies Commission and is not available for inspection by the general public. Secondly, the binding force of shareholder agreements stems from the normal principles of the law of contract. Section 15(6), with its complexities and limitations, governs only the legal status of the Memorandum of Incorporation and the rules; it does not extend to shareholder agreements (see further 4.6 below).

The disadvantage of a shareholder agreement, on the other hand, is that it binds only those shareholders who are party to it. It also does not bind any new shareholders of the company unless they consent to be bound. Moreover, the Act does not provide an overriding mechanism for the alteration of a shareholder agreement (bearing in mind that s 16 applies only to amendments of the Memorandum of Incorporation), and accordingly the default position is that, unless the agreement provides otherwise, the consent of each party to the agreement will be required to amend it.

Shareholder agreements have traditionally proved to be very useful in practice. The new Act, however, makes significant inroads into the practical benefits of shareholder agreements. The Act states that a shareholder agreement must be consistent not only with the Act, but also with the Memorandum of Incorporation of the company. Any inconsistent provision is void to the extent of its inconsistency.[214] Accordingly, under the new Act, the Memorandum of Incorporation of a company takes precedence over shareholder agreements.

This is a crucially important change from the previous regime, where a key purpose of the shareholder agreement was to supplant various provisions of a company's constitution (or articles of association). It was held, under the 1973 Act, that a shareholder agreement (to which the company was a party together with all its shareholders) could validly contain provisions that were contrary to the company's constitution and that those provisions would prevail over the company's constitu-

---

[212] Schedule 5 item 4(3). See further chapter 21: Transitional Arrangements.
[213] A shareholder in this context means 'the holder of a share issued by a company and who is entered as such in the certificated or uncertificated securities register' (s 1 of the Act). In a non-profit company that has voting members, the term 'shareholder' refers to the voting members (s 10(4)).
[214] Section 15(7).

tion.[215] The policy shift on shareholder agreements under the new Act may be expected to have important practical implications for shareholder agreements, and may be anticipated to have an adverse impact on the practical utility and value of shareholder agreements.[216] One such aspect is the protection of minority shareholders by way of shareholder agreements under the previous regime. This was often achieved, for instance, by imposing a higher threshold or a supermajority requirement for shareholder approval of specified minority protected matters. These supermajority voting requirements may now be proscribed under the new Act, where this gives rise to a conflict with the Memorandum of Incorporation or the Act. (However this may now be significantly affected by the draft Companies Amendment Bill, 2010, if it is adopted.[217] See also the discussion of voting agreements below.)

The anti-avoidance provisions in the Act may also impact on shareholder agreements. The anti-avoidance provisions are widely drafted and empower a court to declare any agreement (or transaction, arrangement, resolution or provision of a company's Memorandum or Incorporation or rules) to be primarily or substantially intended to *defeat* or *reduce* the effect of a prohibition or requirement established by an unalterable provision of the Act, and to declare it void to that extent.[218]

It is notable that a shareholder agreement may not be used to alter any 'alterable provisions' of the Act — alterable provisions may be altered only by the company's Memorandum of Incorporation.[219] Where a company's Memorandum of Incorporation has in fact altered the effect of any alterable provisions of the Act, then that company's shareholder agreement must be consistent with the approach of its Memorandum of Incorporation to those 'alterable provisions' that have in fact been altered.[220]

---

[215] See *Gohlke & Schneider v Westies Minerale (Edms) Bpk* 1970 (2) SA 685 (A) 692–3, which stated that an agreement between the company and all its members (or shareholders) to do something (*intra vires* of the company's memorandum of association but) in a manner contrary to the articles of association, would be binding on those members. See also *Russell v Northern Bank Development Corporation Ltd* [1922] 1 WLR 589 where the court held that a company (in its articles of association) could not forgo its statutory right to alter its articles of association by special resolution, but this right could be validly fettered in a shareholder agreement dehors (or outside) the articles (which related to the manner in which the shareholders would exercise their voting rights on a resolution to alter the constitution). The court reasoned that individual shareholders may by contract deal with their own interests as they think fit.

[216] FHI Cassim op cit n 3 at 167–8.

[217] The draft Companies Amendment Bill, 2010, significantly now proposes to create scope for a company's Memorandum of Incorporation to require a higher threshold of more than 75 per cent of the voting rights to approve a special resolution (cl 41*(b)*; cl 2(1)). The Act in its present form permits only a decrease of the threshold requirement for a special resolution to less than 75 per cent, subject to certain provisos (in terms of s 65(10)). See further n 166 above and chapter 9: Governance and Shareholders.

[218] Section 6(1). See further 4.3.2 above and chapter 1: Introduction to the New Companies Act.

[219] Section 1; s 19(1)*(c)*(ii); s 15(2)*(a)*(ii). See further 4.3.2 above.

[220] The force and effect of shareholder agreements of pre-existing companies is dealt with in the draft Companies Amendment Bill, 2010 (cl 115). This proposes to insert a new item in the Transitional Arrangements to the effect that a pre-existing shareholder agreement of a pre-existing company will continue to have the same force and effect for two years after the effective date of the new Act (or until amended), and will prevail in the event of a conflict with the Act or the company's constitution. After the two-year period, the shareholder agreement will have force and effect only to

An interesting issue relates to voting agreements. Voting agreements are used by two or more shareholders to provide for the manner in which they will vote their shares when exercising voting rights. Voting agreements have long been recognised at common law under the previous company law regime. In this regard, it was held that a shareholder's right to vote is a proprietary right that the shareholder may exercise in any way he or she pleases and with regard, not to the company's interests, but to his or her own interests as a shareholder.[221] Shareholders, unlike directors, owe no fiduciary duty to the company to act in the best interests of the company. However, under the new Act, voting agreements may, in certain circumstances and depending on their content, fall foul of the anti-avoidance measure. This applies where the voting agreement is found to be primarily or substantially intended to defeat or even to merely *reduce* the effect of an unalterable provision of the Act.[222] A voting agreement may also be required to comply with the Act and the company's Memorandum of Incorporation (and would be void to the extent of any inconsistency), if the voting agreement falls within the very wide meaning of a shareholder agreement in s 15(7), namely an agreement between the shareholders of a company concerning any matter relating to the company. In view of this very wide definition of a shareholder agreement, it is likely that many voting agreements would fall within its scope and ambit.

4.6 THE LEGAL STATUS OF THE MEMORANDUM OF INCORPORATION AND RULES

4.6.1 Introduction

In terms of s 15(6) of the Act, a company's Memorandum of Incorporation and any company rules are binding as follows:
- between the company and each shareholder,
- between or among the shareholders of the company *inter se*,
- between the company and each director or prescribed officer, in the exercise of his or her functions within the company,
- between the company and any other person serving the company as a member of the audit committee or as a member of a committee of the board, in the exercise of his or her functions within the company.[223]

Section 15(6) thus creates a number of legal relationships, each of which is examined in detail below. Although this section governs the legal status of the Memorandum of Incorporation and the rules, it does not apply to shareholder agreements. The binding force of shareholder agreements derives from the ordinary principles of the law of contract.

The fundamental question arises: What is the legal status of the Memorandum of Incorporation and the rules? In respect of legislation pre-dating s 15(6), the

---

the extent of its consistency with the Act and the company's constitution. See further chapter 21: Transitional Arrangements.

[221] *Sammel v President Brand Gold Mining Co Ltd* 1969 (3) SA 629 (A) 680–1.
[222] Section 6(1). See further 4.3.2 above and chapter 1: Introduction to the New Companies Act.
[223] Section 15(6). The reference to a member of the audit committee is proposed to be deleted by the draft Companies Amendment Bill, 2010 (cl 11).

courts proclaimed that the company's constitution had the legal status of a contract created by statute.[224] This was based both on the history of the relevant section and its wording.[225] Under previous legislation, there was thus a contractual relationship between the company and its shareholders (as well as between the shareholders *inter se*) that was based on the company's constitution. Under the new Act, the wording of s 15(6) fails to specify the legal status of the various relationships based on the Memorandum of Incorporation and the rules.[226] It is submitted that the binding nature of s 15(6) may still be based on a statutory contract, in other words, a contract that derives its binding force from the terms of the statute.[227]

The binding nature of the statutory contract formed by the Memorandum of Incorporation has some unusual features. The most significant feature is that it may be altered unilaterally by the company (acting through its shareholders in general meeting), by way of a special resolution.[228] In other words, the collective body of shareholders is able to alter this statutory contract with the consent of the prescribed majority, and unanimity is not required in order to change the contractual rights and obligations of the individual shareholder under the Memorandum of Incorporation. A further important feature is that in interpreting the Memorandum of Incorporation and the company rules, if any provision read in its context can be reasonably construed to have more than one meaning, the court (or the Companies Commission, the Companies Tribunal or the Takeover Regulation Panel, as the case may be) must prefer the meaning that best promotes the spirit and purpose of the Act, and will best improve the realisation and enjoyment of rights.[229]

The various relationships created by the Memorandum of Incorporation and the rules are discussed in turn below. While the constitution (and now also the rules) continues to be binding between the company and each shareholder, and between

---

[224] Furthermore, the constitution was not to be elevated to a statutory enactment merely because it had the status of a statutory contract. See *Gohlke & Schneider v Westies Minerale (Edms) Bpk* 1970 (2) SA 685 (A); *Hickman v Kent or Romney Marsh Sheep Breeders' Association* [1915] 1 Ch 881; *De Villiers v Jacobsdal Saltworks (Michaelis and De Villiers) (Pty) Ltd* 1959 (3) SA 873 (O).

[225] The wording of s 65(2) of the 1973 Act was that the articles of association were binding 'as if they ... had been signed by each member', which implied a contractual relationship. However, complex difficulties arose with this concept. One such issue was whether the company itself was bound to its articles in view of the fact that, on the wording of s 65(2), the company was not deemed to have signed its articles.

[226] By contrast, the new UK Companies Act 2006 explicitly retains the contractual status of the company's constitution by stating in s 33 that the constitution binds the company and the members 'to the same extent as if there were covenants on the part of the company and of each member to observe it'. The UK Act thus retains the contractual approach but abandons the outdated concept of the deemed signature by the members.

[227] The common law and the history of the section arguably support this contention. From the time that legislation was first drafted for incorporated companies, both in England and in South Africa, the constitution of the incorporated company was based on the method for forming the English unincorporated company by way of deed of settlement, which constituted a *contract* between all the members who signed it (See Paul L Davies op cit n 126 at 65–6).

[228] *Shuttleworth v Cox Brothers & Co (Maidenhead) Ltd* [1927] 2 KB 9 (CA); *Malleson v National Insurance and Guarantee Corp* [1894] 1 Ch 200.

[229] Section 158*(b)*(ii).

shareholders *inter se*, the Act introduces a novel and remarkable aspect. In this regard, the constitution and rules are now also binding between the company and each director, prescribed officer, member of the audit committee and member of a board committee. This is an important extension to the scope of the contract created by s 15(6), which modifies the large body of case law that insisted that the contract was binding only on shareholders in their capacity as shareholders, and that it was not binding between the company and its directors nor between shareholders and directors *qua* directors. Moreover, the new Act makes it abundantly clear that the company itself is bound by its Memorandum of Incorporation and rules. This is a fine improvement on the 1973 Act which, due to its drafting, caused interpretational difficulties on this important point.[230] The Memorandum of Incorporation and rules continue to generally remain unenforceable by outsiders or third parties. These aspects of the contract created by s 15(6) are elucidated below.

4.6.2 The relationship between the company and each shareholder

It is clear from s 15(6)(*a*) that the company is bound to each shareholder and, conversely, that each shareholder is bound to the company by the Memorandum of Incorporation and the company rules. But the Act leaves certain important issues unanswered. The first issue is: Are shareholders bound to the company's constitution and rules only to the extent that the rights conferred or obligations imposed on them affect them in their capacity as shareholders? The second issue relates to the enforcement of the rights of shareholders against the company.

(a) Are shareholders bound only in their capacity as shareholders?

The key question is whether the shareholders are bound to the company's constitution and rules only *qua* (or as) shareholders. Surprisingly, the Act is silent on this fundamental matter which is so important in practice.

At common law, in relation to the 1973 Act, the courts read in the proviso that the company's constitution was only binding on a shareholder (or member) to the extent that the rights and obligations were conferred or imposed on the shareholder *in his or her capacity as a shareholder*.[231] By this is meant that the rights or duties imposed on a shareholder must in some way be connected with the holding of shares.[232] At common law, in order for shareholders to rely on a right conferred by the company's constitution, the right must be conferred on them by virtue of their shareholding in the company and must, moreover, relate to their shareholding in the company.

It is submitted that the common-law position under the 1973 Act should continue in this respect to apply equally to s 15(6) of the new Companies Act. The Memorandum of Incorporation and the company rules should be binding only in respect of those rights granted to, and obligations imposed on, shareholders *qua*

---

[230] See *Hickman v Kent or Romney Marsh Sheep Breeders' Association* [1915] 1 Ch 881. See also n 225 above.
[231] *Hickman v Kent or Romney Marsh Sheep Breeders' Association* [1915] 1 Ch 881; *Eley v Positive Government Security Life Assurance Co* (1876) 1 ExD 88; *Beattie v Beattie Ltd* [1938] 3 All ER 214 (CA); *De Villiers v Jacobsdal Saltworks (Michaelis and De Villiers) (Pty) Ltd* 1959 (3) SA 873 (O).
[232] *Rosslare (Pty) Ltd v Registrar of Companies* 1972 (2) SA 524 (D) 528.

shareholders.[233] Persons who become shareholders in a company should not be bound to do something unrelated to their shareholding in the company by some provision that they would not expect to find in the constitution of that type of company. Nor should the company be bound to do something in favour of a particular shareholder that other shareholders of that type of company would not expect to find in the constitution.[234]

This has vital practical ramifications. For instance, if a clause in the company's constitution appoints a shareholder as attorney of the company for life and the company later ceases to employ the shareholder as attorney, the shareholder will be unable to enforce the clause against the company. The reasoning is that the constitution is binding only to extent that it confers rights on a shareholder *in his or her capacity as a shareholder*, whereas the clause in issue conferred a right on the relevant shareholder *in his capacity as attorney*. As such, it is unenforceable against the company.[235]

However, there may be scope for relying on another common-law principle to circumvent this. A shareholder acting *in his or her capacity as a shareholder* may restrain the company from contravening its constitution, in view of its binding nature. In so doing, shareholders may *indirectly* enforce a right that is granted to them in the constitution *other than* in their capacity as shareholders (for instance, in the example above, the shareholder may restrain the company from breaching its constitution and thereby indirectly enforce his appointment as attorney of the company, which right is clearly granted to him in his capacity as attorney).[236] The limits of this principle are still subject to debate.

To sum up, it is submitted that the above common-law principles continue to apply to s 15(6)*(a)* of the new Act, so that the Memorandum of Incorporation and rules are binding between the company and shareholders only *in their capacity as shareholders*. There are, however, some important exceptions flowing from s 15(6)*(c)*, to the effect that where the Memorandum of Incorporation or the rules grant rights to a shareholder in his or her capacity either as a director, a prescribed officer, a member of the audit committee or a member of a board committee, then these rights will indeed be enforceable against the company, but only in the exercise of their respective functions within the company (see further 4.6.4 below).

---

[233] 'Shareholder' is defined in s 1 of the Act as 'the holder of a share issued by a company and who is entered as such in the certificated or uncertificated securities register'. In this context, a shareholder under the new Act is equivalent to the concept of a 'member' under the previous Act (which used the term 'member' in reference to a registered shareholder).

[234] RP Austin and IM Ramsay *Ford's Principles of Corporations Law* 13 ed (2007) at 196.

[235] See *Eley v Positive Government Security Life Assurance Co* (1876) 1 ExD 88. Under the 1973 Act, where shareholders were granted rights under the company's constitution *in their capacity as directors*, it was held that these rights could not be enforced against the company, on the above basis. The new Act now overrides this, because s 15(6) explicitly declares that the Memorandum of Incorporation is now binding between the company and directors in the exercise of their functions as directors — see further 4.6.4 below.

[236] *Quin & Axtens Ltd v Salmon* [1909] AC 442 (HL); see Lord Wedderburn 'Shareholders' Rights and the Rule in *Foss v Harbottle*' [1957] *CLJ* 193 at 210–15.

Formation of Companies and the Company Constitution

(b) Enforcement by shareholders against the company

The rights granted to a shareholder in terms of the Memorandum of Incorporation and rules are enforceable against the company by a shareholder *qua* shareholder (see *Pender v Lushington*).[237] The usual shareholder remedy for a breach of the constitution is an interdict or a declaratory order, as opposed to damages against the company.[238]

Section 15(6)(a) leaves unanswered, however, the crucial issue of which range of provisions of the Memorandum of Incorporation and rules may be *directly* enforced by a shareholder against the company. There have been several differing views on this matter. The widest view is that every shareholder has a general right to have the company's affairs conducted in accordance with its constitution.[239] But a different view is that a distinction must be drawn between the personal rights of shareholders and corporate rights. According to this view, an individual shareholder may sue only in respect of a provision that confers a personal right on him or her (or it) *qua* shareholder (eg the right to vote at a shareholders' meeting); whereas if a breach involves provisions that merely impose obligations on the company (as opposed to conferring corresponding rights on individual shareholders), the company itself is the proper plaintiff.[240] See in this regard the case of *MacDougall v Gardiner* where the chairman of a shareholders' meeting, in breach of the constitution, rejected a demand for a poll. The court held that this did not constitute an infringement of a shareholder's personal right, but was a mere internal irregularity that consequently could not be directly enforced by the shareholder against the company.

It was thus undecided under the previous company law regime exactly which or what type of constitutional provisions could be directly enforced by a shareholder against the company. Section 15(6) of the new Act regrettably does nothing to clarify this uncertainty in the law.

It is noteworthy in this regard that s 161 of the Act (dealing with the application to protect the rights of securities holders) now provides an alternate legal basis for a shareholder to determine and protect any of his or her (or its) rights in terms of the company's Memorandum of Incorporation or rules, namely by obtaining a declaratory order or any appropriate order necessary to protect any shareholder rights or rectify harm done to the shareholder (see further chapter 16: Shareholder Remedies and Minority Protection).

4.6.3 The relationship between or among the shareholders *inter se*

The Memorandum of Incorporation and rules are binding between the shareholders *inter se* (s 15(6)(b). In other words, each shareholder is bound to every

---

[237] See *Pender v Lushington* (1877) 6 ChD 70 at 80.
[238] *Houldsworth v City of Glasglow Bank* (1880) 5 App Cas 317 (HL); *Pathescope (Union) of SA Ltd v Mallinick* 1927 AD 292.
[239] Lord Wedderburn op cit n 236.
[240] See *MacDougall v Gardiner* (1875) 1 Ch 13 (CA).

other shareholder.[241] The relationship between the shareholders *inter se* is at issue when, for example, a shareholder wishes to sell his or her shares without complying with a right of first refusal or right of pre-emption under the Memorandum of Incorporation (in terms of which shareholders wishing to dispose of their shares must offer them to the other shareholders and not to outsiders, unless the other shareholders first refuse them).

Based on the common law, it is submitted that the complex issue of the enforcement of the Memorandum of Incorporation among the shareholders *inter se* is still unresolved. Of particular importance is the question whether shareholders may enforce the Memorandum of Incorporation against one another *directly*, without the intervention of the company itself. In *Rayfield v Hands*[242] the plaintiff, a shareholder, was permitted a *direct action* against the defendants, who were the sole directors and also shareholders of the company, in order to compel them to take over the plaintiff's shares as provided in the articles. The basis of the direct action must have been that the plaintiff was personally affected by the clause in question, ie a direct action is based on a 'personal and individual right' of the shareholder against other shareholders. If the clause does not affect the plaintiff personally it is arguable that, in accordance with the *obiter dictum* of Lord Herschell in *Welton v Saffery*,[243] a direct action would not be permitted. The plaintiff would instead be required to bring an action through the company.[244]

The Act fails to shed light on whether the Memorandum of Incorporation and the rules bind the shareholders *inter se* only where they are affected specifically *in their capacity as shareholders*. This is an important question in practice. It could, for instance, impact on whether a shareholder may rely on s 15(6) to enforce an obligation imposed by the Memorandum of Incorporation on another shareholder where the obligation affects the other shareholder in his or her capacity as a director of the company. It is submitted that the common-law principles in this respect continue to apply, so that shareholders *inter se* are bound by the Memorandum of Incorporation but only insofar as it affects them *qua* shareholders. Had the drafters of the Act intended for the Memorandum of Incorporation to be binding between shareholders and directors, one would expect the Act to have expressly provided so.

4.6.4 The relationship between the company and each director, prescribed officer, member of the audit committee or member of a board committee, in the exercise of their respective functions within the company[245]

Section 15(6)*(c)* is an entirely new provision that did not form part of the 1973 Act. Under the previous company law regime the constitution of a company,

---

[241] In respect of the common law under the previous regime, see *Wood v Odessa Waterworks Co* (1889) 42 ChD 636; *Automatic Self-Cleansing Filter Syndicate Co Ltd v Cuninghame* [1906] 2 Ch 34.
[242] [1960] 1 Ch 1; [1958] 2 All ER 194; see also *De Villiers v Jacobsdal Saltworks (Michaelis and De Villiers) (Pty) Ltd* 1959 (3) SA 873 (O).
[243] 1897 AC 297 (HL) 315.
[244] See further LCB Gower 'The Contractual Effect of Articles of Association' (1958) 21 *MLR* 401 and LCB Gower '*Rayfield v Hands* — A Postscript and a Drop of Scotch' (1958) 21 *MLR* 657.
[245] The reference to a member of the audit committee is proposed to be deleted by the draft Companies Amendment Bill, 2010 (cl 11).

notably, was not binding between the company and a director in his or her capacity as a director, as laid down by a long line of cases at common law.[246] This is now superseded by s 15(6)*(c)*, which effects considerable changes to the legal position. It is now clear, in terms of s 15(6)*(c)*, that the Memorandum of Incorporation and rules of a company are binding between the company and each of its directors, in the exercise of their functions within the company. A director may now enforce the Memorandum of Incorporation directly against the company and vice versa, to the extent that the Act does not expressly provide otherwise. Prescribed officers,[247] audit committee members and board committee members may do likewise.

It must be emphasised that s 15(6) only binds directors *in the exercise of their functions as directors*. This would boil down to a question of fact in each case. Should the Memorandum of Incorporation or rules confer rights or impose obligations on a director in another capacity, for instance *qua* attorney of the company, the director may not enforce this against the company on the basis of s 15(6). In a similar vein, the Memorandum of Incorporation and rules are binding between the company and prescribed officers, members of the audit committee and members of board committees only in relation to the exercise of their respective functions within the company.[248]

There are important practical implications stemming from the new-found ability of a director to enforce relevant provisions of the Memorandum of Incorporation and the rules directly against the company in terms of s 15(6). Where a director does not have a separate contract of service with the company, he or she no longer has to resort to proving the existence of an *implied* or tacit contract of service that impliedly incorporates the relevant provisions of the company's constitution.[249] Instead, the director may now simply base his or her claim against the company solely and *directly* on a provision of the Memorandum of Incorporation or the rules (for instance, a provision relating to the director's term of office).[250]

---

[246] See *Hickman v Kent or Romney Marsh Sheep Breeders' Association* [1915] 1 Ch 881 and the line of cases following it. *Ross & Co v Coleman* 1920 AD 408 and *Re New British Iron Co* [1898] 1 Ch 324 held that the articles of association as such were not a contract between the company and a director in his capacity as a director.

[247] Prescribed officers are persons who, despite not being directors of the company (and regardless of the title of their office), have general executive authority over the company; general responsibility for the financial management of the company; general responsibility for the management of the legal affairs of the company; general managerial authority over the operations of the company; or otherwise directly or indirectly exercise or significantly influence the exercise of control over the general management of the administration of the whole or a significant portion of the business and activities of the company, irrespective of any title assigned by the company to an office held by that person, or function performed by that person (s 66(10) read with s 1 and regulation 45 of the draft Companies Regulations).

[248] By contrast, the Act does not *expressly* limit the rights of shareholders only to the extent that they are affected *qua* shareholders, in terms of s 15(6)*(a)* and *(b)*. But, as discussed in 4.6.2 and 4.6.3 above, the common law will arguably still apply to this effect.

[249] This occurred, for example, in the cases of *Ross & Co v Coleman* 1920 AD 408 and *Re New British Iron Co* [1898] 1 Ch 324 under the previous company law regime.

[250] As far as directors' remuneration is concerned, it must now be approved by special resolution passed within the previous two years (s 66(9)).

It must be borne in mind, though, that the Memorandum of Incorporation is generally subject to alteration by special resolution in terms of s 16.[251] This effectively amounts to a unilateral alteration of the statutory contract by the company (as discussed in 4.6.1 above). Accordingly, where the company wishes to avoid the enforcement of a right due to a director (or prescribed officer, audit committee member or board committee member, as the case may be) under its Memorandum of Incorporation or rules, its recourse would be to simply delete the relevant provision from its Memorandum of Incorporation by special resolution.[252] The director will in that event be precluded from claiming a remedy against the company, because the rights conferred and the obligations imposed on him or her under the Memorandum of Incorporation are subject to the qualification that they may be altered at any time[253] by special resolution.[254] It is accordingly still strongly advisable for directors to have separate contracts of service with the company, outside of the Memorandum of Incorporation and the rules, to avoid this state of affairs.

Even where the director enters into a contract of service with the company, the company at common law may not be restrained from exercising its statutory power to alter in its *Memorandum of Incorporation*[255] any provisions relating to the director (for example, the director's term of office), regardless of the existence of a separate contract of service. The advantage of the contract of service in such cases is that where the company then proceeds to act on its Memorandum of Incorporation, as altered, the director will indeed have a remedy based on breach of the *contract of service*.[256]

It is noteworthy that a director may be removed from office at any time by ordinary resolution, despite anything to the contrary in the Memorandum of Incorporation, the rules, any agreement between the director and the company or even any agreement between the director and any shareholders.[257] The director consequently is not entitled to prevent his or her removal even where he or she had

---

[251] An exception applies to entrenched provisions (in terms of s 15(2)(*b*) and (*c*)).

[252] See eg *De Villiers v Jacobsdal Saltworks (Michaelis & De Villiers) (Pty) Ltd* 1959 (3) SA 873 (O); see FHI Cassim op cit n 3 at 167.

[253] See *De Villiers v Jacobsdal Saltworks (Michaelis and De Villiers) Pty (Ltd)* (supra); *Shuttleworth v Cox Brothers & Co (Maidenhead) Ltd* [1927] 2 KB 9 (CA); *Ross & Co v Coleman* 1920 AD 408. Although these cases related to implied contracts of service that were based on the company's constitution, the same principle may be extended to s 15(6)(*c*).

[254] However this may be subject to other relevant provisions of the Memorandum of Incorporation, such as a provision regulating the effect of an alteration of the Memorandum of Incorporation on the rights of the director.

[255] At common law a company could not be restrained from altering its constitution, even though it would constitute a breach of contract for the company to act on the altered constitution (*Southern Foundries (1926) Ltd v Shirlaw* [1940] AC 701, [1940] 2 All ER 445 (HL); *De Villiers v Jacobsdal Saltworks (Michaelis & De Villiers) (Pty) Ltd* (supra) SA 873 (O); *Allen v Gold Reefs of West Africa Ltd* [1900] 1 Ch 656 (CA)).

[256] See eg *De Villiers v Jacobsdal Saltworks (Michaelis & De Villiers) Pty (Ltd)* (supra); *Southern Foundries (1926) Ltd v Shirlaw* (supra), based on common law. *Shirlaw's* case also held obiter that the company could not be restrained from acting on the altered constitution and the only remedy available to the director would be damages for breach of contract.

[257] Section 71(1).

Formation of Companies and the Company Constitution

entered into a separate contract of service. But where the separate contract of service is breached by his or her premature removal from office, the director will at least have a contractual remedy against the company for damages for breach of contract.[258]

There are other relevant provisions in the Act relating to a director's failure to comply with the Memorandum of Incorporation. For instance, where a director (or prescribed officer, member of a board committee or member of the audit committee)[259] breaches any provision of the company's Memorandum of Incorporation, he or she may be held liable in accordance with the principles of the law of delict for any loss, damages or costs caused to the company.[260] Directors may also be in breach of their fiduciary duties and the duty of care and skill should they fail to act in accordance with the Memorandum of Incorporation.[261]

4.7 PRE-INCORPORATION CONTRACTS[262]

4.7.1 Introduction

(a) Significance of pre-incorporation contracts and the common-law hurdles

Companies are frequently formed for a specific purpose, in order to acquire certain assets, business opportunities or other benefits. Before expending funds on incorporating and registering a company, the promoters of the company naturally desire the assurance that the company would indeed be able to reap those benefits or acquire those assets upon its incorporation. Investors are also more assured when investing in a venture in which the promoter has already made the necessary legal arrangements to acquire the assets or benefits for which the company is formed. Promoters, in practice, tend to regard the incorporation of a company as one of the last formalities in the promotion of a company. There is thus a need for binding legal arrangements *prior* to the incorporation of the company.

There are, however, certain common-law hurdles to overcome. At common law, a company cannot be a party to a contract *prior* to its incorporation, since the company comes into existence only upon its incorporation. No reliance may be placed at common law on agency principles, because it is logically impossible for a person (the promoter) to act as an agent for a non-existent principal (the non-existent company that is yet to be formed).

Furthermore, if an 'agent' purports to enter into a 'contract' on a company's behalf, prior to the formation of the company, the company once formed is unable to ratify the contract. The reason is that ratification operates retrospectively to the time that the agent had entered into the contract and thus to a time at which the

---

[258] The director may also rely on any other right to damages or other compensation that he or she may have at common law or otherwise (s 71(9)). See further chapter 10: Governance and the Board of Directors.
[259] Section 77(1).
[260] Section 77(2).
[261] See chapter 12: The Duties and the Liability of Directors.
[262] See Maleka Femida Cassim 'Pre-Incorporation Contracts: The Reform of Section 35 of the Companies Act' (2007) 124(2) *SALJ* 364, from which much of this section on pre-incorporation contracts is derived.

company was not in existence.[263] At common law, not only will the contract be a nullity, but in addition the 'agent' could be held personally liable on the contract.[264]

(b) The main methods of contracting on behalf of a company to be formed

Section 21 of the Act accordingly provides a legislative solution to overcome the hurdle of the non-ratification rule at common law.[265] It facilitates a form of statutory agency. The purpose of s 21 is to put persons (or promoters[266]), acting as agents, in a position to contract on behalf of the company, even though the company does not yet exist.[267] It does so by permitting the company, once formed, to *ratify* a pre-incorporation contract entered into by an agent.

The solution of statutory agency was first formulated in s 71 of the Companies Act 46 of 1926, and then amended by s 35 of the 1973 Act. Section 21 of the new Act now significantly overhauls and reforms the statutory solution to pre-incorporation contracts concluded by agents.

Besides s 21 of the Act, the other important method of contracting on behalf of a company to be formed is the common law *stipulatio alteri* (contract for the benefit of a third party).[268] Here the promoter contracts in his or her own name, as a *principal*, for the benefit of the company to be formed. In contrast, a promoter who relies on a s 21 pre-incorporation contract evidently acts in the capacity of an *agent* on behalf of the company to be formed. The two methods, although superficially quite similar, are nevertheless separate and distinct.

The question inevitably arises whether s 21 pre-incorporation contracts will continue to be important in view of readily available 'shelf' companies. In this regard, a very useful practical alternative to incorporating and registering a new company from scratch is the purchase of a company off-the-shelf, from an agency providing this service. The use of a shelf company is particularly convenient where the promoters wish to expedite the process of setting up a business. After purchasing a shelf company, the promoters would file with the Companies Com-

---

[263] Laid down in *Kelner v Baxter* [1866] LR 2 CP 174, and accepted by the Appellate Division in South African law in *McCullogh v Fernwood Estate Ltd* 1920 AD 204.

[264] *Kelner v Baxter* [1866] LR 2 CP 174. However, the agent's personal liability appears to depend on the parties' intention and the proper interpretation of the contract. South African common law seems to follow the 'rule of construction' approach (where the personal liability of the promoter depends on the parties' intention) as opposed to the 'rule of law' approach (in which the agent's personal liability is automatic). *Nordis Construction Co (Pty) Ltd v Theron, Burke & Isaac* 1972 (2) SA 535 (D) applied the rule of construction approach and was followed in *Terblanche v Nothnagel* 1975 (4) SA 405 (C) and *Indrieri v Du Preez* 1989 (2) SA 721 (C). It has been held occasionally that the rule of law approach should be applied, e g *Gompels v Skodawerke of Prague* 1942 TPD 167; *Van Eeden v Sasol Pensioenfonds* 1975 (2) SA 167 (O) 180H; *Gardner v Richardt* 1974 (3) SA 768 (C).

[265] That is, that a company at common law cannot *ratify* a pre-incorporation contract purportedly made prior to the company's formation by an agent on behalf of the company.

[266] It is noteworthy that the Act does not use the term 'promoter' and instead simply uses the word 'person'.

[267] See eg *Build-a-Brick BK v Eskom* 1996 (1) SA 115 (O) in respect of s 35 of the 1973 Act.

[268] *McCullogh v Fernwood Estate Ltd* 1920 AD 204.

mission the necessary notices to change the registered office of the company, its name, the directors, provisions of the Memorandum of Incorporation and so on.

The use of shelf companies was widespread under the previous company law regime. Despite the expected improvements to the company registration process under the new regime, the practice of using shelf companies may be expected to continue. Promoters consequently have the option of simply acquiring a company off the shelf and thereafter contracting in its name, without the need for a pre-incorporation contract. It is nevertheless expected that, despite these possibilities, pre-incorporation contracts — and the provisions relating to pre-incorporation contracts — will continue to play an increasingly important role in the corporate world.

4.7.2 Section 21 pre-incorporation contracts

(a) General

As stated above, s 21 of the Act provides a statutory solution to overcome the hurdle of the non-ratification rule at common law. In this regard, it enables persons, acting as agents, to contract on behalf of non-existent companies that are yet to be formed, and furthermore enables companies on their formation to *ratify* such pre-incorporation contracts. Section 21, like its predecessor, effectively permits a form of statutory agency.

To elaborate, s 21(1) of the Act enables a person to 'enter into a written agreement in the name of, or purport to act in the name of, or on behalf of,' an entity that is yet to be incorporated and come into existence. This must be read in conjunction with the definition of a 'pre-incorporation contract' in s 1 of the Act. Section 1 defines a pre-incorporation contract as an 'agreement' entered into before the incorporation of a company by a person who purports to act in the name of, or on behalf of, the company, with the intention or understanding that the company will be incorporated, and would thereafter be bound by the agreement. The term 'agreement' is in turn widely defined to include a contract or an arrangement or understanding between or among two or more parties that 'purports' to create rights and obligations between or among those parties.[269]

It is evident from these provisions that a s 21 pre-incorporation contract must be a *written* agreement.[270] The agreement is entered into *before* the company comes into existence. It is entered into by a third party and a person (or promoter[271]), in his or her capacity as an *agent*,[272] who 'purports' to act in the name of or on behalf of the company. Since the company is not yet in existence, it clearly cannot have a person acting on its behalf — for this reason the Act refers to a person who

---

[269] Section 1.
[270] Although s 21(1) of the Act requires a s 21 pre-incorporation contract to be a written agreement, the definition of a pre-incorporation contract in terms of s 1 of the Act fails to specify that the agreement must be in writing.
[271] It is noteworthy that the Act does not use the term 'promoter' and instead simply uses the word 'person'. For the sake of convenience the term promoter (or agent) will be used in this discussion.
[272] Section 21 seems to apply only where the promoter purports to act as an agent as opposed to acting as a principal. However, the section does not use this word. It would have removed some uncertainty had it done so. See further below.

'purports' to act on its behalf. Once the company is incorporated and comes into existence, it may *ratify* the pre-incorporation contract entered into by the promoter. Once ratified, the pre-incorporation contract becomes enforceable against the company.

Strictly speaking, a s 21 pre-incorporation 'contract' is not really a contract at all (between the company and the third party) until such time as the company ratifies it. Until that point the company is not party to it and it cannot therefore amount to a contract by definition.[273] It is instead an inchoate or a nascent contract. For this reason the term 'agreement' is defined expansively, as discussed above, to include an 'arrangement' or 'understanding' between or among two or more parties that 'purports' to create rights and obligations between or among those parties.[274]

An important issue is the formalities for pre-incorporation contracts. The sole formality for a s 21 pre-incorporation contract is that it must be in writing. This is a welcome formality that was introduced only after criticism of the Companies Bill in its original form.[275] Written pre-incorporation agreements provide certainty. They also ensure that the board of directors of the company receives full and proper disclosure of the terms of the pre-incorporation agreement before ratifying it and that there are no disputes over the terms of the contract.

In contrast with the previous company law regime, the other burdensome formalities for statutory pre-incorporation contracts have fortunately been jettisoned. Most importantly, such contracts need no longer be lodged or filed at the Companies Commission. This removes a major disadvantage that was formerly associated with the publicity and public scrutiny of statutory pre-incorporation contracts under the 1973 Act. Nor do pre-incorporation contracts have to be notarially certified — this formality was removed by the Corporate Laws Amendment Act 24 of 2006.[276] Unlike the 1973 Act in terms of which the promoter had to 'profess' to act for a company not yet incorporated, s 21 now removes this formality and simply states that the promoter 'purports' to act for an entity yet to be incorporated. There is no longer a need to 'profess' or declare to be acting on behalf of a company that is yet to be formed.[277]

---

[273] AJ Kerr 'Contracting for a Company Not Yet Incorporated' (1975) *SALJ* 365, 366; MA Maloney 'Pre-Incorporation Transactions: A Statutory Solution?' (1985) 10 *Canadian Business Law Journal* 409, 415.

[274] A better way of resolving the difficulty may have been to define pre-incorporation contracts as 'purported' contracts, as is done in the New Zealand Companies Act 1993 and the British Columbia Business Corporations Act [SBC 2002] (see Maleka Femida Cassim op cit n 262 at 395).

[275] The formality of a written agreement was not initially required (see the provisions of the draft Companies Bill, 2007 (GN 166 *GG* 29630 of 12 February 2007) and the Companies Bill 2008 [B 61-2008]). This was criticised by Maleka Femida Cassim op cit n 262 at 394–5 and 399, and it was fortunately later prescribed by the Companies Bill [B 61D–2008].

[276] Section 8.

[277] However, this must be seen in the light of s 32(6) and (7) which enables a court to impose personal liability (for any liability or obligation of the company) on any person acting on behalf of a company who misrepresents, whether by act or by omission, the true legal status of the company. In view of s 32 the promoter should inform the other party that the company is not yet in existence. But there is the possibility of contending that s 32(6) and (7) applies only to a person acting on behalf of

It is noteworthy that s 21 apparently applies only where the promoter acts as an *agent* on behalf of or in the name of the company to be formed. It does not appear to apply where the promoter contracts in his or her own name, as *principal*, for the benefit of the company to be formed in terms of the common-law *stipulatio alteri*.[278] One would wish that the section had made this clearer. It nevertheless appears to be quite likely that the *stipulatio alteri* will continue to be governed by the common-law principles and will continue to serve as the other main device or method for pre-incorporation contracts. The application of the *stipulatio alteri* will undoubtedly continue to be beneficial. However, it means that in certain cases difficulties may still be encountered in determining whether a promoter intended to act as an agent or as a principal under a pre-incorporation contract, due to uncertainty concerning the guiding criteria.

Section 21, notably, deals not only with pre-incorporation agreements, but also extends to any other 'action' purported to have been 'made or done' in the name of or on behalf of a company that is yet to be incorporated.

(b) Ratification of a section 21 contract

A pre-incorporation contract becomes enforceable against the company, in terms of s 21 of the Act, once it is ratified by the company.

The company may ratify it, but must do so within three months after its incorporation. The power to ratify pre-incorporation contracts lies with the board of directors of the company.[279] The board may either ratify or reject a pre-incorporation contract, and may do so completely, partially or even conditionally.[280]

Should the board fail to either ratify or reject a pre-incorporation contract (or 'other action purported to have been made or done' in the name of the company or on its behalf) within the three-month period after the company's incorporation, then the company is 'regarded to have ratified' it. In other words, there is a *deemed ratification* in the event that the company fails to act within the three-month

---

a company as opposed to a person *purporting* to act on behalf on a company. Significantly, the draft Companies Amendment Bill, 2010 (cl 21) now proposes to repeal s 32(6).

[278] The confusing wording in s 35 of the 1973 Act that the promoter must profess to act as 'agent or *trustee*' [emphasis added] has fortunately now been abolished. This wording previously created confusion as to whether s 35 applied to the *stipulatio alteri*, because a 'trustee' generally acts as a principal and not as an agent. See eg *Ex parte Vickerman* 1935 CPD 429; *McCullogh v Fernwood Estate Ltd* 1920 AD 204.

[279] It is a generally advisable policy decision to leave ratification of pre-incorporation contracts in the hands of the board of directors (as was suggested by Maleka Femida Cassim op cit n 262 at 383–5) and, as such, constitutes an improvement to the original provision in clause 18(2) of the draft Companies Bill, 2007 (GN 166 *GG* 29630 of 12 February 2007). But the section still creates uncertainty insofar as it fails to deal with the issue of implied ratification or ratification by conduct (see further Maleka Femida Cassim op cit n 262 at 383–5).

[280] Section 21(4). In terms of regulation 41 of the draft Companies Regulations, if the board has completely or partially rejected or ratified a pre-incorporation contract, the company must within five business days file a notice of its decision in form CoR 41 and deliver a copy of the notice to each party to the contract.

period.[281] The concept of a deemed ratification is an innovative aspect of the new Companies Act.

To the extent that a pre-incorporation contract has been ratified or is deemed to have been ratified, the agreement[282] is enforceable against the company. Moreover, the liability of the agent in respect of the agreement (or action) is discharged upon ratification (see further below).

Section 21(6)(a) of the Act states that, once ratified, 'the agreement is as enforceable against the company as if the company had been a party to the agreement when it was made.' The question arises whether this wording lends retrospective effect to pre-incorporation contracts. This is an important issue in practice because it determines the point at which the company obtains rights and incurs obligations under the contract. For instance, it would determine the time when the profits of a business that is being sold under a pre-incorporation contract accrue to the company.[283] Ideally, pre-incorporation contracts ought indeed to be retrospective, with the retrospectivity extending to the date that the contract was *entered into* by the agent and the third party, as opposed to the date that the company was *incorporated*. Attributing retrospectivity to s 21 would be in line with the concept of ratification at common law.

The wording of s 21(6)(a) (above), which is based on the wording of the equivalent statutory provisions in many other jurisdictions, has unfortunately proved to be problematic and controversial, in that it fails to go far enough to evince a clear and unambiguous legislative intention of the retrospectivity of pre-incorporation contracts. One view is that the contract can be deemed to have been made no earlier than the time of *incorporation* of the company. The opposing view is that ratification in such terms gives the contract legal effect from the time it was *entered into* by the agent and the third party, and not only from the (later) time of the incorporation of the company. The drafters of the Act would have done well to have gone beyond the wording adopted in s 21(6)(a) so as to provide a clear and unambiguous provision that the company is bound retrospectively from the date the pre-incorporation contract was *entered into* by the agent and the third party.[284] As it happens, this issue remains unsettled under the Act.

(c) Liability of the promoter for a section 21 contract

The Act introduces the concept of the promoter's liability for pre-incorporation contracts.[285] This is a laudable reform of the underpinning policy approach adopted to pre-incorporation contracts in South African law.

---

[281] Although the concept of a deemed ratification may have its benefits, particularly from the point of view of the third party, it may also result in harsh and inflexible effects for the company to the extent that it stipulates a cut-off time without explicitly requiring that the board should have had knowledge of the pre-incorporation contract or action.

[282] This provision does not apply to pre-incorporation 'actions' (s 21(6)(a)).

[283] *Peak Lode Gold Mining Company v Union Government* 1932 TPD 48; R Jooste 'When do pre-incorporation contracts have retrospective effect?' 1998 *SALJ* 507 at 507.

[284] See Maleka Femida Cassim op cit n 262 at 388–9 and the authorities cited therein.

[285] See the discussion of the statutory warranty-type approach to promoter liability for pre-incorporation contracts, as compared and contrasted with the personal liability-type approach, in Maleka Femida Cassim op cit n 262.

In terms of s 21(2), the promoter is jointly and severally liable for *liabilities* created in terms of the pre-incorporation contract in two circumstances:

- if the company is not subsequently incorporated, or
- if the company, once incorporated, rejects any part of the pre-incorporation contract (or action).

To the extent that a pre-incorporation contract (or action) is ratified, whether this be an actual or a deemed ratification, the liability of the promoter is discharged and the agreement is instead enforceable against the company.[286]

A logical exception is made to the promoter's liability where the company, once incorporated, enters into an agreement on the same terms as the pre-incorporation contract or in substitution for it.[287] In other words, if the pre-incorporation contract is not ratified, but is instead novated or substituted by a new contract between the third party and the company, then the promoter is released from liability despite the company's failure to ratify the pre-incorporation contract. This is both logical and reasonable.[288]

By providing for promoter liability for s 21 pre-incorporation contracts, the Act undertakes a fundamental adjustment in the balance of the conflicting rights and liabilities of the company, the promoter and the third party. To elaborate, the former policy approach under the 1973 Act was effectively the protection of the company and the agent, at the expense of the third party (that is, the party with whom the agent purported to contract on behalf of the company). In practice this often operated to the detriment of the third party. For instance, if the company was never incorporated or if the company decided against ratifying the pre-incorporation contract, the 'contract' simply lapsed and (in the absence of an express provision to the contrary) the agent incurred no liability to the third party, who was consequently burdened with the risk of non-incorporation and/or non-ratification. This was criticised as being skewed in 'fail[ing] to afford justice to the third party' and being out of step with modern trends. It was contended that a 'complete, modern and comprehensive solution' should be adopted with 'a greater share of the risk of non-incorporation and/or non-ratification' falling on the promoter.[289] This in effect is what s 21 does, by imposing liability on the promoter in the event of non-incorporation or non-ratification of the pre-incorporation contract.

The question arises: With whom is the promoter 'jointly and severally liable' in terms of s 21(2)? The wording of s 21(2) read with s 21(1) provides that the promoter who enters into a pre-incorporation contract in the name of or on behalf of a company to be formed, is jointly and severally liable with 'any other such person' for liabilities created in terms of the pre-incorporation contract. The meaning of the phrase 'any other such person' is vague in this context. Perhaps the intention of the drafters is to cater for the situation where there is more than one promoter of a company that is yet to be formed. In this regard, in practice there is often more than one promoter or even a group of promoters. In some cases it is not

---

[286] Section 21(6)(*b*).
[287] Section 21(3). This provision does not apply to pre-incorporation 'actions'.
[288] Maleka Femida Cassim op cit n 262 at 377–8.
[289] Maleka Femida Cassim op cit n 262 at 365, 368–89, 398.

even the promoter him- or herself who signs the pre-incorporation contract, but an agent, employee, accountant or even a family member of the promoter. It is in the interests of fairness and equity that liability should not be confined merely to the signatory of the pre-incorporation contract in these instances; instead, liability under the (as yet unratified) pre-incorporation contract ought properly to be imposed also on all the other co-promoters jointly and severally.[290]

Such an interpretation of the section would also counter the potential for abuse of the signatory of the pre-incorporation contract in situations where the promoters-turned-executive-directors initially had an understanding among themselves that the pre-incorporation contract would be ratified by the company upon its formation, but subsequently in their capacity as directors, without legal justification refuse to ratify it. In such circumstances, it would be unfair to the particular promoter who signed the pre-incorporation contract to be held solely liable, since the breach occurred through no fault of his or her own.

Section 21 regrettably leaves open the potential for abuse by a 'fly-by-night company'. This essentially involves an opportunistic ratification or sham incorporation. Here the promoter, in the realisation that a pre-incorporation contract is no longer beneficial, procures a shell company or a company with little capital or assets to ratify the contract. The result is that the third party is merely left with a fruitless or meaningless right of action for breach of contract against a company without any assets. In this way, the promoter effectively escapes liability for the pre-incorporation contract. The unscrupulous promoter might take advantage of this loophole in circumstances where he or she no longer wishes the company to be bound by a particular pre-incorporation contract, for instance, due to changes in market conditions rendering the pre-incorporation contract unprofitable or due to the subsequent availability of a more favourable transaction. The fly-by-night company thus enables promoters to speculate at the expense of third parties, by having a genuine company ratify favourable pre-incorporation contracts, but avoiding liability on unfavourable ones by having them ratified by a fly-by-night company.[291]

Section 21(7) of the Act provides that a promoter, who bears any liability for a rejected pre-incorporation contract (or action), may assert a claim against the company for any benefit it has received, or is entitled to receive, in terms of the agreement (or action). It is noteworthy that the promoter's claim in terms of this provision lies against the company and not against the third party to the contract. This may prevent the unjustified enrichment of the company at the expense of the promoter, for instance where the company received real or personal property under a rejected pre-incorporation contract for which the promoter is liable.

It is not an automatic legal consequence that a promoter who is personally liable for *liabilities* under a pre-incorporation contract is also able to take the initiative of

---

[290] See further Maleka Femida Cassim op cit n 262 at 376–7.
[291] The court could perhaps pierce the corporate veil in these circumstances and impose liability for the company's breach of contract on the promoter. See further *Botha v Van Niekerk* 1983 (3) SA 513 (W). Although the court in *Botha v Van Niekerk* refused to pierce the veil, a future court may differ from *Botha v Van Niekerk* on this issue. See also s 163(4) of the Act dealing with the unconscionable abuse of the juristic personality of a company and chapter 2: The Legal Concept of a Company.

enforcing personal liability against the third party.[292] In other words, personal liability for the liabilities does not invariably mean that the promoter is entitled also to the *benefits* of the contract or to exact performance of the contract. Unlike the equivalent statutory provisions in many other jurisdictions, s 21(2) is silent on whether the personally liable promoter may demand the benefits of the contract from the third party.

(d) Other important issues

The Act is similarly silent on the rights of the parties during the interim period between the execution of the pre-incorporation contract and the company's ratification of it. Of particular practical significance is the question whether the third party may unilaterally withdraw from a pre-incorporation contract prior to its ratification and, if not, how and by whom this is to be enforced. These issues are simply and disappointingly left unresolved in s 21 of the Act.

A further interesting issue is whether a promoter is able to contract out of his or her liability under s 21. It is significant that the draft Companies Bill, 2007[293] expressly permitted the promoter to contract out of his or her liability under a pre-incorporation contract. But notably, this provision has since been deleted and does not form part of the Act. The implication is that the legislature did not intend the promoter to have the power to contract out of his or her liability. It would of course ultimately be for the court to decide this vital issue. The anti-avoidance provisions in terms of s 6(1) of the Act may be quite significant in this regard.[294]

A valuable provision that has regrettably been omitted from s 21 is the judicial discretion empowering the court to fine-tune the balance between the liability of the company and that of the promoter, by apportioning liability between them, where it would be just and equitable in a particular case. This judicial discretion would be very useful in enabling the court to counter many of the abuses to which pre-incorporation contracts are subject and to draw a proper balance between the interests of the parties concerned. Although earlier drafts of the Companies Bill included this provision,[295] it is regrettable and unfortunate that it was omitted from the final version of the Act.

Turning briefly to the Transitional Arrangements, s 21 does not apply to pre-existing companies.[296] This is because companies that are already incorporated would clearly not enter into pre-incorporation contracts. Furthermore, any pending company registrations, that were already filed under the 1973 Act by the time that the new Act came into effect, must be concluded under the 1973 Act with the effect that those companies are regarded as 'pre-existing companies'[297] to which s 21 will not apply.

---

[292] See eg *Gardner v Richardt* 1974 (3) SA 768 (C) 770; see also *Braymist v Wise Finance Co Ltd* [2002] Ch 273 where this question came before the court in the context of s 36C of the UK Companies Act 1985.
[293] Clause 18(1) of the draft Companies Bill, 2007 (GN 166 *GG* 29630 of 12 February 2007).
[294] See further 4.3.2 above and chapter 1: Introduction to the New Companies Act.
[295] See Companies Bill, 2008 [B61–2008].
[296] Schedule 5 item 5.
[297] Schedule 5 item 3(1) and (3). See further chapter 21: Transitional Arrangements.

4.7.3 The *stipulatio alteri* or contract for the benefit of a third party

The *stipulatio alteri* is a common-law device, arising from Roman-Dutch law, by which two parties contract with each other for the benefit of a third party. Both parties contract in their capacity as principals and not as agents.

It was held in the leading case of *McCullogh v Fernwood Estate Ltd*[298] that in a *stipulatio alteri*, the third party need not be in existence at the date of the contract. *McCullogh's* case held further that the *stipulatio alteri* may be used by a promoter to stipulate in favour of an unformed company that he or she is engaged in bringing into existence. The likelihood is that under the new Act, the *stipulatio alteri* may continue to be used as an alternative method for pre-incorporation contracts, where the promoter (or trustee) acts as a *principal*.

In a *stipulatio alteri*, the promoter (known also as the stipulator or promisee in this context) enters into a contract with the other party (termed the promisor) for the benefit of the company yet to be formed (the third party in the context of the *stipulatio alteri*). It is essential that the promoter or trustee must act as a principal and not as an agent. In other words, the promoter contracts in his or her own name and not in the name of the company. It is this factor that distinguishes the *stipulatio alteri* from statutory agency in terms of s 21 of the Act. Accordingly, in a *stipulatio alteri* the promoter enters into the pre-incorporation contract as a principal, whereas in a s 21 pre-incorporation contract the promoter apparently acts as an agent on behalf of the company.

Under the *stipulatio alteri* the company, once incorporated, has an election to accept or adopt the benefit of the contract.[299] The company must make its election within the time limit stated in the contract or, if there is no stated time limit, then within a reasonable time depending on the facts of the case.[300] The company's acceptance must generally be communicated to the promisor, whether expressly or tacitly and in any manner generally used for acceptance. Upon acceptance by the company, it becomes a party to the contract with the promisor.[301]

Consequently, the company is not bound by the contract unless and until it elects to adopt the benefit of the contract. Effectively, the contract between the promoter and the promisor creates an offer to the company, which the company (once incorporated) may accept and thereby become a party to the contract.[302] A new contractual relationship then comes into being between the promisor and the

---

[298] 1920 AD 204.

[299] Note that it is incorrect to refer to the acceptance by the company as ratification. This is because ratification only applies in the context of agency (*Sentrale Kunsmis Korporasie (Edms) Bpk v NKP Kunsmisverspreiders (Edms) Bpk* 1970 (3) SA 367 (A) 394).

[300] *Bagradi v Cavendish Transport Co (Pty) Ltd* 1957 (1) SA 663 (D) 668.

[301] At this point the contract between the promoter and the promisor is often terminated, as all the obligations between them will generally have been discharged. However, if there are remaining terms that apply as between the promoter and the promisor, then the contract between them may continue.

[302] *McCullogh v Fernwood Estate Ltd* 1920 AD 204 at 205–6.

company. If the company accepts the benefit, it must also accept all the consequent obligations and other terms of the contract.[303]

Until such time as the company makes its election, the parties to the contract are the promoter and the promisor. During that time, the promisor cannot unilaterally withdraw from or cancel the contract. Should the promisor attempt to do so, the promoter may obtain an interdict against him or her to prevent the promisor from doing any act that has the effect of nullifying his or her undertaking.[304] Failing an interdict, and if the promisor repudiates the contract, the promoter may claim damages for breach of contract.[305] However, specific performance (in respect of an obligation ultimately to be due to the company) will not be granted in favour of the promoter, unless the terms of the contract so provide.[306]

From the perspective of the company, the disadvantage of the *stipulatio alteri* is that, prior to acceptance by the company, the promoter and the promisor may mutually cancel the contract.[307] This is because the promoter acts as a principal. The mutual cancellation of the contract, whether prior to the formation of the company or prior to the election by the company, clearly has the effect of depriving the company of the benefit of the contract.

An important question is whether the promoter is personally liable in the event that the company is not incorporated or if the company chooses not to adopt the benefit of the contract. Unless the contract so provides, the promoter does not become personally liable on the contract.[308] Provided that the contract does not state otherwise, the contract simply lapses in these circumstances. Accordingly, the promisor would usually be well advised to ensure that the particular *stipulatio alteri* agreement indeed provides for the personal liability of the promoter. Furthermore, where the company fails to adopt the benefit of the contract, the promoter is not automatically entitled to step into the shoes of the company and insist on accepting the benefit of the contract for him- or herself or to personally exact performance of the contract, save where the contract so provides.[309]

There are no formalities for the *stipulatio alteri* other than those imposed by the general law of contract for the relevant transaction.

It is likely that s 21 of the Act does not curtail the use of the *stipulatio alteri* as a device for entering into pre-incorporation contracts, as discussed above. The retention of the common-law *stipulatio alteri* as a method for contracting for the benefit of a company yet to be formed, is commendable. It does, however, mean that problems may continue to be encountered under the new Act, in determining which type of contract was entered into. This issue caused substantial difficulty

---

[303] *McCullogh v Fernwood Estate Ltd* (supra) at 206. Whether the adoption of the benefit of the *stipulatio alteri* operates retrospectively is an unsettled area of law. In practice, the ideal situation would be to include a term in the contract that either provides for or prohibits retrospectivity.
[304] *African Universal Stores Ltd v Dean* 1926 CPD 390 at 395; *Semer v Retief and Berman* 1948 (1) SA 182 (C).
[305] *Bagradi v Cavendish Transport Co (Pty) Ltd* 1957 (1) SA 663 (D).
[306] *Gardner v Richardt* 1974 (3) SA 768 (C); *Nine Hundred Umgeni Road (Pty) Ltd v Bali* 1986 (1) SA 1 (A).
[307] *Crookes v Watson* 1956 (1) SA 277 (A).
[308] *Gardner v Richardt* (supra); *Nine Hundred Umgeni Road Ltd v Bali* (supra).
[309] Ibid.

under the previous company law regime in cases where the wording of the contract was ambiguous. The question whether the parties have entered into a *stipulatio alteri*, in which the promoter acts as a principal, or whether they have entered into a s 21 pre-incorporation contract, in which the promoter apparently acts as an agent for the company, has important practical implications. Different consequences may flow from each of the two types of contract, as discussed above. For instance, while the promoter under a s 21 pre-incorporation contract is personally liable for the liabilities, the promoter in a *stipulatio alteri* is only personally liable if the contract so provides; and whereas s 21 pre-incorporation contracts are apparently retrospective, the issue of the retrospectivity of the *stipulatio alteri* is less clear. Under the previous company law regime, the difficulty in determining which type of contract was involved was largely occasioned by uncertainty concerning the guiding criteria. The deciding factor was held to be the intention of the parties to the particular contract, which depended on the facts of the case, and was determined from the terms of the contract and the surrounding circumstances.[310]

Besides s 21 of the Act and the *stipulatio alteri*, there are certain other methods on which a promoter may rely. Included among these is an offer made to the promoter 'or his (or her) nominee'[311] or the cession of an option.[312]

There is no reason why these common-law methods should not continue to apply.

---

[310] *Martian Entertainments (Pty) Ltd v Berger* 1949 (4) SA 583 (E) at 589–91. See further *Sentrale Kunsmis Korporasie (Edms) Bpk v NKP Kunsmisverspreiders (Edms) Bpk* 1970 (3) SA 367 (A) 394; *McCullogh v Fernwood Estate* 1920 AD 204, and *Ex parte Vickerman* 1935 CPD 429 for the position and guiding criteria under the 1973 Act and the Companies Act 46 of 1926.
[311] *Visser v Van Tonder* 1986 (2) SA 500 (T) 502.
[312] *Trever Investments (Pty) Ltd v Friedhelm Investments (Pty) Ltd* 1982 (1) SA 7 (A) 16.

CHAPTER 5

CORPORATE CAPACITY, AGENCY AND THE TURQUAND RULE

Farouk HI Cassim

5.1	LEGAL CAPACITY OF THE COMPANY	154
	5.1.1 Introduction	154
	(a) Historical development	154
	(b) The object of the *ultra vires* doctrine	155
	(c) The legal consequences of an *ultra vires* contract	155
	(d) The failure of the *ultra vires* doctrine	156
	(e) The reform of the *ultra vires* doctrine	157
	5.1.2 Legal capacity under the Act (ss 19 and 20)	158
	5.1.3 Restricting the company's capacity under the Act: Overview	159
	5.1.4 Further discussion of the effect of s 20(1)(*a*)(i)	161
	5.1.5 The internal consequences of an *ultra vires* act	161
	5.1.6 Ratification (s 20(2) and (3))	162
	5.1.7 The shareholder's claim for damages (s 20(6))	163
	5.1.8 The shareholders' right to restrain an unauthorised act (s 20(4) and (5))	164
	5.1.9 The protection of the *bona fide* third party	165
	5.1.10 The requirements of good faith and actual knowledge (s 20(5)(*a*) and (*b*))	166
	5.1.11 Conclusion	167
5.2	THE DOCTRINE OF CONSTRUCTIVE NOTICE	168
5.3	THE TURQUAND RULE (IE THE PRESUMPTION OF COMPLIANCE WITH FORMAL AND PROCEDURAL REQUIREMENTS)	169
	5.3.1 The common law	169
	5.3.2 The Turquand Rule and the Act (s 20(7) and (8))	171
5.4	REPRESENTATION AND THE AUTHORITY OF THE DIRECTORS	173
	5.4.1 Actual authority	174
	5.4.2 Ostensible authority	174
	(a) Requirements for ostensible authority	175
	(b) Ostensible authority and breach of fiduciary duty	176
	5.4.3 Usual authority	176
	5.4.4 Ratification	178

5.1 LEGAL CAPACITY OF THE COMPANY

5.1.1 Introduction

(a) Historical development

In order to understand the neoteric approach to corporate capacity, it is essential to examine, albeit briefly, the *ultra vires*[1] doctrine and to have regard to its historical development. This would also provide some insight into and an appreciation of the nature of the intractable problem of reforming the *ultra vires* doctrine. The doctrine has undoubtedly exerted a very strong influence on corporate law philosophy in general.

For a contract to be binding and enforceable against a company, apart from having to comply with the legal formalities for a valid contract, it was always necessary for two requirements to be fulfilled. First, the company must have had the legal capacity to enter into the contract; and secondly, the director or officer representing the company must have had authority to enter into the contract on behalf of the company. Both capacity and authority were essential prerequisites for a binding contract. Capacity and authority, although linked, are quite different legal concepts. Capacity in this context means the legal competency and the powers of the company, while authority refers to the power of a company's director or officer or other individual to act on behalf of the company. Authority may be regarded as delegated power.

The legal capacity of a company under the previous company law regime was determined by the main object of the company as set out in the objects clause of its memorandum of association.[2] The clause would specify the purposes for which the company was formed. The objects clause was taken to define the existence of the company as a legal person. According to the *ultra vires* doctrine, a company existed in law only for the purposes of the object stated in the objects clause of its memorandum of association. This included any objects that were reasonably incidental or ancillary to the company's main object. Beyond these limits, a company had no legal existence.

Consequently, if a company, in performing some act or in entering into some contract or transaction, had exceeded its legal capacity as determined from its objects clause, the company ceased to exist as a legal person for the purposes of that contract. It followed that such a contract was absolutely null and void and could not be ratified even by the unanimous assent of all its shareholders. In this statement lies the kernel of the *ultra vires* doctrine as expounded in *Ashbury Railway Carriage and Iron Co v Riche*.[3]

In *Re Horsley & Weight Ltd*[4] the court reaffirmed the long-standing principle that a company had legal capacity to do only those acts that its objects clause empowered it to do or that were reasonably incidental or consequential to it. An

---

[1] By *ultra vires* is literally meant, beyond or outside the powers.
[2] Section 52(1)(*b*) of the Companies Act 61 of 1973 (hereafter 'the 1973 Act') made it mandatory for a company to state its main object in the objects clause of its memorandum of association.
[3] (1875) LR 7 HL 653; *Rolled Steel Products (Holdings) Ltd v British Steel Corporation* [1985] 3 All ER 52.
[4] [1982] 3 All ER 1045 (CA) 1050–1.

ultra vires contract, being a complete nullity, could not become *intra vires* by reason of ratification, lapse of time, acquiescence or delay.[5]

From this brief discussion so far, an *ultra vires* act may be defined as some act or transaction entered into by the company which, although not unlawful or contrary to public policy, is beyond the legitimate powers of the company.[6]

The term '*ultra vires*' must be confined to those transactions that were null and void simply because they fall outside the scope of the company's powers or activities, as stated in its constitution. It is incorrect to refer to an illegal transaction[7] or an unauthorised act[8] as being *ultra vires*.[9] To be *ultra vires*, the transaction in question must be one that is outside the capacity of the company and not merely one that is in excess of the powers or authority of the company's representative.

(b) The object of the ultra vires doctrine

The object of the *ultra vires* doctrine as stated in *Ashbury Railway Carriage and Iron Co v Riche*[10] was twofold: First, to protect investors and shareholders of the company so that they would know the purposes for which their money could be used; and secondly, to protect creditors of the company. Shareholders and creditors were, in theory, able to assess the risk of buying shares in the company or dealing with the company simply from the main object of the company.[11] The protection of shareholders and creditors was at the time, and still is, regarded as being of great importance to company law. This included the object of ensuring that the funds of a company were not dissipated on activities not authorised by the constitution of the company. In modern company law, perhaps more effective means of protecting shareholders, creditors and investors may have been developed, but the objectives remain the same.

(c) The legal consequences of an ultra vires contract

The legal consequences of an *ultra vires* contract went further than merely rendering the contract null and void. This was merely the external consequence[12] of an *ultra vires* contract, namely that the contract was absolutely null and void. The contract could not be enforced by either the company or the other party to the contract. But apart from the external consequences, there were also two important internal consequences to every *ultra vires* contract that still remain relevant to modern company law and to the Companies Act 71 of 2008 (hereafter 'the Act'). By 'internal' consequences

---

[5] *York Corporation v Henry Leetham & Sons Ltd* [1924] 1 Ch 557; *Central Transportation Co v Pullman's Palace Car* 139 US 24 60 (1890).
[6] See FHI Cassim 'The Rise, Fall and Reform of the *Ultra Vires* Doctrine' (1998) 10 *SA Merc LJ* 293.
[7] See *Brady v Brady* [1988] BCLC 579 (HL).
[8] *Aveling Barford v Perion Ltd* [1989] BCLC 626 at 631 (ChD).
[9] See Brown-Wilkinson LJ in *Rolled Steel Products (Holdings) Ltd v British Steel Corporation* [1985] 3 All ER 52.
[10] (1875) LR 7 HL 653.
[11] *Cotman v Brougham* [1918] AC 514 (HL) 520.
[12] By the 'external' consequence is meant the legal position between the company and the other party to the contract.

is meant the consequences that arise between the company, its directors and its shareholders.

The first internal consequence is that in every *ultra vires* contract entered into by the directors or other company representative acting on behalf of the company, the directors could not possibly have had authority to enter into the contract, since a director or an agent could never have authority that exceeds the legal capacity of the company (or principal). The errant director concerned would necessarily be in breach of the fiduciary duty not to exceed his or her authority. To put it differently, if the company does not have legal capacity (ie the power to enter into the contract), its directors or other agent could not possibly have had authority to enter into the contract on behalf of the company. The directors' authority must obviously be limited by the company's capacity. It follows that the directors would inevitably have exceeded their authority and would as a result be liable to the company for damages for breach of fiduciary duty not to exceed their authority.[13] Every director is under a legal duty not to act beyond the limits of his or her authority.[14] The liability of the directors arises irrespective of any fault on the part of the directors.

The second internal consequence of an *ultra vires* contract was that, since the company in entering into an *ultra vires* contract would have failed to comply with the requirements of its constitution, every shareholder of the company was entitled at common law to institute legal proceedings to restrain the company from entering into or performing an *ultra vires* contract. The constitution of the company formed and still forms the basis of a statutory contractual relationship between the company and its shareholders.[15] Apart from statute, the company's memorandum and articles of association were long held at common law to constitute a contract between the company and its shareholders.[16]

The *ultra vires* doctrine consequently played, and continues to play, a very definite role in internal disputes between the shareholders, directors and the company. Moreover, a company that was unable to fulfil its main object could be wound up on the grounds that winding-up was 'just and equitable' given the failure of the company's substratum.[17]

To sum up: Historically, there were thus two facets to every *ultra vires* contract that remain relevant to this day, namely, the external consequence that the contract was null and void, and the internal consequences that the directors would incur liability for breach of fiduciary duty and that the shareholders were entitled to restrain the company from entering into or performing an *ultra vires* contract.

(d) The failure of the ultra vires doctrine

Companies were easily able to circumvent the *ultra vires* doctrine by specifying in detail and as widely as possible in their objects clauses all the business activities the company might conceivably wish to pursue, together with a comprehensive

---

[13] See further chapter 12: The Duties and the Liability of Directors and s 77(3)(*a*).
[14] *Cullerne v London and Suburban General Permanent Building Society* (1890) 25 QBD 485.
[15] See s 65(2) of the 1973 Act and s 15(6) of the Act. See further chapter 4: Formation of Companies and the Company Constitution, where this is discussed in detail.
[16] *Hickman v Kent or Romney Marsh Sheep Breeders' Association* [1915] Ch 881.
[17] Section 344(*h*) of the 1973 Act.

and detailed catalogue of ancillary powers.[18] Each clause was typically designated an independent objects clause, with the result that a company could have legal capacity to carry on every conceivable type of business activity. Lord Wrenbury in *Cotman v Brougham*[19] observed that the point had been reached where the function of the objects clause was 'not to specify, not to disclose, but to bury beneath a mass of words the real object or objects of the company with the intent that every conceivable form of activity shall be found included somewhere within its terms'. Instead of disclosing the company's main business activities, the objects clause concealed it.

Drafting techniques thus enabled companies to evade the *ultra vires* doctrine. In consequence of the width of objects clauses, the *ultra vires* doctrine developed into an illusory protection for the shareholders and a pitfall for unwary third parties dealing with the company.[20] The facts of *Re Jon Beauforte (London) Ltd*[21] vividly illustrate how absolutely correct these remarks (of the Cohen Committee) were.

The acceptance by the House of Lords in *Cotman v Brougham* (supra) of the validity of the independent objects clause was taken even further in *Bell Houses Ltd v City Wall Properties Ltd*,[22] where the court accepted the validity of a subjective objects clause. A subjective objects clause typically empowered the board of directors to carry on any trade or business whatsoever which, in the opinion of the board, could advantageously be carried on by the company in connection with any business of the company. In accepting the validity of this type of objects clause, the court deprived the *ultra vires* doctrine of all its remaining vitality. It was consequently remarked that '[t]he victory of the subjective objects clause must be the beginning of the end for ultra vires'.[23] *Bell Houses Ltd v City Wall Properties Ltd* reduced the *ultra vires* doctrine to obsolescence. This doctrine no longer served any positive or useful purpose.

(e) The reform of the ultra vires doctrine

After the decision of the court in *Bell Houses Ltd v City Wall Properties Ltd* (supra), almost all common-law jurisdictions that had adopted the *ultra vires* doctrine abandoned or reformed the doctrine by statutory amendment. In South African law this was done by s 36 of the Companies Act 61 of 1973 (hereafter 'the 1973 Act'). Section 36 did not abolish the *ultra vires* doctrine entirely. Instead, it abolished only the external consequences of an *ultra vires* contract while preserving its internal consequences. It accordingly remained mandatory for a company to state its object(s) in the main objects clause of its memorandum of association.[24]

---

[18] See FHI Cassim op cit n 6 at 295.
[19] [1918] AC 514 (HL) 520 at 523.
[20] Report of the Committee on Company Law Amendment (the Cohen Committee) Cmnd 6659 (June 1945) para 12.
[21] (1953) Ch 131.
[22] [1966] 2 All ER 674 (CA).
[23] KW Wedderburn 'The death of ultra vires' (1966) 29 *MLR* 673 at 676.
[24] Section 36 is briefly discussed here as the approach it adopts is relevant to the Companies Act of 2008.

In terms of s 36 of the 1973 Act, an *ultra vires* contract was no longer void by reason only of a lack of capacity or a lack of authority on the part of the directors to enter into an *ultra vires* contract on behalf of the company. The directors' lack of authority did not affect the validity of the contract, provided that such a lack of authority arose only from a lack of capacity. Externally, the *ultra vires* contract was valid and binding between the company and the other party to the contract (ie the third party); either party to the contract could enforce it.

This was reinforced by a statutory estoppel that precluded both the company and the third party from asserting or relying, in any legal proceedings, on such a lack of capacity, power or authority. The basic theme of s 36, which as we shall see later is also adopted by the new Act, is that if a company, in legal proceedings against the third party, cannot assert or rely on its lack of capacity, then its lack of capacity cannot be proved. The dispute must then be resolved as if the lack of capacity did not exist.[25]

Under s 36 of the 1973 Act (unlike s 20(5) of the new Act), the knowledge, whether actual or constructive, of the third party that the contract was beyond the capacity of the company, was deemed to be irrelevant. It was also not a requirement that the third party should act in good faith.

The internal consequences of an *ultra vires* contract were, however, preserved by s 36 of the 1973 Act. As between the company, its directors or shareholders, the directors would still be liable to the company for breach of fiduciary duty not to exceed their authority, and shareholders of the company were entitled to restrain the company or its directors from entering into an *ultra vires* contract. But an important change was that once the contract was concluded, shareholders lost their right to restrain performance of the contract. The basis was that the contract, in terms of s 36, was no longer void. Furthermore, the statutory estoppel in s 36 precluded reliance on or assertion of a lack of capacity in any legal proceedings. In this event (ie once the contract was concluded), the liability of the directors for breach of fiduciary duty would still apply to render the miscreant directors liable in damages to the company for any loss suffered as a result of the unauthorised contract.

5.1.2 Legal capacity under the Act (ss 19 and 20)

The modern approach to the legal capacity of a company is that it is archaic and outdated to restrict a company to a specific business activity. In line with this approach, the Act provides that, unless a company's Memorandum of Incorporation provides otherwise[26] a company has the legal capacity and the powers of an individual.[27] This does not necessarily mean that a company may do everything that a natural person may do, although the converse is also true. There are certain acts that by their very nature a metaphysical entity, such as a company, cannot do. The usual examples are to enter into a contract of marriage, to exercise a right to vote, or to have a right of audience in a superior court. A company cannot appear in person in a superior court, unless it is represented by a duly qualified legal

---

[25] FHI Cassim op cit n 6 at 307.
[26] Section 19(1)*(b)*(ii).
[27] Section 19(1)*(b)*. This takes us right back to 17th century England when in the case of *Sutton's Hospital* (1612) 10 Co Rep 23a it was held that a charter company had the capacity of a natural person.

practitioner.[28] Standing up in court and arguing a case is not something that a juristic person is capable of doing.[29]

Section 19(1)*(b)*, in providing that a company has all the legal powers and capacity of an individual, follows the approach adopted in other common-law jurisdictions. For instance, in Australian law, s 161 of the Corporations Laws 1989 states that a company is to have the legal capacity and powers of a natural person despite any restrictions or prohibitions on the exercise of its powers in its memorandum of association. According to s 16(1) of the New Zealand Companies Act 1993 all companies have full capacity to carry on or undertake any business or activity and for this purpose are given full rights, powers and privileges. The Canada Business Corporations Act 1985 confers on companies the capacity of a natural person. Section 31 of the UK Companies Act 2006 states that, unless a company's articles of association specifically restrict the objects of the company, its objects are unrestricted.

Equally importantly, it is no longer mandatory in terms of the Act for a company to have an objects clause in its Memorandum of Incorporation.[30] This alone removes much of the legal complexity surrounding the determination of the main object of the company, its ancillary objects, and their development into the main object of the company, as provided for in s 33(2) of the 1973 Act.[31] In terms of s 33(2) of the 1973 Act, a company's main object and hence its capacity could change by operation of law in accordance with changes in the main business of the company. These unnecessary legal complexities have now been removed by making an objects clause optional. There is no longer any need for an objects clause to broaden the capacity of a company.

5.1.3 Restricting the company's capacity under the Act: Overview

Although companies generally have unrestricted legal capacity under the new Act, a company's Memorandum of Incorporation may, on an optional basis, impose restrictions, limitations, or qualifications on its purposes, powers or activities (s 20(1)). When a company restricts its objects, it follows that its powers cannot be exercised for a purpose that conflicts with such restrictions. This would not only be *ultra vires*, it would of necessity be beyond the authority of its directors (as explained in 5.1.1*(c)* above), hence the need for s 20(1)*(a)*. In terms of s 20(1)*(a)*, such restrictions however have no effect on the validity of the contract between the company and the other party to the contract (that is to say, externally). The contract remains valid and binding on both the company and the other party, subject to s 20(5). The company's lack of legal capacity will not necessarily invalidate the contract. This is further discussed below.

---

[28] *Lees Import and Export (Pvt) Ltd v Zimbabwe Banking Corporation Ltd* 1999 (4) SA 1119 (ZS); *Yates Investments (Pty) Ltd v Commissioner for Inland Revenue* 1956 (1) SA 364 (A); *Manong & Associates (Pty) Ltd v Minister of Public Works* 2010 (2) SA 167 (SCA) para 4. See further chapter 2: The Legal Concept of a Company.

[29] See MP Larkin and FHI Cassim in 1999 *Annual Survey of South African Law* at 409–411. See also s 19(1)*(b)*(i).

[30] This does not apply to a non-profit company, which would have to set out at least one object in its Memorandum of Incorporation. See further chapter 3: Types of Companies.

[31] See FHI Cassim op cit n 6 at 309–10.

Moreover, as with s 36 of the 1973 Act (discussed in 5.1.1*(e)* above), the directors' lack of authority resulting from a lack of capacity does not inevitably affect the validity of the contract. This is explicitly provided in s 20(1)*(a)*(ii), which states that no action of a company is void by reason *only* that, as a consequence of a limitation, restriction or qualification on the purposes, powers or activities of the company as specified in its Memorandum of Incorporation, the directors had no authority to authorise the action by the company. The underlying basis of this provision is the same as under s 36 of the 1973 Act (as discussed above), namely the directors' lack of authority must arise only from a lack of capacity. There must be no other reason for such a lack of authority.[32] Where this requirement is met, the contract or action will remain valid. (Section 20(1)*(a)* is further discussed in 5.1.4 below.)

As under s 36 of the 1973 Act, the new s 20(1)*(b)* contains a statutory estoppel that precludes either the company or the other party to the contract from relying on the limitation, restriction or qualification on the company's purposes, powers or activities, in order to assert that the contract is void. Consequently, the issue of non-compliance with the restrictions on the capacity of the company cannot be raised between the company and the other party to the contract (ie externally), although it may be raised internally as between the company, its directors and shareholders.

The *ultra vires* doctrine is preserved internally as a form of shareholder protection and protection for the company. This is not very different from s 36 of the 1973 Act. The directors would still incur liability to the company for breach of fiduciary duty, and the shareholders (and others, as discussed below) would still be entitled in certain circumstances to restrain the directors from entering into the contract.

It is clear from this discussion that the Act abolishes the *ultra vires* doctrine externally, but has preserved it internally to the extent that a lack of capacity may be raised only as between the company, its directors and its shareholders. The internal consequences of an *ultra vires* contract enable shareholders of a company to exercise some control over the activities of its directors and to restrain them from entering into an *ultra vires* contract. The old legal principles relating to the consequences of an *ultra vires* contract have retained both their relevance as well as their importance. In fact, they are enhanced as a result of being codified in statute. The Act adopts the approach advocated as long ago as 1945 by the Cohen Committee,[33] which recommended that *ultra vires* should be abrogated as far as outsiders are concerned but internally as between the company, its shareholders and directors, it should be preserved. The Committee stated:[34] ' . . . every company . . . should have as regards third parties the same powers as an individual . . . .'

---

[32] If the directors do not have authority for a reason other than (or a reason additional to) a lack of capacity on the part of the company, then the contract is not binding on the company, even against a *bona fide* third party, unless the unauthorised act is ratified by the shareholders of the company. As a result of s 20(1)*(a)*(ii) a contract for which the directors had no authority as a result of a lack of capacity on the part of the company may become binding on the company without the need for any ratification.

[33] Report of the Committee on Company Law Amendment, 1945, Cmnd 6659 para 12.

[34] Para 12.

Even though a company's Memorandum of Incorporation may impose restrictions on the capacity of a company, these restrictions operate in effect as though they were restrictions on the authority of the directors to enter into certain types of contracts on behalf of the company. The question of capacity has in this way become a question of authority, which is very much a live issue. The *ultra vires* doctrine operates now as an internal control mechanism. A breach of these restrictions or limitations is, in some ways, nothing more than a breach of the company's Memorandum of Incorporation, which in turn is a breach of the fiduciary and statutory duties of the directors of the company.[35]

5.1.4 Further discussion of the effect of s 20(1)*(a)*(i)

Section 20(1)*(a)*(i) states that no action of a company is void by reason only that the action was prohibited by a limitation, restriction or qualification on the purposes, powers or activities of the company. This provision is widely drafted.

The conceptual difficulty that immediately arises is that an act or action cannot be that of the company if, due to a limitation, restriction or qualification in its Memorandum of Incorporation, the company does not have the capacity to enter into a contract that is inconsistent with these restrictions. How can it be an 'action of the company'?[36] It is arguable that this conceptual difficulty may be overcome by reliance on the organic theory that treats the acts of the board of directors or shareholders in general meeting as acts of the company.[37]

The word 'only' in s 20(1)*(a)*(i) serves the useful purpose of excluding from the ambit of the section any contract that is illegal or unlawful. The wording of s 20(1)*(a)*(i) puts it beyond doubt that the section applies to an action or contract of the company that is void by reason *only* that it was prohibited by a limitation, restriction or qualification on the company's purposes, powers or activities in its Memorandum of Incorporation. If the action or contract in question is void because it is illegal or unlawful or there is any other additional ground for the nullity of the contract, s 20(1) will not apply to validate such a contract. Such a contract would fall outside the scope of s 20(1). This was also the position under s 36 of the 1973 Act.

The word 'action' in s 20(1)*(a)* is wider than a 'transaction' entered into by the company. An 'action' would include contractual activity as well as a unilateral non-commercial activity such as a donation to a charity or political party. In *International Sales and Agencies Ltd v Marcus*[38] and *Re Halt Garage (1964) Ltd*[39] it was stated that a gratuitous disposition of a company's assets may or may not be a 'transaction', but it is submitted that it would most likely be an 'action' of the company.

5.1.5 The internal consequences of an *ultra vires* act

As stated above, s 20(1)*(b)*(i) and (ii) preserves the internal consequences of an *ultra vires* contract. It permits the issue of capacity to be raised in proceedings

---
[35] See s 77(3)*(a)* and chapter 12: The Duties and the Liability of Directors.
[36] See FHI Cassim op cit n 6 at 308–9.
[37] See *Rolled Steel Products (Holdings) Ltd v British Steel Corporation* (supra).
[38] [1982] 3 All ER 551.
[39] [1982] 3 All ER 1016 (ChD) 1024.

between: *(a)* the company and its shareholders, directors or prescribed officers; or *(b)* between the shareholders and directors or prescribed officers of the company.

Two comments may be made with regard to this provision. First, it is now extended to include prescribed officers. This extension is new in our law. Secondly, it may be noted that, apart from this extension, s 20(1)*(b)*(i) and (ii) is virtually identical to the wording of the exception in s 36 of the 1973 Act.[40] As with s 36 of the 1973 Act, reference is made twice to the shareholders and directors of the company.[41] There is a very definite reason for this wording, namely that s 20(1)*(b)*(i) is an implicit reference to the action instituted by the company against the miscreant director for breach of fiduciary duty owed to the company[42] and the action (by the shareholders, directors or prescribed officers) to restrain the company from acting in contravention of the constitutional restriction on its capacity; whereas s 20(1)*(b)*(ii) is an implicit reference to the shareholder action to restrain the directors or prescribed officers from doing any act in contravention of the limitation, restriction or qualification in the company's Memorandum of Incorporation. This preserves the internal consequences of an *ultra vires* action. The internal remedies are discussed in more detail below.

5.1.6   Ratification (s 20(2) and (3))

Section 20(2) states that, if a company's Memorandum of Incorporation limits, restricts or qualifies the purposes, powers or activities of the company, or limits the authority of the directors to perform an act on behalf of the company, the shareholders may, by special resolution, ratify any action of the company or the directors that is inconsistent with any such limit, restriction or qualification. But no action of the company may be ratified if it is in contravention of the Act (s 20(3)).

It is noteworthy that s 20(2) refers to the directors of the company without any reference to the prescribed officers of the company. Consequently, the unauthorised act of a prescribed officer may not be ratified by special resolution in terms of s 20(2). The relevant act must be an act of the company or its directors. It is also notable that s 20(2) does not explicitly require the limitation of the authority of the directors to result *only* from the company's lack of capacity.

Section 20(2) is modelled on s 35 of the UK Companies Act 1985, as amended by s 108 of the Companies Act 1989, which similarly enables an *ultra vires* transaction to be ratified by a special resolution.[43] Section 20(2) of our Companies Act thus overrules *Ashbury Railway Carriage and Iron Co v Riche* (discussed above in 5.1.1*(a)*) which laid down the principle that, since an *ultra vires* contract is an absolute nullity, it could not be ratified even by the unanimous assent of all the shareholders of the company.

---

[40] Viz '... except as between the company and its members or directors, or as between its members and directors ...'.
[41] See SJ Naudé 'Company Contracts: The Effect of Section 36 of the New Act' (1974) 91 *SALJ* 315.
[42] In certain circumstances shareholders or other interested persons may be entitled to enforce this duty on behalf of the company by way of a derivative action.
[43] See FHI Cassim op cit n 6 at 301–2.

It is significant that s 35(3) of the UK Companies Act 1985 provided, until its repeal by s 39 of the UK Companies Act 2006, that such a special resolution would not affect any liability incurred by the directors for breach of fiduciary duty. Relief from the directors' liability for breach of fiduciary duty had to be ratified by a second, separate special resolution. There was thus a double special resolution requirement, ie a special resolution to ratify the *ultra vires* transaction and a further, separate special resolution to absolve the directors from liability incurred as a result of the transaction.

In comparison, s 20(2) of the Companies Act of 2008 specifically refers to a special resolution to ratify '... any action by the *company* or the *directors* ...' [emphasis added]. This suggests that the special resolution is, as in English law, intended to ratify the *ultra vires* act of the *company*, so that it becomes fully binding on the *company*. The section refers also to any action by the *directors*, that is inconsistent with any such limit, restriction or qualification. This suggests that the special resolution may also ratify the directors' breach of fiduciary duty in failing to comply with the limitation, restriction or qualification in the company's Memorandum of Incorporation. The important question that is left unanswered in s 20(2) is whether both the *ultra vires* action by the company as well as the directors' breach of fiduciary duty may be ratified by the shareholders in one special resolution, or whether a further, second and separate special resolution is required. It is arguable though, that once the *ultra vires* action by the company is ratified by special resolution, it is no longer *ultra vires* or unauthorised, thereby retroactively relieving the directors from liability for breach of fiduciary duty. Ratification operates retroactively to authorise and adopt the act in question as an act of the company. Unlike the UK Companies Act, it appears therefore that only one special resolution is required by s 20(2) of the new Act. Section 20(2) and s 20(6) could certainly have been more carefully drafted to remove doubt or uncertainty over the issue. In practice, the solution would be to draft the relevant special resolution so that it refers to the ratification of both the action of the company and the action of the directors.

The clear wording of s 35(3) of the UK Companies Act 1985 had left no room for doubt on the issue. Unsurprisingly, the UK Companies Act 2006 has repealed s 35(3) and, together with it, the requirement of a double special resolution, with the result that the directors' breach of fiduciary duty is now ratifiable by a mere ordinary resolution of a disinterested majority of the shareholders[44] or, alternatively, by the unanimous assent of all the shareholders. Ironically, our new Companies Act has adopted obsolete statutory provisions that two years ago were discarded in England by the UK Companies Act of 2006.

5.1.7 The shareholder's claim for damages (s 20(6))

Section 20(6) of the Act provides that each shareholder of a company has a claim for damages against any person who fraudulently or due to gross negligence[45]

---

[44] See s 239(1) and (4) of the UK Companies Act 2006.
[45] The Companies Amendment Bill, 2010 (cl 14) proposes to amend this provision by deleting the words 'fraudulently or due to gross negligence' and substituting the expression 'knowingly, wilfully,

causes the company to do anything inconsistent with: *(a)* the Companies Act, or *(b)* a limitation, restriction or qualification contemplated in s 20, unless it has been ratified by a special resolution of the shareholders in terms of s 20(2). Accordingly, ratification will exclude the shareholder's remedy under s 20(6).[46]

5.1.8 The shareholders' right to restrain an unauthorised act (s 20(4) and (5))

As discussed above, the *ultra vires* doctrine has not been abandoned in its entirety: the internal consequences of an *ultra vires* act have been preserved, even though these consequences may now have developed into issues of fiduciary duties and shareholder rights.

One of the internal consequences is that the directors would be in breach of their fiduciary duty in entering into a contract that is inconsistent with a limitation, restriction or qualification on the company's powers, purposes or activities as specified in its Memorandum of Incorporation. This internal consequence and the possibility of its ratification are discussed in 5.1.6 above. It is notable that the right of the company to seek damages against the directors for breach of fiduciary duty does not form part of s 20 itself. For this, one would have to rely on the principles relating to the liability of directors, particularly s 77(3)*(a)* and s 77(2)*(a)*.[47]

The second internal consequence that is relevant here is that the shareholders have a right to institute legal proceedings to prevent the company or its directors from contravening the relevant provisions of its Memorandum of Incorporation. This shareholder action is preserved in s 20(5) of the Act.

Section 20(5) provides that one or more shareholders, directors or prescribed officers may take proceedings to restrain the company or the directors from doing anything inconsistent with a limitation, restriction or qualification on the purposes, powers or activities of the company as specified in its Memorandum of Incorporation. This is subject to s 20(5)*(a)* and *(b)*, which is discussed in 5.1.9 below. Section 20(4), on the other hand, provides that one or more shareholders, directors or prescribed officers of a company, or a trade union representing employees of the company, may institute proceedings[48] to restrain the company from doing anything inconsistent with the Act.

A few matters may be noted about s 20(4) and (5). First, s 20(4) applies to prescribed officers and to a trade union representing employees of the company, although it does not refer to employees not represented by a trade union. Section 20(5), in contrast, does not contain any reference to a trade union or employee representative. Secondly, s 20(5) refers to proceedings to 'restrain' the company or its directors. This section does not confer on the plaintiff a right to claim damages

---

intentionally, fraudulently or due to gross negligence'. The effect would be to considerably widen the scope of s 20(6).

[46] The remedy provided for in s 20(6) is distinct from, and in addition to, the shareholders' right to institute a derivative action under s 165 of the Act.

[47] See further chapter 12: The Duties and the Liability of Directors.

[48] The Companies Amendment Bill, 2010 proposes to amend this section to delete the reference to proceedings and to refer instead to an application of the High Court for an appropriate order. The same applies to s 20(5).

from the miscreant directors. For this, one would have to rely on s 20(6) (discussed above) or s 218(2).[49]

Thirdly, s 20(5) does not distinguish between executed and executory contracts. Under s 36 of the 1973 Act it was thought that the shareholder action to restrain an *ultra vires* contract had to be brought *before* the contract had been concluded, because once the contract was concluded it was no longer void (as discussed in 5.1.1*(e)* above). The wording of s 20(5) does not appear to warrant a similar distinction. It would therefore appear that s 20(5) may, subject to s 20(5)*(a)* and *(b)*, permit a shareholder action to restrain the conclusion or the *performance* of an *ultra vires* contract. By comparison, in English law specific provision was made in s 35(2) of the Companies Act 1985 (as amended in 1989),[50] that shareholders could only restrain an *ultra vires* contract if the contract had not given rise to any legal obligation on the part of the company. The shareholder restraining action (or injunction) had to be brought before the contract was concluded. While this protected the rights of third parties, it had the distinct disadvantage of severely restricting a shareholder's right to restrain an *ultra vires* contract.

5.1.9 The protection of the *bona fide* third party

Section 20(5) of the Act is, however, subject to the right to damages of a third party who: *(a)* obtained the rights in good faith, and *(b)* did not have actual knowledge of the particular limit, restriction or qualification.

According to this section, if the third party (ie the other party to the contract) is in good faith *and* without actual (not constructive) knowledge of a constitutional limitation, restriction or qualification on the purposes, powers or activities of the company, he or she will be entitled to damages in the event of a restraining action under s 20(5). Such a restraining action will not prejudice any rights that the third party may have to damages. But, of course, the third party will not have a right to specific performance of the contract in the event of a restraining action in terms of s 20(5).

If, on the other hand, the third party is not in good faith *or* has actual knowledge of the limitation, restriction or qualification on the company's capacity (as further discussed below), so that he or she knows and appreciates the fact that the company has failed to comply with a constitutional restriction on its capacity, the third party loses his or her rights to damages where the contract (or 'action') is restrained. In this event, the third party would not be able to enforce the transaction against the company, nor will he or she be able to claim damages from the company. From this it follows that a *mala fide* third party would be entitled to his or her rights in respect of the contract only if there is no intervening legal action in terms of s 20(5).

The important change made here is that, unlike s 36 of the 1973 Act which, as pointed out above in 5.1.1*(e)*, disregarded the *mala fides* or the knowledge of the third party that the contract was *ultra vires*, under s 20(5)*(a)* and *(b)* the third

---

[49] Section 77(2)*(a)* and (3)*(a)* (discussed above) relates to the company's remedy against the errant directors.

[50] Before this provision was repealed and replaced by ss 39 and 40 of the UK Companies Act 2006.

party's actual knowledge and good faith are of fundamental importance insofar as his or her rights to damages are concerned. Under s 20 and particularly s 20(5), actual knowledge and *mala fides* are irrelevant only if there is no restraining action under s 20(5). There is also the possibility of a special resolution in terms of s 20(2) that would render the contract, transaction or other action of the company fully binding on the company and may preclude the possibility of a shareholder restraining action under s 20(5).

It must be pointed out that, in view of the requirements of s 20(5)*(a)* and *(b)* of good faith and a lack of actual knowledge of the limitation, restriction or qualification in the company's Memorandum of Incorporation, it would make no difference to the application of s 20 that the third party is a director, shareholder or other insider of the company. In view of the requirements of this subsection, there is no longer any need to explicitly exclude insiders from the protection of s 20.

5.1.10 The requirements of good faith and actual knowledge (s 20(5)*(a)* and *(b)*)

The new approach, as stated above, is that for a third party to preserve his or her rights to damages against the company in the event of a restraining action under s 20(5) (by a shareholder, director or prescribed officer to prevent the company or its directors from doing anything inconsistent with its Memorandum of Incorporation), the third party must satisfy two requirements: *(a)* he or she must have obtained his or her rights in good faith, and *(b)* he or she must not have had actual knowledge of the limitation, restriction or qualification on the company's purposes, powers or activities in its Memorandum of Incorporation.

In short, if the third party is in bad faith *or* if he or she knows of the restriction in the company's constitution, he or she will not be protected should there be a restraining action by a shareholder, director or prescribed officer. The third party must be in good faith at the time that he or she obtained the relevant rights.

In English law, the courts were leaning towards the view that where third parties had actual knowledge of a limitation in the company's constitution, for instance where they had read the company's constitution, they would not be protected even though they had failed to appreciate or understand the significance of its provisions.[51] The Jenkins Committee,[52] on the other hand, took the view that third parties ought not to be deprived of protection if they had honestly and reasonably failed to appreciate that the contract was beyond the capacity of the company.

The wording of s 20(5)*(a)* and *(b)* is perhaps a rejection of the decision in *International Sales and Agencies Ltd v Marcus*[53] that a lack of good faith is to be found either in actual knowledge or where it can be shown that the third party could not, in view of all the circumstances, have been unaware. This objective standard was rejected by Nourse LJ in *Barclays Bank Ltd v TOSG Trust Fund*.[54]

---

[51] See FHI Cassim op cit n 6 at 299–300.
[52] Report of the Company Law Committee Cmnd 1749 (1962) para 42*(c)*.
[53] [1982] 3 All ER 551.
[54] (1984) BCLC 1 at 17.

Reasonableness is not a necessary ingredient of good faith. This would require the introduction of an objective standard into a subjective concept. The court held that a person acts in good faith if he or she acts genuinely and honestly in the circumstances of the case. The court stated further that a defence based on absence of notice or knowledge is not available to someone who has not acted genuinely and honestly in his or her dealings with the company. Knowledge and good faith, although two separate concepts, are often inseparable (at 18C).

To sum up: It is clear from the wording of s 20(5)*(a)* and *(b)* that actual knowledge and good faith are two separate requirements. Actual knowledge of a restriction on the purposes, powers or activities of a company is not necessarily tantamount to bad faith. Both actual knowledge and good faith are required for the preservation of the third party's rights to damages — an absence of any one of these requirements would result in a loss of the right to damages under s 20(5).

For third parties to be deprived of the protection of s 20(5) on the basis of actual knowledge, they must know of the limitation. It is not clear whether they must also understand and appreciate the significance of the limitation. If the third party has inspected the company's Memorandum of Incorporation and is consequently aware of the limitation or restriction but fails to understand it or to interpret it properly, he or she may nevertheless still be deprived of the protection of s 20(5) (ie he or she will lose the right to claim damages from the company, on the basis of actual knowledge of the limitation). On the other hand, the fact that the third party has no actual knowledge of the limitation does not necessarily mean that he or she is in good faith. This, for instance, would apply to someone who is wilfully blind or displays a wilful diligence in ignorance. Such persons would be deprived of their rights to damages under s 20(5) on the basis of a lack of good faith.

A difficulty that arises under s 20(5) is who exactly has the burden of proving good faith or lack of actual knowledge. It would have removed much uncertainty on this score had the Act followed the precedent of s 40(2)*(b)*(ii) of the UK Companies Act 2006, which states with admirable clarity that a person is presumed to have acted in good faith unless the contrary is proved. Section 40(2)*(b)*(iii) of the UK Companies Act also clearly provides that a person is not to be regarded as acting in bad faith by reason only of his knowing that an act is beyond the powers of the directors under the company's constitution.

5.1.11 Conclusion

A company that prefers to avoid the complex provisions of s 20 could simply decide not to impose any restrictions on its capacity in its Memorandum of Incorporation. In this event, neither the external nor the internal operation of the *ultra vires* doctrine would apply to the company, which would have the capacity of an individual. It would have the capacity to enter into any legal contract insofar as juristic persons are capable of doing so.

Section 20 is not a model of clarity. It does not provide a clear, unambiguous solution to the problem of capacity and the effect of constitutional restrictions on the authority of the directors of the company.

5.2 THE DOCTRINE OF CONSTRUCTIVE NOTICE

According to the common-law doctrine of constructive notice, as laid down in 1857 in *Ernest v Nicholls*,[55] persons dealing with a company were deemed to be aware of the contents of the constitution and other public documents of the company that were lodged with the Registrar of Companies and were open to public inspection whether they had read these documents or not.[56]

Following modern company law trends in other common-law jurisdictions, the doctrine of constructive notice has finally been abolished by s 19(4) of the Act. This provision states that, subject to s 19(5), a person must not be regarded as having notice or knowledge of the contents of any document relating to a company merely because the document has been filed or is accessible for inspection at an office of the company.

Having abandoned the doctrine of constructive notice, s 19(5) reintroduces a muted version of the doctrine which applies in two specific circumstances. First, s 19(5) provides that a person is deemed to know of any 'special conditions' that apply to the company, provided that the company had drawn attention to these 'special conditions' in its Notice of Incorporation (or Notice of Amendment).[57]

The second instance where the doctrine of constructive notice applies is in the case of a personal liability company. Persons dealing with such a company are deemed to be aware of the effect of the directors' and former directors' joint and several liability for debts and liabilities of the company 'contracted'[58] during their periods of office. The rationale of this particular provision is obscure.

---

[55] (1857) 6 HL Cas 401.

[56] The Dickerson Report ('Proposals for a New Business Corporations Law for Canada' (1971) vol 1 para 8.4 at 28) in considering the abolition of this judge-made rule stated:

'It may be that prudent people do inspect public documents in their own interests. That, however, is a far cry from imposing upon them as a matter of course a legal duty to do so and that is the effect of the doctrine of constructive notice.'

[57] As a result of the uncertainty concerning the meaning and scope of a 'special condition', the Companies Amendment Bill, 2010 proposes to delete the reference to a special condition, and to substitute for it a procedural or restrictive requirement impeding the amendment of any particular provision of the company's Memorandum of Incorporation. Moreover, the Bill proposes that the doctrine of constructive notice under s 19(5) will apply also to prohibitions of the amendment of any particular provisions of the company's Memorandum of Incorporation (cl 11 and 13). In terms of the Bill, not only must the Notice of Incorporation draw attention to these provisions, but additionally the company must have immediately after its name, the suffix 'RF' (thought to be an abbreviation for a 'ring-fenced' company). The suffix 'RF' is intended to draw attention to the fact that there are restrictive requirements or prohibitions on the amendment of the constitution of the company. See further chapter 4: Formation of Companies and the Company Constitution.

[58] See *Fundstrust (Pty) Ltd (In Liquidation) v Van Deventer* 1997 (1) SA 710 (A) which held that the joint and several liability of the directors of such a company is limited to debts and liabilities 'contracted' during their periods of office. It does not include tax liability, delictual liability or liability under the Insolvency Act 24 of 1936, which are not 'contracted'. See further chapter 3: Types of Companies.

5.3 THE TURQUAND RULE (IE THE PRESUMPTION OF COMPLIANCE WITH FORMAL AND PROCEDURAL REQUIREMENTS)

5.3.1 The common law

The Turquand Rule was historically formulated as an exception to the doctrine of constructive notice. It was originally designed to mitigate the severe effects of the doctrine of constructive notice. The Turquand Rule (also known as the 'indoor management rule', ie those dealing with a company are not affected by the company's indoor management rules or by the company's internal irregularities) is derived from the seminal case of *Royal British Bank v Turquand*[59] which was concerned with restrictions placed by the constitution of a company on the authority of the directors of the company to contract on its behalf.

The Turquand Rule protects *bona fide* third parties who are not aware of any internal irregularities that affect the validity of their contracts with the company. Provided that they are in good faith, third parties are protected by the rule, which entitles them to assume that all the company's internal formalities required for a valid contract have been complied with. A third party acting in good faith is under no duty to enquire whether the company has complied with its internal formalities and procedural requirements. The basis of the Turquand Rule is that *bona fide* third parties should not be prejudiced by a company's failure to comply with its own internal procedures and formal requirements. The Turquand Rule is justified on the basis of business convenience — business dealings with a company would be very difficult, if not hazardous, if third parties were required to enquire into the internal affairs of a company.

Typical internal formalities are the company's compliance with such matters as the quorum requirements for shareholders' meetings or board meetings, the period of notice for such meetings, the voting procedure at meetings and the constitutional limitations on the authority of persons representing the company. A third party dealing with the company may simply assume that the company has complied with these internal formalities unless he or she knows or suspects that they have not been complied with.

The practical effect of the Turquand Rule is that it prevents a company from escaping liability under an otherwise valid contract solely on the grounds that some internal formality or procedure was not complied with. Proof by the company that it has failed to fulfil its own internal formalities is not sufficient basis for escaping liability under the contract.

The facts of *Royal British Bank v Turquand*[60] best illustrate the rule itself. In this case, the articles of association of the company authorised its board of directors to borrow money, provided that the board obtained the prior approval by ordinary resolution of the shareholders of the company. The board borrowed money from the Royal British Bank without obtaining the approval of the shareholders of the company. The Royal British Bank had no knowledge of this fact. The court ruled that, even though the board had failed to comply with the

---

[59] (1856) 6 E & B 327, 119 ER 886.
[60] Supra.

company's articles of association, the company was nevertheless bound by the loan taken from the Royal British Bank. The approval of the shareholders as stipulated in the company's articles of association was an internal formality. The Bank, which was in good faith, was entitled to assume that this internal formality had been duly fulfilled.

The Turquand Rule is not concerned only with limitations on the authority of the directors of the company. The rule applies to all internal irregularities that take place in the management of the company. At common law, the rule applies also to a defective appointment of a director or officer of the company.[61] The court however found it unnecessary to decide this point. The case was instead decided on the basis of implied authority.

But the rule does not protect a third party who knows[62] that an internal formality has not been complied with, or a third party who *suspects* that the internal formality has not been complied with but deliberately shuts his or her eyes or turns a blind eye. In *Morris v Kanssen*[63] the court stated that a person cannot 'presume in his own favour that things are rightly done if inquiry that he ought to make would tell him that they were wrongly done'.

In *Northside Developments (Pty) Ltd v Registrar-General*[64] the court affirmed that a third party who lacks knowledge but is nevertheless suspicious that an internal irregularity may have taken place, cannot rely on the Turquand Rule. The circumstances of the third party in this case were such that he ought to have made inquiry. The court stated (at 619):

> If the nature of the transaction is such as to excite a reasonable apprehension that the transaction is entered into for purposes apparently unrelated to the company's business, it will put the person dealing with the company upon inquiry.

If a third party is put on inquiry, he or she must make inquiry. The more unusual the transaction, the greater the need to make inquiry.[65]

Significantly, the Turquand Rule does not protect a third party who relies on a forged document.[66] In *Ruben's* case the plaintiff had lent money to the secretary of the defendant company on the security of a share certificate that had been issued to the plaintiff certifying that the plaintiff was the registered transferee of certain shares. The secretary had issued the share certificate without any authority to do so, after forging the signatures of two directors, and thereafter affixing the company's seal to it. The plaintiff sued the defendant for damages after the company had refused to register him as the holder of the shares. The court held that, since the defendant company had not held out the company secretary as having authority to issue the share certificate, the company was not bound by his act. The Turquand Rule did not apply to the forged share certificate. The forged share certificate was a pure nullity.

---

[61] *Morris v Kanssen* [1946] AC 459.
[62] *Howard v Patent Ivory Manufacturing Co* (1888) 38 ChD 156.
[63] Supra at 475.
[64] (1990) 8 ACLC 611.
[65] *Underwood Ltd v Bank of Liverpool and Martins* [1924] KB 775 (CA).
[66] *Ruben v Great Fingall Consolidated* [1906] AC 439 (HL).

The Turquand Rule is intended for the protection of outsiders who have no means of knowing whether the internal formalities and procedures required under the company's constitution have been complied with. On this basis, directors and other insiders may not rely on the rule.[67] The directors of a company are taken to know that the company's internal formalities have not been complied with.[68] It is the duty of directors to look after the affairs of the company and to ensure that its transactions are regular. Directors are not entitled to assume that internal formalities have been complied with when, due to their very own neglect, these internal formalities have not in fact been complied with.[69]

In *Hely-Hutchinson v Brayhead Ltd*[70] the court distinguished between a director acting in his or her capacity as a director and a director who is acting, not as a director, but as an outsider contracting with the company. The court suggested that in the latter instance the director may rely on the Turquand Rule. This attempt to narrow down the rule that insiders may not rely on the Turquand Rule draws a distinction between inside and outside transactions.

The question must also inevitably arise whether the Turquand Rule is merely an application of agency principles and particularly of ostensible authority, or whether it is an independent and special rule of company law that imposes liability on the company for unauthorised transactions independently of estoppel and ostensible authority. In South African law, the weight of authority[71] leans towards the view that the Turquand Rule is an independent rule of company law. The Turquand Rule in South African law would thus impose liability on the company for unauthorised contracts where all that was lacking was compliance with internal formalities. Estoppel requirements consequently need not be satisfied in order to rely on the Turquand Rule (discussed in 5.4 below).

In English law, by contrast, the common-law Turquand Rule became interwoven with estoppel or ostensible authority as a result of the decision in *Freeman & Lockyer v Buckhurst Park Properties (Mangal) Ltd*.[72] The same applies to Australian law.[73]

5.3.2 The Turquand Rule and the Act (s 20(7) and (8))

Section 20(7) of the Act states that a person dealing with a company in good faith, other than a director, prescribed officer or shareholder of the company, is entitled to presume that the company, in making any decision in the exercise of its powers, has complied with all the formal and procedural requirements in terms of the Act, its Memorandum of Incorporation and any rules of the company unless, in the circumstances, the person knew or 'reasonably ought to have known' of any

---

[67] *Morris v Kanssen* (supra); *Smith v Hennicker-Major & Co* [2002] 2 BCLC 655.
[68] *Howard v Patent Ivory Manufacturing Co* (1888) 38 ChD 156.
[69] *Morris v Kanssen* (supra).
[70] [1967] 3 All ER 98 (CA).
[71] See *The Mine Workers' Union v Prinsloo* (1948) 3 SA 831 (A) and the *obiter dicta* in *Farren v Sun Service SA Photo Trip Management (Pty) Ltd* 2004 (2) SA 146 (C) that the Turquand Rule is independent of estoppel or ostensible authority.
[72] [1964] 1 All ER 630 (CA).
[73] *Northside Developments (Pty) Ltd v Registrar-General* (supra).

failure by the company to comply with any such requirement. This is a statutory formulation of what in essence is the common-law Turquand Rule, as discussed above.

Section 20(7) also encapsulates the common-law rule that, if the third party is a director, prescribed officer or shareholder of the company, he or she will not be protected by s 20(7). The basis of this exception, as explained above, is that a director or prescribed officer and even a shareholder ought reasonably to have known of non-compliance with the company's internal procedures and formalities. They have access to the company's records and minutes of meetings. Even a shareholder has more effective means of information than an outsider, in the form of notices of meetings and proposed resolutions to be submitted for approval at shareholders' meetings.

Section 20(8) preserves the Turquand Rule as developed at common law. It provides that s 20(7) must be construed concurrently with, and not in substitution for, the common-law principle relating to the presumed validity of the actions of the company in the exercise of its powers. This is of course a reference to the common-law Turquand Rule. From this, it follows that s 20(7) would, like the common-law Turquand Rule, probably not apply to forgeries (discussed above). There is now in our law both a common-law as well as a statutory indoor management rule.

The difficulty, however, is that s 20(7) is not properly aligned with the common-law formulation of the Turquand Rule. The common-law Turquand Rule, as stated above, would not protect a third party who knew or *suspected* that an internal formality or procedure had not been complied with. In striking contrast, s 20(7) goes much further than this, in excluding a third party who '*reasonably ought*' [emphasis added] to have known of non-compliance with a formality. In this respect, s 128(4) of the Australian Corporations Law 2001 unambiguously states that a third party may not assume that internal formalities have been complied with if he or she '. . . knew or *suspected* [my emphasis] that the assumption was incorrect' at the time of his or her dealings with the company. It is this sort of provision that ought perhaps to have been adopted by s 20(7) of the Companies Act.

As a result of the wording of s 20(7) in excluding third parties who reasonably ought to know of non-compliance with internal formalities, difficult distinctions would have to be drawn between being 'put on inquiry' and 'ought to know'.[74] This provision would be understandable if it were aimed only at precluding reliance on s 20(7) by a director, a prescribed officer or a shareholder, but this is clearly not the intent of the provision. With respect, a much more lucid provision is to be found in s 19 of the Canada Business Corporations Act 1995, which excludes reliance on this presumption by an insider who 'has or ought to have by virtue of his position with or relationship to the corporation knowledge to the contrary'.

---

[74] See FHI Cassim op cit n 6 at 314; *Northside Developments (Pty) Ltd v Registrar-General* (1990) 170 CLR 146.

It is significant that the common-law Turquand Rule is not confined to companies only. The courts have extended the rule to trusts, technikons and trade unions. The rule is growing in importance but perhaps, with the abolition of the doctrine of constructive notice, there could be less of a need for an 'indoor management rule'. This is not to suggest in any way that the Turquand Rule is no longer of any importance. There is also nothing odd in preserving the indoor management rule while abolishing the doctrine of constructive notice. English law adopted this approach years ago.

One important consequence of the abolition of the doctrine of constructive notice that must be emphasised here, is that the common-law Turquand Rule and s 20(7) would now, unlike the past, apply even where a special resolution is required as an internal formality to some matter. Since there is no longer any constructive notice of special resolutions filed by the company with the Companies Commission, it follows that there is no longer any obstacle to applying s 20(7) or the Turquand Rule to a special resolution required by the Act or the company's Memorandum of Incorporation to validate a particular act of management.

5.4 REPRESENTATION AND THE AUTHORITY OF THE DIRECTORS

A company is an artificial person that cannot act on its own. It acts only through the medium of its directors and officers. Accordingly, s 66(1) of the Act states that the business and affairs of a company *must* [emphasis added] be managed by or under the direction of its board, which has the authority to exercise all the powers and perform any of the functions of the company, except to the extent that the Act or the company's Memorandum of Incorporation provides otherwise. This provision imposes a mandatory duty on the board of directors to manage the business of the company. It also confers on the board the authority to exercise all the powers of the company subject to the company's Memorandum of Incorporation.

The board of directors would in practice normally delegate its powers to manage the business of the company to individual directors and officers of the company, and particularly to the managing director of the company. If such persons enter into contracts on behalf of the company, whether or not the company would be bound by such contracts must depend on the principles of agency law, which require such individuals to have authority to contract on behalf of the company. Authority is a concept of agency law.

According to agency law, if an agent contracts with a third party on behalf of the company, the contract will bind the third party and the principal (ie the company) as if concluded personally by them. The agent is a mere intermediary or conduit. He or she acquires no rights nor incurs any liability under the contract unless the contrary is agreed upon by the parties.[75] Once the contract with the third party is concluded, the agent falls out of the picture.

The same applies where a director contracts on behalf of the company. For the director or any other agent, for that matter, to do so, he or she must have authority to act on behalf of the company. Such authority may be actual authority, usual

---

[75] As for instance in the case of a *del credere* agent.

authority or ostensible authority, or it may be authority given *ex post facto* in the form of ratification by the company of an unauthorised contract entered into by the director.

5.4.1 Actual authority

Actual authority consists of express authority and implied authority. Express authority is authority given in so many words, either orally or in writing. As we have seen above, where express authority is subject to compliance with some internal formality, the common-law Turquand Rule and now s 20(7) of the Act would entitle a *bona fide* party to assume that this formality has been duly complied with, unless he or she knew or ought reasonably to have known that it has not.

Implied authority is authority given not in so many words, but which arises as a reasonable inference from the conduct of the principal. It may also be authority that is necessary or reasonably incidental to the performance of the agent's express authority.

In *Freeman and Lockyer v Buckhurst Park Properties (Mangal) Ltd*[76] Diplock LJ stated that actual authority is:

> ... a legal relationship between principal and agent created by a consensual agreement to which they alone are parties ... Nevertheless, if the agent does enter into a contract pursuant to the 'actual' authority, it does create contractual rights and liabilities between the principal and the contractor.

In *Hopkins v TL Dallas Group Ltd*[77] the court likewise stated that the authority of an agent 'is actual (express or implied) where it results from a manifestation of consent that he should represent or act for the principal expressly or impliedly made by the principal to the agent himself'. This authority extends to doing 'whatever is necessary for, or ordinarily incidental to, the effective execution of his actual authority'. The court stated further that the grant of actual authority should be implied as being subject to a condition that it is to be exercised honestly and on behalf of the principal.

A third way in which implied authority may arise is discussed under 'usual authority' below in 5.4.3.

5.4.2 Ostensible authority

Ostensible authority (also known as apparent authority or agency by estoppel) is no authority at all; it is an oxymoron or contradiction in terms. It is based on an estoppel.

Ostensible authority is the authority of an agent as it appears to others. It may exceed or extend actual authority[78] (see below). This may apply where, for instance, the company or its board of directors 'hold out' a particular director as having authority in certain circumstances to contract on behalf of the company.[79]

---

[76] [1964] 1 All ER 630 (CA) 644F.
[77] [2005] 1 BCLC 543 (Ch) 572*g*.
[78] *Hely-Hutchinson v Brayhead Ltd* [1967] 2 All ER 14 (CA).
[79] *Freeman and Lockyer v Buckhurst Properties (Mangal) Ltd* (supra).

Actual authority and ostensible authority are quite independent of one another. Generally they coexist and coincide, although either may exist without the other and their respective scopes may be different.[80]

Ostensible authority arises where the principal has made a representation, whether by words or conduct, to the third party that the agent has the requisite authority to act on his or her behalf, and if the third party has reasonably relied on this representation, the principal will be estopped from denying the authority of the agent.

The representation must be made by the principal and not only by the agent, otherwise anyone would be bound by the acts of a self-appointed agent or director.

(a) Requirements for ostensible authority

In *Freeman and Lockyer v Buckhurst Park Properties (Mangal) Ltd*,[81] Diplock LJ stated:

> An 'apparent' or 'ostensible' authority, on the other hand, is a legal relationship between the principal and the contractor, created by a representation, made by the principal to the contractor, intended to be, and in fact acted on by the contractor that the agent has authority to enter on behalf of the principal into a contract of a kind within the scope of the 'apparent' authority, so as to render the principal liable to perform any obligation imposed on him by such contract ... The representation, when acted on by the contractor by entering into a contract with the agent, operates as an estoppel preventing the principal from asserting that he is not bound by the contract. It is irrelevant whether the agent had actual authority to enter into the contract.

Three requirements, according to *Freeman's* case, must be fulfilled for ostensible authority:

- First, a representation must have been made to the third party that the agent has authority to enter into a contract of the kind sought to be enforced.
- Secondly, such representation must be made by a person or persons who have actual authority to manage the company's business either generally or in respect of the matters to which the contract relates.
- Thirdly, the third party must have been induced by the representation to enter into the contract, ie he or she must have relied on it. The representation must have been the proximate cause of the third party entering into the contract.

In *Freeman's* case, the court also stressed the importance of the doctrine of constructive notice and the requirement that the company should have had capacity to enter into the contract. Since the doctrine of constructive notice has been abolished, this point is no longer relevant; as regards capacity or *ultra vires*, this has been examined above in the context of constitutional limitations of the powers of the company and the directors. This fourth requirement is also no longer relevant. The three requirements for ostensible authority, as laid down in *Freeman's* case, amount to saying that such authority arises where the board of directors has made a representation, whether by words or conduct, that a particular director or company officer has authority to bind the company to certain kinds of contracts that fall

---

[80] *Per* Diplock LJ in *Freeman and Lockyer v Buckhurst Park Properties (Mangal) Ltd* (supra).
[81] Supra at 644F.

within the scope of his or her ostensible or apparent authority even though such contracts fall outside the scope of his or her actual authority. In this way, ostensible authority may extend actual authority.

In *NBS Bank Ltd v Cape Produce Co (Pty) Ltd*[82] the court, in approving of *Freeman's* case, laid down six requirements for ostensible authority as opposed to the three requirements set out in *Freeman's* case, namely:

- a representation whether by words or by conduct,
- made by the principal (ie someone with actual authority),
- in a form such that the principal should reasonably have expected that outsiders would act on the strength of the representation,
- reliance by the third party,
- such reliance must be reasonable, and
- there must be consequent prejudice to the third party.

The onus of establishing these requirements lies on the third party.[83]

(b) Ostensible authority and breach of fiduciary duty

From the point of view of the third party, it makes no difference whether the agent has actual or ostensible authority, because the principal will in any event be bound to the third party. It makes an important difference, however, between the principal and the agent. As ostensible authority is no authority at all, the agent will be liable to the principal for breach of fiduciary duty not to exceed his authority. In contrast, implied authority is actual authority; thus no action for breach of fiduciary duty would lie against the agent in this case.

If, however, the principal is not bound to the third party at all, on the basis of a lack of authority (including ostensible authority), the third party may have a delictual action against the director or agent based on misrepresentation or an action for breach of warranty of authority. In the latter event, the director or agent is not liable on the contract. The measure of damages is that the agent must put the third party in the same position as if the principal had been bound by the contract.

5.4.3 Usual authority

It must be emphasised at the outset that usual authority may form part of implied authority, in which event it is referred to as implied usual authority; or it may be restricted usual authority, in which event it may form the basis for ostensible authority.

The importance of usual authority in company law arises from the fact that the position or office occupied by a company officer who is an employee of the company may determine the extent of his or her authority. To put it differently, the authority of the agent may flow from the office held by the particular company officer in question.

The appointment of a person as the managing director or company secretary may carry with it implied usual authority to do whatever falls within the usual

---
[82] 2002 (1) SA 396 (SCA) para 26.
[83] *IPF Nominees (Pty) Ltd v Nedcor Bank Ltd (Basfour 130 (Pty) Ltd, Third Party)* 2002 (5) SA 101 (W) 122 I–J.

scope of that office. Thus in *Hely-Hutchinson v Brayhead*[84] R, the chairman of the company, also acted as the *de facto* managing director of the company without ever having been formally appointed as such. The board of directors of the company acquiesced in R's conduct in acting first and then reporting afterwards to the board. R entered into an agreement on behalf of the company under which he committed the company to giving a guarantee and an indemnity in respect of certain transactions previously entered into by the parties. The board of directors of the company subsequently refused to honour these undertakings on the ground that R had no authority to give the undertakings on behalf of the company. The court decided that, as chairman of the board of directors, R had no implied usual authority to enter into the agreements, but he did have such authority in his capacity as a *de facto* managing director and in the acquiescence by the board in his conduct.[85]

A managing director or chief executive director has very wide implied usual authority to contract on behalf of the company. In *SA Securities Ltd v Nicholas*[86] the court stated that the mere fact of appointing a person as managing director gives him certain implied powers. Anyone dealing *bona fide* with the managing director is entitled to assume that the managing director has all the powers which his or her position as such ostensibly would give him or her. On the other hand, the chairperson of the board of directors or an ordinary director does not have wide usual authority to contract on the company's behalf.[87]

In *Panorama Developments (Guildford) Ltd v Fidelis Furnishing Fabrics Ltd*[88] the court held that a company secretary is an officer of the company with extensive duties and responsibilities. He is no longer a mere clerk, but the chief administrative officer of the company. He is entitled to sign contracts connected with the administrative side of a company's affairs, such as employing staff and hiring chauffeur-driven cars required for the purposes of the company's business. All these things may be regarded as part of the usual authority of a company secretary.

Where company officers act within the scope of their usual authority, the company may in certain circumstances still be bound by their acts even though the company may have restricted the scope of their usual authority. Such restricted usual authority would not form part of implied authority. The basis of liability in such cases may consequently be ostensible authority, provided that the prerequisites for such authority (as discussed above) are satisfied.

---

[84] Supra.
[85] Another instance of a *de facto* managing director arose in *Freeman and Lockyer v Buckhurst Park Properties* (supra). In this case the act of the managing director in hiring a firm of architects to perform certain architectural services for the company was held to be binding on the company. The basis of liability in this case was however ostensible authority.
[86] 1911 TPD 450.
[87] *Wolpert v Uitzigt Properties (Pty) Ltd* 1961 (2) SA 257 (W). See also *NBS Bank Ltd v Cape Produce Co (Pty) Ltd* (supra).
[88] [1971] 3 All ER 16 (CA).

5.4.4 Ratification

Ratification, as discussed above, is a retroactive conferral of authority by the principal or the company. In effect, the company or principal forgives the agent and adopts the unauthorised contract, usually with retrospective effect. If ratified, the contract becomes fully binding with retrospective effect on the company.

CHAPTER 6

GROUPS OF COMPANIES AND RELATED PERSONS

Richard Jooste

6.1	GENERAL	179
6.2	THE HOLDING/SUBSIDIARY RELATIONSHIP	183
6.3	DIRECTORS' FIDUCIARY DUTIES AND THE HOLDING/ SUBSIDIARY RELATIONSHIP	190
6.4	THE 'RELATED' AND 'INTERRELATED' CONCEPTS	193
	6.4.1 The 'related' relationship	193
	(a) Two individuals	194
	(b) An individual and a juristic person	194
	(c) Two juristic persons	194
	(d) Control	194

6.1 GENERAL

Where two or more companies are in a holding/subsidiary relationship with each other (the meaning of which is explained below), the companies are referred to as a 'group of companies'.[1]

The nature of the group is that:

> [Its] basic characteristic is that the management of the different and independent holding and subsidiary companies comprising the group, is co-ordinated in such a way that they are managed on a central and unified basis in the interests of the group as a whole. This management on a unified basis is possible because of the control, implicit in the holding/ subsidiary company relationship, which the holding company exercises over the subsidiary or subsidiaries. This control makes it possible that the group is managed as an economic unit, in the sense that the different holding and subsidiary companies no longer carry out their commercial activities on a footing of complete economic independence.[2]

This economic interrelationship and control can lead to the 'camouflaging' of

---

[1] See definition of 'group of companies' in s 1. In the draft Companies Amendment Bill, 2010 the definition is amended, increasing the scope of the definition. It provides:

'"group of companies" means two or more companies that are related or inter-related as a result of one or more relationships contemplated in section 2(1)*(c)*(i) or (ii);'

[2] DH Botha 'Recognition of the group concept in company law' (1982) 15 *De Jure* 107 at 108.

'economic reality' and abuse,[3] which has necessitated legislative intervention. The following are examples of how the legislature has intervened (these control provisions are merely listed here and are dealt with in detail elsewhere in the book):

- Group and consolidated financial statements are required in respect of a group of companies.[4]
- The auditor of a holding company has the right to access all current and former financial statements of any subsidiary of that holding company and is entitled to require from the directors or officers of the holding company or subsidiary any information and explanations in connection with any such statements and in connection with the accounting records, books and documents of the subsidiary as necessary for the performance of the auditor's duties.[5]
- The annual financial statements of a company must include a report by the directors with respect to the state of affairs, the business and profit or loss of the company, or of the group of companies, if the company is part of a group.[6]
- In certain instances,[7] the 'solvency' requirement[8] must be met. In applying the solvency and liquidity test, the assets and liabilities of the group of which the company is a part, must be taken into account.[9]
- Where shares are issued by a company to certain persons, shareholder approval is generally required.[10] Such persons include the holding companies and subsidiary companies of the company issuing the shares.[11]
- Section 48 regulates, inter alia, the situation where a company acquires shares in its holding company.
- A company may not directly or indirectly pay any fine that may be imposed on a director of the company or of its holding or subsidiary company, who has been convicted of an offence in terms of any national legislation.[12]
- In certain circumstances, where a company offers to holders of the company's securities, securities in the company or any other company within the same group of companies, a prospectus is required.[13]

The fact that the legislature has had to intervene does not, of course, mean that there is anything inherently wrong with the group structure. In fact, on the contrary, '[on] the basis of such control, group structures commonly provide commercial, financial and organisational advantages for the group as a whole'.[14]

---

[3] See D Bhana 'The Company Law implications of conferring a power on a subsidiary to acquire the shares of its holding company' (2006) 17 *Stell LR* 232 at 233.
[4] Section 30 read with the definition of 'financial statement' in s 1 of the Act.
[5] Section 93(1)*(b)*.
[6] Section 30(3)*(b)* of the Act.
[7] For example, ss 44(3)*(b)*; 45(3)*(b)*; 46(1)*(b)*; 47(2)*(a)*; 48(2)*(a)*.
[8] See s 4 of the Act.
[9] See the requirement regarding a member of a group of companies in s 4(1)*(a)*.
[10] See s 41 of the Act.
[11] See s 41 of the Act.
[12] Section 78(3) read with the definition of related company in s 2(1)*(c)*.
[13] See s 95 of the Act.
[14] Bhana op cit n 3 at 233.

It is to be noted that legislative intervention has been necessary because the common law has not developed sufficiently to cope with the problems arising in the group situation.[15] This is due to the fact that:

> [The] common law was founded in the principle of the separate legal personality of each company and did not, in its inception, anticipate the emergence of 'groups of companies'. Moreover, as the phenomenon of groups and their associated problems of camouflage and abuse began to unfold, it appears that real concerns of commercial fairness and equity played little role in the common law development of company law on this front. The law consequently failed to appreciate fully the significance of group relationships particularly in terms of the propensity for camouflage and abuse and therefore failed to address the issue effectively.[16]

The legislative intervention referred to earlier does not, however, interfere with the foundational principle of the separate legal personality of each company in a group. In other words, the fact that the Companies Act 71 of 2008 (hereafter 'the Act), through its inclusion of control provisions[17] 'attaches consequences to the exercise of control by a holding company over its subsidiary cannot be regarded in any way as a denial of the separate legal personalities of the companies involved'.[18] Thus the fact that the requirement of group annual financial statements recognises the group as a single entity does not mean that the holding and subsidiary companies lose their separate legal personalities.[19]

The courts have often referred to a group.[20] However, they have made it clear that:

- the group is not 'a separate independent persona apart from the personae of the independent constituent companies comprising the group',[21]
- there is no separate persona which represents the interests of the different companies in the group that exists side by side with the personae of the different companies in the group.[22]

---

[15] It must be noted that what is of relevance here is not the 'piercing of the corporate veil' of companies in a group in terms of the common law or those instances where a company in a group acts as an agent on behalf of another company in the group or where companies in a group operate as a partnership in pursuing some group enterprise.

[16] Bhana op cit n 3 at 234.

[17] See list above.

[18] See Botha op cit n 2 at 110.

[19] Ibid.

[20] See *Hull v Turf Mines* 1906 TS 68 at 77; *Robinson v Randfontein Estates Gold Mining Co Ltd* 1921 AD 168 at 196; *R v Milne & Erleigh (7)* 1951 (1) SA 791 (A) 810–12, 827–8; *Goode, Durrant & Murray Ltd v Hewitt & Cornell NNO* 1961 (4) SA 286 (N) 291; *S v Heller (2)* 1964 (1) SA 524 (W) 525, 527, 533–5; *Langeberg Koöperasie Bpk v Inverdoorn Farming & Trading Co Ltd* 1965 (2) SA 597 (A) 603, 604, 606; *S v de Jager* 1965 (2) SA 616 (A) 619.

[21] Botha op cit n 2 at 111. See *Rex v Milne & Erleigh* (supra) at 827, 828; *Goode, Durrant & Murray Ltd v Hewitt & Cornell* (supra); *Langeberg Koöperasie Bpk v Inverdoorn Farming & Trading Co Ltd* (supra) at 606, 607; *Harold Holdsworth & Co (Wakefield) Ltd v Caddies* [1955] 1 All ER 725 at 734; *Charterbridge Corporation Ltd v Lloyds Bank Ltd* [1970] Ch 62 at 74; *Lonrho Ltd v Shell Petroleum (CA)* [1980] 2 WLR 367 at 374–5; *The Albazero* [1975] 3 All ER 21 (CA); and the Australian decisions *Walker v Wimborne* (1976) 50 ALJR 446 at 449; *Industrial Equity Ltd v Blackburn* (1978) 52 ALJR 89 at 93.

[22] See *Rex v Milne & Erleigh* (supra) at 827F–H. See also *Langeberg Koöperasie v Inverdoorn Farming & Trading Co* (supra) at 606E–G where it was stated that a company in a group, despite its

As has been pointed out:[23]

> Lord Denning has expressed the view that there is a general tendency, evidenced by the statutory requirement for group accounts, more readily to ignore the separate legal entities of companies within a group, especially in the case of wholly owned subsidiaries.[24] Lord Roskill has suggested that where 'a group is in truth the party interested and injured, the law should not be too astute not to recognise the realities of the position.[25]

In *Ritz Hotel Ltd v Charles of the Ritz Ltd*[26] Nicholas JA referred with approval to a passage in the judgment of Lord Denning MR in *DHN Food Distributors Ltd v London Borough of Tower Hamlets*[27] where that learned judge, after quoting with approval a passage in Gower saying that 'there is evidence of a general tendency to ignore the separate legal entities of various companies within a group, and to look instead at the economic entity of the whole group', added:

> This is especially the case when a parent company owns all the shares of the subsidiaries, so much so that it can control every movement of the subsidiaries. These subsidiaries are bound hand and foot to the parent company and must do just what the parent says.[28]

The decision in *DHN Food Distributors Ltd v London Borough of Tower Hamlets*[29] would seem to have been the high-water mark of this approach. In that case the Court of Appeal held that, for the purposes of the case, a holding company could be treated as the owner of property that it has placed in one of its subsidiary companies, and that it was therefore entitled to claim compensation for disruption of its business as a consequence of an expropriation of that property. Subsequently, however, the correctness of that decision has been questioned in a number of cases.[30]

---

group membership '. . . nevertheless had a personality of its own . . . with interests of its own'. See also *Charterbridge Corporation Ltd v Lloyds Bank Ltd* [1970] Ch 62 at 74E–F) where Pennycuick J rejected the contention that a transaction should be viewed from its benefit for a group of companies as a whole. He stated that 'each company in the group is a separate legal entity and the directors of a particular company are not entitled to sacrifice the interest of that company. This becomes apparent when one considers the case where the particular company has separate creditors', and as Botha (op cit n 2 at 111) says, '[t]o this may be added where the particular company possesses separate shareholders, especially non-controlling shareholders.'

[23] See MS Blackman et al *Commentary on the Companies Act* vol 1 (2002) (Revision Service 3, 2006) at 4-142–4-143.

[24] *Littlewoods Mail Order Stores Ltd v McGregor* [1969] 3 All ER 855 at 860, [1969] 1 WLR 1241 (CA) 1254; *DHN Food Distributors Ltd v London Borough of Tower Hamlets* [1976] 3 All ER 462 at 467, [1976] 1 WLR 852 (CA) 860; *Ritz Hotel Ltd v Charles of the Ritz Ltd* 1988 (3) SA 290 (A) 314–15.

[25] Per Roskill LJ in *The Albazero* [1977] AC 774 at 807, [1975] 3 All ER 21 (CA) 41.

[26] 1988 (3) SA 290 (A) 314–16.

[27] [1976] 3 All ER 462 at 467, [1976] 1 WLR 852 (CA) 860.

[28] Nicholas JA went on to say that, in the light of the judgments in *Revlon Inc v Cripps and Lee Ltd* 1980 FSR 85 (CA), approved by the Court of Appeal ibid 99ff, '. . . it may become necessary to reconsider *Adcock-Ingram Laboratories Ltd v Lennon Ltd* 1983 (2) SA 350 (T) where I held that use of a trade mark by a wholly owned subsidiary of the registered proprietor was not use by the proprietor'. See also D Milo 'The liability of a holding company for the debts of its subsidiary: Is Salomon still alive and well?' (1998) 115 *SALJ* 318.

[29] [1976] 3 All ER 462, [1976] 1 WLR 852 (CA) 860.

[30] See *Woolfson v Strathclyde Regional Council* 1978 SC 90 (HL) 96; *Briggs v James Hardie & Co Pty Ltd* [1989] 16 NSWLR 549 CA (NSW) 752; *National Dock Labour Board v Pinn & Wheeler Ltd*

It is doubtful whether the statutory requirement for group accounts evidences the general tendency referred to by Lord Denning,[31] although the wording or purpose[32] of a statute[33] or a contract[34] may permit a holding and a subsidiary company to be treated as one entity.[35] Just because a group of companies effectively forms one economic unit does not mean that the separate identities of the companies must be ignored.'[36]

6.2 THE HOLDING/SUBSIDIARY RELATIONSHIP

The definitions of 'holding company' and 'subsidiary' are of vital importance because, as was seen above, the holding/subsidiary relationship brings with it the existence of a group of companies and accordingly the possible application of numerous provisions of the Act.

For ease of reference, the relevant provisions are set out here in full.

Section 1 of the Act provides that:

'holding company' in relation to a subsidiary, means a juristic person or undertaking that controls that subsidiary.[37]
'subsidiary' has the meaning determined in accordance with section 3.

Section 3 provides:

3 Subsidiary relationships
(1) A company is —
(a) a subsidiary of another juristic person if that juristic person, one or more other subsidiaries of that juristic person, or one or more nominees of that juristic person or any of its subsidiaries, alone or in any combination —

[1989] BCLC 647 at 650; *State Bank of Victoria v Parry* (1990) 2 ACSR 15 SC (WA); *Pioneer Concrete Services Ltd v Yelnah Pty Ltd* (1986) 11 ACLR 108 SC (NSW).

[31] See *Industrial Equity Ltd v Blackburn* (1977) 137 CLR 567 (HC of A) 575, 577; *State Bank of Victoria v Parry* (1990) 2 ACSR 15 SC (WA); *Woolfson v Strathclyde Regional Council* (supra); *Adams v Cape Industries plc* [1990] 1 Ch 433, [1991] 1 All ER 929 (CA).

[32] See *Adams v Cape Industries plc* [1990] 1 Ch 433 at 536, [1991] 1 All ER 929 (CA) 1019; *DHN Food Distributors Ltd v London Borough of Tower Hamlets* [1976] 3 All ER 462, [1976] 1 WLR 852 (CA).

[33] See *Dimbleby & Sons Ltd v National Union of Journalists* [1984] 1 All ER 751 at 758, [1984] 1 WLR 427 (HL) 435.

[34] See *Industrial Equity Ltd v Blackburn* (1977) 137 CLR 567 (HC of A) 577; *Adams v Cape Industries plc* [1990] 1 Ch 433 at 532–9, [1991] 1 All ER 929 (CA) 1016–22; *Harold Holdsworth & Co (Wakefield) Ltd v Caddies* [1955] 1 All ER 725, [1955] 1 WLR 352 HL (SC) and *Dithaba Platinum (Pty) Ltd v Econovaal Ltd* 1985 (4) SA 615 (T) 625.

[35] See *Adams v Cape Industries plc* [1990] 1 Ch 433 at 536, [1991] 1 All ER 929 (CA) 1016.

[36] *Bank of Tokyo Ltd v Karoon* [1987] AC 45 at 64, [1986] 3 All ER 468 (CA) 486; *Woolfson v Strathclyde Regional Council* 1978 SC 90 (HL) 96; *National Dock Labour Board v Pinn & Wheeler Ltd* [1989] BCLC 647 at 650; *Adams v Cape Industries plc* [1990] 1 Ch 433 at 532–9, [1991] 1 All ER 929 (CA) 1016–22; *State Bank of Victoria v Parry* (1990) 2 ACSR 15 SC (WA); *Dithaba Platinum (Pty) Ltd v Econovaal Ltd* 1985 (4) SA 615 (T) 625; *Briggs v James Hardie & Co Pty Ltd* [1989] 16 NSWLR 549 CA (NSW) 576–7; *Quintex Australia Finance Ltd v Schroeders Australia Ltd* (1990) 3 ACSR 267 SC (NSW) 269; *Wambach v Maizecor Industries (Edms) Bpk* 1993 (2) SA 669 (A) 675; *Macadamia Finance Bpk v De Wet* 1993 (2) SA 743 (A) 748; *EBBW Vale UDC v S Wales Traffic Area Licensing Authority* [1951] 2 KB 366, [1951] 1 All ER 806 (CA).

[37] The draft Companies Amendment Bill, 2010 amends the definition to read:
'"holding company", in relation to a subsidiary, means a juristic person that controls that subsidiary as a result of any circumstances contemplated in section 2(2)*(a)* or 3(1)*(a)*;'

(i) is or are directly or indirectly able to exercise, or control the exercise of, a majority of the general voting rights associated with issued securities of that company, whether pursuant to a shareholder agreement or otherwise; or

(ii) has or have the right to appoint or elect, or control the appointment or election of, directors of that company who control a majority of the votes at a meeting of the board; or

(b) a wholly owned subsidiary of another juristic person if all of the general voting rights associated with issued securities of the company are held or controlled, alone or in any combination, by persons contemplated in paragraph (a).

(2) For the purpose of determining whether a person controls all or a majority of the general voting rights associated with issued securities of a company —

(a) voting rights that are exercisable only in certain circumstances are to be taken into account only —

(i) when those circumstances have arisen, and for so long as they continue; or

(ii) when those circumstances are under the control of the person holding the voting rights;

(b) voting rights that are exercisable only on the instructions or with the consent or concurrence of another person are to be treated as being held by a nominee for that other person; and

(c) voting rights held by —

(i) a person as nominee for another person are to be treated as held by that other person; or

(ii) a person in a fiduciary capacity are to be treated as held by the beneficiary of those voting rights.

(3) For the purposes of subsection (2), 'hold', or any derivative of it, refers to the registered or direct or indirect beneficial holder of securities conferring a right to vote.

The holding/subsidiary relationship is based on control of the subsidiary company by the holding company either at board meeting or general meeting level.

The relationship exists if the holding company itself controls the subsidiary, or does so through other subsidiaries or in combination with other subsidiaries.[38] The following possibilities present themselves to make Company S a subsidiary of Company H:

- Company H itself controls Company S,
- Company H together with one or more of its subsidiaries controls Company S,
- one or more of Company H's subsidiaries control Company S. (It will be recognised that, if a subsidiary of Company H controls Company S, then Company S will have two holding companies.)

The above possibilities also exist if the control is exercised through the nominees of Company H and/or its subsidiaries.[39]

By 'control' at board meeting level is meant having the right to appoint or elect, or control the appointment or election of, directors of that company who control a majority of the votes at a meeting of the board.[40]

By 'control' at general meeting level is meant the ability to directly or indirectly exercise, or control the exercise of, a majority of the general voting rights

---

[38] Section 3(1)(a).
[39] Section 3(1)(a).
[40] Section 3(1)(a)(ii).

associated with issued securities of that company, whether pursuant to a shareholder agreement or otherwise.[41]

A company is a wholly owned subsidiary of another juristic person if all of the general voting rights associated with issued securities of the company are held or controlled, alone or in any combination, by that juristic person, one or more other subsidiaries of that juristic person, or one or more nominees of that juristic person or any of its subsidiaries.[42]

Important points relating to the holding/subsidiary definition are:

- As was the case in the Companies Act 61 of 1973 (hereafter 'the 1973 Act')[43] there appears to be no doubt that the definition of the holding/subsidiary relationship is exhaustive.
- With regard to control at board level, what is important is the right to appoint or remove directors holding a majority of the voting rights at board meetings, rather than the right to appoint the majority of directors in terms of a head count. This caters for situations where the directors have differential voting rights at board meetings.[44] Thus, A (Pty) Ltd could permit a maximum of five directors, three appointed by B Limited, with one vote each, one appointed by C Limited, also with one vote, and one appointed by D Limited, with five votes. D Limited would then exercise five of the nine votes and would therefore become the holding company. Note that even though B Limited appoints the majority of the directors, it is not the holding company of A (Pty) Ltd, as its appointees do not hold the majority of the voting rights at directors' meetings.[45]

  As it is the exercise of voting rights that is vital, the chairperson's ability to exercise a casting vote may be decisive in determining whether or not a company is a subsidiary. If, for example, the directors carry equal voting rights, but P Ltd is entitled to appoint half of the directors and nominate the chairperson (and assuming that there must be an even number of directors), if the chairperson is entitled to a casting vote, then the company will become a subsidiary of P Ltd. Where the chairpersonship rotates annually, this would lead to the bizarre situation where the holding/subsidiary relationship would alternate every year.[46]
- It is clear from the definition that the number of shares held is not a criterion in determining the holding/subsidiary relationship. It is all about voting rights. The effect of this is that if, for example, Company S has 1 250 000 ordinary A shares with voting rights in issue, held by Company H, and 2 000 000 ordinary

---

[41] Section 3(1)(a)(i).
[42] Section 3(1)(b).
[43] See *Sage Holdings Ltd v The Unisec Group Ltd* 1982 (1) SA 337 (W) 350, accepted on appeal in *Unisec Group Ltd v Sage Holdings Ltd* 1986 (3) SA 259 (T) 271.
[44] See GK Everingham and RD Jooste 'A critical analysis of the new definition of the holding-subsidiary relationship' (1994) 7 (2) *De Ratione* 5. This article deals with the holding/subsidiary definition in the 1973 Act.
[45] Ibid.
[46] Ibid.

B shares without voting rights held by Company X, Company S would be a subsidiary of Company H.

Also, assume, for example, that Company S has 5 000 000 issued ordinary shares and that the Memorandum of Incorporation provides that all shares carry one vote, but for holdings above 100 000 shares, the additional shares carry one vote for every five shares held. Assume further that Company H holds 3 600 000 shares, with all the remaining shareholders holding 100 000 shares or fewer.

Total shares in issue:	5 000 000
Total votes in issue:	
Major shareholder (Company H) (100 000 + 3 500 000/5)	800 000
'Minority' shareholders (5 000 000 − 3 600 000)	1 400 000
	2 200 000

Thus Company H would hold more than 50% of the shares, but only 36,4% of the voting rights, therefore failing to be the holding company of Company S.

With such a voting structure, the total number of votes in issue will depend on the size of the holdings of the various shareholders. Any holdings above the ceiling will have their voting rights diluted; the extent of the dilution (and hence the reduction in available votes) will therefore affect the total exercisable votes.

In the example above, if there is another large shareholder (Company D) with 1 000 000 shares, the picture would change as follows:

Total shares in issue:	5 000 000
Total votes in issue:	
Major shareholder (Company H)	800 000
Second large shareholder (Company D) (100 000 + 900 000/5	280 000
'Minority' shareholders	
(5 000 000 − 3 600 000 − 1 000 000)	400 000
	1 480 000

Thus the peculiar situation arises that the presence of a second major shareholder reduces the total exercisable votes to such an extent that Company H now exercises a majority of the votes despite the effect of dilution on its holding, and has become the holding company of Company S.[47]

- Section 3(2)(a) of the Act provides that voting rights that are exercisable only in certain circumstances are to be taken into account only when those circumstances have arisen, and for as long as they continue; or when those circumstances are under the control of the person holding the voting rights.

In *Unisec Group Ltd v Sage Holdings Ltd*[48] it was held that, if H Ltd held options to acquire shares in S (Pty) Ltd, then, for the purpose of the definition of subsidiary in the 1973 Act before its substitution by s 1(b) of the Companies Amendment Act 82 of 1992, H Ltd had to be attributed with the voting power attaching to those shares despite the fact that it did not, and might never, hold

---
[47] Example adapted from example used in the article by Everingham & Jooste op cit n 44.
[48] 1986 (3) SA 259 (T).

those shares. It was thus possible for H Ltd, through membership of S (Pty) Ltd[49] and potential control of the composition of S (Pty) Ltd's board of directors through the holding of share options, to be S (Pty) Ltd's holding company. The court arrived at this conclusion by interpreting the words 'some power (to) appoint' in s 1(3)(b) of the old definition[50] liberally so as to include a potential power to appoint; it rejected the argument that 'some power to appoint' covered only an 'actual one-step power'.[51]

It seems 'that the change of wording in the new definition (omitting the reference to 'some power') in the Act excludes potential voting power, flowing from the holding of share options, from the reckoning in the determination of voting control'.[52]

However, it is submitted that evasion of the holding/subsidiary relationship and its undesirable consequences cannot be achieved simply through the use of options. The dicta of the learned Innes CJ in *Dadoo Ltd v Krugersdorp Municipal Council*[53] must be borne in mind. After referring to the fact that parties may genuinely arrange their affairs so as to remain outside the provisions of a statute and that such a transaction would not be rendered illegitimate by the mere fact that the parties intended to avoid the operation of the law, the Chief Justice said:[54]

> An attempted evasion, however, may proceed on other lines. The transaction contemplated may in truth be within the provisions of the statute, but the parties may call it by a name or cloak it in a guise, calculated to escape those provisions. Such a transaction would be *in fraudem legis*; the Court would strip off its form and disclose its real nature, and the law would operate.

And at 547 he is reported as follows:

> ... a transaction is *in fraudem legis* when it is designedly disguised so as to escape the provisions of the law, but falls in truth within these provisions. Thus stated, the rule is merely a branch of the fundamental doctrine that the law regards the substance rather than the form of things — a doctrine common, one would think, to every system of jurisprudence and conveniently expressed in the maxim *plus valet quod agitur quam simulate concipitur.*

---

[49] Membership was a requirement at that time.
[50] Section 1(3)(b) of the 1973 Act provided at that time that '... the composition of a company's board of directors shall be deemed to be controlled by another company, if that other company may, by the exercise of some power, without the consent or concurrence of any other person, appoint or remove the majority of the directors ...'
[51] The court did, however, qualify its finding by stressing that the power must not be too remote and, accordingly, it was not in every case that the voting power attaching to the shares would be taken into account. In referring to share options that would not be taken into account, the court cited as examples 'a non-negotiable option to acquire 51% of the share capital of a company for some unrealistic number of millions of rands by a company of modest means, or one which is hedged in with so many conditions precedent of such a nature that it is rendered wholly impracticable in a commercial sense' (Everingham & Jooste op cit n 44. *Unisec Group Ltd v Sage Holdings Ltd* 1986 (3) SA 259 (T) 275).
[52] Ibid.
[53] 1920 AD 530.
[54] 1920 AD 530 at 548.

The de-subsidiarisation scheme (using options) in the *Unisec* case[55] also failed on the basis of the *fraus legis* doctrine, Innes CJ's dicta, above, being quoted with approval. The scheme was found to be no more than a façade and a sham. Devised to carry out an unlawful object and thus 'conceived in sin', the court regarded the project as having been 'born in sin'. The court preferred 'the fundamental truth to a hollow superstructure'.[56]

It must be borne in mind that attempts to avoid the holding/subsidiary relationship could be thwarted through the application of s 6(1) of the Act.

- Voting rights held by a person as nominee for another person are to be treated as held by that other person.[57]
- Voting rights held by a person in a fiduciary capacity are to be treated as held by the beneficiary of those voting rights.[58]

A trustee of a trust is an obvious example of a person acting in a fiduciary capacity. Accordingly, where the trustee holds voting rights associated with issued securities of a company, those voting rights are to be treated as held by the beneficiary of those voting rights.

It appears that what is envisaged here is the situation where a trustee in his or her capacity as such holds securities in a Company S. Company H, a beneficiary of the trust, either has a vested right to the securities and/or to the income from the securities. By 'vested' here is meant an unconditional right even though enjoyment may be postponed. So if Company H's right to the income and/or securities is conditional on the happening of some event, for example, the exercise of the trustee's discretion, then Company H does not have a vested right but a 'contingent' right and accordingly is not a beneficiary for the purposes of the holding/subsidiary definition.

If there are no trust beneficiaries with a vested right to the securities and/or the income, then it appears that the trust, being a juristic person,[59] may be construed as the holding company of Company S.[60] This would in fact appear to be the only situation in which a trust could be a holding company. This of course does not sit well, because the trust has no beneficial interest in the voting rights.

- Section 3(2)*(b)* provides that voting rights that are exercisable only on the instructions or with the consent or concurrence of another person are to be treated as being held by a nominee for that other person.

Section 3(2)*(b)* has the following effect, among other things. Assume Company A and Company B, with the concurrence of each other, can exercise the majority of the voting rights in Company S. This means, according to s 3(2)*(b)*, that in respect of the voting rights in Company S, Company B holds

---

[55] *Unisec Group Ltd v Sage Holdings Ltd* 1986 (3) SA 259 (T).
[56] *Unisec Group Ltd v Sage Holdings Ltd* (supra) at 282.
[57] Section 3(2)*(c)*(i).
[58] Section 3(2)*(c)*(ii).
[59] See definition of 'juristic person' in s 1 of the Act.
[60] The definition of 'holding company' in s 1 of the Act does envisage the possibility of a juristic person other than a company being a 'holding company'. See also the reference to 'juristic person' in s 3(1) of the Act.

the voting rights as nominee for Company A and vice versa, ie Company A holds the voting rights as nominee for Company B. This means that Company S is a subsidiary of both Company A and Company B.

- Not only voting rights attaching to shares in a company come into the reckoning in determining the holding/subsidiary relationship. This is clear from the reference to 'securities' and not 'shares' in s 3. Accordingly, voting rights attaching to 'debt instruments'[61] must also be taken into account. It is thus possible, for example, for a company to be the holding company of another company through the holding of the majority of the voting rights in that other company, which voting rights are attached to debentures in that other company.
- Voting power attaching to shares held by moneylenders as security for money lent, is to be taken into the reckoning in determining the holding/subsidiary relationship. In terms of the definition of subsidiary in the 1973 Act, prior to its substitution in 1992, such voting rights were excluded. The absence of such an exclusion in the new Act's definition is mystifying. 'Surely it is not the legislature's intention that, for example, a bank could become the holding company of another company as a result of the holding of shares in that company as security for money lent to the company.'[62] It appears, however, that the terms of the bank's security could be such that the bank acquires the voting power attached to the shares held.[63]
- Voting rights held through a shareholder agreement are expressly stated to be included in the determination of the holding/subsidiary relationship.[64]
- Whereas it is possible for a juristic person or undertaking other than a company to be a 'holding company', the same is not true of a 'subsidiary', which must be a company.[65] This is the converse of the position in the 1973 Act in terms of which only a company, but not an undertaking, could be a holding company, but an 'undertaking' could be a subsidiary of another company.[66] It must be pointed out, however, that despite the fact that the definition of 'holding company' in relation to a subsidiary expressly includes an 'undertaking', s 3, which appears to be exhaustive, only envisages a juristic person being a holding company. Thus only an 'undertaking' which is a juristic person could be a holding company.[67] The problem is that the meaning of

---

[61] See s 43.
[62] Everingham & Jooste op cit n 44.
[63] See *Marais v Ruskin* 1985 (4) SA 659 (A). 'South African banks appear to have accepted this to be the case — it is now usual to encounter a note within a bank's accounting policies to the effect that entities over which the bank (or its subsidiaries) have acquired control in the course of lending activities are not consolidated.' (See Everingham & Jooste op cit n 44.)
[64] See s 3(1)(*a*)(i) of the Act.
[65] See the definition of 'holding company' and 'subsidiary' in s 1 of the Act, and s 3(1) of the Act. Section 3(1) begins with the words '(1) A company is . . .'
[66] See the definitions of 'holding company' and 'subsidiary company' in s 1(1) and 1(3)(*c*) of the 1973 Act.
[67] It is to be noted that the draft Companies Amendment Bill, 2010 removes the reference to 'undertaking' in the definition of 'holding company'.

'undertaking' is not clear; it is not defined in the Act. A partnership cannot be a holding company because a partnership is not a juristic person.
- The fact that an undertaking controlled by a company cannot be a subsidiary of the company, unlike the position in terms of the 1973 Act, is mystifying. It means that unincorporated enterprises can be used as a means of:

> ... keeping borrowings off the balance sheet of the investor(s) in such enterprises. Increasingly, it has become the practice to conduct business as an unincorporated joint venture or partnership, in terms of which the joint venture or partnership agreement confers a controlling interest on one of the investors. The joint venture or partnership might incur substantial liabilities; however, none of the investors would reflect these liabilities, or even their share thereof in their balance sheets.[68]

All that needs to be shown is the investment in the joint venture/partnership. The definition in the 1973 Act attempted to deem such enterprises to be subsidiaries of the investor holding the majority of the voting rights. Accordingly, they fell within the scope of s 288 of the 1973 Act and consequently had to be consolidated (unless one of the exemptions of ss 291 or 289 applied).
- A trust cannot be a subsidiary. It can only be a holding company. This is clear from a reading of the definition of 'subsidiary' in s 1 of the Act with s 3 of the Act. The same goes for a close corporation: it cannot be a subsidiary.
- A close corporation, being a juristic person, can be a holding company.

6.3 DIRECTORS' FIDUCIARY DUTIES AND THE HOLDING/ SUBSIDIARY RELATIONSHIP

A group of companies is not a separate legal persona and the directors of the companies in the group owe no duties to the group.[69] They only owe duties to their own respective companies.[70] So a company cannot compel a director of its subsidiary to look to the group when exercising his or her discretion.[71] If acting in the interests of the group would be acting in the company's interests, that would be in order, particularly if it is in the interests of minority shareholders.[72]

---

[68] See Everingham & Jooste op cit n 44.
[69] *R v Milne and Erleigh (7)* 1951 (1) SA 791 (A) 828. See generally, DH Botha 'Holding and subsidiary companies: Fiduciary duties of directors' (1983) 16 *De Jure* 234, (1984) 17 *De Jure* 167. Regarding the situation where a director is also a director of its subsidiary, see the King Code of Corporate Governance Principles for South Africa 2009 (Chapter 2) and also the JSE Listings Requirements. See also regarding the duty of a director in such a situation, s 72(2)(*b*)(ii) of the Act, and chapter 12: The Duties and Liability of Directors.
[70] *R v Milne and Erleigh* (supra). See *Walker v Wimborne* (1976) 137 CLR 1 at 6–7 (HC of A); *Linter Group Ltd v Goldberg* (1992) 7 ACSR 580 at 620–3 SC (Vic); *Charterbridge Corporation Ltd v Lloyds Bank Ltd* [1970] Ch 62; [1969] 2 All ER 1185; *Lipschitz v Landmark Consolidated (Pty) Ltd* 1979 (2) SA 482 (W) 488.
[71] *Pergamon Press Ltd v Maxwell* [1970] 2 All ER 809; *ANZ Executors & Trustee Company Ltd v Qintex Australia Ltd* (1990) 2 ACSR 676 SC (Qld); MS Blackman et al *Commentary on the Companies Act* vol 2 (2002) (Revision Service 7, 2010) at 8–53.
[72] An illustration of this is *Charterbridge Corporation Ltd v Lloyds Bank Ltd* [1970] Ch 62; [1969] 2 All ER 1185, where it was accepted that the giving of a guarantee by a company to secure the overdraft of another company within the same group was in the interests of the company giving the guarantee.

However, as Blackman says:[73]

> ... but what is required is that the transaction be judged according to the interests of their company, and, in particular, with regard to the interests of the minority shareholders in their company. The concept of the financial stability of the group as a whole does not necessarily show that a particular company within the group has received value in return for a transaction which it entered into for such an end; always vital are the particular circumstances and the fact that each company within a group of companies retains its own legal personality.[74]

In this regard the courts have sometimes applied an objective test: whether 'an intelligent and honest man in the position of a director of the company concerned, could, in the whole of the existing circumstances, have reasonably believed that the transactions were for the benefit of the company'.[75] However, as Blackman says:[76]

> The better view is that the test is, as always, a subjective one: namely, whether the directors *bona fide* believed that they were acting in the interests of their company.[77] And where the

---

[73] Blackman et al op cit n 71 at 8–54.

[74] *Swanee's Boerdery (Edms) Bpk (in liquidation) v Trust Bank of Africa Ltd* 1986 (2) SA 850 (A) 860. In *Walker v Wimborne* (1976) 137 CLR 1 at 6–7 (HC of A) Mason J said: 'To speak of the companies as being members of a group is something of a misnomer ... In [the case of a group] the payment of money by company A to company B to enable company B to carry on its business may have derivative benefits for company A as a shareholder in company B if that company is enabled to trade profitably or realise its assets to advantage. Even so the transaction is one which must be viewed from the standpoint of company A and judged according to the criterion of the interests of that company ... Indeed the emphasis given by the primary judge to the circumstance that the group derived a benefit from the transaction tended to obscure the fundamental principles that each of the companies was a separate and independent legal entity, and that it was the duty of the directors ... to consult [the] interests [of the company] and its interests alone in deciding whether payments should be made to other companies.' See *Solaglass Finance Co (Pty) Ltd v Commissioner for Inland Revenue* 1991 (2) SA 257 (A), where the majority held that a wholly owned subsidiary acting as the banker or financier of the group, could not deduct from its taxable income irrevocable loans which it had made to subsidiaries in the group. This was because these moneys had not been 'exclusively laid out or expended for the purposes of trade'.

[75] Formulated by Pennycuick J in *Charterbridge Corporation Ltd v Lloyds Bank Ltd* [1970] Ch 62 at 74; [1969] 2 All ER 1185 at 1194. This test has been applied in the case of groups in a number of Australian cases: see *Reid Murray Holdings v David Murray Holdings Pty Ltd* (1972) 5 SASR 386 at 402; *Australian National Industries Ltd v Greater Pacific Investments Pty Ltd* (1992) 7 ACSR 176 SC (NSW); *Jenkins v Enterprise Gold Mines NL* (1991) 6 ACSR 539 SC (WA); *Equiticorp Financial Services Ltd v Equiticorp Financial Services Ltd* (1992) 9 ACSR 199 SC (NSW). See Blackman et al op cit n 71 at 8–54.

[76] Blackman et al op cit n 71 at 8–54.

[77] See *Equiticorp Finance Ltd v Bank of New Zealand* (1993) 11 ACSR 642 CA (NSW), where Clarke and Cripps JA said (at 726–7): 'Although we are content to deal with the issues in the case upon the basis of the test proposed by Pennycuick J in *Charterbridge Corporation Ltd v Lloyds Bank Ltd* [1970] Ch 62; [1969] 2 All ER 1185 we should indicate that we have reservations about the test proposed ... The directors are bound to exercise their powers, *bona fide*, in what they consider is in the interests of the company and not for any collateral purpose. Whether they did so or not is a question of fact ... Accordingly there seems to us to be difficulties in substituting an objective test (How would an intelligent and honest man have acted?) for the factual question raised in the proceedings. It may be that if a director bluntly states that he or she did not consider the interests of the particular company at all and solely had regard to the interests of the group, then difficulties would arise in resolving that factual question. But the position will rarely be such a black and white one and it would usually be possible to discern whether in deciding to take certain action for the

directors did not consider the interests of their company, the court — rather than then applying the objective test — ought simply to conclude that the directors acted in breach of duty.

A director of a company owes no fiduciary duties to its holding company. 'Nominee directors' are accordingly, as the courts have said, in a precarious position.[78]

> Although there is authority for the proposition that where the company's articles provide the appointment of directors to represent the interests of shareholders with particular interests, such directors may act to further those interests (on the theory that it is in the interests of the company that they do so), this principles, even if correct, clearly has no application in the case of the directors of a subsidiary whose board is appointed by its holding company.[79]

The position of directors of a company vis-à-vis the company's subsidiary depends on whether the subsidiary has an independent board.[80] If it is independent, neither the holding company nor its directors owe the subsidiary fiduciary duties.[81] However, 'where a holding company places its nominees on the board of the subsidiary, the holding company, and hence its directors, must 'behave with scrupulous fairness to the minority shareholders and to avoid imposing on their nominees the alternative of disregarding their instructions or betraying the interests of the minority'.[82] In other words, while neither the directors of a holding

---

benefit of the group the directors perceived, and were justified in their perception, that in so doing they were acting for the benefit of the particular company. On the other hand it may be possible to discern that the directors embarked on a course to support the group unconcerned about the detrimental effect of the action of the particular company or were prepared to sacrifice that company for the good of the other companies in the group. A careful analysis of the factual situation will usually reveal the answer to the factual question posed although no doubt on some occasions the problem may very well be a difficult one.' . . . But see *Liniton v Telenet Pty Ltd* (1998) 30 ACSR 465 at 472 CA (NSW) where it was pointed out that 'the *Charterbridge* test' had been applied many times in Australia and it was held that, since the respondent itself had adopted it, the case should be decided by an application of that test.

[78] See *Equiticorp Finance Ltd v Bank of New Zealand* (1993) 11 ACSR 642 CA (NSW), where as Blackman et al op cit n 71 at 8–55 point out, Clarke and Cripps JA said (at 727–8): 'We are mindful of the fact that Pennycuick J [in *Charterbridge Corporation Ltd v Lloyds Bank Ltd* [1970] Ch 62 at 74; [1969] 2 All ER 1185 at 1194] was not substituting the objective test for the subjective one which had traditionally been applied. In his view the occasion to apply the objective test only arose when it was clear that the directors had not considered the interests of the relevant company at all. In a sense he proposed a legal test to be applied only in limited cases to avoid what he regarded as an absurd situation. Nonetheless we have reservations about this means of resolving those difficulties. A preferable view may be that where the directors have failed to consider the interests of the relevant company they should be found to have committed a breach of duty. If, however, the transaction was, objectively viewed, in the interests of the company, then no consequences would flow from the breach. Such an inquiry would not require the court to consider how the hypothetical and intelligent director would have acted. On the contrary it would accept that a finding of breach of duty flows from a failure to consider the interests of the company and would then direct attention at the consequences of the breach.'

[79] Blackman et al op cit n 71 at 8–56.
[80] Ibid.
[81] *Lindgren v L & P Estates Ltd* [1968] Ch 572. See Blackman et al op cit n 71 at 8–56.
[82] *Per* Viscount Simonds in *Scottish Co-operative Wholesale Society Ltd v Meyer* [1959] AC 324 at 341; [1958] 3 All ER 66 71 (HL). And see *Kuwait Asia Bank EC v National Mutual Life Nominees Ltd* [1991] 1 AC 187; [1990] 3 All ER 404 (PC) where it was held that directors nominated by a shareholder who employed them are, when acting as directors of the company, agents of the company, and not of the person who nominated them, so that that person is not liable for their acts

company nor the holding company itself stands in a fiduciary relationship to its subsidiary, they do owe it a duty not to fetter or otherwise undermine the independence of its directors.'[83]

If the board of the subsidiary is not independent:

> ... the general principle is that a person who procures the election of a board of directors under circumstances which make it impossible for them to exercise an independent judgment, must ... observe the utmost good faith in his dealings with the company, which he has, of set purpose, deprived of independent advice — a duty that arises from the circumstances which he has chosen to bring about.[84]

And where the holding company in fact conducts the business of the subsidiary, it must act fairly in regard to the interests of the subsidiary.[85]

6.4 THE 'RELATED' AND 'INTERRELATED' CONCEPTS

The Act, apart from the holding/subsidiary relationship, also recognises what are termed 'related' and 'interrelated' relationships between persons and makes certain provisions applicable if such relationships exist.

The rationale for such recognition appears to be that, if a company transacts with another person and they are related or interrelated, they might not act at arm's length, and might accordingly act to the detriment of the company and its creditors and/or members. For example, if a company makes a loan to a director of the company, the requirements of s 45 of the Act must be met. Similarly, s 45 applies if the loan is to a person 'related' to the director. The interrelated relationship becomes particularly important in relation to the 'group' concept, the proper functioning of the provisions relating to the duties of directors to disclose conflicts with the company, and to the proper application of the takeover regulations.

It is, of course, possible that the parties to the transaction who are related or interrelated may be acting quite independently and at arm's length, and accordingly the Act[86] empowers the court, the Takeover Regulation Panel and the Companies Tribunal to exempt any person from the application of a provision of the Act that would apply to that person because of the relationship.

As will be seen, the definitions of 'related' and 'interrelated' persons are wide and it may not always be 'factually or legally simple to determine whether companies are related or interrelated, especially in complex group structures'.[87] Section 2(3), referred to above, may also have an ameliorating role to play in this regard.

6.4.1 The 'related' relationship

Section 1 of the Act provides that '"related", when used in respect of two persons, means persons who are connected to one another in any manner contemplated in section 2(1)(*a*) to *(c)*'.

---

either as employer or principal. But it was accepted (at 222–3; at 424) that the position would be otherwise if the shareholder exploited its influence over the directors it nominated and interfered with the affairs of the company.

[83] Ibid.
[84] *Robinson v Randfontein Estates Gold Mining Co Ltd* 1921 AD 168 at 196–7.
[85] *Nicholas v Soundcraft Electronics Ltd* [1993] BCLC 360 at 364–5 (CA).
[86] See s 2(3).
[87] See J Yeats and RD Jooste 'Financial assistance — A new approach' (2009) 126 *SALJ* 566 at 576.

Section 2(1) distinguishes between the 'related' relationships between:
- two individuals,
- an individual and a juristic person, and
- two juristic persons.

(a) Two individuals

An individual is related to another individual if they are:
- 'married or live together in a relationship similar to a marriage', or
- 'separated by no more than two degrees of natural or adopted consanguinity or affinity'.[88]

To determine the degree of consanguinity between two relatives, one must count up from the one relative to the nearest common ancestor and then continue counting down to the other relative. Relatives of a person separated by no more than two degrees of consanguinity are thus the person's parents and children (first degree) and brothers, sisters, grandchildren and grandparents (second degree). Such persons are included whether the relationship arises naturally, through adoption or through marriage (affinity). For example, brothers, sisters, parents and grandparents through adoption are included, as are grandparents-in-law, parents-in-law, brothers-in-law and sisters-in-law.

(b) An individual and a juristic person

An individual is related to a juristic person 'if the individual directly or indirectly controls the juristic person'.[89]

The 'control' envisaged[90] is the same as the control envisaged where one juristic person controls another juristic person, which is dealt with below.

(c) Two juristic persons

A juristic person is related to another juristic person if:
- either of them directly or indirectly controls the other, or the business of the other,
- either is a subsidiary of the other, or
- a person directly or indirectly controls each of them, or the business of each of them.[91]

(d) Control

(i) *Control of a company*

A person controls a company if:

(1) that person is a subsidiary of that company,[92]

---

[88] Section 2(1)(*a*)(i) and (ii).
[89] Section 2(1)(*b*).
[90] See s 2(2).
[91] Section 2(1)(*c*).
[92] See s 2(*a*)(i).

Groups of Companies and Related Persons

(2) that person, together with any related or inter-related person is —[93]
- directly or indirectly able to exercise or control the exercise of a majority of the voting rights associated with securities of that company, whether pursuant to a shareholder agreement or otherwise, or
- has the right to appoint or elect, or control the appointment or election of, directors of that company who control a majority of the votes at a meeting of the board,

(3) that person has the ability to materially influence the policy of the company in a manner comparable to a person who, in ordinary commercial practice, would be able to exercise an element of control referred to in (1) and (2).[94]

It will be recognised that point (2) above is virtually identical to the voting control required for the holding/subsidiary relationship to exist.[95] A difference is that, in relation to the holding/subsidiary relationship, s 3(1)(a)(i) refers to 'a majority of the general voting rights', whereas s 2(2)(ii)(aa) does not use the word 'general'. Also, s 3(1)(a)(i) refers to 'voting rights associated with *issued* securities' whereas s 2(2)(ii)(aa) does not use the word 'issued'. It is doubtful whether anything turns on this difference in wording.

In determining whether a person controls all or a majority of the general voting rights in a company for the purposes of the holding/subsidiary definition, s 3(2) provides:

. . .

(a) voting rights that are exercisable only in certain circumstances are to be taken into account only —
  (i) when those circumstances have arisen, and for so long as they continue; or
  (ii) when those circumstances are under the control of the person holding the voting rights;
(b) voting rights that are exercisable only on the instructions or with the consent or concurrence of another person are to be treated as being held by a nominee for that other person; and
(c) voting rights held by —
  (i) a person as nominee for another person are to be treated as held by that other person; or
  (ii) a person in a fiduciary capacity are to be treated as held by the beneficiary of those voting rights.

It will be recognised that there is no similar provision to s 3(2) in s 2. The rationale for this is unclear and its omission may be an oversight.

(ii) *Control of a close corporation*

A person controls a close corporation if that person owns the majority of members' interest, or controls directly, or has the right to control, the majority of members' votes in the close corporation.[96]

---

[93] See s 2(a)(ii)(aa) and (bb).
[94] See s 2(d).
[95] See s 3(1)(a)(i) and (ii). See 6.2 above.
[96] Section 2(2)(b).

Control also exists if that person has the ability to materially influence the policy of the close corporation in a manner comparable to a person who, in ordinary commercial practice, would be able to exercise an element of control referred to in the last paragraph.[97]

(iii) *Control of a trust*

A person controls a trust if that person has the ability to control the majority of the votes of the trustees or to appoint the majority of the trustees, or to appoint or change the majority of the beneficiaries of the trust.[98]

Control also exists if that person has the ability to materially influence the policy of the trust in a manner comparable to a person who, in ordinary commercial practice, would be able to exercise an element of control referred to in the last paragraph.[99]

6.4.2 The 'interrelated' relationship

Section 1 of the Act provides that 'inter-related, *[sic]* when used in respect of three or more persons, means persons who are related to one another in a series of relationships, as contemplated in section 2(1)*(d)*'.

Unfortunately, there is no section 2(1)*(d)* in the Act. The draft Companies Amendment Bill, 2010 recognises this and, to rectify the situation, the definition of 'interrelated' has been amended in the Bill to read as follows:

> inter-related' *[sic]*, when used in respect of three or more persons, means persons who are related to one another in a linked series of relationships, such that two of the persons are related in a manner contemplated in section 2(1), and one of them is related to the third in any such manner, and so forth in an unbroken series.

So, for example, if Company X is related to Company Y and Company Y is related to Mr A and Mr A is related to Mr B and Mr B is related to Trust C and Trust C is related to Close Corporation D, then Company X, Company Y, Mr A, Mr B, Trust C and Close Corporation D are interrelated persons.

---

[97] Section 2(2)*(c)*.
[98] Section 2(2)*(c)*.
[99] Section 2(2)*(c)*.

CHAPTER 7

SHARES, SECURITIES AND TRANSFER

Richard Jooste and Jacqueline Yeats*

7.1	GENERAL	197
7.2	NATURE OF A SHARE	198
7.3	CLASSES OF SHARES	199
	(a) Preference shares	200
	(b) Redeemable shares	203
	(c) Ordinary shares	204
	(d) Deferred shares	204
7.4	AUTHORISATION FOR SHARES	204
7.5	AUTHORITY TO ISSUE SHARES	205
7.6	CONSIDERATION FOR SHARES	207
7.7	CAPITALISATION SHARES	210
7.8	DEBT INSTRUMENTS	212
7.9	OPTIONS FOR SUBSCRIPTION OF SECURITIES	217
7.10	REGISTRATION AND TRANSFER OF SECURITIES	218
	7.10.1 Certificated and uncertificated securities	218
	7.10.2 Equal status of securities	218
	7.10.3 'Certificated' securities	218
	(a) Register of certificated securities	218
	(b) Security certificates	220
	(c) Transfer of certificated securities	221
	(d) Beneficial interest in certificated securities	227
	7.10.4 'Uncertificated' securities	232
	(a) Introduction	232
	(b) Registration of uncertificated securities	233
	(c) Transfer of uncertificated securities	235
	(d) Security by cession *in securitatem debiti*	237
	(e) Substitution	237
	(f) Liability relating to uncertificated securities	238
	(g) Beneficial interest in uncertificated securities	239

7.1 GENERAL

The activities of a company are financed through the issue by the company of securities in the company (usually shares) or by borrowings by the company. In

---

* Richard Jooste authored sections 7.1 to 7.10.3 and Jacqueline Yeats authored section 7.10.4.

this way funds are made available to the company through investments made in securities in the company or by loans made to the company.

The monies raised by a company through the issue of shares can be referred to as the 'share capital' of the company although, unlike in the old Companies Act 61 of 1973 (hereafter 'the 1973 Act'), this is not a term used in the new Companies Act 71 of 2008 (hereafter 'the Act'). The 1973 Act required the proceeds on the issue of par value shares to be transferred to a 'share capital account' and the proceeds on the issue of no par value shares to a 'stated capital account'.[1] Where par value shares were issued at a premium, ie above the par value of the shares, the premium referred to as the 'share premium' had to be transferred to a 'share premium account'. Changes to these accounts were strictly controlled. The provisions in the 1973 Act relating to these accounts are foreign to the new Act.

A distinction is drawn in the Act between 'authorised' and 'issued' shares of a company. The 'authorised' shares are the shares which the company is entitled by its memorandum of incorporation to issue, but which have not yet been issued. The 'issued' shares are shares that are authorised and issued.

7.2 NATURE OF A SHARE

The proprietary interest that a person holds in a company is a 'share'. The company as a separate legal person is capable of owning assets. Accordingly, ownership of the assets resides in the company and the holding of a share in the company does not entitle the shareholder to ownership or part or joint ownership of its assets. A share is accordingly defined in the Act[2] as 'one of the units into which the proprietary interest in a profit company is divided'.

The nature of a share has been addressed by the courts. In *Bradbury v English Sewing Cotton Co Ltd*[3] Lord Wrenbury said:

> A share ... is a fractional part of the [share] capital. It confers upon the holder [certain rights] to a proportionate part of the assets of the corporation, whether by way of dividend or distribution of assets in winding up. It forms, however, a separate right of property. The capital is the property of the corporation. The share ... is the property of the corporator.

In *Cooper v Boyes*[4] Van Zyl J said:

> [T]here is no simple definition of a share. The various definitions emphasise a complex of characteristics which are peculiar to it. The gist thereof is that a share represents an interest in a company, which interest consists of a complex of personal rights which may, as an incorporeal movable entity, be negated or otherwise disposed of. It is certainly not a consumable article, such as money, even though a money value can be placed on it. Nor can it, by any analogy, be likened to a debt ... The fact that the value of a share in a company may fluctuate for a great variety of reasons, or that it may be affected by all manner of eventualities which befall the company, such as liquidation, cannot change its essential nature ... There is, of course, no reason why it cannot be bequeathed by way of a usufruct. The usufructuary will have the right to receive dividends or other benefits accruing to the shares, subject thereto that, on termination of the usufruct, the share itself must devolve upon the heir as ultimate beneficiary in whom the ownership vests.

---

[1] The meaning of par and no par value shares is dealt with in 7.2 below.
[2] See s 1.
[3] [1923] AC 744 (HL) 746.
[4] 1994 (4) SA 521 (C) 535.

Fidelis Oditah explains the legal nature of a share as follows:[5]

> Shares are a bundle of intangible property rights shareholders receive from the company in return for their contribution of cash or non-cash assets to the company. Shares define and allocate *(a)* income rights ie rights of participation in the company's cashflow, usually in the form of dividend; *(b)* the incidence of the risk of loss, usually in the form of priority rights in relation to capital; and *(c)* power of control, principally through voting rights. Shares are classified according to income, capital and control rights. The definition and allocation of these rights is an integral part of shares. By reason of ownership of a share, a shareholder becomes the owner of an intangible property right in a company made up of income, capital and voting rights, all determined by the terms of the issue of the share, the company's Memorandum of Incorporation, the general law and applicable statutes of the place (ie country) of incorporation of the company. Shares are the units into which shareholders' rights of participation in the company's cash flow, management and on a return of capital, are divided.

In considering the nature of a share, it must be noted that:

- A share issued by a company is regarded as movable property.[6] It is transferable in any manner provided by or recognised by the Act or other legislation.[7]
- A share does not have a label or indicator of value. Under the 1973 Act it was possible to have shares with no label of value, known as 'no par value' shares and also shares with a label of value, known as 'par' or 'nominal' value shares, for example, a 'R10 share'. The danger of this was that the par value could be misleading if the actual value was different from the par value and hence the concept of par value was dropped in the new Act. There was no fundamental difference between a par value and a no par value share.
- The term 'security' is wider than 'share'. In terms of s 1 of the Act, 'securities' has the meaning set out in s 1 of the Securities Services Act 36 of 2004 and includes shares held in a private company. 'Securities' includes, for example, options and debt instruments.[8]

7.3 CLASSES OF SHARES

The basic presumption is that all shares enjoy equal rights.[9] However, it is possible for a company to have shares with different rights, preferences, limitations and terms, in which case the company has 'classes' of shares. Generally, the division of shares into various classes is based on the nature of the rights they give with regard to dividends and participation in a distribution on liquidation, and voting rights. But this is not necessarily always true. For example, where all the company's shares carry the same rights with regard to dividends and return of capital, some of them may have conversion rights, eg the right to convert the shares into shares of another class. A company has almost unlimited freedom to

---

[5] 'Takeovers, Share Exchanges and the Meaning of Loss' (1996) 112 *LQR* 424 at 426–7.
[6] See s 35(1).
[7] Ibid.
[8] See s 43, which is dealt with below. The definition of 'securities' is set out below in 7.8, which deals with debt instruments.
[9] See s 36(1). *Birch v Cropper* (1889) 14 App Cas 525 (HL) 543.

create the capital structure it desires, and in so doing to structure the rights of each of its various classes of shares in an almost infinite variety of ways.

All the shares of any particular class authorised by a company have preferences, rights, limitations and other terms that are identical to those of other shares of the same class, except to the extent that the company's Memorandum of Incorporation provides otherwise.[10]

Shares have traditionally been divided, according to the rights attached to them, into three main types or classes of shares: *(a)* preference shares, which may or may not be redeemable preference shares, *(b)* ordinary shares, and *(c)* deferred shares.

(a) Preference shares

Where the rights of classes of shares differ on the basis of rights to priority with regard to dividends and/or return of capital, the class or classes that enjoy preference rights are referred to as 'preference' shares. The shares that enjoy no preferred rights are referred to as 'ordinary' shares.

It is only possible therefore for preference shares to exist 'by way of juxtaposition with other shares'.[11] They have some preference or priority over ordinary shares.

It has been held[12] that:

> ... either with regard to dividend or with regard to the rights in winding-up, the express gift or attachment of preferential rights to preference shares, on their creation, is, *prima facie*, a definition of the whole of their rights in that respect, and negatives any further or other right to which, but for the specified rights, they would have been entitled.

However, it has been held that that construction 'must be applied with caution, and the memorandum must be examined to see whether they contain any indication that preferential rights are not intended to be exhaustive'.[13] The onus of proving that they are not exhaustive is upon the preference shareholders who allege that they have further and better rights.[14]

It is usual for preference shares to carry a preferential right to dividend. Unless, which is rarely the case, they are entitled to their preference dividend on the making of a profit by the company, the holders of preference shares are entitled to claim their preference dividend only if both sufficient assets are available for such distribution and the dividend has been declared in the manner provided by the memorandum or rules.[15]

Preference shareholders do not have any right to participate in surplus profits unless the right to do so is conferred, in which case the preference shares are known as 'participating preference shares'. Therefore, unless there is provision to

---
[10] Section 37(1). It is to be noted that the draft Companies Amendment Bill, 2010 proposes to delete the wording beginning with 'except' to the end of s 37(1).
[11] Barrett J in *Re Capel Finance* (2005) 52 ACSR 601 at 605.
[12] *Re National Telephone Co* [1914] 1 Ch 755 at 764 *per* Sargant J.
[13] *Anglo-Transvaal Collieries Ltd v SA Mutual Life Assurance Society* 1977 (3) SA 631 (T) 638.
[14] *Donaldson Investments (Pty) Ltd v Anglo-Transvaal Collieries Ltd: SA Mutual Life Assurance Society Intervening* 1979 (3) SA 713 (W) 727.
[15] *Bond v Barrow Haematite Steel Co* [1902] 1 Ch 353; [1900–3] All ER Rep 484.

the contrary, the participation of preference shares in the distribution of profits is restricted to the fixed percentage dividend to which they are entitled.[16] The preference in dividend rights thus operates both as a priority over other shares and as a limitation on dividend participation. Participating preference shares, then, entitle their holders to the fixed percentage preference dividend and to a share in the residual distributable profits.

'Cumulative preference shares' give the holder a prior right to both arrear and current preference dividends. This means that, if the monies applicable to dividends in one year are not sufficient to pay the preference dividend, the deficiency, including arrears, must be made good at a subsequent dividend distribution before anything is paid as dividend to the holders of other shares ranking after such preference shares.

The general presumption is that, if the conditions of issue are silent in this regard, preference shares are cumulative, ie if preference shares confer preferential rights in respect of dividend, the dividend is *prima facie* cumulative.[17]

When a preference dividend has been declared, the preference shareholder's claim to it is that of a creditor. This is also so where the company's memorandum or rules provide that the preference shareholders have a right to their preference dividend and to arrear dividends if the company makes a profit. The dividends become a debt due by the company on the making of a sufficient profit and do not become a debt due by the company only when declared.[18]

Where dividends must first be declared before they can be claimed, which is usually the case, the holders of cumulative preference shares have no preference on liquidation in respect of arrear, but undeclared, dividends.[19] However, this is only the *prima facie* position, because the memorandum or rules may provide that, in a winding-up, preference shareholders are to be paid arrear dividends before capital is repaid to the ordinary shareholders. If the memorandum or rules provide that arrear preference dividends must be paid out on liquidation, such payment must be made out of the available surplus proceeds of assets irrespective of whether the dividends have been declared and irrespective of whether the said surplus represents revenue profits or capital, ie whether or not there were any profits out of which the dividends could have been paid before winding-up.[20] If there has been no express extension of the right of preference shareholders to arrears to date of payment, they are entitled to such arrears up to the date of the winding-up.[21]

---

[16] *Will v United Lankat Plantations Co Ltd* [1914] AC 11 (HL), which judgment is based on the rule that the provisions setting out the rights attached to shares are deemed to be exhaustive (*inclusio unius est exclusio alterius*). See also *Scottish Insurance Corporation Ltd v Wilsons and Clyde Coal Co Ltd* [1949] AC 462; [1949] 1 All ER 1068 (HL).
[17] *Ferguson and Forrester Ltd v Buchanan* [1920] SC 154 (Ct Sess); *Henry v Great Northern Railway Co* (1857) 1 De G & J 606; 44 ER 858; *Webb v Earle* (1857) LR 20 Eq 556.
[18] See *Bishop v Smyrna and Cassaba Railway Co (No 2)* [1895] 2 Ch 265.
[19] *Re Catalinas Warehouse & Mole Co Ltd* [1947] 1 All ER 51; *Re Roberts & Cooper Ltd* [1929] 2 Ch 383; *Re W Foster & Son Ltd* [1942] 1 All ER 314.
[20] *Re EW Savory Ltd* [1951] 2 All ER 1036; *Re Springbok Agricultural Estates Ltd* [1920] 1 Ch 563; *Re Wharfedale Brewery Co Ltd* [1952] Ch 913; [1952] 2 All ER 635.
[21] *Re EW Savory Ltd* (supra).

In the absence of an express stipulation that shares enjoying a preference with regard to dividends also enjoy a preference with regard to repayment of capital on liquidation, the preference and ordinary shareholders share in the capital on a *pro rata* basis.[22] Thus, *prima facie* a preference share gives only a preferential right to dividend.

On liquidation, if there is a surplus after capital has been repaid, preference and ordinary shareholders will share equally in the surplus in proportion to their respective shareholdings. This is the case whether the surplus represents capital or profits.[23]

Preference shareholders' rights may, however, be restricted. For example, their rights to surplus assets may be restricted to surplus assets exclusive of reserves of undistributed profits[24] that could have been distributed by way of dividend to the ordinary shareholders.[25] However, it would seem that the mere fact that the preference shareholders' rights to dividend are restricted to a preference dividend (ie they are not participating preference shares with regard to dividend) is, in itself, not sufficient to disentitle them from participating in all the surplus assets on winding-up.[26]

The value of preference shares with a preference to return of capital on winding-up would appear to have been undermined by s 46 of the Act. Section 46 empowers a company to make distributions to its shareholders by virtue of their

---

[22] *Ex parte Betty: in re First Mutual Investment Trust Ltd* 1974 (1) SA 127 (W) 129; *South African Mutual Life Assurance Society v Anglo-Transvaal Collieries Ltd* 1973 (3) SA 642 (A) 656; *Donaldson Investments (Pty) Ltd v Anglo-Transvaal Collieries Ltd* 1980 (4) SA 204 (T) 214–15.

[23] *Birch v Cropper, re Bridgewater Navigation Co* (1889) 14 App Cas 525 (HL).

[24] As Blackman et al point out (see *Commentary on the Companies Act* vol 1 (2002) 5–179 in *Donaldson Investments (Pty) Ltd v Anglo-Transvaal Collieries Ltd: SA Mutual Life Assurance Society Intervening* 1979 (3) SA 713 (W) 730 Preiss J held that where the capital of a company consists of shares and they are sold before or in the course of liquidation, the difference between the price of their acquisition and the price realised is classifiable as a profit, albeit a capital profit. This view was rejected by Myburgh J in *Donaldson Investments (Pty) Ltd v Anglo-Transvaal Collieries Ltd* 1980 (4) SA 204 (T) 214, who held that the mere fact that shares have increased in value does not convert those specific shares from surplus assets to profits, and that their increase in value cannot be regarded as profits: the shares are capital assets. In *Donaldson Investments (Pty) Ltd v Anglo-Transvaal Collieries Ltd* 1983 (3) SA 96 (A) 114–15 Galgut AJA found it unnecessary to express an opinion as to whether or not an increase in the value of shares constitutes a capital profit, ie as to which view, that of Preiss J or that of Myburgh J, is correct.

[25] *Donaldson Investments (Pty) Ltd v Anglo-Transvaal Collieries Ltd* 1980 (4) SA 204 (T) 214; *Birch v Cropper, re Bridgewater Navigation Co* (supra); *Dimbula Valley (Ceylon) Tea Co Ltd v Laurie* [1961] Ch 353; [1961] 1 All ER 769; *Donaldson Investments (Pty) Ltd v Anglo-Transvaal Collieries Ltd: SA Mutual Life Assurance Society Intervening* (supra) at 727.

[26] *Dimbula Valley (Ceylon) Tea Co Ltd v Laurie* (supra); *Donaldson Investments (Pty) Ltd v Anglo-Transvaal Collieries Ltd* (supra); Cf *Donaldson (Pty) Ltd v Anglo-Transvaal Collieries Ltd: SA Mutual Life Assurance Society Intervening* (supra) at 727. In *Donaldson Investments (Pty) Ltd v Anglo-Transvaal Collieries Ltd* 1983 (3) SA 96 (A) 114–15 Galgut AJA considered counsel's argument to the effect that once a company is placed in liquidation, the distinction between profits and capital assets falls away because in a winding-up there is no room for an investigation into which of the company's assets are derived from profits and which of them are simply assets of the company. He said that '[a]s a result of my reading of the cases I incline to the view that it cannot be said that, as between shareholders, the undeclared profits of a company necessarily cease to be such in a winding-up.'

shareholding, subject to a liquidity and solvency test.[27] This test merely prohibits payments if, after the distribution, the fairly valued assets of the company would be less than the liabilities of the company. In addition, s 48 empowers a company to repurchase its shares, provided that the same liquidity and solvency tests are satisfied. In both instances the rights of preference shareholders are not considered. This is contrary to the position in some other jurisdictions where companies have been empowered to make distributions and repurchases subject to liquidity and solvency tests. The solvency test is satisfied only if the company's net assets exceed both its liabilities and the amount that would be needed, if the company were wound up, to satisfy the preferent rights of shareholders whose preferent rights are superior to those receiving the distribution or whose shares are to be repurchased.[28]

(b) Redeemable shares

Section 37(5) of the Act provides that a company's Memorandum of Incorporation may establish, for any class of shares, terms that provide for shares of that class to be redeemable subject to the requirements of ss 46 and 48 (the latter provisions are dealt with later):

- at the option of the company, the shareholder, or another person at any time, or upon the occurrence of any specified contingency,
- for cash, indebtedness, securities or other property,
- at prices and in amounts specified, or determined in accordance with a formula, or
- subject to any other terms set out in the company's Memorandum of Incorporation.

A redemption of shares is a repurchase of the shares[29] made in terms of a right to purchase or to sell conferred on the company or the holder of the shares as a term of the issue.

Redeemable shares are not restricted to redeemable *preference* shares as was the case under the 1973 Act.[30]

---

[27] Section 46 read with s 4.
[28] See, for example, s 52(4) of the New Zealand Companies Act 1993.
[29] See *Re Handevel Pty Ltd* (1983) 8 ACLR 44 50–1 SC (Vic). And see *Lord Provost Magistrates of the City of Edinburgh v British Linen Bank* [1913] AC 133 at 138–9, 141–2 (HL).
[30] Prof LCB Gower refers to this restriction as follows: 'The main reason for restricting the power to issue redeemable shares to preference shares was, no doubt, that the possibilities of abuse are less in this case since they do not normally afford voting control of the company or fluctuate in value to the same extent as equity shares. But since there is no definition of "preference shares" for the purpose of [the section] it would appear to cover any shares which afford a preference either as regards dividends or capital. Hence it could be used to issue redeemable shares which because of their rights to further participation in either or both of income and capital confer a considerable slice of equity (and, indeed, of the votes). If the section is intended to limit redeemable shares to non-equity shares, it has achieved its purpose only because advantage has not in practice been taken of it in relation to equity shares. The only worthwhile purpose that the word "preference" seems to serve is that it ensures that the company has other, non-redeemable, shares and therefore helps to avoid the complications which occur when a company finds itself without any shareholders.' See *The Purchase by a Company of its Own Shares, A Consultative Document* (1980) Cmnd 7944 Part II 'The Purchase by a Company of its Own Shares', by Prof LCB Gower para 4.

(c) Ordinary shares

The term 'ordinary shares' describes shares that are fully participating as to dividends, capital and surplus assets on winding-up. Where there are preference shares, ordinary shares confer on their holders the residue of the rights with regard to dividend and/or repayment of capital.

(d) Deferred shares

A deferred share is rarely found. It is a share bearing the restriction that no dividend can be paid to the shareholder in a particular year unless the ordinary shareholders are first paid a certain amount for that year. Deferred shares have in the past usually been issued as remuneration for promoters for services rendered in the formation of the company (founders' shares) or to persons who have sold assets, including a business as a going concern, to the company (vendors' shares). Thus, founders' or vendors' shares are usually issued as fully paid for consideration other than cash.[31] Although all founders' shares are not necessarily deferred shares, in the past they usually were. They were also usually shares of a small nominal amount which, although deferred in priority as to dividends, entitled holders to the whole or a large percentage of the surplus profits remaining after the 'ordinary shareholders' had received their minimum dividend.[32]

7.4 AUTHORISATION FOR SHARES

The Act provides[33] that a company's Memorandum of Incorporation:

- must set out the classes of shares, and the number of shares of each class, that the company is authorised to issue,
- must set out, with respect to each class of shares:
  - a distinguishing designation for that class, and
  - the preferences, rights, limitations and other terms associated with that class, but may set out a class of shares without specifying the associated preferences, rights, limitations or other terms of that class for which the board of the company must determine the associated preferences, rights, limitations or other terms, and
- may authorise a stated number of unclassified shares, which are subject to classification by the board of the company and which must not be issued until the board of the company has determined the associated preferences, rights, limitations or other terms.

The authorisation and classification of shares, the numbers of authorised shares of each class, and the preferences, rights, limitations and other terms associated with each class of shares, as set out in a company's Memorandum of Incorporation, may be changed only by:[34]

- an amendment of the Memorandum of Incorporation by special resolution of the shareholders, or

---

[31] *Holaway v Allighan* 1950 (3) SA 542 (W); see also *Broomberg v Hilewitz* 1970 (3) SA 568 (W).
[32] See Blackman et al op cit n 24 at 5–181.
[33] See s 36.
[34] See s 36(2).

- the board of the company, except to the extent that the Memorandum of Incorporation provides otherwise.

Except to the extent that a company's Memorandum of Incorporation provides otherwise, the company's board may:[35]

- increase or decrease the number of authorised shares of any class of shares,
- reclassify any classified shares that have been authorised but not issued,
- classify any unclassified shares that have been authorised but are not issued, or
- determine the preferences, rights, limitations or other terms of shares in a class subject to determination by the board.

If the board of a company acts in any one of these ways, the company must file a Notice of Amendment of its Memorandum of Incorporation, setting out the changes effected by the board.

7.5 AUTHORITY TO ISSUE SHARES

The board of directors of a company is given the authority by s 38, generally,[36] to issue shares. This is a shift from the position under the 1973 Act, which generally required the approval of the shareholders.[37] The shift in position is questionable. The provisions in the 1973 Act (s 221) were introduced on the recommendation of the Van Wyk de Vries Commission.[38] The Commission found that there was 'a strong body of opinion to the effect that directors should not have unlimited powers, whether derived from the articles or a resolution by the company in meeting, to issue shares'.[39] It pointed out that:

> ... the issue by the company of further shares is a matter which directly affects the interests of each holder of shares in that company and is in this respect distinguishable from ordinary managerial acts by the directors performed in carrying on the business of the company.[40]

Thus, there 'seems to be justification for imposing a curb on unlimited powers of directors in this respect'.[41]

In terms of s 38(1) of the Act, the board of a company may resolve to issue shares of the company at any time, but only within the classes, and to the extent, that the shares have been authorised by or in terms of the company's Memorandum of Incorporation, in accordance with s 36.

If a company issues shares that have not been authorised in accordance with s 36, or in excess of the number of authorised shares of any particular class, the issuance of those shares may be retroactively authorised in accordance with s 36.[42]

---

[35] See s 36(3).
[36] There are exceptions — see s 41 — which are dealt with below.
[37] See s 221 of the 1973 Act.
[38] *Commission of Enquiry into the Companies Act* Main Report RP 45/1970 para 44.40 and recommendation 101.
[39] Ibid.
[40] Ibid.
[41] Ibid.
[42] Section 38(2). It is to be noted that, in terms of the draft Companies Amendment Bill, 2010 it is proposed that the retroactive authorisation must be within 60 business days after the date on which the shares were issued.

If a resolution seeking to retroactively authorise an issue of shares is not adopted when it is put to a vote:
  (a) the share issue is a nullity to the extent that it exceeds any authorisation;
  (b) the company must return to any person the fair value of the consideration received by the company in respect of that share issue to the extent that it is nullified, together with interest in accordance with the Prescribed Rate of Interest Act, 1975 (Act No. 55 of 1975), from the date on which the consideration for the shares was received by the company, until the date on which the company complies with this paragraph;
  (c) any certificate evidencing a share so issued and nullified, and any entry in a securities register in respect of such an issue, is void; and
  (d) a director of the company is liable to the extent set out in section 77(3)(e)(i) if the director —
      (i) was present at a meeting when the board approved the issue of any unauthorised shares, or participated in the making of such a decision in terms of section 74; and
      (ii) failed to vote against the issue of those shares, despite knowing that the shares had not been authorised in accordance with section 36.[43]

Although the general position under the new Act is that the board has the authority to issue shares and does not need to seek shareholder approval, there are instances, set out in s 41, where shareholder approval by special resolution is required for the issue of shares and securities convertible into shares and the grant of options to take up securities. Such approval is required where the issue of the shares, securities or options is to:

• a director, future director, prescribed officer, or future prescribed officer of the company or his or her nominee, or
• a person related or interrelated to the company, or to a director or prescribed officer of the company or his or her nominee.[44]

Requiring shareholder approval in these two instances is clearly desirable because of the board's potential conflict of interest. There are, however, situations where conflict of interest is not a concern and, accordingly, no shareholder approval is required in these two instances if the issue is:
  (a) under an agreement underwriting the shares, securities or rights;
  (b) in the exercise of a pre-emptive right to be offered and to subscribe shares, as contemplated in section 39;
  (c) in proportion to existing holdings, and on the same terms and conditions as have been offered to all the shareholders of the company or to all the shareholders of the class or classes of shares being issued;
  (d) pursuant to an employee share scheme that satisfies the requirement of section 97; or
  (e) pursuant to an offer to the public, as defined in section 95(1)(h), read with section 96.[45]

Where an issue by a company of shares, securities convertible into shares, or rights exercisable for shares involves a significant number of shares, it is desirable that the approval of shareholders be obtained because of the possible resultant change in control of the company. This appears to be the rationale behind s 41(3): shareholder approval is required where the issue is in a transaction, or a series of integrated transactions if the voting power of the class of shares that are issued or

---
[43] Section 38(3).
[44] Section 41(1).
[45] Section 41(2).

issuable as a result of the transaction or series of integrated transactions will be equal to or exceed 30% of the voting power of all the shares of that class held by shareholders immediately before the transaction or series of transactions.

Section 41(4) enlarges on s 41(3) by providing that:

(a) for purposes of determining the voting power of shares issued and issuable as a result of a transaction or series of integrated transactions, the voting power of shares is the greater of —
 (i) the voting power of the shares to be issued; or
 (ii) the voting power of the shares that would be issued after giving effect to the conversion of convertible shares and other securities and the exercise of rights to be issued;
(b) a series of transactions is integrated if —
 (i) consummation of one transaction is made contingent on consummation of one or more of the other transactions; or
 (ii) the transactions are entered into within a 12-month period, and involve the same parties, or related persons; and —
  (aa) they involve the acquisition or disposal of an interest in one particular company or asset; or
  (bb) taken together, they lead to substantial involvement in a business activity that did not previously form part of the company's principal activity.

A director who was present at the board meeting at which an issue by the company referred to in s 41 was approved without complying with s 41 can incur personal liability for any loss, damages or costs incurred as a result. The director will incur liability if he or she failed to vote on the issue despite knowing that the issue was inconsistent with s 41 (s 41(5)).

A company may not issue shares to itself.[46]

7.6 CONSIDERATION FOR SHARES

If the board of directors of a company could issue shares for any consideration, existing shareholders could potentially be prejudiced through a watering down in the value of their shares if the shares are issued for an inadequate consideration. Accordingly, s 40 of the Act provides that the board may issue shares only:

(a) for adequate consideration to the company, as determined by the board;
(b) in terms of conversion rights associated with previously issued securities of the company; or
(c) as capitalisation shares, as contemplated in section 47.[47]

However, in the past the courts have been reluctant to inquire closely into the value of such consideration unless it was obviously inadequate or there was evidence of fraud or of an absence of any *bona fide* valuation of the consideration.[48]

This approach by the courts has been incorporated into the Act by s 40(3), which provides that 'the adequacy of consideration for any shares may not be challenged on any basis other than in terms of section 76, read with section 77(2)'. Section 76 places various duties on directors, including the duty to avoid a conflict

---

[46] Section 35(3).
[47] See below at 7.7.
[48] *Ooregum Gold Mining Co of India v Roper* [1892] AC 125 (HL) 136–7.

of interests; to act in good faith, for a proper purpose and in the best interests of the company; and to act with due care, skill and diligence. It follows from the reference to s 76 read with s 77(2) that the board's determination of the adequacy of the consideration for shares may only be challenged on the basis that the determination of the adequacy of the consideration constitutes a breach of one or more of these duties.

Once the consideration approved by the board has been received, s 40(4) provides that:

- the shares in question are fully paid, and
- the company must issue those shares and cause the name of the holder to be entered in the company's securities register in accordance with Part E of Chapter 2 of the Act.

In terms of s 1 of the Act, 'consideration':

> means anything of value given and accepted in exchange for any property, service, act, omission or forbearance or any other thing of value, including —
> *(a)* any money, property, negotiable instrument, securities, investment credit facility, token or ticket;
> *(b)* any labour, barter or similar exchange of one thing for another; or
> *(c)* any other thing, undertaking, promise, agreement or assurance, irrespective of its apparent or intrinsic value, or whether it is transferred directly or indirectly.

It appears that restrictions in the Memorandum of Incorporation on the type of consideration permissible have no validity.

Despite the unlimited power that the board has regarding the type of consideration, s 40 does provide certain safeguards where the company does not receive the consideration immediately on the issue of the shares. The idea is to permit the company to issue the shares, but to require the shares to be held in trust for the subscribing party and to restrict:

- transfer of the shares to the subscribing party,
- the exercise of voting rights and appraisal rights set out in s 164, associated with the shares in question, and
- distributions by the company in respect of the shares held in trust.

The general scheme of s 40 is therefore to permit the subscriber to enjoy the benefits attached to the shares only to the extent that the consideration for the shares has actually been received by the company, unless the trust agreement provides otherwise.

The actual provisions of s 40 setting out these safeguards can be paraphrased as follows:

- Where the consideration takes the form of an instrument that is not negotiable,[49] or is in the form of an agreement for future services, future benefits or future payment, the consideration is regarded as having been received by the

---

[49] It is to be noted that the draft Companies Amendment Bill, 2010 does not refer here to a situation where the form of consideration is not negotiable, but to a situation where the value of the consideration cannot be realised until a date after the time the shares are to be issued.

company at any time only to the extent that the instrument is negotiable[50] by the company; or that the subscribing party to the agreement has fulfilled its obligations in terms of the agreement. Upon receiving the instrument or entering into the agreement, the company must issue the shares immediately and cause the issued shares to be transferred to a third party, to be held in trust and later transferred to the subscribing party in accordance with the trust agreement.[51]

- Except to the extent that a trust agreement referred to above provides otherwise:
  - voting rights, and appraisal rights set out in s 164, associated with shares that have been issued but are held in trust may not be exercised,
  - any pre-emptive rights associated with shares that have been issued but are held in trust may be exercised only to the extent that the instrument has become negotiable by the company or the subscribing party has fulfilled its obligations under the agreement,
  - any distribution with respect to shares that have been issued but are held in trust must be paid or credited by the company to the subscribing party, to the extent that the instrument has become negotiable by the company or the subscribing party has fulfilled its obligations under the agreement; and may be credited against the remaining value at that time of any services still to be performed by the subscribing party, any future payment remaining due, or the benefits still to be received by the company, and
  - shares that have been issued but are held in trust may not be transferred by or at the direction of the subscribing party unless the company has expressly consented to the transfer in advance,
  - shares that have been issued but are held in trust may be transferred to the subscribing party on a quarterly basis, to the extent that the instrument has become negotiable by the company or the subscribing party has fulfilled its obligations under the agreement,
  - shares that have been issued but are held in trust must be transferred to the subscribing party when the instrument has become negotiable by the company, or upon satisfaction of all the subscribing party's obligations in terms of the agreement, and
  - shares that have been issued but are held in trust to the extent that the instrument is dishonoured after becoming negotiable, or that the subscribing party has failed to fulfil its obligations under the agreement, must be returned to the company and cancelled, on demand by the company.[52] A company may not make such a demand unless a negotiable instrument is dishonoured after becoming negotiable by the company or, in the case of an agreement, the subscribing party has failed to fulfil any obligation in terms

---

[50] Ibid. The consideration in terms of the draft Companies Amendment Bill, 2010 is only regarded as having been recovered when the consideration is realised.
[51] See s 40(5).
[52] See s 40(6).

of the agreement for a period of at least 40 business days after the date on which the obligation was due to be fulfilled.[53]

7.7 CAPITALISATION SHARES

Instead of distributing profits to its shareholders by way of a cash dividend, the board of a company may, except to the extent that the company's Memorandum of Incorporation provides otherwise, capitalise the profits and issue authorised shares to the shareholders as capitalisation shares[54] on a *pro rata* basis.[55] This appears to be what is intended by s 47(1) of the Act, although there is no definition of 'capitalisation shares' and no reference to 'profits' that would clarify that capitalisation shares are shares arising on the capitalisation of profits. This construction does, however, seem to be implied and any other interpretation would not make sense.

Issuing the capitalisation shares on a *pro rata* basis means no shareholders can be prejudiced by the issue.

It is not a requirement that capitalisation shares issued to a shareholder should be of the same class as the shares already held by the shareholder. They may be of a different class.[56]

When resolving to award a capitalisation share, the board may at the same time resolve to permit any shareholder who is entitled to receive such an award, to elect instead to receive a cash payment, at a value determined by the board.[57] However, the board of a company may not resolve to offer a cash payment in lieu of awarding a capitalisation share unless the board has considered the solvency and liquidity test, as required by s 46, on the assumption that every such shareholder would elect to receive cash; and is satisfied that the company would satisfy the solvency and liquidity test immediately upon the completion of the distribution.[58] The latter requirement is aimed at the protection of creditors.[59] A cash payment in lieu of awarding a capitalisation share is a 'distribution', as defined in s 1 of the Act, and accordingly must comply with the provisions of s 46 in their entirety.[60] It is not clear therefore why s 47(2) does not simply require compliance with the entire s 46 instead of with just one of its aspects.

It appears that the Act only permits the issue of capitalisation shares and not an issue of debentures.[61] This was permitted by the common law.[62]

---

[53] Section 40(6).
[54] Formerly these new shares were known as 'bonus shares' but the name was misleading, implying that such shares were a gift from the company, which they were not.
[55] See s 47(1)*(a)*.
[56] Section 47(1)*(b)*.
[57] Section 47(1)*(e)*.
[58] Section 47(2).
[59] The solvency and liquidity test is set out in s 4 of the Act and is dealt with in chapter 8: Corporate Finance under 8.1.4.
[60] Section 46 is aimed at the protection of creditors and is dealt with in chapter 8: Corporate Finance.
[61] Section 47 only refers to shares.
[62] See *Wood v Odessa Waterworks Co* (1889) 42 ChD 636.

In *Commissioner for Inland Revenue v Collins*[63] Innes CJ explained the effect of a capitalisation issue as follows:

> The company has parted with no assets — no money or moneys worth — and the shareholders have received none. The profits dealt with remain in the business as they were before. The only difference is that as they have become portion of the capital they are represented by shares; but these shares do not increase the holder's interest in the company; that also remains exactly what it was before. The distribution being *pro rata* his interest in the old capital plus the undivided profits under the old holding was exactly the same as his interest in the increased capital under the new holding. The total assets of the company have not changed, and his original share represented the same proportion of the then issue as his increased shares do of the increased issue. The intrinsic value of each new share is therefore lower than the intrinsic value of each share before the increase of capital ... [T]he new certificates simply increase the number of shares with consequent dilution of the value of each share.

A capitalisation issue is in essence the declaration of a dividend out of profits combined with the application of that dividend, on behalf of the shareholders entitled to participate in it, in paying up shares to be allotted and issued to them in satisfaction of their rights of participation.[64] As a general rule only that which can be distributed as dividends out of profits can be capitalised.[65] A reserve fund constituted as a result of a revaluation of unrealised fixed assets, made in good faith by competent valuers and which is not likely to be liable to short-term fluctuations, may be capitalised.[66]

The issue and acceptance of capitalisation shares involves a relationship between the company and its shareholders analogous to a contractual relationship. When the resolution authorising the issue has been passed, each shareholder becomes entitled to be issued the appropriate number of shares by that company.[67]

Where capitalisation shares are issued in the mistaken belief that there are profits available for dividend, the issue is void[68] and any dividend paid in respect of those shares can be reclaimed by the company. A declaration that a capitalisation issue is void does not, however, place in jeopardy innocent third parties who have in the meanwhile purchased the shares. Such persons are entitled as against the company to rely on the share certificates relating to the shares, their title to the shares deriving, not from the void issue itself, but from estoppel.[69]

---

[63] 1923 AD 347 at 363–4. See also *Commissioners of Inland Revenue v Blott* [1921] 2 AC 171 (HL); *RA Hill v Permanent Trustee Co of New South Wales Ltd* [1930] AC 720; [1930] All ER Rep 87 (PC).

[64] *Dimbula Valley (Ceylon) Tea Co Ltd v Laurie* [1961] Ch 353 at 372; [1961] 1 All ER 769 at 780. In *Dibowitz v Commissioner for Inland Revenue* 1952 (1) SA 55 (A) 60, it was held that the nominal value of a capitalisation share awarded to a shareholder 'cannot be described in the ordinary meaning of words as "profits distributed", for no profits are distributed when [capitalisation] shares are awarded, even although those shares are issued as a result of the resolution of the company to capitalise undivided profits'. See also *Commissioner for Inland Revenue v Legal & General Assurance Society Ltd* 1963 (2) SA 876 (A).

[65] *Dimbula Valley (Ceylon) Tea Co Ltd v Laurie* (supra).

[66] *Dimbula Valley (Ceylon) Tea Co Ltd v Laurie* (supra).

[67] *Re Cleveland Trust plc* [1991] BCLC 424 at 434.

[68] *Re Cleveland Trust plc* (supra).

[69] *Re Cleveland Trust plc* (supra) at 436–7.

7.8 DEBT INSTRUMENTS

'Debt instruments' are governed by s 43 of the Act.

Section 43(1)*(a)* provides that, for the purposes of s 43:

'debt instrument' —
  (i) includes any securities other than the shares of a company, irrespective of whether or not issued in terms of a security document, such as a trust deed; but
  (ii) does not include promissory notes and loans, whether constituting an encumbrance on the assets of the company or not;

Section 1 of the Act provides that 'securities' has the meaning set out in s 1 of the Securities Services Act, 2004, and includes shares held in a private company.[70]

Section 1 of the Securities Services Act provides:

'securities' —
(a) Means —
  (i) shares, stocks and depository receipts in public companies and other equivalent equities, other than shares in a share block company as defined in the Share Blocks Control Act, 1980 (Act No. 59 of 1980);
  (ii) notes;
  (iii) derivative instruments;
  (iv) bonds;
  (v) debentures;
  (vi) participatory interests in a collective investments scheme as defined in the Collective Investments Schemes Control Act, 2002 (Act No. 45 of 2002), and units or any other form of participation in a foreign collective investment scheme approved by the Registrar of Collective Investment Schemes in terms of section 65 of that Act;
  (vii) units or any other form of participation in a collective investment scheme licensed or registered in a foreign country;
  (viii) instruments based on an index;
  (ix) the securities contemplated in subparagraphs (i) to (viii) that are listed on an external exchange; and
  (x) an instrument similar to one or more of the securities contemplated in subparagraphs (i) to (ix) declared by the registrar by notice in the *Gazette* to be a security for the purposes of this Act;
  (xi) rights in the securities referred to in subparagraphs (i) to (x);
(b) excludes —
  (i) money market instruments except for the purposes of Chapter IV; and
  (ii) any security contemplated in paragraph *(a)* specified by the registrar by notice in the *Gazette*.

The issue of 'debt instruments' by a company is a means of obtaining funds other than by the issue of shares. Thus the issue by a company of any security other than a share is an issue of debt instruments. The only qualification is that a debt instrument does not include 'promissory notes and loans'. It is submitted that the securities other than shares referred to in s 43(1)*(a)* of the Act include debentures and the various hybrid securities (see the definition of 'securities' above) that have

---

[70] The draft Companies Amendment Bill, 2010 proposes the following definition of 'securities': 'securities' means —
  (a) any share issued, or authorised to be issued, by a profit company; or
  (b) anything falling within the meaning of 'securities' asset out *[sic]* in section 1 of the Securities Services Act, 2004 (Act No. 36 of 2004).

sprung up in recent years. These instruments have the characteristics of both a share and a debt, as well as the common feature of making the holder thereof a creditor of the company. There are of course significant differences between a shareholder and a creditor of a company with regard to rights against the company, the ranking of claims on insolvency of the company and taxation of the return on the security, with dividends (the return on a share) in most cases being exempt from tax, and interest (the return on a hybrid) in most cases being taxable.

Neither the 1973 Act nor the new Act defines what a 'debenture' is.

The courts have consistently said that there is in fact no precise definition of a 'debenture'.[71] In *British India Steam Navigation Co v Inland Revenue Commissioner*[72] Grove J said debenture is 'a word which has no defined signification in the present state of the English language', and Lindley J said that 'what the correct meaning of "debenture" is I do not know'.

A debenture, the courts have said, is essentially a written acknowledgement of indebtedness,[73] irrespective of its form, executed by the company.[74] In *Edmonds v Blaina Furnaces Co*[75] Chitty J said:

> I have seen debentures of various kinds and classes, and it is a mistake to say that to be debentures the instruments must be issued and numbered seriatim. I have even seen a single debenture issued to one man. There is nothing in the section requiring that more than one instrument be issued . . . No doubt as a rule the instruments called debentures are issued so that each person gets his own document and can deal with it separately . . . [B]ut it would be unreasonable to hold that because the obligation to pay and the security in favour of several persons is contained in one single document, therefore the instrument is not within the protection of the section.

A debenture may (but need not) include terms providing for the indebtedness to be

---

[71] *Edmonds v Blaina Furnaces Company* (1887) 36 ChD 215; *British India Steam Navigation Co v Inland Revenue Commissioner* (1881) 7 QBD 165 at 172–3; *Levy v Abercorris Slate & Slab Co* (1887) 37 ChD 260; *Coetzee v Rand Sporting Club* 1918 WLD 74 at 76; *Lemon v Austin Friars Investment Trust* [1926] Ch 1 17; [1925] All ER Rep 255 (CA); *R v Findlater* [1939] 1 All ER 82 85 (CA); *Knightsbridge Estates Trust Ltd v Byrne* [1940] AC 613 at 621–3; [1940] 2 All ER 401 405–6 (HL); *Handevel Pty Ltd v Comptroller of Stamps* (1986) 10 ACLR 207 at 218 (HC of A); *Austral Mining Construction Pty Ltd v NZI Capital Corporation Ltd* (1991) 4 ACSR 57 at 58 SC (Qld); *Re SH & Co (Realisations) 1990 Ltd* [1993] BCLC 1309 at 1317–8.

[72] (1881) 7 QBD 165 at 171, 172.

[73] *Edmonds v Blaina Furnaces Co* (1887) 36 ChD 215; *Levy v Abercorris Slate & Slab Co* (1887) 37 ChD 260 at 264; *Coetzee v Rand Sporting Club* 1918 WLD 74 at 76–7; *Randfontein Estates Gold Mining Co Ltd v Custodian of Enemy Property* 1923 AD 576 at 580.

[74] *Edmonds v Blaina Furnaces Co* (supra); *British India Steam Navigation Co v Inland Revenue Commissioner* (1881) 7 QBD 165; *Levy v Abercorris Slate & Slab Co* (1887) 37 ChD 260 at 264; *Coetzee v Rand Sporting Club* 1 (supra). See also *Topham v Greenside Glazed Fire-Brick Co* (1887) 37 ChD 281 at 292; *Randfontein Estates Gold Mining Co Ltd v Custodian of Enemy Property* (supra); *Handevel Pty Ltd v Comptroller of Stamps* (1986) 10 ACLR 207 at 218 (HC of A); *Re Bauer Securities Ltd* (1990) 4 ACSR 328 at 333 SC (Qld); *Austral Mining Construction Pty Ltd v NZI Capital Corporation Ltd* (1991) 4 ACSR 57 at 58, 61 SC (Qld).

[75] (1887) 36 ChD 215 at 221.

secured by a charge over property of the company.[76] In *Levy v Abercorris Slate & Slab Co*[77] Chitty J said:

> In my opinion a debenture means a document which either creates a debt or acknowledges it, and any document which fulfils either of these conditions is a 'debenture'. I cannot find any precise legal definition of the term, it is not either in law or commerce a strictly technical term, or what is called a term of art. It must be 'issued', but 'issued' is not a technical term, it is a mercantile term well understood; 'issue' here means the delivery over by the company to the person who has the charge . . .

Every document creating or acknowledging a debt of a company is not necessarily a debenture. The term would not include a negotiable instrument and many other documents in which the company agrees to pay a sum of money; and it has never been suggested that a promise in writing by a company to purchase shares at a future date amounts to a debenture in the ordinary sense of the term, nor that a specific mortgage of land to secure a future obligation to purchase property amounts to a debenture according to its ordinary meaning.[78]

A debenture holder is a particular kind of creditor.[79] The holder is a creditor of the company for the amount of the loan and interest, whose rights are defined by the terms of the issue read with the provisions of the Act.

The terms of issue of debentures usually provide that they are repayable or redeemable at a fixed future date, or between specified dates, at their nominal value, unless the terms of the issue stipulate that a premium is payable on redemption in addition to the nominal value.

Prior to the 2008 Act, instead of issuing debentures that each represent a separate debt, a single debt could be created and debenture stock certificates issued to the subscribers in such amounts as each wanted, subject usually to a prescribed minimum amount. The holder of a debenture stock certificate was, then, a participant with others in the whole stock, and he or she could (subject to any restrictions imposed by the stock conditions) sell and transfer any fraction of the amount issued to them.[80] The difference between a mortgage bond and debenture stock was that, while the former was a specific mortgage for a definite amount according, of course, to the terms of the charge in each case, the latter only made the holder a participant with others in the whole of the stock. There appears to be no reason why a debt instrument in the form of debenture stock cannot be issued in terms of the new Act.

---

[76] *Re Bauer Securities Ltd* (1990) (supra); *Edmonds v Blaina Furnaces Co* (supra); *Handevel Pty Ltd v Comptroller of Stamps* (supra); *Austral Mining Construction Pty Ltd v NZI Capital Corporation Ltd* (supra); *Re SH & Co (Realisations) 1990 Ltd* [1993] BCLC 1309 at 1317–18.

[77] (1887) 37 ChD 260 at 264.

[78] *Handevel Pty Ltd v Comptroller of Stamps* (1986) 10 ACLR 207 at 218 (HC of A); *Austral Mining Construction Pty Ltd v NZI Capital Corporation Ltd* (1991) 4 ACSR 57 at 61 SC (Qld); *Knightsbridge Estates Trust Ltd v Byrne* [1940] AC 613; [1940] 2 All ER 401 (HL).

[79] See eg *Randfontein Estates Gold Mining Co Ltd v Custodian of Enemy Property* 1923 AD 576 at 580; *Coetzee v Rand Sporting Club* 1918 WLD 74 at 76–7.

[80] In *Gower's Principles of Modern Company Law* 6 ed (1997) 325 it is said that '[a] further advantage is that, whereas with a series of debentures with a charge on the company's assets it will be necessary to say expressly in each debenture that it is one of a series each ranking *pari passu* in respect of the charge, debenture stock achieves that result without express provision'.

Where there are a great number of debenture holders and the company contracts with each debenture holder to repay the principal sum and interest until repayment, and gives each debenture holder security over its assets for that amount to rank *pari passu* as between the individual debenture holders, difficulties could arise. If the company wishes to modify the security, dispose of any of the mortgaged assets, or depart in any way from the terms of its undertaking with the individual debenture holders, it can do so only with the consent of all the debenture holders concerned. This problem can be solved by the introduction of a trust deed by which trustees are appointed to represent the interests of the debenture holders. The trust deed creates mortgages over the company's assets in favour of the trustees, empowers the trustees to consent on the debenture holders' behalf to minor departures by the company from the terms of the loan, and authorises the trustees to call meetings of the lenders to decide whether to authorise the trustees to enforce the security when a case arises for doing so, or to agree to a modification of their rights or their securities when the company is unable to meet its obligations in full. Because the company contracts with each individual debenture holder to pay the principal of the loan and interest, the debenture holder is a creditor of the company, even if the debentures are payable to bearer, and consequently he or she can exercise all the legal remedies available to a creditor to recover what is individually owed to him or her. However, only the trustees can enforce the security.[81]

Prior to the new Act, a further step could have been taken that presumably may still be taken.[82] The company may contract with the trustees to repay the loan and to pay interest on it until repayment. These payments are to be made either to the trustees on behalf of the debenture holders, or directly to the debenture holders themselves in proportion to their individual subscriptions. The subscribers are, in turn, provided with debenture stock certificates issued by the company, which evidence their respective rights to a proportionate share of the total amount of the loan equal to the amount they have individually subscribed. But there is no contract by the company with these debenture stockholders to repay the amounts that they have individually advanced. Where this is done, the debenture stockholders are not creditors of the company, even where the company has contracted with trustees in the trust deed to pay the principal of the loan and the interest directly to the debenture stockholders. The trustees are the creditors of the company for the whole amount of the loan plus interest and the cost of performing their functions that the company agreed to defray, and the debenture stockholders are equal beneficiaries under the trust. Consequently, the debenture stockholders' remedies are primarily against the trustees; but by suing them to compel them to enforce their contractual rights against the company and to realise the security vested in them, a debenture stockholder can indirectly enforce the same remedies against the company as a debenture holder can otherwise enforce directly.

The board of a company may authorise the company to issue a secured or

---

[81] See Blackman et al op cit n 32 at 5–334–5–335.
[82] See Blackman et al op cit n 32 at 5–335 and generally, RR Pennington *Company Law* 7 ed (1995) 556–8.

unsecured debt instrument at any time, except to the extent provided otherwise by the company's Memorandum of Incorporation[83] and must determine whether each such debt instrument is secured or unsecured.[84] Every security document[85] must in fact clearly indicate, on its first page, whether the relevant debt instrument is secured or unsecured.[86] There is no restriction on the manner in which a debt instrument is secured.

Except to the extent that a company's Memorandum of Incorporation provides otherwise, a debt instrument issued by the company may grant special privileges regarding:

(a) attending and voting at general meetings and the appointment of directors; or

(b) allotment of securities, redemption by the company, or substitution of the debt instrument for shares of the company, provided that the securities to be allotted or substituted in terms of any such privilege, are authorised by or in terms of the company's Memorandum of Incorporation. . . .[87]

A company may appoint any person, including a juristic person, as trustee for the holders of the company's debt instruments.[88] Such a person may not be a director or prescribed officer of the company, or a person related or interrelated to the company, a director or a prescribed officer; and must not have any interest in, or relationship with, the company that might conflict with the duties of a trustee.[89]

The board must be satisfied that the person has the requisite knowledge and experience to carry out the duties of a trustee.[90]

A new trustee appointed for the purpose of this section must be approved by the holders of at least 75 per cent of the value of debt instruments who are present at a meeting called for that purpose.[91]

Section 43(7) provides that:

[a]ny provision contained in a trust deed for securing any debt instruments, or in any agreement with the holders of any debt instruments secured by a trust deed, is void to the extent that it would exempt a trustee from, or indemnify a trustee against, liability for breach of trust, or failure to exercise the degree of care and diligence required of the prudent and careful person, having regard to the provisions of the trust deed respecting the powers, authorities or discretions of the trustee.

Section 43(7) does not, however, invalidate any release that has been validly given in respect of anything done or omitted to be done by a trustee before the giving of the release.[92] Nor does it invalidate any provision of a debt instrument —

---

[83] Section 43(2)*(a)*.
[84] Section 43(2)*(b)*.
[85] 'security document' includes any document by which a debt instrument is offered or proposed to be offered, embodying the terms and conditions of the debt instrument, including, but not limited to, a trust deed or certificate.
[86] Section 43(2)*(b)*.
[87] Section 43(3).
[88] Section 43(5).
[89] Ibid.
[90] Ibid.
[91] Section 43(6).
[92] Section 43(8).

(i) enabling a release to be given with the consent of the majority of not less than three fourths in value of the holders of debt instruments present and voting at a meeting called for the purpose; and
(ii) with respect to a specific act or omission, or of the trustee dying or ceasing to act.[93]

7.9 OPTIONS FOR SUBSCRIPTION OF SECURITIES

A company may contract that it will issue securities to a person who desires to take them up in the future. This contract confers a contractual right on the holder to require, at the appropriate time, the company to allot and issue to him or her the agreed number of securities. The option will specify the time or times when, and the exercise price at which, the option may be exercised.

An option holder has been considered to be a contingent creditor.[94]

Section 42(1) of the Act provides that a company may issue options for the allotment or subscription of authorised shares or other securities of the company. Section 42(2) then provides that the board of a company must determine the consideration or other benefit for which, and the terms upon which options are issued, and the related shares or other securities are to be issued.

To obviate the need to pass more than one resolution, s 42(3) provides that a decision by the board that the company may issue any options, constitutes also the decision of the board to issue any authorised shares or other securities for which the options may be exercised. In addition, a decision by the board to issue any securities convertible into shares of any class constitutes also the decision of the board to issue the authorised shares into which the securities may be converted.

The authority to issue the options referred to in s 42 appears to rest with the board. This is apparent from the wording of s 42(3), although the reference to 'the company' in s 42(1) implies that the authority lies with the shareholders in general meeting. It seems, however, judging from the wording in s 42(2) and (3), that this is just a case of sloppy draftsmanship and that 'A company' in s 42(1) was intended to be 'The board of a company'.

Where the Memorandum of Incorporation of a company has not authorised the shares that are the subject matter of an option, or the shares into which any securities which are the subject matter of an option may be converted, a director of the company may be liable for any loss, damages or costs sustained by the company as a result of the lack of authority.[95] The director is liable if he or she has voted in favour of the board resolution approving the granting of the option.[96]

There is no restriction in s 42 on the authority of the board of directors to grant options to themselves or other persons related to them. This is highly questionable because of the potential for abuse. The 1973 Act (s 223) required a special resolution of the company in order to grant options to directors (s 42(1)).

---

[93] Section 43(8).
[94] *Re Companie de Electricidad de la Provincia de Buenos Aires Ltd* [1980] Ch 146; [1978] 3 All ER 668. But see *Re BDC Investments Ltd* (1987) 13 ACLR 201 at 203–4 SC (NSW), where this was doubted.
[95] Section 42(4).
[96] Ibid.

7.10 REGISTRATION AND TRANSFER OF SECURITIES

7.10.1 Certificated and uncertificated securities

Shares must be 'certificated' (ie evidenced by a certificate[97]) or 'uncertificated'.[98] 'Uncertificated' securities are defined in s 1 of the Act as meaning 'any securities defined as such in section 29 of the Securities Services Act 2004 . . .'. Section 29 of the Securities Services Act defines uncertificated securities as securities that are not evidenced by a certificate or written instrument and that are transferable by entry without a written instrument. In terms of s 29 of that Act 'entry' includes electronic recordings. Insofar as the definition of 'securities' in the Securities Services Act is concerned, s 29 defines 'securities' as certificated and uncertificated securities and money market instruments.

7.10.2 Equal status of securities

Except to the extent that the Act expressly provides otherwise:

(a) the rights and obligations of security holders are not different solely on the basis of their respective securities being certificated or uncertificated; and
(b) any provision of this Act applies with respect to any uncertificated securities in the same manner as it applies to certificated securities.[99]

7.10.3 'Certificated' securities

(a) Register of certificated securities

Every profit company must maintain a securities register or its equivalent in the prescribed form, as required by s 50.[100]

In terms of the regulations[101] read with s 50 of the Act, the securities register must be kept in one of the official languages of South Africa and must comprise:[102]

- for every class of authorised securities, a record of:
  - the number of securities authorised, and the date of authorisation,
  - the total number of securities of that class that have been issued, reacquired or surrendered to the company, and
  - the number of issued securities of that class that are held in uncertificated form,
- in respect of every issuance, reacquisition or surrender of securities of any particular class, entries showing:
  - the date on which the securities were issued, reacquired or surrendered to the company,
  - the distinguishing number or numbers of any certificated securities issued, reacquired or surrendered to the company,

---

[97] See s 49(1).
[98] Ibid.
[99] See s 49(3).
[100] See s 24(4)(a) and s 50(1).
[101] See Regulation 36 of the draft Companies Regulations.
[102] See Regulation 36(1) of the draft Companies Regulations.

- the consideration for which the securities were issued or reacquired by, or surrendered to the company, and
- the name and identity number of the person to, from or by whom the securities were issued, reacquired or surrendered, as the case may be,
• for every class of authorised securities, at any time:
  - the number of securities of that class that are available to be issued, and
  - the number of securities of that class that are the subject of options or conversion rights which, if exercised, would require securities of that class to be issued.

The company's securities register must also include:[103]

- in respect of each person to whom the company has issued securities, or to whom securities of the company have been transferred:
  - the person's name and business or residential address, and the person's e-mail address, if available,
  - an identifying number that is unique to that person,
  - in respect of each issue of securities to that person, the consideration for which the securities were issued, and
  - in respect of each issue or transfer of securities to that person:
    - the date on which the securities were issued or transferred to the person,
    - the number and class of securities issued or transferred to the person,
    - the distinguishing number or numbers of the securities issued or transferred to the person, if the securities are held in certificated form,
  - the date on which any securities that had been issued or transferred to the person were subsequently:
    - transferred by that person, or by operation of law, to another person, or
    - reacquired by, or surrendered to, the company in terms of any provision of the Act or the Memorandum of Incorporation, and
  - at any time, the total number of securities of that class held by the person.

If a company contemplated in s 56(7) has received any disclosure of a beneficial interest referred to in that section,[104] the securities register of that company, despite any additional requirements that may be imposed by a central securities depository (CSD), must also include[105] a record of all such disclosures. This should include the following information for any securities in respect of which a disclosure was made:

- the name and unique identifying number of the registered holder of the securities,
- a reference number to the relevant entry in the company's securities register at which the issue of those securities to the registered holder is recorded,
- the number, class and, in the case of certificated securities, the distinguishing numbers of the securities, and

---

[103] See Regulation 36(2) of the draft Companies Regulations.
[104] See below at 7.10.3(*d*).
[105] See Regulation 36(3) of the draft Companies Regulations.

- the name, unique identifying number, business or residential address, and e-mail address, if available, of each person who holds a beneficial interest in the securities, and the extent of each such person's interest in the securities.

The securities register must be kept in such a manner as:[106]

- to provide indexed access to all relevant entries for any one person,
- to provide adequate precautions against:
  ○ theft, loss or intentional or accidental damage or destruction, and
  ○ falsification, and
- to facilitate the discovery of any falsification.

If the company keeps its securities register in electronic form, the company must:

- provide adequate precautions against loss of the records as a result of damage to, or failure of, the media on which the records are kept, and
- ensure that the records are at all times capable of being retrieved to a readable and printable form, including by converting the records from legacy to later storage media, or software, to the extent necessary from time to time.[107]

Any entry in a securities register pertaining to a person who has ceased to hold securities of the company must be kept for seven years after that person last held any securities of the company. After that period, the company may dispose of the records.

Where certificated securities have been placed in trust[108] or where their transfer is restricted,[109] the register must reflect the number of, and prescribed circumstances relating to, such securities.[110]

Unless all the shares of a company rank equally for all purposes, the company's shares, or each class of shares, and any other securities, must be distinguished by an appropriate numbering system.[111]

A securities register maintained in accordance with the Act is sufficient proof of the facts recorded in it, in the absence of evidence to the contrary.[112]

(b) Security certificates

A certificate evidencing any certificated securities of a company must state the following:[113]

    (i) the name of the issuing company;
   (ii) the name of the person to whom the securities were issued;
  (iii) the number and class of shares and the designation of the series, if any, evidenced by that certificate; and
  (iv) any restriction on the transfer[114] of the securities evidenced by that certificate.

---

[106] See Regulation 36(5) of the draft Companies Regulations.
[107] Regulation 36(6) of the draft Companies Regulations.
[108] See s 40(6)(d).
[109] See (c) and (e) below.
[110] See s 50(2)(b) (iii) of the Act.
[111] See s 50(5).
[112] Section 50(c).
[113] See s 51(1).
[114] See (c) and (e) below.

It is to be noted that, if any share certificate issued by a pre-existing company fails to satisfy the above requirements, it is not regarded as a contravention of the Act and does not invalidate the share certificate.[115]

A security certificate must be signed by two persons authorised by the company's board. This acts as proof that the named security holder owns the securities, in the absence of evidence to the contrary.[116]

A signature may be affixed to or placed on the certificate by autographic, mechanical or electronic means.[117] A certificate remains valid despite the subsequent departure from office of any person who signed it.[118] If all the shares of a company rank equally for all purposes, and are therefore not distinguished by a numbering system, each certificate issued in respect of those shares must be distinguished by a numbering system. In addition, if the share has been transferred, the certificate must be endorsed with a reference number or similar device that will enable each preceding holder of the share in succession to be identified.[119]

(c) Transfer of certificated securities

Securities in a company can be acquired directly from the company by way of issue and allotment to the acquirer. They may also be acquired by transfer from the holder thereof.

(i) Issue and allotment

A contract to acquire securities in a company from the company is not a contract of purchase, but a contract referred to as a contract of 'subscription' or 'allocation'.[120]

An issue and allotment of securities pursuant to an offer to the public is governed by the Act.[121] Otherwise the common-law rules of contract apply, which means that no particular form of agreement is required, and the contract may be effected in any manner in which a contract may be concluded. It may be either written or oral and either express or implied.[122]

In accordance with the general principles of contract, the subscriber applies to the company for securities. This is the offer. The company then allots the securities to the subscriber. The allotment is the acceptance of the offer and the contract is

---

[115] Section 51(1)(a) read with item 6(4) of Schedule 5. On a strict reading this only applies to a share certificate and not generally to all security certificates. Section 51(1)(a) refers to 'securities' but item 6(4) of Schedule 5 refers only to 'shares'.
[116] Section 51(1)(b).
[117] Section 51(2).
[118] Section 51(3).
[119] Section 51(4).
[120] *Moosa v Lalloo* 1957 (4) SA 207 (D) 219.
[121] See Chapter 4 of the Act.
[122] *Re New Theatre Co Ltd (Bloxam's Case)* (1864) 33 LJ Ch 574; *Re Universal Non-Tariff Fire Insurance Co (Ritso's Case)* (1877) 4 ChD 774 (CA); *Moosa v Lalloo* (supra) at 219.

concluded when the acceptance comes to the notice of the subscriber,[123] or when the acceptance is posted.[124]

As far as the term 'issue' is concerned, it has been held that 'inasmuch as the term "issue" is used, it must be taken as meaning something distinct from allotment, as importing that some subsequent act has been done whereby the title of the allottee becomes complete . . .'.[125] It is doubtful whether the mere issue of the share certificates, without placing the subscriber on the register of members, is sufficient to constitute an 'issue' of the shares.[126] The better view[127] is that it is:

> . . . only upon issue, as distinct from allotment, that individual shares come into existence as separate items of property, a process which logically must include entry in the share register for without such entry there will not have been . . . 'the investing of the shareholder with complete control over the shares'.[128]

(ii) Transfer

The Act says very little about the transfer of certificated securities. Section 35(1) of the Act says that '[a] share issued by a company is movable property, transferable in any manner provided for or recognised by this Act or other legislation'. Section 51 of the Act, which is headed 'Registration and transfer of certificated securities', simply provides regarding transfer that 'a company must enter in its securities register every transfer of any certificated securities'[129] but must do so only if the transfer '*(a)* is evidenced by a proper instrument of transfer that has been delivered to the company; or *(b)* was effected by operation of law'.[130] Section 51(1)*(a)* (iv) also implies that restrictions can be placed on the transfer of the securities.

It therefore appears that, if a purchaser of securities delivers to the company a valid agreement for the purchase thereof (not in any particular form), the purchaser can, subject to any restrictions on the transferability of the securities, demand that the company registers the transfer of the securities in his or her name in accordance with s 51(5).[131]

It is not expressly provided that the company must issue new securities certificates to the purchaser, but this seems to be implied by s 51. It is also not expressly

---

[123] *Ex parte The Master: In re Niagara Ltd* 1913 TPD 38; *Pretorius v Natal South Sea Investment Trust Ltd* 1965 (3) SA 410 (W).
[124] *Cape Explosives Works Ltd v South African Oil and Fat Industries Ltd* 1921 CPD 244; *Kergeulen Sealing and Whaling Co Ltd v Commissioner of Inland Revenue* 1939 AD 487, 503–5. The applicant must, however, have agreed to the use of the post and accordingly, if there is no such agreement, there is no acceptance unless the applicant actually receives it (*Botha v Myburgh* 1923 CPD 482).
[125] See *LAWSA* 4 Part 1 Companies 257 (MS Blackman).
[126] Ibid.
[127] Ibid.
[128] *Federal Commissioner of Taxation v St Helens Farm (ACT) Pty Ltd* (1980) 146 CLR 336 (HC of A) 425–6.
[129] See s 51(5).
[130] Section 51(6).
[131] Registration of transfer would likewise be required on the death or insolvency of a shareholder as the securities are transmitted by operation of law to the executor or trustee of the deceased or insolvent estate, as the case may be. No instrument of transfer is required (s 51(6)*(b)*). The executor or trustee would have to prove death or insolvency and valid appointment.

provided that the securities certificates held by the seller must be delivered with the instrument of transfer, although the requirement that a proper instrument of transfer be delivered implies that this is required. It would of course make sense if this was the case.

When a purchaser enters into an agreement with the seller of securities in a company, the seller cedes the rights attached to the securities to the purchaser. The rights are therefore transferred by cession. Mere consensus is sufficient for a valid cession of the rights attached to a security.[132] Delivery of the security certificate is not a requirement for the validity of the cession of rights arising out of securities.[133] Delivery is simply evidence that the cession has taken place.[134] It is, however, the intention of the parties 'that determines when the rights are ceded; and no doubt in most cases that intention is present when, and only when, the share [security] certificates together with a signed blank transfer form are delivered by the seller to the purchaser'.[135]

In the case of shares, although cession has taken place, it does not, it appears, make the purchaser a shareholder in the company. This view is based on the definition of 'shareholder' in s 1 of the Act, which provides:

> 'shareholder', subject to section 57(1),[136] means the holder of a share issued by a company and who is entered as such in the certificated or uncertificated securities register, as the case may be.

It appears that it is only once the purchaser is registered as the shareholder in the company's securities register that he or she can exercise the rights attaching to the shares. Until registration it seems that:

> ... the transferor holds the shares and the rights deriving from the shares for the exclusive benefit of the transferee. The transferor will have to act in accordance with the instructions of the transferee as the beneficial holder and owner of the shares.[137]

As seen above, the purchaser has the right to registration.[138]

The position regarding the holders of securities other than shares is unclear. For example, can the cessionary of a debenture in a company who is not registered in the securities register exercise the rights attached to the debenture? There is nothing in the Act that says the purchaser of a security other than a share is only the holder thereof if transfer thereof is entered in the securities register in terms of s 51(5).

- *Transferability of shares*

The general rule is that shareholders have the right to deal freely with their

---

[132] *Botha v Fick* 1995 (2) SA 750 (A).
[133] Ibid.
[134] Ibid.
[135] Blackman *LAWSA* vol 4 part 1 para 229.
[136] Section 57(1) provides:
  '(1) In this Part, 'shareholder' means a person who is entitled to exercise any voting rights in relation to a company, irrespective of the form, title or nature of the securities to which those voting rights are attached.'
[137] See Cilliers and Benade 3 ed *Corporate Law* para 18.16.
[138] See s 51(5). There must be delivered to the company a proper instrument of transfer (s 51(6)(*a*)).

shares.[139] However, the Memorandum of Incorporation or the rules of a company may restrict transferability of its securities.[140] In the case of private companies such restriction is of course obligatory.[141]

The courts are, however, reluctant to restrict transferability and accordingly the rule is that provisions limiting transferability must be restrictively interpreted.[142] In the absence of express provision to the contrary, restrictions are interpreted so as to apply only to transfers to non-shareholders.[143]

As far as the reasons for restricting transferability are concerned, the view is that 'in the case of the statutory requirement that the transferability of shares in a private company be restricted, the object would seem to be that of protecting the public and restricting speculation. As far as the company (whether private or public) is concerned, restrictions are usually imposed to allow existing shareholders a measure of control over the identity of the company's shareholders, to maintain an existing pattern of control, or to prevent one or more shareholders from obtaining control by purchase from other shareholders.'[144]

The transfer of securities in the face of a restriction is ineffective.[145] However, there is some debate as to what 'transfer' means:

> On one view, the member is prevented (unless he complies with the provisions in the restriction) from transferring beneficial ownership of the shares; on the other view, it is merely the right to have the transfer registered that is denied.[146]

This is a matter of proper interpretation. The better view is that:

> ... in most cases at least, and especially in the case of private companies, the intention can only sensibly be understood to be that of restricting the transfer of the beneficial ownership of the shares, and this would appear to be the approach of our courts.[147]

A common restriction on transferability is making the right of transfer subject to a *right of pre-emption*. Usually this involves a provision that a member who wishes

---

[139] See *Re Smith, Knight & Co, Weston's Case* (1868) 4 Ch App 20, 27; *Safeguard Industrial Investments Ltd v National Westminster Bank* [1980] 3 All ER 849 (C) 860. Regarding the transferability of shares, see also chapter 3: Types of Companies.
[140] This is implied in s 51(1)(a)(iv).
[141] See s 8(2)(b)(bb). See *Smuts v Booyens; Markplaas (Edms) Bpk v Booyens* 2001 (4) SA 15 (SCA).
[142] See *Greenhalgh v Mallard* [1943] 2 All ER 234 at 237 (CA); *Delavenne v Broadhurst* [1931] 1 Ch 234; *Re Smith & Fawcett Ltd* [1942] Ch 304; [1942] 1 All ER 542 (CA); *Moodie v W & J Shepherd (Bookbinders) Ltd* [1949] 2 All ER 1044 (HL); *Greenacre v Falkirk Iron Co Ltd* 1953 (4) SA 289 (N); *Re Swaledale Cleaners Ltd* [1968] 3 All ER 619 at 622 (CA); *Estate Milne v Donohoe Investments (Pty) Ltd* 1967 (2) SA 359 (A); *Bellairs v Hodnett* 1978 (1) SA 1109 (A) 1139; *Commercial Grain Producers Association v Tobacco Sales Ltd* 1983 (1) SA 826 (ZS) 830.
[143] See *Re Smith & Fawcett Ltd* (supra); *Greenacre v Falkirk Iron Co Ltd* (supra). In *Estate Milne v Donohoe Investments (Pty) Ltd* (supra) restrictions were placed on transfers between members.
[144] See Blackman et al op cit n 32 at 5–184.
[145] *Lombard v Suid-Afrikaanse Vroue-Federasie, Transvaal* 1968 (3) SA 473 (A); *Smuts v Booyens; Markplaas (Edms) Bpk v Booyens* 2001 (4) SA 15 (SCA).
[146] See Blackman et al op cit n 32.
[147] Blackman et al op cit n 32. See *Lyle & Scott Ltd v Scott's Trustees* [1959] AC 763; [1959] 2 All ER 661 (HL); *Lombard v Suid-Afrikaanse Vroue-Federasie, Transvaal* (supra) at 484–5; *Swart v Cilliers* 1976 (2) PH E10; *United Trust (Pty) Ltd v SA Milling Co* 1959 (2) SA 426 (W).

to dispose of his or her shares must first offer them to the other shareholders *pro rata* to their existing shareholdings at a price to be determined in a prescribed way.[148]

It appears that 'transfer' in this context will usually be understood to mean or include the cession of shareholders' rights, otherwise a shareholder could evade a restriction on transferability.[149] In *Lyle & Scott Ltd v Scott's Trustees*[150] Lord Keith said:[151]

> I think that a shareholder who has transferred, or pretended to transfer, the beneficial interest in a share to a purchaser for value is merely endeavouring by subterfuge to escape from the peremptory provisions of the article . . . A sale of a share is a sale of the beneficial rights that it confers, and to sell or purport to sell the beneficial rights without the title to the share is, in my opinion, a plain breach of the provision of [the article].[152]

If the Memorandum of Incorporation empowers the directors to allocate the shares among such shareholders of the company as the directors decide, the directors do not have to allocate the shares to the bidding shareholders in proportion to their shareholding. In fact, a bidding shareholder need not be allocated any shares:[153]

> Such a power to allocate shares among the members is more akin to a power to refuse to register a transfer than a power to allot new shares; the duty of the directors is to refrain from acting in order to obtain some private advantage or to gain some objective other than that for which the power was conferred.[154]

A shareholder is not bound to sell his or her shares to the members unless one or more of them agree to take up all the shares offered.[155]

Where a shareholder ignores a pre-emption right and sells his or her shares, the sale to the purchaser is valid. However, the shareholder cannot cede his or her rights to the purchaser in terms of the sale. The purported cession of the rights to the purchaser is invalid:[156]

---

[148] *Borland's Trustee v Steel Brothers & Co Ltd* [1901] Ch 279; *Phillips v Manufacturer's Securities Ltd* (1917) 16 LT 290; (1917) 86 LJ Ch 305 (CA); *Dean v Prince* [1954] Ch 409; [1954] 1 All ER 749 (CA); see also *Larsen v Hansen* 1944 2 PH E8 (C) and cf *Konyn v Viedge Bros (Pty) Ltd* 1961 (2) SA 816 (E); *Estate Milne v Donohoe Investments (Pty) Ltd* 1967 (2) SA 359 (A); *Bellairs v Hodnett* 1978 (1) SA 1109 (A) 1134–9. The price at which other shareholders may acquire the shares may be fixed or may be left to the valuation of or determination by a third party, eg the company's auditor. If the provision giving the pre-emption right provides that the third party's valuation is to be accepted as conclusive, the seller and the purchaser of the shares are bound by the valuation in the absence of fraud or collusion or a mistake amounting to a material departure from their instructions. The fact that the auditor to whom a valuation is entrusted is also a shareholder does not preclude him or her from doing the valuing, provided he or she exercises an honest judgment (*Estate Milne v Donohoe Investments* (supra)).
[149] See Blackman et al op cit n 32 at 5–186.
[150] [1959] AC 763; [1959] 2 All ER 661 (HL).
[151] [1959] AC 763 at 785; [1959] 2 All ER 661 at 672 (HL).
[152] *Lombard v Suid-Afrikaanse Vroue-Federasie, Transvaal* 1968 (3) SA 473 (A) 484–5; *Smuts v Booyens; Markplaas (Edms) Bpk v Booyens* 2001 (4) SA 15 (SCA).
[153] See Blackman et al op cit n 32 at 5–187; *TC Newman (Pty) Ltd v DHA Rural (Qld) Pty Ltd* (1987) 2 ACLR 257 SC (Qld).
[154] Ibid.
[155] *Ocean Coal Co Ltd v Powell Duffryn Steam Coal Co Ltd* [1932] 1 Ch 654; [1932] All ER Rep 845; *Sindler NO v Gees* 2006 (5) SA 501 (C).
[156] *Smuts v Booyens; Markplaas (Edms) Bpk v Booyens* (supra) at 21–2.

The purchaser is left with an action for damages against the member and, perhaps, if the other members do not agree to take up all the shares offered (and the member is nevertheless bound to sell to them those shares which they agree to take up), a right to claim cession of the balance of the shares.[157]

Normally (depending on the wording of the Memorandum of Incorporation), a right of pre-emption would not apply in a situation where a company is buying back its own shares.[158] 'Mostly such a clause is addressed to a "bilateral transaction" in that it contemplates the continuing existence and ownership of the shares which is not the case with a buy-back. The shares, on a buy-back, must be cancelled.'[159]

A company's Memorandum of Incorporation may give the directors the power to refuse to register a transfer, without having to give reasons for their refusal.[160]

However, in *Re Smith & Fawcett Ltd*,[161] 'usually thought to represent the high point in the abdication by the courts of responsibility to review the discretion vested in the directors to refuse registration',[162] Lord Greene MR said:

> [t]he principles to be applied in cases where the articles of a company confer a discretion on directors with regard to the acceptance of transfer of shares are, for the present purposes, free from doubt. They must exercise their discretion *bona fide* in what they consider — not what a court may consider — is in the interests of the company, and not for any collateral purpose.

- *Security by cession* in securitatem debiti

Shares can be used to secure a debt. This is done by cession *in securitatem debiti*, which may be done in two ways:

  ○ the shareholder can pledge his or her rights to the cessionary, or
  ○ the shareholder can cede them out-and-out to the cessionary subject to the condition that they will be ceded back to him or her on repayment of the debt.[163]

Whether the cession is a pledge or an out-and-out cession depends on the intention of the parties.

Both forms of cessions *in securitatem debiti* can be effected by delivering a share certificate with a signed blank transfer form, which effectively cedes to the cessionary all the rights accruing from the share to the cedent.[164] Although

---

[157] Blackman et al op cit n 32 at 5–192–1.
[158] See *Lion Nathan Australia Pty Ltd v Coopers Brewery Ltd* 2006 56 ACSR (FCA) 163; Blackman et al op cit n 32 at 5–192–2 .
[159] Blackman et al op cit 5–192–2.
[160] See generally JE Parkinson 'Restrictions on Transfer and Small Companies' (1981) *New LJ* 1084; Andrew Borrowdale 'The Directors' Power to Refuse Registration of Shares' (1985) 9 *SA Company LJ* 68.
[161] *Re Smith & Fawcett Ltd* [1942] Ch 304; [1942] 1 All ER 542 (CA).
[162] Blackman et al op cit n 32 at 5–195.
[163] *Alexander v Standard Merchant Bank* 1978 (4) SA 730 (W) 739–40; *Bank of Lisbon and South Africa Ltd v The Master* 1987 (1) SA 276 (A); *Trust Bank of Africa Ltd v Standard Bank of South Africa Ltd* 1968 (3) SA 166 (A) 173–4; *Holzman v Knights Engineering and Precision Works (Pty) Ltd* 1979 (2) SA 784 (W).
[164] Blackman et al op cit n 32 at 5–369.

delivery of the share certificate to the cessionary is not required to constitute a valid cession,[165] it may be vital evidence of the cession.[166]

(d) Beneficial interest in certificated securities

- *'Nominee' holdings*

To the extent that the Memorandum of Incorporation does not provide otherwise, it is possible for a person to hold securities in his or her name on behalf of someone else.[167] This person is referred to as the 'nominee' of the latter. The person on whose behalf the shares are held by the nominee has often been referred to as the beneficial owner of the securities. However, it has been pointed out that the term 'beneficial owner' is:

> ... juristically speaking, not wholly accurate, but it is a convenient and well-used label to denote the person in whom, as between himself and the registered shareholder, the benefit of the bundle of rights constituting the share vests.[168]

As Blackman says:[169]

> the term comes from English law where the registered member holds the shares in trust for the beneficial owner. But in our law, where there is no distinction between legal and beneficial or equitable ownership, the rights attaching to the share vest in the 'beneficial owner', and in him alone. Hence it is more accurate to refer to him as the 'owner' of the shares. And, in our law, the nominee as such is not the trustee, but is the agent, of the 'beneficial owner'.

In the 2008 Act the 'owner' is referred to as the holder of the beneficial interest in the securities.[170]

- *Meaning of beneficial interest*

Section 1 of the Act defines 'beneficial interest' as follows:

> **'beneficial interest'**, when used in relation to a company's securities, means the right or entitlement of a person, through ownership, agreement, relationship or otherwise, alone or together with another person to —
> (a) receive or participate in any distribution in respect of the company's securities;
> (b) exercise or cause to be exercised, in the ordinary course, any or all of the rights attaching to the company's securities; or
> (c) dispose or direct the disposition of the company's securities, or any part of a distribution in respect of the securities,
> but does not include any interest held by a person in a unit trust or collective investment scheme in terms of the Collective Investment Schemes Act, 2002 (Act No. 45 of 2002).

- *Disclosure by nominees*

There could be various reasons why a person may wish to use a nominee to hold his or her securities. It could be, for example, to keep their holding confidential. The reason for doing so could be legitimate, but the lack of transparency it creates

---

[165] *Botha v Fick* 1995 (2) SA 750 (A). See *Lief v Dettmann* 1964 (4) SA 252 (A) 271.
[166] *Botha v Fick* (supra).
[167] Section 56(1).
[168] *Per* Corbett JA in *Standard Bank of South Africa Ltd v Ocean Commodities Inc* 1983 (1) SA 276 (A) 289; and see *Oakland Nominees (Pty) Ltd v Gelria Mining & Investment Co (Pty) Ltd* 1976 (1) SA 441 (A) 453.
[169] Blackman et al op cit n 32 at 5–172.
[170] See s 56.

could lead to undesirable cover-ups of, for example, insider trading and unlawful competition. It is also undesirable that a company should be 'unable to communicate with its real shareholders or should be kept ignorant of a build-up of shareholding towards a take-over of control'.[171] It is because of such potential mischief that the Act requires disclosure by nominees of those for whom they are holding their shares.

When the provision in the 1973 Act[172] governing disclosure of nominee holdings was inserted,[173] the following reasons in the memorandum on the objects of the Bill[174] were given for requiring disclosure of the beneficial interest holder:

> Large volumes of shares in public companies are held by nominee companies on behalf of their clients. The proliferation of nominee companies resulted in [about] 35% of shares on the JSE being held by nominee companies. Furthermore over 50% of the shares in some 157 companies listed on the JSE are held by nominee companies.
>
> Problems arising out of this situation are, for instance, that insider trading becomes impossible to detect; minority shareholders are unable to detect a change of controlling shareholder and could be prejudiced if a new controlling shareholder is an asset-stripper or, at least, someone in whom they don't have confidence; the board and shareholders ought to be able to be forewarned of a hostile takeover; competition legislation is virtually impossible to administer; a company itself does not know who a large percentage of its shareholders is and communication with all shareholders is virtually impossible.
>
> An obligation on nominee companies to identify beneficial shareholders is essential in the maintenance of free, fair and acceptably regulated securities markets. It is wholly consistent also with South Africa's progress from a secretive and narrowly empowered society to an open market democracy where transparency and accountability have become of paramount importance. South Africa's obligations in international markets and the growing trend towards disclosure in these markets also compel legislative support for the principle of transparency of shareholdings.

The Act provides that, if a security of a public company is registered in the name of a person who is not the holder of the beneficial interest in all the securities in the same company held by that person, that registered holder of security must disclose —

  (a) the identity of the person on whose behalf that security is held; and
  (b) the number and class of securities held for such person with a beneficial interest.[175]

The information required must —

  (a) be disclosed in writing to the company within five business days after the end of every month;[176] and

---

[171] Cilliers and Benade op cit n 137 para 15.14.
[172] Section 140A.
[173] By the Companies Amendment Act 37 of 1999.
[174] B 17D–99.
[175] Section 56(3). Note that the draft Companies Amendment Bill, 2010 proposes changing what is in the second bullet (s 56(3)(b)) to the following: 'the identity of each person with a beneficial interest in the securities so held, the number and class of securities held for each such person with a beneficial interest, and the extent of each such beneficial interest'.
[176] The 1973 Act required that disclosure had to be made only at the end of every three-month period (see s 140A(3) of the 1973 Act), thus jeopardising the effectiveness of the disclosure, for example exposing a build-up of shareholding to effect a takeover bid. See Blackman et al n 32 at 5–408.

(b) otherwise be provided on payment of a prescribed fee charged by the registered holder of securities.[177]

A company that knows or has reasonable cause to believe that any of its securities are held by one person for the beneficial interest of another may, by notice in writing, require either of those persons to —

(a) confirm or deny that fact;
(b) provide particulars of the extent of the beneficial interest held during the three years preceding the date of the notice; and
(c) disclose the identity of each person with a beneficial interest in the securities held by that person.[178]

This information must be provided not later than ten business days after receipt of the notice.[179]

A company that is subject to the Takeover Regulations must —

(a) establish and maintain a register of the disclosures made in terms of this section; and
(b) publish in its annual financial statements, if it is required to have such statements audited,[180] a list of the persons who hold beneficial interests equal to or in excess of 5 per cent of the total number of securities of that class issued by the company, together with the extent of those beneficial interests.[181]

In addition to the above requirements, it should be noted that the draft Companies Regulations provide:[182]

- If a company has received any disclosure of a beneficial interest, the securities register of that company, despite any additional requirements that may be imposed by a central securities depository, must also include a record of all such disclosures, including the following information for any securities in respect of which a disclosure was made —
    - the name and unique identifying number of the registered holder of the securities,
    - a reference number to the relevant entry in the company's securities register at which the issue of those securities to the registered holder is recorded,
    - the number, class and, in the case of certificated securities, the distinguishing numbers of the securities, and
    - the name, unique identifying number, business or residential address, and e-mail address if available, of each person who holds a beneficial interest in the securities, and the extent of each such person's interest in the securities.

---

[177] Section 56(4).
[178] Section 56(5).
[179] Section 56(6).
[180] In terms of s 30(2).
[181] Section 56(7).
[182] See Regulation 36 of the draft Companies Regulations.

- The securities register required to be kept by the Act and this regulation must be kept in such a manner as —
  - to provide indexed access to all relevant entries for any one person,
  - to provide adequate precautions against theft, loss or intentional or accidental damage or destruction, and falsification, and
  - to facilitate the discovery of any falsification.
- Any entry in a securities register pertaining to a person who has ceased to hold securities of the company may be disposed of seven years after that person last held any securities of the company.

It is clear that where a person holds shares in a company on behalf of another person, ie as a nominee, then the person on behalf of whom the shares are held has a beneficial interest in the shares. In addition, however, the Act (s 56(2)) sets out circumstances in which a person is to be regarded as having a beneficial interest in a security in a public company.[183] Section 56(2) is clearly a deeming provision. It provides:

> (2) A person is regarded to have a beneficial interest in a security of a public company if the security is held *nomine officii* by another person on that first person's behalf, or if that first person —
> (a) is married in community of property to a person who has a beneficial interest in that security;
> (b) is the parent of a minor child who has a beneficial interest in that security;
> (c) acts in terms of an agreement with another person who has a beneficial interest in that security, and the agreement is in respect of the co-operation between them for the acquisition, disposal or any other matter relating to a beneficial interest in that security;
> (d) is the holding company of a company that has a beneficial interest in that security;
> (e) is entitled to exercise or control the exercise of the majority of the voting rights at general meetings of a juristic person that has a beneficial interest in that security; or
> (f) gives directions or instructions to a juristic person that has a beneficial interest in that security, and its directors or the trustees are accustomed to act in accordance with that person's directions or instructions.

Section 56(2) thus sets out seven situations in which a person is to be regarded as having a beneficial interest in a security of a public company. The first is where the security is held *nomine officii*[184] by a person on behalf of another and the others are those envisaged in s 56(2)(a) to (f).

It will be recognised that in none of the circumstances envisaged by s 56(2)(a) to (f) is disclosure in terms of s 56(3) necessary. This is because s 56(3) only requires disclosure by the registered holder of the securities where that holder does not have a beneficial interest in all the securities held by that person, and in all the situations in s 56(2)(a) to (f) the registered holder *does* have a beneficial interest. By way of illustration:

- Section 56(2)(a) says that if A and B are married in community of property and A is the registered holder of securities of company Y and has a beneficial interest in the securities held, then B also has a beneficial interest in those

---
[183] Section 56(2).
[184] For example, where shares are held by a trustee of an insolvent estate.

securities. No disclosure of B's beneficial interest is required by A because A has a beneficial interest in the securities.
- Section 56(2)*(b)* says that if X's minor child has a beneficial interest in and is the registered holder of a security, X also has a beneficial interest in that security. No disclosure is required by the minor child because disclosure in terms of s 56(3) is only required by a non-beneficial interest holder.
- Section 56(2)*(c)* says that if company X and company Y have an agreement relating to a beneficial interest in a security of company Z and company Y is the registered shareholder of, and a beneficial interest holder in, company Z, then both company X and company Y have a beneficial interest in company Z. Therefore, no disclosure of company X's beneficial interest is required by company Y.
- Section 56(2)*(d)* says that if a company is the registered holder of and has a beneficial interest in a security, then the company's holding company also has a beneficial interest in that security. As both the holding and subsidiary companies have a beneficial interest, no disclosure is required in terms of s 56(3).
- Section 56(2)*(e)* says that if company X controls the majority of the voting rights at general meetings of company Y and company Y is the registered shareholder of, and has a beneficial interest in, a security of company Z, then company X and company Y both have beneficial interests in the security. Therefore no disclosure of company X's beneficial interest in the security by company Y is required.
- Section 56(2)*(f)* says that if company Y's directors act in accordance with company X's directions and company Y is the registered shareholder of, and has a beneficial interest in, a security of company Z, then company X and company Y both have beneficial interests in the security. Therefore no disclosure of company X's beneficial interest is required by company Y.

It is difficult to understand why in these circumstances no disclosure is required. In all these circumstances the holder of the beneficial interest in the shares who is not the registered shareholder has or could have control over the registered shareholder. Surely, for the reasons given earlier, it is imperative therefore that the former's identity should be disclosed?[185]

It will be recognised that, if the registered holder of securities in a company is the nominee/agent of the person other than the 'first person' referred to in s 56(2), then the nominee/agent would have to disclose those persons referred to in s 56(2) who are regarded as having a beneficial interest in the securities. For example, if Company X controls the exercise of the majority of the voting rights in Company Y, and Company N holds securities in Company Z as Company Y's nominee (and has no beneficial interest in the securities of Company Z), then Company N would have to disclose that both Company X and Company Y are beneficial interest holders in those securities. Section 56(2) requires disclosure because Company Y does not have a beneficial interest in the securities.

---

[185] A similar problem exists in the 1973 Act. See s 140A thereof. See Blackman et al op cit n 32 at 5–406–5–407.

It is incongruous that disclosure only becomes necessary if the nominee is interposed.

It will be observed that the circumstances set out in s 56(2) deeming a person to have a beneficial interest in a security could become relevant in other parts of the Act. They are:

- section 26(1) (access to company records)
- section 30(2)(ii)(AA) and (BB) (audit requirement)
- section 31(1) (access to financial statements)
- section 50(2)*(b)*(iv) (securities register)
- section 75(2)*(b)*(i) and s 75(3) (directors' personal financial interests)
- section 117(1)*(c)* (definition of 'affected transaction')
- section 117(1)*(d)* (definition of 'holder')
- section 122(1)*(a)* and *(b)* and s 122(4) (required disclosure concerning certain transactions)
- section 123(2)*(a)* (ii) (mandatory offers).

7.10.4 'Uncertificated' securities

(a) Introduction

As has been stated above,[186] any securities issued by a company must be either evidenced by a certificate ('certificated') or uncertificated. If they are uncertificated, the company must not issue certificates evidencing or purporting to evidence title to those securities.[187] Except to the extent that the Act provides otherwise, the rights and obligations of security holders are not different solely on the basis that the securities are certificated or uncertificated. Furthermore, any provision in the Act applies in the same manner to both certificated and uncertificated securities.[188] It may thus be assumed that in all other respects the principles and provisions discussed above in relation to certificated securities apply equally to uncertificated securities.

This part of the chapter deals with the provisions of the Act that are peculiar to uncertificated securities. Sections 52 to 55 of the Act apply only to uncertificated securities and prevail in the event of a conflict between those sections and any other provision of the Act, any other law, the common law, the company's Memorandum of Incorporation, or any agreement.[189]

In order to understand the specific provisions of the Act dealing with uncertificated securities, it is necessary to have some general understanding of the electronic settlement system used in the listed securities environment and the manner in which it functions. In 1997 the JSE Limited launched an electronic settlement

---

[186] See 7.10.1.
[187] There is an exception to this rule regarding substitution of securities, which is to be found in s 49(6) read with s 54 and that is discussed in more detail in 7.10.5*(e)* below. Uncertificated securities may be withdrawn from the uncertificated securities register and certificates issued evidencing those securities, ie, the uncertificated securities are substituted with certificated securities.
[188] See s 49(3).
[189] See s 49(4).

system called STRATE[190] (hereafter 'Strate') to replace the existing system that entailed the manual settlement of listed share transactions. The structure that was put in place to facilitate the Strate system basically operates as follows: the main role-player and custodian of the system is a body known as the Central Securities Depository (CSD). Its function is to oversee, control and manage the dematerialisation[191] process, the electronic settlement system and the conduct of the other role-players.[192] The CSD holds electronic records of all dematerialised (uncertificated) shares. The other major role-players are the Central Securities Depository Participants (commonly known as 'CSDPs' or 'participants').[193] Strate Ltd (an unlisted public company) is the approved CSD and only participants may liaise directly with Strate. Participants had to qualify for their status as such by meeting certain criteria laid down by Strate. The participants are mainly banking institutions.[194] They keep and manage electronic share accounts for investors and brokers. These accounts can be kept either in the name of the investor or his or her broker, or in the name of the participant on behalf of the investor or broker.

Under Strate, investors may elect whether they want to establish and conduct a relationship directly with a participant of their choice or whether they want to have an account with a broker. If they opt for the former, they will open a share account with the participant that will be either in their own name or the name of a nominee. If they opt for the latter, the broker will keep a share account for the investor reflecting the shares held. The account will be either in the investor's own name or in the name of a nominee. The broker will then interact with the participant on behalf of the investor. It is not possible for an investor to deal directly with the CSD because the latter deals only with participants. It is important to note that exchange transactions generally, as well as the holding, transfer and registration of uncertificated securities, are also governed by the Securities Services Act[195] and consistency with the provisions of that legislation in the Companies Act is therefore extremely important.[196]

(b) *Registration of uncertificated securities*

If a company has issued uncertificated securities or has issued securities that have ceased to be certificated (because they have been dematerialised in accordance with s 49(5) and Strate), the Act provides that a record must be administered and

---

[190] STRATE is an acronym for Share Transactions Totally Electronic.
[191] Dematerialisation is a technical term for the replacement of paper share certificates with electronic records to enable the Strate system to operate. Once a share has been dematerialised it is an uncertificated share. Of course, uncertificated shares may also be issued as such initially, in which case dematerialisation is not required.
[192] Clarke G 'The CSD Rules' *STRATE Talking* 6, 1.
[193] In s 1 of the Act the terms 'central securities depository' and 'participant' are defined as having the meaning set out in s 1 of the Securities Services Act 36 of 2004.
[194] Approved participants include ABSA, FNB, Nedbank, Standard Bank and Computershare.
[195] Act 36 of 2004.
[196] See Maria Vermaas 'The reform of the law of uncertificated securities in South African company law' 2010 *Acta Juridica* 87 at 92.

maintained by a participant or the CSD[197] in the prescribed form as the company's uncertificated securities register.[198] The uncertificated securities register:
- forms part of the company's securities register, and
- must contain with respect to all the company's uncertificated securities any details determined by the rules of the CSD,[199] as well as:
  o the names and addresses of the persons to whom the securities were issued,
  o the number of securities issued to each of them,
  o the number of, and prescribed circumstances relating to, any securities that —
    ▪ have been placed in trust as contemplated in s 40(6)(d), or
    ▪ whose transfer has been restricted,
  o in the case of securities contemplated in s 43 —
    ▪ the number of those securities issued and outstanding, or
    ▪ the names and addresses of the registered owner of the security and any holders of a beneficial interest in the security, and
  o any other prescribed information.

An uncertificated securities register maintained in accordance with the Act is sufficient proof of the facts recorded in it, in the absence of any evidence to the contrary.[200] In a number of provisions relating to uncertificated securities, reference is made to *(a)* a 'participant or CSD' as alternatives to one another, and *(b)* to details or procedures determined by 'the rules of the CSD'. According to Vermaas[201] this reflects the intention of the legislature to enable the CSD to determine and prescribe the settlement model to be used in the Strate system. The current holding and transfer model utilised by Strate in South Africa is based on a subregister system prescribed by the 1973 Act.[202] This system has certain drawbacks.[203] The Act therefore attempts to move away from the restrictive approach of prescribing a specific holding and transfer model for the market and, by including the type of references mentioned above in key provisions, give the CSD the flexibility to determine the specific holding and transfer model. This must, however, take place through the prescribed rule-making process as set out in the Securities Services Act 2004.[204] Vermaas points out that the CSD would only be able to migrate from a subregister model to its chosen model:

---

[197] Vermaas op cit n 196 at 92.
[198] The 'uncertificated securities register' is defined in s1 of the Act as 'the record of uncertificated securities administered and maintained by a participant or CSD, as determined in accordance with the rules of a CSD, and which forms part of the relevant company's securities register maintained in terms of part E of Chapter 2.'
[199] Section 50(3)(b)(ii). These details are contained in the Strate Rules, which were initially published in GN 2190 of 1999, *GG* 20476 of 23 September 1999, and which have been periodically updated and amended since.
[200] See s 50(4).
[201] Vermaas op cit n 196.
[202] See s 91A of the 1973 Act.
[203] See further Vermaas op cit n 196 at 94–6 where she discusses direct v indirect, centralised v fragmented and transparent v non-transparent systems.
[204] Act 36 of 2004, s 61.

... when the South African financial market is ready for such an implementation ... Under the new Act the choice of system is delegated to the CSD for specification in the CSD rules. It is believed that the choice would be best captured in CSD rules, as the rules may require adjustment to accommodate market changes ... It is believed that the CSD has developed over the last decade a core of expertise and understanding which can discharge this function successfully ... [A]t the same time, it is very clear that the existing body of law, rules and administrative practices must be regularly examined to ensure that these do not fail to provide adequate and effective regulation.[205]

In terms of s 52 of the Act, at the request of a company and on payment of a prescribed fee (if any), a participant or the CSD[206] must furnish that company with all details of its uncertificated securities reflected in the uncertificated securities register. If a person wants to inspect an uncertificated securities register, he or she may only do so through the relevant company in terms of s 26 (which regulates access to company records) and in accordance with the rules of the CSD. Within five business days after the date of a request for inspection, a company must produce a record of the uncertificated securities register, which must reflect at least the details referred to in s 50(3)*(b)* as at the close of business on the day on which the request for inspection was made. (The five business day period was presumably set as a result of the fact that under the Strate system it takes five days to finally and irrevocably settle a trade.)

Each person for whom uncertificated securities are held in an uncertificated securities register must be provided, free of charge, with a regular statement at prescribed intervals setting out the number and identity of the uncertificated securities held on that person's behalf.[207]

(c) *Transfer of uncertificated securities*

Section 53 provides that the transfer of uncertificated securities in an uncertificated securities register may be effected only by a participant or a CSD.[208] Furthermore, the transfer may be effected only 'on receipt of an instruction to transfer sent and properly authenticated in terms of the rules of a CSD'[209] or an order of a court[210] and in accordance with s 53 of the Act and the rules of the CSD. Section 53 further provides that transfer of ownership in any uncertificated securities must be effected by:

(a) debiting the account in the uncertificated securities register from which the transfer is effected; and

(b) crediting the account in the uncertificated securities register to which the transfer is effected,

---

[205] Vermaas op cit n 196 at 101–2.
[206] As explained, whether it is the participant or the CSD that must do so will ultimately be determined by the rules of the CSD.
[207] Once again, whether this obligation rests on a participant or the CSD will depend on the rules of the CSD (see s 52(4)). Any charge or service fee which may be imposed for the statement in accordance with the regulations will be for the account of the relevant company (see s 52(4)*(c)* read with s 52(5)).
[208] See Vermaas op cit n 196.
[209] See s 53(1)*(b)*(i). The rules referred to here are the Strate Rules as amended from time to time.
[210] See s 53(1)*(b)*(ii).

in accordance with the rules of a central securities depository.[211]

By way of explanation, the transfer takes place in practice as follows: When a trade has been completed, brokers will signal via Strate the participant for the seller, and the bank, as the CSDP. The banker and the participant will each review their respective ability to settle the trade. In order to do so, each of them must receive either a specific mandate from an investor or be in possession of a valid mandate to settle. The participant for the seller will check whether it is in the possession of the securities and, if so, these will be electronically flagged for settlement. Once this is done, the shares cannot be withdrawn prior to settlement. They are electronically frozen. The bank acting on behalf of the buyer will examine the buyer's account balance to determine whether there are sufficient funds available to settle the trade. If so, the seller's scrip balance is frozen. The banks will then be electronically signalled for payment. While the buyer's bank account is debited, the seller's account will be credited for payment of the transaction. The relevant participants debit the seller's share account and credit the buyer's share account. In this way the trade will be settled finally and irrevocably five working days after it has taken place.[212]

It is very important to note that a transfer of ownership, which takes place as described above in terms of s 53 of the Act, occurs despite any fraud, illegality or insolvency that may affect the relevant uncertificated securities or have resulted in the transfer being effected. It is only a transferee who was party to or had knowledge of the fraud, illegality or insolvency that may not rely on this provision — in all other circumstances the transfer of ownership will be valid and cannot be challenged or reversed.[213] Furthermore, a court may not order the name of a transferee contemplated in this section to be removed from an uncertificated securities register (ie the transferee in a transfer tainted by fraud or illegality) unless the transferee was a party to or had knowledge of the fraud or illegality as contemplated in s 53(4). It is worth noting that 'insolvency' has been omitted from s 53(5) although it does appear in s 53(4), to which section 53(5) refers. Presumably this means that a court may not order the name of a transferee to be removed from the uncertificated securities register unless the transferee had knowledge of the fraud or illegality, and that knowledge of any insolvency affecting the transfer is irrelevant. The court will not remove the name of the transferee notwithstanding knowledge of such insolvency.

The protection of the good faith transferee is one of the cornerstones of the Strate system. This protection (which existed under the 1973 Act) has been extended to cover insolvency and 'makes the electronic register sacrosanct'.[214] Apparently the rationale behind the inclusion of insolvency as an added protective measure arose from concerns for the position of the transferee in the event of

---

[211] See s 53(2).
[212] See 'The Second Investor's Guide to STRATE', an investor information document issued by the JSE Limited.
[213] See, however, s 55, which deals with liability relating to uncertificated securities, including damages for direct loss suffered as a result of unlawful action.
[214] See Vermaas op cit n 196 at 87.

insolvency of a participant or other intermediary.[215] However, there is nothing in the Act indicating that it is limited to the insolvency of these parties and it will therefore arguably extend to protection in the event of the insolvency of the seller or the purchaser. This may result in unforeseen consequences, especially regarding the question of which section will prevail in the event of a conflict between these sections and any other provision of any other law, for example, the law of insolvency.[216]

Section 53(6) states that nothing in s 53 prejudices the power of a participant or a CSD to effect a transfer to a person to whom the right to any uncertificated securities of any company has been transmitted by operation of law. It is not entirely clear what is meant by 'the right to any uncertificated securities'. Presumably this refers to rights other than ownership, such as the right of the executor of an estate to have the securities transferred to him or her in that capacity so that the exectutor can deal with them further as directed in terms of the will of the deceased and the law relating to the administration of estates.

(d) Security by cession in securitatem debiti

As was explained above, shares can be used to secure a debt. When one is dealing with uncertificated shares there is obviously no share certificate that can be delivered to effect the cession. Although it is noted that delivery is not vital to secure cession, it may be vital evidence of cession.[217] Furthermore, and very importantly, given the rules protecting the good faith transferee, once shares that were supposed to be ceded *in securitatem debiti* have been transferred, the transfer is final and irrevocable. The transfer cannot be reversed, not even by a court order, unless the transferee was *mala fide*. It is therefore a particularly risky system for a cessionary. To address this, s 43 of the Securities Services Act 2004 provides that a pledge or cession to secure a debt must be effected by entry in the account of:

(a) the pledgor in favour of the pledgee specifying the name of the pledgee, the interest in the securities pledged and the date; or

(b) the cedent in favour of the cessionary specifying the name of the cessionary, interest in the securities ceded and the date, as the case may be.

Such interest in securities may not be transferred except with the written consent of the pledgee or cessionary.[218]

(e) Substitution

An investor may, at any time, withdraw all or some of the uncertificated securities that he or she holds in an uncertificated securities register and obtain a certificate in respect of the withdrawn securities. In essence, this amounts to a 'rematerialisation' of the securities if they had previously been certificated and then were dematerialised in terms of Strate. Alternatively, it could be an initial 'materialisa-

---

[215] The word 'intermediary' is used as a general term that includes all account holders between the issuing company and the end investor. On this point see, further, Vermaas op cit n 196 at 88.
[216] See s 49(4).
[217] *Botha v Fick* 1995 (2) SA 750 (A). See also 7.10.3(e) above.
[218] The Strate Rules (notably rules 5.15, 6.7.4 and 7.8) place similar obligations on participants.

tion' of the securities if they were not initially issued in certificated form. In order to do so, the investor must notify the relevant participant or the CSD, which must notify the relevant company to provide the requested certificate and remove the details of the uncertificated securities from the uncertificated securities register. After receiving such a notice from a participant or the CSD, a company must immediately enter the relevant person's name and details of his or her holding of securities in its (certificated) securities register and indicate on the register that the withdrawn securities are no longer held in uncertificated form. Furthermore, within ten business days after receiving the notice, the company must prepare and deliver a certificate in respect of those securities to the relevant person and must also notify the CSD that the securities are no longer held in uncertificated form. The company may charge the holder a reasonable fee to cover the actual costs of issuing the certificate. Section 49(6) specifically provides that, as from the date on which previously uncertificated securities become certificated, ss 52 to 55 of the Act cease to apply to those securities and transfer of ownership in those securities can no longer be effected by a participant or the CSD while the securities remain in certificated form.

(f) Liability relating to uncertificated securities

Section 55(1) of the Act stipulates that a person who takes any unlawful action that results in any of the following occurring in a securities register:

   (a) the name of any person remains in, is entered in, or is removed or omitted;
   (b) the number of uncertificated securities is increased, reduced, or remains unaltered; or
   (c) the description of any uncertificated securities is changed,
   is liable to any person who has suffered any direct loss or damage arising out of that action.[219]

Section 55(2) provides that a person who gives an instruction to transfer uncertificated securities must warrant the legality and correctness of that instruction and also indemnify the company and the participant or the CSD required to effect the transfer against any claim and direct loss or damage arising from such a transfer by virtue of the (presumably, incorrectness or illegality) of that instruction.

Section 55(3) provides for an indemnity by a participant or a CSD. If a transfer of securities was effected by the participant or the CSD:

- without instruction, or
- in accordance with an instruction that was not sent and properly authenticated in terms of the rules of a CSD, or
- in a manner inconsistent with an instruction that was sent and properly authenticated in terms of the rules of a CSD, the participant or CSD must indemnify:
- a company against any claim and any direct loss or damage suffered by or arising out of a transfer of securities, and
- any other person against any direct loss or damage arising out of a transfer of any uncertificated securities.

---

[219] This provision presumably serves to ameliorate the potentially prejudicial effect of s 53(4) and (5).

(g) Beneficial interest in uncertificated securities

The issue of determining and reporting who has a beneficial interest in uncertificated securities may prove to be more challenging than when the same provisions laid down in s 56 (as discussed in the section on securities registration and transfer in chapter 6) are applied to certificated securities. The reason for this stems mainly from the South African Strate system in general[220] and the different forms that registration may take. Thus, an investor who holds 100 shares in a listed entity may have registered that interest in a number of ways: *(a)* in his or her own name, *(b)* in the name of a nominee in an account held with his or her broker or in his or her own name or in the name of a nominee, or *(c)* in the name of a participant if held directly with a participant. In the event that he or she held the shares with a broker, those shares will be reflected in the register maintained by the (broker's) chosen participant either in the name of the investor, in the name of the broker, or in the name of the broker's nominee. Ultimately, the holding of the securities is registered in the CSD, which opens securities accounts for participants.

This potential range of registration options is covered by s 56(3) in that any registered holder (like the nominee company of a CSD) who is not the holder of the beneficial interest in all the securities held by that person (being the nominee company) must disclose details in relation to the identity of the person on whose behalf it holds the securities (ie the various investors) as well as the number and class of securities held for each person. This information must be disclosed in writing to the company within five business days after the end of every month and otherwise be provided on payment of a fee charged by the registered holder of the securities.

Furthermore, all companies that have issued uncertificated securities will fall within the meaning of 'regulated company' as set out in s 117(1) because they will be public companies as contemplated in s 118(1)*(a)*. This, in turn, means the company must establish and maintain a register of disclosures as contemplated by s 56, and publish in its annual financial statements[221] a list of persons who hold beneficial interests equal to or in excess of 5 per cent of the total number of securities of that class issued by the company, together with the extent of those beneficial interests.[222] To the extent that they are not discussed here, the other provisions of the Act relating to a beneficial interest in securities (and the disclosure thereof) and which are examined in relation to certificated securities apply *mutatis mutandis* to uncertificated securities.[223]

---

[220] Vermaas op cit n 196 at 94.
[221] Which, as a public company, it will be required to have audited in terms of s 30(2).
[222] See s 56(7)*(b)*.
[223] See 7.10.4 above on 'uncertificated' securities.

CHAPTER 8

CORPORATE FINANCE

Richard Jooste

8.1	DISTRIBUTIONS		241
	8.1.1	General	241
	8.1.2	The definition of 'distribution'	242
	8.1.3	Authorisation of a distribution	246
	8.1.4	The solvency and liquidity requirement	246
	8.1.5	Enforcement of distribution	259
	8.1.6	Directors' liability for unlawful distributions	259
	8.1.7	Recovery of unlawful distributions from shareholders	263
	8.1.8	Dividends out of profits	263
8.2	REPURCHASES (BUY-BACKS)		268
	8.2.1	General	268
	8.2.2	Redemptions and repurchases	272
	8.2.3	Regulation of repurchases by the Act	272
		(a) Section 48	272
		(b) Reference to s 46	274
		(c) 'Acquire'	274
		(d) Conflict with Memorandum of Incorporation	275
		(e) Requirements for a repurchase	276
	8.2.4	Enforceability of agreement to acquire shares	279
	8.2.5	Directors' liability	280
	8.2.6	Treasury shares	280
8.3	ACQUISITION BY A COMPANY OF SHARES IN ITS HOLDING COMPANY (INDIRECT REPURCHASES)		282
	8.3.1	Reference to s 46	282
	8.3.2	'Limit'	283
	8.3.3	Requirement of s 48(3)	284
	8.3.4	Section 46 (distributions) applicable	284
	8.3.5	Directors' liability	284
	8.3.6	Non-applicability of s 48(4) and (5)	285
	8.3.7	Voting rights not exercisable	285
	8.3.8	Rationale for acquisition	285
8.4	FINANCIAL ASSISTANCE FOR THE ACQUISITION OF SECURITIES		287
	8.4.1	Background	287
	8.4.2	Section 44	288
	8.4.3	The meaning of 'financial assistance'	289

	8.4.4	The meaning of 'for the purpose of or in connection with'	297
	8.4.5	Purchase of or subscription for securities	299
	8.4.6	Authority for provision of financial assistance	301
	8.4.7	Requirements of ss 44(3) and (4)	302
		(a) The special resolution requirement	302
		(b) The solvency and liquidity test	303
		(c) Fair and reasonable terms	303
	8.4.8	Extension to a 'related or inter-related' company	306
	8.4.9	Consequences of contravention of s 44	306
		(a) Voidness	306
		(b) Statutory Turquand Rule	306
		(c) Criminal consequences	308
		(d) Liability of directors	308
8.5	FINANCIAL ASSISTANCE TO DIRECTORS ET AL		310
	8.5.1	Introduction	310
	8.5.2	Section 45	311
	8.5.3	Financial assistance	312
	8.5.4	Who must be financially assisted?	316
	8.5.5	The requirements of s 45	318
	8.5.6	The consequences of contravening s 45	321
	8.5.7	Disclosure in the annual financial statements	325

8.1 DISTRIBUTIONS

8.1.1 General

Regarding distributions by a company to its shareholders it must be borne in mind that:

> shareholders have an expectation, but not a right, to receive a return on the capital they contributed to the company by sharing in its profits during its existence. They also have a residual or reversionary interest in the company's net assets upon its dissolution, but no right to repayment of their contributions while the company exists.[1]

The distribution by a company of its assets to its shareholders, whether they be in the form of cash or otherwise, ought to be carefully regulated by any legal system intent on protecting the interests of creditors and minority shareholders of the company. Until 1999 such protection was largely provided by the maintenance of capital principle, which manifested itself in various ways. Most significantly, it was unlawful for a company to acquire its own shares or shares in its holding company. Also, the distribution of funds to shareholders other than those representing legally distributable profits usually required a court order. In 1999 this all changed with far-reaching amendments to the Companies Act 61 of 1973 (hereafter 'the 1973 Act').[2] The maintenance of capital principle was effectively abolished; companies were permitted to acquire their own shares and shares in their holding companies, and the distinction between a company's profits and other

---

[1] K van der Linde 'The regulation of distributions to shareholders in the Companies Act 2008' (2009) 3 *TSAR* 484.
[2] See the Companies Amendment Act 37 of 1999.

funds was removed. The distribution of funds was allowed provided, inter alia, that the company's solvency and liquidity were not placed in jeopardy and, in the case of a buy-back or a purchase of shares in the holding company, in addition, a special resolution was required.

The new Companies Act 71 of 2008 (hereafter 'the Act') follows a similar approach, but the provisions are significantly different from those of the 1973 Act.

The Act does not deal separately with the different types of distributions. Section 48 deals specifically with the acquisition by a company of its own shares and shares in its holding company, while distributions, generally, are dealt with in s 46 of the Act. The definition of 'distribution' in s 1 of the Act includes a transfer of the consideration for the acquisition by a company of its own shares or shares in any company in its 'group'. Accordingly, acquisitions by a company of its own shares or shares in its holding company are governed by both s 46 and s 48. Sections 46 and 48 are not, however, the only relevant provisions governing distributions. For example, the liability of directors in this context is dealt with in s 77. The Act provides that all shares of a class must be treated equally, unless the Memorandum of Incorporation provides otherwise.[3] It also provides that the Memorandum of Incorporation may entitle the shareholders to 'distributions' calculated in specific ways[4] and may provide for preferences as to distributions or liquidation rights in respect of different classes of shares.[5]

8.1.2 The definition of 'distribution'

All distributions governed by the Act are encapsulated in the definition of 'distribution' contained in the Act.[6]

---

[3] Section 37(1).
[4] Section 37(5)(c).
[5] Section 37(5)(d).
[6] See s 1 where 'distribution' is defined as 'a direct or indirect —
  (a) transfer by a company of money or other property of the company, other than its own shares, to or for the benefit of one more [an 'or' is inserted between 'one' and 'more' by the draft Companies Amendment Bill, 2010] holders of any of the shares of that company or of another company within the same group of companies, whether —
    (i) in the form of a dividend;
    (ii) as a payment in lieu of a capitalisation share, as contemplated in section 47;
    (iii) is ['as' has been substituted for 'is' by the draft Companies Amendment Bill, 2010] consideration for the acquisition —
      (aa) by the company of any of its shares, as contemplated in section 48; or
      (bb) by any company within the same group of companies, of any shares of a company within that group of companies; or
    (iv) otherwise in respect of any of the shares of that company or of another company within the same group of companies, subject to section 164(19);
  (b) incurrence of a debt or other obligation by a company for the benefit of one or more holders of any of the shares of that company or of another company within the same group of companies; or
  (c) forgiveness or waiver by a company of a debt or other obligation owed to the company by one more [an 'or' is inserted before 'more' by the draft Companies Amendment Bill, 2010] holders of any of the shares of that company or of another company within the same group of companies,
but does not include any such action taken upon the final liquidation of the company;'

The definition is broken down into essentially three types of distribution:
- a transfer of money or other property,[7]
- the incurrence of an obligation,[8] and
- the forgiveness or waiver of an obligation.[9]

Each of these is a distribution, whether made directly or indirectly.[10] The definition expressly excludes liquidation distributions, which has prompted the comment that the 'reason for this is that in a liquidation the surplus assets will be distributed to shareholders only once the debts have been paid, obviating the need for creditor protection. This exclusion provides welcome clarity.'[11]

The first type of distribution is a direct or indirect transfer, by a company, of money or other company property, other than its own shares, to or for the benefit of one or more of its shareholders or the shareholders of another company within the same group of companies. A number of specific inclusions are provided. The generality of the last inclusion (para *(a)*(iv)), together with the use of the term 'means' at the beginning of the definition, indicates that this is an exhaustive list of distributions that can be effected by way of a transfer of money or property.[12]

The inclusions are:
- dividends,
- payments in lieu of capitalisation shares,
- consideration for the acquisition by a company of its own shares,
- consideration for the acquisition by any company in a group of shares of another company in the group, and
- transfers by a company in respect of any of the shares of that company or of another company within the same group.[13]

There is no definition of 'dividend' in the Act. Ordinarily, when one uses the term 'dividend', one is referring to a distribution by a company of profits of the company. As nothing in the provisions governing distributions turns on the distinction between transfers of profits and other transfers, it is not clear why the definition of 'distribution' draws a distinction between transfers in the form of a dividend[14] and transfers otherwise in respect of shares.[15]

---
[7] Section 1 under 'distribution' para *(a)*.
[8] Section 1 under 'distribution' para *(b)*.
[9] Section 1 under 'distribution' para *(c)*.
[10] See the introductory words of the definition in s 1 *sv* 'distribution'.
[11] Van der Linde op cit n 1 at 486.
[12] Ibid.
[13] Section 1 under 'distribution' para *(a)*(iv) read with s 164(19). A 'surrender' of shares under the appraisal remedy is not regarded as an acquisition of shares. See s 48(1).
[14] Paragraph *(a)*(i) of the definition.
[15] Paragraph *(a)*(iv) of the definition. As Van der Linde says (op cit n 1 at 487):
'Under the capital maintenance doctrine a dividend in this sense (ie a distribution of profit) represents the only way in which a return on share capital can lawfully be paid by a company... In view of the move away from the common-law rules the need for a distinction between dividends and the residual category of other transfers in respect of shares is questionable. It would make sense to include a definition of the term 'dividend' in order to facilitate distinguishing between proportionate and non-proportionate distributions, as is the case in the New Zealand Companies Act (see s 53(1) of the New Zealand Companies Act), and to then impose different

The board may, when issuing capitalisation shares, if permitted by its Memorandum of Incorporation, offer shareholders a cash payment as an alternative to the capitalisation shares.[16] Such a cash alternative will qualify as a distribution.[17]

Where a company transfers money or other property as consideration for the acquisition by the company of its own shares or shares in any other company in its group, such transfer is a distribution.[18] Accordingly, all provisions governing distributions, and s 48 (with a notable exception[19]) governing such acquisitions, will apply.

Companies can, in terms of the Act, issue redeemable shares[20] and the redemption thereof requires compliance with the distribution and acquisition provisions of ss 46 and 48.[21] There is no special provision, as there was in the 1973 Act,[22] governing the redemption of shares. Treating a redemption by a company of its own shares the same as an acquisition by a company of its own shares obviously makes sense.

It appears that, where a company, in terms of a court order,[23] is required to restore to a shareholder any part of the consideration that the shareholder paid for the shares or its equivalent value, the company would be making a distribution, as defined. This would be a transfer by the company 'otherwise in respect of any shares of that company' (para *(a)*(iv) of the definition of distribution in s 1 of the Act).[24]

As pointed out,[25] the conversion of shares into debt instruments is not expressly regarded as a distribution. It only requires compliance with the Memorandum of Incorporation.[26] This is unfortunate, as a conversion may affect the interests of creditors in the same way as a distribution.[27] It may be that a conversion is a distribution regarded as a transfer 'otherwise in respect of any of the shares of that company or of another company within the same group of companies'.[28] It may also qualify as the 'incurrence of a debt or other obligation by a company for the

---

shareholder authorisation requirements for dividends and other distributions. However, the Companies Act 2008 does not require shareholder approval for any kind of distribution, so nothing turns on whether a transfer can be classified under one of the specific examples.'

[16] Section 47(3)*(a)*. See earlier.
[17] Section 1 under 'distribution' para *(a)*(ii).
[18] See para *(a)*(iii) of the definition of 'distribution'.
[19] Section 48 governs the acquisition by a company of shares in its holding company but not acquisitions by the company of shares in any other company in its group.
[20] Of any class and not only preference shares.
[21] See s 37(5)*(b)*.
[22] Section 98.
[23] That is, in terms of s 163(2)*(g)* of the Act.
[24] Van der Linde (op cit n 1 at 488) is of the view that this transfer is possibly also a distribution pursuant to an acquisition by the company of its own shares. This no doubt would be true if the court, as is likely, orders a surrender by the shareholder of the shares in question, which it can do. Section 163(2)*(g)* does not talk of an 'acquisition' but it does provide that the court can impose 'conditions', which no doubt would include the surrender of the shares.
[25] See Van der Linde op cit n 1 at 489.
[26] See s 37(4)*(b)*.
[27] Van der Linde op cit n 1 at 489. She says '[t]his is why conversions are also regarded as distributions under s 6.03*(b)* of the American Model Business Corporation Act.'
[28] Section 1 under 'distribution' para *(a)*(iv). See Van der Linde op cit n 1 at 489.

benefit of one or more holders of any of the shares of that company or of another company within the same group of companies'.[29]

The making of a demand, tendering of shares and payment by a company to a shareholder in terms of the appraisal remedy provision does not constitute a 'distribution'.[30] Why this distinction is drawn is unclear. As has been pointed out,[31] the distinction is difficult to justify.

> This exclusion has the effect that shareholders who insist on being paid for their shares as a result of their dissent with certain corporate actions may receive payment in competition with creditors. Although the company 'may' approach the court to vary its obligations if it can prove that its liquidity (but not its solvency) will be impaired, it is not obliged to do so. A shareholder relying on the appraisal remedy need not even prove prejudice as a result of the intended corporate action.[32] Yet the Companies Act 2008 affords such a shareholder the same status as a creditor, while payment due to a shareholder who succeeded under the oppression remedy will be regarded as a distribution . . . I think that this disparate regulation of procedures with the same basic objective, namely to protect shareholders from being locked into a company, is difficult to justify.[33]

A distribution is made by the company by incurring a debt or obligation in favour of its own shareholder or a shareholder of another company in the group.[34]

It is unclear as to 'whether the incurring of a non-monetary obligation by a company, for example to render a service or to refrain from doing something, will also constitute a distribution and, if so, how it will be quantified'.[35]

The definition of 'distribution' in the Act does not only cover distributions by a company to its own shareholders but also to holders of shares in any company within the same group of companies.[36]

The entire implications of this extension of the definition to the group context are unclear, as is the rationale.[37] The strange result of this extension is that the payment made by a company when purchasing further shares in its subsidiary would be a 'distribution' as defined. Why such a payment should be regulated as a distribution is unfathomable considering that such an acquisition poses no risk.[38]

As a distribution may be made 'directly or indirectly'[39] it appears that it may be that the same distribution may be regarded as a distribution by more than one company in the group. Say S (Pty) Ltd makes a payment to the shareholders of its holding company H Ltd. S (Pty) Ltd will have made a distribution to shareholders of another company in the group. The same payment can also be seen as an

---

[29] Section 1 under 'distribution' para *(b)*; see Van der Linde op cit n 1 at 489.
[30] See s 164(19) of the Act read with para *(a)*(iv) of the definition of 'distribution'.
[31] Van der Linde op cit n 1 at 489.
[32] See Beukes 'An introduction to the appraisal remedy as proposed in the Companies Bill: Triggering actions and the differences between the appraisal remedy and existing shareholder remedies' 2008 *SA Merc LJ* 479 at 492.
[33] Ibid.
[34] Section 1 under 'distribution' para *(b)*.
[35] Van der Linde op cit n 1 at 489.
[36] See paras *(a)*, *(b)* and *(c)* of the definition. There appears to be no other jurisdiction with such a general group extension. See Van der Linde op cit n 1 at 491.
[37] The Explanatory Memorandum does not explain the reason for the extension.
[38] See MS Blackman et al *Commentary on the Companies Act* vol 1 (Revision Service 6) 5–99.
[39] See the definition of 'distribution' in s 1 of the Act.

indirect transfer by H Ltd to its own shareholders. Applying the requirements for distributions to such instances may be problematic.[40]

8.1.3 Authorisation of a distribution

A distribution by a company must be authorised by the company's board of directors, unless the distribution is pursuant to an existing obligation of the company or a court order.[41]

No shareholder approval of any kind is required for a distribution. It also appears that the Memorandum of Incorporation cannot validly impose any prohibitions, conditions or requirements relating to distributions.[42] This means provisions in the Memorandum of Incorporation that prohibit certain distributions or acquisitions altogether or permit them only if certain conditions are met, are ineffective. This is borne out by a reading of s 15(2)(a)(ii) of the Act and the definition of 'alterable provision' in s 1 of the Act. Section 15(2)(a)(ii) provides:

> The Memorandum of Incorporation of —
> (a) any company may include any provision —
> ...
> (ii) altering the effect of any alterable provision of this Act.

An 'alterable provision' means:[43]

> a provision of this Act in which it is *expressly* contemplated that its effect on a particular company may be negated, restricted, limited, qualified, extended, or otherwise altered in substance or effect by that company's Memorandum of Incorporation. (emphasis added)

An examination of s 46 shows that this section is not an alterable provision. There is nothing in s 46 that 'expressly contemplate[s]' that the effect of s 46 may be 'negated, restricted, limited, qualified, extended, or otherwise altered in substance or effect by' a company's Memorandum of Incorporation.[44]

It is doubtful whether the legislature intended the Memorandum of Incorporation to be nullified in this way. Why should a company not, for example, in its Memorandum of Incorporation, prohibit the paying of dividends out of anything other than profits? A clarifying amendment is called for.[45]

8.1.4 The solvency and liquidity requirement

In an effort to safeguard creditors and minority shareholders of a company, the company's board of directors must not make any proposed distribution unless:

---

[40] Van der Linde op cit n 1 at 491.
[41] See s 46(1)(a)(ii).
[42] For a contrary view see Van der Linde op cit n 1 at 492.
[43] See s 1 of the Act.
[44] Section 46 is unlike, for example, sections 44 and 45 of the Act, which are 'alterable provisions'. Section 44 'expressly contemplates' that a company's Memorandum of Incorporation may override the company's ability to assist in a subscription for its shares, which is permitted by s 44 subject to the requirements of the section. This is clear from the words 'Except to the extent that the Memorandum of Incorporation of a company provides otherwise . . .' in s 44(2) (see also s 44(4)). Section 45, which deals with, inter alia, the giving of financial assistance by a company to its directors, is similarly an alterable provision with the same wording as s 44.
[45] The position in the Act may be contrasted with, for example, s 59(1) of the New Zealand Companies Act 105 of 1993 which requires a buy-back to be expressly permitted by the company's constitution.

- it has applied the solvency and liquidity test, and
- it has acknowledged, by resolution, that it has reasonably concluded that the company will satisfy the test immediately after completion of the proposed distribution.[46]

These requirements must be met whether the distribution is pursuant to a board resolution, an existing obligation or a court order.

When more than 120 business days have passed since the board's acknowledgement that it has applied the solvency and liquidity test and it has reasonably concluded that the company will satisfy the test, and the company has not yet completed the distribution, the board is required to reconsider the solvency and liquidity test with respect to the remaining distribution to be made.[47] The company may not proceed with or continue a distribution unless the board adopts a further resolution acknowledging that it has applied the solvency and liquidity test and has reasonably concluded that the company will satisfy it.[48]

As has been pointed out,[49] the implication of this formulation is that, once the first acknowledgement has been made, periodic testing must take place irrespective of when the company intends proceeding or continuing with the distribution.[50]

Once an acknowledgement is made (whether an initial or a subsequent one) the company is required to proceed with the distribution. As Van der Linde says,[51] this means a company may have to proceed with and complete a distribution on the basis of the directors' acknowledgement even when it appears, within the 120-day period, that the company no longer satisfies the test. It is strange that the company is obliged to proceed with what is in effect an unlawful distribution, merely based on the board's formal acknowledgement.[52]

The solvency and liquidity requirements have different theoretical justifications:

---

[46] Section 46(1)*(b)* and *(c)*. The solvency and liquidity requirement is set out in s 4 of the Act. For a comprehensive article analysing the solvency and liquidity test see K van der Linde 'The solvency and liquidity approach in the Companies Act 2008' (2009) 2 *TSAR* 224. See also Murphy 'Equity insolvency and the new Model Business Corporation Act' (1981) *University of Richmond Law Review* 839 at 847–50; Grainger 'Assessing liabilities for a declaration of solvency: another view' (1984) *Company Lawyer* 290 at 290–1.
[47] Section 46(3)*(a)*.
[48] Section 46(3)*(b)*. This provision is based on s 6.40*(e)*(3) of the American Model Business Corporation Act.
[49] Van der Linde takes the view that 'the provision should be reformulated so that a reconsideration and acknowledgement is required only when the company is about to proceed with a distribution and more than 120 days have lapsed since the previous consideration.'
[50] Van der Linde op cit n 46 at 239.
[51] Op cit n 46 at 239.
[52] See Van der Linde op cit n 46 at 239. She says:

'I recommend that a company should be prohibited from proceeding with a distribution if the directors are no longer satisfied that the company's financial situation allows it. In such a case the shareholder should not be able to enforce her claim, despite the existence of a current acknowledgement by the directors. My proposal does not obviate the need for a formal reconsideration by the directors, but merely attaches less weight to the acknowledgement.'

[t]he solvency element gives advance recognition to the ultimate priority that creditors enjoy over shareholders upon dissolution of the company by preventing the company from favouring its shareholders through a partial liquidation. The justification for a liquidity element is that it addresses the fundamental expectation of creditors to be paid on time and also fits in well with the representation a company is said to make when it incurs debt, namely that it reasonably expects to be able to pay as and when the debt becomes due.[53] It would be unfair to allow a company which has made an implied representation of liquidity to subsequently compromise that liquidity by making distributions to shareholders.[54]

The solvency and liquidity test is set out in s 4 of the Act. It is not only a prerequisite for all distributions, but is also required if a company gives financial assistance in connection with the acquisition of its shares,[55] makes a loan or gives other financial assistance to its directors,[56] or amalgamates or merges with another company.[57] Actually, two aspects are involved — a solvency aspect (or test) and a liquidity aspect (or test).

Section 4 provides as follows:

4 (1) For any purpose of this Act, a company satisfies the solvency and liquidity test at a particular time if, considering all reasonably foreseeable financial circumstances of the company at that time —
 (a) the assets of the company or, if the company is a member of a group of companies, the aggregate assets of the company, as fairly valued, equal or exceed the liabilities of the company or, if the company is a member of a group of companies, the aggregate liabilities of the company, as fairly valued;[58] and
 (b) it appears that the company will be able to pay its debts as they become due in the ordinary course of business for a period of —
  (i) 12 months[59] after the date on which the test is considered; or
  (ii) in the case of a distribution contemplated in paragraph (a) of the definition of 'distribution' in section 1, 12 months following that distribution.
 (2) For the purposes contemplated in subsection (1) —
(a) any financial information to be considered concerning the company must be based on —
  (i) accounting records that satisfy the requirements of section 28;[60]
  (ii) financial statements that satisfy the requirements of section 29;[61]
(b) subject to paragraph (c), the board or any other person applying the solvency and liquidity test to a company —

---

[53] Van der Linde op cit n 46 at 226. See *Ex parte De Villiers NNO: in re Carbon Developments (Pty) Ltd (in liquidation)* 1993 (1) SA 493 (A) 504.
[54] Van der Linde op cit n 46 at 240.
[55] Section 44.
[56] Section 45.
[57] Section 113(1).
[58] It is to be noted that the draft Companies Amendment Bill proposes substituting s 4(1)(a) with the following:
 '(a) the assets of the company or, in the case of a holding company, the consolidated assets of the company, as fairly valued, equal or exceed the liabilities of the company or, in the case of a holding company, the consolidated liabilities of the company, as fairly valued; and'
[59] Providing a specific time period does provide an element of certainty for the board of directors, but it will not benefit creditors whose claims against the company are enforceable after the 12-month period has expired.
[60] Section 28 requires accounting records to be accurate and complete.
[61] Section 29 prescribes compliance with financial reporting standards.

(i) must consider a fair valuation of the company's assets and liabilities, including any reasonably foreseeable contingent assets and liabilities, irrespective of whether or not arising as a result of the proposed distribution, or otherwise; and

(ii) may consider any other valuation of the company's assets and liabilities that is reasonable in the circumstances; and

(c) unless the Memorandum of Incorporation of the company provides otherwise, a person applying the test in respect of a distribution contemplated in paragraph *(a)* of the definition of 'distribution' in section 1 is not to be regarded as a liability any amount that would be required, if the company were to be liquidated at the time of the distribution, to satisfy the preferential rights upon liquidation of shareholders whose preferential rights upon liquidation are superior to the preferential rights upon liquidation of those receiving the distribution.

The solvency aspect of the test is satisfied whenever the assets[62] would exceed or equal the liabilities[63] following a distribution. 'No provision is made for a solvency margin except in limited circumstances where the liquidation preferences of preference shareholders must be taken into account.'[64]

The solvency and liquidity test is met if 'it reasonably appears that the company will satisfy the solvency and liquidity test'[65] and the board has acknowledged that 'it has applied the solvency and liquidity test' and 'has ... reasonably concluded that the company will satisfy the solvency and liquidity test'.[66] In regard to this wording two issues arise:

First, is the solvency and liquidity of the company a purely objective test, ie would a hypothetical reasonable board have been satisfied with the solvency and liquidity of the company; or is the test both objective and subjective, ie would a hypothetical reasonable board with the knowledge, skill and experience of the particular board in question, have been reasonably satisfied with the solvency and liquidity of the company? The subjective/objective test takes into account the knowledge, skill and experience in reasonably concluding that the company will satisfy the solvency and liquidity test. The objective test, on the other hand, disregards these subjective factors. An analogy can perhaps be drawn with the test as to whether a director has acted with due care and diligence in a particular respect. In this regard, s 76(3)*(c)*(ii) of the Act provides that a director:

... must exercise the powers and perform the functions of director —
...
(c) with the degree of care, skill and diligence that may reasonably be expected of a person —
(i) carrying out the same functions in relation to the company as those carried out by that director; and

---

[62] 'Asset' is not defined in the Act, but it is in the draft Companies Amendment Bill, 2010, as follows:
'"asset" means a resource controlled by an entity as a result of past events, and from which future economic benefits are expected to flow;'

[63] It is to be noted that the draft Companies Amendment Bill, 2010 defines 'liability'. It provides:
'"liability" means a present obligation of an entity arising from past events, the settlement of which is expected to result in an outflow from the entity of resources embodying economic benefits;'

[64] Van der Linde op cit n 46 at 228. See s 4(2)*(c)* and below regarding preferential rights of preference shareholders.

[65] Section 46(1)*(b)*.

[66] Section 46(1)*(c)*.

(ii) having the general knowledge, skill and experience of that director.

This is a subjective/objective test. It is submitted that the test in the present context is purely objective.[67] It appears that, if the legislature intended that the subjective factors mentioned above should be taken into account, it would have said so.

A second issue regarding the solvency and liquidity test in the context of distributions is that in s 44 and s 45 the test appears to be different to the one applicable to distributions. Section 44 deals, inter alia, with a company assisting in the acquisition of its shares, and s 45, inter alia, with a company giving loans or financial assistance to its directors. In both instances the transaction must meet certain requirements, one of which is that 'the board is satisfied' that 'the company would be in compliance with the solvency and liquidity test'.[68] Here it could be argued that the wording 'the board is satisfied' is purely subjective. As long as the board is satisfied, no matter how unreasonable that satisfaction may be, the requirement is met.[69] If this is so, it is difficult to rationalise why the test in s 44 and s 45 should be different to the one applicable to distributions.[70] One would expect consistency in this regard.

It will be recognised that the actual insolvency of the company after the distribution has been made will be of concern to creditors. Creditors of the company 'are affected by the actual solvency or liquidity of the company rather than by the accuracy of predictions or assumptions'.[71] Accordingly, the validity of a distribution and the liability of shareholders to return to the company an invalid distribution should be based on the actual solvency and liquidity of the company. The liability of directors could be based on whether they made reasonable predictions. This, however, is not the position in the Act — neither the solvency nor the liquidity aspects of the test are based on actual solvency and liquidity, but on predictions.[72]

Clearly, whether or not the test is objective or subjective or a combination of both, the board must make proper enquiry.

Section 4 is not very helpful in determining how such enquiry must be carried out apart from requiring that:

---

[67] As Van der Linde says (op cit n 46 at 235):
'This paragraph does not state to whom this should be reasonably apparent, so it can be assumed that the test must be applied from the perspective of an objective bystander.'

[68] See s 44(3)*(b)*(i) and s 45(3)*(b)*(ii).

[69] The board must, in satisfying itself, of course, comply with the requirements of s 4(2), which do contain an element of 'reasonableness'. See in this regard the word 'fair' in s 4(2)*(b)*(i) and the word 'reasonable' in s 4(2)*(b)*(ii).

[70] See also s 47(2)*(a)*, s 47(2)*(b)*, s 113(4)*(a)* and *(b)* for other differences in the way the solvency and liquidity test is to be applied.

[71] Van der Linde op cit n 46 at 236.

[72] The position in terms of the Act can be contrasted with California (see ss 500–2 of the California Corporations Code), New Zealand (see s 56(1) of the New Zealand Companies Act) and the American Model Business Corporation Act (see s 6.40) where 'the lawfulness of a distribution depends on the corporation's actual compliance with the restrictions when the distribution is made. However, additional factors are relevant to determine liability for an unlawful distribution' (Van der Linde op cit n 46 at 236).

- any financial information considered in the enquiry must be based on accounting records and financial statements satisfying the requirements of the Act,
- the board must consider a fair valuation of the company's assets and liabilities, including any reasonably foreseeable contingent assets and liabilities, irrespective of whether or not arising as a result of the proposed distribution, or otherwise; and may consider any other valuation of the company's assets and liabilities that is reasonable in the circumstances.[73]

When making such inquiry the board may, no doubt, rely on others, unless they have actual knowledge, or ought in the circumstances to have had grounds for the suspicion, that such reliance is unwarranted. The American Revised Model Business Corporation Act 1984 states that:

> [t]he board of directors may base a determination that a distribution is not prohibited under s 6.40*(c)* either on financial statements prepared on the basis of accounting practices and principles that are reasonable in the circumstances, or on a fair valuation or other method that is reasonable in the circumstances.[74]

In exercising their judgment, the directors are entitled to rely on information, opinions, reports and statements prepared by others.[75]

As to the liquidity test in s 6.40*(c)*(1) of this Act, the official comment made with the publication of the Act[76] explains that:

> [i]n most cases involving a corporation operating as a going concern in the normal course, information generally available will make it quite apparent that no particular inquiry concerning the equity insolvency test is needed ... While neither a balance sheet nor an income statement can be conclusive as to this test, the existence of significant shareholders' equity and normal operating conditions are of themselves a strong indication that no issue should arise under that test.

The absence of any qualification in the most recent auditor's opinion coupled with a lack of subsequent adverse events, 'would normally be decisive'. It is only when circumstances indicate that the corporation is encountering difficulties or is in an uncertain position concerning its liquidity and operations that the board of directors may need to address the issue. Because overall judgment is required, 'no one or more "bright line" tests can be employed'. However:

> certain judgments or assumptions as to the future course of the corporation's business are customarily justified, absent clear evidence to the contrary. These include the likelihood that *(a)* based on existing and contemplated demand for the corporation's products or services, it

---

[73] As Van der Linde says: '[I]t is difficult to conceive of circumstances where a valuation of the company's assets that is not a fair valuation would nevertheless be "reasonable in the circumstances"' (op cit n 46 at 231).

[74] Section 640*(d)*.

[75] Under s 8.30*(b)*. Section 8.30, which deals with general standards for directors, provides (in s 8.30*(b)*) that, in discharging his duties, a director is entitled to rely on information, opinions, reports, or statements, including financial statements and other financial data, if prepared or presented by: (1) one or more officers or employees of the corporation whom the director reasonably believes to be reliable and competent in the matters presented; (2) legal counsel, public accountants, or other persons as to matters the director reasonably believes are within the person's professional or expert competence; or (3) a committee of the board of directors of which he is not a member if the director reasonably believes the committee merits confidence.'

[76] See Blackman et al op cit n 38 at 5–120.

will be able to generate funds over a period of time sufficient to satisfy its existing and reasonably anticipated obligations as they mature, and *(b)* the indebtedness which matures in the near-term will be refinanced where, on the basis of the corporation's financial condition and future prospects and the general availability of credit to businesses similarly situated, it is reasonable to assume that such financing may be accomplished.[77]

In regard to contingent liabilities:

> [R]easonable judgment as to the likelihood, amount, and time of any recovery against the corporation, after giving consideration to the extent to which the corporation is insured or otherwise protected against loss, may be utilized ... There may be occasions when it would be useful to consider a cash flow analysis, based on a business forecast and budget, covering a sufficient period of time to permit a conclusion that known obligations of the corporation can reasonably be expected to be satisfied over the period of time that they will mature.[78]

As to the solvency or balance-sheet test, the official comment[79] explains[80] that 'the determination of a corporation's assets and liabilities and the choice of the permissible basis on which to do so', is left to the judgment of the board of directors. In making this judgment, 'the board may rely[81] upon opinions, reports, or statements, including financial statements and other financial data prepared or presented by public accountants or others'. It 'may make judgments about accounting matters, giving full effect to its right to rely upon professional or expert advice'. In all circumstances, it is 'entitled to rely upon reasonably current financial statements prepared on the basis of generally accepted accounting principles, unless aware that it would be unreasonable to so because of newly-discovered or subsequently arising facts or circumstances'.

Section 6.40*(d)* does not mandate the use of generally accepted accounting principles. It only requires the use of accounting practices and principles that are 'reasonable in the circumstances'. It specifically permits 'determinations to be made ... on the basis of a fair valuation or other method that is reasonable in the circumstances'.[82] Thus it authorises departures from historical cost accounting, and the use of the appraisal and current value methods to determine the amount available for distribution.

> No particular method of valuation is prescribed, since different methods may have validity depending upon the circumstances, including the type of enterprise and the purpose for which the determination is made ... In most cases, a fair valuation method or a going

---

[77] The directors, the official comments states, 'should not, of course, be held responsible as a matter of hindsight for unforeseen developments. This is particularly true with respect to assumptions as to the ability of the corporation's business to repay long-term obligations which do not mature for several years, since the primary focus of the directors' decision to make a distribution should normally be on the corporation's prospects and obligations in the shorter term, unless special factors concerning the corporation's prospects require the taking of a longer term perspective.'

[78] Blackman et al op cit n 38 at 5–122.

[79] On the balance sheet test in s 6.40*(c)*(2).

[80] See Blackman et al op cit n 38 at 5–121.

[81] Under s 8.30*(b)*.

[82] Section 6.40*(d)* also refers to some 'other method that is reasonable in the circumstances'. This phrase is intended to comprehend within s 6.40*(c)*(2) the wide variety of possibilities that might not be considered to fall under '[the] "fair valuation" or "current value" method but might be reasonable in the circumstances of a particular case'.

concern basis would be appropriate if it is believed that the enterprise will continue as a going concern.

As Blackman says,[83] ordinarily assets should not be selectively revalued. The corporation should consider the value of all its material assets, whether or not reflected in the financial statements (eg a valuable executory contract), and it should consider and, to the extent appropriate and possible, revalue, all material obligations.

The UK Companies Act 1985 permits a private company to pay for the purchase of its shares out of its capital.[84] Section 173(3) specifies, as one condition for this, that the directors must make a statutory declaration stating inter alia that, 'having made full inquiry into the affairs and prospects of the company, they have formed the opinion' that, immediately following the payment, there will be no grounds on which the company could then be found unable to pay its debts, and, having regard to their intentions with respect to the management of the company's business during the year following the payment, and to the amount and character of the financial resources that will in their view be available to it during that year, the company will be able to continue to carry on business as a going concern (and will accordingly be able to pay its debts as they fall due) throughout that year.

The New Zealand Companies Act 1993 provides that, in determining whether the value of a company's assets is greater than the value of its liabilities, including contingent liabilities, the directors must have regard to *(a)* the most recent financial statements of the company; and *(b)* all other circumstances that the directors know or ought to know affect, or may affect, the value of the company's assets and the value of the company's liabilities. They may rely on the valuations of assets or estimates of liabilities that are reasonable in the circumstances.[85] A director acting in good faith, who makes proper inquiry where the need for inquiry is indicated by the circumstances, and who has no actual knowledge that such reliance is unwarranted,[86] may, when exercising powers or performing duties as a director, rely on reports, statements and financial data and other information prepared or supplied, and on professional or expert advice given, by an employee, a professional adviser, and any other director or committee of directors in the circumstances specified.[87]

In determining a company's assets and liabilities, s 4 of the Companies Act of 2008 requires that 'any reasonably foreseeable contingent assets and liabilities' must be taken into account.[88] Including *contingent* assets and liabilities is necessary to give a true picture of a company's solvency and liquidity position.

---

[83] Blackman et al op cit n 38 at 5–121.

[84] Section 171. See now s 709, UK Companies Act 2006.

[85] Section 4(2). Regarding the New Zealand position see *Re DML Resources Ltd (In Liquidation)* 2004 3 NZLR 490 (HC).

[86] Section 138(2) of the New Zealand Companies Act 1993.

[87] A director may rely on *(a)* an employee of the company whom the director believes on reasonable grounds to be reliable and competent in relation to the matters concerned; *(b)* a professional adviser or expert in relation to matters which the directors believe on reasonable grounds to be within the person's professional or expert competence; *(c)* any other director or committee of directors upon which the director did not serve in relation to matters within the director's or committee's designated authority: s 138(1) of the New Zealand Companies Act 1993.

[88] Section 4(2)*(b)*(i) of the Act.

A contingent liability is one that will only become due and payable on the happening of an event which may or may not occur. A contingent asset is a claim to an asset the vesting of which is conditional on the happening of an event that may or may not occur. Of course the event may not occur. Accordingly, the question must be the likelihood of the contingent event occurring and, if likely to occur, the time when it is likely to occur.

In order for a liability to be a contingent liability there must be a *vinculum juris* between the claimant and the company. By '*vinculum juris*' is meant 'a legal obligation which creates a right enforceable in a court of law'.[89] It is essential that there be an actually existing *vinculum juris*.[90] It has been held that contingent liabilities include unliquidated claims for damages.[91]

The inclusion of reasonably foreseeable contingent assets and liabilities 'irrespective of whether or not arising as a result of the proposed distribution or otherwise'[92] is confusing. As has been pointed out:[93]

> [f]irstly, it is not clear how contingent assets would arise from a distribution. Secondly, it appears to conflict with the principle that the solvency and liquidity test must be satisfied immediately after completing the distribution or other transaction. Once a distribution has been made or completed, the liability will have been extinguished, thus removing the need to include it as a liability. Perhaps this requirement is intended for the situation where a distribution takes the form of the incurring of a debt or obligation that is not immediately enforceable. In such a case the solvency and liquidity test must be satisfied when the distribution is authorised.[94] If the authorisation itself will not create a debt or obligation, it would make sense to include the proposed distribution as a contingent liability.

In dealing with the solvency aspect of the test, claims in respect of previously authorised distributions that have not yet been fully completed, clearly must be taken into account as liabilities. However, regarding the liquidity aspect 'it is arguable that they cannot be regarded as debts due in the ordinary course of business for purposes of the liquidity element because they are enforceable only while the company is solvent and able to pay its debts'.[95]

In Australia the test for insolvency of a company has for a long time been whether the company is unable to pay its debts as they become due and payable.[96] What the courts have held in this regard is therefore useful in determining the meaning of the liquidity aspect of the solvency and liquidity test in s 4 of the Act.[97] The Australian courts have held that whether a company is unable to pay its

---

[89] See *Kyle v Maritz & Pieterse Inc* [2002] 3 All SA 223 (T) 226.

[90] *Wiseman v Ace Table Soccer (Pty) Ltd* 1991 (4) SA 171 (W) 176; *Holzman v Knights Engineering and Precision Works (Pty) Ltd* 1979 (2) SA 784 (W) 787.

[91] Section 4(2)(*b*)(ii).

[92] Section 4(2)(*b*)(ii).

[93] Van der Linde op cit n 46 at 231.

[94] Section 46(4)(*b*). The requirement cannot apply if the obligation is immediately enforceable, as intended in s 46(4)(*a*).

[95] Van der Linde op cit n 46 at 231. Section 6.40(*g*) of the American Model Business Corporation Act expressly provides that such claims must be disregarded. 'This is a useful exclusion, given the uncertainty as to whether such claims can ever be regarded as debts due in the ordinary course of a company's business' (Van der Linde op cit n 46 at 232).

[96] See s 95 of the Bankruptcy Act (1924–1960) (Cth); and s 95A of the Corporations Law.

[97] See Blackman et al op cit n 38 at 5–124–5–126.

debts as they fall due is always a question of fact to be decided as a matter of commercial reality in the light of all the circumstances of the case, and not merely by looking at the accounts and making a mechanical comparison of assets and liabilities.[98] The position must be viewed as it would be by someone operating in a practical business environment.[99] This requires a consideration of the company's financial condition in its entirety, including the nature and circumstances of its activities, its assets and liabilities and their nature, cash on hand, moneys procurable within a relatively short time (relative, that is, to the nature and amount of the debts and to the circumstances of the company, including the nature of its business) by the sale of assets, or by way of loan and mortgage or pledge of assets, or by raising capital.[100] The size of any deficiency between assets and liabilities of the company is a factor that can be taken into account, for it may be indicative of a company that, on relevant dates, could not reasonably be expected to be able to pay its debts as and when they become due.[101]

The courts have also held that, in addition, account must be taken of:

> ... all the cash resources available to the company, including credit resources, ... and in determining those credit resources there are to be taken into account the times extended to the company to pay its creditors, on the one hand, and the times within which it will receive payment of debts owing to it on the other hand.[102]

Or, at least, the times within which the company might reasonably expect to receive payments of debts owing to it.[103] It would, for example, be relevant that the company was at the relevant time 'advantaged by stricter arrangements for obtaining payment from its debtors than the more indulgent trading terms that its creditors were prepared to extend to it'.[104] In the case of a solvent company, it will be necessary to take into account moneys procurable by the sale of assets, or by obtaining sufficient credit, within a relatively short time, relative that is to the

---

[98] *Wiseman v Ace Table Soccer (Pty) Ltd* 1991 (4) SA 171 (W) 180–1; *Dunn v Shapowloff* (1978) 3 ACLR 775 CA (NSW); *Taylor v Australian and New Zealand Banking Group Ltd* (1988) 13 ACLR 780, 783 SC (Vic); *Taylor v Carrol* (1991) 6 ACSR 255 at 259 SC (Qld); *Levi v Guerlini* (1997) 24 ACSR 159 at 163–4 SA (WA); *Credit Corporation Australia Pty Ltd v Atkins* (1999) 30 ACSR 727 at 742 (Fed C of A).

[99] *Brooks v Heritage Hotel Adelaide Pty Ltd* (1996) 20 ACSR 61 at 65 SC (SA); *Taylor v Australian and New Zealand Banking Group Ltd* (supra) at 784; *Re New World Alliance Pty Ltd; Syncotes Pty Ltd v Baseler (No 2)* (1994) 51 FCR 425.

[100] *Levi v Guerlini* (supra); *Dunn v Shapowloff* (supra); *3M Australia Pty Ltd v Kemish* (1986) 10 ACLR 371 SC (NSW); *Taylor v Australian and New Zealand Banking Group Ltd* (supra) at 783; *Taylor v Carrol* (supra) at 251; *Standard Chartered Bank of Australia Ltd v Antico (Nos 1 and 2)* (1995) 18 ACSR 1 SC (NSW); *Credit Corporation Australia Pty Ltd v Atkins* (supra); *Sandell v Porter* (1966) 115 CLR 666 at 670 (HC of A).

[101] *Credit Corporation Australia Pty Ltd v Atkins* (supra) at 758; *Sycotex Pty Ltd v Baseler* (1994) 13 ACSR 766 at 776 (Fed C of A); *TCN Channel Nine Pty Ltd v Scotney* (1995) 18 ACSR 393 at 397 (Fed C of A).

[102] O'Bryan J in *Heide Pty Ltd v Lester* (1990) 3 ACSR 159 at 165 SC (Vic).

[103] See *Levi v Guerlini* (1997) 24 ACSR 159 at 164 SC (WA); *Calzaturificio Zenith Pty Ltd v New South Wales Leather & Trading Co Pty Ltd* [1970] VR 605 at 605–9; *Taylor v Australian and New Zealand Banking Group Ltd* (1988) 13 ACLR 780 at 783 SC (Vic); *Pioneer Concrete (Vic) Ptd Ltd v Stule* (1996) 20 ACSR 475 at 478 SC (Vic).

[104] Per Thomas J in *Taylor v Carrol* (1991) 6 ACSR 255 at 259 SC (Qld).

nature and amount of the liabilities in question.[105] 'To give recognition of such facts involves nothing more than to take into account the reality of the trading position.'[106]

In *Taylors Industrial Flooring Ltd v M & H Plant Hire (Manchester) Ltd*[107] Scott J said:

> Something more must be proved than simply that the company has not paid a debt; the circumstances surrounding the non-payment must justify the inference that the company is unable to pay its debts as they fall due, eg a series of dishonoured cheques might justify that inference.[108]

Nor can the inference be drawn merely from the fact that the company's financial statements reflect an excess of liabilities over assets. It has been held in *Wiseman v Ace Table Soccer (Pty) Ltd*[109] that, where the company's financial statements reflected an excess of liabilities over assets, the applicant was 'in effect seeking to draw an inference from the financial statements that the respondent is unable to pay its debts', when 'it was only as a result of an exceptional factor of depreciation' permitted by the Receiver of Revenue that the 'net income [had] changed to a net loss'. The court held that, although assets may have been depreciated to a nil value in the books of the company, it did not follow that those assets were valueless. He held that the company was not unable to pay its debts. On the contrary, it was 'alive and well'.

The test is whether the company will be able to pay its debts 'as they become due in the ordinary course of business'. The courts have distinguished between the phrase 'in the ordinary course of business'[110] and the phrase 'in the ordinary course of that business'.[111] The test for determining whether a transaction was 'in the ordinary course of business' is an objective one, namely whether, having regard to the terms of the transaction and the circumstances under which it was entered into, the transaction was one which would normally have been entered into by solvent businessmen.[112] The test for 'in the ordinary course of that business', however, 'introduces the necessity of an enquiry into the kind of business in question, and the usual or ordinary business transactions of a business of that kind'.[113]

In regard to whether the rights of preference shareholders must be taken into account as liabilities in applying the solvency test, s 4(2)*(c)* of the Act provides that:

---

[105] See *Re Kolback Group Ltd* (1991) 4 ACSR 165 at 169 SC (NSW).
[106] *Per* Thomas J in *Taylor v Carrol* (supra); *Pioneer Concrete (Vic) Pty Ltd v Stule* (supra); *Levi v Guerlini* (supra).
[107] *Per* Scott J in *Taylors Industrial Flooring Ltd v M & H Plant Hire (Manchester) Ltd* [1990] BCC 44 at 46–7.
[108] *Taylors Industrial Flooring Ltd v M & H Plant Hire (Manchester) Ltd* (supra) at 46–7.
[109] 1991 (4) SA 171 (W) 180–1 *per* Claasen AJ.
[110] In s 29(1) of the Insolvency Act 24 of 1936.
[111] In s 34(1) of the Insolvency Act.
[112] See *Joosab v Ensor NO* 1966 (1) SA 319 (A) 326–7; *Hendriks, NO v Swanepoel* 1962 (4) SA 338 (A) 345.
[113] *Per* Botha J in *Joosab v Ensor NO* (supra) at 326–7.

... unless the Memorandum of Incorporation of the company provides otherwise, a *person* applying the insolvency test in respect of a distribution contemplated in paragraph *(a)* of the definition of 'distribution' in section 1 is *not to be regarded* as a liability any amount that would be required, if the company were to be liquidated at the time of the distribution, to satisfy the preferential rights upon liquidation of shareholders whose preferential rights upon liquidation are superior to the preferential rights upon liquidation of those receiving the distribution[114] (emphasis added).

Preference shareholders are accordingly left out in the cold. Their preferential rights will be meaningless, because all the company's net assets may be returned to its ordinary shareholders (provided the Act's requirements are met).

This exclusion relating to preferential rights only applies to transfers referred to in paragraph *(a)* of the definition of 'distribution' and not to an incurrence of a debt referred to in paragraph *(b)* or the forgiveness or waiver of a debt referred to in paragraph *(c)*.[115] The rationale for this is not clear.

If a distribution is by way of a transfer in terms of paragraph *(a)* of the definition, the preferential rights of preference shareholders must be taken into account if the Memorandum of Incorporation so requires. The inference to be drawn from s 4(2)*(c)* is that, in the case of a distribution by way of the incurrence of a debt (paragraph *(b)* of the definition) or the forgiveness or waiver of a debt (paragraph *(c)* of the definition), the preferential rights will have to be taken into account even if the Memorandum of Incorporation does not require such rights to be taken into account.[116]

Section 4(2)*(c)* does not make reference to fixed preferential returns on shares ranking ahead of those in respect of which a distribution is made. It only deals with the preferential rights on liquidation. Accordingly, there is some uncertainty as to whether such returns should be taken into account. It is to be noted that the preferential rights of preference shareholders are taken into account in the New Zealand Companies Act 105 of 1993, which provides in s 52(4):

(a) Debts include fixed preferential returns on shares ranking ahead of those in respect of which:
a distribution is made (except where that fixed preferential return is expressed in the constitution as being subject to the power of the directors to make distributions), but does not include debts arising by reason of the authorisation; . . .

The time when the solvency and liquidity test must be satisfied is generally 'immediately after completing the proposed distribution'.[117] However, there is an exception in regard to the incurrence of a debt, in which case satisfaction of the

---

[114] Although this provision applies to both the solvency and the liquidity aspects of the test, it is clear that it can only apply to the solvency aspect. This is so because liquidation rights are not debts due in the ordinary course of business. It will be noted that the wording in s 4(2)*(c)* is inept. As can be seen from the italicised words, the provision refers to a 'person' as a 'liability'. This is rectified in the draft Companies Amendment Bill, 2010.
[115] See s 4(2)*(c)*. See also s 1 under 'distribution' paras *(a)*, *(b)* and *(c)*.
[116] Protection for preference shareholders is provided in these circumstances in New Zealand (s 52(4)*(b)* of the New Zealand Companies Act 105 of 1993), California (s 502 of the California Corporations Code) and the American Model Business Corporation Act (s 6.40*(c)*(2) of the revised American Model Business Corporation Act 1984. See also s 170*(a)* of the Delaware General Corporation Law, Title 8).
[117] See s 46(1)*(b)*.

test is required 'at the time that the board resolves that the company may incur that debt'.[118] The test does not have to be met when the company satisfies the debt unless the board resolution provides otherwise.[119] The prudence of this exception is questionable considering that the solvency and liquidity of the company could, to the detriment of creditors, deteriorate between the date of authorisation of the incurrence of the debt and the date of satisfaction of the debt.

Where a company making a distribution is part of a group of companies,[120] the solvency test involves looking not only at the company's assets and liabilities, but at the assets and liabilities of all the companies in the group.[121]

The justification for this requirement 'is questionable'.[122] It would mean that the group assets:

> ... have to be taken into account whenever a group company makes a distribution and not only when it makes a distribution to the shareholders of another company in the group. This seems to be an unnecessary complication that will make unjustified inroads into the separate legal personality of a subsidiary making a simple distribution to its own shareholders who, it must be remembered, might not even include the holding company.[123] The financial position of a group of companies hardly seems relevant where a subsidiary is making a distribution to its shareholders other than the holding company or if the holding company does not hold any shares in the subsidiary. Similarly, the financial position of a subsidiary in which the holding company holds no shares or only a relatively low percentage of shares should not be relevant when the holding company makes a distribution.[124]

The group concept, whatever its role may be, clearly only has relevance in s 4 with regard to the solvency aspect of the test. It is not relevant to the liquidity aspect. It is not clear why this should be so.[125]

One should not lose sight of the fact that schemes aimed at circumventing the solvency test could be set aside by the court on application by the Companies and Intellectual Property Commission ('the Companies Commission') or the Takeover Regulation Panel ('the Panel') (s 6(1) of the Act). It is hoped, however, that suitable amendments to s 4(1)(a) will be made so as to avoid having to resort to such a time-wasting and resource-consuming procedure, the outcome of which is

---

[118] See s 46(4)(a).

[119] See s 46(4)(b).

[120] See s 1 of the Act for the definition of 'group of companies' which is 'two or more companies that share a holding company or subsidiary relationship'.

[121] See s 4(1)(a). It is to be noted that the draft Companies Amendment Bill, 2010 proposes the substitution for s 4(1)(a) of the following:

'(a) the assets of the company or, in the case of a holding company, the consolidated assets of the company, as fairly valued, equal or exceed the liabilities of the company or, in the case of a holding company, the consolidated liabilities of the company, as fairly valued; and'

This will eliminate the difficulty posed below, although the term 'consolidated' should be defined.

[122] See Van der Linde op cit n 46 at 227.

[123] In terms of the definition of 'subsidiary' in s 1 and the deeming provision in s 3 it is not required that the holding company or its other subsidiaries hold any shares in the subsidiary. The holding company could, for example, enjoy this status by virtue of its ability to control the majority of the board; see s 3.

[124] Van der Linde op cit n 46 at 227.

[125] See Van der Linde op cit n 46 at 228.

uncertain. It is also to be noted that the application to court cannot be made directly by a creditor but must go through the Companies Commission or the Panel.

8.1.5 Enforcement of distribution

When the board of a company has acknowledged by resolution its successful application of the solvency and liquidity test, the company is required to proceed with the distribution, subject only to the requirement of a reconsideration of the test if the distribution has not been completed within 120 business days.[126]

The inference here is that, once the required acknowledgement is made by the board, the distribution becomes enforceable by those to whom the proposed distribution is to be made. If this construction is correct, however, it appears to conflict with s 46(1)*(b)*, which provides that a distribution must not be made unless the solvency and liquidity test is satisfied immediately after completing the proposed distribution.[127] Such construction makes s 46(1)*(b)* of no effect and s 46(1)*(c)* could have stood by itself.[128]

This clearly makes no sense and a clarifying amendment is necessary. These issues have not been addressed in the Companies Amendment Bill, 2010.

8.1.6 Directors' liability for unlawful distributions

The effect of s 46(6) read with s 77(3)*(e)*(vi) of the Act is to make directors liable[129] to a certain extent in respect of unlawful distributions.

Section 46(6) provides as follows:

> (6) A director of a company is liable to the extent set out in section 77(3)*(e)*(vi) if the director —
> *(a)* was present at the meeting when the board approved a distribution as contemplated in this section, or participated in the making of such a decision in terms of section 74; and
> *(b)* failed to vote against the distribution, despite knowing that the distribution was contrary to this section.

Section 77(3)*(e)*(vi) provides as follows:

> '(3) A director of a company is liable for any loss, damages or costs sustained by the company as a direct or indirect consequence of the director having —
> . . .
> *(e)* been present at a meeting, or participated in the making of a decision in terms of section 74, and failed to vote against —
> . . .
> (vi) a resolution approving a distribution, despite knowing that the distribution was contrary to section 46, subject to subsection (4).

The meaning of 'director' for the purposes of the liability provision (s 77) is enlarged to include an alternate director, a prescribed officer, and a person who is a member of a committee of a board of the company, or of the audit committee of the company,

---

[126] Section 46(2), read with s 46(3).
[127] See Van der Linde op cit n 1 at 494.
[128] Ibid.
[129] The liability is joint and several liability (s 77(6)).

irrespective of whether or not the person is also a member of the company's board.[130] However, as liability can only arise if the person in question participated in a board resolution, only a director in the usual sense of the word can be liable.[131]

A director is also liable in terms of s 77(3)(e)(vii) if he or she had:

(e) been present at a meeting, or participated in the making of a decision in terms of section 74, and failed to vote against —

. . .

(vii) the acquisition by the company of any of its shares, or the shares of its holding company, despite knowing that the acquisition was contrary to section 46 or 48.

It follows that, where a company acquires its own shares unlawfully and makes a distribution pursuant thereto, unlawfully, a director who participated in the acquisition and distribution will be liable under two subsections of s 77(3)(e).[132] In this regard it appears that the reference in s 77(3)(e)(vii) to an 'acquisition' that 'was contrary to section 46 or section 48' is inappropriate, because s 46 only deals with 'distributions'. The passing of the consideration pursuant to an acquisition is a 'distribution'[133] but the acquisition itself is not.

Liability of a director only arises if the director participates in the relevant resolution 'knowing' that the distribution was unlawful.[134] In this regard s 1 of the Act provides for an extended meaning of 'knowing'. It provides:

' "knowing", "knowingly" or "knows", when used with respect to a person, and in relation to a particular matter, means that the person either —
(a) had actual knowledge of that[135] matter;
(b) was in a position in which the person reasonably ought to have —
　(i) had actual knowledge;
　(ii) investigated the matter to an extent that would have provided the person with actual knowledge; or
　(iii) taken other measures which, if taken, would reasonably be expected to have provided the person with actual knowledge of the matter.

It appears that, if a director does not 'participate' in the resolution approving of a distribution but does 'participate' in the resolution acknowledging that the solvency and liquidity test has been successfully applied, the director incurs no liability. It is only participation in the resolution approving of the distribution that gives rise to liability.[136] Also, no liability can arise in terms of s 46 out of a distribution pursuant to an existing legal obligation or court order,[137] because liability is premised on there having been a board resolution approving the distribution. This is so despite the fact that the solvency and liquidity test needs to be applied in such a case.[138]

---

[130] See s 77(1).
[131] See Van der Linde op cit n 1 at 495.
[132] Although clearly the same loss can only be recovered once.
[133] See the definition of 'distribution' in s 1 of the Act.
[134] See ss 46(6)(b) and 77(3)(e)(vii).
[135] The draft Companies Amendment Bill, 2010 changes 'that' to 'the'.
[136] See ss 46(6) and 77(3)(e). See also Van der Linde op cit n 1 at 496.
[137] See s 46(1)(a)(i).
[138] See Van der Linde op cit n 1 at 496.

There are two limitations placed on a director's liability.[139] The liability of a director arises only if:
- immediately after making *all* of the distribution, the company does not satisfy the solvency and liquidity test, and
- it was unreasonable at the time of the resolution to come to the conclusion that the company would satisfy the solvency and liquidity test after making the distribution.[140]

Strangely, it appears that no liability can arise out of a partial implementation of a distribution. This is apparent from the word 'all' in s 77(4)(*a*)(i).

If the board of a company has made a decision contrary to s 46, the company, or any director who has been or may be held liable, may apply to a court for an order setting aside the decision.[141] The court may make an order setting aside the decision in whole or in part, absolutely or conditionally and any further order that is just and equitable in the circumstances, including an order:
- to rectify the decision, reverse any transaction, or restore any consideration paid or benefit received by any person in terms of the decision of the board,[142] and
- requiring the company to indemnify any director who has been or may be held liable, including indemnification for the costs of the proceedings.[143]

Where there is actual knowledge on the part of the director that a distribution is unlawful, it is unlikely that a court would order the indemnification referred to in the second bullet above.

Relief from liability

Section 77(9) may provide a director with relief. It provides:

> (9) In any proceedings against a director, other than for wilful misconduct or wilful breach of trust, the court may relieve the director, either wholly or partly, from any liability set out in this section, on any terms the court considers just if it appears to the court that —
> (a) the director is or may be liable, but has acted honestly and reasonably; or
> (b) having regard to all the circumstances of the case, including those connected with the appointment of the director, it would be fair to excuse the director.

A director who has reason to apprehend that a claim may be made alleging that the director is liable, other than for wilful misconduct or wilful breach of trust, may apply to a court for relief. The court may grant relief to the director if the director has acted honestly and reasonably or, having regard to the circumstances, it would be fair to excuse the director.

Prescription

The proceedings to recover any loss, damages or costs 'may not be commenced more than three years after the act or omission that gave rise to the liability'.[144]

---

[139] See s 77(4)(*a*).
[140] Ibid.
[141] Section 77(5)(*a*).
[142] Section 77(5)(*b*)(ii)(*bb*).
[143] Section 77(5)(*b*)(ii)(*bb*).
[144] Section 77(7).

The wording in s 77(7) is different from the wording in s 12 of the Prescription Act 68 of 1969, which states that the three-year prescription period for extinction of a debt shall begin to run as soon as the debt is due and that a debt shall not be deemed to be due until the creditor has knowledge of the identity of the debtor and of the facts from which the debt arises. The commencement dates of the three-year period in these two pieces of legislation may be different and it is not clear which would prevail in the event of such a conflict.

A further problem arises in connection with the commencement date of the prescription period in s 77(7). The problem arises because of the provisions of s 218(1) of the new Act. Section 218(1) provides:

> Nothing in this Act renders void an agreement, resolution or provision of an agreement, resolution, Memorandum of Incorporation or rules of a company that is prohibited, void, voidable or may be declared unlawful in terms of this Act, unless a court declares that agreement, resolution or provision to be void.

It appears from s 218(1) that the directors' liability only arises once the relevant resolution has been declared void, yet the three-year prescription period runs from the date of the act or omission that gave rise to the liability. Is one to understand from this that the taking of a prohibited resolution marks the beginning of the three-year period, but that the liability attached to that transgression only arises once the court has declared the resolution void, ie possibly three years or more (depending on the length of the case) after the act has occurred? How does this interact with the potential common-law liability based on the directors' duties of care and skill in a prohibited act of this nature — does liability arise at the time of the act (as one would expect and as seems to be the case in terms of s 77(2)(*a*)) which would mean that this occurs at a different point in time than the statutory liability?[145]

Limit on amount of damages, loss and costs
Section 77(4)(*b*) provides for a limit on the amount for which a director can be liable. It provides:

> (4) The liability of a director in terms of subsection (3)(*e*)(vi) as a consequence of the director having failed to vote against a distribution in contravention of section 46 —
> *(a)* arises only if —
>   (i) immediately after making all of the distribution contemplated in a resolution in terms of section 46, the company does not satisfy the solvency and liquidity test; and
>   (ii) it was unreasonable at the time of the decision to conclude that the company would satisfy the solvency and liquidity test after making the relevant distribution; and
> *(b)* does not exceed, in aggregate, the difference between —
>   (i) the amount by which the value of the distribution exceeded the amount that could

---

[145] The proposed amendment to s 218 by the Companies Amendment Bill, 2010 does not clarify this issue. The amended s 218(1) provides as follows:

'(1) Nothing in this Act renders void an agreement, resolution or provision of an agreement, resolution, Memorandum of Incorporation or rules of a company that is prohibited, **[void,]** voidable or that may be declared unlawful in terms of this Act, unless a court [declares] has made a declaration to that effect regarding that agreement, resolution or provision **[to be void]**.'

have been distributed without causing the company to fail to satisfy the solvency and liquidity test; and
(ii) the amount, if any, recovered by the company from persons to whom the distribution was made.

It appears that this means that, if the distribution is R100, the lawful amount is R80 and the amount recovered by the company is R7, then the amount a director can be liable for is R13.

The liability of a director extends to liability for:

- costs of all parties in the proceedings unless the proceedings are abandoned, or exculpate the director,[146] and
- any amount distributed that is not otherwise recoverable.[147]

It appears that the director is liable for these amounts independently of the limit set out above.[148]

8.1.7 Recovery of unlawful distributions from shareholders

The Act does not expressly provide that a shareholder to whom an unlawful distribution has been made is liable to return such distribution.

However, being unlawful, the distribution would be invalid and recovery would be possible in terms of the common law irrespective of the *bona fides* of the shareholder.[149]

8.1.8 Dividends out of profits

The Act draws no distinction between the distribution of profits and any other distributions. However, the Memorandum of Incorporation may require dividends to be paid only out of profits. In such a case, unless the Memorandum of Incorporation defines the term 'profits', it appears that the case law remains relevant.

In this regard the following 'rules' have been devised by the courts:[150]

- Profits earned before a company is incorporated (pre-incorporation profits) constitute capital.[151]
- Dividends received by a holding company from a subsidiary which have been paid out of profits earned by the subsidiary prior to the holding company acquiring the subsidiary (pre-acquisition profits) are not income earned but have been paid as part of the purchase price.[152]
- The profits of a subsidiary are not profits which the subsidiary's holding

---

[146] See s 77(8)(*a*).
[147] See s 77(8)(*b*).
[148] That is, the limit imposed by s 77(4)(*b*)(i).
[149] See Van der Linde op cit n 1 at 499, 500.
[150] See Blackman et al op cit n 38 at 5–140–5–147.
[151] See Blackman et al op cit n 38 at 5–147.
[152] See *Marra Developments Ltd v BW Rofe Pty Ltd* (1977) 3 ACLR 185 at 204 CA (NSW); *Shearer (Inspector of Taxes) v Bercain Ltd* [1980] 3 All ER 295 at 312.

company can treat as its own profits.[153] This flows from the basic principle that a company is a separate legal entity.[154]
- The position with regard to 'retained profits' prior to the Act (and presumably still the position) was as follows:[155]

> [a] company may retain revenue profits from past periods in such a form as will, subject to such increment or diminution as trading in the next or later periods may bring, leave them immediately available to base a dividend, eg where they are retained as undistributed profits.[156] If the company retains profits as a reserve for a particular purpose, the general rule is that such earmarked reserves remain undivided profits applicable for the same purposes as profits earned during the current financial period.[157] Therefore, even where in the company's accounts profits have been transferred to reserves for specific purposes, such as the replacement of fixed assets or future tax payments or the depreciation of goodwill, if the purposes for which those reserves fail, or the profits are not required for those purposes, they may be re-transferred in order to pay dividends.[158] If, however, the articles require a reserve fund of a certain amount to be set aside for a particular purpose before any dividend is declared, no part of the fund can be distributed as dividend unless the articles are altered.[159] Furthermore, profits carried to reserve will not be available for dividend where the company has, in effect, capitalised them[160] by applying them so as to replace capital previously lost[161] or to replace the loss in value of a capital asset arising from depreciation.[162] But where a company has merely applied a reserve to write out of its books an asset previously appearing in its accounts, eg goodwill,[163] and that asset in fact retained a value (ie capital has not in fact been lost), the company may, on electing to write the asset back into its accounts, restore the profits to the reserve fund and use them to pay dividends, provided that the company has not finally and irrevocably capitalised the profits.[164] If a company elects to apply profits in paying up unissued shares as capitalisation shares, those profits will, of course, be capitalised and so cease to be available for dividend.

---

[153] *Industrial Equity Ltd v Blackburn* (1977) 137 CLR 567 at 575–8; (1977) 3 ACLR 89 at 96–98 (HC of A); *Marra Developments Ltd v BW Rofe Pty Ltd* (supra).
[154] Ibid.
[155] See Blackman et al op cit n 38 at 5–146–5–147.
[156] *Federal Commissioner of Taxation v Miller Anderson Ltd* (1946) 73 CLR 341 at 373–374 (HC of A); *Marra Developments Ltd v BW Rofe Pty Ltd* (supra) at 198.
[157] In *Federal Commissioner of Taxation v Miller Anderson Ltd* (supra) at 373 Dixon J said the directors 'may in some way earmark the profit or part of it as a reserve or provision for a special purpose and thus distinguish it by placing it in an accounting category so that to withdraw it and make it available for distribution would require a new and affirmative decision'.
[158] *Re Bridgewater Navigation Co* [1891] 2 Ch 317 at 327; [1891–94] All ER Rep 174–7; *Stapley v Read Bros Ltd* [1924] 2 Ch 1; [1924] All ER Rep 421.
[159] *Re Eastern and Australian SS Co* [1893] WN 31.
[160] *Re Hoare & Co Ltd* [1904] 2 Ch 208; [1904–7] All ER Rep 635 (CA); *Federal Commissioner of Taxation v Miller Anderson Ltd* (supra) at 373; and see *Genville Pastoral Co Pty Ltd v Commissioner of Taxation of Commonwealth of Australia* (1963) 109 CLR 199 at 207 (HC of A); *Marra Developments Ltd v BW Rofe Pty Ltd* (supra) at 198.
[161] *Re Hoare & Co Ltd* (supra) at 653; *Genville Pastoral Co Pty Ltd v Commissioner of Taxation of Commonwealth of Australia* (supra) at 207–8; *Marra Developments Ltd v BW Rofe Pty Ltd* (supra).
[162] *Re Bridgewater Navigation Co* [1891] 2 Ch 317; [1891–94] All ER Rep 174; *Marra Developments Ltd v BW Rofe Pty Ltd* (supra) at 198.
[163] *Stapley v Read Bros Ltd* [1924] 2 Ch 1; [1924] All ER Rep 421; *Marra Developments Ltd v BW Rofe Pty Ltd* (supra) at 198–9.
[164] *Stapley v Read Bros Ltd* (supra) at 421; *Federal Commissioner of Taxation v Miller Anderson Ltd* (supra) at 373; *Marra Developments Ltd v BW Rofe Pty Ltd* (supra) at 198–9. Unless and until the

- Capital profits, realised or unrealised, are not distributable without reference to the result of 'the whole accounts fairly taken for the year, capital, as well as profit and loss'.[165] Consideration must therefore be given to the financial position of the company as a whole.[166] Accordingly, while dividends may in proper cases be paid out of revenue profits despite there having been a depreciation of capital, any loss that may possibly have been incurred on other fixed assets, as well as any net loss on the company's trading activities during the financial year in question, must be brought into account against the realised capital profit in question.[167] It has been held that the only losses that need to be set off are those suffered during the trading period when the profit is made,[168] but there is also authority suggesting that all past losses must be set off.[169]
- It has been held that it is permissible to take into account an unrealised increase in the value of the company's fixed assets.[170] It would appear, however, that the Memorandum of Incorporation would have to authorise such distribution; appreciation must be of a permanent nature in the sense that it is

---

fund is in fact capitalised, it retains its characteristic of a distributable profit: *Re Bates* [1928] Ch 682; *RA Hill v Permanent Trustee Co of New South Wales Ltd* [1930] AC 720; [1930] All ER Rep 87 (PC).

[165] Per Byrne J in *Foster v New Trinidad Lake Asphalt Co Ltd* [1901] 1 Ch 208 at 212–13. And see *Wall v London & Provincial Trust Ltd* [1920] 1 Ch 45; [1920] 2 Ch 582 (CA).

[166] *Foster v New Trinidad Lake Asphalt Co Ltd* (supra); *Lubbock v British Bank of South America* [1892] 2 Ch 198; *Cross v Imperial Continental Gas Association* [1923] 2 Ch 553 at 565; [1923] All ER Rep 628 at 633; *Australian Oil and Exploration Ltd v Lachberg* (1958) 101 CLR 119 at 133 (HC of A); *Marra Developments Ltd v BW Rofe Pty Ltd* (supra) at 197, 198, 212; *QBE Insurance Group Ltd v Australian Securities Commission* (1992) 8 ACSR 631 at 648 (Fed C of A).

[167] *Foster v New Trinidad Lake Asphalt Co Ltd* (supra); *Marra Developments Ltd v BW Rofe Pty Ltd* (supra) at 198. Where the amount of depreciation of a capital asset has been written off and treated as a deduction from profits in previous accounts, a subsequent appreciation in the value of the asset may be treated as a profit in the same way as any other appreciation of a capital asset: *Bishop v Smyrna & Cassaba Railway Co (No 2)* [1895] 2 Ch 596. And see *Stapley v Read Bros Ltd* [1924] 2 Ch 1; [1924] All ER Rep 421, where it was held that, failing provisions to the contrary in the articles, a company may write back to profit account so much of the depreciation written off goodwill (which the company had in fact retained) as has proved to have been in excess of the proper requirements.

[168] See *Ammonia Soda Co Ltd v Chamberlain* [1918] 1 Ch 266 at 289; [1916–1917] All ER Rep 708 at 714 (CA).

[169] See *Australian Oil and Exploration Ltd v Lachberg* (1958) (supra); *Marra Developments Ltd v BW Rofe Pty Ltd* (supra) at 197, 198, 212; *QBE Insurance Group Ltd v Australian Securities Commission* (1992) 8 ACSR 631 at 648 (Fed C of A).

[170] *Dimbula Valley (Ceylon) Tea Co Ltd v Laurie* [1961] Ch 353; [1961] 1 All ER 769; *Re New Zealand Flock & Textiles* [1976] 1 NZLR 192; *Blackburn v Industrial Equity Ltd* (1976) 2 ACLR 8; *Industrial Equity Ltd v Blackburn* (1977) 2 ACLR 421 CA (NSW); (1977) 137 CLR 567; (1977) 3 ACLR 89 (HC of A); *Marra Developments Ltd v BW Rofe Pty Ltd* (supra) at 197; *QBE Insurance Group Ltd v Australian Securities Commission* (supra) at 648. In *Westburn Sugar Refineries Ltd v Inland Revenue Commissions* 1960 SLT 297 the Scottish court decided to the contrary.

not liable to short-term fluctuations,[171] and the valuation resulting in the surplus has been made in good faith by competent valuers.[172]
- The profit made on the disposal of fixed assets is distributable subject to the Memorandum of Incorporation.[173]
- Dividends may be, and usually are, based upon the company's revenue or trading profits. The profits are net of revenue expenses[174] and depreciation in the value of circulating assets.[175] Unless the Memorandum of Incorporation provides otherwise, all losses suffered in earlier periods may be disregarded. A dividend may thus be paid out of the company's revenue or trading profits of a period without having to write off past trading losses[176] and a deficiency in the company's capital need not be recouped out of such profits.[177]
- In determining what revenue profits are, a distinction is drawn[178] between 'fixed assets'[179] and 'circulating or current assets'.[180] As has been held:

> '[C]apital' is fixed in the sense of being invested in assets intended to be retained by the company more or less permanently and used for producing income ... [Circulating capital] is a portion of the subscribed capital of the company intended to be used by being temporarily parted with and circulated in business, in the form of money, goods or other assets, and which, or the proceeds of which, are intended to return to the company with an increment, and are intended to be used again, and again and to always return with some accretion.[181]

- Realised and unrealised profits on current assets may be taken into account. Losses in previous periods in respect of fixed or capital assets, and losses to

---

[171] *QBE Insurance Group Ltd v Australian Securities Commission* (supra) at 648.
[172] *Dimbula Valley (Ceylon) Tea Co Ltd v Laurie* [1961] (supra) at 372–3; [1961] 1 All ER 769 at 780–1.
[173] *Lubbock v British Bank of South America* (supra).
[174] *Re County Marine Insurance Co (Rance's Case)* (1870) LR 6 Ch App 104; *Bloxam v Metropolitan Railway Co* (1868) 3 Ch App Cas 337; *Ashton & Co Ltd v Honey* (1907) 23 TLR 253.
[175] *Ammonia Soda Co Ltd v Chamberlain* [1918] 1 Ch 266; [1916–17] All ER Rep 708 (CA).
[176] *Marra Developments Ltd v BW Rofe Pty Ltd* (1977) 3 ACLR 185 198 CA (NSW); *Re National Bank of Wales Ltd* [1899] 2 Ch 629 at 669; [1895–99] All ER Rep 715 721 (CA), affd *sub nom Dovey v Cory* [1901] AC 477; [1895–99] All ER Rep 724 (HL); *Ammonia Soda Ltd v Chamberlain* (supra).
[177] *Ammonia Soda Co Ltd v Chamberlain* (supra) at 292–3, 296–8; [1916–17] All ER Rep 708 at 716, 717–19 (CA); *Lee v Neuchatel Asphalte Co* (1889) 41 ChD 1 at 22–3; [1886–90] All ER Rep 947 953–4 (CA); *Verner v General & Commercial Investment Trust* [1894] 2 Ch 239 at 264–5 (CA); *Re National Bank of Wales Ltd* [1899] 2 Ch 629; [1895–99] All ER Rep 715 (CA), affd *sub nom Dovey v Cory* (supra).
[178] *Ammonia Soda Co v Chamberlain* (supra) at 286–7; See *Lee v Neuchatel Asphalte Co* (supra); *John Smith & Sons v Moore* [1921] 2 AC 13 at 19–20 (HL); *Commissioner for Inland Revenue v George Forest Timber Co Ltd* 1924 AD 516; *Sekretaris van Binnelandse Inkomste v Aveling* 1978 (1) SA 862 (A); *Bourke's Estate v Commissioner for Inland Revenue* 1991 (1) SA 661 (A) 672–3; *Commissioner for Inland Revenue v Pick 'n Pay Employee Share Purchase Trust* 1992 (4) SA 39 (A); *Wilmer v McNamara & Co Ltd* [1895] 2 Ch 245; *Verner v General & Commercial Investment Trust* [1894] 2 Ch 239 (CA); *Re Kingston Cotton Mill Co (No 2)* [1896] 1 Ch 331, [1896] 2 Ch 279 (CA).
[179] Assets retained as such in order to produce income.
[180] Assets that are manufactured or purchased with the object of converting them into cash at a profit.
[181] Swinfen Eady in *Ammonia Soda Co v Chamberlain* (supra) at 713.

such assets during the current period, need not be taken into account.[182] Providing out of profits for the depreciation of fixed assets is not required, eg the company's plant and machinery,[183] or for a drop in value of its property[184] or goodwill[185] or for irrecoverable investments or long-term loans.[186] A wasting fixed asset, such as a licence, does not need to be provided for capital replacement before paying a dividend.[187] In *Bagot Pneumatic Tyre Co v Clipper Pneumatic Tyre Co*[188] Romer LJ held that, before arriving at the amount of profits 'available for dividend' it was only right and honest that provision should have been made for depreciation of wasting assets, such as licences, although the directors probably could not be compelled to do so. Depreciation[189] and losses of circulating current assets must, however, be taken into account.[190] Earnings after commencement of winding-up are capital and not income.[191]

- The following *dicta* from the cases must also be borne in mind when addressing the question of what is revenue profit:
  - 'There is nothing at all in the Act about how dividends are to be paid, nor how profits are to be reckoned; all that is left, and very judiciously and properly left, to the commercial world. It is not a subject for an Act of Parliament to say how accounts are to be kept; what is to be put into a capital account, what into an income account is left to men of business.'[192]
  - 'I do not think it desirable for any tribunal to do that which Parliament has abstained from doing — that is, to formulate precise rules for the guidance or embarrassment of business men *[sic]* in the conduct of business affairs.'[193]

---

[182] *Lee v Neuchatel Asphalte Co* (1889) 41 ChD 1, [1886–90] All ER Rep 947 (CA); *Re Kingston Cotton Mill Co (No 2)* [1896] 1 Ch 331, [1896] 2 Ch 279 (CA); *Verner v General & Commercial Investment Trust* [1894] 2 Ch 239 at 265 (CA); *Bond v Barrow Haematite Steel Co* [1902] 1 Ch 353, [1900–3] All ER Rep 484.
[183] *Bolton v Natal Land and Colonization Co* [1892] 2 Ch 124.
[184] *Bolton v Natal Land and Colonization Co* (supra).
[185] *Wilmer v McNamara & Co Ltd* [1895] 2 Ch 245.
[186] *Bolton v Natal Land and Colonization Co* (supra); *Verner v General & Commercial Investment Trust* [1894] 2 Ch 239 (CA); *Bishop v Smyrna & Cassaba Railway Co (No 2)* [1895] 2 Ch 596.
[187] *Lee v Neuchatel Asphalte Co* (supra).
[188] [1902] 1 Ch 146 159 (CA).
[189] This is because, if the depreciation of circulating assets were not taken into account, the profit reflected as the revenue profit would be fictitious. In depreciating the circulating assets, the company is reflecting trading losses.
[190] *Verner v General & Commercial Investment Trust* (supra) at 266; *Re National Bank of Wales Ltd* [1899] 2 Ch 629; [1895–99] All ER Rep 715 (CA), affd *sub nom Dovey v Cory* [1901] AC 477 at 493–4; [1895–99] All ER Rep 724 at 727 (HL); *Bond v Barrow Haematite Steel Co* at 366; [1900–3] All ER Rep 484–90.
[191] *Bishop v Smyrna & Cassaba Railway Co (No 2)* (supra) at 596.
[192] Lindley LJ in *Lee v Neuchatel Asphalte Co* (1889) 41 ChD 1 at 21; [1886–90] All ER Rep 947 at 952 (CA).
[193] *Dovey v Cory* (supra) *per* Lord MacNaghten.

○ 'The mode and manner in which a business is carried on, and what is usual or the reverse, may have a considerable influence in determining the question what may be treated as profits and what as capital. Even the distinction between fixed and floating capital, which may be appropriate enough in an abstract treatise like Adam Smith's "Wealth of Nations", may with reference to a concrete case, be quite inappropriate.'[194]

It must also be borne in mind that although the memorandum may not define 'profits' it may place restrictions on what constitutes profits 'available for dividend', eg the memorandum may restrict the distribution of certain types of profit.[195]

8.2 REPURCHASES (BUY-BACKS)

8.2.1 General

Before an amendment to the 1973 Act in 1999[196] a company could not acquire its own shares even if permitted to do so by its memorandum of association or articles of association. This was established in *Trevor v Whitworth*[197] and until 1999 was a fundamental part of our law. As stated in *Trevor v Whitworth*,[198] the prohibition had two purposes: *(a)* to protect creditors, and *(b)* to protect the company's shareholders by preventing a company from trafficking in its own shares.[199]

In *Trevor v Whitworth* additional reasons for the prohibition were advanced by individual judges. Lords Herschell[200] and Macnaghten[201] could find no legitimate purposes for which the power could be used. Lord Watson[202] held that a company could not become a member of itself and further held that a company could not legally either resell the shares, as this would be *ultra vires*, or cancel them, as this would be a reduction of capital. Lord Macnaghten[203] also expressed concern with the effect of the practice on control of the company, suggesting that it would be disastrous to allow managing directors to buy out inquisitive or troublesome critics.[204]

To prevent avoidance of this prohibition through a subsidiary of a company purchasing shares in the company, such purchases were also prohibited.[205] The prohibition was, however, rejected in most states in the US and this approach was

---

[194] *Dovey v Cory* (supra) at 486–7 per Lord Halsbury LC.
[195] *Quadrangle Investments (Pty) Ltd v Witind Holdings Ltd* 1975 (1) SA 572 (A); *Dent v London Tramways Co* (1990) 16 ChD 334; *Wall v London & Provincial Trust Ltd* [1920] 1 Ch 45; [1920] 2 Ch 582 (CA); *Marra Developments Ltd v BW Rofe Pty Ltd* (1977) 3 ACLR 185 at 197 CA (NSW).
[196] See ss 9–12 of Act 37 of 1999.
[197] (1887) 12 App Cas 409 (HL).
[198] Supra at 416.
[199] See also *Sage Holdings Ltd v The Unisec Group Ltd* 1982 (1) SA 337 (W) 348–9; *Unisec Group Ltd v Sage Holdings Ltd* 1986 (3) SA 259 (T) 265.
[200] At 417.
[201] At 437–8.
[202] At 428.
[203] At 435.
[204] See Eilis Magner 'The power of a company to purchase its own shares: A comparative approach' (1984) 2 *C&SLJ* 79 at 80.
[205] See s 39 of the 1973 Act.

Corporate Finance 269

later followed in Canada,[206] the UK,[207] Australia,[208] New Zealand[209] and finally South Africa.

In the Memorandum on the Objects of the Companies Amendment Bill, 1999[210] ('Memorandum to the Bill') the following reasons were given for the amendment of the Companies Act to permit a company to acquire its own shares:

> The principles of capital maintenance have undergone significant changes in almost all countries. The modern notion of capital maintenance is that companies may reduce capital, including the acquisition of their own shares, but subject to solvency and liquidity criteria. This has the advantage of affording protection to creditors whilst at the same time giving flexibility to companies to achieve sound commercial objectives. These aspects of flexibility and achievement of sound commercial objects have become extremely important since South Africa's re-entry into the global market.
>
> In this regard it should be pointed out that our financial markets have lately entered into derivative activities on a large scale and the Johannesburg Stock Exchange (JSE) [sic] and SAFEX are rapidly becoming more complex and sophisticated. Markets have weakened considerably and this can be attributed to, inter alia, market manipulations by international banks and other speculators with unlimited financial resources. This factor alone poses a fundamental danger to our economy.
>
> There are inherent dangers in the impact of speculative derivative, futures and currency trading activities which are taking place in virtually all developed investment markets and now also in South Africa. These activities if taking place in an unscrupulous way, can easily suppress the price of shares on the stock market. South Africa has now become a magnet for profitable trading by these speculators. This has resulted in the decline in the value of most leading South African shares. Acquiring control of sound companies through these methods could lead to significant job losses and businesses closing down due to asset stripping and other irregular activities.
>
> One of the accepted defences against this negative action in the international market place [sic] is the ability of strong companies to repurchase and cancel their own issued shares which levels the playing field in relation to those speculators wishing to reduce the value of [a] company's shares by indiscriminate market activities. Legislation in most of the EEC, US and other developed markets permits the repurchase of a company's issued share capital, subject to solvency and liquidity criteria.
>
> Allowing a company to acquire its own shares to support the market of its shares, thus preserving for its shareholders the value of their shares, is but one advantage. There are several other advantages. It is particularly useful in relation to employee share schemes enabling the shares of employees to be repurchased on their ceasing to be employed by the

---

[206] Beginning with the Business Corporations Act 1970 (Ont) s 39. See *Select Committee of the Ontario Legislative Assembly, Interim Report on Company Law* (the Lawrence Committee), Toronto 1967 para 5.2; RW Dickerson, JL Howard and L Getz, *Proposals for a New Business Corporations Law for Canada*, Ministry of Supply and Services, Ottawa (1971) vol 1 (the Dickerson Committee) paras 121–34. And see Canada Business Corporations Act, R.S.C. 1985 ss 33–36.

[207] Companies Act 1981. See *The Purchase by a Company of its Own Shares, A Consultative Document* (1980) Cmnd 7944 (report by Prof LCB Gower, Research Advisor on Company Law to the Department of Trade). See Companies Act 1985 ss 162–181. See also *Report of Committee to Review the Functioning of Financial Institutions* (1980) Cmnd 7937 (the Wilson Committee), where it was suggested that repurchase be permitted as a device to promote business development.

[208] See *Companies and Securities Law Review Committee: Report to Ministerial Council, A Company's Purchase of its Own Shares*, Sept 1987. And see Corporations Law 1989 ss 257A–257J.

[209] See Company Law Reform and Restatement Report No 9, Wellington, 1989. See New Zealand Companies Act 1993 ss 58–67C.

[210] B17D–99.

company; it provides a means to avert a hostile take-over; it provides a means whereby a shareholder, or the estate of a deceased shareholder, in a company whose shares are not listed, can find a buyer.

With regard to this explanation the following comment is pertinent:

> Two of the reasons for repurchases mentioned here are relatively non-contentious: where the company's shares are not listed, it provides a means whereby a shareholder, or the estate of a deceased shareholder, can find a buyer; and it enables the company itself to purchase the shares of its employees. However, the main thrust of this explanation would appear to be the need to provide an effective means for market manipulation and for the frustration of takeovers, justified by distrust of market forces, suspicion of international 'brands' and foreign investors, and a theory that repurchases — a form of partial liquidation — will prevent job losses.[211]

As the same commentators say,[212] because a repurchase is a distribution of the company's assets, a reorganisation of issued share capital (and accordingly a change in ownership) and a transfer of shares, 'it invites all the abuses associated with each of these three functions'. In fact, it may involve abuses of all three of these functions[213] and may impact on corporate governance, takeover regulation, creditor protection, discrimination between shareholders, oppression of minorities and the proper functioning of the securities market.[214]

Robert Dugan accordingly sums up by saying that:

> [t]his use of company assets subverts the statutory scheme of corporate governance, contravenes the expectations of most investors, places management in a severe conflict of interest and, according to most studies, does not enhance the market value of the firm.[215]

Some of the justifications for a share repurchase that have been suggested[216] are:

- share repurchases are useful where a company has an employee share incentive scheme because they enable the company to purchase employees' shares when they leave their employment;
- share repurchases can be usefully utilised to buy out dissident shareholders;
- share repurchases enable a company to return surplus funds to shareholders who can then make other more profitable investments;
- share repurchases can be used to maintain or achieve what is perceived to be a desirable debt-equity ratio;
- where a company has a number of shareholders with small shareholdings, the

---

[211] Blackman et al op cit n 38 at 5–49.
[212] See Blackman et al op cit n 38 at 5–45.
[213] Robert Dugan 'Repurchase of Own Shares for New Zealand' (1987) 17 *Victoria Univ of Wellington LR* 179 at 180, who gives the example of management buy-outs involving repurchases, where the massive distributions involved threaten the company's financial stability, the purpose is to enable existing management to acquire control for themselves, the terms are dictated on the basis of inside information, and their execution effectively freezes out minority shareholders. See Blackman et al op cit n 38 at 5–45.
[214] See Blackman et al op cit n 38 at 5–45.
[215] Robert Dugan op cit n 213 at 198.
[216] See Blackman et al op cit n 38 at 5–49–5–61 for a comprehensive analysis and criticism of the reasons used to justify the purposes of repurchases. See also the Memorandum to the Bill quoted in 8.2.1 above.

administrative overheads that this causes can be reduced by the company buying out these 'odd-lots' without incurring any material cost;
- share repurchases, it is sometimes suggested, are a 'good investment' for a company whose shares are considered to be undervalued. As Clarke puts it, this is really 'a form of double talk'[217] because:

  > [a]fter the repurchase, the funds used for it will no longer be in the company or, in any sense, invested in its business operations. If the directors are right about the market's undervaluation, the repurchase serves only to transfer wealth from the shareholders who sell to those who do not.[218]

- a share repurchase:

  > assists companies engaging in takeovers and mergers by enabling them to take shares off the market to be reissued as consideration in takeovers and mergers without dramatically increasing the company's issued shares. The purpose of this exercise is to prevent dilution of the equity of the non-selling shareholders, usually a matter of concern only for the controlling shareholders.[219]

- as seen in the Memorandum to the Bill quoted above, a purpose of a repurchase in a takeover situation is that 'it provides a means to avert a hostile takeover'. As has been stated, the repurchase may have a number of strategic purposes:

  (1) Repurchases may increase the percentage of the target's shares owned by management or its supporters.
  (2) A repurchase may raise the price of the target's shares above the offer price, forcing the bidder to increase its offer or abandon its bid.
  (3) By means of repurchase, the target company may seek to rid itself of the liquid assets which makes it an attractive target in the first place, or to make itself an unattractive target by increasing its debt-equity ratio.
  (4) Repurchase may also be resorted to where the target dilutes the voting power of a threatening block of shares by issuing new shares to a 'white knight', and grants the white knight an option to require the company to repurchase the shares at an advantageous price, or, by repurchasing shares, increases the voting strength of the shares issued to the white knight.
  (5) The repurchased shares may come from the bidder itself, which may agree, on payment to it of a substantial premium over the market price unavailable to the other shareholders, as a condition of the sale to terminate its effort to control the

---

[217] See RC Clarke *Corporate Law* (1986) 627; Blackman et al op cit n 38 at 5–35; Marvin A Chirelstein 'Optional dividends: Taxing the repurchase of common stock' (1969) 78 *Yale LJ* 739 at 744–5 says: 'The meaning of "investment" in this context is not always clear, but most writers appear to have nothing more in mind than that a distribution of excess working capital is the obvious and appropriate course to follow when attractive internal investment opportunities are lacking. Used this way the term "investment" seems to refer only to the *de facto* adjustment of individual portfolios ... ie the contraction of the company's equity base and to the accompanying increase in earnings per share on the reduced number of shares outstanding. It is difficult to perceive any other meaning ... [C]ash assets are reduced precisely because a profitable opportunity for internal assets acquisition is lacking, and the corporation's equity is diminished correspondingly. Although stock repurchasing increases the earnings per share, there is no real increase in the earnings available for distribution. The contrast with investment in conventional operating assets is evident.'
[218] Blackman et al op cit n 38 at 5–55.
[219] Ibid.

target (usually referred to as a 'greenmail', 'green' as in the dollar bill, 'mail' as in blackmail).[220]

- repurchases assist management in a buy-out of control of their company. Repurchases facilitate:

    ... management buy-outs by reducing (at company expense) the number of shares that have to be acquired to gain control of the company. They will usually also reduce liquidity of the outstanding shares, thus depressing the price of those shares and placing the remaining shareholders under coercion to sell.[221]

8.2.2 Redemptions and repurchases

A distinction is drawn in company legislation and practice between 'redemptions' and 'repurchases'/'buy-backs' of shares. Both involve the return to a company of shares the company has issued to shareholders. In return, the company will pay money or transfer assets to the shareholder(s) concerned. With a redemption, the company acquires shares in accordance with a contract contained either in its Memorandum of Incorporation or in the terms of the issue of the shares. A 'repurchase'/'buy-back', on the other hand, is a transaction entered into between a company and one or more of its shareholders in terms of which it is agreed that the company will acquire their shares. The distinction:

> thus turns on whether the company takes back its shares in accordance with rights attaching to the shares themselves (redemptions), or in accordance with a separate contract entered into between it and the shareholders concerned (repurchases or buy-backs).[222]

8.2.3 Regulation of repurchases by the Act

(a) Section 48

A company acquiring its own shares must comply with s 48 of the Act. Section 48 provides as follows:

48 Company or subsidiary acquiring company's shares

(1) The making of a demand, tendering of shares and payment by a company to a shareholder in terms of a shareholder's appraisal rights set out in section 164 do not constitute an acquisition of its shares by the company within the meaning of this section.

(2)[223] Subject to subsection (3) —

(a) a company may acquire its own shares, if the decision to do so satisfies the requirements of section 46; and

(b) any subsidiary of a company may acquire shares of that company, but —

---

[220] Blackman et al op cit n 38 at 5–59.
[221] Blackman et al op cit n 38 at 5–61.
[222] Blackman et al op cit n 38 at 5–43.
[223] Note that the draft Companies Amendment Bill, 2010 proposes the substitution in subsection (2), for the opening phrase, for paragraph (a), and for the opening phrase of paragraph (b), of the following:

'(2) Subject to subsections (3) and (8), and if the decision to do so satisfied the requirements of section 46 —

(a) the board of a company may determine that the company will acquire a number of its own shares; and

(b) the board of a subsidiary company may determine that it will acquire shares of its holding company, but —'

(i) not more than 10%, in aggregate, of the number of issued shares of any class of shares of a company may be held by, or for the benefit of, all of the subsidiaries of that company, taken together; and

(ii) no voting rights attached to those shares may be exercised while the shares are held by the subsidiary, and it remains a subsidiary of the company whose shares it holds.

(3) Despite any provision of any law, agreement, order or the Memorandum of Incorporation of a company, the company may not acquire its own shares, and a subsidiary of a company may not acquire shares of that company, if, as a result of that acquisition, there would no longer be any shares of the company in issue other than —

(a) shares held by one or more subsidiaries of the company; or

(b) convertible or redeemable shares.

(4) An agreement with a company providing for the acquisition by the company of shares issued by it is enforceable against the company, subject to subsections (2) and (3).

(5) If a company alleges that, as a result of the operation of subsection (2) or (3), it is unable to fulfil its obligations in terms of an agreement contemplated in subsection (4) —

(a) the company must apply to a court for an order in terms of paragraph *(c)*;

(b) the company has the burden of proving that fulfilment of its obligations would put it in breach of subsections (2) or (3); and

(c) if the court is satisfied that the company is prevented from fulfilling its obligations pursuant to the agreement, the court may make an order that —

(i) is just and equitable, having regard to the financial circumstances of the company; and

(ii) ensures that the person to whom the company is required to make a payment in terms of the agreement is paid at the earliest possible date compatible with the company satisfying its other financial obligations as they fall due and payable.

(6) If a company acquires any shares contrary to section 46, or this section, the company may, not more than two years after the acquisition, apply to a court for an order reversing the acquisition, and the court may order —

(a) the person from whom the shares were acquired to return the amount paid by the company; and

(b) the company to issue to that person an equivalent number of shares of the same class as those acquired.

(7) A director of a company is liable to the extent set out in section 77(3)*(e)*(vii) if the director —

(a) was present at the meeting when the board approved an acquisition of shares contemplated in this section, or participated in the making of such a decision in terms of section 74; and

(b) failed to vote against the acquisition of shares, despite knowing that the acquisition was contrary to this section or section 46.

The draft Companies Amendment Bill, 2010 proposes the addition of a s 8, as follows:

(8) A decision by the board of a company contemplated in subsection (2)*(a)* —

(a) must be approved by a special resolution of the shareholders of the company if any shares are to be acquired by the company from a director or prescribed officer of the company, or a person related to a director or prescribed officer of the company; and

(b) is subject to the requirements of sections 114 and 115 if, considered alone, or together with other transactions in an integrated series of transactions, it involves the acquisition by the company of more than 5% of the issued shares of any particular class of the company's shares.

(b) Reference to s 46

Section 48 provides that, if a company is to acquire its own shares, it may only do so 'if the decision to do so satisfies the requirements of section 46'.[224] As has been pointed out[225] the cross-reference to s 46 in s 48 is 'unnecessary and confusing' because s 46 states the requirements for 'distributions' and not for 'decisions'.[226] It is to be noted that the proposed amendment in the draft Companies Amendment Bill, 2010 does not eliminate this confusion. The cross-reference creates the impression that a decision to make a repurchase requires the company to be solvent and liquid at the time of making the decision. This does not make sense, because the decision can do no harm — it is the distribution pursuant to the decision that is potentially harmful and it is immediately after the distribution that the solvency and liquidity test should be satisfied.[227] The reference to s 46 in s 48 should therefore be removed.[228]

(c) 'Acquire'

Section 48 of the Act refers to the 'acquisition' by a company of its own shares. The term 'acquisition' is, however, a misnomer because it indicates that the acquiring company holds the shares. This is not possible, because a company cannot acquire rights against itself.[229] In any event, s 35(5) of the Act makes it clear that the shares acquired by the company no longer, on acquisition, retain the status of issued shares, but have the same status as shares that have been authorised but not issued. It follows that the direct acquisition by a company of 'treasury' shares[230] is not possible, although a limited acquisition thereof is possible through the company's subsidiaries.[231]

It is not clear whether the acquisition by a company of its own shares by gift or inheritance is covered by s 48. Clearly there is no 'distribution', as defined, involved, and on that basis s 46 has no application. However, if such acquisition falls within the purview of the term 'acquire' in s 48(2)(*a*), then s 46 would have to be complied with. Such compliance does not make sense. In fact, s 48 in its entirety seems geared towards an acquisition by a company of its own shares or shares in its group involving a distribution of some consideration, which, of course, is absent in the case of an acquisition through a gift or inheritance. If an acquisition through a gift or inheritance is included for the purposes of s 48(2)(*a*),

---

[224] Section 48(2)(*a*).
[225] See K van der Linde op cit n 1 at 492.
[226] Ibid. The draft Companies Amendment Bill, 2010 proposes that s 48(2)(*a*) reads as follows:
  '(2) Subject to subsections (3) and (8), and if the decision to do so satisfies the requirements of section 46 —
  (*a*) the board of a company may determine that the company will acquire a number of its own shares, and; . . .'
[227] K van der Linde op cit n 1 at 492.
[228] Ibid.
[229] See Blackman et al op cit n 38 at 5–43.
[230] See 8.2.6 on treasury shares.
[231] See further below.

then the shares would have to be 'cancelled' in terms of s 35(5)*(a)*, which refers to an acquisition contemplated in s 48. This makes no sense.[232]

In terms of the new Act, companies can issue redeemable shares of any class (and not only preference shares, as was the case under the 1973 Act). The redemption of these shares is treated as an acquisition by a company of its own shares, which must comply with ss 46 and 48.[233] There is no special provision, as there was in the 1973 Act,[234] governing the redemption of shares.

(d) Conflict with Memorandum of Incorporation

It appears, although this is by no means clear, that an acquisition which complies with the relevant requirements of ss 46 and 48, as the case may be, is valid even if it conflicts with the Memorandum of Incorporation.[235] Thus provisions in the Memorandum of Incorporation that prohibit acquisitions partially or altogether or permit them only if certain conditions are met, are ineffective. This is borne out by a reading of s 15(2)*(a)*(ii) of the Act and the definition of 'alterable provision' in s 1. Section 15(2)*(a)*(ii) provides:

> (2) The Memorandum of Incorporation of any company may —
> *(a)* include any provision —
> . . .
> (ii) altering the effect of any alterable provision of this Act;

An 'alterable provision' means (s 1 of the Act):

> a provision of this Act in which it is expressly contemplated that its effect on a particular company may be negated, restricted, limited, qualified, extended, or otherwise altered in substance or effect by that company's Memorandum of Incorporation.

An examination of s 48 shows that it is not an alterable provision. There is nothing in s 48 that 'expressly contemplate[s]' that the effect of s 48 may be 'negated, restricted, limited, qualified, extended, or otherwise altered in substance or effect by' a company's Memorandum of Incorporation.[236]

It is doubtful whether the legislature intended the Memorandum of Incorporation to be nullified in this way. Why should a company not, for example, in its

---

[232] It is of note that s 37 of the Canada Business Corporations Act, R.S.C. 1985 expressly permits the acquisition of its shares by a company by gift and no provision is made for the cancellation of the shares.
[233] Section 37(5)*(b)*.
[234] Section 98.
[235] For a contrary view see Van der Linde op cit n 1 at 492.
[236] Thus s 48 is unlike, for example, ss 44 and 45 of the Act, which are 'alterable provisions'. Section 44 'expressly contemplates' that a company's Memorandum of Incorporation may override the company's ability to assist in a subscription for its shares, which is permitted by s 44 subject to the requirements of the section. This is clear from the words 'Except to the extent that the Memorandum of Incorporation of a company provides otherwise . . .' in s 44(2) (see also s 44(4)). Section 45, which deals with, inter alia, the giving of financial assistance by a company to its directors, is similarly an alterable provision with the same wording as s 44.

Memorandum, prohibit repurchases or add to the requirements of s 48 in some way? A clarifying amendment is called for.[237]

(e) Requirements for a repurchase

Repurchases necessitate compliance with the following requirements:

- Compliance with the requirements for 'distributions'. The requirements include compliance with the solvency and liquidity test. These requirements, which are set out in s 46, are dealt with in detail earlier in this chapter.
- The board of directors of a company needs no authorisation from the shareholders of the company to make a distribution pursuant to a repurchase. A board resolution suffices, unless the acquisition is pursuant to an existing legal obligation of the company, or a court order, in which case no board resolution is required.[238]

It is highly questionable whether the shareholders should be excluded from the making of such a significant decision. Their interests, and not only those of the creditors, are also at stake.[239] As Cassim says[240] with regard to buy-backs:

> A share repurchase entails a change in the ownership of the company's shares, and . . . may thus be used to change control of a company or, for that matter, to prevent a change of control; or it may be used to manipulate the market price of the company's shares. Share repurchases clearly have a . . . potential for unequal treatment of shareholders. In short, the share repurchase power may be abused and it may, unless safeguards are provided, enable one group of shareholders to obtain an unfair advantage over other shareholders . . . It is not enough to protect creditors — shareholders and the investing public must also be protected. This is clearly acknowledged and recognised in the JSE Securities Exchange Listings Requirements on share repurchase.

Not only does the new Act exclude shareholders from deciding on a buy-back, it also contains no provisions aimed at informing shareholders as to the merits or demerits of an offer to acquire their shares. No circulars in a prescribed form, like those required by the 1973 Act,[241] have to be sent to all shareholders when an offer for their shares is made.[242] No distinction is drawn in the Act between general and selective offers[243] and so no special safeguards have been enacted, aimed at the potential mischief inherent in selective offers. As Cassim says in relation to the provisions of the previous Act (which were far more protective of shareholders than the new provisions):

> The safeguards provided by our Companies Act are not only inadequate; they are clearly rudimentary, and require further thought and analysis. The provisions of the Act relating to selective share repurchases leave too much scope for mischief. Specific statutory

---

[237] The position in the current Act may be contrasted with, for example, s 59(1) of the New Zealand Companies Act 105 of 1993, which requires a buy-back to be expressly permitted by the company's constitution.
[238] See s 46(1)(*a*) of the Act and the cross-reference to s 46 in s 48.
[239] In the 1973 Act a special resolution was required (see s 85(1) of the 1973 Act).
[240] See FHI Cassim 'The reform of company law and the capital maintenance concept' (2005) 122 *SALJ* 283 at 287–8.
[241] See s 87 of the 1973 Act.
[242] In the case of listed shares the JSE Listings Requirements would of course be applicable.
[243] Unlike s 87 of the previous Act.

safeguards must be provided to guard against the very real danger of abuse here. It is not a sufficient safeguard that at common law the directors have a fiduciary duty to act *bona fide* in the best interests of the company, or that it may not be a proper exercise of their powers for directors to repurchase shares of the company with the primary motive of perpetuating themselves in office.

It is to be noted that the draft Companies Amendment Bill, 2010 proposes the insertion of a further subsection (s 48(8), see 8.2.3(*a*) above), which provides that, if a company is to repurchase shares from a director or prescribed officer of the company, or a person related to a director or prescribed officer of the company, a board resolution does not suffice. The decision by the board must be approved by special resolution.

This requirement, which is aimed at preventing directors from abusing their positions to benefit themselves, goes some way towards limiting the dangers referred to above.

The proposed new s 48(8) also provides that if a repurchase, considered alone or together with other transactions in an integrated series of transactions, involves the acquisition by the company of more than 5% of the issued shares of any particular class of the company's shares, then ss 114 and 115 must be complied with.[244]

These proposals are made, it appears, because there is a conflict between s 48 and s 114.

Section 48 allows the company to acquire its own shares, provided that it satisfies the solvency and liquidity test. It is silent on who within the company may make that decision, although the necessary implication of s 48(7) — which imposes liability on directors — is that the board of directors has authority to cause the company to exercise its power under s 48.

Section 114 allows the board to propose and — if approved — implement a scheme of arrangement which, among other things, might involve a share buy-back. This proposal requires a special resolution, is subject to court review if more than 15% vote against it, and gives rise to appraisal rights.

The thinking behind the new s 48(8) appears to be to reconcile the requirements of s 48 and s 114, because why can the board alone make a share buy-back decision in terms of s 48, but a special resolution is required to approve a share buy-back in terms of s 114?

It seems that the distinction is that s 48 is designed to deal with casual, or one-off, decisions to reacquire shares on a scale that does not amount to a restructuring of the company's capital structure, while s 114 is designed to address wholesale fundamental changes to the company's capital structure.

But the proposed new section appears to indicate that that distinction is not clearly expressed, creating a potential for arbitrage. A company could misuse s 48 to avoid the onerous standards of s 114 (and all those in Chapter 5 of the Act). Furthermore, since the board would determine the price at which the company would reacquire the shares, there is potential for abuse if the shares are acquired from a director or a prescribed officer.

---

[244] Section 48(8)(*b*).

At the same time, the reasoning appears to be that it is desirable to retain distinct schemes for the different purposes, and to allow the board to act without a special resolution, in respect of the matters for which s 48 was intended, unless a director or officer may benefit from the decision.

Regarding the provision in the proposed s 48(8)*(b)* that a decision by the board of a company to acquire a number of its own shares can be 'considered alone, or together with other transactions in an integrated series of transactions', it is to be noted that s 41(4)*(b)* provides that a series of transactions is integrated if:

(i) consummation of one transaction is made contingent on consummation of one or more of the other transactions; or
(ii) the transactions are entered into within a 12-month period, and involve the same parties, or related persons; and —
   (aa) they involve the acquisition or disposal of an interest in one particular company or asset; or
   (bb) taken together, they lead to substantial involvement in a business activity that did not previously form part of the company's principal activity.

This provision is, however, only applicable in the context of s 41 and is not made applicable in the context of the proposed new s 48(8).

- The repurchase by a company of its own shares must not result in the only shareholders being one or more of its subsidiaries.[245] This is understandable, because it would clash with the limit on the number of shares that the subsidiaries of a company may hold in the company.[246] This requirement is of course unnecessary, because the limit would prevent this from happening anyway.
- An acquisition by a company of its own shares must not result in the company whose shares are acquired being left with only 'convertible or redeemable' shares.[247] In this regard, s 37(5) provides:

(5) Subject to any other law, a company's Memorandum of Incorporation may establish, for any particular class of shares, preferences, rights, limitations or other terms that —
. . .
(b) provide for shares of that class to be redeemable, subject to the requirements of sections 46 and 48, or convertible, as specified in the Memorandum of Incorporation —
   (i) at the option of the company, the shareholder, or another person at any time, or upon the occurrence of any specified contingency;
   (ii) for cash, indebtedness, securities, or other property;
   (iii) at prices and in amounts specified, or determined in accordance with a formula; or
   (iv) subject to any other terms set out in the company's Memorandum of Incorporation.

A 'convertible share' is a 'convertible security'[248] and 'convertible securities' are defined as follows in s 1 of the Act:[249]

---

[245] Section 48(3)*(a)*.
[246] See 8.3.2 below.
[247] Section 48(3)*(b)*.
[248] See definition of 'securities' in s 1 of the Act.
[249] The definition in s 1 of the Act has been substituted by the draft Companies Amendment Bill, 2010 by the following:

'convertible securities' means any securities of a company that may, by their terms, be converted into other securities of the company, including —
   (a) any non-voting securities issued by a company and which will become voting securities —
      (i) on the happening of a designated event; or
      (ii) if the holder of those securities so elects at some time after acquiring them; and
   (b) options to acquire securities to be issued by the company, irrespective of whether or not those securities may be voting securities, or non-voting securities contemplated in paragraph (a).

8.2.4 Enforceability of agreement to acquire shares

An agreement with a company providing for the acquisition by the company of shares issued by it is enforceable against the company.[250] Such enforceability is subject to the qualification that the agreement is not enforceable if the company would fall foul of the solvency and liquidity requirement or if the acquisition would result in there being no longer any shares of the company in existence other than shares held by the company's subsidiaries or convertible or redeemable shares.[251]

If a company alleges that it is unable to fulfil its obligations in terms of the agreement because it is unable to meet this qualification, the company must apply to a court and prove that fulfilment of its obligations would put it in breach of these requirements.[252] If the court is satisfied that the company is prevented from fulfilling its obligations pursuant to the agreement, the court may make an order that:

- is just and equitable, having regard to the financial circumstances of the company, and
- ensures that the person to whom the company is required to make a payment in terms of the agreement is paid at the earliest possible date that is compatible with the company satisfying its other financial obligations as they fall due and payable.[253]

If a company acquires shares contrary to s 48 (which governs repurchase) and s 46 (which governs distributions) the company may,[254] not more than two years after the acquisition, apply to a court for an order reversing the acquisition, and the court may order:

' "convertible" when used in relation to any securities of a company, means securities that may, by their terms, be converted into other securities of the company, including —
   (a) any non-voting securities issued by the company and which will become voting securities —
      (i) on the happening of a designated event; or
      (ii) if the holder of those securities so elects at some time after acquiring them; and
   (b) options to acquire securities to be issued by the company, irrespective of whether those securities may be voting securities, or non-voting securities contemplated in paragraph (a);'

[250] Section 48(4).
[251] Section 48(4) read with s 48(2) and s 48(3).
[252] Section 48(5).
[253] Ibid. It appears that such a person will rank concurrently with other creditors if the company is liquidated (see Van der Linde op cit n 1 at 495).
[254] The draft Companies Amendment Bill, 2010 proposes changing the word 'may' to 'must'.

- the person from whom the shares were acquired to return the amount paid by the company, and
- the company to issue to that person an equivalent number of shares of the same class as those acquired.

8.2.5 Directors' liability

A director of a company is liable for any loss, damages or costs sustained by the company as a direct or indirect consequence of the director being party to the acquisition by the company of its own shares despite knowing that the acquisition was contrary to s 46 or s 48.[255] The liability arises if the director was present at the meeting when the board approved the acquisition and failed to vote against the acquisition knowing that the acquisition was contrary to s 48 or s 46.[256]

As an acquisition by a company of its own shares involves a distribution, the acquisition can give rise to liability on the part of a director in terms of s 48(7) read with s 77(3)*(e)*(vi) and also s 46(6) read with s 77(3)*(e)*(vii). It appears that the two liabilities are the same, with two exceptions:

- in the case of an acquisition, the liability is wider in that the director is not only liable if the distribution does not meet the solvency and liquidity requirement, but also if the acquisition results in the requirement in s 48(3) not being met (ie the acquisition leaves the company with only shares held by its subsidiaries or only convertible or redeemable shares),[257] and
- in the case of an acquisition, the limit in s 77(4)*(b)*[258] does not apply, whereas it does in the case of a distribution.[259]

The liability provisions relating to a distribution have been dealt with under 8.1.6 and so will not be repeated here.

8.2.6 Treasury shares

Treasury shares are shares acquired by a company by way of repurchase, surrender, donation, inheritance or similar method[260] which, instead of being cancelled on their reacquisition, are held by the company until reissue or resale.

---

[255] Section 48(7) read with s 77(3)*(e)*(vii).
[256] Section 48(7).
[257] This requirement is dealt with earlier in 8.1 on distributions.
[258] Section 77(4)*(b)* provides:
 '(4) The liability of a director in terms of subsection (3)*(e)*(vi) as a consequence of the director having failed to vote against a distribution in contravention of section 46 —
 . . .
 (b) does not exceed, in aggregate, the difference between —
   (i) the amount by which the value of the distribution exceeded the amount that could have been distributed without causing the company to fail to satisfy the solvency and liquidity test; and
   (ii) the amount, if any, recovered by the company from persons to whom the distribution was made.'
[259] This limit has been dealt with earlier in 8.1.6*(c)*. It may be that this difference was not intended. See Van der Linde op cit n 1 at 499.
[260] See FHI Cassim 'The challenge of treasury shares' (2010) *SALJ* 137. See also FHI Cassim 'The repurchase by a company of its own shares: The concept of treasury shares' (2003) *SALJ* 137.

Although the Act does not permit the direct holding by a company of treasury shares, as pointed out in 8.2.3(c) above, the company may, to a limited extent, do so through a subsidiary or subsidiaries (see 8.3 below).

The acquisition of treasury shares does not reduce the number of the issued shares of the company, nor does the sale of treasury shares by the company increase the number of issued shares. Treasury shares are treated as the property of the corporation, to be disposed of by the company on such terms as it chooses. They may be sold at any price. They carry no voting rights or rights to dividends, nor the right to participate in a distribution of assets on a winding-up.

Being resaleable, treasury shares appear to be assets of the company. However, they are no more assets of the company than authorised but unissued shares of the company and therefore cannot properly be taken into account in calculating 'net assets' of the company or the profits available for distribution as dividends.[261] When a company is in decline, so too are its treasury shares, which then become very difficult, if not impossible, to sell.[262] Treasury shares, rather than being a corporate asset, really only represent 'an opportunity to acquire new assets for the corporate treasury by creating new obligations' and to show them as an asset on the company's balance sheet is 'a fiction, however admirable'.[263] As has been said:[264]

> [t]reasury shares are indeed a masterpiece of legal magic, the creation of something out of nothing ... Their existence as issued shares is a pure fiction, a figure of speech to explain certain special rules and privileges as to their re-issue *[sic]*.

What they really are, are authorised shares that may be reissued free of some of the restrictions or formalities of an original issue of shares regarding prospectuses, allotment requirements or pre-emptive rights.[265] Treasury shares are thus:

> not shares in the strict sense of the word. They carry no voting or dividend rights; they cannot be counted for purposes of determining a quorum or be reflected as an asset in the balance sheet of the company; they are merely a possible source of additional funds.[266]

Regarding the use of treasury shares in other jurisdictions, the position in Australia, New Zealand and Canada is similar to the position in South Africa. The American Model Business Corporation Act of 1979 has rendered treasury shares redundant by requiring reacquired shares to be restored to the status of authorised but unissued shares or, in certain circumstances, to be cancelled and eliminated

---

[261] See *Borg v International Silver Co* 11 Fed (2d) 147 (1925). Generally accepted accounting practice does not permit a holding company to show treasury shares as an asset in its own balance sheet or the group's consolidated balance sheet (see AC416). See also GS Hills 'Federal taxation v corporation law' (1936–37) 12 *Wisconsin LR* 280, 289; FHI Cassim op cit n 260 at 138; Blackman et al op cit n 38 at 5–72–5–73.
[262] FHI Cassim 'The repurchase by a company of its own shares: The concept of treasury shares' (2003) *SALJ* at 138.
[263] Hand J in *Borg v International Silver Co* (supra) at 150.
[264] See HW Ballantine *Ballantine on Corporations* rev ed (1946) para 260 at 615.
[265] *Ballantine* op cit n 264 para 260 at 615–6. See also FHI Cassim op cit n 262 at 139.
[266] FHI Cassim op cit n 262 at 139.

from authorised shares.[267] Treasury shares are currently permitted in Singapore, Malaysia, the United Kingdom and the European Union.[268]

The view is taken by some that treasury shares provide distinct advantages: they afford companies flexibility in managing their capital structure and in adjusting their debt-equity ratio, reduce or avoid the cost of raising new capital, and are also useful for employee share schemes.[269] It is argued that, based on the UK's experience:

> complex legislation to curtail the potential abuse of treasure *[sic]* shares is unnecessary. All that is required in order to reap the much needed flexibility which treasury shares would inject into our developing economy are a few simple and surprisingly uncomplicated statutory provisions.[270]

8.3 ACQUISITION BY A COMPANY OF SHARES IN ITS HOLDING COMPANY (INDIRECT REPURCHASES)

Until the 1973 Act was amended in 1999,[271] the Companies Act prohibited a company from being a member of its holding company.[272] This prohibition was aimed at preventing an indirect return of capital to shareholders and the indirect trafficking in its shares by a holding company.

The amendment to the 1973 Act in 1999 made it possible for subsidiaries of a holding company to acquire shares in the holding company subject to certain requirements.[273]

Subject to what is said below, the current Act also permits such acquisitions. Section 48(2)*(b)* of the Act provides that a company may acquire shares in the company's holding company subject to certain conditions and requirements. Although s 48(2)*(b)* refers to 'the company', it is implied in the provision dealing with directors' liability (s 48(7)) that the board has the authority to make such an acquisition.[274] The comments made earlier regarding the non-involvement of the shareholders of a company in making the decision to acquire shares in itself are also relevant here. It is to be noted that the special requirements laid down in the new s 48(8) proposed in the draft Companies Amendment Bill, 2010 do not apply where a company acquires shares in its holding company.[275]

8.3.1 Reference to s 46

As mentioned in 8.2.3*(b)* above, s 48 provides that, if a company is to acquire shares in its holding company, it may only do so 'if the decision to do so satisfies the requirements of section 46'.[276] As has been pointed out[277] the cross-reference

---

[267] See FHI Cassim op cit n 262.
[268] Ibid. This article provides a very useful survey of the position in the various jurisdictions.
[269] Ibid.
[270] Ibid.
[271] See the Companies Amendment Act 37 of 1999.
[272] See s 39.
[273] See s 89 of the 1973 Act.
[274] The draft Companies Amendment Bill, 2010 amends s 48(2)*(b)* to make this clear.
[275] See 8.2.3 for the discussion of the new s 48(8) proposed by the draft Companies Amendment Bill, 2010.
[276] Section 48(2)*(b)*.

to s 46 in s 48 is 'unnecessary and confusing' because s 46 states the requirement for 'distributions' and not for 'decisions'.[278] The cross-reference creates the impression that a decision to make such an acquisition requires the company to be solvent and liquid at the time of making the decision. This does not make sense, because the decision can do no harm — it is the distribution pursuant to the decision that is potentially harmful and it is immediately after the distribution that the solvency and liquidity test should be satisfied.[279] The reference to s 46 and s 48 should therefore be removed.[280] Unfortunately, this is not done in the draft Companies Amendment Bill, 2010.

8.3.2 'Limit'

Section 48(2)(b) provides that any subsidiary of a company may acquire shares in that company, but subject to a limit set out in s 48(2)(b)(i). The limit is that:

> any subsidiary of a company may acquire shares of that company, but —
> (i) not more than 10%, in aggregate, of the number of issued shares of any class of shares of a company may be held by, or for the benefit of, all of the subsidiaries of that company, taken together.

There is uncertainty regarding this limit. Is the limit 10 per cent of each class, or 10 per cent of the total shares, irrespective of class of share? For example: Company X has three classes of shares, A shares, B shares and C shares. One hundred of each have been issued. Is the maximum limit on the number of shares that subsidiaries of company X can acquire in Company X (i) ten A shares, ten B shares and ten C shares, or (ii) 30 shares, irrespective of their class?[281]

It is clear from s 48(2)(b)(i) that, in determining the number of shares held by subsidiaries in their holding company, shares acquired by the subsidiaries before they became subsidiaries of the holding company must be taken into account.[282] In the 1973 Act, the view was taken that such shares did not have to be taken into account.[283]

It appears that shares acquired by a subsidiary as a trustee or in a representative capacity must be taken into account in determining the percentage holding, which is anomalous.[284]

It also appears that shares acquired by subsidiaries in their holding company by

---

[277] See Van der Linde op cit n 1 at 492; see also 8.2.3(b) above.
[278] Van der Linde op cit n 1 at 492. It is to be noted that the proposed amendment in the draft Companies Amendment Bill, 2010 does not eliminate this confusion. The draft Bill proposes that s 48(2)(a) reads as follows:
   '(2) Subject to subsections (3) and (8), and if the decision to do so satisfies the requirements of section 46—
   (a) the board of a company may determine that the company will acquire a number of its own shares; and . . .'
[279] Ibid.
[280] Ibid.
[281] In terms of the 1973 Act (s 89) the answer was the latter.
[282] Cf HE Wainer 'The New Companies Act: Peculiarities and Anomalies' 2009 *SALJ* 806 at 821.
[283] See Blackman et al op cit n 38 at 5–98.
[284] The same anomaly was found in s 89 of the 1973 Act.

way of a capitalisation issue must be taken into account in determining whether the 10 per cent limit has been exceeded.[285]

8.3.3 Requirement of s 48(3)

Section 48(3) provides that, despite any provision of any law, agreement, order or the Memorandum of Incorporation of a company, the company may not acquire its own shares, and a subsidiary of a company may not acquire shares of that company if, as a result of that acquisition, there would no longer be any shares of the company in issue other than:

- shares held by one or more subsidiaries of the company, or
- convertible or redeemable shares.

The requirement in the second bullet makes no sense in relation to a company acquiring shares in its holding company. If a subsidiary acquires shares in the holding company from another shareholder, the company's shares remain the same. If the shares are issued by the holding company to the subsidiary, that simply increases the company's shares. So it is difficult to see how the acquisition can have the result envisaged in the second bullet.

8.3.4 Section 46 (distributions) applicable

The definition of 'distribution' in s 1 of the Act includes a transfer of money or other property by a company as consideration for the acquisition of shares in a company in the same group of companies as the transferring company. A 'group of companies' means 'two or more companies that share a holding company or subsidiary relationship'.[286] Accordingly, s 46 governing 'distributions' applies to the distribution made by a company pursuant to an acquisition by the company of shares in its holding company. This also seems to be what is intended by s 48(2)*(b)*, although the reference to 'decision' in s 48(2)*(b)* is confusing, because s 46 deals only with distributions and not with decisions. Section 46 is dealt with earlier in this chapter (see 8.1).

8.3.5 Directors' liability

Where a company acquires shares in its holding company unlawfully or makes a distribution pursuant to such an acquisition unlawfully, directors of the acquiring company incur liability in terms of s 48(7) or s 46(6) respectively. The liability is for any loss, damages or costs sustained by the company as a direct or indirect consequence of the director being party to the distribution or acquisition despite knowing that the acquisition or distribution was unlawful. The liability arises if the director was a party to the resolution approving the acquisition or distribution

---

[285] It may be noted that nowhere has it been explained how the limit of 10 per cent was arrived at. In this regard one sees that, in the initial draft Companies Amendment Bill preceding the Companies Amendment Act 37 of 1999, the Co-ordinating Research Institute for Corporate Law originally proposed a general prohibition on a subsidiary's acquiring its holding company's shares except to a nominal extent of 1 per cent of the issued share capital of the holding company. The published proposed amendment, which was adopted in the current s 89, recommended a 10 per cent limitation (GN 724 *GG* 18868 of 8 May 1998). This modification was not explained.

[286] See definition in s 1 of the Act.

and failed to vote against it knowing that the acquisition or distribution was unlawful.

The limit on liability in terms of s 77(4) applies. It is the difference between 'the amount by which the value of the distribution exceeded the amount that could have been distributed without causing the company to fail the solvency and liquidity test' and 'the amount, if any, recovered by the company from persons to whom the distribution was made'.

8.3.6 Non-applicability of s 48(4) and (5)

It is to be noted that the provisions of s 48(4) and (5) which, as was seen above, apply to the acquisition by a company of its own shares, do not apply to the acquisition by a company of shares in its holding company. The agreement referred to in s 48(4) and (5) is an agreement providing only for the acquisition by a company of shares in itself. It is difficult to discern why this should be the case, ie why does it not also refer to an acquisition by a company of shares in its holding company?

8.3.7 Voting rights not exercisable

The voting rights attaching to the shares held by subsidiaries in their holding company present a problem.

Although a company can acquire shares in its holding company, the voting rights attaching to the shares are not exercisable. Section 48(2)(b)(ii) provides:

> **48.** (2) Subject to subsection (3) —
> . . .
> (b) any subsidiary of a company may acquire shares of that company, but —
> . . .
> > (ii) no voting rights attached to those shares may be exercised while the shares are held by the subsidiary, and it remains a subsidiary of the company whose shares it holds.

The problem arises in this regard: section 48(2)(b)(ii) only neutralises the votes of shares held by a subsidiary in a holding company in respect of those shares acquired by the subsidiary when it was a subsidiary. It does not cover any shares the subsidiary may have acquired in the holding company before it became the holding company of that subsidiary.[287] It is unlikely that this discrepancy was intended.

8.3.8 Rationale for acquisition

A question that arises is: why would a subsidiary want to acquire shares in its holding company?[288] This question is important, considering the dangers of allowing a company to traffic in its own shares. As Coetzee J said in *The Unisec Group Ltd v Sage Holdings Ltd*:[289]

> The rapid development of the group of companies-concept since the first world war *[sic]* produced a mixed bag of results. The group usually consists of one or more pyramids of

---
[287] HE Wainer op cit n 282 at 821–2.
[288] See Blackman et al op cit n 38 at 5–101–5–102.
[289] 1986 (3) SA 259 (T) 265–6.

interrelated companies in which all or the majority of the shares of some are held by others with the parent or holding company at the apex. Economic and administrative advantages flow from this arrangement, on the one hand, but, on the other, it is clearly capable of abuse, particularly in regard to the important principle that a company may not traffic in its own shares. Through this principle, the group concept drives a coach and horses. In addition, the true financial state of the holding company can be effectively masked from the eyes of its shareholders and indeed distorted in the separate accounts of the companies in the group.

Coetzee J pointed out that a purchase of shares by a wholly owned subsidiary of its holding company's shares 'cannot possibly have any income or investment advantage for [the holding company], as opposed to a purely speculative one by trafficking in them'. He said that, although he had 'always regarded [this] as beyond doubt', and 'would have been content with the mere statement of this self-evident fact', the 'insistence to the contrary of both counsel for the appellants throughout the hearing of this appeal', compelled him 'to demonstrate the obvious'.

He pointed out that, if a wholly owned subsidiary purchases shares of its holding company, and the holding company distributes dividends, if the subsidiary, then, in turn, redistributes this to its holding company, the process, if repeated, will result in the whole of the original dividend declared by the holding company being paid to its other shareholders. This, the learned judge said, demonstrates that the dividends that the holding company receives from its subsidiary are *part of* and *not* additional to its original ... distributable income which did not increase as a result of the "investment" by [the subsidiary] in [its holding company's] shares', hence 'no *extra* income' for the holding company is generated by its subsidiary's 'investment'. As this investment cannot produce *extra* income for [the holding company], the holding company's accounts 'will reflect the untruth' as to its distributable income, unless the holding company's and subsidiary's accounts are consolidated. 'It is therefore illusory and totally misleading' to think of the money spent by the subsidiary in its holding company's shares as 'a good investment' either by the subsidiary or by the holding company. The additional dividends that the other shareholders of the holding company receive 'results from what is in effect a reduction of capital which may or may not be advantageous to them in the long term'.

Thus the purchase presents no economic benefit for the holding company 'save to speculate, through [its subsidiary], with its own shares'. In addition, if shareholders of the holding company were directors of it, they could, 'without expending their own money', obtain control of the holding company. The learned judge concluded:

> The possibility of evil and mischief which lurks in the above catalogue is manifest. Although in this example a wholly owned subsidiary is posited, exactly the same mischief results in the case of a partially owned subsidiary, only to a lesser degree, which will be commensurate with the percentage of its shares owned by [the holding company]. The principle remains the same. The mischief which, in the absence of statutory control, may flow from [such an] arrangement can be succinctly stated as: (1) The trafficking by a company in its own shares. (2) The reduction of its capital, not by special resolution of the members, but by executive action of its directors. (3) The sterilisation of funds which are available to it for capital investment. (4) The entrenchment of the directors' control of [the holding company]. (5) The misleading picture presented by the final accounts of [the holding company] which might very well be a gross distortion of the truth without being, technically, inaccurate.

What is more[290] 'although Coetzee J said that where the subsidiary is not a wholly owned subsidiary "the same mischief results ... only to a lesser degree", this ignores the fact that further mischief may occur, namely, oppression of the minority shareholders of the subsidiary. Funds of their company are used, not in the conduct of its business, but to pay out shareholders of its holding company. It would seem that purchases by their company of its holding company's shares will inevitably constitute "unfairly prejudicial, unjust or inequitable" conduct (of the grossest kind) in terms of s 252 — except perhaps where the subsidiary is able to speculate successfully in its holding company's shares.'

8.4 FINANCIAL ASSISTANCE FOR THE ACQUISITION OF SECURITIES

8.4.1 Background

In general terms, s 44 of the Act regulates the situation where a company provides financial assistance for the acquisition of the company's securities.

The Jenkins Committee said[291] that the mischief at which such a provision is aimed is the abuse that becomes possible when persons, with insufficient funds or credit facilities of their own, purchase the shares of a company out of borrowed funds and, after gaining control of the company, use the funds of the company to pay for the shares acquired by them. If the speculation fails, the company will suffer loss, for it will have received either an inadequate security or an illusory consideration or *quid pro quo* when parting with its funds. But even if the venture is successful, so that actual loss is avoided, the interests of the creditors and minority shareholders will nevertheless have been subjected to an unwarranted and illegitimate risk. The object of such a provision is simply to ensure that corporate funds are used for proper corporate purposes. A person who purchases shares in a company must do so out of his or her own funds and not by misusing the funds of the company.[292] In *Chaston v SWP Group plc,*[293] Arden LJ stated: '[T]he general mischief, however, remains the same, namely that the resources of the target company and its subsidiaries should not be used directly or indirectly to assist the purchaser financially to make the acquisition'.

In *Lewis v Oneanate (Pty) Ltd*[294] Nicholas AJA said:

> The object of a provision such as 38(1) is the protection of creditors of a company, who have a right to look to its paid-up capital as the fund out of which their debts are to be discharged ... The purpose of the Legislature was to avoid that fund being employed or depleted or exposed to possible risk in consequence of transactions concluded for the purpose of or in connection with the purchase of its shares.[295]

In England, the Greene Committee,[296] on whose recommendation the regulation

---

[290] See Blackman et al op cit n 38 at 5–102.
[291] Report of the Company Law Committee ('the Jenkins Committee') Cmnd 1749 of 1962.
[292] See FHI Cassim 'The reform of company law and the capital maintenance concept' (2005) 122 *SALJ* 283 at 290–2.
[293] [2003] 1 BCLC 675 (CA) at 686 para 31(i).
[294] 1992 (4) SA 811 (A) 818. See also *Peters NNO v Schoeman* 2001 (1) SA 872 (SCA).
[295] Quoted with approval by Van Heerden JA in *Gardner v Margo* 2006 (6) SA 33 (SCA).
[296] English Company Law Reform Committee (1926) Cmnd 2657 para 173 p 62.

was first introduced, had examined these abuses. It thought that such an arrangement offended against the spirit, if not the letter, of the law that prohibited a company from trafficking in its own shares. The Committee's recommendation that such financial assistance should be prohibited was given statutory recognition in s 54 of the UK Companies Act of 1948.[297] Substantially the same provision as s 54 was enacted into South African company law by s 86(*bis*)(2) of the 1926 Companies Act. It was re-enacted, with minor amendments, in s 38 of the 1973 Act and subsequently amended by s 9 of the Corporate Laws Amendment Act 24 of 2006.

A liberal approach was adopted in the 2006 Amendment Act when a further exception to the prohibition in s 38 was added to facilitate black economic empowerment (BEE).

A similar liberal approach has been adopted in s 44 of the Companies Act of 2008, although the formulation of s 44 is different from s 38 of the 1973 Act.

8.4.2 Section 44

Section 44 provides:

> **44** (1) In this section, "financial assistance" does not include lending money in the ordinary course of business by a company whose primary business is the lending of money.
>
> (2) To the extent that the Memorandum of Incorporation of a company provides otherwise, the board may authorise the company to provide financial assistance by way of a loan, guarantee, the provision of security or otherwise to any person for the purpose of, or in connection with, the subscription of any option, or any securities, issued or to be issued by the company or a related or inter-related company, or for the purchase of any securities of the company or a related or inter-related company, subject to subsections (3) and (4).
>
> (3) Despite any provision of a company's Memorandum of Incorporation to the contrary, the board may not authorise any financial assistance contemplated in subsection (2), unless —
> (*a*) the particular provision of financial assistance is —
> (i) pursuant to an employee share scheme that satisfies the requirements of section 97; or
> (ii) pursuant to a special resolution of the shareholders, adopted within the previous two years, which approved such assistance either for the specific recipient, or generally for a category of potential recipients, and the specific recipient falls within that category; and
> (*b*) the board is satisfied that —
> (i) immediately after providing the financial assistance, the company would satisfy the solvency and liquidity test; and
> (ii) the terms under which the financial assistance is proposed to be given are fair and reasonable to the company.
>
> (4) In addition to satisfying the requirements of subsection (3), the board must ensure that any conditions or restrictions respecting the granting of financial assistance set out in the company's Memorandum of Incorporation have been satisfied.
>
> (5) A decision by the board of a company to provide financial assistance contemplated in subsection (2), or an agreement with respect to the provision of any such assistance, is void to the extent that the provision of that assistance would be inconsistent with —
> (*a*) this section; or

---

[297] The provision was later replaced by provisions in the Companies Act 1981 and consolidated in ss 151–8 of the Companies Act 1985. The prohibition against a company giving financial assistance for the acquisition of its own shares is now located in s 678 of the Companies Act 2006.

(b) a prohibition, condition or requirement contemplated in subsection (4).

(6) If a resolution or an agreement has been declared void in terms of subsection (5) read with section 218(1), a director of a company is liable to the extent set out in section 77(3)*(e)*(iv) if the director —
(a) was present at the meeting when the board approved the resolution or agreement, or participated in the making of such a decision in terms of section 74; and
(b) failed to vote against the resolution or agreement, despite knowing that the provision of financial assistance was inconsistent with this section or a prohibition, condition or requirement contemplated in subsection (4).

8.4.3 The meaning of 'financial assistance'

The only assistance[298] provided by the Act in determining the meaning of 'financial assistance' is that:

- financial assistance does not include lending money in the ordinary course of business by a company whose primary business is the lending of money,[299]
- financial assistance includes a loan, guarantee, the provision of security or otherwise.[300]

Like s 44 of the Act, s 38 of the 1973 Act also covered financial assistance 'by means of a loan, guarantee, the provision of security or otherwise'[301] and it was held in relation thereto that the words 'or otherwise' were not to be construed *eiusdem generis* with 'loan, guarantee, the provision of security'.[302] Nothing further was stated in s 38 as to what constituted 'financial assistance' within the meaning of the section.[303]

'Financial assistance' is not a term capable of precise legal definition and it has been held that it is clearly unwise for the legislature to lay down a precise definition of this term.[304] The absence of a clear definition means, however, that the section can give rise to uncertainties and ambiguities and has the potential to bring innocuous transactions into play.[305]

In *Charterhouse Investments Trust Ltd v Tempest Diesel Ltd*[306] Hoffman J said:

---

[298] In regard to interpretation of the Act generally, s 5 thereof states that it must be interpreted in a manner that gives effect to the purposes set out in s 7. Section 7, in turn, lists some of the most fundamental underlying principles of the new legislation. Section 7(2) permits a court interpreting or applying the legislation to consider, to the extent appropriate, foreign company law. In light hereof, although the South African case law dealing with s 38 will most certainly remain relevant and applicable, courts should also look to the foreign jurisdictions from which certain of the new terms and concepts have been drawn as an aid to their proper interpretation.
[299] Section 44(1).
[300] Section 44(2).
[301] Section 38 also referred to the provision of financial assistance 'directly or indirectly', a term not used in s 44. It is unlikely that anything turns on the omission.
[302] *Gradwell (Pty) Ltd v Rostra Printers Ltd* 1959 (4) SA 419 (A) 425.
[303] Section 152 of the UK Companies Act 1985 contains a fairly comprehensive definition of 'financial assistance'. See ss 677(1), 687(2) and 681 of the Companies Act 2006.
[304] See Toulson LJ in *Anglo Petroleum Ltd v TFB (Mortgages) Ltd* [2008] 1 BCLC 185 (CA) at para 26 pp 190–1.
[305] Ibid.
[306] [1986] 1 BCLC 1. See also *Chaston v SWP Group plc* [2003] 1 BCLC 675 (CA) 682–92 where a due diligence test was done on the company whose shares were being acquired and the company's

> There is no definition of giving financial assistance in the section, although some examples are given. The words have no technical meaning and their frame of reference is in my judgment the language of ordinary commerce. One must examine the commercial realities of the transaction and decide whether it can properly be described as giving financial assistance by the company, bearing in mind that the section is a penal one and should not be strained to cover transactions which are not fairly within it.

It will be recognised that 'assistance' involves something in the nature of aid or help.[307] It cannot exist in a vacuum: it must be given to someone.[308]

For the assistance to qualify, the assistance must be 'financial'.[309] Therefore, providing documents or information relating to the transaction in question, responding to requests for information relating thereto, providing access for the purpose of inspection of records, restructuring of the board of directors and concluding *bona fide* service contracts[310] all involve co-operation by the company with the parties to the transaction, but do not constitute 'financial assistance'.[311] By facilitating a transaction (for example, by serving as a vehicle or conduit for the transmission of money to a party to the transaction), a company does not give 'financial assistance'.[312]

In *Lewis v Oneanate (Pty) Ltd*[313] all the shares of the company were sold. Part of the purchase price was to be paid in cash and the balance was to be paid over a period of 'three to five years'. In order to secure the unpaid balance, the company was to pass a bond in favour of the seller over immovable property that was to be transferred to the company; and it was assumed by the court (the matter came before the court by way of an exception to the seller's particulars of claim) that the bond over the property would be passed at the same time that the property was transferred to the company. The Appellate Division held that this would not amount to the giving of financial assistance:

> If the course outlined above should be adopted, this will not result in giving of financial assistance . . . in contravention of s 38(1). Although the passing of a bond constitutes the provision of security, it will not in the special circumstances of this case amount to the giving of financial assistance. It will not bind any of the assets which will be held by the company at the moment immediately prior to the passing of the bond. Unless the amount of the mortgage debt exceeds the realisable value of [the property to be transferred to the company] (as to which there is nothing alleged in the particular claim), the company's financial position will in no way be altered by the transaction, and it will not be exposed to any possible risk in consequence of it. The simultaneous registration will no doubt facilitate

---

subsidiary paid the professional fees in respect thereof. Such payment was held to be 'financial assistance'.

[307] *Sterileair (Pty) Ltd v Papallo* (1998) 29 ACSR 461 at 466.
[308] *Sterileair (Pty) Ltd v Papallo* (supra).
[309] *Armour Hick Northern Ltd v Armour Trust Ltd* [1980] 3 All ER 833 (Ch) at 837–8; *London Ranch (Pty) Ltd v Hyreb Estate (Pty) Ltd* 1963 (2) SA 570 (E); *Chaston v SWP Group plc* [2002] EWCA Civ 1999, [2003] B.C.C. 140.
[310] *Albert v Papenfus* 1964 (2) SA 713 (E); *Parlett v Guppys (Bridport) Ltd* [1996] 2 BCLS 34.
[311] *Burton v Palmer* (1980) 5 ACLR 481 CA (NSW) 490–3. See also *British Commonwealth Holdings plc v Barclays Bank plc* [1996] 1 All ER 381.
[312] *Gray v Thesing Vastgoed BV* 1987 (1) SA 744 (A); *Lewis v Oneanate (Pty) Ltd* 1992 (4) SA 811 (A) 818.
[313] 1992 (4) SA 811 (A).

the purchase of the shares, but it is [the transferor of the property] who will be giving the financial assistance . . .[314]

There is no financial assistance provided when the direct object of the transaction is simply to give to another what he or she is in any event entitled to,[315] even where the transaction involves a net transfer of value from the company.[316] So, for example, the proper distribution of a dividend is not financial assistance.[317] In *Re Wellington Publishing Co Ltd*[318] Quilliam J said:

> The expression 'financial assistance' is an indefinite one and it is beyond normal experience to regard the expression as applying to the payment of a dividend. The payment of a dividend is part of the normal functions of a company, and indeed, in the final analysis is probably as much the reason for the company's existence as is the earning of profits the reason for an individual trader being in business.

Nor does the ordinary payment of a debt that is due and payable constitute financial assistance, even if such payment is a condition of the share sale:[319] — 'where a debt is presently due and payable and the debtor can have no answer to the creditor's demand for payment, it would be straining the language to hold that by paying the debt the debtor gives the creditor financial assistance'.[320] Even if the repayment of the debt was not made in the ordinary course of business but solely to facilitate the purchase of the shares, there is no financial assistance within the meaning of the section.[321]

Financial assistance is also not given where the seller of the shares is given security by the company for the repayment of a loan made by him or her to the company — the object being the continuation of the loan.[322]

---

[314] *Lewis v Oneanate (Pty) Ltd* 1992 (4) SA 811 (A) 818.
[315] *Gradwell (Pty) Ltd v Rostra Printers Ltd* 1959 (4) SA 419 (A) 426; *Lipschitz NO v UDC Bank Ltd* 1979 (1) SA 789 (A) 800; *Rossfield Group Operations (Pty) Ltd v Austral Group Ltd* 1981 QdR 279 at 286; *Augusto v Socieda de Angolana de Commercio International Limitada (Sacilda)* 1998 (4) SA 124 (NM); *Gardner v Margo* 2006 (6) SA 33 (SCA) at paras [45]–[48].
[316] *Charterhouse Investments Trust Ltd v Tempest Diesel Ltd* [1986] 1 BCLC 1 at 10.
[317] *Novick v Comair Holdings Ltd* 1979 (2) SA 116 (W); *Re Wellington Publishing Co Ltd* [1973] 1 NZLR 133 at 136; *Coleman v Myers* [1977] 2 NZLR 225 CA (NZ) 378; *Rossfield Group Operations (Pty) Ltd v Austral Group Ltd* 1981 QdR 279 at 286; *Brady v Brady* [1989] AC 755 at 783.
[318] [1973] 1 NZLR 133 at 136. See also *Chaston v SWP Group plc* [2003] 1 BCLC 675 (CA) 689 and *Belmont Finance Corp Ltd v Williams Furniture Ltd (No 2)* [1980] 1 All ER 393 (CA) where the court rejected the argument that financial assistance cannot be given without a detriment to the company being acquired.
[319] *Gradwell (Pty) Ltd v Rostra Printers Ltd* 1959 (4) SA 419 (A) 425; *Augusto v Socieda de Angolana de Commercio International Limitada (Sacilda)* (supra); *MT Realisations v Digital Equipment* [2003] 2 BCLC 117 (CA).
[320] Per Schreiner JA in *Gradwell (Pty) Ltd v Rostra Printers Ltd* (supra) at 426. See also *Belmont Finance Corp v Williams Furniture Ltd (No 2)* (supra) at 401–2; *Armour Hick Northern Ltd v Armour Trust Ltd* [1980] 3 All ER 833 (Ch) 837.
[321] See *Augusto v Socieda de Angolana de Commercio International Limitada (Sacilda)* (supra) at 130.
[322] *Karnovsky v Hyams* 1961 (2) SA 368 (W) 371–2; *Bay Loan Investment (Pty) Ltd v Bay View (Pty) Ltd* 1972 (2) SA 313 (C); *Lomcord Agencies (Pty) Ltd v Amalgamated Construction Co (Pty) Ltd* 1976 (3) SA 86 (D); and cf *Straiton v Cleanwell Dry Cleaners (Pty) Ltd* 1960 (1) SA 355 (SR). See also *Lipschitz v UDC Bank Ltd NO* 1979 (1) SA 789 (A).

In *Gardner v Margo*[323] Van Heerden JA said:

> In *Lipschitz NO v UDC Bank Ltd* ... this court appears to have accepted the distinction drawn by Schreiner JA in *Gradwell (Pty) Ltd v Rostra Printers Ltd* ... between the 'ultimate goal' of the transaction in question and its 'direct object', and to accept that it is only the direct object of the transaction that is relevant. If the direct object is not the provision of financial assistance by the company for the purpose of or in connection with a purchase of its shares, then it is irrelevant that the ultimate goal of the transaction was to enable a person to purchase such shares.

Accordingly, for example, where a company passed a bond over its property with the direct object of securing, or raising money to pay off or reduce, the seller's loan account, this will not amount to the giving of financial assistance even if the ultimate goal of the transaction had been to facilitate the purchaser's acquisition of the shares by rendering it unnecessary for him or her to purchase the loan account along with the shares.[324]

In *Gardner* a mandate was given by a Mr Joubert (J) to Mr Gardner (G) to sell a large number of J's shares in OTR Mining Ltd (OTR). OTR was party to the agreement in terms of which it guaranteed a certain amount for the shares. J later ceded his rights in terms of the agreement to a Mr Margo. A dispute arose as to the precise amount that J was entitled to in terms of the mandate, which required a determination by the court of the terms of the agreement. It was also contended that OTR's guarantee was a breach of the provisions of s 38 of the 1973 Companies Act.

It was held by the court[325] that, in terms of the agreement, J was entitled to 40 cents per share and the proceeds over and above that were to be paid to OTR. The contention was given short shrift by the court. Van Heerden JA held:[326]

> In *Lewis v Oneanate (Pty) Ltd* 1992 (4) SA 811 (A) Nicholas JJA stated that: 'The object of a provision such as section 38(1) is the protection of the creditors of a company, who have a right to look to its paid-up capital as the fund out of which their debts are to be discharged ... The purpose of the Legislature was to avoid that fund being employed or depleted or exposed to possible risk in consequence of transactions concluded for the purpose of or in connection with the purchase of its shares.' Although the prohibition against the giving of financial assistance is couched in very wide and general terms: 'There has ... been a tendency, in the light of the extremely wide terms of the prohibition considered in conjunction with the circumstance that contravention of the section constitutes a criminal offence, to give close attention to the underlying purpose of the prohibition and the real mischief at which it was aimed ... and, with that in mind, to adopt what JC Beuthin has described [in (1973) *SALJ* at 213] as 'a much narrower approach to the section'. In *Lipschitz NO v UDC Bank Ltd* ... this court appears to have accepted the distinction drawn by Schreiner JA in *Gradwell (Pty) Ltd v Rostra Printers Ltd* ... between the 'ultimate goal' of the transaction in

---

[323] 2006 (6) SA 33 (SCA) at para 45. For a critical analysis of *Gardner v Margo* see Rehana Cassim and Maleka Femida Cassim '*Gardner v Margo*: A misapplication of section 38 of the Companies Act' (2007) 124 *SALJ* 37 who submit that the SCA incorrectly conflated and consequently misapplied the two vital elements of s 38, namely the giving of financial assistance and the purpose for which it is given.

[324] *Gradwell (Pty) Ltd v Rostra Printers* 1959 (4) SA 419 (A) 425 426; *Lipschitz NO v UDC Bank Ltd* 1979 (1) SA 789 (A) 799.

[325] Van Heerden JA handed down the judgment, with Scott, Zulman, Maya and Cachalia concurring.

[326] At 243[45]–[48].

question and its 'direct object', and to accept that it is only the direct object of the transaction that is relevant. If the direct object is not the provision of financial assistance by the company for the purpose of or in connection with a purchase of its shares, then it is irrelevant that the ultimate goal of the transaction was to enable a person to purchase such shares. Moreover, financial assistance within the meaning of section 38(1) is given only when the direct object of the transaction is to assist another financially — the section 38 prohibition is not contravened when the direct object of the transactions is merely to give another that to which he or she is already entitled. As was submitted by Margo's counsel, the guarantee given by OTR to Joubert was not intended to provide financial assistance to anyone in respect of the purchase of OTR shares. The direct object of the guarantee was to provide Joubert with some security for that to which he was entitled in terms of the mandate, ie part of the proceeds of the shares to be sold on his behalf by Gardner. In my view, the guarantee does not fall foul of section 38(1) of the Companies Act and counsel for the appellants (once again, wisely) did not press this point at all.

The judgment raises a number of questions.

It is true, as Van Heerden JA says, that the guarantee was to provide Joubert with some security for that to which he was entitled in terms of the mandate. But does that mean that OTR was not contravening s 38? If a bank makes a loan to a purchaser to enable the purchaser to buy shares in a company and the company gives security for the repayment of the loan, surely the company was contravening s 38 and it cannot be argued that the direct object of the provision of security was to protect the bank and therefore there was no contravention? Is the company in both cases not, without any prior obligation (unrelated to the purchase), facilitating the purchase of the shares? Van Heerden JA said that 'the section 38 prohibition is not contravened when the direct object of the transaction is merely to give to another that to which he or she is already entitled' (see quote above). Is the implication that by giving the guarantee, OTR was merely giving to J that to which he was already entitled? If so, surely that was not the case? Was J entitled to a guarantee from OTR? Is the rationale that J was 'entitled' to the guarantee because OTR was to receive the proceeds of the sale of the shares over and above 40 cents per share? Even if this is the argument, was there not still a contravention of s 38?

Despite the acceptance by the court of the 'narrow approach' to the application of s 38 (see the quote above), even if it is accepted that the purpose of the guarantee was not for the purchase of the shares, was it not 'in connection with' the purchase of the shares? It is true that the courts have taken a very narrow view of the meaning of 'in connection with', as the following dictum of Miller JA in *Lipschitz NO v UDC Bank*[327] indicates:

> The words 'in connection with' appear to have been inserted in order to cover a situation where, although the actual purpose of the company in giving financial assistance might not have been established, its conduct nevertheless stood in such close relationship to the purchase of its shares that, substantially if not precisely, its conduct was similar to that of a company which gave the forbidden assistance with the purpose described in the section. In short, the alternative was inserted merely to close possible loopholes; it was not intended by such insertion to create a different type of offence, or a lesser offence, or to prohibit conduct which was not substantially similar to the conduct prohibited by the main provision charac-

---

[327] 1979 (1) SA 789 (A) 804–805.

terised by the words 'for the purpose of'. Obviously, it is not possible to define the exact extent of the enlargement of the scope of the prohibition by the addition of the words in question; the facts of each case will determine whether the established 'connection' with the purchase of shares constitutes conduct which the Legislature was concerned to prohibit.

Notwithstanding this narrow interpretation of the wording, does the situation in question not fall clearly within its confines?

Van Heerden JA refers (see quote earlier) with approval to *Lewis v Oneanate* where Nicholas AJA states as the purpose of s 38 the avoidance of, inter alia, exposing the company 'to possible risk in consequence of transactions concluded for the purpose of or in connection with the purchase of the shares'. Did the guarantee that OTR provided not clearly expose OTR to such risk?[328]

After the judgment by Schreiner JA in *Gradwell (Pty) Ltd v Rostra Printers Ltd*,[329] it was for a time fairly generally accepted that the *ratio* of that judgment was that, in deciding whether financial assistance had been given, the test was whether the company had been made poorer — a test which became known as the 'impoverishment test'. This test was applied in a number of cases.[330]

The impoverishment test came in for a great deal of criticism and was much debated.[331] In *Lipschitz NO v UDC Bank Ltd*[332] Miller JA referred to the criticism that had been levelled against s 38 and held that, valid as it might have been, there was no latitude for curtailment by the courts of the scope of the section. He said he was not convinced of the generality of the acceptance of the impoverishment test and that the judgment of Schreiner JA in *Gradwell's* case[333] did not justify such acceptance.[334] Such an interpretation, he said, unduly narrowed and restricted the terms of the section which 'expressly and unequivocally includes within the meaning of "financial assistance" acts not necessarily nor even probably involving impoverishment of the company or the employment at all of its "pecuniary resources".' He said:

> [the] giving by a company of a guarantee, or the provision by it of security, does not *per se* involve the actual or even probably disbursement or employment of the company's funds . . . yet, if such guarantee or security was provided by the company and if it were to be

---

[328] Perhaps there is more to the facts of the case and/or the court's reasoning than is expressed in the judgment, which might throw more light on the rationale for the decision. Counsel's reluctance to pursue the issue may have some bearing on the manner in which the court dealt with it. See further R Cassim & MF Cassim op cit n 323 at 37.

[329] 1959 (4) SA 419 (A).

[330] See *Miller v Muller* 1965 (4) SA 458 (C); *Bay Loan Investment (Pty) Ltd v Bay View (Pty) Ltd* 1972 (2) SA 313 (C); *Lomcord Agencies (Pty) Ltd v Amalgamated Construction Co (Pty) Ltd* 1976 (3) SA 86 (D); *Evrard v Ross* 1977 (2) SA 311 (D). A test very similar to the impoverishment test was referred to in *Burton v Palmer* [1980] 2 NSWLR 878 (SC) as the reduction or diminution of resources test.

[331] See IB Murray ' "Financial assistance" by company in connection with purchase of its shares' (1960) 77 *SALJ* 17 381; RC Beuthin 'Section 86*bis* — A new test for "financial assistance" ' (1973) *SALJ* 211.

[332] 1979 (1) SA 789 (A).

[333] *Lipschitz NO v UDC Bank Ltd* 1979 (1) SA 789 (A).

[334] *Lipschitz NO v UDC Bank Ltd* (supra) at 800. See also *Darvall v North Sydney Brick & Tile Co Ltd* [1989] 16 NSWLR 260; (1989) 15 ACLR 230 CA (NSW); *Milburn v Pivot Ltd* (1997) 149 ALR 439, 25 ACSR 237. But cf *Tallglen Pty Ltd v Optus Communications Pty Ltd* (1998) 28 ACSR 610.

established that it was provided for the purpose of or in connection with the purchase of the company's shares, the section would be shown to have been contravened whether or not such guarantee or security actually rendered or was likely to render the company poorer, for the section expressly provided that the giving of a guarantee for the provision of security constituted financial assistance. Clearly, the purpose of the Legislature in specifically including the giving of a guarantee and the provision of security in the concept of 'financial assistance' was to guard also against a company's merely exposing its funds to possible risk (as distinct from actually employing or depleting its funds) for the purpose of or in connection with the purpose of its shares.

Miller JA then said:

> I have no doubt that in certain cases, depending largely upon the form which the alleged financial assistance is said to have taken, the impoverishment test might be a helpful guide and might often yield a clear and decisive answer to the question whether financial assistance was given by the company.[335] But in other cases, of which I have given examples, the inquiry envisaged by the impoverishment test might not only be unhelpful but entirely irrelevant to the question whether what was done constituted financial assistance, although the state of the finances of the company and of other persons involved in the transactions, and other related circumstances, might indeed be relevant to and helpful in deciding a different question, namely, whether such assistance as was given was in truth given for the purpose of or in connection with the purchase of the company's shares.

It is clear from the judgment in *Lipschitz NO v UDC Bank Ltd* that, where the transaction in question consisted of a loan, a guarantee, or the provision of security, the impoverishment test was irrelevant, because these transactions were explicitly prohibited by s 38 irrespective of whether the company was or had not been rendered any poorer by the transaction in question.

In *Lewis v Oneanate (Pty) Ltd*[336] Nicholas AJA (giving the judgment of the Appellate Division and quoting Miller JA on some of the points) said the following propositions could be extracted from *Lipschitz* in regard to financial assistance:

1. The prohibition against the giving of financial assistance is couched in very wide terms. It relates to 'any' financial assistance, whether given 'directly or indirectly' and it relates to such assistance not only when it is given for the purpose of the purchase of or subscription for any shares in the company, but also when it is given 'in connection with' such purchase or subscription.
2. The prohibition contains two main elements — the giving of financial assistance, and the purpose for which it is given. Although the two elements are linked to form a single prohibition, they are vitally different in concept.
3. There is no comprehensive definition of 'financial assistance' in the section or elsewhere in the Act. From time to time various tests have been formulated by the courts as a guide to a proper answer to the question whether what a company has done in a given case constitutes the giving of 'financial assistance' within the meaning of the section.
4. One such test is the so-called 'impoverishment test', which asks the question, has the company become poorer as a result of what it did for the purpose of or in connection with the purchases of its shares?

---

[335] Cf *per* Lord Denning MR in *Wallersteiner v Moir* [1974] 3 All ER 217 (CA).
[336] 1992 (4) SA 811 (A) 816–17.

5. The application of the impoverishment test is not always appropriate.[337] In some cases the test may be a helpful guide and may often yield a clear and decisive answer to the problem. In other cases it may be not only unhelpful but irrelevant.
6. The section provides that the giving of a guarantee or the provision of security constitutes the giving of financial assistance. In such case, if the giving of the guarantee or the providing of the security is shown to be for the purpose of or in connection with the purchase of the company's shares, the section would be contravened, whether or not such guarantee or security actually renders or is likely to render the company poorer.

It has been held that the issue is whether 'in a practical business sense' financial assistance was given for the purpose of or in connection with the acquisition of the shares.[338]

Where an agreement is not genuine but is disguised in order to hide the true agreement (which is to provide financial assistance), the court will give effect to the true position, for example, where a company creates a fictitious debt to the seller[339] or enters into a fictitious service contract with the seller.[340]

Financial assistance will also have been given where the company purchased an asset at an inflated price or where the asset was not required for the purposes of its business,[341] even if a fair price was paid.[342] Where, however, the asset is bought by the company in the ordinary course of business in the genuine belief that the purchase is a good commercial proposition and the seller subsequently uses the proceeds to purchase shares in the company, there would be no financial assistance.[343]

Where it is a condition of a share sale that the company whose shares are being sold will pay an excessive rental to the seller in respect of a lease agreement between the company and the seller, financial assistance will have been given.[344]

The prohibition in s 38 is 'not confined to financial assistance to the purchaser'.[345] It is directed at financial assistance given to any person, provided that it

---

[337] In Australia the essence of financial assistance is that the company has 'diminished its financial resources, including future resources, in connection with the sale and purchase of its shares' (Hutley JA in *Burton v Palmer* [1980] 2 NSWLR 878 881. See also *Tallglen Pty Ltd v Optus Communications Pty Ltd* (1998) 28 ACSR 610 613–21; *Milburn v Pivot Ltd* (1997) 149 ALR 439, 25 ACSR 237.)
[338] *Sterileair (Pty) Ltd v Papallo* (1998) 29 ACSR 461 at 468. But *Cashmere Pacific Ltd v NZ Dairy Board* [1996] 1 NZLR 218 at 224.
[339] *Albert v Papenfus* 1964 (2) SA 713 (E); *Gray v Thesing Vastgoed BV* 1987 (1) SA 744 (A).
[340] *Goss v EC Goss & Co (Pty) Ltd* 1970 (1) SA 602 (D).
[341] *Gradwell (Pty) Ltd v Rostra Printers Ltd* 1959 (4) SA 419 (A) 425.
[342] *S v Hepker* 1973 (1) SA 472 (W) 479.
[343] *Belmont Finance Corp Ltd v Williams Furniture Ltd (No 2)* [1980] 1 All ER 393 (CA).
[344] See *Dyment v Boyden* [2004] 2 BCLC 423 ChD; [2005] 1 BCLC 163 (CA). In this case the court found that on the facts there had been no financial assistance 'for the purpose' of the acquisition.
[345] *EH Dey (Pty) Ltd v Dey* 1966 VR 464 at 470; *Jacobson v Liquidator of M Bulkin & Co Ltd* 1976 (3) SA 781 (T) 787–8; *Armour Hick Northern Ltd v Armour Trust Ltd* [1980] 3 All ER 833 (Ch) 837; *Re Myer Retail Investments Pty Ltd* (1983) 8 ACLR 102 SC (ACT); *Darvall v North Sydney Brick & Tile Co Ltd* (1987) 12 ACLR 537 SC (NSW) 559; *Ryan v Independent Steels Pty Ltd* (1988) 13 ACLR 379 SC (Vic); *Mercato Holdings v Crown Corp Ltd* [1989] 3 NZLR 704 at 708.

is for the purpose of a purchase of shares or in connection with a purchase of shares.[346]

8.4.4 The meaning of 'for the purpose of or in connection with'

Section 44 of the Act, like its predecessor in the 1973 Act, s 38, regulates the provision of financial assistance 'for the purpose of' or 'in connection with' the acquisition of the securities referred to.

In *Lipschitz NO v UDC Bank Ltd*,[347] Miller JA said, in relation to s 38 of the 1973 Act:

> [t]he prohibition in the section comprises two main elements; one is the giving of financial assistance, the other is the purpose for which it is given (or the 'in connection with' provisions). The two elements are linked to form a single prohibition, but although so linked they are vitally different in concept.

The impoverishment test, although not the sole test to determine what is meant by 'financial assistance',[348] may be relevant and helpful in deciding whether such assistance was given 'for the purpose of or in connection with' the purchase of the company's shares.[349] Knowing the financial position of the company and of others involved may also be useful in this regard.[350]

A distinction must be drawn between the 'purpose' and the 'motive' or 'reason' why a purpose is formed.[351] Motive is not the same as purpose.[352] Thus in *Brady v Brady*[353] the UK's House of Lords said:

> [i]f one postulates the case of a bidder for control of a public company financing his bid from the company's own funds, the obvious mischief at which the section is aimed, the immediate purpose which it is sought to achieve is that of completing the purchase and vesting control of the company in the bidder. The reasons why that course is considered desirable may be many and varied. The company may have fallen on hard times so that a change of management is considered necessary to avert disaster. It may merely be thought, and no doubt would be thought by the purchaser and the directors whom he nominates once he has control, that the business of the company will be more profitable under his management than it was heretofore ... but ... the purpose and the only purpose of the financial assistance is and remains that of enabling the shares to be acquired and the financial or commercial advantages flowing from the acquisition, are a by-product of it rather than independent purpose of which the assistance can properly be considered to be an incident.

---

[346] *EH Dey (Pty) Ltd v Dey* (supra); *Jacobson v Liquidator of M Bulkin & Co Ltd* (supra); *Armour Hick Northern Ltd v Armour Trust Ltd* [1980] 3 All ER 833 (Ch) 837; *Re Myer Retail Investments Pty Ltd* (supra); *Darvall v North Sydney Brick & Tile Co Ltd* (supra); *Ryan v Independent Steels Pty Ltd* (supra); *Mercato Holdings v Crown Corp Ltd* (supra) at 708. See also *Sterileair (Pty) Ltd v Papallo* (supra) at 466–8. See Rehana Cassim and Maleka Femida Cassim '*Gardner v Margo*: A misapplication of Section 38 of the Companies Act' (2007) 124 *SALJ* 37.
[347] 1979 (1) SA 789 (A) 799. See also *Sterileair (Pty) Ltd v Papallo* (supra) at 461.
[348] Ibid.
[349] *Lipschitz NO v UDC Bank Ltd* 1979 (1) SA 789 (A) 800; *Zentland Holdings (Pty) Ltd v Saambou Nasionale Bouvereniging* 1979 (4) SA 574 (C) 578; *Lewis v Oneanate (Pty) Ltd* 1992 (4) SA 811 (A).
[350] *Lipschitz NO v UDC Bank Ltd* (supra) at 800; *Zentland Holdings (Pty) Ltd v Saambou Nasionale Bouvereniging* (supra); *Lewis v Oneanate (Pty) Ltd* (supra).
[351] *Brady v Brady* [1988] 2 All ER 617 (HL) 633.
[352] *Independent Steels (Pty) Ltd v Ryan* (1989) 15 ACLR 518 SC (Vic) 524.
[353] [1988] 2 All ER 617 (HL) 633.

It is uncertain whether by 'purpose' is meant 'sole purpose'. In *Lipschitz NO v UDC Bank Ltd*[354] the question was raised but left unanswered because it was not necessary to deal with the issue.[355]

The meaning of the words 'in connection with' was dealt with by the Appellate Division in *Lipschitz NO v UDC Bank Ltd*.[356] As mentioned before regarding Miller JA's dictum in *Lipschitz*, the court said the meaning of the words was profoundly affected by the concept 'for the purpose of' to which it was an alternative. The words appeared to have been inserted to cover a situation where, although the actual purpose of the company in giving financial assistance might not have been established, the conduct of the company nevertheless stood in such close relationship to the purchase of its shares that substantially, if not precisely, its conduct was similar to that of a company that was giving the forbidden assistance with the purpose described in the section. The words had been inserted merely to close possible loopholes and not to create a different type of offence, or a lesser offence, or to prohibit conduct that was not substantially similar to the conduct prohibited by the main provision characterised by the words 'for the purpose of'. The exact extent of the enlargement of the scope of the prohibition could obviously not be defined, everything depending upon the facts peculiar to each individual case. However, it could be said that, where the purpose of the company was something other than the purchase of its shares, there would in general be little room for a finding that the act had nevertheless been performed 'in connection with' the purchase of shares.

The court gave the following example. Company A, for its own purposes, guarantees B's overdraft at a bank so as to enable B to carry on his business of manufacturing certain equipment which Company A necessarily requires for its business and which equipment it purchases from B. Company A knows at the time of giving the guarantee that B, who has confidence in the stability and management of his company, intends to invest in shares in Company A the surplus profits he will make as a result of being able to continue his manufacturing business by reason of the overdraft facilities made available to him by virtue of A's guarantee. The guarantee given by A clearly amounts to the giving of financial assistance to B, but not at all for the purpose of the purchase of the company's shares; its purpose, clearly established, was to enable B to continue producing the equipment required by A. In such a case there would be no room for finding that, because A knew of B's ultimate intention regarding the purchase of shares in the company, the financial assistance given by A, although not given for the purpose of purchasing shares but for a different purpose, was nevertheless 'in connection' with the purchase of shares and was therefore in contravention of the section.

---

[354] 1979 (1) SA 789 (A) 800.
[355] In Australia it is sufficient if a subsidiary's purpose is to facilitate the purchase of the shares. That means the purpose requirement is satisfied. See *Saltergate Insurance Co Ltd v Knight* [1982] 1 NSWLR 369 at 378; cf *Darvall v North Sydney Brick & Tile Co Ltd* (1987) 12 ACLR 537 SC (NSW). In the UK the position is not entirely clear. See *Belmont Finance Corp Ltd v Williams Furniture Ltd (No 2)* [1980] 1 All ER 393 (CA). In New Zealand it appears that it does not have to be the sole purpose. See *Cashmere Pacific Ltd v NZ Dairy Board* [1996] 1 NZLR 218 224.
[356] 1979 (1) SA 789 (A) 804–5; cf *Darvall v North Sydney Brick & Tile Co Ltd* (supra).

Where a seller's credit loan account was being sold as well as his or her shares, it was held in relation to s 38 of the 1973 Act that financial assistance by the company to purchase the loan account would not infringe s 38, even though it facilitated the purchase of the shares.[357] In such circumstances the financial assistance could not be construed as being 'in connection with' the purchase of the shares.[358] Nor was s 38 contravened where, through a reciprocal arrangement, Company A gave financial assistance for the purchase of shares in Company B and Company B gave financial assistance for the purchase of shares in Company A.[359]

8.4.5 Purchase of or subscription for securities

Section 44 regulates financial assistance for the 'purchase' of or 'subscription' for 'securities', which means that s 44 is wider in its scope of operation than s 38 of the 1973 Act, which referred only to 'shares'.

Section 1 of the Act provides that 'securities' has the meaning set out in s 1 of the Securities Services Act.[360] Section 1 of that Act provides the following definition:

'securities' —
(a) means —
  (i) shares, stocks and depository receipts in public companies and other equivalent equities, other than shares in a share block company as defined in the Share Blocks Control Act, 1980 (Act No 59 of 1980);
  (ii) notes;
  (iii) derivative instruments;
  (iv) bonds;
  (v) debentures;
  (vi) participatory interests in a collective investment scheme as defined in the Collective Investment Schemes Control Act, 2002 (Act No. 45 of 2002), and units or any other form of participation in a foreign collective investment scheme approved by the Registrar of Collective Investment Schemes in terms of section 65 of that Act;
  (vii) units or any other form of participation in a collective investment scheme licensed or registered in a foreign country;
  (viii) instruments based on an index;
  (ix) the securities contemplated in subparagraphs (i) to (viii) that are listed on an external exchange; and
  (x) an instrument similar to one or more of the securities contemplated in subparagraphs (i) to (ix) declared by the registrar by notice in the *Gazette* to be a security for the purposes of this Act;
  (xi) rights in the securities referred to in subparagraphs (i) to (x);
(b) excludes —
  (i) money market instruments except for the purposes of Chapter IV;
  (ii) any security contemplated in paragraph *(a)* specified by the registrar by notice in the *Gazette*.

The reference to 'purchase' and 'subscription' makes it clear that s 44 applies where a company:

---
[357] *Lipschitz NO v UDC Bank Ltd* 1979 (1) SA 789 (A) 806.
[358] *Lipschitz NO v UDC Bank Ltd* (supra).
[359] *Lipschitz NO v UDC Bank Ltd* (supra).
[360] Act 36 of 2004.

- assists a person in purchasing a security in the company from the holder of the security, and
- assists a person in acquiring a security in the company from the company itself (in other words, where the person subscribes to the company for the security).

Section 44 is only concerned with a purchase or a subscription. If the financial assistance relates to any other transaction, the section is not operative. Accordingly, where the financial assistance relates to the cancellation of a share sale[361] the section is not contravened.

Whether a 'subscription' includes an exchange of shares is uncertain.[362] In a different context, namely the definition of 'offer' in s 142 of the 1973 Act, in relation to an offer of shares to the public requiring a prospectus, the Supreme Court of Appeal has held that 'subscription' includes an exchange of shares.[363] The inclusion of an exchange of shares in s 44 could have far-reaching implications for, inter alia, certain BEE transactions. Thus it has been said, in relation to s 38 of the 1973 Act, that:[364]

> [a] somewhat disturbing implication of the decision of the Supreme Court of Appeal in *Gold Fields* is that there is no reason why its definition of a 'subscription' should not apply to s 38, or for that matter to any other section of the Act in which the word appears. Should the prohibition against a company giving financial assistance for the subscription of its shares be extended to apply to a share exchange transaction, this would have a severe impact on some of the black empowerment transactions which have recently taken place, and which have been justified as being in the public interest. The problem of access to capital in empowerment transactions has of late been addressed by way of elaborate financing structures. These structures are multi-layered and complex, with the result that the parties frequently run the risk of contravening s 38. Depending on its particular financing structures, it is quite conceivable that an empowerment transaction may be seen to have effected a share exchange. Extending the meaning of a 'subscription' to include a share exchange would thus heighten the risk of such a transaction being declared void as a contravention of s 38. This result was surely not intended by the legislature.

In *Johnson v Johnson*,[365] as a result of a dispute between the two shareholders of a company, the minority shareholder's shares were converted into redeemable preference shares and were redeemed, and the company paid the shareholder a large amount for a restraint of trade undertaking. It was held that no contravention of s 38 had taken place since there had been no purchase of or subscription for shares.

Section 38 of the 1973 Act governed financial assistance for the purchase of a subscription for shares 'made or to be made', indicating that whether the assistance was given before or after the purchase or subscription did not matter. No such wording appears in s 44 of the current Act. However, it is submitted that these words in s 38 were redundant, ie the section would have had its desired

---

[361] See *Pires v American Fruit Market (Pty) Ltd* 1952 (2) SA 337 (T).
[362] See Blackman et al op cit n 38 at 4–65.
[363] See *Gold Fields Ltd v Harmony Gold Mining Co Ltd* 2005 (2) SA 506 (SCA).
[364] See MF Cassim *'Gold Fields v Harmony:* A lost opportunity to clarify section 145 of the Companies Act' (2005) *SALJ* 269 at 274–5.
[365] 1983 (2) SA 324 (W); see also *Harrison v Harrison* 1952 (3) SA 417 (N).

effect without them, and that s 44 will apply whether or not the purchase or subscription has been made at the time of the assistance.

The prohibition in s 44(2) of the Act relates to securities 'issued or to be issued' by the company concerned. These words were possibly included to counter the technical argument that financial assistance for the purchase of shares not yet in existence is not assistance for obtaining shares of the company.[366]

Section 44 also applies to financial assistance provided for the subscription of any 'option'.[367] However, the section only applies in relation to options where a 'subscription' is involved and not a 'purchase'. It is not clear what the rationale is for this distinction. Furthermore, s 44 does not state what the options are in respect of. The wording is wide enough to cover options to acquire any property of the company.

8.4.6 Authority for provision of financial assistance

The opening words of s 44(2) are: 'To the extent that the Memorandum of Incorporation of a company provides otherwise, the board may authorise' the provision of financial assistance as envisaged by s 44.

The wording 'To the extent that the Memorandum of Incorporation of a company provides otherwise' is confusing. Better wording is to be found in s 45(2) in relation to financial assistance to directors, namely, 'Except to the extent that the Memorandum of Incorporation of a company provides otherwise', followed by a list of conditions for the provision of loans to directors.[368]

Section 44(2) gives the authority to provide financial assistance to the board of directors. However, the opening words of s 44(2) (referred to in the previous paragraph) indicate the legislature's intention that the Memorandum of Incorporation may remove or substitute the board's authority (for example by the authority of the members in general meeting) or qualify or restrict it in some way. This is borne out by s 44(4), which provides that the board must ensure that 'any conditions or restrictions respecting the granting of financial assistance set out in the company's Memorandum of Incorporation have been satisfied'.

The authority to provide financial assistance is subject to satisfaction of the requirements of s 44(3) and (4), which are dealt with below.

---

[366] J Yeats and R Jooste 'Financial assistance – a new approach' (2009) *SALJ* 566 at 575.

[367] It is not clear whether s 38 of the 1973 Act prohibited financial assistance for the purchase of an option to purchase or subscribe for shares. It is arguable that the words 'directly or indirectly' in s 38(1) of the 1973 Act had the effect, inter alia, of including options. It may be, however, that this was only the case if the option was exercised and there was actually a purchase. If there was no exercise of the option and therefore no ensuing purchase, it is arguable that there was no contravention. On the other hand, it may be arguable that what is important is the purpose of the assistance, and if the purpose was to assist in the purchase of the option, the purpose was indirectly to assist in the purchase of the shares and the fact that the option was never exercised was irrelevant. The more precise wording of s 44(2) of the Act has also put paid to this uncertainty. In the past similar problems of interpretation existed in relation to debentures convertible to shares, ie whether financial assistance in regard to such instruments was prohibited or not. Fortunately the definition of 'securities' in the new Act has settled this debate as the definition specifically provides that securities means, inter alia, debentures. (See Yeats & Jooste op cit n 366 at 574.)

[368] See Yeats & Jooste op cit n 366 at 572. The draft Companies Amendment Bill, 2010 proposes the substitution of such wording.

8.4.7 Requirements of s 44(3) and (4)

Irrespective of what the Memorandum of Incorporation may say, financial assistance is prohibited unless the requirements set out in s 44(3) and (4) are met. The requirements are:

- the particular provision of financial assistance must be pursuant to an employee share scheme that satisfies the requirements of section 97,[369] or pursuant to a special resolution of the shareholders, adopted within the previous two years, which approved such assistance either for the specific recipient, or generally for a category of potential recipients, and the specific recipient falls within that category,[370]
- the board must be satisfied that immediately after providing the financial assistance, the company would satisfy the solvency and liquidity test,
- the board must be satisfied that the terms under which the financial assistance is proposed to be given are fair and reasonable to the company,[371] and
- the board must ensure that any conditions or restrictions respecting the granting of financial assistance set out in the company's Memorandum of Incorporation have been satisfied.[372]

It is of note that two of the specifically exempted transactions contained in the 1973 Act, namely the making of loans to *bona fide* employees[373] and the provision of financial assistance for the acquisition of shares in a company by the company or its subsidiary,[374] have not been repeated in the current Act. In these circumstances, a company will therefore have to comply with the general requirements of a special resolution, the solvency and liquidity test, as well as the 'fair and reasonable' determination. This makes the requirements more onerous than they were before.[375]

(a) The special resolution requirement

The financial assistance must either be pursuant to a s 97 employee share scheme, or to a special resolution adopted within the previous two years that approved such assistance for a specific recipient or generally for a category of potential recipients (and the specific recipient falls within that category).[376]

As has been pointed out,[377] what may prove to be problematic is the resolution approving financial assistance generally for a category of potential recipients. Needless to say, the special resolution requirement will have administrative and cost implications for companies (especially large public companies and listed companies). A pragmatic board may therefore decide to propose a suitably drafted resolution at, for example, the annual general meeting every two years. The

---

[369] Section 44(3)*(a)*(i).
[370] Section 44(3)*(a)*(ii).
[371] Section 44(3)*(b)*.
[372] Section 44(4).
[373] Section 38(2)*(c)*.
[374] Section 38(2)*(d)*.
[375] Yeats & Jooste op cit n 366 at 580.
[376] Section 44(3)*(a)*.
[377] Yeats & Jooste op cit n 366 at 579.

question then arises whether a category or categories of potential recipients may be so widely framed so as to effectively give the board the discretion whether to provide the assistance or not without consulting the shareholders again. So, for example, would it satisfy the requirements of s 44(3) and (4) if the shareholders resolve that the company may provide financial assistance to any person if, in the opinion of the directors, the provision of such financial assistance would serve to further the BEE objectives of the company? This possibility would largely remove the protection ostensibly afforded to shareholders by the resolution requirement, because in these circumstances the board will be able to provide financial assistance without obtaining shareholder approval. However, nothing that appears from the section militates against such an interpretation, nor is there anything in the Act that prevents the passing of a number of such 'boilerplate' resolutions, widely framed, in respect of a number of different categories of recipients every two years as a matter of course.[378]

(b) The solvency and liquidity test

The second requirement, embodying the 'solvency and liquidity test', is governed by s 4 of the Act. The test has been dealt with in detail in 8.1.4 and will not be repeated here.

The solvency and liquidity test must be satisfied immediately after providing the financial assistance.

(c) Fair and reasonable terms

The board of directors may not authorise any financial assistance unless it is satisfied that 'the terms under which the assistance is proposed to be given are fair and reasonable to the company'.[379] It will be recognised that this requirement makes the Act tougher to negotiate than s 38 of the 1973 Act. As a result of the exception to s 38 introduced by the amendment in 2006, as long as there was a special resolution and the solvency and liquidity criteria were met, there was no contravention of s 38 even if the terms under which the assistance was given were not fair and reasonable to the company. As has been said[380] the change is to be welcomed, although it is not clear what is meant by 'the terms under which the assistance is proposed' being 'fair and reasonable to the company'. Does it mean that, viewed from a commercial perspective, the transaction, whatever it might be, will benefit the company? In other words, must there be a reasonable *quid pro quo*? Or does it simply mean that the company is provided with 'fair and reasonable' security? If the latter, and this needs to be clarified, it may be appropriate to include the provisions of s 37(3)*(c)* of the 1973 Act. Section 37 regulates loans and security provided by a company on behalf of its holding company or fellow subsidiary. Section 37(3)*(a)* imposes liability on a director or officer of the company where the 'terms or conditions' of the loan or the provision of security

---

[378] It is to be noted that the previous version of this section as contained in the Companies Bill, 2007 provided for an identical resolution to be valid for a period of five years. The reduced period therefore represents improved protection in at least this respect.
[379] See third bullet above under 8.4.7.
[380] See Yeats & Jooste op cit n 366 at 576–7.

'were not fair to the company or failed to provide reasonable protection for its business interests'. Section 37(3)*(c)* enlarges on what is meant here by providing that:

> [i]nquiring ... whether or not any terms or conditions were fair to the company or failed to provide reasonable protection for its business interests, regard shall be had, without prejudice to the generality of the enquiry, to —
> (i) whether, in view of the financial position of the parties, the loan should have been made or the security should have been provided at all;
> (ii) in the case of a loan, whether security has been or should in the circumstances have been provided therefor, and whether any security provided therefor is adequate;
> (iii) the consideration for the loan or security, including any interest or other benefit received therefor;
> (iv) the term of the loan or security; and
> (v) the manner of repayment of the loan or discharge of the security.

It may also be appropriate to exclude this requirement where all the members of the company have consented to the assistance.[381]

It is to be noted[382] that the provision in the New Zealand Companies Act 1993 dealing with financial assistance also requires the terms and conditions under which the assistance is given to be fair and reasonable to the company[383] but in addition that 'giving the assistance is in the best interests of the company'.[384]

The relevant part of section 76 of the New Zealand Companies Act reads as follows:

> (2) A company may give financial assistance ... if the board has previously resolved that —
> *(a)* The company should provide the assistance; and
> *(b)* Giving the assistance is in the best interests of the company; and
> *(c)* The terms and conditions under which the assistance is given are fair and reasonable to the company.
> (3) The resolution must set out in full the grounds for the directors' conclusions.

The fact that the 'fair and reasonable terms' requirement in the New Zealand Companies Act is preceded by the requirement that the assistance must also be in the best interests of the company provides some context for the phrase, which we do not currently have (there is no 'best interests of the company' requirement in the Act). One can reason that, while 'best interests' is aimed at protecting the shareholders of the company, 'fair and reasonable terms' is possibly aimed at protecting its creditors. However, this raises the question whether, in our interpretation of the phrase, we must assume that the drafters have intentionally omitted the 'best interest' requirement from the South African legislation. If so, does this mean that 'fair and reasonable' is intended to serve as a protection mechanism for both creditors and shareholders, or that the focus here is on the protection of creditors rather than shareholders of the company?[385]

---

[381] See s 37(5) of the 1973 Act. Yeats & Jooste op cit n 366 at 577.
[382] See Yeats & Jooste op cit n 366 at 577.
[383] Section 76(2)*(c)*.
[384] Section 76(2)*(b)*.
[385] See Yeats & Jooste op cit n 366 at 578.

It is of note[386] that s 60(3) of the New Zealand Companies Act requires that a general offer by a company to acquire its own shares may be made only if the board has resolved that the acquisition is in the best interests of the company and that the terms and price of the offer are fair and reasonable to the company. In relation to this requirement and to the requirements with regard to financial assistance (which also include, in the current context, a board resolution that giving the assistance is of benefit to those shareholders not receiving the assistance and that the terms and conditions under which the assistance is given are fair and reasonable to those shareholders not receiving the assistance) David Jones, a New Zealand author,[387] has commented as follows:

> In exercising the power to repurchase the shares of a company, directors of the company must to do so in good faith, and in what each director considers to be in the best interests of the company, as required by the duty of loyalty imposed on each director by the 1993 Act. An interesting issue is whether the duty of loyalty subsumes the requirements of s 60(3) [this subsection includes the best interests and fair and reasonable requirements] . . . In large part it probably does so.

With respect to the financial assistance requirements, Jones states that:

> As with the power of the board to repurchase shares, the directors of a company in exercising the power to provide financial assistance must do so in what each director considers to be the best interests of the company, as required by the duty of loyalty imposed on each director by the 1993 Act. It is difficult to give guidance to directors in these circumstances as to what additional considerations are required of them to be satisfied that the assistance is of benefit to shareholders not receiving the assistance and the terms and conditions of the assistance are fair and reasonable to those shareholders. The better view is that if the directors satisfy the duty of loyalty in resolving to give the financial assistance, then they will probably satisfy these additional requirements.[388]

The directors' duty of loyalty to which the author refers is the duty contained in s 131(1) of the New Zealand Companies Act, which requires a director to act in good faith in what the director believes to be in the best interests of the company. According to Jones this preserves the common-law duty of loyalty.[389] The Act, in s 91(1)*(b)* also spells out the duty of a director to 'act honestly and in good faith, and in a manner the director reasonably believes to be in the best interests of, and for the benefit of, the company'. It seems therefore that in the South African context one could possibly make the same statement in relation to the interplay between directors' duties and what is required of the board under s 44 of the Act — if a director satisfies the requirements of s 91(1)*(b)* in deciding whether to grant financial assistance, he or she will probably satisfy any additional requirements posed by s 44. If this is correct, the only rationale for the inclusion of the 'fair and reasonable' criterion in s 44(3)*(b)*(ii) seems to be the possible liability of a director to the company or its shareholders created in s 44(6) of the Act.[390]

---

[386] Ibid.
[387] See David O Jones *Company Law in New Zealand – A Guide to the Companies Act 1993* (1993) 34.
[388] Ibid.
[389] Ibid.
[390] Yeats & Jooste op cit n 366 at 579.

It is of note[391] that the same 'fair and reasonable' requirement that appeared in s 45, which deals with loans or other financial assistance to directors, was included in the Companies Bill, 2007, but deleted from the Companies Act of 2008 in terms of the amendments agreed to and made by the Portfolio Committee, probably at least partly as a result of the public comments received in this regard. It is not clear why the two sections are dealt with differently.

8.4.8 Extension to a 'related or inter-related' company

Section 44 of the Act applies not only to financial assistance by a company for the acquisition of securities in itself but also securities in 'a related or inter-related *[sic]* company'.[392] This goes much further than s 38 of the 1973 Act, which only covered financial assistance by a company for the acquisition of shares in itself or its holding company. An obvious illustrative example of the new extended ambit of s 44 is that, whereas in the 1973 Act there was no bar to a company providing financial assistance for the purchase of shares in its subsidiary or a fellow subsidiary, these transactions now fall squarely within the ambit of s 44.

8.4.9 Consequences of contravention of s 44

(a) Voidness

Section 44(5) of the Act provides that a board decision or agreement to provide financial assistance is void to the extent that the provision of that assistance would be inconsistent either with s 44 or with any conditions or restrictions in respect of the granting of financial assistance set out in the Memorandum of Incorporation of the company.

(b) Statutory Turquand Rule

What adds to the confusion regarding the voidness of a transaction that contravenes s 44 is the 'statutory Turquand Rule' in s 20(7) and (8). The Turquand Rule is a rule of common law,[393] which is generally expressed by saying that a person dealing with a company in good faith is entitled to assume that all internal formalities or acts of management have been duly performed and carried out by the company. Section 20(7) and (8) of the Act provides:

> (7) A person dealing with a company in good faith, other than a director, prescribed officer or shareholder of the company, is entitled to presume that the company, in making any decision in the exercise of its powers, has complied with all of the formal and procedural requirements in terms of this Act, its Memorandum of Incorporation and any rules of the company unless, in the circumstances, the person knew or reasonably ought to have known of any failure by the company to comply with any such requirement.

---

[391] Yeats & Jooste op cit n 366 at 579.
[392] See s 2 of the Act as to what constitutes a 'related or inter-related person'. See chapter 6: Groups of Companies and Related Persons in this regard.
[393] *Royal British Bank v Turquand* (1855) 5 E and B 248; affirmed (1856) 6 E and B 327; [1843–60] All ER Rep 435.

(8) Subsection (7) must be construed concurrently with, and not in substitution for, any relevant common law principle relating to the presumed validity of the actions of a company in the exercise of its powers.

The effect of s 20(7) appears to be that where a company, for example, contracts to provide financial assistance to a third party to enable that third party to acquire shares in the company and the board of directors has failed to satisfy itself, as required by s 44(3)*(b)*(ii) of the Act, that 'the terms under which the assistance is proposed to be given are fair and reasonable to the company', or the board has agreed to provide financial assistance in conflict with conditions or restrictions in respect of the granting of financial assistance (as set out in the Memorandum of Incorporation of the company), the third party is protected and can presume that the company has complied with all the formal and procedural requirements of the legislation.[394]

Section 44(5) of the Act explicitly states that a board decision or agreement to provide financial assistance is void to the extent that the provision of that assistance would be inconsistent either with s 44 or with any conditions or restrictions regarding the granting of financial assistance in the Memorandum of Incorporation of the company. It is not clear how s 20(7) and s 44(5) are intended to work together. If the agreement is void the third party is not protected. This confusion is compounded by the fact that, although s 20(7) provides that the third party may presume compliance with the Act, it does not specify what the legal effect of this presumption is on the validity of the transaction in question. Furthermore, the reference in s 20(8) to the fact that s 20(7) should be construed concurrently with 'any common law principle relating to the presumed validity of the actions of a company in the exercise of its powers' is puzzling. The relevant common-law principle which springs to mind is the doctrine of estoppel, but it is hard to fathom why it would be necessary to prove estoppel when it is far easier to use s 20(7) and hence why (and how) these constructs would be used in conjunction with one another. It also raises the question whether the application of the Turquand Rule under common law is excluded by the statutory provision or whether, under

---

[394] Note that once the third party becomes a shareholder in terms of the Act, he or she loses the protection of s 20(7). In s 1 of the Act 'shareholder' is defined as 'the holder of a share issued by a company and who is entered as such in the certificated or uncertificated company register, as the case may be'. Thus it is fair to state that the problem sketched in the example is self-limiting. There will come a point in the third party's dealings with the company when he or she is no longer entitled to presume that the company has complied with all the formal and procedural requirements of the Act. However, at the time that he or she initially deals with the company (and when the board must consider the terms of the assistance), he or she is an ordinary third party who is not privy to the internal workings of the company. This raises the question whether, when they in fact do become a shareholder, they are deemed to have knowledge of whether company decisions prior to their becoming a shareholder complied with the Act or the Memorandum of Incorporation in the manner contemplated or not, ie do they lose the protection of s 20(7) retrospectively?

s 20(8), it could be used instead of or in conjunction with s 20(7),[395] notwithstanding the apparent negation of the doctrine of constructive notice by s 19.[396]

(c) Criminal consequences

The 1973 Act made a contravention of s 38 a criminal offence.[397] Section 44 of the Act, on the other hand, contains no criminal liability provision. A punitive sanction that appears possible is a fine of an administrative nature flowing from a failure to comply with a compliance notice issued by the Companies and Intellectual Property Commission ('the Companies Commission') established in terms of s 185 of the Act.[398] It has been submitted[399] that, although the decriminalisation of companies legislation in many respects is an appropriate and positive development, the threat of potential criminal liability for directors was an effective deterrent in certain contexts and the criminal liability provision should have been retained for the purposes of sections such as this one. Commercially, the potential gain to be made by a company or individuals where financial assistance is provided otherwise than in accordance with the section, may well exceed the maximum administrative fine. If the criminal sanction has been removed, this means there is less legal imperative for compliance especially if, as discussed above, it is not the contravention of the Act but the court ruling that makes the tainted transaction void.

(d) Liability of directors

Section 38 of the 1973 Act imposes no civil liability on the directors of a company responsible for a contravention of s 38 by the company.

In the new Act, s 44(6) read with s 77(3)(e)(iv) provides that a director is liable for any loss, damages or costs sustained by the company as a direct or indirect consequence of the director having been present at a meeting, or participated in

---

[395] Section 20(7) and (8) should be read with s 19(4) and (5), which provides:
'(4) Subject to subsection (5), a person must not be regarded as having received notice or knowledge of the contents of any document relating to a company merely because the document —
(a) has been filed; or
(b) is accessible for inspection at an office of the company.
(5) A person must be regarded as having received notice and knowledge of —
(a) any provision of a company's Memorandum of Incorporation contemplated in section 15(2)(b) if the company's Notice of Incorporation or a Notice of Amendment has drawn attention to the provision, as contemplated in section 13(3); or
(b) the effect of subsection (3) on a personal liability company.'

[396] This approach seems to indicate that the drafters rejected the idea of the modern formulation of the Turquand Rule as an extension of the doctrine of estoppel. The modern formulation holds that all the rule does is to temper the doctrine of constructive notice. The rule simply prevents the company from arguing that a third party is precluded from relying on estoppel due to their deemed knowledge of the internal requirement in question. See in this regard MS Blackman et al op cit n 38.

[397] See s 38(3) of the 1973 Act.

[398] See s 171 of the Act. An administrative fine can be imposed by the court in an amount not exceeding the greater of 10 per cent of the respondent's annual turnover during the preceding financial year and an amount to be prescribed by the Minister by way of regulation subject to a maximum fine of R1 000 000. See s 175(1) of the Act. The constitutionality of the administrative fine may be questionable.

[399] See Yeats & Jooste op cit n 366 at 584.

the making of a decision adopted by written consent of a majority of the directors, and failing to vote against the provision of financial assistance as contemplated in s 44, despite knowing that the provision of such financial assistance was inconsistent with the requirements of the section, to the extent that the resolution or agreement has been declared void in terms of s 44(5) read with s 218(1).

It appears that subjective knowledge on the part of the director is a requirement. This can be contrasted with s 77(4)*(a)*, which deals with the liability of a director who has failed to vote against a distribution in contravention of s 46. In terms of that section, liability arises only if the company does not satisfy the liquidity and solvency test and 'it was unreasonable at the time of the decision to conclude that the company would satisfy the liquidity and solvency test' — clearly an objective test. It is not apparent what the reason for the discrepancy between these sections is, but the effect is arguably to make it more difficult to hold a director liable for a contravention of s 44 than of s 45.

Section 77(7) provides that proceedings to recover any loss, damages or costs for which a person is or may be held liable in terms of the section may not be commenced more than three years after the act or omission that gave rise to the liability. This constitutes a type of 'statute of limitations' provision as far as actions against directors and prescribed officers of a company are concerned. What is of note is the difference between the wording of this subsection and provisions of the Prescription Act,[400] which state that a three-year prescription period for extinction of a debt shall begin to run as soon as the debt is due and that a debt shall not be deemed to be due until the creditor has knowledge of the identity of the debtor and of the facts from which the debt arises.[401] It is therefore quite conceivable that the commencement dates of the three-year period in these two pieces of legislation may be different and it is not clear which would prevail in the event of such a conflict.[402]

The confusion regarding the voidness of a transaction contravening s 44 referred to above also continues in this section. In terms of s 77(3)*(e)*(iv) it appears that the directors' liability only arises once the relevant resolution or agreement has been declared void, yet the three-year prescription period runs from the date of the act or omission that gave rise to the liability. Is one to understand from this that the taking of a prohibited resolution marks the beginning of the three-year period, but that the liability attached to that transgression only arises once the court has declared the resolution void, ie possibly three years or more (depending on the length of the case) after the act has occurred? How does this interact with the potential common-law liability based on the directors' duties of care and skill in a prohibited act of this nature — does liability arise at the time of the act (as one would expect and as seems to be the case in terms of s 77(2)*(a)*), which would mean that this occurs at a different point in time than the statutory liability? Does common-law liability still exist in this context irrespective of

---

[400] Act 68 of 1969.
[401] Section 12.
[402] See Yeats & Jooste op cit n 366 at 585.

whether the act giving rise to such liability is ultimately declared void in terms of s 77(3)*(e)*(iv) or not?

It would seem that the simplest way for a director to avoid liability in terms of this section would be not to attend the meeting or participate in the making of the decision at all if he or she is uncertain whether the requirements of s 44 will be complied with or not, or if he or she would prefer not to vote against a particular resolution for political reasons.[403]

Section 40(4) of the Companies Bill, 2007 imposed liability on the director responsible for the contravention to compensate not only the company, but also any shareholder for any loss, damages or costs that the shareholder may have sustained or incurred in relation to the transaction. (It was unclear whether this meant that a shareholder could bring an action based on a drop in the value of his or her shares brought about by the contravention.) Furthermore, the meaning of s 40(4)(i)*(b)* was unclear. The provision stated that a director, 'may be held as responsible as the company, in terms of this Act, for the contravention'. There was no indication of what responsibility of the company the provision was referring to. In the Companies Act of 2008 s 44 is silent on the issue. However, s 20(6) states that:

> (6) Each shareholder of a company has a claim for damages against any person who causes the company to do anything inconsistent with —
> *(a)* this Act; or
> *(b)* a limitation, restriction or qualification contemplated in this section, unless that action has been ratified by the shareholders in terms of subsection (2).

This presumably means that a shareholder has a claim for damages against a director who causes the company to provide financial assistance in a manner inconsistent with the provisions of s 44. In addition, s 218(2) states that:

> (2) Any person who contravenes any provision of this Act is liable to any other person for any loss or damage suffered by that person as a result of that contravention.

This constitutes grounds for a claim against a director for a s 44 contravention, but also once again raises the question of whether a shareholder could bring an action based on a drop in the value of his or her shares brought about by the contravention.

It is unfortunate that liability is not extended to the directors of the holding company of the company contravening the s 44. After all, they are usually the main culprits.

8.5 FINANCIAL ASSISTANCE TO DIRECTORS ET AL[404]

8.5.1 Introduction

Those in control of a company's finances are in a position of power, a position that has the potential for abuse, particularly where the company provides the controllers with loans or security. Recognising the potential for abuse, the 1973 Act contained a number of provisions:

---

[403] See Yeats & Jooste op cit n 366 at 586.
[404] See also chapter 10. See R Jooste 'Financial assistance to directors — the Companies Act 71 of 2008' 2010 *Acta Juridica* 165.

- prohibiting certain loans and provisions of security (s 226);[405]
- imposing a strict liability on directors in certain circumstances (s 37);
- requiring special disclosure in the annual financial statements of certain transactions (ss 37, 295 and 296).

The corresponding (but by no means equivalent) provisions of the new Act appear in s 45 and s 30(4)(a) read with s 30(6). Section 45 attempts to regulate certain transactions by prohibiting them unless certain requirements are satisfied. Section 30(4)(a) read with s 30(6) requires disclosure in a company's financial statements of the particulars of some of these transactions.

A comparison of the provisions of the 1973 Act and the new Act aimed at preventing abuse of the powerful position of directors indicates that in some respects the proposed new provisions are more stringent than the old, but that in other respects the converse is true. The new provisions cast their tentacles far wider, drawing in a far more extensive range of transactions, as well as parties to such transactions, to which the provisions apply. The extent of this range is such that a vigilant, law-abiding company will be faced with an onerous task in assuring itself that it has complied with the law. It is submitted that the net has been cast too wide, capturing situations that are no threat to the company in question, situations that do not involve any potential abuse of the powerful position of directors. On the other hand, the liability provisions are too heavily weighted in favour of directors, and the confusing powers of the court to relieve recalcitrant directors are unfounded. An analysis of the new provisions also brings to light a host of problems of interpretation not apparently envisaged by the legislature. Legislative amendment is clearly necessary to address the situation.

8.5.2 Section 45

Section 45 regulates the giving of financial assistance by a company to its directors but also to its prescribed officers and certain related and interrelated companies.

For ease of reference, s 45 is quoted in full:

45 (1) In this section, 'financial assistance' —
(a) includes lending money, guaranteeing a loan or other obligation, and securing any debt or obligation; but
(b) does not include —
  (i) lending money in the ordinary course of business by a company whose primary business is the lending of money;
  (ii) an accountable advance to meet —
    (aa) legal expenses in relation to a matter concerning the company; or
    (bb) anticipated expenses to be incurred by the person on behalf of the company; or
  (iii) an amount to defray the person's expenses for removal at the company's request.

(2) Except to the extent that the Memorandum of Incorporation of a company provides otherwise, the board may authorize the company to provide direct or indirect financial assistance to a director or prescribed officer of the company or of a related or inter-related company, or to a related or inter-related company or corporation, or to a member of a related

---
[405] For an analysis of s 226 see R Jooste 'Loans to directors — an analysis of section 226 of the Companies Act' 2000 *SALJ* 269.

or inter-related corporation, or to a person related to any such company, corporation, director, prescribed officer or member, subject to subsections (3) and (4).

(3) Despite any provision of a company's Memorandum of Incorporation to the contrary, the board may not authorize any financial assistance contemplated in subsection (2), unless —
  (a) the particular provision of financial assistance is —
    (i) pursuant to an employee share scheme that satisfies the requirements of section 97; or
    (ii) pursuant to a special resolution of the shareholders, adopted within the previous 2 years, which approved such assistance either for the specific recipient, or generally for a category of potential recipients, and the specific recipient falls within that category, and
  (b) the board is satisfied that immediately after providing the financial assistance, the company would satisfy the solvency and liquidity test.

(4) In addition to satisfying the requirements of subsection (3), the board must ensure that any conditions or restrictions respecting the granting of financial assistance set out in the company's Memorandum of Incorporation have been satisfied.

(5) If the board of a company adopts a resolution to do anything contemplated in subsection (2), the company must provide written notice of that resolution to all shareholders, unless every shareholder is also a director of the company, and to any trade union representing its employees —
  (a) within 10 business days after the board adopts the resolution, if the total value of all loans, debts, obligations or assistance contemplated in that resolution, together with any previous such resolution during the financial year, exceeds one-tenth of 1% of the company's net worth at the time of the resolution; or
  (b) within 30 business days after the end of the financial year, in any other case.

(6) A resolution by the board of a company to provide financial assistance contemplated in subsection (2), or an agreement with respect to the provision of any such assistance, is void to the extent that the provision of that assistance would be inconsistent with —
  (a) this section; or
  (b) a prohibition, condition or requirement contemplated in subsection (4).

(7) If a resolution or an agreement has been declared void in terms of subsection (6) read with section 218(1), a director of a company is liable to the extent set out in section 77(3)*(e)*(v) if the director —
  (a) was present at the meeting when the board approved the resolution or agreement, or participated in the making of such a decision in terms of section 74; and
  (b) failed to vote against the resolution or agreement, despite knowing that the provision of financial assistance was inconsistent with this section or a prohibition, condition or requirement contemplated in subsection (4).

8.5.3 Financial assistance

What is immediately apparent when one compares s 45 of the new Act with s 226 of the 1973 Act is that s 45 covers a wider range of transactions than s 226 did.

Section 226 covered loans and the provision of security[406] and s 226(1A) provided that:
  (a) 'loan' includes —
    (i) a loan of money, shares, debentures or any other property; and
    (ii) any credit extended by a company, where the debt concerned is not payable or being paid in accordance with normal business practice in respect of the payment of debts of the same kind.

---

[406] Section 226(1).

(c) 'security' includes a guarantee.

Section 45 of the new Act governs the provision of 'financial assistance' and provides for a number of inclusions and exclusions.[407] The use of the word 'includes' in s 45(1)*(a)* indicates that the types of transactions referred to are not an exhaustive list of what constitutes financial assistance. If the list was intended to be exhaustive, one would have expected the term 'means' to have been used instead of 'includes'. The term 'financial assistance' is wide ranging and accordingly s 45 is generally[408] more extensive in its ambit than s 226. Transactions such as donations, sales at discounted prices and leases at favourable rentals would be covered by s 45 but not by s 226.[409] It will be recognised that the extension of abnormal credit, which was included in the definition of a 'loan' in s 226,[410] is clearly 'financial assistance' and would accordingly be covered by s 45 of the new Act.

Financial assistance for the purposes of s 45 does not include 'an amount to defray the person's expenses for removal at the company's request'.[411] The reasoning behind this is not clear. Is the removal in question a forced removal from office by the shareholders or the board as envisaged by s 71 of the Act? But this does not sound like a removal 'at the company's request'. It appears that what the legislature possibly has in mind is a removal in terms of an amicable settlement with the director before the expiration of his or her period of office and not a forced removal in terms of s 71. If so, it is unclear what expenses are envisaged; perhaps relocation expenses are included. If the provision is referring to a forced removal in terms of s 71, it is foreseeable that difficulties may also arise regarding which expenses the legislature has in mind. How close must the connection be between the expenses and the removal to qualify? Presumably costs of legal representation would be covered. It is also not clear whether expenses only qualify for exemption if there is an actual removal or whether expenses incurred in successfully negating an attempt at removal also qualify. These are vague issues that need to be clarified. A further (perhaps minor) point is that in this exemption the financial assistance in question is referred to as an 'amount' whereas in all other instances the financial assistance refers to a transaction, for example, a loan. This needs to be attended to.

Where s 226 of the 1973 Act was perhaps wider than s 45 of the new Act was in respect of a loan of something other than money. It could be argued that in certain

---

[407] See the definition of 'financial assistance' in s 45(1).
[408] See below for a possible exception.
[409] If the price or rental was, however, nominal, so as to evade the law, then such a contract could have been construed as a loan and accordingly would have been covered by s 226. As was said in *Treasurer-General v Lippert* (1880) 1SC 291 (*per* Smith J), 'the court should look to what a transaction is intended to be, and really is, rather than to what it is described as being'. In other words, if a transaction is designedly disguised so as to escape the provisions of the law but actually falls within those provisions, it is *in fraudem legis* and will be considered to be within the provisions of the law (*Dadoo Ltd v Krugersdorp Municipal Council* 1920 AD 530; *S v Pouroulis* 1993 (4) SA 575 (W) 590–595).
[410] See s 226(1A)(ii).
[411] Section 45(1)*(b)*(iii).

cases such a loan is not financial assistance. For example, if a company allows a director the free use of the company's yacht,[412] this was covered by s 226,[413] but it is arguable that it is not financial assistance for the purposes of s 45.

The precise ambit of 'financial assistance' for the purposes of s 45 is not clear. A similar problem arose in relation to s 38 of the 1973 Act which made it unlawful for a company to assist financially in the acquisition of its own shares or shares in its holding company 'by means of a loan, guarantee, the provision of security or otherwise'.[414] A fair amount of case law built up with regard to what fell within the ambit of the words 'or otherwise' in s 38, which may have a role to play in determining the scope of financial assistance in s 45. It must of course be borne in mind that financial assistance in the context of s 38 was more limited than it is in s 45 because, to fall foul of s 38, it had to be for the purpose of or in connection with the acquisition of shares. For s 45 to operate the objective of the assistance is, of course, irrelevant. It will also be observed that s 45 does not use the words 'or otherwise' but that does not, it is submitted, give s 45 a narrower scope than s 38 of the 1973 Act. This view is based on the suggestion above that the list of transactions in s 45(1)*(a)* is not exhaustive.

Section 45(2) refers to 'direct or indirect financial assistance' whereas s 226(1) referred to the making of a loan 'directly or indirectly'.[415] In *S v Pouroulis*[416] the court said[417] in relation to s 226 that the prohibited indirect ways of giving a loan to a director did not include any transaction which did not result in a contract of a loan between the lending company and a borrower who was disqualified in relation to such company. It followed, the court held, that the prohibition did not extend to the use of a conduit, such as where a company made a loan to the wife or a close relative of a director with the intention that the director should indirectly receive a benefit through the wife or relative.[418] Accordingly, in *S v Pouroulis*[419] it was held that where a subsidiary makes a loan to its holding company to enable the holding company to make a loan to a company, X, controlled by a director of the subsidiary, the subsidiary had not contravened s 226 by 'indirectly' making a loan to X.[420] It will be seen below, in dealing with the recipients of the financial assistance to whom s 45(2) applies, that a loan to the wife or a close relative of a director is covered by s 45.[421] In those circumstances where the conduit used to benefit a director indirectly is not a recipient referred to in s 45(2), it appears that

---

[412] Such free use would constitute a loan for use (*commodatum*).
[413] Section 226(1A)(i) expressly included a loan of any property and not only money.
[414] Similar wording is to be found in s 44(2), the new Act's counterpart to s 38 of the 1973 Act.
[415] It is of note that s 44 of the new Act, which deals with financial assistance for the acquisition of shares, does not use the term 'direct or indirect financial assistance' or 'directly or indirectly'. The reason for this is unclear as s 44 and s 45 mirror each other in many other respects.
[416] 1993 (4) SA 575 (W).
[417] At 660.
[418] See *Pouroulis* at 591, rejecting the view of Phillip M Meskin (ed) *Henochsberg on the Companies Act* 4 ed (1994) vol 1 at 433.
[419] Supra at 596–598.
[420] Note that the court incorrectly said that the holding company's loan would contravene s 226. This would be so only if the holding company itself had a holding company (see s 226(1)*(a)*(iii)).
[421] Such a person is 'related' to the director. See below.

s 45(2) could nevertheless still apply on the basis that the director is the recipient of indirect financial assistance. It could be argued that the rationale in *Pouroulis* is not applicable because of the generality of the term 'financial assistance' used in s 45 but not in s 226.

Excluded from the definition of 'financial assistance' in s 45 is 'lending money in the ordinary course of business by a company whose primary business is the lending of money'.[422] Exempted from the prohibitions in s 226 was 'anything done *bona fide* in the ordinary course of the business of a company actually and regularly carrying on the business of the making of loans or the provision of security'.[423] A comparison of the proposed and current provisions shows three differences:

- Good faith (*bona fides*) was relevant in s 226 but is not relevant in s 45. Theoretically this means that if a loan is made in bad faith and meets the other requirements of the proposed provision, it is nevertheless excluded from the prohibition in s 45.
- The extent of the business in question was irrelevant in s 226. In s 45 the exclusion only operates if it is the 'primary' business which presumably means 'the greater part of the business'.
- For the exclusion in s 45 to operate it is not a requirement that the business must be 'actually and regularly' carried on. This was a requirement of s 226.

Also excluded from the meaning of 'financial assistance' in s 45 are 'accountable advances' to cover 'legal expenses in relation to a matter concerning the company' or 'anticipated expenses to be incurred by the person on behalf of the company'.[424] The qualification that the advance must be 'accountable' is significant as it appears to mean that if the person involved does not have to account for how the advance is expended it is 'financial assistance' within the meaning of s 45 (and understandably so). Section 226 was confusing in this regard. Advances of this kind, whether 'accountable' or not, did not fall within the ambit of the prohibited transactions in s 226(1), yet s 226(2)*(b)* exempted from the prohibitions in s 226(1) 'anything done to provide any director or manager with funds to meet expenditure incurred or to be incurred by him for the purposes of the company concerned'. Section 226(2)*(b)* thus purported to exempt from s 226 a transaction that was not prohibited in the first place! It is of note that the exemption in s 226(2)*(b)* was not an outright exemption. It was subject to the requirement of prior general meeting approval or repayment within six months of the next annual general meeting.[425] The exclusion in s 45*(b)*(ii), under discussion, is an outright exclusion — there are no strings attached, which is understandable considering that the expenses have to be fully accounted for. It is commendable that 'non-accountable' advances are covered by s 45 as they present an obvious opportunity for abuse; that such advances escaped regulation by s 226 was a serious flaw in the provision.

---

[422] See s 45(1)*(b)*(i).
[423] See s 226(2)*(c)* of the 1973 Act.
[424] Section 45*(b)*(ii).
[425] Section 226(3).

8.5.4 Who must be financially assisted?

Who are the recipients of the financial assistance to which s 45 applies? As can be seen in s 45(2), the provision does not only cover directors. Again, s 45 is wider in this respect than s 226. The recipients include, in addition to a director, inter alia, a 'prescribed officer'. A 'prescribed officer', in terms of s 1, 'means the holder of an office, within a company, that has been designated by the Minister in terms of section 66(11)'. At the time of writing, such designation has not been effected. The 1973 Act[426] defined an 'officer' in the following terms: ' "officer", in relation to a company, includes any managing director, manager or secretary thereof but excludes a secretary which is a body corporate'. A distinction was thus drawn between a manager and a secretary, indicating that a secretary was not a manager. It is likely that the Minister will designate the same persons as 'prescribed officers'. If so this would mean that s 45 is wider than s 226 which covered only directors and managers and not secretaries. The extension is to be welcomed as it is possible that in certain instances the position of a secretary might be abused.

The persons who may not be financially assisted in terms of s 45(2), unless the requirements of s 45 are satisfied, are described as follows, using Company X as the company providing the assistance:

(1) a director or prescribed officer of Company X;
(2) a director or prescribed officer of a company related or interrelated to Company X;
(3) a company or corporation that is related to or inter-related to Company X;
(4) a member of a corporation that is related to or inter-related to Company X;
(5) a person related to Company X or related to any of the persons in (1) to (4) above.

The 'related' and 'inter-related' relationships referred to in (2) to (5) above are defined in s 2 of the Act and are dealt with in chapter 6: Groups of Companies and Related Persons.

It will be recognised immediately that s 45(2) is aimed not only at financial assistance given to individuals but also to certain companies and corporations as well. The same applied in s 226 but not to the same extent. Section 226 extended its tentacles to companies and other body corporates controlled by directors or officers. Section 37 of the 1973 Act complemented s 226 by regulating loans to and the provision of security by a company on behalf of its holding company or fellow subsidiary. The regulation in s 226 was different to that of s 37, taking the form of prohibitions (subject to various exemptions) whereas s 37 contained no prohibitions but required disclosure in the annual financial statements and liability for damages on the part of the responsible directors and officers in the event that the terms of the loan or provision of security were 'not fair to the company or failed to provide reasonable protection for its business interests'.[427]

As can be seen from the wide definition of 'related' and 'inter-related' persons,[428] read with s 45(2), the new Act casts its net much wider than s 226 and s 37. The extent of its operation is tempered to some extent by s 2(3) which

---

[426] See s 1.
[427] Section 37(3)(*a*).
[428] See chapter 6: Groups of Companies and Related Persons.

enables a court, the Companies Tribunal or the Panel to exempt any person from the operation of s 45 if there is sufficient evidence that the 'related' or 'inter-related' relationship is such that the person acts independently of the related or inter-related person. It follows that if, for example, a company makes a loan to its subsidiary, or to a director thereof (his sole directorship), because the company acts independently of the subsidiary (and the director), it is possible that the company could be exempted from the operation of s 45 by invoking s 2(3). However, it may not always prove to be factually or legally simple to determine whether companies are related or inter-related, especially in complex group structures. Although s 2(3) provides relief, the onus remains on the company to prove it is acting independently and, even if such an application is not made or proves unnecessary, the directors will need to apply their minds to determine whether a particular transaction falls within the ambit of s 45 or not. This may prove to be difficult, time-consuming and expensive for the company and may make the practical application of s 45 challenging, without necessarily providing significant additional protection for creditors and shareholders.

A loophole in s 226 existed where a loan (for example) was made to a trust of which a director of a company was a beneficiary. If the director was also a trustee of the trust, then s 226 applied because the loan had been made to the trustee (if only one) or the trustees jointly.[429] If, however, the director was not also a trustee, then, applying *Pouroulis*,[430] s 226 was not applicable (in other words, the loan had not been made indirectly to the director).

Turning to s 45, a different situation presents itself. A trust is a juristic person for the purposes of the new Act.[431] Accordingly, when the loan is made it is to the trust and not to the trustees. If a company makes a loan to the trust and a director of the company controls[432] the trust, then s 45 will apply, because the director is related to the trust.[433] It is clear that the director does not have to be a trustee in order to be related to the trust, although the most likely relationship would be where he or she is a trustee.

If the director is a beneficiary of the trust but does not control it, the director and the trust are not 'related persons'[434] and accordingly, if the company makes a loan to the trust, the trust is not one of the recipients in s 45(2) (referred to in (2) to (5) above). However, it may be argued that, in such a case, the company is providing the director with indirect financial assistance and, accordingly, the issues of control of the trust and whether or not the director is related or inter-related to the trust are irrelevant.

---

[429] The 1973 Act did not deem a trust to be a juristic person.
[430] See earlier.
[431] See s 1, definition of 'juristic person'.
[432] The director controls the trust for the purposes of s 2 of the new Act in two situations: (i) if the director 'has the ability to control the majority of the votes of the trustees to appoint the majority of the trustees, or to appoint or change the majority of the beneficiaries of the trust' (s 2(2)*(c)*); or (ii) if the director 'has the ability to materially influence the policy of the juristic person in a manner comparable to a person who, in ordinary commercial practice, can exercise an element of control referred to in (i)' (s 2(2)*(c)–(d)*).
[433] See s 2(1)*(b)*.
[434] See s 2(1)*(b)*.

If s 45 is applicable in this situation, there seems to be no reason why it should not also be applicable in the following situation:

> *Company X makes a loan to Company Y. None of the relationships or inter-relationships referred to in s 45(2) exist between the two companies. A director of Company X is a shareholder of Company Y. None of the relationships or inter-relationships referred to in s 45(2) exist between the director and Company Y.*

By reason of the director's shareholding in Company Y, it appears that, on the basis of the reasoning in the previous paragraph, Company X is providing the director with indirect financial assistance and s 45 applies. If this is so, the ludicrous situation arises that every time a company makes a loan to another company, it must check to see if any of its directors is a shareholder of the other company, in order to ascertain whether it has to comply with s 45. In fact the ambit of s 45 is so extensive as a result of the wide definitions of the 'related' and 'inter-related' relationships in s 2 that companies are, in any event, in all situations where they have entered into a transaction constituting financial assistance, going to be put to extensive enquiries to determine if s 45 is applicable. However, it may be the case, as in this example, that because Company X is acting independently of Company Y, Company X can invoke s 2(3) in order to be exempted from the operation of s 45(2).

It will be recognised that if the director is not a shareholder of Company Y, but rather a director, s 45 does not apply. Because the director is not related or inter-related to Company Y, Company Y is not one of the recipients referred to in s 45(2), and the loan is not indirect assistance to the director him- or herself, so s 45(2) cannot apply.

8.5.5 The requirements of s 45

A number of requirements or conditions must be satisfied to avoid a contravention of s 45, despite anything to the contrary contained in the Memorandum of Incorporation.[435] The requirements or conditions are those prescribed by s 45 and the Memorandum of Incorporation.[436] The Memorandum of Incorporation may also prohibit or restrict the provision of financial assistance generally or particular transactions that constitute financial assistance.[437]

In explaining why s 226 of the 1973 Act permitted the transactions prohibited by s 226 in certain circumstances, Stegmann J held in *S v Pouroulis*[438] that exceptions are provided 'presumably on the basis that in the excepted circumstances there are sufficient safeguards to establish a likelihood that the use of the company's assets for the benefit of its directors or managers or of companies controlled by them, will also be of benefit to the company and not at its expense.'

In summary, the requirements of s 45 that must be met in order to avoid a contravention of the section are:

---

[435] See s 45(3).
[436] See s 45(4).
[437] See s 45(2) and (4).
[438] 1993 (4) SA 575 (W) 589E.

- the financial assistance must be pursuant to an employee share scheme[439] or pursuant to a special resolution;[440]
- the 'solvency' and 'liquidity' test must be satisfied;[441] and
- written notice to shareholders and any trade union representing its employees must be given by the board if it adopts a resolution to provide financial assistance.[442]

When one compares the requirements of s 45 with s 44 (financial assistance for the acquisition of shares[443]) what is noticeable is that s 44 (but not s 45) has as one of its requirements that 'the board is satisfied that ... the terms under which the financial assistance is proposed to be given are fair and reasonable to the company'. It is difficult to discern why this requirement does not also appear in s 45. The requirement seems to be equally important in both the s 44 and s 45 contexts. Of course, if the financial assistance to a director is for the acquisition of shares, then s 44 applies and the 'fair and reasonable' requirement will have to be satisfied.

What immediately stands out when one compares the requirements for exemption from the prohibition in s 45 and the exemptions in s 226 and s 37 is that in all circumstances s 45(3)(b) requires compliance with the solvency and liquidity test. This test did not feature at all in s 226 and s 37 of the 1973 Act.

The solvency and liquidity test is set out in s 4 of the new Act and is dealt with earlier in this chapter.

It is of note that s 45(3)(b) provides that the *board must be satisfied* that the solvency and liquidity test is complied with. Does this mean that the test is met as long as the directors are satisfied that the test has been met, even if from an objective standpoint such satisfaction is not reasonable? In other words, is the test whether or not the board is satisfied a subjective test? An indication that the test requires some objectivity is the reference to 'all reasonably foreseeable financial circumstances' in s 4(1) and the requirements of s 4(2)(b) which provides:

(2) For the purposes contemplated in subsection (1) —
...
(b) subject to paragraph (c), the board or any other person applying the solvency and liquidity test to a company —
  (i) must consider a fair valuation of the company's assets and liabilities, including any reasonably foreseeable contingent assets and liabilities, irrespective of whether or not arising as a result of the proposed distribution, or otherwise; and
  (ii) may consider any other valuation of the company's assets and liabilities that is reasonable in the circumstances; ...

The 'employee share scheme' requirement is more onerous than the corresponding exemption in s 226(2)(d). Section 226(2)(d) exempted 'the provision of money or making of loans by a company for the purposes contemplated in section 38(2)(b)

---

[439] Section 45(3)(a)(i). The scheme must satisfy the requirements of s 97.
[440] Section 45(3)(a)(ii). The special resolution must have been adopted within the previous two years and must have approved such assistance for the specific recipient, or generally for a category of potential recipients, and the specific recipient falls within that category.
[441] Section 45(3)(b)(i).
[442] Section 45(5).
[443] See 8.4 above.

and *(c)*'. Section 38 was the provision prohibiting a company from providing financial assistance for the acquisition of its shares or those of its holding company. Section 38(2)*(b)* exempted:

> the provision by a company, in accordance with any scheme for the time being in force, of money for the subscription for or purchase of shares of the company or its holding company by trustees to be held by or for the benefit of employees of the company, including any director holding a salaried employment or office in the company.

Section 38(2)*(c)* exempted:

> the making by a company of loans to persons, other than directors, bona fide in the employment of the company with a view to enabling those persons to purchase or subscribe for shares of the company or its holding company to be held by themselves as owners.

The 'employee share scheme' requirement in s 45 is more onerous in that, firstly, the requirements laid down by s 97 must be complied with[444] in order for the scheme to qualify, whereas no such qualification was required by s 226. Secondly, s 45 does not go beyond an employee share scheme the way s 38(2)*(c)* did. Thus a loan, for example, by a company to one of its managers[445] to assist the manager in acquiring shares in the company was exempted outright by s 38(2)*(c)* but still required a special resolution for the purposes of s 45.

Where the financial assistance is not pursuant to an employee share scheme it must in all instances[446] be 'pursuant to a special resolution of the shareholders, adopted within the previous 2 years, which approved such assistance either for the specific recipient, or generally for a category of potential recipients, and the specific recipient falls within that category.'[447] The special resolution does not have to be passed at a formal meeting. It may be passed by way of a 'round robin' resolution voted for by the majority required at a formal meeting.[448] The special resolution must be passed *prior* to the provision of financial assistance. This is clear from the wording 'adopted within the previous 2 years' in s 45(3)*(a)*(ii). Thus ratification is not possible. The special resolution does not have to specify the specific recipients as long as it specifies the category of potential recipients. It appears, however, that the resolution must specify the type of financial assistance and cannot leave it to the discretion of the directors to decide on the type. This is apparent from the wording '... the particular provision of financial assistance is ... pursuant to a special resolution ... which approved such assistance' in s 45(3)*(a)*(ii). What may prove to be problematic is the resolution approving financial assistance generally for a category of potential recipients. Needless to say, this requirement will have administration and cost implications for companies (especially large public companies and listed companies). A pragmatic board may therefore decide to propose a suitably drafted resolution at, for example, the annual general meeting every two years. The question then arises whether a

---

[444] Section 97 requires that to qualify as an employee share scheme for the purposes of s 45, a company must, inter alia, appoint a compliance officer who is responsible for the administration of the scheme and who is required to comply with various duties laid down by s 97.

[445] It is assumed that a 'manager' will be designated as a 'prescribed officer'. See 8.5.4 above.

[446] Section 45 is unlike s 226 which provides for certain exemptions that required less than a special resolution (see the exemptions in s 226(2)*(b)* and *(e)*).

[447] Section 45(3)*(a)*(ii).

[448] See s 60 of the Act. This, of course, was not permitted by the 1973 Act.

category or categories of potential recipients may be so widely framed as to effectively give the board the discretion whether to provide the assistance or not without consulting the shareholders again. So, for example, would it satisfy the requirements of the section if the shareholders were to resolve that the company may provide financial assistance to any person if, in the opinion of the directors, the provision of such financial assistance would serve to further the BEE objectives of the company? If so, this would largely remove the protection ostensibly afforded to shareholders by the resolution requirement. However, there is nothing in the section which militates against such an interpretation, nor is there anything in the Act which prevents the passing of a number of such 'boilerplate' resolutions, widely framed, in respect of a number of different categories of recipients every two years as a matter of course.[449]

The requirement in s 45(5) regarding notice by the board of a company to the company's shareholders and any trade union representing its employees is one that must be complied with in all circumstances. It is not clear why notice to the shareholders is required, considering that if a special resolution is required (ie if the financial assistance is not pursuant to an employee share scheme), the shareholders will in any event have to be given notice of the meeting at which the shareholders will be called upon to vote on the special resolution.[450] The rationale for the differentiation in s 45(3)*(a)* and *(b)* calling for different periods of notice, depending on the company's 'net worth' is unclear. It is unsatisfactory that 'net worth' is not defined. The requirement of notice to any trade union representing the company's employees is an illustration of the legislature's apparent recognition that the body of employees of a company also constitutes a stakeholder whose interests must be taken into account in certain circumstances for good corporate governance purposes. Thus the company's shareholders are not in all instances regarded as the only constituency whose interests must be taken into account.

8.5.6 The consequences of contravening s 45

A contravention of s 45 has no criminal consequences, in keeping with the clear policy evident in the new Act to decriminalise company law (which is questionable especially in the context of s 45).[451] The 1973 Act made a contravention of s 37 and s 226 a criminal offence.[452]

---

[449] The points made in this paragraph regarding a resolution approving financial assistance generally are also made by J Yeats and R Jooste in 'Financial assistance — a new approach' 2009 *SALJ* 566. See 8.4.5 above.

[450] Notice of meetings is dealt with in s 62 of the new Act. Section 62(1) requires at least 15 business days' notice in the case of a public company or a non-profit company that has voting members, and 10 business days' notice in any other case. A company's Memorandum of Incorporation may provide for longer minimum notice periods (s 62(2)).

[451] A punitive sanction that appears possible is a fine of an administrative nature flowing from a failure to comply with a compliance notice issued by the Companies and Intellectual Property Commission established in terms of s 185 of the Act (see s 171 of the Act). An administrative fine can be imposed by the court in an amount not exceeding the greater of 10 per cent of the respondent's annual turnover during the preceding financial year and R1 000 000 (see s 175(1) of the Act). Whether such a fine will prove to be sufficient deterrent is questionable. The constitutionality of the fine may also be questionable.

[452] See s 37(2) and s 226(4)*(b)*.

Section 45(6) provides that 'a resolution by the board to provide financial assistance' or 'an agreement with respect to the provision of any such assistance' is 'void to the extent that the provision of that assistance would be inconsistent with':

- section 45; or
- a prohibition, condition or requirement regarding financial assistance in the company's Memorandum of Incorporation.[453]

Section 45(7) imposes liability on any director who was present at the meeting when the board approved the resolution or agreement, or where no formal board meeting was held, participated in the making of such a decision by way of a 'round robin' resolution.[454] The liability arises if the director failed to vote against the resolution, despite *knowing* that the provision of financial assistance was inconsistent with s 45 or the company's Memorandum of Incorporation.[455] Liability accordingly hinges on a subjective enquiry into the director's knowledge at the relevant time.

The liability of directors for breach of s 45 is liability for any loss, damages or costs sustained by the company as a direct or indirect consequence of the voidness of the resolution or agreement.[456]

If the board of a company has made a decision contrary to s 45 the company, or any director who has been or may be held liable, may apply to a court for an order setting aside the decision.[457] The court may make an order setting aside the decision in whole or in part, absolutely or conditionally, and may make any further order that is just and equitable in the circumstances, including an order:

- to rectify the decision, reverse any transaction, or restore any consideration paid or benefit received by any person in terms of the decision of the board;[458] and
- requiring the company to indemnify any director who has been or may be held liable in terms of this section, including indemnification for the costs of the proceedings under this subsection.[459]

The rationale for the order in the last bullet is difficult to comprehend. As seen above, a prerequisite for liability is *knowledge* on the part of the director at the time of voting on the resolution that the financial assistance was inconsistent with s 44 or the company's Memorandum of Incorporation.[460] Why should a director be indemnified when he or she knew of such inconsistency and yet failed to vote against the resolution?

---

[453] Section 45(6).
[454] Section 74 of the Bill permits 'round robin' resolutions.
[455] Section 45(7)(*b*). See also s 77(3)(*e*)(iv).
[456] Section 45(7) read with s 77(3)(*e*)(v).
[457] Section 77(5)(*a*).
[458] Section 77(5)(*b*)(ii)(*bb*).
[459] Section 77(5)(*b*)(ii)(*bb*).
[460] Section 45(7)(*b*). See also s 77(3)(*e*)(iv).

For the same reason it is difficult to understand s 77(9) which provides:

In any proceedings against a director, other than for wilful misconduct or wilful breach of trust, the court may relieve the director, either wholly or partly, from any liability set out in this section, on any terms the court considers just if it appears to the court that —
(a) the director is or may be liable, but has acted honestly and reasonably; or
(b) having regard to all the circumstances of the case, including those connected with the appointment of the director, it would be fair to excuse the director.

Again, why should a director be indemnified when he or she knew of the inconsistency and yet failed to vote against the resolution? Regarding s 77(9)(a), how can such conduct be honest and reasonable? In addition, if the director has such knowledge at the time that the resolution is voted on, is there not *ipso facto* 'wilful misconduct or wilful breach of trust'? Regarding s 77(9)(b) it is also by no means clear what 'circumstances of the case, including those connected with the appointment of the director'[461] justify excusing such director from liability.

Similar misgivings arise in relation to the reference to s 77(9) in s 77(10). Section 77(10) provides:

A director who has reason to apprehend that a claim may be made alleging that the director is liable, other than for wilful misconduct or wilful breach of trust, may apply to a court for relief, and the court may grant relief to the director on the same grounds as if the matter had come before the court in terms of subsection (9).

The above analysis of the liability provisions with their indemnification and relief provisions leaves one wondering whether there is a serious attempt to impose liability. The directors' lobby has obviously been hard at work. This clearly does not bode well for good corporate governance.

The proceedings to recover any loss, damages or costs may not commence more than three years after the act or omission that gave rise to the liability.[462] Regarding the prescription of a claim there are problems which are the same as those arising in the context of s 44 (financial assistance for the acquisition of securities). These problems are discussed in 8.4.9(d) above and are not repeated here.

It would seem that the simplest way for a director to avoid liability in terms of this section would be not to attend the meeting or participate in the making of the decision at all if he or she is uncertain whether the requirements of s 44 will be complied with or not, or if he or she would prefer not to vote against a particular resolution for political reasons. If the decision is not taken at a formal meeting but by way of a round robin resolution and a director refrains from voting, it appears from s 45(7)(a) that the director will not incur liability. A counter to this may be that by being presented with the round robin resolution the director has 'participated in the making of such a decision' as specified in s 45(7)(a). One must also not lose sight of a director's general duties to the company, breach of which could give rise to liability.

Section 45 read with s 77(3)(v) imposes only liability for damages, costs and loss to the company. Section 226 of the 1973 Act extended the liability to 'any other person who had no actual knowledge of the contravention. . . .'[463] Sight

---
[461] Section 77(9)(b).
[462] Section 77(7).
[463] Section 226(4)(a).

must not, however, be lost of s 20(6)*(a)* of the new Act which provides that a '[s]hareholder of a company has a claim for damages against any person who fraudulently or due to gross negligence causes the company to do anything inconsistent with' the Act or the company's Memorandum of Incorporation.[464] A contravention of s 45 by a company could accordingly give rise to a claim for damages by a shareholder of the company against any person who fraudulently or due to gross negligence[465] causes the company to do anything inconsistent with s 45. A director's liability to the company, not being dependent on fraud or gross negligence, is a stricter liability than liability to shareholders. It is unclear why liability should differ in this way. Loss to the shareholders is as serious as loss to the company. Presumably a director who has voted against the contravening transaction could not be said to have 'caused' the contravention and therefore no liability to shareholders could arise. It is to be noted that the three-year prescription period in s 77(7) has no application to liability in terms of s 20(6). Accordingly the prescription of the claim will be governed by the Prescription Act. Therefore, the problems related to prescription of a claim by the company referred to above do not arise. Presumably shareholders could claim for a decrease in the value of their shares resulting from the fraud or negligence of the culprit.

Section 20(6) of the new Act is narrower than s 226(4)*(c)* of the 1973 Act in that the latter but not the former extends a liability claim to any person and not only to shareholders. However, s 218(2) of the new Act does extend liability to any person, providing that '[a]ny person who contravenes any provision of the Act is liable to any other person for any loss or damage suffered by that person as a result of that contravention'. No requirement of fraud or gross negligence is required, as in s 20(6)*(a)*, and it appears that where the claimant is a shareholder there is a conflict between s 20(6)*(a)* and s 218(2). Again, as is the case with liability in terms of s 20(6), the prescription provision in s 77(7) has no application to liability in terms of s 218(2), and accordingly prescription will be governed by the Prescription Act and the problems referred to above do not arise.

It will be recognised that, because of the wide range of possible recipients of the financial assistance covered by s 45, the transaction may be with a third person who is unaware that the transaction contravenes s 45. Does the law provide any protection for such person? Can such person prevent the transaction from being declared void? In this regard see 8.4.9*(b)* above where the same considerations applicable there are applicable here.

How does the voidness of a transaction envisaged by s 45 impact on related transactions? Take as an example a simplified version of the facts in *Kirsten v Bankorp Ltd*.[466] X makes a loan to company A. It is a term of the loan contract that company A will lend the money thus borrowed by it to company B, which is controlled by one of the company A's directors. The loan made to Company B contravenes s 45 and is accordingly void. How does the contravention of s 45 affect the loan by X to company A?

---

[464] Where there is inconsistency with the Memorandum there is no liability if the action has been ratified by the shareholders by special resolution (s 45(6)*(b)*).
[465] Fraud or gross negligence are not requirements of s 226(4)*(c)* of the 1973 Act.
[466] 1993 (4) SA 649 (C).

In *Kirsten* the court found that the loan by Company A to Company B was a contravention of s 226 of the 1973 Act and the loan by X to Company A was not affected by the contravention, unless it could be shown that X knew that company A intended to lend the money it borrowed in contravention of s 226. The court held that X was entitled to presume that company A would act lawfully, which in *Kirsten* meant obtaining the necessary consent or special resolution required by s 226(2)*(a)*. It would seem, based on the rationale in *Kirsten*, that the loan by X to Company A would not be affected by the contravention of s 45 of the new Act.

8.5.7 Disclosure in the annual financial statements

The 1973 Act contained a number of provisions requiring special disclosure of some of the loans and provisions of security exempted from the prohibitions in s 226.[467] The 1973 Act also required special disclosure of loans and provisions of security by a company to its holding company and fellow subsidiaries[468] as well as loans and the provisions of security by a company to persons before they became directors or managers of the company.[469]

The new Act also contains disclosure provisions. A company which is required to be audited is required in terms of s 30(4) to include in its annual financial statements 'particulars showing . . . the remuneration, as defined in subsection (5), and benefits received by each director, or individual holding any prescribed office in the company'.[470] The definition of 'remuneration', which is in s 30(6), includes, inter alia:

(f) financial assistance to a director, past director or future director, or person related to any of them, for the subscription of shares, as contemplated in section 44; and

(g) with respect to any loan or other financial assistance by the company to a director, past director or future director, or a person related to any of them, or any loan made by a third party to any such person, as contemplated in section 45, if the company is a guarantor of that loan, the value of —
 (i) any interest deferred, waived or forgiven; or
 (ii) the difference in value between —
  (aa) the interest that would reasonably be charged in comparable circumstances at fair market rates in an arm's length transaction; and
  (bb) the interest actually charged to the borrower, if less.

It appears from these disclosure requirements that not all the provisions of financial assistance covered by s 45 have to be disclosed. Firstly, the provision of financial assistance to a prescribed officer is not included. Secondly, difficulty arises with the interpretation of s 30(6)*(g)*. This provision expressly refers to any loan or other financial assistance as well as a guarantee by a company of a loan to a director, among others. However, it is clear from s 30(6)*(g)* read with s 30(4) that what must be disclosed in the annual financial statements is the value of *interest*, either interest deferred, waived or forgiven,[471] or notional interest.[472] The

---

[467] See s 295 which required special disclosure of the loans and provisions of security exempt in terms of s 226(2)*(b)* and *(e)*.
[468] See s 37.
[469] See s 296.
[470] Section 30(4)*(a)*.
[471] Section 30(6)*(g)*(i).
[472] Section 30(6)*(g)*(ii).

problem is that 'interest' relates to a loan. It does not relate to any other type of financial assistance, including a guarantee. So if the financial assistance is a guarantee or something other than a loan, there is nothing to disclose. A possible interpretation in relation to a guarantee, perhaps, is that the interest referred to is not interest deferred, waived or forgiven by the company providing the guarantee but by the person making the loan. For example, if a lender makes a loan to a director of Company A and defers, waives or forgives any interest or charges a lower than fair market rate of interest and Company A guarantees the repayment of the loan, then Company A is required to disclose in its annual financial statements the interest deferred, waived or forgiven or the difference between the interest charged by the lender and the interest that would have been charged if it had been charged at a fair market rate, as the case may be. The difficulty with this interpretation is, of course, that it is odd that disclosure is not required where the director has to pay interest at a fair market rate. If Company A is guaranteeing repayment of the loan why does that make a difference? The company is exposed in either event. And why should Company A have to disclose the difference between the interest charged on the loan and the interest that would have been charged if it had been charged at a fair market rate when it is not the lender? This interpretation, of course, also does not explain how financial assistance, other than a loan or guarantee, can be brought within the purview of the disclosure provision.

CHAPTER 9

GOVERNANCE AND SHAREHOLDERS

Rehana Cassim

9.1	INTRODUCTION	329
9.2	SHAREHOLDERS	329
	9.2.1 Securities register	329
	9.2.2 Definition of a 'shareholder'	330
	9.2.3 Shareholders and members	331
	9.2.4 Beneficial and registered shareholders	331
	(a) Beneficial interest	331
	(b) Disclosure of beneficial shareholders	333
	(c) Register of disclosures	334
	(d) Voting by beneficial shareholders	334
	(e) Notices and proxy appointments	335
9.3	RECORD DATE FOR DETERMINING SHAREHOLDER RIGHTS	335
9.4	INSTANCES WHERE COMPLIANCE WITH FORMALITIES IS NOT REQUIRED	336
	9.4.1 Unanimous assent at common law	336
	9.4.2 Companies with one shareholder	338
	9.4.3 Companies in which every shareholder is also a director	338
9.5	PROXIES	339
	9.5.1 Persons who may be appointed as proxies	339
	9.5.2 Procedure to appoint a proxy	339
	9.5.3 Validity of the proxy appointment	340
	9.5.4 Delivery of notices to proxy	340
	9.5.5 Voting	340
	9.5.6 Revocation of the proxy appointment	341
	9.5.7 Company-sponsored invitations to appoint a proxy	342
9.6	SHAREHOLDERS' MEETINGS	343
	9.6.1 The definition of a 'shareholders' meeting'	343
	9.6.2 Distinction between a shareholders' meeting and an annual general meeting	343
9.7	CONVENING A SHAREHOLDERS' MEETING	344
	9.7.1 Persons who may convene a shareholders' meeting	344
	9.7.2 Instances when a company must hold a shareholders' meeting	345
	(a) When the board of directors is required by the Act or the Memorandum of Incorporation to refer a matter to the shareholders for decision	345
	(b) Whenever required in terms of s 70(3) to fill a vacancy on the board	346

		(c) When one or more written and signed demands for a shareholders' meeting are delivered to the company	346
		(d) When an AGM of the shareholders is required to be convened...	347
		(e) Whenever required by the company's Memorandum of Incorporation	347
	9.7.3	Company with one shareholder	348
	9.7.4	Failure to convene a meeting	348
		(a) Power of authorised persons and the Companies Tribunal to convene meetings.............................	348
		(b) Power of courts to convene meetings.................	348
9.8	NOTICE OF MEETINGS...		349
	9.8.1	Period of notice...	349
	9.8.2	Content of notice..	349
	9.8.3	Failure to give notice and defects in the notice	351
9.9	CONDUCT OF SHAREHOLDERS' MEETINGS....................		352
	9.9.1	Location of shareholders' meetings	352
	9.9.2	Attending and participating in a shareholders' meeting	352
	9.9.3	Electronic communication.................................	352
9.10	VOTING AT MEETINGS		353
	9.10.1	Show of hands and poll	353
	9.10.2	Voting agreements.......................................	354
9.11	CHAIRPERSON AT MEETINGS		355
9.12	QUORUM..		355
	9.12.1	Quorum for a meeting to commence	356
	9.12.2	Quorum for a matter at the meeting to be considered	356
	9.12.3	Quorum once a meeting has commenced	356
	9.12.4	Quorum where a company has more than two shareholders	357
9.13	POSTPONEMENT AND ADJOURNMENT OF MEETINGS		357
	9.13.1	Postponement where quorum is not present	357
	9.13.2	Notice of a postponed or adjourned meeting	358
	9.13.3	Deemed quorum	358
	9.13.4	Voluntary adjournments of meetings......................	358
	9.13.5	Period of adjournment	359
9.14	SHAREHOLDER RESOLUTIONS		359
	9.14.1	Proposing a resolution	359
	9.14.2	Ordinary resolutions.....................................	360
	9.14.3	Special resolutions	360
9.15	WRITTEN RESOLUTIONS		362
	9.15.1	Consent of shareholders required..........................	362
	9.15.2	Support required for written resolutions	363
	9.15.3	Time within which the consent must be obtained	364
	9.15.4	Electronic communication.................................	364
	9.15.5	Restrictions	364
	9.15.6	Informing shareholders of the written resolution............	365
9.16	COMPANY RECORDS		365

9.16.1	Records...	365
9.16.2	Access to records	367
9.16.3	Exercising the right to access the information contained in the company's records	369
9.16.4	Failure to accommodate a request for access to company records	370
9.16.5	Location of company records	371

9.1 INTRODUCTION

The governance of companies is addressed in Part F of Chapter 2 of the Companies Act 71 of 2008 (hereafter 'the Act'). The two main organs of a company are the board of directors and the shareholders in a shareholders' meeting. Certain substantive decisions regarding the management of the company are reserved for the shareholders. A shareholders' meeting is the focus of decision making by the shareholders. The classic description of the relationship between the bodies constituting a company is that of Greer LJ, as stated in *John Shaw and Sons (Salford) Ltd v Shaw*:[1]

> A company is an entity distinct alike from its shareholders and its directors. Some of its powers may, according to its articles, be exercised by directors, certain other powers may be reserved for the shareholders in general meeting. If powers of management are vested in the directors, they and they alone can exercise these powers. The only way in which the general body of the shareholders can control the exercise of the powers vested by the articles in the directors is by altering their articles, or, if opportunity arises under the articles, by refusing to re-elect the directors of whose actions they disapprove. They cannot themselves usurp the powers which by the articles are vested in the directors any more than the directors can usurp the powers vested by the articles in the general body of shareholders.[2]

The Act sets out procedural rules relating to the convening of shareholders' meetings, the provision of notice of meetings, attendance at meetings, the conduct of meetings, the passing of resolutions and voting at meetings. It is essential that these formalities be complied with so that the business transacted at a shareholders' meeting is not open to being impugned afterwards due to non-compliance or irregularities in the proceedings, although in some instances compliance with some formalities is not required. These issues are discussed in this chapter.

9.2 SHAREHOLDERS

9.2.1 Securities register

Every company must establish a register of its issued securities in the prescribed form and maintain its securities register in accordance with the prescribed standards.[3] The securities register must contain certain prescribed information in

---

[1] [1935] 2 KB 113 (CA), approved in *Letseng Diamonds Ltd v JCI Ltd; Trinity Asset Management (Pty) Ltd v Investec Bank Ltd* 2007 (5) SA 564 (W).

[2] At 134.

[3] Section 50(1). Regulation 36 of the draft Companies Regulations sets out in detail the information that must be included in the securities register. 'Securities' is defined in the Act as having the meaning set out in s 1 of the Securities Services Act 36 of 2004 and includes shares held in a private company. The draft Companies Amendment Bill, 2010 widens the definition of 'securities' in s 1 so

relation to each class of securities that has been issued.[4] Securities issued by a company may be either certificated, which means that they are evidenced by a certificate, or uncertificated, in which case the company may not issue certificates evidencing or purporting to evidence title to those securities.[5] In order to be a shareholder of a company, a person must hold at least one share issued by a company and must be entered as a shareholder in the securities register of the company, be it the certificated or the uncertificated securities register.[6]

9.2.2 Definition of a 'shareholder'

Section 1 of the Act defines a shareholder to mean 'the holder of a share issued by a company and who is entered as such in the certificated or uncertificated securities register, as the case may be'. This definition of a shareholder is subject to s 57(1) of the Act, which contains a specific definition of a 'shareholder' that applies only to Part F of Chapter 2 of the Act, dealing with the governance of companies. Under s 57(1) a shareholder means 'a person who is entitled to exercise any voting rights in relation to a company, irrespective of the form, title or nature of the securities to which those voting rights are attached'. The very wide definition of a 'shareholder' in s 57(1) of the Act differs from the narrower definition in s 1 of the Act and could give rise to practical difficulties.

---

as to include any share issued, or authorised to be issued, by a profit company. Section 1 of the Securities Services Act defines 'securities' as meaning, inter alia, shares, stocks and depository receipts in public companies and other equivalent equities (other than shares in a share block company), notes, derivative instruments, bonds, debentures, participatory interests in a collective investment scheme and instruments based on an index.

[4] In terms of s 50(2), the following information must be contained in the securities register:
  (a) the total number of securities that are held in uncertificated form;
  (b) with respect to certificated securities —
    (i) the names and addresses of the persons to whom the securities were issued;
    (ii) the number of securities issued to each of them;
    (iii) the number of and prescribed circumstances relating to any securities that have been placed in trust as contemplated in s 40(6)(d) or whose transfer has been restricted;
    (iv) in the case of securities other than shares (contemplated in s 43) —
      (aa) the number of those securities issued and outstanding; or
      (bb) the names and addresses of the registered owner of the security and any holders of a beneficial interest in the security; and
    (v) any other prescribed information.

The reference to 'or' in (aa) above should read 'and'. This is to be amended in the draft Companies Amendment Bill, 2010 (cl 32).

[5] Section 49(2). See ss 51–55 of the Act on the registration and transfer of certificated and uncertificated securities and the liability relating to uncertificated securities. See further chapter 7: Shares, Securities and Transfer on uncertificated securities.

[6] If a company has issued uncertificated securities or has issued securities that have ceased to be certificated, a record must be administered and maintained by a participant or central securities depository (CSD) in the prescribed form, as the company's uncertificated securities register, and this forms part of that company's securities register (s 50(3)). For a detailed exposition of uncertificated securities in our law, see Maria Vermaas 'The reform of the law of uncertificated securities in South African company law' 2010 Acta Juridica 87. See further chapter 7: Shares, Securities and Transfer on the securities register of a company.

9.2.3 Shareholders and members

The terms 'shareholder' and 'member' have traditionally been used interchangeably,[7] but the Act now does away with this interchangeability of the terms. The Act does not use the term 'member' in respect of a shareholder of the company, whether registered or not. The term 'member' is reserved for use in respect of non-profit companies.[8] Section 1 of the Act states that the term 'member', when used in reference to a non-profit company, means a person who holds membership in and has specified rights in respect of that non-profit company, as contemplated in item 4 of Schedule 1.

9.2.4 Beneficial and registered shareholders

(a) Beneficial interest

Except to the extent that a company's Memorandum of Incorporation provides otherwise, a company's issued securities may be held by, and be registered in the name of one person for the beneficial interest of another person.[9] Thus the right to be on the register is independent of the ownership of the shares.[10] The beneficial shareholder is entitled to the rights attached to the share while the registered shareholder is the person in whose name the share happens to be registered. Such a person is also known as a nominee, defined as 'a person that acts as the registered holder of securities or an interest in securities on behalf of other persons'.[11] In *Oakland Nominees (Pty) Ltd v Gelria Mining & Investment Co (Pty) Ltd*[12] the then Appellate Division explained the concepts of nominee and beneficial shareholders as follows:

> A nominee is an agent with limited authority: he holds shares in name only. He does this on behalf of his nominator or principal, from whom he takes his instructions . . . The principal, whose name does not appear on the register, is usually described as the 'beneficial owner'. This is not, juristically speaking, wholly accurate; but it is a convenient and well-understood

---

[7] This was not entirely accurate because traditionally a person was regarded as being a member only once they were registered in the register of members. A person may acquire shares in a company as a beneficial owner through a nominee, without being registered as a member. Thus a person could have been a shareholder but not necessarily a member of a company. This is discussed further below.

[8] A non-profit company is not required to have members, but its Memorandum of Incorporation may make provision for it to have members (see item 4(1) of Schedule 1). The draft Companies Amendment Bill, 2010 proposes to expand the definition of a 'member' so that a 'member' when used in reference to: (i) a close corporation, has the meaning set out in s 1 of the Close Corporations Act 69 of 1984; (ii) a non-profit company, means a person who holds membership in and specified rights in respect of that non-profit company, as contemplated in item 4 of Schedule 2 (this should read 'Schedule 1'); or (iii) any other entity means a person who is a constituent part of that entity (see cl 2(1)(*t*) of the draft Companies Amendment Bill, 2010).

[9] Section 56(1).

[10] *Jeffery v Pollak and Freemantle* 1938 AD 1 at 18; *Davis v Buffelsfontein Gold Mining Co Ltd* 1967 (4) SA 631 (W) 633.

[11] See s 1 of the Act and s 1 of the Securities Services Act 36 of 2004.

[12] 1976 (1) SA 441 (A).

label. Ownership of shares does not depend upon registration. On the other hand, the company recognises only its registered shareholders.[13]

The term 'beneficial interest' is defined in s 1 of the Act to mean:

> the right or entitlement of a person, through ownership, agreement, relationship or otherwise, alone or together with another person to —
> (a) receive or participate in any distribution in respect of the company's securities;
> (b) exercise or cause to be exercised, in the ordinary course, any or all of the rights attaching to the company's securities; or
> (c) dispose or direct the disposition of the company's securities, or any part of a distribution in respect of the securities,
> but does not include any interest held by a person in a unit trust or collective investment scheme in terms of the Collective Investment Schemes Act, 2002 (Act No. 45 of 2002).

Section 56(2) of the Act provides for a wider definition of 'beneficial interest' in certain instances where securities are issued by a public company. Under s 56(2) of the Act a person is deemed to:

> have a beneficial interest in a security of a public company if the security is held *nomine officii* by another person on that first person's behalf or if that first person —
> (a) is married in community of property to a person who has a beneficial interest in that security;
> (b) is the parent of a minor child who has a beneficial interest in that security;
> (c) acts in terms of an agreement with another person who has a beneficial interest in that security, and the agreement is in respect of the co-operation between them for the acquisition, disposal or any other matter relating to a beneficial interest in that security;
> (d) is the holding company of a company that has a beneficial interest in that security;
> (e) is entitled to exercise or control the exercise of the majority of the voting rights at general meetings of a juristic person that has a beneficial interest in that security; or
> (f) gives directions or instructions to a juristic person that has a beneficial interest in that security, and its directors or the trustees are accustomed to act in accordance with that person's directions or instructions.[14]

There are several reasons why a person would not want the shares of a company to be registered in his or her own name. One reason may be that they wish to keep their identity unknown. Another reason may be where the directors of a company would refuse the registration of the transfer of shares and in order to circumvent this refusal, the seller of the shares could become the registered shareholder while the purchaser would accordingly be the beneficial shareholder. Another example is where an investor in shares acts as the registered shareholder for numerous investors in a number of different shares.[15]

The company is not obliged to take notice of the fact that the registered shareholder holds the shares as nominee on behalf of another. As Corbett JA stated in *Standard Bank of South Africa Ltd v Ocean Commodities Inc*[16] 'it is the policy of the law that a company should concern itself only with the registered owner of

---

[13] At 453. See also *Sammel v President Brand Gold Mining Co Ltd* 1969 (3) SA 629 (A) 666 and *Standard Bank of South Africa Ltd v Ocean Commodities Inc* 1983 (1) SA 276 (A) 289.
[14] See s 56(2). See further chapter 7: Shares, Securities and Transfer.
[15] Cilliers and Benade *Corporate Law* 3 ed (2000) para 15.09 p 242.
[16] 1983 (1) SA 276 (A).

the shares'.[17] But there are good reasons why the identity of the beneficial owner of the shares in a public company should be accessible to those who wish to know. Some problems that may arise out of shares being held by registered shareholders is that insider trading becomes very difficult to detect; minority shareholders are unable to detect a change of the controlling shareholder; the board of directors and shareholders are not in a position where they may be forewarned of a hostile takeover; competition legislation is difficult to administer; a company itself does not know who a large percentage of its shareholders are, and communication with all shareholders is virtually impossible.[18]

(b) Disclosure of beneficial shareholders

The disclosure of beneficial shareholders protects the management of the company and to some extent the shareholders too, by, for instance, making them aware of who is building up a stake in the company.[19] Disclosure thus functions as an early warning device about potential takeover bids.[20] Disclosure also protects the public, because it promotes market transparency and maintains a free and fair regulated securities market.[21]

Accordingly, in terms of s 56(3) of the Act, if a security of a public company is registered in the name of a person who is not the holder of the beneficial interest in all the securities in the same company held by that person, that registered holder of the security is required to disclose the identity of the person on whose behalf the security is held and the number and class of securities held for each such person with a beneficial interest.[22] The extent of such beneficial interest is not required to be disclosed.[23]

This information must be disclosed in writing to the company within five business days after the end of every month or, as required, be provided on payment of a prescribed fee charged by the registered holder of securities.[24] In contrast, under the Companies Act of 1973 (hereafter 'the 1973 Act') disclosure had to be made only at the end of every three-month period.[25] This delay in the disclosure could have reduced the efficacy of the disclosure requirement.[26] It also enabled a person to acquire a substantial shareholding in a company and to

---

[17] At 289. See also *Sammel v President Brand Gold Mining Co Ltd* 1969 (3) SA 629 (A) 666 and *Oakland Nominees (Pty) Ltd v Gelria Mining & Investment Co (Pty) Ltd* 1976 (1) SA 441 (A) 453.
[18] See the *Memorandum on the Objects of the Companies Bill, 2008*, Companies Bill [B 17D–99] at 30, and see further chapter 7: Shares, Securities and Transfer.
[19] Paul L Davies *Gower and Davies' Principles of Modern Company Law* 8 ed (2008) at 923.
[20] Ibid.
[21] Ibid. See also the *Memorandum on the Objects of the Companies Amendment Bill, 2008* (n 18 above) at 30.
[22] Section 56(3).
[23] The draft Companies Amendment Bill, 2010 proposes to amend s 56(3)*(b)* to provide that the extent of the beneficial interest must also be disclosed to the company (see cl 34*(a)* of the draft Companies Amendment Bill, 2010). This would make s 56(3)*(b)* consistent with s 56(5)*(b)* of the Act.
[24] Section 56(4).
[25] See s 140A(3) of the 1973 Act.
[26] MS Blackman et al *Commentary on the Companies Act* vol 1 (2002) (Revision Service 7, 2010) at 5–408.

disclose this fact only three months after the acquisition of the shares. If properly timed, this would have effectively concealed a takeover bid.[27] The disclosure requirement has thus been tightened up under the Act.

The draft Companies Amendment Bill, 2010 proposes to amend the disclosure requirement by requiring disclosure to be made within five business days after the end of every month during which a change has occurred in the information relating to beneficial shareholding.[28] Accordingly, under the Bill, if there is nothing new to disclose, disclosure would not have to be made. But this is subject to the rules of a central securities depository (CSD) — disclosure would have to be made more promptly or frequently should the rules of a CSD so provide.[29]

Any company that knows or has reasonable cause to believe that any of its securities are held by one person for the beneficial interest of another, may by notice in writing require either of those persons to: *(a)* confirm or deny that fact; *(b)* provide particulars of the extent of the beneficial interest held during the three years preceding the date of the notice, and *(c)* disclose the identity of each person with a beneficial interest in the securities held by that person.[30] This information must be provided not later than ten business days after receipt of the notice.

(c) Register of disclosures

A register of the disclosures made in terms of s 56 regarding the beneficial interests in securities must be established and maintained by a company that falls within the meaning of 'regulated company' as set out in s 117(1)*(i)* of the Act.[31] In addition, such a company must publish in its annual financial statements (if it is required to have such statements audited) a list of the persons who hold beneficial interests equal to or in excess of 5 per cent of the total number of securities of that class issued by the company, together with the extent of those beneficial interests.[32] The securities register of a regulated company must include a record of all such disclosures of beneficial interests.[33]

The disclosure of beneficial shareholders is consistent with this country's progress from a secretive and narrowly empowered society to an open-market democracy where transparency and accountability are now of paramount importance.[34]

(d) Voting by beneficial shareholders

May a beneficial shareholder vote at a shareholders' meeting? The draft Companies Amendment Bill, 2010 addresses this issue in cl 34*(c)* by providing that a

---

[27] Ibid.
[28] See cl 34*(b)* of the draft Companies Amendment Bill, 2010.
[29] Clause 34*(b)* of the draft Companies Amendment Bill, 2010.
[30] Section 56(5).
[31] A regulated company is one to which the Takeover Regulations apply. It is defined in s 117(1)*(i)* of the Act as meaning a company to which Part B, Part C and the Takeover Regulations apply, as determined in accordance with s 118(1) and (2).
[32] Section 56(7).
[33] See further Regulation 36(3) of the draft Companies Regulations on the register of disclosures, and chapter 7: Shares, Securities and Transfer.
[34] See the *Memorandum on the Objects of the Companies Amendment Bill* (n 18 above) at 30.

beneficial shareholder may vote in a matter at a shareholders' meeting only to the extent that the beneficial interest includes the right to vote on the matter and the person's name appears on the company's register of disclosures as the holder of a beneficial interest, or the person holds a proxy appointment in respect of that matter from the registered holder of those securities.

(e) Notices and proxy appointments

Regarding the sending of notices of shareholders' meetings to the beneficial shareholder, the draft Companies Amendment Bill, 2010 provides that the registered shareholder must deliver notices of meetings to the beneficial shareholder within two business days after receiving the notice from the company.[35] In addition:

> [A] person who has a beneficial interest in any securities that are entitled to be voted on a matter at a meeting of a company's shareholders may demand a proxy appointment from the registered holder of those securities, to the extent of that person's beneficial interest, by delivering such a demand to the registered holder, in writing, or as required by the applicable requirements of a central securities depository.[36]

9.3 RECORD DATE FOR DETERMINING SHAREHOLDER RIGHTS

It is important for a company to be able to establish who is entitled to receive notice of a shareholders' meeting and to vote on resolutions, particularly when the shares of the company are constantly being traded. For this purpose, s 59(1) of the Act makes provision for the board of directors to set a record date for determining which shareholders are entitled to receive notice of a meeting and to participate in and vote at a meeting. In addition, the record date must be set for the purpose of determining which shareholders are to decide any matter by written consent (as contemplated in s 60) or electronic communication; to exercise pre-emptive rights (as contemplated in s 39); to receive a distribution, or to be allotted or exercise other rights.[37]

The record date must not be set too far in advance of the meeting because, if shares are traded between the record date and the date of the meeting, persons who are no longer shareholders at the date of the meeting would be entitled to vote and those who have become shareholders after the record date would not be entitled to vote (save by instructing the shareholder on record how to vote).[38] Some jurisdictions address this problem by share-blocking in public listed companies, that is, prohibiting trading between the record date and the date of the meeting. Share-blocking does have its disadvantages and is in fact prohibited in the European Union.[39] In the United Kingdom the record date is set very close to the meeting date — it may not be more than 48 hours before the time fixed for the meeting —

---

[35] See cl 34(c) of the draft Companies Amendment Bill, 2010.
[36] Ibid.
[37] Section 59(1).
[38] Paul L Davies op cit n 19 at 464.
[39] See Article 7(1)(b) of Directive 2007/36/EC of the European Parliament and of the Council of 11 July 2007 on the exercise of certain rights of shareholders in listed companies.

in order to minimise the effect of trading in public listed companies once the record date has been set.[40]

The Act has not adopted the share-blocking approach, but has instead emulated the approach adopted in the UK of setting the record date close to the meeting. In terms of s 59(2)(a)(ii) of the Act the record date may not be more than ten business days before the date on which the event or action for which the record date is set is scheduled to occur. It must be conceded that, if the record date is set at ten business days before a meeting, there may be some misallocation of voting rights if shares are traded between the record date and the date of the meeting. Note that the record date may not be earlier than the date on which it is determined, ie it may not be retrospective.[41]

The record date must be published to the shareholders in a manner that satisfies any prescribed requirements.[42] Should the board of directors fail to determine a record date for any action or event, unless the Memorandum of Incorporation or rules provide otherwise, the record date would be, in the case of a meeting, the latest date by which the company is required to give notice to the shareholders of that meeting,[43] or, in any other event, the date of the action or event.[44]

9.4 INSTANCES WHERE COMPLIANCE WITH FORMALITIES IS NOT REQUIRED

9.4.1 Unanimous assent at common law

At common law, the doctrine of unanimous assent permits informal methods of giving shareholder consent. This doctrine allows shareholders to take decisions by unanimous agreement without the need for a formal meeting or without having to observe all the formalities which shareholders' meetings usually entail, such as the giving of notice.[45] Decisions may be taken by unanimous assent provided all the shareholders are fully aware of what is being done and they have all assented to it.[46] The principle of unanimous assent was expounded in *In re Duomatic Ltd*[47] as follows:

> ... where it can be shown that all shareholders who have a right to attend and vote at a general meeting of the company assent to some matter which a general meeting of the

---

[40] See regulation 41(1) of the Uncertificated Securities Regulations 2001 (SI 2001/3755).
[41] Section 59(2)(a)(i).
[42] Section 59(2)(b).
[43] In terms of s 62(1), notices of meetings must be given at least 15 business days before the meeting is to begin in the case of a public company or a non-profit company that has voting members, and ten business days before the meeting is to begin, in any other case.
[44] Section 59(3).
[45] See *Sugden v Beaconhurst Dairies (Pty) Ltd* 1963 (2) SA 174 (E) 180–1; *Dublin v Diner* 1964 (1) SA 799 (D) 801; *Gohlke & Schneider v Westies Minerale (Edms) Bpk* 1970 (2) SA 685 (A) 693–4; *Advance Seed Co (Edms) Bpk v Marrok Plase (Edms) Bpk* 1974 (4) SA 127 (NC); *Quadrangle Investments (Pty) Ltd v Witind Holdings Ltd* 1975 (1) SA 572 (A); *Swanee's Boerdery (Edms) Bpk (in Liquidation) v Trust Bank of Africa Ltd* 1986 (2) SA 850 (A) 858; *Levy v Zalrut Investments (Pty) Ltd* 1986 (4) SA 479 (W) 485; *Transcash SWD (Pty) Ltd v Smith* 1994 (2) SA 295 (C) 302 and *Parker & Cooper Ltd v Reading* [1926] 1 Ch 975 at 984.
[46] *EIC Services Ltd v Phipps* [2004] 2 BCLC 589 para 135.
[47] [1969] 2 Ch 365.

company could carry into effect, that assent is as binding as a resolution in general meeting would be.[48]

As the court in *EIC Services Ltd v Phipps*[49] said, whether the approval is given in advance or after the event, whether it is characterised as agreement, ratification, waiver, or estoppel, and whether the shareholders give their consent in different ways or at different times, is irrelevant for the purposes of unanimous assent.[50]

The then Appellate Division in *Gohlke & Schneider v Westies Minerale (Edms) Bpk*[51] stated that the holding of a general meeting is merely the formal machinery for securing the assent of shareholders and if the assent of all the shareholders is otherwise obtained, there is no reason why this should not be just as effective.[52] The Appellate Division asserted further that the principle is a sound one that gives effect to the substance rather than the mere form of the shareholders' assent.[53] The doctrine of unanimous assent is particularly useful in small companies as it permits shareholders to make decisions informally without the need to hold a meeting or without having to observe all the formalities that shareholders' meetings usually entail.

In *Salomon v Salomon and Co Ltd*[54] Lord Davey stated that '... the company is bound in a matter *intra vires* by the unanimous agreement of its members'.[55] The principle of unanimous assent may not be used to do something that the shareholders do not have the power to do in a shareholders' meeting, nor can it be relied on to obtain an illegal outcome.[56] In *Quadrangle Investments (Pty) Ltd v Witind Holdings Ltd*[57] the then Appellate Division held that a dividend declared by a company in contravention of a condition contained in its memorandum of association (which could lawfully have been contained in its articles of association instead of its memorandum) was not valid nor validated simply because all the shareholders had unanimously assented to it.[58]

It is not clear whether the doctrine of unanimous assent may be used to give

---

[48] *Per* Buckley J at 373.
[49] [2004] 2 BCLC 589 para 135.
[50] See also *Sugden v Beaconhurst Dairies (Pty) Ltd* (supra) at 181 and *Parker & Cooper Ltd v Reading* (supra), where the respective courts stated that it did not matter whether the assent was given simultaneously or at different times.
[51] 1970 (2) SA 685 (A).
[52] At 693 and 694. In this case the Appellate Division held that the shareholders of a company could validly appoint a director to the board without any formal meeting being held by virtue of their unanimous assent, as evidenced by a contract signed by all of them.
[53] At 694.
[54] [1897] AC 22.
[55] At 57. See also *Gohlke & Schneider v Westies Minerale (Edms) Bpk* 1970 (2) SA 685 (A) 693, where this dictum was approved, and *Parker & Cooper Ltd v Reading* [1926] 1 Ch 975 at 984, where the court stated that 'where the transaction is *intra vires* and honest, and especially if it is for the benefit of the company, it cannot be upset if the assent of all the corporators is given to it'.
[56] *Quadrangle Investments (Pty) Ltd v Witind Holdings Ltd* 1975 (1) SA 572 (A) 582; *Re New Cedos Engineering Co Ltd* [1994] 1 BCLC 797 at 813–15.
[57] 1975 (1) SA 572 (A) 582.
[58] The court was however dealing with a special condition contained in the memorandum of association that had applied to the company.

authority to litigate.[59] There has also been much controversy and debate on whether it may be used where a special resolution is required.[60]

9.4.2 Companies with one shareholder

Where a profit company (other than a state-owned company) has only one shareholder, that shareholder may exercise any of or all the voting rights pertaining to that company at any time, without complying with the formalities of notice or any internal formalities, except to the extent that the company's Memorandum of Incorporation provides otherwise.[61] Furthermore, ss 59 to 65 of the Act would not apply to the governance of that company.[62]

9.4.3 Companies in which every shareholder is also a director

If every shareholder of a company (other than a state-owned company) is also a director of that company, in terms of s 57(4) of the Act any matter that is required to be referred by the board of directors to the shareholders for a decision may be decided by the shareholders at any time after being referred by the board, without notice or compliance with any other internal formalities, except to the extent that the Memorandum of Incorporation provides otherwise. But this is subject to the following requirements being fulfilled:

- every such person must have been present at the board meeting when the matter was referred to them in their capacity as shareholders,
- sufficient persons must be present in their capacity as shareholders to satisfy the quorum requirements set out in s 64 of the Act,[63] and
- a resolution adopted by such persons in their capacity as shareholders must have at least the support that would have been required for it to be adopted as an ordinary or a special resolution, as the case may be, at a properly constituted shareholders' meeting.

Section 57(4) is very useful in small companies where the shareholders and the directors are the same persons. By permitting the board meeting and the shareholders' meeting to be rolled into one, the section conveniently disposes of unnecessary and superfluous compliance with internal formalities. But s 57(4) does distinguish between decisions taken in the capacity of a director and those taken in the capacity of a shareholder in that, when acting in the capacity of a shareholder, such persons are not subject to the provisions of ss 73 to 78 of the Act relating to the duties, obligations, liabilities and indemnification of directors.[64]

---

[59] See *L Taylor & Kie (Edms) Bpk v Grabe* 1976 (3) SA 75 (T).

[60] While arguments have been made in favour of each view, the predominant view seems to be that the doctrine of unanimous assent may not be used to pass a special resolution. See *Gohlke & Schneider v Westies Minerale (Edms) Bpk* (supra) at 692–3 and *Quadrangle Investments (Pty) Ltd v Witind Holdings Ltd* (supra) at 581.

[61] Section 57(2)(a).

[62] These provisions relate to shareholders' meetings, notices of meetings and resolutions.

[63] It is not clear why this requirement is necessary since the first requirement states that all shareholders must have been present at the board meeting when the matter was referred to them in the first instance.

[64] See s 57(4)(b).

9.5 PROXIES

A shareholder is not obliged to attend a shareholders' meeting personally and to personally vote on resolutions. He or she may instead appoint a proxy to attend, participate in, speak and vote on his or her behalf at a shareholders' meeting.[65] A proxy is an authorisation to exercise voting rights given by a shareholder to another person.[66] In the context of meetings of companies, the word 'proxy' is used indiscriminately by the authorities to describe both the person appointed to represent a shareholder at a meeting and the instrument by which such a person is appointed and authorised to exercise voting rights.[67] A proxy may also be appointed by a shareholder to give or withhold written consent on his or her behalf to a written resolution contemplated in s 60 of the Act.[68] Proxy appointments are essential and very useful because in practice many shareholders do not attend meetings. Note that the appointment of a proxy is not in itself a vote until it is actually acted upon, ie until the vote is actually cast.[69]

9.5.1 Persons who may be appointed as proxies

Any individual may be appointed as a proxy, including an individual who is not a shareholder of the company.[70] A shareholder may appoint more than one proxy to exercise voting rights attached to different shares held by him or her. Except to the extent that the Memorandum of Incorporation provides otherwise, there is no limit to the number of proxies that may be appointed and a shareholder may appoint two or more persons concurrently as proxies.[71] Under s 189(1) of the 1973 Act a shareholder of a private company was not entitled to appoint more than one proxy, unless the articles of association had provided otherwise. Under the new Act this restriction no longer applies (save to the extent that the Memorandum of Incorporation provides otherwise).

Except to the extent that the Memorandum of Incorporation provides otherwise, a proxy may delegate his or her authority to act on behalf of a shareholder to another person, subject to any restrictions set out in the instrument appointing the proxy.[72]

9.5.2 Procedure to appoint a proxy

A proxy appointment must be in writing and must be dated and signed by the shareholder appointing the proxy.[73] Except to the extent that the Memorandum of Incorporation of a company provides otherwise, a copy of the instrument appointing a proxy must be delivered to the company, or to any other person on behalf of

---

[65] Section 58(1)(*a*).
[66] *Nuwe Suid-Afrikaanse Prinsipale Beleggings (Edms) Bpk v Saambou Holdings Ltd* 1992 (4) SA 387 (W) 390.
[67] Ibid.
[68] Section 58(1)(*b*).
[69] *Nuwe Suid-Afrikaanse Prinsipale Beleggings (Edms) Bpk v Saambou Holdings Ltd* 1992 (4) SA 387 (W) 391.
[70] Section 58(1).
[71] Section 58(3)(*a*).
[72] Section 58(3)(*b*).
[73] Section 58(2)(*a*).

the company, before the proxy exercises any rights of the shareholder at a shareholders' meeting.[74] Under s 6(11)*(b)*(i) of the Act, if a document, record or statement is required to be delivered, it may be delivered electronically, provided it is delivered in a manner and form such that it can conveniently be printed by the company within a reasonable time and at a reasonable cost. In terms of this provision, the proxy instrument may be delivered to the company electronically.

The Act does not stipulate a time period within which the proxy appointment must be delivered to the company. Under s 189(3)*(a)* of the 1973 Act the articles of association of a company could not require a proxy appointment to be received by the company more than 48 hours before the meeting. Most articles of association usually provided that the instrument appointing a proxy had to be deposited not less than 48 hours before the time for holding the meeting, failing which the proxy instrument would be treated as invalid.[75] The object of imposing this deadline was to afford an opportunity for the proxy forms to be scrutinised before the proxies voted at the meeting. No such time period has been enacted under the Act, so presumably the proxy appointments may be handed in at the meeting.[76]

9.5.3 Validity of the proxy appointment

A proxy appointment remains valid for one year after the date on which it was signed, or for any longer or shorter period expressly set out in the appointment.[77] This period of appointment is subject to the proxy appointment not being revoked by the shareholder[78] or expiring at an earlier period.[79]

9.5.4 Delivery of notices to proxy

If the instrument appointing a proxy or proxies has been delivered to the company, for so long as that appointment remains in effect, any notice required to be delivered by the company to the shareholder in terms of the Act or the company's Memorandum of Incorporation must be delivered to the shareholder and not to the proxy or proxies. Notices are only to be delivered to the proxy or proxies if the shareholder has directed the company in writing to do so and has paid any reasonable fee charged by the company for doing so.[80]

9.5.5 Voting

Section 58(7) of the Act provides that a proxy is entitled to exercise, or abstain from exercising, any voting right of the shareholder without direction, except to the extent that the Memorandum of Incorporation or the instrument appointing the

---

[74] Section 58(3)*(c)*.
[75] See for instance Article 51 of Table A of Schedule 1 to the 1973 Act (articles for a public company having a share capital) and Article 52 of Table B of Schedule 1 to the 1973 Act (articles for a private company having a share capital).
[76] See *Du Preez v Garber: In re Die Boerebank Bpk* 1963 (1) SA 806 (W) 817 and *In re Dorman Long & Co Ltd* [1934] Ch 635 at 662–4.
[77] Section 58(2)*(b)*.
[78] See s 58(4)*(c)*.
[79] This would occur where the proxy appointment is intended to expire at the end of the meeting at which it was intended to be used, in terms of s 58(8)*(d)*.
[80] Section 58(6).

proxy provides otherwise. In other words, a proxy may vote as he or she thinks fit, unless the Memorandum of Incorporation provides otherwise or unless the shareholder in question has indicated, on the proxy form, the manner in which the proxy should vote.

A shareholder may instruct a proxy to vote for or against a resolution or to abstain from voting altogether. A proxy may be a 'three way' proxy, where the agent is given the choice to vote either for or against a resolution or to abstain from voting; a 'two way' proxy, which permits the agent to vote either for or against a particular resolution, or a 'one way' proxy, which does not give the agent any discretion regarding the manner in which he or she is to vote.

Should a proxy vote contrary to the shareholder's instructions, the vote may not be rejected as between the company and the shareholder and would be binding.[81] But on the basis of the well-established principles of the law of agency, as between the proxy and the shareholder, the shareholder (the principal) would have a contractual remedy for damages (where damages can be proved) against the proxy (the agent) for breach of contract.[82]

A proxy may vote on a poll, and on a poll he or she is entitled to exercise all the voting rights attached to the shares held or represented by the shareholder in question.[83] Under the 1973 Act a proxy was not permitted to vote on a show of hands, unless the articles of association had permitted this,[84] but the current Act does not expressly permit or forbid a proxy from voting on a show of hands. It is submitted that from this it follows that a proxy may now probably vote on a show of hands.

9.5.6 Revocation of the proxy appointment

Irrespective of the form of instrument used to appoint a proxy, the proxy appointment is revocable unless it expressly states otherwise.[85] If the appointment is revocable, a shareholder may revoke it by cancelling the appointment in writing or making a later inconsistent appointment of a proxy (ie appointing a different person as the proxy), and delivering a copy of the revocation instrument to the originally appointed proxy and to the company.[86]

The revocation of a proxy instrument constitutes a complete and final cancellation of the proxy's authority to act on behalf of the shareholder. The revocation is effective as of the later of the date stated in the revocation instrument, if any, or the date on which the revocation instrument is delivered to the proxy and to the company.[87]

A proxy appointment may be suspended at any time and to the extent that the shareholder chooses to act directly and in person to exercise any of his or her

---

[81] *Nuwe Suid-Afrikaanse Prinsipale Beleggings (Edms) Bpk v Saambou Holdings Ltd* 1992 (4) SA 387 (W) 391.
[82] Ibid; *Cousins v International Brick Co Ltd* [1931] 2 Ch 90 at 104.
[83] Section 63(5).
[84] See s 189(1) of the 1973 Act.
[85] Section 58(4)(*b*).
[86] Section 58(4)(*c*).
[87] Section 58(5).

rights as a shareholder.[88] The guiding principle is that every proxy is subject to an implied condition that the proxy should only be used if the shareholder is unable to attend the meeting. Accordingly, if a shareholder were to attend the meeting and vote at the meeting, the proxy appointment would be impliedly revoked.[89]

9.5.7 Company-sponsored invitations to appoint a proxy

In terms of s 58(8) of the Act, a company may invite shareholders to appoint a proxy from a list of names provided by the company. If the company issues an invitation to shareholders to appoint one or more persons named by the company as a proxy, or supplies a form of instrument for appointing a proxy, the invitation must be sent to every shareholder who is entitled to notice of the meeting at which the proxy is intended to be exercised.

The invitation or form of instrument supplied by the company for the purpose of appointing a proxy must bear a reasonably prominent summary of the rights established by s 58(8) of the Act.[90] As to what constitutes 'reasonably prominent' is a question of fact and depends on the circumstances of the particular case.[91] In *Abromowitz v Pretoria District Rural Licensing Board*[92] the court said the word 'prominent' has as a synonym the word 'conspicuous', which means 'easily seen' or 'manifest'.[93] This means the summary of the rights that is to appear on the proxy form must be legible and easily seen or manifest, compared to the other terms on the invitation or appointment form.

A shareholder is not bound to appoint one of the persons named by the company as a proxy in the prepared proxy form. Accordingly, the invitation or appointment form must contain adequate blank space immediately preceding the name(s) of any person(s) named in it, to enable a shareholder to write in the name of a proxy chosen by him or her and, if they desire, the name of an alternative proxy of their choice. In addition, the invitation or appointment form must provide adequate space for the shareholder to indicate whether the appointed proxy is to vote in favour of or against any resolution(s) to be put at the meeting or to abstain from voting.[94] These requirements would not apply if the company were to merely supply a generally available standard form of proxy appointment on request by a shareholder.[95]

The proxy appointment remains valid only until the end of the meeting at which it was intended to be used (unless it is revoked earlier by the shareholder).[96] The company may not require the proxy appointment to be made irrevocable.[97]

---

[88] Section 58(4)(*a*).
[89] *Cousins v International Brick Co Ltd* (supra) at 102.
[90] Section 58(8)(*b*)(i).
[91] Galgut, Jennifer, A Kunst, Piet Delport and Quintus Vorster *Henochsberg on the Companies Act* vol 1 5 ed (1994) (Service Issue 31, June 2010) at 355.
[92] 1938 TPD 478.
[93] At 480.
[94] Section 58(8)(*b*). See also 9.5.5 above on voting.
[95] Section 58(9).
[96] Section 58(8)(*d*). This does not apply if the company merely supplies a generally available standard form of proxy appointment on request by a shareholder (s 58(9)).
[97] Section 58(8)(*c*).

The rationale of these provisions is to prevent directors from attempting to secure at the meeting a majority that would support their policies by the device of inviting only selected shareholders to appoint proxies or ensuring that the proxies are those from whom they expect a favourable response.[98]

9.6 SHAREHOLDERS' MEETINGS

9.6.1 The definition of a 'shareholders' meeting'

A 'shareholders [sic] meeting' is defined in s 1 of the Act as meaning, with respect to any particular matter concerning a company, 'a meeting of those holders of that company's issued securities who are entitled to exercise voting rights in relation to that matter'. Shareholders' meetings are held in order to provide shareholders with an opportunity to debate and vote on matters affecting the company.[99]

The Act gives shareholders at a shareholders' meeting some substantive constitutional and managerial powers. Some of these powers include the power to amend the Memorandum of Incorporation;[100] the power to vote on and approve a rule made by the board of directors relating to the governance of the company;[101] the power to remove directors;[102] the power to fill vacancies on the board of directors,[103] and the power to approve the disposal of all or the greater part of the company's assets or undertaking.[104]

9.6.2 Distinction between a shareholders' meeting and an annual general meeting

A distinction is drawn in the Act between a shareholders' meeting and an annual general meeting (AGM). Both are meetings of the shareholders, but an AGM is one which is held once a year and at which particular business is required to be conducted. A public company is required to convene an AGM, but the Act sensibly no longer makes it mandatory for a private company to do so.[105] The minimum business that must be transacted at an AGM must comprise the following:

- the presentation of the directors' report,[106] the audited financial statements for the immediately preceding financial year and an audit committee report,
- the election of directors, to the extent required by the Act or the company's Memorandum of Incorporation,
- the appointment of an auditor for the ensuing financial year and the appointment of an audit committee, and

---

[98] Galgut, Jennifer A Kunst et al op cit n 91 at 356; Paul L Davies op cit n 19 at 457.
[99] *Byng v London Life Association Ltd* [1990] Ch 170 at 183.
[100] Section 16(1)*(c)*.
[101] Section 15(4) and (5).
[102] Section 71(1).
[103] Section 70(3)*(b)*.
[104] Section 112(2)*(a)*.
[105] See s 61(7).
[106] The directors' report deals with the state of affairs of the company, the business and profit or loss of the company (or of the group of companies if the company is part of a group), including any matter material for the shareholders to appreciate the company's state of affairs, and any prescribed information (see s 30(3)*(b)* of the Act).

- any matters raised by the shareholders, with or without advance notice to the company.[107]

The words 'at a minimum' in s 61(8) make it clear that the business transacted at an AGM may go beyond the matters listed above, provided the business is properly put before the shareholders.

The AGM is a key mechanism for promoting transparency and accountability in the management of the company's affairs.[108] It is a forum for conveying information to shareholders and also provides a safeguard to shareholders: it gives them an opportunity to question the directors on the company's financial statements, the directors' report and various other issues relating to the company's affairs that must be transacted at the AGM.[109]

The shareholders are also able to raise any matters of their own at the AGM, without having to give advance notice to the company of these matters, and to express their views on matters relating to the company's affairs. It would seem that even a single shareholder may raise a matter of their own at the AGM without providing advance notice to the company and without having to give the board of directors an opportunity to prepare a response to such matter. This illustrates the wide powers given to shareholders at the AGM.

In practice, though, the AGM does not always successfully achieve these objects. The shareholders of public companies, particularly listed companies, are usually widely dispersed throughout the country and indeed the world, and many shareholders do not attend the AGM due to it being impractical to do so.[110] Accordingly, most shareholders, particularly institutional investors, decide on their votes before the meeting and simply appoint proxies to vote on resolutions at meetings.[111] Thus in practice the AGM is not always the forum for debating, information exchange and decision making that it was intended to be.[112]

9.7 CONVENING A SHAREHOLDERS' MEETING

9.7.1 Persons who may convene a shareholders' meeting

The board of directors or any other person specified in the company's Memorandum of Incorporation or rules may at any time convene a shareholders' meeting.[113]

The power given to the board of directors to call a shareholders' meeting is a fiduciary power and must be exercised in good faith and in the interests of the company as a whole.[114] The right to participate in a meeting and the right to vote are rights inherent in the ownership of shares, and it is thus not competent for the

---

[107] Section 61(8).
[108] *Modern Company Law for a Competitive Economy: Company General Meetings and Shareholder Communication* (URN 99/1144) (London: DTI, 1999) para 3.
[109] Ibid; Blackman et al op cit n 26 at 7–10.
[110] *Modern Company Law for a Competitive Economy: Company General Meetings and Shareholder Communication* (URN 99/1144) (London: DTI, 1999) para 19.
[111] Ibid para 20.
[112] Ibid.
[113] Section 61(1).
[114] *Umfolozi Co-operative Sugar Planters Ltd v St Lucia Sugar Farms (Pty) Ltd* 1983 (1) SA 792 (N) 796, 798; *Pergamon Press Ltd v Maxwell* [1970] 1 WLR 1167 at 1171–2.

board of directors to frustrate or impede that right by either not holding a shareholders' meeting or holding it at a time and a place that make it very difficult for some shareholders to attend.[115] This proposition would clearly not apply where a shareholder is in prison or overseas or finds it inconvenient to attend the meeting at the specified time and place.[116] But in general, directors have a fiduciary duty to convene shareholders' meetings at a time and a place that make it possible for all shareholders of the company to attend.[117]

9.7.2 Instances when a company must hold a shareholders' meeting

A company must hold a shareholders' meeting in the following instances:

(a) When the board of directors is required by the Act or the Memorandum of Incorporation to refer a matter to the shareholders for decision[118]

A shareholders' meeting must be called when the board of directors is required, by the Act or the Memorandum of Incorporation, to refer a matter to the shareholders for decision. Unless the Act or the Memorandum of Incorporation empowers the directors to do so, directors may not refer matters that are within their power to a shareholders' meeting and thereby enable the shareholders to deal with such matters.[119] In *John Shaw and Sons (Salford) Ltd v Shaw*[120] the court described this aspect of the relationship and the division of powers between directors and shareholders as follows:

> If powers of management are vested in the directors, they and they alone can exercise these powers. The only way in which the general body of the shareholders can control the exercise of the powers vested by the articles in the directors is by altering their articles, or, if opportunity arises under the articles, by refusing to re-elect the directors of whose actions they disapprove. They cannot themselves usurp the powers which by the articles are vested in the directors any more than the directors can usurp the powers vested by the articles in the general body of shareholders.[121]

---

[115] *Albert E Touchet Inc v Touchet* 163 NE 184 (Mass. 1928) 188, approved in *Smith v Sadler* [1997] NSWSC 525.
[116] *Smith v Sadler* (supra).
[117] Ibid.
[118] Section 61(2)(*a*).
[119] *John Shaw and Sons (Salford) Ltd v Shaw* [1935] 2 KB 113 (CA); *Letseng Diamonds Ltd v JCI Ltd; Trinity Asset Management (Pty) Ltd v Investec Bank Ltd* 2007 (5) SA 564 (W) para 16; *Automatic Self-Cleansing Filter Syndicate Co Ltd v Cuninghame* [1906] 2 Ch 34; *Hogg v Cramphorn Ltd* [1967] Ch 254; *Bamford v Bamford* [1970] Ch 212; *Winthrop Investments Ltd v Winns Ltd* [1975] 2 NSWLR 666 (CA) (NSW) 673–4; *Smith v Croft (No 2)* [1988] Ch 114.
[120] [1935] 2 KB 113 (CA).
[121] At 134. But the shareholders may intrude upon the powers of the board of directors in certain instances. For instance, where the board of directors for some reason (such as a deadlock among the directors) cannot or will not exercise the powers vested in them, the shareholders in a shareholders' meeting may do so. Another instance would be when certain powers have been reserved for the board of directors but the particular act is voidable because the board has exceeded or abused its powers (see for example *Ben-Tovim v Ben-Tovim* 2001 (3) SA 1074 (C) 1085–6 and *Barron v Potter* [1914] 1 Ch 895). These are the default powers of a shareholders' meeting.

(b) Whenever required in terms of s 70(3) to fill a vacancy on the board[122]

If a vacancy arises on the board (other than as a result of an *ex officio* director ceasing to hold that office) it must be filled by a new appointment if the director had been appointed by a person named in or determined in terms of the Memorandum of Incorporation, or by a new election.[123] The election must be conducted at the next AGM of the company if the company is required to hold such meetings. If the company is not required to hold AGMs, then the vacancy must be filled within six months after it arose, either at a shareholders' meeting called for the purpose of electing the director, or by a written polling of all the shareholders who are entitled to vote in the election of that director.[124]

If, as a result of a vacancy arising on the board of directors, there are no remaining directors of a company, any shareholder who is entitled to vote in the election of a director may convene a meeting for the purpose of such an election.[125]

(c) When one or more written and signed demands for a shareholders' meeting are delivered to the company[126]

The board of directors or any other person specified in the company's Memorandum of Incorporation or rules must call a shareholders' meeting if one or more written and signed demands for such a meeting are delivered to the company by the shareholders. The aggregate of the demands for substantially the same purpose must be made and signed by holders of at least 10 per cent of the voting rights entitled to be exercised in relation to the matter proposed to be considered at the meeting. The Memorandum of Incorporation may specify a lower but not a higher threshold.[127]

It may be to the advantage of small shareholders in public companies if the Memorandum of Incorporation were to specify a lower percentage for demanding a meeting because small individual shareholders of public companies may find it difficult and expensive to enlist the support of a sufficient number of fellow individual shareholders to reach the 10 per cent threshold required to demand a meeting. Reaching the threshold of 10 per cent may not be as difficult in public companies where the support of only a few institutional shareholders may be required to reach the 10 per cent threshold for demanding a meeting. In contrast, a lower threshold has been specified in the Australian Corporations Act 50 of 2001, where the directors of a company are required to call a shareholders' meeting on the request of shareholders with at least 5 per cent of the votes that may be cast at the meeting.[128]

---

[122] Section 61(2)*(b)*.
[123] Section 70(3).
[124] Section 70(3)*(b)*.
[125] Section 70(4).
[126] Section 61(2)*(c)*(i) read with s 61(3).
[127] Section 61(3)–(4).
[128] See s 249D of the Australian Corporations Act 50 of 2001.

Even though shareholders are given a right to demand a meeting, the company or any shareholder of the company may apply to court for an order setting aside the demand for a meeting on the grounds that the demand is frivolous, or calls for a meeting for no other purpose than to reconsider a matter that has already been decided by the shareholders, or is otherwise vexatious.[129] The Act empowers a court to determine whether a meeting demanded by shareholders may proceed, and thus gives the courts a wide discretion to determine whether a meeting validly called by the shareholders may in fact proceed.

At any time before the commencement of a shareholders' meeting called by means of a demand, a shareholder who had submitted a demand for that meeting may withdraw the demand.[130] The company must cancel the meeting if, as a result of one or more demands being withdrawn, the voting rights of any remaining shareholders continuing to demand the meeting, in aggregate, fall below the minimum percentage of voting rights required to call a meeting.[131]

To be valid, the demand must describe the specific purpose for which the meeting is proposed.[132] Matters not stated in the demand may not be dealt with at the meeting.[133]

(d) When an AGM of the shareholders is required to be convened[134]

A public company must convene an AGM of its shareholders no more than 18 months after the company's date of incorporation. Thereafter, it is required to convene an AGM once in every calendar year, but no more than 15 months after the date of the previous AGM, or within such an extended time permitted by the Companies Tribunal on good cause being shown.[135]

As is the case in the UK, under the Act it is not mandatory for a private company to convene an AGM.[136] Under the 1973 Act every company was required to hold an AGM, but under the new Act it is now mandatory for public companies only to hold an AGM.

(e) Whenever required by the company's Memorandum of Incorporation[137]

The Memorandum of Incorporation may specify certain instances when a company must hold a shareholders' meeting.

---

[129] Section 61(5).
[130] Section 61(6)*(a)*.
[131] Section 61(6)*(b)*.
[132] Section 61(3)*(a)*.
[133] *Ball v Metal Industries Ltd* 1957 SC 315.
[134] Section 61(2)*(c)*(i) read with s 61(7).
[135] Section 61(7). In *Cohen Brothers v Samuels* 1906 TS 221 at 224 Innes CJ commented, in regard to defining the phrase 'good cause', as follows: 'In the nature of things it is hardly possible, and certainly undesirable, for the Court to attempt to do so. No general rule which the wit of man could devise would be likely to cover all the varying circumstances which may arise in applications of this nature. We can only deal with each application on its merits, and decide in each case whether good cause has been shown.'
[136] See s 336(1) of the UK Companies Act 2006.
[137] Section 61(2)*(c)*(ii).

9.7.3 Company with one shareholder

As discussed earlier, if a profit company (other than a state-owned company) has only one shareholder, that shareholder may exercise any of or all the voting rights pertaining to that company at any time, without complying with the formalities of notice or any internal formalities, except to the extent that the company's Memorandum of Incorporation provides otherwise.[138] Sections 59 to 65 of the Act, relating to shareholders' meetings, notices of meetings and resolutions of shareholders, would not apply to the governance of that company. Moreover, s 75(2)*(b)* of the Act provides that s 75 of the Act, dealing with the disclosure of directors' personal financial interests, would not apply to a company or its director if one person holds all of the beneficial interests of all of the issued securities of the company and is the only director of that company.

9.7.4 Failure to convene a meeting

(a) *Power of authorised persons and the Companies Tribunal to convene meetings*

In terms of s 61(11)*(a)* of the Act, if a company is unable to convene a shareholders' meeting (including an AGM) because it does not have any directors, or because all its directors are incapacitated, any other person authorised by the Memorandum of Incorporation may convene the meeting.

Under s 61(11)*(b)*, if no person has been authorised by the Memorandum of Incorporation to convene a meeting, the Companies Tribunal, on request by any shareholder, may issue an administrative order for a shareholders' meeting to be convened on a date, and subject to any terms, that the Tribunal considers appropriate in the circumstances.

(b) *Power of courts to convene meetings*

Under s 61(12) of the Act, where a company fails to convene a meeting for any reason other than that contemplated in s 61(11), at a time (i) required in accordance with its Memorandum of Incorporation; (ii) when required by demand by the shareholders, or (iii) within the time period required for a public company to convene an AGM, a shareholder may apply to court for an order requiring the company to convene a meeting on a date, and subject to any terms that the court considers appropriate in the circumstances.[139]

However, the general policy of the courts has been not to interfere with the internal domestic affairs of the company where the company ought to be able to regulate its own affairs by appropriate resolutions of a majority of shareholders.[140] For example, in *Yende v Orlando Coal Distributors (Pty) Ltd*[141] the court refused to order the holding of a meeting where, despite disputes between the shareholders, there was nothing preventing the shareholders from requisitioning a general meeting in accordance with the provisions of the Act. The power given to a court

---
[138] Section 57(2)*(a)*.
[139] Section 61(12).
[140] *Yende v Orlando Coal Distributors (Pty) Ltd* 1961 (3) SA 314 (W) 316.
[141] 1961 (3) SA 314 (W).

to call a meeting is generally only exercised by the court in exceptional circumstances.[142]

The company must compensate a shareholder who applies to the Companies Tribunal under s 61(11) or to court under s 61(12) for the costs of those proceedings.[143]

A failure by a company to hold a shareholders' meeting would affect neither the existence of the company, nor the validity of any action taken by the company.[144]

9.8 NOTICE OF MEETINGS

A company must deliver a notice of each shareholders' meeting in the prescribed manner and form to all the shareholders of the company as at the record date.[145]

A notice may be transmitted electronically directly to a shareholder in such a manner and form that enables it to be conveniently printed by the recipient within a reasonable time and at a reasonable cost.[146]

9.8.1 Period of notice

In the case of a public company or a non-profit company that has voting members, the notice of each shareholders' meeting must be delivered at least 15 business days before the meeting is to begin. In any other case the notice must be delivered at least ten business days before the meeting is to begin.[147]

A company's Memorandum of Incorporation may provide for a longer minimum notice period, but, unlike the 1973 Act, no provision has been made in the Act permitting shareholders to call a meeting on a shorter notice period or to waive the notice period altogether.[148] Presumably, the shareholders may be able to agree to a shorter notice period or to waive the notice period altogether in terms of the common-law doctrine of unanimous assent. It is arguable, however, that short notice may fall within the scope and ambit of s 62(4), and particularly s 62(4)(d) of the Act.

9.8.2 Content of notice

The notice must be in writing and must include certain information, namely:

(a) the date, time and place for the meeting, and the record date for the meeting;

---

[142] *Otto v Klipvlei Diamond Areas (Pty) Ltd* 1958 (2) SA 437 (T) 441.
[143] Section 61(13).
[144] Section 61(14).
[145] Section 62(1).
[146] Section 6(10).
[147] Section 62(1). According to s 5(3) of the Act, where a particular number of 'business days' is provided for between the happening of one event and another, the number of days is calculated by:
   (a) excluding the day on which the first such event occurs;
   (b) including the day on or by which the second event is to occur; and
   (c) excluding any public holiday, Saturday or Sunday that falls on or between the days contemplated in paragraphs (a) and (b), respectively.
[148] Under the 1973 Act a meeting could be called on a shorter period of notice than the prescribed period if agreed to by a majority in number of the shareholders having a right to attend and vote at the meeting who held not less than 95 per cent of the total voting rights of all the shareholders of the company (s 186(2)(a)). Notice could even be waived altogether if so agreed in writing before or at the meeting, by all the shareholders of the company (s 186(2)(b)).

(b) the general purpose of the meeting, as well as any specific purpose for which a meeting may have been demanded by the shareholders (if applicable);

(c) a copy of any proposed resolution of which the company has received notice, and which is to be considered at the meeting, and a notice of the percentage of voting rights that would be required for that resolution to be adopted;

(d) a reasonably prominent statement that:
   (i) a shareholder entitled to attend and vote at the meeting is entitled to appoint a proxy to attend, participate in and vote at the meeting in the place of the shareholder, or two or more proxies if the Memorandum of Incorporation so permits;
   (ii) a proxy need not be a shareholder of the company; and
   (iii) s 63(1) of the Companies Act requires that participants at the meeting provide satisfactory identification.[149]

In the case of an AGM of a company the notice must include a summarised form of the financial statements to be presented, as well as directions on how to obtain a copy of the complete annual financial statements for the preceding financial year.[150]

For the shareholders to be in a position to decide whether to attend the meeting, to vote for or against the proposed resolutions or to appoint a proxy to vote on their behalf, or not to take any such action but simply to leave it to the majority of the shareholders to decide on the resolutions, they must have sufficient information to be able to come to an 'intelligent conclusion on the matter on which they were asked to vote'.[151] This right arises from a term implied in the company contract.[152] In *Trinity Asset Management (Pty) Ltd v Investec Bank Ltd*[153] the Supreme Court of Appeal held that shareholders were entitled to interdict a meeting from proceeding where a circular sent to the shareholders on the issues to be voted on at a shareholders' meeting contained inaccurate information. The court ruled as follows:

> It is clear that a shareholder's right to information regarding a proposition to be voted on at a general meeting has developed and been extended down the years, particularly since the practice of giving proxies has become so widespread . . . a shareholder's right to receive the necessary information arises from an implied term in the company contract. Regard being had to the fact that an individual shareholder will be bound by the votes of the majority, it must follow that the shareholder's rights extend not only to his or her being furnished with the necessary information but that all his or her fellow shareholders also receive such information. It also follows that a shareholder has the right flowing from the company contract to insist that he or she and his or her fellow shareholders do not receive information

---

[149] Section 62(3).
[150] Section 62(3)*(d)*.
[151] *Trinity Asset Management (Pty) Ltd v Investec Bank Ltd* 2009 (4) SA 89 (SCA) para 22. See also *Sammel v President Brand Gold Mining Co Ltd* 1969 (3) SA 629 (A) 674–7 and *Williamson v Durban City Council* 1977 (3) SA 342 (D) 348.
[152] *Trinity Asset Management (Pty) Ltd v Investec Bank Ltd* (supra). See also *Bulfin v Bebarfald's Ltd* (1932) 38 SR (NSW) 423 at 440–1.
[153] *Trinity Asset Management* (supra).

which is inaccurate and to enforce such right by applying for an interdict to prevent a meeting from proceeding.[154]

9.8.3 Failure to give notice and defects in the notice
Section 62(4) of the Act provides as follows:
> If a company fails to give the required notice of a shareholders *[sic]* meeting, or if there was a material defect in the giving of the notice, the meeting may proceed, subject to subsection (5), if all of the persons who are entitled to exercise voting rights in respect of each item on the agenda of the meeting —
> *(a)* acknowledge actual receipt of the notice;
> *(b)* are present at the meeting;
> *(c)* waive notice of the meeting; or
> *(d)* in the case of a material defect in the manner and form of giving notice, ratify the defective notice.

This section is ambiguous and could well be interpreted to be that subsections *(a)* to *(d)* are disjunctive and not conjunctive. This is particularly so in view of the word 'or' used in the section.

Note than an immaterial defect in the form or manner of giving notice, or an accidental or inadvertent failure in the delivery of notice to any particular shareholders to whom it was addressed, would not invalidate any action taken at the meeting.[155] But in the case of a material defect in the form or manner of giving notice, the defect must be ratified by all the persons who are entitled to exercise voting rights in respect of each item on the agenda.[156]

If the material defect in the form or manner of giving notice relates only to one or more particular matters on the agenda for the meeting, such matter or matters may be severed from the agenda, and the notice would remain valid with respect to any remaining matters on the agenda.[157] However, the meeting may proceed to consider a severed matter if the defective notice in respect of that matter were ratified by all the shareholders.[158]

A shareholder who is present at a meeting[159] has a right to allege a material defect in the form of notice for a particular item on the agenda for the meeting, and to participate in the determination whether to waive the requirements for notice, or ratify a defective notice.[160] A shareholder who is present at a meeting is deemed to have received or waived notice of the meeting,[161] and to have waived any right based on an actual or alleged material defect in the notice of the meeting, except to the extent that he or she alleges a material defect in the form of the

---
[154] Para 36.
[155] Section 62(6).
[156] Section 62(4)*(d)*.
[157] Section 62(5)*(a)*.
[158] Section 62(5)*(b)*.
[159] The phrase 'present at a meeting' is defined in s 1 of the Act as meaning 'to be present in person, or able to participate in the meeting by electronic communication, or to be represented by a proxy who is present in person or able to participate in the meeting by electronic communication'.
[160] Section 62(7)*(b)*.
[161] Section 62(7)*(a)*.

notice and participates in the determination whether to waive the requirements for notice or ratify the defect.[162]

9.9 CONDUCT OF SHAREHOLDERS' MEETINGS

9.9.1 Location of shareholders' meetings

Except to the extent that the Memorandum of Incorporation provides otherwise, the board of directors of the company may determine the location for any shareholders' meeting, which shareholders' meeting may be held in South Africa or even in any foreign country.[163]

9.9.2 Attending and participating in a shareholders' meeting

All shareholders have a right not only to vote at a meeting, but also to hear and be heard in any debate at the meeting.[164] Before a person attends or participates in a shareholders' meeting, he or she must present reasonably satisfactory identification, and the chairperson of the meeting must be reasonably satisfied that the right of that person to participate and vote, either as a shareholder or as a proxy for a shareholder, has been reasonably verified.[165]

9.9.3 Electronic communication

A company may make provision for a shareholders' meeting to be conducted by electronic communication, or for one or more shareholders, or proxies for shareholders, to participate by electronic communication in all or part of a shareholders' meeting that is being held in person.[166] This is subject to the proviso that all participants are able to communicate concurrently with each other without an intermediary, and are able to participate reasonably effectively in the meeting.[167] Permitting shareholders to participate in meetings electronically and to vote electronically would encourage them to play a more active role in the company's affairs and would promote shareholder activism. Flexibility is maintained by permitting shareholders' meetings to be held electronically while at the same time permitting a company in its Memorandum of Incorporation to restrict electronic meetings if it so chooses.[168]

If a company makes provision for participation in a meeting by means of electronic communication, the notice of that meeting must inform shareholders of this fact and must provide any necessary information to enable shareholders or their proxies to access the available medium or means of electronic communication.[169] Access to the medium or means of electronic communication is at the

---

[162] Section 62(7)(c).
[163] Section 61(9).
[164] *Byng v London Life Association Ltd* [1990] Ch 170 at 188.
[165] Section 63(1).
[166] Section 63(2).
[167] Section 63(2)(b).
[168] See s 63(2).
[169] Section 63(3)(a).

expense of the shareholder or proxy (except to the extent that the company determines otherwise).[170]

In respect of public companies, every shareholders' meeting must be reasonably accessible within South Africa for electronic participation by shareholders, irrespective of whether the meeting is held in South Africa or elsewhere.[171] In the particular context of this section, one wonders what 'reasonably accessible' means.

9.10 VOTING AT MEETINGS

9.10.1 Show of hands and poll

Voting at a meeting may take place by a show of hands or on a poll. On a show of hands, any person present and entitled to exercise voting rights has only one vote, irrespective of the number of shares held by that person.[172] It is a head count — not a value count. A shareholder may exercise or abstain from exercising his or her vote at their discretion. In terms of this procedure voters in favour of a motion are asked to raise their hand and are counted and voters against a motion are asked to do the same. Each voter is counted once only, irrespective of the number of shares held by him or her. The chairperson then announces whether the motion is carried or lost.

Voting on a show of hands has the advantage of being a fast and simple process of taking uncontroversial decisions quickly.[173] But a disadvantage of this method of voting is that it may produce a different result from that which would be produced by voting on a poll, because a shareholder's full voting power is not used when voting on a show of hands. In contrast, when voting on a poll, weighted voting rights may be exercised. For instance, in *In re Horbury Bridge Coal, Iron, and Waggon Company*,[174] on voting on a show of hands on an ordinary resolution, three voters together holding 50 shares had voted in favour of the motion while two voters together holding 65 shares had voted against the motion. A poll had not been demanded, but the chairman declared that those who had voted against the motion had won as a result of which the motion had failed. The court held that the result of the motion had to be determined on a show of hands, without counting shares, because a poll had not been demanded, and that weighted voting rights were not available on a show of hands. Accordingly, those voting in favour of the motion had won.

A further, less critical, disadvantage of voting on a show of hands is that, where a resolution is controversial, this may have the effect of disguising the level of opposition to the resolution.[175] For instance, a resolution may be passed on a show of hands by 80 in favour of the resolution and 20 against it, but if a poll were taken it would have been clear, for instance, that 500 votes were in favour of the

---

[170] Section 63(3)*(b)*.
[171] Section 61(10).
[172] Section 63(4).
[173] Paul L Davies op cit n 19 at 461.
[174] (1879) LR 11 ChD 109.
[175] Paul L Davies op cit n 19 at 461.

resolution and 400 against it.[176] Voting on a show of hands is also not confidential. The vote of a shareholder voting on a show of hands could easily be influenced by the manner in which other shareholders vote at the meeting.

In order to counter these disadvantages, shareholders should be given the right to demand that voting takes place on a poll. Section 63(5) of the Act accordingly provides that on a poll, any shareholder, including his or her proxy present at the meeting, is entitled to exercise all the voting rights attached to the shares held or represented by that person. While the 1973 Act permitted shareholders to demand a poll in certain instances,[177] the current Act has oddly failed to indicate how and when a poll may be demanded at a meeting. This oversight is to be rectified by the draft Companies Amendment Bill, 2010, which provides that, despite any provision of a company's Memorandum of Incorporation or agreement to the contrary, a polled vote must be held on any particular matter to be voted on at a meeting if a demand for such a vote is made by (i) at least five persons having the right to vote on that matter (either as a shareholder or as a proxy representing the shareholder), or (ii) a person who is, or persons who together are, entitled as a shareholder or as a proxy representing a shareholder, to exercise at least 10 per cent of the voting rights entitled to be voted on that matter.[178]

The procedure for voting on a poll is that voting papers are given to the shareholders present, who indicate whether their vote is in favour of or against the motion. Since a shareholder is entitled to exercise all the voting rights attached to his or her shares, the number of shares in respect of which he or she is voting must be indicated on the voting paper. Scrutineers are appointed to examine and count the votes and to eliminate 'spoilt' votes, ie those voting papers that have not been properly completed. When the votes have been counted, the chairperson is informed of the result and he or she declares the result of the poll to the meeting.[179] An advantage of voting on a poll is that the vote is concealed from the other shareholders, but there is, of course, a record of how each individual shareholder has voted.

9.10.2 Voting agreements

A shareholder's right to vote is a proprietary right of his or her shareholding, and when they vote for or against a particular resolution, they vote as persons that owe no fiduciary duty to the company. They are exercising a right of property. Accordingly, a shareholder's right to vote may be exercised in their own interests and not necessarily in the company's interests.[180] Directors, on the other hand, owe a fiduciary duty to the company to act in good faith and in what they consider will best serve the interests of the company.[181]

---

[176] Ibid at 461–2.
[177] See s 198 of the 1973 Act.
[178] See cl 39(c) of the draft Companies Amendment Bill, 2010.
[179] RP Austin and IM Ramsay *Ford's Principles of Corporations Law* 13 ed (2007) para 7.530 p 297.
[180] *Sammel v President Brand Gold Mining Co Ltd* 1969 (3) SA 629 (A) 680; *Rentekor (Pty) Ltd v Rheeder and Berman* 1988 (4) SA 469 (T) 497–8; *Ben-Tovim v Ben-Tovim* 2001 (3) SA 1074 (C) 1088; *Pender v Lushington* (1877) 6 ChD 70.
[181] *Coronation Syndicate Ltd v Lilienfeld and New Fortuna Co Ltd* 1903 TS 489.

There are, however, limitations to a shareholder's right to vote in any way he or she pleases. In *Porteus v Kelly*[182] the court stated that 'shareholders may vote at a meeting of a company in favour of their own interests provided that it is in an ordinary legitimate manner on a matter within the scope of the company's powers'.[183] A majority may not oppressively and fraudulently use their votes to defraud a minority.[184] In *Sammel v President Brand Gold Mining Co Ltd*[185] the Supreme Court of Appeal stressed that, while a shareholder may exercise his or her vote in his or her own interests, this does not entitle the majority to use their voting power to discriminate between themselves and the minority shareholders so as to give themselves an advantage at the expense of the minority.

Note that a director, in his or her capacity as a shareholder of a company, may vote at a shareholders' meeting as he or she pleases, and may act entirely in their personal interests without taking any account of any conflicting interests of the company, provided they are not guilty of fraud or oppression of minority shareholders.[186]

9.11 CHAIRPERSON AT MEETINGS

The Act does not deal with the appointment of a chairperson at a shareholders' meeting. Presumably this would be dealt with in the company's Memorandum of Incorporation. Generally, the chairperson of the board of directors acts as the chairperson of the shareholders' meeting, or alternatively a shareholder may be elected at the meeting to chair the meeting.

The chairperson plays an important role at a meeting. It is his or her duty to preserve order at the meeting and to ensure that the proceedings are conducted in a proper manner.[187] He or she must act honestly and fairly to the interests of all parties and in the best interests of the company.[188] The chairperson has a fiduciary duty to act objectively.[189] Note that the chairperson owes a duty to the meeting and not to the board of directors, even if he or she is a director.[190]

9.12 QUORUM

A quorum is the minimum number of qualified persons whose presence at a meeting is necessary before any business may be validly transacted at the meeting. The Act specifies two quorum requirements: one must be satisfied in order for a

---

[182] 1975 (1) SA 219 (W).
[183] At 222.
[184] *Porteus v Kelly* 1975 (1) SA 219 (W) 222. See also *Gundelfinger v African Textile Manufacturers Ltd* 1939 AD 314 at 326.
[185] 1969 (3) SA 629 (A) 680.
[186] *Gundelfinger v African Textile Manufacturers Ltd* (supra); *Ben-Tovim v Ben-Tovim* (supra); *North-West Transportation Co Ltd v Beatty* (1887) 12 App Cas 589 (PC); *Northern Counties Securities Ltd v Jackson & Steeple Ltd* [1974] 2 All ER 625 (Ch).
[187] See *National Dwellings Society v Sykes* [1894] 3 Ch 159 at 162; *Berman v Chairman, Cape Provincial Council* 1961 (2) SA 412 (C) 416 and *Jonker v Ackerman* 1979 (3) SA 575 (O) 583–4.
[188] *Blair v Consolidated Enfield Corp* (1995) 128 DLR (4th) 73 para 47.
[189] *South African Broadcasting Corporation Ltd v Mpofu* [2009] 4 All SA 169 (GSJ).
[190] *The Second Consolidated Trust Ltd v Ceylon Amalgamated Tea & Rubber Estates Ltd* [1943] 2 All ER 567.

shareholders' meeting to commence, and the other for a matter at the meeting to be considered.

9.12.1 Quorum for a meeting to commence

A shareholders' meeting may not commence until sufficient persons are present at the meeting to exercise, in aggregate, at least 25 per cent of all the voting rights that are entitled to be exercised in respect of at least one matter to be decided at the meeting.[191] A company's Memorandum of Incorporation may specify a higher or even a lower percentage in place of the 25 per cent required for a meeting to commence.[192]

9.12.2 Quorum for a matter at the meeting to be considered

A matter to be decided at a shareholders' meeting may not begin to be considered unless sufficient persons are present at the meeting to exercise, in aggregate, at least 25 per cent of all the voting rights that are entitled to be exercised on that particular matter at the time the matter is called on the agenda.[193] The Memorandum of Incorporation may specify a higher or a lower threshold in this regard.

9.12.3 Quorum once a meeting has commenced

Section 64(9) of the Act states that, unless the Memorandum of Incorporation or rules provide otherwise, after a quorum has been established for a meeting or for a matter to be considered at a meeting, the meeting may continue, or the matter may be considered, if at least one shareholder with voting rights entitled to be exercised at the meeting, or on that matter, is present at the meeting.

This means that once the quorum requirements for a meeting to commence or for a matter to be considered at a meeting have been satisfied, should one or more shareholders leave the meeting resulting in the number of shareholders present at the meeting to be reduced below the minimum number required to constitute a quorum, the meeting may nevertheless continue and a matter may nevertheless be considered at the meeting as long as at least one shareholder with voting rights entitled to be exercised at the meeting is still present at the meeting. In terms of the Act this is the default position; should the Memorandum of Incorporation or rules provide otherwise, it would seem that the quorum must be present throughout the meeting for the meeting to continue or for a matter to be considered at the meeting.

In *Henderson v James Louttit & Co Ltd*[194] the court took the view, *obiter*, that a quorum must not only be present at the commencement of the meeting, but also at the time when the business is transacted. In the course of the judgment it was stated by the court:

> [It] would be a highly inconvenient, not to say unnatural meaning to attribute to it [the article] to hold that all that is necessary to the validity of the proceedings is, that at the

---

[191] Section 64(1)(*a*).
[192] Section 64(2).
[193] Section 64(1)(*b*).
[194] (1894) 21 Rettie 674.

earliest stage of the meeting a quorum should be present, but that after the real business of the meeting is started and under consideration the quorum might go away.[195]

In *Hartley Baird Ltd*[196] the articles of association of a company similarly provided that 'No business shall be transacted at any general meeting unless a quorum is present when the meeting proceeds to business . . .'. The court refused to follow the dictum in *Henderson v James Louttit & Co Ltd* on the basis that it was an *obiter dictum*. The court held that this provision in the articles of association meant that, if a quorum was present at the beginning of a meeting, the subsequent departure of a shareholder reducing the meeting to below the number required for a quorum would not invalidate the proceedings of the meeting after such departure.

It is submitted that it may be inconsistent with the quorum requirements set out in s 64 of the Act to require a quorum to be present at the beginning of a meeting but not once the real business of the meeting is under consideration. Furthermore, s 64(9) is problematic in that it could result in only one shareholder making a decision that would bind the company and all the other shareholders. However, flexibility is maintained in that the Memorandum of Incorporation or rules may provide that the requisite quorum must be present throughout the meeting in order for the meeting to continue or for a matter to be considered at the meeting. Since the statutory provision could lead to an unfair and inequitable result, it may be advisable for a company to provide in its Memorandum of Incorporation that the quorum must be present throughout the meeting for the meeting to continue or for a matter to be considered at the meeting.

9.12.4 Quorum where a company has more than two shareholders

If a company has more than two shareholders, a meeting may not begin, or a matter begin to be debated, unless at least three shareholders are present at the meeting, provided that the quorum requirements for a meeting to begin and for a matter to be debated as specified in the Act or the Memorandum of Incorporation (if different) are satisfied.[197]

9.13 POSTPONEMENT AND ADJOURNMENT OF MEETINGS

An adjournment of a meeting is the suspension of the business of the meeting with the intention of continuing the meeting at a later time, while a postponement of a meeting entails deferring the date of a meeting before it is held.

9.13.1 Postponement where quorum is not present

If a quorum for a meeting to commence is not present within one hour after the appointed time for the commencement of the meeting, the meeting is postponed without motion, vote or further notice, for one week.[198] This is an alterable or

---

[195] At 676.
[196] [1955] Ch 143.
[197] Section 64(3).
[198] Section 64(4)*(a)*.

default provision of the Act, which may be modified by the company's Memorandum of Incorporation or rules.[199]

If the quorum for a matter to be debated at the meeting is not present within one hour after the appointed time for a meeting to commence, and if there is other business on the agenda of the meeting, the consideration of that matter may be postponed to a later time in the meeting without motion or vote. However, if there is no other business on the agenda of the meeting, then the meeting must be adjourned for one week, without motion or vote.[200] The Memorandum of Incorporation or rules may alter the one-hour limit or the one-week period.[201]

Where a meeting cannot commence due to the absence of a quorum, the chairperson of the meeting may extend the one-hour limit for a reasonable period on the ground that exceptional circumstances affecting weather, transport or electronic communication may have impeded the ability of the shareholders to be present at the meeting. Such extension of time must be reasonable. A further ground would be that one or more particular shareholders who are delayed have communicated their intention to attend the meeting, and those shareholders, together with others in attendance, would satisfy the quorum requirements.[202]

9.13.2 Notice of a postponed or adjourned meeting

A company is not required to give further notice of a meeting that is postponed or adjourned unless the location for the meeting is different from the location of the postponed or adjourned meeting, or is different from the location announced at the time of the adjournment, in the case of an adjourned meeting.[203]

9.13.3 Deemed quorum

If at the time appointed for a postponed meeting to begin, or for an adjourned meeting to resume, a quorum is still not present, then the shareholders of the company who are present in person or by proxy will be deemed to constitute a quorum.[204]

9.13.4 Voluntary adjournments of meetings

A shareholders' meeting or the consideration of any matter being debated at the meeting, may be adjourned from time to time without further notice, on a motion supported by persons entitled to exercise, in the aggregate, a majority of the voting rights —

(a) held by all of the persons who are present at the meeting at the time; and

---

[199] Section 64(6)(b).
[200] Section 64(4).
[201] Section 64(6)(b).
[202] Section 64(5).
[203] Section 64(7). The reason why further notice is not required of an adjourned meeting is that an adjourned meeting is simply a continuation of the original meeting, and only the business of the original meeting may be considered at the adjourned meeting (see *McLaren v Thomson* [1917] 2 Ch 261 (CA) at 264–5).
[204] Section 64(8).

(b) that are entitled to be exercised on at least one matter remaining on the agenda of the matter, or on the matter under debate, as the case may be.[205]

The adjournment of the meeting or the consideration of the matter being debated at the meeting may be either to a fixed time and place or 'until further notice', as agreed at the meeting.[206] A further notice need only be given to shareholders if the meeting determined that the adjournment was 'until further notice'.[207]

9.13.5 Period of adjournment

A meeting may not be adjourned beyond the earlier of a date that is 120 business days after the record date (determined in accordance with s 59) or a date that is 60 business days after the date on which the adjournment occurred.[208]

However, a company's Memorandum of Incorporation may provide for different maximum periods of adjournment of meetings or even for unlimited adjournment of meetings.[209]

9.14 SHAREHOLDER RESOLUTIONS

Matters that are raised for decision at a meeting are framed as resolutions and are put to the vote by the shareholders. Shareholder resolutions are an ordinary resolution or a special resolution.[210]

9.14.1 Proposing a resolution

The board of directors may propose a resolution to be considered by the shareholders.[211] The board may also determine whether that resolution will be considered at a meeting, or by vote or written consent without a meeting in terms of s 60 of the Act.[212]

The Act gives wide powers to shareholders to propose resolutions. Any two shareholders of a company may propose a resolution concerning any matter in respect of which they are each entitled to exercise voting rights.[213] When proposing a resolution, the shareholders may require the resolution to be submitted to shareholders for consideration at a shareholders' meeting convened by written demand in terms of s 61(3), or at the next shareholders' meeting, or by written consent without a meeting in terms of s 60 of the Act.[214]

A resolution proposed by the shareholders must be expressed with sufficient clarity and specificity and must be accompanied by sufficient information or explanatory material to enable a shareholder who is entitled to vote on the resolution to determine whether to participate in the meeting and to seek to

---
[205] Section 64(10).
[206] Section 64(11).
[207] Ibid.
[208] Section 64(12).
[209] Section 64(13).
[210] Section 65(1).
[211] Section 65(2).
[212] Ibid.
[213] Section 65(3)*(a)*.
[214] Section 65(3)*(b)*.

influence the outcome of the vote on the resolution.[215] Before the start of the meeting at which a resolution will be considered, if a shareholder or director believes that the form of the resolution does not meet these requirements, he or she may seek leave to apply to court for an order restraining the company from putting the proposed resolution to a vote until the necessary requirements have been satisfied.[216] The shareholder or director in question may also require the company or the shareholders who proposed the resolution, as the case may be, to take appropriate steps to amend the resolution so that it complies with the necessary requirements, and to compensate him or her for the costs of the proceedings, if successful.[217] Once a resolution has been approved it may not be challenged or impugned by any person in any forum on the grounds that it did not meet the necessary requirements.[218]

9.14.2 Ordinary resolutions

For an ordinary resolution to be approved by the shareholders, it must be supported by more than 50 per cent of the voting rights exercised on the resolution.[219] If the requisite support is not obtained then the resolution is not adopted.

Save for an ordinary resolution for the removal of a director in terms of s 71 of the Act, a company's Memorandum of Incorporation may require a higher percentage of voting rights to approve an ordinary resolution, or one or more higher percentages of voting rights to approve ordinary resolutions concerning one or more particular matters, provided that there must at all times be a margin of at least ten percentage points between the requirements for approval of an ordinary resolution and of a special resolution, on any matter.[220]

9.14.3 Special resolutions

For a special resolution to be approved by shareholders it must be supported by at least 75 per cent of the voting rights exercised on the resolution.[221]

For the first time in our corporate law history the Act provides that a company's Memorandum of Incorporation may permit a lower percentage of voting rights to approve any special resolution, or one or more lower percentages of voting rights to approve special resolutions concerning one or more particular matters, provided that there must at all times be a margin of at least ten percentage points between the requirements for approval of an ordinary resolution and of a special resolution, on any matter.[222] While a lower percentage of voting rights to approve a special resolution is permitted, a higher percentage of voting rights is presently not permitted.

---

[215] Section 65(4).
[216] Section 65(5)(a).
[217] Section 65(5)(b).
[218] Section 65(6).
[219] See the definition of an 'ordinary resolution' in s 1 and s 65(7). This means 50% + 1.
[220] Section 65(8).
[221] Section 65(9).
[222] Section 65(9).

However, the draft Companies Amendment Bill, 2010 proposes to amend this provision to permit a 'different' percentage of voting rights to approve any special resolution or one or more 'different' percentages of voting rights to approve special resolutions concerning one or more particular matters.[223] This would mean that a higher percentage of voting rights would be permitted to approve a special resolution, but this is subject to the proviso that there must at all times be a margin of at least ten percentage points between the highest established requirement for approval of an ordinary resolution on any matter and the lowest established requirement for approval of a special resolution on any matter.[224]

A special resolution is required to be passed for the most important decisions relating to the company's affairs. Section 65(11) of the Act sets out the matters for which a special resolution is required, namely:

- to amend the company's Memorandum of Incorporation to the extent required by s 16(1)*(c)*,
- to approve the voluntary winding-up of the company, as contemplated in s 80(1), or
- to approve any proposed fundamental transaction to the extent required by Part A of Chapter 5, viz a disposal of all or the greater part of a company's assets or undertaking, an amalgamation, a merger and a scheme of arrangement.[225]

This list of matters for which a special resolution is required as set out in s 65(11) of the Act is clearly incomplete. The draft Companies Amendment Bill, 2010 remedies this by expanding on the list to include in s 65(11) the following matters for which a special resolution is required:[226]

- to ratify a consolidated revision of the Memorandum of Incorporation, as contemplated in s 18(1)*(b)*,
- to ratify actions by the company or directors in excess of their authority, as contemplated in s 20(2),
- to amend the company's Memorandum of Incorporation to the extent required by s 36(2)*(a)*, that is, to change the authorisation and classification of shares, the numbers of authorised shares of each class, and the preferences, rights, limitations and other terms associated with each class of shares as set out in the Memorandum of Incorporation,
- to approve an issue of shares or grant of rights in the circumstances contemplated in s 41(1),
- to authorise the board of directors to grant financial assistance in the circumstances contemplated in s 44(3)*(a)*(ii) (for the purpose of, or in connection

---

[223] See cl 41*(b)* of the draft Companies Amendment Bill, 2010.
[224] See cl 41*(c)* of the draft Companies Amendment Bill, 2010. This would mean that a 100 per cent approval may be required for a special resolution if the Memorandum of Incorporation so provides. The draft Companies Amendment Bill, 2010 further amends the definition of a 'special resolution' in s 1 to mean, in the case of a juristic person other than a company, a decision by the owner or owners of that person, or by another authorised person, that requires the highest level of support in order to be adopted, in terms of the relevant law under which that juristic person was incorporated.
[225] See ss 112(2)*(a)* and 115(2).
[226] See cl 41*(d)* of the draft Companies Amendment Bill, 2010.

with, the subscription or purchase of the company's securities), or s 45(3)(*a*)(ii) (to provide loans or other financial assistance to directors or prescribed officers),
- to authorise the basis for the remuneration of the directors of a profit company, as required by s 66(9), and
- to approve an application to transfer the registration of the company to a foreign jurisdiction as contemplated in s 82(5).

In addition, a special resolution is required by s 41(3) of the Act, ie to approve an issue of shares, securities convertible into shares or rights exercisable for shares in a transaction, or a series of integrated transactions, if the voting power of the class of shares that are issued or issuable as a result of the transaction or series of integrated transactions will be equal to or will exceed 30 per cent of the voting power of all the shares of that class held by shareholders immediately before the transaction or series of transactions.

A company's Memorandum of Incorporation may require a special resolution to approve any other matter not contemplated in s 65(11).[227]

It is important to note that the Act does not make provision for any additional notice or quorum requirements for special resolutions. The 1973 Act required all special resolutions to be registered with the Registrar of Companies in order to be effective,[228] but this is no longer a requirement under the current Act. In some instances, the filing of a special resolution with the Companies and Intellectual Property Commission ('the Companies Commission') is required, but this is not the same as the registration of a special resolution.[229] There is no longer any constructive notice of special resolutions filed with the Companies Commission.

9.15 WRITTEN RESOLUTIONS

Instead of holding a formal meeting, under s 60 of the Act the shareholders may consent in writing to decisions that could be voted on at a shareholders' meeting. Such decisions have the same effect as if they had been approved by voting at a meeting.[230] Since the procedure circumvents both the procedural formality of convening a meeting and substantive discussion, it reflects a prudent approach to decision making,[231] and provides companies with a quick and efficient means of passing resolutions.

9.15.1 Consent of shareholders required

The written resolution must be submitted for consideration to the shareholders entitled to exercise voting rights in relation to the resolution.[232] It is not necessary to seek out the consent of every shareholder to the written resolution, but the

---
[227] Section 65(12).
[228] See ss 200 and 203 of the 1973 Act.
[229] For example, a special resolution providing for the voluntary winding-up of a company must be filed with the Companies Commission, together with the prescribed notice and filing fee (see s 80(2)).
[230] Section 60(2)(*b*).
[231] *Southern Witwatersrand Exploration Co Ltd v Bisichi Mining plc* 1998 (4) SA 767 (W) 776.
[232] Section 60(1)(*a*).

consent of only those shareholders who are entitled to exercise voting rights in relation to the resolution is required.

Section 60(2)(a) provides that the written resolution will be adopted if it is 'supported by persons entitled to exercise sufficient voting rights for it to have been adopted as an ordinary or special resolution at a properly constituted shareholders' meeting'. The wording implies that the resolution will not be adopted if it is not supported by sufficient shareholders to form a quorum for a shareholders' meeting.[233]

9.15.2 Support required for written resolutions

In the United Kingdom, the Company Law Review Steering Group recommended in 2001 that the requirement of unanimity for passing written resolutions be replaced by a requirement that ordinary resolutions should be supported by a simple majority of those entitled to vote, while a special resolution should be supported by a majority of 75 per cent of those entitled to vote.[234] It was reasoned that the written resolution procedure would be more useful and greatly improved with a lower requisite majority, so that a minority shareholder could not block a written resolution where he or she would be easily outvoted at a meeting.[235] The UK Companies Act 2006 subsequently adopted these recommendations and unanimity is no longer a requirement for written resolutions.[236]

Section 60 of our Companies Act is similar in this respect to the equivalent sections of the UK Companies Act 2006 that deal with written resolutions. Section 60 is a statutory enactment of the common-law principle of unanimous assent, but a vital difference is that, unlike the position at common law, unanimous assent is not required for the written resolution to be adopted. Section 60(2)(a) provides that, for a written resolution to be adopted, it must be supported by persons entitled to exercise sufficient voting rights for it to have been adopted as an ordinary or a special resolution, as the case may be, at a properly constituted shareholders' meeting. In other words, the resolution must be adopted by the same percentage of support as is required to pass a resolution at a meeting.

Note that decisions requiring an ordinary resolution as well as a special resolution may be passed by means of a written resolution. As previously discussed, a company's Memorandum of Incorporation may require a different percentage of voting rights than 50 per cent plus one to approve an ordinary resolution and 75 per cent to approve a special resolution, provided that there is at all times a margin of at least 10 percentage points between the requirements for approval of an ordinary resolution and a special resolution.[237]

An important difference between voting on a written resolution and voting at a meeting is that, in the case of a meeting, the percentage figures refer to those who

---

[233] See *Re New Cedos Engineering Co Ltd* [1994] 1 BCLC 797 at 813–5.
[234] See *Modern Company Law for a Competitive Economy: Final Report* vol 1 (URN 01/942) (London: DTI, 1999) para 4.3.
[235] Ibid.
[236] See s 282(2) and s 283(3) of the UK Companies Act 2006.
[237] Section 65(8) and (9).

vote (whether in person or by proxy)[238] whereas in the case of a written resolution the percentage figures refer to those who are entitled to vote.[239] The implication is that the consent of a higher percentage of the shareholders needs to be obtained to pass a written resolution compared to passing a resolution at a meeting, where ordinarily fewer than half the shareholders attend (whether in person or by proxy).[240] This is a disadvantage of passing a written resolution, but the advantages of not having to call a meeting may well outweigh this disadvantage.

9.15.3 Time within which the consent must be obtained

The resolution must be voted on in writing by the shareholders within 20 business days after the resolution was submitted to them.[241] Accordingly, if the necessary support for the resolution is not obtained by that date, the resolution will lapse. Should a shareholder assent to the written resolution after the expiry of 20 business days, the assent would be ineffective.

9.15.4 Electronic communication

Unlike the equivalent provision permitting directors to make decisions without convening a meeting (contained in s 74 of the Act), which specifically provides that the written consent of the directors may be given in person or by electronic communication, s 60 does not explicitly make provision for the consent of the shareholders to be provided by electronic communication. But presumably the written resolution may be circulated to the shareholders electronically by virtue of s 6(11)*(b)*(i) of the Act. This section provides that, if a document, record or statement (other than a notice) is required to be published, provided or delivered, it may be done so electronically, provided it is done in a manner and form that allows it to be conveniently printed by the recipient within a reasonable time and at a reasonable cost.

9.15.5 Restrictions

The election of a director that may be conducted at a shareholders' meeting 'may instead be conducted by written polling of all of the shareholders entitled to exercise voting rights in relation to the election of that director'.[242]

One restriction on the use of written resolutions is that a director may not be removed in terms of s 71(1) of the Act by a written resolution of the shareholders

---

[238] See s 65(7), which, in relation to passing ordinary resolutions at a meeting, refers to the support required by 'more than 50% of the voting rights exercised on the resolution'. Similarly, s 65(9), in relation to passing special resolutions at a meeting, refers to the support required by 'at least 75% of the voting rights exercised on the resolution'.
[239] See s 60(2)*(a)*, which, in relation to passing a written resolution, refers to the support required by 'persons entitled to exercise sufficient voting rights' for it to have been adopted as an ordinary or a special resolution, at a properly constituted shareholders' meeting.
[240] Paul L Davies op cit n 19 at 417.
[241] Section 60(1)*(b)*.
[242] Section 60(3).

without the holding of a meeting.[243] If the resolution were to be passed in this way, it would deprive the director in question of the opportunity to present his or her case before the meeting.

Another restriction is that no business of a company that is required to be conducted at the company's AGM (in terms of the Act or the Memorandum of Incorporation) may be conducted by a written resolution of the shareholders without the holding of a meeting.[244]

9.15.6 Informing shareholders of the written resolution

It is important for shareholders to be kept fully informed of the written resolution that was passed. Accordingly, s 60(4) of the Act provides that the company must deliver a statement describing the results of the vote, consent process or election to every shareholder who was entitled to vote or consent to the resolution, or vote in the election of the director, as the case may be, within ten business days after the company has adopted the written resolution, or conducted an election of directors by written resolution.[245]

9.16 COMPANY RECORDS

9.16.1 Records

Every company is required to maintain certain documents, accounts, books, writing, records and other information for a period of seven years (or any longer period specified in any applicable public regulation).[246] If a company has existed for a shorter period than seven years, it is required to retain its records for that shorter time.[247] Note that the draft Companies Regulations require a company's Memorandum of Incorporation (as amended from time to time), registration certificate, register of directors and securities register to be kept indefinitely.[248] It may be that a company for tax purposes may have to keep its records for a period longer than the seven years required by the Act. The records must be kept in

---

[243] See the Hearings on Companies Bill [B 61–2008]: Department's Response (3), comprising the response by the Department of Trade and Industry (DTI) to the public comments on the Bill, issued to the Portfolio Committee on Trade and Industry, 22 August 2008, at 33.
[244] Section 60(5).
[245] Section 60(4).
[246] Section 24(1)(b). A 'public regulation' is widely defined in s 1 of the Act to mean any national, provincial or local government legislation or subordinate legislation, or any licence, tariff, directive or similar authorisation issued by a regulatory authority or pursuant to any statutory authority.
[247] Section 24(2). Under item 7(8)(a) of Schedule 5 of the Act a pre-existing company would not contravene the Act should it fail to maintain any record for the duration of the period required by s 24(1) if the company disposed of that record before the effective date of the Act and, at the time it disposed of the record, it was not required, under any public regulation, to maintain that record. See further chapter 21: Transitional Arrangements.
[248] Regulation 24(1). This would presumably include a members' register in the case of a non-profit company. If a company keeps its securities register in electronic form, it must provide adequate precautions against loss of the records as a result of damage to, or failure of, the media on which the records are kept. It must also ensure that the records are always capable of being retrieved to a readable and printable form (see Regulation 36(6) of the draft Companies Regulations).

written form, or another form or manner that allows that information to be converted into written form within a reasonable time.[249]

In terms of s 24(3) every company must maintain the following records:

- a copy of its Memorandum of Incorporation, and any amendments or alterations to it and any rules of the company made in terms of s 15(3) to (5),
- a record of its directors, containing the prescribed information required by s 24(5), including details of past directors (for a period of seven years after the person ceases to be a director),
- copies of all reports presented at an AGM of the company (for a period of seven years after the date of any such meeting),
- copies of all annual financial statements required by the Act (for seven years after the date on which each such particular statements were issued),
- copies of all accounting records[250] required by the Act (for the current financial year and for the previous seven completed financial years of the company),
- notices and minutes of all shareholders' meetings, including all resolutions adopted by the shareholders, and any document that was made available by the company to the shareholders in relation to each resolution, for seven years after the date on which each resolution was adopted,
- copies of any written communications sent generally by the company to all holders of any class of the company's securities (for a period of seven years after the date on which each such communication was issued), and
- minutes of all meetings and resolutions of directors or directors' committees or the audit committee (if any) (for a period of seven years after the date of each meeting or the date on which each such resolution was adopted).

Every profit company is also required to maintain a securities register.[251] The draft Companies Amendment Bill, 2010 requires non-profit companies that have members to maintain a members' register.[252] A company must also maintain the records required in terms of s 85 of the Act (dealing with the records of its company secretaries and auditors), if applicable.[253] In addition, the draft Companies Amendment Bill, 2010 requires every company to maintain the company's registration certificate.[254]

---

[249] Section 24(1)(a).
[250] The draft Companies Amendment Bill, 2010 (cl 2(1)(a)) defines 'accounting records' as meaning information in written or electronic form concerning the financial affairs of a company as required in terms of the Act, including, but not limited to, purchase and sales records, general and subsidiary ledgers and other documents and books used in the preparation of financial statements.
[251] Section 24(4)(a).
[252] Clause 16(c) of the draft Companies Amendment Bill, 2010.
[253] Section 24(4)(b).
[254] Clause 16(c) of the draft Companies Amendment Bill, 2010.

9.16.2 Access to records

Under s 26(1)*(a)* of the Act, a person who holds or has a beneficial interest in any securities issued by a company has a right to inspect and copy the following records:[255]

- the Memorandum of Incorporation, and any amendments or alterations to it and any rules of the company made in terms of s 15(3) to (5), as referred to in s 24(3)*(a)*,
- the record of directors, as referred to in s 24(3)*(b)*,
- all reports presented at an AGM of the company, as referred to in s 24(3)*(c)*(i),
- the annual financial statements of the company, as referred to in s 24(3)*(c)*(ii),
- notices and minutes of shareholders' meetings, including resolutions adopted by the shareholders and any document that was made available by the company to the shareholders in relation to each resolution, as referred to in s 24(3)*(d)*,
- any written communications sent generally by the company to all holders of any class of the company's securities, as referred to in s 24(3)*(e)*,
- the securities register of a profit company and members' register of a non-profit company that has members, as referred to in s 24(4)*(a)*, and
- the records required in terms of s 85 of the Act, ie the record of the company's company secretaries and auditors (if applicable to the company), as referred to in s 24(4)*(b)*.[256]

The rights under s 26(1) of the Act are conferred on persons who hold a beneficial interest in securities issued by a company and not to registered holders of securities who are not also the beneficial holders of the securities.[257] But note that the Memorandum of Incorporation of a company may make provision for additional information rights of any person with regard to information that pertains to the company.[258] This is subject to the proviso that no right may negate or diminish any mandatory protection of any record under Part 3 of the Promotion of Access to Information Act 2 of 2000 (PAIA).[259] The rights of access to company records set out in s 26 of the Act are in addition to, and not in substitution of, any rights a

---

[255] The draft Companies Amendment Bill, 2010 gives members of a non-profit company the same rights as persons who hold a beneficial interest in any securities issued by the company to access these records. In this regard, references to shareholders' meetings and to communications sent to holders of a company's securities in s 24 of the Act must be regarded as meaning a meeting of members of the non-profit company and communications sent to members of the non-profit company (see cl 17 of the draft Companies Amendment Bill, 2010).
[256] Clause 17 of the draft Companies Amendment Bill, 2010 has omitted to include this item in its list of records to which shareholders have access.
[257] The draft Companies Amendment Bill, 2010 extends the rights given under s 26(1) to inspect or copy the records of a company to members of a non-profit company.
[258] This is permitted by s 26(1)*(b)* and s 26(2) of the Act.
[259] Section 26(2). Part 3 of PAIA deals with the access to records of private bodies, and in particular ss 62 to 70 deal with grounds for refusal of access to records. Section 68 deals with the grounds for refusal of access to commercial information of a private body.

person may have to information in terms of s 32 of the Constitution of the Republic of South Africa, 1996,[260] PAIA or any other public regulation.[261]

If there is any inconsistency between the Act and PAIA, then the provisions of both Acts apply concurrently to the extent that it is possible to apply and comply with one of the inconsistent provisions without contravening the second. To the extent that it is impossible to apply or comply with one of the inconsistent provisions without contravening the second, then the provisions of PAIA will prevail.[262]

In *Clutchco (Pty) Ltd v Davis*[263] the Supreme Court of Appeal examined the right of access of shareholders to company information. The respondent, a shareholder of a private company, had sought access to the company's books of first accounting entry, such as its cash book, ledgers, journals and invoice books. He claimed that he needed access to these records to value his shares for purposes of selling them, and contended that he needed access to the underlying financial records because he suspected that the audited financial statements were inaccurate. The court *a quo* had permitted the respondent's application under PAIA. It was against this order that the appellant, the company, lodged an appeal.

The Supreme Court of Appeal confirmed that, while a shareholder does have a right to receive copies of the company's annual financial statements and to obtain copies of the minutes of the company's general meetings, he does not have an automatic right to a company's accounting records, or a right to inspect the minutes of directors' meetings and managers' meetings. It was for this reason that the respondent had sought access to the company's accounting records in terms of s 50(1)(*a*) of PAIA[264] read with s 32 of the Constitution of the Republic of South Africa, 1996. Section 50(1)(*a*) of PAIA provides that a requester must be given access to any record of a private body if that record is 'required' for the exercise or protection of any rights. The Supreme Court of Appeal assumed, without deciding, that the right of a shareholder to value his or her shareholding in order to fix an appropriate selling price amounted to a 'right' for purposes of s 50(1)(*a*) of PAIA. The court ruled that the word 'required' in s 50(1)(*a*) of PAIA does not mean

---

[260] Section 32 of the Constitution of the Republic of South Africa, 1996 provides as follows:
'(1) Everyone has the right of access to —
   (a) any information held by the State; and
   (b) any information that is held by another person and that is required for the exercise or protection of any rights.
(2) National legislation must be enacted to give effect to this right, and may provide for reasonable measures to alleviate the administrative and financial burden on the State.'
The national legislation contemplated in s 32(2) of the Constitution is PAIA.

[261] Section 26(4).

[262] See s 5(4)(*b*)(i)(*cc*) of the Act.

[263] 2005 (3) SA 486 (SCA).

[264] Section 50(1)(*a*) of PAIA provides as follows:
'(1) A requester must be given access to any record of a private body if —
   (a) that record is required for the exercise or protection of any rights;
   (b) that person complies with the procedural requirements in this Act relating to a request for access to that record; and
   (c) access to that record is not refused in terms of any ground for refusal contemplated in Chapter 4 of this Part.'

necessity, but means 'reasonably required' for the exercise or protection of any rights, 'provided that it is understood to connote a substantial advantage or an element of need'.[265]

The Supreme Court of Appeal found that the 1973 Act was replete with provisions designed to protect the interests of shareholders,[266] and opined that the machinery established by legislation and the common law for the protection of shareholders is not to be taken lightly or be disregarded.[267] The court ruled that, in enacting PAIA, Parliament could not have intended that the books of a company, great or small, should be thrown open to shareholders on a whiff of impropriety or on the grounds that relatively minor errors or irregularities had occurred, and that a far more substantial foundation would be required.[268] The court was not persuaded that the respondent had succeeded in laying such a foundation and found that he had failed to show that the access he had sought was required for the exercise or protection of the rights he had asserted.[269]

The decision in *Clutcho* shows that our courts have adopted a restrictive approach to the right to access to information in private hands. But perhaps the decision in *Clutchco* is not in line with the modern trend of transparency in company affairs.[270] The respondent's purpose in obtaining access to the company's books of first accounting entry was to ascertain the value of his shares that he intended to sell, and not, for instance, for purposes of disclosing confidential information to competitors.[271] Interestingly, the Supreme Court of Appeal stated, without deciding the issue, that there might exist special circumstances in which a court would, in terms of s 252 of the 1973 Act (now s 163 of the current Act) (relief from oppressive or prejudicial conduct) grant some form of access to company information to a shareholder who complained of oppressive conduct by the company.[272]

9.16.3 Exercising the right to access the information contained in the company's records

The right to information provided by s 26 may be exercised by direct request made to the company in the prescribed manner, either in person or through an attorney or other personal representative designated in writing, or in accordance with PAIA. The rights must be exercised during business hours for reasonable periods.

---

[265] Paras 11–13. See also *Institute for Democracy in South Africa v African National Congress* 2005 (5) SA 39 (C) where the court accepted that the phrase 'required for the exercise or protection of any rights' in s 50(1)(a) of PAIA does not mean 'necessity' but means 'reasonably required' for the exercise or protection of any rights (paras 34–5).
[266] Para 15.
[267] Para 17.
[268] Ibid.
[269] Para 18.
[270] See FHI Cassim 'Company Law (including Close Corporations)' *Annual Survey of South African Law* (2005) 466 at 481.
[271] Ibid.
[272] Para 14.

Under s 26(3) of the Act, the members' register and the register of directors are open to inspection by any 'member', free of charge. The draft Companies Amendment Bill, 2010 gives persons who hold a beneficial interest in securities issued by a profit company and members of a non-profit company a right to inspect and copy the records of the company without any charge, or upon payment of no more than the prescribed maximum charge for a copy of the records.[273]

Under s 26(3) of the Act, persons who are not members of a company must pay R100 for each inspection of the members' register and the register of directors. The draft Companies Amendment Bill, 2010 does not specify the amount of the fee and provides that a person who does not hold a beneficial interest in any securities issued by a profit company or who is not a member of a non-profit company has a right to inspect the securities register of a profit company or members' register of a non-profit company or the register of directors, upon payment of an amount not exceeding the prescribed maximum fee for any such inspection.[274] No provision is made for such persons to make a copy of the records, and the right is limited merely to that of an inspection of the records.

A right of access to any record held by a company is not perfected until a request to exercise that right has been made to the company in terms of Regulation 26(4) of the draft Companies Regulations, and the right of access to the information has been confirmed in accordance with PAIA.[275] Under draft Regulation 26(4), a person seeking to exercise a right of access to any record held by a company must make a written request to do so, as contemplated in s 26(1)*(c)* of the Act,[276] by delivering a completed Request for Access to Information form to the company[277] and any further documents or other material required in terms of PAIA. A perfected right of access to any information held by a company may be exercised only during the company's normal business hours.[278]

9.16.4 Failure to accommodate a request for access to company records

It is an offence for a company to fail to accommodate any reasonable request for access, or to unreasonably refuse access, to any record that a person has a right to inspect or copy, or to otherwise impede, interfere with, or attempt to frustrate, the reasonable exercise by any person of their right to access to the company records.[279]

---

[273] See cl 17*(a)* of the draft Companies Amendment Bill, 2010.
[274] Ibid.
[275] Regulation 26(3) of the draft Companies Regulations.
[276] That is, by direct request made to the company either in person or through an attorney or other personal representative designated in writing.
[277] Form CoR 26.
[278] Regulation 26(5) of the draft Companies Regulations.
[279] Section 26(6). The draft Companies Amendment Bill, 2010 also makes it an offence for a company to fail to accommodate a reasonable request for access to the financial statements or related information rights under s 31 of the Act, or to impede, interfere with or attempt to frustrate, the reasonable exercise by any person of access to the financial statements or related information rights under s 31 of the Act (cl 17*(c)*). A person convicted of an offence in terms of the Act is liable to a fine

9.16.5 Location of company records

A company's records must be accessible at or from the company's registered office or another location or locations within South Africa. A company is required to file a notice setting out the location or locations at which any particular records are kept or from which they are accessible if those records are not kept at or made accessible from the company's registered office or are moved from one location to another.[280]

---

or to imprisonment for a period not exceeding 12 months, or to both a fine and imprisonment (s 216(b)).
[280] Section 25.

CHAPTER 10

GOVERNANCE AND THE BOARD OF DIRECTORS

Rehana Cassim

10.1	INTRODUCTION	375
10.2	WHO IS A 'DIRECTOR'?	375
	10.2.1 Definition of a 'director'	375
	(a) 'includes'	375
	(b) 'occupying the position of a director'	376
	(c) 'by whatever name designated'	376
	(d) 'as contemplated in section 66'	376
	(i) Director appointed in terms of the Memorandum of Incorporation	376
	(ii) *Ex officio* director	376
	(iii) Alternate director	377
	(iv) A director elected by the shareholders	377
	(e) In addition, the following types of directors are recognised in our law:	378
	(i) *De jure* director	378
	(ii) Temporary director	378
	(iii) Nominee director	378
	(iv) Puppet director	379
	(v) *De facto* director	380
	(vi) Shadow director	381
	(vii) Executive, non-executive and independent directors	383
10.3	THE LEGAL POSITION OF DIRECTORS	383
	10.3.1 Directors as agents	384
	10.3.2 Directors as trustees	384
	10.3.3 Directors as managing partners	385
	10.3.4 *Sui generis*	386
10.4	PRESCRIBED OFFICERS	386
10.5	OFFICE BEARERS OF THE COMPANY	387
	10.5.1 Manager	387
	10.5.2 Managing director	388
	10.5.3 Chairperson of the board of directors	388
	10.5.4 Company secretary	389
	10.5.5 Auditor	391

10.6	NUMBER OF DIRECTORS		392
	10.6.1	Minimum number of directors	392
	10.6.2	Company with one director	392
	10.6.3	Failure to have the required number of directors	393
10.7	APPOINTMENT OF DIRECTORS		393
	10.7.1	Initial appointment of directors	393
	10.7.2	Subsequent appointments	393
		(a) Appointments by a person named in the Memorandum of Incorporation	393
		(b) Appointments by the shareholders	394
		(c) Appointments by the board of directors or other stakeholders or outsiders	394
		(d) Other appointments	395
	10.7.3	Consent to be a director	395
10.8	TERMS OF APPOINTMENT		395
10.9	RECORD OF DIRECTORS		396
	10.9.1	Information to be contained in the record of directors	396
	10.9.2	Retention of record of directors	397
	10.9.3	Location of record of directors	397
	10.9.4	Inspection of record of directors	397
	10.9.5	Failure by the company to accommodate a request for access	399
10.10	COMPANY RULES		399
10.11	INELIGIBILITY AND DISQUALIFICATION OF PERSONS TO BE DIRECTORS		399
	10.11.1	Application of s 69 of the Act	399
	10.11.2	Qualifications	399
	10.11.3	Distinguishing ineligibility from disqualification	400
	10.11.4	Grounds of ineligibility	400
	10.11.5	Grounds of disqualification	400
	10.11.6	Consequences of ineligibility and disqualification	402
	10.11.7	Exemptions from disqualification	402
		(a) Exercise of the court's discretion	402
		(b) Statutory exemption from disqualification	403
	10.11.8	Duration of disqualification	404
	10.11.9	Public register	404
10.12	DELINQUENT DIRECTORS AND DIRECTORS ON PROBATION		404
	10.12.1	*Locus standi*	404
	10.12.2	Grounds of delinquency	405
	10.12.3	Grounds of probation	406
	10.12.4	Terms of the order and conditions	406
	10.12.5	Application to suspend or set aside the order of delinquency or probation	407
10.13	VACANCIES ON THE BOARD OF DIRECTORS		408
	10.13.1	Instances when a vacancy arises	408
	10.13.2	Filling of a vacancy	408
10.14	REMOVAL OF DIRECTORS		409

10.14.1	Removal by the shareholders	409
10.14.2	Removal by the board of directors	410
10.14.3	Notice	410
10.14.4	Presentation	411
10.14.5	Ordinary resolution	411
10.14.6	Loaded voting rights	412
10.14.7	Application to court to review the board's determination	414
10.14.8	Breach of contract and damages	414
10.15	RETIREMENT FROM OFFICE	415
10.16	RESIGNATION OF DIRECTORS	415
10.17	REMUNERATION OF DIRECTORS	416
10.17.1	No automatic right to remuneration	416
10.17.2	Remuneration may be prohibited by Memorandum of Incorporation	417
10.17.3	Special resolution required	417
10.17.4	Remuneration not contingent on company earning sufficient profits	418
10.17.5	Disclosure of remuneration in annual financial statements	418
10.18	BOARD COMMITTEES	418
10.18.1	Appointment of committees	418
10.18.2	Members of committees	419
10.18.3	Compulsory committees	419
	(a) Audit committee	419
	(b) Social and ethics committee	420
10.18.4	Recommended committees	422
10.19	BOARD MEETINGS	422
10.19.1	Calling a meeting	422
10.19.2	Notice	423
10.19.3	Quorum	424
10.19.4	Voting	424
10.19.5	Minutes and resolutions	425
10.19.6	Electronic communications	426
10.20	DECISIONS TAKEN WITHOUT CONVENING A MEETING	426
10.21	LOANS OR OTHER FINANCIAL ASSISTANCE TO DIRECTORS	427
10.21.1	Meaning of 'financial assistance'	428
10.21.2	Exceptions	428
10.21.3	Provision of financial assistance	428
10.21.4	'Direct or indirect' financial assistance	429
10.21.5	Conditions for the authorisation of financial assistance	429
10.21.6	Notice	430
10.21.7	Consequences of contravening s 45	430
	(a) Void resolution or agreement	430
	(b) Liability of directors	431
10.21.8	Disclosure in the annual financial statements	431

10.1 INTRODUCTION

Section 66(1) of the Companies Act 71 of 2008 (hereafter 'the Act') states that the business and affairs of a company must be managed by or under the direction of its board of directors, which has the authority to exercise all the powers and perform any of the functions of the company, except to the extent that the Act or the company's Memorandum of Incorporation provides otherwise.

This provision is highly significant in that, for the first time in our Companies Act, the board of directors has been given a legal duty and responsibility to manage the affairs of a company. Previously, under the Companies Act 61 of 1973 (hereafter 'the 1973 Act'), the board of directors did not enjoy original powers to manage the company's business, with the result that the power to manage the company's affairs had to be delegated to the board of directors by the members in general meeting or by the constitution of the company. Section 66(1) of the Act is a concession to reality by acknowledging that the very basis for the appointment of a board of directors is the management of the company's business. But, notably, the board's powers may be curtailed by the Act or the Memorandum of Incorporation.

The Act sets out rules relating to the appointment of directors, grounds of ineligibility and disqualification of persons to be directors, the removal of directors, the procedure to declare directors delinquent or under a probation order, board committees, board meetings, resolutions of directors, remuneration of directors, and the provision of loans and other financial assistance to directors. These issues are discussed in this chapter.

10.2 WHO IS A 'DIRECTOR'?

Given the crucial role directors play in managing the affairs of a company, it is imperative to identify the directors of a company and the scope of their role within the company. In general, the law is concerned with rendering directors responsible because they have the power to manage the company's business and to make vital decisions relating to the running of the company. Higher standards are continually being expected of directors, as evidenced by the Act, the King Report on Governance for South Africa 2009 ('the King III Report') and the King Code of Governance for South Africa 2009 ('the Code'). In these circumstances certain individuals may wish to evade being formally classified as a director. Accordingly, identifying the directors of a company is important in establishing the accountability of individuals in relation to their conduct in managing the affairs of the company.

10.2.1 Definition of a 'director'

A 'director' is defined in s 1 of the Act as 'a member of the board of a company, as contemplated in section 66, or an alternate director of a company and includes any person occupying the position of a director or alternate director, by whatever name designated'.

(a) 'includes'

The word 'includes' in the definition of a 'director' indicates that the definition of a 'director' is inclusive and not exhaustive. This means that the formalities are not crucial in attempting to identify those persons who are directors of a particular company,[1] and that the meaning of 'director' must be derived from the words of the Act as a whole.[2] The definition is intended to apply to all directors that are formally appointed as directors as well as to persons such as *de facto* directors who are not formally appointed as directors.

(b) 'occupying the position of a director'

The court in *Corporate Affairs Commission v Drysdale*[3] explained that the phrase 'occupying the position of a director' denotes one who acts in the position of a director, with or without lawful authority, while the phrase 'holds an office' denotes one who is the lawful holder of the office.[4] In line with this statement, since the definition of a 'director' in s 1 of the Act employs the words 'occupying the position of a director', it implies that for the purposes of the Act a person who is not formally appointed as a director of a company may nevertheless be deemed to be a director if he or she occupies the position of a director, whether with or without lawful authority.

(c) 'by whatever name designated'

These words are crucial since they make it clear that certain persons are to be regarded as directors even though they may be designated a different name. Thus title is not the determining factor in determining whether someone is a director. For instance, it is possible for someone to be a director even though he or she is described as a manager. The court in *Re Mea Corporation Ltd*[5] asserted that it matters not what a person calls himself, but what he does, that determines whether he is a director of a company.

(d) 'as contemplated in section 66'

Section 66 of the Act recognises the following types of directors:

(i) *Director appointed in terms of the Memorandum of Incorporation*

A director may be appointed by any person who is named in, or determined in terms of, the Memorandum of Incorporation.[6] This is discussed further below in 10.7.2.

(ii) Ex officio *director*

An *ex officio* director refers to a person who is a director of a company as a consequence of holding some other office, title, designation or similar status.[7] He or she has all the powers and functions of any other director of the company,

---

[1] John de Lacy 'The Concept of a Company Director: Time for a new expanded and unified statutory concept' (May 2006) *Journal of Business Law* 267 at 269.
[2] *Re Lo-Line Electric Motors Ltd* [1988] Ch 477 at 489; *Corporate Affairs Commission v Drysdale* (1978) 141 CLR 236 at 255.
[3] (1978) 141 CLR 236.
[4] At 242.
[5] [2007] BCC 288 para 82.
[6] Section 66(4)(*a*)(i).
[7] Section 66(4)(*a*)(ii).

except to the extent that these are restricted by the Memorandum of Incorporation.[8] It follows that an *ex officio* director has all the duties and is subject to all the liabilities of any other director of the company.[9] But no person may serve as an *ex officio* director should he or she be or become ineligible or disqualified to be a director under s 69 of the Act.[10]

(iii) *Alternate director*

The definition of a 'director' in s 1 makes specific reference to an 'alternate director'. An alternate director is defined in s 1 of the Act as meaning 'a person elected or appointed to serve, as the occasion requires, as a member of the board of a company in substitution for a particular elected or appointed director of that company'. Alternate directors serve a useful purpose. For instance, they allow a director who is ill or has other commitments to ensure that his or her influence is still maintained at board level through an alternate director when they are unable to be present. Notably, an alternate director may only be appointed if the Memorandum of Incorporation makes provision for a director to nominate an alternate director to act in his or her stead.[11]

The extent of the alternate director's powers and other terms relating to his or her appointment would depend on the provisions contained in the Memorandum of Incorporation. Generally, alternate directors are in the eyes of the law in the same position as any other director. They are recognised by the courts as independent directors in their own right such that they alone are responsible for their own actions after their appointment — they do not serve as agents of their appointers when serving as alternate directors.[12] While an alternate director only enjoys the powers that his or her appointer enjoyed, he or she is subject to all the duties a director owes to his or her company and must exercise and discharge all the powers and functions of a director.[13]

An alternate director ceases to hold office whenever the director who appointed him or her ceases to be a director, or gives notice to the company secretary that the alternate director is no longer representing him or her.[14]

(iv) *A director elected by the shareholders*

Each director of a company, except the first directors, a director appointed in terms of the Memorandum of Incorporation and an *ex officio* director, must be elected by the shareholders, to serve as a director of the company for an indefinite term or for a term set out in the Memorandum of Incorporation.[15]

In terms of s 66(4)*(b)* of the Act, in the case of a profit company (other than a state-owned company) the Memorandum of Incorporation must provide for the

---
[8] Section 66(5)*(b)*(i).
[9] Section 66(5)*(b)*(ii).
[10] Section 66(5)*(a)*.
[11] See s 66(4)*(a)*(iii).
[12] *Australian Securities & Investment Commission v Doyle* [2001] WASC 187.
[13] *Markwell Bros Pty Ltd v CPN Diesels (Qld) Pty Ltd* (1982) 7 ACLR 425 SC (Qld) 433.
[14] MS Blackman et al *Commentary on the Companies Act* vol 1 (2002) (Revision Service 7, 2010) at 8–12.
[15] Section 68(1).

election by shareholders of 'at least' 50 per cent of the directors, and 50 per cent of any alternate directors. The words 'at least' in s 66(4)*(b)* indicate that the Memorandum of Incorporation may provide that a higher percentage of directors must be elected by the shareholders. A company could, for instance, require the election of all its directors by its shareholders. Alternatively, a company could, for example, require 50 per cent (or less) of its directors to be appointed by parties other than the shareholders, such as the board of directors, other stakeholders or outsiders. This is discussed further below in 10.7.2.

(e) In addition, the following types of directors are recognised in our law:

(i) De jure *director*

A *de jure* director simply means a person validly and formally appointed to the position of a company director who has freely consented to that appointment.[16]

(ii) *Temporary director*

Unless the Memorandum of Incorporation provides otherwise, the board of directors may appoint a person who would satisfy the requirements for election as a director to fill a vacancy and serve as a director on a temporary basis, until such time as the vacancy has been filled by a director that is elected by the shareholders.[17] Such a temporary director would have all the powers, functions and duties, and be subject to all of the liabilities, of any other director of the company.[18]

(iii) *Nominee director*

A nominee director is a *de jure* director who owes his or her nomination as a director to a shareholder or other third party such as a bank or financier. Generally, a nominee director is appointed by a shareholder who controls sufficient voting power in the company to represent his or her interests.[19] Nominee directors may, for example, represent a major shareholder, a class of shareholders or debenture holders, a significant creditor or an employee group.[20]

Nominee directors are useful in certain situations, for instance where a significant shareholder agrees to subscribe for shares in a company on the condition that he or she has representation on the board of directors, or where a significant shareholder lacks the time or expertise to serve as a director personally, and accordingly wishes to appoint a nominee to act on his or her behalf.

While the practice of appointing a nominee director to represent the interests of the person who nominated him or her is legally recognised, the presence of a nominee director may well lead to a potential conflict of interests should the

---

[16] *Re Hydrodam (Corby) Ltd* [1994] BCC 161 at 162.
[17] Section 68(3).
[18] Ibid.
[19] *S v Shaban* 1965 (4) SA 646 (W) 651; *Boulting v Association of Cinematograph, Television and Allied Technicians* [1963] 2 QB 606 at 626.
[20] E Boros 'The duties of nominee and multiple directors: Part 1' (1989) 10 *Company Lawyer* 211 at 211.

interests of the company not coincide with those of the nominator.[21] Where the interests of the company and those of the nominator conflict, the nominee is placed in a difficult position. In carrying out his or her duties and functions as a director, a nominee director is in law obliged to serve the interests of the company to the exclusion of the interests of any nominator, employer or principal.[22] He or she may not fetter their vote as a director, and as a director may not be subject to the control of any employer or principal other than the company.[23] Lord Denning MR in *Boulting v Association of Cinematograph, Television and Allied Technicians*[24] described the position of a nominee director as follows:

> [T]ake a nominee director, that is, a director of a company who is nominated by a large shareholder to represent his interests. There is nothing wrong in it. It is done every day. Nothing wrong, that is, so long as the director is left free to exercise his best judgment in the interests of the company which he serves. But if he is put upon terms that he is bound to act in the affairs of the company in accordance with the directions of his patron, it is beyond doubt unlawful (see *Kregor v. Hollins* (1913) 109 L.T. 225, 228, C.A. by Avory J.), or if he agrees to subordinate the interests of the company to the interests of his patron, it is conduct oppressive to the other shareholders for which the patron can be brought to book: see *Scottish Co-operative Wholesale Society Ltd v Meyer* [1959] A.C. 324, 341, 363, 366, 367.[25]

(iv) *Puppet director*

A nominee director must be distinguished from a puppet director. A puppet director is a person who has been placed on the board of directors with the intention that he or she should blindly follow the instructions of his or her controller.[26] In *S v Shaban*[27] the court stated that '[o]ur law does not know the complete puppet who pretends to take part in the management of a company whilst having no idea what it is to which he puts his signature. It is utterly foreign to the basic concepts of our law and the Courts will punish it as fraud'.[28]

A puppet director will not escape liability for breach of a fiduciary duty by laying the blame on the person who put him or her into office and pulled the strings.[29] In *S v De Jager*[30] the court held that a director who had resigned and had secured the appointment of a puppet in his place was nevertheless still bound by the fiduciary and other duties of a director. Thus the 'puppet master' will also not escape liability for the duties of a director and will not escape liability on the ground that he or she was not formally appointed to the office of director.[31]

---

[21] *Scottish Co-operative Wholesale Society Ltd v Meyer* [1959] AC 324 at 366–7.
[22] *Fisheries Development Corporation of SA Ltd v Jorgensen; Fisheries Development Corporation of SA Ltd v AWJ Investments (Pty) Ltd* 1980 (4) SA 156 (W) 163.
[23] Ibid.
[24] [1963] 2 QB 606.
[25] At 626–7.
[26] *S v Shaban* 1965 (4) SA 646 (W) 652–3.
[27] 1965 (4) SA 646 (W).
[28] At 652. See also *Sage Holdings Ltd v The Unisec Group Ltd* 1982 (1) SA 337 (W) 354.
[29] *S v Hepker* 1973 (1) SA 472 (W) 484.
[30] 1964 (2) SA 616 (A).
[31] *S v Hepker* (supra) at 484.

(v) De facto *director*

A *de facto* director is a person who claims to act and purports to act as a director, without having been so appointed validly or at all.[32]

In order to establish whether a person is a *de facto* director of a company it must be proved that he or she had undertaken functions in relation to the company that could properly be discharged only by a director.[33] It is necessary for the person alleged to be a *de facto* director to have participated in directing the affairs of the company on an equal footing with the other directors and not in a subordinate role.[34] A *de facto* director must be shown to have exercised 'real influence' in the corporate decision-making process of the company.[35] A *de facto* director does not have to be held out by the company as a director[36] but, being held out as a director may be important evidence in support of the conclusion that the person did in fact act as a director.[37] In *Secretary of State for Trade and Industry v Tjolle*[38] the court declined to formulate a single test to determine whether a person is a *de facto* director. The court emphasised that all relevant factors must be taken into account in determining this issue. The Court of Appeal in *Re Kaytech International plc; Portier v Secretary of State for Trade and Industry*[39] endorsed this approach.

As mentioned above, a person could also be a *de facto* director where he or she was not validly appointed, ie that person was appointed to a directorship, but there is either a defect in the initial appointment of that person as a director or a defect appears at a later stage.[40] In such a case either the initial appointment is not legal (ie not *de jure*) or the original *de jure* director is rendered into a *de facto* director when the defect occurs. For instance, in *In re Canadian Land Reclaiming & Colonizing Co*[41] two persons had accepted directorships of a company in which the qualification for serving as a director in terms of the company's constitution was the holding of 100 shares in the company. Both persons had acted as directors of the company for some time but had never held any shares in the company. The Court of Appeal held that their appointment as directors nevertheless rendered them *de facto* directors of the company.

The words 'occupying the position of a director' in the definition of a 'director' in s 1 make it clear that a *de facto* director would constitute a director for the purposes of the Act. Accordingly, a 'director' may not escape his or her duties

---

[32] *Re Hydrodam (Corby) Ltd* [1994] BCC 161 at 162, 163.
[33] It is not sufficient to show that he or she had been engaged in the management of the company's affairs or had undertaken tasks in relation to its business that could properly be performed by a manager below board level (*Re Hydrodam (Corby) Ltd* (supra) at 163).
[34] *Gemma Ltd v Davies* [2008] BCC 812 para 40; *Secretary of State for Trade and Industry v Hollier* [2007] BCC 11 paras 68–9 and para 81.
[35] *Re Kaytech International plc; Portier v Secretary of State for Trade and Industry* [1999] BCC 390 at 402; *Gemma Ltd v Davies* (supra) para 40.
[36] Ibid.
[37] *Secretary of State for Trade and Industry v Hollier* (supra) para 66.
[38] [1998] BCC 282 at 290.
[39] [1999] BCC 390 at 402.
[40] See *R v Mall* 1959 (4) SA 607 (N) 624.
[41] [1880] 14 ChD 660.

simply because he or she has not been formally or validly appointed as a director. A *de facto* director is subject to the fiduciary and other duties of a director.[42]

(vi) *Shadow director*

In English law a 'shadow director' is defined as 'a person in accordance with whose directions or instructions the directors of the company are accustomed to act'.[43] As the name indicates, a shadow director 'lurks in the shadows', sheltering behind others who he or she claims are the only directors of the company to the exclusion of him- or herself.[44] He or she is not held out as a director by the company, but exercises power from the shadows.[45] While concealment is not a prerequisite,[46] in practice, most shadow directors would want to remain anonymous.[47] Should only a minority of the company's directors be accustomed to act in accordance with a person's instructions or directions this would not be sufficient to make that person a shadow director.[48]

In *Re Hydrodam (Corby) Ltd*[49] the court stated that, to establish that a defendant is a shadow director of a company, it is necessary to allege and prove:

> (1) [W]ho are the directors of the company, whether de facto or de jure; (2) that the defendant directed those directors how to act in relation to the company or that he was one of the persons who did so; (3) that those directors acted in accordance with such directions; and (4) that they were accustomed so to act. What is needed is, first, a board of directors claiming and purporting to act as such; and, secondly, a pattern of behaviour in which the board did not exercise any discretion or judgment of its own, but acted in accordance with the directions of others.[50]

The concept of a shadow director emerged to prevent the use of intermediaries acting as directors as a façade for the real exercise of power within the company.[51] Even though the Act does not explicitly define the concept of a shadow director, the definition of a 'director' in s 1 of the Act is wide enough to include a shadow director because of the phrase 'occupying the position of a director'. Shadow

---

[42] See for example *Shepherds Investment Ltd v Walters* [2007] 2 BCLC 207, where the court held that a *de facto* director had acted in breach of the no conflict duty in setting up a competing business and exploiting and diverting business opportunities that had belonged to the company for his own benefit. For further examples see *Statek Corp v Alford* [2008] BCC 266 and *Primlake Ltd v Matthews Associates* [2007] EWHC 1227 (Ch). See further chapter 12: The Duties and the Liability of Directors.
[43] See s 251(1) of the UK Companies Act 2006.
[44] *Re Hydrodam (Corby) Ltd* [1994] BCC 161 at 163.
[45] Ibid.
[46] *Secretary of State for Trade & Industry v Deverell* [2001] Ch 340 at 355.
[47] Some reasons why shadow directors would want to remain anonymous are that they wish to avoid being subject to certain of the duties or liabilities imposed on directors (such as liability for wrongful trading if the company fails), or because they have been disqualified from being validly appointed as a director.
[48] *Kuwait Asia Bank EC v National Mutual Life Nominees Ltd* [1991] AC 187 (PC) at 223.
[49] [1994] BCC 161.
[50] At 163.
[51] John de Lacy 'The Concept of a Company Director: Time for a new expanded and unified statutory concept' (May 2006) *Journal of Business Law* 267 at 291.

directors have been recognised in our common law, even if they have not been referred to as 'shadow directors'.[52]

Under s 251(2) of the UK Companies Act 2006 a person is not to be regarded as a shadow director by reason only that the directors act on advice given by him or her in a professional capacity. In the Australian Corporations Act 50 of 2002 the definition of a 'director' extends to a person who is not validly appointed as a director, but in accordance with whose instructions or wishes the directors of the company are accustomed to act.[53] Like the UK Companies Act 2006, s 9 of the Australian Corporations Act 50 of 2002 expressly states that a person is not a shadow director merely because the directors act on advice given by the person in the proper performance of functions attaching to the person's professional capacity, or the person's business relationship with the directors or the company. In a similar vein, s 1(2) of the 1973 Act provided that a person would not be deemed to be 'a person in accordance with whose directions or instructions the directors of a company are accustomed to act by reason only that the directors of the company act on advice given by him in a professional capacity'. The Act contains no similar provision — an omission that could cause difficulties in practice.

It is possible for a parent company to be a shadow director of its subsidiaries.[54] In *Re Hydrodam (Corby) Ltd*[55] the court held that, if a parent company is a shadow director of one of its subsidiaries, it does not necessarily follow that the directors of the parent company must also be shadow directors of the subsidiary. If the directors of the parent company as a collective body give instructions to the directors of the subsidiary company, who are accustomed to act in accordance with such directions, the result would be to constitute the parent company, but not its directors, a shadow director of the subsidiary company.[56] The court in *Re Hydrodam (Corby) Ltd* stated that the reason is that when the directors of the parent company give the instructions to the directors of the subsidiary company they do so as agents for the parent company, or more accurately, as the appropriate organ of the parent company.[57]

A *de facto* director and a shadow director are often confused and must be distinguished from each other. In *Re Hydrodam (Corby) Ltd* the court stated that the concepts of a *de facto* and a shadow director do not overlap but are alternatives, and in most cases are mutually exclusive. While a *de facto* director is one who claims to act and purports to act as a director, although not validly appointed as such, a shadow director does not claim or purport to act as a director, but in fact claims not to be a director.[58] A *de facto* director assumes functions that only a *de jure* director could properly perform, but a shadow director instructs the directors

---

[52] See for example *S v De Jager* 1965 (2) SA 616 (A), where two directors of a company had resigned and had appointed two persons as directors, who had acted simply on their instructions. It was held that even though the directors in question had formally resigned as directors they nevertheless had continued to be directors for the purposes of the fiduciary duties of a director.
[53] Section 9 of the Australian Corporations Act 50 of 2002.
[54] *Re Hydrodam (Corby) Ltd* [1994] BCC 161.
[55] Ibid.
[56] At 164.
[57] Ibid.
[58] *Re Hydrodam (Corby) Ltd* (supra) at 163.

(whether *de jure* or *de facto*) on how to act in relation to the company's affairs so that they become accustomed so to act. A shadow director does not act on an equal footing with the board of directors, as a *de facto* or *de jure* director would do, but instead is a superior who instructs or directs the directors.[59]

But the distinction between a *de facto* director and a shadow director is not always patent. For instance, in *Re Kaytech International plc; Portier v Secretary of State for Trade and Industry*[60] the court reasoned that the distinction between a *de facto* director and a shadow director is not always clear-cut because the influence of a person may be concealed at times and quite open at other times. In *Secretary of State for Trade and Industry v Deverell*[61] the Court of Appeal appeared to have merged the concepts of a *de facto* director and a shadow director — an approach that has been strongly criticised.[62] In *Secretary of State for Trade and Industry v Hollier*[63] the court stated that *de facto* directorships and shadow directorships are alternatives, but accepted that there may be cases, particularly where a person's influence was partly concealed and partly open, where it may not be entirely straightforward which of the two descriptions is most apposite.[64]

(vii) *Executive, non-executive and independent directors*

The Act does not distinguish between executive, non-executive and independent directors, but an important distinction is made between these types of directors in practice and in the King III Report and the Code, which are discussed in chapter 11: Corporate Governance.

10.3 THE LEGAL POSITION OF DIRECTORS

Since a company is a juristic person it can function only through human agency. It acts through its members in general meetings, and through its directors and employees. The day-to-day running of a company is the responsibility of the board of directors. The precise nature of the legal relationship between the company and a director is still a controversial question and several views have been expressed on this issue. Among other things, directors have been described as agents for the company,[65] trustees of the company,[66] and as managing partners.[67] As discussed below, none of these labels are entirely appropriate or correct.

---

[59] See Chris Noonan and Susan Watson 'The nature of shadow directorship: ad hoc statutory intervention or core Company law principle?' 2006 *Journal of Business Law* 763 at 772.

[60] [1999] BCC 390 at 402.

[61] [2001] Ch 340.

[62] See for instance Stephen Griffin 'Problems in the identification of a company director' (2003) 54 *Northern Ireland Legal Quarterly* 43; Chris Noonan and Susan Watson (op cit n 59).

[63] [2007] BCC 11.

[64] Para 81.

[65] See *Ferguson v Wilson* (1866) 2 Ch App 77 at 89; *Kuwait Asia Bank EC v National Mutual Life Nominees Ltd* [1991] AC 187 (PC) at 217–18.

[66] *Re Exchange Banking Co (Flitcroft's Case)* (1882) LR 21 ChD 519 at 525; *Selangor United Rubber Estates Ltd v Cradock (No 3)* [1968] 1 WLR 1555 at 1574–7.

[67] *Re Forest of Dean Coal Mining Co* (1878) LR 10 Ch 450 at 453; *Re Faure Electric Accumulator Co* (1889) LR 40 ChD 141 at 151; *Automatic Self-Cleansing Filter Syndicate Co Ltd v Cuninghame* [1906] 2 Ch 34 at 45.

10.3.1 Directors as agents

In some respects the relationship of a director to the company is analogous to that of an agent. For instance, a director, like an agent, acts for the benefit of some other person, that is, the company, and not for his or her own benefit, and when they contract on behalf of the company, they do not incur liability, unless they act outside their powers, or expressly or impliedly assume liability.[68] But under the Act the analogy of a director to an agent is not as strong as it may have been under the 1973 Act. Previously, a director did not enjoy original powers to act and, like an agent, his or her power to act arose from and was limited by the powers conferred on him or her. But s 66(1) of the Act now confers original powers and duties on directors. Thus the position of a director has changed considerably under the Act.

10.3.2 Directors as trustees

The legal position of a director as a fiduciary developed historically in England around the trust concept. The description of a director as a trustee thus played a useful role in English law at one stage. The position of a director is analogous to that of a trustee in that a director, like a trustee, stands in a fiduciary relationship to the company in the performance of his or her duties, and acts for the benefit of some other person, and not for his or her own benefit.[69] Furthermore, as in the case of a trustee, the property that is under the control of a director must be applied for the specified purposes of the company and for its benefit.[70]

But the description of a director as a trustee is not appropriate in South African law because in South African law trust property in vested in the trustee, but the property which directors are bound to administer is not vested in them but in the company itself, ie directors do not own any part of the property of the company.[71] Also, the courts do not apply the same strict standards of care and skill to directors as are applied to trustees.[72] In *Daniels t/as Deloitte Haskins & Sells v AWA Ltd*[73] New Zealand's New South Wales Court of Appeal stated that:

> [W]hile the duty of a trustee is to exercise a degree of restraint and conservatism in investment judgments, the duty of a director may be to display entrepreneurial flair and accept commercial risks to produce a sufficient return on the capital invested.[74]

In *In re City Equitable Fire Insurance Co Ltd*[75] it was stated that, while directors, like trustees, stand in a fiduciary relationship to the company in the performance of their duties, the analogy with trustees provides little indication as to what

---

[68] *Ferguson v Wilson* (1866) 2 Ch App 77 at 89; Blackman et al op cit n 14 at 8–9.
[69] *Re City Equitable Fire Insurance Co Ltd* [1925] Ch 407 at 426.
[70] *Selangor United Rubber Estates Ltd v Cradock (No 3)* [1968] 1 WLR 1555 at 1575.
[71] *Dadoo Ltd v Krugersdorp Municipal Council* 1920 AD 530 at 550–1; *Re Faure Electric Accumulator Co* (1889) LR 40 ChD 141 at 150; *Macaura v Northern Assurance Co Ltd* [1925] AC 619 (HL(Ir)); *Mulkana Corp NL (in liq) v Bank of New South Wales* (1983) 8 ACLR 278 SC (NSW) 282–3.
[72] *Re Faure Electric Accumulator Co* (supra) at 151; *Mulkana Corp NL (in liq) v Bank of New South Wales* (supra) at 284–5.
[73] (1995) 37 NSWLR 438.
[74] At 494.
[75] [1925] Ch 407 at 426.

precisely their fiduciary duties are. The court in *Mulkana Corp NL (in liq) v Bank of New South Wales*[76] commented on the analogy of directors as trustees as follows:

> [W]hile directors are not properly speaking, trustees, but fiduciary agents, the range of duties and obligations to which they are subject, or which are imposed upon them, include duties or obligations which place them, in relation to moneys or property which are in their possession, or over which they have control, in a position analogous to, although not identical with, that of trustees. Their position is not identical, since, for example, directors are not subject to the limitations on investment to which trustees normally are subject, but it is analogous since, just as, in such a case, trustees would be liable to recoup the trust for any loss, directors who misapply, or are parties to the misapplication of, funds or other property of the company, are, subject, to the court's powers to relieve them from so doing, liable to recoup the company for any loss thereby sustained.[77]

10.3.3 Directors as managing partners

Directors have also been described as managing partners.[78] The position of directors is analogous to managing partners in that they are empowered to manage a business.[79]

But, unlike managing partners, directors do not necessarily have a financial interest in the business, and even where they do hold shares in the company they are not, as directors, liable for the company's debts.[80]

The analogy of directors as managing partners is strong in the case of a personal liability company, where the directors and past directors are jointly and severally liable, together with the company, for the debts and liabilities of the company contracted during their periods of office. The analogy is also strong in the case of domestic companies or quasi-partnerships, ie companies that are very near to partnerships and which the courts have for certain purposes treated as if they were partnerships.[81] But again, there are differences in that directors owe their duties to the company and not to their fellow directors; each director alone has no power to

---

[76] (1983) 8 ACLR 278 SC (NSW).

[77] At 279.

[78] *Re Forest of Dean Coal Mining Co* (1878) LR 10 Ch 450 at 453; *Re Faure Electric Accumulator Co* (1889) LR 40 ChD 141 at 151; *Automatic Self-Cleansing Filter Syndicate Co Ltd v Cuninghame* [1906] 2 Ch 34 at 45.

[79] Blackman et al op cit n 14 at 8–9.

[80] Ibid at 8–10.

[81] By domestic companies in this context is meant small, usually family-owned-type companies. Domestic companies are formed on the basis of a personal relationship involving shared purposes, co-operation and mutual confidence, an agreement or understanding that some or all of the shareholders shall participate in the conduct of the business and a restriction on the shareholders' rights to transfer their shares (see *Roderick v AB Jackson (Pty) Ltd; Roderick v Bremco (Pty) Ltd* [2007] JOL 20079 (C)). A particular personal relationship of confidence and trust arises in a domestic company, which is similar to that which exists between partners in regard to partnership business (see *In re Yenidje Tobacco Co Ltd* [1916] 2 Ch 426 (CA); *Moosa, NO v Mavjee Bhawan (Pty) Ltd* 1967 (3) SA 131 (T) 137–8; *Emphy v Pacer Properties (Pty) Ltd* [1979] 2 All SA 35 (D) 36 and *Apco Africa (Pty) Ltd v Apco Worldwide Inc* 2008 (5) SA 615 (SCA) paras 18–19)). See further chapter 2: The Legal Concept of a Company.

bind the other directors or the company unless authorised to do so, and the powers of the directors are limited by restrictions in the Memorandum of Incorporation.[82]

10.3.4 *Sui generis*

It is evident from the above discussion that directors cannot properly be categorised as agents, trustees or managing partners, but that they occupy a unique position.[83] In other words, the legal relationship of a director is *sui generis*: it stands in a class of its own. It cannot be determined by reference to a single legal relationship, but must be determined by reference to the facts of each case.[84] In *Cohen v Segal*[85] the court concisely summed up the legal relationship of directors as follows:

> Directors are from time to time spoken of as agents, trustees or managing partners of a company, but such expressions are not used as exhaustive of the powers and responsibilities of those persons, but only as indicating useful points of view from which they may for the moment and for the particular purpose be considered, points of view at which, for the moment, they seem to be falling within the category of the suggested kind. It is not meant that they belong to the category, but that it is useful for the purpose of the moment to observe that they fall, *pro tanto*, within the principles which govern that particular class. . . .[86]

10.4 PRESCRIBED OFFICERS

A 'prescribed officer' is defined in s 1 of the Act as meaning the 'holder of an office, within a company, that has been designated by the Minister in terms of section 66(11)'.[87] In terms of s 66(10) the Minister may make regulations designating any specific function or functions within a company to constitute a prescribed office for the purposes of the Act.

In terms of Regulation 45 of the draft Companies Regulations a person is designated a 'prescribed officer' of a company if, despite not being a director of the company, that person:

(a) has general executive authority over the company (such as a President, Chief Executive Officer, Managing Director, Executive Director or similar office holder) by whatever title the office is designated; or

(b) has general responsibility for the financial management of the company (such as a Treasurer, Chief Financial Officer, Chief Accounting Officer, or similar office holder) by whatever title the office is designated; or

(c) has general responsibility for management of the legal affairs of the company (such as a General Secretary, General Counsel or similar officer holder) by whatever title the office is designated; or

---

[82] Blackman et al op cit n 14 at 8–11.
[83] See *Regal (Hastings) Ltd v Gulliver* [1967] 2 AC 134 at 147, [1942] 1 All ER 378.
[84] *Regal (Hastings) Ltd v Gulliver* (supra) at 147.
[85] 1970 (3) SA 702 (W).
[86] At 706.
[87] The reference to 'section 66(11)' ought to be a reference to 'section 66(10)'. This is corrected in the draft Companies Amendment Bill, 2010 (cl 2(1)*(x)*), which defines a 'prescribed officer' as 'a person who, within a company, performs any function that has been designated by the Minister in terms of section 66(10)'.

(d) has general managerial authority over the operations of the company (such as a Chief Operating Officer or similar office holder) by whatever title the office is designated; or
(e) otherwise directly or indirectly exercises, or significantly influences the exercise of, control over the general management and administration of the whole or a significant portion of the business and activities of the company, irrespective of any title assigned by the company to an office held by that person, or function performed by that person.

It is evident from the above list that a wide group of persons have been designated as prescribed officers of a company. Notably, certain provisions of the Act which apply to directors also apply to the prescribed officers of the company.[88] The object is to ensure that prescribed officers are subject to the same strict duties and accountability as directors.

10.5 OFFICE BEARERS OF THE COMPANY

10.5.1 Manager

The position of a director is not to be equated to that of a manager. As stated by the court in *R v Mall*,[89] there are fundamental differences between the position of a director and that of a manager:

> There is, however, a material difference between the situation of a director and that of a manager. Directors are required by statute; they are essential to a company, and their functions and duties are defined by law. They are appointed by the shareholders and are vested with the management and control of the company. They represent the company, and there is a degree of permanence attaching to their position. They act as a body, save so far as powers are lawfully delegated. Their identity, the law intends, should be undoubted and easily discoverable from the company's records. To regard as a director a person with no appointment, a person meddling in the company's affairs, runs counter to the whole idea of company law.
>
> A manager, on the other hand, is an employee of the company and his services are engaged by the directors; he is not legally essential to the company, his contract may be of a formal nature or otherwise; his position may be inferred from conduct, and he may continue in employment for a long time or a short time. His position is not defined by law, indeed he may be a general manager, manager of a department, office manager or whatsoever. It is always a question of fact what he is and what his functions are, which may be easy or not easy of proof.[90]

A further difference between directors and managers is that directors are accountable to the shareholders for the company's performance and may be removed from office by the shareholders, while managers are usually appointed and dismissed by the directors and do not interact with the shareholders.[91]

---

[88] For instance, s 69 of the Act, which sets out the grounds of ineligibility and disqualification of directors, also applies to prescribed officers. In addition, ss 75 (directors' personal financial interests), 76 (standards of directors' conduct) and 77 (liability of directors and prescribed officers) of the Act apply to directors and to prescribed officers.
[89] 1959 (4) SA 607 (N).
[90] At 622–3, referred to with approval in *L Suzman (Rand) Ltd v Yamoyani* (2) 1972 (1) SA 109 (W) 112–13.
[91] D Davis et al *Companies and Other Business Structures in South Africa* (2009) 81.

A director must also be distinguished from a consultant. A consultant is engaged by the company to perform specific functions, while a director is engaged in the affairs of the company generally.[92]

10.5.2 Managing director

The term 'managing director' is applied to a director who is vested by the board of directors with all or a substantial part of its general powers of the control of the affairs of the company.[93] The courts have taken different views on the role of a managing director. In *In re Newspaper Proprietary Syndicate Ltd*[94] the court stated that 'a managing director is only an ordinary director entrusted with some special powers'.[95] Other courts have regarded a managing director as a manager who happens also to be a director,[96] while in *Southern Foundries (1926) Ltd v Shirlaw*[97] the court stated that the positions of a director and that of a managing director 'involve different qualifications, duties and responsibilities'.[98] These differing views illustrate that the functions of a managing director are not fixed by law, but depend on the specific terms of his or her appointment.

Generally, a managing director is the direct and immediate representative of the board of directors, and acts within his or her ostensible (or usual) authority to bind the company in its dealings with other parties.[99] As the chief executive who is in charge, under the board of directors, of the daily running of the company, the managing director's task is to supervise the work of other managers and the daily running of the company. In this regard, he or she is usually the highest-paid employee of the company.[100]

As a result of s 66(1) of the Act it is no longer necessary for the Memorandum of Incorporation to confer express power to appoint a managing director.

10.5.3 Chairperson of the board of directors

The Memorandum of Incorporation may make provision for the directors to elect a chairperson of their meetings and to determine the period for which he or she is to hold office. Generally, in the absence of a specific mandate or authorisation by the company in the Memorandum of Incorporation or otherwise, the position of the chairperson of the board of directors differs little from that of an ordinary director, and the chairperson usually does not have any additional powers merely by virtue of his or her chairpersonship.[101] But the chairperson's position is an important one in that he or she is obliged at board meetings 'to preserve order, and to take care that the proceedings are conducted in a proper manner, and that the

---

[92] *Mistmorn Pty Ltd (in liq) v Yasseen* (1996) 21 ACSR 173.
[93] *Morseby White v Rangeland Ltd* 1952 (4) SA 285 (SR) 286–7. See also *Kuter v South African Pharmacy Board* 1954 (2) SA 423 (T) 425–6.
[94] [1900] 2 Ch 349.
[95] At 350.
[96] *Anderson v James Sutherland (Peterhead) Ltd* 1941 SC 203 at 217.
[97] [1940] AC 701.
[98] At 712.
[99] *Morseby White v Rangeland Ltd* (supra) at 287.
[100] RP Austin and IM Ramsay *Ford's Principles of Corporations Law* 13 ed (2007) para 7.264 p 262.
[101] *Wolpert v Uitzigt Properties (Pty) Ltd* 1961 (2) SA 257 (W) 266.

sense of the meeting is properly ascertained with regard to any question which is properly before the meeting'.[102] The chairperson has a fiduciary duty to act objectively.[103] He or she must be satisfied that the meeting has been properly convened and constituted, that the provisions of the Act and the Memorandum of Incorporation are complied with and that the business is properly put before the meeting.

As regards voting at board meetings in terms of the Act, in the case of a tied vote, except to the extent that the Memorandum of Incorporation provides otherwise, the chairperson has a casting vote only if he or she did not have or cast a vote initially.[104]

The King III Report and the Code lay down some important principles relevant to the role and function of the chairperson of the board of directors. See further chapter 11: Corporate Governance.

10.5.4 Company secretary

The secretary of a company is ordinarily the chief administrative officer of the company. Whereas in the past the company secretary fulfilled 'a very humble role'[105] and was regarded as a mere servant who was required to do what he or she was told, today the company secretary has grown in importance in the role he or she plays in the company's affairs. As the court in the English case of *Panorama Developments (Guildford) Ltd v Fidelis Furnishing Fabrics Ltd*[106] stated:

> ... times have changed. A company secretary is a much more important person nowadays than he was in 1887. He is an officer of the company with extensive duties and responsibilities. This appears not only in the modern Companies Acts, but also by the role which he plays in the day-to-day business of companies. He is no longer a mere clerk. He regularly makes representations on behalf of the company and enters into contracts on its behalf which come within the day-to-day running of the company's business.[107]

The Act makes it mandatory for every public company and state-owned company to appoint a company secretary (this is subject to certain exemptions).[108] It is not mandatory for a private company, personal liability company and non-profit company to appoint a company secretary, save to the extent that the company's Memorandum of Incorporation provides otherwise.[109] Every company that appoints a company secretary must maintain a record of its company secretaries.[110]

The first company secretary may be appointed by the incorporators of the company or, within 40 business days after the incorporation of the company, by

---

[102] *National Dwellings Society v Sykes* [1894] 3 Ch 159 at 162. See further *Berman v Chairman, Cape Provincial Council* 1961 (2) SA 412 (C) 416 and *Jonker v Ackerman* 1979 (3) SA 575 (O) 583–4.
[103] *South African Broadcasting Corporation Ltd v Mpofu* [2009] 4 All SA 169 (GSJ).
[104] Section 73(5)*(e)*.
[105] *Barnett, Hoares & Co v South London Tramways Co* (1887) 18 QBD 815 at 817.
[106] [1971] 2 QB 711.
[107] At 716–17.
[108] Section 84(4)*(a)* read with s 86(1).
[109] Section 34(2) read with s 84(1)*(c)*.
[110] Section 85.

either the directors of the company or by means of an ordinary resolution passed by the holders of the company's securities.[111] A juristic person or partnership may be appointed as the company secretary.[112]

The company secretary must be a person knowledgeable or experienced in relevant laws as a company secretary.[113] He or she must be a permanent resident of South Africa and must remain so while serving as the company secretary.[114] The disqualifications relating to the appointment of a director set out in s 69(8) of the Act apply equally to the appointment of a company secretary.[115] The company secretary is accountable to the board of directors, and his or her duties include, but are not restricted to the following:

(a) providing the directors of the company collectively and individually with guidance as to their duties, responsibilities and powers;
(b) making the directors aware of any law relevant to or affecting the company;
(c) reporting to the company's board any failure on the part of the company or a director to comply with the Memorandum of Incorporation or rules of the company or this Act;
(d) ensuring that minutes of all shareholders' meetings, board meetings and the meetings of any committees of the directors, or of the company's audit committee, are properly recorded in accordance with this Act;
(e) certifying in the company's annual financial statements whether the company has filed required returns and notices in terms of this Act, and whether all such returns and notices appear to be true, correct and up to date;
(f) ensuring that a copy of the company's annual financial statements is sent, in accordance with this Act, to every person who is entitled to it; and
(g) carrying out the functions of a person designated in terms of section 33(3).[116]

From the above list of the secretary's duties, it is evident that the secretary has a vital role to play in assisting the board to ensure proper corporate governance. The King III Report and the Code set out some pertinent principles relating to the role of the company secretary.[117]

---

[111] Section 86(3). Within 60 business days after a vacancy arises in the office of company secretary the board of directors is required to fill the vacancy by appointing a person whom the directors consider to have the requisite knowledge and experience.

[112] This is subject to the provisos that every employee of that juristic person who provides company secretary services, or partner and employee of that partnership, as the case may be, is not disqualified to serve as a director of a company, and at least one employee of that juristic person or one partner or employee of that partnership, as the case may be, is knowledgeable or experienced in the relevant laws as a company secretary and is a permanent resident of South Africa (see s 87(1)).

[113] Section 86(1).
[114] Section 86(2).
[115] Section 84(5).
[116] Section 88(2). In terms of s 33(3) each company is required to designate a director, employee or other person who is responsible for the company's compliance with the requirements of Part C of the Act (Transparency, accountability and integrity of companies) and Chapter 3 (Enhanced accountability and transparency) (should Chapter 3 apply to the company).
[117] See further chapter 11: Corporate Governance and chapter 13: The Auditor, Financial Records and Reporting on the company secretary.

10.5.5 Auditor

A public company and a state-owned company are required to appoint an auditor upon their incorporation and each year at their annual general meeting.[118] A firm of auditors may be appointed to hold the office of auditor.[119]

Before a company's financial statements are submitted to the members they must be audited by an auditor. The annual financial statements of a public company must comply with International Financial Reporting Standards. The function of the auditor is to ensure that the financial information relating to the company's affairs, as prepared by the directors, fairly and accurately reflects the company's financial position. The purpose of an audit is firstly, to protect the company itself from the consequences of undetected errors or wrongdoing, and secondly, to provide shareholders with reliable intelligence to enable them to scrutinise the conduct of the company's affairs.[120] It would clearly be open to abuse if the shareholders did not receive any report on the financial stewardship of their investment save from those to whom the stewardship has been entrusted.[121]

The auditor is not a functionary of the company and when he or she carries out their duties, they are not acting on behalf of the company or in its name; even though they have been appointed by the company they act independently.[122] In performing his or her duties, an auditor must act with reasonable care and skill.[123] The content of an auditor's duty to use reasonable care and skill was regarded as being well described in *In re Kingston Cotton Mill Co (No 2)*[124] in 1896 when Lopes LJ stated that an auditor 'is a watchdog, not a bloodhound'.[125] But although auditors are not 'bloodhounds' and are not bound to be detectives or to approach their work with suspicion or with a foregone conclusion that there is something wrong, they are supposed to bring to their task a high capacity to perceive financial irregularities.[126] They are entitled to assume that the company's employees are honest, but their training and experience should be such that they should recognise opportunities for fraud and error and should make appropriate inquiries.[127]

Under s 90(1)(a) of the Act, to be appointed as an auditor of a company, a person or firm must be registered as an auditor with the Independent Regulatory Board for Auditors established by the Auditing Profession Act 26 of 2005. As already mentioned, the auditor must be independent of the company and may not be a director, a prescribed officer or an employee of the company, or a consultant who has engaged for more than a year in the maintenance of any of the company's

---

[118] Section 90(1).
[119] Section 90(3).
[120] *Caparo Industries plc v Dickman* [1990] 1 All ER 568 at 583.
[121] *Caparo Industries plc v Dickman* [1989] 1 All ER 798 at 804.
[122] *Powertech Industries Ltd v Mayberry* 1996 (2) SA 742 (W) 746.
[123] *Tonkwane Sawmill Co Ltd v Filmalter* 1975 (2) SA 453 (W); *Pacific Acceptance Corporation Ltd v Forsyth* (1970) 92 WN (NSW) 29 at 50; *In re London and General Bank: Ex parte Theobald (No 2)* [1895] 2 Ch 673 at 682–3.
[124] [1896] 2 Ch 279 at 288.
[125] At 288. See also *Tonkwane Sawmill Co Ltd v Filmalter* (supra).
[126] RP Austin and IM Ramsay op cit n 100 at para 10.550 p 617.
[127] Ibid.

financial records or the preparation of any of its financial statements.[128] The auditor may also not be a person who, by him- or herself or with a partner or employees, habitually or regularly performs the duties of accountant or bookkeeper or performs related secretarial work for the company.[129] The disqualifications relating to the appointment of a director set out in s 69(8) of the Act apply equally to the appointment of the auditor.[130] The same individual may not serve as the auditor of a company for more than five consecutive financial years.[131]

The auditor of a company has a right of access at all times to the accounting records,[132] books and documents of the company and its subsidiaries and is entitled to require from the directors or prescribed officers of the company and its subsidiaries any information and explanations necessary for the performance of his or her duties. In addition, he or she is entitled to attend any shareholders' meetings, to receive notices and other communications relating to any shareholders' meeting and to be heard at any shareholders' meeting on any part of the business of the meeting that concerns his or her duties and functions.[133] See further chapter 13: The Auditor, Financial Records and Reporting on the role and functions of the auditor.

10.6 NUMBER OF DIRECTORS

10.6.1 Minimum number of directors

A private company and a personal liability company must appoint at least one director, while a public company and a non-profit company must appoint at least three directors.[134] This is subject to the Memorandum of Incorporation, which may require a company to have a higher minimum number of directors.[135]

10.6.2 Company with one director

Where a profit company (other than a state-owned company) has only one director, that director may exercise any power or perform any function of the board at

---

[128] Section 90(2)(b).
[129] See further s 90(2)(b) for further disqualifications relating to the appointment of an auditor.
[130] Section 84(5).
[131] Section 92(1).
[132] The draft Companies Amendment Bill, 2010 defines 'accounting records' as meaning information in written or electronic form concerning the financial affairs of a company as required in terms of the Companies Act, including, but not limited to, purchase and sales records, general and subsidiary ledgers and other documents and books used in the preparation of financial statements (see cl 2(1)(a)).
[133] Section 93.
[134] Section 66(2).
[135] Clause 42 of the draft Companies Amendment Bill, 2010 has amended this provision to provide that the number of directors of a private company, a personal liability company, a public company or a non-profit company is in addition to the minimum number of directors that the company is required to have to satisfy any requirement to appoint an audit committee or a social and ethics committee as contemplated in s 72(4) of the Companies Act. Both the audit committee and the social and ethics committee are required to comprise three directors, at a minimum. The implication of cl 42 of the draft Companies Amendment Bill, 2010 is that those companies that are required to have an audit committee and/or a social and ethics committee would have to have at least three or even six directors in addition to the minimum required number of directors. This does seem rather onerous.

any time, without notice or compliance with any other internal formalities (except to the extent that the Memorandum of Incorporation provides otherwise).[136] The company is also exempt from the application of various provisions of the Act.[137]

10.6.3 Failure to have the required number of directors

If the number of incorporators of a company, together with any *ex officio* directors and directors to be appointed in terms of the Memorandum of Incorporation, is fewer than the minimum number of required directors, the board of directors must call a shareholders' meeting within 40 business days after the company has been incorporated, for the purpose of electing sufficient directors to fill all the vacancies on the board.[138]

Notably, a failure by a company to have the required minimum number of directors would not limit or negate the board's authority or invalidate anything done by the board or the company.[139]

10.7 APPOINTMENT OF DIRECTORS

10.7.1 Initial appointment of directors

The first directors of a company are the incorporators of the company, and such persons serve as directors of the company until the minimum number of required directors (in terms of the Act or the Memorandum of Incorporation) has been appointed or elected.[140]

10.7.2 Subsequent appointments

(a) Appointments by a person named in the Memorandum of Incorporation

As discussed previously, a director may be appointed by a person named in, or determined in terms of, the Memorandum of Incorporation.[141] Where the authority to appoint a director is vested in a third party, that third party is not under any obligation to appoint as a director the most suitable person for the position. This was clearly expressed in *Kuwait Asia Bank EC v National Mutual Life Nominees Ltd* as follows:

> [I]n the absence of fraud or bad faith ... a shareholder or other person who controls the appointment of a director owes no duty to creditors of the company to take reasonable care to see that directors so appointed discharge their duties as directors with due diligence and competence.[142]

---

[136] Section 57(3)(*a*).
[137] Section 57(3)(*b*). For instance, s 71(3)–(7) (removal of directors), s 73 (board meetings) and s 74 (directors acting other than at a meeting) do not apply to the governance of that company.
[138] Section 67(2).
[139] Section 66(11).
[140] Section 67(1).
[141] Section 66(4)(*a*)(i). See also *Gohlke & Schneider v Westies Minerale (Edms) Bpk* 1970 (2) SA 685 (A) and *Kuwait Asia Bank EC v National Mutual Life Nominees Ltd* [1991] AC 187 (PC) at 220–1.
[142] Supra at 221.

(b) Appointments by the shareholders

Each director, other than the first directors, a director appointed in terms of the Memorandum of Incorporation and an *ex officio* director, must be elected by the shareholders, to serve as a director of the company for an indefinite term or for a term set out in the Memorandum of Incorporation.[143] Unless the Memorandum of Incorporation provides otherwise, the election is to be conducted as a series of votes, and each director is to be appointed by a separate resolution.[144] The series of votes would continue until all vacancies on the board at that time have been filled. Having separate voting for each candidate prevents a block of candidates being voted on together, which would compel a shareholder who wishes to vote for one candidate of the block to vote for all the candidates even though there may be one or more candidates whom he or she does not want to elect as directors.[145] But note that the Memorandum of Incorporation may make provision for two or more candidates to be elected as directors by way of a single resolution.

The Act does not make provision for cumulative voting.[146] A shareholder may only exercise his or her right to vote once, and the vacancy would be filled if a majority of the voting rights exercised support the candidate.[147] The general rule is that shareholders may vote for a director in their own interests, even if their interests conflict with those of the company, and they are under no obligation to choose the person most suitable to be a director.[148] Of course it is in a shareholder's interests to ensure that the director he or she supports is competent, but there is no duty to vote in this way.[149]

(c) Appointments by the board of directors or other stakeholders or outsiders

As discussed previously, in terms of s 66(4)*(b)*, in the case of a profit company (other than a state-owned company) the Memorandum of Incorporation must provide for the election by shareholders of at least 50 per cent of the directors and 50 per cent of any alternate directors. This implies that a company could require 50 per cent or less of its directors to be appointed by parties other than the shareholders, such as the board of directors, or other stakeholders or outsiders. Where the power to appoint directors is vested in the board of directors it is a

---

[143] Section 68(1). Clause 43 of the draft Companies Amendment Bill, 2010 makes it clear that the election of directors under s 68 applies to directors of profit companies only.

[144] Section 68(2)*(a)*.

[145] *Aitchison v Dench* 1964 (2) SA 515 (T) 516–17.

[146] Cumulative voting is where each shareholder receives a number of votes equal to the number of votes attached to his or her shares, multiplied by the number of directors to be appointed. The shareholder may cast his or her votes in favour of one candidate or distribute them among the candidates. By focusing all their votes on one candidate, a group of minority shareholders would be able to elect a director against the wishes of the majority group, thus ensuring that they do not remain unrepresented on the board. Cumulative voting thus ensures minority representation. It is useful to a minority when it combines a substantial number of shares and when there are several directors to be appointed.

[147] Section 68(2)*(b)*.

[148] *Re HR Harmer Ltd* [1959] 1 WLR 62 at 82; *Kuwait Asia Bank EC v National Mutual Life Nominees Ltd* (supra) at 221.

[149] *Kuwait Asia Bank EC v National Mutual Life Nominees Ltd* (supra) at 221.

fiduciary power and must be exercised in good faith in the interests of the company and not for any improper or collateral purpose.[150]

(d) Other appointments

As previously discussed, provision is made in the Act for the appointment of *ex officio* directors, alternate directors, temporary directors and nominee directors.

10.7.3 Consent to be a director

In order for a person to be a director of a company, a written consent to serve as a director must be delivered to the company.[151] A person will not become a director of a company if this consent is not delivered to the company. This obviously does not apply to *de facto* and shadow directors.

An election or appointment of a person as a director would be a nullity if at the time of the election or appointment that person was ineligible or disqualified from being a director.[152]

Within ten business days after a person becomes a director of the company (or ceases to be a director of the company), the company is required to file a notice with the Companies and Intellectual Property Commission ('the Companies Commission') to this effect.[153]

10.8 TERMS OF APPOINTMENT

A director is not as such an employee or servant of the company, but may be employed by the company as an employee in terms of a separate contract of service.[154] Thus the terms upon which directors hold office may be contained either in the Memorandum of Incorporation or in a service contract that exists outside of, and is unconnected to, the Memorandum of Incorporation. This would not affect the nature of the person's office as a director, and he or she would be an employee in addition to, and independently of, holding the office of director.[155] The dismissal of a director as an employee does not of itself result in the termination of his or her office as a director. Should the company breach the contract, s 71 of the Act, like s 220 of the 1973 Act, would preserve the director's right to claim damages for breach of contract.

Under the 1973 Act the articles of association of a company did not create a contract between the company and a director in his or her capacity as such.[156] For a director who had been removed from office to have an action for damages

---
[150] Blackman et al op cit n 14 at 8–243; RP Austin and IM Ramsay op cit n 100 at para 7.170 p 235. For the law relating to a director's fiduciary duty to exercise his or her powers for a proper purpose, refer to chapter 12: The Duties and the Liability of Directors.
[151] Section 66(7).
[152] Section 66(6). Section 69 of the Act sets out those instances when a person would be ineligible or disqualified from being a director. This is discussed below in 10.11.
[153] Section 70(6).
[154] *Diner v Dublin* 1962 (4) SA 36 (N) 41; *Moriarty v Regent's Garage & Engineering Co Ltd* [1921] 1 KB 423 at 445–6; *Re Lee, Behrens & Co Ltd* [1932] 2 Ch 46 at 53.
[155] *Diner v Dublin* (supra) at 41; *Van Tonder v Pienaar* 1982 (2) SA 336 (SE).
[156] See for instance *De Villiers v Jacobsdal Saltworks (Michaelis and De Villiers) (Pty) Ltd* 1959 (3) SA 873 (O); *Beattie v E&F Beattie Ltd* [1938] Ch 708 and *Southern Foundries (1926) Ltd v Shirlaw*

against the company, it was necessary for that director to have a separate contract of service with the company binding it to hold his or her position for a fixed term or not to terminate his or her office or to compensate him or her if he or she were removed from office. But in terms of s 15(6) of the Act, the Memorandum of Incorporation now constitutes a contract between the company and the director.[157] This means that, should the company breach the provisions of the Memorandum of Incorporation relating to a director, the director would have a contractual claim against the company based solely on the Memorandum of Incorporation.

Regarding the term of office of a director, s 68(1) of the Act provides that each director of a company, other than the first directors, a director appointed in terms of the Memorandum of Incorporation and an *ex officio* director, must be elected by the persons entitled to exercise voting rights in such an election, to serve for an indefinite term or for a term as set out in the Memorandum of Incorporation. It is questionable whether it is advisable for a person to remain in the position of a director for an indefinite term, because this may affect his or her independence as a director and may not accord with good corporate governance practices. The problem is compounded in the case of an independent non-executive director, who must not only be independent in fact but must also be perceived to be independent in the perception of a reasonably informed outsider.[158] Of course, even if a director is appointed for an indefinite term, he or she may nevertheless be removed as a director by ordinary resolution at any time in terms of s 71 of the Act.

10.9 RECORD OF DIRECTORS

Every company is required to maintain a record of its directors.

10.9.1 Information to be contained in the record of directors

The information that must be contained in the record of directors includes details of the company's directors, such as full names and any former names of the directors;[159] identity number or, failing that, date of birth; nationality and passport number (if the person is not of South African nationality); occupation; date of their most recent election or appointment as a director of the company; name and registration number of every other company of which the person is a director and in the case of a foreign company, the nationality of that company, and any other prescribed information.[160]

Regulation 25(1) of the draft Companies Regulations further requires the company's record of directors to include, with respect to each director of the company, the name and registration number of any company of which a person related to

---

[1940] AC 701. In light of s 15(6) of the Act the position has changed. See further chapter 4: Formation of Companies and the Company Constitution.

[157] See further chapter 4: Formation of Companies and the Company Constitution.

[158] See further on independent non-executive directors the King III Report discussed in chapter 11: Corporate Governance.

[159] In order to protect personal privacy, the Minister of Trade and Industry may exempt categories of names as formerly used by any person before attaining majority, or by persons who have been adopted, married, divorced or widowed, or in other circumstances prescribed by the Minister (s 24(6)).

[160] Section 24(5).

that director is a director or prescribed officer; the address for service of documents for that director, and in the case of a company that is required to have an audit committee, the professional qualifications (if any) and previous experience of the director.

Note that it is no longer necessary to provide details of a director's residential address.[161] An address for service of documents for each director would suffice. Keeping a director's residential address away from the public record would protect his or her personal privacy and would prevent harassment and abuse of directors.

The record of directors must include details relating to the company's current directors as well as its past directors. With respect to the company's past directors, the information relating to those directors must be compiled as of the date those directors had ceased to be directors of the company.[162] The information must be retained by the company for a period of seven years after such directors have ceased to be directors of the company.[163]

10.9.2 Retention of record of directors

Under s 24(1)(b) of the Act any records that a company is required to keep in terms of the Act or any other public regulation must be retained for seven years, or any longer period of time specified in any other applicable public regulation. If a company has existed for fewer than seven years then it is required to retain its records for that shorter time.[164] But Regulation 24(1)(c) of the draft Companies Regulations requires the record of directors to be retained by the company indefinitely.

10.9.3 Location of record of directors

The record of directors must be accessible at the company's registered office or another location or locations within South Africa.[165] A company must file a notice setting out the location or locations where the records are kept if they are not kept at the registered office, or are moved from one location to another.

10.9.4 Inspection of record of directors

Under s 26(3) of the Act the register of directors is open to inspection by any 'member' free of charge. The draft Companies Amendment Bill, 2010 gives persons who hold a beneficial interest[166] in securities issued by a profit company and members of a non-profit company a right to inspect and copy the register of

---

[161] Under s 215 of the 1973 Act it was mandatory for the register of directors to state every director's residential address.
[162] Regulation 25(2)(b) of the draft Companies Regulations.
[163] Section 24(3)(b). See cl 16 of the draft Companies Amendment Bill, 2010.
[164] Section 24(2).
[165] Section 25.
[166] 'Beneficial interest', as defined in s 1 of the Act, means the right or entitlement of a person, through ownership, agreement, relationship or otherwise, alone or together with another person, to receive or participate in any distribution in respect of the company's securities; to exercise or cause to be exercised, in the ordinary course, any or all of the rights attaching to the company's securities, or to dispose or direct the disposition of the company's securities, or any part of a distribution in

directors without any charge, or upon payment of no more than the prescribed maximum charge for a copy of the records.[167] The right to inspect and copy the register of directors is conferred on persons who hold a beneficial interest in securities issued by a company and not to registered holders of securities who are not also the beneficial holders of the securities. But note that the Memorandum of Incorporation of a company may make provision for additional information rights of any person with regard to information that pertains to the company.[168] This is subject to the proviso that no right may negate or diminish any mandatory protection of any record under Part 3 of the Promotion of Access to Information Act 2 of 2000 (PAIA).[169]

Under s 26(3) of the Act, persons who are not members of a company must pay R100 for each inspection of the register of directors. The draft Companies Amendment Bill, 2010 does not specify the amount of the fee and provides that a person who does not hold a beneficial interest in any securities issued by a profit company or who is not a member of a non-profit company has a right to inspect the register of directors upon payment of an amount not exceeding the prescribed maximum fee for any such inspection.[170] No provision is made for such persons to make a copy of the records, and the right is limited merely to that of an inspection of the register of directors.

The right to inspect and copy the directors' register may be exercised by direct request made to the company in the prescribed manner, either in person or through an attorney or other personal representative designated in writing, or in accordance with PAIA.[171]

A right of access to any record held by a company is not perfected until a request to exercise that right has been made to the company in terms of Regulation 26(4) of the draft Companies Regulations, and the right of access to the information has been confirmed in accordance with PAIA.[172] In terms of Regulation 26(4), a person seeking to exercise a right of access to any record held by a company must make a written request to do so, as contemplated in s 26(1)(c) of the Act,[173] by delivering a completed Request for Access to Information form to the company[174] and any further documents or other material required in terms of PAIA.

---

respect of the securities. It does not include any interest held by a person in a unit trust or collective investment scheme in terms of the Collective Investment Schemes Act 45 of 2002.

[167] See cl 17(a) of the draft Companies Amendment Bill, 2010.

[168] This is permitted by s 26(1)(b) and s 26(2) of the Act. See cl 17 of the draft Companies Amendment Bill, 2010 which renumbers the provisions of s 26 of the Act.

[169] Section 26(2). Part 3 of PAIA deals with the access to records of private bodies, and in particular ss 62 to 70 deal with grounds for refusal of access to records. Section 68 deals with the grounds for refusal of access to commercial information of a private body.

[170] See cl 17(a) of the draft Companies Amendment Bill, 2010.

[171] See s 26(1)(c) of the Act. This section is renumbered as s 26(4) in the draft Companies Amendment Bill, 2010.

[172] Regulation 26(3) of the draft Companies Regulations.

[173] That is, by direct request made to the company either in person or through an attorney or other personal representative designated in writing.

[174] Form CoR 26.

A perfected right of access to any information held by a company may be exercised only during the company's normal business hours.[175]

10.9.5 Failure by the company to accommodate a request for access

It is an offence for a company to fail to accommodate any reasonable request for access, or to unreasonably refuse access, to any record that a person has a right to inspect or copy, or to otherwise impede, interfere with, or attempt to frustrate, the reasonable exercise by any person of their rights of access to the company's records.[176]

10.10 COMPANY RULES

Unless prohibited by the Memorandum of Incorporation, the board of directors may make, amend or repeal any necessary or incidental rules relating to the governance of the company in respect of matters that are not addressed in the Act or the Memorandum of Incorporation.[177] Such rules must be consistent with the Act and the Memorandum of Incorporation, failing which they will be void to the extent of the inconsistency.[178] See further chapter 4: Formation of Companies and the Company Constitution, on company rules.

10.11 INELIGIBILITY AND DISQUALIFICATION OF PERSONS TO BE DIRECTORS

10.11.1 Application of s 69 of the Act

The provisions of s 69 of the Act setting out the grounds of ineligibility and disqualification of directors apply not only to directors and alternate directors, but also to prescribed officers and persons who are members of the company's board committees or audit committee, irrespective of whether or not such persons are also members of the company's board of directors.[179]

10.11.2 Qualifications

The Act does not prescribe minimum qualifications for a director, such as those relating to the education and training of directors, but instead imposes criteria that disqualify a person from being a director. The reason for not imposing minimum qualifications is that these are regarded as being an internal company policy

---

[175] Regulation 26(5) of the draft Companies Regulations. See cl 17 of the draft Companies Amendment Bill, 2010.
[176] Section 26(6). A person convicted of an offence in terms of the Act is liable to a fine or to imprisonment for a period not exceeding 12 months, or to both a fine and imprisonment (s 216*(b)*). Note the renumbering of the provisions of s 26 by cl 17 of the draft Companies Amendment Bill, 2010.
[177] Section 15(3).
[178] Section 15(4)*(a)*.
[179] Section 69(1).

issue.[180] The Memorandum of Incorporation may, however, on an optional basis, impose minimum qualifications to be met by directors of a particular company.[181]

The Act does not impose a share qualification requirement on directors either and accordingly, being a shareholder is not a formal condition of being a director. But the Memorandum of Incorporation may well impose a share qualification requirement and may require directors to hold a specified number of shares in the company to qualify as directors of the company.

10.11.3 Distinguishing ineligibility from disqualification

The difference between a person who is ineligible to be a director and one who is disqualified from being a director is that a disqualification is not absolute and a court has a discretion to permit a disqualified person to accept an appointment as a director, but no such flexibility is permitted with respect to ineligible persons, who are absolutely prohibited from being a director.

10.11.4 Grounds of ineligibility

The following persons are ineligible to be directors of a company:[182]

- a juristic person,[183]
- an unemancipated minor[184] or person under a similar legal disability,[185]
- any person who does not satisfy any minimum qualification set out in the Memorandum of Incorporation in terms of s 69(6)(b), and
- any person disqualified in terms of any additional ground of ineligibility set out in the Memorandum of Incorporation in terms of s 69(6)(a).

10.11.5 Grounds of disqualification

The following persons are disqualified from being directors of a company:[186]

(i) a person prohibited by a court of law from becoming a director,
(ii) a person declared to be delinquent by a court of law,[187]
(iii) an unrehabilitated insolvent,
(iv) a person prohibited in terms of any public regulation to be a director of a company,

---

[180] See the Hearings on Companies Bill [B61–2008]: Department's Response (3), comprising the response by the Department of Trade and Industry to the public comments on the Bill, issued to the Portfolio Committee on Trade and Industry, 22 August 2008, at 42.
[181] Section 69(6).
[182] Section 69(7).
[183] For example, a company or a close corporation is a juristic person and cannot be appointed as a director.
[184] A person is a minor until he or she attains the age of 18 (see s 17 of the Children's Act 38 of 2005). Regarding an unemancipated minor, doubts have been expressed whether emancipation would in fact have the effect of removing the disqualification of the minor (*Ex parte Velkes* 1963 (3) SA 584 (C)).
[185] For example, a person who has been declared by a court of law to be incapable of managing his or her affairs.
[186] Section 69(8).
[187] A person may be declared to be delinquent by a court of law in terms of s 162 of the Act or in terms of s 47 of the Close Corporations Act 69 of 1984.

(v) a person removed from an office of trust on the grounds of misconduct involving dishonesty, and
(vi) a person convicted, in South Africa or elsewhere, and imprisoned without the option of a fine or fined more than the prescribed amount,[188] for theft, fraud, forgery, perjury or other offences as specified in s 69(8)*(b)*(iv) of the Act.

The offences specified in s 69(8)*(b)*(iv) are:

- an offence involving fraud, misrepresentation or dishonesty,
- an offence in connection with the promotion, formation or management of a company, and
- an offence under the Companies Act, the Insolvency Act 24 of 1936, the Close Corporations Act 69 of 1984, the Competition Act 89 of 1998, the Financial Intelligence Centre Act 38 of 2001, the Securities Services Act 36 of 2004 or Chapter 2 of the Prevention and Combating of Corruption Activities Act 12 of 2004.

Regarding the offences involving dishonesty, 'dishonesty' means a disposition to deceive, defraud or steal, and involves an element of fraud. An 'offence involving dishonesty' is an offence of which actual dishonesty is an element or ingredient, whether the offence is one under the common law or under a statute.[189] For example, in *Nusca v Da Ponte*[190] the court held that illicit diamond dealing was an offence involving dishonesty and that a person convicted of such an offence could not be a director of a company without the authority of the court.

As with the grounds of ineligibility, the Memorandum of Incorporation may impose additional grounds for the disqualification of directors. For example, the Memorandum of Incorporation may provide that a director will be disqualified from being a director should he or she absent themselves from meetings of directors for more than six months without the permission of the board of directors; or becomes interested in any contract or proposed contract with the company and fails to declare his or her interest therein, or holds any other office of profit without the consent of the company in general meeting.

These provisions are not designed to punish the individual, but to:

> ... protect the public and to prevent the corporate structure from being used to the financial detriment of investors, shareholders, creditors and persons dealing with the company. In its operation it is calculated to act as a safeguard against the corporate structure being used by individuals in a manner which is contrary to proper commercial standards.[191]

But, as Nicolas Browne-Wilkinson V-C stated in *Re Lo-Line Electric Motors Ltd*,[192] disqualification does involve a substantial interference with the freedom of

---

[188] The prescribed minimum value of the fine has been prescribed by Regulation 46(2) of the draft Companies Regulations, and is presently an amount of R1 000.
[189] *Ex parte Bennett* 1978 (2) SA 380 (W) at 383–4; *Nusca v Da Ponte* 1994 (3) SA 251 (BG) at 258–9.
[190] 1994 (3) SA 251 (BG).
[191] *Re Magna Alloys & Research Pty Ltd* (1975) 1 ACLR 203 SC (NSW) 205.
[192] [1988] Ch 477 at 486.

the individual. It also carries with it a degree of stigma for anyone who is disqualified.[193]

10.11.6 Consequences of ineligibility and disqualification

An ineligible or disqualified person may not be appointed or elected a director of the company, or consent to be appointed or elected a director, or act as a director of a company.[194] It follows that, should a person become ineligible or disqualified while serving as a director of a company, he or she would cease to be a director with immediate effect (subject to s 70(2) of the Act).[195] Needless to say, a company may not knowingly permit an ineligible or disqualified person to serve or act as a director.[196]

10.11.7 Exemptions from disqualification

(a) Exercise of the court's discretion

A court has an unfettered discretion to exempt a person from the application of grounds (iii) to (vi) set out in para 10.11.5 above.[197] A Court of Appeal will only interfere with the decision if it is satisfied that the discretion was not exercised properly.[198] In exercising its discretion, a court would take into account the fact that the object of the grounds of disqualification is not to punish the director in question, but to protect the interests of shareholders and the public, and to ensure that these interests are not endangered in any way.[199]

An unrehabilitated insolvent who wishes to serve as a director of a company would be required, in his or her application, to place before the court a full statement and explanation of the circumstances giving rise to his or her sequestration and other business failures.[200] In exercising its discretion, a court would consider whether in the circumstances there are exceptional circumstances that make the applicant a fit and proper person to be appointed a director despite the fact that he or she is an unrehabilitated insolvent.[201] Again, the rationale for disqualifying an unrehabilitated insolvent from serving as a director is not punitive, but is intended to protect the public from reckless action that could cause it to suffer financial loss.[202]

Where a person is disqualified by reason of having committed an offence under ground (vi) listed in para 10.11.5 above, the factors to be taken into account by a

---

[193] *Re Westminister Property Management Ltd, Official Receiver v Stern* [2001] BCC 121 at 143.
[194] Section 69(2).
[195] Section 69(4). The draft Companies Amendment Bill, 2010 (cl 44(*a*)) provides that a person who becomes ineligible or disqualified while serving as a director, alternate director, prescribed officer or board committee member ceases to be entitled to continue to act as such, subject to s 70(2).
[196] Section 69(3).
[197] Section 69(11).
[198] *Ex parte Harrod* 1954 (4) SA 28 (SR) 30; *Ex parte Schreuder* 1965 (2) SA 174 (O); *Ex parte K* 1971 (4) SA 289 (D) 291–2; *Ex parte Tayob* 1990 (3) SA 715 (T) 717.
[199] *Ex parte Harrod* (supra) at 30; *Ex parte Schreuder* 1974 (2) SA 358 (O) 361; *Nusca v Da Ponte* 1994 (3) SA 251 (BG) at 262.
[200] *Ex parte Dworsky* 1970 (2) SA 293 (T) 295–6.
[201] Ibid at 295.
[202] *Re Altim Pty Ltd* [1968] 2 NSWLR 762 at 764.

court cannot be stated exhaustively, because each case depends on its own facts.[203] In general, some of the factors that a court would take into account in exercising its discretion are the applicant's general character; his or her conduct since the offence and whether he or she has shown that they have reformed; the nature of the offence and circumstances under which it was committed; the length of time between the conviction and the application; the attitude of the shareholders and whether they support the application; the interests of shareholders, creditors and employees and the risk to them and the public; the applicant's honesty and competency, and the hardship resulting to the applicant and his or her personal and family business interests.[204]

A court would exercise some leniency where a director of a private company is affected as opposed to a public company, because with a public company the chances of more people being affected by an unscrupulous or dishonest director are greater than in the case of a private company.[205] The fundamental question is whether in all the circumstances the applicant has satisfied the court that the defect of character no longer exists and that he or she has rehabilitated him- or herself and measures up to the high standards required of directors.[206]

(b) Statutory exemption from disqualification

Despite being disqualified in terms of s 69(8)(*b*)(iii) or (iv), that is, on the basis of the removal from an office of trust on the grounds of misconduct involving dishonesty or on the basis of a conviction in South Africa or elsewhere, a person may act as a director of a private company if he or she is the sole shareholder of the company or the other shareholders are related to him or her[207] and have consented in writing to his or her appointment as a director of the company.[208]

While this provision protects shareholders from the risk of financial loss due to misconduct, theft, fraud, forgery, perjury or an offence committed by a director specified in s 69(8)(*b*)(iv) of the Act, it exposes other stakeholders of a private company (such as employees and creditors) to the risk of such conduct by the director in question.[209] It also permits dishonest persons to be appointed a director of a small family-owned private company.[210]

---

[203] *Ex parte Schreuder* 1974 (2) SA 358 (O) 362.
[204] *Ex parte Tayob* 1989 (2) SA 282 (T) 288; *NUCSA v Da Ponte* (supra) at 262–3; *Re Magna Alloys & Research Pty Ltd* (supra) at 205; *Commission for Corporate Affairs (WA) v Ekamper* (1987) 12 ACLR 519 SC (WA).
[205] *Ex parte Barron* 1977 (3) SA 1099 (C) at 1100; *Nusca v Da Ponte* (supra) at 262.
[206] *Ex parte Schreuder* 1974 (2) SA 358 (O) 361; *Ex parte Tayob* 1989 (2) SA 282 (T) 287; *Ex parte Tayob* 1990 (3) SA 715 (T) 720; *Nusca v Da Ponte* (supra) at 262.
[207] Refer to s 2 of the Act for the definition of 'related persons'.
[208] Section 69(12).
[209] See the Hearings on the Companies Bill [B61–2008]: submission by the Institute of Directors in Southern Africa (IoD) and the King Committee to the Portfolio Committee on Trade and Industry (11 August 2008) at 11 and the Hearings on the Companies Bill [B61–2008]: submission by Pricewaterhouse Coopers to the Portfolio Committee on Trade and Industry (12 August 2008) para 2.25.
[210] Clause 44(*b*) of the draft Companies Amendment Bill, 2010 amends s 69(12) to provide that the right of a person to be a director in terms of s 69(12) would terminate automatically upon any subsequent conviction or loss of office contemplated in s 69(8)(*b*)(iii) or (iv).

10.11.8 Duration of disqualification

A disqualification under grounds (v) and (vi) set out in para 10.11.5 above ends at the later of five years after the date of removal from office or the completion of any sentence imposed for the relevant offence, as the case may be, or at the end of any extension of the disqualification, as determined by a court of law.[211]

The Companies Commission may apply to court at any time before the expiry of a person's disqualification for an extension of the disqualification under grounds (v) and (vi) set out in para 10.11.5 above, which the court, in its discretion, may grant for no more than five years at a time should it find that an extension is necessary to protect the public, having regard to the conduct of that person up to the time of the application.[212]

10.11.9 Public register

The Companies Commission is required to establish and maintain a public register of persons who are disqualified from serving as a director, or who are subject to an order of probation, in terms of a court order, pursuant to the Act or any other law.[213]

10.12 DELINQUENT DIRECTORS AND DIRECTORS ON PROBATION

Under the Act an application may be made to court to declare a director delinquent or to have him or her placed under an order of probation. This is a significant innovation in the Companies Act of 2008.

10.12.1 *Locus standi*

A wide range of persons may apply to court for an order declaring a director delinquent or placing him or her under probation. These are a company, a shareholder, a director, a company secretary or prescribed officer of a company, a registered trade union that represents employees of a company or other employee representative, the Companies Commission and the Takeover Regulation Panel.[214] In addition, any organ of State responsible for the administration of any legislation may bring an application to declare a director delinquent.[215]

The application may be brought not only against a present director of a company but also against a former director, ie a person who had been a director within the 24 months immediately preceding the application.[216]

It is important to guard against abuse by those persons with *locus standi* making these applications, because such persons may well use this mechanism to lodge vexatious claims, which may result in damage being caused to the reputation of directors.

---

[211] Section 69(9).
[212] Section 69(8).
[213] Section 69(13).
[214] Specific grounds of delinquency or probation are available to each of these persons with *locus standi*, as set out in s 162(2) and (3).
[215] See s 162(4).
[216] Section 162(2)(a).

10.12.2 Grounds of delinquency[217]

A court must make an order declaring a person to be a delinquent director if, inter alia, the person:

- served or agreed to serve as a director, or acted in the capacity of a director or prescribed officer, while ineligible or disqualified to be a director,[218]
- while under an order of probation, acted as a director in a manner that contravened that order,
- while a director, grossly abused the position of a director,
- while a director, contrary to s 76(2)(a) of the Act, took personal advantage of information or an opportunity, or intentionally or by gross negligence inflicted harm upon the company or a subsidiary of the company,[219]
- while a director, acted in a manner that amounted to gross negligence, wilful misconduct or breach of trust in relation to the performance of their functions within, and duties to, the company or in a manner contemplated in s 77(3)(a), (b) or (c) of the Act;[220]
- has repeatedly been subject to a compliance notice (or similar enforcement mechanism) or has at least twice been personally convicted of an offence or subjected to an administrative fine or penalty, in terms of any legislation, or
- within a period of five years was a director of one or more companies or a managing member of one or more close corporations, or controlled or participated in the control of a juristic person, irrespective of whether concurrently, sequentially or at unrelated times, that were convicted of an offence or subjected to an administrative fine or similar penalty in terms of any legislation.[221]

---

[217] Section 162(5)(a)–(f).
[218] This ground does not apply if the person were acting under the protection of a court order contemplated in s 69(11) or as a director as contemplated in s 69(12).
[219] Section 76(2)(a) prohibits a director from using his or her position or any information obtained while acting in the capacity of a director, to gain an advantage for him- or herself or for another person other than the company or a wholly owned subsidiary of the company, or to knowingly cause harm to the company or a subsidiary of the company.
[220] In terms of s 77(3)(a), a director may not act in the company's name, sign anything on behalf of the company or purport to bind the company or authorise the taking of any action by the company while knowing that he or she lacks the authority to do so. Section 77(3)(b) prohibits a director from acquiescing in the carrying on of the company's business despite knowing that the business was being conducted in a reckless manner, as prohibited by s 22(1) of the Act. Under s 77(3)(c) a director may not be a party to an act or omission by the company while knowing that that act or omission was calculated to defraud a creditor, employee or shareholder of the company or had another fraudulent purpose.
[221] In order for this ground to apply it is further required that:
  (i) the person in question must have been a director of each such company, or a managing member of each such close corporation or was responsible for the management or each such juristic person, at the time of the contravention that resulted in the conviction, administrative fine or other penalty; and
  (ii) the court must be satisfied that the declaration of delinquency is justified, having regard to the nature of the contraventions, and the person's conduct in relation to the management, business or property of any company, close corporation or juristic person at the time.

10.12.3 Grounds of probation[222]

A court may make an order placing a person under probation if the person:

- while a director, was present at a meeting[223] and failed to vote against a resolution despite the inability of the company to satisfy the solvency and liquidity test, contrary to the Act,
- while a director, acted in a manner materially inconsistent with the duties of a director,
- while a director, acted in or supported a decision of the company to act in a manner that was oppressive or unfairly prejudicial in terms of s 163 of the Act;[224] or
- within any period of ten years after the effective date,[225] was a director of more than one company or a managing member of more than one close corporation (be it concurrently, sequentially or at unrelated times), and during that time two or more of those companies or close corporations had each failed to pay all their creditors or meet all their obligations (except under a business rescue plan resulting from a resolution of the board of directors in terms of s 129 of the Act or a compromise with creditors in terms of s 155 of the Act).[226]

10.12.4 Terms of the order and conditions

The effect of an order of delinquency is that a person is disqualified to be a director of a company.[227] An order of delinquency may under certain circumstances be unconditional and subsist for the lifetime of the delinquent director, or it may be conditional and subsist for seven years or longer, as determined by the court.[228]

---

[222] Section 162(7)(a)–(b).

[223] The phrase 'present at a meeting' is defined in s 1 of the Act as meaning to be present in person, or to be able to participate in the meeting by electronic communication, or to be represented by a proxy who is present in person or able to participate in the meeting by electronic communication.

[224] In terms of s 162(8)(a) of the Act a court may declare a person under probation under this ground only if it is satisfied that the declaration is justified, having regard to the circumstances of the company's or close corporation's conduct, if applicable, and the person's conduct in relation to the management, business or property of the company or close corporation at the time.

[225] The 'effective date' is defined in s 1 of the Act as the date when a provision came into operation in terms of s 225 of the Act. Section 225 provides that the Act comes into operation on a date fixed by the President by proclamation in the *Government Gazette* and may not be earlier than one year following the date on which the President assented to the Act. This ten-year period would appear to be arbitrary.

[226] In terms of s 162(8)(b) of the Act a court may declare a person under probation under this ground only if it is satisfied that the manner in which the company or close corporation was managed was wholly or partly responsible for it failing to meet its obligations, and that the declaration is justified, having regard to the circumstances of the company or close corporation's failure, and the person's conduct in relation to the management, business or property of the company or close corporation at the time.

[227] Section 69(8)(a).

[228] Section 162(6). Where a director is declared to be delinquent on the basis that he or she served as a director while ineligible or disqualified, or on the basis that he or she, while under an order of probation acted as a director in a manner that contravened that order (as contemplated in s 162(5)(a) and (b)), the declaration of delinquency would be unconditional and would subsist for the lifetime of the person. A declaration of delinquency under the remaining grounds of delinquency may be subject

A person who has been placed under probation may not serve as a director except to the extent permitted by the order of probation.[229] The probation order may be subject to any conditions the court considers appropriate and generally subsists for a period not exceeding five years.[230]

Some of the conditions that the court may impose on the order of delinquency or probation are that the director concerned is required to undertake a designated programme of remedial education relevant to the nature of his or her conduct as a director, or to carry out a designated programme of community service. A court may also order the director concerned to pay compensation to any person adversely affected by his or her conduct as a director, to the extent that such a victim does not otherwise have a legal basis to claim compensation. A further condition the court may impose on an order of probation is that the person concerned be supervised by a mentor in any future participation as a director while the order remains in force, or be limited to serving as a director of a private company, or of a company of which that person is the sole shareholder.[231]

10.12.5 Application to suspend or set aside the order of delinquency or probation

Save for certain instances,[232] a delinquent director may, after three years, apply to court to suspend the order of delinquency and to substitute for it an order of probation (with or without conditions).[233] If the order of delinquency is suspended, it may be set aside by the court after two years of suspension.[234]

A person who is subject to an order of probation may apply to court to set aside the order of probation, at any time more than two years after it was made.[235]

On considering these applications, a court may not grant the order applied for unless the applicant has satisfied any conditions attached to the order. A court may grant the order if, having regard to the circumstances leading to the original order, and the conduct of the applicant in the ensuing period, the court is satisfied that the applicant has demonstrated satisfactory progress towards rehabilitation and there is a reasonable prospect that the applicant would be able to serve successfully as a director of a company in the future.[236]

---

to any conditions that the court considers appropriate (including conditions limiting the application of the declaration to one or more particular categories of companies), and subsists for seven years from the date of the order or a longer period, as determined by the court.

[229] Section 69(5).
[230] Section 162(9).
[231] Section 162(10).
[232] An application to court to suspend an order of delinquency or to set aside the order may not be brought where a director served as a director while ineligible or disqualified, or, while under an order of probation acted as a director in a manner that contravened that order, as contemplated in s 162(5)(*a*) and (*b*).
[233] Section 162(11).
[234] Section 162(11)(*b*)(i).
[235] Section 162(11)(*b*)(ii).
[236] Section 162(12).

10.13 VACANCIES ON THE BOARD OF DIRECTORS

10.13.1 Instances when a vacancy arises

A person ceases to be a director and a vacancy arises on the board of directors in the following circumstances:[237]

- when a fixed term of office as a director, as specified in the Memorandum of Incorporation, expires,
- upon resignation or death,
- in the case of an *ex officio* director, where he or she ceases to hold the office, title, designation or similar status that entitled him or her to be an *ex officio* director,
- if the person becomes incapacitated to the extent that he or she is unable to perform the functions of a director and is unlikely to regain that capacity within a reasonable time,
- if the person is declared delinquent by a court or is placed on probation under conditions that are inconsistent with continuing to be a director of the company,
- where the person becomes ineligible or disqualified from being a director, and
- where the person is removed as a director by the shareholders, or the board of directors[238] or a court order.

10.13.2 Filling of a vacancy

Within ten business days after a person ceases to be a director of the company, the company is required to file a notice with the Companies Commission to this effect.[239]

Once a vacancy arises on the board (other than as a result of an *ex officio* director ceasing to hold that office) it must be filled by a new appointment if the director had been appointed by a person named in or determined in terms of the Memorandum of Incorporation, or by a new election.[240] The election must be conducted at the next annual general meeting of the company if the company is required to hold such meetings. If the company is not required to hold annual general meetings, then the vacancy must be filled within six months after it arose, either at a shareholders' meeting called for the purpose of electing the director, or by a written polling of all the shareholders who are entitled to vote in the election of that director.[241] If, as a result of a vacancy arising on the board of directors there are no remaining directors of a company, any shareholder who is entitled to vote in

---

[237] Section 70(1).
[238] Where the board of directors removes a director, the director in question may apply to court within 20 business days to review the board's determination (s 71(5)). Should the board remove a director, a vacancy on the board would not arise until the later of the expiry of the time for filing the application for review in terms of s 71(5) or the granting of an order by the court on such an application, but the director would be suspended from office during this time (s 70(2)).
[239] Section 70(6).
[240] Section 70(3).
[241] Section 70(3)*(b)*.

the election of a director may convene a meeting for the purpose of such an election.[242]

Unless the Memorandum of Incorporation provides otherwise, the board of directors may also appoint a person who satisfies the requirements for election as a director to fill a vacancy and serve as a director on a temporary basis until the vacancy has been filled by election.[243]

10.14 REMOVAL OF DIRECTORS

A director may be removed from office by the shareholders or the board of directors at any time. This is a powerful weapon in the hands of the shareholders. The right to remove a director is in addition to the right to place a director under probation or to have him declared a delinquent director under s 162 of the Act.[244]

10.14.1 Removal by the shareholders

In terms of s 71 of the Act, a director may be removed by the shareholders at a shareholders' meeting. Notably, the ability of the shareholders to remove a director applies despite anything to the contrary contained in the company's Memorandum of Incorporation or rules, or an agreement between a company and a director, or even an agreement between any shareholders and a director.[245]

Accordingly, s 71 overrides a provision in the company's Memorandum of Incorporation, any rules or an agreement between the company and a director not to remove a particular director. Thus the position of a director may not be effectively entrenched in these documents. Further, unlike the equivalent s 220 of the 1973 Act, s 71 applies despite any agreement between the shareholders and a director not to remove that director. Under s 220 of the 1973 Act, an agreement between the shareholders and a director not to remove the director from office was valid and enforceable, and a director was able to interdict or restrain the shareholders from voting for his or her removal as a director in breach of the shareholder agreement.[246] Significantly, this is no longer the position under s 71 of the current Act, which applies '[d]espite anything to the contrary' in an agreement 'between any shareholders and a director'.[247]

However, if the shareholder agreement not to remove a particular director is between the shareholders among themselves and not with the director, then it could possibly fall outside the scope of s 71, and may bind the shareholders among themselves not to vote for the removal of that director.[248] But notably the validity of this agreement would be subject to s 15(7) of the Act, which permits

---

[242] Section 70(4).
[243] Section 68(3).
[244] Section 71(10).
[245] Section 71(1).
[246] See *Stewart v Schwab* 1956 (4) SA 791 (T) 793–4 where it was held that while s 220 of the 1973 Act may apply to agreements between the company and a director not to remove the director, it did not apply to agreements between the shareholders and a director not to remove that director, and that such agreements had to be honoured by the shareholders. This was followed in *Amoils v Fuel Transport (Pty) Ltd* 1978 (4) SA 343 (W) 347.
[247] Section 71(1).
[248] Davis et al op cit n 91 at 97.

the shareholders to enter into any agreement with one another concerning any matter relating to the company, but requires any such agreement to be consistent with the Act and the Memorandum of Incorporation, failing which such inconsistent provision would be void to the extent of the inconsistency.

A provision in a company's Memorandum of Incorporation that gives a director a right to prevent an otherwise valid resolution from having any force or effect, is invalid insofar as it conflicts with the right of the shareholders to remove a director by ordinary resolution.[249] In other words, a provision in the Memorandum of Incorporation of a company in terms of which a director has a power to veto any resolution may not take effect to prevent his or her removal by a resolution duly adopted.[250]

10.14.2 Removal by the board of directors

The board of directors may remove a director if a company has more than two directors and:

- a shareholder or director alleges that a director has become ineligible or disqualified in terms of s 69 of the Act to be a director (other than on the grounds contemplated in s 69(8)(*a*)),
- a shareholder or director alleges that a director has become incapacitated to the extent that he or she is unable to perform his or her functions, and is unlikely to regain that capacity within a reasonable time, or
- a shareholder or director alleges that a director has neglected or has been derelict in the performance of his or her functions.[251]

These provisions do not apply where a company has fewer than three directors. In such a case any director or shareholder may apply to the Companies Tribunal to determine the director's removal from office.[252]

There is no explicit provision in the Act on whether additional grounds for the removal of a director may be specified, but presumably this may be done.

10.14.3 Notice

Before the resolution is put to the vote by the shareholders or the board of directors, the director in question must be given notice of the meeting and a copy of the proposed resolution to remove him or her from office. The period of the notice to be given to the director where the resolution is to be voted on by the shareholders must be at least equivalent to that which a shareholder is entitled to receive when a shareholders' meeting is convened.[253]

---

[249] Blackman et al op cit n 14 at 8–283.
[250] *Swerdlow v Cohen* 1977 (1) SA 178 (W); 1977 (3) SA 1050 (T).
[251] Section 71(3).
[252] Section 71(8).
[253] Section 71(2). Unless the Memorandum of Incorporation provides for longer minimum periods, the required periods of notice for a shareholders' meeting are as follows:
    (i) in the case of a public company or a non-profit company that has voting members, 15 business days before the meeting is to begin,
    (ii) in any other case, ten business days before the meeting is to begin (s 62(1)).

Where the resolution to remove the director is to be considered by the board of directors, the resolution must be accompanied by a statement setting out the reasons for the resolution, with sufficient specificity to reasonably permit the director in question to prepare and present a response.[254] Where a director is removed by the shareholders it is not a requirement that the director must be provided with a statement setting out the reasons for the resolution to remove him or her as a director.

10.14.4 Presentation

As discussed above, the director in question must be given a reasonable opportunity to make a presentation to the shareholders' meeting or to the board of directors (in person or through a representative), as the case may be, before the resolution is put to the vote.[255] The object of this presentation is to prevent a director from being removed on an impulsive vote and without having had a proper opportunity to state his or her case.

10.14.5 Ordinary resolution

Removal of a director must be by ordinary resolution of a company in a shareholders' meeting, or by a resolution of the board of directors.

For an ordinary resolution to be approved by the shareholders, it must be supported by more than 50 per cent of the voting rights exercised on the resolution. Section 65(8) of the Act, which provides that the Memorandum of Incorporation may specify a higher percentage of voting rights to approve an ordinary resolution, prohibits this option in respect of an ordinary resolution to be passed for the removal of a director under s 71 of the Act. If this were not the case, it would be possible for a company to frustrate or impede the shareholders' right to remove a director by specifying a higher percentage for the removal of a director.

The resolution to remove a director may not be informally passed in terms of s 60 of the Act, ie in writing by the shareholders without holding a meeting, or by means of a round robin resolution of the directors in terms of s 74 of the Act. If the resolution were to be passed in this way, it would deprive the director in question of the opportunity to present his or her case before the meeting.

Shareholders may ordinarily exercise their vote in any way they please because their right to vote is a proprietary right. Accordingly, a resolution by the general meeting to remove a director from office may not be impeached on the ground that it was not passed in good faith in the interests of the company.[256]

However, where the board of directors exercises the power to remove a director, it must do so in the best interests of the company and not for an improper purpose or for ulterior reasons.[257] But in *Lee v Chou Wen Hsien*[258] the court held that, while each director concurring in the removal of a director must act in accordance with what he or she believes to be in the best interests of the company and that

---
[254] Section 71(4)(*a*).
[255] Section 71(2)(*b*) and s 71(4)(*b*).
[256] Blackman et al op cit n 14 at 8–285.
[257] *Lee v Chou Wen Hsien* [1984] 1 WLR 1202 at 1206.
[258] [1984] 1 WLR 1202.

they may not properly concur for ulterior reasons of their own, it does not follow that the director sought to be removed would remain a director of the board simply because one or more of the directors had acted from an ulterior motive in removing that director. Those directors that exercised their power to remove a director for an improper purpose or for ulterior reasons could be in breach of their fiduciary duties. As discussed below in 10.14.7, where the board of directors has voted to remove a director, the director may apply to court to review the board's decision.[259] The fact that one or more directors exercised their powers to remove a director for an improper purpose or for ulterior reasons is a factor that will most probably be taken into account by the court in such an application.

10.14.6 Loaded voting rights

Under s 73(5)(c) of the Act, each director has one vote on a matter before the board, except to the extent that the Memorandum of Incorporation provides otherwise. Thus, it is possible for directors to have loaded votes, which means that more voting rights may be attached to some shares than to others. This raises the question whether a director who holds or controls shares with loaded votes would be able to prevent his or her removal by ensuring that the loaded votes are all cast against the resolution to remove him or her from office, which would have the effect of there not being a majority in favour of the resolution.

In *Bushell v Faith*[260] the constitution of a private company provided that, in the event of a resolution being proposed at a general meeting of the company for the removal of a director, any shares held by that director would carry three votes per share. The company's 300 shares were held equally between the plaintiff, the defendant (the plaintiff's brother) and their sister. The plaintiff and the defendant were the company's only directors. The two sisters, being dissatisfied with their brother's conduct as a director, purported to remove him from office. They both voted for his removal, but he voted against it. A dispute arose as to whether the resolution had been passed or defeated — the plaintiff contended that it had been passed by 200 votes to 100, while the defendant contended that, in accordance with the provisions of the constitution of the company, his 100 shares carried 300 votes, and that therefore the resolution had been defeated by 300 votes to 200. It was held by the majority of the House of Lords that the resolution seeking to remove the defendant from office had indeed been defeated by the weighted votes exercised by the defendant. The conclusion which emerges from *Bushell v Faith* is that the statutory provision for the removal of a director could well be frustrated by a provision in the company's constitution attaching increased votes to a director's shares on a resolution to remove him or her, thus enabling him or her always to defeat such a resolution.[261]

---

[259] See s 71(5).
[260] [1970] AC 1099.
[261] Paul L Davies *Gower and Davies' Principles of Modern Company Law* 8 ed (2008) 390. In *Swerdlow v Cohen* 1977 (3) SA 1050 (T) the court discussed the *ratio* of *Bushell v Faith* but found that it was unnecessary to examine the validity of the decision because the decision could be distinguished on the basis that the issue in *Swerdlow v Cohen* was not one where a provision of the

As regards permitting loaded votes in the Memorandum of Incorporation, s 73(5)*(c)* of the Act does not distinguish between public and private companies, and it seems that both entities may make provision for loaded votes in their respective Memorandums of Incorporation. This is contrary to the position under the 1973 Act, where a public company was not permitted to issue shares with loaded votes, but a private company was permitted to do so.[262] Section 195(1) of the 1973 Act provided that, if the share capital of a public company was divided into shares of par value, the votes of a member had to bear the same proportion to the total votes in the company as the nominal value of his or her shares bore to the nominal value of all the shares issued by the company. If the share capital was divided into shares of no par value, then a member had only one vote in respect of each share. A distinction between par value and no par value shares is no longer made under the current Act and such a provision is no longer applicable. On the one hand, while it appears that loaded votes are permissible in both public and private companies under the Act, on the other hand it is arguable that the company in question in *Bushell v Faith* was a small private company and thus the *ratio* of this case as regards the removal of directors should be confined to private companies only.[263]

But attention must be drawn to the significance of s 71(1) of the Act, which provides that a director may be removed from office *despite anything to the contrary* in the Memorandum of Incorporation or rules, or any agreement between a company and a director or between any shareholders and a director. This provision makes it clear that the legislature intended to override methods designed to ensure that a director could not be removed from office. Thus the notion of weighted votes being applicable to a resolution to remove a director may be challenged on the basis that it is contrary to the intention of the legislature in s 71 of the Act and may well be a device *in fraudem legis*. As the dissenting minority in *Bushell v Faith* said, while some shares may carry a greater voting power than others, and on a resolution to remove a director shares would carry the voting power they possess, the notion of loaded voting rights being exercised in this instance introduces a device that has the effect of making a director irremovable and of circumventing the statutory section making provision for his or her removal from office.[264] Additionally, attention must be drawn to s 6(1) of the Act, that may have the effect of striking down such loaded voting rights in the particular context of s 71 of the Act.

---

company's constitution had been formulated with the express purpose of circumventing the statutory provision permitting the removal of a director.
[262] See s 195(1) and (2) of the 1973 Act; see also *Swerdlow v Cohen* 1977 (1) SA 178 (W) 184.
[263] The decision of *Bushell v Faith* may possibly be justified in small private companies, which are in effect an incorporated partnership or a 'quasi-partnership', where it is not unreasonable for each 'partner' to be entitled (as under partnership law) to participate in the management of the firm in the absence of his or her agreement to the contrary and to protect themselves against removal by their fellow partners (see Paul L Davies op cit n 261 at 391).
[264] *Per* Lord Morris of Borth-y-Gest, at 1106. For commentary on the decision in *Bushell v Faith*, see RC Beuthin 'A director firmly in the saddle' (1969) 86 *SALJ* 489; A Hyman 'Weighted votes' 1977 *SA Company LJ* D–5–D–15 and 'Weighted votes again' 1977 *SA Company LJ* D17—D–20, and A Preiss 'Prevention of the statutory removal of directors' 1983 *Modern Business Law* 111.

10.14.7 Application to court to review the board's determination

Where the board has voted to remove a director, the director may apply to court to review the board's decision.[265] The application to court must be brought by the aggrieved director within 20 business days of the board's decision.[266]

Should the board decide that none of the applicable grounds for removal of the director in question apply, any director who voted otherwise on the resolution, or any shareholder, may apply to court to review the board's determination.[267] The court may either confirm the board's determination not to remove the director in question, or remove the director from office if the court is satisfied that there are grounds for his or her removal.[268] Should the court confirm the board's decision not to remove the director in question, the applicant in question would be required to compensate the company and any other party for costs incurred in terms of the application.[269] Should the court reverse the board's decision not to remove the director in question, then the applicant would not be required to compensate the company or any other party for the costs incurred in terms of the application.

Removal of a director by the shareholders is not subject to review by a court.

10.14.8 Breach of contract and damages

While directors are not entitled to prevent their own removal, they are entitled to pursue any right they may have at common law or otherwise to apply to court for damages or other compensation for loss of office as a director or loss of any other office as a consequence of being removed as a director.[270] In other words, where the director's removal from office constitutes a breach of contract on the part of the company or where the company has contracted to compensate the director in the event of his or her removal from office, the director in question may claim damages or other compensation from the company.[271]

As discussed previously, under the 1973 Act, the articles of association of a company did not create a contract between the company and a director in his or her capacity as such. Thus, for a director who had been removed from office to have an action for damages against the company, it was necessary for that director to have had a separate contract of service with the company binding it to hold the director's position for a fixed term or not to terminate their office or to compensate them if they were removed from office.[272] But in terms of s 15(6) of the new Act, the Memorandum of Incorporation is now binding between the company and a director. Accordingly, a director who has been removed from office under s 71 of

---

[265] Under s 71(5) this application may also be brought by the person who appointed that director in terms of the Memorandum of Incorporation, as contemplated in s 66(4)(*a*)(i).
[266] Section 71(5).
[267] Section 71(6)(*a*).
[268] Section 71(6)(*b*).
[269] Section 71(7).
[270] Section 71(9).
[271] Blackman et al op cit n 14 at 8–285.
[272] See for instance *De Villiers v Jacobsdal Saltworks (Michaelis and De Villiers) (Pty) Ltd* 1959 (3) SA 873 (O); *Beattie v E&F Beattie Ltd* [1938] Ch 708 and *Southern Foundries (1926) Ltd v Shirlaw* [1940] AC 701. In light of s 15(6) of the current Act the position has changed. See further chapter 4: Formation of Companies and the Company Constitution.

the Act would have a legal remedy based on a breach of a provision of the Memorandum of Incorporation. In other words, contractual claims based solely on the company's Memorandum of Incorporation are now permissible and it is no longer essential for a director to have a separate contract of service in order to apply to court for damages or other compensation for loss of office as a director or loss of any other office as a consequence of being removed as a director.

10.15 RETIREMENT FROM OFFICE

The company's constitution usually makes provision for the retirement of the directors, and typically provides that all directors shall retire from office at the first annual general meeting, and that at the annual general meeting in every subsequent year a third of the directors (or if their number is not three or a multiple of three, the nearest to a third) shall retire.[273] Alternatively, the company's constitution may provide that the company in general meeting may from time to time determine the terms of office and the manner of retirement.[274] It is also usually provided in the constitution that the directors to retire in every year shall be those who have been the longest in office since their last election. However, regarding persons who became directors on the same day, those to retire shall be determined by lot, unless they agree otherwise among themselves.[275] The constitution may provide further that a retiring director will be eligible for re-election.[276]

10.16 RESIGNATION OF DIRECTORS

Director may terminate there office simply by tendering their resignation, and depending on the requirements of the Memorandum of Incorporation, they may do so by giving written or oral notice to the company or the board of directors.[277] Resignation is taken to be a final unilateral act, and therefore (unless the Memorandum of Incorporation or a contract between the director and the company provides otherwise) it takes effect when it is tendered. Thus the concurrence or acceptance of the resignation by the company is not required to terminate the appointment of the director.[278] However, in *Harding v Standard Bank of South Africa Ltd*[279] the court stated that, where the company's constitution requires written notice of resignation to be given by a director, an oral notice would become effective only upon acceptance by the company. Once having given notice

---

[273] Refer to Article 66 of Table A of Schedule 1 to the 1973 Act (articles for a public company having a share capital).
[274] See Article 67 of Table B of Schedule 1 to the 1973 Act (articles for a private company having a share capital).
[275] Refer to Article 67 of Table A of Schedule 1 to the 1973 Act (articles for a public company having a share capital).
[276] Refer to Article 68 of Table A of Schedule 1 to the 1973 Act (articles for a public company having a share capital) and Article 67 of Table B of Schedule 1 (articles for a private company having a share capital).
[277] *Harding and Others NNO v Standard Bank of South Africa Ltd* 2004 (6) SA 464 (C) 469.
[278] *Rosebank Television & Appliance Co (Pty) Ltd v Orbit Sales Corp (Pty) Ltd* 1969 (1) SA 300 (T) 302. See further *Symington v Pretoria-Oos Privaat Hospitaal Bedryfs (Pty) Ltd* 2005 (5) SA 550 (SCA) para 18.
[279] 2004 (6) SA 464 (C) 469.

of his or her resignation, a director is not entitled to withdraw it unilaterally and may do so only with the consent of those entitled to appoint a new director.[280]

In *CMS Dolphin Ltd v Simonet*[281] the court made it clear that a director's right to resign from office is not a fiduciary power. This implies that a director is entitled to resign from the company even if his or her resignation may have a disastrous effect on the business or reputation of the company.[282] Unless restricted by contract, a director may resign from the company at any time 'with complete immunity because freedom of employment and encouragement of competition generally dictate that such persons can leave their corporation at any time and go into a competing business'.[283] However, the position would be different where the entire board of directors of a public company listed on the JSE resigns simultaneously, as occurred in the case of *Minister of Water Affairs and Forestry v Stilfontein Gold Mining Co Ltd*.[284] The court in this case held that the board of directors was under a duty to act *bona fide* in the interests of the company, and that by resigning en masse (in order to evade complying with certain legal duties imposed on the company by a High Court order enforcing a ministerial directive relating to preventing water pollution for which they would ultimately be responsible), they had failed to comply with this duty because what they had achieved by resigning was to incapacitate themselves from discharging their duties towards the company and its members.[285]

A director who has contracted to serve the company for a fixed period may resign before the termination of that period, but he or she will be liable to the company for damages for any loss the company has suffered as a result of the premature termination of his or her services.[286]

Where directors resign to put puppet directors in their place and then continue to control the company, their resignation is a sham and will be disregarded.[287]

10.17 REMUNERATION OF DIRECTORS

10.17.1 No automatic right to remuneration

A director *qua* director is not an employee of the company and accordingly is not entitled to the standard rights flowing from an employment contract.[288] It follows that a director is not entitled to be remunerated for his or her services as a director simply because he or she has been appointed as a director.[289] Of course, if a

---

[280] *Glossop v Glossop* [1907] 2 Ch 370 at 374–5.
[281] [2001] 2 BCLC 704.
[282] At 733.
[283] *Raines v Toney* 313 SW2d 802 (1958) 809 (a judgment of the Supreme Court of Arkansas), approved in *Canadian Aero Service Ltd v O'Malley* (1973) 40 DLR (3d) 371 (SCC) at 386.
[284] 2006 (5) SA 333 (W).
[285] Paragraph 16.6.
[286] *Southern Foundries (1926) Ltd v Shirlaw* [1940] AC 701 at 722.
[287] *S v De Jager* 1965 (2) SA 616 (A) 622–3.
[288] *In re Beeton & Co Ltd* [1913] 2 Ch 279.
[289] See *Hutton v West Cork Railway Co* (1883) 23 ChD 654 (CA) at 672; *In re George Newman & Co* [1895] 1 Ch 674 (CA) 686; *Phillips v Base Metals Exploration Syndicate Ltd (in Liquidation)* 1911 TPD 403 at 406; *Brown v Nanco (Pty) Ltd* 1976 (3) SA 832 (W) 834; *Guinness plc v Saunders* [1990] 2 AC 663 (HL).

director enters into a contract of employment with the company then he or she would be entitled to those rights that flow from the employment contract and they would stand in the position of both an employee and a director in relation to the company.[290] But in the position of a director, he or she is not automatically entitled to be remunerated for their services as a director.

10.17.2 Remuneration may be prohibited by Memorandum of Incorporation

Under the Act a company may pay remuneration to a director for his or her services as a director, unless this is prohibited by the Memorandum of Incorporation.[291] Should the Memorandum of Incorporation prohibit the payment of remuneration, a director is not entitled to remuneration for his or her services and the board of directors may not cause the company to pay remuneration to the directors.[292] Should the directors remunerate themselves out of the company's funds in circumstances where they are not entitled to be remunerated, they are bound to account to the company for it and to pay damages.[293] This rule is thought to stem from the rule that a person in a fiduciary position is not entitled to use their office to profit themselves, unless they have the consent of a majority of the shareholders.[294]

10.17.3 Special resolution required

Notably, remuneration may be paid only in accordance with a special resolution approved by the shareholders within the previous two years.[295] Accordingly, the decision whether or not a director is to be remunerated is placed in the hands of the shareholders, and not in the hands of the board of directors or any other party. The rationale for the onerous requirement of a special resolution being necessary to approve the remuneration is presumably to encourage good corporate governance and to curtail excessive remuneration.

Based on the wording of s 66(9) of the Act, the shareholder approval must be given within the previous two years and may not be given retrospectively. Companies would accordingly have to ensure that a special resolution is passed prior to any remuneration being paid to a director and that this special resolution is updated at least every two years. This is to ensure that the remuneration paid to a director is paid in accordance with a special resolution that is not older than two years. Remuneration paid without such a special resolution would be invalidly paid and should therefore be recoverable by the company or the liquidator.

---

[290] *Lee v Lee's Air Farming Ltd* [1960] 3 All ER 420 (PC).
[291] Section 66(8).
[292] *Hutton v West Cork Railway Co* (supra); *Guinness plc v Saunders* (supra) at 692.
[293] *In re George Newman & Co* (supra); *Re Halt Garage (1964) Ltd* [1982] 3 All ER 1016 (ChD) at 1023.
[294] *Guinness plc v Saunders* (supra) 692.
[295] Section 66(9).

10.17.4 Remuneration not contingent on company earning sufficient profits

Unless express provision is made to the contrary, there is no presumption that directors' remuneration is contingent on the company earning sufficient profits.[296] If a director is entitled to be remunerated, that remuneration is a debt owed by the company. Should the company be wound up, the director may claim the remuneration owed to him or her in competition with the company's ordinary creditors.[297]

10.17.5 Disclosure of remuneration in annual financial statements

With regard to those companies that are required to have their annual financial statements audited in terms of the Act, the annual financial statements must include particulars showing the remuneration and benefits received by each director (or individual holding any prescribed office in the company).[298]

In public listed companies the controversy over the remuneration packages of directors and senior executives has been a core issue in the corporate governance debate. The King III Report makes some important recommendations regarding the remuneration of directors and senior executives. See further chapter 11: Corporate Governance.

10.18 BOARD COMMITTEES

10.18.1 Appointment of committees

Except to the extent that the Memorandum of Incorporation provides otherwise, the board of directors may appoint any number of committees and may delegate any of its authority to a committee.[299] But note that the Act provides in s 72(3) that the creation of a board committee, delegation of any power to a committee or action taken by a committee does not alone satisfy or constitute compliance by a director with his or her required duty to the company, as set out in s 76 of the Act.[300] This meant that board of directors remains liable for the proper performance of the duty delegated. In other words, while the board may delegate its powers to a committee, it cannot abdicate its legal responsibility for the conduct of the committee. This was concisely stated in *Barlows Manufacturing Co Ltd v RN Barrie (Pty) Ltd*[301] as follows:

---

[296] *Re Halt Garage (1964) Ltd* (supra) 1038.
[297] *Markham v South African Finance & Industrial Co Ltd* 1962 (3) SA 669 (A).
[298] Section 30(4)(a). In terms of s 30(6), for purposes of the disclosure in the annual financial statements 'remuneration' includes fees paid to directors for services rendered by them, including any amount paid to a person in respect of the person's accepting the office of director; salaries; bonuses; performance-related payments; expense allowances (to the extent that the director is not required to account for the allowance); contributions paid under certain pension schemes; the value of any option or any right for subscription of securities given to a director in terms of s 42 of the Act; financial assistance given for subscription of securities to a director in terms of s 44 of the Act, and the value of any deferred, waived, forgiven or reduced interest in terms of any loan or other financial assistance given by a company to a director in terms of s 45 of the Act, where the company is a guarantor of that loan.
[299] Section 72(1).
[300] Section 76 of the Act sets out the standards of directors' conduct.
[301] 1990 (4) SA 608 (C).

Governance and the Board of Directors

A director owes a fiduciary duty to his company. He cannot, while he is a director, divest himself of that duty. It is something which is inextricably tied to the office. In the exercise of this duty the director may delegate some or even all of his powers of controlling the company but he cannot, without violating what I regard as a fundamental principle of company law, delegate his duty ... He may delegate but he may not abdicate. The board must retain ultimate control.[302]

A similar sentiment is expressed in s 94(10) of the Act with regard to the audit committee. The section provides as follows:

Neither the appointment nor the duties of an audit committee reduce the functions and duties of the board or the directors of the company, except with respect to the appointment, fees and terms of engagement of the auditor.

10.18.2 Members of committees

Unless the Memorandum of Incorporation or a resolution establishing a committee provides otherwise, a board committee may consist of persons who are not directors of the company, provided they are not ineligible or disqualified from being directors.[303] Non-director members are useful in that they may bring knowledge and expertise to board committees that is lacking among the director members of the committees. Except to the extent that the Memorandum of Incorporation or a resolution establishing a committee provides otherwise, such non-director members of a committee do not have any right to vote on matters to be decided by the committee.[304]

Unless the Memorandum of Incorporation or a resolution establishing a committee provides otherwise, a committee may consult with or receive advice from any person and has the full authority of the board in respect of a matter referred to it.[305] This latter provision means that the board of directors is entitled to delegate any authority in its discretion to a board committee.

Section 76(1) of the Act, dealing with the standards of directors' conduct, provides that a 'director', for the purposes of s 76, includes a member of a board committee or of the audit committee of a company, *irrespective of whether or not the person is also a member of the company's board of directors*. Thus, significantly, s 76(1) of the Act places the same standards of conduct and liability on non-director members of a board committee and the audit committee as if they were directors of the company.

10.18.3 Compulsory committees

(a) Audit committee

While a company may generally determine its own number and type of committees, s 84(4)*(c)* of the Act requires a public company and a state-owned company

---
[302] At 610–11.
[303] Section 72(2)*(a)*(i).
[304] Section 72(2)*(a)*(ii).
[305] Section 72(2)*(b)* and *(c)*.

to appoint an audit committee (this is subject to certain exemptions).[306] In addition, any other company may voluntarily decide to have an audit committee.[307]

The Act requires the audit committee to be elected at the annual general meeting.[308] It should comprise at least three members who must be directors of the company who satisfy the prescribed minimum qualification requirements for members of an audit committee.[309] Certain persons are excluded from being members of the audit committee, such as persons who are involved in the day-to-day management of the company's business; a prescribed officer, full-time employee, material suppliers or customers of the company; and persons related to such persons.[310]

Section 76(1) of the Act provides that the standards of directors' conduct set out in s 76 of the Act also apply to members of the audit committee. But each member of the audit committee is required to be a director, and would in any case be subject to the duties set out in s 76 of the Act.

The duties of the audit committee are set out in some detail in s 94(7) of the Act. Note that s 94(10) of the Act provides that the appointment and duties of an audit committee will not reduce the functions and duties of the board or the directors of the company, except with respect to the appointment, fees and terms of engagement of the auditor. Thus, save for the appointment, fees and terms of engagement of the auditor, the audit committee is accountable to the board of directors.[311]

(b) Social and ethics committee

In terms of s 72(4) of the Act the Minister may prescribe that certain categories of companies must have a social and ethics committee, if it deems it desirable in the public interest, having regard to the annual turnover, the size of the workforce or the nature and extent of the activities of such companies.[312] Regulation 50 of the draft Companies Regulations requires a public company and a state-owned company to appoint a social and ethics committee.

In certain circumstances a company that falls within a category of companies that is required to appoint a social and ethics committee may apply to the Companies Tribunal for an exemption from this requirement.[313]

---

[306] If a company is a subsidiary of another company that has an audit committee and the audit committee of that other company will perform the requisite audit functions on behalf of that subsidiary company, that company is not required to appoint an audit committee (s 94(2)).
[307] See s 34(2) and s 94(2) of the Act.
[308] Section 94(2).
[309] Section 94(2) and (4).
[310] Section 94(4)(b).
[311] See further chapter 13: The Auditor, Financial Records and Reporting.
[312] Under the draft Companies Amendment Bill, 2010, the Minister may also prescribe the functions to be performed by the social and ethics committees as well as the rules governing the composition and conduct of such committees (see cl 45(a) of the Bill).
[313] Under cl 45(b) of the draft Companies Amendment Bill, 2010, the Companies Tribunal may grant an exemption from the requirement to have a social and ethics committee if the Tribunal is satisfied that the company is required in terms of other legislation to have, and does have, some form of formal mechanism within its structures that substantially performs the functions that would otherwise be performed by the social and ethics committee, or that it is not reasonably necessary in the public interest to require the company to have a social and ethics committee, having regard to the

The committee must comprise at least three directors of the company.[314] Furthermore, the board of directors is required to appoint a social and ethics advisory panel to assist the committee.[315] A wide range of persons must comprise the advisory panel, such as some of the company's employees, members of professions related to social and ethical matters,[316] and persons who represent the community and public interest, having regard to the location and nature of the company's activities and the consumers of its products or services. Certain persons are excluded from being members of the advisory panel, such as persons who are disqualified in terms of the Act from being a director or prescribed officer of the company; persons involved in the day-to-day management of the company's business; a prescribed officer, full-time executive employee, material suppliers or customers of the company; an office bearer of a registered trade union representing employees of the company, and persons related to such persons.[317] Thus executive directors may not be members of the social and ethics advisory panel.

The functions of the committee are wide ranging. Its main function is that of monitoring the company's activities, having regard to relevant legislation, other legal requirements or prevailing codes of best practice in the field of social and economic development;[318] good corporate citizenship;[319] the environment, health and public safety; consumer relationships, and labour and employment.[320] It is also required to consult with the social and ethics advisory panel with regard to matters within the mandate of the committee; to draw matters within its mandate to the attention of the board of directors, and to report annually to the shareholders at the company's annual general meeting on the matters within its mandate.[321]

The social and ethics committee is empowered to require from any director,

---

nature and extent of the company's activities. Should the Tribunal grant the exemption, it would be valid for five years, or a shorter period as the Tribunal may determine. This is subject to the Tribunal not setting the exemption aside. The Companies Commission may, on its own initiative or on request by a shareholder or a person who was granted standing by the Tribunal at the hearing of the exemption application, apply to the Tribunal to set aside an exemption on the ground that the basis on which the exemption was granted no longer applies (see cl 45*(b)* of the draft Companies Amendment Bill, 2010).

[314] Regulation 50(6) of the draft Companies Regulations.

[315] See Regulation 50(7) of the draft Companies Regulations.

[316] These professions include, but are not limited to, anthropology or psychology, education, environmental assessment, health, sociology or social services, law, theology or ethics (see Regulation 50(7) of the draft Companies Regulations).

[317] See Regulation 50(8) of the draft Companies Regulations.

[318] This includes the company's standing in terms of the goals and purposes of the ten principles set out in the United Nations Global Compact Principles; the OECD (Organisation for Economic Co-operation and Development) recommendations regarding corruption; the Employment Equity Act 55 of 1998 and the Broad-Based Black Economic Empowerment Act 53 of 2003.

[319] This includes the company's promotion of equality, prevention of unfair discrimination and reduction of corruption; its contribution to the development of the communities in which its activities are predominantly conducted or within which its products or services are predominantly marketed and its record of sponsorship, donations and charity.

[320] This includes the company's standing in the International Labour Organization Protocol on decent work and working conditions; the company's employment relationships and its contribution towards the educational development of its employees.

[321] See Regulation 50(12) of the draft Companies Regulations.

prescribed officer or employee of the company any information or explanation necessary for the performance of the committee's functions; to attend any shareholders' meeting, and to receive all notices and other communications relating to any shareholders' meeting. The committee is also entitled to be heard at any shareholders' meeting on any part of the business of the meeting that concerns its functions.[322]

The wide-ranging functions and the powers given to the social and ethics committee to carry out its functions are evidence of the strong emphasis the new Act places on identifying and managing social and ethical issues in companies.[323] See further the discussion on the social and ethics committee in chapter 12: The Duties and the Liability of Directors and the enlightened shareholder value approach.

10.18.4 Recommended committees

The King III Report recommends that companies should appoint the following committees:

- an audit committee — to oversee the internal audit (mandatory in terms of the Act for public and state-owned companies),
- a remuneration committee — to assist the board of directors in setting and administering remuneration policies,
- a nomination committee — to assist with the process of identifying suitable candidates for the board of directors, and
- a risk management committee — to assist the board of directors in carrying out its risk responsibilities.

See further chapter 11: Corporate Governance.

10.19 BOARD MEETINGS

Directors exercise their powers by passing resolutions at board meetings. These meetings must be properly convened. Proper notice must be given to all the directors and a quorum must be present at the meetings.[324]

10.19.1 Calling a meeting

A director authorised by the board may call a board meeting at any time. Subject to the Memorandum of Incorporation, which may specify a higher or a lower number of directors, a meeting must be called if required by at least 25 per cent of

---

[322] See cl 45(b) of the draft Companies Amendment Bill, 2010.

[323] The company is required to pay all the expenses reasonably incurred by its social and ethics committee. These expenses may include the costs of the fees of any consultant or specialist who may be engaged by the committee in the performance of its functions (see cl 45(b) of the draft Companies Amendment Bill, 2010). Under cl 45(b) of the draft Companies Amendment Bill, 2010, if a company fails to appoint a social and ethics committee, s 84(6) and (7) of the Companies Act would apply to that company. Under s 84(6) the Companies Commission may take steps to convene a meeting to appoint a social and ethics committee and may assess a *pro rata* share of the costs of convening the meeting to the directors who knowingly permitted the company to fail to appoint a social and ethics committee.

[324] *Burnstein v Yale* 1958 (1) SA 768 (W) 771; *Majola Investments (Pty) Ltd v Uitzigt Properties (Pty) Ltd* 1961 (4) SA 705 (T) 710; *Van Tonder v Pienaar* 1982 (2) SA 336 (SE) 341.

the directors where the board has 12 or more members, or by at least two directors where the board has fewer than 12 members.[325] The Act does not make provision for a single director to call a meeting.

As previously discussed, where a profit company (other than a state-owned company) has only one director, the provisions of the Act relating to board meetings do not apply to the governance of that company.[326]

10.19.2 Notice

The form of notice and the notice period may be determined by the board of directors, provided there is compliance with the Memorandum of Incorporation and the rules of the company.[327]

A board meeting may not be convened without notice being given to all the directors.[328] But, except to the extent that the Memorandum of Incorporation provides otherwise, if all the directors of the company acknowledge actual receipt of the notice, are present at the meeting or waive notice of the meeting, the meeting may proceed even if the company had failed to give the notice of the meeting, or if there was a defect in the giving of the notice.[329]

Where no specific time limits are prescribed in the Memorandum of Incorporation for the calling of board meetings, fair and reasonable notice of the meeting must be given to every director who is within reach.[330] This does not mean that a valid meeting cannot be held if notice has not been given to one or more directors who were inaccessible, for example, through being indisposed or overseas.[331] The general rule is that the more contentious the business of the meeting, the greater the inaccessibility needed before notice to a director may be dispensed with.[332]

The question before the court in *South African Broadcasting Corporation Ltd v Mpofu*[333] was whether a resolution passed at a meeting of the board of directors of the South African Broadcasting Corporation, the appellant, to suspend the respondent, the Group Chief Executive Officer, had been valid. The respondent and two other executive directors had been notified of a meeting on one minute's notice, and the respondent and the two executive directors were then called into the meeting for a short period. The respondent addressed the meeting, whereafter he

---

[325] Section 73(1).
[326] See s 57(3)*(b)*.
[327] Section 73(4)*(a)*.
[328] Section 73(4)*(b)*.
[329] Section 73(5)*(a)*.
[330] *African Organic Fertilizers and Associated Industries Ltd v Premier Fertilizers Ltd* 1948 (3) SA 233 (N) 241; *Burnstein v Yale* (supra) at 771. In order to determine what constitutes fair and reasonable notice, the circumstances of each case must be looked at in the context of the company's structure, practice and affairs (*African Organic Fertilizers and Associated Industries Ltd v Premier Fertilizers Ltd* (supra) at 241).
[331] *African Organic Fertilizers and Associated Industries Ltd v Premier Fertilizers Ltd* (supra) at 240; *Majola Investments (Pty) Ltd v Uitzigt Properties (Pty) Ltd* 1961 (4) SA 705 (T) 710; *Young v Ladies' Imperial Club Ltd* [1920] 2 KB 523 (CA) 528.
[332] *African Organic Fertilizers and Associated Industries Ltd v Premier Fertilizers Ltd* (supra) at 241; *Burnstein v Yale* 1958 (1) SA 768 (W) 771; *Transcash SWD (Pty) Ltd v Smith* 1994 (2) SA 295 (C) 304–5.
[333] [2009] 4 All SA 169 (GSJ).

was asked, together with the two executive directors, to leave the meeting. In their absence, a decision was taken by the board of directors to suspend the respondent.

In evaluating whether the decision of the board of directors was valid, the court reiterated that fair and reasonable notice to attend a directors' meeting depends on the circumstances and on the structure, practice and affairs of the company.[334] The court found that a notice period of one minute in this case constituted insufficient and improper notice. Also, only four of the 12 non-executive directors were present at the meeting, and the others were present via teleconference. The court held that this was not a satisfactory situation where a matter of the suspension of the chief executive officer was being deliberated, and that in the circumstances the haste was unnecessary since a board meeting had already been scheduled for the next day.

The court held further that it was not in accordance with proper corporate governance to keep directors out of a board meeting and then allow them in for a selected period, and when the vote is to be taken to remove them from the meeting.[335] It found that the board's chairperson had unilaterally and without proper deliberation with all the board members made a decision to exclude the respondent from a large portion of the meeting based on a perceived conflict of interest, and concluded that all of these circumstances did not make it possible to hold that there had been a properly convened meeting of the board of directors. Consequently the business transacted at the meeting was not valid.[336]

It is generally not strictly necessary for the business to be transacted at the meeting to be specified in the notice of the meeting, but this is often done, because in practice it is regarded as being prudent to do so.[337]

10.19.3 Quorum

Except to the extent that the Memorandum of Incorporation provides otherwise, the quorum for board meetings is a majority of directors.[338] A quorum must consist of directors who are capable of voting on the business before the board, otherwise there will not be a quorum.[339] Moreover, a quorum must be a disinterested quorum: a director who has an interest in a matter may not vote on the matter.[340]

10.19.4 Voting

Each director has one vote on a matter before the board, except to the extent that the Memorandum of Incorporation provides otherwise.[341] Thus, as discussed in 10.14.6 above, it is possible for directors to have loaded votes, which means that

---

[334] Paragraph 39.
[335] Paragraph 41.
[336] Ibid.
[337] *Rentekor (Pty) Ltd v Rheeder and Berman* 1988 (4) SA 469 (T) 495–6.
[338] Section 73(5)(*b*).
[339] *Re Greymouth Point Elizabeth Railway & Coal Co Ltd* [1904] 1 Ch 32 at 34.
[340] Refer to s 75 of the Act. See further chapter 12: The Duties and the Liability of Directors.
[341] Section 73(5)(*c*).

greater voting rights may be attached to some shares than to others. The approval of a resolution requires a majority of the votes cast.[342]

Except to the extent that the Memorandum of Incorporation provides otherwise, in the case of a tied vote, the chairperson has a casting vote only if he or she did not have or cast a vote initially, but in any other case the matter being voted upon will fail, ie it will not be passed.[343]

A director may not be prevented from voting on a matter by his or her co-directors.[344] Should he or she be prevented from voting on a matter, the resolution will be assailable[345] (ie may be set aside as invalid by a court). A company is entitled to the benefit of the collective wisdom of all the directors present at the meeting, and not merely to that of the majority. Accordingly, the minority of directors are entitled to all the relevant information relating to a decision to be made, time to consider the matter and an opportunity to state their views, even though they may ultimately have to submit to a majority decision.[346]

Directors may not bind themselves by a voting agreement under which they bind themselves to vote in accordance with the directions and instructions of some other person.[347] This would be contrary to their fiduciary duty not to fetter their discretion.[348]

10.19.5 Minutes and resolutions

A company must keep minutes of its board and committee meetings.[349] The minutes must include every resolution adopted by the board and any declarations given by notice or made by a director regarding his or her personal financial interests in a matter in terms of s 75 of the Act.[350] Resolutions adopted by the board must be dated and sequentially numbered and are effective as of the date of the resolution, unless the resolution states otherwise.[351]

Every company must maintain the minutes of all meetings and resolutions of directors or directors' committees (or the audit committee, if any) for a period of seven years after the date of each meeting or the date on which each resolution was adopted.[352] These records must be accessible from the company's registered office or another location or locations within South Africa.[353] A company must file

---

[342] Section 73(5)(d).
[343] Section 73(5)(e).
[344] *Robinson v Imroth* 1917 WLD 159 at 169–73.
[345] *Novick v Comair Holdings Ltd* 1979 (2) SA 116 (W) 128.
[346] *Robinson v Imroth* (supra) at 171; *Novick v Comair Holdings Ltd* (supra) at 128; *Van Tonder v Pienaar* 1982 (2) SA 336 (SE) 341; *Transcash SWD (Pty) Ltd v Smith* 1994 (2) SA 295 (C) 305–6; *South African Broadcasting Corporation Ltd v Mpofu* [2009] 4 All SA 169 (GSJ).
[347] *Coronation Syndicate Ltd v Lilienfeld and New Fortuna Co Ltd* 1903 TS 489; *Boulting v Association of Cinematograph, Television and Allied Technicians* [1963] 2 QB 606 at 626–7.
[348] See further chapter 12: The Duties and the Liability of Directors.
[349] Section 73(6).
[350] Section 73(6).
[351] Section 73(7).
[352] Section 24(3)(f).
[353] Section 25(1).

a notice setting out the location or locations where the records are kept if they are not kept at its registered office, or are moved from one location to another.[354]

Minutes of directors' meetings are not open for inspection by members of the company unless the Memorandum of Incorporation permits this. But it is unlikely that such inspection would be permitted, because it would be potentially damaging to the company to permit confidential information concerning its affairs to become known to outsiders, such as its competitors (for instance, a member of the company could also be a member of the company's competitor).[355]

The minutes of a meeting or resolutions signed by the chairperson of the meeting, or by the chairperson of the next board meeting, constitute evidence of the proceedings of that meeting or adoption of that resolution, as the case may be.[356]

10.19.6 Electronic communications

For the purposes of board meetings it is not essential that members of the board meet physically in the same room. Board meetings may be conducted electronically, or one or more directors may participate in a meeting by way of electronic communication.[357] This is subject to the proviso that all participants are able to communicate concurrently with each other without an intermediary, and are able to participate effectively in the meeting.[358] Flexibility is maintained by permitting board meetings to be held electronically while at the same time permitting a company in its Memorandum of Incorporation to restrict electronic meetings if it so chooses.[359]

10.20 DECISIONS TAKEN WITHOUT CONVENING A MEETING

Instead of holding a formal meeting, the directors may consent in writing to decisions that could be voted on at a board meeting, in terms of a resolution informally known as a 'round robin' resolution.[360] Such decisions have the same effect as if they had been approved by voting at a meeting.[361]

The term 'round robin' usually refers to a document in which the names of the subscribers are arranged in a circle so as to disguise the order in which they have signed, but in corporate decision-making the term is more generally applied and

---

[354] Section 25(2).
[355] Galgut, Jennifer A Kunst, Piet Delport and Quintus Vorster *Henochsberg on the Companies Act* vol 1 5 ed (1994) (Service Issue 31, June 2010) at 455.
[356] Section 73(8).
[357] Section 73(3). Section 1 of the Act states that 'electronic communication' has the meaning set out in s 1 of the Electronic Communications and Transactions Act 25 of 2002 (ECTA). Section 1 of ECTA defines 'electronic communication' as meaning a 'communication by means of data messages'. 'Data messages' is defined in s 1 of ECTA as meaning 'data generated, sent, received or stored by electronic means and includes —
  (a) voice, where the voice is used in an automated transaction; and
  (b) a stored record'.
[358] Section 73(3).
[359] Ibid.
[360] Section 74. See *Southern Witwatersrand Exploration Co Ltd v Bisichi Mining plc* 1998 (4) SA 767 (W) 776.
[361] Section 74(2).

the sequence in which the document is signed is not relevant.[362] Since the procedure circumvents not only the procedural formality of convening a meeting, but also substantive discussion, it reflects a less formal approach to decision-making.

Decisions may be taken by means of a round robin resolution only if every director has received notice of the matter to be decided.[363]

Under the 1973 Act the consent of *all* the directors was required to pass a round robin resolution, but under the new Act, unless the Memorandum of Incorporation provides otherwise, board decisions may be adopted by the written consent of a majority of the directors only.[364] Notably, this ignores the principle that the minority of directors should be entitled to the opportunity to persuade the majority of the directors to their view by means of discussion (even though they may ultimately have to submit to a majority decision).[365]

The written consent may be given in person or by electronic communication.[366] A round robin resolution will usually comprise a single piece of paper containing the resolution and all the directors' signatures, but in *Southern Witwatersrand Exploration Co Ltd v Bisichi Mining plc*[367] the court stated that there was no reason in principle why this should be so, and that a round robin resolution may exist in more than one part, ie comprise more than one piece of paper.[368]

10.21 LOANS OR OTHER FINANCIAL ASSISTANCE TO DIRECTORS

Given that directors have control over the company's day-to-day activities and are able to exert a strong influence on their company or a company under their company's control, they are in a good position to effect loan transactions or other financial assistance for their own benefit.[369] History has shown that, from time to time, directors have given in to the temptation to do so. Accordingly, the provision of loans or other financial assistance to directors by their company has for a long time either been prohibited or subject to statutory regulation.[370]

The provision of loans or other financial assistance to directors is regulated by s 45 of the Act. The purpose of s 45 was succinctly stated by Goldblatt AJ in *Standard Bank of SA Ltd v Neugarten*,[371] in relation to s 226 of the 1973 Act (the predecessor of s 45 in the current Act) as follows:

> The clear purpose of s 226 of the Act is to prevent directors or managers of a company acting in their own interests and against the interests of shareholders by burdening the

---
[362] *Southern Witwatersrand Exploration Co Ltd v Bisichi Mining plc* (supra) at 777.
[363] Section 74(1).
[364] Ibid.
[365] See *Robinson v Imroth* 1917 WLD 159 at 171; *Novick v Comair Holdings Ltd* 1979 (2) SA 116 (W) 128; *Van Tonder v Pienaar* 1982 (2) SA 336 (SE) 341; *Transcash SWD (Pty) Ltd v Smith* 1994 (2) SA 295 (C) 305–6.
[366] Section 74(1).
[367] 1998 (4) SA 767 (W).
[368] At 778. In this case the court held that a resolution constituted by two faxes that together contained the signatures of all the directors was valid.
[369] Paul L Davies op cit n 261 at 550.
[370] Ibid.
[371] 1988 (1) SA 652 (W).

company with obligations which are not for its benefit but are for the benefit of another company and/or for the benefit of its directors and/or managers.[372]

Section 45 also aims to prevent abuse of control where the company has a holding company, by preventing directors of that holding company from using their control of the company to benefit themselves or the directors of other subsidiaries of the holding company.[373]

10.21.1 Meaning of 'financial assistance'

In terms of s 45 '"financial assistance" includes lending money, guaranteeing a loan or other obligation, and securing any debt or obligation'.[374] The word 'includes' in s 45 indicates that 'financial assistance' for the purposes of s 45 may be wider than the lending of money, guaranteeing a loan or other obligation and securing a debt or obligation.

10.21.2 Exceptions[375]

Certain transactions do not constitute 'financial assistance' under s 45. First, loans made in the ordinary course of business by a company whose primary business is the lending of money do not constitute financial assistance. The words 'primary business' indicate that it is not sufficient if the business of lending money is only a small part of the company's business; in order for the exception to apply the business of lending money must be the main or a substantial part of the company's business.

Secondly, an accountable advance to meet legal expenses in relation to a matter concerning the company, or anticipated expenses to be incurred by the person on behalf of the company also do not constitute financial assistance.

And finally, under s 45 an amount to defray the expenses for removal (see s 45(1)(b)(iii)) at the company's request would not constitute financial assistance.

10.21.3 Provision of financial assistance

Under s 45(2) of the Act, except to the extent that the Memorandum of Incorporation provides otherwise, the board of directors may authorise the company to provide direct or indirect financial assistance to:

- a director or prescribed officer of the company,
- a director or prescribed officer of a related or interrelated company,
- a related or interrelated company or corporation,
- a member of a related or interrelated corporation, or
- a person related to any such company, corporation, director, prescribed officer or member.[376]

---

[372] At 658. See also *Bevray Investments (Edms) Bpk v Boland Bank Bpk* 1993 (3) SA 597 (A) 606.
[373] Blackman et al op cit n 14 at 8–306–8–307. See further Richard Jooste 'Loans to directors: an analysis of section 226 of the Companies Act' (2000) 12 *SA Merc LJ* 269 and Richard Jooste 'Financial assistance to directors — the Companies Act 71 of 2008' 2010 *Acta Juridica* 165.
[374] Section 45(1)(a).
[375] See s 45(1)(b).
[376] Refer to s 2 of the Act for the meaning of a 'related' and an 'inter-related' *[sic]* company.

Section 45 deals with loans or other financial assistance being provided not only to directors, but also to prescribed officers of the company or of a related or an interrelated company, as well as to certain companies and corporations.

The provision of financial assistance under s 45 is subject to certain conditions being met, as discussed below at 10.21.5.

10.21.4 'Direct or indirect' financial assistance

Section 45(2) provides that the board may authorise the company to provide 'direct or indirect' financial assistance, provided certain conditions are met. In *S v Pouroulis*[377] the court held that the words 'direct or indirect' (in reference to s 226 of the 1973 Act, the predecessor to s 45 of the Act) emphasise that the prohibition applies whether the loan is constituted by a payment made by the lender to the borrower directly (for example, where the lender advances money to the borrower directly) or indirectly, upon the borrower becoming obliged to repay to the lender a sum of money that has become a loan from the lender to the borrower in any of a number of possible indirect ways (for example, where the lender makes a payment directly to a creditor of the intended borrower and thereby simultaneously makes a loan to the borrower indirectly).[378]

10.21.5 Conditions for the authorisation of financial assistance

As mentioned above, before the particular financial assistance is authorised, certain conditions must be met. These are as follows:

- the financial assistance must be provided pursuant to an employee share scheme that satisfies the requirements of s 97 of the Act, or
- the financial assistance must be provided pursuant to a special resolution of the shareholders, adopted within the previous two years, which approved the financial assistance either for the specific recipient or generally for a category of potential recipients and the specific recipient falls within that category, and
- the board of directors must be satisfied that immediately after providing the financial assistance the company would satisfy the solvency and liquidity test,[379] and
- any conditions or restrictions relating to the granting of financial assistance set out in the Memorandum of Incorporation must be satisfied.[380]

It is noteworthy that an ordinary resolution of the shareholders would not suffice, and that a special resolution must be passed. Note that the special resolution must be passed prior to the provision of the financial assistance, ie within the previous two years of the financial assistance being provided. The words 'adopted within the previous two years' in s 45(3)*(a)*(ii) seem to indicate that ratification of the special resolution is not possible. The special resolution may specify the specific

---

[377] 1993 (4) SA 575 (W) 601.
[378] See also *Kirsten v Bankorp Ltd* 1993 (4) SA 649 (C) 660–1.
[379] Refer to s 4 of the Act for the solvency and liquidity test. The draft Companies Amendment Bill, 2010 inserts an additional condition, which requires the board of directors to be satisfied that the terms under which the financial assistance is proposed to be given are fair and reasonable to the company (see cl 29*(a)* of the Bill).
[380] Section 45(3) and (4).

recipient or it may simply specify the category of potential recipients (but the specific recipient must fall within that category).

10.21.6 Notice

Should the board of directors adopt a resolution to provide financial assistance under s 45(2), the company must provide written notice of that resolution to all shareholders of the company (unless every shareholder is also a director of the company). In addition, written notice of the resolution must be provided to any trade union representing the company's employees.[381]

If the total value of all loans, debts, obligations or assistance contemplated in the resolution authorising the company to provide the financial assistance, together with any previous such resolution during the financial year, exceeds a tenth of 1 per cent of the company's net worth at the time of the resolution, the notice of the resolution must be provided to the shareholders and trade unions within ten business days after the board of directors adopts the resolution. In all other instances, the notice must be provided within 30 business days after the end of the company's financial year.[382]

The requirement of giving notice to trade unions representing the company's employees indicates that the legislature recognises the employees of a company as being a stakeholder whose interests must be taken into account in certain circumstances for good corporate governance purposes.[383]

10.21.7 Consequences of contravening s 45

If s 45 of the Act is contravened no criminal liability will ensue, but the following consequences will arise:

(a) Void resolution or agreement

A resolution authorising the company to provide financial assistance under s 45 of the Act, or an agreement with respect to the provision of any such assistance, will be void to the extent that the provision of that assistance is inconsistent with s 45 or any prohibition, condition or requirement provided in the Memorandum of Incorporation.[384] Section 45(6) must be read together with s 218(1) of the Act, which provides that an agreement or resolution or provision of an agreement or resolution will not be void unless a court declares it to be void.[385]

Since s 45 is enacted to protect companies, shareholders and creditors from a misapplication of the company's funds, it seems implicit in the section that the company would have a right to recover the amount of the loan made by it in

---

[381] Section 45(5).
[382] Ibid.
[383] Richard Jooste 'Financial assistance to directors — the Companies Act 71 of 2008' 2010 *Acta Juridica* 165 at 179.
[384] Section 45(6).
[385] Under the draft Companies Amendment Bill, 2010 (cl 29(b)) there is no longer the need to first have the resolution or agreement declared void under s 218 of the Companies Act.

contravention of s 45 from the director or prescribed officer or relevant person concerned.[386]

(b) Liability of directors

If a resolution or agreement with respect to the provision of financial assistance has been declared void by a court in terms of s 45(6) of the Act read with s 218(1) of the Act,[387] a director of a company will be liable to the extent set out in s 77(3)(*e*)(v) of the Act for any loss, damages or costs sustained by the company if the director was present at the meeting when the board of directors approved the resolution or agreement or participated in a round robin resolution approving the resolution, and he or she failed to vote against the resolution or agreement, despite knowing that the provision of the financial assistance was inconsistent with s 45 or with a prohibition, condition or requirement provided in the Memorandum of Incorporation.[388] The liability of a director would thus depend on whether he or she knew that the provision of the financial assistance was inconsistent with s 45 or with a prohibition, condition or requirement provided in the Memorandum of Incorporation.

In addition to his or her liability under s 45, the director concerned may also incur liability to the company on the ground of breach of his or her fiduciary duties or the duty of care and skill.[389]

10.21.8 Disclosure in the annual financial statements

Not all the provisions of financial assistance dealt with in s 45 are required to be disclosed in the annual financial statements. With respect to a loan or other financial assistance by a company to a director, past director or future director, or a person related to any of them, or any loan made by a third party to any such person, as contemplated in s 45, if the company is a guarantor of that loan, the annual financial statements of the company must include details of the value of:

- any interest deferred, waived or forgiven, or
- the difference in value between the interest that would reasonably be charged in comparable circumstances at fair market rates in an arm's length transaction and the interest actually charged to the borrower, if less.[390]

---

[386] Blackman et al op cit n 14 at 8–315.
[387] As mentioned above, under the draft Companies Amendment Bill, 2010 (cl 29*(b)*) there is no longer the need to first have the resolution or agreement declared void under s 218 of the Act.
[388] Section 45(7).
[389] Blackman et al op cit n 14 at 8–316.
[390] Section 30(4)*(a)* read with s 30(6)*(g)*. See further on this issue Richard Jooste op cit n 383 at 186–7.

CHAPTER 11

CORPORATE GOVERNANCE

Rehana Cassim

11.1 INTRODUCTION 432
11.2 APPLICATION 434
11.3 PHILOSOPHY OF 'APPLY OR EXPLAIN' 434
11.4 PRINCIPLES AND RECOMMENDATIONS OF THE KING III REPORT AND THE CODE.. 435
    11.4.1 Ethical leadership and corporate citizenship............... 435
    11.4.2 Boards and directors...................................... 437
        (a) Types of directors..................................... 437
        (b) The responsibilities of the board of directors 438
        (c) Composition of the board 439
        (d) Board appointment 440
        (e) Board meetings 441
        (f) Board committees 441
        (g) Group boards 442
        (h) Induction and training................................. 443
        (i) Performance assessment.............................. 443
        (j) Remuneration 443
        (k) The chairperson 444
        (l) The chief executive officer (CEO)..................... 444
        (m) The company secretary............................... 444
    11.4.3 Audit committees 445
    11.4.4 The governance of risk................................... 446
    11.4.5 The governance of information technology (IT) 447
    11.4.6 Compliance with laws, rules, codes and standards 448
    11.4.7 Internal audit 448
    11.4.8 Governing stakeholder relationships 449
        (a) Stakeholder-inclusive approach....................... 449
        (b) Shareholder activism and shareholder apathy.......... 451
        (c) Dispute resolution 454
    11.4.9 Integrated reporting and disclosure 457
11.5 CONCLUSION 457

11.1 INTRODUCTION

Corporate governance is concerned with the structures and processes associated with management, decision making and control in organisations.[1] It relates to the

---
[1] Tom Wixley and Geoff Everingham *Corporate Governance* 2 ed (2005) 1.

way in which companies are directed and controlled and the principles and practices that are regarded as appropriate conduct by directors and managers.[2] The function of corporate governance practices is essentially nothing other than a performance management system to ascertain or assist directors on whether they have discharged their duties.

Good corporate governance is essentially about effective, responsible leadership. Responsible leadership is characterised by the ethical values of responsibility, accountability, fairness and transparency, which values underpin good corporate governance. In *South African Broadcasting Corporation Ltd v Mpofu*[3] the court stressed that integrity is a key principle underpinning good corporate governance, and that 'good corporate governance is based on a clear code of ethical behaviour and personal integrity exercised by the board, where communications are shared openly'.[4] Practising sound corporate governance is essential for the well-being of a company and is in the best interests of the growth of South Africa's economy, particularly in attracting new investments.[5]

In 1994 the King Committee, formed at the instance of the Institute of Directors in Southern Africa, published the King Report on Corporate Governance, which contained a Code of Corporate Practices and Conduct. This report was updated and superseded in 2001 by the King Report on Corporate Governance for South Africa ('King II Report'), which also contained a Code of Corporate Practices and Conduct. The King Report on Governance for South Africa 2009 ('the King III Report') and the King Code of Governance for South Africa 2009 ('the Code'), which came into effect on 1 March 2010, have now replaced the King II Report and Code of Corporate Practices and Conduct.

The King III Report was prompted by changes in international governance trends and the changes and reforms implemented by the Companies Act 71 of 2008 (hereafter 'the Act'). One of the very purposes of the Act, as embodied in s 7*(b)*, is to encourage transparency and high standards of corporate governance as a means of promoting the development of the South African economy. This purpose encourages an interaction between the King III Report and the Act.[6]

The King III Report, which sets out a number of key corporate governance principles, must be read together with the Code, which sets out best practice recommendations on how to carry out each principle. The Code regulates directors and their conduct not only with a view to complying with the minimum statutory standard, but also to seek to adhere to the best available practice that may be relevant to the company in its particular circumstances.[7] The Institute of Directors in Southern Africa issues Practice Notes to the King III Report. These notes are intended to provide guidance to entities on implementing the key principles and

---

[2] See Mervyn King 'The synergies and interaction between King III and the Companies Act 71 of 2008' 2010 *Acta Juridica* 446 at 447.

[3] [2009] 4 All SA 169 (GSJ).

[4] Paragraph 64.

[5] *Minister of Water Affairs and Forestry v Stilfontein Gold Mining Co Ltd* 2006 (5) SA 333 (W) para 16.7.

[6] See Mervyn King op cit n 2 at 447.

[7] *South African Broadcasting Corporation Ltd v Mpofu* [2009] 4 All SA 169 (GSJ) para 29.

should be read together with the principles contained in the King III Report. Some of the main principles and recommendations of the King III Report and the Code are discussed in this chapter.

11.2 APPLICATION

The King III Report and the Code apply to all entities incorporated in and resident in South Africa, regardless of the manner and form of incorporation or establishment and whether such establishment is in the public, private or non-profit sectors.[8] In contrast, the King II Report only applied to certain categories of business enterprises, namely listed companies, financial institutions and public sector enterprises, while companies falling outside these categories were merely required to consider the application of the King II Report insofar as it was applicable.

The USA codified a significant part of its corporate governance provisions in the Sarbanes-Oxley Act 2002 and legal sanctions are applied for non-compliance with this Act.[9] In South Africa, compliance with the King III Report and the Code is mandatory for companies listed on the JSE,[10] but for all other entities there is no statutory obligation to comply with the King III Report and the Code. While corporate governance practices in South Africa may be voluntary, note that they are highly recommended and have considerable persuasive force. Commonwealth countries and the European Union states have also not legislated their corporate governance practices and adopt a similar approach to that adopted in South Africa.

11.3 PHILOSOPHY OF 'APPLY OR EXPLAIN'

Instead of the 'comply or else' regime adopted by the USA, South Africa has adopted an 'apply or explain' philosophy.[11] This philosophy must be distinguished from the 'comply or explain' approach previously adopted in the King II Report.

The drafters of the King III Report were of the view that the 'comply or explain' approach denotes a mindless response to corporate governance recommendations, whereas the 'apply or explain' regime shows appreciation of the fact that it is often not a case of whether to comply or not, but rather to consider how the principles and recommendations may be applied.[12] The idea is to discourage a 'tick box' approach. The 'apply or explain' approach requires more consideration and explanation of what has actually been done to implement the principles of corporate governance. All entities should make a positive statement to the shareholders about how the principles have been applied or not.

For instance, in following the 'apply or explain' approach, the board of directors may conclude that to follow a recommendation would not, in the particular circumstances, be in the best interests of the company, and it may decide to apply the recommendation differently or to apply a different practice but nevertheless achieve the objective of the overarching corporate governance principles. Explain-

---

[8] King III Report at 17.
[9] The Sarbanes-Oxley Act 2002 applies to all companies with securities traded publicly in the USA.
[10] See paras 7.F.5–7.F.6 and para 8.63(a) of the JSE Listings Requirements.
[11] King III Report, preface, at 7.
[12] Ibid.

ing how the corporate governance recommendations were applied, or the reasons for not applying them, would result in compliance.[13]

Significantly, the new Act incorporates certain issues of corporate governance. Accordingly, the language used in the King III Report has been carefully chosen in that the word 'must' is used in the King III Report to indicate a legal requirement.[14] In other words, the word 'must' is used with regard to a principle or practice where that principle or practice is in line with the Act. Where the application of the Report would result in good corporate governance the word 'should' has been used.[15] Thus where the word 'should' is used in regard to a recommendation, such recommendation is not contained in the Act.[16] Accordingly, compliance with the King III Report would result in compliance with the Act with regard to governance, but the converse would not apply.[17]

11.4 PRINCIPLES AND RECOMMENDATIONS OF THE KING III REPORT AND THE CODE

The King III Report provides guidance on the following aspects related to corporate governance:

- ethical leadership and corporate citizenship,
- boards and directors,
- audit committees,
- the governance of risk,
- the governance of information technology,
- compliance with laws, codes, rules and standards,
- internal audit,
- governing stakeholder relationships, and
- integrated reporting and disclosure.

The Report is divided into nine chapters. Each of the principles contained in the Report is set out in the Code, together with the recommended practices relating to each principle. Some of the main principles and practices of the King III Report are discussed below.

11.4.1 Ethical leadership and corporate citizenship

The underlying philosophy of the King III Report revolves around leadership, sustainability and corporate citizenship.[18]

On the issue of leadership, the King III Report requires the board of directors to provide effective leadership based on an ethical foundation.[19] Ethics or integrity is the foundation of and very reason for corporate governance. An ethical corporate culture constitutes more than social philanthropy or charitable donations.[20] The

---

[13] Ibid.
[14] King III Report, preface, at 17.
[15] Ibid.
[16] See Mervyn King op cit n 2 at 447.
[17] Ibid.
[18] King III Report, preface, at 10.
[19] Principle 1.1 of the King III Report.
[20] King III Report para 9 p 20.

reasoning behind the ethics of corporate governance, which requires the board of directors to ensure that the company is run ethically, is that, as this is achieved, the company would earn the necessary approval from those affected by and affecting its operations.[21] Ethical leaders should consider the short- and long-term impact of the strategy on the company, society and the environment and should take account of the company's impact on internal and external stakeholders. Certain categories of companies are required to establish a social and ethics committee under s 72(4) of the Act.

The board should set the values to which the company will adhere and these values should be incorporated in a code of conduct (Code 1.1.7). The board should ensure that all decisions and actions are based on the four values underpinning good corporate governance, namely responsibility, accountability, fairness and transparency, and should ensure that each director adheres to the duties of a director.[22] The board should, in addition, ensure that its conduct and that of management aligns to the set values and is adhered to in all aspects of its business (Code 1.1.8).

As part of developing an ethical foundation, the board should ensure that the company's ethical performance is assessed, monitored, reported and disclosed (Code 1.3.8). The ultimate object of assessment, reporting and disclosure is to improve the company's ethical culture by enhancing its ethical performance. Assessing, reporting and disclosure of its ethical performance should thus enable users of ethics reports to form opinions and make decisions based on disclosed and verified information.[23]

Sustainability is a primary moral and economic imperative of the 21st century.[24] It means having regard to the impact of a company's business operations on the economic life of the community in which it operates, and includes environmental, social and governance issues. Sustainability considerations are rooted in the Constitution of the Republic of South Africa, 1996, which imposes responsibilities upon individuals and juristic persons for the realisation of the most fundamental rights.[25] For sustainability to become integrated into the company, effective leadership is required.

On the issue of corporate citizenship, the board should ensure that the company is, and is seen to be, a responsible corporate citizen.[26] Responsible corporate citizenship implies an ethical relationship of responsibility between the company and the society in which it operates.[27] This means the board should consider not only the financial performance of the company, but also the impact of the company's operations on society and the environment (Code 1.2.1). As a responsible

---

[21] King III report para 12 p 21.
[22] Ibid para 14 p 21.
[23] Ibid para 53 p 27.
[24] King III Report, preface, at 11.
[25] Ibid.
[26] Principle 1.2 of the King III Report. See *Minister of Water Affairs and Forestry v Stilfontein Gold Mining Co Ltd* 2006 (5) SA 333 (W) para 16.9.
[27] King III Report, para 19 p 22.

corporate citizen, the company should protect, enhance and invest in the well-being of the economy, society and the environment.[28]

11.4.2 Boards and directors

(a) *Types of directors*

The King III Report differentiates between executive and non-executive directors. An executive director is involved in the day-to-day management of the company. He or she is in the full-time salaried employ of the company[29] and is generally under a contract of service with the company. A non-executive director, on the other hand, is a part-time director. He or she is not involved in the management of the company, but plays an important role in providing objective judgment, independent of management, on issues facing the company.[30] Generally, non-executive directors contribute to the development of management strategies and monitor the activities of the executive directors.

In *Fisheries Development Corporation of SA Ltd v Jorgensen; Fisheries Development Corporation of SA Ltd v AWJ Investments (Pty) Ltd*[31] the court stated that non-executive directors are not bound to give continuous attention to the affairs of the company. Their duties are of an intermittent nature, to be performed at periodical board meetings and at any other meetings that may require their attention. It is expected of non-executive directors to attend board and board committee meetings and to acquire and maintain a broad knowledge of the economic environment, industry and business of the company.[32] The role of non-executive directors and the independence that they are believed to bring to the board of directors have been a consistent theme of corporate governance theories, policies and programmes.[33]

An independent non-executive director is a director who is required to be independent in character and judgment. There should be no relationships or circumstances that are likely to affect, or could appear to affect, their independence.[34] By independence is meant the absence of undue influence and bias that could be affected by the intensity of the relationship between the director and the company, rather than any particular fact such as length of service or age.[35] Not only should the director be independent in fact, but he or she should also appear or be perceived to be independent in the perception of a reasonably informed outsider.[36] The King III Report[37] defines an independent non-executive director as a non-executive director who:

---

[28] King III Report para 19 p 22.
[29] Annex 2.2 of the King III Report.
[30] Annex 2.3 of the King III Report. See *Fisheries Development Corporation of SA Ltd v Jorgensen; Fisheries Development Corporation of SA Ltd v AWJ Investments (Pty) Ltd* 1980 (4) SA 156 (W) 165.
[31] 1980 (4) SA 156 (W) 165.
[32] King III Report para 83 p 41.
[33] MS Blackman et al *Commentary on the Companies Act* vol 2 (2002) (Revision Service 7, 2010) at 8–13.
[34] King III Report para 66 p 38.
[35] Ibid.
[36] Ibid para 65 p 38.
[37] Ibid para 67 p 38.

- is not a representative of a shareholder who has the ability to control or significantly influence management or the board,
- does not have a direct or indirect interest in the company that exceeds 5 per cent of the group's total number of shares in issue,
- does not have a direct or indirect interest in the company that is less than 5 per cent of the group's total number of shares in issue, but is material to his or her personal wealth,
- has not been employed by the company or the group of which it currently forms part in any executive capacity, or been appointed as the designated auditor or partner in the group's external audit firm, or as a senior legal adviser in the preceding three financial years,
- is not a member of the immediate family of an individual who is, or has, during the preceding three financial years, been employed by the company or the group in an executive capacity,
- is not a professional adviser to the company or the group, other than as a director,
- is free from any business or other relationship (contractual or statutory) that could be seen by an objective outsider to interfere materially with the individual's capacity to act in an independent manner, such as being a director of a material customer of or supplier to the company, and
- does not receive remuneration contingent upon the performance of the company.

The King III Report recommends that independent directors undergo an evaluation of their independence by the chairperson of the board every year. It suggests that independence be assessed by weighing all relevant factors that may impair independence.

The Report suggests further that any term beyond nine years for an independent non-executive director should be subject to a particularly rigorous review by the board of directors, of not only the performance of the director but also the factors that may impair his or her independence at that time.[38] The review should also take into account the need for refreshing the board. However, this does not mean that an independent non-executive director may not serve for longer than nine years. He or she may serve for longer if, after the independence assessment by the board of directors, there are no relationships or circumstances that are likely to affect, or that appear to affect, his or her judgment.[39] The King III Report recommends further that the assessment should show that the director's independence of character and judgment is not in any way affected or impaired by the length of his or her service, and a statement to this effect should be included in the integrated report.[40]

(b) The responsibilities of the board of directors

The King III Report and the Code deal extensively with the responsibilities of the board of directors. The Report confirms that it is for the board of directors to act as

---
[38] King III Report para 77 p 40.
[39] Ibid para 78 p 40.
[40] Ibid.

the focal point and custodian of corporate governance.[41] As the court in *South African Broadcasting Corporation Ltd v Mpofu*[42] stressed, good corporate governance (particularly in state-owned enterprises) is ultimately about effective leadership. The court stressed further that an organisation depends on its board of directors to provide it with direction.[43] The board should ensure that the company is, and is seen to be, a responsible corporate citizen[44] and should provide effective leadership based on an ethical foundation.[45] It is responsible for the strategic direction and the control of the company.[46] Furthermore, the board of directors should act in the best interests of the company.[47] The Report recommends that every board should have a charter setting out its responsibilities and should meet as often as required to fulfil its duties, but preferably at least four times per year.[48]

The board of directors should strive to achieve the appropriate balance between its various stakeholder groupings, and is urged to take into account, as far as possible, the legitimate interests and expectations of its stakeholders when making decisions in the best interests of the company.[49] The King III Report requires the board to ensure the integrity of the company's integrated report, which should be prepared annually and should convey adequate information regarding the company's financial and sustainability performance.[50] Integrated reporting enables stakeholders to better assess the economic value of a company.

The board should furthermore ensure that the company complies with applicable laws and that it also considers adherence to non-binding rules, codes and standards.[51] The board should be responsible for the governance of both risk[52] and information technology,[53] and should ensure that there is an effective risk-based internal audit.[54] In addition, the board should be responsible for dispute resolution and should ensure that disputes are resolved as effectively, efficiently and expeditiously as possible.[55]

(c) Composition of the board

There are generally two types of board structures: unitary boards and two-tier boards. A two-tier board comprises both a management board and a supervisory board. The task of running the company is entrusted to the management board, which is composed of executive directors (appointed by the supervisory board). The supervisory board, which is composed of non-executive directors that are

---

[41] Principle 2.1 of the King III Report.
[42] [2009] 4 All SA 169 (GSJ) para 60.
[43] Ibid.
[44] Principle 1.2 of the King III Report.
[45] Principle 1.1 of the King III Report.
[46] King III Report para 7 p 20.
[47] Principle 2.14 of the King III Report.
[48] Paragraph 1 at 29.
[49] Principle 8.3 of the King III Report.
[50] Principle 9.1 of the King III Report.
[51] Principle 6.1 of the King III Report.
[52] Principle 4.1 of the King III Report.
[53] Principle 5.1 of the King III Report.
[54] Principle 2.10 of the King III Report.
[55] Principle 8.6 of the King III Report.

elected by the shareholders and in some cases by the employees, monitors how the management board discharges its functions. Both employees and shareholders are represented on the supervisory board. The two-tier board structure results in a more defined separation between the management and the supervisory functions. Members of the one board may not sit as members of the other board. In Germany,[56] Austria, the Netherlands and Denmark, for example, a two-tier board is mandatory for public companies.

A unitary board, on the other hand, is composed of both executive and non-executive directors who interact directly with each other. The unitary board is the norm in Britain, the USA and the Commonwealth. The King III Report expresses the view that, given the positive interaction and diversity of views that occur between individuals of different backgrounds, experiences and skills, the unitary board structure with executive directors and non-executive directors interacting in a working group is more appropriate for South African companies.[57]

The King III Report states that there should be a balance of power and authority in the board and that no one individual or block of individuals should have sufficient power to be able to dominate the board's decision making.[58] There should be a majority of non-executive directors on the board and the majority should be independent, because this reduces the possibility of conflicts of interests and promotes objectivity.[59] The Code (2.18.5) recommends that every board should have a minimum of two executive directors, being the chief executive officer and the director responsible for the finance function.

In determining the number of directors that should serve on the board, the collective knowledge, skills, experiences and resources required for conducting the business of the board should be taken into consideration (Code 2.18.3). Every board should consider whether its size, diversity and demographics make it effective (Code 2.18.4).

Regarding the rotation of the directors on the board, it is recommended that at least a third of the non-executive directors should rotate every year (Code 2.18.6) and that any independent non-executive director serving for longer than nine years be subjected to a rigorous review of his or her independence and performance by the board (Code 2.18.8).

(d) Board appointment

The King III Report calls for the procedures for the appointment of directors to be formal and transparent.[60] The Code recommends that the nomination committee should assist with the process of identifying suitable members of the board (Code

---

[56] In most German public companies, a third of the members of the supervisory board are required to be elected by the employees of the company while the other two-thirds are elected by the shareholders. Thus the supervisory board in Germany plays an important role in encouraging worker participation in management (see Derek French, Stephen W Mayson and Christopher L Ryan *Mayson, French & Ryan on Company Law* 26 ed (2009) para 15.2.4 p 425).
[57] King III Report para 62 p 38.
[58] See Principle 2.18 and para 63 p 38 of the King III Report.
[59] King III Report para 64 p 38.
[60] Principle 2.19 of the King III Report and para 80 p 40.

2.19.1). It suggests further that background and reference checks should be performed before the nomination and appointment of directors (Code 2.19.2). Full disclosure regarding each individual director should be made to enable shareholders to make their own assessment of the directors (Code 2.19.4).

(e) Board meetings

It is recommended that the board meets as often as is required to fulfil its duties, but that board meetings should be held at least four times per year (Code 2.1.2).

Non-executive directors should meet from time to time without the presence of any executive directors to consider the performance and actions of executive management.[61]

(f) Board committees

While the board may delegate certain functions to well-structured committees, it must do so without abdicating its own responsibilities.[62] This is in any event required by the Act.[63] The board should critically apply its collective mind to the recommendations and the reports of all its committees before approving such recommendations.[64] Formal terms of reference should be established and approved for each committee of the board (Code 2.23.1).

Public and state-owned companies must appoint an audit committee, but all other companies may voluntarily appoint an audit committee (Code 2.23.4 and 2.23.5). The audit committee is responsible for overseeing the internal audit and is an integral component of the risk management process.[65] Its members should be suitably skilled and experienced independent non-executive directors.[66] The audit committee is an important committee that plays a central role in corporate governance.

Companies should also establish a risk committee to assist the board in carrying out its risk responsibilities.[67] The risk committee should consider the risk management policy and it should also plan and monitor the risk management process (Code 4.3.2.1). In addition, a remuneration committee should assist the board of directors in setting and administering remuneration policies (Code 2.25.2), and a nomination committee should assist with the process of identifying suitable members for the board of directors (Code 2.19.1). It is recommended that the board also considers the establishment of a governance committee, an information technology steering committee and a sustainability committee.[68] It may be onerous for smaller companies to set up all these committees. The King III Report accordingly provides that small companies need not establish formal committees

---

[61] Annex 2.3 of the King III Report.
[62] Principle 2.23 of the King III Report.
[63] See s 76(3)–(5) of the Act.
[64] King III Report para 137 p 47.
[65] Principles 3.7 and 3.8 of the King III Report.
[66] Principle 3.2 of the King III Report.
[67] Principle 4.3 of the King III Report.
[68] King III Report para 130 p 46.

to perform the recommended functions, but they should ensure that these functions are appropriately addressed by the board.[69]

The Code (2.23.7) recommends that committees (other than the risk committee, which should comprise executive and non-executive directors) should comprise a majority of non-executive directors, the majority of which should be independent.

Committees should be free to take independent outside professional advice at the cost of the company subject to an approved process being followed (Code 2.23.9). External parties may be present at committee meetings by invitation, but may not vote on the committee.[70] This is in accordance with s 72(2) of the Act, which provides that, except to the extent that the Memorandum of Incorporation or a resolution establishing a committee provides otherwise, non-director members of a committee do not have any right to vote on matters to be decided by the committee. Section 76(1) of the Act, dealing with the standards of directors' conduct, provides that a 'director', for the purposes of s 76, includes a member of a board committee or of the audit committee[71] of a company, *irrespective* of whether or not the person is also a member of the company's board of directors. Thus non-directors serving as members on committees should be aware of s 76(1) of the Act, which places the same standards of conduct and liability on such individuals as if they were directors.

(g) Group boards

The King III Report recommends that a governance framework be agreed upon between a group and the boards of its subsidiaries.[72] Where a subsidiary company is listed on a stock exchange, special attention must be paid to the rules of the relevant stock exchange and the requirement that all shareholders must be treated equally. In particular, attention should be given to compliance with the relevant rules relating to inside information.[73]

The King III Report emphasises that a holding company must recognise and respect the fiduciary duties of the directors of the subsidiary company and particularly the duty to act in the best interests of the subsidiary company at all times, whether or not the director has been nominated to the board of the subsidiary company by the holding company.[74] This in any event is a fiduciary duty of the directors of the company. The Report clarifies that it is acceptable for the chairperson or chief executive officer of a subsidiary company to be appointed as a director on the holding company's board, but emphasises that the fiduciary duties of the director are owed to the company to which he or she has been appointed.[75]

The implementation and adoption of policies, processes or procedures of the holding company in the operations of the subsidiary company should be consid-

---

[69] King III Report para 130 p 46.
[70] Ibid para 132 p 46.
[71] Each member of the audit committee is required to be a director, and would in any case be subject to the duties set out in s 76 of the Act.
[72] Principle 2.24 of the King III Report.
[73] King III Report para 140 p 47.
[74] Ibid para 142 p 48.
[75] Ibid para 144 p 48.

ered and approved by the subsidiary company, if the subsidiary company's board considers it appropriate.[76] The subsidiary company should disclose this adoption and implementation in its integrated report.[77]

(h) Induction and training

It is recommended that the board of directors ensures that a formal induction programme is established for new directors, and that continuing professional development programmes are implemented (Code§ 2.20.1 and 2.20.3). The induction and ongoing training programmes should incorporate an overview of any changes to applicable laws, rules, codes and standards (Code 6.2.1). The mentorship of inexperienced directors by experienced directors is encouraged (Code 2.20.2). The King III Report suggests that incompetent or unsuitable directors should be removed as directors, taking relevant legal and other requirements into consideration.[78]

(i) Performance assessment

The King III Report requires the board, its committees and individual directors to be evaluated on an annual basis.[79] The evaluations should be performed by the chairperson or an independent provider (Code 2.22.2). The nomination for reappointment of a director at the annual general meeting is not an automatic process — it should occur after the proper evaluation of the performance and attendance of the director in question (Code 2.22.5). An overview of the appraisal process, its results and action plans is required to be disclosed in the integrated report (Code 2.22.4).

(j) Remuneration

The King III Report deals with the remuneration of directors and senior executives in some detail. The remuneration packages of directors in listed public companies have been a central issue in the corporate governance debate. The King III Report recommends that companies should remunerate directors and executives fairly and responsibly.[80] Companies should disclose the remuneration of each individual director and certain senior executives in its annual remuneration report (which is included in the integrated report).[81] The Code suggests that the remuneration committee should assist the board in setting and administering remuneration policies (Code 2.25.2). It is suggested further that shareholders should approve the company's remuneration policy[82] and that they should pass a non-binding advisory vote on the company's annual remuneration policy (Code 2.27.1). Note that,

---

[76] King III Report para 145 p 48.
[77] Ibid.
[78] Ibid para 94 p 43.
[79] Principle 2.22 of the King III Report.
[80] Principle 2.25 of the King III Report.
[81] Principle 2.26 of the King III Report.
[82] Principle 2.27 of the King III Report.

in terms of the Act, shareholders are required to approve the remuneration to be paid to directors by a special resolution passed within the previous two years.[83]

Bonuses, severance and retirement benefits, and share-based and other long-term incentive arrangements for directors are dealt with in detail in the King III Report.[84]

(k) The chairperson

The King III Report requires the board of directors to elect as a chairperson someone who is an independent non-executive director.[85] It recommends that the chief executive officer of the company should not also fufil the role of the chairperson[86] as this leads to excessive concentration of power in one person. A lead independent director should be appointed in cases where an executive chairperson is appointed or where the chairperson is not independent or free of conflicts of interest (Code 2.16.3). The role of a lead independent director is to support the chairperson and the board and to provide leadership and advice to the board, without detracting from the authority of the chairperson.[87] The board should elect a chairperson on an annual basis (Code 2.16.1). The chairperson's ability to add value, and his or her performance against what is expected of their role and function, should be assessed annually (Code 2.16.6).

(l) The chief executive officer (CEO)

The board should appoint a CEO, who would serve as the chief representative of the company.[88] The collective responsibilities of management vest in the CEO, who ultimately bears responsibility for all management functions. The Report suggests that the board should delegate to management via the CEO, who in turn should delegate to those reporting to him or her.[89]

(m) The company secretary

The Report recommends that the board should be assisted by a competent, suitably qualified and experienced secretary.[90] As the gatekeeper of good governance, it is important for the secretary to maintain an arm's-length relationship with the board of directors (Code 2.21.3). The company secretary should not be a director of the company (Code 2.21.4). The secretary is required, inter alia, to provide guidance to the board on the duties of the directors and good governance, and to assist with the evaluation of the board, its committees as well as individual directors. The secretary should also assist the nominations committee in the appointment of the directors of the company (see Code 2.21.5–13).

---

[83] Section 66(9) of the Act. See further chapter 10: Governance and the Board of Directors.
[84] King III Report paras 157–79 pp 49–52.
[85] Principle 2.16 of the King III Report.
[86] Ibid.
[87] See Annex 2.1 of the King III Report.
[88] Principle 2.17 and para 56 p 37 of the King III Report.
[89] King III Report para 48 p 36.
[90] Principle 2.21 of the King III Report.

11.4.3 Audit committees

The King III Report requires the board of directors to ensure that the company has an effective and independent audit committee.[91] An independent audit committee plays a central role in corporate governance and is vital to ensure the integrity of integrated reporting and internal financial controls and to identify and manage financial risks.[92]

The Report requires listed and state-owned companies to establish an audit committee.[93] The shareholders must elect the members of the audit committee at each annual general meeting.[94] Private companies, non-profit companies and personal liability companies may voluntarily appoint an audit committee and define its composition, purpose and duties in the Memorandum of Incorporation (Code 3.1.2).[95] The audit committee should meet as often as is necessary to perform its functions, but it is recommended that it meets at least twice a year (Code 3.1.4). It should also meet with internal and external auditors at least once a year without management being present (Code 3.1.5).

The audit committee should comprise at least three members (Code 3.2.2)[96] who should be suitably skilled and experienced independent non-executive directors.[97] Section 94(4) of the Act prescribes further requirements to qualify as a member of the audit committee.[98] The chairperson of the board of directors should not be the chairperson of or a member of the audit committee (Code 3.2.3). This is because the chairperson of the board of directors has a strategic and comprehensive role to play in guiding the board and cannot simultaneously lead and participate objectively in the audit committee.[99] But he or she may attend audit

---

[91] Principle 3.1 of the King III Report.
[92] King III Report para 1 p 56.
[93] Ibid para 3 p 56.
[94] Ibid. Under s 94(2) of the Act this does not apply where a company is a subsidiary company of another company that has an audit committee and the audit committee of the holding company will perform the functions required to be performed by the audit committee on behalf of that subsidiary company.
[95] See s 94(2) read with s 34(2) of the Act.
[96] See s 94(2) of the Act.
[97] Principle 3.2 of the King III Report.
[98] Under s 94(4) of the Act, a member of an audit committee must be a director of the company who satisfies any minimum qualification requirements set out by the Minister of Trade and Industry as being necessary to ensure that the committee comprises persons with adequate relevant knowledge and experience to equip the committee to perform its functions. Furthermore, a member of the audit committee must not be: (i) involved in the day-to-day management of the company's business or have been so involved at any time during the previous financial year; (ii) a prescribed officer, or full-time employee of the company or another related or inter-related company, or have been such an officer or employee at any time during the previous three financial years; (iii) a material supplier or customer of the company, such that a reasonable and informed third party would conclude in the circumstances that the integrity, impartiality or objectivity of that director is compromised by that relationship; or (iv) related to any person who falls within any of the criteria set out in (i), (ii) or (iii) above.
[99] King III Report para 11 p 57.

committee meetings by invitation.[100] The chairperson of the audit committee should be an independent non-executive director.[101]

Some of the functions of the audit committee are to oversee the integrity of the integrated report for which the board of directors is responsible;[102] oversee the internal audit;[103] form an integral component of the company's risk management process;[104] recommend the appointment of the external auditor, and oversee the external audit process.[105] The audit committee should report to the board of directors and shareholders on how it has discharged its duties.[106] Section 94(7) of the Act sets out further duties of the audit committee.[107]

11.4.4 The governance of risk

The King III Report requires that the board of directors be responsible for the governance of risk and determine the levels of risk tolerance that the company is able to bear in the pursuit of its objectives.[108] 'Risk' is defined as the taking of risk for reward.[109] The board of directors should determine the levels of risk tolerance at least once a year. It should review these limits during periods of increased uncertainty or any adverse changes in the business environment.[110]

It is recommended that the board's responsibility for risk governance be expressed in the board charter (Code 4.1.3). In addition, the board's responsibility for risk governance should manifest in a documented risk management policy and plan (Code 4.1.5), which should be widely distributed throughout the company and reviewed by the board at least once a year (Code 4.1.7 and 4.1.8). The board should also comment in the integrated report on the effectiveness of the system and process of risk management (Code 4.1.2).

A risk committee or audit committee should assist the board in carrying out its risk responsibilities.[111] The risk committee should have at least three members and should include executive and non-executive directors (Code 4.3.2.2 and 4.3.2.3). The committee should comprise people with adequate risk management skills and experience to equip the committee to perform its functions, and may invite independent risk management experts to attend its meetings, if necessary.[112] It should convene at least twice a year (Code 4.3.2.4).

---

[100] King III Report para 11 p 57.
[101] Principle 3.3 of the King III Report.
[102] Principle 3.4 of the King III Report.
[103] Principle 3.7 of the King III Report. The audit committee should assist the board in approving the disclosure of sustainability issues in the integrated report by ensuring that the information is reliable and that no conflicts or differences arise when compared with the financial results (King III Report para 35 p 60).
[104] Principle 3.8 of the King III Report.
[105] Principle 3.9 of the King III Report.
[106] Principle 3.10 of the King III Report.
[107] See further chapter 13: The Auditor, Financial Records and Reporting.
[108] Principles 4.1 and 4.2 of the King III Report.
[109] King III Report para 11 p 74.
[110] Ibid.
[111] Principle 4.3 of the King III Report.
[112] King III Report para 20 p 75.

Regarding risk disclosure, the King III Report recommends that the board of directors should ensure that there are processes in place that enable complete, timely, relevant, accurate and accessible risk disclosure to stakeholders.[113] Undue, unexpected or unusual risks should be disclosed in the integrated report (Code 4.10.1). The board should also disclose its view on the effectiveness of the risk management process in the integrated report (Code 4.10.2).

11.4.5 The governance of information technology (IT)

The governance of IT is dealt with for the first time in the King III Report. As acknowledged by the King III Report, IT has become an integral part of doing business and is fundamental to support, sustain and grow the business.[114] The King III Report states that IT governance is not an isolated discipline, but an integral part of overall corporate governance.[115]

Information technology governance can be considered as a framework that supports effective and efficient management of IT resources to facilitate the achievement of a company's strategic objectives.[116] The IT governance framework should include the relevant structures, processes and mechanisms to enable IT to deliver value to the business and to mitigate IT risks.[117] It should focus on the governance of the information as well as the governance of technology.[118]

The King III Report requires the board of directors to be responsible for IT governance.[119] The board may appoint an IT steering committee or similar forum to assist with its governance of IT.[120] It is recommended that the chief executive officer appoints a chief information officer (CIO) to be responsible for the management of IT (Code 5.3.3). There is an increased risk to organisations that embrace IT and directors should ensure that reasonable steps have been taken to govern IT.

As part of the IT governance framework, the board of directors should ensure that an IT governance charter and policies are established and implemented (Code 5.1.2). The board should also monitor and evaluate significant IT investments and expenditure.[121] The King III Report recommends further that companies understand and manage the risks, benefits and constraints of IT[122] and suggests that IT should form an integral part of the company's risk management.[123] Companies must comply with the applicable IT laws and consider adherence to applicable IT rules, codes, standards, guidelines and leading practices.[124]

---

[113] Principle 4.10 of the King III Report.
[114] King III Report para 1 p 82.
[115] Ibid para 6 p 82.
[116] Ibid para 2 p 82.
[117] Ibid para 3 p 82.
[118] Ibid para 7 p 82.
[119] Principle 5.1 of the King III Report.
[120] King III Report para 18 p 83.
[121] Principle 5.4 of the King III Report.
[122] King III Report para 1 p 82.
[123] Principle 5.5 of the King III Report.
[124] King III Report para 33 p 85.

11.4.6 Compliance with laws, rules, codes and standards

The King III Report requires the board of directors to ensure that the company complies with all applicable and relevant laws and that it considers adherence to non-binding rules, codes and standards.[125] A compliance culture should be encouraged through leadership, establishing the appropriate structures, education and training, communication and the measurement of key performance indicators relevant to compliance.[126] The board has a duty to take the necessary steps to ensure the identification of laws, rules, codes and standards that apply to the company.[127] Details must be disclosed by the board in its integrated report on how it has discharged its responsibility to establish an effective compliance framework and processes (Code 6.1.8).

The King III Report goes so far as to require the board and each individual director to have a working understanding of the effect of the applicable laws, rules, codes and standards on the company and its business.[128] Directors should sufficiently familiarise themselves with the general content of applicable laws, rules, codes and standards to be able to adequately discharge their fiduciary duties and their duty of care, skill and diligence in the best interests of the company (Code 6.2.2).

Compliance risk, which is the risk of damage arising from non-adherence to the law and regulations, to the company's business model, objectives, reputation, going concern, stakeholder relationships or sustainability, should form an integral part of the company's risk management process.[129]

The King III Report suggests that the board delegates to management the implementation of an effective compliance framework and processes.[130] An independent, suitably skilled compliance officer may be appointed (Code 6.4.6). He or she should have access to, and interact regularly on, strategic compliance matters with the board and/or appropriate board committee and executive management (Code 6.4.7). Although the chief executive officer may appoint a compliance officer to assist in the execution of the compliance function, note that accountability to the board of directors remains with the chief executive officer.[131]

11.4.7 Internal audit

The King III Report requires the board of directors to ensure that there is an effective risk-based internal audit.[132] An internal audit should evaluate the company's governance processes, perform an objective assessment of the effectiveness of risk management and the internal control framework, systematically analyse and evaluate business processes and associated controls, and provide a source of information, as appropriate, regarding instances of fraud, corruption, unethical

---

[125] Principle 6.1 of the King III Report.
[126] King III Report para 21 p 91.
[127] Ibid para 11 p 90.
[128] Principle 6.2 of the King III Report.
[129] Principle 6.3 and King III Report para 14 p 90.
[130] Principle 6.4 of the King III Report.
[131] King III Report para 23 p 91.
[132] Principle 7.1 of the King III Report.

behaviour and irregularities (Code 7.1.2). An internal audit plays an important role in providing assurance to the board regarding the effectiveness of the system of internal controls and risk management of the company.[133]

It is suggested that an internal audit charter be formally defined and approved by the board of directors (Code 7.1.3), and that at a minimum the internal audit function should adhere to the Institute of Internal Auditors' Standards for the Professional Practice of Internal Auditing and Code of Ethics (Code 7.1.4).

The King III Report recommends further that the internal audit should provide a written assessment of the effectiveness of the company's system of internal control and risk management.[134] It is the audit committee that should be responsible for overseeing the internal audit.[135]

11.4.8 Governing stakeholder relationships

(a) Stakeholder-inclusive approach

The King III Report adheres to the 'triple context' or integrated approach, which acknowledges that companies should act with economic, social and environmental responsibility.[136] Directors should consider the economic, social and environmental factors when they manage a company. Thus the Report advocates the notion that the board of directors is responsible not merely for the company's financial bottomline, but rather for the company's performance within the triple context in which it operates ('triple bottomline').[137]

There are two main schools of thought relating to the question of in whose interests the company should be managed. The enlightened shareholder value approach holds that directors must have regard to the longer-term interests of shareholders, as opposed to the immediate term and, where appropriate, must have regard to the need to ensure productive relationships with all stakeholders. However, it is ultimately the shareholders' interests that retain primacy. In other words, directors may prioritise the interests of other stakeholders only if this would promote the success of the company for the benefit of the shareholders in general. Stakeholders are any group that could affect the company's operations or could be affected by the company's operations. This would include shareholders, institutional investors, creditors, lenders, suppliers, customers, regulators, employees, trade unions, the media, analysts, consumers, society in general, communities, auditors and potential investors. The list is not exhaustive.

The pluralist approach, on the other hand, holds the view that companies have a social responsibility to society and that shareholders are just one constituency among many. Directors must consider the interests not only of shareholders, but of all stakeholders in the company. This approach asserts that directors have a legal duty to balance the interests of shareholders and stakeholders, and must give independent value to the interests of stakeholders, whose interests are not subordi-

---
[133] King III Report para 12 p 95.
[134] Principle 7.3 of the King III Report.
[135] Principle 7.4 of the King III Report.
[136] Paragraph 18 p 22.
[137] Paragraph 16 p 22.

nate to those of shareholders. While the enlightened shareholder value approach is a profit-maximising approach, the pluralist approach is a profit-sacrificing, social responsibility approach. See further chapter 12: The Duties and the Liability of Directors on the pluralist and the enlightened shareholder value approach.

The approach adopted by the King III Report is a stakeholder-inclusive corporate governance approach. The stakeholder-inclusive approach recognises that a company has many stakeholders that could affect it in the achievement of its strategy and long-term sustained growth.[138] In terms of the stakeholder-inclusive approach, the legitimate interests and expectations of stakeholders are considered when making decisions in the best interests of the company.[139] An interest or expectation of a stakeholder is considered to be legitimate if a reasonable and informed outsider would conclude it to be valid and justifiable in the circumstances on a legal, moral or ethical basis.[140] The integration and trade-offs between various stakeholders are then made on a case-by-case basis, to serve the best interests of the company.[141] In terms of this approach, the shareholder does not have a predetermined place of precedence over other stakeholders, but the interests of the shareholder or any other stakeholder may be afforded precedence based on what is believed to serve the best interests of the company at that point.[142]

Note that under the stakeholder-inclusive approach, the legitimate interests and expectations of stakeholders are considered insofar as it would be in the best interests of the *company*, and not merely as an instrument to serve the interests of the shareholder, ie as an end rather than as a means to an end.[143] In contrast, in terms of the enlightened shareholder value approach, the legitimate interests and expectations of stakeholders have only an instrumental value and stakeholders are considered only to the extent that it would be in the interests of shareholders to do so.[144] From a corporate governance point of view, the stakeholder-inclusive approach extends the interests of a company to include stakeholders.

The King III Report thus recommends that the board of directors strives to achieve the appropriate balance between its various stakeholder groupings, in the best interests of the company.[145] The Report acknowledges that this does not mean that a company should and could always treat all stakeholders equally, because some stakeholders may be more significant to the company in particular circumstances and it is not always possible to promote the interests of all stakeholders in all corporate decisions. However, the Report emphasises that it is important that stakeholders have confidence that the board would consider their legitimate inter-

---

[138] King III Report para 6 p 100.
[139] Ibid para 4 p 100. The best interests of the company must be interpreted within the parameters of the company as a sustainable enterprise and the company as a responsible corporate citizen.
[140] Ibid para 5 p 100.
[141] King III Report, preface, p 13.
[142] Ibid.
[143] Ibid.
[144] Ibid.
[145] Paragraph 23 p 102. See the Code 8.3.1.

ests and expectations in an appropriate manner and be guided by what is in the best interests of the company.[146]

The King III Report is of the view that the board cannot unilaterally achieve successful interaction with the company's stakeholders. Stakeholders should actively support constructive engagement and the principles of good governance, take a longer-term view and not be solely focused on advancing their own interests.[147]

The Report opines that transparent and effective communication with stakeholders is essential for building and maintaining trust and confidence.[148] It emphasises that a stakeholder-inclusive approach aims to stimulate appropriate dialogue between the company and its stakeholders, which could enhance or restore stakeholder confidence, remove tensions, relieve pressure on the company's reputation and offer opportunities to align expectations, ideas and opinions on issues.[149] The Report thus recommends that companies implement processes to promote appropriate disclosure; that companies use communication channels that are accessible to its stakeholders, and that the board adopts communication guidelines that support a responsible communication programme.[150]

The King III Report notes that stakeholders' perceptions affect a company's reputation and emphasises the fact that there is a growing awareness of the importance of the company's reputation to its economic value.[151] In light of the impact that stakeholder perceptions may have on a company's reputation, the King III Report asserts that companies should realise that stakeholder interests and expectations, even if not considered warranted or legitimate, should be dealt with and cannot be ignored.[152] Accordingly, the Report recommends that the board of directors should be the ultimate custodian of the corporate reputation and stakeholder relationships and that the company's reputation and linkage with stakeholder relationships should be a regular item on the agenda of board meetings.[153] In addition, it is recommended that management should develop, for adoption by the board, a strategy and suitable policies for the management of the board's relations with all stakeholder groupings.[154]

(b) *Shareholder activism and shareholder apathy*

One implication of the right to vote being a right of property is that shareholders may choose not to exercise their right to vote at all. But if shareholders are

---

[146] Paragraph 24 p 102. The King III Report recommends that the board of directors should identify from time to time important stakeholder groupings, as well as their legitimate interests and expectations, relevant to the company's strategic objectives and long-term sustainability (see King III Report para 7 p 100). It suggests further that the board of directors should consider from time to time whether it is appropriate to publish its stakeholder policies and a list of its stakeholder groupings that it intends to deal with on a proactive basis, and the method of engagement (see King III Report paras 11–12 p 101).
[147] Paragraphs 25–6 p 102–3.
[148] Principle 8.5 of the King III Report.
[149] Paragraph 29 p 103.
[150] Paragraphs 32–4 p 103–4. See the Code 8.5.1–8.5.4.
[151] Paragraph 1 p 100.
[152] Paragraph 3 p 100.
[153] Paragraph 4 p 100. See the Code 8.1.1–8.1.3.
[154] Paragraph 10 p 101. See the Code 8.2.1–8.2.6.

passive, it undermines good levels of compliance by management. To encourage shareholder activism, an environment should be created where shareholders are not mere speculators, but owners concerned with the well-being of the company in which they hold shares, constantly checking whether the directors are practising good corporate governance.[155]

There are a number of reasons for shareholder apathy. One reason is said to be the perception among shareholders that their efforts in exercising their right to vote will not bring about any noticeable change or compliance with corporate governance principles. Adolf Berle and Gardiner Means, who documented the rise of the modern corporation in the USA, identified this problem many years ago as being attributable to the separation of ownership and control.[156] As Berle and Means note, the traditional view that the profits of a company should go to the providers of its capital originated at a time when individual businesspeople provided the capital for the enterprise and also directed the enterprise, so that profits went to a single owner who combined the functions of ownership and control of an enterprise. In many private companies the directors and the shareholders are the same persons, but in large public companies providing capital to business and controlling the business have developed into two different functions. Ownership and control are thus split — the control and management of large public companies are left in the hands of the board of directors, while ownership of the shares rests with the shareholders. The separation of ownership and control has the potential to cause a divergence between the interests of the shareholders and the managers of the company without there being any effective check on the power of the directors.

Furthermore, the wide spread of ownership of shares results in no single shareholder or group of shareholders being able to exercise effective control over the directors. As a result, shareholders tend to be passive or indifferent, which results in the directors tending to do as they please. Thus the absence of shareholder activism undermines appropriate levels of managerial compliance.[157] The relationship between management and shareholders is at the core of the corporate governance debate.

Another reason for shareholder apathy is said to be due to their lack of knowledge of their legal rights and powers.[158] Shareholders would be in a position to be actively involved if they had the knowledge to determine whether or not the directors were complying with principles of good corporate governance. If shareholders are unhappy with what the directors are doing, instead of engaging in efforts to ensure compliance with corporate governance and attempting to per-

---

[155] Conrad Rademeyer and Johan Holtzhausen 'King II, corporate governance and shareholder activism' (2003) 120 *SALJ* 767 at 768.
[156] See Adolf A Berle and Gardiner C Means *The Modern Corporation and Private Property* (1931).
[157] See further George J Stigler and Claire Friedland 'The literature of economics: The case of Berle and Means' (1983) 26 *Journal of Law and Economics* 237; Eugene F Fama and Michael C Jensen 'Separation of ownership and control' (1983) 26 *Journal of Law and Economics* 301 and William W Bratton 'Berle and Means reconsidered at the century's turn' (2001) 26 *Journal of Corporation Law* 737.
[158] Conrad Rademeyer and Johan Holtzhausen op cit n 155 at 769.

suade the directors to change their conduct or their course of action, they tend to simply sell their shares.[159] Moreover, attending shareholder meetings, particularly those of listed public companies, where shareholders are often widely dispersed throughout the country and the world, entails travel expenses and the loss of productive work hours.[160] Thus the costs of becoming more actively involved may discourage shareholders from being more actively involved in the conduct of the affairs of the company.

Institutional investors are recognised as having an essential role to play in achieving successful corporate governance in South Africa. Institutional investors have the resources, the capabilities and the expertise to properly scrutinise company management.[161] It may be possible for large institutional shareholders to control sufficient shares to overcome the separation of ownership and control in large public companies and have a direct influence on management.[162] The King III Report states that recent experience indicates that market failures in relation to governance are in part due to an absence of active institutional investors.[163] As the King II Report pointed out, the majority of shareowners in South Africa are institutional investors, and accordingly focus should be placed on the actions of institutional shareowners.[164] In line with this, the King III Report strongly recommends that institutional investors be encouraged to vote and engage with companies, or require their agents through mandates to vote and engage with the company.[165] The King Committee is of the view that a code should be drafted to specifically set out the expectations pertaining to institutional investors to ensure that companies apply the principles and recommended practices effectively.[166] The King Committee also agrees with the recommendation of the Organisation for Economic Cooperation and Development (OECD) that shareholders be allowed to consult with each other on issues concerning basic shareholder rights.[167]

The King III Report further recommends that the board of directors should encourage shareholders to attend annual general meetings and other company meetings, at which all the directors should be present.[168] The Report suggests that the board considers adopting informal processes such as direct contact with

---

[159] Derek French, Stephen W Mayson and Christopher L Ryan op cit n 56 para 15.2.6 p 427.
[160] George P Kobler 'Shareholder voting over the Internet: A proposal for increasing shareholder participation in corporate governance' (1998) 49 *Alabama LR* 673 at 675; Conrad Rademeyer and Johan Holtzhausen op cit n 155 at 770.
[161] Institutional investors are organisations that pool large sums of money and invest those sums in companies on behalf of others. They include banks, insurance companies, retirement or pension funds, hedge funds and mutual funds. Their role in the economy is to act as highly specialised investors on behalf of others.
[162] Derek French, Stephen W Mayson and Christopher L Ryan op cit n 56 para 15.2.7 p 428.
[163] King III Report, preface, at 10.
[164] Section 6, chapter 6, para 2.
[165] King III Report, preface, at 10.
[166] Ibid.
[167] But this is subject to exceptions to prevent abuse of the types that usually arise in amalgamations, schemes of arrangements, takeovers, mergers and the disposal of the greater part of the assets of a company (King III Report, preface, at 10).
[168] Paragraph 18 p 102. See the Code 8.2.4.

shareholders and utilising websites, advertising and press releases.[169] Creating a corporate website that provides for the online publication of corporate information and reports, the posting of proposals that would be considered and discussed at meetings, and permitting shareholders to post messages and responses to information would also improve the information flow and communication among shareholders and between shareholders and management.[170] This would encourage shareholder activism and increase management's responsiveness to shareholder issues.[171]

There are various provisions in the Act that encourage shareholder activism. There is now an emphasis on trying to ensure that shareholders attend meetings, which have been generally poorly attended, so that such meetings serve as an effective counterbalance to the board of directors. For instance, the Act provides that the quorum at a shareholders' meeting is 25 per cent of all the voting rights that are entitled to be exercised in respect of a matter to be decided at that meeting.[172] Under the Companies Act 61 of 1973 the quorum was three members entitled to vote in the case of a public company and two members entitled to vote in the case of a private company.[173] The increased quorum requirement will ensure that more shareholders attend shareholders' meetings because it would encourage companies to actively pursue and convince shareholders to attend shareholders' meetings or to provide proxies so that the quorum requirements are fulfilled.

The use of IT not only encourages shareholder activism, but also reduces the costs that inhibit shareholder activism. For instance, s 63(2) of the Act permits meetings to be held electronically and for shareholders to participate via electronic communication in a shareholders' meeting. This would encourage shareholder activism, because it saves on travelling time and the expense of attending a shareholders' meeting in person, and facilitates participation and voting at meetings. It also permits management to receive more information on shareholder concerns because more shareholders would be able to participate in the meeting.[174] In addition, permitting proxy forms to be submitted electronically[175] results in proxies being used more often and more effectively and would certainly go some way towards promoting shareholder activism.

(c) Dispute resolution

Alternative dispute resolution (ADR) has become a worldwide trend in resolving disputes. The King III Report has recognised that ADR is a vital element of good corporate governance. As the Report points out, ADR has been a most effective and efficient methodology to address the costly and time-consuming features associated with more formal litigation.[176] The ADR procedures take into account

---

[169] Paragraph 19 p 102. See the Code 8.2.5.
[170] See George P Kobler op cit n 160 at 697.
[171] Ibid.
[172] Section 64(1).
[173] Section 190 of the Companies Act 61 of 1973.
[174] George P Kobler op cit n 160 at 699.
[175] See s 58 of the Act read with s 6(11).
[176] Paragraph 39 p 104.

the needs of both parties and strive to achieve flexible solutions that may help to preserve relationships. Alternative dispute resolution processes may thus be used as a tool to manage and preserve stakeholder relationships and to resolve disputes quickly and inexpensively.

The King III Report requires the board of directors to ensure that disputes are resolved as effectively, efficiently and expeditiously as possible.[177] The successful resolution of disputes entails choosing a dispute resolution method that best serves the interests of the company. Consideration must be given to the preservation of business relationships, and cost-dispute resolution in particular must be cost effective and must not be a drain on the finances and resources of the company.[178]

It is suggested that the board of directors should adopt formal dispute resolution processes for internal disputes (disputes within a company) and external disputes (disputes between the company and outside entities or individuals) (Code 8.6.1) and that the board should select appropriate individuals to represent the company in alternative dispute resolution processes (Code 8.6.2). Internal disputes may be addressed by recourse to the provisions of the Act and by ensuring that internal dispute resolution systems are in place and function effectively.[179] External disputes may be referred to arbitration or to a court, but these may not always be the most effective means of resolving external disputes.[180]

The King III Report suggests that mediation may be a more appropriate channel to resolve disputes where interests of the disputing parties need to be addressed and where commercial relationships need to be preserved and even enhanced.[181] The Report defines 'mediation' as 'a process where parties in dispute involve the services of an acceptable, impartial and neutral third party to assist them in negotiating a resolution to their dispute, by way of a settlement agreement'.[182] A mediator does not have any independent authority and does not render a decision; all decision-making powers in regard to the dispute remain with the parties.[183] Conciliation, on the other hand, is also a structured negotiation process involving the services of an impartial third party, but in addition to playing the role of a mediator, a conciliator makes a formal recommendation to the parties as to how the dispute can be resolved.[184]

Some of the factors that should be taken into account in selecting an appropriate dispute resolution process, as recommended by the King III Report, are:[185]

- *The time available to resolve the dispute*

Where there is limited time available to resolve a dispute, ADR methods, particularly mediation, may be appropriate because they could be concluded within a

---

[177] Principle 8.6 of the King III Report.
[178] King III Report para 38 p 104.
[179] Ibid para 42 p 104.
[180] Ibid para 43 p 105.
[181] Ibid.
[182] Ibid para 50 p 105.
[183] Ibid.
[184] Ibid para 51 p 105.
[185] Ibid para 53 p 105–6.

limited period of time (sometimes even a day), whereas in formal proceedings, particularly court proceedings, the procedure often lasts for a few years.

- *Principle and precedent*

Where the issue in dispute involves a matter of principle and where the company wishes to obtain a resolution that will be binding in relation to similar disputes in the future (ie set a precedent), court proceedings, rather than ADR, may be a better method to resolve the dispute.

- *Business relationships*

Where relationships and especially continuing business relationships are an issue, mediation or conciliation may be preferable to litigation, as these processes are designed to produce a solution that will be satisfactory to both parties.

- *Expert recommendation*

Where the parties require an expert to assist them to devise a solution to their dispute, a recommendation from an expert in the context of conciliation proceedings would be appropriate.

- *Confidentiality*

Alternative dispute resolution processes may be conducted privately, thus ensuring that the parties' dispute remains confidential, should they desire such confidentiality.

- *Rights and interests*

Mediation and conciliation, unlike court proceedings, would allow the respective needs and interests, both current and future, of both parties to be considered in finding a settlement for their dispute. Thus, where forward-looking solutions are required for a particular dispute and where the dispute involves a continuing relationship between the parties, mediation and conciliation would be preferable to an adjudicative method of dispute resolution.

In line with the strong modern trend of attempting to resolve disputes by means of alternative dispute resolution procedures as opposed to court procedures, the Act has established a Companies Tribunal to assist in dispute resolution processes. One of the functions of the Companies Tribunal is to serve as a forum for voluntary alternative dispute resolution through mediation, conciliation or arbitration in matters arising under the Act.[186] The Companies Tribunal is an independent body that has jurisdiction throughout South Africa.[187] The matters referred to the Companies Tribunal are heard by a panel of members and the decision of the majority of members of the Tribunal is regarded as the decision of the Tribunal.[188]

---

[186] See s 156(*a*), s 166 and s 195(1)(*b*) of the Act. Other functions of the Companies Tribunal are to adjudicate in relation to any application made to it in terms of the Act (s 195(1)(*a*)) and to perform any other functions assigned to it by the Act or any other Act enforced by the Companies and Intellectual Property Commission (s 195(1)(*c*)).
[187] Section 193(1) of the Act.
[188] Section 195(6) of the Act.

The decision of a panel on a matter referred to it must be in writing and must include reasons for the decision.[189]

11.4.9 Integrated reporting and disclosure

The board of directors should ensure the integrity of the company's integrated report.[190] Integrated reporting means a holistic and integrated representation of the company's performance in terms of both its finances and its sustainability.[191] The integrated report should be prepared every year, and should convey adequate information regarding the company's financial and sustainability performance (Code 9.1.3 and 9.1.4). It should also focus on substance over form (Code 9.1.5).

Sustainability reporting and disclosure should be integrated with the company's financial reporting.[192] The annual financial statements should be included in the integrated report, and the board should include a commentary on the company's financial results. This commentary should include information to enable a stakeholder to make an informed assessment of the company's economic value.[193] The board should ensure that the positive and negative impacts of the company's operations and plans to improve the positives and eradicate or ameliorate the negatives in the financial year ahead are conveyed in the integrated report (Code 9.2.4).

The King III Report emphasises that companies should recognise that the principle of transparency in reporting sustainability information is a critical element of effective reporting.[194] The central consideration is whether the information provided has allowed stakeholders to understand the key issues affecting the company and the effect the company's operation has had on the economic, social and environmental well-being of the community, both positive and negative.[195]

Sustainability reporting and disclosure should be independently assured.[196] The general oversight and reporting of sustainability should be delegated by the board of directors to the audit committee, which should assist the board by reviewing the integrated report to ensure that the information contained therein is reliable and that it does not contradict the financial aspects of the integrated report (Code 9.3.1 and 9.3.2).[197]

11.5 CONCLUSION

There is no doubt that corporate governance is a key element in improving economic efficiency and growth as well as enhancing investor confidence. The King III Report and the Code provide useful guidance to directors on how to direct and control the business of the company and make decisions on behalf of the

---

[189] Section 195(5) of the Act. See further chapter 17: Enforcement and Regulatory Agencies, on the role and function of the Companies Tribunal in voluntary resolution of disputes under the Act.
[190] Principle 9.1 of the King III Report.
[191] King III Report para 1 p 108.
[192] Principle 9.2 of the King III Report.
[193] King III Report paras 8–9 p 109.
[194] Paragraph 13 p 109.
[195] Ibid.
[196] Principle 9.3 of the King III Report.
[197] See further chapter 13: The Auditor, Financial Records and Reporting.

company. As discussed, the purpose of the Act (as embodied in s 7(b)) of encouraging transparency and high standards of corporate governance as a means of promoting the development of the South African economy, would encourage an interaction between the King III Report and the Act, which complement each other and ought to be read and applied together.

CHAPTER 12

THE DUTIES AND THE LIABILITY OF DIRECTORS

Farouk HI Cassim

12.1 INTRODUCTION 461
    12.1.1 General 461
    12.1.2 The partial codification of directors' duties 461
12.2 THE FIDUCIARY DUTIES OF COMPANY DIRECTORS: GENERAL 463
    12.2.1 Who owes fiduciary duties to the company? 463
    12.2.2 Who is a fiduciary? 465
    12.2.3 To whom do the directors owe their fiduciary duties? 467
    12.2.4 The duty to act in the best interests of the company in terms of s 76(3)(b) of the Act 467
    12.2.5 The pluralist and the enlightened shareholder value approach. 469
        (a) The King Code of Governance for South Africa 2009... 473
        (b) Section 72(4): The social and ethics committee 474
        (c) The functions of the social and ethics committee 474
12.3 THE FIDUCIARY DUTIES OF DIRECTORS AND THE STANDARDS OF DIRECTORS' CONDUCT 475
    12.3.1 The duty to act in good faith and in the best interests of the company 475
    12.3.2 Proper purpose 477
        (a) General 477
        (b) Section 38 of the Act and proper purpose 479
    12.3.3 The duty to exercise an independent judgment 480
    12.3.4 The duty to act within their powers 483
12.4 CONFLICT OF INTEREST 485
    12.4.1 The common law 485
        (a) The no-profit rule 487
        (b) The corporate opportunity rule 489
        (c) Illustrative cases on the corporate opportunity rule 491
            (i) *Cook v Deeks* 491
            (ii) *Robinson v Randfontein Estates Gold Mining Co Ltd* 492
            (iii) *Industrial Development Consultants Ltd v Cooley* 492
            (iv) *Canadian Aero Services Ltd v O'Malley* 493
            (v) *Bhullar v Bhullar* 494

		(vi) *Da Silva v CH Chemicals (Pty) Ltd*	495
	(d)	Summary	497
	(e)	The post-resignation duties of directors	497
12.4.2	The Act and the duty to avoid a conflict of interest		500
	(a)	Section 76(2)(a): The duty to avoid a conflict of interest	500
	(b)	Section 76(2)(b): The duty to communicate information to the company	503
12.5	DUTY OF CARE, SKILL AND DILIGENCE (s 76(3)(c))		504
12.5.1	The common law prior to the Act		504
12.5.2	Section 76(3)(c) of the Act and the duty of care and skill		508
12.5.3	Delegation		510
	(a)	Common-law principles	510
	(b)	Section 76(4) and (5) of the Act	511
12.5.4	The business judgment rule (a safe harbour from liability for directors) (s 76(4))		513
12.6	THE DISCLOSURE OF THE DIRECTOR'S PERSONAL FINANCIAL INTERESTS (SECTION 75)		515
12.6.1	Introduction		515
12.6.2	Section 75(5): Proposed transactions		516
	(a)	What must be disclosed	517
	(b)	Disclose and recuse	519
12.6.3	Section 75(6): Declaration of an interest in existing contracts		519
12.6.4	General notice in advance		520
12.6.5	Disclosure to whom?		520
12.6.6	Where no declaration of interests is necessary		520
12.6.7	Failure to comply with s 75		521
12.7	INDEMNIFICATION AND DIRECTORS' AND OFFICERS' INSURANCE		521
12.7.1	Introduction		521
12.7.2	Section 78(1) to (8): Exemptions, indemnities and insurance		522
12.7.3	Exemption from duty or liability		523
12.7.4	Indemnification		523
	(a)	When an indemnity is prohibited (s 78(6))	523
	(b)	When an indemnity is permissible (s 78(5))	524
	(c)	Advances and indemnities to defend legal proceedings (s 78(4))	524
12.7.5	Payment of fines and penalties		525
12.7.6	Directors' and officers' liability insurance		525
12.7.7	Restitution		526
12.8	RATIFICATION, CONDONATION AND RELIEF		526
12.8.1	Relief by the court		526
12.8.2	Ratification by the shareholders		528
12.9	THE LIABILITY OF DIRECTORS AND PRESCRIBED OFFICERS		530
12.9.1	Breach of fiduciary duty (s 77(2)(a))		531

12.9.2   Breach of the duty of care and skill or other provisions 531
12.9.3   Liability under section 77(3)............................ 532
12.10 FRAUDULENT, RECKLESS AND INSOLVENT TRADING
      (SECTION 22)... 534
   12.10.1 Introduction 534
   12.10.2 Fraudulent or reckless trading........................ 535
   12.10.3 Insolvent trading 538
            (a)   General 538
            (b)   The requirements of s 22(1)*(b)* 539
   12.10.4 The other requirements of s 22(1)*(a)* and *(b)* 541

12.1   INTRODUCTION

12.1.1   General

The common-law duties of directors are the fiduciary duties of good faith, honesty and loyalty. In addition, directors have the duty to exercise reasonable care and skill, which is not a fiduciary duty. The fiduciary duties of directors are of fundamental importance to any developed corporate law system. Under the Companies Act, the fiduciary duties of directors are mandatory, prescriptive and unalterable, and apply to all companies. Their object is to raise the standards of corporate and directorial behaviour. A further reason for imposing these duties on directors is deterrence.[1] The fiduciary duties are protective of the company and its shareholders and indeed even of the public interest.

The fiduciary duties of directors are now of even greater importance, because for the first time in our corporate law history the Companies Act confers on the board of directors a new statutory power and duty to manage the business of the company. In this regard, see s 66(1)) of the Companies Act 71 of 2008 (hereafter 'the Act'). Since this original power is derived from statute instead of the constitution of the company, it is subject to shareholder control to a much lesser extent than has hitherto been the case.

In the common-law jurisdictions, including South Africa, the fiduciary duties of directors have since the 18th and 19th centuries been judicially created and developed, mainly in English law, on a case-by-case basis. Their exact contours and limits are still uncertain. In short, the fiduciary duties are never static — they are dynamic and are still evolving. One hopes that nothing in the new Act will freeze or stifle judicial development of the fiduciary duties. It is essential for the courts to be given room to develop these fiduciary duties gradually so that the duties are suitably adapted to meet constantly changing circumstances.

12.1.2   The partial codification of directors' duties

One very significant innovation of the Act is that, for the first time in our corporate law regime, the fiduciary duties of directors (including senior employees or top-level management and prescribed officers) and the duty to exercise reasonable

---

[1] W Bishop and DD Prentice 'Some legal and economic aspects of fiduciary remuneration' (1983) 46 *MLR* 289.

care and skill have been partially codified[2] or set out in a statute. The object of the partial codification of directors' duties is to make the law clearer and more accessible, particularly for directors. The advantages and disadvantages of codification, namely certainty and accessibility on the one hand, against flexibility on the other hand, have long been debated. The advantages of codification are intended to apply in full force to the partial codification of directors' duties. In the United Kingdom, in a survey done by the UK Institute of Directors, it was found that many directors do not even know what their fiduciary duties are and to whom these duties are owed.[3] A further reason for legislative interference in the fiduciary duties of directors as developed by the courts is that it presents an opportunity for the legislature to rectify and resolve some of the conflicting judicial decisions and dicta on these fiduciary duties. The common-law principles relating to the directors' fiduciary duties are preserved, with the result that there is a great deal of overlap between the two sources of these duties. There is now in our law an uneasy and uncertain combination of statutory law and still evolving judicial precedent. The 'statutory statement of directors' duties' (as it is called in the UK) adopts a 'one size fits all' approach.

The partial codification of directors' duties is not by any means an original idea; it simply follows the trend set in the UK and other common-law jurisdictions such as Australia, New Zealand, Ghana, Malaysia and Singapore, and brings South African company law in line with this approach.

As stated above, the justification for the statutory statement of directors' conduct and for interfering in a well-developed body of case law on the fiduciary duties is that it will provide much needed clarification of and accessibility to these duties, so that the directors of a company know what is expected of them. Directors, it is said, need no longer search in the law reports for the complex and inaccessible decisions of the courts relating to their fiduciary duties. However, a statement of this nature reflects merely the theory underlying the statutory standard of directors' conduct; the reality is quite different. It is doubtful whether the partial codification of directors' duties will make our law more certain. As set out in ss 75 and 76 of the Act, these duties are couched in terms that are not free from ambiguity. Furthermore, there is no attempt to resolve the existing defects in the law and the current conflicting case law, particularly on corporate opportunities and the duty of a nominee director to exercise an independent judgment in the best interests of the company. The failure to resolve existing defects and conflicts in the law could be attributed to the intention of the legislature that the statutory statement of directors' duties be declaratory of the common law. If so, it may perhaps have gone too far in the wrong direction in merely restating the law. Section 76 is, moreover, not properly aligned with the common law.

As the Act stands, a golden opportunity to resolve some of the present uncertainty and conflicting judicial decisions has been lost. The statutory statement of directors' conduct cannot be properly understood without knowledge of the common law. It regrettably provides arcane rather than clear and simple guidelines that

---

[2] It is not an exhaustive, comprehensive or fully self-contained code of fiduciary duties.
[3] *Modernising Company Law* (2002) CM 5553–1, para 3.2 at 26.

are easily intelligible and informative to company directors and other users of company law (as was intended). More than before, it is now going to be difficult to get the legal profession to agree not only on what the directors' fiduciary duties are, but also on the exact contours of these duties.

12.2 THE FIDUCIARY DUTIES OF COMPANY DIRECTORS: GENERAL

In examining the fiduciary duties of directors, it is important to bear in mind that these duties are largely derived from English law. This has been stated by the courts on many occasions. For instance, in *Fisheries Development Corporation of SA Ltd v Jorgensen; Fisheries Development Corporation of SA Ltd v AWJ Investments (Pty) Ltd*[4] the court stated: 'The essential principles of this branch of our company law are however the same as those in English law and the English law cases provide a valuable guide'. Likewise, in *Le Roux Hotel Management (Pty) Ltd v E Rand (Pty) Ltd (FBC Fidelity Bank Ltd (Under Curatorship), Intervening)*[5] the court stated: 'This progressive approach in South African company law was not based on any precedent in the English Companies Act, the usual source of inspiration for matters relating to companies.' Historically there have been, and to a lesser extent now continue to be, strong links between South African corporate law and English law.

12.2.1 Who owes fiduciary duties to the company?

The directors of a company are fiduciaries who owe fiduciary duties to the company of which they are directors. There are of course many types of directors. Directors may be said to be the persons responsible for the management of the affairs of a company. But the legal definition of a 'director' of a company differs vastly from this description of a director. Section 1 of the Act contains an open-ended, non-exhaustive definition of a director, which is both tautologous and unhelpful.[6]

Section 1 states that a '"director" means a member of the board of a company, as contemplated in s 66, or an alternate director and includes any person occupying the position of director or alternate director, by whatever name designated'. This is an inadequate definition, because all it does is provide that certain persons may be regarded as directors, even though designated or described by a different name.

The definition of a director in s 1 of the Act is wide enough to include most types of directors, such as executive and non-executive directors, *de facto* and *de jure* directors, alternate directors, nominee directors, *ex officio* directors and also shadow directors. A shadow director would for instance be someone who, although not formally appointed as a director, is a retired director or a person who has resigned as director but who is still able to give instructions (from the shadows) to the board or to puppet directors appointed by him or her to carry out

---

[4] 1980 (4) SA 156 (W) 165.
[5] 2001 (2) SA 727 (C) para 37 at 738.
[6] See chapter 10: Governance and the Board of Directors for a detailed discussion.

his or her instructions relating to the management of the affairs of the company.[7] The definition of a director may be even wider than intended, because if the board is accustomed to act in accordance with the advice and instructions of a professional person given his or her professional capacity, that person may well be regarded as 'occupying the position of director ...'. This possibility arises because s 1 of the Act fails to adopt s 1(2) of the Companies Act 61 of 1973 (hereafter 'the 1973 Act') which explicitly excludes from the definition of a director a person who gives advice or instructions to the board in a professional capacity. The UK Companies Act 2006 similarly excludes such professional persons from the definition of a director.[8]

Thus all types of directors (mentioned above) are subject to the fiduciary duties of a director. The Act states that *ex officio* directors have all the duties of and are subject to all the liabilities of any other director of the company, irrespective of the company's Memorandum of Incorporation.[9] An *ex officio* director means a person who holds office as a director of the company as a result of holding some other office, title, designation or similar status specified in the company's Memorandum of Incorporation. An alternate director also falls within the definition of a director in s 1 of the Act and his or her duties are also no different from those of any other director.[10] An alternate director is defined (in s 1 of the Act) as a person elected or appointed to serve, as the occasion requires, as a member of the board of a company in substitution for a particular elected or appointed director. Thus an alternate director may serve a useful purpose as a substitute director when a director is unable to attend board meetings, and as such is subject to the same duties that a director owes to his or her company.[11] A person may not serve as an *ex officio* director or an alternate director if that person is disqualified or ineligible to hold office as a director in terms of s 69.[12]

Likewise, no distinction is drawn between executive and non-executive directors.[13] In *Howard v Herrigel* the court stated '[a]t common law, once a person accepts an appointment as a director, he becomes a fiduciary in relation to the company and is obliged to display the utmost good faith towards the company and in his dealings on its behalf'.[14] Executive and non-executive directors have the same fiduciary duties in law.[15]

The fiduciary and other statutory duties of a director are not, however, limited to directors only. The duties extend to senior employees or a senior manager of a

---

[7] *S v Shaban* 1965 (4) SA 646 (W). A shadow director is a person occupying the position of director within the scope and ambit of the definition of a director in s 1 of the Act.

[8] See s 251(2) of the UK Companies Act 2006, which states that a person is not to be regarded as a shadow director by reason only that the directors act on advice given by him in a professional capacity.

[9] Section 66(4)(*a*)(ii) read with s 66(5)(*b*)(ii).

[10] See ss 75(1), 76(1), 77(1), which apply to all directors, including alternate directors.

[11] MS Blackman et al *Commentary on the Companies Act* vol 2 (2002) at 8–12.

[12] Section 66(5)(*a*) and s 66(6).

[13] *Howard v Herrigel* 1991 (2) SA 660 (A) 678A.

[14] At 678.

[15] The duty of care and skill expected of executive and non-executive directors does, however, differ (see below).

The Duties and the Liability of Directors

division of the company.[16] The Act further extends these statutory duties to prescribed officers[17] and members of an audit committee or a board committee, even if the prescribed officers or members of these committees are not members of the company's board of directors (s 76(1)*(a)* and *(b)*)[18] and even if they do not have the right to vote at board level. The underlying rationale of this approach is that board committees and particularly the audit committee play an increasingly important role in the functioning of corporate boards. The fiduciary and the new statutory duties of directors should therefore apply also to members of board committees and the audit committee. But the consequence of this approach is that persons who may be non-directors have onerous duties thrust on them even though they do not have decision-making powers. The adage is 'no power without responsibility' and 'with greater power goes greater responsibility', but here it is a case of greater responsibility without greater power.

12.2.2 Who is a fiduciary?

The following question inevitably arises: who is a fiduciary and what are the criteria that render a person a fiduciary? Fiduciaries may include trustees, agents, partners, directors and attorneys. The content of the duty varies, depending on the nature of the relationship between the parties. There is no magic in the term 'fiduciary duty';[19] nor is there a closed list of fiduciary relationships,[20] or a comprehensive definition of who a fiduciary is. In *English v Dedham Vale Properties Ltd*[21] Slade J ruled that the classes of fiduciary relationships are never closed. Fiduciaries are not limited to a fixed number of defined relationships.

The hallmark of a fiduciary relationship is a relationship of trust and confidence. A fiduciary can be said to be someone who acts on behalf of and in the interests of another person.[22] A fiduciary would, for instance, control the assets of another or exercise power to act on behalf of another. In *Bristol and West Building Society v Mothew*[23] the court stated that a fiduciary is someone who undertakes to act for or on behalf of another in circumstances that give rise to a relationship of trust and confidence between the parties.

Typically, in fiduciary relationships, one party is vulnerable or is at the mercy of another party's discretion. In *Hospital Products Limited v United States Surgical*

---

[16] Laskin J in *Canadian Aero Service Ltd v O'Malley* (1973) 40 DLR (3d) 371 (SCC) 381; *Phillips v Fieldstone Africa (Pty) Ltd* 2004 (3) SA 465 (SCA); *Volvo (Southern Africa) (Pty) Ltd v Yssel* 2009 (6) SA 531 (SCA).

[17] See chapter 10: Governance and the Board of Directors for a discussion of who the prescribed officers are. Section 1 defines prescribed officers as the holders of an office within a company that has been designated by the Minister in terms of s 66(11) (*sic*). The reference should be to s 66(10) — a cross-reference error that is to be rectified by cl 2(1)*(x)* of the Companies Amendment Bill, 2010.

[18] See also s 75(1) and s 77(1).

[19] *Phillips v Fieldstone Africa (Pty) Ltd* 2004 (3) SA 465 (SCA) 477H.

[20] *Volvo (Southern Africa) (Pty) Ltd v Yssel* 2009 (6) SA 531 (SCA).

[21] [1978] WLR 93 (ChD) 110.

[22] See Blackman et al op cit n 11 at 8–31.

[23] [1998] Ch 1 at 18.

Corporation[24] the court stated that a fiduciary relationship may arise because on the facts a person has been appointed to act for the benefit of another whose appointment carries powers that could be exercised to the detriment of another. A fiduciary has a special opportunity to exercise power or discretion to the detriment of another, who is vulnerable to abuse by the fiduciary. The court further stated that the critical feature of fiduciary relationships is that the fiduciary undertakes to act for or on behalf of or in the interests of another, in the exercise of a power or discretion that will affect the interests of that other person. A contractual relationship is not an indispensable feature of a fiduciary relationship.[25]

To sum up: there appear to be three elements to a fiduciary relationship, namely: *(a)* a fiduciary has some discretion or power, *(b)* a fiduciary is able to unilaterally exercise that power or discretion so as to affect the beneficiary's legal or practical interests, and *(c)* the beneficiary is vulnerable to or at the mercy of the fiduciary.[26]

The fiduciary relationship requires the fiduciary to act in good faith and in the interests of the beneficiary. A number of duties apply to the fiduciary relationship and they are aimed at ensuring that a fiduciary does not abuse the fiduciary relationship of trust and confidence.[27]

The general principle is clear: a director is a fiduciary and as such his or her paramount and overarching duty is to act in good faith and for the benefit of his or her company. This basic duty of loyalty is unbending, inflexible and '. . . must be applied inexorably by [the] court'[28] This is designed to ensure that a fiduciary does not abuse his or her position of trust. For this reason a lax attitude towards the observance of fiduciary duties must be avoided. The courts must continue to insist on a strict and scrupulous observance of fiduciary duties.

Fiduciary duties were developed in English law on the analogy of trust law and the similarities with trustees because a director, like a trustee, manages the business of another person, ie the company, and confronts a similar conflict of interest and duty. Despite the similarities, a director is not a trustee. Unlike English law, a trustee in South African trust law is the legal owner of trust property because a trust does not enjoy separate legal personality. In contrast, a director is not the legal owner of property or other assets belonging to the company.[29] Furthermore, unlike a trustee who is expected to cautiously preserve the trust assets, a director is normally expected to take commercial risks on behalf of the company. In *Daniels t/as Deloitte Haskins & Sells v AWA Ltd*[30] the court remarked that 'while the duty of a trustee is to exercise a degree of restraint and conservatism in investment judgments, the duty of a director may be to display entrepreneurial flair and accept commercial risks to produce a sufficient return on the

---

[24] (1984) 156 CLR 41 at 96–7 (HC of A), referred to with approval in *Volvo (Southern Africa (Pty) Ltd v Yssel* 2009 (6) SA 531 (SCA).
[25] *Volvo v Yssel* (supra).
[26] *Frame v Smith* (1987) 42 DLR (4th) 81 at 98.
[27] Blackman et al op cit n 11 at 8–34.
[28] *Parker v McKenna* (1874) LR 10 Ch 96 at 124–5.
[29] *Dadoo Ltd v Krugersdorp Municipal Council* 1920 AD 530. 'A director is in no sense a trustee' Vaughan Williams J in *Re Kingston Cotton Mill CO (No 2)* [1896] 1 Ch 331 at 345, [1896] 2 Ch 279 (CA).
[30] (1995) 37 NSWLR 438 at 494.

capital invested'. The most that may be said is that a director has trustee-like duties. The relationship between a director and a company is best seen as being *sui generis*. It is simply a distinct and independent category of fiduciary relationship.[31]

12.2.3 To whom do the directors owe their fiduciary duties?

'To say that a man is a fiduciary only begins analysis; it gives direction to further inquiry. To whom is he a fiduciary? What obligations does he owe as a fiduciary? In what respect has he failed to discharge his obligations?'[32]

The fundamental and paramount or overarching duty of company directors is to act *bona fide* in what they consider — not what the court may consider — to be in the interests of the company as a whole, and not for a collateral purpose.[33] Traditionally, directors have been required to manage the business of the company in the interests of its shareholders and to maximise profits for the benefit of shareholders. The courts have always insisted that directors must exercise their powers *bona fide* in what they believe — and not what a court may consider — to be in the best interests of the company.

The basic goal of the directors of a company is the success of the company and the collective best interests of the shareholders of the company. In *Cohen v Segal*[34] the court stated: 'They [ie the directors] (my insertion) occupy a fiduciary position towards the company and must exercise their powers *bona fide* solely for the benefit of a company as a whole and not for an ulterior motive'. Directors must consider both the short-term and the long-term consequences of their actions.

The question arises whether the position remains the same under the new Act. This is considered in 12.2.4 and 12.2.5 below.

12.2.4 The duty to act in the best interests of the company in terms of s 76(3)*(b)* of the Act

The common-law principle that a director must act in the best interests of the company is codified in s 76(3)*(b)* of the new Act, which states that a director of a company, when acting in that capacity, must exercise the powers and perform the functions of director '. . . in the best interests of the company'. The wording of this provision removes any doubt that the directors of a company owe their duty to the company and the company alone. The problematic part of this otherwise lucid provision is the meaning of the word 'company'.

Since the word 'company' is not defined for the purposes of s 76(3)*(b)*,[35] it consequently follows that the common-law meaning attributed to this word must apply to s 76(3)*(b)*. At common law, there is copious authority for the view that the word 'company' in this context refers not to the legal entity itself, but rather to

---

[31] *Robinson v Randfontein Estates Gold Mining Co Ltd* 1921 AD 168; *Du Plessis NO v Phelps* 1995 (4) SA 165 (C).
[32] *Per* Frankfurter J in *SEC v Chenery Corporation* 318 US 80 (1943) at 85–6.
[33] *Re Smith & Fawcett Ltd* [1942] Ch 304 at 306 (CA).
[34] 1970 (3) SA 702 (W) 706.
[35] The word 'company' is defined in s 1 of the Act as 'a juristic person incorporated in terms of the Act'. This definition is of little relevance in the particular context of s 76(3)*(b)*.

the interests of the collective body of present and future shareholders. 'A requirement to benefit an artificial entity as an end in itself, would be irrational and futile, since a non-real entity is incapable of experiencing well-being'.[36] A company as an artificial legal entity cannot have any interests. In *Greenhalgh v Arderne Cinemas Ltd*[37] the court stated that the phrase 'company as a whole' does not mean the commercial entity as distinct from the shareholders. It means the shareholders or incorporators as a general body.[38]

It is thus trite law that the directors owe their duty to the 'company' as a whole, by which is meant the collective body of shareholders including future shareholders.[39] The word 'company' in this context is merely a synonym for the shareholders of the company. In appropriate circumstances, the directors are fully entitled to balance short-term considerations affecting the present shareholders against the long-term considerations that affect future shareholders. Another way of expressing the same principle is that directors must act for the benefit of existing shareholders, having regard to their future interests as well as their existing interests.[40] As stated above, the interests of the 'company' are not confined simply to the present body of shareholders — it includes the interests of future shareholders. The reference to future shareholders emphasises the need for directors to take into account long-term considerations rather than only committing themselves to short-term considerations.[41] Directors are consequently not obliged to maximise profits to satisfy short-term demands for dividends at the expense of growth and profitability over a longer period. They have a discretion concerning the time-scale over which existing shareholders may benefit.[42]

It is for the directors to decide what is in the best interests of shareholders, but in so doing they must act fairly between the shareholders. Thus in *Parke v Daily News Ltd*[43] it was held that directors could not make voluntary redundancy payments to employees of a company because this was not in the short- or long-term interests of the company, which was being wound up.[44] The clear implication of the common-law principle that directors owe their fiduciary duties to the company, ie the collective body of shareholders, whether present or future shareholders, is that they do not owe their fiduciary duties to individual shareholders;[45] or to creditors of the company while the company is a going concern;[46]

---

[36] JE Parkinson *Corporate power and responsibility: Issues in the theory of company law* (Oxford 1993) at 76–77.
[37] [1951] Ch 286 at 291; [1950] 2 All ER 1120 at 1126E.
[38] See also *Brady v Brady* [1988] BCLC 20 (CA); and *Gaiman v National Association for Mental Health* [1970] 2 All ER 362.
[39] *Miller v Bain Sub Nom Pantone 485 Ltd* [2002] BCLC 266 (ChD).
[40] RP Austin and IM Ramsay *Ford's Principles of Corporations Law* 13 ed (2007) para 8.095 at 357.
[41] LCB Gower 'Corporate control: The battle for the Berkeley' (1954–55) 668 *Harv LR* 1176 at 1184.
[42] See Parkinson op cit n 36 at 81.
[43] [1962] 2 All ER 929 (ChD).
[44] See also *Hutton v West Cork Railway Co* (1883) 23 ChD 654 (CA); *Parke v Daily News Ltd* was reversed in England by s 719 and s 309 of the Companies Act 1985, but ironically its *ratio* still applies to South African law.
[45] *Percival v Wright* [1902] 2 Ch 421 (ChD).

or even to employees of the company.[47] All these principles continue to apply to our corporate law regime as the Act has effected no change in the law in this respect (see further below).

At common law, a director of a subsidiary company did not owe any fiduciary duty to its parent or holding company or to the group of companies of which the subsidiary formed a part.[48] As discussed below, s 76(2) may have modified this common-law principle.

A further crucial implication of the principle that directors owe their fiduciary duties to the 'company' is that, since the duties are owed to the company only, the company alone is entitled to enforce these duties against errant directors. Hence the importance of the new derivative action instituted in terms of s 165 on behalf of the company by a shareholder or other director of the company. Where the company incurs a loss as a result of a director's breach of fiduciary duty, only the company may sue in respect of that loss. A shareholder cannot claim from the errant director for a loss he or she may have incurred as a result of a fall in the value of his or her shares caused by the director's breach of fiduciary duty.[49]

In *Prudential Assurance Co Ltd v Newman Industries Ltd (No 2)*[50] Prudential, an institutional investor, sued two directors of Newman Industries Ltd who, in breach of their fiduciary duty to the company, had issued a circular that had misled the shareholders into approving a purchase above market value by Newman Industries Ltd of the assets of another company in which certain directors of Newman Industries Ltd had an interest. It was held that the shareholders could not personally recover damages from the directors because it was not them, but the company in which they had held the shares, that had suffered the damage. The shareholders' loss was merely a reflection of the loss suffered by the company: the loss suffered by the shareholders was through the company as a result of a fall in the value of their shares. The shares themselves were not directly affected by the wrongdoing, as the shareholders still had their shares. The shareholders should have sued derivatively and not personally, as directors owe their fiduciary duties to the company and not to its shareholders.

12.2.5 The pluralist and the enlightened shareholder value approach

As stated in 12.2.3 and 12.2.4 above, both at common law as well as in terms of s 76(3)*(b)* of the Act, a director is required to act in the best interests of the 'company', by which is meant the collective interests of present and future shareholders. Section 76(3)*(b)* is cast in mandatory terms.

---

[46] *Multinational Gas and Petrochemical Co v Multinational Gas and Petrochemical Services Ltd* [1983] 2 All ER 653 (CA).
[47] *Hutton v West Cork Railway Co* (supra); *Parke v Daily News Ltd* (supra).
[48] *Charterbridge Corporation Ltd v Lloyds Bank Ltd* [1969] 2 All ER 1185; *Linderen v L & P Estates Co Ltd* [1968] All ER 917.
[49] *Stein v Blake (No 2)* [1998] 1 All ER 724; *Johnson v Gore Wood & Co* [2001] 1 BCLC 313 (HL); [2002] 2 AC 1. See chapter 16: Shareholder Remedies and Minority Protection for a detailed discussion.
[50] [1982] 1 All ER 354 (CA).

The clear implication of this common-law and statutory principle is that the interests of stakeholders other than the shareholders of the company have received no formal, legal recognition under the Act.[51]

This yet again raises the enduring issue whether a company is just another business entity or whether it is an integral part of society. Does modern corporate law still insist that the fundamental purpose of a company is wealth creation or profit maximisation? Should the directors, especially of large listed companies, be required to manage a company only for the benefit of shareholders, or should they be required also to act in the interests of other stakeholders such as employees of the company, its creditors, customers, suppliers, the environment and the interests of the local community in which the company functions? The crux of the matter is whether the directors should be allowed to be public-spirited with corporate funds that do not belong to them. It is because the funds do not belong to the directors that the courts have insisted that charitable donations must be *bona fide* and reasonably incidental to the business of the company and for its benefit.[52]

The two different approaches to this issue are known as the 'stakeholder' or 'pluralist' approach and the 'enlightened shareholder value' approach. The pluralist approach emphasises that a socially responsible company[53] would consider the impact of its activities on its stakeholders. In *AP Smith Manufacturing Co v Barlow*,[54] in deciding that a charitable donation made by a company was validly made, the court stated *obiter* that '. . . modern conditions require that corporations acknowledge and discharge social as well as private responsibilities as members of the communities within which they operate'. The pluralist approach asserts that non-shareholder stakeholders are an important constituency of a company and that shareholders are merely one of its several constituencies. According to the pluralist approach, the directors should ignore shareholder interests in favour of stakeholder interests where this would be in the interests of the company in its extended sense.[55]

These issues hark back to the famous debate in the 1930s between Professor Adolf A Berle and Professor E Merrick Dodd Jr, which still remains relevant to modern company law. Professor Berle was of the view that powers granted to a company or its management are exercisable only for the benefit of the shareholders of the company. The sole object or function of a company is to make a profit for its shareholders, who are the ultimate beneficiaries of a company and the providers of its capital. Supporters of this school of thought assert that companies pay tax to ensure that social and environmental concerns are taken care of.[56] Professor Dodd, on the other hand, rejected the view that the only object of a

---

[51] Except for the social and ethics committee (discussed below).
[52] *Evans v Brunner Mond & Company Ltd* [1921] ChD 359; *Re Lee Behrens & Co Ltd* [1932] 2 Ch 46.
[53] By which is generally meant a company that integrates social and environmental issues in its business activities and interacts with stakeholders. A socially responsible company is one that is engaged in the solution of society's major problems.
[54] 98 A2d 581 (NJ 1953) at 586.
[55] See Rehana Cassim and Femida Cassim 'The Reform of Corporate Law in South Africa' (2005) *International Company and Commercial Law Review* 411 at 411–12.
[56] A Berle 'Corporate powers as powers in trust' (1931) 44 *Harv LR* 1049.

company is to make a profit for its shareholders, and the assertion that it is not the function or business of a company to rectify social ills. In his view, profit maximisation is not the sole object of a company.[57] According to Professor Dodd, a company is an economic institution performing a social service as well as a profit-making function. Companies have, it is contended, wider responsibilities that extend beyond their shareholders:

> No doubt it is to a large extent true that an attempt by business managers to take into consideration the welfare of employees and customers (and under modern industrial conditions the two classes are largely the same) will in the long run increase the profits of stockholders.[58]

The issue has been debated until the present time.[59] A factor that is relevant to the debate and must not be overlooked is that a wide diversity of stakeholder and other economic interests is found in large public companies. It must clearly be a very difficult task to expect the directors of a company to weigh up competing and conflicting stakeholder interests.

It thus remains controversial whether the directors of a company should take into account the interests of stakeholders, all of whom are generally affected in one way or another by the activities of the company. However, the issue is not whether the directors 'should' or 'may' but whether they 'must' take stakeholder interests into account.

The law appears to have been settled in both the USA as well as the UK that non-shareholder interests *may* be taken into account but only if, in so doing, the interests of the company, ie of its shareholders as a collective body, is thereby served. This in effect is tantamount to saying that profit maximisation still remains the ultimate goal of a company and that stakeholder interests may be taken into account only if doing so promotes the interests of shareholders of the company in the long term. In the event of a conflict between the interests of shareholders and stakeholders, it is the interests of shareholders that must prevail. In other words, shareholders retain primacy. Profit-sacrificing corporate social responsibility, which entails the voluntary sacrifice of profits to confer benefits on other stakeholder groups, is acceptable to a much lesser extent than the view advocated by the pluralist approach.

The 'enlightened shareholder value' approach requires directors to maximise profits for the benefit of shareholders, but permits directors to take stakeholder interests into account provided that this is subordinate to profit-maximisation and the interests of shareholders. Company directors must consider the importance of fostering and nurturing a good, positive relationship with stakeholders, because this ultimately promotes the interests of the company. The company benefits from the improved retention of employees, customers and suppliers and it enhances the goodwill and the image of the company in the local community in which it operates. The modern neoteric approach is that it makes good business sense for

---

[57] E Merrick Dodd, Jr 'For whom are corporate managers trustees?' (1931–32) 45 *Harv LR* 1145 at 1147–8.
[58] Dodd op cit n 57 at 1156.
[59] See AA Sommer, Jr 'Whom should the corporation serve? The Berle-Dodd debate revisited sixty years later' 16 *Delaware Journal of Corporate Law* 33.

companies to embrace wider social responsibilities. It also takes cognisance of the fact that the very character of large public companies has changed from a purely economic entity to one that also has social functions to fulfil. But this is more of a corporate governance issue than an issue of the fiduciary duties of the directors of a company.

In contrast, the pluralist approach requires companies to promote stakeholder interests as an end in itself rather than as a means to an end, ie as a proper and valid object in itself. Independent value is required to be given to the interests of stakeholders, which are not subordinate to the interests of shareholders. Directors should be willing where necessary to sacrifice shareholder profits in order to promote the interests and the well-being of other stakeholders in the company.

Apart from some European countries, very few jurisdictions have adopted the pluralist approach. Section 172(1) of the UK Companies Act 2006 adopts the enlightened shareholder value approach by requiring directors acting in good faith and in the best interests of the company to promote the success of the company for the benefit of the company as a whole. According to this section, the shareholders of a company are its primary beneficiaries. In fulfilling this duty, the directors should insofar as is practicable have regard to the likely consequences of any decision in the long term. They must also have regard to the interests of employees of the company; the need to foster the company's business relationships with suppliers, customers and others; the impact of the company's operations on the community and the environment; the desirability of maintaining a reputation for high standards of business conduct; and the need to act fairly between the shareholders. This list of factors to be taken into account, as set out in s 172(1)*(a)* to *(f)* of the UK Companies Act 2006, is non-exhaustive. Nothing is said in s 172 of the order of priority of the various factors and the weight to be given to each. The directors may take these factors into account provided they honestly believe they are acting in the best interests of the shareholders. But since the duty of the directors is owed to the company, the duty is not directly enforceable by any of the stakeholders referred to in s 172. The section thus comes very close to imposing an unenforceable duty on the directors of the company. It is also clear from s 172 that the duty to consider stakeholder interests is subordinate to the success of the company, ie the interests of the shareholders as a whole. The section thus adopts the enlightened shareholder value approach.

The common-law principles laid down by the courts many decades ago are not very different from the enlightened shareholder value approach. For instance, in *Dodge v Ford Motor Co*[60] the court proclaimed that a company's prime object is to make a profit for its shareholders. The directors of a company may not reduce these profits in order to benefit the public, thereby making the interests of shareholders incidental to the interests of the public. In *Hutton v West Cork Railway Co*[61] the board of directors of a company that was being wound up proposed to give gratuities to corporate officers for loss of employment. The court held these payments to be *ultra vires*. In the classic words of Bowen LJ:

---

[60] 204 Mich 495; 170 NW 668 (1919).
[61] (1883) 23 ChD 654 (CA) 673.

[C]harity has no business to sit at boards of directors qua charity. There is, however, a kind of charitable dealing which is for the interests of those who practice it, and to that extent and in that garb (I admit not a very philanthropic garb) charity may sit at the board, but for no other purpose ... The law does not say that there are to be no cakes and ale, but that there are to be no cakes and ale except such as are required for the benefit of the company.[62]

This principle is, as stated above, not very different from the modern enlightened shareholder value approach. Corporate altruism and corporate philanthropy are acceptable only if expected to benefit the company and its shareholders. Directors are allowed to have a social conscience only if it is in the interests of the company. The courts have, however, tended to give this principle an increasingly liberal interpretation. In *Teck Corp Ltd v Millar*[63] Berger J commented that the traditional legal principles must yield to the facts of modern life. 'If today the directors of a company were to consider the interests of employees no one would argue that in so doing they were not acting bona fide in the interests of the company itself.' It is submitted that, provided the directors do not entirely disregard the interests of shareholders, a South African court would accept the wisdom of the dictum in *Teck Corp Ltd v Millar*. It is a glaring corporate law anomaly in modern times to insist that the interests of employees do not form part of the interests of the company. In any event, a number of provisions of the new Act confer wide-ranging powers on trade unions and employee representatives in specific instances. These developments show that the legal principles laid down by the courts in the 19th century have not continued unchanged.

(a) The King Code of Governance for South Africa 2009

Stakeholder interests, as stated above, have received no formal legal recognition under the Act as a constituency of a company. The promotion and protection of stakeholder interests have been left to specific legislation such as the Labour Relations Act 66 of 1995 (ss 78–94), the environmental laws, the Broad-Based Black Economic Empowerment Act 53 of 2003 and the new Consumer Protection Act 68 of 2008. There is, in addition, on a voluntary rather than on a mandatory basis, the King Code of Governance for South Africa 2009 ('the Code') which has a stakeholder — inclusive corporate governance approach[64] . The Code strongly emphasises the importance of stakeholder interests and the triple bottomline or integrated approach that requires companies to have regard to social, economic and environmental concerns. But unlike its predecessor, the Code is not confined to listed companies only. The Code now applies to all business entities. It remains a recommended or voluntary code of best practices, unlike the US Sarbanes-Oxley Act 2002, which is legally enforceable. The result is that the promotion of stakeholder interests remains permissive.

---

[62] *Per* Bowen LJ in *Hutton v West Cork Railway Co* (1883) 23 ChD 654 (CA) 673.
[63] (1972) 33 DLR (3d) 288 (BCSC) 313–14.
[64] See further chapter 11: Corporate Governance.

(b) Section 72(4): The social and ethics committee

Section 72(4) of the Act[65] requires every public company (whether listed or not) and every state-owned company to appoint a social and ethics committee as well as a social and ethics advisory panel, unless the company is a subsidiary of a holding company that already has a social and ethics committee that would perform the prescribed functions on behalf of the subsidiary company, or it is exempted by the Companies Tribunal from the requirement to appoint a social and ethics committee.[66]

Section 72(4) also applies to a significant private company if it is desirable in the public interest to appoint a social and ethics committee and advisory panel, having regard to *(a)* its annual turnover, *(b)* the size of its workforce, or *(c)* the nature and extent of its activities. In terms of s 72(4), the Minister may prescribe by regulation that a company or a category of companies must have a social and ethics committee. However, the section does not prescribe any functions for the social and ethics committee; this is done instead by Regulation 50(12) of the draft Companies Regulations.

The social and ethics committee must comprise a minimum of three independent non-executive directors who are not disqualified from holding office as directors of a company. Regulation 50(7) requires the board of directors of a company to appoint a social and ethics advisory panel to assist the social and ethics committee. The panel must comprise a number of members equal to the number of members of the social and ethics committee. The members of the advisory panel must be drawn from employees of the company and registered members of a profession entitled to practise in a field directly related to the functions of the social and ethics committee, such as an anthropologist, a psychologist or a person engaged in sociology or the social services, education, environmental assessment, law, theology, ethics or health. Also included in this list are representatives of the community and of the public interest, who must not be directors or employees of the company.

(c) The functions of the social and ethics committee

The function of the social and ethics committee is to monitor the company's activities, having regard to any relevant legislation, such as the Broad-Based Black Economic Empowerment Act 53 of 2003, or prevailing codes of best practice, such as the United Nations Global Compact Principles and the recommendations of the Organisation of Economic Co-operation and Development on corruption.

The social and ethics committee must, in terms of Regulation 50(12) of the draft Companies Regulations, also monitor the company's activities with regard to good corporate citizenship (ie corporate social responsibility, as discussed above in 12.2.4 and 12.2.5), including:

---

[65] Read with Regulation 50 of the draft Companies Regulations, GN 1664 of 2009, *GG* 32832 of 22 December 2009.

[66] Clause 45*(b)* of the draft Companies Amendment Bill, 2010 enables the Companies Tribunal to exempt a company in certain circumstances from appointing a social and ethics committee for a period of five years.

- the company's promotion of equality and the prevention of unfair discrimination,
- contribution to the development of the communities in which the company's activities are predominantly conducted,
- its record of sponsorship, donations and charitable giving,
- the environment, health and public safety,
- consumer relationships, and
- labour and employment.

This is in effect the legislative adoption of the enlightened shareholder value approach and of corporate social responsibility. The problem with this particular regulation is that it could very easily be turned into a mere box-ticking exercise.

Moreover, a further problem with this regulation is that, as in the case of s 172(1) of the UK Companies Act 2006 (discussed above in 12.2.5), no legal duty is directly owed to any of the stakeholders referred to in Regulation 50(12). The provisions of this regulation are consequently unenforceable by stakeholders, unless they are able to rely on a derivative action brought in terms of s 165 (see chapter 16: Shareholder Remedies and Minority Protection) by someone who has the necessary legal standing to institute proceedings, such as a shareholder, director, prescribed officer, trade union, an employee representative or a person who has the leave of the court. Even if that person may have the requisite legal standing, it is doubtful whether the proceedings would 'protect the legal interests of the company' as is required by s 165(1). At worst, failure to appoint a social and ethics committee could be the subject of a compliance notice. For further discussion of the social and ethics committee, see chapter 10: Governance and the Board of Directors.

12.3 THE FIDUCIARY DUTIES OF DIRECTORS AND THE STANDARDS OF DIRECTORS' CONDUCT

The duties of directors are now derived from two sources, namely the Act and the common law as found in the decisions of the courts.

Section 76(3)*(a)* and *(b)* states that, subject to s 76(4) and (5), a director of a company, when acting in that capacity, must exercise the powers and perform the functions of director:
- in good faith and for a proper purpose, and
- in the best interests of the company.

At common law, the duty to act in good faith and in the best interests of the company is the overarching fiduciary duty of directors from which all the other fiduciary duties flow. These duties are discussed in turn below. As stated above, the standards of directors' conduct prescribed by s 76 apply to all directors, including an alternate director, prescribed officers, and members of a board committee or audit committee, irrespective of whether or not such persons are also members of the company's board of directors.

12.3.1 The duty to act in good faith and in the best interests of the company

The fundamental duty of good faith is now imposed by both the common law as well as the Act. 'It is a well-established rule of common law that directors have a fiduciary duty to exercise their powers in good faith and in the best interests of the company'.[67]

In *Re Smith & Fawcett Ltd*[68] the court laid down the long-standing and oft-quoted legal principle that the directors are bound to exercise the powers conferred upon them *bona fide* in what *they* [emphasis added] consider — not what a court may consider — is in the interests of the company. A director's duty is thus to act in what he or she in good faith honestly considers to be in the best interests of the company.

Honesty is subjective. A breach of this duty consequently requires subjective awareness of wrongdoing. The directors of a company have more knowledge, time and expertise at their disposal to evaluate the best interests of the company than judges.[69] The courts will not assume that thay can act as a kind of supervisory board over directors' decisions that are honestly arrived at within the powers of their management.[70] In *Hogg v Cramphorn Ltd*[71] it was likewise stated that it was not for the courts to review the merits of a decision of the directors honestly arrived at.[72]

The duty of honesty and good faith is the paramount and overarching duty of a director of a company. Section 76(3)(a) couples the duty of good faith with the duty of a director to exercise his or her powers for a proper purpose. The test of good faith is subjective and not objective, since the question is whether the director honestly believed that he or she acted in the interests of the company. The issue is about the director's state of mind.[73]

But there are limits to the subjective test. The absence of a reasonable ground for believing that the director is acting in the interests of the company may be the basis for finding lack of good faith.[74] In *Shuttleworth v Cox* the court stressed that the best interests of the company are not assessed by the court itself; instead, the test is whether a reasonable man would have regarded the act of the directors to be in the best interests of the company. This was also emphasised in *Teck Corp Ltd v Millar*[75] where the court stated that there must be reasonable grounds for the directors' belief that they were acting in the best interests of the company. So too in *Extrasure Travel Insurances Ltd v Scattergood*[76] the court ruled that there must be reasonable grounds for the belief of the directors that they were acting in the interests of the company. The test as formulated in *Charterbridge Corporation*

---

[67] *Da Silva v CH Chemicals (Pty) Ltd* 2008 (6) SA 620 (SCA) para 13, 627B.
[68] [1942] Ch 304 at 306.
[69] *Darvall v North Sydney Brick & Tile Co Ltd* (1989) 15 ACLR 230 SC (NSW).
[70] Ibid.
[71] [1967] Ch 254 at 268.
[72] In *Carlen v Drury* (1812) Ves & B54 it was said that it was not for the courts to review or judge the merits of a business decision made by the company.
[73] *Greenhalgh v Ardene Cinemas* [1950] 2 All ER 1120 (CA); *Regentcrest plc v Cohen* [2001] 1 BCLC 80 at 104.
[74] Scrutton LJ in *Shuttleworth v Cox Bros & Co (Maidenhead) Ltd* [1927] 2 KB 9 at 23; [1926] All ER Rep 498 (CA) 506; *Gething v Kilner* [1972] 1 WLR 337 at 342; [1972] 1 All ER 1166 at 1170.
[75] (1972) 33 DLR (3d) 288 (BCSC).
[76] [2003] 1 BCLC 598 at 619.

Ltd v Lloyd's Bank[77] is whether an intelligent and honest person in the position of the director could in the whole of the circumstances have reasonably believed that he or she was acting in the interest of the company.

By way of illustration, in *Neptune (Vehicle Washing Equipment) Ltd v Fitzgerald (No 2)*[78] it was held that, quite apart from any issue of self-dealing, the sole director of a company had not acted in the interests of the company by arranging for the company to make gratuitous or redundancy payments to him on the termination of his service contract with the company. The director was acting in his own, rather than in the company's interests.[79]

It may be noted at this stage, that s 76(4) of the Act, which adopts the US Business Judgment Rule (discussed in 12.5.4 below) applies also to the directors' duty to act in the best interests of the company.

12.3.2 Proper purpose

(a) General

It is not enough for the directors to exercise their powers for the benefit of what they believe is the best interests of the company. Section 76(3)(a) requires that the directors must also exercise their powers for a 'proper purpose'. 'Proper purpose' is not defined, but at common law it has always been taken to mean that directors must exercise their powers for the purpose for which the power was given to them and not for a collateral or ulterior purpose.

There are thus two duties referred to in s 76(3)(a), namely, good faith and proper purpose. These are separate and distinct, and yet cumulative, with the result that even if the directors have subjectively acted honestly in the interests of the company, they could yet objectively be in breach of their duty to exercise their powers for a proper purpose.

Section 76(3)(a) is declaratory of the common law and effects no change in this aspect of the common-law fiduciary duties of directors. The section does, however, serve the very useful purpose of removing any doubt relating to the existence of this particular fiduciary duty instead of regarding it, as some authorities do, as an aspect of the director's duty of good faith.[80] The legal principles relating to the 'proper purpose' duty are in effect an attempt by the courts to control or restrain the exercise by directors of the discretionary powers conferred on them.

The director's duty to exercise powers for a 'proper purpose' is thus now both a statutory and a common-law obligation. It is an abuse of power for a director to exercise his or her powers for a purpose other than the purpose for which the power was conferred on him or her. The existence of subjective good faith is insufficient to save the purported exercise of a power, if the power was exercised

---

[77] [1970] Ch 62 at 74.
[78] [1995] 1 BCLC 352 (ChD).
[79] See also *Re W & M Roith Ltd* [1967] 1 All ER 427.
[80] See in this respect, *Teck Corp Ltd v Millar* (1972) 33 DLR (3d) 288 (BCSC).

for a collateral purpose.[81] Unlike the duty of good faith, which is subjective, the test for 'proper purpose' is objective.[82]

In *Hogg v Cramphorn Ltd*[83] the directors of a company, which was a family concern, in order to forestall a hostile takeover bid by a person whom they honestly and genuinely believed to be inexperienced and unsuitable, allotted unissued preference shares that, contrary to the constitution of the company, carried special voting rights of ten votes per share. The shares were allotted to the trustees of a trust established for the benefit of the employees of the company. It was expected that the trustees, who were allies of the directors, would cast their votes in support of the directors rather than the takeover bidder. An interest-free loan was extended to the trust, to enable the trustees to pay for the shares. Even though the directors had honestly believed in good faith that the takeover would be contrary to the best interests of the company, its employees and customers, the court ruled that the directors had improperly exercised their power to issue shares. It was irrelevant that they had acted in good faith and in the interests of the company. The court found that the primary purpose of the allotment of the shares was not to raise share capital required for the company, but to ensure that the directors retained control of the company. The power to issue shares is a fiduciary power, which in this case was exercised for an improper purpose. The court held, however, that the invalid allotment of shares was ratifiable by the members in general meeting.

The court emphasised that it was unconstitutional for the directors to exercise their power to issue shares of the company for the purpose of defeating a takeover bid, or for the purpose of destroying an existing majority or to create a new majority.

A similar improper exercise of a power to issue shares also took place in *Howard Smith Ltd v Ampol Petroleum Ltd*[84] where, unlike the situation in *Hogg v Cramphorn Ltd*, the board of directors of RW Miller (Holdings) Ltd was in favour of a higher takeover bid by Howard Smith Ltd, whom they preferred to a competing and lower takeover bid made by a majority shareholder, Ampol Petroleum Ltd and another company. The board consequently allotted further shares to Howard Smith Ltd in order to dilute the majority shareholding of Ampol Petroleum Ltd and to ensure the success of the takeover bid made by Howard Smith Ltd. In setting aside the allotment of shares to Howard Smith Ltd, the court stated that it was unconstitutional for directors to use their fiduciary powers over the shares of a company for the purpose of destroying an existing majority or creating a new one which did not previously exist. This applies even if the directors believed in good faith that they were acting in the best interests of the company and even though there was no desire by the directors to obtain a personal advantage for themselves or to retain their position as directors of the company. The legal principle is clear: the directors of a company must not interfere with the constitutional right of shareholders to decide the fate of a takeover bid.

---

[81] *Darvall v North Sydney Brick & Tile Co Ltd* (1989) 15 ACLR 230 SC (NSW).
[82] *Hogg v Cramphorn Ltd* [1967] Ch 254; see also *Extrasure Travel Insurances Ltd v Scattergood* [2003] 1 BCLC 598 at 613.
[83] Supra.
[84] [1974] AC 821 (PC).

In *Howard Smith Ltd v Ampol Petroleum Ltd* there was both a desire to raise further share capital or finance for the company as well as a desire to defeat a takeover bid made by Ampol Petroleum. The court found on the facts that it was the latter purpose that was the primary or substantial purpose of the issue of further shares, and set aside the allotment of shares.

In *Punt v Symons & Co Ltd*[85] the directors had issued shares to their friends and supporters with the object of creating a sufficient majority to enable them to pass a special resolution to alter the constitution of the company to deprive certain shareholders of special rights conferred on them by the company's constitution. In *Piercy v Mills*[86] the directors had likewise issued further shares to create a sufficient majority to enable them to resist the election of additional directors that would have resulted in the incumbent directors becoming a minority on the board. In both cases, the directors were held to have exercised their powers for an improper purpose. An issue of shares in order to distort the balance of voting power is an improper exercise of the power to issue shares.[87]

It is not an easy task to identify from the facts of a particular case the purpose for which a director has exercised his or her power. Where there are multiple purposes for the exercise of a power, the court must determine what the substantial or dominant purpose was. If the dominant purpose is found to be improper, the court must regard the exercise of the power as being voidable.[88] For the exercise of the power to be valid, the impermissible purpose must not be causative.[89]

In *Extrasure Travel Insurances Ltd v Scattergood*[90] the court stated that the law relating to proper purpose is clear. It is not necessary to prove that a director was dishonest or that the director knew that he or she was pursuing a collateral purpose. There is a four-step test to be applied by the court. The court must:

- identify the particular power that is being challenged,
- identify the proper purpose for which the power was given to the directors,
- identify the substantial purpose for which the power was in fact exercised, and
- decide whether the purpose was proper.

(b) Section 38 of the Act and proper purpose

Section 38(1) of the Act confers on the board of directors the power to issue shares. This power, as stated above, is a fiduciary power that must be exercised *bona fide* for a proper purpose and not for a collateral purpose. In view of s 38, this particular fiduciary duty assumes greater importance. The common-law principles (discussed above) continue to be relevant, particularly the view enunciated by Buckley J in *Hogg v Cramphorn Ltd*[91] where the court, referring with approval

---

[85] [1903] 2 Ch 506.
[86] [1920] 1 Ch 77.
[87] *Gaiman v National Association for Mental Health* [1970] 2 All ER 362.
[88] *Mills v Mills* (1938) 60 CLR 150 at 185 (HC of A); *Howard Smith Ltd v Ampol Petroleum Ltd* [1974] AC 821 (PC); *Teck Corp Ltd v Millar* (1972) 33 DLR (3d) 288 (BCSC); *Bamford v Bamford* (1969) 1 All ER 969 (CA).
[89] *Mills v Mills* (supra).
[90] [2003] 1 BCLC 598 (ChD) 619.
[91] *Hogg v Cramphorn Ltd* [1967] Ch 254 at 267.

to *Punt v Symons*, reaffirmed the principle that the directors' power to issue shares is given to them primarily for the purpose of raising capital when required for the purposes of the company.

Where the directors' exercise of their powers is improper and is consequently set aside, the directors will be jointly and severally liable to compensate the company for any loss suffered in consequence of the improper exercise of the power.[92]

It must be stressed in this particular context that s 77(2)(a) of the Act provides that a director will be held liable in accordance with the principles of the common law relating to a breach of a fiduciary duty by the director as contemplated in s 76(3)(a) (ie the duty to act in good faith and for a proper purpose). See further 12.9 below.

12.3.3 The duty to exercise an independent judgment

The common-law principle is clear: in the exercise of their powers and in deciding what is in the best interests of the company, the directors must exercise an independent and unfettered discretion.[93] Directors must consider the affairs of the company in an unbiased and objective manner. Accordingly, a voting agreement under which a director binds him- or herself to vote or to exercise his or her powers in accordance with the instructions of some other person, thereby fettering the director's discretion, will not be enforced by the court. The effect of such a voting agreement, if it were binding, would be that the directors thereby disable themselves from acting honestly in what they believe to be the best interests of the company.[94]

The duty to exercise an independent judgment is seen by some commentators as merely an aspect of the directors' duty to act *bona fide* in the interests of the company. This perhaps explains why this specific common-law duty is not explicitly referred to in s 76, and more specifically, in s 76(2) and (3). On this basis, the duty to exercise an independent judgment continues to form part of the fiduciary and statutory duties of directors.

As a general principle, a director cannot bind him- or herself in the present on how to vote in future. It is irrelevant to this duty whether or not the director is deriving any personal benefit from such an agreement. In *Fulham Football Club Ltd v Cabra Estates Plc*,[95] where a football club and its directors undertook in return for a substantial payment to vote in a particular way, the court rejected the contention that the board of directors may never make a contract by which they bind themselves to the future exercise of their powers in a particular way, even though the contract as a whole is manifestly for the benefit of the company. The

---

[92] See *Re Lands Allotment Co Ltd* (1894) Ch 616 (CA) and *Bishopsgate Investment Management Ltd (In liquidation) v Maxwell (No 2)* [1994] 1 All ER 261 (CA), where a director was held to be in breach of his fiduciary duty in giving away company assets for no consideration to a private company of which he was a director.

[93] See *Kregor v Hollins* (1913) 109 LT 225 (KB and CA).

[94] Andrew Keay 'The duty of directors to exercise an independent judgment' (2008) 29 *The Company Lawyer* (No 10) 290.

[95] [1994] 1 BCLC 363 (Ch and CA).

directors were in this case binding themselves under a commercial contract which had conferred benefits on the company and which at the time they had honestly believed was in the best interests of the company. The Australian case of *Thorby v Goldberg*,[96] which *Fulham Football Club Ltd v Cabra Estates Plc* followed, is to a similar effect.

Moreover, a company cannot simply escape from a binding contractual obligation that has willingly been undertaken by its directors on the basis of their alleged failure to exercise an independent judgment. There is of course a distinction between the situation where the entire board of directors has entered into such an agreement and one where an individual director has done so. The former may in certain circumstances be beyond reproach, as shown in the *Fulham Football Club* case.

The duty to exercise an independent judgment is particularly important to nominee directors, ie persons who are appointed by a nominator to represent his or her interests at board meetings. A nominee director is a lawfully elected director appointed to the board of directors by a creditor, a financier or a significant shareholder who controls sufficient voting power for this purpose. For instance, a holding company may appoint a nominee director to the board of directors of a subsidiary company or, to take another common example, it may be agreed that a bank that has financed a company may appoint a representative to that company's board of directors. The nominee director is expected to represent the interests of the nominator. This means that a nominee director is undertaking a duty to a person other than the company in addition to the fiduciary duty that he or she owes to the company.

A nominee director may even be expected to report to his or her nominator on any developments that may affect the interests of the nominator. The problem becomes more acute when it is borne in mind that a nominee director is entitled, like any other director, to inspect the documents of the company, and that he or she may have the same right of access to information relating to the company. Yet, the legal principle as laid down by the courts is that nominee directors are under a duty to act in the interests of the company of which they are directors instead of the interests of their nominator.[97]

The practice of appointing nominee directors is widespread. The courts have ruled that there is nothing inherently dishonest or improper about nominee directors. In most cases no harm is done to the company mainly because the interests of the nominator often coincide with, or conform to, those of the company, to the extent that they both desire the company to prosper. This enables nominee directors to comply with their duties both to the company as well as to their nominators. When, however, the interests of the company clash with those of the nominator there is a manifest conflict of interest that puts the nominee director in an invidious position.[98]

---

[96] (1964) 112 CLR 597.
[97] *Kuwait Asia Bank EC v National Mutual Life Nominees Ltd* (1991) 1 AC 187 (PC).
[98] See *Scottish Co-operative Wholesale Society Ltd v Meyer* [1958] 2 All ER 66 (HL), the facts of which clearly illustrate the nature of the problem and the dilemma of the nominee director.

In *Boulting v Association of Cinematograph, Television and Allied Technicians*[99] Lord Denning MR stated:

> Or take a nominee director, that is, a director of a company who is nominated by a large shareholder to represent his interests. There is nothing wrong in that. It is done every day. Nothing wrong, that is, so long as the director is left free to exercise his best judgment in the interests of the company he serves. But if he is put on terms that he is bound to act in the affairs of the company in accordance with the directions of his patron, it is beyond doubt unlawful . . . or if he agrees to subordinate the interests of the company to the interests of his patron, it is conduct oppressive to the other shareholders for which the patron can be brought to book.

Similarly, in *Fisheries Development Corporation of SA Ltd v Jorgensen; Fisheries Development Corporation of SA Ltd v AWJ Investments (Pty) Ltd*[100] the court stated that a director's duty is to exercise an independent judgment and to take decisions according to the best interests of the company. Even though nominee directors may in fact be representing the interests of the persons who nominated them, they are in law obliged to serve the interests of the company to the exclusion of the interests of their nominators. As directors, they cannot be subject to the control of any employer or principal other than the company. In short, a director may not serve two masters as this gives rise to conflicting loyalties.

It is clear from the decisions of the courts that the general legal principle is that once the nominee becomes a member of the board of directors of a company, he or she is subject to the duty to serve the interests of the company rather than the interests of his or her nominator. A duty to consult the nominator is, however, not incompatible with the nominee director's duty to exercise an independent judgment in the best interests of the company. The nominee director must, however, be left free to exercise his or her judgment *bona fide* in the interests of the company.

The relevant legal principles are as follows: A nominee director may, without being in breach of fiduciary duty to the company, take the interests of his or her nominator into account, provided that the nominee director's decisions as a director are in what he or she genuinely considers to be in the best interests of the company.[101]

A more flexible approach to the duty of a nominee director to exercise an independent judgment has been adopted in Australian and New Zealand law. This flexible approach may well influence the courts in South Africa to take into account the commercial realities of the practice of appointing nominee directors, and to adopt a similar flexible approach rather than a strict rigid approach to nominee directors. The trend in these jurisdictions is for companies to draw up proper guidelines for the relationship between the nominee director and the company, particularly with regard to the disclosure of confidential information and the duty to avoid a conflict of interest.

For now, the legal principle nevertheless remains that the nominee director must exercise an independent judgment for the benefit of the company. Nominee directors must not blindly follow the judgment or the instructions of those who

---

[99] [1963] 1 All ER 716 (CA) 723.
[100] 1980 (4) SA 156 (W) 163.
[101] *Re Neath Rugby Ltd (No 2); Hawkes v Cuddy (No 2)* [2009] 2 BCLC 427.

have appointed them. Certainly a nominee director may not be a 'dummy' or a 'puppet'. Thus in *S v Shaban*[102] the court cautioned that 'puppets' cannot be lawfully employed in our company law system. By 'puppets' the court meant persons placed on the board of directors of a company who pretend to have taken part in resolutions of which they know nothing, or persons who pretend to have taken part in the management of a company while having no idea what they have signed. On the other hand, the practice of appointing nominee directors is not a hollow pretence. It is consequently vital to distinguish a nominee director from a puppet director, whose appointment is not lawful.

In *Selangor United Rubber Estates Ltd v Cradock (No 3)*[103] two nominee directors, in disregard of their fiduciary duties, had exercised no volition or discretion of their own, preferring instead to put themselves in the hands of their controller. They were said to be mere puppets and were as such held liable for the improper use by their controller of funds belonging to the company.

As regards any expectation of the nominator that the nominee director would convey relevant corporate information to him or her, this is curtailed to a large extent by s 76(2)*(a)*(i) and (ii) of the Act which prohibits a director from using any information obtained in his or her capacity as a director to gain an advantage for a person other than the company or a wholly owned subsidiary of the company (discussed in 12.4.2*(a)* below) or to knowingly cause harm to the company or its subsidiary.

As previously stated, there is no specific reference in the Act to the duty of a director not to fetter his or her discretion or, conversely, a duty to exercise an independent judgment. This is because this duty is essentially an aspect of the fundamental duty of a director to act *bona fide* in the best interests of the company, as provided in s 76(3)*(a)* and *(b)* of the Act.

The common-law principles discussed above continue to be relevant to South African law. A director consequently must not enter into an agreement under which he or she undertakes to act in accordance with the instructions of his or her nominator.

12.3.4 The duty to act within their powers

At common law, directors are under a distinct fiduciary duty not to exceed their powers or the limits of their authority. One aspect of this duty is that they may not enter into an *ultra vires* contract on behalf of the company or a contract that is illegal. At common law, since a company could not itself enter into such transactions, it inevitably followed that its directors likewise could not possibly have the power to do so, because an agent cannot have authority to enter into a contract that exceeds the legal capacity of the principal.[104]

The *ultra vires* doctrine was however abolished by s 36 of the 1973 Act.[105] Section 19(1)*(b)* of the new Act takes this further by conferring on companies all the legal powers and the capacity of an individual subject to the company's

---

[102] 1965 (4) SA 646 (W) 651.
[103] [1968] 2 All ER 1073 (ChD).
[104] See *Ashbury Railway Carriage and Iron Co v Riche* (1875) LR 7 HL 653.
[105] See FHI Cassim 'The rise, fall and reform of the *ultra vires* doctrine' (1998) 10 *SA Merc LJ* 293.

Memorandum of Incorporation.[106] If a company's Memorandum of Incorporation limits, restricts or qualifies the powers or the activities of the company, the directors of the company would be acting beyond their powers by entering into a contract that is inconsistent with such a provision. They would consequently incur liability to the company for breach of their fiduciary duty, unless their act has been ratified by a special resolution of the company's shareholders (s 20(2)). However, a contract that contravenes of the Act may not be ratified (s 20(3)).

In *Cullerne v London and Suburban General Permanent Building Society*[107] the court ruled that, if directors exceed the powers conferred on them by the company, they would be liable to the company for breach of their fiduciary duty. Similarly, if a director has made payments as a result of transactions that are beyond the capacity of the company, he or she may be called upon to compensate the company. This liability for a breach of fiduciary duty arises irrespective of the *bona fides* of the director in question[108] or any fault on his or her part.

Once again there is no explicit reference in s 76 of the Act to this fiduciary duty as a separate and distinct duty. This duty is nevertheless an aspect of the fiduciary duty of directors to exercise their powers in good faith for a proper purpose and in the best interests of the company, as provided in s 76(3)*(a)* and *(b)*.

It is notable that there is a distinction between a lack of authority and abuse of authority (ie where a power is exercised for a collateral purpose or an improper purpose), which of course also results in a lack of authority.

Where a director disregards a constitutional limitation on his or her authority, a number of relevant statutory provisions may be triggered. Section 77(2)*(a)* imposes liability on a director in accordance with the principles of the common law relating to breach of fiduciary duty for any loss, damages or costs sustained by the company as a result of a breach of duty. It follows that, if directors disregard a constitutional limitation on their authority to act on behalf of the company, they could incur liability to the company for any loss, damages or costs sustained by the company as a result of their failure to act within the constitutional limits of their authority. A director may also be held liable in accordance with the principles of the common law relating to delict for any loss, damages or costs sustained by a company as a consequence of any breach by a director of (among other things) any provision of the company's Memorandum of Incorporation.

Moreover, s 77(3)*(a)* imposes liability on a director for any loss, damages or costs sustained by a company as a direct or indirect consequence of the director having done some act in the name of the company, signed anything on behalf of the company, or purported to bind the company or authorise the taking of any action by or on behalf of the company despite knowing that he or she lacked the authority to do so.

Also relevant here is s 20(6) of the Act, which confers a right on each shareholder to claim damages from any person who fraudulently or due to gross negligence causes the company to do anything inconsistent with the Act or with a

---

[106] This topic is more fully discussed in chapter 5: Corporate Capacity, Agency and the Turquand Rule.
[107] (1890) 25 QBD 485.
[108] *Re Lands Allotment Company* (1894) 1 Ch 616 (CA).

The Duties and the Liability of Directors

limitation, restriction or qualification of the powers and activities of the company unless this is ratified by a special resolution of the shareholders of the company.

In Australian law, in *R v Byrnes*[109] the court held that, where directors enter into an unauthorised transaction, when they knew or ought to have known that they had no authority to enter into the transaction, they would thereby be making an improper use of their position as directors. Based on the persuasive authority of *R v Byrnes*, it may be stated that, if a director has knowingly entered into an unauthorised transaction on behalf of the company, there is a strong possibility of the court finding that the director has contravened the statutory duties under s 76(3)*(a)* or *(b)* of the Companies Act.

The duty of directors to avoid a conflict of interest is also a fiduciary and statutory duty. It is discussed separately below.

12.4 CONFLICT OF INTEREST

12.4.1 The common law

The duty to avoid a conflict of interest is one of the most important fiduciary duties of directors. Before turning to the new Act, a discussion of the relevant common-law principles that continue to be relevant is essential to obtain a proper understanding of the new statutory provisions relating to this duty.

The company law principles in this area of the law have been heavily influenced by trust law and particularly by the case of *Keech v Sanford*.[110] As fiduciaries, company directors are under a fiduciary duty to avoid placing themselves in a position in which their duties to the company conflict with their personal interests. Directors may furthermore not, without the informed consent of the company, make a profit or retain a profit made by them in the course of and by means of their office as directors, ie while performing their duties as directors. This test ensures that the profit made by directors that derives from their position as directors are disgorged by them. The duty to avoid a conflict of interest is undoubtedly the core duty of a fiduciary. It requires the director to account for any profit he or she has received in breach of this fiduciary duty.[111]

The rule is an inflexible one that must be applied inexorably by a court.[112] In *Sibex Construction (SA) (Pty) Ltd v Injectaseal CC*[113] the court observed that:

> [a]n examination of the case law in this court and in the courts of other jurisdictions on the fiduciary duties of directors and senior officers shows the pervasiveness of a strict ethic in this area of law. Persons in positions of trust may be less tempted to place themselves in a position where duty conflicts with interest if the courts recognised and enforced the strict ethic in this area of the law.

This fundamental and inflexible legal principle was enunciated as long ago as 1854 in *Aberdeen Railway Co v Blaikie Bros*,[114] where the court stated:

---

[109] (1995) 183 CLR 501. See Austin & Ramsay op cit n 40 para 9.280 at 475.
[110] (1726) Sel. Cas. Ch 61.
[111] *Imageview Management Ltd v Jack* [2009] BCLC 725 at 739 (CA).
[112] *Parker v Mckenna* (1874) LR 10 Ch App 96 at 124.
[113] 1988 (2) SA 54 (T) at 66D.
[114] (1854) 1 Macq 461 at 471.

> [It] is a rule of universal application that no one having such duties to discharge, shall be allowed to enter into engagements in which he has or can have, a personal interest conflicting, or which possibly may conflict, with the interests of those whom he is bound to protect. So strictly is this principle adhered to, that no question is allowed to be raised as to the fairness or unfairness of a contract so entered into.

In *Boardman v Phipps*[115] the court explained the phrase 'possibly may conflict' in the above extract from *Aberdeen Railway Co v Blaikie Bros* to mean where a reasonable man looking at the relevant facts and circumstances of the particular case would think that there was a real sensible possibility of conflict. This test was applied in *Bhullar v Bhullar*.[116]

In *Aberdeen Railway Co v Blaikie Bros* the court referred to a conflict of '*interest*' [emphasis added], but the principle applies also to a conflicting *duty*.[117] A director may also not place himself, without the consent of the company, in a situation in which he or she has conflicting duties to some other person. This may arise in multiple directorships, where a director is also a director of another company, or in the case of a nominee director. (See the discussion above on nominee directors and the duty to exercise an independent judgment.)[118] The rule (duty to avoid a conflict of interest) does not depend on fraud or absence of good faith or whether the company has incurred a loss as a result of a breach of fiduciary duty. The liability to account arises from the mere fact of a profit having been made by the director.[119]

In *Robinson v Randfontein Estates Gold Mining Co Ltd*[120] the court likewise proclaimed that no one who has a duty to perform shall place himself in a situation where their interests conflict with their duty. A director must be precluded from being swayed by his or her personal interests. The objective of the no-profit rule is to preclude directors from misusing or making improper use of their position as directors for their own personal advantage.[121]

There are two separate and independent but closely related legal principles that apply here: *(a)* a duty to avoid a conflict of personal interests (the no-conflict rule), and *(b)* a duty not to make a profit from the fiduciary's position as a director (known as the no-profit rule).[122] In *Bray v Ford*[123] Lord Herschell expressed the rule as follows:

> It is an inflexible rule of a Court of Equity that a person in a fiduciary position ... is not, unless otherwise expressly provided, entitled to make a profit [no-profit rule] [my insertion];

---

[115] [1966] 3 All ER 721 at 756H.
[116] *Sub Nom Re Bhullar Bros Ltd* [2003] 2 BCLC 241.
[117] Lord Denning in *Boulting v Association of Cinematograph, Television and Allied Technicians* (1963) 1 All ER 716 (CA) 723.
[118] See also Blackman et al op cit n 11 at 8–111: '[a] director may not place himself in a position in which he has, or can have, a personal interest or duty to another, conflicting, or which may possibly conflict with his duties to the company'.
[119] *Regal (Hastings) Ltd v Gulliver* [1942] 1 All ER 378 at 385–6.
[120] 1921 AD 168 at 178–9.
[121] *Chan v Zacharia* (1984) 154 CLR 178 at 198.
[122] See *Re Allied Business & Financial Consultants Ltd Sub Nom O'Donnell v Shanahan* [2009] 2 BCLC 666 (CA); see also *Ultraframe (UK) Ltd v Fielding* [2005] EWHC 1638 (Ch).
[123] [1896] AC 44 at 51–2.

he is not allowed to put himself in a position where his interest and duty conflict [no-conflict rule] [my insertion].

The distinction between the 'no-conflict' rule and the 'no-profit' rule is not always easy to identify and there are a number of reported decisions where the distinction has not been rigidly observed. In some cases, both rules apply.[124] As the two rules are separate and distinct, either rule or both may apply. The two rules are nevertheless different in concept.

The rationale of both the 'no-conflict' and the 'no-profit' rule is to underpin the fiduciary's duty of undivided loyalty to his or her beneficiary.[125] The strict application of the two rules enhances their deterrent effect.

(a) The no-profit rule[126]

According to the no-profit rule directors may not retain any profit made by them in their capacity as directors while performing their duties as a director. Profits made by reason of and in the course of their office as a director must be disgorged, unless the majority of shareholders in general meeting have consented to the director making the profit. The rule applies even if the company could not itself have made the profit, that is to say, even if the director had not made the profit at the expense of the company. It must, however, be emphasised that 'profit' in this context is not confined to money, but includes every gain or advantage obtained by a miscreant director.[127]

The strict application of the no-profit rule is best illustrated by the leading case of *Regal (Hastings) Ltd v Gulliver*.[128] The facts of this seminal case, which has been followed many times in many jurisdictions, are as follows:

Regal (Hastings) Ltd (hereafter 'R Co') owned a cinema. The directors resolved to acquire two further cinemas with the intention of selling all three cinemas as a going concern. For this purpose, R Co formed a subsidiary ('Hastings Amalgamated Cinemas Ltd') (hereafter 'A Co') to acquire the cinemas. The directors of R Co were also the directors of A Co. The owner of the cinemas was prepared only to lease but not to sell the cinemas to A Co and then too, only if the directors of R Co either gave their personal guarantee for the payment of the rent (which the directors were not willing to furnish) or if A Co had an issued and paid-up share capital of £5 000. R Co simply did not have the resources to acquire more than 2 000 shares of £1 each in A Co. Consequently, four of the five directors of R Co decided to subscribe for 2 000 shares of £1 each in A Co. The balance of 1 000 shares was taken up by R Co's attorney and an outsider. Having thus acquired the minimum £5 000 share capital, A Co thereafter duly obtained the leases to the two cinemas. A few weeks later, all the shares in R Co and A Co were sold. The four directors of R Co sold their shares in A Co at a profit. After the conclusion of this

---

[124] See for instance *Re Allied Business and Financial Consultants Ltd Sub Nom O'Donnell v Shanahan* (supra) 372.
[125] *Re Allied Business and Financial Consultants Ltd* (supra).
[126] This entire discussion of the no-profit rule and the corporate opportunity rule remains directly relevant to the Companies Act of 2008.
[127] *Robinson v Randfontein Estates Gold Mining Co Ltd* 1921 AD 168.
[128] [1942] 1 All ER 378 (HL); [1967] AC 134.

transaction, the new controllers of R Co instituted a derivative action on behalf of R Co, demanding that the four former directors of R Co account to R Co for the profits they had made on the sale of their shares in A Co. The House of Lords ruled that the defendants, the four former directors of R Co, were accountable to R Co for the profits made by them on the sale of the shares in A Co, as the profits had been made by them in their capacity as directors of R Co, in the course of performing their duties as directors of R Co. The opportunity to acquire the shares in A Co had come to them only because they were directors of R Co, which also gave them access to all relevant information regarding the value of the shares in A Co, including its financial statements. It was irrelevant that due to its lack of financial resources, R Co was unable to take for itself the opportunity to acquire the shares in A Co. The fact that the profits made by the defendants were not made at the expense of R Co was likewise irrelevant to the directors' duty to account, nor was it relevant that the defendants had acted in good faith and in the interests of R Co, and that there had been no fraud. The liability to account arises from the mere fact of the profit having been made. No matter how honest and well intentioned the defendants may have been, they remained under the duty to account for the profits made by them.

Ironically, the company's attorney and the outsider who had also purchased shares in A Co were able to keep the profits made by them on the sale of their shares in A Co, since they owed no fiduciary duty to the company. Even more ironically, the defendants would have been permitted to retain the profits made by them had they complied with the formality of obtaining the consent of the majority of the shareholders in general meeting to keeping the profits made by them. This formality would have presented no difficulty as the defendants were in fact the majority shareholders of R Co.[129]

The result of the decision in *Regal (Hastings) Ltd v Gulliver* was that the new purchasers of the shares of R Co had received an undeserved windfall or discount. Theirs was not a meritorious claim. An equitable principle was, in effect, taken to an unfair and inequitable conclusion.

The no-profit rule and the no-conflict rule were reaffirmed in *Phillips v Fieldstone*[130] as strict rules that allow little room for exception. The rule extends not only to actual conflicts of interest, but also to situations in which there is a real sensible possibility of conflict, as emphasised in *Aberdeen Railway Co v Blaikie Bros.*[131] The defences open to a fiduciary who is in breach of his or her trust are very limited — only the free consent of the principal after full disclosure would suffice.[132]

The Supreme Court of Appeal in *Phillips v Fieldstone*[133] stated in accordance

---

[129] The extent to which the approval of the majority of the shareholders or ratification by them of the profit made by a director may now relieve them of liability to account in terms of the new Act raises different issues.
[130] 2004 (3) SA 465 (SCA) 479 para 31.
[131] Supra, discussed in 12.4.1.
[132] *Robinson v Randfontein Estates Gold Mining Co* 1921 AD 168; *Regal (Hastings) v Gulliver* (supra).
[133] Supra.

with the principles laid down in *Regal (Hastings) Ltd v Gulliver* that once a breach of fiduciary duty has occurred, it is of no relevance that the company has suffered no loss or damage, or that the profit was not made at the expense of the company; nor is it relevant that the company could not have made use of the opportunity or the information. The court furthermore accepted that the duty of the fiduciary to avoid a conflict of interest may extend beyond the term of his or her employment (discussed in 12.4.1(*e*) below). The court declared that all the principles enunciated above were consistent with *Robinson v Randfontein Estates Gold Mining Co* and '. . . should be approved by this Court'.[134]

The no-profit rule must be distinguished from the corporate opportunity rule.

(b) The corporate opportunity rule

In sharp contrast to the no-profit rule is the corporate opportunity rule that prohibits a director from usurping any contract, information or other opportunity that properly belongs to the company and that came to him or her as director of the company. Since the opportunity belongs to the company, it is a breach of fiduciary duty for a director to divert the opportunity to him- or herself. Until recently, the courts regarded the corporate opportunity rule as an aspect of the no-profit rule or the rule against secret profits.[135] But in the recent decision of the Supreme Court of Appeal in *Da Silva v CH Chemicals (Pty) Ltd*[136] the court acknowledged the corporate opportunity rule by stating:

> A consequence of the rule is that a director is in certain circumstances obliged to acquire an economic opportunity for the company if it is acquired at all. Such an opportunity is said to be a 'corporate opportunity' or one which is the 'property' of the company.'[137]

The court also opined that, while any attempt at an all-embracing definition is likely to prove a fruitless task, a corporate opportunity is one that the company was actively pursuing or one that can be said to fall within the company's 'existing or prospective business activities', or that is related to the operations of the company within the scope of its business or that falls within its line of business.[138] It is of no consequence that the opportunity would not or could not have been taken up by the company — the opportunity would, according to *Da Silva v CH Chemicals (Pty) Ltd*, remain a corporate opportunity.

The leading cases relating to the corporate opportunity rule vividly illustrate the scope of the rule but, before turning to the cases, a few broad principles may usefully be noted here.

The corporate opportunity rule is particularly well developed in the USA where it has long been laid down that no director may exploit for him- or herself a business opportunity that in fairness belongs to the company of which he or she is a director. Since it is a requirement of the rule that the company must have had a legitimate interest in the opportunity, the US courts developed 'a line of business' test which lays down that, if the opportunity is closely related to the business that

---

[134] At para 33 at p 480G.
[135] See Blackman et al op cit n 11 at 8–164.
[136] 2008 (6) SA 620 (SCA) 627 para 18.
[137] See also *Phillips v Fieldstone Africa* 2004 (3) SA 465 (SCA) 482E.
[138] At para 19.

the company is engaged in or that it expects to be engaged in, the opportunity is a corporate one.[139] The 'line of business test' was thought to be too narrow. It was consequently extended to apply to an opportunity that is naturally in the line of the company's business or is closely associated with it or one that the company has decided to pursue.[140] In these circumstances, the director's duty is to acquire the opportunity for the company and not for him- or herself, although this will depend on the particular relationship between the director and the company and the circumstances in which the opportunity came to the director.

It seems therefore that the opportunity must not only be in the line of the business of the company or be closely associated with it, but in addition, the company must have been justifiably relying on the director to acquire it for the company, eg where the director has a general mandate from the company to acquire business opportunities for the company,[141] or where he or she is authorised to obtain a specific opportunity for the company. It was the US case of *Lagarde v Anniston Lime & Stone Company*[142] that established the 'interest' or 'expectancy' test.[143]

In *Canadian Aero Services Ltd v O'Malley*[144] the court stated that a director or senior officer may not usurp or divert for himself, or for another person or another company with which he [or she] is associated, a maturing business opportunity which his [or her] company is actively pursuing. In determining a breach of the corporate opportunity rule or the duty to avoid a conflict of interest, some of the factors to be taken into account are the position held by the defendant, the nature of the corporate opportunity, its ripeness, the circumstances in which it was obtained and the director's position in relation to it.[145]

A corporate opportunity is seen in law to be a corporate asset that belongs to the company.[146] The corporate opportunity rule is not, however, confined to property or assets only — it extends to confidential corporate information which a director has used to make a profit for him- or herself. This is exactly what the defendants did in *Boardman v Phipps*.[147] The defendants had in this case acquired confidential information belonging to a trust, which they exploited for their own profit. They were held liable to disgorge the profits that they had made from the transaction. In *Sibex Construction (SA) (Pty) Ltd v Injectaseal CC*[148] the court similarly held that directors may not use confidential information obtained by virtue of their office as directors to acquire a business opportunity for themselves. The legal principle that emerges from these authorities is that a fiduciary may not use confidential information obtained as a fiduciary for purposes that are detri-

---

[139] *Guth v Loft Inc* 5 A 2d 503 (1939).
[140] *Canadian Aero Service Ltd v O'Mallley* (1973) 40 DLR (3d) 371 (SCC) — discussed below.
[141] The facts of *Olifants Tin 'B' Syndicate v De Jager* 1912 TPD 301 illustrate this principle vividly.
[142] 28 So 199 (Ala.1899).
[143] See RC Beuthin 'Corporate opportunities and the no-profit rule' (1978) 85 *SALJ* 458.
[144] Supra.
[145] At 391.
[146] *CMS Dolphin Ltd v Simonet* [2001] 2 BCLC 704.
[147] [1966] 3 All ER 721 (HL); [1967] 2 AC 46.
[148] 1988 (2) SA 54 (T).

mental to the company. In *Cranleigh Precision Engineering (Pty) Ltd v Bryant*[149] a managing director had used confidential information obtained as managing director to set up a rival business after resigning as managing director. He was held liable to the company for breach of fiduciary duty.[150]

The misuse of a corporate opportunity may also be analysed in terms of the no-conflict rule or the no-profit rule, as has been done in English law.[151] The basis of this approach is that, historically, the corporate opportunity rule is derived from the rule that a director must avoid a conflict of duty and personal interest.

(c) Illustrative cases on the corporate opportunity rule

This section discusses a few relevant cases to illustrate the corporate opportunity rule. The cases are also used to show the critical distinction between the corporate opportunity rule and the no-profit rule.

(i) Cook v Deeks

The classic illustration of a corporate opportunity is *Cook v Deeks*.[152] In this case, three of the four directors who were also equal shareholders of T Co, a railway construction company, decided to appropriate for themselves a new, lucrative construction contract that was expected to be offered to T Co by the Canadian Pacific Railway Co, which had previous dealings with T Co. T Co had in the past built railway lines for the Canadian Pacific Railway Co. The new contract involved the continuation of a railway line that had already been laid by T Co. Instead of obtaining the new construction contract for T Co, the defendants obtained the contract for themselves to the exclusion of T Co. They thereafter sought, at a general meeting of the shareholders of T Co, to obtain approval of what they had done by passing a resolution in terms of which T Co declared that it had no interest in the new construction contract from the Canadian Pacific Railway Co. The defendants were able to pass the resolution as a result of their 75 per cent shareholding in the company. The court ruled that the benefit of the contract belonged to T Co and that the resolution passed by the company was of no effect. Directors, the court said, could not validly use their voting power to divert an opportunity to themselves. The court proclaimed[153] that men who assumed the complete control of a company's business must remember that they are not at liberty to sacrifice the interest which they are bound to protect, and, while ostensibly acting for the company, divert in their own favour business that should properly belong to the company they represent. The benefit of the contract thus belonged to the company. The court held further that directors holding a majority of the votes are not permitted to make a gift to themselves. To do this would be to allow the majority to oppress the minority shareholders.[154] The defendants were in

---

[149] [1965] 1 WLR 1293.
[150] These common-law principles are relevant to s 76(2)(a) of the Act, which is discussed below.
[151] *Ultraframe (UK) Ltd v Fielding* [2005] EWHC 1638 (Ch).
[152] [1916] 1 AC 554 (PC).
[153] At 563.
[154] At 564.

this case making a gift of corporate assets to themselves. The new contract should have been dealt with as an asset of the company, which is what it was.

The importance of the distinction between the no-profit rule and the corporate opportunity rule is that the no-profit rule requires the consent of a majority of the shareholders for a director to retain the profit made by him or her. The corporate opportunity rule, on the other hand, requires the unanimous approval of the shareholders for a director to take the opportunity for him- or herself.[155] *Cook v Deeks* illustrates that even a 75 per cent majority approval for a director to take a corporate opportunity for him- or herself is not sufficient.

(ii) Robinson v Randfontein Estates Gold Mining Co Ltd

In *Robinson v Randfontein Estates Gold Mining Co Ltd*[156] Robinson, a director and chairperson of the board of directors of the plaintiff company, had purchased a farm for himself through an agent when the company, which had been keen to purchase the farm, could not reach finality with the sellers. Robinson then sold the farm to the company at a massive profit. The court held that the company was entitled to claim from Robinson the profit made by him on the basis that, where a man stands in a position of confidence in relation to another, involving a duty to protect the interests of that other, he is not permitted to make a secret profit at the expense of the other or to place himself in a position where his interests conflict with his duty.

The vital difference between *Robinson v Randfontein Estates Gold Mining Co Ltd* and *Regal (Hastings) Ltd v Gulliver*[157] (which, as discussed in 12.4.1(*a*), is the classic example of the no-profit rule) is that in *Regal (Hastings)* the company simply did not have the funds to subscribe for more shares in A Co, whereas in *Robinson v Randfontein Estates Gold Mining Co Ltd* the company had a definite interest in acquiring the farm for itself — it was actively pursuing that opportunity. The same may be said of the new construction contract that was expected to be offered to the company in *Cook v Deeks*. The contract, furthermore, in both *Cook v Deeks* and *Robinson v Randfontein Estates Gold Mining Co Ltd* was in the line of the business of the company.

(iii) Industrial Developments Consultants Ltd v Cooley

In *Industrial Development Consultants Ltd v Cooley*[158] the court was arguably faced with the corporate opportunity rule rather than the no-profit rule. The facts of this case were as follows: The defendant, an architect and managing director of the plaintiff company, had entered into negotiations with the Eastern Gas Board to secure certain valuable construction contracts for the plaintiff company. The Eastern Gas Board was not prepared to enter into any business with the plaintiff company, but a year later the board approached the defendant in his private capacity and offered the contract personally to him. The defendant thereupon, on the pretext of ill health, resigned as managing director of the defendant company

---

[155] *Canada Safeway Ltd v Thompson* (1952) 2 DLR 591; RC Beuthin op cit n 138.
[156] 1921 AD 168.
[157] Supra.
[158] [1972] 2 All ER 162.

and took for himself the contract offered by the Eastern Gas Board. The contract in question was substantially the same contract that the plaintiff company had been attempting to obtain for itself in the previous year. The defendant was held to be accountable to the plaintiff company for the profits made by him on the contract with the Eastern Gas Board. The court found that the defendant had placed himself in a position in which his duty to the company had conflicted with his personal interests. He had one capacity at the time and that was as managing director of the plaintiff company. Information which came to him while he was managing director was information which he had a duty to convey to the plaintiff company. The fact that he had resigned as managing director was irrelevant; it did not relieve him of his fiduciary duty to avoid a conflict of interest, because the opportunity had come to him while he was a managing director of the plaintiff company. It was consequently an opportunity that belonged to the company.

The actual basis of the decision was the no-conflict rule and the fact that the defendant had used for himself information that had come to him in his capacity as a managing director. But it is cogently arguable that *Industrial Development Consultants Ltd v Cooley* concerned a corporate opportunity that belonged to the company, as there had been no decision by the board of directors of the plaintiff company to abandon the possibility of obtaining the contract from the Eastern Gas Board. The company could thus still be said to be pursuing the opportunity, thereby rendering the defendant's action a breach of the corporate opportunity rule.

(iv) *Canadian Aero Services Ltd v O'Malley*

In *Canadian Aero Services Ltd v O'Malley*[159] O'Malley and 'Z', a respected specialist in geodesy, were senior officers[160] although not directors of Canadian Aero Services Ltd ('Canaero'). O'Malley and Z had unsuccessfully attempted on behalf of Canaero to obtain a contract to carry out a topographical survey and mapping services of a certain part of Guyana. They had subsequently resigned from Canaero and had formed their own surveying company which was awarded the contract sought by Canaero. This was achieved only as a result of business contacts made by the defendants while performing services on behalf of Canaero. The defendants were held to be in a fiduciary relationship to Canaero, which the court stated had betokened loyalty, good faith and avoidance of a conflict of duty and self-interest.[161] As fiduciaries, they were liable to Canaero for breach of fiduciary duty in diverting to themselves or another person or a company with whom they were associated a maturing business opportunity that the company was actively pursuing. The court held that the defendants could not usurp a corporate opportunity even after their resignation, if their resignation had been prompted by a desire to acquire for themselves the opportunity sought by the company.[162] The court swept aside the argument that it was the company formed by the defendants,

---

[159] (1973) 40 DLR (3d) 371 (SCC).
[160] O'Malley was president and Chief Executive of Canaero while Z was an executive vice-president.
[161] At 382.
[162] Ibid.

and not the defendants personally, that had signed the contract in question. The defendants had on the facts diverted to themselves a maturing business opportunity belonging to the plaintiff company.

The fact that the defendants were not directors did not matter, because senior officers such as a keyperson or top management are under the same fiduciary duties as those imposed on directors.[163] It is significant that the liability of the defendants did not depend upon proof by Canaero that, had it not been for the defendants' intervention, Canaero would have obtained the Guyana contract.[164]

(v) *Bhullar v Bhullar*

A strict approach was adopted in *Bhullar v Bhullar*,[165] which approved of and followed *Industrial Development Consultants Ltd v Cooley*.[166] The court strongly reaffirmed that the no-profit rule and the no-conflict rule remain universal and inflexible.[167]

In this case, two directors of Bhullar Bros Ltd ('B Co'), a family-controlled property investment company, had learnt that property adjacent to that owned by B Co had become available for purchase. They purchased the property for themselves through the medium of a company controlled by them, without informing B Co of the opportunity. Shareholders holding 50 per cent of the shares of B Co instituted legal proceedings within the scope of s 459 of the Companies Act of 1985,[168] alleging that the manner in which the affairs of B Co had been conducted had constituted unfair prejudice arising from a breach of fiduciary duty. The appellants (who were the respondents in the court *a quo*) contended on appeal that the relations between the two groups of shareholders, each holding 50 per cent of the shares of B Co, had been deteriorating for some time and had broken down. The appellants had been told by the petitioners at a board meeting that they had no desire that any further properties be acquired by B Co. This was accepted in principle by the appellants. The parties had in fact decided to wind down the company's business and to go their own separate ways.

The court ruled that the appellants were in breach of their fiduciary duty. Following *Industrial Development Consultants Ltd v Cooley*,[169] the court found that the appellants had only one capacity in which they were carrying on business at the material time, namely as directors of B Co.[170] In that capacity, they were in a fiduciary relationship with B Co. Since the company was still trading at the material time, it would have been 'worthwhile' for it to acquire further property. The property was commercially attractive to the company given its proximity to

---

[163] This was followed and applied in *Volvo (Southern Africa) (Pty) Ltd v Yssel* 2009 (6) SA 531 (SCA).
[164] At 392.
[165] [2003] 2 BCLC 241 (CA). *Bhullar v Bhullar* may usefully be compared and contrasted with the approach of the court in *Bellairs v Hodnett* 1978 (1) SA 1109 (A).
[166] Supra.
[167] Paragraph 31.
[168] Substituted now by s 994 of the UK Companies Act 2006 which deals with unfairly prejudicial conduct.
[169] Supra.
[170] Paragraph 40.

its business premises. Whether or not the company would have taken the opportunity was beside the point. The existence of the opportunity and the information relating to it were relevant to the company. As in *Industrial Development Consultants Ltd v Cooley*,[171] the appellants were under a duty to communicate it to the company.[172] The appellants were consequently accountable to B Co for the profit made by them. They were ordered to transfer the property to B Co at cost.

Both *Bhullar v Bhullar* and *Industrial Development Consultants Ltd v Cooley* adopt the view that the fact that the company would not or could not avail itself of the opportunity is not of direct relevance to the liability of a director for breach of fiduciary duty in usurping that opportunity for him- or herself. *Bhullar v Bhullar* appears to have extended the criteria for identifying a corporate opportunity. There was no emphasis in the case on a maturing corporate opportunity nor any improper dealing with property belonging to the company.[173] The appellants had instead diverted to themselves an opportunity in circumstances where there was 'a real possibility of a conflict of interest'.[174]

The difficulty with the judgment in *Bhullar v Bhullar* is that the court did not consider the possibility of the corporate opportunity having ceased to be such when the petitioners had informed the appellants that they had no desire that any further properties be purchased by B Co, which was accepted by the appellants. This is tantamount to a decision of the board of directors of B Co to reject any further opportunities to purchase property for the company.

(vi) Da Silva v CH Chemicals (Pty) Ltd

The facts of *Da Silva v CH Chemicals (Pty) Ltd*[175] were as follows: Resinex, a company engaged in the distribution of chemical and plastic products, wished to enter the South African market, and was contemplating either entering into a joint venture with the respondent, CH Chemicals ('CHC'), or alternatively, establishing its own business in South Africa in competition with CHC. The first appellant, Da Silva, the managing director of CHC, had handled its negotiations with Resinex. Resinex subsequently informed Da Silva that it had decided against collaborating with CHC and would instead enter the South African market on its own by setting up two South African subsidiaries. Resinex offered Da Silva a position as the managing director of these subsidiaries. Da Silva did not inform CHC of the offer at that stage, but continued to negotiate with Resinex on behalf of CHC. Eventually Da Silva accepted the offer made by Resinex, and they entered into an agreement under which Da Silva was to establish the two South African subsidiaries of Resinex (a holding company and a trading company), Da Silva was to be the managing director of both companies, future acquisitions by the Resinex group in the territory would be directed through the said holding company, and Da Silva would be allocated a 25 per cent interest in the said holding company. During his notice period with CHC, Da Silva acquired two shelf companies which subse-

---

[171] Supra.
[172] Paragraph 41.
[173] See para 27.
[174] See *Aberdeen Railway Co v Baikie Bros*, discussed in 12.4.1 above.
[175] 2008 (6) SA 620 (SCA).

quently became the two subsidiaries of Resinex. Da Silva was appointed a director of both companies and hired premises for the two companies. During his notice period, Da Silva also purchased and then sold on behalf of the trading subsidiary of Resinex three containers of LLDPE, a plastic product (the 'LLDPE transaction'). The respondent instituted action against Da Silva for breach of fiduciary duty for which it sought disgorgement of profits and damages.

The Supreme Court of Appeal held that directors may not make a secret profit or otherwise place themselves in a position where their fiduciary duties conflict with their personal interests. A consequence of the rule is that a director is in certain circumstances obliged to acquire an economic opportunity for the company, if it is acquired at all. Such an opportunity is said to be a 'corporate opportunity' or one which is the 'property' of the company. If it is acquired by the director, not for the company but for him- or herself, the law will refuse to give effect to the director's intention and will treat the acquisition as having been made for the company.[176] The LLDPE transaction was quite straightforward: the court found that it was not a breach of fiduciary duty for a managing director serving his notice period merely to incorporate a company that, in the future, would compete with his existing employer (in this case the two Resinex subsidiaries) or to obtain premises for the future companies (as Da Silva had done), as these actions amount merely to preparatory steps taken to enable the director to obtain alternative employment.[177] However, by purchasing and selling the containers of LLDPE on behalf of the Resinex subsidiaries, while still serving his notice period with CHC, Da Silva had clearly breached his fiduciary duty to CHC. This was because any transaction involving the purchase and sale of plastic products fell within the scope of the business of CHC.[178] The court thus found that Da Silva had clearly violated the corporate opportunity rule in respect of the LLDPE transaction.

The more challenging and controversial question before the Supreme Court of Appeal was, however, whether Da Silva had breached his fiduciary duty to CHC in relation to the Resinex transaction. CHC alleged that Da Silva, by agreeing to set up the subsidiaries of Resinex in South Africa and to be appointed as their managing director, had exploited an opportunity belonging to CHC to establish some form of collaboration with Resinex in South Africa. The court examined the nature of the agreement between Da Silva and Resinex and held that it was not one of a joint business venture, but was instead a contract of employment or at least analogous to one.[179] On this basis, the court reasoned that the transaction between Da Silva and Resinex was not the same transaction pursued by CHC but rather the antithesis of what CHC had pursued. The court elaborated by stating that, when Resinex had decided to extend its operation to South Africa, it had had two choices: either to enter the market in competition with CHC or to do so in collaboration with CHC — it was either one or the other. While CHC had pursued the latter transaction, Da Silva had pursued the former transaction. The Supreme

---

[176] Paragraph 18.
[177] Paragraphs 54 and 55.
[178] Paragraph 55.
[179] Paragraphs 29 and 37.

Court of Appeal accordingly concluded that Da Silva had not breached his fiduciary duty to CHC insofar as the Resinex transaction was concerned.

The decision of the court on the Resinex transaction is open to criticism. Maleka Femida Cassim[180] questions the decision on three grounds:

> With respect, the judgment of the Supreme Court of Appeal may be criticized on three grounds. First, the court's analysis of the corporate opportunity doctrine is debatable. Secondly, the court concluded its analysis after interrogating the corporate opportunity rule, but failed to consider the no-profit rule. Thirdly, the court did not take account of the broader rule that a director may not place himself in a position of *conflict of interest*. These criticisms will be discussed in turn.
>
> . . .
>
> Moreover the finding of the court in relation to the Resinex transaction is questionable. One wonders whether the court based its decision on a distinction without a difference by stating that while the opportunity open to CHC was one for a joint venture or other form of collaboration, the opportunity open to Da Silva was one of employment, and accordingly did not amount to the appropriation of the same opportunity that belonged to the company.

See further Maleka Femida Cassim[181] for a detailed elucidation of these criticisms.

(d) Summary

This brief discussion of the common-law fiduciary duty of a director to avoid a conflict of interest shows that there are several rules that apply to this fiduciary duty. There is a duty to avoid a conflict of interest and duty, a duty to avoid a conflict of duties, and the no-profit rule and the corporate opportunity rule. There is a considerable overlap between these various rules. All these common-law principles developed by the courts continue to be relevant to the statutory standards of directors' conduct under the Act. Before proceeding to the statutory standards of directors' conduct, a brief discussion of the issue of the post-resignation duties of directors is apt.

(e) The post-resignation duties of directors

A director cannot, by resigning, divest him- or herself of the fiduciary duty not to usurp a corporate opportunity.[182] The fiduciary duty to avoid a conflict of interest cannot be evaded simply by resigning. The underlying basis of the liability of a director who exploits a corporate opportunity after his resignation is that the opportunity belongs to the company and the director is thereby appropriating for himself an opportunity that belongs to the company. In *CMS Dolphin Ltd v Simonet*,[183] the court ruled that a director will not escape liability by first resigning before seeking to exploit an opportunity that the company was actively pursuing, or one within the scope of the company's business activities of which the director

---

[180] Maleka Femida Cassim '*Da Silva v C H Chemicals (Pty) Ltd:* Fiduciary duties of resigning directors' 2009 *SALJ* 61 at 65. I am indebted to Femida for her comments and insight on *Da Silva* which I have incorporated here.
[181] Maleka Femida Cassim op cit n 180.
[182] *Canadian Aero Services v O'Malley* (1973) 40 DLR (3d) 371 (SCC); *Industrial Development Consultants Ltd v Cooley* [1972] 2 All ER 162; Blackman et al op cit n 11 at 8–174.
[183] [2001] 2 BCLC 704.

became aware in the course of performing his duties, but had deliberately concealed from the company.

This is an issue with which the court has been increasingly confronted.[184] The issue arose in *Industrial Development Consultants Ltd v Cooley*[185] and in *Canadian Aero Services v O'Malley*[186] where the court expounded[187] the principle that a director is precluded from exploiting a corporate opportunity where his resignation '... may fairly be said to have been prompted or influenced by a wish to acquire for himself the opportunity sought by the company, or where it was his position with the company rather than a fresh initiative that led him to the opportunity he later acquired'. If, on the other hand, the opportunity arose after the resignation of the director or is one of which the director had been unaware prior to his or her resignation, the director is at liberty to exploit it for him- or herself in the absence of any explicit contractual restraints.[188]

Two well-established general legal principles must be carefully balanced, namely the freedom of individuals or directors of a company to use for their own purposes their own expertise, experience and entrepreneurial skills even if acquired during the period of their office as director, and the fiduciary duty of loyalty and good faith of directors. The common-law principle now enshrined in s 22 of the Bill of Rights is that all persons should in the interests of society be productive and be permitted to engage in trade and commerce or their professions.[189]

The general policy of the law is not to impose undue restraint on post-resignation activities.[190] But this does not mean that this broad principle must in every case override the fiduciary duty of a director to act in the best interests of the company and to avoid a conflict of interest and duty.

The general principle is that, subject to restraints in a contract of service and on the provisions of the company's constitution, a director may resign simply by tendering his or her resignation even though this may not be in the best interests of the company and irrespective of the damage his or her resignation may cause to the company.[191] Resignation is a unilateral act that is not dependent on the concurrence of the company.[192] It consequently follows that, if the director's motive for resigning is found not to be for the purpose of exploiting a corporate opportunity for him- or herself, the resignation will not be in breach of his or her fiduciary duty to the company. In *Island Export Finance Ltd v Umunna*[193] the

---

[184] See Rehana Cassim 'Post-resignation duties of directors: The application of the fiduciary duty not to misappropriate corporate opportunities' (2008) 125 *SALJ* 731.
[185] Supra. See 12.4.1(*c*) above.
[186] Supra. See 12.4.1(*c*) above
[187] At 382.
[188] See *Da Silva v CH Chemicals (Pty) Ltd* (supra) at para 20. See 12.4.1(*c*) above.
[189] *Reddy v Siemens Telecommunications (Pty) Ltd* 2007 (2) SA 486 (SCA); *Da Silva v C H Chemicals* (supra) at 628 para 20.
[190] *Da Silva v C H Chemicals* (supra); *Island Export Finance Ltd v Umunna* [1986] BCLC 460.
[191] *CMS Dolphin Ltd v Simonet* (supra). See 12.4.1(*b*) above.
[192] *Symington v Pretoria-Oos Privaat Hospitaal Bedryfs (Pty) Ltd* 2005 (5) SA 550 (SCA); FHI Cassim 2005 *Annual Survey of SA Law* 477–9.
[193] [1986] BCLC 460.

court found that, since the managing director's motive for resigning was due to dissatisfaction with his role as a managing director and a desire to branch out on his own, he had committed no breach of fiduciary duty in resigning. The managing director was consequently permitted to retain profits that he had made from similar contracts he had entered into after his resignation.

In *Foster Bryant Surveying Ltd v Bryant and Savernake Property Consultants*[194] the respondent had resigned as a director of a surveying company after relations between himself and a fellow director, who was a chartered surveyor, had broken down. During his notice period, the respondent was invited by an important client to perform the services of a chartered surveyor for them after he had served his notice period, and he undertook to do so. The Court of Appeal, upholding the decision of the court of first instance, found that the respondent, by undertaking to work for a client of the company, was not in breach of his fiduciary duty to the company.

The basis of the decision was that the respondent's resignation had not been prompted by any ulterior motive or desire to appropriate for himself a corporate opportunity belonging to the company. The respondent had been neither dishonest nor disloyal to the company. His resignation had been caused by the hostile and truculent behaviour of a fellow director. The court stated[195] that, unlike in *O'Malley* or *Cooley*, the respondent was not a 'faithless fiduciary'. He had not deliberately resigned to evade his fiduciary duties. Of particular importance to the decision of the court was the fact that the respondent had already resigned when he was offered the opportunity to render services to the client of the company.

In *Da Silva v CH Chemicals (Pty) Ltd*[196] the court approved of and applied the relevant legal principles discussed above. The court reaffirmed that a director will not escape liability by first resigning before seeking to exploit an opportunity which the company was actively pursuing, or one within the scope of the company's business activities which the director had become aware of in the performance of his or her duties as a director. But if the opportunity did not fall within the scope of the company's business or is one that arose only after the resignation of the director, he or she would be free in the absence of contractual restraint to exploit it to the full. The director may then resign and set up business in competition with his or her former company or obtain employment with a competing company. The general policy of the courts is not to impose undue restraints on post-resignation activities.[197] Much of this is clearly in harmony with the decisions of the courts in English law.

In summary, as suggested in *Foster Bryant Surveying Ltd v Bryant and Savernake Property Consultants*, a pragmatic solution based on common sense and the merits of the particular case must be adopted.

The following guiding principles extracted from the cases relating to the post-resignation duties of a director have been suggested by Rehana Cassim:[198] Direc-

---

[194] [2007] EWCA Civ 200; [2007] 2 BCLC 239.
[195] At para 57.
[196] Supra.
[197] Paragraphs 20 and 21.
[198] See Rehana Cassim op cit n 184 at 731.

tors will be held accountable to their company for the appropriation of a corporate opportunity that occurs after their resignation where:
- they resign to personally take up a maturing business opportunity that the company was actively pursuing, or
- they pursue an opportunity which their company is unable to take, without the company having finally abandoned the opportunity, or
- their resignation is prompted or influenced by a desire to acquire the opportunity for themselves, or
- their position with the company led them to the opportunity, which they subsequently acquired after their resignation.

It appears that the courts are leaning towards a more flexible and merits-based approach.

12.4.2 The Act and the duty to avoid a conflict of interest

The aforegoing common law provides the background against which the new provisions of the Act pertaining to the fiduciary duty to avoid a conflict of interest may be properly understood. It must also be reiterated that s 77(2) (discussed in 12.3.2*(b)* and 12.3.4 above and in 12.9 below) preserves the common-law principles relating to the liability of 'directors' for any damages or costs sustained by the company in consequence of any breach of a duty contemplated in ss 75, 76(2), 76(3)*(a)*, *(b)* or *(c)*. Regrettably, this statutory provision is not a model of clear draftsmanship since it is not free from ambiguity. Superimposed on these common-law fiduciary duties are the new statutory duties embodied in ss 75 and 76. Section 76(3) preserves the director's duty to act in good faith and in the best interests of the company *and* the duty to exercise reasonable care, skill and diligence in the performance of his or her duties. Because the statutory duties are not properly aligned with the common-law duties, they inevitably have the effect of modifying the common-law duties.

Section 76(3)*(a)* and *(b)* was discussed above in 12.2.4 and 12.3. Here only the statutory provisions relating to an avoidance of a conflict of interest and duty are discussed.

(a) Section 76(2)(a): The duty to avoid a conflict of interest

Section 76(2)*(a)*(i) and (ii) states that a director (in the extended sense) of a company must not use the position of director, or any information obtained while acting in the capacity of director:

(i) to gain an advantage for the director, or for another person other than the company or a wholly-owned subsidiary of the company; or

(ii) to knowingly cause harm to the company or a subsidiary of the company.

It would seem that the fact that the company has not incurred any loss nor suffered any damage may not be relevant to s 76(2)*(a)*(i) and (ii).

Underlying this section is the director's duty of loyalty and fidelity and the duty of directors not to make a profit out of their position as directors. Directors may not utilise information that has come to them as directors of the company for their personal advantage, or for any other person except the company or a wholly owned subsidiary of the company. They may also not use this information to knowingly cause 'harm' to the company or its subsidiary. The section is wide enough to include both a duty to avoid a conflict of interest and a conflict of duties, as discussed above in 12.4.1.

The inclusion of a subsidiary represents an important extension of the common-law principle. At common law, a director of a holding company does not owe any fiduciary duty to its subsidiary. There is no general principle that all companies in a group of companies are to be regarded as one or as one single economic unit. Each company in a group of companies is as a general principle regarded as a separate legal entity with its own rights and liabilities,[199] unless the court decides to pierce the veil of corporate personality or this is done by the legislature.

Moreover, s 76(2)(a) does not explicitly require the use of the position of director or any information obtained as director to be improper, but it is submitted that the whole underlying sense of the section is that it is improper to use the office of director or information obtained as director to gain an advantage for oneself or to knowingly cause harm to the company or its subsidiary.

Section 76(2)(a)(i) codifies the common-law 'no-profit' rule (as discussed above in 12.4.1) and imposes a mandatory and positive duty on directors to avoid a conflict of interest. The case law and common-law principles related to this fiduciary duty are preserved. *Regal (Hastings) v Gulliver*,[200] *Robinson v Randfontein Estates Gold Mining Co*,[201] *Da Silva v CH Chemicals*[202] and the legal principles relating to the no-profit rule as adumbrated in *Phillips v Fieldstone*[203] continue to be relevant.

But while s 76(2)(a) may have encapsulated the common-law no-profit rule, what is left implicit is the corporate opportunity rule. It is submitted, however, that s 76(2)(a)(i) and (ii) is wide enough to apply to both the no-profit rule and the corporate opportunity rule. There is nothing in the section to indicate otherwise. Arguably both rules have been implicitly encapsulated in s 76(2)(a)(i) and (ii). This would also include the post-resignation duties of directors (as discussed above in 12.4.1(e)).

The section could undoubtedly have been drafted more clearly. By way of comparison, s 175(1) of the UK Companies Act 2006 states with admirable clarity that '[a] director of a company must avoid a situation in which he has, or can have, a direct or indirect interest that conflicts, or possibly may conflict, with the interests of the company'. Section 175(2) of that Act leaves no room for doubt that the exploitation of corporate information or a corporate opportunity fall within the purview of the prohibition. There is even an express provision providing that the directors' fiduciary duty to avoid a conflict of interest, including the corporate opportunity rule, continues to apply to a director who has ceased to be a director (s 170(2)). Section 175(7) of the UK Companies Act 2006 explicitly provides that any reference to a conflict of interest in s 175 includes a duty to avoid a conflict of

---
[199] *Adams v Cape Industries plc* [1990] Ch 433 (CA).
[200] Supra. See 12.4.1(a) above.
[201] Supra.
[202] Supra.
[203] Supra. See 12.4.1(a) above.

interest and duty, as well as a conflict of duties (ie a conflict between various duties of that director or a conflict of duty and duty, as it has been termed).

In order for s 76(2)*(a)*(i) and (ii) of the Act to apply, the following requirements must be satisfied:[204]

- the defendant must be a director, prescribed officer, or an alternate or a *de facto* director or a member of a board committee or of the audit committee,
- the information or advantage obtained (if any) must have come to the director while acting in his or her capacity as such or by reason of his or her position in the company as director,
- the director must have used his or her position as director or information obtained in his or her capacity as a director either to gain an advantage or to knowingly cause harm to the company or its subsidiary,
- such advantage (where applicable) must have been obtained for the director or for some other person (other than the company or its wholly owned subsidiary).[205]

Section 76(2)*(a)*(i) and (ii) is aimed at deterring directors from misusing corporate information or their position as directors in order to profit or to benefit from it. The section would deter any self-dealing that directors may be tempted to engage in. The section does not, however, refer to the 'indirect' use of the information or the status of a director.

The most obvious example of a contravention of this section would occur where a director uses inside information, ie confidential price-sensitive information, to make a gain for him- or herself. Another useful application of the section would arise where nominee directors have a duty to convey information relating to the company to their nominator. This may now entail a contravention of s 76(2)*(a)*(i) and (ii) (see the discussion above in 12.3.3 on nominee directors). *Cook v Deeks*[206] is also a typical example of a case that would fall within the ambit of s 76(2)*(a)*(i) and (ii). Another instance arises in the case of multiple directorships. Persons who are directors of two or more competing companies may not use information conveyed to them as director of one company for the benefit of another company of which they are also a director. Undoubtedly they would also fall within the ambit of s 76(2)*(a)*(i) and (ii).

An important issue, fundamental to s 76(2)*(a)*(ii), is whether a court would interpret the section as setting an objective standard, or whether it would look at the subjective belief of a director to determine whether he or she had knowingly caused harm to the company or its subsidiary. 'Knowingly' is very widely defined in s 1 of the Act to mean that a person either:

  (a) had actual knowledge of that matter;
  (b) was in a position in which the person *reasonably* [emphasis added] ought to have —
    (i) had actual knowledge;
    (ii) investigated the matter to an extent that would have provided the person with actual knowledge; or

---

[204] See *Chew v R* (1992) 173 CLR 626.
[205] See Austin & Ramsay op cit n 40 para 89.200 at 473.
[206] Supra. See 12.4.1*(c)* above.

(iii) taken other measures which, if taken, would reasonably be expected to have provided the person with actual knowledge of the matter.[207]

This definition of the word 'knowingly' points to an objective and not a subjective determination.

A crucial point in issue is whether a director or an officer would contravene s 76(2)(a)(i) if he or she honestly intended to act in the best interests of the company, ie with the intention of benefiting the company. It is submitted that the section would lose much of its effectiveness if the courts did apply a subjective test. In *Regal (Hastings) v Gulliver*[208] the directors had made a profit, or, to use the language of s 76(2)(a)(i), had gained an 'advantage' from the sale of their shares in the subsidiary company and, even though they had acted *bona fide* for the benefit of Regal (Hastings) Ltd, were held accountable for the profit made by them. It is submitted that the same would apply in terms of s 76(2)(a)(i). The directors would be in breach of this section despite their *bona fides*.

The section is drafted in terms that are wider than the common-law duty of a director to avoid a conflict of interest and duty, and the director's duty not to make a secret profit. It is the task of the courts to determine the interaction between the new statutory duties and the common-law fiduciary duty and to reconcile these parallel duties. In theory but hardly likely in practice, the statutory duty in terms of s 76(2)(a) and the common-law fiduciary duty to avoid a conflict of interest should reinforce one another. The same may be said of the other statutory and common-law fiduciary duties. The wording of s 76(2)(a)(i) and (ii) certainly creates scope for the courts to develop a much needed wider and more effective provision to deter directorial misconduct and abuse of power.

(b) Section 76(2)(b): The duty to communicate information to the company

Section 76(2)(b) of the Act states that a director of a company must:

(b) communicate to the board at the earliest practicable opportunity *any* [emphasis added] information that comes to the director's attention, unless the director —
  (i) reasonably believes that the information is —
    (aa) immaterial to the company; or
    (bb) generally available to the public, or known to the other directors; or
  (ii) is bound not to disclose that information by a legal or ethical obligation of confidentiality.

This section is premised on the underpinning common-law principle that the directors are the custodians and treasurers of corporate information. Section 76(2)(b) imposes a mandatory duty on a director to communicate to the board of directors at the earliest practicable opportunity *any* information that comes to the director's attention, unless the director reasonably believes that the information is immaterial to the company, generally available to the public, or known to the other directors. However, directors are exempt from disclosing such information if they

---

[207] The definition of 'knowingly' applies only to s 76(2)(a)(ii); it does not apply to s 76(2)(a)(i), which applies to any advantage gained, irrespective of whether innocently, negligently or in good faith.
[208] Supra. See 12.4.1(a) above.

are bound by a legal or ethical obligation of confidentiality that forbids them from doing so. Directors are protected, however, if they fail to disclose relevant information in the reasonable belief that the information is immaterial or public or known to the other directors, even if this is not in fact the case.

Section 76(2)*(b)* is an omnibus provision that requires directors to convey material corporate information to the company. Even though the section requires 'any' information to be communicated to the company, this is sensibly pruned down by requiring the information:

- to be material to the company, or
- not to be generally available to the public, or
- not to be already known to the directors, or
- not to be information that is protected from disclosure by a legal or ethical duty.

In a nutshell, the information required to be communicated to the company would essentially be relevant corporate information of a sensitive nature. The information that comes to the attention of the director need not be confidential information, nor need it be information that comes to the director in his or her capacity as a director. The section refers to 'any' information.

Section 76(2)*(b)* attempts in effect to impose an ethical standard on directors. Its *raison d'être* is simply that information is the property of the company,[209] and that, as custodians of corporate information, directors may not misuse it for their own purposes. This is the correct approach, because corporate information is nowadays regarded as one of the company's most valuable commodities. Section 76(2)*(b)* also encompasses the common-law 'fair-dealing' rule[210] — a director must disclose, unasked, any information he or she has acquired when acting for the company that is likely to influence the company's decisions and which he or she knows that those acting on behalf of the company do not already possess.

The duty to communicate relevant information to the board of directors is an integral part of the directors' fiduciary duty of loyalty, good faith and the avoidance of a conflict of interest. Section 76(2)*(b)* also complements s 76(2)*(a)*(i) and (ii). The latter prohibits the use of corporate information to gain an advantage or to inflict some harm on the company. Section 76(2)*(b)* completes this prohibition by positively requiring a director to communicate information to his or her company.

The information to be communicated to the company must in some way be concerned with the company or at least be relevant to it in some way. The section fails to specify how the information should have come to the director. The information need not necessarily come to the director in his or her capacity as director. For instance, if it came to the director by unlawful means, it is unclear whether it must still be communicated to the company.

12.5 DUTY OF CARE, SKILL AND DILIGENCE (s 76(3)*(c)*)

12.5.1 The common law prior to the Act

A brief discussion of the common law prior to the new Act is once again of importance in gaining a proper understanding of s 76(3)*(c)* of the Act, which relates to the director's duty to exercise reasonable care, skill and diligence.

---

[209] *Boardman v Phipps* (supra). See 12.4.1 above.
[210] Blackman et al op cit n 11 at 8–124.

The broad general principle is clear: directors are liable for negligence in the performance of their duties. The issue is the extent to which the directors, whether executive or non-executive directors, are liable for loss caused to the company by their incompetence or carelessness.

In striking contrast to the directors' fiduciary duty of good faith, honesty and the avoidance of a conflict of interest, which have been rigorously enforced, the courts have adopted a very lenient attitude to the positive duty of a director to exercise reasonable care, skill and diligence in the performance of his or her duties. However, in recent years, at least in other jurisdictions, a more rigorous approach has been adopted.

The duty of care, skill and diligence, which is not a fiduciary duty but is based on delictual or Aquilian liability for negligence,[211] has been formulated by the courts in largely subjective terms, that depend on the skill, experience and the ability of the particular director in question. The consequence has been that a very low or a lenient standard of care was required of directors. The duty was couched in undemanding terms. Directors were expected to exercise only that degree or level of care and skill that they were capable of, so that the more inexperienced or incompetent a director was, the lower the standard of care expected of him or her. According to this subjective test of care and skill, it is the director's ignorance or inexperience that protects him or her from liability, since the less the director knows, the less is expected of him or her.[212]

Unlike a professional person, a director is not required by law to have any special qualifications for his or her office. Directors are not members of a professional body, and no objective standard of skill is thus applicable to directors. It is also very difficult to formulate a single objective standard that will apply to all directors of all companies, ranging from small owner-managed companies to large multinational ones. Not only are there different types of companies, there are also different types of directors. An executive director will naturally be expected to know more than a non-executive director about the internal affairs of a company. Consequently the duty of care and skill must depend on the type of company, the type of director, senior manager or employee, and his or her particular skills and knowledge, position in the company and responsibilities.

There clearly are practical difficulties in prescribing an appropriate and acceptable standard of care and skill for company directors across the board. At common law, a director was required, in the performance of his or her duties, to exercise the care and skill that may be expected of a person with *his or her* knowledge and experience. In *Re Brazilian Rubber Plantations & Estates Ltd*[213] the directors were unsuccessfully sued for losses as a result of their disastrous speculation in rubber plantations in Brazil. The directors had based their decision to invest in rubber plantations on a false and fraudulent report on the output of rubber plantations. In dismissing the proceedings, the courts held that a director's duty is

---

[211] *Ex parte Lebowa Development Corporation Ltd* 1989 (3) SA 71 (T); *Du Plessis NO v Phelps* 1995 (4) SA 165 (C).
[212] See FHI Cassim 'Fraudulent or reckless trading and s 424 of the Companies Act of 1973' (1981) 98 *SALJ* 162.
[213] [1911] Ch 425 (CA) 437.

to act with such care as is reasonably to be expected from him, having regard to *his* knowledge and experience.[214] The court stated that a director is not bound to bring any special qualifications to his office. He may undertake the management of a rubber company in complete ignorance of anything connected with rubber, without incurring responsibility for the mistakes which may result from such ignorance. On the other hand, if he is acquainted with the rubber business, he must give the company the benefit of his knowledge when transacting the company's business. More importantly, it was held that a director is not liable for damage caused by errors of judgment (ie for imprudence).

Built into the test of care and skill laid down by the court is a bias in favour of the inexperienced director. At the same time, it subjects the more experienced director to a higher risk of liability for the failure to exercise reasonable care and skill.

Before proceeding further, it is important to bear in mind that care and skill are not the same thing. In *Daniels v Anderson*[215] the court stated that skill refers to the knowledge and experience that a director brings to his office. Skill perhaps means the technical competence of a director, while care is the manner in which the skill is applied. Care may be objectively assessed, but skill varies from person to person. Care and skill are different, although the line between them is not always easy to draw.

In *Re City Equitable Fire Insurance Co Ltd*[216] the company had suffered a huge shortfall in its funds as a result of which its managing director was convicted of fraud. The liquidator of the company sought to hold the other directors of the company liable for their failure to detect the fraud of the managing director. In this the liquidator was successful, as the court found the directors to have been negligent. They were, however, protected from liability by a provision in the constitution of the company. In approving the subjective test laid down in *Re Brazilian Rubber Plantations & Estates Ltd*,[217] the court in its classic judgment laid down three basic legal propositions, which over 50 years later were simply adopted without critical examination in *Fisheries Development Corporation of SA Ltd v Jorgensen; Fisheries Development Corporation of SA Ltd v AWJ Investments (Pty) Ltd*.[218] The court in this case simply ignored the fact that *Re City Equitable Fire Insurance Co* had been decided at a time when directors were honorary directors or figureheads appointed as directors more because of their title and status than their business acumen. The modern director is quite a different person altogether, usually with a superior grasp of commercial matters.

The three legal propositions laid down in *Re City Equitable Fire Insurance Co*, which are relevant to a proper understanding of s 76(3)*(c)* of the Act, are as follows:

---

[214] This principle was laid down in *Lagunas Nitrate Co v Lagunas Syndicate* [1899] 2 Ch 392.
[215] (1995) 13 ACLC 614 (CA (NSW)) 665.
[216] [1925] Ch 407.
[217] Supra.
[218] 1980 (4) SA 156 (W).

- First, a director need not exhibit in the performance of his or her duties a greater degree of skill than may reasonably be expected from a person of *his or her* [emphasis added] knowledge and experience.

  This legal principle leaves no doubt that the standard is not that of a reasonable director. It clearly is a subjective standard. The director of a life insurance company does not guarantee, for instance, that he or she has the skill of an actuary or a physician. Directors are not liable for mere errors of judgment.

- Secondly, a director is not bound to give continuous attention to the affairs of the company. His or her duties are of an intermittent nature to be performed at periodical board meetings.

  This legal principle is more relevant to non-executive directors who may not be required by their contract or by the terms of their appointment to attend all board meetings. But in modern times, this second principle no longer reflects what is expected even of a non-executive director.

- Thirdly, in respect of all duties that, having regard to the exigencies of business and the articles of association, may properly be left to some official, a director is, in the absence of grounds for suspicion, justified in trusting that official to perform such duties honestly.

  A director is thus entitled, in the absence of grounds for suspicion, to rely on the company's accountant, auditor or attorney or other such persons to perform their functions properly and honestly. Unquestioning reliance on others is however not acceptable.[219]

Both English and South African law have adopted the attitude that the directors need not have any special qualifications for their office. But unlike South African law, English law has imposed a more rigorous duty of care on the directors of a company. This new trend was not adopted in South African common law. In *Fisheries Development Corporation of SA Ltd v Jorgensen*[220] the court distinguished between the executive and the non-executive director,[221] stating that the non-executive director is not liable for mere errors of judgment; he is not required to have any special business acumen, expertise, singular ability, intelligence or even experience in the business of the company. But he must not be indifferent nor shelter behind culpable ignorance of the company's affairs, and nor must he accept information or advice blindly even if this is given by an apparently suitably qualified person.

The approach of the common-law jurisdictions may be contrasted by reference to s 8–30b of the US Model Business Corporation Act 1984 (as revised through 2002) which states that the members of the board of directors or a committee 'shall discharge their duties with the care that a person in a like position would reasonably believe appropriate under similar circumstances'. This entails an objective standard which at the same time recognises the different nature and extent of the responsibilities and duties imposed on the directors of a particular

---

[219] *Re Equitable Life Assurance Society v Human* [2002] 1 AC 408.
[220] Supra.
[221] An executive director may be under a duty to exercise a higher standard of care arising from the terms, whether express or implied, of his [or her] contract of service with the company.

company. In the USA the liability of directors for failure to exercise reasonable care and skill depends on the business judgment rule (discussed in 12.5.4 below).

Likewise, s 117 of the Canada Business Corporations Act, 1985 adopts an objective approach in providing that 'a director shall exercise that degree of care, diligence and skill which a reasonably prudent person would exercise in comparable circumstances'.

The common-law standard of care imposed by the courts in South African law under the previous company law regime is manifestly inadequate in modern times to protect shareholders from the carelessness and the negligence of the directors of a company. As the court stated in *Daniels t/as Deloitte Haskins & Sells v AWA Ltd*,[222] it is no longer appropriate to judge directors' conduct by the subjective tests that were applied in outdated precedents. The court suggested that a more objective approach to the director's duty to exercise care and skill is appropriate.

In South African law, it was s 40*(c)* and *(d)* of the Banks Amendment Act 19 of 2003 that led the way towards legislating a more rigorous and less subjective duty of care and skill for the directors, the manager, the chief executive and the secretary of a bank.[223] The new Companies Act of 2008 continues this trend.

12.5.2 Section 76(3)*(c)* of the Act and the duty of care and skill

The new Act tightens up the director's duty of care and skill. The statutory amendments to this common-law duty correctly reflect the modern commercial fact that nowadays a company director, particularly of a listed company, is often a highly skilled professional with considerable business experience. Section 76(3)*(c)* also reflects more closely contemporary attitudes towards the management of the company and corporate governance best practices.

Section 76(3)*(c)* of the Act states the following:

> (3) Subject to subsections (4) and (5), a director of a company, when acting in that capacity, must exercise the powers and perform the functions of director —
> . . .
> *(c)* with the degree of care, skill and diligence that may reasonably be expected of a person —
> (i) carrying out the same functions in relation to the company as those carried out by that director; and
> (ii) having the general knowledge, skill and experience of *that* [emphasis added] director.

The wording of the section suggests that 'care' is different from 'diligence'. Section 76(3)*(c)*(i) and (ii) requires a director to exercise the reasonable care, skill and diligence that would be exercised by a person carrying out the same functions as the director and with the same general knowledge, skill and diligence that the director has.

The standard of care and skill prescribed by the section is not entirely objective. The subjective standard at common law remains as part of the test of care and skill. Section 76(3)*(c)* introduces a twofold or dual or hybrid standard that is partly objective and partly subjective. The test or standard is objective to the extent that

---

[222] (1995) 37 NSWLR 438.
[223] See MP Larkin and FHI Cassim 2004 *Annual Survey of SA Law* 551.

the first limb of the section, ie 76(3)*(c)*(i), requires a director to exercise the degree of care, skill and diligence that may reasonably be expected of a person carrying out the same functions as the director. The standard is that of a reasonable person and not that of a reasonable director. On the other hand, the test in s 76(3) is subjective to the extent that the second limb, ie s 76(3)*(c)*(ii), requires that the knowledge, skill and experience of the director in question should also be taken into account. If the director has any special skill or is more experienced or knowledgeable, his or her conduct will be gauged or measured against this higher subjective standard.

The wording of s 76(3)*(c)*(i) and (ii) makes it clear that the objective standard prescribed by the section is the minimum standard with which all directors are expected to comply. Since the standard is an objective one, it is not limited by the lack of knowledge or experience or the ignorance of the particular director. Section 76(3)*(c)*(i) also implies that there will now be a distinction between an executive and a non-executive director and that a different standard of care and skill may be expected of a non-executive director (note the statutory wording 'carrying out the same functions . . . as those carried out by that director').

Section 76(3)*(c)*(i) imposes a standard of care that is fair and equitable insofar as it is assessed against the standard that may reasonably be expected to be exercised by a person in a like position under like circumstances. The effect of s 76(3)*(c)*(ii) is that the more skilled, knowledgeable and experienced the director is, the higher the level of care and skill he or she must exercise. On the other hand, the more inexperienced he or she is, the less the level of care and skill expected of him or her, provided that he or she does exercise reasonable care and skill. As stated above, this is the objective minimum standard of care, skill and diligence with which every director must comply.

The subjective standard of skill, knowledge and experience is taken into account only when it increases or improves the objective standard of care or skill expected of a reasonable director. If the skill or knowledge of the particular director exceeds that of a reasonably diligent person, the higher level of knowledge, skill and experience must be taken into account in deciding whether the particular director has exercised reasonable care and skill and has complied with the requirements of s 76(3)*(c)*.

The objective standard is thus a flexible and reasonable one, which is essential, because directors are not a homogeneous group. In *Dorchester Finance Co Ltd v Stebbing*[224] two of the three directors of the company were qualified accountants with business experience. They were held liable for their negligence in signing blank cheques without enquiry. This had enabled the managing director to misappropriate the funds of the company. As professional persons, a higher standard of care was expected of them. Similarly, in *Re D'Jan of London Ltd*[225] it was held that a director who had signed a fire insurance proposal form containing the wrong

---

[224] [1989] BCLC 498 (Ch).
[225] [1994] 1 BCLC 561 (Ch).

answers without reading its contents had been negligent, particularly because the proposal form had been filled in, not by the director himself, but by the insurance broker.

In determining the degree of care, skill and diligence that may reasonably be expected of a director, the courts will in all likelihood take into account the nature of the company, the nature of the decision in question, the position of the director and the nature of the responsibilities undertaken by him or her.[226] But it must be emphasised that directors are not required to take all possible care — only reasonable care is required of them. Directors are not infallible. They will make mistakes, but provided they exercise reasonable care and skill, they will not incur liability for negligence.

By 'diligence' under s 76(3)(c) is probably meant attending properly to one's duties. These would include devoting attention to the company's affairs and the proper supervision and ongoing mentoring of other company officers and employers. It would naturally entail regular attendance at board meetings. Failure to attend board meetings without a reasonable excuse for non-attendance would now, unlike in the past, very likely be seen as a failure to exercise reasonable care and diligence.

Failure to attend board meetings without a good reason is increasingly seen as irresponsible behaviour. Another instance of a failure to act diligently is to be found in *Re Barings plc (No 5)*,[227] which was decided under the UK Directors Disqualification Act 1986, where the court opined that directors collectively and individually had a continuing duty to acquire and maintain sufficient knowledge and understanding of the company's business to enable them properly to discharge their duties as directors.

12.5.3 Delegation

(a) Common-law principles

It is inevitable, particularly in large companies, that the directors would delegate certain functions and tasks to employees of the company and rely on the advice of experts employed by the company. Delegation to auditors, accountants and managers is an essential part of the way in which the business of large companies is conducted. In *Dovey v Cory*[228] the court stated that '[t]he business of life could not go on if people could not trust those who are put into a position of trust for the express purpose of attending to details of management'.[229]

In *Re City Equitable Fire Insurance Co Ltd*[230] the third legal proposition laid down by the court (see 12.5.1 above) was as follows:

> In respect of all duties that, having regard to the exigencies of business, and the articles of association, may properly be left to some official, a director is, in the absence of grounds for suspicion, justified in trusting that official to perform such duties honestly.

---

[226] This is explicitly required by s 157 of the New Zealand Companies Act of 1995.
[227] (*Sub Nom Baker v Secretary of State for Trade and Industry*) [1999] 1 BCLC 433.
[228] [1901] AC 477 (HL) 485–6.
[229] See also *Huckerby v Elliott* [1970] 1 All ER 189 at 194.
[230] [1925] Ch 407 at 429.

The Duties and the Liability of Directors

This principle was approved in *Fisheries Development Corporation of SA Ltd v Jorgensen; Fisheries Development Corporation of SA Ltd v AWJ Investments (Pty) Ltd*[231] where the court stated:

> [i]n respect of all duties that may properly be left to some official, a director is in the absence of grounds for suspicion, justified in trusting that official to perform such duties honestly. He is entitled to accept and rely on the judgment, information and advice of the management unless there are proper reasons for querying such. Similarly, he is not bound to examine entries in the company's books ... obviously, a director exercising reasonable care would not accept information and advice blindly.

Even though directors may rely on and delegate some of their functions and duties, they remain legally responsible for the proper performance of these tasks.[232] Directors, it is said, may delegate but may not abdicate their responsibilities, ie they cannot avoid accountability simply by delegating authority to some other person. Directors must carry out their supervisory and monitoring duties — they must supervise the discharge of the delegated functions.

(b) Section 76(4) and (5) of the Act

The common-law principles (discussed above in *(a)*) have been modernised, expanded and codified in s 76(4) and (5) of the Act. In essence, s 76(4)*(b)* and (5) provides that directors may now rely on the performance of an employee, a professional person, an expert, or a board committee, provided that they reasonably believe that such persons are reliable and competent or merit confidence. Directors may also rely on a person to whom the board has reasonably delegated the authority or duty to perform a delegable function of the board. The effect of s 76(4) and (5) is that, provided the requirements of the section are complied with, directors are entitled to rely on the performance of such persons, as well as information, opinions, recommendations, reports or statements prepared by them.

Section 76(4)*(b)* and (5) states that, in respect of any particular matter arising in the exercise of the powers or the performance of the functions of a director, a particular director is entitled to rely on:

(a) the performance by one or more of the employees of the company whom the director reasonably believes to be reliable and competent in the functions performed or in the information, opinions, reports or statements provided by them. Section 76(5)*(a)* implies that the director must at least have read the report or the statement in question or must in some way be familiar with it.
(b) legal counsel, accountants and other professional persons retained by the company, the board, or a committee as to matters involving skills or expertise that the director reasonably believes (i) fall within that person's professional or expert competence; or (ii) are matters as to which the particular person merits confidence (s 76(5)*(b)*).
(c) a committee of the board of which the director is not a member, unless he or she has reason to believe that the actions of the committee do not merit

---
[231] 1980 (4) SA 156 (W) 166.
[232] *Re Barings plc (No 5)* [1999] 1 BCLC 433.

confidence (s 76(5)*(c)*). This would clearly include the audit committee, although it is not restricted to the audit committee only.

In each of the instances set out in s 76(5)*(a)* to *(c)* there is a strong underlying theme that there must be a *reasonable* [emphasis added] belief in the reliability and competence of those who have been assigned the particular task or duty. The same applies to a committee that 'merits confidence', that is to say, there must be a reasonable belief in the competence and the reliability of the committee. The criteria of competence and reliability form the quintessence of the phrase 'merit confidence' in s 76(5)*(b)*(ii) and *(c)*. This provision is modelled on s 8.30*(e)* of the US Model Business Corporation Act which also uses the expression 'merits confidence'.

The gist of s 76(4)*(b)* and (5) is that, since directors must always act in good faith and in the interests of the company, they must not have had any knowledge that makes their reliance on employees, professional persons and board committees unwarranted or unreasonable.

According to s 76(4)*(b)*(ii), apart from relying on the performance of any of the persons referred to in s 76(5)*(a)* to *(c)*, the director is also entitled to rely on the information, opinions, recommendations, reports or statements, including financial statements and financial data, prepared or presented by the persons referred to in s 76(5)*(a)* to *(c)*. A report of the auditor of the company, an engineer or a valuator would obviously fall within the ambit of this provision.

A further group of persons whom a director may rely on (in terms of s 76(4)*(b)*(i)*(bb)*) are persons to whom the board may reasonably have delegated, whether formally or informally by course of conduct, the authority or duty to perform one or more of the functions of the board that are delegable under the applicable law.

If directors have complied with the requirements of s 76(4)*(b)* and (5), they will then not incur liability for the actions of persons on whom they have placed their reliance. Thus a director would not be liable for his or her reliance on a delegate to whom the board had reasonably delegated the authority to perform a delegable board function. Similarly, if legal counsel incorrectly advises that a particular contract is valid or if the company auditor incorrectly states that the company is solvent and liquid, the director will not incur liability for the error or the loss caused to the company. But, as stated above, the director's reliance on the competence of any persons referred to in s 76(5) must be warranted. If the director knows a delegate to be incompetent or dishonest, his or her reliance on that person would be unreasonable, with the result that he or she could incur liability for the wrongdoing of the delegate. Reliance on the delegate must be in good faith and in the reasonable belief that the delegate or employee in question is competent and reliable. In the case of a board committee it must 'merit confidence' and in the case of a professional person it must either be a matter within his or her professional or expert competence or it must 'merit confidence' (ie the director must be justified in his or her belief that the person or committee is competent and reliable). While the director is not explicitly required to make proper inquiries before relying on an employee, professional person or board committee, he or she must not act blindly. If the circumstances require it, the director must make inquiry.

12.5.4 The business judgment rule (a safe harbour from liability for directors) (s 76(4))

Section 76(4) encompasses a new US-style business judgment rule that has been adopted in Australia[233] and Hong Kong but rejected in the UK and New Zealand. The rule has applied in the USA for over 160 years. It is a rule of restraint that prevents a court from interfering, with the benefit of hindsight, in honest and reasonable business decisions of the directors of the company. Under the Act, the business judgment rule will have the practical effect of countering or alleviating the new less subjective and more rigorous duty of directors to exercise reasonable care, skill and diligence in the performance of their duties.

According to s 76(4)(a), in respect of any particular matter arising in the exercise of the powers or the performance of the functions of director, a particular director of the company is deemed or presumed to have exercised his or her powers or performed his or her functions in the best interests of the company and with reasonable care, skill and diligence (as contemplated in s 76(3)(b) and (c)) if:[234]

  (i) the director has taken reasonably diligent steps to become informed about the matter;
  (ii) either —
   (aa) the director had no material personal financial interest in the subject matter of the decision, and had no reasonable basis to know that any related person had a personal financial interest in the matter; or
   (bb) the director complied with the requirements of section 75 with respect to any interest contemplated in subparagraph (aa); and
  (iii) the director made a decision, or supported the decision of a committee or the board, with regard to that matter, and the director had a rational basis for believing, and did believe, that the decision was in the best interests of the company.

Accordingly, the first requirement is that the decision must be an informed one, and, secondly, the director must have no 'personal financial interest', that is to say, he or she must not be self-dealing, or alternatively, the director must in accordance with s 75 make due and proper disclosure. The interest in the matter could be his or her own or that of a related person. Thirdly, the director must have had a rational basis for believing and did believe that the decision was in the best interests of the company.

A few important matters need to be noted with regard to the third requirement (s 76(4)(a)(iii)). First, the test of rationality is objective. An objectively irrational decision is not protected by s 76(4). Secondly, the requirement of rationality is a pivotal ingredient of the business judgment rule. The decision made by the directors must be a reasonable one — if it is, the court will not substitute its own decision for that of the board. The underlying basis of this requirement is that an irrational decision is indicative of bad faith. In *Shuttleworth v Cox Brothers &*

---
[233] Section 180(2) of the Corporations Act 2001.
[234] Section 76(4)(a) of the Act.

Co (Maidenhead) Ltd[235] the court stated that, while it is not the business of the court to manage the affairs of the company, the absence of any reasonable ground for deciding that a certain course of action is for the benefit of the company may be a ground for finding lack of good faith.

Section 76(4)*(a)* thus protects only informed and reasonable business decisions. The business judgment rule creates a 'safe harbour' for a director who makes an informed and reasonable business judgment or decision. If the requirements of s 76(4)*(a)* are satisfied, a director will not be liable for honest and reasonable mistakes or honest errors of judgment that he or she may have made in managing the business of the company. The director will, in accordance with s 76(4)*(a)*, be deemed to have complied with his or her duty to act in the best interests of the company (as required by s 76(3)*(b)*) and the duty of reasonable care, skill and diligence (as required by s 76(3)*(c)*).

What is not clear from s 76(4) is who exactly bears the onus of establishing the requirements of the section as set out in s 76(4)*(a)*(i) to (iii). It is not an explicit requirement of s 76(4)*(a)* that the director must have exercised his or her powers for a proper purpose as required by s 76(3)*(a)*, unless this duty is treated by the court as an aspect of the duty to act in good faith and in the best interests of the company. Section 76(4)*(a)*, however, specifically refers only to paras *(b)* and *(c)* of sub-s (3), and makes no mention of para *(a)* of sub-s (3).

To summarise, there are three requirements for a director to be protected by the business judgment rule contained in s 76(4)*(a)*:

- he or she must have made an informed decision,
- there must have been no self-dealing or, alternatively, there must have been proper disclosure of any material personal financial interest of the director or a related person (see further 12.6 below), and
- there must be a rational basis for believing that the director was acting in the best interests of the company.

On compliance with these three requirements, the merits and the wisdom of business decisions fall outside the scope of judicial review. The courts are not business experts. They do not have the expertise to review the commercial merits of business decisions. It has thus been said that in the USA, except in a flagrant case of bad judgment or when there is evidence of bad faith, the courts do not attempt to second-guess the directors on the substantive soundness of business decisions made by them.[236] Thus, when the business judgment rule is applicable, the courts will not impose its own judgment regarding the merits of the matter on the directors.

The business judgment rule encourages innovation and risk-taking by protecting certain business decisions and other acts of the directors. Moreover, unlike the US rule and the Australian Corporations Act, 2001, s 76(4)*(a)* is not strictly confined to business decisions and business judgments only. The scope of the section is much wider, to the extent that it applies to the exercise by the directors

---

[235] [1927] 2 KB 9 (CA) 23.
[236] C Hansen 'The ALI corporate governance project: of the duty of due care and the business judgment rule' (1986) 41 *Bus Law* 1257.

of any power or the performance by them of any of their functions. If the directors have acted honestly and reasonably and the requirements of s 76(4)(a) have been fulfilled, they will not incur liability for errors of judgment or for poor business decisions even if subsequent events show that the decision of the directors or the board has had a disastrous effect on the company. But fraudulent or dishonest business decisions are quite obviously not protected.

By way of illustration, a decision by the directors of a company to sell the business of the company at a price that subsequently turns out to be undervalued will be protected by the business judgment rule provided that its requirements are satisfied, and the directors will incur no liability for their decision. The same will apply if the directors of the company relied on valuators to estimate the value of the company's business, provided that their reliance on the valuators' opinion was reasonable in the circumstances.[237]

In *Smith v Van Gorkum*, the court decided that, on the facts, the directors had not adequately informed themselves of the value of the company's business. The court found that the board of directors of Trans Union Corporation had been inadequately informed in their approval of a cash-out merger for the company. Their approval was not the product of an informed decision. The business judgment rule is predicated on diligence and reasonable care. In this case, the directors had approved the sale of the company's business at a board meeting that had lasted a mere two hours, during which Van Gorkum, the chief executive, had not even disclosed or discussed the basis on which he had arrived at the valuation of the company's shares. Van Gorkum had made a mere twenty-minute presentation to the board. A decision to sell the business of the company is a fundamentally important decision for the directors to make. Yet the board in this case uncritically accepted the recommendations of senior management of the price at which the company's business should be sold. The board had thus patently failed to inform themselves adequately of the intrinsic value of the company's shares.

12.6 THE DISCLOSURE OF THE DIRECTOR'S PERSONAL FINANCIAL INTERESTS (SECTION 75)

12.6.1 Introduction

The no-conflict rule (as discussed above in 12.4.1) requires that directors avoid putting themselves in a situation in which their personal interests conflict or may possibly conflict with their duties to the company.[238] The most obvious form of conflict of interest and duty situation, or self-dealing, arises where a director has a material interest in a contract entered into by his or her company. In this situation, the no-profit rule will also apply (see 12.4.1(a) above), so that both the no-conflict and the no-profit rules are relevant here.

There is moreover a real possibility of directors abusing their position as directors whenever they enter into a contract with their company. It consequently makes sense to subject such contracts to additional restrictions and safeguards.

---

[237] *Smith v Van Gorkum* 488 A 2d 858 (Del. Supr. 1985).
[238] *Brey v Ford* [1896] AC 44; *Aberdeen Railway Co v Blaikie Bros* (1854) 1 Macq 461, both discussed above in 12.4.1.

To prevent the abuse of the fiduciary powers of a director, the courts had long ago laid down the rule that, where a director contracts with his or her company, the contract is voidable at the option of the company.[239] A director would then be liable to account to the company for any profits made by him or her unless the contract had been approved or ratified by the shareholders. This common-law principle proved to be inconvenient for both the company and the director. It was consequently accepted that the common-law principle would not apply if the constitution of the company (ie the articles of association of the company) permitted the directors to enter into contracts with their company subject to disclosure of their interest in the contract to the board of directors, as opposed to obtaining the approval of the members in general meeting that was required at common law.

The detailed and lengthy statutory provisions relating to the disclosure by directors of their interest in a contract or a proposed contract entered into by their company were located in ss 234 to 241 of the 1973 Act. Failure to comply with these statutory provisions constituted a criminal offence — an indication of the importance attached to the common-law duty of a director to avoid such a conflict of interest and duty.

Section 75 of the new Act, consisting of eight subsections, replaces ss 234 to 241 of the 1973 Act.

12.6.2 Section 75(5): Proposed transactions

The general principle is straightforward: a director (in the extended sense)[240] is required by s 75(5) to disclose any 'personal financial interest' that he or she or a related person has in respect of a matter to be considered at a meeting of the board of directors. This declaration or disclosure of the director's interest in the matter must be made before it is considered by the board of directors (s 75(5)). The meaning of the phrase 'personal financial interest' lies at the very core of s 75.

A 'personal financial interest' is defined in s 1 of the Act to mean 'a *direct* [emphasis added] material interest of that person, of a financial, monetary or economic nature, or to which a monetary value may be attributed'. An interest held by a person in a unit trust or collective investment scheme is excluded from this definition, unless that person has direct control over the investment decisions of that fund or investment. The director's interest must be a 'direct' material interest, not an indirect one. Since, however, the interest of a person related to the director who is known by the director to hold a personal financial interest falls within the ambit of s 75(5), the omission of the word 'indirect' may be less significant in practice.

The financial interest must not only be a direct one, it must also be material. While a 'material' interest is not defined in s 75, it is defined in s 1, which states that:

---

[239] *North-West Transportation Co Ltd v Beatty* (1887) 12 App Cas 589 (PC); *Aberdeen Railway Co v Blaikie Bros*, discussed in 12.4.1.
[240] The extended meaning of director has been discussed above. The draft Companies Amendment Bill, 2010 (cl 46) proposes to delete the reference to members of the audit committee for the purposes of s 75.

'material' when used as an adjective, means significant in the particular circumstances to a degree that is —
(a) of consequence in determining the matter; or
(b) might reasonably affect a person's judgment or decision-making in the matter.

In view of this definition, there are no hard and fast rules as to when a financial interest would be 'material'. The word 'material' is clearly not an exact concept that can be accurately defined; its meaning will depend on the particular facts and circumstances. However, what may be confidently stated is that the interest must be a significant and not a trivial one. The *de minimis* rule will thus apply.

What exactly is meant by an 'interest' remains to be seen. It has been left to the courts to decide what financial interests will fall within the ambit of the section. It is clear from the definition of a 'personal financial interest' that a director need not be a party to the matter in order to have an 'interest' in the matter. A shareholding that is not insignificant or immaterial in a company that is contracting with the company of which he or she is a director will probably fall within the scope of s 75(5) if the director directly or indirectly 'controls' the former company (as determined in accordance with s 2 of the Act and the definition of 'related persons'). Likewise, a director's interest in his or her own service contract which is to be considered by the board (or the remuneration committee) has been held in English law to be an interest that must be disclosed.[241] All non-pecuniary interests are excluded from s 75. In *Hospital Products Ltd v United States Surgical Corp*[242] it was stated that a material financial interest is likely to be one that would give rise to a real or sensible possibility of conflict of interest.[243]

Section 75(5) is triggered when a director or related person (to the knowledge of the director) has a direct material financial interest in a matter to be considered by the board of directors.[244] The section requires disclosure rather than approval of the director's personal financial interest in the matter to be decided by the board. If s 75(5) is complied with, and the board duly makes a decision or approves of the transaction or agreement, or if it is ratified by ordinary resolution of the shareholders, the decision, transaction or agreement will be valid despite any personal financial interest of a director or a related person (s 75(7)).

Section 75(8) provides that a court, on application by an interested person, may declare valid a transaction or agreement approved by the board or the shareholders, as the case may be, despite a failure by the director to comply with the requirements of s 75.

(a) What must be disclosed

In terms of s 75(5)*(a)* to *(c)* the following matters must be disclosed by the directors:

---

[241] *Runciman v Walter Runciman plc* [1992] BCLC 1084.
[242] (1984) 156 CLR 41.
[243] See s 182(6)*(a)* of the UK Companies Act 2006 which states this as a specific requirement of the section.
[244] For the meaning of 'related persons' see generally ss 1 and 2 of the Act and chapter 6: Groups of Companies and Related Persons. An important amendment is proposed by the draft Companies Amendment Bill, 2010 (cl 46) in that 'related persons' in the context of s 75 also includes a second company of which the relevant director (or related person) is also a director or a close corporation of which he or she is a member.

- the personal financial interest that he or she or a related person has and its general nature, before the matter is considered at the meeting,
- any material information relating to the matter and known by him or her (this must be disclosed at the meeting),
- any observations or pertinent insights relating to the matter. These may — not must — be disclosed if requested by the other directors.

In English law, the courts have insisted on strict compliance with the equivalent requirements of s 182 of the UK Companies Act 2006.[245] It is very likely that the strict English law approach will also be adopted by our courts. Disclosure in terms of s 75(5) must of course be made before the company enters into the transaction or the particular matter in question. The manner of disclosure is not prescribed. While disclosure of the general nature of the interest (s 75(5)(*a*)) requires prior notice, it seems that this could be prior written or oral notification — either would suffice (see further s 75(4), discussed below in 12.6.3). Disclosure of material information and observations or insights relating to the matter may be disclosed at the meeting itself (see s 75(5)(*b*) and *(c)* read with *(d)*).

As stated above, s 75(5) is intentionally limited to a proposed matter 'to be' considered at a board meeting. The underpinning rationale is that, if the board is informed of a director's interest in a proposed matter or transaction, it is then free to decide whether and on what terms to enter into the transaction.[246]

In order to disclose a personal financial interest of a related person, the director must obviously have been aware of or have known about it. But s 1 of the Act defines 'knowing', 'knowingly' or 'knows' very widely:

> when used with respect to a person, and in relation to a particular matter, means that the person either —
> *(a)* had actual knowledge of that matter;
> *(b)* was in a position in which the person reasonably ought to have —
>   (i) had actual knowledge;
>   (ii) investigated the matter to an extent that would have provided the person with actual knowledge; or
>   (iii) taken other measures which, if taken, would reasonably be expected to have provided the person with actual knowledge of the matter.

In some circumstances, as specified above, constructive knowledge would thus suffice.

It is unclear whether the section will apply to a material personal financial interest held by a director through a company that is not a related person. It is also uncertain whether disclosure must be made at a board meeting or whether disclosure to a committee of the board will suffice. It is suggested that the reference in s 76(5) to 'a meeting of the board' indicates that disclosure to a board committee as opposed to the board itself will not comply with s 76(5).[247]

Section 75(5)(*a*) and *(b)* requires that the director must disclose his or her interest and its general nature and any material information relating to the matter. This does not seem to require disclosure of the extent of the director's interest in

---
[245] *Movitex Ltd v Bulfield* [1988] BCLC 104 (ChD).
[246] This was the explanation given by the Attorney-General in England.
[247] *Guinness plc v Saunders* [1988] 2 All ER 940 (CA).

the proposed matter.[248] All that is required is disclosure of the fact of the interest held by him or her and its *'general nature'* [emphasis added] but not necessarily its extent. Any material information relating to the matter, rather than the interest held by the director, must be disclosed. In English law, the courts have insisted on 'full and frank' disclosure.[249] Perhaps the proper approach is that the amount of detail disclosed depends in each case on the nature of the contract or matter to be considered at the board meeting and the context in which it arises.[250] By the same token, sufficient detail should be disclosed to enable the board to assess the benefit that the director may reap — a mere suggestion or mere statement that the director has an interest may not suffice.[251]

(b) Disclose and recuse

Having made the disclosure, the director, if present at the meeting, must leave the meeting immediately thereafter and may not take part in the consideration of the matter, save to disclose to the meeting any material information and any observations or pertinent insights relating to the matter, as discussed above (s 75(5)*(d)* and *(e)*). These provisions embody the new 'disclose and recuse' approach. The director's departure from the meeting does not affect the quorum for the meeting as he or she is deemed for this purpose to be present at the meeting. But, for voting purposes and for determining whether the resolution has sufficient support for its adoption, he or she is regarded as being absent (s 75(5)*(f)*(i) and (ii)).

The director must not execute any document on behalf of the company in relation to the matter, unless he or she is specifically requested or directed to do so by the board (s 75(5)*(g)*).

12.6.3 Section 75(6): Declaration of an interest in existing contracts

If a director, or a related person to the knowledge of the director, acquires any personal financial interest in an agreement or other matter in which the company has a material interest, after the agreement or matter was approved by the company, the director must in terms of s 75(6) 'promptly' disclose to the board of directors (or to shareholders in the case of a company that has only one director who is not the sole beneficial securities holder) the nature and extent of the interest and the material circumstances relating to the acquisition of the interest. One can only assume that by 'promptly' in this context is meant that disclosure must be made as soon as is reasonably practicable after the acquisition of the interest.

Section 75(6) refers to a 'personal financial interest' of the director or related person, which is defined in s 1 to mean a *material* [emphasis added] financial interest. But disclosure is to be made in terms of s 75(6) only if the *company* has a 'material' interest in the agreement or the matter. No such requirement is pre-

---

[248] See in this respect s 75(6), which distinctly requires disclosure of the nature and extent of the director's interest. The same applies to s 75(4).
[249] *Ultraframe (UK) Ltd v Fielding* [2005] EWHC 1638 (Ch); see also *Neptune (Vehicle Washing Equipment) Ltd v Fitzgerald (No 2)* [1995] BCC 1000 at 1016; *Movitex Ltd v Bulfield* [1988] BCLC 104, discussed in 12.6.2.
[250] *Gray v New Augarita Porcupine Mines Ltd* (1952) 3 DLR 1 at 14.
[251] *Camelot Resources Ltd v MacDonald* (1994) 14 ACSR 437.

scribed by s 75(5) which, as discussed above in 12.6.2, applies to interests held in a proposed transaction as opposed to an existing transaction.

12.6.4 General notice in advance

Section 75(4) provides that a director may at any time disclose any personal financial interest in advance, by delivering to the board of directors (or shareholders in the case of a board consisting of one director who is not the sole beneficial securities holder) a general notice or a standing notice in writing that states the nature and the extent of his or her interest, to be used generally for the purposes of s 75. The general notice remains operative until it has been changed or withdrawn by the director by written notice (s 75(4)). This particular provision does not refer, either expressly or impliedly, to an interest which to the knowledge of the director is held by a related person.

There is no explicit provision in s 75 that notice may be given in electronic form, but perhaps s 6(10) may apply here to permit such notice to be given in this form.

12.6.5 Disclosure to whom?

Disclosure must be made to the board of directors. In *Guinness plc v Saunders*[252] the court held that disclosure must be made to the board of directors; disclosure to a board committee is not sufficient (see further 12.6.2 above.)

In the case of a private company with one director,[253] disclosure will entail disclosure to oneself. To avoid this ludicrous situation, s 75(3) provides that if the sole director of the company is not also the sole beneficial securities holder of the company, disclosure of the nature and extent of the director's (or related person's) personal financial interest must be made to the shareholders of the company, and their approval must be obtained by way of an ordinary resolution (s 75(3)(a) and (b)). The same applies where a director or related person acquires a personal financial interest in the matter after its approval by the company. Here too disclosure must be made to the shareholders (s 75(6)). See further the above discussion of s 75(6) in 12.6.3.

12.6.6 Where no declaration of interests is necessary

According to s 75(2) of the Act, no declaration of personal financial interests is required in the following circumstances:

- in respect of decisions generally affecting all the directors in their capacity as directors,
- in respect of decisions generally affecting a class of persons of which the director is a member, unless the only members of that class are the director or a person related or interrelated to him or her,[254]

---

[252] (1988) 2 All ER 940 (CA) 944 (see 12.6.2 above).
[253] A company with one director can only be a private company.
[254] There is no longer any definition of interrelated persons. The draft Companies Bill defined this term, but the definition was strangely removed from the Act itself. The draft Companies Amendment Bill, 2010 now proposes to remedy this.

- in respect of a proposal to remove that director from office in terms of s 71, or
- where one person holds all the beneficial interests of all the issued securities of the company and that person is the sole director of the company.

A possible solution in the last instance is to have an express provision in the Companies Act that, in this event, the director's personal financial interest must be recorded in the minutes of a board meeting.[255] Since there is no such provision in our Companies Act, the effect of s 75(2)(b)(i) and (ii) is that a sole director and shareholder is not subject to the statutory duty to disclose his or her personal interests under s 75. A sole director who is also the sole shareholder will fall outside the scope of s 75.

12.6.7 Failure to comply with s 75

As pointed out above, if the decision, transaction or agreement is approved by the board of directors (or shareholders, as the case may be) on compliance with the disclosure requirements of s 75, it is valid despite any personal financial interest of a director (s 75(7)). Section 75(7) also provides scope for ratification by ordinary resolution of the shareholders. This will seemingly apply where a transaction has been approved without the requisite disclosure by the director — in these circumstances the shareholders may later ratify the transaction, presumably after disclosure is made. On the other hand, on a failure by a director to comply with the disclosure requirements of s 75, it may still be possible for the court on application by any interested person to declare the transaction, decision or agreement that had been approved by the board of directors or the shareholders, as the case may be, to be a valid decision, agreement or transaction — despite the director's failure to disclose the relevant interest (s 75(8)).

As regards the miscreant director who has failed to declare a personal financial interest held by him or her or a related person, logically the director will be in breach of his or her fiduciary duty to avoid a conflict of interest, unless the transaction is ratified by ordinary resolution of the shareholders.

12.7 INDEMNIFICATION AND DIRECTORS' AND OFFICERS' INSURANCE

12.7.1 Introduction

There are three important methods that companies have relied on in the past in order to limit the extent to which their directors are exposed to personal liability for negligence, breach of fiduciary duty, breach of trust or other default in the performance of their duties. First, companies have inserted provisions in their constitutions that have exempted directors from liability for negligence, breach of fiduciary duty or breach of trust.[256] Secondly, indemnities were given to directors that protected them from loss as a result of some default, breach of duty or negligence. A third method was to effect and to pay for directors' liability insurance, which indemnified a director from liability arising out of his or her service to

---

[255] See *Runciman v Walter Runciman plc* [1992] BCLC 1084, discussed in 12.6.2. But see s 57(3).
[256] See *Re Brazilian Rubber Plantations & Estates Ltd* [1911] Ch 425 (CA) and *Re City Equitable Fire Insurance Co Ltd* (1925) Ch 407 (discussed in 12.5.1 above).

the company. The extent to which these methods are valid and permissible has a direct effect on the effectiveness of the fiduciary and statutory duties imposed on directors.

Their main justification is that, without these mechanisms, it would be difficult for companies to find suitable persons willing to serve as directors. The Greene Committee in the UK[257] rejected this assertion on the basis that there was no foundation for it. There nevertheless remains a need to carefully balance two conflicting underpinning policies: on the one hand, to encourage persons to accept office as directors, and on the other hand, to protect companies and shareholders from the effects of the wrongful acts of the directors of a company. Now that the Act provides a more effective means of enforcing the duties of directors and a more effective derivative action (in s 165), the need for such protective measures for directors is perceived to have been magnified. Directors may now face the real possibility of more derivative actions being instituted against them personally by disgruntled minority shareholders and others, including shareholder activists, which they may have to defend at their own cost. Hence the importance of s 78 of the Act.

To curtail abuse and ensure that directors did not with impunity flout their fiduciary and statutory duties, s 247 of the 1973 Act declared all such provisions void, whether contained in a contract with the company or in the constitution of the company. The section was amended in 1998[258] to enable a company to effect insurance to protect itself against liability for the negligence, default, or breach of duty or trust of any director or officer of the company. This provision protected the company and not the director, who could not validly be indemnified against liability for his or her own negligence, default or breach of duty or trust. Section 247(2) did however permit a company to indemnify a director against any liability incurred by the director in successfully defending any legal proceedings, whether criminal or civil, instituted against him or her.

12.7.2 Section 78(1) to (8): Exemptions, indemnities and insurance

Section 78 of the Act is an important supplement to the fiduciary duties and the statutory liability of directors of companies.

Section 78 in essence prohibits, subject to certain exceptions, any exemptions or indemnities for directors. 'Directors' is used in the extended sense of the word to include an alternate director and even a 'former' director. A 'former' director is not defined in the Act, but presumably the section will apply to directors who have resigned or vacated their office as directors after having committed during their periods of office a breach of duty or trust, negligence, or were in default in some way in the performance of their duties. Section 78 also applies to members of a board committee or an audit committee and to prescribed officers of the company, whether or not they are directors. The section will presumably apply to nominee directors, but it is uncertain to what extent it will apply to an indemnity given to the nominee director by his or her nominator, as opposed to one given by the company.

---

[257] Company Law Amendment Committee Cmnd 2657 (1925–26) paras 46–7.
[258] By s 12 of the Companies Amendment Act 35 of 1998.

The Duties and the Liability of Directors

Although it must await judicial clarification, there appears to be nothing in s 78 or s 78(6) that prevents a nominee or any other director from being indemnified against liability by someone other than the company.

12.7.3 Exemption from duty or liability

Section 78(2) provides that, subject to s 78(4) to (6), a provision in an agreement, the Memorandum of Incorporation, the rules or a resolution of the company, whether express or implied, is void to the extent that it directly or indirectly purports to:

- relieve a director of a duty contemplated in s 75 or s 76 (discussed in 12.3 to 12.6 above) (ie a failure to disclose a personal financial interest in a matter considered by the company, or a breach of the standards of directors' conduct, including a fiduciary or a statutory duty) — this provision reinforces the mandatory nature of these duties,
- relieve a director of any liability contemplated in s 77, or
- negate, limit or restrict any legal consequences arising from an act or omission that constitutes wilful misconduct or wilful breach of trust on the part of the director.

The prohibition in s 78(2) applies to the company's Memorandum of Incorporation and its rules, but also extends to a separate agreement outside the company's Memorandum of Incorporation. This wide prohibition is pruned down by permitting a company in certain circumstances to indemnify a director and to purchase insurance protection for its directors and officers. In this regard, this section (s 78(2)) is subject to s 78(4), (5) and (6), discussed below in 12.7.4.

12.7.4 Indemnification

(a) When an indemnity is prohibited (s 78(6))

While s 78(2) prohibits certain exemptions or exclusions from duties and liability, s 78(6) prohibits the indemnification by a company of its directors in certain circumstances. The section states that a company may not indemnify a director in respect of the following:

- any liability arising in terms of s 77(3)*(a)*, *(b)* or *(c)* (ie knowingly acting without authority on behalf of the company; acquiescing in the fraudulent or reckless conduct of the company's business or trading in insolvent circumstances contrary to s 22; knowingly being a party to conduct calculated to defraud a creditor, employee or shareholder of the company or for another fraudulent purpose),
- liability arising from wilful misconduct or wilful breach of trust on the part of the director (this provision is perfectly sensible, because there is no good reason why a company should pay for the wilful misconduct of a miscreant director), or
- any fine contemplated in s 78(3), which provides that a company may not directly or indirectly pay any fine that may be imposed on the director of the company or of a related company who has been convicted of any offence in terms of any national legislation.

(b) When an indemnity is permissible (s 78(5))

Subject to the above exceptions of s 78(6) and to any contrary provisions of the company's Memorandum of Incorporation, s 78(5) permits indemnification of *any* [emphasis added] liability incurred by a director. This means there is now a considerably wider scope for the indemnification of the directors (and prescribed officers) of a company.

(c) Advances and indemnities to defend legal proceedings (s 78(4))

Section 78(4) states that, except to the extent that the company's Memorandum of Incorporation provides otherwise, the company may advance expenses to a director to defend any legal proceedings that arise out of the director's service to the company, and may directly or indirectly indemnify a director in respect of such litigation expenses, irrespective of whether or not the company has advanced these expenses, if the legal proceedings:

- have subsequently been abandoned or exculpate the director, or
- relate to liability for which the company may indemnify the director in terms of s 78(5) and (6).

Section 78(4) and (5) is particularly relevant to derivative actions instituted against a director. Presumably, s 78(4) applies to both civil and criminal proceedings, and perhaps also to legal proceedings brought by the Companies and Intellectual Property Commission ('the Companies Commission') in the exercise of its considerable powers.

It is interesting that advances of expenses or indemnities permitted by s 78(4) are not subject to the approval or the consent of the shareholders of the company, although an indemnity may be prohibited by the company's Memorandum of Incorporation. A welcome change, however, in the new statutory provisions is that, unlike under the 1973 Act,[259] companies may now make a loan in advance to directors to allow them to meet their legal costs to defend litigation arising out of their service with the company. This will include the fees of legal counsel. Legal costs frequently involve substantial amounts of money. It is not required that the company should wait until the court has made its decision in the legal proceedings. To put it differently, while an indemnity is generally retrospective, an advance to pay legal costs is prospective.[260]

Section 78(4)*(b)* permits a company to indemnify a director for litigation expenses, irrespective of whether or not it actually advances the expenses. Where the company does in fact advance the expenses then, if the decision of the court is unfavourable to the director, with the result that the director has not successfully defended the legal proceedings, the money advanced to him or her by the company must be repaid to the company — unless the proceedings concerned an indemnifiable liability (under s 78(5) and (6)) or were abandoned. On the other hand, if the director has successfully defended the legal proceedings, the director

---

[259] Section 247 of the 1973 Act (discussed in 12.7.1 above).
[260] See the official text of the US Model Business Corporation Act s 8–103.

may retain the money advanced to him or her as part of the indemnity that was granted to him or her (see s 78(4)(*b*)).[261]

Section 78(4) does not go so far as s 119(3) of the Canada Business Corporations Act 1985, which imposes a mandatory statutory duty on a company to indemnify a director who has acted in good faith and has been substantially successful on the merits in his defence of the legal action instituted against him.[262] Mandatory indemnification of reasonable legal expenses incurred by a director in successfully defending legal proceedings instituted against a director of the company is also required by s 8.52 of the US Model Business Corporation Act.[263] This applies only in the absence of any contrary provision in the company's constitution.

It should be noted that there is no distinct or explicit requirement in s 78(4) of the Act that the director's ability to repay the advance must be taken into consideration before the advance is made. The safeguard, however, is that the directors, in approving the advance, are under a fiduciary duty to act in good faith and in the interests of the company.

12.7.5 Payment of fines and penalties

Section 78(3) prohibits a company from directly or indirectly paying any fine that may be imposed on a director of the company, or of a related company, who has been convicted of an offence in terms of any national legislation.[264]

This provision is commendable. There is no reason, for instance, for a company to pay a fine imposed on a director for contravening the insider trading provisions of the Securities Services Act 36 of 2004. The glaring defect of s 78(3) is that it is unnecessarily narrow in being confined to a fine levied in terms only of any national legislation. The section excludes, without any apparent good reason, administrative fines levied by a regulatory authority. Administrative fines ought to have been brought within the purview of the provision.

12.7.6 Directors' and officers' liability insurance

A company may purchase and maintain insurance on behalf of a director (in the extended sense) or prescribed officer of the company during their periods of office to protect them against liability incurred in their capacity as directors or prescribed officers of the company. This type of insurance is known in other jurisdictions as 'directors and officers liability insurance' (D&O insurance). It confers protection on the directors and prescribed officers against liability or expenses for which a company is permitted to indemnify a director. Insurance policies of this nature may also provide protection to the directors and prescribed officers in the event of

---

[261] RP Austin, HAJ Ford and I Ramsay *Company directors; principles of law and corporate governance* (2005) para 17–13 at 655.
[262] This in effect means that a director would be entitled to an indemnity even if he was not fully exonerated but is exonerated to a large extent — a difficult question of degree.
[263] As revised through 2002.
[264] The draft Companies Amendment Bill, 2010 (cl 48) proposes the creation of an exception to this provision for private or personal liability companies having either a sole shareholder who is also the sole director, or having related individuals as the only shareholders and directors.

the company being unable to honour the indemnification payments it has undertaken. The D&O liability insurance policies must of course provide insurance cover only for those matters that are statutorily permissible. This type of policy usually affords insurance cover for damages for an error, a negligent or misleading statement, or breach of duty, but may not protect against liability arising from a fraudulent, dishonest or an illegal act or against wilful default or a wilful breach of a duty owed to the company.

Section 78(7) thus provides that, unless the company's Memorandum of Incorporation provides otherwise, a company may purchase insurance to protect a director against any liability or expenses for which the company is permitted to indemnify a director in accordance with s 78(5). The section thus permits insurance not against all liability, but against such liability or expenses for which it is permitted to indemnify a director (or prescribed officer).

In terms of s 78(7)(b), the company may also effect insurance to protect itself against the expenses that it is allowed to advance to a director or indemnify a director (under s 78(4)(a) and (b)) or to protect itself against any indemnifiable liability (under s 78(5) and (6)).[265] It is to be noted that, while s 78(7) explicitly refers to the purchase by a company of an insurance policy, there is no specific reference to maintaining the insurance policy by, for instance, paying the premiums for the policy. This needlessly creates uncertainty where there should be none.

12.7.7 Restitution

Section 78(8) provides that a company is entitled to claim restitution from a director of the company or of a related company for any money paid directly or indirectly by the company to the director or to some other person on behalf of the director, in any manner inconsistent with s 78.

In conclusion, it is clear from this discussion that, if directors of companies really desire to avoid liability incurred in the performance of their duties, their best form of action will be to comply with their fiduciary and statutory duties.

12.8 RATIFICATION, CONDONATION AND RELIEF

12.8.1 Relief by the court

Section 77(9)(a) and (b) states that:

> (9) In any proceedings against a director, other than for wilful misconduct or wilful breach of trust, the court may relieve the director, either wholly or partly, from any liability set out in this section, on any terms the court considers just if it appears to the court that—
> (a) the director is or may be liable, but has acted honestly and reasonably; or
> (b) having regard to all the circumstances of the case, including those connected with the appointment of the director, it would be fair to excuse the director.

This is supplemented by s 77(10) which enables a director, who has reason to apprehend that a claim may be made against him or her[266] alleging that he or she is

---
[265] The draft Companies Amendment Bill, 2010 (cl 48) proposes to widen this so that companies may effect insurance to protect themselves against any other contingency as well.
[266] For example, a claim that could result in a derivative action against him or her.

liable, to lodge an anticipatory application to a court for relief. The court may grant relief on the same grounds as if the matter had come before the court in terms of s 77(9). Section 77(10), like s 77(9), does not apply to wilful misconduct or a wilful breach of trust.

There are two grounds for relief, whether under s 77(9) or s 77(10):

- the director must have acted honestly and reasonably, or
- the circumstances must be such that he or she ought fairly to be excused from liability under s 77 for his or her negligence, breach of duty or other default that does not amount to wilful misconduct or wilful breach of trust.

It seems that either, and not both, of these requirements need be fulfilled. In contrast, under the 1973 Act, both requirements had to be satisfied. It is suggested that s 77(9) ought preferably to be read in the same way, so that the court should refuse to grant relief where, even if the director had acted honestly and reasonably, the circumstances are such that he or she ought not to be excused. The court has a discretion whether to grant relief. It may grant relief on such terms as it considers just, and may relieve the director from liability wholly or partially.

Section 77(9) of the Act is, in several respects, similar but not identical to s 248 of the 1973 Act, which it replaces. Section 248 also required that the director must have acted honestly and reasonably. But, unlike s 248, the new s 77(9) and (10) no longer applies to the auditor of the company.

Regal (Hastings) Ltd v Gulliver, where the issue of relief by the court was not actually raised, offers an excellent example of a case that is appropriate for the exercise of the court's discretion under s 77(9).[267] In *Ex parte Lebowa Development Corporation Ltd*[268] the court held that s 248 of the 1973 Act did not empower a court to relieve a director from any liability resulting from fraudulent conduct on his part, nor did s 248 apply to granting relief to a director or officer against a claim by a third party, such as a creditor of the company. Section 248 empowered the court to grant relief against a claim by the company only. In the case of gross negligence, reasonableness may virtually never be found.[269] These principles will in all probability continue to apply to s 77(9) and (10) of the Act.

In *PNC Telecom plc v Thomas*[270] a director had, without having acted fraudulently, placed himself in a position of conflict of interest and duty. He was held to have failed to act reasonably 'in the way in which a man of affairs . . . dealing with his own affairs with reasonable care and circumspection could reasonably be expected to act in such a case'.[271] In *PNC Telecom plc v Thomas*[272] the court accepted that, under the equivalent section in the UK Companies Act 1985 (s 727(1); now s 1157 of the UK Companies Act 2006), a director may act reasonably even though he has been negligent. This, of course, will apply equally to s 77(9) of the Act.

---

[267] See 12.4.1(*a*) above for the facts of the case.
[268] 1989 (3) SA 71 (T) 107.
[269] *Ex parte Lebowa Development Corp Ltd* (supra) at 109.
[270] [2008] 2 BCLC 95 (ChD).
[271] This is the test laid down by Buckley J in *In Re Duomatic Ltd* [1969] 1 All ER 161 (ChD).
[272] At para 94.

In *In Re Duomatic Ltd*[273] the court found that a director who had agreed to make an unauthorised severance payment to a fellow director had acted unreasonably and ought not to be excused because he had failed to take legal advice on whether the severance payment could properly be claimed. In *Re D'Jan of London Ltd*[274] the court aptly summarised the dilemma in stating that it may seem odd that a person who had been found to be negligent, which entailed failing to exercise reasonable care, could ever satisfy a court that he had acted reasonably.[275]

It must be emphasised that s 77(9)(a) requires a director to act both honestly and reasonably. It is most unlikely that s 77(9) will apply to a director who, in contravention of s 22 read with s 77(3)(b), had knowingly acquiesced in the conduct of the company's business in a manner prohibited by s 22, namely fraudulent, reckless or grossly negligent conduct of the company's business.[276] Gross negligence cannot be reasonable conduct within the scope of s 77(9)(a).[277]

There are conflicting decisions on the issue whether the equivalent and comparable statutory provisions in the UK and Australia are restricted to proceedings between the company and its directors, or whether the provisions also apply to legal proceedings instituted by someone other than the company. As stated above, in *Ex parte Lebowa Development Corporation Ltd* the court ruled that the predecessor to s 77(9) applied only to proceedings between the company and its directors. The section had no application to proceedings between a director and a third party.[278] The Australian approach adopted in *Daniels t/as Deloitte Haskins & Sells v AWA Ltd*[279] is that the equivalent section does apply to legal proceedings between the director of the company and a third party. It remains to be seen which approach will be adopted by the courts in the application of s 77(9) of the Act. However, to the extent that s 77(9) enables a court to relieve a director from 'any liability set out in this section' (ie s 77), the section will apparently apply only to proceedings between the company and its directors. Section 218(2) of the Act must also be kept in mind in this context, in that it provides that any person who contravenes any provision of the Act is liable to any other person for loss or damage suffered by that person as a result.

12.8.2 Ratification by the shareholders

The common-law principles relating to the ratification by the shareholders of a breach by a director of his or her fiduciary duties may have been preserved by the Act. There is no explicit provision that these legal principles no longer apply. Consequently, it appears that the question of whether or not a breach of duty is ratifiable by the shareholders may depend on judicial precedent (save where this would conflict with the Act).

---

[273] [1969] 1 All ER 161 (ChD).
[274] [1994] 1 BCLC 561 at 564.
[275] This is attributable to the subjective nature of honesty.
[276] See *Ex parte Lebowa Development Corporation Ltd* (discussed in 12.8.1 above).
[277] See also *Re Produce Marketing Consortium Ltd (No 2)* [1989] BCLC 520 (ChD).
[278] This was the approach adopted in *Customs and Excise Commissioners v Hedon Alpha Ltd* [1981] 2 All ER 697 (CA).
[279] (1995) 37 NSWLR 438.

A breach of fiduciary duty may sometimes be ratified after full disclosure, by ordinary resolution of the shareholders of the company. Ratification requires full and frank disclosure.[280] At common law, not all breaches of fiduciary duty are ratifiable. However, the distinction between ratifiable and unratifiable breaches of fiduciary duty has not always been clearly drawn by the courts.

Ratification must not be confused with a blanket release that releases a director from any liability that he or she may incur.[281] Rather, ratification is a condonation by the company of a specific breach of fiduciary duty that takes place after the occurrence of that breach. A blanket release is invalid and could fall foul of s 78(2) of the Act (see 12.7.3 above).

Some breaches of fiduciary duty are ratifiable by majority consent of the shareholders. In *Regal (Hastings) Ltd v Gulliver*,[282] which concerned a breach of the no-profit rule, it was held obiter that the breach was ratifiable by ordinary resolution. Likewise, a director's failure to exercise his or her powers for a proper purpose (discussed above in 12.3.2) is ratifiable by an ordinary resolution of the shareholders of the company.[283]

In *Pavlides v Jensen*,[284] where the directors were alleged to have negligently sold an asbestos mine at a gross undervalue to an associated company, it was held that negligence was ratifiable. There was no evidence of fraud or personal benefit in this case. The decision is confined to mere negligence and does not extend to gross negligence or recklessness, which is not ratifiable at common law.

An act of a director in excess of his or her authority is also ratifiable at common law by ordinary resolution, provided that it does not in contravene some limitation, restriction or qualification in the company's Memorandum of Incorporation to the purposes, powers or activities of the company or a limitation on the authority of directors, in which event the unauthorised act will be subject to the provisions of s 20 and particularly s 20(2) of the Act.[285]

Turning to acts that are not ratifiable, an illegal act or a fraudulent act, or one that infringes the personal rights of an individual shareholder, is not ratifiable at all. *Cook v Deeks*[286] illustrates that usurping a corporate opportunity that belongs to the company is not ratifiable even by a 75 per cent majority of the shareholders. It might have been different had there been unanimous approval of all the shareholders of the company. The majority of shareholders could not, however, approve of the directors misappropriating a corporate opportunity that belonged to the company.

It remains to be seen whether a breach of a statutory duty in s 76(2) (ie the improper use of information or the position of director, as discussed above in 12.4.2 or a failure to communicate information to the company) or a failure to

---

[280] *Phosphate of Lime Co v Green* (1871) LR 7 CP 43.
[281] See Blackman et al op cit n 11 at 8–205.
[282] Supra. See 12.4.1(*a*) above.
[283] See *Hogg v Cramphorn Ltd* [1967] Ch 24 where an issue of shares for the improper purpose of defeating a takeover bid was held to be ratifiable. See also *Bamford v Bamford* [1969] 1 All ER 969 (CA).
[284] (1956) Ch 565.
[285] See chapter 5: Corporate Capacity, Agency and the Turquand Rule.
[286] [1916] 1 AC 554 (PC) (discussed in 12.4.1(*c*)).

exercise reasonable care, skill and diligence, as required by s 76(3), might be ratifiable by an ordinary resolution of the shareholders of the company. It is arguable that, since these statutory duties to a large extent embody the common-law duties of a director, they should be ratifiable in accordance with the common-law principles laid down by the courts.

12.9 THE LIABILITY OF DIRECTORS AND PRESCRIBED OFFICERS

Section 77(1) to (10), which sets out the liability of the directors and prescribed officers of a company, applies also to alternate directors, members of the audit committee, or a committee of the board, irrespective of whether or not such persons are members of the board of directors of the company. Section 77 is supplemented by s 218(2) of the Act, which states that any person who has contravened any provision of the Act is liable to any other person for any loss or damage suffered by that person as a result of that contravention. The repetition of the word 'any' in s 218(2) underscores its very wide ambit.

Section 20(6) of the Act is also relevant in this context. This section (discussed in chapter 5: Corporate Capacity, Agency and the Turquand Rule) provides as follows:

> (6) Each shareholder of a company has a claim for damages against any person who fraudulently or due to gross negligence causes the company to do anything inconsistent with —
> *(a)* this Act; or
> *(b)* a limitation, restriction or qualification contemplated in this section, unless that action has been ratified by the shareholders in terms of subsection (2).

In terms of s 20(6) each shareholder of a company has a claim for damages against any person who fraudulently or due to gross negligence causes the company to do anything inconsistent with the Act or a limitation, restriction or qualification in the company's Memorandum of Incorporation on its purposes, powers or activities (or a limitation on the authority of the directors), unless this is ratified by special resolution. It must be stressed that, in terms of s 20(3), an act that contravenes of the Companies Act may not be ratified.

It must also be borne in mind that s 78(2) (as discussed above in 12.7.3) renders void any provision in the company's Memorandum of Incorporation or rules or in any agreement or resolution of a company, whether express or implied, to the extent that it directly or indirectly purports to relieve a director of liability contemplated in s 77. The director's liability cannot be eliminated or limited in this way. But, on the other hand, s 77(9) confers on the court a discretion to relieve a director from liability if he or she has acted honestly and reasonably or ought fairly to be excused from liability, in respect of conduct which is not wilful misconduct or a wilful breach of trust (see 12.8.1 above).

The liability of a person in terms of s 77 is joint and several with that of any other person who is also liable for the same act (s 77(6)). But proceedings to recover any loss, damages or costs for which a person is or may be held liable in terms of s 77 are subject to a three-year period of prescription (s 77(7)). Section 77(8) provides that a person who is liable under s 77 is also jointly and severally liable to pay the costs of all the parties incurred in court proceedings to enforce liability in terms of s 77, unless the proceedings are abandoned or exculpate such person. This would also include liability to restore to the company any amount improperly paid by the company as a consequence of the impugned act and not recoverable by the company in terms of the Act.

Section 77(2) to (5) sets out the liability of a director of a company. This is as follows:

12.9.1 Breach of fiduciary duty

A director may be held liable in accordance with the principles of the common law relating to breach of a fiduciary duty, for any loss, damages or costs sustained by the company as a consequence of any breach by a director of a duty contemplated in s 75 (disclosure of a director's personal financial interests), s 76(2) (improper use of position or corporate information and failure to communicate relevant information to the company), or s 76(3)*(a)* or *(b)* (duty to act in good faith and for a proper purpose and in the best interests of the company), discussed in 12.2.4, 12.3.1 and 12.3.2 above.

Section 77(2)*(a)* links the statutory duties with the common-law fiduciary duties. The problem, however, with this particular provision is that, while it applies to liability for 'any loss, damages or costs sustained by a company', it does not provide for the disgorgement of profits made by a director in breach of the no-profit rule, which applies even where the profit is not made at the expense of the company. This is clearly illustrated by the facts of the seminal case of *Regal (Hastings) Ltd v Gulliver* (discussed at length in 12.4.1*(a)* above), where directors were required to disgorge profits made by them even though the company had suffered no loss and may have benefitted from the act of the directors.

The ambiguity in s 77(2)*(a)* in failing to provide explicitly for disgorgement of profits creates unnecessary uncertainty in this regard. It is arguable that, since liability is imposed in accordance with the common-law principles relating to a breach of fiduciary duty, the above scenario in *Regal Hastings* would fall within the ambit of liability under the new company law regime. It would be unthinkable for directors to be allowed to retain profits made in such circumstances.

12.9.2 Breach of the duty of care and skill or other provisions

In terms of s 77(2)*(b)* a director will be liable in accordance with the principles of the common law relating to delict for any loss, damages or costs sustained by the company as a consequence of any breach by the director of:

- a duty contemplated in s 76(3)*(c)* (failure to exercise reasonable care, skill and diligence — see 12.5 above) — this preserves the traditional common-law principles insofar as delictual liability is imposed for breach of the director's duty of care and skill,
- any provision of the Act not otherwise mentioned in s 77, or
- any provision of the company's Memorandum of Incorporation.

The duties referred to in s 77(2)*(a)* and *(b)* are owed to the company, not to its shareholders. Consequently, it is the company that must proceed against the miscreant director in terms of these provisions. If a shareholder (or other interested person) wishes to seek redress in respect of these corporate wrongs, a derivative action will have to be instituted by him or her.

12.9.3 Liability under section 77(3)

A director is liable for any loss, damages or costs sustained by the company as a direct or indirect consequence of having:

(a) acted in the name of the company, or signed anything on behalf of the company, or purported to bind the company or authorise the taking of any action by or on behalf of the company, despite knowing that he or she lacked authority to do so;[287]

(b) acquiesced in the conduct of the company's business fraudulently or recklessly or trading under insolvent circumstances contrary to s 22(1) (this ground of liability is discussed in more detail below in 12.10);

(c) been a party to an act or omission by the company despite knowing that the act or omission was calculated to defraud a creditor, an employee or a shareholder of the company, or had another fraudulent purpose;

(d) knowingly signed, consented to or authorised the publication of any financial statements that were false or misleading in a material respect, or a prospectus or a written statement contemplated in s 101 that contained an 'untrue statement' (as defined in s 95), or a statement to the effect that a person had consented to be a director when no such consent had been given (in each of these circumstances, the director must have known that the statement was false, misleading or untrue, as the case may be (subject to s 104(3)); or

(e) attended a meeting or participated in the making of a decision (in terms of s 74)[288] and failed to vote against any one of the resolutions or actions proposed to be taken in the following eight circumstances:

  (i) the issue of any unauthorised shares, despite knowing that the shares had not been authorised (in terms of s 36),

  (ii) the issue of authorised securities, despite knowing that the issue was in contravention of s 41 (ie without the prescribed shareholder approval and special resolutions required by s 41),

  (iii) the granting of options in terms of s 42(4), despite 'knowing'[289] that the shares for which the options could be exercised, or the shares into which any securities could be converted, were unauthorised in terms of s 36,

  (iv) the provision of financial assistance to any person for the *'acquisition'*[290] of securities, despite knowing that such financial assistance was

---

[287] 'Knowing' is very widely defined in s 1 to mean actual knowledge or knowledge which he or she reasonably ought to have had or reasonably ought to have investigated to the extent that would have provided him or her with actual knowledge or to have taken other measures that would reasonably be expected to have provided him or her with actual knowledge.

[288] According to which a decision need not be made at a formal meeting of the board. It could be adopted by the written consent of the majority of the board given either personally or by electronic communication.

[289] See the wide definition in s 1 of 'knowing'.

[290] 'Acquisition' is much wider than a 'purchase' or 'subscription' for the securities of a company referred to in s 44(2).

inconsistent with the requirements of s 44 or the company's Memorandum of Incorporation,
(v) the provision of financial assistance to a director, despite knowing that it was inconsistent with the requirements of s 45 or the company's Memorandum of Incorporation,
(vi) a resolution approving of a distribution, despite knowing that it had failed to comply with the requirements of s 46 (this is, however, subject to s 77(4) of the Act, discussed immediately below),
(vii) the acquisition by a company of its own shares or the shares of its holding company, despite knowing that it was in contravention of the requirements of a valid distribution in s 46 or the requirements in s 48 for a valid share repurchase, or
(viii) the allotment of shares, despite knowing that it was contrary to the requirements of any provision of Chapter 4 of the Act (relating to offers to the public for the securities of the company).

In respect of wrongful distributions, s 77(4) qualifies the liability of the directors and prescribed officers under s 77(3)(e)(vi) for wrongful distributions made in contravention of s 46. In terms of s 46 read with s 77(3)(e)(vi), a director is liable for a wrongful distribution if he or she was present at the board meeting that had approved of the distribution or had participated in the making of the decision and had failed to vote against the distribution, despite knowing that the distribution was contrary to the requirements of s 46. Essentially, this will entail a failure to satisfy the solvency and liquidity test immediately after completing the proposed distribution (s 46(1)(b)). According to s 77(4)(a)(ii) liability arises only if it was also unreasonable at the time of the decision to conclude that the company would satisfy the solvency and liquidity test after the distribution had been made. It consequently follows that, provided there were reasonable grounds at the time of the decision for concluding that the company would satisfy the solvency and liquidity test, the directors will not incur liability to the company even if the company was not in fact solvent and/or liquid.

Section 77(4)(b) limits the liability of the directors for a wrongful distribution to the difference between, on the one hand, the amount by which the value of the distribution had exceeded the amount that could validly have been distributed without causing the company to fail to satisfy the solvency and liquidity test and, on the other hand, the amount, if any, that was recovered by the company from the persons to whom the distribution was made (s 77(4)(b)(i) and (ii)).

A further matter may be stressed here. Section 77(5) provides that, where the board of directors has made a decision that contravened the Companies Act as contemplated in s 77(3)(e) (as discussed above), either the company[291] or any director who has been or may be held liable in terms of s 77(3)(e) is entitled to apply to court for an order setting aside the decision of the board. The court has the discretion to make an order setting aside the decision of the board in whole or in part, absolutely or conditionally, and to make any further order that is just and equitable in the circumstances, and could even require the company *inter alia* to

---

[291] Depending on the circumstances, this may have to be done by way of a derivative action.

indemnify a director who may be held liable in terms of s 77(3)*(e)*, including indemnification for the costs of the proceedings under s 77.

12.10 FRAUDULENT, RECKLESS AND INSOLVENT TRADING (SECTION 22)

12.10.1 Introduction

Section 22(1) of the Act states that a company must not —

(a) carry on its business recklessly, with gross negligence, with intent to defraud any person or for any fraudulent purpose; or
(b) trade under insolvent circumstances.

Section 77(3)*(b)* states that a director of a company is liable for any loss, damages or costs sustained by the company as a direct or indirect consequence of the director having 'acquiesced in the carrying on of the company's business despite knowing that it was being conducted in a manner prohibited by s 22(1)'. In terms of s 78(6), a company may not indemnify a director in respect of any liability arising from s 77(3)*(b)*. Moreover, s 162(5)*(c)*(iv)*(bb)* provides that a court must make an order declaring a person to be a delinquent director if the person acted in a manner contemplated in s 77(3)*(b)*.[292] Fraudulent, reckless or insolvent trading will consequently result in a director being held personally liable to the company for loss, damages or costs directly or indirectly sustained by the company (where the director knew it was contrary to s 22(1)), as well as being declared a delinquent director, which will thereby disqualify him or her from holding office as a director subject to such conditions as the court deems appropriate for a period of seven years or longer, as determined by the court (s 162(6)*(b)*(i) and (ii) read with s 69(8)).

Additionally, s 214(1)*(c)*(i)[293] imposes criminal sanctions on a person who was knowingly a party to conduct prohibited by s 22(1). The offence is punishable by a fine or imprisonment for a period not exceeding ten years, or both (s 216*(a)*). Section 214(1)*(c)*(ii) makes it an offence to knowingly be a party to an act or omission by a business calculated to defraud a creditor, employee or the holder of securities of the company, or with another fraudulent purpose.

A further statutory provision that must not be overlooked in this context is s 218(2), which provides that any person who contravenes any provision of the Act is liable to any other person for any loss or damage suffered by that person as a result of that contravention. The wide scope and ambit of this section has already been emphasised elsewhere in this chapter (see 12.9). Creditors, in particular, will be entitled to such redress from the company or its directors for fraudulent, reckless or insolvent trading.

All these statutory provisions heavily underscore the gravity of a contravention of s 22(1). No director should treat s 22 lightly.

---

[292] The word 'directors', as has already been pointed out, is used in s 77 in its extended sense to include an alternate director, prescribed officer or a member of a committee of the board or the audit committee even if such persons are not directors.
[293] The Companies Amendment Bill, 2010 proposes to amend s 214 by deleting s 214(1)*(c)*(i).

To return to s 22, the section prohibits not only fraudulent or reckless trading (s 22(1)(a)) but also trading under insolvent circumstances (s 22(1)(b)). The first limb of s 22 is very similar to s 424 of the 1973 Act, but the second limb that prohibits insolvent trading is new. Both limbs are discussed below in turn.

12.10.2 Fraudulent or reckless trading

In view of the similarity of the wording of s 22 and s 424 of the 1973 Act, a brief discussion of the most important and relevant aspects of s 424 will be useful in gaining a proper perspective of s 22.

Section 424(1) of the 1973 Act provided that:

> [w]hen it appears, whether it be in a winding-up, judicial management or otherwise, that any business of the company was or is being carried on recklessly or with intent to defraud creditors of the company or creditors of any other person or for any fraudulent purpose, the Court may, on the application of the Master, the liquidator, the judicial manager, any creditor or member or contributory of the company, declare that any person who was knowingly a party to the carrying on of the business in the manner aforesaid, shall be personally responsible, without any limitation of liability, for all or any of the debts or other liabilities of the company as the Court may direct.

It is noteworthy at the outset that in a number of respects, s 22 is wider than s 424 of the 1973 Act.

Section 22 of the Act, like s 424 of the 1973 Act, is not confined to a winding-up of the company. It will apply to a company that is still a going concern, irrespective of whether it is being wound up or not.

Section 424 of the 1973 Act applied to two types of wrongful trading, which may be referred to as fraudulent trading and reckless trading. Section 22 of the new Act adds a further type of wrongful trading, which is referred to as 'insolvent trading'. Section 22 also widens reckless trading to include 'grossly negligent' trading. While both s 424 and s 22 are powerful weapons in deterring the abuse of limited liability, it remains essential to strike a balance between the risk of a company going insolvent and the need to promote the success of the company.

The object of s 424, and the same applies to s 22, is twofold: first, to render liable all persons, not only directors, who 'knowingly' participate or acquiesce[294] in the fraudulent or reckless conduct of the company's business, and secondly, to provide a meaningful remedy for the abuses at which s 424 or s 22 are directed.[295]

Section 22, like s 424, supplements but does not replace any common-law remedy that may apply to the same set of facts and circumstances, and does not relieve the company from liability to pay its debts.

For liability to arise under s 22 or s 77(3)(b), the business of the company must have been carried on (a) fraudulently or recklessly or with gross negligence, (b) to the knowledge of the wrongdoer, and (c) with the acquiescence of the wrongdoer or for criminal liability to arise the wrongdoer must have been a party to such conduct of the company's business — see s 214(1)(c)(i). The wording of

---

[294] 'Acquiesce' may be wider than 'being a party'. It may mean simply permitting the conduct and doing nothing or taking no steps to deter it.
[295] See *Pressma Services (Pty) Ltd v Schuttler* 1990 (2) SA 411 (C) 417E.

s 22(1)(a) (although not s 22(1)(b)) suggests that the section applies even where the company is still in a sound financial position, and far from insolvency.

Unlike s 424 of the 1973 Act, which confers *locus standi* only on a specific list of persons and relates only to the liability of the wrongdoer for the debts of the company, s 218(2) of the Act confers on any person who has suffered any loss or damage the additional remedy of a right of action against someone who has contravened any relevant provision of the Act.

Section 214(1)(c) of the new Act requires that the defendant, in order to be found guilty of an offence, be 'knowingly' a 'party' to the fraudulent or reckless conduct prohibited by s 22(1)(a) (or to trading under insolvent circumstances in terms of s 22(1)(b)). Similarly, s 77(3)(b) requires a director, in order to be held liable for the company's loss or damages, to have 'knowingly' acquiesced in the conduct of the company's business in a manner contrary to s 22(1). Knowledge or 'knowingly' under s 424 of the 1973 Act meant knowledge of the facts from which the conclusion may properly be drawn that the business of the company was or is being fraudulently or recklessly conducted. It was not necessary to have had actual knowledge of the legal consequences of those facts.[296] Likewise, in *Philotex v Snyman*[297] it was held that the word 'knowingly' in the context of s 424 of the 1973 Act did not entail knowledge of the legal consequences of the facts. 'Knowingly' did not necessarily mean consciousness of recklessness. In contrast, s 1 of the new Act states that 'knowingly', 'knowing' or 'knows':

> when used with respect to a person, and in relation to a particular matter, means that the person either —
> *(a)* had actual knowledge of that matter;
> *(b)* was in a position in which the person reasonably ought to have —
>   (i) had actual knowledge [of the matter];
>   (ii) investigated the matter to an extent that would have provided the person with actual knowledge; or
>   (iii) taken other measures which, if taken, would reasonably be expected to have provided the person with actual knowledge of the matter.

Thus, under the new Act a person who could have acquired knowledge by the exercise of reasonable diligence will fall within the scope of s 77(3)(b) and s 214(1)(c). Knowledge will be imputed to him in the circumstances set out above.

But knowledge alone is not sufficient. In addition to knowledge, the offence in s 214(1)(c) requires the defendant to be a 'party' to the conduct prohibited by s 22(1), while liability in terms of s 77(3)(b) requires the director to have 'acquiesced' in the carrying on of the company's business despite knowing that it was being conducted in a manner prohibited by s 22(1). This means that the wrongdoer must have taken part in or concurred in the fraudulent or reckless trading of the company.[298] . It is not necessary to take positive steps in the conduct of the company's business — it is enough to support or concur in the company's business. The wrongdoer's supine attitude may in certain circumstances amount to

---

[296] *Howard v Herrigel* 1991 (2) SA 660 (A) 674.
[297] 1998 (2) SA 138 (SCA) 143.
[298] *Re Maidstone Building Provisions Ltd* [1971] 3 All ER 363 (Ch); *Howard v Herrigel* (supra), discussed in 12.2.1.

concurrence in the wrongful conduct.[299] Likewise, in *Nel v McArthur*[300] the court approved and applied the principle that to be a 'party' to the conduct of the company's business, no positive steps need be taken. But an auditor of a company cannot be a 'party' to the carrying on of a company's business merely by virtue of performing his or her duties as an auditor.[301] However, a *de facto* director, and perhaps even a shadow director, will come within the ambit of the prohibition.

A single isolated act of dishonesty committed by those responsible for managing the affairs of the company has been held by the courts to be a sufficient basis for the imposition of personal liability on such persons.[302] In *In Re Gerald Cooper Chemicals*[303] the court stated '[i]t does not matter . . . that only one creditor was defrauded, and by one transaction provided that the transaction can properly be described as a fraud on a creditor perpetrated in the course of carrying on business.'

By the same token, in *Morphitis v Bernasconi*[304] the court ruled that the fact that one person may have been defrauded in the course of a company's business does not necessarily mean that the business of the company was carried on with the intention to defraud creditors. However, 'carrying on business' is not synonymous with 'actively carrying on business'.[305]

Fundamental to s 22 is the issue of when the business of the company can be said to be carried on 'recklessly, with gross negligence, with intent to defraud any person or for any fraudulent purpose' within the meaning of s 22(1)(a).

In practice, there is seldom direct evidence of the dishonest or fraudulent intention of the defendant. Fraudulent intention is invariably proved by inference. The inference sought to be drawn must be consistent with the proved facts.[306] The guiding principle laid down many years ago by Maugham J in *Re William Leitch Bros Ltd*[307] is that:

> If a company continues to carry on business and to incur debts at a time when there is to the knowledge of the directors no reasonable prospect of the creditors ever receiving payment of those debts, it is, in general, a proper inference that the company is carrying on business with intent to defraud.

This principle in effect distinguishes factual insolvency from commercial insolvency. To put it differently, factual insolvency relates to the insolvency of the company in the sense of liabilities exceeding assets, ie balance sheet insolvency, while commercial insolvency relates to liquidity, or the company's ability to pay its debts as they

---

[299] *Philotex v Snyman* (supra), discussed in 12.10.2).
[300] 2003 (4) SA 142 (T).
[301] *Powertech Industries Ltd v Mayberry* 1996 (2) SA 742 (W).
[302] *In re Gerald Cooper Chemicals Ltd* [1978] 2 All ER 49 at 53; *Gordon and Rennie v Standard Merchant Bank Ltd* 1984 (2) SA 519 (C); FHI Cassim 'Fraudulent or 'reckless' trading and section 424 of the Companies Act (1981) 98 *SALJ* 162 at 163; Blackman et al *Commentary on the Companies Act* vol 3 14–533.
[303] [1978] Ch 262 at 268.
[304] [2003] 2 BCLC 53.
[305] *In re Sarflax Ltd* [1979] 1 All ER 529.
[306] *Triptomania Twee (Pty) Ltd v Connolly* 2003 (3) SA 558 (C) 570C.
[307] [1932] All ER 892 at 895.

become due in the ordinary course of business. Commercial insolvency is simply illiquidity, ie the company is unable to pay its debts as they fall due, even though its assets may equal or exceed its liabilities (cash flow insolvency).

'Recklessly' in s 424 is used in contradistinction to the term 'fraudulently'.[308] In this context, 'recklessly' implies the existence of an objective standard of care that would be observed by the reasonable man in the conduct of the business of the company. A departure from that standard constitutes negligence (or *culpa*); a more serious departure from that standard constitutes gross negligence (*culpa lata*).[309] There is more than ample authority that 'recklessly' in s 424 means gross negligence.[310] The same will arguably apply to s 22(1)(*a*) of the new Act. Recklessness is not an error of judgment — it is rather a disregard for the consequences of one's actions.

In considering whether the business of the company has been carried on 'recklessly', the court must have regard to the scope of the operations of the company, the role, functions and powers of the directors, the amount of the debts involved, the extent of the company's financial difficulties, and the prospects, if any, of recovery.[311]

Recklessness is not to be lightly found.[312] Sometimes, reckless trading may be established by proof of a lack of any genuine concern for the prosperity of the company.[313] The test of recklessness is partly objective to the extent that the defendant's actions are measured against the standard of a reasonable man, and partly subjective insofar as the defendant's knowledge is taken into account.[314] Actual dishonesty is not an essential element of 'recklessness'.

12.10.3 Insolvent trading

(a) General

Section 22(1)(*b*) prohibits a company from trading under insolvent circumstances. It imposes a statutory duty on the directors of a company to avoid insolvent trading. There are thus two separate grounds stated in s 22(1)(*a*) and (*b*), any one of which will trigger the section, namely, fraudulent or reckless trading, or trading under insolvent circumstances. Trading under insolvent circumstances is not necessarily fraudulent trading, although it may in certain circumstances be reckless trading.

The genesis of s 22(1)(*b*) is to be found in the finding of the Report of the Company Law Committee (Jenkins Committee (UK))[315] that a widespread criticism of the UK Companies Act 1948 was that it had failed to deal adequately with

---

[308] *Ex parte Lebowa Development Corporation Ltd* 1989 (3) SA 71 (T) 111C.
[309] Ibid.
[310] See *Philotex v Snyman* 1998 (2) SA 138 (SCA).
[311] *Fisheries Development Corporation of SA Ltd v Jorgensen; Fisheries Development Corporation of SA Ltd v AWJ Investments (Pty) Ltd* 1980 (4) SA 156 (W) 170B–C, referred to with approval in *Philotex v Snyman* (supra) 144B.
[312] *Philotex v Snyman* (supra).
[313] *Anderson v Dickson* 1985 (1) SA 93 (N).
[314] *Philotex v Snyman* (supra).
[315] Cmnd 1749 (1962) para 497.

the situation arising from fraud and incompetence on the part of directors, particularly directors of insolvent companies. The Jenkins Committee recommended that fraudulent trading be extended to reckless trading, irrespective of whether or not the company was being wound up.[316]

The Cork Report[317] was of the view that 'it is right that it should be an offence to carry on a business dishonestly and right that, in the absence of dishonesty, no offence should be committed'. The Cork Committee went on to state that, where the question is not the punishment of an offender but the provision of a civil remedy for those who have suffered financial loss, a requirement that dishonesty be proved is inappropriate. More importantly and more directly to the point, the Cork Committee recommended that:

> ... if the directors at any time consider the company to be insolvent, they should have a duty to take immediate steps for the company to be placed in receivership, administration or liquidation. Failure to do so will normally expose any director who is party to the company's continued trading to civil liability ... .[318]

Consequently, the underpinning objective of s 22(1)*(b)* is to deter directors from abusing the privilege of limited liability at the expense of creditors. On this basis, the new approach is that directors should be held liable to creditors if they knew or ought to have known that there was no reasonable prospect that the company would avoid going into insolvent liquidation. A proper balance must be struck so that the directors are not penalised with unnecessarily harsh penalties. This would merely induce them, perhaps, to place the company under business rescue when there is no real need for it.

The duty to cease trading is a novel and modern approach to the protection of creditors and the public. This new duty discourages directors and companies from continuing to trade at the expense of creditors. As a result of limited liability, directors in the past suffered no additional losses as a result of continuing to trade instead of winding up the company or placing it under judicial management, or its modern equivalent, business rescue. This led to irresponsible trading and the chasing of rainbows at the cost of creditors. The threat of personal liability and criminal sanctions is now an inducement to companies and directors to avoid further loss to creditors arising from the persistent continuation of the business of a company that is known to them to be insolvent.

Directors who ignore s 22(1)*(b)* run a grave risk of being declared delinquent directors and of being held personally liable for loss or damage suffered by some other person as a result of a contravention of s 22. They may also be held liable for loss, damages or costs sustained by the company as a result of their 'knowing' acquiescence in the contravention. As stated above, in 12.10.2, a contravention of s 22 will also attract criminal penalties. There is ample deterrence in these statutory provisions.

(b) The requirements of s 22(1)(b)

As stated immediately above, s 22(1)*(b)* imposes a statutory duty to stop trading when the company is in 'insolvent' circumstances.

---
[316] Paragraph 503*(b)* and *(c)*.
[317] Insolvency Law and Practice: Report of the Review Committee Cmnd 8558 (1982) para 1777.
[318] Paragraph 1786.

A major difficulty with this provision is that it fails to define what exactly 'insolvent' circumstances are. Is this a reference to balance sheet insolvency (factual insolvency) or to cash flow or equity insolvency (commerical insolvency), ie an inability to pay debts as they become due in the ordinary course of business? In *Rosenbach & Co (Pty) Ltd v Singh's Bazaar (Pty) Ltd*[319] the court stated that the true test of a company's insolvency was not whether the company's liabilities exceeded its assets, but whether it was able to pay its debts, ie factual insolvency as opposed to commercial insolvency. This was rejected in *Ex parte Lebowa Development Corporation Ltd*[320] but was approved in *Ex parte De Villiers NNO: In re Carbon Developments (Pty) Ltd (In Liquidation)*.[321]

It has been left to the draft Companies Regulations[322] to provide some clarity on the issue. Regulation 21[323] states that, if a company, at any particular time, is trading in circumstances in which its 'liabilities exceed its assets', the company must file a notice to that effect and thereafter file quarterly renewals of that notice until such time as the company's assets equal or exceed its liabilities.

This draft regulation defines insolvency as balance sheet insolvency, ie liabilities exceeding assets. The regulation does not expressly specify what type of liabilities should be taken into account — whether they should be gross or net liabilities, and whether contingent liabilities should be taken into account. For the purposes of s 22, and particularly s 22(1)(b), the solvency and liquidity test as set out in s 4 could be relevant, namely:

> 4. (1) For any purpose of this Act, a company satisfies the solvency and liquidity test at a particular time if, considering all reasonably foreseeable financial circumstances of the company at that time —
> (a) the assets of the company or, if the company is a member of a group of companies, the aggregate assets of the company, as fairly valued, equal or exceed the liabilities of the company or, if the company is a member of a group of companies, the aggregate liabilities of the company, as fairly valued; and
> (b) it appears that the company will be able to pay its debts as they become due in the ordinary course of business for a period of —
> (i) 12 months after the date on which the test is considered; or
> (ii) in the case of a distribution contemplated in paragraph (a) of the definition of 'distribution' in section 1, 12 months following that distribution.

Directors of the company are best advised to regularly monitor the company's financial status to determine its solvency and liquidity. If the company is in near insolvent circumstances, their most appropriate step would be to place the company under business rescue and thereby obtain the benefit of a temporary moratorium.[324] For this purpose they have access to the financial statements of the company, including its profit and loss accounts and other accounting records that must be maintained by companies. In the case of public companies, the directors would also have the benefit of guidance and information provided by professional

---

[319] 1962 (4) SA 593 (D) 596–7.
[320] 1989 (3) SA 71 (T) 95–7.
[321] 1993 (1) SA 493 (A).
[322] GN 1664 *GG* 32832 of 22 December 2010.
[323] Which at the time of writing is still in draft form.
[324] See chapter 18: Business Rescue and Compromises.

advisers. Directors must, in brief, acquaint themselves with the company's financial position. They can no longer safely remain in ignorance of the financial affairs of the company.

It nevertheless remains crucial to s 22(1)*(b)* for directors to be able to identify and recognise the stage at which the insolvency of the company is imminent. For instance, in *Re Purpoint Ltd*,[325] the company's financial position was precarious even at the time when it commenced trading. It had no capital base, its assets had been purchased with bank loans or acquired by hire-puchase, and it had the burden of paying a salary to its director. But when the company was later unable to meet its trade debts as they fell due, the director ought to have realised that the company could not avoid going into insolvent liquidation.

Whenever a company is in financial difficulties, the directors have a difficult decision to make: whether to close down and go into liquidation,[326] or whether to continue trading in the hope of turning the corner. If the directors decide to close down immediately and cause the company to go into early liquidation, they may be criticised on other grounds. In this situation they are in a real and unenviable dilemma.[327] There is also clearly a risk of the court resolving the issue with the benefit of hindsight.

12.10.4 The other requirements of s 22(1)*(a)* and *(b)*

Section 22(2) states that, if the Companies Commission has reasonable grounds to believe that a company is engaging in conduct prohibited by s 22(1), it may issue a notice to the company to show cause why the company should be permitted to continue carrying on its business, or to trade, as the case may be. The company has 20 business days in which to satisfy the Companies Commission that it is not engaging in conduct that is prohibited by s 22(1), ie fraudulent, reckless or insolvent trading.

Where a company fails to respond within 20 business days or fails to satisfy the Companies Commission that it is not contravening s 22(1), the Companies Commission may issue a compliance notice to the company requiring it to cease carrying on its business or trading. This in effect is a 'stop trading' notice.[328]

Section 22(2) thus confers on the Companies Commission the power to determine whether the company is engaging in fraudulent, reckless or insolvent trading.

---

[325] [1991] BCLC 491.
[326] Or under business rescue.
[327] See *Singer v Beckett, Sub Nom Continental Assurance Co of London plc (In Liquidation)* [2007] 2 BCLC 287 (ChD).
[328] See ss 171–175 for the consequences and other related matters of a compliance notice, from which it is clear that failing to comply with a compliance notice will have severe consequences for the company.

CHAPTER 13

THE AUDITOR, FINANCIAL RECORDS AND REPORTING

Joanne Shev and Richard Jooste*

13.1	INTRODUCTION	543
13.2	FINANCIAL RECORDS AND FINANCIAL STATEMENTS	544
	13.2.1 Accounting records	544
	13.2.2 Financial statements and financial reporting standards	545
	13.2.3 Financial year	547
	13.2.4 Annual financial statements	548
	13.2.5 Access to financial statements or related information	549
	13.2.6 Financial Reporting Standards Council	549
	13.2.7 Responsibility for financial statements	549
13.3	ANNUAL RETURN	550
13.4	AUDIT AND INDEPENDENT REVIEW	550
13.5	THE AUDITOR	553
	13.5.1 Appointment	553
	13.5.2 Resignation or removal of auditors and vacancies	554
	13.5.3 Rotation of auditors	555
	13.5.4 Rights and restricted functions of auditors	555
13.6	THE AUDITING PROFESSION ACT	556
	13.6.1 Registration as registered auditors	556
	13.6.2 Registered auditor's duties in relation to an audit	558
13.7	AUDIT COMMITTEE	560
	13.7.1 Appointment of the audit committee	560
	13.7.2 Duties of the audit committee	560
13.8	COMPANY SECRETARY	562
	13.8.1 Appointment of the company secretary	562
	13.8.2 Duties of the company secretary	562
	13.8.3 Resignation or removal of the company secretary	563
	13.8.4 Registration of the company secretary	563
13.9	THE KING III REPORT AND CORPORATE GOVERNANCE	563
	13.9.1 The King III Report	564
	13.9.2 Audit committees	564
	13.9.3 Company secretary	564
	13.9.4 Integrated reporting and disclosure	565

---

* Joanne Shev authored sections 13.1 to 13.9. Richard Jooste authored section 13.10.

13.10 AUDITORS' LIABILITY...	566
13.10.1 Criminal liability..	566
13.10.2 Civil liability to client and third parties...................	568
(a) Civil liability to the client...........................	568
(i) Duties to the client.............................	568
(ii) Reasonable care and skill......................	568
(iii) Grounds for liability to the client	570
(b) Civil liability to third parties	573
(i) The common law..............................	573
(ii) Legislative intervention	577
(iii) Current position...............................	578
13.10.3 Auditors' liability and 'reportable irregularities'............	584
(a) Reportable irregularities............................	585
(b) Criminal and civil liability	588
13.10.4 Disciplinary liability......................................	589

13.1 INTRODUCTION

The integrity of financial information, the credibility of the external audit, and good corporate governance, in general, have come under the spotlight globally in recent years due to numerous corporate scandals and collapses. As part of the corporate law reform in South Africa, the Corporate Laws Amendment Act 24 of 2006 (hereafter 'the Corporate Laws Amendment Act') took interim measures to legislate those provisions considered urgent. Prior to the Corporate Laws Amendment Act, limited legislation existed in relation to good corporate governance. Most of the guidance in this area was included in the King Report on Corporate Governance which, at the time, included recommendations only and not legislation. The provisions of the Corporate Laws Amendment Act included the introduction of legislation addressing audit committees for public interest companies,[1] the function of audit committees,[2] the rotation of auditors to preserve the auditor's independence,[3] restrictions on non-audit services by the auditor,[4] and general requirements for the preparation of financial statements.[5]

The Companies Act 71 of 2008 (hereafter 'the Act') adopts some of the provisions introduced in the Corporate Laws Amendment Act, amends others and implements additional legislation with respect to the integrity of financial information, the external auditor, the external audit, audit committees and the company secretary.

---

[1] Section 269A of the Corporate Laws Amendment Act.
[2] Section 270A of the Corporate Laws Amendment Act.
[3] Section 274A of the Corporate Laws Amendment Act.
[4] Section 275A of the Corporate Laws Amendment Act.
[5] Section 285A of the Corporate Laws Amendment Act.

13.2 FINANCIAL RECORDS AND FINANCIAL STATEMENTS

13.2.1 Accounting records

Accounting records form part of the company records.[6] A company must maintain accurate and complete accounting records — in one of the official languages of South Africa — to discharge its legal obligations with respect to the preparation of financial statements. These records must be kept at, or be accessible from, the company's registered office.[7]

It is an offence for a company or person to falsify any of its accounting records, or for a company to allow any person to do so. In addition, it is an offence for a company, with an intention to deceive or mislead any person, to fail to maintain:

- accurate and complete records, or
- records in any prescribed manner and form.[8]

The accounting records of a company must include:[9]

- a register of the company's non-current assets, including, for each asset:
  ○ the date and cost of acquisition,
  ○ the reason for, and the date, amount and basis of, revaluation, if any,
  ○ the date of disposal, consideration received for it and the name of the person to whom it was transferred, and
  ○ a register of any loan by the company to a shareholder, director, prescribed officer or employee of the company, or to any person related to any of them, including the amount borrowed, the interest rate, and the terms of repayment;
- a record of any property held by the company:
  ○ in a fiduciary capacity, or
  ○ in any capacity or manner contemplated, in terms of a lay-by agreement, in s 65(2) of the Consumer Protection Act 68 of 2008;
- a record of all liabilities and obligations of the company, including but not limited to:
  ○ a register of any loan to the company from a shareholder, director, prescribed officer or an employee of the company, or from a person related to any of them, including the amount borrowed, the interest rate, and the terms of repayment,
  ○ a register of any guarantee granted by the company in respect of an obligation to a third party incurred by a shareholder, director, prescribed officer or employee of the company, or by a person related to any of them, including the amount guaranteed, the interest rate, the terms of repayment, and the circumstances in which the company may be called upon to honour the guarantee,
  ○ a register of contractual obligations due to be performed in the future, recording for each such obligation the date on which it was undertaken, the

---
[6] Section 24(3)(c)(iii) of the Act.
[7] Section 28(1) and (2) of the Act.
[8] Section 28(3) and (4) of the Act.
[9] Regulation 27(3) of the draft Companies Regulations.

person to whom the obligation is owed, the estimated cost of discharging the obligation and the date on which it is due to be discharged;
- a record of any inventory, statements of the annual inventory count, and records to enable the determination of the value of inventory at the financial year-end; and
- a record of the company's revenue and expenditures, including:
  - daily records of all receipts and payments, in sufficient detail to enable the nature of the transactions and, except in the case of cash transactions, the names of the parties to the transactions to be identified,
  - daily records of all purchases and sales of goods on credit, and services received and rendered on credit, in sufficient detail to enable the nature of those goods or services and the parties to the transactions to be identified, and
  - statements of every account maintained in a financial institution in the name of the company, or in any name under which the company carries on its activities, together with vouchers or other supporting documentation for all transactions recorded on any such statement.

In addition to the requirements set out above, a non-profit company must maintain a register of revenue received from donations, grants and members' fees, or in terms of any funding contracts or arrangements with any party.[10]

The accounting records must be safeguarded against falsification, theft, loss and intentional or accidental damage or destruction. A company may maintain its accounting record in an electronic format if it provides adequate precautions against loss of the records as a result of damage to, or failure of, the medium in which the records are stored. It must also be possible to retrieve the electronic records in a readable and printable format at all times.[11]

13.2.2 Financial statements and financial reporting standards

A company's accounting records are used as a basis for the preparation of its financial statements, which must:[12]

- satisfy the financial reporting standards as to form and content;
- present the state of affairs and business of the company fairly, and explain the transactions and financial position of the business;
- present the company's assets, liabilities, equity, income and expenses, and any other prescribed information;
- set out the date on which the statements were published, and the accounting period to which the statements apply;
- have a prominent notice on the first page of the statements indicating:
  - whether the statements have been audited, independently reviewed, or have not been audited or independently reviewed, and
  - the name and professional designation, if any, of the individual who prepared, or supervised the preparation of, those statements; and

---

[10] Regulation 27(4) of the draft Companies Regulations.
[11] Regulation 27(5) and (6) of the draft Companies Regulations.
[12] Section 29(1) and (2) of the Act.

- not be false, misleading or incomplete in any material respect.

Any person party to the preparation, approval, dissemination or publication of financial statements or a summary thereof, knowing that these statements or the summarised version do not comply with these requirements, is guilty of an offence.[13]

The need for certain companies to comply with financial reporting standards was first legislated without scope for departure in the Corporate Laws Amendment Act.[14] This reduced the opportunity for 'creative accounting' by companies, which has contributed to corporate scandals and resulted in the defrauding of investors, creditors and other stakeholders. The primary reason for compliance with financial reporting standards is to achieve consistency in the preparation of company financial statements. This leads to financial statements being comparable from one year to the next and across different companies. Furthermore, as South Africa has harmonised its standards with International Financial Reporting Standards (IFRS), financial statements are often comparable between countries.

Regulation 28 of the draft Companies Regulations proposes prescribed financial reporting standards. These standards must promote sound and consistent accounting practices, which are in accordance with IFRS or IFRS for Small and Medium Enterprises (IFRS for SMEs), as adopted by the International Accounting Standards Board (IASB). The prescribed financial reporting standards are as follows:[15]

Category of company	Applicable financial reporting standard
State-owned companies	IFRS, but in the case of any conflict with any requirements in terms of the Public Finance Management Act 1 of 1999, the Public Audit Act 25 of 2004, or other applicable national legislation, the latter prevails.
Public companies listed on an exchange	IFRS, but in the case of any conflict with the applicable listing requirements of the relevant exchange, the latter prevails.
Public companies not listed on an exchange	IFRS
Profit companies, other than public companies, that are required in terms of Regulation 29(1)(a) to have their annual financial statements audited	IFRS
Profit companies that are required in terms of Regulation 30(2)(b) to have their annual financial statements independently reviewed	IFRS for SMEs
Profit companies that are required in terms of Regulation 30(2)(a) to have their annual financial statements independently compiled and reported, or are exempt from having their annual financial statements audited or independently reviewed	No prescribed financial reporting standard.

---

[13] Sections 29(6) and 214 of the Act.
[14] Section 36 of the Corporate Laws Amendment Act.
[15] Regulation 28(2) of the draft Companies Regulations.

Non-profit companies, other than public companies, that are required in terms of Regulation 29(1)(a) to have their annual financial statements audited	IFRS, but in the case of any conflict with any requirements in terms of the Public Finance Management Act 1 of 1999, the Public Audit Act 25 of 2004, or other applicable national legislation, the latter prevails.
Non-profit companies, other than public companies, that are required in terms of Regulation 29(1)(b) to have their annual financial statements audited	IFRS
Non-profit companies that are required in terms of Regulation 30(2)(b) to have their annual financial statements independently reviewed	IFRS for SMEs
Non-profit companies that are required in terms of Regulation 30(2)(a) to have their annual financial statements independently compiled and reported	No prescribed financial reporting standard.

Reporting standards differ for the various company categories. More rigorous standards are required for some companies, such as those in which there is a public interest. Consequently, most public and state-owned companies are required to prepare financial statements in accordance with IFRS, whereas many private companies are subject to less stringent standards, such as IFRS for SMEs.

A company may provide a summary of the financial statements, but the first page of the summary must state prominently:[16]

- that it is a summary, and identify the summarised financial statements,
- whether or not the financial statements that have been summarised were audited or independently reviewed,
- the name and professional designation, if any, of the individual who prepared, or supervised the preparation of, the financial statements that have been summarised, and
- the steps required to obtain a copy of the financial statements that have been summarised.

The term 'financial statement' is defined broadly in the Act and includes not only annual, provisional, group and consolidated financial statements, but also interim or preliminary reports and the financial information in a circular, prospectus or provisional announcement of results.[17]

13.2.3 Financial year

A company must have a financial year, which is its annual accounting period. The financial year-end is the date stated in the Notice of Incorporation. The first financial year of a company begins on the registration date of the company's incorporation and ends no later than 15 months thereafter.[18] Any changes to the

---
[16] Section 29(3) of the Act.
[17] Section 1 of the Act.
[18] Section 27(1) and (2) of the Act.

year-end date may not result in a financial year extending more than 15 months after the end of the preceding financial year.[19]

13.2.4 Annual financial statements

A company must prepare annual financial statements within six months after the end of its financial year.[20]

The annual financial statements must:[21]
- include an auditor's report, if audited;
- include a directors' report with respect to the state of affairs, the business and profit or loss of the company, or of the group of companies if the company is part of a group, including:
  - any matter material for the shareholders to appreciate the company's state of affairs, and
  - any prescribed information;
- be approved by the board and signed by an authorised director; and
- be presented at the first shareholders' meeting after the statements have been approved by the board.

The annual financial statements of a company that is required in terms of the Act to have its annual financial statements audited must disclose remuneration and benefits received or receivable by a director or prescribed officer of the company or attributable to the rendering of services to the company, or a company within the same group of companies, including:[22]

- fees, salaries, bonuses and performance-related payments;
- expense allowances, to the extent that the director is not required to account for these,
- the value of any option or right given directly or indirectly to a director, past director or future director, or person related to any of them;
- financial assistance to a director, past director or future director, or person related to any of them for the subscription of options or securities, or the purchase of securities;
- with respect to any financial assistance by the company to a director, past director or future director, or a person related to any of them, or any loan made by a third party to any such person, if the company is a guarantor of that loan, the value of:
  - any interest deferred, waived or forgiven, or
  - the difference in value between the interest that would reasonably be charged in comparable circumstances at fair market rates in an arm's length transaction and the interest actually charged to the borrower, if less;
- the amount of any pensions paid or payable to current or past directors, current or past prescribed officers, or to a pension scheme on their behalf;
- the amount of any compensation paid in respect of loss of office to current or past directors, or current or past prescribed officers;

---

[19] Section 27(4)(c) of the Act.
[20] Section 30(1) of the Act.
[21] Section 30(3) of the Act.
[22] Section 30(4)–(6) of the Act.

- the number and class of any securities issued to a director or prescribed officer, or to any person related to them, and the consideration received by the company for those securities; and
- details of service contracts of current directors and prescribed officers.

The remuneration of executive directors is a contentious issue. Many feel that executive directors and prescribed officers receive excessive remuneration. The detailed disclosure of these amounts is aimed at enhancing the transparency of directors' remuneration and benefits.

13.2.5 Access to financial statements or related information

In addition to the right of access to company records set out in s 26 of the Act, a person who holds or has a beneficial interest in any securities of a company is entitled to:[23]

- receive a notice of the publication of any annual financial statements of the company, setting out the steps to obtain a copy thereof, and
- receive, on demand, without charge, one copy of any annual financial statements of the company.

13.2.6 Financial Reporting Standards Council

Section 203(1) of the Act establishes the Financial Reporting Standards Council (FRSC), which replaces the Accounting Practices Board for the purpose of:[24]

- receiving and considering any relevant information relating to the reliability of, and compliance with, financial reporting standards and adapting international reporting standards for local circumstances,
- advising the Minister on matters relating to financial reporting standards, and
- consulting with the Minister on the setting of regulations establishing financial reporting standards, which promote sound and consistent[25] accounting practices in accordance with IFRS of the IASB.[26]

13.2.7 Responsibility for financial statements

The directors of the company are ultimately responsible for the preparation of the financial statements. They may delegate this task, but are not allowed to abdicate responsibility for it. The external auditor or independent reviewer reports on these financial statements. To avoid compromising the independence of an external auditor or independent reviewer, he or she should not prepare the financial statements upon which he or she is reporting. An audit firm may be requested to perform a compilation engagement and to audit the financial statements it has compiled. This would constitute a self-review threat to the auditor's independence, as an auditor would be reporting on his or her own work.[27] This threat can

---
[23] Section 31 of the Act.
[24] Section 204 of the Act.
[25] Standards may vary for different categories of company.
[26] Section 29(5)(*b*) of the Act.
[27] SAICA Code of Professional Conduct, para 290 at 166.

be reduced by assigning the compilation engagement to members of the audit firm who do not form part of the audit team.

13.3 ANNUAL RETURN

A company that:[28]
- is required in terms of the Act[29] to have its annual financial statements audited in a particular year must file a copy of those statements as a supplement to its annual return;
- has voluntarily had its annual financial statements audited must, at the option of the company, either:
    ○ file a copy of those audited statements as a supplement to its annual return, or
    ○ file a financial accountability supplement to its annual return; or
- is not required in terms of the Act[30] to have its annual financial statements audited in a particular year, and has not voluntarily had those statements audited, must file a financial accountability supplement to its annual return.

13.4 AUDIT AND INDEPENDENT REVIEW

The Companies Act 61 of 1973 (hereafter 'the 1973 Act') required all companies to have a financial statement audit, whereas the new Companies Act requires only certain companies to have a financial statement audit. The annual financial statements of a public company must be audited.[31] Taking into account the desirability in the public interest of the integrity of financial statements and having regard to the economic and social significance of a company,[32] the proposed draft Companies Regulations also require an audit of the annual financial statements of the following companies:[33]

- a private company, in the ordinary course of its activities, holding assets in a fiduciary capacity in the conduct of its primary activity or incidental to its primary activity in any manner contemplated, in terms of a lay-by agreement, in s 65(2) of the Consumer Protection Act 2008, for a broad group of persons not related to the company;
- a non-profit company:
    ○ incorporated directly or indirectly by the state, a state organ, a state-owned company, an international entity, a foreign state entity or a foreign company,
    ○ incorporated primarily to perform a statutory or regulatory function in terms of any legislation, or to carry out a public function at the initiation or

---

[28] Section 33 of the Act and Regulation 32(3) of the draft Companies Regulations.
[29] This provision would also apply if an audit was required in terms of the draft Companies Regulations.
[30] This provision would also apply if an audit was required in terms of the draft Companies Regulations.
[31] The financial statements of a state-owned company must also be audited, as per Regulation 29(1) of the draft Companies Regulations.
[32] Section 30(2) of the Act.
[33] Regulation 29(1) of the draft Companies Regulations.

direction of a state organ, a state-owned company, an international entity, a foreign state entity, or
- soliciting or accepting donations from the general public if its assets or current expenditures, as reported on its annual financial statements, for the immediately preceding year exceeded R60 million or R120 million, respectively; or
* any company required in terms of a compliance notice to have its most recent annual financial statements audited on the grounds that the activities of the company in the previous year raise a reasonable apprehension of potentially adverse consequences to the public, which cannot be put to rest without the performance of an audit.

The financial statements of companies not requiring an audit must be either audited voluntarily[34] or independently reviewed. An independent review takes one of three forms:[35]

* a compilation engagement,
* an agreed-upon procedures engagement in accordance with ISRS 4400, an International Standard on Related Services, or
* a review engagement in terms of ISRE 2400, an International Standard on Review Engagements.

The form of the engagement determines the level of assurance provided. Audit and review engagements in terms of ISRE 2400 are assurance engagements, whereas compilation engagements and agreed-upon procedures engagements are non-assurance engagements. Assurance is the confidence which the auditor or independent reviewer adds to the information being reported upon. An audit involves comprehensive testing to gather sufficient appropriate audit evidence for the auditor to express an opinion on the fair presentation of the financial statements. This opinion provides reasonable assurance rather than certainty regarding the fair presentation of the financial statements, as the auditor performs test checks and does not examine every transaction. A review engagement, in terms of ISRE 2400, involves less comprehensive procedures than an audit, resulting in moderate assurance being expressed by the independent reviewer on the fair presentation of the financial statements. An agreed-upon procedures engagement involves the performance of specific procedures agreed upon by the parties to the agreement, whereas a compilation engagement requires the use of accounting skills to compile financial information. No opinion is expressed by the independent reviewer or compiler performing an agreed-upon procedures engagement or a compilation engagement, respectively.

After concluding that an independent review is appropriate, the form of independent review required is determined by the magnitude of the company's assets and turnover, as follows:[36]

---

[34] Clause 20*(c)* of the draft Companies Amendment Bill, 2010 proposes a voluntary audit as required in terms of the company's Memorandum of Incorporation, a shareholder resolution or a board resolution.
[35] Regulation 30(2) of the draft Companies Regulations.
[36] Regulation 30(2) of the draft Companies Regulations.

Form of engagement	Reporting standard	Assets		Turnover
Review	ISRE 2400	≥ R100 million[1]	or	≥ R200 million[1]
Agreed-upon procedures	ISRS 4400	< R5 million[2]	and	≥ R20 million[2] and < R200 million[1]
Agreed-upon procedures	ISRS 4400	≥ R5 million[2] and < R100 million[1]	and	≥ R20 million[2] and < R200 million[1]
Agreed-upon procedures	ISRS 4400	≥ R5 million[2] and < R100 million[1]	and	< R20 million[2]
Compilation	None	< R5 million[2]	and	< R20 million[2]

[1] Average for the three immediately preceding years based on figures reported in the annual financial statements.
[2] As reported in the annual financial statements for the immediately preceding year.

An independent review must be performed by an independent accounting professional, who is a member in good standing of a professional body that is a member of the International Federation of Accountants (IFAC), for example, the South African Institute of Chartered Accountants (SAICA). An independent accounting professional is a person who does not have a financial interest in the company or a related or interrelated company, and is not:[37]

- involved in the day-to-day management of the company's business nor has been so involved in the previous three years,
- a prescribed officer or full-time executive employee of the company, a related company or interrelated company, or has not been such an officer or employee during the previous three financial years,
- a material customer or supplier of the company, such that a reasonable and informed third party would conclude that the integrity, impartiality or objectivity of that professional is compromised by that relationship, or
- a related person of any of the abovementioned persons.

A private company is exempt from the audit or independent review requirement, assuming that this is not required in terms of any other laws, a court order or an agreement, provided that:[38]

- one person holds, or has all of the beneficial interest in, all the securities issued by the company;[39] or
- every person who is a holder, or has a beneficial interest in, any securities

---

[37] Regulation 30(3)(*d*) of the draft Companies Regulations.
[38] The Companies Amendment Bill, 2010 proposes (cl 20) that these provisions in s 30(2) of the Act be replaced with the following:

'(2A) Except to the extent required by any other law or agreement, a private company is exempt from the requirements in this section to have its annual financial statements audited or independently reviewed, and from the requirements of subsection (3)(*d*), if every person who is a holder of, or has a beneficial interest in, any securities issued by the company is also a director of the company.'

[39] Section 30(2)(*bb*)(AA) of the Act.

issued by the company is also a director of the company, unless the company's only director has been:[40]
- removed from an office of trust, on the grounds of misconduct involving dishonesty, or
- has been convicted and imprisoned without the option of a fine, or fined more than the prescribed amount, for theft, fraud, forgery, perjury or an offence:
  - involving fraud, misrepresentation or dishonesty,
  - in connection with the formation, promotion or management of a company,
  - in connection with the appointment or election of a company director, board committee member, audit committee member, or prescribed officer who is ineligible or disqualified for the position,
  - in connection with any act as a director of the company, or in the case of a person who was a director of the company in the preceding 24 months, as a board committee member, audit committee member, or prescribed officer, which exceeds the limits of a probation under which that person is placed in terms of s 162 of the Act or s 47 of the Close Corporations Act 69 of 1984 (hereafter 'the Close Corporations Act'), or
  - under the Act, the Insolvency Act 24 of 1936, the Close Corporations Act, the Competition Act 89 of 1998, the Financial Intelligence Centre Act 38 of 2001 (FICA), the Securities Services Act 36 of 2004, or Chapter 2 of the Prevention and Combating of Corrupt Activities Act 12 of 2004 (PRECCA).

13.5 THE AUDITOR

13.5.1 Appointment

Section 90(1) requires every public or state-owned company to appoint an auditor upon incorporation and each year at its annual general meeting (AGM).[41]

To be appointed as a company auditor, a person or firm must be a registered auditor and must be acceptable to the company's audit committee as being independent of the company.[42] In addition, the person, firm or a related person must not be, or have been at any time during the five financial years immediately preceding the date of appointment:[43]

- disqualified in terms of s 69(8) of the Act to serve as a director of the company,
- a director or prescribed officer of the company,
- an employee or consultant of the company who was or has been engaged for more than one year in the maintenance of any of the company's financial records or the preparation of any of its financial statements,

---

[40] Sections 30(2)(*bb*)(BB) and 69(12) of the Act.
[41] Clause 53 of the draft Companies Amendment Bill, 2010 also requires an auditor to be appointed annually by a company requiring an audit voluntarily, in terms of its Memorandum of Incorporation, or by any private company, personal liability company or non-profit company required by the Act to have its annual financial statements audited.
[42] Section 90(2)(*a*) and *(c)* of the Act.
[43] Sections 84(5) and 90(2)(*b*) of the Act.

- a director, officer or employee of a person appointed as company secretary, or
- a person who, alone or with a partner or employees, habitually or regularly performs the duties of accountant or bookkeeper, or performs related secretarial work, for the company.

If a company appoints a firm as auditor, the individual determined by that firm, in terms of s 44(1) of the Auditing Profession Act 25 of 2005 (hereafter 'the Auditing Profession Act'), is responsible for performing the functions of auditor and must satisfy these requirements.[44]

When an auditor is not appointed by the company, as required upon registration of the company's incorporation, the directors of the company must appoint the first auditor of the company within 40 business days after the company's date of incorporation. The first auditor of a company holds office until the conclusion of the first AGM of the company. If a company's AGM does not appoint or reappoint an auditor, the directors must fill the vacancy within 40 business days after the date of the meeting.[45]

A retiring auditor may be automatically reappointed at an AGM without any resolution being passed, unless:[46]

- the retiring auditor is no longer qualified for appointment, or is no longer willing to accept appointment and has notified the company,
- rotation of auditors is required in terms of s 92 of the Act,
- the audit committee objects to the reappointment, or
- the company has notice of an intended resolution to appoint some other person or persons in place of the retiring auditor.

13.5.2 Resignation or removal of auditors and vacancies

The resignation of an auditor is effective when the notice is filed.[47]

Clause 54 of the draft Companies Amendment Bill, 2010 proposes that an auditor may resign by giving the company one month's written notice, or, with the approval of the board, less than one month's notice. It also proposes that, if the auditor is removed from office by the board, the auditor may require the company to include a statement in the directors' report in the annual financial statements, relating to that financial year, setting out the auditor's contention as to the circumstances that resulted in the removal.

When a vacancy arises in the office of auditor of a company, the board of the company:[48]

- must appoint a new auditor within 40 business days, if there had been only one incumbent auditor of the company, and
- may appoint a new auditor at any time, if there had been more than one incumbent, but while any such vacancy continues, the surviving or continuing auditor may act as auditor of the company.

---

[44] Section 90(3) of the Act.
[45] Section 90(4) and (5) of the Act.
[46] Section 90(6) of the Act.
[47] Section 91(1) of the Act.
[48] Section 91(2) of the Act.

Before making an appointment:[49]

- the board must propose to the company's audit committee, within 15 business days after the vacancy occurs, the name of at least one registered auditor to be considered for appointment as the new auditor, and
- may proceed to make an appointment of the proposed registered auditor if, within five business days after delivering the proposal, the audit committee does not give notice in writing to the board rejecting the proposed auditor.

If a company appoints a firm as its auditor, any change in the composition of the members of that firm does not by itself create a vacancy in the office of auditor for that year, unless by comparison with the membership of the firm at the time of its latest appointment, fewer than half of the members remain.[50]

13.5.3 Rotation of auditors

Rotation of auditors was introduced to enhance the independence of auditors. It is the individual serving as auditor or designated auditor[51] who is required to rotate and not the audit firm.

No individual may serve as auditor or designated auditor of a company for more than five consecutive financial years. If an individual has served as auditor or designated auditor of a company for two or more consecutive financial years and then ceases to be the auditor or designated auditor, that individual may not be appointed again as the auditor or designated auditor of that company until after the expiry of at least two further financial years.[52]

When a company appoints two or more persons as joint auditors, the company must manage the rotation requirements to ensure that not all the joint auditors relinquish office in the same year.[53]

13.5.4 Rights and restricted functions of auditors

The auditor of a company has the right of access to:[54]

- the accounting records and all books and documents of the company, and is entitled to require from the directors or prescribed officers of the company any information and explanations necessary for the performance of the auditor's duties, and
- all current and former financial statements of any subsidiary, as auditor of the holding company, and is entitled to require from the directors or officers of the holding company or subsidiary any information and explanations in connection with any such statements and in connection with the accounting records, books and documents of the subsidiary as necessary for the performance of the auditor's duties.

---

[49] Section 91(3) of the Act.
[50] Section 91(4) of the Act.
[51] Section 44(1) of the Auditing Profession Act requires a firm appointed as auditor to designate the responsibility and accountability for that audit to an individual registered auditor or auditors within the firm.
[52] Section 92(1) and (2) of the Act.
[53] Section 92(3) of the Act.
[54] Section 93(1)*(a)* and *(b)* of the Act.

An auditor may apply to a court for an appropriate order to enforce these rights and a court may:[55]

- make any order that is just and reasonable to prevent frustration of the auditor's duties by the company or any of its directors, prescribed officers or employees, and
- make an order of costs personally against any director or prescribed officer whom the court has found to have wilfully and knowingly frustrated, or attempted to frustrate, the performance of the auditor's functions.

The auditor is also entitled to:[56]

(i) attend any general shareholders [sic] meeting;
(ii) receive all notices of and other communications relating to any general shareholders meeting; and
(iii) be heard at any general shareholders meeting contemplated in this paragraph on any part of the business of the meeting that concerns the auditor's duties or functions.

Section 93(3) of the Act provides that:

An auditor appointed by a company may not perform any services for that company:
(a) that would place the auditor in a conflict of interest as prescribed or determined by the Independent Regulatory Board for Auditors in terms of section 44(6) of the Auditing Profession Act; or
(b) as may be determined by the company's audit committee in terms of section 94(7)(d).

See further chapter 10: Governance and the Board of Directors.

13.6 THE AUDITING PROFESSION ACT

The Auditing Profession Act 26 of 2005 replaced the Public Accountants' and Auditors' Act 80 of 1991 when it was enacted in 2006. It was introduced in light of several corporate collapses in South Africa and globally, which questioned the credibility of external auditors and the external audit function. The Auditing Profession Act regulates the auditing profession in South Africa and provides for:[57]

- the establishment of the Independent Regulatory Board for Auditors (IRBA),
- the education, training and professional development of registered auditors,
- the accreditation of professional bodies,
- the registration of auditors,
- regulation of the conduct of registered auditors, and
- other related matters.

13.6.1 Registration as registered auditors

Individuals or firms may register as registered auditors. An individual may be registered, if that individual:[58]

---

[55] Section 93(2) of the Act.
[56] Section 93(1)(c) of the Act.
[57] Preamble to the Auditing Profession Act.
[58] Section 37(2) of the Auditing Profession Act.

- has complied with the prescribed education, training and competency requirements for a registered auditor,
- has arranged for his or her continuing professional development in the case where the individual is not a member of an accredited professional body,
- is resident within South Africa, and
- is a fit and proper person to practise the profession.

An individual may not be registered if that individual:[59]

- has at any time been removed from an office of trust because of misconduct,
- has been convicted of theft, fraud, forgery, producing a forged document, perjury, an offence under the Prevention and Combating of Corrupt Activities Act 12 of 2004, or any offence involving dishonesty — other than theft, fraud or forgery, committed prior to 27 April 1994 and associated with political objectives — and has been sentenced to imprisonment without the option of a fine or to a fine exceeding such an amount as may be prescribed by the Minister,
- is for the time being declared by a competent court to be of unsound mind or unable to manage his or her own affairs, or
- is disqualified from registration under a sanction imposed under the Auditing Profession Act.

The IRBA may also decline to register an individual who:[60]

- is an unrehabilitated insolvent,
- has entered into a compromise with creditors, or
- has been provisionally sequestrated.

A firm may be registered if it is:[61]

- a partnership of which all the partners are individuals who are themselves registered auditors;
- a sole proprietor where the proprietor is a registered auditor; or
- a company:
  - that is incorporated and registered as a company under the 1973 Act,[62] with a share capital, and its memorandum of association provides that its directors and past directors are jointly and severally liable, together with the company, for the debts and liabilities of the company that were contracted during their periods of office,
  - that has only individuals who are registered auditors as shareholders,
  - in which every shareholder is a director, and every director is a shareholder, or
  - the articles of association of the company provide that:
    - the company may, without confirmation by a court, purchase on such terms as it may consider expedient, any shares held in the company

---

[59] Section 37(3) of the Auditing Profession Act.
[60] Section 37(5) of the Auditing Profession Act.
[61] Section 38 of the Auditing Profession Act.
[62] This section has not been aligned with the new Companies Act.

and the shares purchased are available for allotment in accordance with the company's Memorandum of Incorporation, and
- a member of the company may not appoint a person who is not a member of the company to act as proxy at any meeting of the company.

A person who is not a registered auditor may not:[63]
- perform any audit unless by order of and under the supervision, direction and control of a registered auditor who takes responsibility for the audit,
- pretend to be, or hold out to be, a registered auditor,
- use the name of any registered auditor,
- use the titles 'public accountant', 'certified public accountant', 'registered accountant and auditor' or 'accountant and auditor in public practice', or
- perform any act indicating or calculated to lead persons to believe that he or she is registered.

A person who is not a registered auditor may:[64]
- use the title 'internal auditor' or 'accountant',
- as a member of a not-for-profit club, institution or association, act as auditor for that club, institution or association, if he or she receives no fee or other consideration for such audit, or
- be appointed by the Auditor-General to carry out on his or her behalf any audit which that person is, in terms of the Public Audit Act 25 of 2004, required to undertake.

Without the consent of the IRBA, a registered auditor may not knowingly employ:[65]
- any person who is, for the time being, suspended from public practice under any provision of the Auditing Profession Act,
- any person who is no longer registered as a registered auditor as a result of the termination or cancellation of that person's registration, or
- any person who applied for registration, but whose application was declined by the IRBA on the grounds of s 37(3) of the Auditing Profession Act.

A registered auditor also may not:[66]
- perform audits unless adequate risk management practices and procedures are in place,
- engage in public practice during any period in respect of which the registered auditor has been suspended from public practice,
- share any profit derived from performing an audit with a person that is not a registered auditor, or
- engage in public practice unless all prescribed fees have been paid.

13.6.2 Registered auditor's duties in relation to an audit

Where an entity appoints a firm to perform an audit, that firm must immediately, after the appointment is made, take a decision as to the individual registered

---
[63] Section 41(2) of the Auditing Profession Act.
[64] Section 41(3) of the Auditing Profession Act.
[65] Section 41(4) of the Auditing Profession Act.
[66] Section 41(6) and (10) of the Auditing Profession Act.

auditor or registered auditors within the firm that is or are responsible and accountable for that audit.[67]

The registered auditor may not, without such qualifications as may be appropriate in the circumstances, express an opinion to the effect that any financial statements or any supplementary information attached thereto fairly present in all material respects the financial position of the entity and the results of its operations and cash flows, in accordance with the basis of accounting and the financial reporting framework as disclosed in the relevant financial statements, unless the registered auditor is satisfied that certain criteria have been met.[68] The criteria to be satisfied are:[69]

- that the audit has been conducted free from any restrictions and in compliance, so far as applicable, with auditing pronouncements,
- that the registered auditor has satisfied him- or herself of the existence of all assets and liabilities shown on the financial statements,
- that proper accounting records in at least one of the official languages of South Africa have been kept for the entity so as to reflect and explain all its transactions and record all its assets and liabilities correctly and adequately,
- that all information, vouchers and other documents, which in the registered auditor's opinion were necessary for the proper performance of the registered auditor's duties, have been obtained,
- that the registered auditor has not had occasion, during the period to which the auditing services relate, to report a reportable irregularity[70] to the IRBA or that, if such an irregularity was reported, the registered auditor has been able, prior to expressing the opinion, to send to the IRBA a notification that he or she was satisfied that no reportable irregularity has taken place or is taking place,
- that the registered auditor has complied with all laws relating to the audit of that entity, and
- that the registered auditor is satisfied as to the fair presentation of the financial statements.

To avoid compromising a registered auditor's independence, if he or she or a member of his or her audit firm is responsible for keeping the books, records or accounts of an entity, the registered auditor must indicate that responsibility when reporting on anything in connection with the business or financial affairs of the

---

[67] Section 44(1) of the Auditing Profession Act.
[68] Section 44(2) of the Auditing Profession Act.
[69] Section 44(3) of the Auditing Profession Act.
[70] A 'reportable irregularity' is defined in s 1 of the Auditing Profession Act as 'any unlawful act or omission committed by any person responsible for the management of the entity, which —
  (a) has caused or is likely to cause material financial loss to the entity or to any partner, member, shareholder, creditor or investor of the entity in respect of his, her or its dealings with that entity; or
  (b) is fraudulent or amounts to theft; or
  (c) represents a material breach of any fiduciary duty owed by such person to the entity or any partner, member, shareholder, creditor or investor of the entity under any law applying to the entity or the conduct or management thereof'.

entity. This does not apply when a registered auditor is only making closing entries, assisting with adjusting entries or framing any financial statements or other document from existing records.[71]

In addition, a registered auditor may not conduct the audit of any financial statements of an entity if he or she has or had a conflict of interest in respect of that entity.[72]

13.7 AUDIT COMMITTEE

13.7.1 Appointment of the audit committee

A public company, a state-owned company or any other company that has voluntarily determined in its Memorandum of Incorporation to have an audit committee must elect a committee comprising at least three members at each AGM, unless:[73]

- the company is a subsidiary of another company that has an audit committee, and
- the audit committee of that other company will perform the required audit committee functions on behalf of that subsidiary company.

Each member of the audit committee must be a director and must not be:[74]

- involved in the day-to-day management of the company's business or have been so involved at any time during the previous financial year,
- a prescribed officer, a full-time employee of the company, or a related or interrelated company, or have been such an officer or employee at any time during the previous three years,
- a material supplier or customer of the company, such that a reasonable and informed third party would conclude in the circumstances that the integrity, impartiality or objectivity of that director is compromised by that relationship, or
- related to any of the abovementioned persons.

13.7.2 Duties of the audit committee

The duties of an audit committee are to:[75]

- nominate, for appointment as auditor of the company, a registered auditor who, in the opinion of the audit committee, is independent of the company,
- determine the auditor's fees and terms of engagement,
- ensure that the auditor's appointment complies with any legislation related to the appointment of auditors, including the Act,
- determine the nature and extent of any non-audit services that the auditor may provide to the company, or that the auditor must not provide to the company or a related company,

---

[71] Section 44(4) and (5) of the Auditing Profession Act.
[72] Section 44(6) of the Auditing Profession Act.
[73] Section 92(2) of the Act.
[74] Section 94(4) of the Act.
[75] Section 94(7) of the Act.

- pre-approve any proposed agreement with the auditor for the provision of non-audit services to the company,
- prepare a report for inclusion in the annual financial statements:
  - describing how the audit committee carried out its functions,
  - stating whether the audit committee is satisfied that the auditor was independent of the company,
  - commenting in any way in which the audit committee considers appropriate on the financial statements, the accounting practices and the internal financial control of the company,
- receive and deal appropriately with any concerns or complaints (whether from within or outside the company or on its own initiative) relating to the accounting practices and internal audit of the company, the content or auditing of the company's financial statements, the internal financial control or any related matter,
- make submissions to the board on any matter concerning the company's accounting policies, financial control, records and reporting, and
- perform other functions determined by the board, including the development and implementation of a policy and plan for a systematic, disciplined approach to evaluate and improve the effectiveness of risk management control and governance processes within the company.

The appointment by a company in general meeting of an auditor other than the one nominated by the audit committee will be valid provided that the proposed auditor is independent of the company.[76] In considering whether the auditor is independent of the company, the audit committee must, in relation to the company and any company forming part of the same group of companies:[77]

- ascertain that the auditor does not receive any direct or indirect remuneration or other benefit from the company, except as auditor or for the rendering of non-audit services, to the extent permitted in terms of Act,
- consider whether the auditor's independence may have been prejudiced as a result of any previous appointment as auditor or with regard to any consultancy, advisory or other work undertaken by the auditor for the company, and
- consider compliance with other criteria relating to independence or conflict of interest as prescribed by the IRBA as established by the Auditing Profession Act.

In terms of s 94(10) of the Act 'neither the appointment nor the duties of an audit committee reduce the functions and duties of the board or the directors of the company, except with respect to the appointment, fees and terms of engagement of the auditor.'

All expenses reasonably incurred by the audit committee, including fees of any consultant or specialist engaged by the audit committee to assist in the performance of its duties, must be paid by the company.[78]

See further chapter 10: Governance and the Board of Directors.

---

[76] Section 94(9) of the Act.
[77] Section 94(8) of the Act.
[78] Section 94(11) of the Act.

13.8 COMPANY SECRETARY

13.8.1 Appointment of the company secretary

All public or state-owned companies must appoint a company secretary, whereas private companies, public liability companies or non-profit companies must appoint a company secretary if required in terms of the company's Memorandum of Incorporation or if the company requires an audit in terms of the Act or the proposed draft Companies Regulations.[79] A company secretary is accountable to the board of the company, must be knowledgeable or experienced in the relevant laws, and must be a permanent resident of South Africa.[80] Every company appointing a company secretary must maintain a register of its company secretaries.[81]

A juristic person or partnership may be appointed company secretary provided that:[82]

- no employee or partner is disqualified from serving as a director of that company in terms of s 69(8) of the Act, and
- at least one employee or partner is resident in South Africa and possesses the required knowledge and experience.

A change in the membership of a juristic person or partnership that holds office as company secretary does not constitute a casual vacancy if these requirements continue to be satisfied. Where these requirements are no longer satisfied, the juristic person or partnership must immediately notify the company directors and will be regarded as having resigned upon giving this notice. Any action taken by a juristic person or partnership in the performance of its functions as company secretary is not invalidated merely because the juristic person or partnership did not qualify to serve as company secretary at the time of the action.

13.8.2 Duties of the company secretary

A company secretary's duties include, but are not limited to:[83]

- providing the directors of the company with guidance as to their duties, responsibilities and powers,
- making the directors aware of any law relevant to or affecting the company,
- reporting to the company's board any failures on the part of the company or a director to comply with the Memorandum of Incorporation or rules of the company or the Act,
- ensuring that the minutes of all shareholder, board, board committee and audit committee meetings are properly recorded,
- certifying in the annual financial statements whether the company has filed required returns and notices in terms of the Act, and whether all such returns and notices appear to be true, correct and up to date,

---

[79] Section 86(1) and (2) of the Act.
[80] Sections 86(1) and 88(1) of the Act.
[81] Section 85(1) of the Act.
[82] Section 87(1) of the Act.
[83] Section 88(2) of the Act.

- ensuring that a copy of the company's annual financial statements is sent to every person who is entitled to it, and
- taking responsibility, if designated by the company, for compliance with Chapter 2 Part C and Chapter 3 of the Act, if applicable to the company.

13.8.3 Resignation or removal of the company secretary

A company secretary may resign by giving the company one month's written notice or giving less than one month's notice, with the approval of the board.[84]

If the company secretary is removed from office by the board, he or she may require the company to include a statement in the directors' report in the annual financial statements, relating to that financial year, setting out the company secretary's contention as to the circumstances that resulted in the removal.[85]

13.8.4 Registration of the company secretary

A company must file a notice of appointment or termination within ten business days of the appointment of a company secretary or after the termination of such appointment. Notice of the appointment of the company's first company secretary may, alternatively, be filed as part of the company's Notice of Incorporation.[86]

See further chapter 10: Governance and the Board of Directors.

13.9 THE KING III REPORT AND CORPORATE GOVERNANCE

Corporate governance is the system whereby entities are managed and controlled.

The King Committee was established in South Africa in 1992 by the Institute of Directors with the objective of making recommendations on the effective implementation of corporate governance in South Africa. The original King Report ('King I') was published in 1994 and a revised report ('King II') in July 2001. King II came into effect for financial years commencing on or after 1 March 2002. A further revision to the King Report, the King Report on Corporate Governance for South Africa 2009 ('the King III Report' or 'King III') came into effect on 1 March 2010.

Although the term 'corporate governance' was coined in the 1980s, King I was the first formal document to address corporate governance in South Africa. It addressed the divergent interests of the owners (eg shareholders) of an entity and the managers of that entity, who act as the owners' agents in the day-to-day management of the business.

In the late 1990s, a number of corporate scandals and corporate collapses resulted in the need for a revised King Report. King II addressed not only the divide in interests between the owners and the management of entities, but also the interests of all stakeholders, including employees, creditors and the general public. In so doing, it accounted for both local and global developments by dealing with the triple bottom line, which expanded a company's responsibilities beyond financial issues to include social and environmental issues.

---

[84] Section 89(1) of the Act.
[85] Section 89(2)–(4) of the Act.
[86] Section 85(3) and (4) of the Act.

13.9.1 The King III Report
The King III Report was introduced due to the corporate law reform in South Africa, which gave rise to the new Companies Act. It deals with changes in governance trends such as the move towards integrated sustainability reporting and applies broadly to all entities, whereas King I and King II applied to limited entities only.

13.9.2 Audit committees
The audit committee plays an important role in ensuring the integrity of integrated reporting and internal financial controls. The King III Report recommends that a company should have an audit committee, even if not required by statute. An effectively functioning audit committee could offer significant advantages for all parties interested in the financial reporting process. These advantages include:
- improving the quality and the enhancing the credibility of the financial reporting process of an undertaking,
- improving the entity's internal control,
- promoting communication between the directors, the external auditors and management,
- strengthening the external auditor's visible independence through which the credibility of the annual financial statements is enhanced, and
- improving the external auditor's performance and the quality of the audit process.

This is achieved by the recommendations of the King III Report in relation to the composition of the audit committee, its duties and responsibilities. To ensure an effectively functioning audit committee, the King III Report recommends that the audit committee should:
- meet at least twice a year,
- meet with the internal and external auditors at least once a year without management in attendance,
- comprise at least three members,
- comprise independent non-executive directors only,
- comprise members who collectively have an understanding of integrated reporting, internal financial controls, the external and internal audit processes, corporate law, risk management, sustainability issues, information technology governance as it relates to integrated reporting, and the governance processes within the company,
- be chaired by an independent non-executive director, and
- not be chaired by the chairperson of the board — however, the chairperson of the board may attend audit committee meetings by invitation.

See further chapter 10: Governance and the Board of Directors.

13.9.3 Company secretary
The company secretary plays a fundamental role in the corporate governance of a company. Accordingly, the King III Report advises that a competent, suitably qualified and experienced person should be appointed to this position. Owing to

the 'gatekeeper' role played by the company secretary, an arm's length relationship should be maintained with the board and its directors. The company secretary should ideally not be a director of the company.

In addition to the duties mentioned in the Act and in 13.8.2 above, the company secretary's role is to:
- provide advice to the board on matters of ethics and good governance,
- assist with the proper and timely compilation of board agendas,
- ensure that the procedures for the appointment of directors are followed and that induction, orientation and development courses take place, and
- assist the board with the annual evaluation of the board, its individual directors and senior management.

See further chapter 10: Governance and the Board of Directors.

13.9.4 Integrated reporting and disclosure

Although King II extended the reporting responsibilities of companies beyond financial reporting to include social and environmental issues, in the majority of cases these additional issues were tagged onto reports without being properly integrated into the reporting. The King III Report recommends integrated reporting that gives a holistic and integrated representation of a company's performance in terms of both its finances and its sustainability.[87] Effective reporting on a company's goals, strategies, and economic, social and environmental issues can assist with the alignment of company and stakeholder interests, which can build and/or restore stakeholder confidence.[88]

An integrated report should be prepared annually by a company and should convey adequate information in respect of the company's operations, the sustainability of the business, the financial results, the results of its operations and the cash flows.[89] It should also include forward-looking information. Substance should prevail over form in the preparation of this report, which should include disclosure which is complete, timely, relevant, accurate, honest, accessible, and comparable with past company performance.[90]

The audit committee's role in integrated reporting is *(a)* to ensure the reliability of the integrated report, and *(b)* to ensure that no contradictions arise between the financial and the sustainability information included in the report.[91]

An integrated report should present financial disclosure, including:
- the annual financial statements,
- commentary by the board on the financial results, including insight into the potential for future value creation and the board's assessment of key risks which may limit those prospects, and

---

[87] King Report on Corporate Governance for South Africa 2009, Principle 9.1.1.
[88] King Report on Corporate Governance for South Africa 2009, Principle 9.1.6.
[89] King Report on Corporate Governance for South Africa 2009, Principle 9.1.5.
[90] King Report on Corporate Governance for South Africa 2009, Principle 9.1.7.
[91] King Report on Corporate Governance for South Africa 2009, Principle 9.1.3.

- disclosure as to whether or not the company is and will continue to be a going concern in the future.

It should also provide sustainability disclosure, including:

- a description of how the company has generated its money, the positive and negative impact of the company's operations on its stakeholders, and any plans to improve the positive impact and eradicate the negative impact in the financial year ahead, and
- reporting on economic, social and environmental issues.

The credibility of financial and sustainability reporting is equally important. Although there is no equivalent for sustainability reporting of the financial reporting standards that apply to financial reporting, the third-generation Global Reporting Initiative guidelines of 2007 are the accepted international standard for sustainability reporting. As a global standard, these guidelines facilitate benchmarking and comparability across companies.[92] Listed companies in South Africa also often take guidance from the JSE Socially Responsible Investment Index (SRI) criteria.[93]

The King III Report recommends that an entity should obtain independent assurance over the sustainability reporting and disclosure in the integrated report.[94] Providing assurance on sustainability reporting has its complexities, because, unlike financial reporting, sustainability information is not subject to set standards. Globally, two assurance standards exist for sustainability:

- AccountAbility's AA 1000 Assurance Standard (AA1000AS), and
- the International Accounting and Auditing Standard Board's International Standard on Assurance Engagements (ISAE 3000), which must be complied with by all auditing professionals in South Africa.[95]

AA1000AS aligns the assurance process with the material concerns of stakeholders in terms of the integrated report as a whole, whereas ISAE 3000 focuses on verifying the accuracy and completeness of information, assessing the performance of the underlying systems, and evaluating compliance with the company's defined scope. These standards are complementary and the King III Report recommends that they be used concurrently.[96]

13.10 AUDITORS' LIABILITY

13.10.1 Criminal liability

In the course of his or her duties, an auditor may incur criminal liability in a number of instances laid down in the Auditing Profession Act. In terms of this Act, an auditor is guilty of an offence if he or she:

---

[92] King Report on Corporate Governance for South Africa 2009, Principle 9.2.16.
[93] King Report on Corporate Governance for South Africa 2009, Principles 9.2.15 and 9.2.16.
[94] King Report on Corporate Governance for South Africa 2009, Principle 9.3.17.
[95] King Report on Corporate Governance for South Africa 2009, Principle 9.3.18.
[96] King Report on Corporate Governance for South Africa 2009, Principle 9.3.18.

The Auditor, Financial Records and Reporting 567

- fails to report a reportable irregularity in accordance with s 45 of the Auditing Profession Act,[97]
- for the purposes of, or in connection with, the audit of any financial statement, knowingly or recklessly expresses an opinion or makes a report or other statement which is false in a material respect,[98]
- contravenes ss 41, 43 or 44 of the Auditing Profession Act relating to public practice,[99]
- contravenes any provision of s 47 of the Auditing Profession Act (which relates to public practice)[100] or obstructs or hinders any person in the performance of functions under s 47,[101]
- having been duly summoned to a disciplinary hearing[102] under s 50 of the Auditing Profession Act, fails, without sufficient cause, to attend at the time and place specified in the summons, or to remain in attendance until excused from further attendance by the chairperson of the disciplinary committee,[103]
- having been called to a disciplinary hearing under s 50 of the Auditing Profession Act, refuses to be sworn or to affirm as a witness or fails without sufficient cause to answer fully and satisfactorily to the best of his or her knowledge and belief all questions lawfully put concerning the subject of the hearing,[104]
- having been called to a disciplinary hearing under s 50 of the Auditing Profession Act and having possession, custody or control of any information, including but not limited to any working papers, statements, correspondence, books or other documents, refuses to produce it when required to do so,[105]
- is a witness before a disciplinary committee and, having been duly sworn or having made an affirmation, gives a false answer to any question lawfully put or makes a false statement on any matter, knowing the answer or statement to be false,[106]

---

[97] Section 52(1) of the Auditing Profession Act. A person convicted of an offence in a court of law under this section is liable to a fine or to imprisonment for a term not exceeding ten years or to both a fine and such imprisonment. The duty to report reportable irregularities and the civil liability flowing therefrom is dealt with in 13.10.3. The criminal liability here, where the registered auditor is a firm, attaches to the individual auditor responsible for the audit (see s 52(2) of the Auditing Profession Act).

[98] Section 52(1) of the Auditing Profession Act.

[99] The penalty is a fine or, in default of payment, imprisonment not exceeding five years, or both a fine and such imprisonment.

[100] Section 54 of the Auditing Profession Act. The penalty is a fine or imprisonment for a period not exceeding one year.

[101] Section 54 of the Auditing Profession Act.

[102] See Chapter V of the Auditing Profession Act regarding disciplinary action and hearings. See also 13.10.4 below regarding disciplinary liability.

[103] Section 53 of the Auditing Profession Act. The penalty is a fine or imprisonment for a period of five years, or both a fine and such imprisonment.

[104] Section 53 of the Auditing Profession Act.

[105] Ibid.

[106] Ibid.

- wilfully hinders any person acting in the capacity of a member of a disciplinary committee in the exercise of any power conferred upon him or her by or under s 51 of the Auditing Profession Act,[107] or
- contravenes any of the following provisions of the Companies Act: s 26(6), s 28(2) and (4), s 29(6), s 213(1), s 214(1) and (3), or s 215(1) and (2).[108]

13.10.2 Civil liability to client and third parties

A clear distinction must be made between an auditor's civil liability to the company that he or she is auditing (the client) and his or her civil liability to third parties. The reason for the distinction is of course that the client has a contract with the auditor, whereas usually there is no contract between the auditor and the third party.

(a) Civil liability to the client

(i) Duties to the client

Auditors may incur civil liability to their client by failing to comply with the statutory duties they owe to the client they are auditing, as well as the additional duties undertaken by them in terms of their contract with the client. The auditor's statutory duties to his or her client are those set out in 13.6.2 above.

Additional duties may include tax advisory and compliance work or consultancy work on aspects of financial management or information systems. In the performance of his or her duties, the auditor must not act maliciously, fraudulently or negligently.

(ii) Reasonable care and skill

As stated above, in carrying out his or her statutory duties, the auditor must not act negligently; in other words, he or she must 'bring to bear on the work he [or she] has to perform that skill, care and caution which a reasonably competent, careful and cautious auditor would use'.[109] The duty to act with 'reasonable care and skill' is a term of the contract implied by law.

The standard of care required of an auditor is not static but must meet changed circumstances. As Moffitt J said in *Pacific Acceptance Corporation Ltd v Forsyth*:[110]

> The legal duty, namely, to audit the accounts with reasonable skill and care, remains the same, but reasonableness and skill in auditing must bring to account and be directed towards the changed circumstances referred to. Reasonable skill and care call for changed standards to meet changed conditions or changed understanding of dangers and, in this sense, standards are more exacting today than in 1896. The audit profession has rightly accepted, and by change in emphasis in their procedures and in some changed procedures have acknow-

---

[107] Section 53 of the Auditing Profession Act.
[108] The penalty for the contravention is a fine or imprisonment not exceeding ten years, or both a fine and imprisonment.
[109] *Per* Lopes LJ in *In re Kingston Cotton Mill Co (2)* [1896] 2 Ch 279 (CA) 288. See also *Tonkwane Sawmill Co Ltd v Filmalter* 1975 (2) SA 453 (W) 455; *Re Thomas Gerrard & Son Ltd* [1967] 2 All ER 525 (Ch) 534.
[110] (1970) 92 WN (NSW) 29 74.

ledged that due skill and care calls for some different approaches. It is not a question of the court requiring higher standards because the profession has adopted higher standards. It is a question of the court applying the law, which by its content expects such reasonable standards as will meet the circumstances of today, including modern conditions of business and knowledge concerning them. However, now as formerly, standards and practices adopted by the profession to meet current circumstances provide a sound guide to the court in determining what is reasonable.

The duty to act with due care and skill does not impose on the auditor a duty to approach the audit suspecting dishonesty. Thus Lopes J said in *In re Kingston Cotton Mill Co (2)*:[111]

> [A]n auditor is not bound to be a detective, or as was said, to approach his work with suspicion or with a foregone conclusion that there is something wrong. He is a watch-dog, but not a bloodhound.

It has been stated:[112]

> [A]n auditor is not to be confined to the mechanics of checking vouchers and making arithmetical computations. His vital task is to take care to see that errors are not made, be they errors of computation, or errors of omission or commission or downright untruths. To perform this task properly he must come to it with an enquiring mind — not suspicious of dishonesty — but suspecting that someone may have made a mistake somewhere and that a check must be made to ensure that there has been none.

Also:

> *Prima facie*, the duty of the auditor is to satisfy himself on material matters by such checks and procedures as are commonly understood to comprise an audit. He does not satisfy himself merely by being content that management is responsible and is satisfied about the matter. Of course, the fact that management is satisfied about some matter may be relevant in aiding to produce an apparent state of regularity which may justify some reduction in the auditor's checks. *Prima facie* the auditor's job is to check material matters for himself from available documents and he does not ordinarily do his job or 'audit' if he merely seeks the assurance of another as to the check that other has made or as to his views as to the effect of documents.
>
> In principle an auditor is really in no different position from any skilled inquirer. To the inquirer in any field, to know by direct examination is surer proof than to believe on the hearsay of others or by inference. The latter and second-best alternatives may well be acceptable if a direct examination is not permissible or the delay, expense or effort that will be occasioned by such examination is out of proportion to the importance of the matter to be proved.[113]

Specialist advice, such as legal advice on a point of law, must be sought when necessary.[114]

---

[111] [1896] 2 Ch 279 (CA) 288–9. In *Pacific Acceptance Corporation Ltd v Forsyth* (1970) 92 WN (NSW) 29 61 Moffitt J remarked with reference to the above quotation: 'These approaches, however, are but what one would expect of a professional auditor who is called upon to do no more than that what is reasonable in the circumstances. In any of a number of fields of human activity it is but the approach to be expected of a person assigned to do a routine check of affairs as against having to make a special inquiry in the light of special circumstances.'
[112] *Tonkwane Sawmill Co Ltd v Filmalter* 1975 (2) SA 453 (W) 455, referring to Lord Denning in *Fomento (Sterling Area) Ltd v Selsdon Fountain Pen Co Ltd* [1958] 1 All ER 11 (HL) 23.
[113] *Pacific Acceptance Corporation Ltd v Forsyth* (supra) at 67–8.
[114] *Fomento (Sterling Area) Ltd v Selsdon Fountain Pen Co Ltd* (supra) at 23.

If an auditor's suspicion is aroused, he or she must conduct further enquiries. As stated by the New Zealand High Court:[115]

> [T]he auditor's basic duty is to plan and carry out the audit of the company cognisant of the possibility of fraud. If and when the auditors discover any irregularity, they must carry out such further tests or make such further inquiries as may be required to be satisfied that, in fact, no irregularity exists. If an irregularity is found to exist they must be satisfied, or take further steps as may be necessary to be satisfied, that the irregularity will not affect the truth of the accounts. If the circumstances are such as to give rise to a reasonable suspicion of fraud, they must necessarily proceed further and either determine that no fraud exists or report their suspicion to the general manager, or the board, or the shareholders of the company, as may be appropriate in the circumstances of the case.

Auditors must be careful to supervise and review the work of employees under them, particularly inexperienced ones — the auditor is responsible for their work.[116]

In determining whether an auditor has acted negligently, the courts have held that they must be careful not to make a scapegoat of the auditor nor to be influenced by hindsight.[117]

(iii) *Grounds for liability to the client*

• *Breach of contract*

An auditor may be liable to the client on the basis of breach of contract, if the following is established:

- a contract exists,
- the auditor has breached the contract,
- the auditor has acted maliciously, fraudulently or negligently in breaching the contract,[118] and
- loss has been suffered by the client as a result of the breach.

In *Thoroughbred Breeders' Association v Price Waterhouse*[119] it was held that the Apportionment of Damages Act 34 of 1956 does not apply to contractual claims. Therefore the auditor cannot raise the negligence of the client in an action brought by the client against the auditor.

In the *Thoroughbred Breeders'* case the appellant, a body not for gain, had employed the respondent firm as its auditors since 1990. During January 1994 the respondent had audited the appellant's financial statements in respect of the year ended 31 October 1993 (the 1993 audit). The appellant alleged that the respondent had in doing so breached the auditing agreement between them by failing to detect

---

[115] *Dairy Containers Ltd v NZI Bank Ltd* [1995] 2 NZLR 30.
[116] *Pacific Acceptance Corporation Ltd v Forsyth* (1970) 92 WN (NSW) 29 79.
[117] *In re City Equitable Fire Insurance Co Ltd* [1925] 1 Ch 407, 503; *In Re London and General Bank (2)* [1895] 2 Ch 673, 687; *Pacific Acceptance Corporation Ltd v Forsyth* (supra) at 61.
[118] In this regard it is to be noted that s 46(2) of the Auditing Profession Act provides:

'(2) In respect of any opinion expressed or report or statement made by a registered auditor in the ordinary course of duties the registered auditor does not incur any liability to a client or any third party, unless it is proved that the opinion was expressed, or the report or statement made, maliciously, fraudulently or pursuant to a negligent performance of the registered auditor's duties.'

[119] 2001 (4) SA 551 (SCA).

(1) that a promissory note with a face value of R138 864 belonging to the appellant had been encashed and the proceeds stolen; and (2) that several substantial sums of cash (in all totalling R143 403,44) had not been deposited for long periods. The undeposited cash had been stolen by the appellant's financial manager, one M, who had subsequently encashed the promissory note to cover the thefts. It was common cause that, after the 1993 audit, M had gone on to steal a further R1 389 801,90 from the appellant before his activities were uncovered. The core of the appellant's case was that, had the respondent properly (that is, with the exercise of reasonable care and not negligently) carried out the 1993 audit, M's activities in respect of the promissory note and the undeposited cash would have been discovered, and his subsequent misappropriation of funds and the resultant losses to the appellant prevented. The appellant accordingly instituted a claim for damages in the amount of R1 389 801,90, plus interest. The respondent denied breaching the audit agreement, alternatively it denied that any breach it might have committed had caused the loss, and raised various other defences based on the fact that the appellant had been aware that M had a previous conviction for theft but had nevertheless employed him in a senior financial position without proper supervision, and thus only had itself to blame. It also pleaded that the appellant's claim had to be reduced because its contributory negligence meant that the Apportionment of Damages Act 34 of 1956 was applicable to its cause of action.

On appeal to the Supreme Court of Appeal the first issue was whether the respondent had breached its auditing agreement with the respondent. The actual terms of the respondent's appointment were never formalised and the relationship between the parties was accordingly governed by such terms as were customary between a client and its auditor (it was in fact common cause that the respondent was bound to conduct its audit 'in accordance with generally accepted auditing standards (GAAS)' and 'with due professional care required of an auditor in public practice'). This meant that the respondent would have been in breach of its obligations if it had been careless in the execution of any aspect of its mandate, measured against the general standards prevailing in the profession at the time. The first enquiry on appeal was thus whether the respondent had been negligent. The next issue was causation, namely, if breach of contract was established, whether it had caused the losses sustained.

The court held that the auditor had been negligent in aspects of the audit and hence in breach of its contract with the company. The company's loss flowed naturally and generally from the auditor's breach and was thus not too remote. The company was itself careless in failing to properly supervise the activities of the financial manager, despite its awareness that he had previously been convicted of theft. Both sets of carelessness thus contributed to the loss. However, the Apportionment of Damages Act 34 of 1956 was not applicable to a contractual claim for damages and accordingly was not available to the auditor to counter or curtail the company's claim. The claim was allowed in full.

- *Delict*

An action can be brought against the auditor by the client on the basis of delict. Here a distinction must be drawn between a common-law delictual action and an action based on a breach of statutory duty.

In determining whether an action can be brought against an auditor on the basis of a breach of statutory duty it will have to be shown that the statutory duty carries with it an implied civil remedy in the event of its breach. Thus, in interpreting the provision imposing the duty, the intention of the legislature to provide a civil remedy must be established.[120] If that intention is established, the company, in relying on the remedy, will have to show that it was one of the persons for whose benefit the remedy was imposed, the damage it suffered was of the kind contemplated by the statute, the auditor's conduct constituted a breach of the duty, and the breach caused or materially contributed to the damage.[121] It will also have to be established that the auditor acted maliciously, fraudulently or negligently.[122]

The common-law delictual action arises through the duty of care imposed on the auditor by virtue of the auditor's relationship with the client.

Therefore, independently of the liability attaching to the auditor on the basis of breach of contract, the client will also have a delictual action in terms of the common law. The client can thus bring action on the basis of either breach of contract or delict. In fact, action can be brought in the alternative (although damages in respect of the loss suffered can be recovered only once).

In order for the auditor to be liable on the basis of delict, it will have to be proved that:

o   the auditor acted negligently, fraudulently or maliciously,[123]
o   the client suffered loss, and
o   the loss was caused by the auditor's malice, fraud or negligence.

- *Pure economic loss*

In an action based on delict or breach of contract, the client may recover pure economic loss as opposed to loss related to physical damage to property.[124] In the case of auditors' liability the loss will invariably, of course, be economic.

- *Measure of damages*

Damages recoverable in an action based on delict are calculated on the basis of what is needed to put the client in the position it would have been in if the delict had not been committed.[125]

Damages recoverable in an action based on breach of contract are calculated on

---

[120] *Knop v Johannesburg City Council* 1995 (2) SA 1 (A); *Lascon Properties (Pty) Ltd v Wadeville Investment Co (Pty) Ltd* 1997 (4) SA 578 (W); *Van der Merwe Burger v Munisipaliteit van Warrenton* 1987 (1) SA 899 (NC); *Minister van Polisie v Ewels* 1975 (3) SA 590 (A); *Da Silva v Coutinho* 1971 (3) SA 123 (A).
[121] *Da Silva v Coutinho* (supra).
[122] See s 46(2) of the Auditing Profession Act quoted in n 118.
[123] Ibid.
[124] *Mukheiber v Raath* 1999 (3) SA 1065 (SCA); *Indac Electronics (Pty) Ltd v Volkskas Bank Ltd* 1992 (1) SA 783 (A); *International Shipping Co (Pty) Ltd v Bentley* 1990 (1) SA 680 (A); *Pilkington Brothers (SA) (Pty) Ltd v Lillicrap, Wassenaar & Partners* 1983 (2) SA 157 (W) 162; 1985 (1) SA 475 (A); *Shell and BP South African Petroleum Refineries v Osborne Panama SA* 1980 (3) SA 653 (D); *Administrateur, Natal v Trust Bank van Afrika Bpk* 1979 (3) SA 824 (A); *Greenfield Engineering Works (Pty) Ltd v NKR Construction (Pty) Ltd* 1978 (4) SA 901 (N) 916.
[125] *Union Government v Warneke* 1911 AD 657 at 665.

the basis of putting the client in the position it would have been in if the contract had been properly carried out.[126]

- *Apportionment of damages*

In delict the contributory negligence of the client can result in an apportionment of damages between the company and the auditor.[127] It has been held that this is not the case in an action based on breach of contract.[128]

(b) Civil liability to third parties

(i) The common law

It is readily apparent that it is not only the client who is interested in the audit of the company. Third parties also may very well be interested. They may wish, for example, to transact with the company, or invest in securities of the company, or make loans to the company. A clean audit report may give them the assurance to do so.

The question, of course, that arises in these circumstances is: what liability does the auditor incur to a third party if the clean audit report should have been qualified and is therefore misleading? Is the auditor liable for the loss that the third party might have suffered as a result of their reliance on the audit report?

In answering this question, one must bear in mind two factors[129] 'which traditionally have caused considerable uncertainty in modern legal systems about the limitation, and even the recognition, of liability for negligent misrepresentation causing mere financial loss'.[130] First, in the famous words of Lord Pearce:[131]

> [Words are] more volatile than deeds. They travel fast and far afield. They are used without being expended . . . Yet they are dangerous and can cause vast financial damage. In the result a good deal of judicial caution has shown itself in the approach to harm caused by words.[132] Secondly, there is the traditional fear that a general remedy not only for physical injury to person or property, but also for mere pecuniary or economic loss, would result in an unmanageably wide liability. It would impose an 'almost intolerable burden on legitimate human activity',[133] lead to unnecessary duplication or multiplicity of actions so that more harm than good would be done by such an extension,[134] and result in overwhelming potential liability which is indeterminate and socially calamitous.

It was these factors that led Cardozo J to deny liability in the New York Court

---

[126] *Dennill v Atkins & Co* 1905 TS 282; *Novick v Benjamin* 1972 (2) SA 842 (A) 857.
[127] See s 1 of the Apportionment of Damages Act 34 of 1956.
[128] *OK Bazaars (1929) Ltd v Stern and Ekermans* 1976 (2) SA 521 (C). In *Thoroughbred Breeders' Association v Price Waterhouse* 1999 (4) SA 968 (W) 1024–5 the correctness of this was questioned by the court *a quo*, which held to the contrary. This aspect of the case was overturned on appeal. See the discussion of the SCA's decision above.
[129] See SJ Naude 'Auditors' liability to third parties' 1979 *MB* 121.
[130] Naude op cit n 129.
[131] *Hedley Byrne & Co Ltd v Heller & Partners Ltd* [1963] 2 All ER 575 (HL) 613I–614A.
[132] See the judgment of Schreiner JA in *Herschel v Mrupe* 1954 (3) SA 464 (A) 477D–478G; DB Hutchison 'Negligent statements: why the reluctance to impose liability?' 1978 *SALJ* 515 at 524–7.
[133] RG McKerron 'Liability for mere pecuniary loss in an action under the *Lex Aquilia*' 1973 *SALJ* 1; see also Hutchison op cit n 132 at 527–31.
[134] *Combrinck Chiropraktiese Kliniek (Edms) Bpk v Datsun Motor Vehicle Distributors (Pty) Ltd* 1972 (4) SA 185 (T) 192.

of Appeals in this oft-quoted statement in *Ultramares Corporation v George A Touche*:[135]

> If liability for negligence exists, a thoughtless slip or blunder, the failure to detect a theft or forgery beneath the cover of deceptive entries may expose accountants *to a liability in an indeterminate amount for an indeterminate time to an indeterminate class*. The hazards of a business conducted on these terms are so extreme as to enkindle doubt whether a flaw may not exist in the implication of a duty that exposes to these consequences.

As Naude says,[136] since the *Ultramares* case, 'the three indeterminates appearing in italics have been repeated in some judgments almost as though they reveal a self-evident truth'. But the attraction and force of the language ought not to lead to uncritical acceptance of that sort of argument.

> It is, of course, substantially a plea in mitigation on behalf of a particular class of defendants [auditors in this case] that they should be altogether excused from liability for their negligent conduct because the consequences are too serious to justify responsibility. It may be regarded as a rather one-sided argument, particularly when it is set up in favour of those who are in business to give advice.[137]

In South Africa the existence of an action for negligent misstatement causing financial loss was first recognised in *Herschel v Mrupe*[138] (the case did not involve an auditor) and followed in a number of other cases since.[139]

Of particular importance was Rumpf CJ's judgment in the *Trust Bank* case in which he recognised the importance of the particular circumstances and policy considerations in deciding whether a legal duty not to make a misstatement to the plaintiff in the particular circumstances was established.[140] At the same time he recognised that reasonable foreseeability of reliance by the third party was also a factor that had to be taken into account. The duty of care here is different to the traditional duty of care doctrine which does not take policy considerations into account, but places all emphasis on foreseeability.[141]

It is of assistance to refer to some of Naude's comments on 'policy considerations',[142] because his comments promote understanding of the legislature's attempts to limit an auditor's liability to third parties. There seems no doubt that Naude's comments had a significant impact on the drafting of the legislation.

Regarding policy considerations, Naude says:

> [The] actual policy considerations involved cannot be neatly listed with any pretension of comprehensiveness . . . The usual considerations referred to in claims for financial loss arise from the traditional fear of an unmanageably wide liability . . . They consist of warnings

---

[135] 74 ALR 1139 at 1145; 225 NY 170; 174 NE 441.
[136] Naude op cit n 129 at 122.
[137] Woodhouse J in *Scott Group Ltd v McFarlane* [1978] 1 *NZLR* 553 (CA) 572.
[138] 1954 (3) SA 464 (A).
[139] See *Suid-Afrikaanse Bantoetrust v Ross en Jacobz* 1977 (3) SA 184 (T); *Administrator, Natal v Bizo* 1978 (2) 256 (N) 261; *Greenfield Engineering Works (Pty) Ltd v NKR Construction (Pty) Ltd* 1978 (4) SA 901 (N); *EG Electric Co (Pty) Ltd v Franklin* 1979 (2) SA 702 (EC); *International Shipping Co (Pty) Ltd v Bentley* 1990 (1) SA 680 (A), and *Standard Chartered Bank of Canada v Nedperm Bank Ltd* 1994 (4) SA 747 (A).
[140] *Administrateur, Natal v Trust Bank van Afrika Bpk* 1979 (3) SA 824 (A) 832H–833C.
[141] See Naude op cit n 129 at 124.
[142] See Naude op cit n 129 at 132–3.

against 'almost intolerable burdens', 'duplication or multiplicity of actins', and 'overwhelming potential liability' which is 'indeterminate', 'socially calamitous' or 'open-ended'. Other signposts involve notions such as 'fair and reasonable' or 'instinctive justice as to what is fair and just' ... Some of these considerations are rather forcefully expressed in pithy statements. There is a danger of over-generalisation in this ...

The great and growing importance of the commercial information contained in companies' annual financial statements, does imply a responsibility for auditors — but not unrestricted liability. By restricting liability within reasonable bounds the law in fact promotes the important social policy of encouraging the flow of commercial information so vital to the operation of the economy. A legal duty to a third party whose intended reliance is not actually known or in the particular circumstances reasonably foreseeable, is not reasonable and is socially counterproductive ...

It is not in the public interest to bring about a situation in which auditors will feel obliged to resort to the device of a general disclaimer negativing liability.[143] This branch of the law should be such that professional persons of integrity can feel confident that they will not be held liable except where it is reasonable to do so in view of their particular situation ...

The simple fact is that every auditor knows perfectly well, or ought at least reasonably to foresee, that annual financial statements are widely used by existing or potential members and creditors for investment or business decisions, sometimes, but by no means necessarily, at the inducement of the client company. In essence this is true of all companies, although there are obvious differences in degree regarding the typical private company, the typical public company and the public listed company, respectively. This knowledge or foreseeability arises purely from the fact that a person is acting as *an auditor*. However, there is no doubt that holding negligent auditors liable on the strength of *this* knowledge or foreseeability simply inferred from their professional position would fly in the face of all the general policy considerations mentioned earlier. It would inhibit the flow of commercial information, and either ruin the profession or lead to a general practice of disclaimer in auditors' reports.

Hence the *knowledge* of the auditor of intended reliance by a third party on annual financial statements referred to in regard to a legal duty, in the absence of which there is no wrongfulness, is an *actual awareness* and not an inference from his or her professional position.

Similarly, it is of fundamental importance that the *reasonable foreseeability* of reliance by the third party on the annual financial statements must be dependent on the *actual circumstances of the particular case* and, again, not be an inference based on the auditor's office or from considerations applying to all auditors generally.

The common-law position as it stands is that a third party bringing a delictual action against the auditor of the company on the basis of negligence will have to establish that:

- the auditor acted negligently in providing a clean audit report when it should have been qualified,
- the auditor owed the third party a duty of care (as stated above, the current duty of care doctrine, contrary to the traditional doctrine, embraces both foreseeability and policy considerations),
- the third party relied on the auditor's negligent misstatement (the unqualified audit report), and
- the third party, as a result, suffered loss (the element of causation).

---

[143] Note that disclaimers are no longer possible. See below in 13.10.2*(b)*(ii).

There has been no reported case in South Africa in which an auditor was sued successfully by a third party for damages caused by the auditor's negligent misstatement. In the only reported case in which such action has been brought by a third party, *International Shipping Co (Pty) Ltd v Bentley*,[144] the appellant, a finance and shipping company, agreed to make certain financial facilities available to the D Group of companies early in 1976. The respondent was appointed auditor to the D Group in November 1977. In March 1979 the respondent issued reports in respect of the financial statements of each of the companies comprising the D Group, as well as the Group financial statements, for the year ended 20 December 1978. In each of these reports, which were not qualified in any way, the respondent stated that he had examined the financial statements in question and that, in his opinion, the statements fairly represented the financial position of the company concerned as at 20 December 1978 and the results of its operations for the period then ended, in the manner required by the Companies Act. The appellant continued to provide these financial facilities until the liquidation of the companies comprising the D Group in April 1981. At the time of such liquidation the total indebtedness of the D Group to the appellant amounted to R977 318, of which the sum of only R593 826 was recovered by the appellant, who thus sustained a loss in the amount of R383 492. The appellant instituted an action for damages against the respondent, alleging that the aforementioned financial statements were materially false and misleading in a number of respects; that in so reporting the respondent had acted fraudulently or, alternatively, negligently towards the appellant, who had relied thereon in reviewing and deciding to maintain and increase the facilities accorded to the D Group; that, had the 1978 financial statements fairly presented the financial position of the D Group and its constituent companies, the appellant would have terminated the facilities and have required the Group to make good its indebtedness to the appellant; and that the loss sustained by the appellant constituted damage for which the respondent was accordingly liable to compensate the appellant. The court held that:

- the financial statements were, to some extent, false and misleading;
- there was no reason for interfering with the court *a quo*'s finding that fraud had not been established but that negligence had been established with regard to some aspects of the financial statements;
- the following facts and considerations established a duty of care:
  - the statutory duty upon the defendant to furnish his report on the financial statements,
  - the nature and context of the relationship between the parties created a direct link between the plaintiff and the defendant,
  - the defendant was aware that, in monitoring and reviewing the facilities of the D Group, the plaintiff would rely upon the financial statements in a serious and business context,
  - there were no considerations of public policy which induced the court to deny liability in the case; and

---

[144] 1990 (1) SA 680 (A).

- the appellant had failed to prove that the auditor's misstatement had both factually and legally caused the loss suffered. Factual causation had been proved but not legal causation. From a legal point of view 'there was not a sufficiently close connection between [the] respondent's negligence and the loss ... for legal liability on respondent's part ...'.[145]

(ii) *Legislative intervention*

The concern about the auditor's liability to third parties being potentially too severe and also too uncertain has led to legislative intervention. First, s 20(9) was introduced into the Public Accountants' and Auditors' Act[146] in an attempt to restrict the liability and to provide certainty. The Auditing Profession Act replaced the Public Accountants' and Auditors' Act in 2004 and the relevant provisions are now to be found in s 46 of that Act. The new provisions are similar to but not exactly the same as the old provisions.

Section 46 of the Auditing Profession Act provides as follows:

Limitation of liability
46. (1)*(a)* The application of this section is limited to an audit performed within the meaning of paragraph *(a)* of the definition of 'audit' in section (1).

(b) Despite section 44(1)*(a)*, for purposes of this section registered auditor means both the individual registered auditor and the firm referred to in that section.

(2) In respect of any opinion expressed or report or statement made by a registered auditor in the ordinary course of duties the registered auditor does not incur any liability to a client or any third party, unless it is proved that the opinion was expressed, or the report or statement made, maliciously, fraudulently or pursuant to a negligent performance of the registered auditor's duties.

(3) Despite subsection (2), a registered auditor incurs liability to third parties who have relied on an opinion, report or statement of that registered auditor for financial loss suffered as a result of having relied thereon, only if it is proved that the opinion was expressed, or the report or statement was made, pursuant to a negligent performance of the registered auditor's duties and the registered auditor —

(a) knew, or could in the particular circumstances reasonably have been expected to know, at the time when the negligence occurred in the performance of the duties pursuant to which the opinion was expressed or the report or statement was made —
   (i) that the opinion, report or statement would be used by a client to induce the third party to act or refrain from acting in some way or to enter into the specific transaction into which the third party entered, or any other transaction of a similar nature, with the client or any other person; or
   (ii) that the third party would rely on the opinion, report or statement for the purpose of acting or refraining from acting in some way or of entering into the specific transaction into which the third party entered, or any other transaction of a similar nature, with the client or any other person; or
(b) in any way represented, at any time after the opinion was expressed or the report or statement was made, to the third party that the opinion, report or statement was correct, while at that time the registered auditor knew or could in the particular circumstances reasonably *have* been expected to know that the third party would rely on that representation for the purpose of acting or refraining from acting in some way or of entering

---

[145] *International Shipping Co (Pty) Ltd v Bentley* 1990 (1) SA 680 (A) 701H.
[146] Act 80 of 1991.

into the specific transaction into which the third party entered, or any other transaction of a similar nature, with the client or any other person.

(4) Nothing in subsections (2) or (3) confers upon any person a right of action against a registered auditor which, but for the provisions of those subsections, the person would not have had.

(5) For the purposes of subsection (3) the fact that a registered auditor performed the functions of a registered auditor is not in itself proof that the registered auditor could reasonably have been expected to know that —

(a) the client would act as contemplated in paragraph *(a)*(i) of that subsection; or

(b) the third party would act as contemplated in paragraph *(a)*(ii) or paragraph *(b)* of that subsection.

(6) Subsections (2) or (3) do not affect any additional or other liability of a registered auditor arising from —

(a) a contract between a third party and the registered auditor; or

(b) any other statutory provision or the common law.

(7) A registered auditor may incur liability to any partner, member, shareholder, creditor or investor of an entity if the registered auditor fails to report a reportable irregularity in accordance with section 45.

(8) A registered auditor may not through an agreement or in any other way limit or reduce the liability that such auditor may incur in terms of this section.

It will be recognised that s 46(3) and (5) of the Auditing Profession Act prescribes the circumstances in which an auditor will owe a duty of care to a third party. Thus these subsections attempt to limit the liability.

It appears from s 46(4) that any limit on liability to the third party in terms of the common law is still applicable, which means that policy considerations must also be taken into account.

(iii) *Current position*

Reading s 46 of the Auditing Profession Act together with the common law, the position appears to be the following:[147] (It is assumed that the company's annual financial statements are misleading; the auditor has been negligent in the performance of his or her duties resulting in a misleading audit report; the third party has relied on the audit report, and, as a result, the third party has suffered loss — all these requirements must be met.)

(1) An auditor is not liable to all third parties who, relying on the annual financial statements, enter into a transaction with the company or anyone else, and suffer financial loss as a result.[148] The fact that the third party is a member of the client company, or that the client is a private company or a public company lodging its annual financial statements with the registrar or a listed company makes no difference. (In this regard it is to be noted that 'third party' is defined in s 1 of the Auditing Profession Act as 'any person other than the client'.) It is also not relevant that the third party has inspected the

---

[147] This summary plus the illustrations are based on Naude's article op cit n 129. It in fact appears that both s 20(9) of the Public Accountants' and Auditors' Act and s 46(2), (3), (4) and (5) of the Auditing Profession Act are based on Naude's article.

[148] See s 46(3) of the Auditing Profession Act.

annual financial statements at the company's registered office, or that those statements have been published.[149]

(2) A duty to the third party not to make a misstatement arises where the auditor, at any time during the performance of his or her duties for the client company, in fact knows that the annual financial statements will be used by his or her client to induce the third party to enter into a specific transaction with the client or any other person.[150]

(3) A duty also arises where the auditor, at any time during the performance of his or her duties for the client company, in fact knows that the third party intends to or would rely on the annual financial statements for the purposes of entering into a specific transaction with the client or any other person.[151]

This is illustrated by Naude's example:[152]

> While performing an audit the auditor is informed by the client company that it is negotiating with X for a loan of R50 000 (or for making a takeover offer to the members), and that X requires the annual financial statements for that purpose. Because of the auditor's negligence he makes an unqualified report on the annual financial statements which materially misstate the financial position of the company. In reliance on them X makes the loan (or a successful takeover offer) and suffers pecuniary loss. The auditor is liable.

As Naude points out,[153] for the legal duty in points (2) and (3) above to arise, it is not necessary that the auditor concerned should be aware of the third party's identity, or know him or her as an individual. It is sufficient that the auditor knows that the annual financial statements will be relied upon by a group or class of persons, and that the particular third party proves to be one of them, even though the auditor has never heard of him or her by name.[154]

Naude illustrates this as follows:[155]

> In the course of the negligent performance of his or her duties, the auditor is told by the client company that the annual financial statements are urgently needed in order to obtain a large loan from 'a bank'. The statements are materially misleading. Relying on them, Bank X later makes a loan and suffers loss. The auditor is liable to Bank X, which was one of several banks approached by the company after the completion of the annual financial statements.

---

[149] See Naude op cit n 129 at 135–7.
[150] See s 46(3)(a) of the Auditing Profession Act. See also *Candler v Crane, Christmas & Co* [1951] 1 All ER 426 (CA) — Lord Denning's dissenting judgment at 434A, which was subsequently approved by the House of Lords in *Hedley Byrne & Co Ltd v Heller & Partners Ltd* [1963] 2 All ER 575 (HL); Naude op cit n 129.
[151] See s 46(3)(b) of the Auditing Profession Act. See also *Perlman v Zoutendyk* 1934 CPD 151; *Candler v Crane, Christmas & Co* (supra); *Hedley Byrne & Co Ltd v Heller & Partners Ltd* (supra); *EG Electric Co (Pty) Ltd v Franklin* 1979 (2) SA 702 (EC); *Dimond Manufacturing Co Ltd v Hamilton* [1969] NZLR 609 (CA); *Scott Group Ltd v McFarlane* [1978] 1 NZLR 553 (CA); *Shatterproof Glass Corporation v Ned James* 466 SW2d 873, 46 ALR (3d) 968; discussed by HR Hahlo in 'Liability of negligent accountants to third parties' 1973 *SALJ* 174; *Rhode Island Hospital Trust National Bank v Swartz* 455 F (2d) 847 (1972); *Haig v Bamford* 72 DLR (3d) 68 (1976); see also unreported case 3955 of 2001 in OFS Provincial Division.
[152] Naude op cit n 129 at 135.
[153] Naude op cit n 129 at 136.
[154] See *Haig, Scott Group, Perlman* and *EG Electric* (supra).
[155] See Naude op cit n 129 at 135.

If the auditor is told that the loan is to be obtained from Bank X, and the bank refuses, but the loan is then made by Bank Y on the strength of the annual financial statements, the auditor is probably not liable to Bank Y.

(4) If the transaction entered into by the third party in reliance on the annual financial statements is not the specific one mentioned in points (2) and (3) above, but a substantially similar one, the negligent auditor would still be liable.

Naude illustrates this as follows:[156]

An auditor negligently conducts an audit and issues an unqualified report on annual financial statements which give a favourable impression of an insolvent company. The auditor was informed that the company intended to exhibit the financial statements to X as a basis for applying for credit for the purchase of goods. But X, in reliance on those statements, buys a substantial block of shares in the company and suffers financial loss as a result. The auditor is not liable to X.

If the auditor was informed that X would be asked to extend credit for the purchase of vacuum cleaners, and credit is extended instead for the purchase of refrigerators, the auditor is liable to X.

If the auditor was informed that X would be asked for a loan to the company of R10 000, and X is in fact asked for and grants a loan of R100 000, the auditor is not liable to X. On the other hand, a loan of R12 000 is not necessarily a different transaction. The question is whether the difference in amount is such that it cannot be regarded as essentially the same transaction.[157]

(5) In the first four points above, the situations have involved annual financial statements. These are of course not the only documents in respect of which liability can arise. Other obvious examples are financial statements made out for a specific purpose, and prospectuses.[158]

As stated by Naude:[159]

[F]rom an auditor's point of view a prospectus is a document requiring caution ... In contrast to annual financial statements, the very purpose of a prospectus is to induce potential investors to subscribe for shares or debentures in the company. This the auditor knows. Hence it is difficult to disagree with the view that he is liable to those who suffer financial loss through investing in the company in reliance on his negligently prepared and misleading report in a prospectus.[160] This implies a duty of care, or a legal duty not to make misstatements in our law, to a wide class of potential investors.

(6) A legal duty also arises where a reasonable auditor, while performing his or her audit duties, would in the particular circumstances of the case have foreseen the reliance on the annual financial statements by the third party. Hence, where the auditor ought to have known in the circumstances that the third party intended to or would rely on the annual financial statements for the purposes of entering into the specific transaction into which he or she had entered, or a similar transaction, with the client company or any other person,

---

[156] Naude op cit n 129 at 136.
[157] Ibid.
[158] Ibid.
[159] Ibid.
[160] See Lord Salmon's judgment in *Anns v London Borough of Merton* [1977] 2 All ER 492 (HL) 512h–513a.

the auditor is liable to the third party for financial loss suffered through reliance on negligent misstatements in those financial statements.[161]

The indeterminate scope of application of the foreseeability test, is left unchecked, is however limited by s 46(5). As Naude says:[162]

[T]he exclusion of reasonably foreseeability for the recognition of a duty is not justified; but it is of fundamental importance that reasonable foreseeability in the particular circumstances should not be inferred from the mere fact that the defendant is an auditor, or from considerations which apply to all auditors . . . This goes to the heart of the danger of an unreasonably and dangerously wide liability of auditors to third parties. In fact, all auditors of all companies know that a variety of third parties rely on annual financial statements for all sorts of transactions, and in this respect the difference between public and private companies is one of degree only.' This is not sufficient for a legal duty which is essential for wrongfulness, and is the effect of s 46(5).

The application of 'foreseeability' in terms of the s 46(3) of the Auditing Profession Act is illustrated by Naude as follows:

Every year, over a long period of time, a company has obtained a large loan from X who has regularly relied on the annual financial statements. The auditor is aware of this established financing pattern. He or she is not informed that X will again be approached. But while performing his or her audit duties, reliance by X on the new annual financial statements for the same purpose is reasonably foreseeable. Hence the auditor owes X a legal duty not to make a misstatement. If he does so negligently and causes X loss, he or she is liable.

(7) An auditor who, at any time after the completion of his or her duties in respect of the annual financial statements of a client company, makes a representation to a third party as to the correctness of those financial statements is liable to the third party if he or she in fact knew, or could in the particular circumstances reasonably have been expected to know, that the third party would rely on those financial statements for the purpose of acting or refraining from acting in some way or of entering into the specific transaction into which the third party entered, or any other transaction of a similar nature, with the client or any other person.[163]

The representation as to the correctness of the annual financial statements can be by word or conduct, and take many forms.[164]

Naude illustrates this as follows:[165]

X asks an auditor for a copy of a client company's completed annual financial statements, informing the auditor that it is needed for purchasing all the company's shares. The auditor shows X a copy, and allows him or her to make extracts therefrom. Those statements are in fact misleading, and the auditor has been negligent in the performance of his or her duties. On the facts the auditor makes an implied representation as to correctness of the annual financial statements, and he or she is liable for loss suffered by X through reliance thereon.

---

[161] See s 46(3)(a) of the Auditing Profession Act.
[162] Naude op cit n 129 at 136–7.
[163] Section 46 of the Auditing Profession Act. See also *Dimond Manufacturing Co Ltd v Hamilton* [1969] NZLR 609 (CA).
[164] Naude op cit n 129 at 137.
[165] Ibid.

A case which the auditing profession may find disconcerting is *Axiam Holdings Ltd v Deloitte & Touche*.[166] In this case the Supreme Court of Appeal addressed the 'representation' referred to in s 20(9)*(b)*(ii) of the Public Accountants' and Auditors' Act, which is virtually identical to s 46(3)*(b)* of the Auditing Professions Act. The majority (Navsa JA handed down the judgment with Howie JA and Jafta JA concurring) held that an auditor may have a duty to warn a third party about the incorrectness of an audit report even if the auditor is unaware of its incorrectness, if the third party can show that the auditor ought reasonably to have known of the incorrectness. In such circumstances, by not warning the third party, the auditor has made the 'representation' referred to in s 20(9)*(b)*(ii).

Navsa J held:[167]

> It must be remembered that we are dealing with a situation where the legal convictions of the community could well consider it unacceptable that an auditing firm which issued a seriously negligent report should escape the legal duty to speak with care concerning that report simply because it was, possibly even negligently, ignorant of the negligence of its report. And what is more, in circumstances in which the latter negligence was something it ought to have known of . . .

It is of note that Cloete JA, Heher JA concurring, disagreed with the judgment of the majority, pertinent points of the dissenting judgment being:

- It was illogical to impose a duty to speak on an auditor who had no reason to believe that what he or she had done might have been negligent.[168]
- You cannot disclose what you do not know, and to hold a person liable for what that person ought to have known was to equate constructive knowledge with actual knowledge, which was unacceptable.[169]
- Public policy dictated that to impose liability on an auditor in these circumstances raised 'the spectre of limitless liability' and would also place an undue and unfair burden on the auditor.[170] Cloete JA said:

> The burden would be undue because the third party is not obliged to rely upon what the auditor has done . . .: the third party can appoint its own auditor, or ask the auditor whether it can rely on the accuracy of the audit already done. The burden would be unfair because should the third party make such an enquiry, the auditor would be entitled to refuse to answer; but if the enquiry is not made, the auditor would be obliged nevertheless to issue a disclaimer (which would reflect on its professional competence, and would be completely unnecessary if it had not been negligent) or would be obliged at its own expense to revisit the audit, on pain of being held liable (perhaps, as in this case, for many millions of rand) to any number of third parties whom the auditor knows or — even worse — ought reasonably to know, will rely on its accuracy. At common law, mere knowledge that the third party did indeed intend to rely on the correctness of the audit or a foreseeable risk that he might, is not

---

[166] 2006 (1) SA 237 (SCA). See R Jooste 'The spectre of indeterminate liability raises its head' 2006 *SALJ* 563.
[167] At para 22.
[168] Paragraph 30.
[169] Ibid. Cloete JA relied in this regard on *Universal Stores Ltd v OK Bazaars (1929) Ltd* 1973 (4) SA 747 (A), reliance which was regarded by the majority as 'misplaced' (para 22).
[170] Paragraph 31.

sufficient to create a legal duty. The same is true of the statue: para (ii) requires a representation in addition to knowledge (actual or constructive).

- What s 20(9)*(b)*(ii) of the PAA [Public Accountants' and Auditors'] Act envisages is that the auditor must, subsequent to the audit, 'take responsibility to the third party for its accuracy'.[171] If silence per se constituted a representation for the purposes of para (ii), then that paragraph would be 'largely ineffective in curbing the mischief — indeterminate liability — at which s 20(9) is aimed'.[172]

The concerns expressed by Cloete JA regarding the consequences flowing from the view taken by the majority of the court are very real ones, and it may be difficult for a court in the future to allay these concerns without adopting a different view to the majority. The view taken by the majority will be disconcerting to the auditing profession, to say the least.

What may be of some consolation to the auditing profession is that it may be difficult for a third party to prove that an auditor, unaware of the incorrectness of the audit opinion, ought reasonably to have become aware of such incorrectness at some time after it was given. As has been said:

> An auditing firm cannot reasonably be expected to review an audit opinion as a matter of course or to perform spot-checks to determine whether or not audit opinions expressed by it in the past were correct. Unless something material occurs which would alert an auditor to the fact that its audit opinion may be incorrect, it may be difficult to persuade a court that the auditor reasonably ought to have become aware of deficiencies in its report after it was prepared.[173]

It must also, of course, be borne in mind that the court in the *Axiam Holdings* case did not rule on Deloitte's liability. It rejected an exception to the appellant's particulars of claim and merely made a finding that a court might, when the matter went to trial, find that liability existed.

(8) Members of the company are third parties.[174]
(9) As Naude says,[175]

> [A] sophisticated third party like a financial institution can in effect create a legal duty to him for his own protection. If he expects that he will have to rely on a company's annual financial statements, he can inform the auditor of the intended reliance. The auditor will then owe that third party a duty when he performs his duties in relation to the financial statements.

(10) An auditor may not escape liability through an agreement or in any other way limit the liability that such auditor may incur on the basis of the above principles. Appending a disclaimer of general liability to the auditor's report would thus not negate any liability to a third party (or to the client for that matter). This is the effect of s 46(8) of the Auditing Profession Act and overrides the common law, which permits disclaimers of liability to third parties (not clients).

---

[171] Paragraph 32.
[172] Ibid.
[173] (2006) 23.5 *Bureau for Mercantile Law Bulletin* 95 at 95.
[174] See definition of 'third party' in s 1 of the Auditing Profession Act.
[175] Naude op cit n 129 at 137.

13.10.3 Auditors' liability and 'reportable irregularities'

An important aspect of corporate governance is the requirement[176] that an auditor of an entity who is satisfied or has reason to believe that a 'reportable irregularity' has taken place or is taking place in respect of that entity must, without delay, send a written report to the IRBA.[177]

Failure may result in liability to 'any partner, member, shareholder, creditor or investor of' the entity being audited.[178] The auditor may not, through an agreement or in any other way, limit or reduce the liability.[179]

A 'reportable irregularity' is defined in s 1 of the Auditing Profession Act as meaning:

> any unlawful act or omission committed by any person responsible for the management of an entity, which —
> (a) has caused *or* is likely to cause material financial loss to the entity or to any partner, member, shareholder, creditor or investor of the entity in respect of his, her or its dealings with that entity; or
> (b) is fraudulent or amounts to theft; or
> (c) represents a material breach of any fiduciary duty owed by such person to the entity or any partner, member, shareholder, creditor or investor of the entity under any law applying to the entity or the conduct or management thereof.

The report must give particulars of the reportable irregularity and must include such other information and particulars as the registered auditor considers appropriate.[180] The auditor must, within three days of sending the report to the IRBA, notify the members of the management board of the entity in writing of the sending of the report.[181] A copy of the report to the IRBA must accompany the notice.[182]

The auditor must, as soon as reasonably possible, but not later than 30 days from the date on which the report was sent to the IRBA:

- take all reasonable measures to discuss the report with the members of the management board of the entity;
- afford the members of the management board of the entity an opportunity to make representations in respect of the report; and
- send another report to the IRBA, which must include a statement that the registered auditor is of the opinion that:
  - no reportable irregularity has taken place or is taking place,
  - the suspected reportable irregularity is no longer taking place and that adequate steps have been taken for the prevention or recovery of any loss as a result thereof, if relevant, or

---

[176] See s 45 of the Auditing Profession Act.
[177] Section 45(1)*(a)* of the Auditing Profession Act. It is to be noted that in certain circumstances the auditor has a duty to report acts or omissions in terms of other legislation, for example the Financial Intelligence Centre Act 38 of 2001 (FICA) and the Prevention and Combating of Corrupt Activities Act (PRECCA).
[178] See s 46(7) of the Auditing Profession Act.
[179] Section 46(8) of the Auditing Profession Act.
[180] Section 45(1)*(b)*of the Auditing Profession Act.
[181] Section 45(2)*(a)*of the Auditing Profession Act.
[182] Section 45(2)*(b)*of the Auditing Profession Act.

○ the reportable irregularity is continuing (detailed particulars and information supporting the statement must be included).[183]

The IRBA must as soon as possible after receipt of a report containing a statement that the reportable irregularity is continuing notify any appropriate regulator in writing of the details of the reportable irregularity to which the report relates and provide it with a copy of the report.[184]

For the purpose of the reports referred to above, a registered auditor may carry out such investigations as he or she may consider necessary and, in performing any duty referred to, he or she must have regard to all the information which comes to his knowledge from any source.[185]

An auditor of an entity that is sequestrated or liquidated also has an obligation to send the above reports to the trustee or liquidator of the entity.[186]

(a) Reportable irregularities

The IRBA has issued a guide on reportable irregularities, entitled 'Reportable Irregularities: A Guide for Registered Auditors'.[187] The relevant paragraphs that support the definition of reportable irregulares in the Auditing Profession Act are as follows (extracts from the definition appear in italics):

4.2 *'has caused or is likely to cause material financial loss to the entity or to any partner, member, shareholder, creditor or investor of the entity in respect of his, her or its dealings with that entity'*

4.2.1 If the unlawful act or omission by any person responsible for the management of the entity has the consequence of causing or being likely to cause material financial loss to any of the parties named then the act or omission is reportable.

4.2.2 If the unlawful act or omission has not or is not likely to cause such financial loss then under this sub-section it is not reportable. The auditor then considers whether or not the act or omission meets the requirements of the other two conditions stipulated in the definition of reportable irregularities. The auditor also considers whether or not he or she should report the act or omission in accordance with any other legislation, for example the Financial Intelligence Centre Act (FICA) or The Prevention and Combating of Corrupt Activities Act (PRECCA) . . .

4.2.3 The measure of materiality should be applied within the context of the absolute financial loss caused by the unlawful act or omission and not the level of materiality as applied for purposes of the audit of the financial statements. The auditor need not determine what the level of materiality is in relation to the financial affairs of any partner, member, shareholder, creditor or investor of the entity, either in their individual capacity or as a group, but considers the material financial loss to the entity or to any

---

[183] Section 45(3) of the Auditing Profession Act.
[184] Section 45(4) of the Auditing Profession Act.
[185] Section 45(5) of the Auditing Profession Act.
[186] Section 45(6) of the Auditing Profession Act.
[187] Issued on 30 June 2006.

partner, member, shareholder, creditor or investor of the entity in respect of his, her or its dealings with that entity.

4.2.4 While it is difficult to set such a materiality level, the auditor considers the relative size of the loss or potential loss with regard to such parties on the basis of the auditor's professional judgment having regard to the nature and value of their collective dealings with the entity.

4.2.5 The auditor may not take into account any benefit that may arise from a reportable irregularity committed by management, for example, where a reportable irregularity arises as a result of the entity's dealings with a creditor but where that creditor is also a debtor of the entity. As a result, it may be inappropriate for an auditor to justify a net position that may result from the entity's collective dealings with that creditor/debtor.

4.3 *'is fraudulent or amounts to theft'*

4.3.1 An unlawful act or omission may itself not give rise to financial loss or potential financial loss, but nonetheless constitutes fraud or amounts to theft. The auditor exercises professional judgment to determine whether an unlawful act or omission constitutes fraud or theft. In cases of uncertainty the auditor may or may not seek professional or legal advice.

4.3.2 Fraud in this context must be considered in the context of the legal definition of fraud. Fraud has been defined as follows: 'Fraud is the unlawful and intentional making of a misrepresentation which causes actual prejudice or which is potentially prejudicial to another'.[188] Fraud involves a deliberate deceit, or action, or omission in order to mislead another party to the other party's prejudice. Likewise, theft must also be considered in the context of the legal definition of theft. Theft has been defined as follows: 'Theft is the unlawful taking of a thing which has value with the intention to deprive the lawful owner or the lawful possessor of that thing.'

4.3.3 While fraud can be difficult to determine from a legal perspective, the auditor takes account of the evidence available and draws a conclusion on the possibility that the act or omission of any person responsible for management of the entity may amount to deceit or misrepresentation intended to cause prejudice to another.

4.4 *'represents a material breach of any fiduciary duty owed by such person to the entity or any partner, member, shareholder, creditor or investor of the entity under any law applying to the entity or the conduct or management thereof'*

4.4.1 A fiduciary duty can generally be defined as the legal duty of a fiduciary to act in the best interests of the beneficiary. In other words, a fiduciary duty is the obligation to act solely for the benefit of another party and to avoid a conflict of interest between his or her own interests and those of the other party.

4.4.2 A person generally comes into a fiduciary relationship when he or she controls the assets of another or holds the power to act. Fiduciaries are

---

[188] *The Law of South Africa* 2 ed vol 6.

expected to be extremely loyal to the person they owe the fiduciary duty to: they must act in good faith on behalf of and for the sole benefit of the person to whom they owe the fiduciary duty and not put their personal interests before the duty, and must not profit from their position as a fiduciary.

4.4.3 Examples of fiduciary relationships include, without being exhaustive:
- a director in respect of his or her relationship to a company,
- a member in respect of his or her relationship to a close corporation,
- an employee in respect of his or her relationship to the employer,
- a partner in respect of his or her relationship to his or her co-partners, and
- a trustee in his or her relationship to the beneficiaries of the trust.

4.4.4 The measure of materiality for a breach of fiduciary duty should be applied within the context of the unlawful act or omission and not the level of materiality as applied for purposes of the audit of the financial statements. Materiality is reviewed in the context of the nature of the breach and not purely in financial terms. The auditor determines the nature of the fiduciary duty and assesses the materiality of the breach having regard to its impact and consequences. The purpose for which the fiduciary duty was established, the impact upon governance within the entity and the consequences for the entity and third parties ought to be considered as well as the high requirement of loyalty and good faith expected of those responsible for management. Only inconsequential and trivial breaches of this form of duty ought to be regarded as non-material. The auditor may or may not seek legal advice in cases of uncertainty.

4.4.5 The key obligations in terms of the directors' fiduciary duties owed toward their company include:
- preventing a conflict of interest,
- not exceeding the limitations of their power,
- maintaining an unfettered discretion, and
- exercising their powers for the purpose for which they were conferred.

4.4.6 Directors should prevent a conflict of interest
A person in a fiduciary position, such as a director, has a legal duty to prevent a conflict arising between his or her own interests and those of the party whom he or she serves. It follows, therefore, that a director may obtain no other advantage from his or her office than that to which he or she is entitled by way of director's remuneration.

4.4.7 Directors may not exceed the limitations of their power (acts ultra vires)
A director has a fiduciary duty to observe limitations of the powers of the company as well as the limits of his or her own authority to act on behalf of the company.

4.4.8 Directors must maintain an unfettered discretion
The directors must consider the affairs of the company in an objective manner and then, in their discretion, act in the best interest of the company.

The following will be noted from an examination of s 45 of the Auditing Profession Act:

- Fraud or theft is a reportable irregularity even though it may not be 'material'.[189] It is not necessary that the fraud or theft caused or is likely to cause any loss.[190]
- 'Reportable irregularities' can be committed only by 'any person responsible for the management of an entity'.[191]
- The material breach of fiduciary duty referred to in the definition of 'reportable irregularity' does not, in order to be classified as a 'reportable irregularity', have to cause loss to anyone.[192] However, if loss is not caused or likely to be caused, the breach may not qualify as being 'material'.
- It is not stated in s 45 that the auditor of an entity only has a duty to report a reportable irregularity if he or she encounters the irregularity during the course of the audit.
- The auditor, in carrying out his or her duty to report in terms of s 45 must have regard to information that he or she acquires from any source and not only information that he or she acquires in the course of his or her audit.[193]
- The auditor must report a reportable irregularity to the IRBA and not first to management as previously required by the Public Accountants' and Auditors' Act, allowing them 30 days to respond. As has been pointed out[194] this could seriously impact on the auditor–client relationship, the more so where the report proves to be unfounded.
- If the irregularity is a breach of the duty of management to act with due care and skill, it will be reportable only if it causes or is likely to cause the material financial loss referred to in the definition of reportable irregularity.[195]

(b) Criminal and civil liability

If an auditor fails to report a reportable irregularity:

- this constitutes an offence,[196] and
- the auditor may incur liability to any partner, member, shareholder, creditor or investor of the entity being audited.[197]

It appears that the civil liability referred to in the second bullet is a strict liability. In other words, it does not have to be shown that the auditor's failure to report was due to malice, fraud or negligence. No doubt liability can arise only if loss is suffered and the loss was caused by the auditor's failure to report.

---

[189] See s 1 of the Auditing Profession Act for a definition of 'reportable irregularity'.
[190] Section 1 of the Auditing Profession Act.
[191] Section 1 of the Auditing Profession Act.
[192] Section 1 of the Auditing Profession Act.
[193] Section 45(5) of the Auditing Profession Act.
[194] See P von Wielligh & H Burger *Accountancy SA* (February 2007) at 18–21.
[195] Paragraph *(a)* of the definition of 'reportable irregularity' in the Auditing Profession Act applies. Paragraph *(c)* is not applicable because the duty to act with due care and skill is not a fiduciary duty.
[196] See s 52(1)*(a)* of the Auditing Profession Act.
[197] See s 46(7) of the Auditing Profession Act.

13.10.4 Disciplinary liability

An auditor (including a firm of auditors) is subject to potential disciplinary action in terms of Chapter V of the Auditing Profession Act if he or she[198] is guilty of improper conduct:

> [I]mproper conduct' means any non-compliance with the Auditing Profession Act or any rules prescribed in terms of the Act or any conduct prescribed as constituting improper conduct.[199]

If found guilty, the disciplinary committee must:[200]

- caution or reprimand the registered auditor,
- impose on the registered auditor a fine not exceeding the amount calculated according to the ratio for five years' imprisonment prescribed in terms of the Adjustment of Fines Act 101 of 1991,
- suspend the right to practice as a registered auditor for a specific period, or
- cancel the registration of the registered auditor concerned and remove his or her name from the register.

The disciplinary committee may impose more than one of these sanctions. A disciplinary committee may order any person who admitted guilt or whose conduct was the subject of a hearing to pay such reasonable costs as have been incurred by an investigating committee and the disciplinary committee in connection with the investigation and hearing in question, or such part thereof as the disciplinary committee considers just.[201]

The IRBA may, if it deems it appropriate, publish the finding and the sanction imposed.[202]

---

[198] A firm is also subject to Chapter V of the Auditing Profession Act.
[199] Section 1 of the Auditing Profession Act.
[200] See s 51(3)(a) of the Auditing Profession Act.
[201] Section 51(4)(b) of the Auditing Profession Act.
[202] Section 51(5) of the Auditing Profession Act.

CHAPTER 14

PUBLIC OFFERINGS OF COMPANY SECURITIES

Jacqueline Yeats

14.1	INTRODUCTION	591
14.2	TYPES OF OFFERS AND THE DISTINCTION BETWEEN LISTED AND UNLISTED SECURITIES	591
	14.2.1 Initial public offering	592
	14.2.2 Primary offering	592
	14.2.3 Secondary offering	592
14.3	GENERAL RESTRICTIONS ON OFFERS TO THE PUBLIC	593
14.4	WHAT CONSTITUTES AN OFFER TO THE PUBLIC?	594
14.5	WHAT DOES NOT CONSTITUTE AN OFFER TO THE PUBLIC?	597
14.6	STANDARDS FOR QUALIFYING EMPLOYEE SHARE SCHEMES	599
14.7	ADVERTISEMENTS RELATING TO OFFERS	601
14.8	PROSPECTUS REQUIREMENTS	601
	14.8.1 The contents of a prospectus	603
	14.8.2 Consent to use name in prospectus	604
	14.8.3 Variation of agreement mentioned in prospectus	604
14.9	SECONDARY OFFERS TO THE PUBLIC	604
14.10	LIABILITY	606
	14.10.1 Liability for untrue statements in the prospectus	606
	14.10.2 Liability of experts and others	609
	14.10.3 Responsibility for untrue statements in the prospectus	609
	14.10.4 Criminal liability	610
14.11	ALLOTMENTS AND ACCEPTANCE OF SUBSCRIPTIONS	611
	14.11.1 Time limits	611
	14.11.2 Restrictions	612
	14.11.3 Voidable allotments	612
	14.11.4 Minimum interval before allotment or acceptance	612
	14.11.5 Conditional allotment if the prospectus states securities to be listed	613

14.1 INTRODUCTION

Chapter 4 of the Companies Act 71 of 2008 (hereafter 'the Act') regulates public offerings of company securities.[1] The principal aim of this legislation is to protect investors by ensuring that they are provided with adequate and accurate information relating to the state of affairs and prospects of a company before they subscribe for or purchase its shares. It does this by prohibiting offers to the public which do not comply with the stringent requirements laid down in the Act. Failure to comply can result in both civil and criminal liability. Thus the Act includes provisions dealing with, among other things:

- the application of Chapter 4,[2]
- definitions of important concepts and terms (such as 'offer to the public'),[3]
- general restrictions on offers to the public,[4]
- types of offers,[5]
- offers that do not constitute offers to the public (and thus do not fall within the purview of the rules and restrictions contained in Chapter 4),[6]
- advertisements relating to offers,[7]
- prospectus requirements,[8]
- potential liability in connection with the prospectus,[9] and
- the allotment of securities.[10]

Chapter 4 of the Act deals with *(a)* offers to the public of securities by a company to raise capital and *(b)* offers to the public by or on behalf of the holders of securities not concerned with the raising of capital. This has not always been the case. In the Companies Act 61 of 1973 (hereafter 'the 1973 Act') these were dealt with in separate parts of the Act as 'offers for sale' and 'offers for subscription' respectively. It is submitted that the way in which the Act now delineates and deals with these categories is simpler and clearer.

14.2 TYPES OF OFFERS AND THE DISTINCTION BETWEEN LISTED AND UNLISTED SECURITIES

Section 99(3) distinguishes between primary and secondary offerings, as well as the securities of a listed and an unlisted entity. These distinctions are new in the context of South African company law insofar as they relate to public offers and go a long way towards clarifying the ambit and application of the statutory

---

[1] The sections dealing with what constitutes a public offer, employee share schemes and criminal liability in this chapter are substantially derived from J Yeats 'Public offerings of company securities: a closer look at certain aspects of Chapter 4 of the Companies Act 71 of 2008' 2010 *Acta Juridica* 117.
[2] Section 95.
[3] Section 95.
[4] Section 99.
[5] Sections 99 and 101.
[6] Section 96.
[7] Section 98.
[8] Section 100.
[9] Sections 104–106.
[10] Sections 107–111.

restrictions. There are basically three types of offers: an initial public offering, a primary offering and a secondary offering. Each type of offer can be made in relation to either listed or unlisted securities and the Act prescribes different requirements in each of these situations.

14.2.1 Initial public offering

An initial public offering (IPO) (which is also a new definition in this specific legislation) means an offer to the public of any securities of a company where no securities of that company have previously been offered to the public, or where all the securities of that company which were previously the subject of an offer to the public have subsequently been reacquired by the company.[11] There is no doubt as to what is required of a company in these circumstances: a prospectus must be produced.[12]

14.2.2 Primary offering

Primary offers (offers made to the public by a company of its own securities or the securities of a company in the same group or of the securities of a proposed merger or amalgamation partner)[13] are divided into offers of listed securities and offers of unlisted securities. A primary offering of listed securities requires compliance with the rules of the relevant exchange (usually the JSE), whereas a primary offering of unlisted securities requires a prospectus that satisfies the requirements of s 100 of the Act.

14.2.3 Secondary offering

Secondary offers (offers made for sale to the public of any securities of a company or its subsidiary, and which are made by or on behalf of a person other than that company or its subsidiary) are also, by implication, divided into offers for the sale of listed securities and offers for the sale of unlisted securities. A secondary offer for the sale of listed securities is regulated by the definition of 'offer to the public'[14] which stipulates that a secondary offer effected through an exchange is not an offer to the public (and the attendant requirements therefore become irrelevant). However, the Act requires a secondary offer of unlisted securities to be accompanied by either the prospectus that accompanied the primary offering (appropriately updated) or a written statement that complies with the requirements of s 101(4) to (6).[15] The written statement is essentially a synopsis of the state of affairs of the company and the particulars of the offer.

These distinctions not only provide legal clarity and certainty as to the relevant requirements, but are also aimed at supplying would-be investors with as much information as they require to make informed investment decisions without placing the primary or secondary offeror under an unreasonable or unnecessary administrative and financial burden in the process. The fact that separate provision is

---

[11] See s 95(1)(e).
[12] See s 99(2).
[13] See s 95(1)(e).
[14] See s 95(h)(ii)(bb).
[15] Section 101(2).

made for offers pertaining to listed and unlisted securities should provide prospective investors with the requisite protection without unnecessary duplication or overregulation in terms of compliance with stock exchange and company law requirements. For example, an offeror making a primary offering of listed securities will not need to produce both a prospectus in terms of the Act and a listing circular which complies with the requirements of the JSE; this would be unnecessarily time consuming and expensive.

14.3 GENERAL RESTRICTIONS ON OFFERS TO THE PUBLIC

The provisions that dictate in which circumstances the restrictions of Chapter 4 will apply appear in s 99 of the Act. There are a number of these:

- A person must not offer to the public any securities of any person unless the second person is a company and, if that company is a foreign company, a copy of its Memorandum of Incorporation must have been filed at least 90 days prior to the public offer being made.[16]
- An initial public offering requires a prospectus.[17]
- Primary offerings of listed securities must comply with exchange requirements.
- Primary offerings of unlisted securities require a registered prospectus that complies with s 100.
- Secondary offerings of securities must comply with the requirements of s 101 (discussed below).
- A person must not issue, distribute, deliver or cause to be issued, distributed or delivered a letter of allocation[18] unless it is accompanied by all the documents that are required[19] and have been filed, in the case of unlisted securities, or approved by the relevant exchange in the case of listed securities.
- A person must not issue, distribute, deliver or cause to be issued, distributed or delivered, any form of application in respect of securities, unless the form is accompanied by a registered prospectus, in the case of a primary offering, or a written statement that satisfies the requirements of s 101, in the case of a secondary offering, and bears on the face of it the date on which the prospectus in respect of those securities was filed.
- The requirements above do not apply where the form of application was issued in connection with a genuine invitation to enter into an underwriting agreement or in relation to securities that were not offered to the public.
- Despite anything contained in its Memorandum of Incorporation, a company may exclude holders of its securities who are not resident in South Africa from any rights offer if the Companies and Intellectual Property Commission ('the

---

[16] See s 99(1).
[17] See s 99(2).
[18] This concept is defined in s 95(1)(f) as 'any document conferring a right to subscribe for shares in terms of a rights offer'.
[19] Regulation 56 prescribes the documents required and the form and process to be adhered to in detail.

Companies Commission') has approved the exclusion in advance on application by the company.[20]
- No person may issue a prospectus or a document that purports to be a prospectus, or a document that may reasonably be misapprehended to be intended as a prospectus, unless it is a registered prospectus.
- A prospectus may not be registered unless the requirements of the Act have been complied with and it has been filed for registration, together with any prescribed documents, within ten business days after the date of that prospectus.
- As soon as the Companies Commission has registered a prospectus, it must send notice of the registration to the person who has filed the prospectus for registration.
- A prospectus may not be issued more than three months after the date of its registration, and if a prospectus is so issued, it is regarded as unregistered.[21]

Note that, in terms of s 95(5), any provision of an agreement is void to the extent that it requires an applicant for securities to waive compliance with a requirement of Chapter 4 of the Act. This means it is not possible to contract out of the requirements set by the Act. Similarly, any provision of an agreement is void to the extent that it purports to affect an applicant for securities with any notice of any agreement, document or matter not specifically referred to in a prospectus or a written statement. This means it is not possible to attribute knowledge of any information to an applicant where he or she has not specifically been referred to that information in the prospectus or written statement as governed by the statute.

14.4 WHAT CONSTITUTES AN OFFER TO THE PUBLIC?

This heading represents one of the most vexing questions in this particular area of company law and is the source of most of the reported cases.[22] The issue is simply that, if an offer constitutes an offer to the public, it falls within the purview of the legislative provisions and thus becomes subject to a substantial body of restrictions and requirements, most notably the requirement to issue a prospectus. Section 95(h) of the Act states that an offer to the public includes an offer of securities to be issued by a company to any section of the public, whether selected as holders of that company's securities or any particular class of property, as clients of the person issuing the prospectus, or in any other manner. However, it does not include an offer made in any of the circumstances contemplated in s 96 or a secondary offer effected through an exchange. Section 96(1) describes and defines offers that are not considered to be offers to the public and is discussed in

---

[20] The grounds for approval are that the number of those persons is insignificant relative to (a) the number of existing holders of the companies securities that are resident in South Africa; and (b) the administrative cost and inconvenience of extending the rights offer to them. The Companies Commission may attach conditions to the approval.

[21] This is presumably because the information in a prospectus can become outdated quite rapidly and the document then no longer serves the purpose for which it was intended, ie to supply would-be investors with accurate, complete and up-to-date information regarding the company in which they intend to acquire securities.

[22] See MS Blackman et al *Commentary on the Companies Act* vol 1 (2002) (Revision Service 7, 2010) at 6-15–6-16-3.

14.5 below. Note that s 95(2) specifically provides that, for the purposes of Chapter 4 of the Act, a person is to be regarded (by or in respect of a company) as being a member of the public, despite that person being a shareholder of the company or a purchaser of goods from the company.

As the definition of 'offer to the public' in the Act is very similar to the definition that appeared in the 1973 Act,[23] the body of case law that has developed around this phrase should still assist the courts in their interpretation of the legislation.[24] Typically the type of factual matrix that presents a problem is one where an offer does not fall squarely into one of the specifically exempted categories and exhibits characteristics that make it difficult to determine whether such an offer is public or private in nature and, consequently, whether the offerees require legislative protection. The most recent case in this regard is that of *Gold Fields Ltd v Harmony Gold Mining Co Ltd*.[25] In this case the court was faced with two fundamental legal issues arising from an offer made by Harmony (a public mining company) to all the shareholders of Gold Fields (also a public mining company) for the former to acquire control of the latter. The content of the offer, simply put, was that Harmony offered to issue and exchange 1275 Harmony shares for one Gold Fields share. The offer was made only to persons who were able to deliver Gold Fields shares. This entitled the Gold Fields shareholders in due course to be allotted new shares in Harmony. Gold Fields contended that the Harmony offer constituted an offer to the public for the subscription of shares as contemplated by s 145 of the 1973 Act which, as such, was prohibited, because it was not accompanied by a prospectus as required by the legislation.

The first issue to be decided by the court centred on the question of whether a share exchange as contemplated qualified as an offer for the 'subscription of shares', because s 145(1) of the 1973 Act makes specific mention of the fact that no person is permitted to make any offer to the public 'for the subscription of shares unless it is accompanied by a prospectus complying with the requirements of this Act . . .'. Nugent JA concluded that the term 'subscription' was not limited to the taking up of shares for cash and relied on, inter alia, *Government Stocks Securities Investment Co Ltd v Christopher*[26] to rule that the word 'subscription' as used in the 1973 Act was not limited to an undertaking to take up shares for cash and that, accordingly, the offer which was structured as a share exchange would also fall within the ambit of the section. It is gratifying to note that s 99 of the Act puts paid to this debate, because no specific mention is made of subscription when the section refers to initial public offerings, primary offers or secondary offers.[27] The definitions of these various terms in s 95 of the Act, similarly, make no mention of the term 'subscription' and refer merely to 'an offer of securities'.

---

[23] Note, however, that the original definition contained in the 1973 Act does not include the 'holders of any particular class of property' or a specific reference to the section itemising offers that do not constitute offers to the public in terms of the Act.
[24] See Blackman et al op cit n 22.
[25] 2005 (2) SA 506 (SCA).
[26] [1956] 1 All ER 490 (CH).
[27] See s 99(2) and (3).

Accordingly, this issue should not need to be addressed by our courts again in the context of public offerings.

The second question, and arguably the more complex one in the Gold Fields decision, was whether the offer as described above, being essentially an offer to a limited (albeit it large and ever-changing) group of offerees, should be construed to be an offer to the public and, by implication, that the intended offerees were entitled to the protection of a prospectus. As is the case in the 1973 Act, the definition of an offer to the public in the Act includes an offer to a 'section of the public', being a group smaller than the public at large. Section 95(1)(h) of the Act stipulates the following:

> (h) **"offer to the public"** —
> (i) includes an offer of securities to be issued by a company to any section of the public, whether selected —
> (aa) as holders of that company's securities;
> (bb) as clients of the person issuing the prospectus;
> (cc) as the holders of any particular class of property; or
> (dd) in any other manner; but
> (ii) does not include —
> (aa) an offer made in any of the circumstances contemplated in section 96; or
> (bb) a secondary offer effected through an exchange;

In deciding this question, the court remarked that:

> an offer that aims to acquire specific private property would not achieve its purpose if it was made to the public for no reason but that the property is in private hands. The offer in the present case is in that category. It is not made to the public but to shareholders in Gold Fields who are not, in that capacity, a mere section of the public at large.[28]

This decision has been the subject of some academic criticism.[29] It would appear that, in future, by virtue of the definition of 'offer to the public' contained in s 95(1)(h)(i) of the Act, such an offer will qualify as a public offer. This is because the definition in question states that an offer to the public includes an offer of securities to be issued by a company to any section of the public whether selected as, inter alia, the holders of any particular class of property or in any other manner. This is a welcome clarification of the legal position in this regard.

There are thus three possibilities: an offer is an offer to the public (because that is its true legal nature and it complies with the definition in the Act), an offer is an exempted non-public offer (because it is specifically exempted in terms of s 96(1), its true legal nature is irrelevant),[30] or an offer is a non-public offer (because, even though it does not fall within the s 96(1) exemptions, that is its true legal nature). Therefore it is quite possible that an offer may qualify as an offer to the public even though it is made to a limited group of persons, because it is an offer to a 'section of the public' as contemplated by the definition in s 95(1)(h). Whether this is the case or not in a specific set of circumstances and whether a particular offer is

---

[28] At 510, para 16.
[29] For a detailed discussion of the case in general, comparable case law in other jurisdictions and particularly criticism of the SCA judgment, see MF Cassim 'Gold Fields v Harmony: A lost opportunity to clarify section 145 of the Companies Act' 2005 SALJ at 269. See also Blackman et al op cit n 22 at 6–15–6–16–3.
[30] Section 96(1)(a).

a public offer, an exempted non-public offer or a non-public offer will no doubt remain a difficult legal question to answer. Each case will need to be decided on its merits to the extent that a particular offer does not constitute an obviously public or obviously exempted or obviously non-public offer.

14.5 WHAT DOES NOT CONSTITUTE AN OFFER TO THE PUBLIC?

Section 96 of the Act lists a number of instances in which offers made are deemed not to be offers to the public and are therefore not expected to meet the prospectus or other requirements of Chapter 4. The exempted offers are as follows:

- Offers made only to:
    - persons whose ordinary business, or part of whose ordinary business, is to deal in securities, whether as principals or agents,
    - the Public Investment Corporation,
    - a person or entity regulated by the Reserve Bank of South Africa,
    - an authorised financial services provider,
    - a financial institution,
    - a wholly owned subsidiary of a person or entity regulated by the Reserve Bank of South Africa, an authorised financial services provider or a financial institution acting as agent in the capacity of portfolio manager for a registered pension fund or as manager for a registered collective investment scheme, or
    - any combination of the persons listed above.[31]
- An offer where the total contemplated acquisition cost of the securities, for any single addressee acting as principal, is equal to or greater than the amount prescribed by the Minister by notice in the *Government Gazette*. The Minister may prescribe a value of not less than R100 000 for the purposes of this section.
- A non-renounceable[32] offer made only to existing holders of the company's securities or persons related to existing holders of the company's securities.
- A rights offer[33] that satisfies the prescribed requirements and where a securities exchange has granted or has agreed to grant a listing for the securities that are the subject of the offer, and the rights offer complies with any relevant requirements of that securities exchange at the time the offer is made.
- An offer made only to a director or prescribed officer of the company, or a person related to a director or prescribed officer, unless the offer is renounceable in favour of a person who is not a director or prescribed officer of the company or a person related to a director or a prescribed officer.
- An offer that pertains to an employee share scheme that satisfies the requirements of s 97.

---

[31] Section 96(1)(a)–(g).
[32] An offer is non-renounceable if the offeree-holder does not have the right to renounce the offer in favour of other persons, ie it can only be accepted by that holder.
[33] A rights offer, in terms of s 95(1)(l), means 'an offer, with or without a right to renounce in favour of other persons, made to any holders of a company's securities for the subscription of any securities of that company, or any other company within the same group of companies'.

- An offer, or one of a series of offers, for subscription, made in writing, and where:
  - no offer in the series is accompanied by or made by means of an advertisement and no selling expenses are incurred in connection with any offer in the series,
  - the issue of securities under any one offer in the series is finalised within six months after the date that the offer was first made,
  - the offer, or series of offers in aggregate, is or are accepted by a maximum of 50 persons acting as principals,
  - the subscription price, including any premium, of the securities issued in respect of the series of offers, does not exceed, in aggregate, an amount prescribed by the Minister by notice in the *Gazette*, which amount may have a maximum value of R100 000 for the purposes of this section, and
  - no similar offer, or offer in a series of offers, has been made by the company within the prescribed period immediately before the offer, or first of a series of offers, as the case may be. The minimum period that the Minister may prescribe is six months.[34]

These are principally the same exemptions as those listed in s 144 of the 1973 Act and any existing case law[35] that directly applies or relates to the interpretation of wording (where the same words have been used in both statutes) may be useful.

Some of the exemptions merit further discussion. A new and interesting addition to the category of exemptions is 'persons whose ordinary business, or part of whose ordinary business, is to deal in securities, whether as principals or agents' (see s 96(1)*(a)*(i)). Presumably the rationale is to avoid the requirement for a prospectus where approaches are being made to brokers or investment firms to assess potential demand as part of a process of 'book-building' prior to making a public offer. Section 96(1)*(c)* of the Act exempts non-renounceable offers made only to existing holders of the company's securities or persons related to existing holders of the company's securities. It is not entirely clear what is contemplated by the term 'related to' in this subsection. The term is used again in s 96(1)*(e)* where offers made only to directors or prescribed officers of the company or a person related to a director or prescribed officer are exempted. The corresponding section in the 1973 Act refers to offers to directors or officers of the company, or 'any close relative of such director or officer'.[36] It would seem, therefore, that 'related to' in this context must be interpreted with reference to the definition of that term as set out in s 2(1) of the Act. Section 2(1) contains a detailed definition as to when individuals are considered to be related (which is linked to natural or adopted consanguinity or affinity) and when individuals and juristic persons are considered to be related (where a relationship is linked to control of the one by the other). At first blush it would seem that this considerably expands the network of permissible offerees in the context of a non-renounceable, exempted offer. Furthermore, it may be expensive and time consuming to determine whether certain

---

[34] Section 96(2)*(b)*.
[35] See Blackman et al op cit n 22 at 6-11–6-15.
[36] See s 144*(f)* of the 1973 Act.

(especially juristic) persons are related or not, as defined in the Act. The same observation applies to the exemption in relation to directors or prescribed officers of the company contained in s 96(1)*(e)* of the Act.

Single one-off offers accepted by a maximum of 50 persons acting as principals are not to be construed as offers to the public, provided that they meet the additional requirements set out in s 96(1)*(g)* of the Act. In essence this exemption is the same as the exemption in s 144*(c)* of the 1973 Act.[37] However, there is an additional requirement — no similar offer or offer in a series of offers must have been made by the company within the period prescribed in terms of s 96(2)*(b)*. In terms of the latter subsection, the Minister, by notice in the *Gazette*, may prescribe a minimum period for the purposes of the said subsection, which must not be less than six months.[38] This new provision is rather interesting. Is the intention here that an offer (or one offer in a series of offers) can be made, provided that it qualifies with regard to the maximum number of principals and the minimum subscription price, and that this will not be construed as an offer to the public even if numerous subsequent offers (each also complying with the prescribed requirements) are made in this fashion, provided that there is a period of at least six months between such offers? If so, it creates the (new) possibility, albeit a convoluted and drawn-out one, of making an offer to the public that exceeds the minimum and maximum requirements prescribed internally in the subsection over a period of time, but which does not require the issue of a prospectus if properly structured from a timing perspective.

Exempted offers also include offers pertaining to employee share schemes that satisfy the requirements of s 97 of the Act.[39] This amendment is dealt with in 14.6 below, as the changes contained in the Act appear to settle questions of law that have previously cropped up in practice regarding offers of shares by foreign companies and the requirement for a prospectus.

14.6 STANDARDS FOR QUALIFYING EMPLOYEE SHARE SCHEMES

One of the problems faced by legal practitioners regarding public offers under the 1973 Act related to employee share schemes conducted by foreign clients to incentivise South African employees. It specifically related to the wording of the exemption and the definitions of 'employee share scheme', 'company' and 'external company'.[40] The critical issue was whether such offers to eligible employees were 'offers to the public' in terms of Chapter VI of the 1973 Act. If so, it was highly unlikely that a company would proceed with the share offers if required to

---

[37] Except for the fact that the exemption in the Act contemplates the possibility that the exempted offer could be one of a series of offers, which series must nevertheless comply with the prescribed limitations and requirements.

[38] The draft Companies Regulations specify 6/12 months (Regulation 52(2)). This error will presumably be rectified in due course.

[39] This is the equivalent of the definition of 'employee share scheme' in s 144A of the 1973 Act.

[40] The legal-technical conundrum is rather complex and, as it has been resolved in the Act, merits no further discussion in this chapter. For a detailed exposition of the problem see Yeats op cit n 1 at 122–124.

go to the expense and effort of issuing a prospectus and otherwise complying with the requirements of ss 145 and 146 of the 1973 Act.[41]

The case law in this regard (both South African and foreign) has proved complex and unpredictable in its application[42] and, accordingly, few foreign listed entities were willing to take this legally uncertain route and chose to incentivise South African employees in more straightforward ways,[43] with the result that the object of the exception (ie to facilitate employee share schemes) was in some instances defeated by a technical drafting error. This anomaly has been resolved in the new Act. Section 96(1)(*f*) determines that an offer is not an offer to the public if it pertains to an employee share scheme that satisfies the requirements of s 97. Section 97, in turn, refers to the appointment of a compliance officer and details to be disclosed in the annual financial statements of the company as well as certain specific filing obligations. Furthermore, s 95(1)(*a*) specifically provides that in Chapter 4 of the Act, 'company' includes a 'foreign company', which, in turn, is defined in s 1 of the Act as an entity incorporated outside the Republic of South Africa, irrespective of whether it is a profit or a non-profit entity or whether it is carrying on profit or non-profit activities within South Africa. This, together with the fact that the reference to the establishment of a scheme by 'a company' together with the use of the more general wording 'pertains to' in s 96(1)(*f*), should now make it possible for foreign companies to offer South African employees shares in an offshore listed holding company in terms of an employee share scheme (as originally intended), without raising concerns regarding the need for a prospectus.

It is also noteworthy that, although s 144A of the 1973 Act stipulated that a compliance officer had to be appointed and allocated certain duties to that person, it contained no provision or sanction as to what the repercussions would be if this did not take place. Accordingly, it was not unheard of for companies to conduct employee share schemes without appointing such a person (thus depriving the employees of the protection intended by the legislation). Section 97(1) of the Act eliminates this problem by stating clearly that an employee share scheme qualifies for the exemptions referred to in the subsection if, inter alia, the company has appointed a compliance officer and the compliance officer has complied with the requirements of the section. The implication is clear — if no compliance officer is appointed, or if he or she does not properly perform his or her duties, the company will not qualify for the exemptions granted in these circumstances, most notably for current purposes, the exemption from complying with the prospectus requirements.

---

[41] It was apparently this kind of consideration that motivated the addition of s 144A of the 1973 Act. See Blackman et al op cit n 22 at 6–11.

[42] See Blackman et al op cit n 22 at 6-3–6-8-6 and the cases cited there.

[43] The determination as to whether such an offer was public or private in nature, notwithstanding the fact that it did not comply with the technical requirement for the relevant exemption, was further complicated by the fact that there were often very large numbers of employees involved was such schemes and that, depending on the terms of a particular scheme, persons entitled to be offered shares were possibly no longer employees of the company.

14.7 ADVERTISEMENTS RELATING TO OFFERS

The Act envisages two scenarios in which an advertisement may be relevant in relation to an offer to the public. Either the offer may actually be made (or presented) by way of advertisement, or the advertisement may merely serve to draw the attention of the public to an offer made by way of a prospectus.

An offer to the public may be made or presented by way of an advertisement if the advertisement satisfies all the requirements of the Act with respect to a registered prospectus.[44] Furthermore, the advertisement will be subject to every provision of the Act relating to the making of a prospectus. An advertisement which serves to draw the attention of the public to an offer made by publishing a prospectus must include a statement clearly stating that it is not a prospectus and indicating where and how a copy of the registered prospectus may be obtained. In addition, it must not contain any untrue statement, or mislead a person reading the advertisement to reasonably believe that it is a prospectus, or be misleading as to any material particular addressed in the prospectus relating to that offer. Finally, such an advertisement is subject to ss 102 to 111 of the Act.[45] In terms of s 98(3)(b), an advertisement drawing attention to an offer to the public is not required to be filed or registered with an exchange and will be regarded as having been intended to be a prospectus, issued by the person responsible for publishing or disseminating the advertisement, if it does not include the statements required by this section, despite any statement to the contrary contained in the advertisement. The effect hereof is that an advertisement is deemed to be a prospectus if it does not comply with the requirements of sections 98, and all the consequences of issuing a non-compliant prospectus[46] will attach to the persons involved in issuing the document.

14.8 PROSPECTUS REQUIREMENTS

Section 100 of the Act deals with prospectus requirements and states, at the outset, that the section does not apply in respect of listed securities[47] (these are subject to the rules and requirements of the exchange on which they are listed) except listed securities that are the subject of an initial public offering.[48] Section 100(2) further provides as follows:

- A prospectus must contain all the information that an investor may reasonably require to assess the assets and liabilities, financial position, profits and losses, cash flow and prospects of the company in which a right or interest is to be acquired, as well as the securities being offered and the rights attached to them. The prospectus must also adhere to the prescribed specifications in legislation.

---

[44] See s 98.
[45] See 14.9–14.11 for a detailed discussion.
[46] For a discussion on liability see 14.10 below.
[47] This is in accordance with the definitions contained in s 95 and s 99(3), which, read together, make a primary offering of listed securities subject to the rules of the exchange and deem a secondary offering of listed securities (effected through an exchange) not to be a public offer, which therefore does not require a prospectus.
[48] See s 99(2).

- The date of registration of a prospectus is the date of the issue of the prospectus unless the contrary is proved.
- A prospectus must not be registered unless there is attached to it a copy of any material agreement as prescribed[49] or, in the case of an unwritten agreement, a memorandum giving full particulars of the agreement.
- If any part of an agreement contemplated above is in a language that is not an official language, a certified translation in an official language of that part must be attached to the agreement.
- A prospectus containing a statement to the effect that the whole or any portion of the issue of the securities offered to the public has been or is being underwritten may not be registered until a copy of the underwriting agreement has been filed, together with the sworn declarations stating that to the best of the deponent's knowledge and belief, the underwriter is and will be in a position to carry out the obligations contemplated in the agreement even if no shares are being applied for.
- The declaration must be sworn by the person named as underwriter or, if the underwriter is a company, by each of two directors of that company (or if it has only one director, by that director).
- If an offer is made in respect of which no prospectus is required in terms of the Act, the copy of the underwriting agreement and sworn declaration must be filed not later than the date of the proposed offer of shares.
- The Companies Commission (or an exchange in the case of listed securities) may, on application,[50] allow required information to be omitted from a prospectus. This will be permitted only if the Companies Commission or exchange is satisfied that publication of the information would be unnecessarily burdensome for the applicant, seriously detrimental to the company whose securities are the subject of the prospectus, or against public interest, and that users will not be unduly prejudiced by the omission.
- As long as an initial public offering or other primary offering to the public of unlisted securities remains open, any person responsible for information in the prospectus must, when that person becomes aware of it:
  ○ correct any error,
  ○ report on any new matter, and
  ○ report on any change of a matter included in the prospectus, provided these are relevant or material in terms of Chapter 4 of the Act.
- A correction or report of this nature must be registered as a supplement to the prospectus, simultaneously published to known recipients of the prospectus and included in future distributions of the prospectus.
- If such a correction or report has been published:
  ○ any person who subscribed for the issue of shares as a result of the offer before the date of that publication may withdraw the subscription by written notice within 20 business days after the date of publication,

---

[49] Draft Regulation 73.
[50] The application must be in writing and accompanied by the prescribed fee. See s 100(10). The Act does not state who will have *locus standi* to bring the application.

Public Offerings of Company Securities 603

- the offeror, upon receipt of a notice of withdrawal, may either accept the withdrawal and restore to the person any consideration already paid, or apply to the court for an order contemplated in s 100(13)(c),
- the court may, on application by the offeror, make any order that is just and equitable in the circumstances, including, but not limited to, an order negating the right of the subscriber to withdraw the offer, or an order to reverse any transaction or restore any consideration paid or benefit received by any person in terms of the offer and the subscription.

14.8.1 The contents of a prospectus

The Act provides in s 100(2)(b) that a prospectus must adhere to the prescribed specifications. In terms of s 1, '"prescribed" means determined, stipulated, required, authorised, permitted or otherwise regulated by a regulation or notice made in terms of [the] Act'. Section 223 deals with the authority of the Minister to make regulations under the Act and the procedure to be followed in this regard. Regulations 58 to 85 of the draft Companies Regulations contain a host of prescribed specifications that deal in detail with the prescribed content and form of a prospectus. These include:

- general requirements relating to form, style and layout,
- signature, date and issue formalities and requirements,
- additional information required if it is the intention to acquire a business undertaking or property,
- access to supporting documents,
- information about the company whose securities are being offered, including very specific details in relation to:
  - name, address and incorporation
  - directors and other office holders
  - history, state of affairs and prospects
  - share capital
  - loans
  - options or preferential rights
  - shares issued otherwise than for cash
  - property acquired or to be acquired
  - amounts paid or payable to promoters
  - commissions paid or payable to underwriters
  - preliminary and issue expenses
  - material contracts
  - interest if directors and promoters,
- information about the offered securities that are being offered, including:
  - purpose of the offer
  - time and date of opening and closing of the offer
  - particulars of the offer
  - minimum subscription,
- statements and reports relating to the offer (which must be included in the prospectus):
  - statement as to adequacy of capital

- report by directors as to material changes
- statement as to listing on stock exchange
- report by auditor of company
- report by auditor where business undertaking to be acquired
- report by auditor where company will acquire subsidiary, and
- (specific) requirements for the prospectus of a mining company.[51]

Part D of the draft Companies Regulations lists different requirements for an intended offer relating to unlisted securities that are in all respects uniform with previously issued securities of the same company and made only to existing holders of that company's securities with a right to renounce the offer in favour of other persons (ie a renounceable rights offer). The requirements are set out in tabular form in Regulation 86 and are far more limited than those for an ordinary prospectus. It is not clear why this distinction has been drawn, but it is presumably for reasons of convenience and cost in circumstances where the legislature does not anticipate that new investors will be at particular risk or require comprehensive protection.

14.8.2 Consent to use name in prospectus

In any prospectus relating to the securities of a company, a person must not name another person as a director or proposed director of that company unless, before registration of that prospectus, the person has consented in writing to act as a director, has not withdrawn the consent, and the return reflecting that person's particulars has been filed. Nor must the prospectus include any statement made by an expert or reference to any statement purporting to be made by an expert, unless the expert consented in writing to the use of that statement before the prospectus was filed, has not withdrawn the consent, and the consent is endorsed on or attached to a copy of the filed prospectus and the prospectus includes a statement that the expert has consented. Equally, the prospectus must not name any person as the auditor, attorney, banker or broker of the company unless it is accompanied by the written consent of the named person agreeing to be named in the stated capacity and to the use of his or her name in the prospectus.

14.8.3 Variation of agreement mentioned in prospectus

For a period of one year after the date of filing a prospectus, a company must not vary or agree to vary any material terms of an agreement referred to in the prospectus, other than in the ordinary course of business. A variation in the terms of an agreement may, however, be made or agreed by the company only if the variation was contemplated and is set out in the prospectus, or if the specific terms of the variation are authorised or ratified by an ordinary resolution adopted at a general shareholders' meeting.[52]

14.9 SECONDARY OFFERS TO THE PUBLIC

Section 101 does not apply to listed securities. A person making a secondary offering must ensure that the offering is accompanied either by the registered

---
[51] See the relevant regulations for more detail.
[52] Section 103.

prospectus that accompanied the primary offering of those securities (together with any revisions required to address material changes since the date of registration of the prospectus) Alternatively, a written statement that satisfies the requirements of s 101 must accompany the offering. The written statement referred to must be dated and signed by the person making the offer or issuing, distributing or publishing the material. If that person is a company, the statement must be dated and signed by every director of the company.

The written statement must:

- not contain any matter other than the particulars required by the section;
- not be in characters smaller or less legible than any characters used in the written offer or any document that accompanies the statement;
- be accompanied by a copy of the last annual financial statements of the company, together with any subsequent interim report or provisional annual financial statements of that company; and
- must contain particulars with respect to the following matters:
  - whether the person making the offer is acting as principal or agent and, if as agent, the name of the principal and address in South Africa where that principal can be served with process, and the nature and extent of the remuneration received or receivable by the agent for the services provided,
  - the date on which and the country in which the company was incorporated and the address of its registered office in South Africa,
  - the classes and number of securities in each class that have been authorised and details as to the rights associated with each class, the number of securities issued for cash, and the number of securities issued for consideration other than cash,
  - dividends paid on each class of security during the previous five financial years and, if no dividend has been paid, a statement to that effect,
  - the total amount of any securities other than shares issued by the company and outstanding at the date of statement together with the rate of interest payable thereon,
  - the names and addresses of the company's directors,
  - whether or not the securities are listed or permission to deal has been granted by an exchange other than the exchange or permission referred to in s 101(1),
  - if the offer relates to units, particulars in respect of the securities represented by the units,
  - the date on which and the prices at which the securities offered were originally offered by the company and were acquired by the person making the offer or by that person's principal,
  - if any securities were issued by the company as partly paid-up shares under the 1973 Act, to what extent they are paid up, and
  - the date of registration of the written statement by the Companies Commission.[53]

---

[53] Section 101(6).

14.10 LIABILITY

All the stringent and detailed requirements laid down in the Act in relation to the prospectus and otherwise and aimed at protecting the investing public would be effectively meaningless if there were no consequences for non-compliance. Therefore the Act imputes personal liability to a range of persons involved in compiling and issuing the prospectus to encourage legal compliance and to provide recourse for investors where they have suffered harm as a result of a failure to comply. The Act distinguishes between:

- liability for untrue statements in the prospectus (for directors, promoters, persons who authorised the issue and persons who made the offer to the public) in s 104,
- liability of experts and others (whose names, material or statements have been included in the prospectus) in s 105,
- responsibility for untrue statements in the prospectus (of all persons, as opposed to liability) in s 106,
- liability in terms of other sections in the Act which is in addition to the liability contemplated in Chapter 4 (such as the liability of a director in s 77(3)(*d*)(ii)),
- liability for untrue statements in terms of the enforcement provisions of the Act (ie criminal liability),[54] and
- liability in terms of s 95(6), which provides that nothing in Chapter 4 'limits any liability that a person may incur under this Act apart from this Chapter, or under any other public regulation, or under the common law'. Thus any additional liability contemplated in these three areas (remainder of Act, public regulation and common law) is specifically preserved.

14.10.1 Liability for untrue statements in the prospectus

Section 104 of the Act governs liability for untrue statements in the prospectus. An 'untrue statement' includes a statement that is misleading in the form and context in which it is made. The ambit of this phrase is therefore quite wide — both false statements and misleading statements fall within the section. Furthermore, an untrue statement is regarded to have been included in a prospectus, written statement or summary directing a person to either a prospectus or a written statement if:

- it is contained in a report or memorandum that appears on the face of one of these documents, or
- it is incorporated by reference in, or is attached to, or accompanies a prospectus, written statement or summary directing a person to either a prospectus or a written statement.

The statement need not therefore appear in the information document itself. This considerably extends the range of information and statements that need to be carefully weighed, considered and tested for veracity by any person who may incur liability in respect thereof. Finally, s 95(4) provides that an omission from a prospectus or a written statement that, in the context, is calculated to mislead by

---
[54] See s 106(1).

omission constitutes the making of an untrue statement, irrespective of whether the Act requires that matter to be included in the prospectus or the written statement. The implication of this provision is that, where information is germane to the investment decision of a member of the public, it must be included notwithstanding the fact that it falls outside one of the categories of information prescribed by the Act and regulations.

If securities are offered to the public for subscription or for sale pursuant to a prospectus, every person who:

- becomes a director,
- consented to be named in the prospectus as a director,
- is a promoter,
- authorised the issue of the prospectus, or
- made that offer to the public,

is liable to compensate any person who acquired securities on the faith of the prospectus for any loss or damage that the person may have sustained as a result of any untrue statement in the prospectus or in any report or memorandum appearing on the face of, issued with, or incorporated by reference in the prospectus. Section 104(2) extends potential liability in the sense that it specifically provides that the liability contemplated in the section is in addition to the liability of a director of the company, as set out in s 77(3)*(d)*(ii).[55]

The available defences are set out in s 104(3). Thus, liability does not attach to a person if:

- with regard to every untrue statement, that person had reasonable grounds to believe, and did up to the time of allotment of the securities or acceptance of the offer believe, that the statement was true,
- with regard to every untrue statement purporting to be a statement by an expert, the untrue statement fairly represented the statement or was a correct and fair copy of or an extract from the report or valuation, and the person had reasonable grounds to believe, and did up to the time of the issue of the prospectus believe, that the expert who had made the statement was competent to make it, had consented to the issue of the prospectus and had not withdrawn that consent before any allotment under the prospectus or the acceptance of the offer,
- any untrue statement purporting to be a statement made by an official person or contained in what purports to be a copy of or an extract from a public official document was a correct and fair representation of the statement or copy of or an extract from the document,

---

[55] The relevant parts of the section provide that a director of a company is liable for any loss, damages or costs sustained by the company as a direct or indirect consequence of the director 'having signed, consented to, or authorised, the publication of a prospectus, or a written statement contemplated in s 101, that contained *(aa)* an 'untrue statement' as defined and described in s 95; or *(bb)* a statement to the effect that a person had consented to be a director of the company, when no such consent had been given, despite knowing that the statement was false, misleading or untrue, as the case may be', but the provisions of s 104(3), read with the changes required by the context, apply to limit the liability of a director in terms of this paragraph.

- that person consented to become a director but subsequently withdrew that consent and the prospectus was issued without his or her consent,
- the prospectus was issued without the knowledge and consent of that person and on becoming aware of its issue, he or she forthwith gave reasonable public notice that it was issued without his or her knowledge or consent, or
- after the issue of the prospectus, on becoming aware of any untrue statement in it, he or she withdrew his or her consent and gave reasonable public notice of his or her withdrawal and the reason for it.

In many respects the provisions of this section of the Act are directly comparable to or the same as those contained in the 1973 Act. Any legal precedent in this regard should therefore continue to provide guidance in an interpretation of these provisions.[56]

If a prospectus names a person as a director (or as having agreed to become a director) and that person has not consented to this or has withdrawn his or her consent before the prospectus is issued, and has not consented to the issue of the prospectus:

- the directors of the company[57] are liable to the extent set out in s 77(3)(*d*)(ii), and
- any other person who authorised or issued the prospectus is liable (together with the directors) to indemnify the incorrectly named person against any damage, cost or expense:
  - arising from so naming him or her, or
  - incurred in defending against any action or legal proceedings brought in respect of having been named.

According to s 104(4), where a director or any other person whose consent is required in connection with any matter contained in the prospectus, including a director, has not given that consent or has withdrawn it before the issue of the prospectus:

- the directors of the company[58] are liable to the extent set out in s 77(3)(*d*)(ii), and
- any other person who authorised or issued the prospectus is liable (together with the directors) to indemnify the incorrectly named person against any damage, cost or expense:
  - arising from the inclusion of that matter, or
  - incurred in defending against any action or legal proceedings brought in respect of such inclusion.

Any person who has satisfied liability under s 104 may recover a contribution (as in cases of contract) from any other person who would have been liable to make the same payment if he or she had been sued separately. This will not, however,

---

[56] See Blackman et al op cit n 22 at 6–32 to 6–42–7 and the cases referred to there.
[57] Except any directors without whose knowledge and consent the prospectus was issued.
[58] Except any directors without whose knowledge and consent the prospectus was issued.

apply if the person who has satisfied liability was guilty of fraudulent misrepresentation and the other person was not.[59]

14.10.2 Liability of experts[60] and others[61]

If a person has consented to the use of his or her name or the inclusion of material in a prospectus, that consent does not make the person liable as someone who has authorised the issue of a prospectus[62] either:

- to compensate anyone purchasing securities on the faith of the prospectus (except in respect of any untrue statement purporting to be made by that person as an expert), or
- to indemnify anyone against liability under s 104(6).[63]

However, despite what is set out above, the position is different where the person in question is purported to be an expert. In that case any untrue statement made will render the expert liable under s 104[64] unless:

- he or she had withdrawn his or her consent in writing before the prospectus was filed for registration,
- between the filing of the prospectus for registration and any allotment in terms thereof to a complainant, the expert became aware of the untrue statement, withdrew his or her consent in writing and gave reasonable public notice of the withdrawal and the reason for it, or
- the expert was competent to make the statement and had reasonable grounds to believe (and did up to the time of allotment or acceptance of the offer believe) that the statement was true.

These defences are available in lieu of any applicable defences in terms of s 104.

14.10.3 Responsibility for untrue statements in the prospectus

The Act distinguishes between *liability* for untrue statements in the prospectus[65] and *responsibility* for untrue statements in the prospectus. Any person who is liable is also responsible for an untrue statement in a prospectus. The fact that the person in question is so responsible makes him or her subject to the enforcement provisions of the Act[66] which deal with criminal liability and are dealt with further in 14.10.4 below.

---

[59] Section 104(6).

[60] In terms of s 95(1)(d), an expert in this context means 'a geologist, engineer, architect, quantity surveyor, valuer, accountant or auditor, or any person who professes to be one of those persons or to have extensive knowledge or experience, or to exercise a special skill which gives or implies authority to a statement made by that person'. Thus the definition is quite wide.

[61] See also s 218(2) which presumably also applies and thus attributes liability in circumstances where a third party has suffered loss or damage as a result of a contravention of any of the provisions of Chapter 4.

[62] That is in terms of s 104(1)(d).

[63] This section deals with recovery of contributions from others where one person has satisfied liability under s 104.

[64] See 14.10.1 above.

[65] Section 104.

[66] Section 106(1).

Note, however, that if a prospectus contains an expert report (or an extract from such a report) which contains an untrue statement and the expert has consented to its inclusion in that form, the expert is solely responsible for that statement.[67] No person is responsible for an untrue statement if the statement was immaterial or if no liability for the untrue statement attaches to the person in terms of s 104(3).[68]

14.10.4 Criminal liability

As pointed out in the preceding paragraph, in terms of s 106(1), if a prospectus contains an untrue statement, every person referred to in s 104(1) or (2)[69] is held to be 'equally responsible in terms of the enforcement provisions of the Act for the untrue statement'. According to Yeats[70] the enforcement provisions referred to are presumably those contained in Chapter 7 of the Act, which deals with remedies and enforcement generally. It is not yet entirely clear how s 106 will operate in relation to those provisions, but it will be interesting to observe to what extent, and how effectively, additional relief can be sought or pressure brought to bear on guilty parties in terms of those provisions. This approach is certainly in line with the stated policy of the drafters to decriminalise company law. In the explanatory memorandum to the Companies Bill the relevant approach and provisions are summarised as follows:[71]

> Generally, the Act uses a system of administrative enforcement in place of criminal sanctions to ensure compliance with the Act. The [Companies] Commission or [Takeover Regulation] Panel may receive complaints from any stakeholder, or may initiate a complaint itself, or act on a matter as directed by the Minister. Following an investigation into a complaint, the Commission or Panel may —
> (a) end the matter;
> (b) urge the parties to attempt voluntary alternative resolution of their dispute;
> (c) advise the complainant of any right they may have to seek a remedy in court;
> (d) commence proceeding in a court on behalf of a complainant, if the complainant so requests;
> (e) refer the matter to another regulator, if there is a possibility that the matter falls within their jurisdiction; or
> (f) issue a compliance notice, but only in respect of a matter for which the complainant does not otherwise have a remedy in a court.
>
> A compliance order may be issued against a company or against an individual if the individual was implicated in the contravention of the Act. A person who has been issued a compliance notice may of course challenge it before the Companies Tribunal, and in court, but failing that, is obliged to satisfy the conditions of the notice. If they fail to do so, the Commission may either apply to a court for an administrative fine, or refer the failure to the

---

[67] Section 106(2).
[68] Section 106(3).
[69] See s 104(1) and (2). These persons are: every person who becomes a director of the company before the issuing of the prospectus and the holding of the first general meeting of the company at which directors are elected or appointed, every person who has consented to be named in the prospectus as a director, or has agreed to become a director either immediately or after an interval of time; every person who is a promoter of the company or every person who authorised the issue of the prospectus or who is, under the Act, deemed to have done so, or every person who has made that offer to the public.
[70] Yeats op cit n 1 at 127.
[71] *Memorandum on the Objects of the Companies Bill, 2008*, Companies Bill [B 61D–2008] at 193.

National Prosecuting Authority as an offence. In the case of a recidivist company that has failed to comply, been fined, and continues to contravene the Act, the Commission or Panel may apply to a court for an order dissolving the company. Finally, to improve corporate accountability, the draft proposes that it will be an offence, punishable by a fine or up to 10 years imprisonment, for a person to sign or agree to a *[sic]* false or misleading financial statements or prospectus, or to be reckless in the conduct of a company's business.

To expand on the last statement in the portion quoted above, s 214(1)*(d)*(ii) of the Act states that a person is guilty of an offence if the person is a party to the preparation, approval, dissemination or publication of a prospectus, or a written statement contemplated in s 101, that contains an 'untrue statement' as defined and described in s 95. Section 214(2), in turn, provides that a person will be a party to the preparation of a document if the document includes or is otherwise based on a scheme, structure or form of words or numbers devised, prepared or recommended by that person; and the scheme, structure or form of words is of such a nature that the person knew, or ought reasonably to have known, that its inclusion or other use in connection with the preparation of the document would cause it to be false or misleading. Finally, in terms of s 216 of the Act, any person convicted of an offence in the case of a contravention relating to an untrue statement as described above is liable to a fine or imprisonment for a maximum period of 12 months, or both.

If all these sections are read together, it would seem therefore that a person who wrongfully makes an untrue statement in a prospectus could be held liable in terms of s 104, s 77(3)*(d)*(ii) (if that person is a director), s 106 and s 214 read with s 216, that is to say, held liable for loss or damages suffered as a result of the untrue statement, held responsible in terms of the enforcement provisions of the Act (whatever form this may take) and (notwithstanding the decriminalisation of almost all the provisions of the Act) be guilty of an offence and thus liable to a fine and/or imprisonment — a veritable plethora of consequences.[72]

14.11 ALLOTMENTS AND ACCEPTANCE OF SUBSCRIPTIONS

Allotment refers to the process of distribution or allocation of shares to subscribers. Only once the share has been allotted (ie allocated or apportioned) to a subscriber can it be issued to him or her. The reason for distinguishing allotment from issue as different phases in the response of the company to the application for subscription from a would-be subscriber is that sometimes an offer is 'oversubscribed'. This means that there are more willing investors than there are shares available for subscription. In the allotment process, the company determines how the shares will be allocated, usually *pro rata* to each applicant in line with the oversubscription.

14.11.1 Time limits

Section 107 sets a time limit for allotment following a public offer. The company must not allot any of the securities offered to the public or accept any subscription for any of those securities more than four months after filing the prospectus for that offer.

---

[72] Yeats op cit n 1 at 127–9.

14.11.2 Restrictions

Section 108 places a number of restrictions on the allotment process:
- a company must not allot any securities or accept any subscription for securities pursuant to a public offer unless:
    - the subscription has been made on an application form that was attached to or accompanied by a prospectus, or
    - it is shown that the applicant was in possession of a prospectus or was aware of its contents at the time of application;
- if the prospectus contained a minimum subscription[73] requirement:
    - a company must not allot any securities pursuant to a public offer unless the minimum amount stated has been paid to and received by the company,
    - the minimum amount must be reckoned exclusively of any amount payable otherwise than in cash,
    - until the minimum amount has been made up, any amount paid on an application must be paid into a separate bank account and may not be used or made available to the company or be used to satisfy its debts;
- if the minimum subscription requirement is not met within 40 days after the issue of the prospectus, all amounts received from applicants must be repaid with interest; or
- if any money is not repaid within 55 business days after the issue of the prospectus, the directors and officers of the company are jointly and severally liable to repay the money (with interest) unless the default was not due to any misconduct or negligence on their part.

14.11.3 Voidable allotments

If an allotment is made in contravention of the s 108 minimum requirement restrictions, and the minimum subscription requirement is not subsequently met, the allotment is voidable at the instance of the applicant. This right applies irrespective of whether the company is in the course of being wound up. If the allotment is declared void, every director of the company and every director of the offeror (if it is a company) is liable to the extent set out in s 77(3)(*e*)(viii). Proceedings to recover loss, damages or costs must be commenced within 20 days after the applicant discovers the contravention or three years after the date of the relevant allotment or acceptance, whichever is earlier.

14.11.4 Minimum interval before allotment or acceptance

No allotment of securities, no acceptance of an offer in respect of securities and no proceedings on applications may be made or taken until the beginning of the third day after that on which the prospectus is first issued (or such later time as is specified in the prospectus). The day on which the prospectus is first issued means

---

[73] This will be the case where the offer is made subject to the condition that a minimum number of subscriptions are received by the offeror. If there is not enough interest among potential investors to meet the minimum subscription requirement, the offeror will not proceed with the offer and any amounts paid must be returned to would-be investors.

that day on which it is first issued as a newspaper advertisement.[74] If it is not issued as a newspaper advertisement before the third day on which it is first issued in another manner, then the first date of issue is the date on which it was first issued in that other manner. A contravention of this subsection does not affect the validity of an allotment or acceptance.[75]

14.11.5 Conditional allotment if the prospectus states securities to be listed

A prospectus stating that application has been made (or will be made) for permission for the securities to be listed on an exchange must not be issued unless:

- an application has been made in accordance with the requirements of the relevant exchange on or before the date of issue of the prospectus, and
- the prospectus names the exchange to which application has been made.

Any allotment of securities pursuant to such a prospectus is subject to the condition that:

- the application is granted, or
- an appeal against its refusal is upheld.[76]

---

[74] See 14.7 for a discussion of advertisements in the context of Chapter 4 of the Act.
[75] Section 110.
[76] Section 111.

CHAPTER 15

FUNDAMENTAL TRANSACTIONS, TAKEOVERS AND OFFERS

Maleka Femida Cassim and Jacqueline Yeats*

15.1	FUNDAMENTAL TRANSACTIONS: GENERAL	616
15.2	AMALGAMATION OR MERGER	617
	15.2.1 Introduction and underpinning policy	617
	15.2.2 Definition and concept of 'amalgamation or merger'	619
	15.2.3 The juridical nature and effect of a merger	621
	15.2.4 The statutory merger procedure	624
	(a) Merger agreement	624
	(b) Solvency and liquidity test	627
	(c) Requisite approvals of the merger (s 115)	628
	(d) Notice to creditors	632
	(e) Implementation of the merger	633
	15.2.5 The requirement of court approval	634
	15.2.6 Appraisal rights of dissenting shareholders	636
	15.2.7 The protective measures for shareholders in the merger procedure	638
	15.2.8 Protective measures for creditors	639
	15.2.9 Types of merger structures: General	639
	15.2.10 'Pooling' type merger	640
	15.2.11 Triangular merger	640
	(a) Structure of the triangular merger	640
	(b) Purpose and advantages of the triangular merger	641
	(c) Merger consideration in a triangular merger	642
	15.2.12 Reverse triangular merger	643
	15.2.13 Cash merger	644
	15.2.14 Freeze-out merger	644
	(a) Purpose of the freeze-out merger	644
	(b) Shareholder voting and structure of freeze-out mergers	645
	(c) The two-step freeze-out merger	647
	15.2.15 Short-form merger	647
15.3	DISPOSAL OF ALL OR THE GREATER PART OF THE ASSETS OR UNDERTAKING	648
	15.3.1 Introduction	648

* Maleka Femida Cassim authored sections 15.1 to 15.3 and Jacqueline Yeats authored sections 15.4 and 15.5.

	15.3.2	Transactions to 'dispose' of 'all or the greater part' of the assets or undertaking	649
		(a) Meaning of 'dispose'.............................	649
		(b) Meaning of 'the greater part'	651
	15.3.3	Approval and other requirements for s 112 disposals	652
		(a) General	652
		(b) Special resolution of the shareholders	654
		(c) Special resolution of the holding company	655
		(d) Takeover Regulation Panel..........................	656
		(e) Court approval	656
		(f) Appraisal rights of dissenting shareholders............	656
		(g) Other	657
	15.3.4	Exemptions	657
15.4	SCHEMES OF ARRANGEMENT...............................		658
	15.4.1	Introduction	658
	15.4.2	Proposal for scheme of arrangement	658
	15.4.3	Background	659
	15.4.4	Approval and other requirements for schemes of arrangement ..	661
		(a) General	661
		(b) Independent expert	662
		(c) Report	662
		(d) Takeover Regulation Panel..........................	663
		(e) Court approval	663
		(f) Appraisal rights of dissenting shareholders............	663
		(g) Other	664
15.5	TAKEOVERS AND OFFERS..................................		664
	15.5.1	General..	664
	15.5.2	Applicable legislation...................................	664
	15.5.3	Key definitions	665
	15.5.4	Application of the Act and the Takeover Regulations........	666
	15.5.5	Regulation of takeovers and offers by the Panel in accordance with the objectives of the Act	667
	15.5.6	Exemption by the Panel.................................	668
	15.5.7	Regulation in the Act	668
	15.5.8	Disclosure of share transactions	669
	15.5.9	Mandatory offers......................................	670
	15.5.10	Compulsory acquisitions and squeeze-out	670
	15.5.11	Comparable and partial offers............................	671
	15.5.12	Restrictions on frustrating action	672
	15.5.13	Prohibited dealings before and during an offer..............	673
	15.5.14	Takeover Regulations...................................	674

15.1 FUNDAMENTAL TRANSACTIONS: GENERAL

Although the Companies Act 71 of 2008 (hereafter 'the Act') does not define the phrase 'fundamental transaction', it provides for three types of fundamental transactions in Part A of Chapter 5. These transactions, which fundamentally alter a company, comprise:

- an amalgamation or merger,
- a disposal of all or the greater part of the assets or undertaking of a company, and
- a scheme of arrangement.

The regulatory regime for fundamental transactions has been comprehensively reformed under the Act to facilitate the creation of business combinations.[1] One of the leading reforms is that the Act introduces the innovative concept of amalgamations or mergers of companies (or the 'statutory merger') in South African law. This is motivated by the object of promoting flexibility and enhancing efficiency in the economy.[2]

Commendably, the new statutory merger is an additional procedure to, and not a substitution for, the three main pre-existing methods for companies wanting to effect business combinations and fundamental transactions under the previous company law regime (namely, the sale of the business of the company as a going concern, the scheme of arrangement, and the takeover offer with compulsory acquisition of securities of the minority).[3] The statutory merger thus provides companies with a further very useful option. An extension of the range of methods for fundamental transactions, each with its own particular nuances, protections, advantages and disadvantages, serves to accommodate differing circumstances, reasons and needs for companies undergoing fundamental transactions.

Closely associated with the new regime for fundamental transactions is the new remedy of appraisal rights for dissenting minority shareholders. The introduction of the appraisal remedy has facilitated a great reduction in the role of the court in fundamental transactions. The appraisal right now functions as the primary protective measure for shareholders in an amalgamation or merger, thereby bypassing the necessity for general court approval of such transactions. In this regard, statutory mergers are not subject to general or automatic court involvement. Instead, court involvement is restricted to certain specified circumstances. This new approach to the requirement of court approval applies equally to disposals of the assets or undertaking of a company under the new Act. The scheme of arrangement procedure has also been reformed, in that the conventional protective measure of judicial sanctioning of schemes of arrangement is now replaced with the appraisal remedy together with the requirement for a report of an independent expert. Accordingly, the protective role and the involvement of the court in fundamental transactions have been considerably reduced under the new Act.

---

[1] *Memorandum on the Objects of the Companies Bill, 2008*, Companies Bill [B 61D–2008] at para 1.2.

[2] *Memorandum on the Objects of the Companies Bill, 2008* op cit n 1 at para 9.

[3] See ss 228, 311–13 and 440K of the Companies Act 61 of 1973 (hereafter 'the 1973 Act').

Fundamental transactions now require court approval only if, in broad terms, there was a significant minority (at least 15 per cent of the exercised voting rights) opposed to the transaction and any of those persons demands that the company seeks court approval, or alternatively, where the court grants leave to a single shareholder to apply for a review of the transaction. The court may set aside such transactions only on the grounds of certain procedural irregularities or a manifestly unfair result.[4]

Another strong policy objective of the Act is to remove or reduce the opportunities for regulatory arbitrage.[5] To the extent that the Act applies substantially uniform[6] approval requirements for the three fundamental transactions (namely, the shareholder approval requirements, the requirements for court approval in specified circumstances and the appraisal rights of dissenting shareholders), this may be expected to reduce the scope for regulatory arbitrage that has typically been a prominent feature of this field of company law.

To the extent that the new Act preserves the scheme of arrangement procedure as a method of effecting fundamental transactions while simultaneously making provision for the statutory merger, it follows the Canadian and New Zealand models. Like the scheme of arrangement, the statutory merger is more suited to friendly or recommended transactions which require the co-operation of the board of directors of the target company, as opposed to hostile transactions where the takeover offer is more appropriate. Substantial changes have been made to the traditional scheme of arrangement, including the abandonment of the traditional safeguards of separate class voting and general judicial sanctioning of schemes of arrangement. However, the merits or wisdom of abandoning the general court approval of schemes of arrangement has been questioned. The court-approved arrangement procedure retains a positive and useful role in Canadian and New Zealand law, which provide for both a court-approved arrangement procedure and a 'court-free' statutory merger.[7] The same model should perhaps have been adopted in South African law as well.

15.2 AMALGAMATION OR MERGER[8]

15.2.1 Introduction and underpinning policy

A radically new concept of the 'amalgamation or merger' is introduced into South African law by the Companies Act of 2008.[9] South African law has never had a

---

[4] Section 115(3)–(7). See further 15.2.5 below.
[5] *Memorandum on the Objects of the Companies Bill, 2008* op cit n 1 at para 1.2.
[6] There are nevertheless some important differences, as discussed further below.
[7] One of the benefits of a court-approved arrangement procedure in these jurisdictions is the avoidance of appraisal rights and the attendant cash drain on companies. See also the discussion of the more flexible and modernised role of the court in arrangements in New Zealand law in Maleka Femida Cassim 'The introduction of the statutory merger in South African corporate law: Majority rule offset by the appraisal right (Part I)' (2008) 20 *South African Mercantile Law Journal* 1 (referred to hereafter as 'Maleka Femida Cassim (Part I)') at 23–4.
[8] The section on amalgamations and mergers in this chapter is largely derived from Maleka Femida Cassim (Part I) op cit n 7 and the activities cited therein; Maleka Femida Cassim 'The introduction of the statutory merger in South African corporate law: Majority rule offset by the appraisal right

statutory merger procedure in its true sense. In broad terms, in an amalgamation or merger,[10] the assets and liabilities of two or more companies are pooled in a single company, which could be either one of the combining companies (referred to as the surviving company) or a newly formed company (referred to as the new company).

The statutory 'amalgamation or merger' is basically a simple, uncomplicated and effective procedure by which two or more companies may merge by agreement, subject to shareholder approval by the shareholders of both (or all) the participating companies (referred to herein as the constituent companies). The 'amalgamation or merger' is a court-free procedure, in that there is no general or automatic need for the approval of the court. The role of the court is instead restricted to certain specified circumstances only.

It is a progressive and modernised procedure that is borrowed from the USA. The new approach of permitting an amalgamation or merger in terms of which the principle of majority rule suffices to fundamentally change the nature of the company will in many ways make it much easier to effect a business combination or fundamental transaction in South Africa. This will assist companies to adapt to changing business conditions in the interests of economic growth and wealth creation.

The statutory merger (or, to be more accurate, 'amalgamation or merger') does, however, represent a significant shift or liberalisation of policy on the part of the legislature between two conflicting underlying policies. On the one hand, there is the value of facilitating the restructuring of businesses in the interests of economic growth, and, on the other hand, there is the interest of shareholders in retaining their investments in companies, coupled with the protection of minority shareholders from discrimination at the hands of the majority. While the Companies Act 61 of 1973 (hereafter 'the 1973 Act') placed considerable emphasis on the latter value, the new Act marks a dramatic shift in policy towards the former value, in line with other jurisdictions that have modernised their corporate law systems.

This change of policy follows a similar trend in the USA, a trend adopted also in Canada and New Zealand. To this extent, the approach of the Act to mergers is in line with foreign trends and the underpinning policy of harmonisation of South African company law with other leading jurisdictions. But it represents a radical departure from our traditional and historical adherence to English company law. In this regard, it is interesting to note that neither English nor Australian law has adopted a court-free statutory merger procedure that as a general principle dispenses with the requirement of court approval.

The modern regulatory emphasis of the Act now is on attaining the appropriate balance of the interests of all the shareholders, so as to avoid either minority oppression by the majority, or minority dictation, which enables recalcitrant

---

(Part II)' (2008) 20 *South African Mercantile Law Journal* 147 (referred to hereafter as 'Maleka Femida Cassim (Part II)'); and Maleka Femida Cassim 'The statutory merger in South African law Part 1' (2008) 16 (2) *JBL* 40 and 'The statutory merger in South African law Part 2' originally to be published in (2008) 16 (3) *JBL*, and the authorities cited therein.

[9] See ss 113, 115 and 116.

[10] Amalgamations or mergers are also known in some jurisdictions as consolidations.

minorities to perversely prevent the improved management of a company that could result from a merger.

The question then arises as to the protection of minority shareholders who disapprove of a merger. The liberalisation in merger policy under the Act is counterbalanced or offset by giving appraisal rights to dissenting shareholders, who have the right to opt out of the company by withdrawing the fair value of their shares in cash through the exercise of their appraisal rights. Dissenters do not generally have recourse to a court of law to prevent or frustrate a merger that has received the due and proper approval of the prescribed shareholder majority (by special resolution), except in certain very limited circumstances where court approval of the merger is a prerequisite.

The appraisal right is thus closely linked to the statutory merger. It is now the prime protective measure for shareholders in a statutory merger. The appraisal right is also an entirely new right introduced in South African company law, although it has been a feature of corporate law in the USA for over a century. The appraisal right is discussed in more detail in chapter 16: Shareholder Remedies and Minority Protection.

15.2.2 Definition and concept of 'amalgamation or merger'

Section 1 of the Act defines an 'amalgamation or merger' as follows:

> [A] transaction, or series of transactions, pursuant to an agreement between two or more companies, resulting in:
> *(a)* the formation of one or more new companies, which together hold all of the assets and liabilities that were held by any of the amalgamating or merging companies immediately before the implementation of the agreement, and the dissolution of each of the amalgamating or merging companies; or
> *(b)* the survival of at least one of the amalgamating or merging companies, with or without the formation of one or more new companies, and the vesting in the surviving company or companies, together with such new companies, of all of the assets and liabilities that were held by any of the amalgamating or merging companies immediately before the implementation of the agreement.

An 'amalgamating or merging company' means a company that is a party to an amalgamation or merger agreement.[11] An 'amalgamated or merged company' is defined as a company that either *(a)* was incorporated pursuant to an amalgamation or merger agreement, or *(b)* was an amalgamating or merging company and continued in existence after the implementation of the amalgamation or merger agreement, and holds any part of the assets and liabilities that were held by any of the amalgamating or merging companies immediately before the implementation of the agreement.[12]

No distinction is drawn by these definitions between a 'merger' and an 'amalgamation'. As appears from the above definition of 'amalgamation or merger', the Act provides for two broad types of 'amalgamation or merger' structures. The first structure is where two (or more) 'amalgamating or merging companies' (referred to herein as the 'constituent companies') fuse into a *new* company, with the result

---
[11] Section 1.
[12] Section 1.

that both the constituent companies are dissolved in the process. The new company is incorporated pursuant to the amalgamation or merger agreement itself and holds *all* the assets and liabilities that were previously held by the two constituent companies. The vesting of such assets and liabilities in the new company (or the 'amalgamated or merged company') takes place automatically, simply by the operation of law, upon effectuation of the merger.[13]

In the second type of structure, one constituent company fuses *into the other constituent company*, resulting in the survival or continuing existence of the latter company (termed the 'surviving company'). The *surviving company holds all* the assets and liabilities that were previously held by the two constituent companies. The first constituent company (termed the 'disappearing company') disappears or is dissolved in the process.

The technical difference between the two structures consequently is that, in the first structure, where an acquiring company (Co A) and a target company (Co T) wish to merge, *both* Co A and Co T are dissolved and a new company, Co N, is created. On the other hand, in the second structure, Co A would *survive* and continue in existence while Co T would be the disappearing company and would be dissolved or deregistered. Accordingly, the first structure results in the fusion of both constituent companies into a new company, whereas the second structure results in the fusion of one constituent company into the other.

The above is, of course, a simplification. The Act also provides for transactions between more than two constituent companies, and creates scope for the survival of more than one company or the formation of more than one new company. It even permits combinations of the two merger structures (whereby the merger results in at least one surviving company as well as the formation of one or more new companies).[14] Amalgamations or mergers could accordingly become quite complex and intricate in structure.

The terms 'amalgamation' or 'merger', as stated above, appear to be regarded as synonymous or interchangeable under the Act, which draws no distinction between these concepts. There is in fact no uniform use of terminology in the various jurisdictions that cater for the concept of a statutory merger.[15] It is notable that a distinction was initially drawn between 'amalgamations' and 'mergers' in the draft Companies Bill, 2007,[16] which referred to the first type of merger structure (that results in the formation of a new company) as an 'amalgamation', and the second structure (that results in a surviving company) as a 'merger'. Curiously, this distinction has not been retained in the Act (with the exception of s 116(7), which distinguishes between a 'newly amalgamated' company and a 'surviving merged' company).[17] But in any event, nothing turns on the distinction

---

[13] See s 116(7) and see further 15.2.3 below.
[14] The definition of an 'amalgamation or merger' in s 1 of the Act is arguably too wide.
[15] The statutory merger procedure is variously termed 'merger', 'amalgamation' and/or 'consolidation' in the jurisdictions that provide for the procedure.
[16] GN 166 of 2007 in *GG* 29630 of 12 Feb 2007 (cl 1).
[17] Whether this indicates an intention to distinguish between an 'amalgamation' and a 'merger', or whether it is merely an overlooked remnant of the draft Companies Bill, 2007, is uncertain.

— apart from the above technical differences, the procedure for and the effect of the transaction are substantially similar, regardless of which of the two structures is used.

In practice the choice between the two structures of an 'amalgamation or merger' will be determined by a number of factors, such as the desire to portray the transaction as a true merger of equals,[18] the need to preserve the goodwill or the identity of one of the constituent companies,[19] the material provisions of the Memorandum of Incorporation of the constituent companies,[20] and the change-of-control provisions in material contracts between a constituent company and third parties.

For the sake of convenience, in the rest of this chapter the term 'merger' is used to refer to an 'amalgamation or merger'.

15.2.3 The juridical nature and effect of a merger

For the sake of simplicity and clarity, the rest of this section on the statutory merger is discussed with reference to a merger of two companies using the *surviving company* structure,[21] ie where one of the constituent merging companies fuses into the other constituent company, resulting in the disappearance of the former company (termed the 'disappearing company') and the survival of the latter company (termed the 'surviving company'), which holds all the assets and liabilities that were previously held by the two constituent companies. The surviving company usually is the 'acquiring company' in the merger, while the disappearing company usually is the 'target company'.

Section 116(7)*(a)* of the Act significantly states that when a merger agreement has been implemented, the 'property' of each constituent merging company '*becomes*' property of the surviving merged company (or the new company, as the case may be). Although the term 'property' is not defined, it will in this context presumably be interpreted in its wide sense to include all property, rights, powers and privileges. Moreover, upon implementation of the merger agreement, the surviving company '*is liable*' for all the obligations of every constituent company (s 116(7)*(b)*).

An important principle emerges from these provisions, namely that the vesting of the assets and liabilities in the surviving company apparently occurs automatically, by *operation of law*. There is consequently no need for compliance with any of the legal formalities associated with transfer (save in terms of s 116(8), as discussed below). The statutory merger thus provides for simplicity and efficiency, with savings in both costs and time.

---

[18] In this case the first structure above (that results in the formation of a new company) may be preferred. It may even involve a more complex structure where the merger results in the new company being the holding company, with each of the constituent merging companies being its separate wholly owned subsidiaries.

[19] This may necessitate the use of a merger *into* the relevant company (which would be the surviving company).

[20] This may determine whether the relevant company must survive or disappear under the transaction.

[21] See 15.2.2 above.

A further important advantage of the statutory merger is that there is apparently no need to formally wind up the disappearing company. It is instead simply deregistered by the Companies and Intellectual Property Commission ('the Companies Commission').[22]

But an attendant disadvantage of the merger procedure is the automatic liability of the acquiring (or surviving) company for all the obligations and liabilities of the disappearing company. This includes unliquidated and contingent liabilities, and even, it seems, liabilities of which the acquiring company was unaware.

The transfer of the property and obligations of the constituent merging companies to the surviving company is, however, subject to s 116(8), the requirements of s 113, any provision of the merger agreement, or any other agreement (s 116(7)).[23] In this regard, an exception to the principle of automatic transfer by operation of law applies in relation to any property that is registered in terms of a public regulation,[24] for instance, immovable property. Where any such property is to be transferred in the course of a merger, the transfer must be registered in the relevant property registry. In this event, a copy of the amalgamation or merger agreement, together with a copy of the filed notice of amalgamation or merger, constitutes sufficient evidence to effect a transfer of the registration of that property.[25]

Further consideration must be given to the vesting in the surviving merged company of the *contractual* rights and obligations of the disappearing company, in terms of agreements between the disappearing company and third parties. Generally, contractual rights and obligations of the disappearing company would vest in the surviving company automatically by operation of law.[26] But it has been submitted that, where a contractual clause specifically provides that the contract will not survive a statutory merger, such a clause would be effective to prevent the vesting of the contract in the surviving merged company. This now seems to emerge also from the (amended and clarified) wording of s 116(7) to the effect that the automatic vesting of the property and obligations of the disappearing company

---

[22] Section 116(5).

[23] Section 116(7). The draft Companies Amendment Bill, 2010 (cl 69) proposes to amend this wording to state that the transfer of the property and obligations is 'in accordance with the provisions of the amalgamation or merger agreement, or any other relevant agreement, but in any case subject to the requirement that each amalgamated or merged company must satisfy the solvency and liquidity test, and subject to sub-s (8), if it is applicable'. In the event of a conflict between s 116(7) and a provision of s 54 of the Banks Act 94 of 1990, with respect to a transaction involving a company that is regulated by that Act, the provisions of the Banks Act prevail (s 116(9) read with cl 2(1)(*b*) of the draft Companies Amendment Bill, 2010).

[24] 'Public regulation' means any national, provincial or local government legislation or subordinate legislation, or any licence, tariff, directive or similar authorisation issued by a regulatory authority or pursuant to any statutory authority (s 1). ('Regulatory authority' means an entity established in terms of national or provincial legislation responsible for regulating an industry, or sector of an industry (s 1)).

[25] Section 116(8).

[26] Generally the vesting of contractual rights and obligations in the surviving company falls within the ambit of s 116(7). The word 'property' in terms of s 116(7)(*a*) would include rights, such as contractual rights, while contractual obligations would fall within the scope of s 116(7)(*b*).

in the surviving merged company is subject to 'any other agreement'.[27] A proper and thorough due diligence is thus essential.

It is further submitted that most contracts that are silent on assignability (and cession) would generally vest in the surviving company in a merger even *without* the consent of the third party. The same would probably apply even where a contract expressly states that it may not be assigned or ceded without the consent of the third party. The basis of this view is that, in a merger, the vesting of the rights and obligations of the disappearing company in the surviving company occurs automatically by operation of law, and not by a process of cession, assignment or novation. Contractual clauses prohibiting cession and assignment are arguably not intended to apply to a transfer by operation of law.

The question arises as to the effect of the wording (in s 116(7) above) that the transfer of the property and obligations of each constituent merging company to the merged company is 'subject to ... the requirements of s 113(1)' and 'any provision of the merger agreement'.[28] This appears to relate to mergers that involve more than one surviving and/or new company, between which the assets and liabilities of the constituent merging companies are distributed or allocated.[29] The implication is that the merger agreement may validly provide for the allocation or distribution, among a number of merged companies, of the assets and liabilities (that prior to the merger were held by the constituent merging companies), subject to compliance with the solvency and liquidity test (s 113(1)) by each such merged company upon implementation of the merger.[30]

It must be stressed that the Act explicitly provides that a merger does not affect any existing liability of any of the constituent companies, or any of their directors, to be prosecuted (that notwithstanding the disappearance or dissolution of the relevant constituent company in the process). A merger also does not affect any civil, criminal or administrative action or proceeding pending by or against a merging company; or any conviction, ruling, order or judgment relating to a merging company. These may therefore continue to be prosecuted or enforced by or against the merged company.[31]

---

[27] It was suggested (by Maleka Femida Cassim (Part I) op cit n 7 at 5–6, in criticising the previous wording of cl 120(5) of the draft Companies Bill, 2007) that such an exception be created in respect of such contracts and agreements with third parties. A second exception to the transfer of contractual rights and obligations by operation of law in a statutory merger may arise in respect of purely personal contracts (see further Maleka Femida Cassim (Part I) op cit n 7 at 5–6 and the authorities cited therein).

[28] Or in terms of the draft Companies Amendment Bill, 2010 (cl 69), 'in accordance with the provisions of the amalgamation or merger agreement', 'but in any case subject to the requirement that each amalgamated or merged company must satisfy the solvency and liquidity test'.

[29] This is contemplated in s 113(2)(*f*), which envisages that the merger agreement may allocate the assets and liabilities of the constituent merging companies among the merged companies.

[30] This is reinforced by the definition of 'amalgamated or merged company' in s 1, which envisages that each merged company may hold *'any part'* — and need not necessarily hold *all* (whether solely or as joint holders with the other merged companies) — of the assets and liabilities that, prior to the merger, were held by the merging companies.

[31] Section 116(6).

15.2.4 The statutory merger procedure

The merger procedure may, for purposes of analysis, be divided into five steps, as follows:

(a) Merger agreement
(b) Solvency and liquidity test
(c) Requisite approvals of the merger
(d) Notice to creditors
(e) Implementation of the merger.

It is noteworthy, at the outset, that the approval of the court is not generally required in the five-step merger procedure, save in certain exceptional circumstances.

The statutory merger procedure applies to mergers between profit companies, including holding and subsidiary companies.[32] Profit companies comprise private companies, public companies, personal liability companies and state-owned companies.[33] In contrast, the draft Companies Bill applied only to mergers involving 'widely held companies' (broadly comparable to public companies under the Act), while 'closely held' companies were required to expressly opt in to the merger provisions subject to the satisfaction of certain criteria.[34] This was criticised on the basis that it often is the shareholders of closely held companies (broadly comparable to private companies under the Act) who have a greater need for the statutory protection and safeguards offered by the merger procedure.[35] The Companies Act has now commendably been widened to include all profit companies in its statutory merger provisions.

The statutory merger provisions do not extend to foreign or external companies that are engaged in statutory mergers with a South African company.[36] Where a company is placed under business rescue, and a merger transaction is pursuant to or contemplated in its business rescue plan as adopted in accordance with Chapter 6 of the Act, the company is exempt from certain aspects of the statutory merger procedure (as pointed out in context below).

Each step of the statutory merger procedure is discussed in turn below.

(a) Merger agreement

The first step is that the companies proposing to merge (ie 'amalgamate or merge') must enter into a written agreement that sets out the terms and manner of effecting

---

[32] Section 113(1).
[33] Section 8(2). For the application of the statutory merger provisions to non-profit companies, see chapter 3: Types of Companies, specifically the discussion on non-profit companies.
[34] Clause 112(3) of the draft Companies Bill, 2007.
[35] Maleka Femida Cassim (Part I) op cit n 7 at 7. (The terminology of 'widely held' and 'closely held' companies is fortunately not part of the Act.)
[36] In this regard, the definition of 'company' in s 1 does not include external companies or foreign companies. Significantly, the provisions on statutory mergers are expected to extend to domesticated companies, as proposed by the draft Companies Amendment Bill, 2010 (see the definition of 'domesticated company' and the proposed amended definition of 'company' in cl 2(1) of the draft Amendment Bill).

the merger.[37] According to s 113(2), the merger agreement must deal with certain specified matters, including:[38]

(a) the proposed Memorandum of Incorporation of any new company that is to be formed by the merger,
(b) the names and identity numbers of the proposed directors of the merged company (or companies),
(c) the manner in which any securities of the constituent merging companies are to be converted into securities of any merged company, or exchanged for other property,
(d) if any securities of any of the merging companies are not to be converted into securities of any merged company, the consideration that those securities holders will receive in addition or instead,
(e) the manner of payment of any consideration instead of the issue of fractional securities of a merged company or of 'any other juristic person the securities of which are to be received' in the merger,
(f) details of the manner in which the assets and liabilities of the constituent merging companies will be allocated among the merged companies on implementation of the merger agreement (this applies to mergers that result in more than one merged company — see 15.2.3 above),
(g) details of any arrangement or strategy necessary to complete the merger, and to provide for the subsequent management and operation of the merged company (or companies), and
(h) the estimated cost of the proposed merger.

Where any securities of a constituent merging company are held by (or on behalf of) another constituent merging company, the merger agreement 'must' provide for such securities to be cancelled when the merger becomes effective, without a repayment of capital. Furthermore, such securities cannot be converted into securities of a merged company.[39] The reason for this provision is that the merged company would otherwise effectively hold shares in itself, and the merger would effectively result in an indirect reduction of the capital of the merged company.

An issue that merits further attention is the merger consideration permitted by this section (s 113(2)). It must be kept in mind that the merger consideration under the merger agreement is usually paid, in effect, to the shareholders of the target or disappearing company, in consideration for their shares in the disappearing company.[40] The issue of the merger consideration is of fundamental importance, because closely linked to it is the assortment or types of merger structures that may be devised under this provision. The Act is widely drafted to provide some flexibility in respect of the form of the merger consideration. This creates latitude and flexibility for merging parties to structure their merger transactions advanta-

---
[37] Section 113(2).
[38] Section 113(2)
[39] Section 113(3).
[40] As stated above, for purposes of simplicity and clarity, this chapter is generally discussed with reference to a merger of two companies using the surviving company structure, whereby the surviving company is usually the acquiring company in the merger and the disappearing company is usually the target company.

geously to suit their differing needs and objectives. As submitted below (see 15.2.9), various types of merger structures are evidently permissible under the Act.

In this regard, the Act clearly encompasses the traditional concept of a merger as a 'pooling' type transaction, under which the two sets of shareholders of the two merging companies continue to participate as shareholders in the surviving merged company, which holds the combined pool of assets and liabilities that were previously held severally by the two merging companies. In a 'pooling' type merger, the shareholders in the target or disappearing company will usually receive their consideration in the form of shares in the acquiring or surviving company. It seems, in this event, that the shares of the target company are automatically *converted*, by operation of law, into shares of the acquiring company on the implementation of the merger agreement.[41] The Act also permits merger consideration to be in the form of other securities,[42] such as debentures of the merged company. The consideration may even consist of the exchange of any 'other property'. But the Act goes further to envisage other types of merger structures and merger consideration. Merger consideration is thus quite wide in scope, thereby giving merging parties lots of options.

This seemingly includes the possibility of shareholders receiving merger consideration in the form of shares in *another company* other than the surviving merged (or new merged entity, as the case may be) (see s 113(2)*(e)* above).[43] This is a vitally significant form of consideration, because it facilitates the very useful triangular merger and reverse triangular merger structures, in which the shareholders frequently receive shares in the *holding* company of the surviving merged company (see further 15.2.11 on triangular mergers and 15.2.12 on reverse triangular mergers).

A *cash* consideration is also evidently permissible in statutory mergers under the Act.[44] The relevant provisions relating to this possibility are quite liberal. This is in contrast with several other jurisdictions where a cash consideration is subjected to stringent restrictions and limitations, in view of the controversy associated with cash mergers. The underpinning policy of paying a cash consideration to the shareholders of the disappearing company is simply that shareholders do not

---

[41] See also the wording of s 113(2)*(c)* and *(e)*.

[42] 'Securities' has the meaning set out in s 1 of the Securities Services Act 36 of 2004, and includes shares held in a private company or shares issued or authorised to be issued by a profit company (s 1 of the Act read with cl 2 of the draft Companies Amendment Bill, 2010).

[43] Section 113(2)*(e)*, which envisages the issue of fractional securities of a 'merged company or of *any other juristic person the securities of which are to be received*' in the merger [emphasis added], may be interpreted to include the issue of securities of *another company* as a merger consideration. See also s 113(2)*(c)* which refers to 'other property'.

[44] See s 113(2)*(d)* read with the definition of 'consideration' in s 1. 'Consideration' is widely defined in s 1 as 'anything of value given and accepted in exchange for any property, service, act, omission or forbearance or any other thing of value, including *(a) any money*, property, negotiable instrument, securities, investment credit facility, token or ticket; *(b)* any labour, barter or similar exchange of one thing for another; or *(c)* any other thing, undertaking, promise, agreement or assurance, irrespective of its apparent or intrinsic value, or whether it is transferred directly or indirectly' [emphasis added].

Fundamental Transactions, Takeovers and Offers

have a vested right to continue to hold their investment as shareholders of the surviving merged entity, but could instead be 'cashed-out'. In this way, shareholders may be compelled under a merger to disinvest from the company. This involves a significant liberalisation of policy in South African law.[45] (See further 15.2.13 on cash mergers and 15.2.14 on freeze-out mergers below.)

(b) Solvency and liquidity test

The second step in the merger procedure is that the board of directors of *each* constituent merging company must consider whether each proposed merged company would satisfy the solvency and liquidity test once the merger agreement is implemented.[46] Compliance with the solvency and liquidity test set out in s 4 of the Act is an essential prerequisite for a merger. Section 4(1) provides as follows:

> **4.** (1) For any purpose of this Act, a company satisfies the solvency and liquidity test at a particular time if, considering all reasonably foreseeable financial circumstances of the company at that time —
> *(a)* the assets of the company or, if the company is a member of a group of companies, the aggregate assets of the company, as fairly valued, equal or exceed the liabilities of the company or, if the company is a member of a group of companies, the aggregate liabilities of the company, as fairly valued; and
> *(b)* it appears that the company will be able to pay its debts as they become due in the ordinary course of business for a period of —
>   (i) 12 months after the date on which the test is considered. . . .[47]

If the board reasonably believes that each proposed merged company would satisfy the solvency and liquidity test, it may submit the merger agreement for consideration at a meeting of the shareholders of that merging company.[48] A notice of the shareholders' meeting must be delivered to each shareholder of each respective merging company,[49] and must include or be accompanied by a copy or summary of the merger agreement and the provisions of ss 115 and 164 of the Act, relating to the required approvals for the transaction and the appraisal rights of dissenting shareholders.[50] This is important, because shareholders may be unaware of their appraisal rights and the procedure for their exercise, or of the provisions regarding court approval.

In view of the need for the co-operation of the board of directors in this procedure, the statutory merger, as stated above, is more suited to friendly or recommended transactions than to hostile transactions.

---

[45] A cash merger thus creates a definite scope for the use of the statutory merger procedure as a means to squeeze out or eliminate the minority shareholders of a company, by compelling them under the merger agreement to exchange their shares for cash.

[46] Section 113(4)*(a)*.

[47] See further s 4 and chapter 8: Corporate Finance. The draft Companies Amendment Bill, 2010 (cl 3) proposes certain important changes to this test. The inappropriate reference to the 'aggregate' assets and liabilities of a company that is a 'member of a group of companies' is proposed to be deleted, and substituted with 'consolidated' assets and liabilities in the case of a 'holding company'. Thus the solvency and liquidity test would take into account the 'consolidated' assets and liabilities of a merging company that is a holding company.

[48] Section 113(4)*(b)* read with s 115.

[49] This presumably includes the holders of non-voting shares.

[50] Section 113(5).

A company that is under business rescue proceedings is exempt from these requirements.[51]

(c) Requisite approvals of the merger (s 115)

The third step in the merger procedure is that the merger must be approved in accordance with s 115 of the Act, failing which it may not be implemented at all. Section 115 applies not only to the statutory merger, but also to disposals of all or the greater part of the assets or undertaking of a company, and to the implementation of schemes of arrangement.[52] Consequently the shareholder approval requirements, the exceptional requirement of court approval and the appraisal rights of dissenting shareholders are largely (although not entirely) the same for all three types of fundamental transactions under the new Act. (This discussion thus pertains to fundamental transactions in general as opposed to mergers alone.)

Importantly, the requisite approval requirements under s 115 apply *despite s 65* (dealing with shareholder resolutions) and despite any contrary provision of a company's Memorandum of Incorporation or any board resolution or resolution of securities holders (see further below). However, an exception is made in respect of a fundamental transaction that is pursuant to or contemplated in an approved business rescue plan for that company.[53]

A number of approvals are required for fundamental transactions.

First, a proposed fundamental transaction must be approved by a special resolution, at a meeting called for that purpose.[54] In the case of a merger, *each* constituent merging company must adopt a special resolution.[55] In contrast, in the case of a disposal of assets or undertaking, it is only the disposing company that must approve the transaction by special resolution.[56] The quorum for the meeting is constituted by the presence of sufficient persons to exercise, in aggregate, at least 25 per cent[57] of all the voting rights that are entitled to be exercised on that matter.[58] A special resolution must be adopted with the support of at least 75 per cent of the voting rights that are exercised on the resolution. It is noteworthy that

---

[51] The exemption applies if the transaction is pursuant to or contemplated in the business rescue plan as adopted in accordance with Chapter 6 of the Act (s 113(6), read with s 113(4) and (5)).

[52] The heading of s 115 is incomplete as it states 'Required approval for transactions contemplated in Part' while omitting to specify the relevant Part. It is presumably intended to refer to Part A of Chapter 5, as appears from the content of s 115.

[53] Section 115(1).

[54] Section 115(2)*(a)*. The requirement of a meeting called for that purpose is apparently an essential requirement, because of the exclusion of s 65 and any contrary provision of the company's Memorandum of Incorporation (s 115(1)).

[55] See s 113(5).

[56] Section 112(2). See further 15.3 below.

[57] It is submitted that the quorum for the meeting may not be decreased or increased in the company's Memorandum of Incorporation, as contemplated in s 64(2). The reason is that s 115(1) expressly states that *despite any provision of a company's Memorandum of Incorporation to the contrary, a merger must be approved in accordance with s 115*.

[58] Shareholders who do not have voting rights to vote in connection with the matter are excluded from the quorum.

both the quorum and the prescribed shareholder approval requirement relate to the percentage of voting rights[59] and not to the percentage of shareholders or shares.

A special resolution, by definition (in s 1), is adopted with the support of at least 75 per cent of the voting rights exercised on the resolution or a lower percentage *as contemplated in s 65(10)*' [emphasis added].[60] The question arises whether a company's Memorandum of Incorporation may validly permit a lower percentage of voting rights (ie below 75 per cent) to approve a special resolution in respect of a fundamental transaction. While the draft Companies Bill, 2007 clearly precluded this,[61] the position under the Act is less clear. It is submitted that, since s 115 applies 'despite s 65' (see above),[62] the effect is that a company is precluded from relying on s 65(10) to reduce the requisite support for a fundamental transaction to anything less than 75 per cent.[63]

The requirement of a special resolution for fundamental transactions constitutes a substantial improvement on the earlier draft of the Companies Bill, 2007, which had stipulated a simple majority (ie over 50 per cent) of the shares voted. This was criticised as being 'inordinately permissive and lenient' and 'fundamentally flawed', on the basis that it was 'heavily weighted in favour of a dominant, majority shareholder' thus resulting in the minority being left vulnerable to oppression by the majority. It was suggested instead that the prescribed shareholder approval threshold should be increased to 75 per cent approval.[64] Commendably, the Act now does just that.

The present shareholder approval requirement ensures a little more adequate protection of minority shareholders, while at the same time preserving flexibility for companies to effect fundamental changes without allowing a troublesome minority to frustrate the merger. It is notable, though, that the approval requirements continue to remain fairly lenient and liberal in comparison with other jurisdictions.[65] Taking into account the potential for shareholder apathy, it is

---

[59] 'Voting rights', with respect to any matter to be decided by a profit company, means the rights of any holder of the company's securities to vote in connection with that matter (s 1).

[60] Section 65(10) states that a company's Memorandum of Incorporation may permit a lower percentage of voting rights to approve a special resolution, provided that there must at all times be a margin of at least 10 percentage points between the requirements for approval of an ordinary resolution, and a special resolution, on any matter. Important changes are proposed by the draft Companies Amendment Bill, 2010, which states that a company's Memorandum of Incorporation may permit a 'different' (as opposed to a 'lower') percentage of voting rights to approve a special resolution, provided that there must at all times be a margin of at least 10 percentage points between the highest established requirement for approval of an ordinary resolution on any matter and the lowest established requirement for approval of a special resolution on any matter (cl 2(1)*(cc)*, cl 41).

[61] See cl 119(1) of the draft Companies Bill, 2007. (This required approval by at least a majority of the shares voted, and this could not be decreased in the company's Memorandum of Incorporation.)

[62] See s 115(1).

[63] By the same token, it cannot be more than 75 per cent.

[64] By Maleka Femida Cassim (Part I) op cit n 7 at 8–11.

[65] For instance, under the Revised American Model Business Corporation Act (s 11.04*(e)*) the requirement is approval by a majority of the votes present at a meeting at which a *quorum* is present, consisting of a *majority* of all the votes entitled to be cast, ie a minimum vote of just over 25 per cent of the total votes of the company would suffice for a merger. Moreover, the corporate laws of most states in the USA generally still implement an *absolute majority* voting requirement based on a percentage of all the *issued (outstanding) shares* of a company, usually 66,6 per cent or 50 per cent

conceivable that in some cases a favourable vote of as little as over 18,75 per cent of the voting rights of the company would suffice for the approval of a fundamental transaction.[66]

The Act significantly does not provide for any form of separate class voting on a merger.

It is important for the purposes of the shareholders' special resolution that any voting rights controlled by an 'acquiring party' or a person related[67] to an acquiring party or one 'acting in concert' with either of them are disqualified from voting and must moreover be excluded from calculating the quorum for the meeting (s 115(4)).[68] The term 'acquiring party' is regrettably not defined.[69] While the phrase 'act in concert' is defined in s 117, that definition does not apply to s 115.[70]

The object of s 115(4) is, commendably, to introduce a minority protection measure in that it would prevent a conflict of interest in an *interested transaction* (as opposed to an arm's length transaction).[71] This is where a party is simultaneously both the *acquiring party* (eg the surviving company in a merger, or the acquiring company in a disposal of assets or undertaking) and a *shareholder in the target company* (eg the disappearing company in a merger, or the disposing company in a disposal of assets or undertaking). In these cases the acquiring party, due to its conflict of interest (given that it is both the acquirer and a shareholder of the target company), is precluded (by s 115(4)) from voting on the target company's special resolution in respect of the transaction. As such, this provision may go a long way towards protecting the minority shareholders of the target company in an interested transaction, where the transaction is not at arm's length and the acquirer stands on both sides of the transaction. This provision may in effect be

---

of all the issued shares, as for instance in Delaware (see s 251*(c)* of the Delaware General Corporation Law, 2001).

[66] Because of shareholder apathy many shareholders, especially in a company with a large number of minority shareholders each with very small shareholdings, do not generally attend meetings, let alone cast their votes. It is consequently possible that, in some cases, a favourable vote of as little as over 18,75 per cent of the company's voting rights (ie 75 per cent of the voting rights at a meeting at which the bare minimum of the quorum of 25 per cent of the voting rights is present) would suffice for the approval of a merger.

[67] See the definition of related persons in s 2 of the Act and chapter 6: Groups of Companies and Related Persons.

[68] Specifically, such voting rights must not be included in calculating the percentage of voting rights: required to be present or actually present, in determining whether the applicable quorum requirements are satisfied; or required to be voted or actually voted in support of a resolution (as proposed by the draft Companies Amendment Bill, 2010 (cl 68)).

[69] The draft Companies Amendment Bill, 2010 now proposes to define 'acquiring party' as follows: '"acquiring party", when used in respect of a transaction or proposed transaction, means a person who, as a result of the transaction, would directly or indirectly acquire or establish direct or indirect control or increased control over all or the greater part of a company, or all or the greater part of the assets or undertaking of a company' (cl 2(1)*(a)*).

[70] The draft Companies Amendment Bill, 2010 (cl 68) now proposes to make the definition in s 117(1)*(b)* applicable to s 115(4). In this regard s 117(1)*(b)* states that 'act in concert', for the purposes of Part B and Part C of Chapter 5 of the Act and the Takeover Regulations, means any action pursuant to an agreement between or among two or more persons, in terms of which any of them co-operate for the purpose of entering into or proposing an affected transaction or offer.

[71] See further 15.2.14 for a more detailed discussion of these concepts.

regarded as a 'majority-of-minority-vote' provision in an interested transaction. (To express it differently, a vote of the majority of the *other* shareholders is required where a transaction is proposed between the company in which they hold shares and one of the existing shareholders of the company.)[72]

Turning to the second approval requirement under s 115, this applies in respect of a disposal of all or the greater part of the assets or undertaking of a company, where the disposing company is a subsidiary of either a South African company or an external company[73] *and* the disposal by the relevant (subsidiary) company will (having regard to the holding company's consolidated financial statements) substantially[74] constitute a disposal of all or the greater part of the assets or undertaking of the holding company. In such circumstances, the transaction additionally requires a similar special resolution by the shareholders of the *holding* company.[75] The special resolution of the holding company must be adopted in the same manner as required for the special resolution of the disposing company itself (as discussed above).

This requirement of a special resolution by the holding company appears to relate only to disposals of all or the greater part of the assets or undertaking of a company in terms of s 112. It must be borne in mind, in this regard, that, even though all the assets or the undertaking of a company may be transferred by way of a merger under s 113, such a transfer does not amount to a '*disposal*' but is instead an automatic transfer by operation of law, as discussed in 15.2.3 above. It is accordingly submitted that the requirement of a special resolution of the holding company applies only in the context of a s 112 disposal (see 15.3.3) and not to the other fundamental transactions. As a matter of policy, this is regrettable, because all the fundamental transactions should be subject to largely similar approval requirements in view of the objective to reduce the opportunities for regulatory arbitrage.[76] Moreover, in the context of triangular mergers, a requirement for a special resolution by the holding company would have served a particularly important protective purpose (see further 15.2.11 on triangular mergers below).

The third approval requirement under s 115 is court approval, to the extent required in the circumstances and manner contemplated in the Act.[77] It is worthy of emphasis that the approval of the court, as stated above, is not a general or automatic requirement for fundamental transactions, but is instead restricted to certain specified circumstances. Where court approval is required, the transaction

---

[72] See further the section on freeze-out mergers in 15.2.14 below.

[73] An 'external company' is defined in s 1 as a foreign company that is carrying on business, or non-profit activities, as the case may be, within South Africa, subject to s 23(2); see further chapter 3: Types of Companies.

[74] The word 'substantially' may be deleted from this provision (see the draft Companies Amendment Bill, 2010 (cl 68)).

[75] Section 115(2)*(b)*. See further 15.3.3 below.

[76] *Memorandum on the Objects of the Companies Bill, 2008* op cit n 1 at para 1.2. A second regrettable inconsistency between statutory mergers and s 112 disposals is that while an exemption is granted to intragroup s 112 disposals from the provisions of the Act, no similar exemption is granted for intragroup amalgamations or mergers (see in this regard 15.2.15 and 15.3.4 below).

[77] In s 115(3)–(6).

may not be implemented until such court approval has been granted. Court approval is discussed separately below in 15.2.5.

Finally, to the extent that Part B and Part C of Chapter 5 and the Takeover Regulations apply to a company, the company may not implement a fundamental transaction unless the Takeover Regulation Panel ('the Panel') has issued a compliance certificate in respect of the transaction or has exempted the transaction.[78]

(d) Notice to creditors

The fourth step of the merger procedure is that, once each merging company has obtained the requisite shareholder approval and other applicable approvals of the merger as discussed above,[79] a notice of the merger must be given, in the prescribed manner and form, to all known creditors[80] of the merging companies.[81]

The Act now provides a remedy for objecting creditors, unlike the draft Companies Bill, 2007, which was criticised for its failure to do so.[82] A creditor may, within 15 business days after delivery of the notice of merger, seek leave to apply to a court for a review of the merger, only on the grounds that the creditor will be materially prejudiced by the merger. It is worth emphasising that this period of 15 business days is calculated from the 'delivery' of the notice to the creditor — not the receipt of the notice by the creditor. A court may grant leave to a creditor to apply for a review of the merger only if it is satisfied (a) that the applicant is acting in good faith; (b) that the merger, if implemented, would materially prejudice the creditor, and (c) that there are no other remedies available to the creditor.[83] The meaning and scope of the phrase 'materially prejudice' is uncertain. It needs judicial interpretation to define its scope and limits.

Until such time as the court has disposed of any such proceedings involving creditors, the merger may not be implemented at all. The implementation of the merger is also subject to the order of the court in any such proceedings.[84]

A company that is under business rescue proceedings is exempt from comply-

---

[78] Section 115(b) read with s 119(4)(b) and (6). The reference to 'compliance notice' in this section of the Act is erroneous and it seems that it was intended to refer to a compliance certificate in terms of s 119(4)(b) (see cl 68 of the draft Companies Amendment Bill, 2010).

[79] Significantly, the draft Companies Amendment Bill, 2010 (cl 69) provides that this fourth step of the merger procedure may be carried out at an earlier stage, ie once each merging company has adopted a special resolution approving the merger. (The requirement that the transaction, by this stage, must have also satisfied all the other applicable requirements under s 115 is proposed to be abolished.)

[80] The draft Companies Amendment Bill, 2010 proposes to define a 'creditor' to mean a person to whom a company is or may become obligated in terms of any liability or other obligation that would be required (in terms of s 4(2)(b)(i)) to be considered by the company if it were applying the solvency and liquidity test (cl 2(1)). 'Liability' is defined by the draft Companies Amendment Bill, 2010 as 'a present obligation of an entity arising from past events, the settlement of which is expected to result in an outflow from the entity of resources embodying economic benefits'.

[81] Section 116(1)(a).

[82] Maleka Femida Cassim (Part I) op cit n 7 at 14.

[83] Section 116(1)(b) and (c).

[84] Section 116(3)(b).

Fundamental Transactions, Takeovers and Offers

ing with this fourth step of the merger procedure.[85] It is also noteworthy that these provisions of the Act specifically apply to mergers only and not to the other fundamental transactions.

(e) Implementation of the merger

The fifth and final step in the merger procedure is the implementation or 'perfection' of the merger. The parties may proceed with the implementation of the merger if no objecting creditors apply to court within the specified 15-day period (as discussed above).[86] If an objecting creditor does, however, seek leave to apply to court for a review of the merger, then the companies concerned may implement the merger only after the court has disposed of the creditor's application, and subject to the order of the court.[87] Legal proceedings by creditors could thus have a considerable impact on the timing and the implementation of a merger.

In order to implement the merger, a notice of amalgamation or merger must be filed with the Companies Commission. It must include the Memorandum of Incorporation of any newly formed company (that is incorporated under the merger agreement) and confirmation that the merger has satisfied the requirements of ss 113 and 115 of the Act, that it has been approved in terms of the Competition Act 89 of 1998, if so required, that it was granted the consent of the Minister of Finance in terms of s 54 of the Banks Act 94 of 1990, if so required, and that it is not subject to further approval by any regulatory authority or any unfulfilled conditions imposed by any law administered by a regulatory authority.[88]

Upon receipt of the notice of amalgamation or merger, the Companies Commission is required to deregister any company that disappears under the merger, without the need for any formal winding-up. The Companies Commission must also issue a registration certificate for each new company (if any) that has been newly incorporated in terms of the merger agreement.[89]

The merger takes effect in accordance with, and subject to any conditions set out in, the merger agreement.[90]

Section 115(9) states that, if a fundamental transaction has been approved, any person to whom assets are or undertaking is to be transferred may, if necessary in the circumstances, apply to a court for an order to give effect to the transaction. This may be an order to effect:

- the transfer of the relevant undertaking, assets and liabilities,
- the allotment and appropriation of any relevant shares or similar interests,
- the transfer of shares from one person to another,

---

[85] Where the merger is pursuant to or contemplated in the company's business rescue plan as adopted in accordance with Chapter 6 of the Act (s 116(2)).
[86] The transaction must also have satisfied all the applicable approval requirements set out in s 115 (see the draft Companies Amendment Bill, 2010 (cl 69)).
[87] Section 116(3).
[88] Section 116(4). ('Regulatory authority' is defined in s 1 as an entity established in terms of national or provincial legislation responsible for regulating an industry, or sector of an industry.)
[89] Section 116(5).
[90] Section 116(6)(*a*).

- the dissolution without winding-up of a company, as contemplated in the transaction,
- any incidental, consequential and supplemental matters that are necessary for the effectiveness and completion of the transaction, or
- any other relief necessary or appropriate to give effect to and properly implement an amalgamation or merger.

15.2.5 The requirement of court approval

The approval of the court is not generally required in the five-step merger procedure. It is only required in certain exceptional circumstances.[91] The governing principle is that, where a proposed fundamental transaction has been approved by the requisite majority of the shareholders of a company, the dissenters are not generally able to prevent or frustrate the fundamental transaction against the wishes of that majority. Instead, their recourse is to rely on their appraisal rights to opt out of the company. It is only in certain specified circumstances that a resolution for a statutory merger or other fundamental transaction may be set aside by the court on the grounds specified by the Act.

This approach to court approval applies equally to all the fundamental transactions, with the effect that schemes of arrangement and disposals of the assets or undertaking of a company will require court approval in the same circumstances as mergers. This, as discussed above, is expected to reduce the scope for regulatory arbitrage in this area of company law. It also constitutes a substantial overhaul of the provisions of the 1973 Act (see further 15.1 above and 15.3 below).

The Act provides that, despite the adoption of the requisite special resolution for a fundamental transaction, there are two circumstances in which a company may not proceed to implement the transaction without the approval of a court.

- First, court approval is required where the special resolution was opposed by at least 15 per cent of the voting rights that were voted on it and any person[92] who had voted against it specifically requires the company to seek court approval.[93] In other words, where the merger resolution receives the support of less than 85 per cent (ie between 75 and 85 per cent support), any person who had voted against it may require the company to apply for court approval. In this event, the company must either treat the resolution as a nullity[94] or, alternatively, apply to the court for approval,[95] in which case the company itself bears the costs of the application.

---

[91] Section 115(2)(c). Court approval is required in the circumstances and manner contemplated in ss 115(3)–(6) of the Act.

[92] A much stricter requirement was imposed by the draft Companies Bill, 2007, in that all the shares voted against the resolution had to *unanimously* require the company to seek court approval. This strict requirement was criticised (by Maleka Femida Cassim (Part II) op cit n 8 at 163), and has now fortunately been relaxed.

[93] Within five business days after the vote (in terms of the draft Companies Amendment Bill, 2010 (cl 68)).

[94] The Act does not specify how the 'company' would treat a resolution as a nullity.

[95] Within ten business days after the vote — see s 115(3)(a) read with s 115(5), and cl 68 of the draft Companies Amendment Bill, 2010.

- Secondly, court approval is required where any shareholder who had voted against the resolution makes a successful application[96] for leave to apply to court for a review of the transaction. This applies regardless of the percentage support for the resolution. The court may grant leave only if it is satisfied that the applicant is in good faith, appears prepared and able to sustain the proceedings, and has alleged facts which, if true, would support an order to set aside the resolution.[97] The costs of the application for court approval in these circumstances would not necessarily be imposed on the company.

It is noteworthy that a person may rely on these court approval provisions only if he or she (or it) had voted against the special resolution in respect of the merger or other fundamental transaction. A mere abstention from voting would not suffice. Shareholders not entitled to vote on the resolution may not rely on this protective measure, nor for that matter on the appraisal remedy.

The court, on reviewing a resolution in either of the above two circumstances, may set it aside only if:[98]

- the resolution is manifestly unfair to any class of holders of the company's securities,[99] or
- the vote was materially tainted by conflict of interest, inadequate disclosure, failure to comply with the Act, the Memorandum of Incorporation or any applicable rules of the company, or other significant and material procedural irregularity.[100]

The judicial interpretation of the scope and ambit of these grounds remains to be seen.

The court approval provisions in s 115 accordingly empower the court to set aside a resolution before it is implemented by the company, and thereby to prevent the merger or other fundamental transaction. This 'remedy' must be distinguished from the appraisal remedy and one must be careful not to confuse the two. The appraisal remedy is concerned with the determination of the fair value of shares in the company, but does not prevent the implementation of the merger. On the other hand, the exceptional requirement of court approval under s 115 is concerned with the review of the merger resolution and the possible setting aside of the transaction. The two remedies complement one another — they apply in different circumstances and they produce different results.

---

[96] Within ten business days after the vote (in terms of the draft Companies Amendment Bill, 2010 (cl 68)).
[97] Section 115(3)(b) read with s 115(6).
[98] Section 115(7).
[99] It is notable that this ground is quite narrowly worded. First, it applies only in the event of unfairness to a 'class' — as opposed to an interest group — of securities holders. This would imply that generally minority shareholders may not be able to rely on this provision to set aside a resolution that is unfair only in relation to the minority shareholders of a class of shares. Secondly, this ground of review is further restricted by the requirement of 'manifest' unfairness. Thirdly, the type of 'unfairness' that would suffice for the purposes of this ground is unclear.
[100] 'Material', when used as an adjective, is defined as significant in the circumstances of a particular matter, to a degree that is of consequence in determining the matter, or might reasonably affect a person's judgment or decision-making in the matter (s 1).

The exceptional requirement of court approval of mergers is undoubtedly an important provision that serves a distinctly different purpose from the appraisal right. It stems mainly from the fact that where there are procedural irregularities or unfairness, the appraisal right is an inappropriate safeguard. The appropriate course of action in this event would instead be for a court to set the transaction aside. Where, for instance, the company has failed to make adequate disclosure to shareholders of sufficient and accurate information to enable them to reach a properly informed decision on how to vote, this may result in the resolution itself (even if adopted by the company) being flawed. The appropriate remedy would therefore be to set the transaction aside and to provide relief to all the shareholders generally. This 'remedy' may be contrasted with the appraisal remedy (which is an exit mechanism and a safeguard against inadequate consideration) which operates on a no-fault basis, where no wrongdoing need be alleged or proved (see further 15.2.6 below).

It is worth noting that the right of shareholders under s 115 to request a court review of a fundamental transaction is in addition to their appraisal rights in terms of s 164.

It must also be borne in mind that the oppression remedy may well provide a further avenue for dissatisfied shareholders seeking a remedy in respect of a fundamental transaction.[101]

15.2.6 Appraisal rights of dissenting shareholders

Closely associated with the new regime for fundamental transactions under the new Act is the innovative remedy of the appraisal rights of dissenting shareholders. In the context of fundamental transactions, the appraisal right is the primary safeguard for shareholders.

The appraisal right applies not only in the context of mergers, but also to disposals of all or the greater part of the assets or undertaking of a company and schemes of arrangement.[102]

The appraisal right is best described as the right of dissenting shareholders, who do not approve of certain triggering events, to opt out of the company by withdrawing the fair value of their shares in cash. Section 115(8) provides that the holder of any voting rights in a company is entitled to seek relief in terms of s 164 (dealing with the appraisal right) if that person *(a)* had notified the company in advance of the intention to oppose the special resolution for the merger (or other fundamental transaction), and *(b)* had been present at the meeting and voted against that special resolution. It is commendable that the third proposed requirement for the exercise of appraisal rights, ie the 'no-appraisal threshold', has been

---

[101] See further chapter 16: Shareholder Remedies and Minority Protection.
[102] Appraisal rights apply also in the event that a special resolution is proposed for the alteration of class rights in terms of the Memorandum of Incorporation in any matter materially adverse to the holders of that class of shares (see further chapter 16: Shareholder Remedies and Minority Protection).

abolished, after strong criticism of this unnecessary and inappropriate cap on the appraisal remedy.[103]

The principal protective measure for shareholders in mergers and fundamental transactions is the appraisal right of dissenting shareholders, and not the sanction of the court. The crux of the appraisal right is that, where a proposed merger or fundamental transaction has received the proper approval of the prescribed shareholder majority, the dissenting shareholders do not generally have recourse to a court of law to object to, prevent or frustrate the transaction (save in certain limited circumstances where court approval of the transaction is required, as discussed in 15.2.5 above). Instead, their recourse is to rely on their appraisal rights to obtain the fair value of their shares from the company, and thus to opt out of the fundamental transaction and indeed opt out of the company.

The US-style appraisal right is a right that is completely new to South African law. It provides dissenting shareholders with a means of exit from the company (particularly where the merger consideration takes the form of securities in the merged company), and a means of challenging the adequacy and fairness of the consideration that they have received (particularly where the merger consideration takes the form of cash).

The appraisal right is thus closely linked to statutory mergers and fundamental transactions. It may be viewed as counterbalancing or offsetting the statutory merger and other fundamental transactions. The appraisal right is a remedy that provides a balance between the rights of the majority shareholders and the rights of the minority shareholders in a company. In this regard, there has been a significant change of policy under the new Act that generally makes it easier for the prescribed majority to effect a fundamental transaction in our law (see 15.1 and 15.2.1 above). The simplicity and leniency of the procedures for mergers and fundamental transactions are consequently counterbalanced or offset by the appraisal rights of the minority shareholders who disapprove of or disagree with the transaction. The importance of the appraisal right is that it enables the dissenting or disgruntled shareholders to *opt out* of the fundamental transaction — but not to prevent it.

It is noteworthy that appraisal rights are granted only to those shareholders who are entitled to vote on the resolution in respect of the merger or fundamental transaction.[104] Dissent rights and appraisal rights would apparently not extend to shareholders who are precluded from voting in terms of s 115(4), nor to shareholders who do not hold 'voting rights' at all. (For a detailed discussion of the appraisal right, refer to chapter 16: Shareholder Remedies and Minority Protection.)

---

[103] Maleka Femida Cassim (Part II) op cit n 8 at 161–4. The 'no-appraisal threshold' had the effect that appraisal rights were available only if the resolution was supported by the holders of less than 75 per cent of the shares entitled to be voted (bearing in mind that the draft Bill required the support of a mere simple majority of the shares voted on the resolution) (see cl 119(7) of the draft Companies Bill, 2007).

[104] Section 115(8).

15.2.7 The protective measures for shareholders in the merger procedure

The new statutory merger procedure will, as stated above, facilitate business combinations and fundamental transactions far more effectively than the previous Act. Indeed, takeovers and fundamental transactions in general are increasingly seen as being beneficial to corporate efficiency, to the economy, and to wealth creation. The regulatory emphasis has now shifted to attaining the appropriate balance of the interests of all the shareholders so as to avoid either minority oppression by the majority or its converse, minority dictation, which enables recalcitrant minorities to perversely obstruct the improved management of a company that could result from a merger.

There are a number of measures and mechanisms for the protection of shareholders. These would of course include other applicable remedies under the Act (such as the oppression remedy). The protective measures for shareholders that are particularly inherent in the statutory merger procedure itself, include the following:

(a) Shareholder approval

Shareholder approval of the merger agreement is a vital safeguard for shareholders. This has been discussed in detail in 15.2.4*(c)* above, including an evaluation of the significance of the new 75 per cent approval threshold, and the importance of s 115(4) as a minority protection measure in an interested transaction.

(b) The appraisal right

Secondly, dissenting shareholders may have recourse to the new appraisal rights to have their shares bought out by the company in cash, at a price reflecting the fair value of the shares, and thereby to opt out of the merger. This effectively constitutes the prime protective measure for shareholders in a merger (see 15.2.6 above).

(c) Court approval

The third protective measure for shareholders is court approval of the merger. Court approval is not a general requirement for statutory mergers, but is required only in certain circumstances, as discussed in 15.2.5 above. The court is empowered, in these circumstances, to set aside a merger resolution and thus to prevent the merger. This 'remedy' must be distinguished from the appraisal remedy, because these two remedies, although complementary, provide different results and apply in different circumstances. (See also 15.2.4 above.)

(d) The role of the board of directors

The Act requires the board of directors to merely consider whether each proposed merged company will satisfy the solvency and liquidity test upon implementation of the merger agreement. If the board reasonably so believes, it may submit the merger agreement for consideration at a shareholders' meeting.[105]

---

[105] Section 113(4). See further 15.2.4*(b)* above.

Unlike some other jurisdictions, the Act does not require the board of directors of a merging company to formally adopt a resolution approving of the merger and stating that it is advisable or in the best interests of the company. However, it is submitted that the fiduciary duties of directors would nonetheless require the directors to honestly and objectively consider whether the merger, including its terms and the merger consideration, is in the best interests of the company. The anticipated new Takeover Regulations are also likely to supplement this.

The Act does not explicitly require any further information to be furnished to the shareholders, nor does it require the directors to give any advice or recommendations to the shareholders. However, the directors' fiduciary duties may possibly require this, as may the anticipated new Takeover Regulations.[106]

15.2.8 Protective measures for creditors

The statutory merger procedure also contains inherent protective measures for the creditors of the merging companies. They clearly require protection, because after the merger the creditors of each of the merging companies would be in competition with one another. This is especially important where the proportion of the claims of a creditor of the one merging company in relation to the value of that merging company's assets is lower than the proportion of the creditor's claim in relation to the value of the assets of the merged company. Creditors' interests are protected by a number of provisions of the statutory merger procedure:

- The first protective measure for creditors lies in the effect of the merger itself, namely that all the liabilities of the constituent merging companies automatically, by operation of law, become liabilities of the surviving company (or new company, as the case may be). This includes unknown and contingent liabilities. In this way creditors' claims are neither extinguished nor wiped out — although they are changed.
- Secondly, creditors' interests are protected by the requirement that a merger may only be effected if each merged company would, upon implementation of the merger, satisfy the solvency and liquidity test.
- Thirdly, written notice of the merger has to be given to all known creditors of the merging companies, thereby ensuring that all creditors are made aware of the proposed merger.
- Fourthly, objecting creditors are now provided with a remedy under the Act (see 15.2.4(*d*) above).

15.2.9 Types of merger structures: General

It is submitted that various types of merger structures are accommodated under the widely drafted provisions of the Act. In this regard, the Act is liberally drafted to make provision for a variety of forms of merger *consideration* (as discussed in 15.2.4(*a*) above). Closely linked to the different forms of merger consideration is a variety of merger structures.

---

[106] In some circumstances, it may even be appropriate for directors to furnish shareholders with a report by an independent expert on the merits of the proposed merger.

The Act thus provides substantial latitude so as to permit an assortment of merger structures, each with its own uses and advantages, thereby catering for different circumstances and differing needs for the statutory merger. A merger under the Act is not limited to the traditional concept of the pooling of two companies into one company. Instead, the Act is drafted widely enough to allow for, inter alia, triangular mergers, reverse triangular mergers, cash mergers and freeze-out mergers. These popular and practically useful merger structures are discussed below.

As mentioned in 15.2.3 above, for the sake of simplicity and for illustrative purposes, the example of a two-party merger involving the 'surviving company' type of structure will be used, ie where one of the constituent merging companies fuses into the other constituent company, resulting in the survival of the latter company (the surviving company), which holds all the assets and liabilities that were previously held by the two constituent companies, and the disappearance of the former company (the disappearing company). The surviving company, as discussed above, usually (but not always) is the 'acquiring company' in the merger, while the disappearing company usually is the 'target company'. The merger consideration in most cases is effectively paid to the shareholders of the target (or disappearing) company, in consideration for their shares in the target company.

15.2.10 'Pooling' type merger

The traditional concept of a 'pooling' type transaction is where two companies are pooled into one company that holds the combined pool of assets and liabilities previously held severally by the two constituent merging companies, and the two sets of shareholders of the two merging companies continue to participate as shareholders in the surviving company (or the newly formed company, as the case may be).

In the traditional 'pooling' type merger, the shareholders of the target (or disappearing) company usually receive *shares* in the acquiring (or surviving) company. In this event, the shares of the disappearing company are conveniently converted automatically, by operation of law, into shares of the surviving company on the implementation of the merger agreement.[107]

The Act also permits merger consideration in the form of other securities,[108] such as debentures of the surviving merged company. The consideration may even include the exchange of any 'other property'.[109] Merger consideration is thus quite wide in scope, consequently giving merging parties a number of different options.

15.2.11 Triangular merger

(a) *Structure of the triangular merger*

A great disadvantage of the statutory merger is the general rule that the liabilities of the target (or disappearing company) automatically become the liabilities of the

---

[107] See also the wording of s 113(2)*(c)* and *(e)*.
[108] As defined in s 1 of the Securities Services Act 36 of 2004, and including shares held in a private company or shares issued or authorised to be issued by a profit company (s 1 of the Act read with cl 2 of the draft Companies Amendment Bill, 2010).
[109] Section 113(2)*(c)*.

acquiring (or surviving) company, as discussed in 15.2.3 above. This may, in practice, discourage many mergers. However, the triangular merger provides a means to get around this issue. One of the primary benefits of the triangular merger structure is that it enables an acquiring company to avoid the assumption of the liabilities of the target company.

As its name suggests, the triangular merger involves three companies. On the target side of the transaction is the target company ('Co T'), while on the acquiring side of the transaction are two companies, being the holding company ('Co H') which is the *would-be* acquirer in the transaction, together with its *wholly owned subsidiary* ('Co S'). Co S is invariably a newly formed company that is formed (by Co H) specifically for the purposes of the merger.

Co S is additionally a shell company, holding no assets or liabilities of its own. Co S functions as an acquisition vehicle in the merger with the target company, so that technically it is the *subsidiary* of the would-be acquirer that is directly a party to the merger and *not the would-be acquirer itself*. In other words, the merger is technically between Co T and Co S; Co H is *not* directly a party to the merger.

The merger between Co T and Co S is structured so that Co T merges into the wholly owned subsidiary Co S. In other words, Co T is the disappearing company, with the result that consequent upon the merger, Co T is effectively absorbed by or 'housed' in Co S. Since Co S was a *shell* company prior to the merger, the effect of the merger is that the business of Co T effectively becomes the business of the wholly owned subsidiary of Co H.

The object of a triangular merger accordingly is that, on the implementation of the merger, in substance (but not in form), the *target company* becomes the *wholly owned subsidiary of Co H*. To express it differently, as a result of the triangular merger, the whole of Co T is effectively absorbed by or 'housed' in the subsidiary (ie Co S).

This type of merger is called a triangular merger because there are three companies involved, two of which are in a holding and subsidiary company relationship. The triangular merger may be contrasted with the standard two-party type of merger, where the disappearing or target company fuses *directly* with the surviving or acquiring company, and is engulfed by or absorbed into the acquiring company. By contrast, in a triangular merger, the target company in substance becomes the *subsidiary* of the (would-be) acquirer.

(b) Purpose and advantages of the triangular merger

The triangular merger is a very popular form of merger structure in the jurisdictions that permit it. It represents a fairly liberal approach. The first advantage of the triangular merger structure, as stated above, is that it enables Co H to acquire and to conduct the business of Co T in a separate wholly owned subsidiary company. It thereby protects the would-be acquirer, Co H, by enabling Co H to ring-fence or isolate Co T's liabilities — including unknown and contingent liabilities — in a separate legal entity. This, quite importantly from a practical point of view, reduces Co H's exposure to the liabilities of Co T pursuant to the merger and thereby effectively neutralises one of the distinct disadvantages associated with the standard two-party merger.

A second advantage of the triangular merger is that neither Co H nor (the business of) Co T need disappear under the merger (as is usually the case in a standard two-party merger, in which at least one constituent company usually disappears pursuant to the merger). The target company's business, customer relationships and goodwill may accordingly be maintained substantially intact and unchanged in the acquisition vehicle, that is, the shell subsidiary (Co S). This is especially convenient where the businesses of Co H and the target company are of a different nature and are best kept separate.

A strong practical reason for the popularity of the triangular merger structure in the USA is that the shareholders of the would-be acquirer (Co H) do not have any voting and appraisal rights on the merger. This is because technically Co H is *not* a party to the merger. (The constituent merging companies are technically and formally only Co T and Co S.) Moreover, the vote of Co S on the triangular merger is a non-contentious matter since Co H, as the holding company, is the sole shareholder of Co S. The triangular merger is used by US companies to their advantage, to avoid the costs of convening a shareholders' meeting of the would-be acquirer Co H and, much more importantly, to avoid the appraisal rights of the shareholders of Co H. Whether this is a suitable policy to be followed in South African law remains to be seen.

It is noteworthy that, while the draft Companies Bill, 2007 provided scope for the shareholders of Co H (ie the parent of the acquiring company) to approve a triangular merger by special resolution,[110] this provision no longer forms part of the Act. (It has now been replaced by s 115(2)*(b)*, which apparently applies only in respect of s 112 disposals of the assets or undertaking of a company, as submitted in 15.2.4*(c)* above). The exclusion of this protective requirement is unfortunate and may have substantial practical ramifications, in that the failure to give voting and appraisal rights to the shareholders of Co H in a triangular merger creates a distinct potential for unfairness to the shareholders of Co H.[111] The anti-avoidance provision in s 6(1) of the Act may be relevant in this regard and could perhaps apply in certain circumstances.[112]

(c) Merger consideration in a triangular merger

The consideration receivable by the shareholders of Co T (as consideration for their shares in the disappearing Co T) is a critical issue. Pursuant to the triangular merger, the shareholders of Co T generally receive either cash or shares in Co H. It must be emphasised that the shares are *in Co H, and not in Co S*. This ensures that on the implementation of the merger, the surviving company (Co S) remains *wholly owned* by Co H.

The crucial point is that the Act seemingly envisages the possibility of merger consideration in the form of shares in *another company* other than the surviving

---

[110] See cl 119(2)*(b)* of the Bill, relating to 'parallel transactions' by the holding company.

[111] See further s 41(3) of the Act, which could potentially provide a safety net for shareholders of the holding company in a triangular merger in certain circumstances. Stock exchange rules could also require a vote of the shareholders of the holding company in a triangular merger.

[112] See chapter 1: Introduction to the New Companies Act.

Fundamental Transactions, Takeovers and Offers

merged company, such as shares in Co H.[113] Consequently, the Act appears to create scope for triangular mergers in South African law. The triangular merger is a welcome procedure in our law and South African companies will, no doubt, regard it as very useful.

The end result of the triangular merger is that Co S remains in existence as the surviving merged company, holding (only) all the assets and liabilities formerly held by Co T, and continuing to remain *a wholly owned subsidiary of Co H*. The former shareholders of Co T, depending on the form of the merger consideration, either become shareholders in Co H or are entirely cashed-out. Thus, in substance, although perhaps not in form, the outcome of the triangular merger is that Co T becomes a wholly owned subsidiary of Co H.

There are, however, some complications and complexities associated with the merger consideration in a triangular merger. These issues are beyond the scope of this chapter.[114]

15.2.12 Reverse triangular merger

The reverse triangular merger procedure is similar in structure to the triangular merger, with the would-be acquirer (Co H) forming a wholly owned subsidiary (Co S), which will act as the acquisition vehicle in the merger with the target (Co T).

The essential difference between the triangular merger and the reverse triangular merger structure is that in the former, Co T merges into Co S, with *Co S* remaining in existence as the surviving company; whereas in the reverse triangular merger, it is Co S that merges into Co T, so that *Co T* (and not the subsidiary Co S) is the surviving company.

This is quite paradoxical. Oddly, the *target* company *survives* in a reverse triangular merger, while the *acquiring* company *disappears*.

The end result of a reverse triangular merger is, first, that Co T becomes a wholly owned subsidiary of Co H. Secondly, Co S, which is a newly formed company that is formed specifically for the purposes of the merger, disappears pursuant to the merger — it thus has a very short lifespan. Thirdly, the former shareholders in Co T (the surviving company) give up their shares in return for the merger consideration, which is usually in the form of cash or shares in Co H. Thus the merger consideration is (also paradoxically) paid to the former shareholders of the *surviving* company (Co T), who give up their shares in return for the merger consideration.

This is a rather illusory and artificial procedure, but is nonetheless permitted by modern merger legislation in the USA. It serves an important purpose in circum-

---

[113] In the context of merger consideration, the Act refers only to the conversion of shares of a constituent merging company into shares of the merged company, without extending this to the conversion into shares of *any other* company. But s 113(2)*(e)*, which envisages the receipt of fractional securities of a 'merged company or of *any other juristic person the securities of which are to be received*' in the merger [emphasis added], suggests that it is permissible for securities of *another company* to be used as a merger consideration. See also s 113(2)*(c)*, which refers to merger consideration in the form of 'other property'. (However, it is regrettable that the wording of the Act on this issue leaves some room for doubt.)

[114] See further Maleka Femida Cassim (Part I) op cit n 7 at 27–32.

stances where the preservation of Co T's corporate personality is vital, for instance, to preserve valuable licences, leases or other valuable contracts of Co T that would not survive the disappearance of Co T under a merger. This would apply, for instance, to contracts between Co T and third parties that, by their very nature or by their express terms, are precluded from being automatically transferred by the operation of law to any other company consequent upon a merger.[115] The reverse triangular merger procedure also encompasses many of the advantages associated with triangular mergers (see 15.2.11 above).

It is submitted that the Act may arguably be interpreted to provide sufficient scope to facilitate reverse triangular mergers in South African law.[116]

However, whether the courts would find the reverse triangular merger structure to be an artificial or an otherwise objectionable form of transaction is yet to be seen. See also the anti-avoidance provisions in terms of s 6(1) of the Act.[117] But on the face of it, and barring a fraudulent or unlawful purpose, there is arguably no reason for it to be condemned as objectionable.

15.2.13 Cash merger

A very significant question in practice is whether the Act permits a cash consideration in a merger. It is crucially important that such a consideration is evidently permissible.[118] The relevant provisions relating to this possibility are liberal, in contrast with several other jurisdictions where a cash consideration is subject to stringent restrictions and limitations.

This is in view of the controversy associated with cash mergers. The underpinning philosophy of paying a cash consideration to the shareholders of the disappearing company is simply that shareholders do not have a vested right to continue to hold their investment as shareholders of the surviving merged entity, but could instead be 'cashed-out'. In this way, shareholders could be compelled to disinvest from the company. A cash merger thus creates a definite scope for the use of the statutory merger procedure as a means to squeeze out or eliminate the minority shareholders of a company, by compelling them under the merger agreement to exchange their shares for cash. This involves a significant liberalisation of merger policy in South African law, notwithstanding the potential benefits associated with 'freeze-out' mergers of this nature.

15.2.14 Freeze-out merger

(a) Purpose of the freeze-out merger

A distinction must be drawn between an arm's length merger and an *interested merger* (or controlled merger). In an interested merger, the acquiring company in the transaction holds an equity interest in the target company, usually as the majority or controlling shareholder of the latter. The controlling shareholder could therefore initiate a *freeze-out merger* between itself as the acquirer and the

---

[115] As discussed in 15.2.3 above.
[116] See further Maleka Femida Cassim (Part II) op cit n 8 at 147–148.
[117] See further chapter 1: Introduction to the New Companies Act.
[118] Section 113(2)*(d)* above read with the definition of 'consideration' in s 1; see 15.2.4*(a)* above.

company as the target, with the purpose of eliminating the minority shareholders in the company.

Pursuant to the freeze-out merger, the former minority shareholders of the company will be eliminated or frozen out, usually in return for a cash consideration or, alternatively, for other property, shares or securities of the controlling shareholder. The controlling shareholder will, in effect, pay the consideration to the minority shareholders, in its capacity as the acquiring party in the freeze-out merger.

A freeze-out merger may thus take the form of a *cash-out merger* where the minority shareholders receive cash as consideration for the elimination of their shares. Indeed, the introduction of cash as a permissible merger consideration enhances the appeal and the popularity of the freeze-out merger.

The controlling shareholder accordingly stands on both sides of a freeze-out transaction, being both the acquiring party and the controlling shareholder of the target. This entails a manifest conflict of interest and a grave risk of oppression of the minority shareholders. Not only is there disparate treatment of the majority and the minority shareholders (who are frozen out of the company), but also, since the controlling shareholder stands on both sides of the transaction, it could have the power to determine the type and the amount of consideration that the minority shareholders will receive in return for the forfeiture of their shares.

The policy issues and the potential for oppression of minority shareholders in freeze-out mergers has long been a controversial issue in the USA and Canada, which now supplement the freeze-out merger by various protective measures designed to ensure fairness to minority shareholders. It is submitted that the Act evidently pre-empts some of these policy issues by introducing a firm minority-protection measure in terms of s 115(4), which, as discussed in 15.2.4*(c)* above, prevents voting rights that are controlled an acquiring party from being voted in respect of a proposed merger. This is explained further below.

(b) *Shareholder voting and structure of freeze-out mergers*

It is submitted that the provisions of the Act provide sufficient latitude to facilitate freeze-out mergers. It is further submitted that a freeze-out merger under the Act may be structured as a two-party merger or perhaps even as a triangular merger.[119]

Dealing first with the two-party freeze-out merger, its structure may be briefly described as follows: The target company is merged directly into its controlling shareholder (which thus acts in the capacity of acquiring company). The minority shareholders of the target company usually receive cash as the consideration for the elimination of their shares in the disappearing target company.[120] The result of the merger is that the minority shareholders of the target company are eliminated.

---

[119] Whether this would be affected by other provisions, for instance, the proposed new Takeover Regulations, remains to be seen.
[120] Since the shares held by the controlling shareholder/acquiring company in the target company seemingly fall within the ambit of s 113(3) — as shares held by one merging company in the other merging company — these shares stand to be cancelled, without repayment of capital or a conversion into shares of the surviving merged company (see 15.2.4*(a)* above).

Section 115(4) will evidently apply to the vote by the target company on the proposed merger. Section 115(4) provides that those voting rights that are controlled by an acquiring party, a person related to an acquiring party, or a person acting in concert with either of them, cannot be voted in respect of a proposed merger or counted for the purposes of the quorum requirement.[121] The object of s 115(4) arguably is to introduce an effective minority protection measure and to prevent a conflict of interest in an interested transaction. In the context of an interested merger (ie where the acquiring party and the target are not at arm's length due to the control by the *acquiring party* of voting shares in the *target company*), the effect of s 115(4) is that the acquiring party is precluded from voting its shares on the target company's resolution in respect of the merger and from being counted for the quorum requirement.

This gives due recognition to and takes cognisance of the acquiring party's conflict of interest, given that it is both the acquirer and a shareholder of the acquired company.[122] Section 115(4) may in effect be regarded as a 'majority-of-minority-vote' provision in an interested merger (see also 15.2.4*(c)*). To put it differently, a vote of the majority of the *minority* (or *other*) shareholders is required where a merger is proposed between the company in which they hold shares and one of the existing shareholders of the company. As such, this provision may go a long way towards protecting the minority shareholders of the target company in an interested merger where the acquirer stands on both sides of the transaction.

Regarding the alternative structure for a freeze-out merger, namely, where it takes the form of a triangular merger, this is in fact the more commonly used mechanism in the USA. A triangular freeze-out merger may perhaps be theoretically permissible under the Act, in view of its inclusion of both cash mergers and triangular mergers. Briefly, a triangular[123] freeze-out merger entails the formation of a wholly owned subsidiary (Co S) by the controlling shareholder of the target company (Co H). Co S functions as the acquisition vehicle in the merger with the target company (Co T). Upon effectuation of the merger of Co T into Co S, the merger consideration payable to the minority shareholders of Co T usually takes the form of cash.[124]

The minority-protection measures of s 115(4) of the Act seem to apply also to a triangular freeze-out merger, so as to preclude the controlling shareholder of the target company (ie Co H) from voting its shares on the target company's resolution in respect of the merger. This is despite the fact that, under this merger structure, the controlling shareholder is *not* formally the *acquiring* party but is

---

[121] See further the discussion of s 115(4) in 15.2.4*(c)* above; see also the discussion of the changes proposed by the draft Companies Amendment Bill, 2010.
[122] Absent this provision, the acquiring party, where it holds sufficient shares in the target company, would have the power to abuse its position by having the target company adopt the merger resolution *merely on the strength of its own vote*, in its capacity as a shareholder of the target company.
[123] Triangular mergers are explained above in 15.2.14.
[124] This may perhaps give rise to issues concerning the equivalent treatment of shareholders of a class.

merely its holding company.[125] On the basis that the acquiring party (Co S) is the wholly owned subsidiary of Co H and, as such, is 'related'[126] to Co H, s 115(4) will preclude Co H from voting any of its shares in the target company in respect of the merger resolution.

Needless to say, the majority-of-minority-vote is a necessary but not a sufficient protection for the minority shareholders in a freeze-out merger. Further effective minority-protection measures are required. These will no doubt in due course form part of the fiduciary duties of directors as developed by the courts, and may also fairly be expected to form part of the new Takeover Regulations.

(c) The two-step freeze-out merger

The two-step freeze-out merger merits a brief mention. The two-step freeze-out merger (or the second-step or back-end freeze-out merger) consists of a *takeover offer as the first step*, followed by a *freeze-out merger as the second step*. The purpose of the first step, namely the takeover offer, is for the offeror to acquire a sufficient number of shares in the offeree company so as to enable it to effect a freeze-out merger as the second step, by voting its newly acquired shares in the offeree/target company in support of the merger resolution. Accordingly in the second step (ie the freeze-out merger), the shares of those minority shareholders who chose not to accept the offer under the first step of the transaction, are acquired by the offeror/acquiring company. In this way the minority shareholders are eliminated from the target company. Even though such a two-step merger initially starts as an arm's length transaction, in the second step of the transaction a freeze-out or a conflict of interest is involved.

The two-step freeze-out merger procedure is likely to be of little use in South African law. This is because the majority-of-minority-vote requirement in s 115(4) of the Act implicitly applies not only to a standard freeze-out merger but also to the two-step merger. (This *precludes* the successful takeover bidder from voting its newly acquired target company shares — that were acquired in the first-step takeover offer — in support of the target company's special resolution on the proposed second-step merger.) Section 115(4) accordingly defeats the very purpose of the first step, that is, to acquire a sufficient number of shares in the offeree/target company so as to be able to single-handedly approve the second-step merger.

This is not necessarily inappropriate as a matter of policy. There are divergent and conflicting policies on the two-step freeze-out merger among different jurisdictions. It is submitted that the conservative approach, which seems to have been implicitly adopted in the Act, is the preferable approach.

15.2.15 Short-form merger

It is a surprising oversight that the Act does not provide for a short-form merger procedure. A short-form merger is a simplified form of merger between a holding

---

[125] See also the proposed definition of 'acquiring party' as proposed by the draft Companies Amendment Bill, 2010 (cl 2(1)).
[126] 'Related' persons are defined in s 2 of the Act. It must be borne in mind that s 115(4) states that those voting rights which are controlled by an acquiring party, a person *'related'* to an acquiring party, or a person acting in concert with either of them are disqualified from voting on the merger.

company and its wholly owned subsidiary (known as a vertical short-form merger) or between two wholly owned subsidiaries of a holding company (known as a horizontal short-form merger). While the Act expressly permits mergers between a holding company and its subsidiary,[127] it surprisingly fails to provide for a special procedure to facilitate such 'intragroup' mergers.

Many other leading jurisdictions permit a simplified short-form merger procedure that dispenses with the requirement of a shareholder resolution by each of the merging companies, so that short-form mergers may instead be effected simply by a resolution of the board of directors of each merging company. This avoids the delay, costs and inconvenience associated with convening a shareholders' meeting, and, more importantly, it avoids the exercise of appraisal rights. The short-form merger procedure in many jurisdictions also dispenses with the requirement of a merger agreement.

It should be borne in mind that the short-form merger is much less controversial than other types of mergers, as it simply involves a parent company and/or its wholly owned subsidiaries. Where the sole shareholder of the wholly owned subsidiary company is the holding company, its favourable vote on the merger would in any event be a non-issue. Moreover, the issues of creditor prejudice and creditor protection are minimised in short-form mergers.

The benefit of a short-form merger procedure is that it enables companies to reorganise their group structures and eliminate subsidiaries that are otherwise kept in existence only to avoid the problem and the expense of getting rid of them. The introduction of a short-form merger would have had clear economic and administrative benefits and would have reduced complexity and compliance costs, all of which are relevant to the underlying objective of company law reform.

It is significant that s 112, which deals with proposals to dispose of all or the greater part of the assets or undertaking of a company, specifically exempts 'intragroup' transactions.[128] One wonders why a similar exemption was not made in the context of mergers, particularly in view of the policy objective of the Act to reduce the opportunity for regulatory arbitrage in the sphere of fundamental transactions.

Finally, it is also noteworthy that many corporate law statutes in the USA eliminate the need for a vote of the shareholders of the acquiring company in what is often known as a 'whale-minnow merger' in the USA. This is a small acquisition, in which the acquiring company does not issue more than a specified percentage of its shares as a merger consideration (usually no more than 20 per cent of the number of issued shares that were in issue prior to the merger). South African law, perhaps for valid policy reasons, does not provide for an equivalent.

15.3 DISPOSAL OF ALL OR THE GREATER PART OF THE ASSETS OR UNDERTAKING

15.3.1 Introduction

Disposals of the all or the greater part of the assets or undertaking of a company, in terms of s 112 of the new Act (referred to loosely in this section as 's 112

---
[127] Section 113(1).
[128] Section 112(1).

disposals'), are subject to very similar approval requirements as amalgamations or mergers (see 15.2.1 and 15.2.4–15.2.6 above). The shareholder approval requirements, the exceptional requirement of court approval and the appraisal rights of dissenting shareholders are largely (although not completely) harmonised for all three types of fundamental transactions under the new Act, as discussed above.[129]

The procedure for s 112 disposals bears many similarities to its predecessor, namely s 228 of the 1973 Act (as amended by the Corporate Laws Amendment Act 24 of 2006). These parallel provisions include the requirement of a special resolution[130] by the disposing company that authorises or ratifies the specific transaction, the requirement in certain circumstances of a special resolution by the holding company of the disposing company, and the exemption of 'intragroup' disposals.[131]

However, the procedure for s 112 disposals under the new Act now also incorporates additional safeguards for dissenting shareholders who are dissatisfied with the transaction. The innovative safeguards comprise court approval of the transaction in specified circumstances, and the appraisal rights of dissenting shareholders. Moreover, in an interested transaction, where a party is simultaneously the acquiring party and a shareholder in the disposing company (ie the company that wishes to dispose of all or the greater part of its assets or undertaking), that party, in view of its conflict of interest, is precluded by the new Act from voting on the special resolution of the disposing company in respect of the proposed transaction.[132]

15.3.2 Transactions to 'dispose' of 'all or the greater part' of the assets or undertaking

Section 112 is triggered only where a company proposes to 'dispose of all or the greater part of its assets or undertaking'. The interpretation of this phrase is of key importance. The meaning of 'dispose' is discussed below, followed by a discussion of the phrase the 'greater part'.

(a) Meaning of 'dispose'

The Act uses the word 'dispose' without defining the range of transactions that fall within the ambit of a 'disposal', in a similar vein to s 228 of the 1973 Act. In view of the similarities in the wording of s 112 of the new Act and s 228 of the 1973 Act, it is submitted that for guidance one may usefully resort to judicial decisions concerning the meaning of the word 'dispose' under the previous regimes.[133]

It has been laid down that the ordinary meaning of the word 'dispose' is 'to part with' or 'to get rid of'. The intended meaning of the word 'dispose', accordingly,

---

[129] Section 115. See 15.1 and 15.2.4–15.2.6 above.
[130] Under the previous regime this requirement was introduced by s 21 of the Corporate Laws Amendment Act 24 of 2006, prior to which an ordinary resolution sufficed for a disposal in terms of s 228 of the 1973 Act.
[131] There are, however, some important differences between the exemption of intragroup disposals under the 1973 Act and that under s 112(1) of the new Act.
[132] Section 115(4).
[133] One may also have regard to s 70*dec*(2) of the Companies Act 46 of 1926, which introduced this provision.

is a transaction that 'would have the effect of permanently depriving the company of its right to ownership of the assets involved'.[134] More recently, the court held that 'dispose' in this context means a disposal in the form of a transfer of ownership.[135] The word 'dispose' in this context is thus given its ordinary meaning,[136] as opposed to any extended meaning.[137]

Based on this interpretation of the word 'dispose', the grant of a right of pre-emption does not fall within the meaning of the section. This is because a right of pre-emption (or a right of first refusal to purchase) is not a 'disposal' of any asset, but merely prevents the company from disposing of its assets pending the fulfilment of a condition.[138] In other words, the grant of a right of pre-emption is not an out-and-out disposal. All that the right of pre-emption does is to preclude the company from selling its undertaking to anyone else until the holder of the right of pre-emption has had the opportunity to exercise the pre-emptive right.

A pledge or cession *in securitatem debiti* similarly does not amount to an out-and-out disposal within the meaning of s 112. It has been held[139] that, in the case of a pledge, the pledgor retains dominium or ownership of the asset, and in the case of a cession *in securitatem debiti*, the cedent retains at least a reversionary right (ie there is an obligation on the cessionary to cede the right back to the cedent once the debt has been repaid). Since the word 'dispose' was found to mean the complete surrender of the assets in question, the court concluded that a pledge or a cession *in securitatem debiti* is not a 'disposal'.[140] However, the court stated further that it may be that, if the debtors abandon their original intention of repaying the debt, thereby causing the right of the cessionary to become absolute, there would then be a 'disposal' within the meaning of the section.[141]

The passing of a mortgage bond over assets is also not a disposal for these purposes because, like a pledge, it is not an absolute disposal of ownership. In *Standard Bank of South Africa Ltd v Hunkydory Investments 188 (Pty) Ltd (No. 2)* the issue before the court was whether the passing of mortgage bonds over the main asset of a company amounted to a disposal of the greater part of its assets (in terms of s 228 of the 1973 Act) that should have been approved by the shareholders. The court held that 'dispose' in this context means a disposal in the form of a transfer of ownership, rather than a transaction that exposes the company's

---

[134] See *Ally v Courtesy Wholesalers (Pty) Ltd* 1996 (3) SA 134 (N) 145D; *Alexander v Standard Merchant Bank Ltd* [1978] 3 All SA 109 (W) 116.
[135] *Standard Bank of South Africa Ltd v Hunkydory Investments 188 (Pty) Ltd (No. 2)* 2010 (1) SA 634 (WCC) at para 21, in relation to s 228 of the 1973 Act.
[136] *Standard Bank of South Africa Ltd v Hunkydory Investments 188 (Pty) Ltd (No. 2)* (supra). The court stated (at para 12) that the ordinary meaning of the phrase 'dispose of' is 'to make over or part with by way of sale or bargain, sell', 'to transfer into new hands or to the control of someone else (as by selling or bargaining away)' or the act of transferring ownership.
[137] The court in *Standard Bank of South Africa Ltd v Hunkydory Investments 188 (Pty) Ltd (No. 2)* (supra) considered the extended meaning of the word 'disposition' in s 1 of the Insolvency Act 24 of 1936 and in ss 340 and 341 of the 1973 Act and found that, while the extended meaning applies in the context of companies which are being wound up, s 228 applied in quite a different context.
[138] *Lindner v National Bakery (Pty) Ltd* 1961 (1) SA 372 (O).
[139] *Alexander v Standard Merchant Bank Ltd* [1978] 3 All SA 109 (W) 120.
[140] *Alexander v Standard Merchant Bank Ltd* (supra) at 116.
[141] *Alexander v Standard Merchant Bank Ltd* (supra) at 120.

assets to the risk of forced disposal because of borrowing.[142] The court accordingly found that the section does not apply to mortgages.

It is consequently submitted that 'dispose' in the context of s 112 similarly means a permanent transfer of the ownership of the assets in question (such as a sale) and does not include a mere encumbrance of the assets, as in a mortgage or pledge, or the grant of a pre-emptive right.[143]

(b) Meaning of 'the greater part'

Section 112 applies only where a company proposes to dispose of all or 'the greater part' of its assets or undertaking. The question must arise as to the meaning of the phrase 'the greater part'.

In this regard, s 112(4) of the Act states that:

> [a]ny part of the undertaking or assets of a company to be disposed of, as contemplated in this section, must be given its *fair market value* [emphasis added] as at the date of the proposal, in accordance with the financial reporting standards.[144]

The intention seems to be that, in determining whether 'the greater part' of the assets or undertaking of a company is being disposed of, the value of the relevant assets or undertaking must be calculated at fair market value as at the date of the proposal.[145]

Although the Act does not specify the scale for 'the greater part' of the assets or undertaking of a company,[146] it is submitted that the scale is tipped where more than 50 per cent of all the company's gross assets or more than 50 per cent of the value of the company's entire undertaking (at fair market value) are disposed of. Once the disposal entails more than 50 per cent of the fair market value of the company's gross assets or entire undertaking, this will trigger the shareholder protective mechanism of a special resolution to approve of the disposal. Accord-

---

[142] *Standard Bank of South Africa Ltd v Hunkydory Investments 188 (Pty) Ltd (No. 2)* 2010 (1) SA 634 (WCC) para 21.

[143] It must be noted, however, that there are some commentators who contend that the exact meaning of 'dispose' is still uncertain and that it does not necessarily entail a permanent divestment of ownership.

[144] The draft Companies Amendment Bill, 2010 (cl 66) proposes to delete the reference to 'financial reporting standards' and substitute for it the words 'as calculated in the prescribed manner'. ('Financial reporting standards', with respect to any particular company's financial statements, means the standards applicable to that company, as prescribed in terms of s 29(4) and (5) (s 1).)

[145] The uncertainty regarding the manner of determination of the 'date of the proposal' will be clarified by the draft Companies Amendment Bill, 2010. The Amendment Bill fortunately now proposes that the date is to be determined in the prescribed manner (presumably as prescribed by regulations in terms of the Act).

[146] Commendably, the draft Companies Amendment Bill, 2010 (cl 2(1)) now proposes to clarify this, by defining 'all or the greater part of the assets or undertaking' to mean, in the case of the company's assets, more than 50 per cent of its gross assets at fair market value, irrespective of its liabilities, or in the case of the company's undertaking, more than 50 per cent of the value of its entire undertaking at fair market value.' ('Asset' is proposed to be defined as a resource controlled by an entity as a result of past events, and from which future economic benefits are expected to flow. 'Liability' is defined by the draft Companies Amendment Bill as a present obligation of an entity arising from past events, the settlement of which is expected to result in an outflow from the entity of resources embodying economic benefits.)

ingly, in determining whether 'the greater part' of the assets or undertaking of a company is being disposed of, what is really required is a calculation of the value of the specific assets or undertaking *in relation to* the value of all of the assets or the entire undertaking of the company.

The method of calculation set out in s 112(4) may be referred to as a quantitative test, which is based on a mathematical asset calculation, that is, the size of the transaction in relation to the company. This may be contrasted with US law and Canadian law, which apply a combination of a qualitative and a quantitative approach.[147]

15.3.3 Approval and other requirements for s 112 disposals

(a) General

Section 112(2) provides that a company may not '*dispose*' of all or the greater part of its assets or undertaking unless:

(a) the disposal has been approved by a special resolution of the shareholders, in accordance with s 115, and
(b) the company has satisfied all other requirements set out in s 115, to the extent that those requirements are applicable to such a disposal by that company.

Section 115(1) in turn states that, despite s 65 and despite any contrary provision of a company's Memorandum of Incorporation or any board resolution or resolution of securities holders, a company may not '*dispose*' of, or '*give effect to an agreement*' or series of agreements to dispose of, all or the greater part of its assets or undertaking unless the disposal has been approved in terms of s 115 (which requires, inter alia, shareholder approval).

Consequently, according to s 112(2) read with s 115(1), unless the transaction has received the requisite shareholder approval, the company may neither '*dispose of*' nor '*give effect to an agreement*' to dispose of all or the greater part of its assets or undertaking. Furthermore, a third party to whom the assets or undertaking of a company are or is to be transferred may apply to a court (in terms of s 115(9)*(a)*) for an order to effect the transfer only if the transaction has been approved. The effect of these provisions accordingly is that if a s 112 disposal has not been approved by the shareholders, then the company is precluded from giving 'effect to' or implementing the transaction, while the third party is precluded from applying to a court for an order 'to effect' or enforce the transaction.

This, moreover, suggests that the controversy concerning the interaction

---

[147] The statutory tests in the USA and Canada distinguish between disposals which are and those which are not in the usual and regular course of business — see the US Revised Model Business Corporation Act, ss 12.01 and 12.02 and the Canada Business Corporations Act, R.S.C. 1985, c C–44, s 189(3). In the Canadian and US jurisprudence, both the qualitative and quantitative approaches are applied. A qualitative approach is based on the character of the assets being sold and the result. It essentially focuses on the nature of the transaction in relation to the regular course of business of the company, and whether the effect of the transaction is to destroy or fundamentally change the nature of the company's business.

between s 228 of the 1973 Act and the Turquand Rule could now be settled.[148] An important practical matter that gave rise to some debate under the previous company law regime was whether an innocent third party purchaser could rely on the Turquand Rule to *enforce* an agreement to dispose of all the assets of a company, even though the requisite shareholder approval had not been obtained and the innocent purchaser had been unaware of this lack of compliance.[149] The above provisions (ie s 115(1) read with ss 115(9) and 112(2)) arguably imply that the Turquand Rule does not operate in the context of s 112 disposals under the new Act since, failing shareholder approval, the transaction must not be effected or implemented (as explained above). However, the Act does not deal with this issue explicitly, and it remains to be seen how the courts will approach the matter.

The further question arises: Does the requirement of shareholder approval relate to the conclusion of the agreement of disposal or does it relate to the implementation of the agreement? In other words, is the agreement itself *binding* without shareholder approval? This is another issue that gave rise to considerable difficulty under the 1973 Act.[150] It is submitted that the the new Act, like the 1973 Act, is unclear in this regard. To elaborate, the words 'give effect to' in s 115(1) (above) apparently refer to the implementation of the agreement, whereas the word 'dispose' in both ss 115(1) and 112(2) (above) has two possible connotations, in that it could be interpreted to relate either 'to the conclusion of an agreement of disposal or to the implementation thereof'.[151] The matter thus remains uncertain and unsettled under the new Act.

The requirements for s 112 disposals are discussed in turn below. These require-

---

[148] It should be pointed out that the Turquand Rule never applied to special resolutions under the 1973 Act, as special resolutions were public documents and third parties were deemed to have constructive notice of them. However, under the new Act, in view of the general abolition of the doctrine of constructive notice (see s 19(4)), third parties are no longer deemed to have constructive knowledge of special resolutions. There is no longer any reason why the Turquand Rule and s 20(7) (the statutory Turquand Rule) should not apply where a special resolution is required as an internal formality. See further the discussion of the Turquand Rule and s 20(7) in chapter 5: Corporate Capacity, Agency and the Turquand Rule.

[149] See *Levy v Zalrut Investments (Pty) Ltd* 1986 (4) SA 479 (W) 487, where it was stated *obiter* that, due to the application of the Turquand Rule (ie that a person dealing with a company in good faith could assume that acts of internal management had been properly performed), the third party could assume that a resolution in terms of s 228 of the 1973 Act had been passed, and therefore the s 228 agreement was enforceable by the third party despite the lack of shareholder approval. See also the contrary decision in *Farren v Sun Service SA Photo Trip Management (Pty) Ltd* 2004 (2) SA 146 (C) which held that the agreement was unenforceable, and that the Turquand Rule was inapplicable to s 228. The court in *Farren's* case stated that, if the Turquand Rule were to apply to s 228, this would nullify the protection of shareholders, which could not have been the intention of the legislature. The court ruled further that the fact that the provisions were embodied in statute gave them far more weight than if they were to be embodied in the constitution of the company.

[150] See eg *Ally v Courtesy Wholesalers (Pty) Ltd* 1996 (3) SA 134 (N). This case favoured the view that the prohibition relates to the implementation rather than the conclusion of the agreement (at 145).

[151] As stated in *Ally v Courtesy Wholesalers (Pty) Ltd* (supra) at 145.

ments apply also to amalgamations or mergers,[152] and have been discussed in detail above in that context. The reader is accordingly cross-referred to the section on amalgamations or mergers where appropriate. It is noteworthy that the approval requirements for s 112 disposals apply not only to an agreement but also to a 'series of agreements'[153] to dispose of all or the greater part of a company's assets or undertaking.

(b) *Special resolution of the shareholders*

A company may not dispose of all or the greater part of its assets or undertaking unless the disposal has been approved by a special resolution of the shareholders.[154] It is the shareholders of the disposing company (ie the company that wishes to dispose of all or the greater part of its assets or undertaking) whose approval is required. The approval of the shareholders of the acquiring company (ie the company that wishes to acquire the relevant assets or undertaking, assuming that the acquirer is a company) is not required by the section. This may be contrasted with an amalgamation or merger, where the shareholders of all the constituent amalgamating or merging companies must approve the transaction.

A special resolution for a s 112 disposal is effective only to the extent that it authorises or ratifies a *specific* transaction.[155] In other words, the directors are prevented from obtaining a general authority to enter into any agreement for the disposal of all or the greater part of the assets or undertaking of a company as they might in future deem advisable.[156] It is also notable that a s 112 transaction may either be authorised or ratified. The section thus creates scope for the authorisation or approval of a transaction in advance of it being made, as well as the ratification of a transaction that has already been entered into by the company. (Importantly, however, the draft Companies Amendment Bill, 2010 proposes to jettison the reference to the ratification of s 112 transactions.[157])

A notice of the shareholders' meeting to consider the resolution for the s 112 disposal must be delivered to each shareholder of the company, within the prescribed time and in the prescribed manner.[158] The notice must include or be accompanied by a written summary of the precise terms of the transaction or series of transactions to be considered at the meeting. It must also include or be accompanied by a written summary of the provisions of ss 115 and 164 of the Act,

---

[152] Section 115. The heading of s 115 is incomplete as it states 'Required approval for transactions contemplated in Part' while omitting to specify the relevant Part. It is presumably intended to refer to Part A of Chapter 5, as appears from the content of s 115.
[153] See s 115(1) and s 112(3).
[154] Section 112(2)(a) and s 115(2)(a) read with s 115(1).
[155] Section 112(5). *Ally v Courtesy Wholesalers (Pty) Ltd* 1996 (3) SA 134 (N) 146 stated that the meaning of 'specific' is 'capable of being exactly named or indicated'. The resolution must thus must authorise a transaction which is either 'exactly named or capable of being so'.
[156] *Lindner v National Bakery (Pty) Ltd* 1961 (1) SA 372 (O) 379 in relation to the previous regimes. The object of the section is evidently that the shareholders are to exercise control over such disposals.
[157] Clause 66 of the draft Companies Amendment Bill, 2010.
[158] This is proposed to be subject to s 62 (regarding notice of meetings). See the draft Companies Amendment Bill, 2010 (cl 66).

relating to the required approvals for the transaction and the appraisal rights of dissenting shareholders.[159] This is important, because shareholders may be unaware of their appraisal rights and how to exercise them, or of the court approval provisions.

The special resolution approving the proposed s 112 disposal must be adopted at a meeting called for that purpose. The quorum for the meeting is constituted by the presence of sufficient persons to exercise, in aggregate, at least 25 per cent of all the voting rights that are entitled to be exercised on that matter.[160] A special resolution must be adopted with the support of at least 75 per cent of the voting rights that are exercised on the resolution.[161] The requirement of a special resolution for s 112 disposals ensures appropriate protection of minority shareholders, while at the same time preserving flexibility for companies to effect fundamental changes without being frustrated by a troublesome minority.[162]

It is important for the purposes of the shareholders' special resolution that any voting rights controlled by an 'acquiring party', or a person related to an acquiring party, or one 'acting in concert' with either of them, are disqualified from voting.[163] It has been submitted[164] that the object of this provision is to introduce a minority protection measure, in that it would prevent a conflict of interest in an interested transaction (as opposed to an arm's-length transaction), where a party is simultaneously both the acquiring party in a s 112 disposal and a shareholder in the disposing company. In these cases the acquiring party, due to its conflict of interest, is precluded from voting its shares on the disposing company's special resolution in respect of the transaction.

See further 15.2.4(c) above for a detailed discussion of the shareholder approval provisions in fundamental transactions, including the quorum requirement, the percentage support for the resolution, the implications of the exclusion of s 65 of the Act in terms of s 115(1), and the minority protection measure in terms of s 115(4).

(c) Special resolution of the holding company

A special resolution of the holding company is required for s 112 disposals only in certain circumstances. It applies in respect of a proposed disposal of all or the greater part of the assets or undertaking of a company that is a *subsidiary* of a South African company or an external company,[165] where the disposal by the relevant subsidiary company will (having regard to the holding company's consolidated financial statements) substantially constitute a disposal of all or the greater part of the assets or undertaking of the holding company. In these circum-

---

[159] Section 112(3).
[160] Section 115(2)(a).
[161] See further 15.2.4(c) above, for a discussion of the provisions of s 65(10) of the Act and other aspects of the shareholder approval provisions.
[162] Maleka Femida Cassim (Part I) op cit n 7 at 8–11.
[163] Section 115(4). See further the discussion of s 115(4) in 15.2.4(c) and 15.2.14 above.
[164] Maleka Femida Cassim (Part II) op cit n 8 at 149–153.
[165] An 'external company' is defined in s 1 as a foreign company that is carrying on business, or non-profit activities, as the case may be, within South Africa, subject to s 23(2). See further chapter 3: Types of Companies.

stances, the transaction is also subject to the approval (by special resolution) of the shareholders of the *holding* company.[166] It must be stressed that such transactions require the approval of both sets of shareholders, ie that of the disposing subsidiary company as well as that of its holding company.[167]

The special resolution of the holding company must be adopted in the same manner as required for the special resolution of the disposing subsidiary company itself.[168] Any voting rights controlled by an acquiring party, a person related to an acquiring party, or a person acting in concert with either of them are similarly disqualified from voting in support of the resolution of the holding company.[169]

This provision serves as a protective measure for the shareholders of the holding company. It gives them both voting rights and appraisal rights in respect of relevant s 112 disposals by its subsidiary company.

(d) Takeover Regulation Panel

To the extent that Part B and Part C of Chapter 5 and the Takeover Regulations apply to a company, the company may not implement a s 112 disposal, unless the Takeover Regulation Panel has issued a compliance certificate in respect of the transaction or has exempted the transaction.[170]

(e) Court approval

The approval of the court is not a general or automatic requirement for s 112 disposals or other fundamental transactions, but is instead restricted to certain specified circumstances.[171] As pointed out (in 15.1 above), this approach to court approval under the new Act now applies also to disposals of all or the greater part of the assets or undertaking of a company, in contrast with the 1973 Act.

For a detailed discussion of court approval of fundamental transactions, including the circumstances in which court approval is required, the grounds on which a court may set aside a resolution in respect of a s 112 disposal, and the distinction and interplay between the 'remedy' of court approval and the appraisal remedy, refer to 15.2.5 above.

(f) Appraisal rights of dissenting shareholders

The appraisal right applies to all the fundamental transactions, including a s 112 disposal. Section 115(8) provides that the holder of any voting rights in a company

---

[166] Section 115(2)(*b*). The word 'substantially' in s 115(2)(*b*)(iii) is proposed to be deleted by the draft Companies Amendment Bill, 2010 (cl 68). A 'special resolution' of an external company means a decision by its owners or another authorised person that requires the highest level of support to be adopted in terms of the relevant law under which the external company was incorporated (cl 2(1)(*cc*) of the draft Companies Amendment Bill, 2010).
[167] Note the use of the word 'and' at the end of paragraphs *(a)* and *(b)* of s 115(2).
[168] That is, by a special resolution adopted by persons entitled to exercise voting rights on such a matter, at a meeting called for that purpose and at which sufficient persons are present to exercise, in aggregate, at least 25 per cent of all of the voting rights that are entitled to be exercised on that matter (s 115(2)(*a*) and *(b)*).
[169] Section 115(4).
[170] Section 115(1)(*b*) read with s 119(4)(*b*) and (6) and the draft Companies Amendment Bill, 2010 (cl 68).
[171] Section 115(2)(*c*). Court approval is required in the circumstances and manner contemplated in s 115(3)–(6) of the Act.

is entitled to seek relief in terms of s 164 (dealing with the dissenting shareholders' appraisal rights) if that person *(a)* had notified the company in advance of the intention to oppose the special resolution for the fundamental transaction, and *(b)* had been present at the meeting and voted against that special resolution. A mere abstention from voting will not suffice. The importance of the appraisal right is that it allows the dissenting shareholders to *opt out* of the fundamental transaction — but not to prevent it.

For a discussion of the appraisal right, see 15.2.6 above and chapter 16: Shareholder Remedies and Minority Protection.

(g) Other

Finally, once a s 112 disposal (or other fundamental transaction) has been approved, any person to whom assets are or an undertaking is to be transferred may, if necessary in the circumstances, apply to a court for an order to give effect to the transaction. This may include (where relevant) an order to effect:

- the transfer of the relevant undertaking, assets and liabilities,
- the allotment and appropriation of any relevant shares or similar interests,
- the transfer of shares from one person to another,
- the dissolution without winding-up of a company, as contemplated in the transaction,
- any other relief necessary or appropriate to give effect to and properly implement an amalgamation or merger, or
- any incidental, consequential and supplemental matters that are necessary for the effectiveness and completion of the transaction.[172]

It is noteworthy that in a s 112 disposal, the parties have to comply with the relevant legal formalities for the transfer of the assets or undertaking. There is no automatic transfer by operation of law, as occurs in the case of a statutory merger which, as discussed in 15.2 above, has the great advantages of the automatic transfer by operation of law of all the property and obligations of the constituent merging companies to the merged company, and the dissolution of the disappearing companies without the need for a formal winding-up.

15.3.4 Exemptions

Certain proposals to dispose of all or the greater part of the assets or undertaking of a company are exempt from the approval and other requirements (of ss 112 and 115) set out above. First, these requirements do not apply to a proposal for a s 112 disposal if the disposal constitutes a transaction that is pursuant to or contemplated in a business rescue plan adopted in accordance with Chapter 6 of the Act.[173]

Secondly, an exemption is granted where a s 112 disposal constitutes a transaction between a wholly owned subsidiary and its holding company.[174] Thirdly, a s 112 disposal is exempt if the disposal constitutes a transaction between or among:

---
[172] Section 115(9).
[173] Section 112(1)*(a)*. See also s 115(1)*(a)*(ii).
[174] Section 112(1)*(b)*.

(i) two or more wholly-owned subsidiaries of the same holding company, or
(ii) a wholly-owned subsidiary of a holding company, on the one hand, and its holding company and one or more wholly-owned subsidiaries of that holding company, on the other hand.[175]

The exemption of these 'intragroup' transactions avoids the unnecessary delay, costs and inconvenience associated with convening a shareholders' meeting and, more importantly, the exercise of appraisal rights. This applies particularly where the disposing company is the wholly owned subsidiary, in which the holding company holds all the voting rights, with the effect that the favourable vote of the wholly owned subsidiary on the transaction (if this were required) would be a non-issue or a superfluous formality.

15.4 SCHEMES OF ARRANGEMENT

15.4.1 Introduction

A scheme of arrangement is a fundamental transaction and as such must comply with the requirements of s 115.[176] However, it must also meet certain requirements peculiar only to schemes of arrangement. The Act has radically reformed the procedure in relation to the scheme of arrangement, most notably by doing away with the two court applications previously required in terms of s 311 of the 1973 Act and (in addition to s 115) introducing new, detailed requirements in relation to the retention of an independent expert by the company and the preparation and circulation of a report by that expert.[177] In the process one of the most attractive features of the use of a scheme of arrangement as a takeover mechanism (namely, the (effectively) lower voting threshold required to engineer a takeover) has also been removed. This aspect will be discussed in more detail below.

15.4.2 Proposal for scheme of arrangement

The board of directors of a company may propose a scheme of arrangement between the company and the holders of any class of its securities. However, the board is prohibited from doing so if the company is in liquidation or in the course of business rescue proceedings in terms of Chapter 6 of the Act.[178] The arrangement may be implemented subject to the required approvals contained in Chapter 5 of the Act being obtained.[179] The arrangement may include a reorganisation of the share capital of the company which can be effected in a variety of ways, namely by way of:

- a consolidation of securities of different classes,
- a division of securities into different classes,

---
[175] Section 112(1)(c).
[176] Section 115(1).
[177] See s 114 generally.
[178] Presumably this is to preserve the integrity of the liquidation and the business rescue processes which are subject to specific rules and procedures.
[179] Section 114(1). See also ss 114(2), 114(3) and 115 in relation to the various approvals and other requirements.

- an expropriation of securities from the holder,[180]
- exchanging any of its securities for other securities,
- a reacquisition by the company of its securities,[181] or
- a combination of the above methods.

Note that this does not constitute a *numerus clausus* of methods for reorganisation of share capital nor of the purposes for which a scheme of arrangement may be utilised as the list is preceded by the words 'may include.' and 'by way of, among other things — '.[182] There is case law to the effect that, when a specific procedure has been laid down for the attainment of something by the (then 1973) Act, the procedure must be complied with and that a scheme of arrangement cannot be utilised instead.[183] To effect the procedure legally, the prescribed procedure had to be used. More recently, it has been held that the scheme of arrangement procedure could legitimately be used to require individual shareholders to participate in certain black empowerment initiatives. The court agreed that, on the facts of the case, the scheme of arrangement procedure was appropriate and that agreement could not practically have been achieved by other convenient means.[184]

There is no reference in this section to the scheme of arrangement being or becoming binding on all the members of the company.[185] This is because the mechanism is no longer necessary — the shareholders and company are bound by virtue of the fact that the requisite special resolution is passed in terms of s 115.

A further change is that the drafters of the Act have physically separated the sections regulating a scheme of arrangement between a company and its shareholders from the sections regulating a compromise between a company and its creditors.[186] Originally these two procedures were intertwined in the same section.[187] It is submitted that this separation of the two concepts is a sensible legislative development.

15.4.3 Background

As was intimated above, the removal of the requirement of the approval of the court constitutes a fundamental departure from the process previously prescribed under the 1973 Act. Section 311 of that Act required:

- an application to the court for leave to convene a scheme meeting to be summoned in such manner as the court directed,
- a majority representing three-fourths (ie 75 per cent) of the votes exercisable by the members or class of members present and voting at the scheme meeting to agree to the arrangement,

---

[180] See the discussion in 15.4.3 which deals with the impact of this particular subsection.
[181] See further 6.11.
[182] Section 114(1).
[183] *Ex parte NBSA Centre Ltd* 1987 (2) SA 783 (W) 796. (*In casu* the prescribed procedure dealt with a capital reduction.)
[184] *Standard Bank Group Ltd and Liberty Group Ltd, Ex parte* [2007] 4 All SA 1298 (W).
[185] As there was in s 311(2) of the 1973 Act.
[186] See s 155.
[187] See Chapter XII of the 1973 Act.

- a second application to court to sanction the results of the scheme meeting, and
- lodgement of the court order with the Registrar and the registration thereof in order to make it effective.

If all the above requirements were met, the arrangement became binding on all the members or the relevant class of members and on the company.[188] This process had two important implications: first, the shareholders of the company enjoyed the automatic protection of the court's scrutiny of the substance of the scheme (as set out in the court papers) as well as the procedures followed at the scheme meeting. Secondly, the majority required to approve the scheme of arrangement was only 75 per cent of the members *present and voting in person or by proxy*. Not only was there no quorum requirement set, but because members who did not attend the meeting or submit proxy forms were disregarded as part of the total shareholding in the company when calculating the number of votes in favour of the scheme of arrangement, the 75 per cent majority could be more easily achieved.[189] This made schemes of arrangement particularly attractive to an offeror who wanted to acquire complete control (ie 100 per cent of the shareholding) of a target company, but was unsure whether it would achieve the requisite 90 per cent majority required to squeeze out minority shareholders in terms of s 440K of the 1973 Act.[190]

To illustrate, offeror A could propose a scheme of arrangement between company B and its members in terms of which the members were paid a scheme consideration of R10 per share. Assume that the court application for leave to convene a scheme meeting was granted and that the scheme of arrangement was approved at the scheme meeting by 75 per cent of the scheme members present and voting. (Note that the approval of, for example, 75 per cent of 50 per cent of the company would be sufficient if only 50 per cent of the shareholders attended the meeting or were represented there. This amounts to approval by 37,5 per cent of the company). If the court then sanctioned the results of the scheme meeting and the order was duly registered, the rest of the shareholders (in this example 62,5 per cent — being those who either attended the meeting and abstained or voted against the scheme, as well as those who did not attend) would be bound by the scheme in terms of the 1973 Act. Thus they would be forced to part with their shares at R10 per share — in essence an expropriation of their property authorised by 37,5 per cent of the shareholders of the company. In this way the offeror could acquire 100 per cent of the shareholding in the company. Had the same offeror

---

[188] See s 311(1) of the 1973 Act.
[189] Note, however, that there was an inherent limitation contained in the section as to the level of support required for the arrangement. Section 311(5) provided that the court, in determining whether the arrangement should be sanctioned, was obliged to have regard to the number of members (or members of a class) present or represented at the meeting and voting in favour of the compromise. However, there was no formal quorum requirement. It is interesting that the court was enjoined to look at the *number* of voters as opposed to what percentage of the voting contingent of the company they represented. Furthermore, it seems that the 1973 Act may have obliged the court to have regard to the number of shareholder attendees *voting in favour*, not the number of attendees generally.
[190] See 15.5.10.

Fundamental Transactions, Takeovers and Offers 661

wanted to obtain control in terms of a general offer to shareholders, 90 per cent of the shareholders would have had to accept his or her offer of R10 per share in order for him or her to oblige the remaining shareholders to sell their shares in order to give him or her complete control.[191]

As it was not originally intended or envisaged by the legislature that s 311 of the 1973 Act would serve purely as a takeover mechanism in this way, a substantive portion of the case law in this area revolves around the issue of whether the scheme in question (namely that the shareholders in the target entity return their shares to the company and get cash in exchange) qualified as a scheme of arrangement within the meaning of the 1973 Act.[192] By using the term 'expropriation', it seems that s 114(1)*(c)* of the Act has put paid to this legal debate. A scheme which amounts to 'taking securities for cash' (ie an offer with the intent to effect a takeover) will now qualify as a scheme of arrangement within the meaning of the Act.[193] The holders of securities have been denuded of the automatic protection of the court by the change in procedure in relation to schemes of arrangement in the Act, but this has been tempered by the fact that the majority threshold to be met in these circumstances is no longer potentially so low. The approval of 75 per cent of the shareholders must be obtained by way of special resolution in terms of s 115.

15.4.4 Approval and other requirements for schemes of arrangement

(a) General

The approval procedure for a scheme of arrangement is now on par with the procedures for other fundamental transactions. Thus, a scheme of arrangement cannot be implemented unless and until it has been approved in terms of s 115 of the Act. Simply put, this means that a scheme of arrangement must be approved by a special resolution at a meeting called for that purpose. The quorum required is the presence of persons sufficient to exercise at least 25 per cent of the voting rights entitled to be exercised on that matter. A special resolution requires the support of at least 75 per cent of the voting rights exercised on that resolution in order to be adopted. (Refer to 15.2.4*(c)* on requisite approvals of the merger

---

[191] See s 440K of the 1973 Act.

[192] See Blackman et al *Commentary on the Companies Act* vol 3 15A–22 to 15A–27.

[193] In the course of this debate the view was taken that, to qualify as an arrangement, there must at least be a rearrangement of the shareholder's rights in the broad sense. An issue to the shareholder of shares in the offeror would qualify as such a rearrangement of rights, as would a share exchange with the option of a cash alternative. However, the total disappearance of a shareholder's rights against a purely monetary consideration would not qualify; this amounted to expropriation in the primary sense. This view was followed in *Ex parte Natal Coal Exploration Co Ltd* 1985 (4) SA 279 (W) where Stegmann J held that expropriation of rights of a shareholder in this sense (ie where a shareholder receives a sum of money as compensation) is, no matter how fair the assessment of the compensation, a concept which falls outside the legitimate sense of the term 'arrangement' in the context of s 311. However, in *Ex parte Suiderland Development Corporation* 1986 (2) SA 442 (C) Van den Heever J held that payment of money to the shareholders whose shares are to be expropriated could qualify as an 'arrangement'. See, however, *Ex parte Mielie-Kip Ltd* 1991 (3) SA 449 (W) 453 where it appears that this line of reasoning has been abandoned altogether.

(s 115) with reference to the statutory merger procedure for a detailed exposition. Although that part of the chapter deals specifically with mergers, the main requirements of s 115 are the same for all fundamental transactions and therefore the observations made there will apply equally to schemes of arrangement.)

The scheme of arrangement may also require the approval of the court in exceptional circumstances. The approval is required where the special resolution was opposed by at least 15 per cent of the voting rights voted on it and any person who had voted against it requires the company to seek court approval. The company bears the costs of this application. The approval of the court is also required where, regardless of the percentage of support for the resolution, any person who voted against the resolution successfully applies for leave to make an application to court for a review of the transaction. For a far more detailed discussion of the process see 15.2.5 above on court approval.

(b) Independent expert

The company must retain an independent expert to compile a report concerning the proposed scheme of arrangement. This is not a specific prerequisite for other fundamental transactions in terms of Chapter 5 of the Act. In terms of s 114(2) the independent expert must meet the following requirements:

(a) The person to be retained must be —
  (i) qualified, and have the competence and experience necessary to —
     (aa) understand the type of arrangement proposed;
     (bb) evaluate the consequences of the arrangement; and
     (cc) assess the effect of the arrangement on the value of securities and on the rights and interests of a holder of any securities, or a creditor of the company; and
  (ii) able to express opinions, exercise judgment and make decisions impartially.
(b) the person to be retained must not —
  (i) have any other relationship with the company or with a proponent of the arrangement, such as would lead a reasonable and informed third party to conclude that the integrity, impartiality or objectivity of that person is compromised by that relationship;
  (ii) have had any relationship contemplated in subparagraph (i) within the immediately preceding two years;
  (iii) be related to a person who has or has had a relationship contemplated in subparagraph (i) or (ii).

(c) Report

The independent expert must prepare a report to the board concerning the proposed arrangement. He or she must cause the report to be distributed to all holders of the company's securities. Section 114(3) states that the report must, *at least*, do the following:

(a) state all prescribed information relevant to the value of the securities affected by the proposed arrangement;
(b) identify every type and class of holders of the company's securities affected by the proposed arrangement;
(c) describe the material effects that the proposed arrangement will have on the rights and interests of the persons mentioned in paragraph *(b)*;
(d) evaluate any material adverse effects of the proposed arrangement against —

(i) the compensation that any of those persons will receive in terms of that arrangement; and
(ii) any reasonably probable beneficial and significant effect of that arrangement on the business and prospects of the company;
(e) state any material interest of any director of the company or trustee for security holders, and state the effect of the arrangement on those interests and persons;
(f) state the effect of the proposed arrangement on the interest and person contemplated in paragraph (e); and
(g) include a copy of sections 115 and 164.

Sections 115 relates to approval for fundamental transactions and s 164 to appraisal rights of dissenting shareholders.

(d) Takeover Regulation Panel

To the extent that Part B and Part C of Chapter 5, as well as the Takeover Regulations apply to a company, the company may not implement a scheme of arrangement unless the Takeover Regulation Panel has issued a compliance certificate in respect of the transaction or has exempted the transaction.[194]

(e) Court approval

As explained above, the approval of the court is not a general or automatic requirement for schemes of arrangement or other fundamental transactions, but is instead restricted to certain specified circumstances.[195]

Refer to 15.2.5 above for a detailed discussion of court approval of fundamental transactions. As was pointed out above, this is one of the cardinal amendments to the scheme of arrangement process. It is noteworthy that the report of the independent expert must contain a copy of s 115, presumably to remind the holders of the company's securities (or alert them if they had been unaware) of their rights in this regard.

(f) Appraisal rights of dissenting shareholders

The appraisal right applies to all the fundamental transactions, including a scheme of arrangement. Section 115(8) provides that the holder of any voting rights in a company is entitled to seek relief in terms of s 164 (dealing with the dissenting shareholders' appraisal rights) if that person (a) had notified the company in advance of the intention to oppose the special resolution for the fundamental transaction, and (b) had been present at the meeting and voted against that special resolution. A mere abstention from voting would not suffice. The importance of the appraisal right is that it allows the dissenting shareholders to *opt out* of the fundamental transaction — but not to prevent it. For a detailed discussion of the appraisal right, refer to chapter 16: Shareholder Remedies and Minority Protection; see also 15.2.6 above on appraisal rights of dissenting shareholders. It is noteworthy that the report of the independent expert must contain a copy of s 164,

---

[194] Section 115(1)(b) read with s 119(4)(b) and (6) and the draft Companies Amendment Bill, 2010 (cl 68).
[195] Section 115(2)(c). Court approval is required in the circumstances and manner contemplated in s 115(3)–(6) of the Act.

again presumably to remind the holders of the company's securities (or alert them if they were unaware) of their rights in this regard.

(g) Other

Finally, once a scheme of arrangement (or other fundamental transaction) has been approved, any person to whom assets are or an undertaking is to be transferred may, if necessary in the circumstances, apply to a court for an order to give effect to the transaction. This may include (where relevant):

- an order to effect the transfer of the relevant undertaking, assets and liabilities,
- the allotment and appropriation of any relevant shares or similar interests,
- the transfer of shares from one person to another,
- the dissolution without winding-up of a company, as contemplated in the transaction, any other relief necessary or appropriate to give effect to and properly implement an amalgamation or merger, or
- any incidental, consequential and supplemental matters that are necessary to effect and complete the transaction.[196]

It is noteworthy that, in a scheme of arrangement (as in a s 112 disposal), the parties would have to comply with the relevant legal formalities for the transfer of the assets (such as securities) or undertaking. There is no automatic transfer by operation of law, as in the case of a statutory merger.

15.5 TAKEOVERS AND OFFERS

15.5.1 General

This area of company law is primarily concerned with transactions which result, or may result, in the acquisition of control or a change in control of a regulated company. These types of transactions (as well as the actions of the parties involved) are carefully regulated to ensure that all shareholders are treated equally and fairly and have equal access to the same information. This serves to protect those shareholders who are not in control of the company (minority shareholders) as well as the integrity of the market. The vast majority of the provisions and regulations dealing with takeovers are aimed at achieving these objectives.

15.5.2 Applicable legislation

The law which applies to takeovers and offers is contained principally in Part B and Part C of the Act and in the Takeover Regulations which are intended to give effect to this part of the Act.[197] The Takeover Regulations are prescribed by the Minister, in consultation with the Takeovers Regulation Panel ('the Panel'). In terms of s 120, they should provide for compliance with (and enforcement of) the provisions of Part B and Part C of the Act, the administration, operation and procedures of the Panel, prescribed fees and levies on certain companies, and any other matters relating to the powers and functions of the Panel. Draft Takeover Regulations dealing with these issues as well as a substantial number of additional

---

[196] Section 115(9).
[197] See s 120.

regulations in connection with Chapter 5 of the Act were published in December 2009.[198] It should be borne in mind that, to some extent, the JSE Listings Requirements also deal with takeovers and offers where one or more of the parties involved is a listed entity, because they contain, for example, requirements relating to disclosure, prohibited dealing, circulars and announcements. However, the focus in this section is on the provisions of the Act and (to a lesser extent) the Takeover Regulations.[199]

15.5.3 Key definitions

To a large extent the law relating to takeovers and offers — and its application in practice — hinges on certain key definitions contained in the Act.[200] Thus, the Act and Takeover Regulations apply to 'an affected transaction' or an 'offer' involving certain types of companies. Obviously it then becomes very important to ascertain whether a particular transaction qualifies as an affected transaction or not, or whether an offer constitutes an offer within the meaning of the definition to establish whether it falls within the ambit of the regulation. This is not always a simple exercise, because offers and transactions can be structured in many complex ways. Two of the most important definitions that need to be considered to establish whether a transaction falls under the auspices of the Panel are the definition of 'affected transaction' and the definition of 'offer'. In terms of s 117(1)(c) an 'affected transaction' means:

 (i) a transaction or series of transactions amounting to the disposal of all or the greater parts of the assets or undertaking of a regulated company as contemplated in section 112, subject to section 118(3);[201]
 (ii) an amalgamation or merger, as contemplated in section 113, if it involves at least one regulated company, subject to section 118(3);
 (iii) a scheme of arrangement between a regulated company and its shareholders, as contemplated in section 114, subject to section 118(3);
 (iv) the acquisition of, or announced intention to acquire, a beneficial interest in any voting securities of a regulated company to the extent and in the circumstances contemplated in section 122(1);
 (v) the announced intention to acquire an beneficial interest in the remaining voting securities of a regulated company not already held by a person or persons acting in concert;
 (vi) a mandatory offer as contemplated in section 123; or
 (vii) compulsory acquisition as contemplated in section 124.

In terms or s 117(1)(f) an 'offer' means a proposal of any sort, including a partial offer, which, if accepted, will result in an affected transaction, other than such a transaction that is exempted in terms of s 118(3). It will be noted that, unless exempted, all fundamental transactions are affected transactions and are therefore

---

[198] GN 1664 of 2009 in *GG* 32832 of 22 December 2009. See Regulations 87–128.
[199] I intend to deal broadly with the relevant Takeover Regulations, but as these are currently in draft form and as it is almost certain that they will change (possibly quite substantially) prior to finalisation, I do not deal with each of them in detail.
[200] See s 117 and Regulations 87 and 88.
[201] Section 118(3) exempts fundamental transactions pursuant to or contemplated in a business rescue plan in terms of Chapter 6 of the Act from the application of Part B and Part C of Chapter 5 and the Takeover Regulations.

subject to the jurisdiction of the Panel. It will also be noted that these definitions contain internal references to other defined terms or sections that can make the legislation and its application to a particular set of facts quite complicated. So, for example, a 'regulated company' is separately defined in s 117(1)*(i)* as a company to which Part B, Part C and the Takeover Regulations apply as determined in accordance with s 118(1) and (2), and to 'act in concert' is defined in 117(1)*(b)* as any action pursuant to an agreement between or among two or more persons, in terms of which any of them co-operate for the purpose of entering into or proposing an affected transaction or offer.[202]

15.5.4 Application of the Act and the Takeover Regulations

The takeover provisions do not apply to all companies; they apply only to 'regulated companies', as determined in accordance with s 118(1) and (2). Section 118 states that the provisions of the Act and the Takeover Regulations will apply with respect to an affected transaction or an offer involving a profit company or its securities if the company is:

- a public company,
- a state-owned company (except if the company has been exempted in terms of s 9), or
- a private company, but only if:
    - more than the prescribed percentage[203] of its issued securities have been transferred (other than between related or interrelated persons) within the 24-month period before the date of a particular affected transaction or offer, or
    - its Memorandum of Incorporation expressly provides that the company and its securities are subject to Part B, Part C and the Takeover Regulations.

Despite the definition of 'affected transaction', Part B, Part C and the Takeover Regulations do not apply to fundamental transactions involving a regulated company if such an affected transaction is pursuant to, or contemplated in, an approved business rescue plan in terms of Chapter 6 of the Act.[204] Furthermore, in the event of a conflict between any provision of Part B, Part C or the Takeover

---

[202] For the purposes of Part B, Part C and the Takeover Regulations, two or more related or interrelated persons are regarded to have acted in concert, unless there is satisfactory evidence that they have acted independently in any particular matter. To make sense of this necessitates an examination of the terms 'related' and 'inter-related' *[sic]* as defined in s 1 of the Act. Furthermore, in terms of s 118(5), a person granted an option to acquire shares with a voting right in a regulated company is presumed to have acted in concert with the grantor of the option, unless the voting right is retained by the grantor. However, such a presumption may be rebutted by evidence to the contrary. The rationale behind identifying parties acting in concert and attributing obligations and responsibilities to them is legislative recognition of the fact that the acquisition and exercise of control of a company is often a joint effort. See further Regulation 90.

[203] The prescribed percentage referred to is regulated by s 118(2), which states that the Minister, after consulting with the Panel, may prescribe a minimum percentage (which may not be less than 10 per cent) of the issued securities of a private company, which will apply in the 24-month period preceding a particular affected transaction as contemplated in s 118(1)*(c)*.

[204] Section 118(3).

Fundamental Transactions, Takeovers and Offers 667

Regulations and any other provision of another public regulation, the conflicting provisions will apply concurrently if this is possible and, to the extent that it is impossible, the provisions of the other public regulation will prevail.[205]

15.5.5 Regulation of takeovers and offers by the Panel in accordance with the objectives of the Act

The Panel must regulate affected transactions in accordance with the Act and the Takeover Regulations. However, the Panel should not have regard to the commercial advantages or disadvantages of any transaction or proposed transaction. The object of the regulation by the Panel is to:

- ensure the integrity of the market place and fairness to the holders of securities of regulated companies,
- ensure the provision of necessary information to the holders of securities of regulated companies to the extent that they require this to make fair and informed decisions,
- ensure the provision of adequate time for regulated companies and holders of their securities to obtain and provide advice with respect to offers, and
- prevent actions by a regulated company that are designed to impede, frustrate, or defeat an offer or the making of fair and informed decisions by the holders of that company's securities.[206]

These are the stated objectives of the Act with regard to takeover regulation and, for the sake of convenience, are hereafter referred to as 'the objectives'.[207]

The Panel is enjoined by the Act to regulate any affected transactional offer (and the conduct of the parties in respect of any transactional offer) in a manner that promotes the objectives.[208] Furthermore, in terms of s 119(2) the regulation and manner of regulation by the Panel must ensure:

(a) that no person may enter into an affected transaction unless that person is ready, able and willing to implement that transaction;
(b) that all holders of —
  (i) any particular class of voting securities of an offeree regulated company are afforded equivalent treatment; and
  (ii) voting securities of an offeree regulated company are afforded equitable treatment, having regard to the circumstances;

---

[205] Section 118(4).
[206] Section 119 (1)(a)–(c).
[207] The predecessor of the Takeover Regulations was the Securities Regulation Code ('the Code') on takeovers and mergers, which came into force on 1 February 1991. The Code contained 11 general principles which were 'to be observed in affected transactions . . . are essentially a codification of acceptable standards of commercial behaviour and . . . have an obvious and universal application'. To illustrate the application of the general principles and designate procedures designed to govern certain types of affected transaction, the Code also contained 36 rules. The stated purpose of the Code was to ensure fair and equal treatment of all holders of relevant securities in relation to affected transactions. Furthermore, it was to provide an orderly framework within which affected transactions were to be conducted. The Code also sought to protect minority shareholders. Some of the provisions in the Act are similar to those in the Code while some are entirely new. Many provisions contained in the Code have been omitted in the new Act.
[208] Section 119(2).

(c) that no relevant information is withheld from the holders of relevant securities; and
(d) that all holders of relevant securities —
  (i) receive the same information from an offeror, potential offeror, or offeree regulated company during the course of an affected transaction, or when an affected transaction is contemplated; and
  (ii) are provided sufficient information, and permitted sufficient time, to enable them to reach a properly informed decision.

Note, however, that this does not prohibit the furnishing of information in confidence by an offeree company to a *bona fide* potential offeror or vice versa, or the issue of circulars by brokers or advisers to any party to the transaction to their own investment clients where the prior approval of the Panel has been obtained.[209] These are acceptable practices.

In carrying out its mandate, the Panel may require the filing of any document with respect to an affected transaction or offer if the document is required to be prepared in terms of Part B, Part C or the Takeover Regulations. The Panel may also issue clearance notices and initiate or receive complaints, conduct investigations and issue compliance notices with respect to any affected transaction or offer.[210]

To the extent necessary to ensure compliance with Part B, Part C or the Takeover Regulations and to fulfil the objectives of the Act, a compliance notice may, inter alia, prohibit or require any action by a person, or order a person to divest an acquired asset or account for profits.[211]

15.5.6 Exemption by the Panel

The Panel may wholly or partially and conditionally or unconditionally exempt an offeror[212] to an affected transaction or an offer from the application of any provision of Part B, Part C or the Takeover Regulations if:

(a) there is no reasonable potential of the affected transaction prejudicing the interests of any existing holder of a regulated company's securities;
(b) the cost of compliance is disproportionate relative to the value of the affected transaction; or
(c) doing so is otherwise reasonable and justifiable in the circumstances having regard to the principles and purposes of this Part, Part C and the Takeover Regulations.[213]

15.5.7 Regulation in the Act

Affected transactions and offers are clearly and directly brought within the ambit of the Act by s 121. This section provides that any person making an offer:

- must comply with all the reporting or approval requirements set out in Part C or the Takeover Regulations (except to the extent that the Panel has exempted them from any requirement), and
- must not give effect to an affected transaction unless the Panel has issued a

---
[209] Section 119(3).
[210] Section 119(4).
[211] Section 119(5).
[212] Section 119(6).
[213] For guidance in this regard see the objectives as stated in s 119.

compliance certificate with respect to the transaction (or granted an exemption for that transaction).

In order to achieve the objectives, the Act contains a number of specific provisions, most of which will be amplified by the Takeover Regulations in due course. As the drafters of the legislation clearly viewed each of these provisions as being important enough to be included in the body of the Act itself, rather than be dealt with by way of regulation, they are briefly discussed below.

15.5.8 Disclosure of share transactions

Any person who acquires a beneficial interest in sufficient securities of a class issued by a regulated company such that, as a result of the acquisition, the person holds a beneficial interest in securities amounting to 5 per cent, 10 per cent, 15 per cent or any further whole multiple of 5 per cent of the issued securities of that company, or who disposes of a beneficial interest in sufficient securities of a class issued by the company such that, as a result of the disposition, the person no longer holds a beneficial interest in securities amounting to a particular multiple of 5 per cent of the issued securities of that class, must notify the company within three business days after he or she has acquired or disposed of such beneficial interest.[214]

In terms of s 122(2) the disclosure requirements apply irrespective of whether:

(a) the person acquires or disposes of any securities —
  (i) directly or indirectly; or
  (ii) individually, or in concert with any other person or persons, or
(b) the stipulated percentage of issued securities is held by that person alone, or in aggregate by that person together with any —
  (i) related or inter-related person; and
  (ii) person who has acted in concert with any other person.

A regulated company that has received a disclosure notice must file a copy with the Panel and report the information to the holders of the relevant class of securities, unless the notice concerned a disposition of less than 1 per cent of the class of securities.[215]

When determining the number of issued securities of a class for the purposes of disclosure, a person is entitled to rely on the most recently published statement by the company, unless he or she knows or has reason to believe that the statement is inaccurate. Further, when determining the number of securities held by a person(s) who has notified the company, to the extent that the person or persons has or have the entire, or a partial or shared beneficial interest in any securities, those interests must be aggregated, irrespective of the nature of the person's interest. In addition, any securities that may be acquired by the person if they exercise any options, conversion privileges or similar rights are to be included. However, when determining the number of securities held by a person who has not had to notify the company, as mentioned, any securities that may be acquired by that other person if

---

[214] Section 122(1).
[215] Section 122(3).

they had exercised any options, conversion privileges or similar rights are to be excluded.[216]

A transaction which requires disclosure in terms of this section constitutes an affected transaction.[217]

15.5.9 Mandatory offers

Section 123 triggers the obligation to make a mandatory offer to acquire securities in a regulated company in certain circumstances. This is a fundamental provision in takeover regulation, because it gives practical effect to the objective of the Act which requires that shareholders in an affected transaction should be treated equally and fairly.[218] The section applies if:

- a regulated company reacquires any voting securities as contemplated in section 48, or
- a person acting alone has acquired a beneficial interest in any voting securities issued by a regulated company (this also applies to two or more related or interrelated persons, or two or more persons acting in concert),
- before that acquisition the person was, or persons together were, able to exercise less than 35 per cent of the voting rights attaching to securities of that company, and
- as a result of that acquisition, together with any other securities already held by the person or persons, they are able to exercise at least 35 per cent of all the voting rights attaching to the securities of that company.

The 35 per cent threshold is determined by the Minister and constitutes a maximum percentage as set out in s 123(5). Note that, in terms of Takeover Regulation 113, in addition to the offeror, each of the persons acting in concert with the offeror has the obligation to extend the offer.

If a reacquisition or an acquisition results in the crossing of the 35 per cent threshold as described above, the person(s) in whom 35 per cent or more of the voting securities beneficially vests must give notice to the holders of the remaining securities within one day after the date of a completed acquisition. The notice must include a statement that they are in a position to exercise at least 35 per cent of all the voting rights attached to securities of that regulated company and the notice must offer to acquire any remaining such securities on terms determined in accordance with the Act and the Takeover Regulations.[219] Thereafter, within one month after giving the s 123 notice, the person(s) must deliver a written offer in compliance with the Takeover Regulations to the holders of the remaining securities to acquire those securities on the terms contemplated.[220]

15.5.10 Compulsory acquisitions and squeeze-out

In terms of s 124, if, within four months of the date of an offer for the acquisition of any class of securities of a regulated company, the offer has been accepted by

---
[216] Section 122(4)*(b)*.
[217] Section 117 (1)*(c)*(iv) and (v).
[218] Section 119(1)*(a)* and (2)*(b)*.
[219] Section 123(3).
[220] Section 123(4).

the holders of at least 90 per cent of that class of securities (other than such securities held before the offer by the offeror, a related or interrelated person, or persons acting in concert, or a nominee or subsidiary of any such person or persons) then within two further months (ie six months after the date of an offer for the acquisition has been accepted), the offeror may notify the holders of the remaining securities of the class that:

- the offer has been accepted to that extent, and
- the offeror desires to acquire all remaining securities of that class.

After giving notice, the offeror is entitled and bound to acquire the securities concerned on the same terms that apply to securities whose holders had accepted the original offer. This process is commonly referred to as a squeeze-out in the sense that the remaining (less than 10 per cent) holders of securities are squeezed out of the company. Section 124(2) provides for circumstances in which a person may apply for a court order to the effect that the offeror is not entitled to acquire the applicant's securities, or imposing different conditions of acquisition. In addition, if the 90 per cent threshold has not been reached by the offeror, the offeror may apply to court for an order authorising him or her to give an acquisition notice as contemplated in s 124. The court may make the order applied for if:[221]

(i) after making reasonable enquiries, the offeror has been unable to trace one or more of the persons holding securities to which the offer relates;
(ii) by virtue of acceptances of the original offer, the securities that are the subject of the application, together with the securities held by the person or persons referred to in subparagraph (i), amount to not less than the minimum specified in subsection (1) [ie 90 per cent];
(iii) the consideration offered is fair and reasonable; and
(iv) the court is satisfied that it is just and equitable to make the order, having regard, in particular, to the number of holders of securities who have been traced but who have not accepted the offer.

Section 124 also operates in reverse, however, by entitling the remaining holders of securities in a regulated company, where an offer has been accepted by at least 90 per cent of the holders of a class of securities, to demand that the offeror acquire all the persons' securities of the class concerned on the same terms and conditions that apply to securities whose holders accepted the original offer.[222]

15.5.11 Comparable and partial offers

If a person makes an offer for any securities of a company that has more than one class of securities, and the offer could result in the person (together with any related or interrelated person or person acting in concert with any of them) holding securities entitling him, her or them to exercise at least 35 per cent of the general voting rights of all issued securities of the company, then a comparable offer must be made for each class of issued securities of that company.[223]

---

[221] Section 124(3)*(b)*.
[222] See s 124(4) and (5).
[223] Section 125(2). See in this regard also Regulation 115.

A partial offer is an offer that, if fully accepted, would result in the offeror[224] holding less than 100 per cent of the voting securities of the company whose securities are the subject of the offer.[225] Section 125(3) states that a person making a partial offer for any class of issued securities of a company must:

(a) make the offer to all of the holders of that class of securities;
(b) if the offer could result in the person, together with any related or inter-related person or person acting in concert with any of them, holding securities of the company entitling the person or persons to exercise more than the prescribed percentage[226] of the general voting rights of all issued securities of the company, make the offer conditional on —
  (i) a specified number of acceptances being received; and
  (ii) the offer being approved by the independent holders of more than 50% of the general voting rights of all issued securities of the company;
(c) state in the offer the precise number of shares offered for, if the offer could result in the person, together with any related or inter-related person or person acting in concert with any of them, holding securities of the company entitling the persons or persons to exercise more than the prescribed percentage, but less than 50%[227] of the general voting rights of all issued securities of the company; and
(d) if the offer could result in the person, together with any related or inter-related person or person acting in concert with any of them, holding securities of the company entitling the persons or persons to exercise more than 50% of the general voting rights of all issued securities of the company —
  (i) include a specific and prominent notice . . . [to this effect]; and
  (ii) include a specific statement setting out the extent to which the person or persons referred to above will be free to acquire further securities in the company without making a general offer, if the offer succeeds to the extent contemplated above.

If a partial offer has been made for a class of securities:

(a) any holder of those securities is entitled to accept the offer in full for the relevant percentage of that person's holding; and
(b) any securities tendered in excess of the relevant percentage must be accepted by the offeror from each holder of securities in the same proportion to the number tendered as will enable the offeror to obtain the total number of shares for which it has offered.[228]

What this means, in essence, is that all offerees must be treated equally; where an offeror seeks to accept additional securities that have been tendered by offerees in order to reach its total target, it must do so *pro rata* in respect of all the offerees who have tendered additional securities.

15.5.12 Restrictions on frustrating action

One of the stated aims of the Panel's regulation is to 'prevent actions by a regulated company designed to impede, frustrate or defeat an offer, or the making of fair and informed decisions by the holders of that company's securities.'[229] To

---
[224] This includes the offeror, alone or together with a related or interrelated person, or a person acting in concert with any of them.
[225] Section 117(1)*(h)*. See also in this regard Regulation 96, which contains further detail regarding the definition of 'partial offer' in the Act and the application of that definition.
[226] Which must be at least 35 per cent.
[227] Thus between 35 and 50 per cent.
[228] Section 125(4).
[229] See s 119(1)*(c)*.

this end the board of directors of a regulated company is subject to certain restrictions which are triggered once it has received a *bona fide* offer or believes that a *bona fide* offer might be imminent. Section 126 provides that the board must not take any action in relation to the affairs of the company that could effectively result in a *bona fide* offer being frustrated or the holders of relevant securities being denied an opportunity to decide on its merits. Furthermore, the board must not:

- issue any authorised but unissued securities,
- issue or grant options in respect of any unissued securities,
- authorise or issue, or permit the authorisation or issue of, any securities carrying rights of conversion into or subscription for other securities,
- sell, dispose of or acquire or agree to do so, assets of a material amount, except in the ordinary course of business,
- enter into contracts otherwise than in the ordinary course of business, or
- make a distribution that is abnormal as to timing and amount.[230]

The board may, however, take any of these actions provided it has the prior written approval of the Panel and the approval of the holders of relevant securities, or provided that the action is taken in terms of a pre-existing obligation or agreement entered into before it received the bona fide offer or believed it to be imminent.[231]

If a regulated company believes that it is subject to a pre-existing obligation, it may apply to the Panel for consent to proceed.[232] This would be the most prudent approach in circumstances where a board of directors finds itself on the horns of a dilemma in that it has a pre-existing contractual obligation to take certain action which directly conflicts with one of the restrictions on frustrating action contained in the Act.

15.5.13 Prohibited dealings before and during an offer

A proposed or possible offer is usually announced on a certain date and runs until a specified closing date as determined in accordance with the terms of the offer, the Takeover Regulations[233] and the requirements of any exchange that may apply. An offer may also be conditional as to acceptance, which means the offeror has determined a minimum percentage level of securities required to be tendered by offerees in order for the offeror to be obliged to accept all tendered securities, ie the offer is made conditional upon a minimum level of acceptance. The period of time from when the announcement is made (or ought to have been made) until the first closing date or, if later, the date when the offer becomes or is declared unconditional as to acceptances (or lapses) is called the 'offer period'.[234]

During an offer, or when one is reasonably in contemplation, an offeror (or person acting in concert with that offeror) must not, if there are favourable conditions attached that are not being extended to all holders of the relevant securities:

---

[230] Blackman et al op cit n 192 at 15A–56.
[231] Section 126(1).
[232] Section 126(2).
[233] See Regulation 103 of the Takeover Regulations with respect to the timeline of an offer.
[234] See s 117(1)(*g*).

- make arrangements with any holders of the relevant securities,
- deal in, or enter into arrangements to deal in, securities of the offeree regulated company, or
- enter into arrangements which involve acceptance of an offer.[235]

During an offer period an offeror (or person acting in concert with that offeror) must not:

- sell any securities in the offeree company unless:
  - the Panel has consented in advance to that sale,
  - the person selling those securities has given at least 24 hours' notice to the public that sales of that type might be made, in the manner and form required by the Takeover Regulations, and
  - the sale is on the same terms and conditions as the offer.

The offeror (or person acting in concert with him or her) must also not acquire any securities in the offeree company after giving the 24 hours' notice referred to above.[236]

If an offer has been announced or posted but has not become or been declared unconditional, and has, as a result, subsequently been withdrawn or has lapsed, the offeror (or any person acting in concert with that offeror) must not, for a period of 12 months thereafter:

- make an offer for the relevant securities of the offeree company, or
- make an acquisition of securities of the offeree company that would require the offeror (or party acting in concert with that offeror) to make a mandatory offer in terms of s 123.[237]

For six months after the closing date of an offer or the date on which the offer became unconditional (whichever is later) the offeror, any person who acted in concert with that offeror, or any person subsequently acting in concert with either of them, must not make a second offer to any holder of securities of the target company, or acquire an interest in any such securities, on more favourable terms than those made under the original offer.[238]

15.5.14 Takeover Regulations

The draft Companies Regulations (in Regulations 87 to 121) contain a host of provisions and rules that apply to takeovers as contemplated in the Act. As previously explained, these will not be dealt with in individual detail as they are subject to probable amendments. Certain of the regulations look very similar to rules which existed under the Securities Regulation Code,[239] while others seem to

---

[235] Section 127(1).
[236] Section 127(2).
[237] Section 127(3). This subsection applies equally to a partial offer whether or not the offer has become or been declared unconditional, but the period of 12 months runs from the date on which that offer became or was declared to be unconditional, or is withdrawn or lapsed, as the case may be.
[238] Section 127(5).
[239] As previously explained, the predecessor of the Takeover Regulations was the Securities Regulation Code ('the Code') on takeovers and mergers, which came into force on 1 February 1991. The Code contained 11 general principles which were 'to be observed in affected transactions ... are

be completely new. Unfortunately the way in which the Takeover Regulations have been included in the draft Companies Regulations is somewhat unstructured, which makes it difficult to develop an understanding of them as a logical and coherent whole. Furthermore, certain regulations refer (as the source of authority for that regulation or otherwise) to sections that do not exist in the Act. Finally, there are a number of issues that require regulation (and which were included in the Securities Regulation Code), but which have not been regulated in either Chapter 5 or the Takeover Regulations. No doubt this will be resolved when a comprehensive and final set of Takeover Regulations is published. For these reasons I deal with each regulation only briefly, spelling out its essence and referring to the specific regulation by number. The relevant regulations are divided into four main parts: Part A — Interpretation and Application, Part B — Fundamental Transactions, Part C — Affected Transactions, and Part D — Takeover Panel Procedures. Each Part is dealt with in turn.

Part A — Interpretation and Application
- Contains a number of definitions to aid in the interpretation of, and lend substance to, Part B and Part C of the Act and the Takeover Regulations generally (Regulations 87–91).

Part B — Fundamental Transactions
- Applies to fundamental transactions generally; the relevant regulations are dealt with in that chapter (Regulations 92–93).

Part C — Affected Transactions
This section of the Takeover Regulations currently deals with the following issues:
- The levels of **confidentiality** to be observed prior to the offer being made. Negotiations must be kept confidential and if there is reasonable suspicion of a leak, price-sensitive information must be published immediately (Regulation 94).
- The manner in which the **approach** must be put forward with a view to an offer being made or when an offer is made (ie it should be unconditional) and the duty of the offeree board to satisfy itself that the offeror will be able to implement the offer (Regulation 95).
- What constitutes a **partial offer** and exceptions in relation to compliance with the legislation in this regard (Regulation 96).
- The specified percentage for a **mandatory offer** (being 35 per cent) (Regulation 97).
- **Cautionary announcements**, including when these should be published, and provision for the equal dissemination of information to securities holders (Regulation 98).

---

essentially a codification of acceptable standards of commercial behaviour and . . . have an obvious and universal application'. To illustrate the application of the general principles and designate procedures designed to govern certain types of affected transaction, the Code also contained 36 rules. The stated purpose of the Code was to ensure fair and equal treatment of all holders of relevant securities in relation to affected transactions. Furthermore, the Code sought to provide an orderly framework within which affected transactions were to be conducted, and also sought to protect minority shareholders.

- When an announcement of a **firm intention to make an offer** needs to be made, the responsibility of the various parties in this regard and the contents of the announcement (Regulation 99).
- **Dealings disclosure and announcements** (the disclosure of allowable dealings during the offer period: when and by whom) (Regulation 100).
- Disclosures and information required in an offeror **circular**, an offeree response circular and a combined circular, as well as details of the documents which must lie for inspection during the offer period (Regulation 102).
- **Timelines** of offers (Regulation 103).
- **Duties of directors of offeree-regulated companies**, including good faith, not resigning during an offer period, disclosure, independence and the number of directors required for an independent board (Regulation 104).
- **Requisite knowledge of independent board members** and what is required to ensure that they have received all necessary information to provide a fully informed opinion (Regulation 105).
- **Independent board of the offeree** to obtain a fair and reasonable opinion and what the board needs to do and consider to express an opinion on an offer or the offer consideration (Regulation 106).
- **Independent expert** required by the Act and Takeover Regulations and details relating to his or her fair and reasonable opinion (Regulation 107).
- **Variation in offers** and approval of amended offer (Regulation 108).
- **Solicitation campaigns** during which the holders of securities in an offeree company are contacted regarding their voting in respect of an offer (Regulation 109).
- **Information to offerors** including the duty to furnish information equally and promptly to all offerors and the right of the offeree company to request information regarding the offeror company and whether there is an undisclosed ultimate offeror behind the offer (Regulation 110).
- **Effect of interests held by non-related persons**, acquisition of control of one non-related person by another related person (making them related persons) and subsequent consequences thereof for purposes of the Act (Regulation 111).
- **Change in control in pyramid** or intermediate pyramid (Regulation 112).
- **Offers by persons acting in concert** — in addition to the offeror, each of the persons acting in concert with the offeror has the obligation to extend an offer in terms of s 123 (Regulation 113).
- **Waiver of right to mandatory offer** possible in certain circumstances, requirements (Regulation 114).
- **Comparable offers** — when a mandatory offer will give rise to same, requirements, offer consideration (Regulation 115).
- **Consensual negotiations** — presumption that *bona fide* offer might be imminent, application of s 126 of the Act, effect of absence of consensual negotiations (Regulation 116).
- **Acquisition of own securities by offeree** requires prior written approval of the Panel and holders of relevant securities or pre-existing obligation or agreement in terms of s 126 (Regulation 117).

Fundamental Transactions, Takeovers and Offers

- **Reinvestment** of consideration offered is permissible subject to certain conditions as per s 119(6)*(c)* of the Act (Regulation 118).
- The Panel will not consent to **sales during offer period** except in limited circumstances and subject to certain requirements (Regulation 119).
- **Waivers — limitation** on offers in six-month period thereafter (Regulation 120).
- **Appointments to board of the offeree company** by the offeror and its concert parties are not permitted during the offer period, nor are they permitted to exercise their votes in securities of the offeree company during the offer period (Regulation 121).

Part D — Takeover Panel Procedures

- General **authority of the Panel** — officers and employees, co-operation with other regulatory bodies (Regulation 122).
- All published **documents to be approved by the Panel** before posting or publication (Regulation 123).
- **Consultations and Rulings** (Regulation 123).
- **Procedure** before the Executive Director and Takeover Special Committee at **hearings** — approach, advice, nature of Rulings, right of review or appeal by court (Regulation 124).
- **Reviews** — application, proceedings, decisions, publication of decisions (Regulation 126).
- **Reporting to the Panel** — compliance requirements, lodging complaints (Regulation 127).
- Panel **services, fees and levies** — advice, consultations, Rulings, document examination, hearings and reviews, fees and party responsible for payment, Panel's discretion to waive or reduce fees, interest payable (Regulation 128).

CHAPTER 16

SHAREHOLDER REMEDIES AND MINORITY PROTECTION

Maleka Femida Cassim

16.1 RELIEF FROM OPPRESSIVE OR PREJUDICIAL CONDUCT..... 680
    16.1.1 Introduction 680
    16.1.2 Applicants who may apply for relief under s 163 681
        (a) Shareholders as applicants 682
        (b) Minority and majority shareholders 683
        (c) Directors as applicants 683
        (d) Related persons 684
        (e) Capacity as shareholder or director................... 684
    16.1.3 Grounds for relief under s 163 686
    16.1.4 Relevant 'conduct' 687
        (a) The result of an act or omission of the company
            (s 163(1)(a)).................................... 687
        (b) The conduct of business (s 163(1)(b)) 688
        (c) The exercise of powers of a director or prescribed officer
            (s 163(1)(c)) 690
        (d) 'Conduct' of 'related persons' 690
    16.1.5 Oppressive, unfairly prejudicial or unfairly disregards interests.. 692
    16.1.6 Available relief under s 163.............................. 695
16.2 THE DERIVATIVE ACTION.................................... 698
    16.2.1 Introduction 698
    16.2.2 Abolition of the common-law derivative action............. 701
    16.2.3 Persons who have standing under s 165 702
    16.2.4 The scope of s 165 and the demand 703
    16.2.5 Application to set aside the demand....................... 705
    16.2.6 The investigation of the demand.......................... 705
    16.2.7 The company's response to the demand 706
    16.2.8 The application to court for leave and the discretion of the court 706
        (a) Good faith (s 165(5)(b)(i)) 708
        (b) Trial of a serious question of material consequence to the company (s 165(5)(b)(ii))...................... 709
        (c) Best interests of the company (s 165(5)(b)(iii)) 710

	16.2.9 Information	714
	16.2.10 Remuneration and expenses; costs; and security for costs	714
	16.2.11 Substituting the person to whom leave is granted	716
	16.2.12 Effect of ratification or approval by shareholders	717
	16.2.13 Permission to discontinue, compromise or settle proceedings	718
16.3	DISSENTING SHAREHOLDERS' APPRAISAL RIGHTS	719
	16.3.1 Introduction and underlying philosophy	719
	16.3.2 Triggers for appraisal rights	721
	16.3.3 The appraisal procedure	722
	(a) Statement of appraisal rights	722
	(b) Notice of objection by dissenting shareholder	722
	(c) Notice of adoption of the resolution	723
	(d) Demand by dissenting shareholder	723
	(e) Offer by the company	726
	(f) Shareholder's acceptance of the offer	726
	(g) Application to court to determine fair value	727
	16.3.4 Flaws and limitations of the appraisal procedure	729
	16.3.5 Determining fair value in appraisal	731
	16.3.6 Alteration of class rights as a trigger for appraisal	732
	(a) Further explanation of the term 'alteration'	735
	(b) 'Alteration' of class rights and the first element of s 164(2)(a)	735
	(c) 'Alteration' of rights and the second element of s 164(2)(a)	737
16.4	APPLICATION TO PROTECT THE RIGHTS OF SECURITIES HOLDERS	739
	16.4.1 General	739
	16.4.1 Meaning of the term 'rights' under section 161	741
16.5	OTHER SHAREHOLDER REMEDIES	742
	16.5.1 Restraining the company from contravening the Act, and damages	742
	16.5.2 The common-law personal action	743
	16.5.3 The 'no reflective loss' principle: overlap between shareholder actions and corporate actions	744
	16.5.4 Other remedies	745

This chapter discusses various shareholder remedies and remedies that constitute significant protective measures for minority shareholders. Included in this chapter are the remedy for relief from oppressive or prejudicial conduct, the derivative action, the appraisal rights of dissenting shareholders, the application to protect the rights of securities holders and various other shareholder remedies. It is noteworthy that some of the shareholder remedies discussed in this chapter are not necessarily restricted only to shareholders or minority shareholders. In some cases persons who are not shareholders may also rely on these remedies, as discussed below.

16.1 RELIEF FROM OPPRESSIVE OR PREJUDICIAL CONDUCT

16.1.1 Introduction

Section 163 of the Companies Act 71 of 2008 (hereafter 'the Act') provides a remedy to a shareholder or director who, in broad terms, complains of oppressive or prejudicial conduct.[1] The section gives the court the power to make any interim or final order it considers fit in the circumstances, including any of a wide, but non-exhaustive, list of orders.

Section 163(1) states that a shareholder or a director of a company may apply to a court for relief if:

(a) any act or omission of the company, or a related person, has had a result that is oppressive or unfairly prejudicial to, or that unfairly disregards the interests of, the applicant;

(b) the business of the company, or a related person, is being or has been carried on or conducted in a manner that is oppressive or unfairly prejudicial to, or that unfairly disregards the interests of, the applicant; or

(c) the powers of a director or prescribed officer of the company, or a person related to the company, are being or have been exercised in a manner that is oppressive or unfairly prejudicial to, or that unfairly disregards the interests of, the applicant.

The applicant's grievance may consequently lie against the following 'conduct':[2]

- (the result of) any act or omission of the company or a related person;
- the conduct or carrying on of the business of the company or related person; or
- the exercise of the powers of a director or prescribed officer of the company or a person related to the company.

In order to succeed, the applicant must prove that the relevant 'conduct' was 'oppressive' or 'unfairly prejudicial' to the applicant or 'unfairly disregards [his or her] interests'. Section 163(1) does not necessarily require that the 'conduct' be unlawful in the sense that it infringes any legal rights of the applicant. It instead enables the court to also take account of the applicant's 'interests' together with wide equitable considerations.

There are accordingly two main elements that the applicant-shareholder or applicant-director must satisfy:

(i) first, relevant 'conduct'; and
(ii) secondly, that the 'conduct' was oppressive, unfairly prejudicial or unfairly disregards the interests of the applicant.

These elements are examined in turn below.

The oppression remedy[3] that is now contained in s 163 has traditionally and

---

[1] A remedy for the abuse of the separate juristic personality of a company is provided for under s 163(4). It is unclear why this remedy forms part of s 163, and why it is not contained in a separate section from the remedy for oppressive or prejudicial conduct. The draft Companies Amendment Bill, 2010 (cl 14) now proposes to include it as part of s 20 of the Act. The remedy for abuse of the separate juristic personality of a company is discussed in chapter 2: The Legal Concept of a Company. The above discussion of s 163 relates only to the remedy for oppressive or prejudicial conduct.

[2] The expression 'conduct' is used in this discussion to refer to these instances.

[3] This remedy is commonly called the 'oppression remedy' but its extent is broader than suggested by this expression.

primarily served the purpose of protecting oppressed minority shareholders (mainly in smaller private companies). It may do so without inevitably setting aside the decisions of the majority shareholders. The need for minority protection arises from the consideration that the business and acts of a company are generally conducted by its board of directors and by its members in general meeting by majority vote. Since shareholders are bound by the resolutions of the company in general meeting, a minority shareholder runs the risk of 'oppression' by majority rule. Shareholders are also at risk of 'oppression' by the directors or managerial power. Company law provides a number of safeguards, and one of the available remedies in such circumstances is the oppression remedy.

By way of background, a leading reason for the predominance of the oppression remedy in smaller private companies or quasi-partnership companies (see further below) is that in this type of company, shareholders commonly play an active role in the affairs of the company. This often results in disputes of a personal nature among the shareholders. Voluntary exit by a disgruntled minority shareholder is very difficult, as a purchaser of a minority stake in a private company may be hard to come by. This is compounded by the restricted transferability of the shares of a private company. By contrast, in public companies, disputes tend to centre on quite different issues and there is greater reliance on other mechanisms to resolve disputes. Notably, disgruntled shareholders in public companies may exit the company much more easily by simply selling their shares, particularly in a listed company which has a ready market for its shares.

However, the oppression remedy is not limited to use by minority shareholders, nor is it limited to smaller private companies. It has furthermore been widened under the new Act to provide *locus standi* not only to shareholders, but also to directors.

16.1.2 Applicants who may apply for relief under s 163

A complaint under s 163 is brought by way of an application to court and not an action. Both shareholders as well as directors may apply for relief under s 163, but not creditors or employees.

A shareholder or director of a company has *locus standi* in respect of 'oppressive or prejudicial conduct',[4] whether by that company or by a person *related* to the company.

The Act thus significantly expands the list of persons who have *locus standi* under the oppression remedy, as contrasted with the Companies Act 61 of 1973 (hereafter 'the 1973 Act'), which provided standing only to shareholders (members) of the relevant company while excluding the directors of the company and the shareholders and directors of related persons.[5] Further matters concerning applicants and standing are discussed below.

---

[4] Although the title of s 163 refers to 'relief from oppressive or prejudicial conduct', s 163 is actually wider in that it additionally covers the unfair disregard of the interests of the applicant. This should be borne in mind where reference is made in this chapter to 'oppressive or prejudicial conduct' of the company.

[5] Section 252 of the 1973 Act.

(a) Shareholders as applicants

A 'shareholder' is defined in the Act as 'the holder of a share issued by a company and who is entered as such in the certificated or uncertificated securities register, as the case may be.'[6] On the basis of this definition, it appears that only a registered shareholder may bring an application in terms of s 163. A holder of a beneficial interest in any shares does not seem to have *locus standi* in terms of the Act. By contrast, the Canada Business Corporations Act explicitly gives standing to both registered holders as well as beneficial owners of securities.[7]

The principle that only a registered shareholder has *locus standi* accords with the case of *Lourenco v Ferela*[8] (decided under the 1973 Act), in which the applicants had inherited shares but had not yet been formally registered as members (or shareholders) of the company and were consequently held to lack standing under the oppression remedy.[9] An exception might, however, be made to this principle in the event that a shareholder, who is entitled to registration as such, has been unable to obtain registration as a shareholder because of opposition or lack of co-operation by the company or his or her (or its) fellow shareholders.[10] (Moreover a nominee, who is the registered shareholder, will have standing and may seek relief to protect the interests of the holder of the beneficial interest in the shares.[11])

In a non-profit company it is the voting members (if any) (and of course also the directors) who have standing to apply for relief under s 163. (See s 10(4) of the Act, which states that in respect of a non-profit company, a reference in the Act to 'a shareholder' is to be regarded as a reference to the voting members of the non-profit company.)

A holder of securities other than shares, or a holder of debt instruments, clearly lacks *locus standi* under the section. It is noteworthy that the Canada Business Corporations Act differs by providing standing to holders of securities generally.[12]

---

[6] Section 1.
[7] Section 238 of the Canada Business Corporations Act, R.S.C. 1985.
[8] *Lourenco v Ferela (Pty) Ltd (No 1)* 1998 (3) SA 281 (T).
[9] In English law, by contrast, s 994(2) of the Companies Act 2006 explicitly extends the right to petition for relief under the oppression remedy to non-members to whom shares have been transferred or transmitted by operation of law. The usual instances of transmission are on death or bankruptcy (Paul L Davies *Gower and Davies' Principles of Modern Company Law* 8 ed (Sweet & Maxwell 2008) 617, 682).
[10] See in this regard *Barnard v Carl Greaves Brokers (Pty) Ltd* 2008 (3) SA 663 (C) at para 41, which was decided under the 1973 Act. The principle laid down in this case may continue to apply to the new Act.
[11] In English law this is the position, it is likely that this will prevail in South African law (see the English case of *Atlasview Ltd v Brightview Ltd* [2004] 2 BCLC 191). It furthermore seems, from the wording of s 163, that an applicant may complain of 'conduct' that occurred *before* the applicant became a shareholder (or director) of the company, provided that the relevant 'conduct' is in fact oppressive or prejudicial to the applicant — such an interpretation would enable a beneficial shareholder to apply for relief under s 163 if the nominee shareholder transfers the shares to him or her (or it) (see the English law case *Lloyd v Casey* [2002] 1 BCLC 454; Paul L Davies op cit n 9 at 683).
[12] Section 238 of the Canada Business Corporations Act, R.S.C. 1985.

(b) Minority and majority shareholders

The oppression remedy operates typically as a mechanism for the protection of minority shareholders. As stated above, it has been used by and large by minority shareholders against majority shareholders. Yet relief has also been granted to a shareholder who could cast precisely half the votes in a general meeting of the company, such that the voting power was equally divided between the applicant and the respondent.[13]

Majority shareholders, as such, are not excluded from relying on the section. In this regard s 163 technically provides *locus standi* generally to any 'shareholder'. It has, however, been held that a majority shareholder or controlling shareholder will not be granted relief under the oppression provisions, on the basis that the majority shareholder is able to use its voting power to eliminate the oppression or prejudice of which it complains.[14] (To put it more accurately, the reason for the denial of a remedy to majority shareholders is not a lack of *locus standi* but is, instead, an absence of 'unfairly' prejudicial conduct to the majority within the meaning of the section. Since the majority shareholder has sufficient voting power to rid itself of the prejudice, the conduct cannot be said to be unfairly prejudicial to it.[15] Perhaps a passive majority, who cannot eliminate oppressive conduct by the minority shareholders, would be entitled to apply for relief under this section.[16])

These principles may now also extend to directors who control a majority of the votes at meetings of the board.

(c) Directors as applicants

Unlike the previous regime, directors are now also entitled to seek relief under s 163 in respect of 'oppressive or prejudicial conduct'. Included in the definition of a 'director' is an alternate director as well any person occupying the position of a director or alternate director, by whatever name that person may be designated.[17] A *de facto* director would consequently also appear to qualify for relief under the section.

One of the favourable consequences of the expansion of legal standing to include directors is that the section now plainly caters for the quasi-partnership type of company which so commonly formed the subject matter of oppression applications under the previous company law regime (see further below).

---

[13] *Benjamin v Elysium Investments (Pty) Ltd* 1960 (3) SA 467 (E); *Livanos v Swartzberg* 1962 (4) SA 395 (W).

[14] *Re Baltic Real Estate (No 2)* [1993] BCLC 503; *Re Legal Costs Negotiators Ltd* [1999] 2 BCLC 171 (ChD and CA); *Re Polyresins Pty Ltd* (1998) 28 ACSR 671. These decisions will probably continue to be of persuasive force, particularly in view of the similarity of s 163 to its predecessors, namely s 252 of the 1973 Act and s 111*bis* of the Companies Act 46 of 1926 (hereafter 'the 1926 Act'), which were based on the equivalent provisions in English law.

[15] Ibid.

[16] RP Austin and IM Ramsay *Ford's Principles of Corporations Law* 13 ed (LexisNexis Butterworths 2007) 708–709; Birds, Boyle, Clark, MacNeil, McCormack, Twigg-Flesner & Villiers *Boyle & Birds' Company Law* 6 ed (Jordan Publishing Ltd 2007) 694; see *Re Legal Costs Negotiators Ltd* [1999] 2 BCLC 171 (ChD and CA) at 179; *Re Baltic Real Estate Ltd (No 1)* [1993] BCLC 499.

[17] Section 1 of the Act.

(d) Related persons

An applicant shareholder or director (as the case may be) may seek relief under s 163 in respect of 'oppressive or prejudicial conduct', whether on the part of the company in which the applicant is a shareholder or director, or a person or entity *related* to the company. It may thus be said that one would generally qualify as an applicant if one is inter alia a shareholder or a director either of the relevant company or of a juristic person *related* to the company.

The concept of a related person, as defined in s 2 of the Act, includes a holding company and subsidiary relationship, as well as the direct or indirect 'control' of another company or its business (or the direct or indirect 'control' of each of them or the business of each of them by a third person).[18]

The extension of *locus standi* to include shareholders (and directors) of related persons constitutes a distinct improvement on the 1973 Act. It takes account of pertinent judicial decisions and the issues that arose from time to time of whether an applicant could complain of the conduct of the affairs of a parent company or, less commonly, the conduct of the affairs of a subsidiary company (see further 16.1.4 below).[19] Section 163 now makes it clear that in appropriate cases, and provided that the other elements of the oppression remedy are satisfied, they may indeed do so.

(e) Capacity as shareholder or director

A noteworthy common-law principle, which applied to both the 1973 Act and the 1926 Act, is that a shareholder (member) could only obtain relief under the oppression remedy where he was prejudiced *in his capacity as* a shareholder.[20] This principle is likely to continue to apply in view of the similarity of the wording of s 163 of the new Act to that of its predecessors, so that a shareholder-applicant may complain of oppressive or prejudicial conduct only where this affects the shareholder *qua* shareholder and a director-applicant only where he or she is affected *qua* director — as opposed to oppression or prejudice in some other capacity, for instance, as a creditor or a tenant.

The question arises as to the interpretation and ambit of this principle. It is submitted that an applicant is affected *qua* shareholder or *qua* director (as the case may be) not only where the applicant's *rights* as a shareholder or director are concerned, but also where the applicant's *interests* as a shareholder or director are in issue.

This appears from the wording of s 163 which grants relief inter alia from conduct that 'unfairly disregards the *interests* of the applicant' [emphasis added].

---

[18] See further s 2 and chapter 6: Groups of Companies and Related Persons.
[19] See eg *Scottish Co-operative Wholesale Society Ltd v Meyer* [1959] AC 324; *Re Dernacourt Investments Pty Ltd* (1990) 20 NSWLR 588; *Re Norvabron Pty Ltd (No 2)* (1986) 11 ACLR 279; *Morgan v 45 Flers Avenue Pty Ltd* (1986) 10 ACLR 692.
[20] *Elder v Elder & Watson* [1952] SC 49 at 61; *Re a Company* [1983] 2 All ER 36 (Ch) at 44; *Aspek Pipe Co (Pty) Ltd v Mauerberger* 1968 (1) SA 517 (C); *Ben-Tovim v Ben-Tovim* 2001 (3) SA 1074 (C). However, insofar as these cases concerned the oppression of a shareholder in his or her capacity as a *director*, this would no longer be as problematic under the new Act since s 163 now provides standing also to directors *qua* directors.

The unfair disregard of the 'interests' of the applicant did not previously form part of the oppression remedy. Its explicit inclusion under the new Act arguably indicates that even where the conduct complained of does not affect any *rights* of the applicant as derived, for instance, from the Act or the company's Memorandum of Incorporation, the applicant will still have *locus standi* if the applicant's *interests* are affected. 'Interests' are wider than 'rights', as discussed in 16.1.5 below, and may include equitable considerations. It is thus submitted that the explicit inclusion of the concept of 'interests' in s 163 will allow the courts to avoid a strict or overly-technical shareholder *qua* shareholder or director *qua* director approach, and instead take account of the wider interests of the applicant.

The novel incorporation of the 'interests' of the applicant in s 163 would also seem to take into consideration the previous judicial decisions and the common-law approach to the principle that a shareholder must be affected *qua* shareholder. While this principle was historically imposed by the courts as a limiting factor to the oppression remedy, it eventually came to be much relaxed by the courts under the previous company law regimes. In this regard, the courts laid down that this principle should not be construed too narrowly or too technically.[21] The principle came to be widely interpreted, even under the prior company law regimes, to take into account not only the 'rights' of the applicant (for instance in terms of the Act or the company's constitution) but also equitable considerations.[22]

It was thus held under the previous Companies Acts that where the prejudice affected the applicants other than in their capacity as shareholders (for instance, as creditors or employees), it could nonetheless be relevant for the purposes of the oppression remedy if it were part and parcel of conduct designed to react unfavourably on the rights of shareholders as such, or in furtherance of a scheme intended to prejudice them as shareholders.[23] These decisions probably remain germane to the new Act.

The quasi-partnership type of case serves as a useful illustration of the distinction between 'rights' and 'interests'. It was the standard or typical case[24] for oppression applications under the previous company law regimes. A quasi-partnership (or owner-managed company) usually involves a small private company that is formed on the basis of an agreement or an understanding or intention that the shareholders will generally all be directors and participate in the management of the company, for instance, because the return on investment is to take the form of directors' remuneration rather than dividends on shares. Where a shareholder in a

---

[21] See eg *O'Neill v Phillips* [1999] 2 All ER 961.

[22] *O'Neill v Phillips* [1999] 2 All ER 961. This case actually concerned the interpretation of the concept of 'unfairness' in the context of the oppression remedy. It was furthermore laid down in *Re A Company (No. 008699 of 1985)* [1986] 2 BCC 99 that the concept of 'unfairness' cuts across the distinction between acts that do and acts that do not infringe rights. The concept of 'unfairness' was thus used to extend the practical application of the principle that a shareholder must be affected *qua* shareholder. (These English law decisions were relevant to s 252 of the 1973 Act and its predecessor, s 111*bis* of the 1926 Act. See further below the discussion on unfairness in 16.1.5.)

[23] *Aspek Pipe Co (Pty) Ltd v Mauerberger* 1968 (1) SA 517 (C) at 525; *O'Neill v Phillips* [1999] 2 BCLC 1 (HL) 15; see also *Gamlestaden Fastigheter AB v Baltic Partners Ltd* [2007] UKPC 26, [2007] Bus LR 1521.

[24] See eg *Barnard v Carl Greaves Brokers (Pty) Ltd* 2008 (3) SA 663 (C) at para 46.

quasi-partnership is subsequently unjustifiably removed from office as a director[25] by the majority shareholders using their voting power, this would not violate his or her *rights* as a shareholder — but it would affect his or her *interests* or expectation *as a shareholder* to receive director's remuneration or to participate in management. As discussed above, where either the 'rights' or the 'interests' of the applicant are affected by the oppressive or prejudicial conduct, this would suffice to satisfy the principle that a shareholder must be affected *qua* shareholder.

In any event the position on quasi-partnerships is now further clarified by the oppression remedy under the new Act, in two respects: first, s 163 explicitly includes the 'interests' of the applicant-shareholder.[26] Secondly, s 163 introduces the innovation that directors now have *locus standi* — so that a minority shareholder in a quasi-partnership who is unjustifiably removed from his or her position on the board contrary to an agreement, understanding or intention, may be seen to be affected *qua* director[27] and may therefore bring an application under s 163 in his or her capacity as a director.

It is noteworthy that it has been held, in relation to the oppression remedy under the English Companies Act 2006, that the 'interests of members' which are alleged to be unfairly prejudiced (in terms of s 994) need not necessarily be interests in their capacity as members (or shareholders), although they must be sufficiently connected with membership.[28]

16.1.3 Grounds for relief under s 163

It may be said, for purposes of convenience, that there are broadly two main elements that an applicant must satisfy in order to obtain relief under s 163:

(i) first, there must be relevant 'conduct' (in the sense of a relevant act or omission, conduct of business, or exercise of powers by a director or prescribed officer of the company or a related person), and
(ii) secondly, such 'conduct' must be oppressive or unfairly prejudicial to the applicant or unfairly disregard the interests of the applicant.

These two limbs of the oppression remedy are discussed in turn in 16.1.4 and 16.1.5 below.

While the applicant under the 1973 Act additionally had to establish that it was just and equitable for the court to make an order under the oppression remedy,[29] this requirement has now been dispensed with. But these factors are still likely to

---

[25] This is usually as a result of personal disputes among the shareholders, for instance, over remuneration or the future objectives of the company.

[26] In this regard, the 'interests' of a shareholder in a small, private quasi-partnership type company may in appropriate circumstances include an expectation that he or she would hold the office of director, as discussed above.

[27] See Paul L Davies op cit n 9 at 690 and the authorities cited therein; *Re Lundie Bros* [1965] 1 WLR 1051; *Re Westbourne Galleries* [1970] 3 All ER 374.

[28] *Gamlestaden Fastigheter AB v Baltic Partners Ltd* [2007] UKPC 26, [2007] Bus LR 1521.

[29] Section 252(3) of the 1973 Act; see also *Ben-Tovim v Ben-Tovim* 2001 (3) SA 1074 (C) 1090; *Donaldson Investments (Pty) Ltd v Anglo-Transvaal Collieries Ltd* 1979 (3) SA 713 (W); *Donaldson Investments (Pty) Ltd v Anglo-Transvaal Collieries Ltd* 1980 (4) SA 204 (T) 209.

Shareholder Remedies and Minority Protection

be effectively considered by the courts and would probably influence the decision of the court.[30]

16.1.4 Relevant 'conduct'

The applicant's complaint of oppression, unfair prejudice or unfair disregard of his or her (or its) interests must lie against one of the following instances of relevant 'conduct':

- the result of any act or omission of the company or a related person,
- the conduct or carrying on of the business of the company or a related person, or
- the exercise of the powers of a director or prescribed officer of the company or a person related to the company.

In view of these wide grounds, this statutory remedy is capable of extending quite broadly over the conduct of corporate affairs generally. Among other things, it embraces control of both shareholders' voting powers and directors' powers. It is notable that the relevant conduct may now emanate either from 'related persons' or from the company itself in which the applicant is a shareholder or director. Important aspects of relevant 'conduct' are discussed further below.

(a) The result of an act or omission of the company (s 163(1)(a))

Where an applicant complains under s 163(1)(*a*) of an act or omission of a company, the focus is on the *result* of the act or omission. It is clear from the wording of the section that what matters is whether the act or omission has had a result that is oppressive or unfairly prejudicial to or unfairly disregards the interests of the applicant. The act or omission in itself is not as relevant as the result of that act or omission.

An 'act or omission of the *company*' (or of a related company)[31] encompasses the resolutions of the board of directors and the acts of the board of directors. It also includes the acts of an individual who has been authorised by the board or to whom the powers of the board have been delegated.[32] An act or omission of the directors may even amount to an 'act or omission of the company' where it is done in breach of a duty owed to the company.[33] The resolutions of shareholders in general meeting are also 'acts of the company'.[34] However, the conduct of a

---

[30] For instance, the just and equitable requirement could be applied where conduct fell within the provision of the *de minimis* principle or where an unjustly prejudicial act was later rectified or balanced by subsequent conduct (*Donaldson Investments (Pty) Ltd v Anglo-Transvaal Collieries Ltd* 1979 (3) SA 713 (W) 718–9; *Donaldson Investments (Pty) Ltd v Anglo-Transvaal Collieries Ltd* 1980 (4) SA 204 (T)).

[31] Relevant 'conduct' by 'related companies' is discussed further below.

[32] Acts of a managing director may perhaps constitute acts of the company.

[33] See MS Blackman et al *Commentary on the Companies Act* Vol 1 (2010) 9–9; *Re Stewarts (Brixton) Ltd* [1985] BCLC 4 at 8. Although these authorities do not relate directly to the new Companies Act of 2008, they may yet be relevant to its interpretation, since they too refer to an act or omission of the company.

[34] See eg *Meyer v Scottish Co-operative Wholesale Society* [1954] SC 381; *Re Unisoft Group Ltd (No 3)* [1994] 1 BCLC 609; Paul L Davies op cit n 9 at 683. But see also *Northern Counties Securities Ltd v Jackson & Steeple Ltd* [1974] 2 All ER 625 which stated that the passing of a

shareholder of its own affairs, even a majority shareholder, cannot be an act or omission of the *company*, for instance a sale of its shares or voting in general meeting.[35]

Section 163(1)*(a)* covers both positive acts as well as omissions. It also applies to continuing conduct as well as isolated acts (in view of the wording '*any* act or omission').

Since the section requires the 'result' of the act or omission to be prejudicial, it seems that no relief will be available in respect of threatened conduct, where the complaint relates to what will be done in the future. For instance, the mere calling of a meeting to pass a resolution to amend the articles of a private company (to the effect that a proposed transfer of shares would be subject to the approval of the directors and would no longer require the unanimous approval of the shareholders) was held not be unfairly prejudicial in itself in the context of s 252 of the 1973 Act,[36] on the basis that it related to threatened conduct.

This may be contrasted with s 459(1) of the English Companies Act 1985 and s 994(1) of the English Companies Act 2006, which refer to an 'actual or proposed' act or omission that 'is or would be' unfairly prejudicial. It is submitted that this is the preferable approach, because there should be no need to wait until the harm has been inflicted.

(b) The conduct of business (s 163(1)(b))

The applicant's complaint of oppression, unfair prejudice or unfair disregard of his or her (or its) interests may, in terms of s 163(1)*(b)*, relate to the manner in which the 'business of the company, or a related person, is being or has been carried on or conducted'. The 1973 Act referred to the conduct of the 'affairs' of the company as opposed to the 'business' of the company. The phrase 'business of the company' is undefined and it remains to be seen whether this will be interpreted differently to the 'affairs' of the company. There are indications in the Act that the 'business' of a company is distinct from its 'affairs'.[37]

The term 'affairs' of the company is very wide. It may include not only external company activity but also internal management.[38] It has been stated (albeit in a different context) that the expression includes all the company's business affairs,

---

resolution by shareholders in general meeting is not an act by the company; see also *Re Astec (BSR) plc* [1998] 2 BCLC 556.

[35] See eg *Scottish Co-operative Wholesale Society Ltd v Meyer* [1959] AC 324; *Re Unisoft Group Ltd (No 3)* [1994] 1 BCLC 609; *Re Legal Costs Negotiators Ltd* [1999] 2 BCLC 171 (Chd and CA). While voting in general meeting is an act of a shareholder in his or her private capacity, the resulting resolution of the company in general meeting amounts to an act of the company. In other words, for an act of the shareholders to constitute an 'act of the company', the shareholders must be in general meeting acting as a collective body. The same applies to a director voting on a directors' resolution.

[36] *Porteus v Kelly* 1975 (1) SA 219 (W) 222; *Investors Mutual Funds Ltd v Empisal (South Africa) Ltd* 1979 (3) SA 170 (W) 177.

[37] See eg s 66(1) which states that '[t]he business and affairs of a company must be managed by or under the direction of its board'; s 128(1)*(b)* which refers to business rescue as including the 'temporary supervision of the company, and of the management of its affairs, business and property'; see also s 141(1).

[38] It may include not only external company activity but also 'internal management and abuses thereof by individuals which tend to oppress others in obtaining their due entitlements from a

goodwill, profits and losses, assets and contracts, its internal management and administration, and its relationships with other companies.[39] In contrast, the 'business' of a company appears to be a narrower term than the 'affairs' of a company. It has been held (albeit in a different context) that the 'business of a company' would encompass a company's external activities as a whole.[40] It has been further stated that the business of a company is not limited to its 'financial affairs'.[41] Whether these interpretations of the 'business' of the company will apply equally in the context of s 163(1)(b) is yet to be seen.

This ground of relevant 'conduct' seems to be wide enough to cover oppressive or prejudicial conduct by any person who is participating in conducting or carrying on the business of the company, regardless of whether he or she does so *de jure* or *de facto*.[42]

It appears from the wording of the section that either the ongoing conduct or the past conduct of the business may form the basis of the complaint (see the wording of s 163(1)(b) which refers to the manner in which the business 'is being or has been' carried on or conducted). But it seems that no relief will be available in respect of threatened conduct of the business, where the complaint relates to what will be done in the future.

It is noteworthy that in terms of s 163(1)(b) the business of a company might in some circumstances be conducted oppressively by way of an omission. Just as the directors can conduct the business oppressively by doing something injurious to the company's interests when they ought not to do it, so it has been held in this regard that the business of the company can be conducted in a manner that is oppressive where the directors are inactive or do nothing to defend its interests when they ought to take some action.[43]

---

properly run company' (*Raymond v Cook* (1998) 29 ACSR 252 (CA)). See also *Australian Securities Commission v Lucas* (1992) 7 ACSR 676; *Re Cumberland Holdings Ltd* (1976) 1 ACLR 361 SC (NSW).

[39] *Breetveldt v Van Zyl* 1972 (1) SA 304 (T), which made the above statement in the context of s 95*bis*(1) of the 1926 Act dealing with the investigation of the 'affairs of a company' by an inspector appointed by the Minister.

[40] *Hardie v Hanson* (1960) 105 CLR 451 (HC of A), in the context of the liability of directors for fraudulent conduct of any business of the company.

[41] This was held in the context of s 424 of the 1973 Act dealing with the liability of directors for fraudulent conduct of any business of the company, in *Body Corporate of Greenwood Scheme v 75/2 Sandown (Pty) Ltd* 1999 (3) SA 480 (W) 486–489. In the context of the liability of directors for fraudulent conduct of any business of the company, *In Re Sarflax Ltd* [1979] 1 All ER 529 (Ch) 534 held that the business of the company does not necessarily involve active trading and may, for instance, involve the realisation of assets and dealing with their proceeds. But to the extent that the relevant statutory provision in that case used the phrase '*any*' business of the company as opposed to the expression the 'business of the company', the decision in *In Re Sarflax* may be inapplicable in the context of the oppression remedy (see *Hardie v Hanson* supra) since 'any' business is clearly wider in meaning.

[42] See the cases of *Re HR Harmer Ltd* [1958] 3 All ER 689 (CA); *Heckmair v Beton & Sandstein Industrieë (Pty) Ltd (2)* 1980 (1) SA 353 (SWA); *Re East West Promotions Ltd* (1986) 10 ACLR 222, which are persuasive authority.

[43] *Scottish Co-operative Wholesale Society Ltd v Meyer* [1959] AC 324 at 367 *per* Lord Denning; see also *Re Legal Costs Negotiators Ltd* [1999] 2 BCLC 171 (Chd and CA) 199. These decisions may continue to have persuasive authority.

(c) The exercise of powers of a director or prescribed officer (s 163(1)(c))

A new ground of relevant 'conduct' that has been introduced by the new Act is the exercise of 'the powers of a director or prescribed officer of the company' or a person related to the company,[44] where such powers are being or have been exercised in a manner that is oppressive or unfairly prejudicial to the applicant or unfairly disregards the interests of the applicant (s 163(1)(c)). This ground will be particularly useful in cases where the relevant exercise of powers by a director or prescribed officer amounts to neither the conduct of the business, nor an act or omission of the company or a related person.

A complaint in terms of s 163(1)(c) may relate either to an ongoing or a past exercise of powers of a director or prescribed officer. This includes the exercise of the powers of an alternate director or any person occupying the position of a director or alternate director (by whatever name that person may be designated), in view of the definition of a 'director' in the Act.[45] Prescribed officers whose powers may form the subject matter of an application on this ground include persons who, despite not being directors of the company (and regardless of the title of their office), have:

- general executive authority over the company (such as a president, chief executive officer, managing director, executive director or similar office holder),
- general responsibility for the financial management of the company (such as a treasurer, chief financial officer, chief accounting officer or similar office holder),
- general responsibility for the management of the legal affairs of the company (such as a general secretary, general counsel or similar office holder),
- general managerial authority over the operations of the company (such as a chief operating officer or similar office holder), or
- otherwise directly or indirectly exercise, or significantly influence the exercise of, control over the general management and administration of the whole or a significant portion of the business and activities of the company, irrespective of any title assigned by the company to an office held by that person, or function performed by that person.[46]

(d) 'Conduct' of 'related persons'

In contrast with the 1973 Act, the relevant 'conduct' under s 163 need not necessarily be that of the company in which the applicant is a shareholder or director (as the case may be), and may instead consist in the 'conduct' of a *'related person'*. This applies to all the above types of relevant 'conduct', namely the acts or omissions of related persons, the conduct of the business of related persons, or

---

[44] The inconsistent wording of s 163(1)(a), (b) and (c) viz 'related person' or 'person related to the company' is open to criticism in that it could create uncertainty as to its precise meaning.

[45] Section 1 of the Act.

[46] Section 66(10) read with s 1 and regulation 45 of the draft Companies Regulations pursuant to the Companies Act, 2008 (Act 71 of 2008) GN 1664 *GG* 32832 of 22 December 2009 (hereafter 'the draft Regulations').

the exercise of powers of the directors or prescribed officers of persons related to the company (provided of course that the 'conduct' in question was oppressive or unfairly prejudicial to the applicant himself or herself or unfairly disregarded the applicant's interests).

The concept of 'related persons' embraces holding company and subsidiary relationships as well as the direct or indirect 'control' by one juristic person of another or its business (or the direct or indirect 'control' of each of them or the business of each of them by a third person).[47] Related persons may also include individuals in certain circumstances, who directly or indirectly 'control' the company. The inclusion of related persons thus significantly widens the scope of the oppression remedy under the Act, thereby narrowing down the possibilities of evasion of the section.

This extension and refinement of the oppression remedy under the new Act addresses the issue that arose from time to time in judicial decisions under the previous regimes of whether and to what extent an applicant could complain of the 'conduct' (or the affairs) of a related company, usually being the holding company or, less commonly, a subsidiary company.[48] For instance in *Scottish Co-operative Wholesale Society Ltd v Meyer*,[49] the society had deliberately used its controlling powers to deprive a subsidiary company of its business of manufacturing rayon, as part of a policy to transfer the business of the subsidiary to one of its own departments. The result was that the subsidiary's business virtually came to a standstill, with a corresponding decline in the value of its shares. Relief was granted in this case to the minority shareholders of the *subsidiary* company based on the consideration that the society had effectively determined the conduct of the subsidiary, since the society's nominees on the board of the subsidiary had acted on their instructions and in their interests as opposed to the interests of the subsidiary company.

Section 163 of the new Act settles the issue that it is now indeed possible for an applicant to obtain relief in appropriate circumstances from the 'conduct' of a holding or subsidiary company or other related persons (provided of course that the applicant is able to establish the oppressive or prejudicial element in relation to that 'conduct').

---

[47] See s 2 of the Act and chapter 6: Groups of Companies and Related Persons. 'Control' is determined in accordance with s 2(2) of the Act, and includes the direct or indirect control of the exercise of a majority of the voting rights of the company, or the right to appoint or elect directors who control a majority of the votes at board meetings (whether alone or together with any related or inter-related person). 'Control' also includes the ability to materially influence the policy of the company.

[48] For instance, where the holding company had appointed the relevant director of the subsidiary company, the issue arose whether his or her conduct could be construed as conduct in the affairs of the holding company. The conduct of 'related' companies arose also where there was a common board of directors. See eg *Scottish Co-operative Wholesale Society Ltd v Meyer* [1959] AC 324; *Re Dernacourt Investments Pty Ltd* (1990) 20 NSWLR 588; *Re Norvabron Pty Ltd (No 2)* (1986) 11 ACLR 279; *Morgan v 45 Flers Avenue Pty Ltd* (1986) 10 ACLR 692. See also *Citybranch Group Ltd, Gross v Rackind* [2004] 4 All ER 735 where the English Court of Appeal accepted that the conduct of a company's affairs can extend to the conduct of the affairs of its subsidiary and vice versa.

[49] [1959] AC 324.

16.1.5 Oppressive, unfairly prejudicial or unfairly disregards interests

This is the second main element that the applicant must establish to obtain relief in terms of s 163, the first element being relevant 'conduct' as discussed in 16.1.4 above. The applicant must prove that the relevant 'conduct' (in the sense of a relevant act or omission, conduct of business, or exercise of powers by a director or prescribed officer of the company or a related person) is 'oppressive or unfairly prejudicial to, or unfairly disregards the interests of, the applicant'. The critical question arises as to the interpretation and meaning of the phrase oppressive, unfairly prejudicial or unfair disregard of the applicant's interests.

It is submitted that these may be considered as alternatives, but may also be read as a compound expression.[50]

They are wide terms and their exact ambit is undefined. In all likelihood a judicial construction will be given (one hopes) to extend rather than to limit the remedy (following the approach under the previous regime).[51] The case law on the meaning of the phrase 'unfairly prejudicial' in the context of s 252 of the 1973 Act, and the term 'oppressive'[52] in s 111*bis* of the 1926 Act, may well continue to apply to s 163, in view of the similarities in wording.[53] However s 163 is much more widely drafted than its predecessors so as to now include the unfair disregard of the interests of the applicant.

It is submitted, based on earlier judicial decisions, that relief would continue to be granted in terms of s 163 if the applicant is able to establish 'a lack of probity or fair dealing, or a visible departure from the standards of fair dealing, or a violation of the conditions of fair play on which every shareholder is entitled to rely. . . . The emphasis is on the unfairness of the conduct complained of. It must be conduct which departs from the accepted standards of fair play, or which amounts to an unfair discrimination against the minority.'[54] The test of the oppression remedy is therefore *unfairness*, as opposed to unlawfulness. Conduct

---

[50] See *Thomas v HW Thomas Ltd* [1984] 1 NZLR 686 CA (NZ); *Re George Raymond Pty Ltd; Salter v Gilbertson* (2000) 18 ACLC 85; *Fexuto Pty Ltd v Bosnjak Holdings Pty Ltd* (2001) 37 ACSR 672, which are persuasive authority.

[51] See *Donaldson Investments (Pty) Ltd v Anglo-Transvaal Collieries Ltd* 1979 (3) SA 713 (W); *Donaldson Investments (Pty) Ltd v Anglo-Transvaal Collieries Ltd* 1980 (4) SA 204 (T); *Livanos v Swartzberg* 1962 (4) SA 395 (W).

[52] The term 'oppressive', which was used in s 111*bis* of the 1926 Act, was abandoned in s 252 of the 1973 Act, despite forming part of the heading of the section, namely 'Member's remedy in case of oppressive or unfairly prejudicial conduct'. Curiously, the term 'oppressive' now reappears in s 163 of the new Act. 'Oppressive' was defined as 'burdensome, harsh and wrongful' in *Scottish Co-operative Wholesale Society Ltd v Meyer* [1959] AC 324, and was said to involve a lack of probity or fair dealing towards a shareholder in *Elder v Elder & Watson* [1952] SC 49 at 60. 'Oppressive' conduct (in terms of s 111*bis*) has a narrower meaning than 'unfairly prejudicial, unjust or inequitable' conduct under s 252 (*Garden Province Investment v Aleph (Pty) Ltd* 1979 (2) SA 525 (D) 531; *Donaldson Investments* (supra) at 718–722).

[53] Indeed in interpreting s 252 of the 1973 Act, the courts similarly had recourse to its predecessor s 111*bis* of the 1926 Act (see *Donaldson Investments (Pty) Ltd v Anglo-Transvaal Collieries Ltd* (supra) at 720–721).

[54] *Donaldson Investments (Pty) Ltd v Anglo-Transvaal Collieries Ltd* 1979 (3) SA 713 (W) at 722, affirmed on appeal 1980 (4) SA 204 (T) and on further appeal 1983 (3) SA 96 (A).

may be unlawful without being unfair or unfair without being unlawful.[55] Conduct may accordingly be 'oppressive or prejudicial' within the meaning of the section, even where it does not violate any '*rights*' of the applicant, for instance, rights in terms of the Act or the company's Memorandum of Incorporation.

This is now made even clearer in the new Act by the innovative inclusion of the unfair disregard of the applicant's '*interests*' (as contrasted with the applicant's '*rights*'). The term 'interests' is wider than 'rights'.[56] It would seem that s 163 has been drafted to include 'interests' in order to underline or emphasise the principle that the oppression remedy is not limited to the strict infringement of legal rights, but that it extends also to the protection of the interests of applicants.[57] The precise meaning of the 'interests' of the applicant in this context is, however, left undefined. It remains to be seen whether it would signify some proprietary right, and whether some financial detriment would be necessary.

The interpretation of the concept of 'unfairness' in the context of the oppression remedy is pivotal. English courts have declared (in respect of the English law equivalent of the oppression remedy, which originally formed the basis of the South African oppression remedy) that the concept of 'unfairness' cuts across the distinction between acts that do and acts that do not infringe rights, and requires the court to have regard also to wide equitable considerations that must be weighed in the balance.[58] Courts may therefore subject the exercise of legal rights to equitable considerations in the context of the oppression remedy. The equitable considerations that the court is required to take into account may, depending on the circumstances, be the expectations (or 'legitimate expectations'[59]) 'arising from the agreements or understandings of the members inter se', so that sometimes (primarily in quasi-partnerships) the collateral agreements or even mere

---

[55] See the English cases *Re a company, ex parte Harries* [1989] BCLC 383 390; *Re Saul D Harrison & Sons plc* [1995] 1 BCLC 14 17 (CA) at 19. *Garden Province Investment v Aleph (Pty) Ltd* 1979 (2) SA 525 (D) at 531 commented that 'unfairly' in the context of the oppression remedy is used in the sense of 'unreasonably' — but the test may be regarded as an essentially ethical one (Blackman et al op cit n 33 at 9–26).

[56] See *Utopia Vakansie-Oorde Bpk v Du Plessis* 1974 (3) SA 148 (A) in which the court laid down the principle (in the context of s 62*quat*(4) of the 1926 Act which concerned the voting rights of preference shareholders) that the concept of 'interests' is much wider than 'rights'. See also the English case *Re A Company (No 00477 of 1986)* [1986] BCLC 376. It was held that shareholders may have different interests even if their rights as shareholders are the same, in *Re Sam Weller and Sons Ltd* [1990] Ch 682.

[57] Section 459 of the English Companies Act 1985 and now s 994(1) of the English Companies Act 2006 also provide for relief where conduct is unfairly prejudicial to the '*interests*' of the applicant. It seems that 'interests' was included in the English statutes for the above reason. English courts have attached some importance to the fact that the statute protects the 'interests' and not merely the 'rights' of applicants (Paul L Davies op cit n 9 at 685).

[58] *Re A Company (No 8699 of 1985)* [1986] BCLC 382, 387; *Re A Company (No 00477 of 1986)* [1986] BCLC 376, 378–9; *Re Saul D Harrison & Sons plc* [1995] 1 BCLC 14, 17 (CA); *O'Neill v Phillips* [1999] 2 All ER 961 (HL), a decision of the House of Lords.

[59] The expression 'legitimate expectations' is best avoided in this context. It may be regarded as the ' "correlative right" to which a relationship between company members may give rise in cases when, on equitable principles, it would be regarded as unfair for a majority to exercise a power conferred upon them by the articles to the prejudice of another member' (*O'Neill v Phillips* [1999] 2 All ER 961 969 (HL)).

understandings between shareholders *inter se* could possibly form the basis of an oppression application.[60] Furthermore, in certain circumstances equitable principles would render it unfair for the majority (or those conducting the business of the company) to exercise their strict legal powers, where this would be to the prejudice of another shareholder[61] (or director).

'Unfairness' has been defined in Australian law as 'conduct that is so unfair that reasonable directors who consider the matter would not have thought the decision fair'.[62] 'Unfairness' has also been stated to connote 'an obligation to act equitably and impartially in the exercise of power and authority'.[63]

The court would grant relief under the oppression remedy when, for instance, the majority shareholders use their 'greater voting power unfairly in order to prejudice' a minority shareholder, or where they act in a manner which does not enable such a shareholder to enjoy a fair participation in the affairs of the company.[64] The courts have also granted relief in the 'standard case' of a quasi-partnership where shareholders have entered into an association on the understanding that each of them will participate in the management of the company but the majority subsequently use their voting power to exclude a member from participation in management, without giving him or her the opportunity to withdraw his or her capital upon reasonable terms.[65]

Although these cases concerned the predecessors to s 163, the concept of 'unfairness' is likely to be similarly interpreted in relation to s 163, as stated above. Moreover the introduction in the Act of the new phrase 'unfair' disregard of the applicant's 'interests', reinforces the principle that s 163(1) may be invoked where interests and equitable considerations, as opposed to legal rights, are in contention.

The words 'unfairly disregards' in this context have been interpreted in Alberta to mean 'to unjustly and without cause . . . pay no attention to, ignore or treat as of no importance the interests of' the applicant.[66]

Despite the wide ambit of s 163, it must be borne in mind that the conduct of the majority shareholders must be evaluated in light of the fundamental corporate law principle, that by becoming a shareholder, one undertakes to be bound by the decisions of the majority shareholders.[67] A minority shareholder accordingly cannot obtain relief merely because he or she (or it) is outvoted on a certain issue, or is constantly outvoted; nor may relief be granted merely on the basis of a loss of confidence in or dissatisfaction with the conduct of the company's affairs.[68] Thus

---

[60] *O'Neill v Phillips* [1999] 2 All ER 961 969 (HL).
[61] *O'Neill v Phillips* [1999] 2 All ER 961 (HL) *per* Lord Hoffman.
[62] *Wayde v NSW Rugby League Ltd* (1985) 3 ACLC 799 at 804, 807.
[63] *Re Alldrew Holdings Ltd v Nibro Holdings* (1993) 16 OR (3d) 718 (Gen Div) 732.
[64] *Aspek Pipe Co (Pty) Ltd v Mauerberger* 1968 (1) SA 517 (C) 527.
[65] *Barnard v Carl Greaves Brokers (Pty) Ltd* 2008 (3) SA 663 (C) para 46, referring with approval to the opinion of Lord Hoffman in *O'Neill v Phillips* [1999] 2 All ER 961 (HL). See also *Bayly v Knowles* 2010 (4) SA 548 (SCA). But see further the discussion on the new position of quasi-partnerships in 16.1.2 above.
[66] *Stech v Davies* (1987) 53 Alta LR (2d) 373 at 379.
[67] *Sammel v President Brand Gold Mining Co Ltd* 1969 (3) SA 629 (A).
[68] Ibid.

not all acts which prejudicially affect shareholders or directors, or which disregard their interests, will entitle them to relief — it must be shown that the 'conduct' is not only prejudicial or disregardful but also that it is *unfairly* so.[69]

Where one is able to readily rid oneself of the alleged prejudice or to put an end to it (for instance, in the capacity of majority shareholder), then one may not complain of unfair prejudice or unfair disregard of one's interests — the court will not intervene, on the basis that there is no *'unfair'* prejudice[70] or *'unfair'* disregard of interests. This principle will now also extend to directors.

The motive underlying the 'conduct' in question will not usually be directly relevant to the enquiry, but it may be of assistance to the court in deciding whether the conduct is oppressive, unfairly prejudicial, or unfairly disregards the applicant's interests.[71]

An application under s 163 may not be based on allegations that an investigation would possibly reveal that the business of the company is being conducted in a manner contrary to the section[72] or that other relevant conduct in terms of s 163 has transpired.

Unlike its predecessor, s 163 no longer contains wording to the effect that the relevant conduct must affect the applicant or 'some part of the members of the company'. This deletion is commendable. It clarifies the previous uncertainty of whether conduct that affected *all* the shareholders *equally* (or in the same way) would fall outside the section.[73]

16.1.6 Available relief under s 163

The court has a discretion under s 163(2) to make *any* interim or final order or orders it thinks fit. The section sets out an extensive, but non-exhaustive,[74] list of possible remedies. The open-ended list of remedies is much more extensive than that under the 1973 Act, and includes the following remedies, some of which are far-reaching:

- An order restraining the conduct of which the applicant complains.
- An order appointing a liquidator, if the company appears to be insolvent. It thus seems that the court's power to appoint a liquidator is qualified, in that this order may be made only where the company appears to be insolvent.
- An order placing the company under supervision and commencing business rescue proceedings, if the court is satisfied that the circumstances set out in s 131(4)(*a*) apply. This order is similarly qualified.

---

[69] See in this regard *Donaldson Investments (Pty) Ltd v Anglo-Transvaal Collieries Ltd* 1980 (4) SA 204 (T).

[70] *Re Baltic Real Estate (No 2)* [1993] BCLC 503; *Re Legal Costs Negotiators Ltd* [1999] 2 BCLC 171 (ChD and CA); *Re Polyresins Pty Ltd* (1998) 28 ACSR 671. See above.

[71] See in relation to the previous Acts *Donaldson Investments (Pty) Ltd v Anglo-Transvaal Collieries Ltd* 1983 (3) SA 96 (A); *Ben-Tovim v Ben-Tovim* 2001 (3) SA 1074 (C); *Aspek Pipe Co (Pty) Ltd v Mauerberger* 1968 (1) SA 517 (C).

[72] *Investors Mutual Funds Ltd v Empisal (South Africa) Ltd* 1979 (3) SA 170 (W).

[73] *Re A Company: Ex parte Glossop* [1988] 1 WLR 1068 (Ch) at 1074–1075; *Scottish Co-operative Wholesale Society Ltd v Meyer* [1959] AC 324.

[74] In this regard s 163(2) uses the word 'including', which indicates that the court is not limited to the list of remedies provided in the section.

- An order to regulate the company's affairs by directing the company to:
  ○ amend its Memorandum of Incorporation, or
  ○ create or amend a unanimous shareholder agreement.

  Where an order directs the company to amend its Memorandum of Incorporation, the company must not make any further amendment to the Memorandum of Incorporation that will alter, limit or negate the effect of the court order, unless and until a court orders otherwise.[75] In the event of an order directing the company to amend its Memorandum of Incorporation, the directors must promptly file a notice of amendment to give effect to the order. The amendment in this case is effected by a resolution of the board of directors of the company as opposed to a special resolution of the shareholders.[76]
- An order directing an issue or exchange of shares.
- An order appointing directors in place of or in addition to all or any of the directors then in office. This overrules the conflicting *obiter dictum* in *Ex parte Avondzon Trust (Edms) Bpk*[77] where the court proclaimed that it did not have the power to appoint directors under the oppression remedy (in terms of s 111*bis* of the 1926 Act).
- An order declaring a director to be delinquent or to place a director under probation (in terms of s 162).
- An order directing the company or any other person to restore to a shareholder any part of the consideration that the shareholder paid for shares, or pay the equivalent value, with or without conditions.
- An order varying or setting aside a transaction or an agreement to which the company is a party and compensating the company or any other party to the transaction or agreement.
- An order requiring the company, within a time specified by the court, to produce to the court or an interested person financial statements in a form required by the Act, or an accounting in any other form the court may determine.
- An order to pay compensation to an aggrieved person, subject to any other law entitling that person to compensation.
- An order directing rectification of the registers or other records of a company. or
- An order for the trial of any issue as determined by the court.

The range of orders that may be made by the court under s 163(2) is very wide.[78] It even includes the making or amendment of a shareholder agreement, as well as the setting aside of agreements or transactions of the company with third parties,

---

[75] Section 163(3).

[76] Section 163(3) read with s 16(4). See further chapter 4: Formation of Companies and the Company Constitution.

[77] 1968 (1) SA 340 (T) 342–343.

[78] In contrast s 252(3) of the 1973 Act provided that '... if the Court considers it just and equitable, the Court may, with a view to bringing to an end the matters complained of, make such order as it thinks fit, whether for regulating the future conduct of the company's affairs or for the purchase of the shares of any members of the company by other members thereof or by the company ...'.

where this amounts to 'conduct' that is oppressive or unfairly prejudicial to the applicant or unfairly disregards the applicant's interests.

Surprisingly, the section fails to refer explicitly to an order to purchase the shares of a shareholder, whether by other shareholders or by the company. Indeed this has been the most common remedy granted in terms of the oppression remedy under the previous company law regime. Nonetheless, this omission probably will not preclude the court from making such an order, as the list of orders under s 163(2) is non-exhaustive and open-ended.

The remedy for oppressive or prejudicial conduct constitutes a flexible mechanism for the protection of minority shareholders and directors. It departs to some extent from the general principle of judicial non-intervention in corporate management. While some of the remedies under s 163(2) involve minimal judicial intervention in corporate management, other remedies may go much further in giving the court the power to change the structure and the governing rules of the company. In this regard, some of the orders leave the company's existing power structure and rules intact, either by assisting the applicant in self-help (for instance, an order for the rectification of the registers or other company records, orders for the production of financial statements, an order restraining the particular conduct, an order for the trial of any issue), or by relieving either the applicant or the company from a particular situation (eg an order directing the company or another person to restore to a shareholder part of the consideration for the shareholder's shares or to pay the equivalent value, an order compensating an aggrieved person, or an order varying or setting aside a transaction or agreement to which the company is a party and compensating the company or any other party). On the other hand, other orders may involve a greater degree of judicial interference in the management of the company, being orders directed at realigning the balance of power established by the constitution (such as those directing an issue or exchange of shares, or appointing directors in place or in addition to the directors in office), or orders that actually change the rules of the company themselves (eg an order regulating the company's affairs by amending its Memorandum of Incorporation or creating or amending a unanimous shareholder agreement).[79]

An applicant who applies for relief from oppressive or prejudicial conduct in terms of s 163 should indicate the general nature of the relief he or she (or it) seeks.[80] The court, however, is not necessarily limited to the relief sought by the applicant, and may grant other, more appropriate relief. This appears from the wording that the court 'may make any . . . order *it considers fit*'.[81]

An oppression application should be brought with the genuine object of obtaining the relief claimed. It has been held to be an abuse of the process of the court to bring an application with the prime object of exerting pressure to achieve a collateral purpose, for instance, where the purpose of the application is to exert pressure on the company to repay a debt to another company in which the

---

[79] See Bruce Welling *Corporate Law in Canada* 2 ed (1991) 559–563.
[80] *Lourenco v Ferela (Pty) Ltd (No 1)* 1998 (3) SA 281 (T); *Re Antigen Laboratories Ltd* [1951] 1 All ER 110 (Ch); *Breetveldt v Van Zyl* 1972 (1) SA 304 (T).
[81] Section 163(2); see also *Heckmair v Beton & Sandstein Industrieë (Pty) Ltd (1)* 1980 (1) SA 350 (SWA); *Re HR Harmer Ltd* [1958] 3 All ER 689 (CA), which may be of persuasive authority.

applicant has an interest.[82] This may also serve as a useful safeguard against vexatious or frivolous applications by minority shareholders.

While the 1973 Act provided that the court had to be satisfied that it was 'just and equitable' to make the order,[83] 'with a view to bringing to an end the matters complained of',[84] this limitation on the court's discretion has now been dispensed with. But to some extent, as discussed above, these factors are still likely to be considered by the courts.[85]

16.2 THE DERIVATIVE ACTION

16.2.1 Introduction

A derivative action is brought by a person on behalf of a company in order to protect the legal interests of the company. Section 165 of the new Act reforms the statutory derivative action and at the same time abolishes the common-law derivative action.

It must be emphasised that a derivative action is brought by another person, such as a shareholder, in order to protect the legal interests *of the company*. The derivative action is so called because the shareholder 'derives' his or her (or its) right of action from that of the company.[86] This is distinct from the situation where shareholders wish to enforce their *own shareholder* rights.[87]

Section 165 is a statutory exception to the principle that where a wrong is done to the company, the 'proper plaintiff' is the company itself. This principle is commonly known as the rule in *Foss v Harbottle*.[88] It is usually the board of directors that has the authority to institute legal proceedings in the name of or on behalf of the company. The Act provides in this regard that the business and affairs of a company must be managed by the board, which has the authority to exercise all the powers and perform any function of the company, except to the extent that

---

[82] *Re Bellador Silk Ltd* [1965] 1 All ER 667 (Ch) at 671–672.

[83] Section 252(3) of the 1973 Act; *Donaldson Investments (Pty) Ltd v Anglo-Transvaal Collieries Ltd* 1979 (3) SA 713 (W) and 1980 (4) SA 204 (T); *Ben-Tovim v Ben-Tovim* 2001 (3) SA 1074 (C); cf *Bader v Weston* 1967 (1) SA 134 (C).

[84] In this regard it was held that the discretion of the court concerning its order was subject to the overriding consideration that the order should aim at bringing to an end the matters complained of (*Ben-Tovim v Ben-Tovim* 2001 (3) SA 1074 (C) in relation to the 1973 Act).

[85] For instance, the just and equitable requirement could be applied where conduct fell within the provision of the *de minimis* principle or where an unjustly prejudicial act was later rectified or balanced by subsequent conduct (*Donaldson Investments (Pty) Ltd v Anglo-Transvaal Collieries Ltd* 1979 (3) SA 713 (W); *Donaldson Investments (Pty) Ltd v Anglo-Transvaal Collieries Ltd* 1980 (4) SA 204 (T)).

[86] This follows US jurisprudence; see *Schiowitz v IOS Ltd* (1971) 23 DLR (3d) 102; see also *Estmanco (Kilner House) v Greater London Council* [1982] 1 WLR 2.

[87] The line between personal actions (where shareholders wished to enforce their own shareholder rights) and derivative actions was unsettled and problematic under the previous company law regime. This problem is perhaps not fully resolved by the new Act. See 16.5.2 below on the personal action.

[88] (1843) 2 Hare 461; 67 ER 189. *Foss v Harbottle* is the leading case on the proper plaintiff rule. The exceptions to the proper plaintiff rule related to the circumstances in which the common-law derivative action could be brought. In view of the abolition of the common-law derivative action by s 165(1), these exceptions are no longer directly relevant.

the Act or the company's Memorandum of Incorporation provides otherwise.[89] There is, however, a well-established common-law exception to this general principle, in that the company in general meeting may intervene in the powers of the board where the board refuses or is unable to institute action on behalf of the company.[90] Consequently, the need to bring a derivative action on behalf of the company will generally arise where the claim is not brought by the company itself.

The classic case (and indeed the way the common-law derivative action initially developed) is where those who commit a wrong against the company are the controllers of the company: for instance, the company is defrauded by its directors who are also the majority shareholders — so the wrongdoers subsequently use their control or influence over the company to prevent the company from instituting legal proceedings against them to remedy the wrong done to the company.[91]

The statutory derivative action is an important minority shareholder protection measure. It shields the minority shareholders from the effects of corporate personality and majority rule. It enables a minority shareholder, who knows of a wrong that is done to the company and unremedied by management (often because they are the wrongdoers), to institute proceedings on behalf of the company.[92]

But the new streamlined statutory derivative action in terms of s 165 is much wider than this and its reach extends beyond instances of wrongdoer control of the company, in contradistinction with the now obsolete common-law derivative action as laid down in *Foss v Harbottle*.[93] Section 165 is available to a wider class of applicants than just minority shareholders. Moreover its use is not limited to wrongs that are committed by the management or the controllers of the company — it even extends to wrongs that are committed by third parties or outsiders (although practically it could be more difficult to bring a claim in such circumstances).[94]

The *Memorandum on the Objects of the Companies Bill, 2008*[95] states that the Companies Act of 2008 codifies and streamlines the right to commence or pursue legal action in the name of the company, and that the statutory action replaces the common-law derivative action. Part of the codification and streamlining process has involved the extension of the statutory derivative action as contrasted with its predecessor, namely s 266 of the 1973 Act. Under the previous company law

---

[89] Section 66(1).
[90] *Alexander Ward & Co Ltd v Samyang Navigation Co Ltd* [1975] 2 All ER 424 (HL). This exception may still be expected to apply under the new company law regime; see Paul L Davies op cit n 9 at 608.
[91] As stated in *Wallersteiner v Moir (No 2)* [1975] 1 All ER 849 (CA), if the company is defrauded by insiders who control its affairs or by directors who hold a majority of the shares, then who can sue for damages? If a board meeting is held, the wrongdoer-directors will not authorise legal action against themselves; and if a general meeting is called for these purposes, they will vote down any resolution that they be sued by the company.
[92] Welling op cit n 79 at 526.
[93] Supra.
[94] This is as a result of the rebuttable presumption in s 165(7) and (8) — see further 16.2.8 below.
[95] *Memorandum on the Objects of the Companies Bill, 2008*, Companies Bill [B 61D–2008] at para 11.

regime, the statutory derivative action was narrower and restricted both the types of wrong as well as the types of wrongdoer. In respect of other causes of action beyond the scope of s 266, shareholders had to fall back on the problematic common-law derivative action. Now, concurrently with the abolition of the common-law action, the statutory action has been expanded and much improved (see further below), particularly with regard to the cause of action, the identity of the wrongdoer, and persons who have legal standing to institute legal proceedings. The problematic common-law concepts of wrongdoer control and the ratifiability principle have been entirely jettisoned under the new regime, and ratification is no longer a bar to any derivative claim.[96]

Section 165 instead provides for a judicial discretion to grant leave to an applicant for derivative proceedings. A key role is accorded to the court under s 165. The section requires a person to apply to the court for leave to bring or to continue proceedings in the name and on behalf of the company, and the court has the discretion to grant or refuse leave, on the basis of guiding criteria stated in the section. The approach that the courts take in exercising their discretion to grant leave is of great consequence and remains to be seen. It is to be hoped that the courts will adopt a permissive approach that will make s 165 more accessible and will promote its use, as opposed to a narrow and restrictive interpretation that will stultify the use of the derivative action. Good and effective legal protection for minority shareholders is fundamental to a developed corporate law system.

Bearing in mind that a derivative action is brought on behalf of the company and not on the applicant's own behalf, potential applicants may be reluctant to make use of the section. The problem of shareholder apathy together with the temptation to be a free-rider, who leaves it to some other person to institute the action, contributes to this. It is an important policy matter that the derivative action is made accessible to applicants and that procedural barriers are reduced. Foremost among these barriers are access to information, which is often under the control of the wrongdoers, and the issue of the applicant's personal liability for the legal costs of the proceedings, which is an important issue since any benefit from the proceedings accrues not to the applicant but to the company (ie to the benefit of all the shareholders of the company).

However, it is an equally important policy consideration that checks and balances be built in, to prevent the abuse of the derivative action. There is a risk of applicants bringing frivolous or vexatious proceedings or of using the section for 'strike suits' or 'greenmail' in order to extract personal benefits for themselves as opposed to the company. The main control measure or safeguard is that the leave of the court is required to commence or continue derivative proceedings.[97] Other control measures are discussed further below.

---

[96] See further 16.2.12 below. Although ratifiability was a bar to the common-law derivative action, ratification was not an obstacle to the statutory derivative action under s 266 of the 1973 Act.

[97] Controls for vexatious claims or frivolous claims include the requirement that a demand must be served on the company, the good faith test, the test of the best interests of the company, the criterion that the proceedings must involve a serious question of material consequence to the company, the possibility of the company having the demand set aside, and the scope for security for costs. Strike suits and greenmail are dealt with below.

16.2.2 Abolition of the common-law derivative action

The new Act abolishes the common-law derivative action,[98] and substitutes a new statutory regime to govern derivative actions. Derivative claims may now be brought only in terms of the Act. Section 165(1) of the Act provides that any right at common law of a person other than a company to bring or prosecute any legal proceedings on behalf of that company is entirely abolished, and that the rights in terms of s 165 replace such abolished rights.

The abolition of the common-law derivative action happily relegates to the history books the notorious rule in *Foss v Harbottle* along with the uncertainties, restrictions and procedural barriers associated with the common-law derivative action.[99] The rule in *Foss v Harbottle*[100] was to the effect that[101] when a wrong is done to the company, only the company may sue for redress (known as the 'proper plaintiff' or 'proper claimant' rule). If the company failed to institute action, a shareholder (member) could in certain circumstances (commonly known as the exceptions to the rule in *Foss v Harbottle*)[102] institute action on behalf of the company by way of the common-law derivative action, but a shareholder could not do so if the alleged wrong or irregularity was one that a simple majority of shareholders could condone or ratify (the 'ratifiability principle').[103] The quandary lay, however, in determining which wrongs and irregularities were ratifiable and which were unratifiable (or non-ratifiable).

The new Act overcomes this hurdle both by abolishing the common-law derivative action and by neutralising the ratifiability principle. Accordingly, ratification is no longer an impediment to any derivative claim under s 165 (see further 16.2.12 below).[104] (The common-law concept of wrongdoer control, in that the

---

[98] In Australia and England the common-law derivative action has similarly been abolished; see s 236(3) of the Australian Corporations Act 2001 and s 260 of the English Companies Act 2006.

[99] As stated by the Van Wyk de Vries Commission of Enquiry into the Companies Act, Main Report RP 45/1970 para 42.10–18, the common-law derivative action was stringently limited by the *Foss v Harbottle* rule, had such a narrow field as to be virtually insignificant, and was beset with procedural difficulties.

[100] (1843) 2 Hare 461, 67 ER 189.

[101] See eg *Edwards v Halliwell* [1950] 2 All ER 1064 (C); *Burland v Earle* [1902] AC 63.

[102] It was widely accepted that a derivative action at common law could be instituted if an unratifiable wrong had been done to the company (in the sense that it could not be ratified or condoned or approved by a simple majority of shareholders), and the wrongdoers controlled the company, so that the company could not or would not institute the action. Such unratifiable wrongs included *inter alia* illegal conduct and 'fraud on the minority'. There is no clear test for 'fraud on the minority' but it is wider than the ordinary concept of fraud and connotes an abuse of power whereby the controllers of the company wrongfully or in breach of duty benefit themselves at the expense of the company and use their control to ensure that no action is brought by the company. The difficulty was to draw the line between wrongs that were ratifiable and those that were unratifiable (or non-ratifiable) (Blackman et al op cit n 33 at 9–101).

[103] The rule in *Foss v Harbottle* was justified by the principles of separate legal personality of the company, as well as majority rule. It took into account the court's refusal to interfere in the internal management of companies, together with the fear of opening the floodgates to a multiplicity of claims.

[104] Ratification was no obstacle to the *statutory* derivative action under s 266 of the 1973 Act, but ratifiability was an obstacle to the *common-law* derivative action.

wrong had to be committed by the controllers of the company, is similarly discarded under s 165.)

However, some of the underlying policy issues of the rule in *Foss v Harbottle* are taken into account in s 165 of the Act, for instance the effect of shareholder ratification or approval in terms of s 165(14) or the question whether the proceedings involve third parties or controllers of the company in terms of the rebuttable presumption in s 165(7) and (8).

16.2.3 Persons who have standing under s 165

The class of applicants who may apply for leave for derivative actions has been substantially widened under s 165. Previously, under the 1973 Act (s 266), it was only members (shareholders) of the relevant company who had *locus standi* to institute a derivative action. Now, under the new regime, s 165 is available to the following categories of applicants:[105]

- shareholders of the company or a related company, as well as persons entitled to be registered as shareholders of the company or a related company,
- directors or prescribed officers of the company or a related company,
- registered trade unions that represent employees of the company, or other representatives of employees of the company, and
- a person who has been granted standing by the court (ie has been granted leave to serve a demand upon the company — see further below). This may be granted only if the court is satisfied that it is necessary or expedient to do so in order to protect a legal right of that person.

Locus standi is given to registered shareholders[106] as well as 'persons entitled to be registered as shareholders'. It is submitted that this will include persons to whom shares have been transferred or transmitted by operation of law even if they are not entered on the securities register, for instance, transmission on death or insolvency. It is further submitted that it may also include cases where persons who are entitled to be registered as shareholders are unable to obtain registration due to an inappropriate refusal by the company or the directors to register the shareholder. This applies particularly to a small quasi-partnership type of company.[107]

Directors and prescribed officers[108] now also have standing under the section.

---

[105] Section 165(2).

[106] In this regard a 'shareholder' is defined in s 1 of the Act as 'the holder of a share issued by a company and who is entered as such in the certificated or uncertificated securities register, as the case may be.' This definition appears to relate to registered shareholders.

[107] See s 51(6) of the Act; see also in this regard ss 260(5)*(c)* and 265(7)*(e)* of the English Companies Act 2006, which extend standing to non-members to whom shares have been transferred or transmitted by operation of law; see further Paul L Davies op cit n 9 at 617.

[108] Prescribed officers are persons who, despite not being directors of the company (and regardless of the title of their office), have general executive authority over the company; general responsibility for the financial management of the company; general responsibility for the management of the legal affairs of the company; general managerial authority over the operations of the company; or otherwise directly or indirectly exercise or significantly influence the exercise of, control over the general management of the administration of the whole or a significant portion of the business and activities of the company, irrespective of any title assigned by the company to an office held by that

This extension is to be welcomed, as directors and prescribed officers have a definite interest in the welfare of the company. They may also be well-versed in the affairs of the company and are therefore best able to identify wrongdoing and to provide the requisite information. Included in the definition of a 'director' is an alternate director as well any person occupying the position of a director or alternate director, by whatever name that person may be designated.[109] Thus a *de facto* director evidently has *locus standi* to bring an application under s 165.

Standing is granted to shareholders, directors and prescribed officers both of the company in question as well as those of 'related companies'. Related companies[110] include holding and subsidiary company relationships, as well as the direct or indirect 'control' by one company of the other or the business of the other (or the direct or indirect 'control' of each of them or the business of each of them by a third person). The extension of *locus standi* to the shareholders, directors and prescribed officers of related companies is laudable. It takes account of the realities of groups of companies and related companies, for example, that shareholders of a holding company may in certain circumstances have a robust interest in preventing harm to its subsidiary by those in control of it.

The inclusion of registered trade unions representing employees of the company and other representatives of employees is striking. Also remarkable is the discretion of the court to grant standing to other persons where it is satisfied that it is necessary or expedient to protect a legal right of that other person. The apparent intention is to create scope for flexibility to permit applicants whose interest does not fit into one of the above specified categories. It remains to be seen in what circumstances the court will regard it as 'necessary or expedient' to grant standing under s 165 to protect legal rights of such other persons. (It ought to be borne in mind that the purpose of the derivative action is to protect the legal interests of the company, as opposed to the legal rights of such 'other persons'. The intention of this provision presumably is that a court may grant standing to other persons whose legal rights are indirectly affected by virtue of a violation of the company's legal interests.)

The right of a person under s 165 (whether to serve a demand on a company or to apply to a court for leave) may be exercised by that person directly, or by the Companies Commission or the Takeover Regulation Panel, or by another person on his or her (or its) behalf in the manner permitted by s 157.[111]

16.2.4 The scope of s 165 and the demand

Section 165(2) provides that an applicant with standing may serve a demand on the company to *commence* or to *continue* legal proceedings, or take *related steps*,

---

person, or function performed by that person (s 66(10) read with s 1 and regulation 45 of the draft Regulations).

[109] Section 1 of the Act.

[110] See s 2 of the Act and chapter 6: Groups of Companies and Related Persons. 'Control' is determined in accordance with s 2(2) of the Act, and includes the direct or indirect control of the exercise of a majority of the voting rights of the company, or the right to appoint or elect directors who control a majority of the votes at board meetings, (whether alone or together with any related or inter-related person). 'Control' also includes the ability to materially influence the policy of the company.

[111] Section 165(16) and s 157.

to protect the legal interests of the company. Various aspects of this provision require attention.

As discussed above, s 165 is concerned with the protection of the legal interests of the *company* as distinct from those of the applicant himself or herself. It may relate to the protection of any 'legal interests' of the company. The term 'legal interests' is undefined, but appears to be wider than the 'rights' of the company. The section is not restricted to any particular type of legal interest or cause of action, nor is there any restriction to any particular class of wrongdoer.

Section 165 thus widens the cause of action and the identity of the true defendant in contrast with its predecessor, s 266 of the 1973 Act. Section 266 applied only in circumstances where the company had suffered damages or loss or had been deprived of any benefit as a result of a wrong, breach of trust or breach of faith that was committed by a director or officer of that company or by a past director or officer while in office. For other types of wrongs or wrongdoers, shareholders previously had to fall back on the common-law derivative action with its numerous disadvantages and complexities. Section 165 of the new Act concurrently abolishes the common-law derivative action and extends the ambit of the statutory action, which may now be depended on to 'protect the legal interests of the company' regardless of the type of legal interest in issue or the identity of the 'wrongdoer' or the other party.

Section 165 consequently goes beyond derivative actions based on a breach of directors' duties. The wrongdoer or the other party may conceivably be the directors, one or more prescribed officers, the majority shareholders or even outsiders (including, but not limited to, those outsiders against whom the controllers of the company decline to act by reason of their association with or interest in the outsider or their wish to shield the outsider). The section now extends to legal proceedings brought by the company against a third party or brought by a third party against the company. It could, however, be more difficult for an applicant to obtain leave for derivative proceedings involving third parties (in view of the rebuttable presumption in terms of s 165(7) and (8) — see 16.2.8 below).

A further important aspect of the section is that it may relate to the *commencement* or the *continuation* of legal proceedings or to *related steps* to protect the legal interests of the company. This, first, allows scope for a person to bring (or defend) derivative proceedings on behalf of the company in the event that the company has failed to *initiate* proceedings. Secondly, it creates scope for a person to intervene in proceedings that the company has already commenced and to *continue* these proceedings as derivative proceedings in the name of and on behalf of the company. Third, it permits a person to take related steps to protect the company's legal interests which could comprise, for instance, settling or compromising legal proceedings on behalf of the company.[112]

These 'legal proceedings' referred to in s 165(2) need not necessarily be proceedings in which the company is the plaintiff. The section includes legal proceedings that are brought *against* the company. (This is implicit from s 165(7)*(a)*(ii)

---

[112] See s 165(7)*(b)*(iii); see also s 236(1) of the Australian Corporations Act 2001 which refers to taking a 'particular step in those proceedings (for example, compromising or settling them)'.

and s 165(7)(*b*)(ii) which refer, respectively, to proceedings by a third party 'against' the company, and the company 'defending' proceedings.) The section consequently creates scope also for a person to defend or intervene in legal proceedings in which the company is the defendant.

Turning to the demand, the requirement that a demand must be served on the company requiring it to commence or continue legal proceedings or to take related steps to protect its legal interests is appropriate. It gives the company the opportunity to reconsider the conduct complained of, and to take suitable remedial action itself to protect its own interests. It is therefore submitted that the demand should be sufficiently specific to apprise the company of the contemplated legal proceedings to be brought (or intervened in or the related steps to be taken) and the grounds for doing so, so that it can be properly evaluated and investigated.[113]

But the demand should not be too technically construed. It should be borne in mind that the applicant at this stage may well be at a disadvantage in not having access to evidence and information on the legal proceedings to be brought. Information about the affairs of the company is generally known to the controllers of the company (who in many cases are also the wrongdoers) and the requisite information may not be easily accessible to the applicant. The applicant, accordingly, should not at this stage be expected to be too specific, particular or technical regarding the cause of action to be brought.[114]

16.2.5 Application to set aside the demand

The company may, within 15 business days, apply to a court to set aside the demand on the ground that it is frivolous or vexatious or without merit.[115] This provision is one of the safeguards directed at protecting the company from frivolous or vexatious demands. As discussed above, it is an important policy consideration that suitable checks and balances be built into the derivative action in order to prevent abuse of the right to bring a derivative action.

16.2.6 The investigation of the demand

Upon receipt of a demand (and on the assumption that it is not set aside by the court on the basis that it is frivolous, vexatious or without merit), the company must appoint an independent and impartial person or committee to investigate the demand. It is vital that the investigator or committee be truly independent and impartial, and that its report be adequately prepared as well as rational and reasonable in its conclusions and recommendations.[116]

The investigator or committee must report to the board on:
- any facts or circumstances that may give rise to a cause of action, or may relate to any proceedings contemplated in the demand,
- the probable costs that would be incurred if the company pursued any such cause of action or continued any such proceedings, and

---
[113] See eg the US case *Allison v General Motors Corp* 604 F Supp 1106, 1117 (D. Del. 1985).
[114] See eg the Canadian cases *Armstrong v Gardner* (1978), 20 OR (2d) 648 (Ont. HC); *Re Northwest Forest Products Ltd* [1975] 4 WWR 724 (BCSC).
[115] Section 165(3).
[116] See s 165(5)(*a*)(ii) and (iii).

- whether it *appears* to be in the best interests of the company to pursue any such cause of action or continue any such proceedings.[117] At this stage the relevant enquiry is whether it *appears* to be in the best interests of the company (as opposed to whether it *is* in the best interests of the company).[118]

Parallels may be drawn between the investigation under the Act and the practice in the USA where companies tend to set up special litigation committees, comprising disinterested and independent directors who are in charge of investigating whether a derivative action is in the best interests of the company.[119]

Court involvement under s 165 occurs only at a later stage, subsequent to the investigation. By contrast, under s 266 of the 1973 Act, court involvement occurred earlier, in that an application was made to the court for the purpose of appointing a provisional *curator ad litem* to conduct the investigation. Furthermore, while the report on the investigation is now made to the board of the company under s 165, it was previously made by the provisional curator *ad litem* to the court on the return day. (If the court confirmed the appointment of the curator on the return day, derivative proceedings under s 266 were then conducted on behalf of the company by the curator; whereas the proceedings are now conducted by the applicant, who has been granted the leave of the court under s 165.)

16.2.7 The company's response to the demand

Within 60 business days after being served with the demand (or such longer time as the court, on application by the company, may permit) the company must either:

- initiate or continue legal proceedings, or take related legal steps to protect its legal interests, as contemplated in the demand, or alternatively,
- serve a notice on the person who made the demand, refusing to comply with it.[120]

16.2.8 The application to court for leave and the discretion of the court

A person who has served a demand on the company, may apply to a court for leave to bring or continue proceedings in the name and on behalf of the company. Three

---

[117] Section 165(4)(*a*).

[118] In contrast, at a later stage when the court considers whether to grant leave to an applicant for derivative proceedings, it must consider whether it *is* in the best interests of the company that such leave be granted (s 165(5)(*b*)).

[119] See the US Revised Model Business Corporation Act (1984), as amended, s 7.44. Section 7.44(*a*) provides that derivative proceedings shall be dismissed by the court on motion by the corporation where the independent committee (or the panel of independent persons appointed by the court or the board of the company by majority vote of independent directors, as the case may be) in good faith and after conducting a reasonable inquiry finds that the maintenance of the derivative action is not in the best interests of the company. In the USA the business judgment rule applies to the decision of the committee, board or panel (as the case may be) and operates to protect its decision whether or not to commence the action by treating it like any other business decision left to the directors to decide (see further below).

[120] Section 165(4)(*b*).

criteria guide the discretion of the court to grant leave. These guiding criteria are discussed in further detail below.

In terms of s 165(5)(a), a person who has made a demand may apply for leave and the court may grant leave only if:[121]

- the company has failed to take any particular step relating to the investigation of the demand and its response to the demand, as discussed in 16.2.6 and 16.2.7 above, or
- the company appointed an investigator or committee who was not independent and impartial, or
- the company accepted a report that was inadequate in its preparation, or was irrational or unreasonable in its conclusions or recommendations, or
- the company acted in a manner that was inconsistent with the reasonable report of an independent, impartial investigator or committee, or
- the company has served a notice refusing to comply with the demand.

In exceptional circumstances, a person may apply to a court for leave to bring proceedings in the name of a company without first making a demand, or without affording the company time to respond to the demand. (This exception in terms of 165(6) refers only to 'bringing' proceedings and not to 'continuing' or 'intervening in' proceedings.) The court may grant leave in such circumstances only if it is satisfied that the delay required for these procedures to be completed may result in irreparable harm to the company, or substantial prejudice to the interests of the applicant or another; that there is a reasonable probability that the company may not act to prevent that harm or prejudice, or to protect the company's interests that the applicant seeks to protect; and that the remaining three criteria for leave[122] are satisfied.

If the company complies with the demand (by initiating or continuing legal proceedings or taking related legal steps to protect the legal interests of the company, as the case may be), then the court will not grant leave to an applicant to sue on behalf of the company. This is logical and sensible. Where the company itself engages in legal proceedings to protect its own legal interests, it will generally be unwarranted to allow an applicant to do so on behalf of the company.

This does, however, give scope for the company to block or frustrate the legal proceedings. To expand on this, where the directors (or those with authority to sue on behalf of the company) are in fact the wrongdoers or wish for some reason to thwart the legal proceedings, they could simply institute a claim in the name of the company without any true intention to earnestly pursue it, by way of an obstructive tactic to avert a successful derivative claim. The solution to this sort of conundrum may be for an applicant to then take steps under s 165 to apply to court for leave to intervene in the proceedings that the company has actually commenced, so as to *continue* the claim as a derivative claim. As discussed above, s 165 commendably creates scope for both the commencement as well as the continuation of proceedings on behalf of the company.

---

[121] Section 165(5)(a). The three guiding criteria in terms of s 165(5)(b) must also be satisfied, as discussed below.
[122] In terms of s 165(5)(b) (discussed below).

Turning to the three criteria to guide the discretion of the court in granting leave, the court may grant leave to the applicant to bring or continue proceedings in the name and on behalf of the company, only if it is satisfied that:[123]
- the applicant is acting in good faith,
- the proceedings involve the trial of a serious question of material consequence to the company, *and*
- it is in the best interests of the company that the applicant be granted leave.

The judicial discretion to grant leave for derivative proceedings must be exercised with reference to these statutory criteria.

Although the interpretation of these criteria by the courts is yet to be seen, the approach that the courts adopt will have a significant impact on the efficacy of the section. It is to be hoped that the courts will adopt a liberal approach that will advance and promote the use of the section, which will also, incidentally, enhance shareholder activism.[124] A narrow or onerous interpretation that would emasculate the derivative action would serve only to frustrate the object of the new statutory provision. The three criteria are considered in turn below.

(a) Good faith (s 165(5)(b)(i))

In considering the good faith criterion, South African courts may well have regard to the Australian approach[125] whereby the courts generally consider two questions:[126] first, whether the applicant genuinely believes that there is a good cause of action that has a reasonable prospect of success, and secondly, whether the applicant has a collateral purpose or is bringing the application in pursuit of a private interest rather than the interests of the company.[127] The question of a collateral purpose is also taken into account in English law.[128] A further important aspect of the good faith criterion is whether there was complicity by the applicant in the matters of which he or she (or it) complains.[129]

An applicant acts for a collateral purpose where the applicant uses a derivative action to pursue his or her (or its) own interests, for instance, where the true objective is to force the defendant directors to arrange for the purchase of their shares,[130] or where the applicants are minority shareholders who participated in

---
[123] Section 165(5)*(b)*.
[124] See the *Memorandum on the Objects of the Companies Bill, 2008* op cit n 95 at para 1.2.4, which states that the new Act should advance shareholder activism.
[125] The above three criteria in terms of s 165(5)*(b)* (including the rebuttable presumption under s 165(7)) are similar to those under the equivalent Australian provision, namely s 237 of the Corporations Act 2001. The latter may accordingly be of assistance in the interpretation of the former.
[126] Austin & Ramsay op cit n 16 at 677; *Maher v Honeysett & Maher Electrical Contractors Pty Ltd* [2005] NSWSC 859.
[127] See eg *Swansson v R A Pratt Properties Pty Ltd* (2002) 42 ACSR 313; *Magafas v Carantinos* [2006] NSWSC 1459.
[128] Paul L Davies op cit n 9 at 618, in the context of the requirement of good faith in the derivative action under s 263 of the UK Companies Act 2006.
[129] Austin & Ramsay op cit n 16 at 676; see eg *Whitwam v Watkin* (1898) 78 LT 188; *Nurcombe v Nurcombe* [1985] 1 WLR 370.
[130] *Goozee v Graphic World Group Holdings Pty Ltd* [2002] NSWSC 640.

and benefited from the wrongdoing and thereafter bring a derivative action for the collateral purpose of drawing attention away from their own wrongdoing.[131]

It seems that where an applicant has nothing obvious to gain by the success of the derivative action, the court may then have reason to be more circumspect in scrutinising the good faith criterion.[132] Good faith may thus be more easily established, for instance, where the applicant is a current shareholder with a substantial shareholding (the value of which will be increased by a successful derivative claim), or where an applicant is a director or officer of the company with a legitimate interest in the welfare and good management of the company.[133] On the other hand, it could be more difficult to show good faith where applicants have only a token shareholding in the company or otherwise have little incentive to sue on behalf of the company.[134]

The good faith criterion may therefore serve to protect the company against frivolous and vexatious claims, and encourage genuine claims that are in the interests of the company.[135]

(b) Trial of a serious question of material consequence to the company (s 165(5)(b)(ii))

This criterion is a further safeguard against frivolous or vexatious claims. Its interpretation is also yet to be seen.

The requirement of a serious question to be tried is construed in Australian law to mean that the applicant need merely establish that the derivative proceedings ought to be commenced or continued, as opposed to actually proving the substantive issues.[136] It is a relatively low threshold in Australian law and is similar to the test used there for interlocutory injunction applications.[137]

In South African law the test of a 'serious question to be tried' has been used in some constitutional cases to determine whether interim relief should be granted.[138] To satisfy the test, the applicant must establish that his or her claim is not frivolous

---

[131] See the English case *Portfolios of Distinction Ltd v Laird* [2004] 2 BCLC 741. See also *Konamaneni v Rolls-Royce Industrial Power (India) Ltd* [2002] 1 WLR 1269 where the derivative action was used as a tactic in a battle for control of the company.
[132] Paul L Davies op cit n 9 at 609; Austin & Ramsay op cit n 16 at 677; *Swansson v R A Pratt Properties Pty Ltd* (2002) 42 ACSR 313.
[133] *Swansson v R A Pratt Properties Pty Ltd* (2002) 42 ACSR 313.
[134] Paul L Davies op cit n 9 at 609; see eg the English case *Harley Street Capital v Tchigirinsky (No 2)* [2006] BCC 209.
[135] Whether the 'clean hands' principle will apply so as to automatically disqualify an applicant under the good faith requirement remains to be seen. (The 'clean hands' principle means that a person has acted in such a way that under the rules of equity it would be unjust to allow a claim brought by him or her to succeed; see eg *Nurcombe v Nurcombe* [1985] 1 WLR 370.) The clean hands principle should arguably not be taken into consideration by the courts. This would also accord with the approach of Australian courts (see *Magafas v Carantinos* [2006] NSWSC 1459).
[136] Austin & Ramsay op cit n 16 at 677.
[137] *Swansson v R A Pratt Properties Pty Ltd* (2002) 42 ACSR 313.
[138] See eg the judgment of Heher J in *Ferreira v Levin* 1995 (2) SA 813 (W); *Reitzer Pharmaceuticals (Pty) Ltd v Registrar of Medicines* 1998 (4) SA 660 (T). (However, other decisions have approached interim interdicts in constitutional matters using the traditional approach that the applicant must show a prima facie right to the relief sought.)

or vexatious, in other words, that there is a serious question to be tried.[139] This may bear some relevance in the interpretation of the phrase 'trial of a serious question of material consequence to the company' in the context of s 165 of the Act.

As to the meaning of the words 'of material consequence to the company', the word 'material', when used as an adjective, is defined in the Act as 'significant in the circumstances of a particular matter, to a degree that is of consequence in determining the matter, or might reasonably affect a person's judgment or decision-making in the matter'.[140]

(c) Best interests of the company (s 165(5)(b)(iii))

The final requirement for the court to grant leave is that it must be satisfied that it is in the best interests of the company that the applicant be granted leave to commence the proposed proceedings or continue the proceedings, as the case may be.[141]

This criterion acknowledges that there may be sound business reasons for companies to decline to pursue legal proceedings, for instance, the loss to the company may have been minor or insignificant, the costs of proceedings may outweigh the potential benefit, the time spent on litigation might be more profitably used elsewhere, or the inability of the wrongdoers to meet the judgment even if the litigation is successful.[142]

The best interests requirement is coupled with a rebuttable presumption. A rebuttable presumption arises that it would *not* be in the best interests of the company to grant leave if it is established that:[143]

- the proceedings are by the company against a third party, or by a third party against the company;
- the company has decided not to bring or defend the proceedings, or to discontinue, settle or compromise the proceedings (as the case may be); *and*
- all of the directors who participated in that decision:[144]
  - acted in good faith for a proper purpose,
  - did not have a personal financial interest in the decision, and were not 'related' to a person who had a personal financial interest in the decision (for instance, a spouse or child of the director or a juristic person 'controlled' directly or indirectly by the director),[145]

---

[139] *Ferreira v Levin* 1995 (2) SA 813 (W) *per* Heher J, relying on the decision of the House of Lords in *American Cyanamid Co v Ethicon Ltd* [1975] AC 396. See also the judgment of Dodson J in *Chief Nchabeleng v Chief Phasha* 1998 (3) SA 578 (LCC).

[140] Section 1.

[141] In contrast the equivalent Canadian provision is that it 'appears to be' in the 'interests' (not best interests) of the company (s 239(2)(c) of Canada Business Corporations Act, RSC 1985). This is a lower standard.

[142] Paul L Davies op cit n 9 at 605–606; Austin & Ramsay op cit n 16 at 677; *Swansson v R A Pratt Properties Pty Ltd* (2002) 42 ACSR 313.

[143] Section 165(7).

[144] Section 165(7)(*c*).

[145] An individual (the director in this case) is 'related' to another individual if they are married, live together in a relationship similar to a marriage, or are separated by no more than two degrees of natural or adopted consanguinity or affinity. An individual is related to a juristic person if the

- informed themselves about the subject matter of the decision to the extent they reasonably believed to be appropriate, and
- reasonably believed that the decision was in the best interests of the company.

These requirements are cumulative and must all be satisfied for the presumption to arise.

For the purposes of the rebuttable presumption, proceedings by or against the company include any appeal from a decision made in proceedings by or against the company.[146] Moreover, a person is a third party for the purposes of the rebuttable presumption if the company and that person are not 'related' or 'inter-related'.[147]

To express it differently, where a wrong is committed against the company by a third party, the rebuttable presumption may apply, so as to make it more difficult to bring derivative proceedings against third parties. On the other hand, the rebuttable presumption will not apply to proceedings between the company and a related (or inter-related) person, with the effect that the court would more easily grant leave for derivative proceedings involving 'related' (or inter-related)[148] persons.

In the case of juristic persons, a 'related' person includes a holding or subsidiary company, as well as a juristic person that directly or indirectly 'controls' the relevant company (or its business) or that is controlled by it. Juristic persons are also related where another person directly or indirectly 'controls' each of them or the business of each of them. An individual who directly or indirectly 'controls' the company is also a related person.[149] 'Control' in this context is defined to mean, in broad terms, the ability to control the exercise of a majority of the voting rights of the company, or the right to appoint or elect directors of the company who control a majority of the votes at board meetings.[150]

---

individual directly or indirectly 'controls' the juristic person (as determined in accordance with s 2(2)). See further s 2 of the Act on 'related' persons and chapter 6: Groups of Companies and Related Persons.

[146] Section 165(8)(*b*).

[147] Section 165(8)(*a*).

[148] Section 1 states that 'inter-related', when used in respect of three or more persons, means persons who are related to one another in a series of relationships as contemplated in s 2(1)(*d*). The Act does not, however, contain a s 2(1)(*d*) — it has been deleted. The draft Companies Amendment Bill, 2010 now proposes to insert a new definition of 'inter-related' as follows: ' "inter-related", when used in respect of three or more persons, means persons who are related to one another in a linked series of relationships, such that two of the persons are related in a manner contemplated in section 2(1), and one of them is related to the third in any such manner, and so forth in an unbroken series' (cl 2(1)(*p*)).

[149] Section 2(1)(*b*) and (*c*).

[150] The concept of 'control' for these purposes is dealt with in s 2(2) of the Act. Briefly, s 2(2)(*a*) states that a person controls a company or its business if (i) that company is its subsidiary; or (ii) that person together with any related or inter-related person, is *(aa)* directly or indirectly able to exercise or control the exercise of a majority of the voting rights associated with securities of that company, whether pursuant to a shareholder agreement or otherwise; or *(bb)* has the right to appoint or elect, or control the appointment or election of, directors of that company who control a majority of the votes at a meeting of the board. A person also controls a company or its business if that person has the ability to materially influence the policy of the company in a manner comparable to a person who, in

In excluding controlling persons and 'related' persons from the benefit of the rebuttable presumption, the Act implicitly recognises that the need to bring a derivative action frequently arises where those in control of the company commit a wrong against it, and subsequently use their control or their influence to prevent the company from proceeding against them. Under s 165, where the wrongdoer controls the company or is related to the company, the wrongdoer will not benefit from the presumption, ie it will *not* be presumed that derivative proceedings against the wrongdoer are contrary to the company's best interests.

It is surprising that the same exclusion from the rebuttable presumption does not apply to the directors of the company. The directors of the company could be regarded as 'third parties' to the company, and not 'related persons', for the purposes of s 165. Directors may consequently benefit from the rebuttable presumption, except where they happen to 'control' the company as well (see the above definition of 'control'). This means that derivative proceedings between a company and its director would be rebuttably presumed to be *contrary* to the best interests of the company, unless the director also 'controls' the company.

This is not an ideal solution. It overlooks the crux of the matter that the derivative action is invariably relied on to protect the company against wrongdoing directors. This is underlined by the fact that the previous statutory derivative action was entirely devoted to wrongdoing by directors and officers (see s 266(1) of the 1973 Act). Where the directors themselves are the wrongdoers, the statutory derivative action should be more (not less) accessible, because this is when the risk of conflicted decision-making by the board or shareholders generally arises. One wonders whether this is an unintended consequence or the result of a deliberate policy decision.

It would have been far better to follow the Australian approach where the directors of a company are indeed regarded as related parties and are consequently *not* third parties to the company for the purposes of the equivalent rebuttable presumption in Australian law.[151] Accordingly, in Australian law derivative proceedings between a company and its director will *not* be presumed to be contrary to the best interests of the company. It is submitted that the same ought to apply to South African law.

Parallels may be drawn between the third limb of the rebuttable presumption (s 165(7)(*c*)) and the business judgment rule.[152] In this regard, as discussed above, the rebuttable presumption that leave is not in the best interests of the company applies only if all of the directors who participated in the decision that the company would not bring, defend or continue legal proceedings against a third party: (i) acted in good faith for a proper purpose; (ii) did not have a personal financial interest in the decision, and were not 'related' to a person who had a personal financial interest in the decision; (iii) informed themselves about the subject matter of the decision to the extent they reasonably believed to be appropriate; *and* (iv) reasonably believed that the decision was in the best interests of

---

ordinary commercial practice, would be able to exercise an element of control (s 2(2)(*d*)). See further chapter 6: Groups of Companies and Related Persons.

[151] Section 273(3) read with s 228 of the Australian Corporations Act 2001.

[152] See s 76(4) of the Act. See further chapter 12: The Duties and the Liability of Directors.

Shareholder Remedies and Minority Protection 713

the company. Its effect is to give some degree of weight to the directors' decision not to bring, defend or continue proceedings against a third party by treating it like any other business judgment or business decision that is normally left to the directors to determine, provided that these four requirements of s 165(7)*(c)* are met. This third limb of the rebuttable presumption takes account of the general principle that the court should not interfere with the internal affairs of companies and with honest and reasonable business decisions of the board of directors of a company. The provision thus constitutes a control for unwarranted interference and unwarranted overriding of the directors' authority to determine whether a company should pursue legal proceedings.

The US derivative action similarly incorporates the US business judgment rule. In this regard, the US Revised Model Business Corporation Act (1984), as amended, provides that if a special litigation committee of *independent* directors, a panel of independent persons appointed by the court or the board of the company by majority vote of independent directors (as the case may be), in *good faith* and after conducting a *reasonable* inquiry, finds that the maintenance of the derivative action is not in the best interests of the corporation, the court shall dismiss the derivative proceedings on motion by the corporation.[153]

The US provision commendably requires the directors who participate in the decision to be independent. Section 165 to some extent achieves a similar effect, by requiring all the directors who participate in the decision to be free of any personal financial interest[154] in the decision and to also be free of any relation (as defined above) to persons with a personal financial interest. However, the concept of independence in the US provision is preferable in that it may be wider. It has been held to mean that the directors must be both 'disinterested', in the sense of not having a personal interest in the transaction in question, as well as 'independent', in the sense of not being influenced in favour of the defendants by reason of personal or other relationships.[155]

To sum up, once the court is satisfied that to grant leave to commence or continue legal proceedings in the name and on behalf of the company is in the best interests of the company (bearing in mind the rebuttable presumption), that the applicant is in good faith, *and* that the proceedings involve the trial of a serious question of material consequence to the company, and provided further that one of the circumstances in terms of s 165(5)*(a)* or (6) above applies, the court may grant leave to the applicant for derivative proceedings.[156] Once the applicant has been granted leave, the applicant is then in a position to commence or continue the derivative proceedings on behalf of the company.

---

[153] Section 7.44(a). However, the effect in the USA may be contrasted with that in South African law. In the USA, where the conclusion of the investigation is that the derivative action is not in the best interests of the company, the proceedings 'shall' be dismissed by the court, whereas in South African law, a rebuttable presumption arises in these circumstances that it is not in the best interests of the company to grant leave for derivative proceedings.
[154] 'Personal financial interest' is defined in s 1 to mean a direct material interest of that person, of a financial, monetary or economic nature, or to which a monetary value may be attributed. See further chapter 12: The Duties and the Liability of Directors.
[155] *Aronson v Lewis*, 473 A.2d 805 (Del. 1984).
[156] Section 165(5)*(b)*.

The court thus has a crucial role in the statutory derivative action, and the approach that the courts adopt in interpreting the statutory criteria specified in s 165 will have a great impact on the effectiveness (or lack thereof) of s 165. Bearing in mind the policy objective of enhanced minority protection,[157] it is suggested that a wide, liberal and flexible approach ought to be favoured over a restrictive one, in order not to stifle a useful minority shareholder remedy.

A final issue is whether the court may entertain other criteria besides those listed in the section. In view of the wording of s 165(5) that the court 'may' (not 'must') grant leave only if the listed criteria are satisfied, it is submitted that there may be scope for the court to consider additional criteria. By contrast, in Australian law (where the statutory provision uses the word 'must'), it has been held that if the prescribed criteria under that Act are satisfied, the court has no discretion and 'must' grant leave.[158] Once again the rationale for the different approach on this issue in terms of s 165 of the Act remains obscure.

16.2.9 Information

A vitally important provision of the Act is that the person to whom leave has been granted is entitled, on giving reasonable notice to the company, to inspect any books of the company for any purpose connected with the legal proceedings.[159]

This takes account of the fact that information about company affairs is generally held by the controllers and directors of the company (who often are the wrongdoers or their supporters in this context), and that the essential information is not necessarily available to the person to whom leave is granted. This section thus ensures that the person to whom leave has been granted has access to relevant information. The right to information is fundamental to the effectiveness of the remedy conferred by s 165.

It is noteworthy that books of the company may only be inspected for a *purpose connected with the legal proceedings*. The question arises what constitutes 'books' of the company. The Act leaves this term undefined. Under the Australian statute, 'books' that may be inspected for these purposes include registers, any other records of information, financial reports or financial records, however compiled, recorded or stored, and documents.[160]

The right to information under s 165 is reinforced by the Promotion of Access to Information Act.[161]

16.2.10 Remuneration and expenses; costs; and security for costs

If a court grants leave to an applicant under s 165, the court must also make an order stating who is liable for the remuneration and expenses of 'the person

---

[157] *Memorandum on the Objects of the Companies Bill, 2008* op cit n 95 at para 1.2.4.
[158] *Maher v Honeysett & Maher Electrical Contractors Pty Ltd* [2005] NSWSC 859; *Magafas v Carantinos* [2006] NSWSC 1459; *Fiduciary Ltd v Morningstar Research Pty Ltd* (2005) 53 ACSR 732.
[159] Section 165(9)(*e*).
[160] Section 9 of the Australian Corporations Act 2001.
[161] Act 2 of 2000.

appointed'.[162] It is not entirely clear who 'the person appointed' refers to. It may be intended to refer to the person who investigated the demand, but this would be problematic in that it does not cover the situations where leave under s 165 is refused, or where a committee is appointed as opposed to a single person. On the other hand 'the person appointed' could perhaps be intended to mean the person who is granted leave (or 'appointed') to commence or continue derivative proceedings on behalf of the company. The latter interpretation will perhaps ensure that a person who brings a well-founded derivative action is not plagued by a lack of funds to maintain the action and an inability to meet the interim expenses until the end of the action.

The order as to who is liable for the remuneration and expenses of the 'person appointed' may be varied by the court at any time. The persons who may be made liable under the order or the varied order are the company, any or all of the parties to the application for leave, or the parties to the derivative proceedings. If the order makes two or more persons liable, it may also determine the nature and extent of the liability of each of those persons.[163]

Turning to costs, a court may make any order it considers appropriate about costs, and may do so at any time. This may arguably create scope for an award of interim costs. The costs order may relate to the application for leave to bring derivative proceedings under s 165 and/or to the actual derivative proceedings themselves that are brought or intervened in pursuant to the grant of leave. (It is noteworthy in this regard that a derivative action involves a two-pronged process: the first step is that a successful application must be made to the court for leave to bring or continue proceedings in the name and on behalf of the company, in terms of s 165, and the second step is the derivative action itself.) The costs order may concern the costs of the following persons: the person who applied for leave or was granted leave, the company, or any other party to the proceedings or the application for leave.[164]

Bearing in mind that the person who is granted leave brings a derivative action for the benefit of the company and does not directly gain from the derivative action, the risk of being burdened with the legal costs could still constitute a strong disincentive even for a potential *bona fide* applicant.

Accordingly, the approach that the courts take towards costs orders could certainly have a substantial effect on the usefulness or efficacy of s 165. It is suggested that the courts need to exercise their discretion in order to promote rather than to curb s 165. Where the statutory criteria for the grant of leave to the applicant are satisfied, the company should arguably be ordered to pay the applicant's costs in relation to the derivative action.[165] In *Wallersteiner v Moir (No 2)*[166] the court cogently stated that, since the derivative claim has the consequence of enforcing the company's rights, where leave is granted it should be the company and not the applicant that is normally liable for the costs of the claim,

---

[162] Section 165(9)(*a*).
[163] Section 165(9).
[164] Section 165(10).
[165] Austin & Ramsay op cit n 16 at 683.
[166] [1975] QB 373 (CA).

even in the event that the litigation is ultimately unsuccessful. (The English court in *Wallersteiner's* case stated further that where the derivative action is a reasonable and prudent course to take, the company should indemnify the applicant for the applicant's own costs and the expenses incurred by the applicant in the course of the derivative proceedings and, additionally, the company should be liable for the costs of the other side (the true defendants) if the derivative action fails.)

A further very useful order is an interim costs order. The possibility of an interim costs order in favour of an applicant who has been granted leave will alleviate the burden on applicants who might otherwise be deterred by concerns about a lack of available funds to finance the costs of maintaining derivative proceedings until the end of the action. The Canadian statute[167] explicitly provides that the court may order the company to pay to the complainant (applicant) interim costs, including legal fees and disbursements (although the applicant may be held accountable for the interim costs on final disposition of the application or the action). Section 165 does not explicitly provide for interim costs orders although, as stated above, it arguably creates scope for such orders.

Turning to security for costs, an order under s 165 may require security for costs.[168] This provision appears to be discretionary in view of the word 'may'. An order that the applicant provide security for costs may be motivated by a desire to protect the interests of the company, and will also prevent vexatious and frivolous proceedings. But its disadvantages are severe and may outweigh its advantages. An order for security for costs could constitute a formidable disincentive for a potential *bona fide* applicant or person to whom leave is granted. It is to be hoped that the courts bear this in mind in exercising their discretion to impose orders for security for costs on persons who apply for leave or are granted leave under s 165. In recognition of this factor, Canadian law specifically provides that the applicant is not to be required to give security for costs in connection with the application for leave or in connection with the action brought pursuant to the grant of leave.[169] Disappointingly, s 165 does not contain an equivalent provision.

The issues of costs, security for costs, and remuneration and expenses will have important practical ramifications for applications under s 165 and derivative actions. In recognition of the impact of these orders, it is to be hoped that the courts will exercise their discretion with regard to such orders in a manner that will promote rather than suppress the efficacy of derivative actions.

16.2.11 Substituting the person to whom leave is granted

Where a court has granted leave to a person for a derivative action under s 165, another person who has *locus standi* may apply to a court at any time for an order that they be substituted for the first person to whom leave was originally granted.

The court may make such an order if it is satisfied that the applicant is acting in good faith and that it is appropriate to make the order in all the circumstances.[170] An order substituting one person for another has the effect that the grant of leave is

---

[167] Section 242(4) of the Canada Business Corporations Act, RSC 1985.
[168] Section 165(11).
[169] Canada Business Corporations Act, RSC 1985, s 242(3).
[170] Section 165(12).

Shareholder Remedies and Minority Protection 717

taken to have been made in favour of the substituting person. If the person who was originally granted leave has already brought the (derivative) proceedings, the substituting person is taken to have brought or intervened in those proceedings.[171]

This provision accordingly enables an applicant to take over existing derivative proceedings if the applicant is in good faith and if it is appropriate in the circumstances. This will be particularly useful where the wrongdoers (for instance, wrongdoing directors), who wish to stifle successful litigation against themselves, are able to persuade a friendly shareholder (or other friendly applicant) to nominally institute derivative proceedings against them without any genuine intention of properly pursuing the proceedings.[172] The solution in these circumstances would be for another applicant to apply to court to take over the existing derivative proceedings by relying on this provision.

16.2.12 Effect of ratification or approval by shareholders

Unlike the common-law derivative action, the statutory derivative action in terms of s 165 is not barred by the possibility of shareholder ratification (or ratifiability) of the wrong.

In this regard, s 165(14) states that if the shareholders of a company have ratified or approved any particular conduct of the company, the ratification or approval does not prevent an applicant from making a demand under s 165, from applying to the court for leave, or from bringing or intervening in proceedings with leave. Furthermore, the ratification or approval will prejudice neither the outcome of an application for leave, nor the outcome of proceedings brought or intervened in with leave.[173] The court, however, may take the ratification or approval into account in making any judgment or order.[174]

By neutralising acts of ratification or approval, a major barrier and difficulty of the common-law procedure is abolished. In this regard, at common law and under the rule in *Foss v Harbottle*, the derivative action was excluded as a mechanism to enforce wrongs that were 'ratifiable' (ie where there was a possibility of ratification of the wrong). However the major quandary was to draw a distinction between ratifiable and non-ratifiable actions. Now, under s 165, where the ratification or approval (or condonation) of the wrong does not arrest or offset the derivative action, there is no longer any need to rely on obscure distinctions between ratifiable and non-ratifiable wrongs. This is certainly to be welcomed.

Ratification or approval under s 165 now is a factor that the court may take into account, as opposed to a mechanical rule that prevents a derivative claim. This fosters flexibility and enables the court to consider each case based on its own facts and merits.[175]

In taking the ratification or approval of shareholders into account under s 165, there are a number of factors that the court may perhaps consider. First, more

---

[171] Section 165(13).
[172] Paul L Davies op cit n 9 at 621.
[173] Section 165(14)*(a)*.
[174] Section 165(14)*(b)*.
[175] Canadian and Australian law adopt similar approaches to ratification (see s 242(1) of the Canada Business Corporations Act, RSC 1985 and s 239 of the Australian Corporations Act 2001).

weight ought to be given to a vote by disinterested shareholders who have no personal interest in the matter. In contrast the courts should be more inclined to disregard shareholder ratifications in which an interested party voted as a shareholder (for instance, where the alleged wrongdoers whose conduct is in question were the majority shareholders, who ratified or approved the conduct). Secondly, the court should also have regard to how well-informed the shareholders were at the time of ratification or approval, and whether they had full disclosure of the facts.

Another factor that the courts might conceivably take into account is whether the character of the act renders it ratifiable or non-ratifiable — this could bring in some aspects of the common-law derivative action, including the cases on fraud on the minority. It is debatable whether the courts would give this construction to s 165(14).

Finally, it is noteworthy that the predecessor to s 165 (ie s 266 of the 1973 Act) similarly applied regardless of any ratification or condonation by the company of the cause of action or the related conduct. However while s 266(4) previously created scope for the court to order that any resolution ratifying or condoning the wrong was of no force or effect, the approach under s 165 is somewhat different. It appears that under s 165 the court will simply sidestep the decision of the majority (by making the derivative action available), rather than striking down the majority's decision as done under the 1973 Act.

16.2.13 Permission to discontinue, compromise or settle proceedings

An additional and fundamental safeguard under s 165 is the requirement to obtain the leave of the court before discontinuing, compromising or settling proceedings that are brought or intervened in with leave under s 165.[176] This vital control measure is designed to counter abuse of the section by shareholders and other applicants.

It reduces the risk of what is known as the 'strike suit' in US law, or the risk of claims of 'greenmail' or 'gold digging'. Here the applicant institutes derivative proceedings with the purpose of blackmailing the management of the company into a settlement of the claim whereby the applicant obtains some private benefit (particularly where the management or directors may be the defendants). In other words the applicant agrees to discontinue the derivative action in exchange for a costly payment in his or her favour or in exchange for a purchase of his or her shares at above market price by the management of the company.[177] This is clearly contrary to the interests of the company, as it occurs at the expense of the company (which would otherwise have benefited from a favourable judgment had the claim proceeded to trial), as well as the other shareholders who are denied the benefit of recovery on the company's behalf.

Since the leave of the court is required before derivative proceedings may be discontinued, settled or compromised, such abuse is curtailed.

---

[176] Section 165(15).
[177] Paul L Davies op cit n 9 at 621.

16.3 DISSENTING SHAREHOLDERS' APPRAISAL RIGHTS[178]

16.3.1 Introduction and underlying philosophy

The appraisal right of dissenting shareholders is a remedy that is completely new to South African law. It has been a feature of US corporate law for over a century and has more recently been adopted in Canada and New Zealand. The appraisal right may best be described as the right of dissenting shareholders who do not approve of certain triggering events to have their shares bought out by the company in cash, at a price reflecting the fair value of the shares, which value may in certain cases be determined judicially.

The appraisal right is not a general right, but is triggered only in certain specified circumstances. Appraisal rights are triggered, in broad terms, where a company passes a special resolution to amend the rights of a class of shares in terms of its Memorandum of Incorporation or to undertake a fundamental transaction. The grant of appraisal rights in these triggering circumstances involves the implicit acknowledgement that such events may have significant and far-reaching consequences for shareholders. This is because the nature of the company as well as the rights of shareholders could be drastically altered. In such circumstances, dissatisfied or dissenting minority shareholders are not compelled to go along with the decision of the (prescribed) majority, but may instead choose to opt out of the company, by withdrawing the fair value of their shares in cash, as a result of the exercise of their appraisal rights.

As a matter of policy, two directly opposing or conflicting values are in issue here. On the one hand, there is a need to provide flexibility for the (prescribed) majority shareholders to fundamentally change or restructure the company and alter investors' rights, in order to adapt to changing business and other conditions. On the other hand, there is the equally important need for minority shareholders to be able to retain their investments in the company together with their expectations of preserving the assets, rights and risks on the basis of which they had invested. In order to balance these conflicting values, fundamental transactions and alterations of class rights are, in the interests of flexibility, subjected to majority rule in that they may be effected with the approval of the prescribed majority; and as a quid pro quo, the disgruntled minority shareholders who disapprove of and dissent from the transaction are granted appraisal rights as an exit strategy, so that effectively they are not compelled to go along with the decision of the prescribed majority. The appraisal right is thus a measure or a remedy that balances the rights and interests of minority shareholders with those of the majority.

There are three important underpinning objects of the appraisal right. Appraisal is traditionally justified as an exit mechanism for dissenters whose expectations have been defeated or disappointed — it gives them the right to withdraw from the

---

[178] The section on appraisal rights in this chapter (16.3) is largely derived from Maleka Femida Cassim 'The introduction of the statutory merger in South African corporate law: Majority rule offset by the appraisal right (Part I)' (2008) 20 *South African Mercantile Law Journal* 1 (referred to hereafter as 'Maleka Femida Cassim (Part I)') and Maleka Femida Cassim 'The introduction of the statutory merger in South African corporate law: Majority rule offset by the appraisal right (Part II)' (2008) 20 *South African Mercantile Law Journal* 147 (referred to hereafter as 'Maleka Femida Cassim (Part II)'), and the authorities cited therein.

company by giving up their shares in exchange for their fair value in cash.[179] The more modern justification, however, is that it is a vital remedy for unfairness, in that minority shareholders who, for instance, are not satisfied with the price offered for their shares, may rely on the appraisal remedy to challenge and dispute the fairness of the offered price.[180] The appraisal right also functions as a check on bad business judgments by directors and controlling shareholders. Where directors, for example, disregard their duty to obtain the best price for the company in a merger,[181] the appraisal right may function as a check on opportunism by directors. This is because the greater the number of dissenting shareholders who wish to exercise their appraisal rights, the more likely it is that the company will reconsider the transaction.

In order for disgruntled shareholders to acquire the right to demand that the company pay them the fair value of their shares they must, on the occurrence of a triggering event, follow the intricate appraisal procedure as set out under s 164 of the Act. Although this is discussed fully below, it is worth emphasising at the outset that a dissenting shareholder becomes entitled to be paid the fair value of his or her (or its) shares only if the dissenter has taken the necessary and mandatory steps to 'perfect' the appraisal right. In this regard, the shareholder must take action as soon as a triggering event is proposed for approval by the general meeting, to make his or her (or its) objection to the proposal known. The dissenter does this by sending a written notice of objection to the company *before* the resolution is put to the vote. Further steps to 'perfect' the appraisal right are that the dissenter must in fact vote against the resolution; thereafter deliver to the company a written demand for the fair value of the shares, once the resolution has been adopted by the company; and comply with all the procedural requirements of the section. The additional requirement that the resolution in question had to be approved by a majority of less than 75 per cent (in terms of the draft Companies Bill),[182] was jettisoned subsequent to strong criticism[183] of this inappropriate 'no-appraisal threshold'. This is a most welcome step in the right direction.

Once the dissenting shareholder's appraisal right has been so perfected, the company should make a written offer to pay the dissenter an amount considered by the directors to be the fair value of the shares. The fair value is determined at the time immediately before the company adopted the relevant resolution that triggered the appraisal right.[184] Should the shareholder consider the company's offer to be inadequate (or the company fail to make any offer at all), the shareholder will be entitled to apply to court for a determination of the fair value of the shares. The involvement of the court in the appraisal procedure is minimal and

---

[179] For instance, in the case of a traditional pooling-type merger. See chapter 15: Fundamental Transactions, Takeovers and Offers.

[180] For example, in the case of a cash merger, where the shareholders are cashed-out. See chapter 15: Fundamental Transactions, Takeovers and Offers.

[181] For instance, if the directors are tempted by various inducements and side-payments offered to them. This would also constitute a breach of fiduciary duty.

[182] GN 166 *Government Gazette* 29630 of 12 February 2007, clause 165(4)(c); see also clause 119(7).

[183] This was strongly suggested by Maleka Femida Cassim (Part II) op cit n 178 at 161–164.

[184] Section 164(16).

occurs only at the final stages of the appraisal procedure, if at all. One of the most appealing features of the appraisal rights is that it is, to a large extent, not a court-driven procedure.

It must be stressed that the shares of a company that are surrendered to the company in the exercise of appraisal rights are not cancelled. Instead they have the status of shares that have been authorised but not issued.[185]

The appraisal procedure is discussed below, together with its problems and limitations. In this regard, the complexity, technicality and inflexibility of the procedural steps are important limitations on its efficacy for shareholders. The attendant time delays and the costs are additional shortcomings that detract from its effectiveness as a shareholder-protection measure.

The other side of the coin, from the perspective of the company, is that the company is obliged to purchase the appraised shares. The potential cash drain on the company to satisfy shareholder demands for appraisal could well result in the abandonment of a triggering transaction that would otherwise have been favourable for the company.[186] Experience in other jurisdictions that have adopted the appraisal remedy shows that the appraisal remedy has not been very successful. Companies tend to be wary of it and tend to view it as a deterrent or obstacle to business combinations or fundamental transactions.

16.3.2 Triggers for appraisal rights

The appraisal right, as stated above, is not a general right but is triggered in certain specified circumstances only. It arises in only four circumstances, three of which relate to fundamental transactions. The appraisal right is triggered where the company proposes to pass a special resolution to:[187]

- dispose of all or the greater part of its assets or undertaking,
- enter into an amalgamation or merger,
- implement a scheme of arrangement, or
- amend its Memorandum of Incorporation by altering the preferences, rights, limitations or other terms of *any* class of its shares in any manner materially adverse to the rights or interests of holders of *that* class of shares (as contemplated in s 37(8)).

For purposes of convenience, the fourth trigger for appraisal is loosely referred to in this chapter as 'alteration of class rights'. This trigger gives rise to a number of difficulties that warrant careful consideration. (See 16.3.6 below on alteration of class rights as a trigger for appraisal.)

It is notable that appraisal rights do not apply in any circumstances relating to a

---

[185] Section 35(5).
[186] See eg Bayless Manning 'The Shareholder's Appraisal Remedy: An Essay for Frank Coker' (1962) 72 *Yale LJ* 223. See also s 164(17) of the Act which provides scope for orders varying the company's obligation to pay the fair value to dissenting shareholders, where such payment will result in the company being unable to pay its debts as they fall due and payable for the ensuing 12 months.
[187] Section 164(2).

transaction, agreement or offer pursuant to a business rescue plan that was approved by shareholders of a company.[188]

A dissenting shareholder is essentially entitled to demand the fair value of his or her shares only if the proposed resolution (above) is ultimately adopted by the company. However the section is activated, according to s 164(2), where a company merely gives notice of a meeting to consider adopting the relevant resolution. The explanation for this earlier time of activation is that a dissatisfied shareholder is required to take action as soon as a triggering event is merely proposed for approval by the general meeting, so as to make his or her (or its) opposition or objection known to the company *before* the resolution is put to the vote.

16.3.3 The appraisal procedure

The appraisal procedure is set out in detail in s 164 of the Companies Act of 2008. Its numerous steps are discussed below.

(a) *Statement of appraisal rights*

When a company gives notice to shareholders of a meeting to consider adopting a resolution to effect one of the triggering events above (viz an alteration of class rights or a fundamental transaction), the notice must include a statement informing shareholders of their rights under s 164.[189]

(b) *Notice of objection by dissenting shareholder*

A dissatisfied or dissenting shareholder may give the company a written notice objecting to the resolution. This must be done at any time before the relevant resolution is to be voted on.[190]

Although the section states that a notice of objection 'may' be given, the importance of this requirement should not be overlooked. A notice of objection is one of the essential prerequisites for the exercise of an appraisal right. Should a shareholder fail to submit a written notice of objection to the company, the shareholder may lose the appraisal right.[191] Accordingly, as soon as one of the triggering events is proposed for approval by the general meeting, the shareholder

---

[188] Section 164(1) read with s 152. Section 164 also does not apply with respect to a conversion of par value or nominal value shares of a pre-existing company in terms of Schedule 5 item 6 and in accordance with the regulations (cl 115 of the draft Companies Amendment Bill, 2010). See further chapter 21: Transitional Arrangements.

[189] Section 164(2). There is some regrettable inconsistency between the various provisions on fundamental transactions. In this regard s 112(3)*(b)*(ii), on proposals to dispose of all or the greater part of the assets or undertaking of the company, requires the notice of the shareholders' meeting to include or be accompanied by a written summary of the provisions of s 164 in a manner that satisfies the prescribed standards. In respect of proposals for amalgamations or mergers, s 113(5)*(b)* requires the notice of the shareholders' meeting to include or be accompanied by a copy or summary of the provisions of s 164 in a manner that satisfies prescribed standards. Section 114(3)*(g)* on proposals for schemes of arrangement requires the report that is distributed to all holders of the company's securities to include, at a minimum, a copy of s 164.

[190] Section 164(3).

[191] See ss 164(5), 37(8) and 115(8).

is best advised to take immediate action to make his or her (or its) objection to the proposed resolution known to the company, by sending a written notice of objection *before* the resolution is actually put to the vote. This is one of the key requirements to invoking the remedy.

The underlying object of the requirement that notices of objection must be given prior to the vote is to alert the company to the number of dissenters, thereby enabling the company to estimate the amount of the cash payment that will be required upon appraisal. As stated above, appraisal demands constitute a potential drain on the cash resources of the company that is obliged to purchase the appraised shares. Indeed, the Act expressly makes provision for the possibility that the company may revoke the adopted resolution after receipt of the dissenters' notices of demand (see further below).[192]

There are two exceptions to the requirement of a notice of objection. First, if the company failed to include a statement of the shareholders' appraisal rights in the notice of the meeting, or secondly, if the company failed to give notice of the meeting at all,[193] then dissenting shareholders do not have to give notices of objection.

(c) Notice of adoption of the resolution

Within ten business days after the company has adopted the relevant resolution (on the assumption that it is adopted), the company must send out notices of the adoption of the resolution. These must be sent to each objecting shareholder who gave the company a written notice of objection, and who has neither withdrawn that notice nor voted in support of the resolution.[194]

If the company fails, however, to send this notice to shareholders, it suffers no adverse consequences *in terms of the Act*.[195]

(d) Demand by dissenting shareholder

A dissenting shareholder is entitled to demand that the company pay him or her (or it) the fair value for all his or her (or its) shares, but only if all the following requirements in terms of the Act have been satisfied:[196]

- first, the shareholder must have sent a notice of objection (subject to the above exceptions),
- secondly, the resolution must subsequently have been adopted by the company,
- thirdly, the shareholder must have voted its shares against the resolution,
- fourthly, the shareholder must have complied with all the procedural requirements of s 164, and
- fifthly, in the case of an amendment to the company's Memorandum of

---

[192] Section 164(9)(c).
[193] Section 164(6).
[194] Section 164(4).
[195] There may, however, be practical consequences eg delays in the delivery to the company of demands by dissenting shareholders.
[196] Section 164(5).

Incorporation to alter class rights, the shareholder must hold shares of a class that is materially and adversely affected by the amendment (see 16.3.6 below).

As previously stated, an appraisal demand was permissible under the draft Companies Bill[197] only if the relevant resolution was adopted with the support of less than 75 per cent of the shares entitled to be voted. A vote that exceeded this 'no-appraisal threshold' bore the consequence that dissenting shareholders were denied appraisal rights. This concept of the 'no-appraisal threshold' was criticised as being 'manifestly and strikingly inappropriate', in view of the underlying object of the appraisal right.[198] Sensibly, this cap on appraisal has since been discarded by the Companies Act.[199]

It is noteworthy that the appraisal right is granted only to those shareholders who are entitled to vote on the relevant resolution. Dissent rights in the event of a fundamental transaction will apparently not extend to shareholders who are precluded from voting on the resolution (in terms of s 115(4)), nor will they extend to shareholders who do not hold any voting rights at all.[200]

Regarding partial dissents, it was suggested[201] that the Companies Bill ought to make it clear that a partial dissent is not permissible, so that a shareholder must dissent in respect of *all* (and not only some of) the shares that it holds in a particular class. This provision prevents shareholders from hedging their bets. Subsequent to this submission, s 164(5) was amended to provide that a dissenting shareholder 'may' demand the fair value 'for *all* of the shares of the company held by that person' [emphasis added]. The word 'all' perhaps indicates that a partial dissent is not permissible.

But by simply stating that the shareholder may demand the fair value 'for *all* of the shares of the company held by that person', s 164(5) fails to distinguish the situation where the appraisal right specifically applies to a particular class of shares (ie an alteration of class rights, where appraisal rights apply only to shares of a class that is materially and adversely affected by the amendment). The question consequently arises: in such circumstances, where a dissenting shareholder holds shares of more than one class, must the dissenter's demand relate to '*all* of the shares of the company held by' it (as per the wording of the section), or

---

[197] GN 166 *Government Gazette* 29630 of 12 February 2007, clause 165(4)(c); see also clause 119(7).

[198] See further Maleka Femida Cassim (Part II) op cit n 178 at 161–164, who states, 'in view of the underlying object of the appraisal right of a dissenting shareholder, the no-appraisal threshold in terms of the Bill is manifestly and strikingly inappropriate' (at 161), and further, that it is 'glaringly out of keeping with the purpose and the justification of the appraisal right' (at 163), and concludes that '[i]t is accordingly submitted that there is no valid justification for the no-appraisal threshold under the Bill: it is inappropriate and ought to be removed from the Bill' (at 163–164).

[199] Unlike certain other jurisdictions, the Act has no market-exception provision or 'market-out' provision that excludes appraisal rights in respect of shares that are traded in a liquid market.

[200] Section 115(4) precludes voting rights that are controlled by an acquiring party, a person related to an acquiring party or a person acting in concert with either of them, from being voted on a resolution in respect of a fundamental transaction (see further chapter 15: Fundamental Transactions, Takeovers and Offers). 'Voting rights' is defined in s 1 of the Act.

[201] Maleka Femida Cassim (Part II) op cit n 178 at 159.

only to those of its shares that fall in the affected class? It is submitted that despite the ambiguous wording of the section, the latter interpretation should be adopted.

A shareholder who satisfies the five requirements above is entitled to demand that the company pay him or her (or it) the fair value for all of his or her shares, and thereby 'perfect' the appraisal right. A demand is made by delivering a written notice to the company. The demand notice must be delivered to the company within 20 business days after the receipt of a notice of adoption of the resolution (or, failing receipt by the shareholder of a notice of adoption of the resolution, within 20 business days after learning that the resolution has been adopted).[202] The demand must state the shareholder's name and address, the number and class of shares in respect of which he or she seeks payment, and a demand for payment of the fair value of those shares.[203]

A shareholder who has sent a demand relinquishes all his or her (or its) other rights in respect of those shares. The shareholder has no further rights in respect of the shares, other than to be paid their fair value.[204] This consequence accords with the approach that the dissenter has thereby elected to opt out of the company with effect from this point, and all that remains is the payment for his or her shares. Despite this, all the shareholder's rights in respect of the shares are reinstated without interruption in three circumstances:[205]

- First, in the event that the dissenter withdraws the demand before the company makes an offer (see below), or allows an offer made by the company to lapse. In this regard, an offer lapses if it has not been accepted within 30 business days after it was made.[206]
- Secondly, in the event that the company fails to make an offer and the shareholder withdraws the demand (The Act does not specify how a shareholder should withdraw the demand.)
- Thirdly, in the event that the company revokes the adopted resolution that gave rise to the shareholder's appraisal rights in the first place.

The Act fails to indicate how the company should revoke a resolution that has already been passed. This may well require a subsequent shareholder resolution, with the attendant costs and inconvenience of once again seeking shareholder approval.[207] One wonders whether it would be valid and enforceable where the agreement itself (eg an amalgamation or merger agreement) or the resolution itself gives the board of directors the power to terminate or to abandon the transaction and revoke the relevant resolution at any time before the effective date, despite prior shareholder approval of it.[208]

---

[202] Section 164(7).
[203] Section 164(8). The draft Companies Amendment Bill, 2010 proposes that the demand must also be delivered to the Takeover Regulation Panel (cl 96).
[204] Section 164(9).
[205] Section 164(9) and (10).
[206] Section 164(12)(b).
[207] The draft Companies Amendment Bill, 2010 (cl 96) now proposes that the company would revoke the resolution by a subsequent special resolution.
[208] This avenue would be particularly useful where the transaction for some reason or another loses its appeal, for instance, where there is a significant number of dissenting shareholders who exercise

It is significant that where the triggering resolution authorised the company to amalgamate or merge with one or more other companies, such that the company whose shares are the subject of appraisal demands has ceased to exist, the obligations of that company under s 164 become the obligations of the amalgamated or merged company.[209]

(e) Offer by the company

Once dissenting shareholders have made their demands, the company must send a written offer to each dissenting shareholder who made a demand. The offer must be sent within five business days after the later of:[210] the day on which the action approved by the resolution is effective, the last day for the receipt of demands,[211] or, if applicable, the day the company received a demand from a shareholder who did not receive a notice of adoption of the resolution.[212]

The offer made by the company must be to pay an amount that the directors consider to be the 'fair value' of the relevant shares. The 'fair value' is determined as at the date on which, and the time immediately before, the company adopted the relevant resolution. The company's offer must also be accompanied by a statement showing how that value was determined.[213] Every offer in respect of shares of the same class or series must be on the same terms.[214]

If the company's offer is not accepted within 30 business days after it was made, the offer lapses.[215] In this event, all the shareholder's rights in respect of the shares are reinstated without interruption.[216]

(f) Shareholder's acceptance of the offer

A shareholder has the discretion to accept or reject the offer made by the company. If a shareholder accepts the offer, the shareholder must tender the relevant share certificates to the company or the company's transfer agent, in the case of shares evidenced by certificates. In the case of uncertificated shares, the shareholder must take the requisite steps (in terms of s 53) to direct the transfer of the shares to the company or its transfer agent.[217]

The company must pay the shareholder the agreed amount within ten business days after the shareholder accepted the offer and complied with the relevant steps

---

their appraisal rights so that the resultant demands on the cash resources of the company render the transaction impracticable, or where an unforeseen disaster causes substantial losses to a merging company. Some jurisdictions expressly empower the board of directors to incorporate provisions of this nature (whether in the contract and/or in the resolution), but the Companies Act of 2008 does not contain such a provision. It is accordingly uncertain whether this would be permissible in South African law.

[209] Or the successor to that company resulting from the amalgamation or merger (s 164(18)).
[210] Section 164(11).
[211] Ie 20 business days after shareholders received notices of adoption of the resolution.
[212] Ie 20 business days after the shareholder learnt of the adoption of the resolution.
[213] Section 164(11); s 164(16).
[214] Section 164(12)(a).
[215] Section 164(12)(b).
[216] Section 164(9) and (10).
[217] Section 165(13)(a).

for the surrender or transfer of the shares to the company.[218] If, however, there are reasonable grounds to believe that payment by the company within this specified period would result in the company being unable to pay its debts as they fall due and payable for the ensuing 12 months, the company may apply to a court for an order varying its obligations.[219] The solvency and liquidity test in s 4 of the Act does not apply in this context.[220]

The shares of a company, which are surrendered to the company in the exercise of appraisal rights, are not cancelled. Rather, they have the same status as shares that have been authorised but not issued.[221]

(g) Application to court to determine fair value

This step of the appraisal procedure applies in the event that the company has failed to make an offer at all, or if the company has made an offer that is considered by a dissenting shareholder to be inadequate, provided that the offer has not lapsed.[222] In these circumstances a dissenting shareholder (who has made a demand) may apply to a court to determine a fair value in respect of the relevant shares, together with an order requiring the company to pay the shareholder the fair value so determined.[223]

Consequently, when the appraisal right is invoked, the involvement of the court is not an inevitable or automatic feature. Court involvement occurs only at the final stages of the appraisal procedure, and in the ideal situation it may even be unnecessary where the company and the dissenter are in accord as to the fair value of the shares. The minimisation of court involvement is one of the most appealing features of the appraisal right.

On an application to the court for judicial appraisal of the shares, all dissenting shareholders who have not accepted an offer from the company must be joined as parties and are bound by the decision of the court. The fair value, as determined by the court, will consequently be inapplicable to those dissenters who accepted the company's offer of fair value. It is the duty of the company to notify each affected dissenting shareholder of the date, place and consequences of the application as well as of their right to participate in the court proceedings. The court may further determine whether any other person is a dissenting shareholder who should be joined as a party.[224]

The court must determine a fair value in respect of the shares of all dissenting shareholders.[225] The fair value must be determined as at the date on which, and time immediately before, the company adopted the resolution that gave rise to the

---

[218] Section 164(13)*(b)*.
[219] In terms of s 164(17); see further below.
[220] Section 164(19).
[221] Section 35(5).
[222] As discussed above, the offer lapses if it is unaccepted within 30 business days after it was made (s 164(12)*(b)*).
[223] Section 16(14).
[224] Section 165(15)*(a)*, *(b)* and *(c)*(i).
[225] Section 164*(c)*(ii).

shareholders' appraisal rights.[226] This impacts on the question whether dissenters may claim a portion of the gains generated by the merger or the transaction itself.[227] However, the Act is silent as to the meaning of the key phrase 'fair value', and on the appropriate method of valuation (see further 16.3.5 below). Commendably, the court has the discretion to appoint one or more appraisers to assist it in determining the fair value of the shares.[228]

Besides determining the fair value of the shares, the court must also make an order:[229]

- requiring the dissenting shareholders to either withdraw their respective demands, in which case each such shareholder is reinstated to its full rights as a shareholder, or to take the necessary steps to surrender or transfer their shares to the company, and
- requiring the company to pay the fair value of their shares to each dissenting shareholder who takes the necessary steps to surrender or transfer the shares to the company, subject to any conditions the court considers necessary to ensure that the company fulfils its obligations under s 164.

It thus seems that upon a judicial appraisal of fair value, each dissenting shareholder has a choice to either accept the court's determination of fair value or, alternatively, to withdraw its demand and be reinstated as a shareholder. It is submitted that the prospect of being saddled with a costs order in respect of the court application would, to some extent, deter potential abuse of this avenue by dissenters.

The court has the discretion to permit a reasonable rate of interest on the amount payable to the dissenting shareholders, from the date that the action approved by the resolution is effective until the date of payment.[230] The underlying purpose is to compensate the dissenting shareholder for the loss of the use of its funds during this period.

In respect of costs orders, the Act provides that the court may make an appropriate order of costs, having regard to any offer made by the company, and the final determination of the fair value by the court.[231] It is to be hoped that costs orders will not be used as a deterrent to judicial appraisal. It must be kept in mind that the valuation of shares creates uncertainty for shareholders and may often yield unpredictable awards, since valuation is not an exact science but merely a

---

[226] Section 164(16).
[227] See further Maleka Femida Cassim (Part II) op cit n 178 at 170.
[228] Section 16415*(c)*(iii)*(aa)*.
[229] Section 164(15)*(c)*(v). The draft Companies Amendment Bill, 2010 (cl 96) proposes to delete the wording 'in which case the shareholder is reinstated to their full rights as a shareholder'. It also proposes to insert the following provision as s 164(15A): 'At any time until the court has made an order contemplated in subsection (15)*(c)*(v), a dissenting shareholder may accept the offer made by the company in terms of subsection (11), in which case — *(a)* that shareholder must comply with the requirements of subsection 13*(a)*; and *(b)* the company must comply with the requirements of subsection 13*(b)*.'
[230] Section 164*(c)*(iii).
[231] Section 164(15)*(c)*(iv).

prediction or an estimate. One hopes that the courts will keep this in mind in exercising their discretion with regard to orders of costs (see further 16.3.4 below).

The Act provides scope for a company to apply to a court for an order varying its obligations, where there are reasonable grounds to believe that payment by the company in accordance with the court order (or payment by a company of the agreed amount that it offered and dissenters accepted) would result in the company being unable to pay its debts as they fall due and payable for the ensuing 12 months. The court may in these circumstances make an order that is just and equitable, having regard to the financial circumstances of the company, and that ensures that the dissenting shareholder is paid at the earliest possible date compatible with the company satisfying its other financial obligations as they fall due and payable.[232]

It is notable that the making of a demand, tendering of shares, and payment by a company to a shareholder in terms of s 164 do not constitute a distribution by the company, or an acquisition of its shares by the company within the meaning of s 48. They are therefore not subject to the provisions of that section, nor to the solvency and liquidity test.[233] Shares of a company that are surrendered to it in the exercise of appraisal rights have the same status as shares that have been authorised but not issued.[234]

Finally, as discussed above, if a shareholder's appraisal rights were triggered by a resolution that authorised the company to amalgamate or merge with one or more other companies, such that the relevant company has ceased to exist, the obligations of that company under s 164 are the obligations of its successor resulting from the amalgamation or merger.[235]

16.3.4 Flaws and limitations of the appraisal procedure

It is evident that the appraisal procedure is complex and technical, involving a number of specified notices, each coupled with a strict prescribed time limit for completion. As discussed above, there are several necessary and mandatory steps to 'perfect' the appraisal right. A shareholder must comply meticulously with each procedural step in order to 'perfect' and to exercise its appraisal right, rendering the appraisal procedure a potential minefield for dissenting shareholders. It is submitted that the procedural limitations detract to a large extent from the effectiveness of the appraisal right as a shareholder protection measure. Not only do the complexity and the rigidity of the procedural steps make it difficult for a shareholder to exercise his or her appraisal rights without legal assistance and attendant

---

[232] Section 164(17).
[233] Section 164(19). Furthermore, s 164 does not apply with respect to the conversion by a pre-existing company of par value or nominal value shares in terms of Schedule 5 item 6 and in accordance with the regulations (cl 115 of draft Companies Amendment Bill, 2010). The draft Companies Amendment Bill, 2010 also proposes to insert, as s 164(20), the following: 'Except to the extent– *(a)* expressly provided in this section; or *(b)* that the Takeover Regulation Panel rules otherwise in a particular case, a payment by a company to a shareholder in terms of this section does not obligate any person to make a comparable offer under section 125 to any other person.'
[234] Section 35(5).
[235] Section 164(18).

legal expenses, but the dissenting shareholder may also lose the appraisal right on a failure to comply with certain procedural steps within the many specified time periods.

The appraisal procedure is, moreover, skewed in favour of the company, in that the company suffers no similar adverse consequences for its non-compliance with its complementary procedural obligations. To expand on this, the shareholder may lose the appraisal right if the shareholder fails to deliver to the company both a written notice of objection and a written demand within the time limits prescribed by the Act. However, if the company fails to send its two requisite notices to the shareholders, namely the notice of the shareholders' meeting to consider the proposed resolution including a statement of the appraisal rights and the notice of the adoption of the resolution, the company suffers no real adverse consequences.[236] Likewise, if the company fails to make a written offer to pay the fair value of their shares to the relevant shareholders, there are once again no adverse consequences for the company.[237] The shareholder, in contrast, is given a strict specified period of only 30 days after the company's written offer (if any) to apply for a judicial determination of the fair value of his or her (or its) shares, after which the offer lapses and the shareholder apparently loses the right to apply for a judicial appraisal.[238]

The imbalance inherent in these provisions is open to criticism. It operates in favour of the company and harshly against the shareholder, resulting in a potential for unfairness to a dissenting shareholder who may lose his or her (or its) appraisal right upon an unwitting failure to comply with one of the many technical and complex steps prescribed by the Act. This is particularly inappropriate in view of the fact that generally the company, but not the dissenting shareholder, will have ready access to and funds for legal representation and proper guidance in complying with the complex procedural steps. While the underlying purpose of the procedural steps may be a worthy one, in that they promote and encourage settlement between the company and the dissenters without necessarily resorting to *judicial* appraisal, it is nonetheless submitted that the balance drawn by the Act between the dissenting minority shareholders and the company may be inappropriate. It is to be hoped that the court will interpret the dissenting shareholders' procedural obligations as flexibly and as leniently as possible, to excuse the shareholders' failure to comply strictly with the prescribed procedure and time periods despite a genuine attempt to do so.

A second problem with appraisal is the delay experienced by dissenting shareholders when exercising their appraisal rights. Once a shareholder sends the written demand to the company, the shareholder loses all further rights in respect

---

[236] In the event of the company's failure to comply with the former requirement, the only consequence is that the shareholder is excused from sending a notice of objection to the company (s 164(6)). Should the company fail to send the latter notice (ie notice of adoption of the resolution), the only consequence is that the shareholder's prescribed 20 business day period (within which to deliver a written demand to the company) starts to run from the day that the shareholder learns of the adoption of the resolution (s 164(7)*(b)*).
[237] See s 164(14)*(a)*.
[238] Section 164(12)*(b)* read with s 164(14)*(b)*.

of those shares other than to be paid their fair value. But the fair value is paid only at the end of the appraisal proceedings (assuming that the shareholder opts for a judicial appraisal of fair value). Until then, the shareholder is deprived of the use of his or her funds.

A third limitation relates to the costs of the appraisal proceedings. The Act provides that the court has the discretion to make an appropriate order of costs, having regard to any offer made by the company and the final determination of the fair value by the court. Although the discretionary nature of the costs order may, to some extent, encourage parties to reach agreement in good faith on the fair value of the shares without unnecessarily or frivolously resorting to the courts, the possibility of being saddled with an adverse costs order may discourage the shareholder from asserting the appraisal right. It must be borne in mind that the valuation of shares is not an exact science but merely a prediction or an estimate. A judicial determination of the fair value creates uncertainty, and a substantial risk that the shareholder's estimate of the fair value may be higher than the valuation made by the court. Fair value is a *range of values* and not a particular figure (as suggested by the wording of s 164(15)*(c)*(ii), which provides that the court must determine '*a*' fair value and not '*the*' fair value). Appraisal could thus be prohibitively costly to a dissenting shareholder. It is to be hoped that the courts will bear these factors in mind in exercising their discretion with regard to costs.

16.3.5 Determining fair value in appraisal

Section 164 requires the court to determine 'a fair value' for the shares of dissenting shareholders.[239] It states that the time for valuation is the date on which, and time immediately before, the company adopted the resolution that gave rise to the shareholders' appraisal rights.[240] It is noteworthy that the reference point for valuation is the adoption of the resolution and not the later date of the effectuation of the relevant corporate action,[241] nor the earlier date of the announcement of the transaction (if any).

The Act does not, however, specify the method of valuation in appraisal proceedings. It must be emphasised that 'fair value' is not necessarily equivalent to market value alone. In many circumstances the market value is not appropriate or reflective of the true worth of the company or the fair value of the shares, for instance where the market is thin or the shares are undervalued on the market or in a depressed market.[242]

Although the issue of the fair price of shares has been considered in South African law in the context of the oppression remedy under s 252 of the 1973 Act and the mandatory acquisition of the shares of minorities under s 440K of the

---

[239] Section 164(15)*(c)*(ii).
[240] Section 164(16).
[241] As in the US Revised Model Business Corporation Act, 1984, as amended, s 13.01(4).
[242] See further Maleka Femida Cassim (Part II) op cit n 178 at 167–171 and the authorities cited therein.

1973 Act, the same factors and considerations do not necessarily apply in cases where the fair value is being assessed for the purposes of the appraisal remedy.[243]

It is suggested with respect that South African courts would have useful resort to and guidance from the well-developed and long-standing judicial experience of the Delaware courts in the interpretation of 'fair value' and in appraisal-valuation methodology. This would be in a similar vein to other jurisdictions that have adopted the appraisal right, such as Canada and New Zealand.[244]

In view of the significance and complexity of appraisal valuation methodology, it is commendable that the Act makes provision for the discretionary appointment by the court of appraisers who will assist the court in determining fair value.[245]

An interesting question is whether shareholders may waive their appraisal rights in advance. This remains to be seen. It is submitted that s 164 is an 'unalterable' provision,[246] so that any attempt to waive or negate appraisal rights in advance, whether in terms of a company's Memorandum of Incorporation or a shareholder agreement or voting agreement, may well be found to be void on the basis of inconsistency with the Act,[247] or it may fall foul of the anti-avoidance provision.[248] The question of the enforceability of a purported advance waiver of appraisal rights is further compounded by the policy issues underlying the appraisal right. It must be kept in mind, in this regard, that appraisal is an express statutory right designed for the fundamentally important policy purpose of protecting minority shareholders (by providing an exit mechanism and by serving as a distinct counterbalance to the liberalisation and leniency of the statutory procedures for fundamental transactions, as discussed in 16.3.1 above), and to function further as a check on the management of a company.[249]

16.3.6 Alteration of class rights as a trigger for appraisal

For purposes of convenience, this trigger for appraisal is loosely referred to herein as 'alteration of class rights'. Section 164, as discussed above, is triggered in four

---

[243] See further Maleka Femida Cassim (Part II) op cit n 178 at 167–168, 176 and the authorities cited therein.

[244] The US Revised Model Business Corporation Act, 1984, as amended. Section 13.01(4) now expressly defines 'fair value' to mean the value of the corporation's shares determined: (i) immediately before the effectuation of the corporate action to which the shareholder objects (it is noteworthy that the reference point is the effectuation of the corporate action and not the earlier date of the shareholder vote on the corporate action or the announcement of the corporate action); (ii) using customary and current valuation concepts and techniques generally employed for similar businesses in the context of the transaction requiring appraisal; and (iii) without discounting for lack of marketability or minority status.

Delaware law now clearly defines the dissenting shareholder's claim as a pro rata claim to the value of the firm as a going concern. Thus the underlying principle of an appraisal proceeding is to value the corporation *itself* and not the shares held by a particular shareholder and, importantly, to value it on a going concern basis rather than on a liquidated basis.

[245] Section 164*(c)*(iii)*(aa)*.

[246] As defined in s 1. See further chapter 4: Formation of Companies and the Company Constitution.

[247] See s 15(1); s 15(7). See further chapter 4: Formation of Companies and the Company Constitution.

[248] Section 6(1). See further chapter 1: Introduction to the New Companies Act and chapter 4: Formation of Companies and the Company Constitution.

[249] Even if an advance waiver of appraisal is found to be permissible in theory, it would give rise to complex issues of the disclosure requirements that are necessary for an effective waiver.

circumstances, one of which is a resolution by the company to 'amend its Memorandum of Incorporation by altering the preferences, rights, limitations or other terms of any class of its shares in any manner materially adverse to the rights or interests of holders of that class of shares, as contemplated in section 37(8)' (s 164(2)(*a*)). Section 37(8), in turn, states that '[i]f the Memorandum of Incorporation of a company has been amended to materially and adversely alter the preferences, rights, limitations or other terms of a class of shares, any holder of those shares is entitled to seek relief in terms of s 164', if that shareholder: (i) notified the company in advance of the intention to oppose the resolution to amend the Memorandum of Incorporation; and (ii) was present at the meeting, and voted against that resolution.

There is a glaring inconsistency between the two provisions above. While s 164(2)(*a*) refers to an alteration that is materially adverse to the rights or '*interests*' of the relevant shareholders, s 37(8) excludes any reference to the interests of the shareholders. The term 'interests' is significantly wider than 'rights'.[250] One wonders whether the discrepancy or inconsistency between s 164(2)(*a*) and s 37(8) is an unintended consequence on the part of the drafters of the Act.

The phrase 'materially adverse to the rights or interests' is undefined and may be expected to spark considerable debate and uncertainty. This is compounded by a second disparity between the two provisions, in that s 37(8) requires the alteration to be *material and adverse*, whereas s 164(2)(*a*) requires it to be *materially adverse* (to rights or interests). The two phrases do not necessarily mean the same thing. This inconsistency in drafting is most regrettable, as the two differing tests will yield contradictory results in certain cases.[251]

It must be kept in mind that this trigger for appraisal applies only where the 'alteration of class rights' is effected by an amendment of the Memorandum of Incorporation. No appraisal rights arise where the board of directors effects a change. It appears, in any event, that the board does not have the power to alter class rights in terms of the Act. Although s 36(2)(*b*), at first blush, seems to permit the board to 'change' the preferences, rights, limitations or other terms of a class of shares, the section restricts the change to a change 'in the manner contemplated in subsection (3)'. Subsection (3), in turn, merely empowers the board to 'determine' the preferences, rights, limitations or other terms of a class of shares as contemplated in s 36(1)(*d*), ie where the company's Memorandum of Incorporation sets out a class of shares without specifying the class rights, for which the board must determine the class rights *before* the shares are issued. Consequently the word 'change' in s 36(2)(*b*) is misleading in this context, and it is submitted that 'alterations of class rights' in terms of the Act may be effected, not by the board, but only by way of an amendment of the Memorandum of Incorporation.

The question arises whether this trigger for appraisal will apply to companies with only one class of shares. It seems that it may be inapplicable to such

---

[250] See *Utopia Vakansie-Oorde Bpk v Du Plessis* 1974 (3) SA 148 (A) 163–4.
[251] The term 'material', when used as an adjective, is defined in s 1 to mean significant in the circumstances of a particular matter, to a degree that is of consequence in determining the matter, or might reasonably affect a person's judgment or decision-making in the matter.

companies. In all likelihood, a 'class' of shareholders will exist only where there is at least one other class of shareholders in existence.[252] The Canadian statute, by contrast, explicitly overrules case law by stating that the right to dissent may be invoked even if a corporation has only one class of shares.[253] There is no such provision in the Companies Act of 2008.

A further important issue is what constitutes the 'preferences, rights, limitations or other terms of any class' of shares. The definition of a class right has in the past been the subject of academic debate. A class right may be interpreted to mean all the rights conferred on any class or, alternatively, only the rights of a class that are specifically unique to that class (ie rights that are not identical to the rights belonging to another class). A middle option was that class rights included the rights unique to a particular class together with the core rights of shareholders (ie voting rights, rights to dividends and rights to participate in surplus assets on a winding-up).[254] Whether this uncertainty will continue to apply to the new Act, in relation to the phrase 'preferences, rights, limitations or other terms of any class' of shares, remains to be seen.[255]

It is submitted that the altered 'rights, preferences, limitations or other terms' of a class of shares may include the core rights of shareholders as to dividends, voting rights, rights to participate in surplus assets on winding-up and priority to return of capital on a winding-up, together with the unique rights, preferences, limitations or other terms that are unique to a particular class. Also explicitly included in Canadian law are redemption rights, rights of transfer or pre-emptive rights, and conversion privileges.[256] There is no authority on whether these terms will be taken into account in South African law, but it is submitted that it is likely that they will now fall within the scope of the phrase 'rights, preferences, limitations or other terms' of a class of shares in the context of s 164, particularly if they are unique to a particular class.[257] Canadian legislation moreover includes an amendment of the Memorandum of Incorporation to increase or decrease the maximum number of authorised shares of a class[258] — but it is submitted that this will not constitute an 'alteration of class rights' or other terms in South African law.

The key question is whether changes to the Memorandum of Incorporation, which do not directly or *formally alter* the rights (or preferences, limitations or other terms) of a class of shares but rather *reduce the value* of those rights, will constitute an *'alteration'* of class rights (or other terms) for the purposes of triggering the appraisal remedy. Closely linked to this is the inclusion of the

---

[252] See eg *Underwood v London Music Hall Ltd* [1901] 2 Ch 309; *Re Mackenzie & Co Ltd* [1916] 2 Ch 450; *Greenhalgh v Arderne Cinemas Ltd* [1946] 1 All ER 512 (CA).
[253] Canada Business Corporations Act, R.S.C. 1985, s 190(2.1); *McConnell v Newco Financial Corporation*, (1979) 8 BLR 180 (BCSC).
[254] Paul L Davies op cit n 9 at 671.
[255] It is pertinent, in this regard, that the former uncertainty related to the wording 'the rights *attached to* any class of shares', whereas the relevant wording under the Act now is the rights *'of'* any class of shares.
[256] Canada Business Corporations Act, R.S.C. 1985, s 176(1)*(c)*.
[257] See eg s 37(5)*(b)*.
[258] Canada Business Corporations Act, R.S.C. 1985, s 176(1)*(a)*.

'interests' of shareholders in terms of s 164(2)*(a)* (albeit, illogically and inconsistently, not in terms of s 37(8)), bearing in mind that 'interests' are wider than 'rights' and may include the full enjoyment of rights as shareholder.[259] This key issue is analysed in detail below. In brief, it will be submitted below that the fundamentally important distinction between a formal alteration of class rights and an alteration of the constitution reducing the value of those rights (without formally changing them) is preserved under the Act. The practical consequence is that where there is a formal improvement of the rights of some *other* class of shares in terms of the Memorandum of Incorporation (eg the voting rights of Class 'B' shares), which has the effect of reducing the value of the rights of the relevant class of shares (eg the Class 'A' shares whose voting power has consequently been diluted), this will fall outside the scope of the section and will not therefore trigger appraisal rights for the relevant class of shareholders (ie Class 'A'). This is further elucidated in detail below.

(a) Further explanation of the term 'alteration'

This discussion analyses in detail the key question posed above, viz would changes to the Memorandum of Incorporation, which do not directly or *formally alter* the rights (or preferences, limitations or other terms) of a class of shares but rather *reduce the value* of those rights, constitute an *'alteration'* of rights (or other terms) for the purposes of triggering the appraisal remedy?

This crucial issue is discussed with reference to the dual requirements of s 164(2)*(a)*. In this regard it may be said, for the purpose of convenience, that there are essentially two prerequisites for the appraisal right under s 164(2)*(a)*, both of which must be satisfied:

(i) first, there must be an amendment of the Memorandum of Incorporation by altering the preferences, rights, limitations or other terms of any class of shares, and
(ii) secondly, the alteration must be in any manner materially adverse (or material and adverse)[260] to the rights or interests of holders of that class of shares.

(b) 'Alteration' of class rights and the first element of s 164(2)(a)

In respect of the first element, ie that there must be an amendment of the Memorandum of Incorporation by altering the preferences, rights, limitations or other terms of any class of shares, under the previous regime the courts gave a restricted, narrow and technical meaning to a variation (or alteration) of rights. It has been laid down that rights are 'varied' (in the context of s 102 of the 1973 Act regulating the variation of rights in respect of shares) when their literal form is actually altered, and not when they are merely rendered less valuable. A distinction is drawn between, on the one hand, varying the formal or actual rights of a class of shares and, on the other hand, amendments to the company's constitution that reduce the value of those rights without formally changing them.

---

[259] *Utopia Vakansie-Oorde Bpk v Du Plessis* 1974 (3) SA 148 (A).
[260] See above.

A variation of class rights at common law was said to entail varying the *'rights'* themselves — as distinguished from merely affecting the shareholders' *'enjoyment of the rights'* while keeping the rights themselves precisely as they were before.[261] To express it differently, a variation of class rights at common law encompasses only *direct* alterations of the rights of a class of shares, in the sense that those rights attached to a particular class of shares are themselves altered. *Indirect* alterations, by contrast, do not suffice at common law ie where an 'alteration' of a class of shares is effected by an amendment of the formal rights of some other class of shares.

It was thus held that the rights of certain ordinary shares (Class 'X') were not varied by the subdivision of other ordinary shares into more voting shares, which had the effect of diluting the voting power of Class 'X'. The basis for this decision was that the voting *rights* of Class 'X' were not themselves literally varied and remained exactly as they were before — only their *enjoyment of the rights* was affected.[262] It was similarly decided that the rights of preference shares were not varied where new preference and ordinary shares had been issued.[263] Another instance is that, in a company with both preference shares and ordinary shares, an issue of preferred ordinary shares with a superior ranking to the ordinary shares, but an inferior ranking to the existing preference shares, was held not to constitute a variation of the rights of either of the existing classes.[264] The operational principle in all these cases is that even though all these changes had an adverse effect on the value of the complaining shareholders' rights, they did not directly vary their formal rights, which had remained the same as before. To elaborate, although an issue of new shares or a subdivision of other shares may change the balance of voting power of the various classes of shares and thereby change the control of the company, it is not considered at common law to constitute a variation of rights because the voting 'right' itself (ie the 'right' to cast a vote) is unaltered and remains exactly as it was before. All that is affected is the holders' 'enjoyment' of the right, since their votes are worth less due to the dilution or diminution of the voting power of their class of shares.[265]

Indirect alterations, or alterations affecting the 'enjoyment' of rights as opposed to the rights themselves, may include a dilution (of voting power or other rights) as well as 'leapfrogging'. 'Leapfrogging' is the increase in or the improvement of

---

[261] *White v Bristol Aeroplane Co Ltd* [1953] 1 All ER 40 (CA); *Re John Smith's Tadcaster Brewery Co* [1953] Ch 308 (CA). See also *Utopia Vakansie-Oorde Bpk v Du Plessis* 1974 (3) SA 148 (A).
[262] *Greenhalgh v Arderne Cinemas Ltd* [1946] 1 All ER 512 (CA). But a dilution of voting power will amount to a variation of a right where the shareholder has a right that requires the balance of voting power to be preserved (*Greenhalgh v Arderne Cinemas Ltd* [1946] 1 All ER 512 (CA); *White v Bristol Aeroplane Co Ltd* [1953] 1 All ER 40 (CA)).
[263] *White v Bristol Aeroplane Co Ltd* [1953] 1 All ER 40 (CA); *Re John Smith's Tadcaster Brewery Co* [1953] Ch 308 (CA).
[264] *Hodge v James Howell & Co* [1958] CLY 446, CA referred to in Paul L Davies op cit n 9 at 669.
[265] *White v Bristol Aeroplane Co Ltd* [1953] 1 All ER 40 (CA); *Re John Smith's Tadcaster Brewery Co* [1953] Ch 308 (CA); *Greenhalgh v Arderne Cinemas Ltd* [1946] 1 All ER 512 (CA). See also *Utopia Vakansie-Oorde Bpk v Du Plessis* 1974 (3) SA 148 (A).

the rights of a competing class of shares, thereby changing the comparative ranking of the classes of shares.[266]

The common-law approach of distinguishing between a formal variation of the 'right' itself as opposed to merely affecting the 'enjoyment of rights', may well be expected to continue to apply to the first element of s 164(2)(a), and more specifically, to the judicial interpretation of the term 'alteration'. Ultimately, of course, this remains subject to a determination of the court under the new Act.

Finally, it must be kept in mind that this trigger for appraisal applies only where an alteration is effected by an amendment to the Memorandum of Incorporation.[267] Where, for instance, a dilution of relative voting power occurs by way of the issue of additional authorised shares, the first element of s 164(2)(a) would be left unsatisfied, since there has been no amendment of the Memorandum of Incorporation at all, with the result that s 164 would not apply at all and the dissenting shareholders would have no appraisal rights.

(c) 'Alteration' of rights and the second element of s 164(2)(a)

Turning to the second element of s 164(2)(a), viz that the alteration must be in any manner materially adverse (or material and adverse)[268] to the rights or interests[269] of holders of that class of shares, the obvious question arises as to the effect of including the *'interests'* of shareholders in s 164(2)(a) (albeit, illogically and inconsistently, not under s 37(8)). As discussed above, it has been held that 'interests' are wider than 'rights' and may include the full *enjoyment* of rights as a shareholder and their protection.[270]

The central enquiry is as follows: by including the concept of 'interests' in s 164(2)(a), is it the intention of the drafters to trigger appraisal rights for a class of shareholders (Class 'A') where a literal alteration of the rights of some *other* class of shares (Class 'B') affects the *'enjoyment* of rights' or the *'interests'* of the former class (Class 'A') by making their class rights less commercially valuable, for instance, by a redistribution of relative voting or other rights or 'leapfrogging'?[271]

---

[266] Welling op cit n 79 at 566–567. Leapfrogging could be effected, for instance, by increasing the rights or privileges of some other class of shares having rights or privileges equal or superior to the shares of the relevant class. It could also be effected by making some other class of shares, having rights or privileges inferior to the shares of the relevant class, equal or superior to the latter shares.

[267] As discussed above, no appraisal rights would arise where a change is effected by the board of directors. In any event, it appears that the board does not have the power to alter class rights in terms of the Act, despite the word 'change' in s 36(2)(b) (see further s 36(3) and s 36(1)(d) and the discussion above).

[268] While s 37(8) requires the alteration to be *material and adverse*, s 164(2)(a) requires it to be *materially adverse* (to rights or interests). As discussed above, they do not necessarily mean the same thing.

[269] As stated above there is a conflict in respect of the term 'interests', in that s 37(8) fails to refer to 'interests' whereas s 164(2)(a) includes 'interests'.

[270] *Utopia Vakansie-Oorde Bpk v Du Plessis* 1974 (3) SA 148 (A) at 163–4 in the context of s 62*quat*(4) of the 1926 Act (concerning the meaning of the phrase a resolution which directly affects any of the rights attached to such shares or the interests of the holders thereof).

[271] See in this regard *Utopia Vakansie-Oorde Bpk v Du Plessis* 1974 (3) SA 148 (A) in relation to whether 'interests' includes the maintenance of voting power.

It is submitted that, on a proper interpretation of the section, this is not the intention of the legislature. Two factors must be borne in mind: First, the section as discussed above has two prerequisites, both of which must be satisfied. Secondly, and more importantly for the purposes of this discussion, both elements must be fulfilled by the *same class* of shareholder.

It is submitted, in this regard, that the literal wording of both s 164(2)*(a)* as well as s 37(8) evidently requires a formal (or literal) alteration of the rights of a particular class itself (ie Class 'A' itself), in order for those (Class 'A') shareholders to qualify for appraisal under the section. To elaborate, s 164(2)*(a)* makes appraisal rights available where the company resolves to 'amend its Memorandum of Incorporation by altering the preferences, rights, limitations or other terms of *any* class of its shares in any manner materially adverse to the rights or interests of holders of *that* class of shares, as contemplated in section 37(8)' [emphasis added]. The word *'that'* seemingly indicates that the only class that could be entitled to appraisal is the class whose rights have been formally altered. Section 37(8), in a similar vein, requires a formal alteration by stating that '[i]f the Memorandum of Incorporation of a company has been amended to materially and adversely alter the preferences, rights, limitations or other terms of *a* class of shares, any holder of *those* shares is entitled to seek relief in terms of s 164' [emphasis added]. The word *'those'* similarly indicates that the class of shares that is entitled to appraisal is the class whose rights have been formally altered — provided, of course, that the alteration has been in a manner materially adverse to their rights or interests.

Thus, a shareholder whose 'interests' are affected in a materially adverse manner may rely on the appraisal right only where its interests have been so affected by a formal alteration of the rights of *its* class of shares. A shareholder of Class 'A', for instance, may not claim appraisal rights based on a formal alteration of the Memorandum of Incorporation that increases the voting rights of Class 'B', in a manner that is materially adverse to its 'interests' in the value and voting power of its Class 'A' shares. To take another example, where there is a subdivision of shares of a competing class (Class 'Z') that has the effect of diluting the voting power of another class of shares (Class 'X'), this may be materially adverse to the *interests* of the Class 'X' shareholders (ie the second element of the appraisal trigger is satisfied), but it does not constitute an amendment of the Memorandum of Incorporation to alter the formal or literal rights or other terms of *'that'* class (Class 'X') of shares (ie the first of the two elements or requirements of s 164(2)*(a)* is left unfulfilled by the Class 'X' shareholders).

Accordingly, despite the inclusion of both rights and 'interests' in s 164(2)*(a)*, the effect of the section arguably is to preclude shareholders from relying on appraisal rights to exit the company where amendments to the Memorandum of Incorporation merely reduce the commercial value of their class rights (or preferences, limitations or other terms) without literally changing them, for instance, a redistribution or dilution of relative voting or other rights, or leapfrogging. What is required instead is an amendment of the Memorandum of Incorporation to literally or formally alter the preferences, rights, limitations or other terms of their class of shares in a manner materially adverse to the rights or interests of holders of that class of shares.

On the other hand, a counterargument may be raised that the inclusion of the term 'interests' in s 164(2)(a) may imply that the drafters intended for a wide interpretation of *'alteration'* to be adopted, so as to guard against both *direct* (or literal) alterations of rights themselves as well as *indirect* alterations that merely affect the 'enjoyment of rights'.[272] However, there are two strong obstacles to this wide interpretation: first, the inconsistency between s 164(2)(a) and s 37(8), which includes neither the term 'interests' nor the phrase 'in any manner', and secondly, the dominant common-law approach to the alteration or variation of rights.[273]

It is notable that the common-law approach to the alteration or variation of rights is supported by a strong line of judicial decisions. Consequently, the circumvention of the decisive common-law approach will be best achieved by an explicit statutory reference to the indirect alterations of class rights as triggers for appraisal, following the lead of the Canada Business Corporations Act. Failing such an explicit reference in the new Companies Act of 2008, the dominant common-law approach will be difficult to overrule.[274]

16.4 APPLICATION TO PROTECT THE RIGHTS OF SECURITIES HOLDERS

16.4.1 General

This is a new remedy introduced by the Act. Its object is to protect the holders of securities of a company. It does so by enabling them not only to seek a declaratory order as to their rights, but also to rectify any harm done to them.

---

[272] This is perhaps supportable by the reference in s 164(2)(a) to an alteration of class rights *'in any manner'* materially adverse — there could be scope for reading the phrase 'in any manner' to mean any manner of *alteration* including indirect alterations that affect the enjoyment of rights. But see further below.

[273] The issue of direct and indirect 'alterations' of class rights is also compounded by s 164(5)(a)(ii), which states that a shareholder may demand fair value if the shareholder 'in the case of an amendment to the company's Memorandum of Incorporation, holds shares of a class that is materially and adversely *affected* by the amendment' [emphasis added]. At first blush, the word 'affected' appears to embrace *indirect* alterations of class rights. For instance, a class of shareholders (Class 'C') may claim to be materially and adversely '*affected*' (in the literal sense of the word) where there is a formal alteration of the rights of some *other* class of shares (Class 'D') that render the rights of Class 'C' shares less valuable, for instance, a redistribution of relative voting rights. But in the technical and legal sense of the word '*affected*', in this context it means affected by a direct alteration of rights (not an indirect alteration), with the result that Class 'C' shareholders are not '*affected*' as such. In this regard, the technical common-law approach to the meaning of 'alteration' or variation of class rights extends also to the term '*affected*'. The dominant view is that the word 'affected' is no different from the word 'varied' or altered, in the context of variations of class rights. It has been held that class rights are 'affected' where the rights themselves are affected and not just their enjoyment (*White v Bristol Aeroplane Co Ltd* [1953] 1 All ER 40 (CA) and *Re John Smith's Tadcaster Brewery Co* [1953] Ch 308 (CA)). It has been further declared that to guard against affecting the enjoyment of rights or the economic interests of shareholders, more explicit wording than 'affected' would have to be used. This common-law principle may be expected to extend to the interpretation of the term 'affected' in the context of s 164(5)(a)(ii). The effect is that, since s 164(5)(a)(ii) omits any explicit reference to the 'interests' of a class, the term 'affected' should be taken to mean a class that is 'affected' by a *direct* alteration of its rights as opposed to a mere reduction in the value of its rights or the enjoyment of its rights (ie its interests).

[274] Canada Business Corporations Act, R.S.C. 1985, s 190(2) read with s 176. See also Welling op cit n 79 at 569–570.

In this regard, s 161 of the Act enables a holder of issued securities of a company to, first, apply to a court for an order determining any of his or her (or its) rights in terms of the Act, the company's Memorandum of Incorporation, any rules of the company, or any applicable debt instrument.[275]

Secondly, a securities holder may also apply for any appropriate order that is necessary to protect any such right.[276] This could include an interdict.

Thirdly, a securities holder may apply under s 161 for any appropriate order necessary to rectify any harm done to him or her (or it):

- by the company, as a consequence of an act or omission that violated any such right or contravened the Act, the Memorandum of Incorporation, rules or applicable debt instrument, or
- by any of its directors, to the extent that they are or may be held liable in terms of s 77 (which deals with the liability of directors and prescribed officers).[277]

This remedy is in addition to any other remedy available to a securities holder, whether in terms of the Act or in terms of the common law, subject to the Act.[278]

This provision, for instance, appears to provide scope for inter alia declaratory orders, interdicts to restrain breaches of relevant rights of securities holders, as well as orders to direct compliance with such rights. This remedy may perhaps be relied on, for example, where there is a wrongful refusal of the right of a shareholder to cast a vote, in which case an appropriate order (depending on the circumstances) could be an interdict to restrain the company from acting on an improperly passed resolution.

Section 161 is not only an innovative provision in South African corporate legislation, but is also particularly remarkable in that it permits direct recourse by a shareholder (or securities holder) against a *director*. This right of recourse, however, is likely to be of limited use, bearing in mind that directors' breaches of the duties and provisions under s 77 will, in the majority of cases, cause harm to the company itself as opposed to its shareholders.[279] But there may be circumstances in which harm is done to a shareholder by a director, in which event the shareholder may be able to seek redress under s 161.

Turning to the scope provided by s 161 for a shareholder to apply for an order to rectify harm that is done to him or her by the *company*, this provision overlaps with the shareholder's personal action at common law. It would probably reduce the practical use of the common-law personal action, except perhaps in so far as damages are claimed (see further 16.5.2 below on the personal action).

In particular, s 161 overlaps with the common-law principles on the enforcement of the Memorandum of Incorporation and rules by shareholders against the

---

[275] Section 161(1)*(a)*.
[276] Section 161(1)*(b)*(i).
[277] Section 161(1)*(b)*(ii).
[278] Section 161(2).
[279] See *Percival v Wright* [1902] 2 Ch 421, which is the leading authority for the proposition that directors' duties are not owed to the shareholders individually. See also *Coleman v Myers* [1977] 2 NZLR 225 CA (NZ) and *Peskin v Anderson* [2001] 1 BCLC 372, which accepted that fiduciary duties may be owed by directors to individual shareholders where a 'special factual relationship' is established between them on the facts of the particular case.

company in terms of s 15(6)*(a)*, which renders the Memorandum of Incorporation and rules binding between the company and each shareholder. (See further chapter 4: Formation of Companies and the Company Constitution). Section 161 thus provides an alternate and perhaps a more effective legal basis for a shareholder to determine and protect his or her rights in terms of the company's Memorandum of Incorporation and rules.

16.4.1 Meaning of the term 'rights' under section 161

Section 161 refers to the 'rights' of securities holders. The question arises as to the meaning and scope of the term 'rights' in this context. The judicial interpretation that is given to the term 'rights' — particularly the 'rights' of a shareholder under the company's Memorandum of Incorporation and rules — could have important practical ramifications.[280]

If the courts adopt the broad view that every shareholder has a general 'right' (based on s 15(6)*(a)* of the Act) to have the Memorandum of Incorporation and rules observed by the company,[281] then a shareholder would be able to seek compliance with or restrain breach of *any* provision of the Memorandum of Incorporation or rules under s 161. This, in effect, is the approach followed by the Canada Business Corporations Act,[282] which explicitly provides for restraining or compliance orders in respect of *any* provision of that Act, the company's constitution or by-laws (or even a unanimous shareholder agreement or the regulations). Should this broad approach be adopted, a further and far-reaching effect could be that a shareholder may rely on s 161 not only to protect the rights that affect the shareholder *in his or her capacity as* a shareholder, but also to indirectly enforce those rights that affect him or her in some other capacity, for instance, as director, employee or creditor, based on the shareholder's general right to seek compliance with the Memorandum of Incorporation and rules.[283]

On the other hand, a restrictive interpretation may be given to the 'rights' of a shareholder under the company's Memorandum of Incorporation and rules, in terms of s 161, so as to include the personal rights of shareholders, but excluding those provisions of the constitution that merely place duties or obligations on the company (regarding rules to be followed in the conduct of the company's affairs) without necessarily conferring any corresponding rights on the shareholders. This narrow interpretation of s 161 will revive the problematic issues that arose at common law under the previous regime, of having to distinguish personal rights from corporate rights. Provisions relating to the convening and the conduct of shareholders' meetings and the selection of board members have especially given rise to difficulties. For instance, while *Pender v Lushington*[284] found that the refusal of the chairman of a shareholders' meeting to recognise the votes attached

---

[280] See also the discussion on the legal status of the Memorandum of Incorporation and rules in chapter 4: Formation of Companies and the Company Constitution.
[281] See Lord Wedderburn 'Shareholders' Rights and the Rule in *Foss v Harbottle*' [1957] *CLJ* 193.
[282] Canada Business Corporations Act, R.S.C. 1985, s 247.
[283] In this regard, s 247 of the Canada Business Corporations Act, R.S.C. 1985, permits a wider class of complainants and even creditors to seek restraining or compliance orders.
[284] (1877) 6 ChD 70 at 80.

to the shares of nominee shareholders was an infringement of their personal shareholder rights, a conflicting and irreconcilable decision of the court in *MacDougall v Gardiner*[285] concluded that the decision of a chairman of a shareholders' meeting to refuse a request for a poll, in breach of the company's constitution, did not amount to an infringement of the shareholders' rights.[286]

It remains to be seen which approach the courts will take to the interpretation of the term 'rights' in the context of s 161, and which provisions of a company's constitution and rules will qualify as shareholder 'rights' under s 161. (See further the discussion of the legal status of the Memorandum of Incorporation and rules in chapter 4: Formation of Companies and the Company Constitution.)

16.5 OTHER SHAREHOLDER REMEDIES

16.5.1 Restraining the company from contravening the Act, and damages

Shareholders have a statutory right under the new Act to restrain the company from violating any provision of the Act. Shareholders also have a statutory right to restrain the company from an *ultra vires* action or transaction.

In this regard, s 20(4) provides that one or more shareholders or directors or prescribed officers of a company, or a trade union representing employees of the company, may take proceedings to restrain the company from doing anything inconsistent with the Act. This is a new provision that had no equivalent under the 1973 Act. It is widely worded. It is noteworthy that it is limited to contraventions of the Act only, and does not encompass contraventions of the company's Memorandum of Incorporation.

Section 20(4) is complemented by s 20(5), which enables one or more shareholders, directors or prescribed officers of a company to take proceedings to restrain the company or the directors from doing anything inconsistent with any limitation, restriction or qualification of the capacity of a company or the authority of the directors in terms of its Memorandum of Incorporation as contemplated in s 20(2). Section 20(5) does not apply to all contraventions of the Memorandum of Incorporation but is limited to provisions dealing with the company's capacity and the authority of its directors. (Section 20(5) is discussed in detail in chapter 5: Corporate Capacity, Agency and the Turquand Rule.)

Each shareholder of a company has a claim for damages, in terms of s 20(6), against any person who fraudulently or due to gross negligence[287] causes the company to do anything inconsistent with the Act (or anything inconsistent with a limitation of the capacity of the company or its directors' authority that has not been ratified by special resolution).[288] Furthermore, any person who contravenes

---

[285] (1875) 1 Ch 13 (CA).
[286] Paul L Davies op cit n 9 at 72.
[287] Or knowingly, wilfully or intentionally (as proposed by the draft Companies Amendment Bill, 2010 (cl 14)).
[288] Section 20(6). Notably, an action in contravention of the Act may not be so ratified (s 20(3)). The shareholder's claim for damages in the context of corporate capacity and *ultra vires* transactions is discussed in detail in chapter 5: Corporate Capacity, Agency and the Turquand Rule.

any provision of the Act is liable, under s 218(2), to any other person for any loss or damage suffered by that person as a result of the contravention.[289]

Section 20(6) provides a remedy for damages, not against the company, but against the person who fraudulently or due to gross negligence causes the company to act inconsistently with the Act. In contrast, s 218(2) creates scope for a claim for damages against any person who contravenes the Act and perhaps even against the company itself, on the basis that an act of the board of directors could constitute an act of the company itself. A second difference between s 20(6) and s 218(2) is that the latter apparently imposes strict liability and applies even if the defendant contravened the Act innocently, as long as the plaintiff suffered damage as a result of the contravention. Section 20(6) on the other hand, requires proof of fraud or gross negligence. A third difference is that, while shareholders have standing to claim damages under both s 20(6) and s 218(2), s 218(2) additionally provides wider standing to 'any other person' who has suffered damage.

The 'no reflective loss' principle may apply to a shareholder's claim for damages under s 218(2) or s 20(6), insofar as the damage caused by the defendant to the plaintiff-shareholder consists in a fall in the value of the plaintiff's shares that is merely reflective of the loss suffered by the company itself as a result of the contravention of the Act (see further 16.5.3 below on the 'no reflective loss' principle).

16.5.2 The common-law personal action

Where a wrong is done to a shareholder and the shareholder consequently wishes to assert his or her (or its) individual shareholder rights, as opposed to the rights of the company, the common-law option of bringing a personal action in his or her own name remains.

The common-law personal action is not abolished by s 165 of the Act. Section 165(1) states that '[a]ny right at common law of a person other than a company to bring or prosecute any legal proceedings *on behalf of that company* is abolished, and the rights in this section are in substitution for such abolished right' [emphasis added]. This provision accordingly abolishes the common-law right of a shareholder to bring legal proceedings on behalf of a company, ie the common-law derivative action, but leaves untouched the shareholder's common-law right to bring legal proceedings in his or her own name to assert his or her own *shareholder* rights (as distinct from those of the company) by way of the personal action. (See however the discussion in 16.5.3 below on the 'no reflective loss' principle.)

A shareholder may accordingly still rely in certain circumstances on a personal action at common law. Under the previous regime personal actions could historically be brought, for instance, to restrain the company from *ultra vires* conduct. Personal actions could also be brought to enforce the rights derived by a shareholder from the constitution of the company in his or her capacity as a shareholder (see the discussion on the legal status of the Memorandum of Incorporation in

---

[289] Section 218(2). The provisions of s 218 do not affect the right to any remedy that a person may otherwise have (s 218(3)).

terms of s 15(6) of the Act in chapter 4: Formation of Companies and the Company Constitution). Personal actions under the previous regime could apply also to certain conduct in contravention of the provisions of the Companies Act or the common law relating to shareholder rights (that could not be ratified by ordinary resolution).

But it is submitted that the personal action at common law is now of much more limited significance. This is particularly so in view of s 20(4) of the new Act, which provides a statutory right to shareholders to restrain the company from violating any provision of the Act, and s 20(5), which provides a statutory right to restrain the company or the directors from *ultra vires* conduct (see 16.5.1 above). Also important is the statutory right to damages in terms of s 218(2), in respect of contraventions of the Act that cause loss or damage to a shareholder (or any other person). The application to protect the rights of securities holders, in terms of s 161, may further reduce the practical usefulness of the common-law personal action (as discussed in 16.4 above). Moreover, in practice, aggrieved shareholders who have grounds for common-law personal actions often have the alternative option of resorting to the more inviting and effective avenue of the oppression remedy in terms of s 163, as discussed in 16.1 above.

16.5.3 The 'no reflective loss' principle: overlap between shareholder actions and corporate actions

The 'no reflective loss' rule applies to the overlap between personal claims of shareholders and derivative (or other corporate) actions. The principle may well extend equally to s 20(6) and s 218(2), as stated in 16.5.1 above.

In this regard, the 'no reflective loss' principle applies where both the company and the shareholder have a claim against the directors (or other persons), based on the same set of facts. Accordingly the shareholder's loss, insofar as this may be a diminution in the value of his or her shares or a loss of dividends, merely reflects the loss suffered by the company. In such cases the shareholder's claim is restricted by the principle that the shareholder cannot recover a loss that is simply reflective of the company's loss.[290] However the 'no reflective loss' rule will not pose an obstacle where the loss suffered by the shareholder and that suffered by the company are distinguishable.[291]

An application of the 'no reflective loss' rule arose, for instance, in *Prudential Assurance Co Ltd v Newman Industries Ltd (No 2)*,[292] where the court decided that the (personal) claim by the shareholders should fail as the only loss they had suffered (as a result of a misrepresentation by the directors in a tricky and misleading circular, in the course of seeking the shareholders' consent to the transaction) was a diminution in the value of their shares, which was simply a reflection of the loss that the company itself had suffered as a result of the wrong done to the company (by the acquisition of certain assets at an overvalue).

---

[290] *Johnson v Gore, Wood & Co* [2002] 2 AC 1 (HL) at 62.
[291] See *Heron International Ltd v Lord Grade* [1983] BCLC 261.
[292] [1981] Ch 257 and 1982 [1] Ch 204 (CA).

See also *Stein v Blake*,[293] where the loss sustained by a shareholder by a diminution in the value of his shares by reason of the misappropriation of the company's assets, was held to be recoverable only by the company and not by the shareholder who had suffered no loss distinct from that suffered by the company.

The rationale for the 'no reflective loss' principle is that it prevents double recovery if the company were also to sue. Moreover, it prevents the individual shareholder from recovering at the expense of the company and its creditors and other shareholders.[294]

It is noteworthy that where both the company and the shareholder have a claim in respect of a breach of a duty owed to both of them arising out of the same set of facts, the 'no reflective loss' principle may apply to preclude recovery by the shareholder even if the company chooses not to exercise its remedy, or if the company settles or compromises for less than it might have done,[295] or if the company is unable to enforce its claim because the defendants have a valid defence against the company (but not against the shareholder).[296]

However, an exception to the 'no reflective loss' rule applies where the company is disabled from pursuing its claim as a result of the wrongful act of the defendant — in these circumstances, provided the shareholder has a separate cause of action, the shareholder should be able to recover damages in full regardless of whether they are for reflective losses.[297]

16.5.4 Other remedies

Finally, it is notable that there are other remedies under the Act which are dealt with in other chapters, as appropriate. For instance, the veil may be pierced in the event of an abuse of the separate juristic personality of a company, solvent companies may be wound-up by court order in certain specified circumstances, and there is the possibility of having errant directors declared by a court to be delinquent or placed under probation. In addition there is, inter alia, the prohibition against fraudulent, reckless or insolvent trading, and the statutory liability of directors as set out in s 77.

---

[293] [1998] 1 All ER 724 (CA).
[294] *Johnson v Gore, Wood & Co* (supra).
[295] *Johnson v Gore, Wood & Co* [2001] 1 BCLC 313 (HL) at 377–378, *per* Lord Millett, differing from the New Zealand case of *Christensen v Scott* [1996] 1 NZLR 273.
[296] *Day v Cook* [2002] BCLC 1 CA; *Barings v Coopers & Lybrand (No 1)* [2002] 1 BCLC 364.
[297] *Giles v Rhind* [2003] Ch 618 CA; *Perry v Day* [2005] BCLC 405.

CHAPTER 17

ENFORCEMENT AND REGULATORY AGENCIES

Maleka Femida Cassim

17.1	INTRODUCTION AND UNDERLYING POLICY	747
17.2	GENERAL PRINCIPLES ON REMEDIES	748
	17.2.1 Extended standing or *locus standi* to apply for remedies	748
	17.2.2 Alternative procedures for addressing complaints or securing rights	750
	17.2.3 Remedies must promote the purpose of the Act	750
	17.2.4 Protection for whistle-blowers	751
	17.2.5 Restraining the company from contravening the Act and damages	753
	17.2.6 Transitional Arrangements	754
17.3	THE REGULATORY AGENCIES	755
	17.3.1 The Companies and Intellectual Property Commission ('the Companies Commission')	755
	(a) Functions of the Companies Commission	757
	(b) Reporting, research and public information	758
	(c) The Commissioner and the Minister	759
	17.3.2 The Companies Tribunal	759
	(a) Functions of the Companies Tribunal	759
	(b) Members of the Companies Tribunal	761
	17.3.3 Confidential information and regulatory agencies (s 212)	761
	17.3.4 Transitional Arrangements for regulatory agencies	762
17.4	COMPLAINTS TO THE COMPANIES COMMISSION (OR TO THE PANEL)	763
	17.4.1 Initiating a complaint	763
	17.4.2 Investigation by the Companies Commission	764
	(a) The Companies Commission's response to a complaint	764
	(b) Powers to support investigations and inspections	765
	17.4.3 Outcome of the investigation	767
	17.4.4 Compliance notice	768
	(a) Issuing a compliance notice	768
	(b) Objection to a compliance notice	769
	(c) Failure to comply with a compliance notice	769
	(d) Administrative fine	770
	(e) Winding-up of the company	771

	17.4.5	Consent order.	771
	17.4.6	Notice of non-referral and referral of complaints to the court.	772
17.5	VOLUNTARY RESOLUTION OF DISPUTES		772
17.6	COMPANIES TRIBUNAL ADJUDICATION PROCEEDINGS		773
17.7	OFFENCES		775
	17.7.1	General	775
	17.7.2	Some specific offences	775
		(a) Breach of confidence	775
		(b) False statements	776
		(c) Reckless conduct	777
		(d) Non-compliance	777
		(e) Hindering the administration of the Act	778
	17.7.3	Penalties	778
17.8	MISCELLANEOUS MATTERS		779
	17.8.1	Civil actions (s 218)	779
	17.8.2	Prescription and double jeopardy (s 219)	779
	17.8.3	Serving documents (s 220)	779
	17.8.4	Proof of facts (s 221)	780
	17.8.5	State liability (s 222)	780

17.1 INTRODUCTION AND UNDERLYING POLICY

One of the key goals of the company law reform process is the establishment of a predictable and effective regulatory environment. This objective is fortified by the stated purpose of the Companies Act 71 of 2008 (hereafter 'the Act') to 'provide a predictable and effective environment for the efficient regulation of companies'.[1] Stemming from this objective is the extensive decriminalisation of company law. Experience under the previous company law regime has shown that criminal sanctions are ineffective as a means of ensuring compliance with the Companies Act, due largely to the failure and reluctance to prosecute for technical offences. Rather than relying on criminal sanctions, the Act relies primarily on a system of administrative enforcement combined with a minimum number of criminal sanctions.[2]

Enforcement takes place through various bodies and by way of various mechanisms, some of which were pre-existent to the Act while others are new. The Act establishes one new institution and adapts or transforms three existing ones.[3] The three transformed regulatory agencies are the Companies and Intellectual Property Commission ('the Companies Commission'), the Takeover Regulation Panel ('the Panel'), which was formerly the Securities Regulation Panel, and the Financial Reporting Standards Council ('the FRSC'), while the entirely new regulatory agency is the Companies Tribunal. The Companies Commission and the Companies Tribunal are discussed in this chapter. (See chapter 15: Fundamental Transactions, Takeovers

---

[1] Section 7(1).
[2] *Memorandum on the Objects of the Companies Bill, 2008*, Companies Bill [B 61D–2008] at para 1.
[3] *Memorandum on the Objects of the Companies Bill, 2008* op cit n 2 at paras 3 and 12.

and Offers, for the Takeover Regulation Panel, and chapter 13: The Auditor, Financial Records and Reporting, for the Financial Standards Reporting Council.)

There are four avenues for addressing complaints on alleged contraventions of the Act or for securing or enforcing rights, namely:[4]
- applying to the High Court,
- filing a complaint with the Companies Commission or the Panel,
- applying to the Companies Tribunal for adjudication, and
- alternative dispute resolution.

These alternative procedures are also dealt with in this chapter.

The inclusion of these other alternatives for addressing complaints or enforcing rights is expected to alleviate the burden on the courts, and save costs, time and other relevant resources. This is coupled with the new approach of reducing court involvement in several areas of the new Act. For instance, the introduction of the appraisal remedy, as the primary protective measure for shareholders in a statutory merger, has facilitated a court-free statutory merger procedure that bypasses any general requirement for court approval of statutory mergers.[5] Similarly, the traditional requirement of general court sanctioning of schemes of arrangement is now replaced with appraisal rights for dissenting shareholders, and court approval is now required only in certain specified circumstances.[6] The High Court nevertheless remains the primary forum for the resolution of disputes and the interpretation and enforcement of the Companies Act.[7]

The new Act preserves several pre-existing remedies, some of which are wider than before, while simultaneously introducing various new remedies and establishing certain new general principles on remedies.[8] These general principles include an extended right of standing to apply for remedies and a regime to protect whistle-blowers. Most of the remedies have been dealt with in other chapters of this book, where appropriate. This section briefly discusses the few remaining remedies and the general principles relating to remedies.[9]

17.2 GENERAL PRINCIPLES ON REMEDIES

17.2.1 Extended standing or *locus standi* to apply for remedies

A novel provision of the Act is the extended right of standing. This applies where applications are made to or matters are brought before a court, the Companies Tribunal, the Panel or the Companies Commission in terms of the Act.

---

[4] See s 156.

[5] Maleka Femida Cassim 'The introduction of the statutory merger in South African corporate law: Majority rule offset by the appraisal right (Part I)' (2008) 20 *South African Mercantile Law Journal* 1 at 19–22.

[6] Maleka Femida Cassim op cit n 5 at 23–4. See also the section on appraisal rights in chapter 16: Shareholder Remedies and Minority Protection.

[7] *Memorandum on the Objects of the Companies Bill, 2008* op cit n 2 at para 3.

[8] *Memorandum on the Objects of the Companies Bill, 2008* op cit n 2 at para 11.

[9] See in this regard the discussion on relief from the abuse of the separate juristic personality of a company in chapter 2: The Legal Concept of a Company; the innovative application to declare a director delinquent or under probation in chapter 10: Governance and the Board of Directors; the prohibition on reckless trading and the liability of directors and prescribed officers in chapter 12: The Duties and the Liability of Directors; disputes concerning the reservation or registration of company names in chapter 4: Formation of Companies and the Company Constitution; and chapter 16: Shareholder Remedies and Minority Protection.

Section 157(1) provides that, where an application may be made to, or a matter may be brought before, a court, the Companies Tribunal, the Panel or the Companies Commission in terms of the Act, the right to do so may be exercised:
- directly by a person contemplated in the relevant provision of the Act,
- by a person acting on his or her (or its) behalf, if they cannot act in their own name,
- by a person acting as a member of, or in the interest of, a group or class of affected persons, or an association[10] acting in the interest of its members, or
- by a person acting in the public interest, with leave of the court.[11]

This broad provision is new to company law and did not form part of the previous Companies Act. It may be compared with the broad approach to *locus standi* in matters relating to the Bill of Rights in terms of s 38 of the Constitution. It also introduces the class action, whereby one or more persons may bring an action in the interest of a class of persons who have a common interest in the same cause of action.[12]

The section furthermore provides that the Companies Commission or the Panel, acting on its own motion and in its absolute discretion, may:
- commence any proceedings in a court in the name of a person who (when filing a complaint with the Companies Commission or the Panel in respect of that matter) made a written request that the Companies Commission or the Panel do so, or
- apply for leave to intervene in any court proceedings arising in terms of the Act, in order to represent any interest that would not otherwise be adequately represented in those proceedings.[13]

---

[10] It is noteworthy that, in terms of the equivalent provision on standing under s 38*(e)* of the Constitution of the Republic of South Africa, 1996, it is irrelevant whether or not an association has separate legal personality and whether or not its constitution authorises such litigation (*South African Association of Personal Injury Lawyers v Heath* 2000 (10) BCLR 1131 (T)).

[11] In respect of the equivalent provision on standing under s 38*(d)* of the Constitution, it has been stated that the courts would take a cautious approach to such applications. The Constitutional Court in *Ferreira v Levin, Vryenhoek v Powell* 1996 (1) SA 984 (CC) laid down relevant factors that would be considered in determining whether an applicant is truly acting in the public interest, including the existence of other reasonable and effective ways to bring the challenge; the nature of the relief sought, including the extent to which it is of general prospective application; the range of persons or groups who may be directly or indirectly affected by any order made by the court, as well as the opportunity that they have had to present evidence and argument to the court.

[12] There are a number of issues and difficulties relating to class actions. In *Permanent Secretary, Department of Welfare, Eastern Cape Provincial Government v Ngxuza* 2001 (4) SA 1184 (SCA), the court recognised the class action in terms of s 38*(c)* of the Constitution and stated that the requisites for such a class action (in terms of s 38 of the Constitution) are that: (i) the class is so numerous that joinder of all its members is impracticable; (ii) there are questions of law and fact common to the class; (iii) the claims of the applicants representing the class are typical of the claims of the rest; and (iv) the applicants through their legal representatives will fairly and adequately protect the interests of the class. The Supreme Court of Appeal also stated that a vital feature of such a class action is that other members of the class, although not formally and individually joined, benefit from and are bound by the outcome of the class action unless they invoke prescribed procedures to opt out of it.

[13] Section 157(2).

Section 157 does not create a right of any person to commence derivative proceedings other than on behalf of a person entitled to make a demand in terms of s 165(2) and in the manner set out in s 165.[14]

17.2.2 Alternative procedures for addressing complaints or securing rights

In terms of s 156, a person with standing may seek to address an alleged contravention of the Act or to enforce a provision or right under the Act, a company's Memorandum of Incorporation or rules, or a transaction or agreement (contemplated in the Act, the company's Memorandum of Incorporation or rules) by:

- attempting to resolve any dispute with or within a company through alternative dispute resolution,
- applying to the Companies Tribunal for adjudication, provided that this is 'in respect of any matter for which such an application is permitted' in terms of the Act,
- applying for appropriate relief to the division of the High Court that has jurisdiction over the matter, or
- filing a complaint with the Companies Commission or the Panel (depending on which body has jurisdiction over the matter) within the time permitted by the Act.

Each of these alternative procedures is discussed in turn below (in 17.4 to 17.6), as are the roles of the Companies Commission and the Companies Tribunal (see 17.3). It is noteworthy, however, that the High Court remains the primary forum for the resolution of disputes and the interpretation and enforcement of the new Companies Act,[15] similarly to the position under the Companies Act 61 of 1973 (hereafter 'the 1973 Act').

17.2.3 Remedies must promote the purpose of the Act

When a court determines a matter brought before it in terms of the Act or when it makes an order contemplated in the Act, it must develop the common law as necessary to improve the realisation and enjoyment of rights established by the Act.[16]

Furthermore, the spirit, purpose and objects of the Act must be promoted by the Companies Commission, the Panel, the Companies Tribunal and/or a court, when determining a matter or making an order in terms of the Act. If any provision of the Act or a document in terms of the Act, read in its context, can be reasonably construed to have more than one meaning, it must prefer the meaning that best promotes the spirit and purpose (as set out in s 7) of the Act, and will best improve the realisation and enjoyment of rights.[17] This section may provide a useful guide for the Companies Commission or the Companies Tribunal in difficult matters brought before it.

---

[14] Section 157(3). See further chapter 16: Shareholder Remedies and Minority Protection.
[15] *Memorandum on the Objects of the Companies Bill, 2008* op cit n 2 at para 3.
[16] Section 158.
[17] Ibid.

The purposes of the Act, in terms of s 7, are as follows:
- to promote compliance with the Bill of Rights as provided for in the Constitution, in the application of company law,
- to promote the development of the South African economy by:
  - encouraging entrepreneurship and enterprise efficiency,
  - creating flexibility and simplicity in the formation and maintenance of companies, and
  - encouraging transparency and high standards of corporate governance as appropriate, given the significant role of enterprises within the social and economic life of the nation,
- to promote innovation and investment in the South African markets,
- to reaffirm the concept of the company as a means of achieving economic and social benefits,
- to continue to provide for the creation and use of companies, in a manner that enhances the economic welfare of South Africa as a partner within the global economy,
- to promote the development of companies within all sectors of the economy, and encourage active participation in economic organisation, management and productivity,
- to create optimum conditions for the aggregation of capital for productive purposes, and for the investment of that capital in enterprises and the spreading of economic risk,
- to provide for the formation, operation and accountability of non-profit companies in a manner designed to promote, support and enhance the capacity of such companies to perform their functions,
- to balance the rights and obligations of shareholders and directors within companies,
- to encourage the efficient and responsible management of companies,
- to provide for the efficient rescue and recovery of financially distressed companies, in a manner that balances the rights and interests of all relevant stakeholders, and
- to provide a predictable and effective environment for the efficient regulation of companies.

17.2.4 Protection for whistle-blowers

A new regime established by s 159 of the Act is the protection of 'whistle-blowers' who disclose irregularities or contraventions of the Act. This has been designed to harmonise with the Protected Disclosures Act 26 of 2000, which affords certain protective measures to employees.[18] The Companies Act, in broad terms, grants protection and safeguards to certain categories of persons who disclose information relating to specified unlawful or irregular conduct on the part of a company or its directors or prescribed officers acting in their capacity as such. It applies also to the disclosure of information relating to external companies.

---

[18] *Memorandum on the Objects of the Companies Bill, 2008* op cit n 2 at para 11.

The following categories of persons who disclose relevant information may benefit from the protection of the section: shareholders, directors, company secretaries, prescribed officers or employees of a company; registered trade unions that represent employees of the company or other representatives of the employees of the company; and suppliers of goods or services to a company, or their employees.[19]

The protective measures apply in the following circumstances:[20]

- if the disclosure of information is made in good faith to the Companies Commission, the Companies Tribunal, the Panel, a regulatory authority, an exchange, a legal adviser, a director, a prescribed officer, a company secretary, an auditor, a board or a committee of the company concerned; *and*
- if the person who makes the disclosure reasonably believed at the time of the disclosure that the information showed or tended to show that a company or external company, or a director or prescribed officer of a company, acting in that capacity, had:
  ○ contravened the Companies Act or a law mentioned in Schedule 4 to the Act,
  ○ failed or was failing to comply with any statutory obligation to which the company was subject,
  ○ engaged in conduct that had endangered or was likely to endanger the health or safety of any individual, or damage the environment,
  ○ unfairly discriminated, or condoned unfair discrimination, against any person, as contemplated in s 9 of the Constitution and the Promotion of Equality and Prevention of Unfair Discrimination Act 4 of 2000, or
  ○ contravened any other legislation in a manner that could expose the company to an actual or contingent risk of liability, or is inherently prejudicial to the interests of the company.

Where a specified person makes a disclosure of information as contemplated above, the following protections are granted to him or her as a 'whistle-blower': First, they have qualified privilege in respect of the disclosure; and secondly, they are immune from any civil, criminal or administrative liability for the disclosure.[21]

The 'whistle-blower' is furthermore entitled to compensation for any damages that he or she may suffer if, *as a result of* their actual disclosure or even a possible disclosure that they are entitled to make, another person engages in conduct with the intent to cause detriment to them, and the conduct causes such detriment.[22] Whistle-blowers are also entitled to compensation for damages if, *as a result of* their actual or possible disclosure, another person makes a threat to cause any detriment to them or to a third party, and either intends them to fear that the threat will be carried out or is reckless as to causing them to fear that the threat will be carried out. It is irrelevant to the enquiry whether or not he or she actually so feared. Such a threat may be made directly or indirectly. It could be express or

---

[19] Section 159(4).
[20] Section 159(3).
[21] Section 159(4).
[22] Section 159(5).

implied, and may be conditional or unconditional.[23] For these purposes, any such conduct or threat (as the case may be) is presumed to have occurred *as a result of* an actual or possible disclosure, unless the person who engaged in the conduct or made the threat can show satisfactory evidence in support of another reason for doing so.[24]

To the extent that s 159 of the Act creates any right or establishes any protection for an 'employee', as defined in the Protected Disclosures Act,[25] the right conferred by s 159 is in addition to the right conferred by the Protected Disclosures Act. For instance, should an employee, on account of having made a disclosure, be subjected to harassment or other occupational detriment by his or her employer, he or she may rely on the Protected Disclosures Act.[26] Moreover, the Protected Disclosures Act applies to a disclosure contemplated in s 159 by an 'employee', irrespective of whether the Protected Disclosures Act would otherwise apply to that disclosure.[27] In the event of an irreconcilable conflict between the Companies Act and the Protected Disclosures Act, it seems that the Companies Act prevails.[28] This is because the list of statutes in s 5(4) that prevail over the Companies Act does not include the Protected Disclosures Act.

Any provision of a company's Memorandum of Incorporation or rules or an agreement is void to the extent that it is inconsistent with s 159 or purports to limit, set aside or negate its effect.[29]

Public companies and state-owned companies must directly or indirectly establish and maintain a system to receive disclosures confidentially, and act on them. They must also routinely publicise the availability of that system to the specified categories of persons contemplated in s 159(4).[30]

17.2.5 Restraining the company from contravening the Act and damages

Section 20(4) and (5), respectively, provides a statutory right to certain categories of persons to restrain the company from violating any provision of the Act, and from *ultra vires* actions.

Section 20(4) states that one or more shareholders, directors or prescribed officers of a company, or a trade union representing employees of the company,

---

[23] Section 159(5).
[24] Section 159(6).
[25] Section 1 of the Protected Disclosures Act 26 of 2000 defines an 'employee' as *(a)* any person, excluding an independent contractor, who works for another person or for the State and who receives, or is entitled to receive, any remuneration; *(b)* any other person who in any manner assists in carrying on or conducting the business of an employer. (In this regard, 'employer' is defined as any person *(a)* who employs or provides work for any other person and who remunerates or expressly or tacitly undertakes to remunerate that other person; or *(b)* who permits any other person in any manner to assist in the carrying on or conducting of his, her or its business, including any person acting on behalf of or on the authority of such employer.)
[26] Section 3 read with s 1 of the Protected Disclosures Act 26 of 2000; see also s 159(1) of the Act.
[27] Section 159(1).
[28] See s 5(4)*(b)*(ii).
[29] Section 159(2).
[30] Section 159(7).

may take proceedings to restrain the company from doing anything inconsistent with the Act. This innovatory provision had no equivalent under the 1973 Act. It is widely worded. It is noteworthy that it is limited to contraventions of the Act and does not apply to contraventions of the company's Memorandum of Incorporation. Section 20(4) is complemented by s 20(5), which enables one or more shareholders, directors or prescribed officers of a company (but not trade unions or employee representatives) to take proceedings to restrain the company or the directors from doing anything inconsistent with any limitation, restriction or qualification on the capacity of a company or the authority of the directors in terms of the Memorandum of Incorporation as contemplated in s 20(2). Section 20(5) does not apply to all contraventions of the Memorandum of Incorporation, but is limited to provisions dealing with the company's capacity and the authority of its directors. Such proceedings in terms of s 20(5) are without prejudice to the rights to damages of a *bona fide* third party who did not have actual knowledge of the limitation, restriction or qualification. (See further chapter 5: Corporate Capacity, Agency and the Turquand Rule for a detailed discussion of s 20(5).)

Turning to damages, it is only shareholders who have *locus standi* to apply for damages in terms of s 20(6), but not the other categories of persons referred to in s 20(4) and (5).[31] (Section 20(6) is consequently discussed in the chapter 16: Shareholder Remedies and Minority Protection.) By contrast, s 218(2) provides *locus standi* to 'any' person, who has suffered any loss or damage as a result of a contravention of the Act, to sue the person who has contravened the Act.[32] Section 218(2) states: 'Any person who contravenes any provision of this Act is liable to any other person for any loss or damage suffered by that person as a result of that contravention.' This provision creates scope for a claim for damages against any person who contravenes the Act, and perhaps even against the company itself on the basis that an act of the board of directors could constitute an act of the company itself. Section 218(2) apparently imposes strict liability and consequently applies even if the defendant had innocently contravened the Act, so long as the plaintiff suffered damages as a result. Section 218(2) is thus wider than s 20(6), which requires proof of fraud or gross negligence.[33]

17.2.6 Transitional Arrangements

The Transitional Arrangements provide for the preservation and continuation of court proceedings and court orders in terms of the 1973 Act. In this regard, any proceedings in any court in terms of that Act, immediately before the effective date (of the new Act), are to be continued in terms of the 1973 Act as if that Act

---

[31] Section 20(6) states that each shareholder of a company has a claim for damages against any person who fraudulently or due to gross negligence causes the company to do anything inconsistent with the Act; or with a limitation, restriction or qualification of the capacity of a company or the authority of the directors that has not been ratified by the shareholders by special resolution in terms of s 20(2). An action in contravention of the Act may not, however, be so ratified (s 20(3)).

[32] Section 218(2). The provisions of s 218 do not affect the right to any remedy that a person may otherwise have (s 218(3)).

[33] Or of knowing, wilful or intentional conduct, as proposed by the draft Companies Amendment Bill, 2010 (cl 14).

had not been repealed. Furthermore, any court order in terms of the 1973 Act, and in force immediately before the effective date, will continue to have the same force and effect as if the 1973 Act had not been repealed, subject to any further order of the court.[34]

Significantly, any person has a right to seek a remedy in terms of the new Act with respect to conduct pertaining to a pre-existing company and occurring *before* the effective date (of the new Act), unless the person had commenced proceedings in a court in respect of the same conduct before the effective date.[35]

The Transitional Arrangements also make provision for the general preservation of regulations,[36] rights and duties, notices and other instruments. In this regard, any right or entitlement enjoyed by or obligation imposed on any person in terms of the previous Act, that had not been spent or fulfilled immediately before the effective date (of the new Act), is still valid in terms of any comparable provision of the new Act, as from the date that the right, entitlement or obligation first arose, subject to the provisions of the Act. Similarly, a notice given or a document served in terms of the 1973 Act is considered as a comparable notice given or a comparable document satisfactorily served in terms of the new Act.[37]

17.3 THE REGULATORY AGENCIES

This section considers the Companies Commission and the Companies Tribunal. The Takeover Regulation Panel is discussed in chapter 15: Fundamental Transactions, Takeovers and Offers, and the Financial Reporting Standards Council in chapter 13: The Auditor, Financial Records and Reporting.

17.3.1 The Companies and Intellectual Property Commission ('the Companies Commission')

The Companies Commission is a juristic person set up as a separate organ of state within the public administration.[38] The Companies Commission is outside the public service. It has jurisdiction throughout the Republic of South Africa, and is independent. It must be impartial and exercise its functions in the most cost-efficient and effective manner and in accordance with the values and principles in s 195 of the Constitution.[39] The Companies Commission, as stated above, is not so much a newly established entity but rather a transformed entity. It is a transformation of CIPRO, the Companies and Intellectual Property Registration Office, which in practice had exercised many of the regulatory functions that were assigned to the Minister and the Registrar of Companies under the 1973 Act.[40]

---

[34] Schedule 5 item 10.
[35] Schedule 5 item 7(7).
[36] Although the heading of item 11 of Schedule 5 refers to 'regulations', 'regulations' are not explicitly referred to in the body of item 11.
[37] Schedule 5 item 11. An order given by an inspector in terms of the 1973 Act, and in effect immediately before the effective date (of the new Act), also continues in effect, subject to the provisions of the new Act. See further chapter 21: Transitional Arrangements.
[38] Section 185(1).
[39] Section 185(2).
[40] *Memorandum on the Objects of the Companies Bill, 2008* op cit n 2 at para 3.

Moreover, the Companies Commission has been granted a significant expansion of the functions and powers previously allocated to CIPRO. Most of the administrative functions that had previously been assigned to the Minister under the 1973 Act (save for *inter alia* the making of regulations and the appointment of the members of the regulatory institutions) are now placed within the jurisdiction of the Companies Commission.[41] The Minister retains the power to issue policy directives to the Companies Commission and to require the Companies Commission to conduct investigations.[42] There is, however, a transitional period for the transfer of power to the Companies Commission.[43]

The objectives of the Companies Commission are as follows:[44]

- the efficient and effective registration of companies and external companies, other juristic persons and intellectual property rights (in terms of the Act and other relevant legislation),
- the maintenance of accurate, up-to-date and relevant information concerning companies, foreign companies, other juristic persons and intellectual property rights, and the provision of that information to the public and other organs of state,
- the promotion of education and awareness of company and intellectual property laws and related matters,
- the promotion of compliance with the Act and other applicable legislation, and
- the efficient, effective and widest possible enforcement of the Act and other legislation listed in Schedule 4.

The legislation to be enforced by the Companies Commission in terms of Schedule 4 includes the following:

- Close Corporations Act 69 of 1984
- Share Blocks Control Act 59 of 1980
- Co-operatives Act 14 of 2005
- Copyright Act 98 of 1978
- Counterfeit Goods Act 37 of 1997
- Designs Act 195 of 1993
- Merchandise Marks Act 17 of 1941
- Patents Act 57 of 1978
- Trade Marks Act 194 of 1993.[45]

---

[41] *Memorandum on the Objects of the Companies Bill, 2008* op cit n 2 at para 3.

[42] Section 190; see further below.

[43] See Schedule 5 item 1(3), which states that, despite any other provision of the Act: *(a)* the Minister, by notice in the *Gazette*, may determine a date on which the Commission may assume the exercise of any particular function or power assigned to it in terms of the Act; and *(b)* until that date, the Commission may not perform that particular function or exercise that particular power; and the Minister has the authority to, and bears the responsibility of, exercising any such function or performing any such power assigned by the Act to the Commission. See further chapter 21: Transitional Arrangements.

[44] Section 186(1).

[45] Also part of Schedule 4 are the Performers Protection Act 11 of 1967, Registration of Copyright in Cinematograph Films Act 62 of 1977, Unauthorised Use of Emblems Act 37 of 1961, 'Vlaglied' Copyright Act 9 of 1974 and Protection of Businesses Act 99 of 1978. The draft Companies

(a) Functions of the Companies Commission

It is a fundamental function of the Companies Commission to enforce the Act,[46] save for matters that are within the jurisdiction of the Panel. The Companies Commission enforces the Act by, inter alia:[47]

- monitoring proper compliance with the Act,
- promoting the voluntary resolution of disputes arising in terms of the Act between a company on the one hand and a shareholder or director on the other, without intervening in or adjudicating any such dispute (see 17.5 below on the voluntary resolution of disputes),
- receiving (or initiating) complaints concerning alleged contraventions of the Act,[48] initiating investigations into complaints, and ensuring prompt and proper investigations (see 17.4 below on complaints to the Companies Commission),
- issuing and enforcing compliance notices, and
- various other means in the course of complaints made to the Companies Commission (as set out in s 187(2); see further 17.4 below).[49]

Another important function of the Companies Commission is the establishment and maintenance of a companies register, as well as any other register in terms of the Act or other relevant legislation. The information in the registers must be made available to the public (and to other organs of state) in an efficient and effective manner. The Companies Commission also registers and deregisters companies, directors, business names and intellectual property rights in accordance with relevant legislation.[50]

Any person may, on payment of the prescribed fee, inspect a document filed under the Act, or obtain from the Companies Commission a copy, certificate or extract of a filed document that is open to inspection, unless the filed document (or any part of it) has been determined to be confidential or to contain confidential information.[51]

The Companies Commission has the further entirely novel function of promoting the reliability of financial statements. Among other things, it must monitor patterns of compliance with financial reporting standards as well as patterns of contraventions, and make recommendations to the Financial Reporting Standards Council on enhancing financial reporting standards.[52]

Amendment Bill, 2010 proposes to add Part A of Chapter 4 of the Consumer Protection Act 19 of 2008 (cl 14).

[46] For the purposes of s 187, the Act includes any legislation listed in Schedule 4 (s 187(1)).

[47] Section 187(2).

[48] The Companies Commission also receives directions from the Minister to investigate alleged contraventions of the Act or other circumstances (s 187(2)(d) read with s 190).

[49] These include negotiating and concluding undertakings and consent orders under s 169(1)(b) and s 173; referring alleged offences in terms of the Act to the National Prosecuting Authority; referring matters to a court and appearing before the court or the Companies Tribunal, as permitted or required by the Act.

[50] Section 187(4).

[51] Section 187(5) and (6); see also 17.3.3 below on confidential information.

[52] Section 186(3).

This new function was previously fulfilled by the Financial Reporting Investigations Panel (FRIP) and the Financial Reporting Standard Council (FRSC) (set up in terms of s 440W and s 440P respectively of the 1973 Act as inserted by the Companies Amendment Act 24 of 2006). Under the 1973 Act the FRSC had the power to set financial reporting standards for 'public interest' companies.[53] A monitoring process for the detection of non-compliance with financial reporting standards was allocated to a monitoring officer,[54] and the investigation of non-compliance with financial reporting standards was the responsibility of the FRIP.[55] Under the new Companies Act, these powers have to some extent been taken over by the Companies Commission, which now assumes the monitoring function. The previous FRIP has now fallen away. The FRSC under the new Act acts in an advisory capacity to the Minister who sets the financial reporting standards.

(b) Reporting, research and public information

The Companies Commission is responsible for recommending to the Minister suitable changes to the law and the administration of the Act to bring it up to date and in line with international best practice. It must also report to the Minister on registration and enforcement activities, and report to and advise the Minister on any other matters referred to it by the Minister or concerning the purposes of the Act.[56]

With regard to public information, the Companies Commission must promote public awareness of company and intellectual property law matters. This includes providing guidance to the public, whether by applying to a court for a declaratory order on the interpretation or application of any provision of the Act, or by issuing explanatory notices outlining its procedures or its non-binding opinions on the interpretation of any provisions of the Act. It must also implement measures for education and information in order to develop public awareness of the Act, and conduct and publish research relating to its mandate and activities.[57]

Provision is also made for relations with other regulatory authorities, including liaising on matters of common interest, referring relevant concerns to other regulatory authorities, exchanging information on specific complaints or investigations, and negotiating agreements to co-ordinate the exercise of jurisdiction over company law matters.[58] It includes liaising with any foreign or international authorities having objects similar to the functions and powers of the Companies Commission.[59] This is intended to promote co-ordination and co-operation between the various regulatory agencies that are now responsible for the enforcement of the Act.

---

[53] Section 440S(1) of the 1973 Act. In terms of s 440U(2) the standards were issued by the Minister on the advice of the FRSC.
[54] Nominated by the Minister in terms of s 440V(2) of the 1973 Act.
[55] Section 440W(2) of the 1973 Act.
[56] See further s 188(1).
[57] See further s 188(2).
[58] Section 188(3). Section 188(3)–(5) deals with the Companies Commission's relations with other regulators.
[59] Section 188(4).

(c) The Commissioner and the Minister

The Commissioner is the person responsible for all matters pertaining to the functions of the Companies Commission. The Commissioner is appointed by the Minister and holds office for an agreed term not exceeding five years, but this is subject to reappointment. The Minister also appoints the Deputy Commissioner of the Companies Commission.[60]

The Minister, as stated above, has the power to issue policy directives to the Companies Commission, with respect to the application, administration and enforcement of the Act, as well as to direct the Companies Commission to conduct investigations. In this regard, the Minister may at any time direct the Companies Commission to investigate an alleged contravention of the Act, or any matter or circumstances relating to the administration of one or more companies in terms of the Act, regardless of whether those circumstances appear at the time to amount to a possible contravention of the Act.[61]

The Minister may also appoint specialist committees to advise him or her on any matter relating to company law or policy, or to advise the Companies Commission on the management of the Companies Commission's resources.[62]

17.3.2 The Companies Tribunal

The Companies Tribunal (or 'the Tribunal') is a newly established body under the Companies Act of 2008. It is an independent organ of state that has jurisdiction throughout South Africa. It must exercise its functions in accordance with the Act and in a transparent manner. It must be impartial, without fear, favour or prejudice.[63]

(a) Functions of the Companies Tribunal

The functions of the Companies Tribunal are set out in the Act as follows:[64]

- First, it must adjudicate in relation to any application that may be made to it in terms of the Act,[65] and make any order provided for in the Act in respect of such an application (see 17.6 below on Companies Tribunal adjudication proceedings).
- Secondly, it serves as a forum for the voluntary resolution of disputes (see 17.5 below on voluntary resolution of disputes).
- Thirdly, it must perform any other function assigned to it under the Act (or any law under Schedule 4).

Included in the mandate of the Companies Tribunal is the review of administrative decisions made by the Companies Commission,[66] such as the review of compliance notices issued by the Commission.

---

[60] Section 189(1) and (2). See further s 189(3)–(4) for the responsibilities and powers of the Commissioner.
[61] Section 190.
[62] Or the performance of any of its functions — see further s 191 and the draft Companies Amendment Bill, 2010 (cl 102).
[63] Section 193(1).
[64] Section 195(1).
[65] See also s 156(b).
[66] *Memorandum on the Objects of the Companies Bill, 2008* op cit n 2 at para 3; see also s 195(7).

The Act does not draw clear distinctions between (i) the 'applications' that may be made to the Companies Tribunal in terms of the Act and in relation to which it may adjudicate (s 195(1)(*a*)), (ii) the function of the Companies Tribunal to review administrative decisions made by the Companies Commission, and (iii) 'other' functions that are assigned to the Companies Tribunal under the Act (s 195(1)(*c*)). It is notable, however, that 'this Act' is defined in s 1 to include the Schedules and regulations. This means that the regulations may be relevant and may clarify which matters the Companies Tribunal may adjudicate. In any event, functions that are assigned to the Companies Tribunal under the various provisions of the Act include the following:

- The Tribunal (or a court or the Panel) may exempt any person from a provision of the Act that would otherwise apply to that person because that person is 'related' or 'inter-related' to another, provided that the person can show that he or she or it acts independently of any related or interrelated person in respect of that matter (s 2(3)).
- A person may apply to the Tribunal for an administrative order exempting an agreement, transaction, arrangement, resolution or provision of a company's Memorandum of Incorporation or rules from any prohibition or requirement established in terms of an unalterable provision of the Act (other than a provision within the jurisdiction of the Panel) (s 6(2)).
- The Companies Commission, a director or a shareholder may apply for an administrative order to set aside a notice of alteration of a company's Memorandum of Incorporation or rules on the basis that the alteration exceeds the authority to correct a patent error or defect (s 17(2)).
- The Tribunal may grant an extension of time for a public company to convene an annual general meeting, on good cause shown (s 61(7)(*b*)).
- The Tribunal may, on a request by a shareholder, issue an administrative order convening a shareholders' meeting, where either there are no directors or all the directors are incapacitated and there is no other person who has been authorised under the company's Memorandum of Incorporation to convene the meeting (s 61(11)).
- Where a company has fewer than three directors, the Tribunal may, on an application by a director or a shareholder, make a determination whether a director is ineligible, disqualified or incapacitated, or has been negligent or derelict (s 71(8)).
- An application may be made to the Tribunal to set aside a notice or a costs assessment issued by the Companies Commission in relation to the convening of a shareholders' meeting to appoint a company secretary, an auditor or an audit committee of a public or state-owned company that has failed to make the appointment (s 84(7)).
- An application may be made to the Tribunal for a determination whether a registered or reserved company name satisfies the requirements of the Act and an administrative order (s 160 read with s 12(3) and s 14(3)).
- An application may be made to the Tribunal to review a compliance notice issued by the Companies Commission and to confirm, modify or cancel all or

part of the notice. The decision of the Companies Tribunal is explicitly subject to any right of review or appeal by a court (s 172).
- Applications may be made to the Tribunal to review decisions of the Companies Commission regarding the confidentiality of, and access to, information that is submitted to the Companies Commission by persons who claim that all or part of the information is confidential (s 212 (4)).

Matters referred to the Companies Tribunal are assigned either to a single member of the Tribunal, to the extent that the Act provides for a matter to be considered by a single member of the Tribunal, or to a panel composed of any three members of the Tribunal, in any other case.[67] A decision of a single member of the Companies Tribunal hearing a matter for adjudication purposes is the decision of the Tribunal.[68] In any other case, the decision of a majority of the members of a panel constitutes the decision of the Tribunal.[69] The decision of a panel on any matter must be in writing and include reasons for the decision.[70]

An order of the Companies Tribunal may be filed in the High Court as an order of the court, in accordance with its rules.[71]

A decision by the Companies Tribunal with respect to a decision, notice or order by the Companies Commission is binding on the Commission, subject to any 'review' by the court (s 195(7)).

(b) Members of the Companies Tribunal

The Companies Tribunal must consist of a chairperson (who may not be reappointed to a second term) and no fewer than ten other members appointed by the Minister, on a full- or part-time basis.[72] The Tribunal must comprise suitably qualified persons with experience in economics, law, commerce, industry or public affairs. There must be sufficient persons with legal training to satisfy these requirements.

The chairman and members must be eligible for membership as set out in s 194 read with s 205. A disqualified person would for instance be an office-bearer of any party or body of a partisan political nature; or a person who is disqualified from serving as a director of a company;[73] or a person who has a personal financial interest, whether personally or through a related person, that may conflict with his or her duties as a member of the Tribunal; or a person who is subject to an order of a competent court holding him or her to be mentally unfit or disordered.[74]

17.3.3 Confidential information and regulatory agencies (s 212)

When a person submits information to an investigator or inspector appointed in terms of the Act or to a regulatory agency (ie the Companies Commission, the

---
[67] Section 195(2).
[68] Section 195(6).
[69] Ibid.
[70] Section 195(5).
[71] Section 195(8).
[72] Section 193(4).
[73] See s 69.
[74] Section 205. See further s 206 on conflicting interests of agency members and s 207 on resignation and removal from office.

Companies Tribunal, the Panel or the Financial Reporting Standards Council), that person may claim that all or part of the information is confidential. Such a claim must be supported by a written statement. The relevant regulatory agency, inspector or investigator (as the case may be) must consider the claim and make a decision on the confidentiality of, and access to, the information. It must also provide written reasons for its decision. A person may object to such a decision in accordance with the procedure in terms of s 172.[75]

The relevant regulatory agency may take confidential information into account when making any ruling, decision or order. If any confidential information would be revealed in the reasons for its decision, the regulatory agency must provide a copy of the proposed reasons to the party claiming confidentiality, at least five business days before publishing those reasons. That party may, within five business days after receiving the copy of the proposed reasons, apply to a court for an appropriate order to protect the confidentiality of the relevant information.[76]

17.3.4 Transitional Arrangements for regulatory agencies

Schedule 5 to the Act states, inter alia, that the registers of companies, external companies, reserved names and delinquent directors, respectively, as maintained by the Companies and Intellectual Property Registration Office in terms of the 1973 Act, are each continued as the register of companies, external companies, reserved names, and directors required to be established by the Companies Commission in terms of the new Act.[77] The registers thus continue to be valid.

Provision is furthermore made for the continued investigation and enforcement of the previous Act. Despite the repeal of the 1973 Act, any investigation by the Minister or the Registrar in terms of the 1973 Act and pending immediately before the effective date (of the new Act) may be continued by the Companies Commission; while those of the Securities Regulation Panel may be continued by the Takeover Regulation Panel.[78]

For a period of three years after the effective date (of the new Act), the Companies Commission may exercise any power of the Registrar[79] while the Takeover Regulation Panel may exercise any power of the Securities Regulation Panel, in terms of the previous Act, to investigate and prosecute any breach of that Act that occurred during the period of three years immediately before the effective date. In addition, a court may make any order that could have been made in the circumstances by a court in terms of the 1973 Act. In exercising this authority, the Companies Commission or the Takeover Regulation Panel must, significantly, conduct the investigation or other matter in accordance with the 1973 Act.[80]

---

[75] See the discussion on s 172, in the context of objections to compliance notices, in 17.4.4 below.
[76] Section 212. The draft Companies Amendment Bill, 2010 proposes to increase this to ten business days (cl 108).
[77] Schedule 5 item 12(9).
[78] Schedule 5 item 13.
[79] Or the Minister, in terms of cl 115(9) of the draft Companies Amendment Bill, 2010.
[80] Schedule 5 item 13. See further chapter 21: Transitional Arrangements.

17.4 COMPLAINTS TO THE COMPANIES COMMISSION (OR TO THE PANEL)

The Companies Act of 2008 extensively decriminalises company law, as discussed above, and generally relies on a system of administrative enforcement in place of criminal sanctions to ensure compliance with the Act. Any person who alleges that his or her (or its) rights have been infringed, or that another has acted inconsistently with the Act, may file a complaint with the Companies Commission or the Panel.

The Panel is dealt with in chapter 15: Fundamental Transactions, Takeovers and Offers, whereas this section focuses on the Companies Commission. However, it should be borne in mind that these provisions apply equally to complaints to the Panel.

17.4.1 Initiating a complaint

'Any person', and not merely securities holders or directors, may file a complaint with the Companies Commission within three years.[81] This is done by filing a written complaint alleging that:[82]

- another person has acted in a manner inconsistent with the Act, or
- that his or her (ie the complainant's) rights, whether under the Act or a company's Memorandum of Incorporation or rules, have been infringed.

There is an inconsistency between the above provision (s 168(1)(b)) and s 156, in that s 156 additionally contemplates the enforcement of a provision or right under a transaction or agreement contemplated in the Act, the company's Memorandum of Incorporation or rules, by the use of one of the alternative procedures set out in s 156, including the filing of a complaint.

Where a complaint concerns a matter within the jurisdiction of the Panel (namely a matter contemplated in the Takeover Regulations; or Part B of Chapter 5 of the Act on the authority of the Panel and the Takeover Regulations; or Part C of Chapter 5 on the regulation of affected transactions and offers), the complaint must be filed with the Panel. All other complaints are filed with the Companies Commission.

A complaint may also be initiated directly by the Companies Commission, whether on its own motion or at the request of another regulatory authority.[83] Furthermore, the Minister may direct the Companies Commission to investigate an alleged contravention of the Act or other specified circumstances (namely, any matter or circumstances with respect to the administration of one or more companies in terms of the Act, whether or not those circumstances appear at the time of the direction to amount to a possible contravention of the Act).[84]

A complaint may not be made to nor initiated by the Companies Commission more than three years after the act or omission that is the cause of the complaint.

---

[81] Section 219.
[82] Section 168(1).
[83] Section 168(2). 'Regulatory authority' means an entity established in terms of national or provincial legislation responsible for regulating an industry, or sector of an industry (s 1).
[84] Section 168(3) read with s 190(2)(b).

In the case of a course of conduct or a continuing practice, the time period of three years is calculated from the date that the conduct or practice ceased.[85] Section 219 caters for the double-jeopardy principle by providing that a complaint may not be prosecuted in terms of the Act against any person who has been a respondent in proceedings under another section of the Act relating substantially to the same conduct.

17.4.2 Investigation by the Companies Commission

(a) The Companies Commission's response to a complaint

The Companies Commission may respond to a complaint (including those initiated by the Companies Commission itself and directions from the Minister) in one of three ways:[86]

- First, (except in the case of a direction from the Minister) it may issue a notice to the complainant, in the prescribed form, indicating that it will not investigate the complaint on the basis that it appears to be frivolous or vexatious or that it does not allege any facts that, if proven, would constitute grounds for a remedy under the Act.
- Secondly, if the Companies Commission thinks it expedient as a means of resolving the matter, it may refer the complainant to the Companies Tribunal or to an accredited entity, with a recommendation that the complainant seek to resolve the matter with the assistance of that agency through alternative dispute resolution.
- Thirdly, in all other cases, the Companies Commission may direct an inspector or investigator[87] to investigate the complaint.

An inspector is any suitable employee of the Companies Commission or other suitable person employed by the state, who is appointed as an inspector by the Commissioner and is issued with a certificate to that effect.[88] The Act provides scope also for appointing an independent investigator, who is to report to both the Companies Commission and the company. In this regard, where a complaint concerns a dispute that is internal to a particular company and does not appear to implicate any party other than the company, the holders of its securities, its directors, committees, prescribed officers, company secretary or auditor, the Companies Commission may submit a proposal to the company seeking an agreement to jointly appoint an independent investigator, at the expense of the company or on a cost-share basis, or alternatively, the Companies Commission may apply to a court for an order appointing an independent investigator at the expense of the company.[89] The Companies Commission may furthermore designate one or more persons to assist an inspector or investigator.[90]

---

[85] Section 219. See further 17.8.2 below.
[86] Section 169(1).
[87] An investigator is a person appointed as such in terms of s 209 (s 1).
[88] Section 209(1).
[89] Section 169(2)(b).
[90] Section 169(2).

In conducting an investigation, an inspector or investigator may investigate any person who is named in the complaint, or who is related to a person named in the complaint, or any person whom the inspector reasonably considers may have information relevant to the investigation of the complaint.[91]

The provisions on investigations may create scope for shareholders who wish to institute proceedings for mismanagement or initiate other remedial action, to obtain the necessary facts or background information required to establish the factual basis of their claim (for instance, derivative proceedings, an application for relief from oppressive or prejudicial conduct or an application to protect the rights of securities holders). The extent to which this section may be used for such purposes will ultimately depend on the manner in which the Companies Commission in practice exercises its discretion to direct an investigation of the complaint (under s 169(1)). This could have important practical consequences as corporate information may not otherwise be available to the shareholder (or securities holder), especially in view of the proclivity of wrongdoers to suppress information that could result in legal proceedings against them. However, a balance must be drawn and, if this provision is to be used at all for such purposes, it should not be misused to badger the management of companies or to embark on fishing expeditions.

(b) Powers to support investigations and inspections

The powers to support investigations and inspections are set out in Part E of Chapter 7 of the Act. Regarding the summons, the Companies Commission has the power to issue a summons to any person who is believed to be able to furnish relevant information, to appear before the Commission or an inspector or independent investigator to be questioned. A summons may also be issued to any person who is believed to have possession or control of any book, document or other object that has a bearing on the subject of the investigation, to deliver or produce it to an inspector or independent investigator.[92] The Act additionally deals with other matters, including the service of the summons, the interrogation and administering of an oath to the person named in the summons, and the retention of a book, document or other object for examination for a period not exceeding two months or such longer period as the court, on good cause shown, may allow.[93]

A person who is questioned in terms of this section must answer each question truthfully and to the best of his or her ability, but they have the right not to answer a self-incriminating question, and must be informed of this right by the person asking the questions. A self-incriminating answer or statement will be inadmissible as evidence in criminal proceedings instituted against them, except in criminal proceedings for perjury or for knowingly providing false information in terms of s 215(2)(*e*).[94]

Turning to entry and search, a warrant to enter and search premises may be issued by a judge of the High Court or a magistrate if, from information on oath or

---

[91] Section 169(3).
[92] Section 176(1).
[93] See further s 176.
[94] See further s 176(4) and (5).

affirmation, there are reasonable grounds for believing that a contravention of the Act has taken place, is taking place, or is likely to take place on or in those premises, or that anything connected with an investigation in terms of the Act is in the possession of, or under the control of, a person who is on or in those premises.[95]

The warrant to enter and search must specifically identify the premises and authorise an inspector or a police officer to enter and search the premises and do anything listed in s 178, which deals with the powers to enter and search.[96] 'Premises' is defined in s 1 of the Act to include land, or any building, structure, vehicle, ship, boat, vessel, aircraft or container. In terms of s 178, a person (inspector or police officer) who has been authorised to enter and search premises may enter the premises; search the premises; search any person on the premises if there are reasonable grounds for believing that he or she has personal possession of an article or document having a bearing on the investigation; or examine any article or document on or in the premises that has a bearing on the investigation. The authorised person may request information about any article or document from the owner of, or person in control of, the premises or from any person who has control of the article or document, or from any other person who may have the information; take extracts from or make copies of any book or document having a bearing on the investigation that is on or in the premises; use any computer system on the premises (or require assistance of any person on the premises to do so) in order to search any data contained in or available to that computer system, or to reproduce any record from that data; or seize any output from that computer for examination and copying. He or she may attach and, if necessary, remove from the premises, for examination and safekeeping, anything that has a bearing on the investigation.[97]

During a search, a person may refuse to permit the inspection or the removal of an article or document on the grounds that it contains privileged information (for instance legal professional privilege). If the owner or person in control of an article or document refuses, on these grounds, to give it to the person conducting the search, the latter person may request the registrar or sheriff of the High Court to attach and remove the article or document for safe custody until the court determines whether or not the information is privileged.[98]

Any person conducting an entry and search must do so with strict regard for

---

[95] Section 177(1). The Act deals further with matters such as the requirements of the warrant; the validity of the warrant and the events that render it invalid (including its expiry one month after the date of issue); the time when it may be executed; and the differing requirements for the execution of the warrant when the owner or the person in control of the premises to be searched is present, and when neither is present (see further s 177).

[96] Section 177(2)(b).

[97] Section 178(1). The provisions of s 176(4) and (5) (on self-incriminating answers and statements, as discussed above) apply to questioning by, and answers or statements made to, an inspector or police officer (s 178(2)).

[98] Section 179(5) and (6). Other provisions on the conduct of entry and search deal inter alia with the general manner of entry and search; the questioning of any person or the removal of anything from the premises; and forced entry during a search (see further s 179).

decency and order, and with regard for each person's right to dignity, freedom, security and privacy.[99]

There are various offences in relation to entry and search. It is an offence to hinder, obstruct or attempt to improperly influence any person exercising a power or performing a duty under the Act;[100] or to improperly frustrate or impede the execution of a warrant to enter and search. By the same token, it is an offence to act contrary to or in excess of a warrant to enter and search; or to enter or search premises without authority. There are also several offences relating to the summons.[101] See further 17.7 below on offences.

17.4.3 Outcome of the investigation

After receiving the report of the inspector or independent investigator, the Companies Commission has several options. The Commission may:[102]

- issue a compliance notice (see further 17.4.4 below),[103]
- refer the matter to the National Prosecuting Authority or other relevant regulatory authority, if the Commission alleges that a person has committed an offence in terms of the Act or any other legislation,[104]
- commence proceedings in a court in the name of the complainant and with the complainant's consent, if the complainant has a right under the Act to apply to court in respect of the relevant matter,
- refer the complaint to the Companies Tribunal or the Panel, if the matter falls within their respective jurisdictions under the Act,
- propose that the complainant and any affected person meet with the Commission or with the Companies Tribunal with a view to resolving the matter by consent order (see further 17.4.5 below),[105]
- issue a notice of non-referral to the complainant, with a statement advising the complainant of any rights they may have under the Act to seek a remedy in court (see 17.4.6 below), and
- excuse any person as a respondent in the complaint, if the Commission considers it reasonable to do so, having regard to the person's conduct and the degree to which the person has co-operated with the Commission in the investigation.

The Companies Commission, in its sole discretion, may publish the report of the inspector or independent investigator. Irrespective of whether it publishes the

---

[99] Section 179(1).
[100] Section 215(1).
[101] Section 215(2).
[102] Section 170(1).
[103] In the case of a complaint to the Takeover Regulation Panel regarding a matter within its jurisdiction, it is the Executive Director who may issue a compliance notice (upon referral of the matter to him or her by the Panel).
[104] In terms of s 219(2), a complaint may not be prosecuted in terms of the Act against any person that is, or has been, a respondent in proceedings under another section of the Act relating substantially to the same conduct.
[105] This applies only to complaints to the Companies Commission and not to complaints to the Takeover Regulation Panel.

report, the Companies Commission must deliver a copy of the report to the complainant (or any regulatory authority that requested the initiation of the complaint), any person who was a subject of the investigation and any court, if requested or ordered to do so by the court. Any other person implicated in the report, any holder of securities and any creditor of the company that was the subject of the report is also entitled to a copy of the report on payment of the prescribed fee.[106]

17.4.4 Compliance notice

Once a complaint has been investigated and the report of the inspector or independent investigator has been received by the Companies Commission, the Commission has several options, one of which is to issue a compliance notice, as discussed above.[107] This is an important and innovative provision of the Act. A compliance notice may only be issued if an alleged contravention could not otherwise be addressed by an application to a court or to the Companies Tribunal.[108] Failure to comply with a compliance notice may have severe consequences.

(a) Issuing a compliance notice

A compliance notice may be issued to any person (whether a company or an individual) that the Companies Commission, on reasonable grounds, believes:

- has contravened the Act, or
- assented to, was implicated in, or directly or indirectly benefited from, a contravention of the Act.[109]

Significantly, the Commission may issue a compliance notice only if an alleged contravention could not otherwise be addressed by an application to a court or to the Companies Tribunal in terms of the Act.[110]

A compliance notice may require such a person to:[111]

- cease, correct or reverse any action in contravention of the Act,
- take any action required by the Act,
- restore assets or their value to a company or to any other person,
- provide a community service,[112] or
- take any other steps reasonably related to the contravention and designed to rectify its effect.

The compliance notice must be in the prescribed form and set out the person or association to whom it applies, the provision of the Act that has been contravened, and details of the nature and extent of the contravention. It must also specify the

---

[106] Section 170(2).
[107] Section 170(1)(g).
[108] Section 171(1).
[109] Section 171(1). When issuing a compliance notice to a 'regulated person or entity' the Companies Commission 'must send a copy of the notice to the regulatory authority that granted a licence or similar authority to that regulated person or entity, and in terms of which that person is authorised to conduct business' (s 171(3)).
[110] Section 171(1).
[111] Section 171(2).
[112] This applies only to a notice issued by the Companies Commission (not the Panel).

Enforcement and Regulatory Agencies 769

steps that must be taken and the period within which this must be done, together with the penalty that may be imposed for failure to do so.[113]

In the event that the requirements of the compliance notice have been satisfied, the Companies Commission must issue a compliance certificate.[114]

A compliance notice generally remains in force until a compliance certificate has been issued by the Companies Commission upon satisfaction of its requirements. But a compliance notice may also be set aside by the Companies Tribunal or by a court, upon a review of the notice.[115]

(b) Objection to a compliance notice

A person who has been issued with a compliance notice may challenge it before the Companies Tribunal or a court. In this regard, that person may apply to have the notice reviewed within 15 business days after receiving it or such longer period as may be allowed on good cause shown.[116]

After considering any representations by the applicant and any other relevant information, the Companies Tribunal or the court (as the case may be) may confirm, modify or cancel all or part of the compliance notice.[117] A decision by the Companies Tribunal is binding but is subject to 'any right of *review* or *appeal* by a court' [emphasis added] (s 172(4)).

Regarding the issue of the review or appeal of the decision of the Companies Tribunal on this matter, it appears that the Tribunal's decision may be appealed only by the person who was issued with the compliance notice, and that the Companies Commission itself may not appeal. A review of the Tribunal's decision, on the other hand, may seemingly be initiated either by the Companies Commission or by the person who was issued with the compliance notice. The Companies Commission thus has a right only to apply for a review of, but not for a right to appeal against, a decision of the Companies Tribunal. This appears from s 172(4) above read with s 195(7), which states that a decision by the Companies Tribunal with respect to a decision, notice or order by the Companies Commission is binding on the Commission, subject to any '*review*' by the court.

Failing a successful objection to a compliance notice, the person who has been issued with the notice is obliged to satisfy its terms and requirements.

(c) Failure to comply with a compliance notice

In the event that a person fails to comply with a compliance notice, the Companies Commission may apply to a court for the imposition of an administrative fine. Alternatively, the Companies Commission may refer the matter to the National Prosecuting Authority for prosecution as an offence (in terms of s 214(3)).[118] The

---

[113] Section 171(4).
[114] Section 171(6).
[115] Section 171(5). In the case of a compliance notice issued by the Executive Director of the Panel, it is the Takeover Special Committee or a court that may set aside the notice upon a review of it.
[116] Section 172(1).
[117] Section 172(2).
[118] Section 214(3) makes it an offence to fail to satisfy a compliance notice. But no person may be prosecuted for such an offence in respect of a particular compliance notice where the Companies

Companies Commission may not, however, do both in respect of a failure to comply with any particular compliance notice.[119]

It is notable that, even though the new Act by and large uses a system of administrative enforcement rather than criminal sanctions to ensure compliance, the system of administrative enforcement may itself ultimately result in criminal sanctions. Central to the system of administrative enforcement by the Companies Commission is the complaints procedure coupled with the compliance notice. Since the failure to satisfy a compliance notice is an offence in itself, the complaints procedure may eventually result in a criminal prosecution. However, unlike the 1973 Act with its extensive criminal offences, a criminal prosecution for a failure to satisfy a compliance notice is a matter of last resort. Moreover, the Companies Commission may in these circumstances opt instead to apply to a court for an administrative fine, which would bypass any prosecution for the offence.

(d) Administrative fine

A court may (on application by the Companies Commission or the Panel, as the case may be) impose an administrative fine only for failure to comply with a compliance notice.

The administrative fine may not exceed the greater of 10 per cent of the respondent's turnover[120] for the period during which the company failed to comply with the compliance notice, and the maximum prescribed[121] by the Minister by way of regulation. The prescribed maximum administrative fine must be not less than R1 million, and is currently set by the draft Companies Regulations at the amount of R1 million.[122]

When determining the appropriate amount of an appropriate administrative fine, the court must consider the following factors:

- the nature, duration, gravity and extent of the contravention,
- any loss or damage suffered as a result,
- the behaviour of the respondent,
- the market circumstances in which the contravention took place,
- the level of profit derived from the contravention,
- the degree to which the respondent has co-operated with the Companies Commission (or the Panel, as the case may be) and the court, and

---

Commission has applied to a court (in terms of s 171(7)(*a*)) for the imposition of an administrative fine in respect of that person's failure to comply with that notice.

[119] Section 171(7).

[120] As determined in the prescribed manner (s 175(3)). The method of calculating turnover is as set out in General Notice 253 of 2001 promulgated in terms of s 6(1) of the Competition Act 1998 (regulation 175 of the draft Companies Regulations Pursuant to the Companies Act, 2008 (Act No. 71 of 2008) GN 1664 *GG* 32832 of 22 December 2009 (hereafter 'the draft Companies Regulations')).

[121] Section 175(1).

[122] Section 175(5) and Regulation 174 of the draft Companies Regulations.

- whether the respondent has previously been found to be in contravention of the Act.[123]

Administrative fines are paid into the National Revenue Fund.[124]

(e) Winding-up of the company

Where a company has engaged in fraudulent or otherwise illegal conduct, in respect of which a conviction for an offence or an administrative fine was imposed, and the company again engages in substantially the same conduct within the ensuing five years and furthermore fails to comply with a compliance notice issued by the Companies Commission in respect of that conduct, then the court may order the (solvent) company to be wound up on an application by the Companies Commission.

To elaborate, the Act states that where a company, its directors or prescribed officers or other persons in control of the company are acting or have acted in a manner that is fraudulent or otherwise illegal, and the Companies Commission (or the Panel) has issued a compliance notice in respect of that conduct, with which the company has failed to comply, then the Companies Commission (or the Panel) may apply to a court for an order that the solvent company be wound up. However, such an application may be made only if, within the previous five years, enforcement procedures in terms of the Act (or the Close Corporations Act 1984) were taken against the company, its directors or prescribed officers, or other persons in control of the company for substantially the same conduct, resulting in an administrative fine or conviction for an offence.[125] This is intended to function as a measure to deal with recidivist companies that repeatedly commit offences.[126]

17.4.5 Consent order

Where a matter has been investigated and the Companies Commission and the respondent (but not necessarily the complainant) have agreed on a resolution of the complaint, the Companies Commission may record the resolution in the form of an order. If the person who is the subject of the complaint consents to that order, the Companies Commission may apply to the High Court to have it confirmed as a consent order, in terms of its rules.[127] The court may make the order as agreed and proposed in the application, or may indicate any changes that must be made to the draft order, or may refuse to make the order. Where the court confirms a consent order, this may include an award of damages. Unless the consent order includes an award of damages to a person, that person is not precluded from applying for an award of civil damages.[128]

---

[123] Section 175(2).
[124] Referred to in s 213 of the Constitution (s 175(4)).
[125] Section 81(1)(f). See further chapter 19: Winding-up.
[126] *Memorandum on the Objects of the Companies Bill, 2008* op cit n 2 at para 12.
[127] Section 173(1). The consent order provisions apply only to complaints to the Companies Commission and not to complaints to the Panel.
[128] Section 173(2) read with s 167(2) to (4).

Although the Act does not require the consent of the complainant for a consent order, the complainant's consent is required for an award of damages.[129] This may be justified on the basis that, where an award of damages is included in a consent order, this would preclude the complainant from commencing a civil action for damages.

The consent order process is expected to promote the expeditious resolution and settlement of disputes.

17.4.6 Notice of non-referral and referral of complaints to the court

In the event that the Companies Commission issues a notice of non-referral in response to a complaint, the complainant is entitled to apply for leave to refer the matter directly to a court. But no complaint may be referred directly to a court in respect of a person who has been excused as a respondent (in terms of s 170(1)*(a)*, as discussed in 17.4.3 above).[130] The court may grant leave only if it appears that the applicant has no other available remedy in terms of the Act.[131]

If after granting leave and conducting a hearing, the court finds that the respondent has indeed contravened the Act, the court may require the Companies Commission to issue a compliance notice to address that contravention. Alternatively, the court may make any other order contemplated in the Act that is just and reasonable in the circumstances.[132]

17.5 VOLUNTARY RESOLUTION OF DISPUTES

One of the alternative procedures provided by the Act for resolving complaints or securing rights is alternative dispute resolution. Alternative dispute resolution or the voluntary resolution of disputes is dealt with in Part C of Chapter 7 of the Act. Alternative dispute resolution for these purposes means conciliation, mediation or arbitration.[133]

A person may refer a matter for resolution by mediation, conciliation or arbitration as an alternative to applying for relief to a court or filing a complaint with the Companies Commission.[134] This applies to disputes 'with or within a company'.[135] The matter may be referred either to the Companies Tribunal or to an accredited entity for alternative dispute resolution.[136] The Act does not explicitly

---

[129] Regulation 142 of the draft Companies Regulations.
[130] Section 174(1).
[131] Section 174(2)*(a)*.
[132] Section 174(2).
[133] Section 156*(a)* read with s 166(1) and (2).
[134] Section 166(1).
[135] Section 156*(a)*. This states that a person with standing may seek to address an alleged contravention of the Act or to enforce a provision or right under the Act, a company's Memorandum of Incorporation or rules, or a transaction or agreement contemplated in the Act, the company's Memorandum of Incorporation or rules, by attempting to resolve any dispute with or within a company through alternative dispute resolution.
[136] Section 166(1). The draft Companies Amendment Bill, 2010 (cl 97) proposes to add that it may also be referred to any other person. An 'accredited entity' means (i) an organ of state or entity established by a public regulation that is mandated, among other things, to perform mediation, conciliation or arbitration, and has been designated by the Minister, after consulting the Companies

Enforcement and Regulatory Agencies 773

require the consent of the other party to alternative dispute resolution, but the voluntary nature of alternative dispute resolution necessitates the consent of both parties.

It is clear that successful alternative dispute resolution requires both parties to the dispute to participate in the process in good faith. Where the Companies Tribunal or the accredited entity (as the case may be) concludes that either party to the conciliation, mediation or arbitration is not participating in that process in good faith, or that there is no reasonable probability of the parties resolving their dispute through that process, the Companies Tribunal or accredited entity must issue a certificate in the prescribed form stating that the process has failed.[137]

On the other hand, where dispute resolution is successful, this may result in a consent order. To elaborate, where the Companies Tribunal or the accredited entity has resolved a dispute or has assisted the parties to resolve a dispute, it may record the resolution of that dispute in the form of an order. Provided that the parties to the dispute consent to that order, the Companies Tribunal or accredited entity may submit it to a court to be confirmed as a consent order, in terms of its rules.[138] On hearing an application for a consent order, the court may make the order as agreed and proposed in the application, or it may indicate any changes that must be made to the draft order before it will be made an order of the court or, alternatively, the court may refuse to make the order.[139] Where the court confirms a consent order, this may also include an award of damages. Unless the consent order includes an award of damages to a person, that person is not precluded from applying for an award of civil damages.[140]

17.6 COMPANIES TRIBUNAL ADJUDICATION PROCEEDINGS

The option of applying to the Companies Tribunal for adjudication is another of the alternative procedures available under the Act for addressing complaints or securing rights.[141] A distinction must be drawn between alternate dispute resolution before the Companies Tribunal and adjudication proceedings before the Companies Tribunal. It is apparent from s 195(1) that these are two separate and distinct dispute resolution procedures.

Any person with standing to apply for remedies may apply to the Companies Tribunal for adjudication 'in respect of any matter for which such an application is permitted in terms of this Act' (s 156*(b)*); and the Companies Tribunal may adjudicate 'in relation to any application that may be made to it in terms of this Act, and make any order provided for in this Act in respect of such an application'

Commission, as an accredited entity; and/or (ii) a juristic person or association of persons accredited by the Commission. In this regard, the Commission may accredit, with or without conditions, a juristic person or an association that functions predominantly to provide conciliation, mediation or arbitration services; has the demonstrated capacity to perform such services within the context of company law; and satisfies the prescribed requirements for accreditation (as prescribed by the Minister, after consulting the Commission) (s 166(3)–(5)).

[137] Section 166(2).
[138] Section 167(1).
[139] Section 167(2).
[140] Section 167(3).
[141] Section 156.

(s 195(1)). '[T]his Act' is defined in s 1 to include the Schedules and the regulations — the regulations may accordingly also be relevant in determining which matters may be adjudicated. See further the discussion in 17.3.2 above on the Companies Tribunal and the functions assigned to the Companies Tribunal by the various provisions of the Act.

Adjudication proceedings must be conducted by the Companies Tribunal expeditiously and in accordance with the principles of natural justice. The Companies Tribunal may conduct adjudication proceedings informally.[142] At the conclusion of adjudication proceedings, the presiding member must issue a decision together with written reasons for it.[143]

The powers of the Companies Tribunal at an adjudication hearing include the powers to direct or summon any person to appear at any specified time and place; to question any person under oath or affirmation; to summon or order any person to produce any book, document or item necessary for the purposes of the hearing, or to perform any other act in relation to the Act; and to give directions prohibiting or restricting the publication of any evidence given to the Tribunal.[144] The Companies Tribunal may determine any matter of procedure for an adjudication hearing, with due regard to the circumstances of the case and subject to the requirements of the applicable section of the Act.[145]

The persons who may participate in an adjudication hearing are the Companies Commission, the applicant or complainant, and any other person who has a material interest in the hearing, unless that interest is adequately represented by another participant. These persons may participate in the hearing either in person or through a representative. They may put questions to witnesses and inspect any books, documents or items presented at the hearing.[146]

Turning to witnesses, every person who gives evidence before the Companies Tribunal at an adjudication hearing must answer any relevant questions. The law regarding the privilege of a witness in a criminal case in a court of law applies to persons who provide information at an adjudication hearing. During an adjudication hearing the Companies Tribunal may order a person to answer any question or to produce any article or document, subject to the provisions of the Act relating to self-incriminating answers or statements.[147] In this regard, a person is not obliged to answer any question if the answer is self-incriminating, and must be informed of this right by the person asking the questions. A self-incriminating answer or statement will be inadmissible as evidence in criminal proceedings instituted against that person in any court, except in criminal proceedings for perjury or the offence of knowingly providing false information to the Companies Tribunal

---

[142] Section 180(1). If the adjudication proceedings are open to the public, the Companies Tribunal may exclude members of the public or specific persons or categories of persons from attending, if evidence to be presented is confidential information that cannot otherwise be protected; or if the proper conduct of the hearing requires it; or for any other reason that would be justifiable in civil proceedings in a High Court (s 186(2)).

[143] Section 180(3). See also 17.3.2 on the Companies Tribunal above.

[144] Section 182.

[145] Section 183.

[146] Section 181.

[147] Section 184.

(under s 215 (2)(e)), and then only to the extent that the answer or statement is relevant to prove the offence.[148] See further section 17.7 below on offences, and specifically the offence of hindering the administration of the Act (17.7.2(e)).

17.7 OFFENCES

17.7.1 General

A guiding policy principle for the Companies Act of 2008 is that company law should be decriminalised where possible,[149] in order to promote predictability, effectiveness and efficiency in the regulation of companies. This is buttressed by the stated purpose of the Act to provide a predictable and effective environment for the efficient regulation of companies.[150] Rather than relying on extensive criminal sanctions in the vein of the 1973 Act, the new Act relies primarily on a system of administrative enforcement, as discussed above. This is expected to enhance and improve compliance with the Act. Criminal sanctions in the context of company law have been found to be ineffective for various reasons, and the trend internationally is to replace criminal sanctions with more meaningful sanctions.

There are, however, a number of offences under the Act. The Act is not completely devoid of criminal sanctions. These offences include the falsification of certain records or documents; publishing or providing untrue, false or misleading information in specified circumstances (eg in a prospectus); and fraudulent or reckless trading. The accounting and reporting requirements of the Act are also subject to criminal sanctions. Failure to satisfy the conditions of a compliance notice is an offence, as is refusal to respond to a summons or give evidence, commit perjury, and similar matters relating to hindering the administration of the Act. Other offences discussed in earlier chapters include those relating to the use of the company name and registration number (s 32); the failure by a company to keep accurate and complete accounting records in the prescribed manner and form, with intent to deceive or mislead (s 28(3)); and access to company records (s 26).

In order to improve corporate accountability,[151] a more stringent penalty is imposed for certain offences, of up to ten years' imprisonment or a fine or both. These offences include (knowingly) signing or agreeing to a false, misleading or untrue financial statement or prospectus.

17.7.2 Some specific offences

(a) Breach of confidence

It is an offence to disclose any confidential information obtained in carrying out any function in terms of the Act, or as a result of initiating a complaint or participating in any proceedings in terms of the Act.[152]

---

[148] Section 176(4) and (5).
[149] *Memorandum on the Objects of the Companies Bill, 2008* op cit n 2 at para 1.
[150] Section 7(l).
[151] *Memorandum on the Objects of the Companies Bill, 2008* op cit n 2 at para 12.
[152] Section 213(1). This is subject to certain exceptions in terms of s 213(2).

Any person convicted of the offence of breach of confidence is liable to a fine or to imprisonment for a period of up to ten years, or to both a fine and imprisonment.[153]

(b) False statements

There are a number of offences relating to false statements. The falsification of any accounting records of a company is an offence, and any person who is a party to such falsification is guilty of an offence.[154]

It is also an offence to knowingly provide false or misleading information, with a fraudulent purpose, in any circumstances in which the Act requires a person to provide information or to give notice to another person.[155]

To be a party to the preparation, approval, dissemination or publication of financial statements or summaries to the extent set out in s 29(6) is an offence,[156] ie in the case of financial statements, knowing that those statements do not comply with the requirements of s 29(1) or that they are materially false or misleading; and in the case of a summary, knowing that the summary does not comply with the requirements of s 29(3) or is materially false or misleading, or that the statements that it summarises do not comply with the requirements of s 29(1) or are materially false or misleading.

'Untrue statements' in a prospectus or a written statement attract criminal penalties if one is a party to the preparation, approval, dissemination or publication of such a prospectus or written statement.[157]

For the purposes of these two offences, a person is a *party* to the preparation of such a document if the document includes or is otherwise based on a scheme, structure or form of words or numbers devised, prepared or recommended by that person; and the scheme, structure or form of words is of such a nature that the person knew, or ought reasonably to have known, that its inclusion or other use in connection with the preparation of the document would cause the document to be false or misleading.[158]

A person who is convicted of any of the above offences relating to false statements is liable to a fine or to imprisonment for a period not exceeding ten years, or to both a fine and imprisonment.[159] The severity of this penalty is designed to improve corporate accountability.

---

[153] Section 216*(a)*.
[154] Section 214(1)*(a)*. See also s 28(3)*(b)*.
[155] Section 214(1)*(b)*.
[156] Section 214(1)*(d)*(i). The draft Companies Amendment Bill, 2010 (cl 109) proposes to delete this provision from s 214, but it will continue to form part of s 29(6).
[157] Section 214(1)*(d)*(ii). See also ss 95 and 101.
[158] Section 214(2).
[159] Section 216*(a)*.

Enforcement and Regulatory Agencies

(c) Reckless conduct

Turning to reckless trading or reckless conduct, it is a criminal offence for a person to knowingly[160] be a party to conduct prohibited by s 22(1), ie carrying on a company's business recklessly, with gross negligence, with intent to defraud any person or for any fraudulent purpose; or trading under insolvent circumstances.[161]

It is also an offence to knowingly[162] be a party to an act or omission by a business that is calculated to defraud a creditor, employee or security holder of the company, or with another fraudulent purpose.[163]

A person who is convicted of any of these offences is similarly liable to a fine or to imprisonment for a period of up to ten years, or to both a fine and imprisonment.[164]

(d) Non-compliance

The failure to satisfy a compliance notice issued in terms of the Act is an offence. This may result in a criminal prosecution, unless the Companies Commission or the Panel (as the case may be) has applied to a court for the imposition of an administrative fine.[165] (See also the discussion on compliance notices above at 17.4.4.)

The penalty for this offence is a fine or imprisonment for a period not exceeding 12 months, or both a fine and imprisonment.[166]

It is notable that even though the new Act by and large uses a system of administrative enforcement rather than criminal sanctions to ensure compliance, the system of administrative enforcement may itself ultimately result in criminal sanctions, as discussed above. Central to the system of administrative enforcement by the Companies Commission is the complaints procedure coupled with the compliance notice. Since the failure to satisfy a compliance notice is an offence in itself, the complaints procedure could ultimately result in criminal prosecution. However, unlike the 1973 Act with its extensive criminal offences, a criminal prosecution for a failure to satisfy a compliance notice is a matter of last resort. Moreover, the Companies Commission may in these circumstances opt instead to apply to a court for an administrative fine, which would bypass any prosecution for the offence.

---

[160] In terms of s 1 of the Act, the term 'knowingly' means 'that the person either *(a)* had actual knowledge of that matter; or *(b)* was in a position in which the person reasonably ought to have: (i) had actual knowledge; or (ii) investigated the matter to an extent that would have provided the person with actual knowledge; or (iii) taken other measures which, if taken, would reasonably be expected to have provided the person with actual knowledge of the matter.'

[161] The draft Companies Amendment Bill, 2010 proposes to repeal this provision, ie 214(1)*(c)*(i).

[162] See n 160 above for the definition of the term 'knowingly' under s 1 of the Act.

[163] Section 214(1)*(c)*(ii).

[164] Section 216*(a)*. The draft Companies Amendment Bill, 2010 proposes to insert additional offences relating to the general restriction on offers to the public under s 99 of the Act. A person who contravenes s 99(1)–(5) or (8)–(9) and, if that person is a company, every director and prescribed officer of the company who knowingly was a party to the contravention, is guilty of an offence, and is liable to any other person for any losses sustained as a consequence of that contravention (cl 109).

[165] Section 214(3). See also s 171(7), as discussed above.

[166] Section 216.

(e) Hindering the administration of the Act

It is an offence to hinder, obstruct or improperly attempt to influence the Companies Commission, the Panel, the Companies Tribunal, an inspector or investigator, or a court when any of them is exercising a power or performing a duty under the Act.[167] A person commits an offence if that person:[168]

- does anything calculated to improperly influence the Companies Commission, the Panel, the Companies Tribunal, an inspector or an investigator concerning any matter connected with an investigation,
- does anything calculated to improperly influence the Companies Tribunal in any matter before it,
- anticipates any findings of the Companies Commission, the Panel, the Companies Tribunal, an inspector or investigator in a way that is calculated to improperly influence the proceedings or findings,
- does anything in connection with an investigation or hearing that would have been contempt of court if the proceedings had occurred in a court of law,
- refuses to attend when summoned, or after attending, refuses to answer any question or produce any document as required by the summons (other than as contemplated in s 176*(a)*),[169]
- knowingly provides false information to the Companies Commission, the Panel, the Companies Tribunal, an inspector or an investigator,
- improperly frustrates or impedes the execution of a warrant to enter and search, or attempts to do so,
- acts contrary to or in excess of a warrant to enter and search, and
- without authority, but claiming to have authority, enters or searches premises or attaches or removes an article or document.

These offences carry a penalty of a fine or imprisonment for a period not exceeding 12 months, or both a fine and imprisonment.[170]

17.7.3 Penalties

The general penalty for a person convicted of an offence in terms of the Act is a fine or imprisonment for a period not exceeding 12 months, or both a fine and imprisonment.[171] However certain offences, as pointed out above, carry a more stringent penalty consisting of a fine or imprisonment for a period of up to ten years, or both a fine and imprisonment. These offences are breach of confidence (in terms of s 213(1)) or offences involving false statements or reckless conduct (in terms of s 214(1)).

Despite anything to the contrary contained in any other law, a Magistrate's Court has jurisdiction to impose any of the above penalties.[172]

---

[167] Section 215(1).
[168] Section 215(2).
[169] The reference to s 176*(a)* is incorrect; it is submitted that the reference ought to be to s 176(4)*(a)*.
[170] Section 216.
[171] Ibid.
[172] Section 217.

17.8 MISCELLANEOUS MATTERS
17.8.1 Civil actions (s 218)[173]

Section 218(1) of the Act states:

> Nothing in this Act renders void an agreement, resolution or provision of an agreement, resolution, Memorandum of Incorporation or rules of a company that is prohibited, void, voidable or may be declared unlawful in terms of this Act, unless a court declares that agreement, resolution or provision to be void.

The draft Companies Amendment Bill, 2010, significantly proposes to remove the reference to a 'void' agreement, resolution or provision. This is a sensible measure, as a declaration of voidness by a court should not be required where a provision is void *ab initio* in terms of the Act. However, the Bill does not go far enough. Section 218(1) is now proposed to read as follows:

> Nothing in this Act renders void an agreement, resolution or provision of an agreement, resolution, Memorandum of Incorporation or rules of a company that is prohibited, voidable or that may be declared unlawful in terms of this Act, unless a court has made a declaration to that effect regarding that agreement, resolution or provision.[174]

The effect of s 218(1) is that an agreement, a resolution or a provision of a company's Memorandum of Incorporation or rules, that either is prohibited or voidable or may be declared unlawful, would only be void when a court declares it to be void. Parallels may be drawn between this provision and s 65(1) of the Competition Act.[175] However, unlike the Competition Tribunal which is empowered to declare agreements to be void in terms of the Competition Act, the Companies Tribunal may not make declarations of voidness under the equivalent provision in terms of s 218(1) of the Companies Act.

17.8.2 Prescription and double jeopardy (s 219)

A complaint in terms of the Act may not be initiated by or made to the Companies Commission or the Panel more than three years after the act or omission that is the cause of the complaint. In the case of a course of conduct or a continuing practice, the time period of three years is calculated from the date that the conduct or practice ceased.[176]

Section 219 also provides for a double-jeopardy principle, in that a complaint may not be prosecuted in terms of the Act against any person who has been a respondent in proceedings under another section of the Act relating substantially to the same conduct.[177]

17.8.3 Serving documents (s 220)

Unless otherwise provided in the Act, a notice, order or other document that must be served on a person in terms of the Act, will have been properly served when it

---

[173] Section 218(2) is discussed in 17.2.5 above and in chapter 16: Shareholder Remedies and Minority Protection.
[174] Clause 110.
[175] Section 65(1) of the Competition Act 89 of 1998 states: 'Nothing in this Act renders void a provision of an agreement that, in terms of this Act, is prohibited or may be declared void, unless the Competition Tribunal or Competition Appeal Court declares that provision to be void.'
[176] Section 219(1).
[177] Section 219(2).

has been delivered to that person or sent by registered mail to that person's last known address.

17.8.4 Proof of facts (s 221)

In any proceedings in terms of the Act, if it is proved that a false statement, entry or record or false information appears in or on a book, document, plan, drawing or computer storage medium, the person who kept that item must be presumed to have made the statement, entry, record or information unless the contrary is proved.

Such a statement, entry, record or information is admissible in evidence as an admission of the facts in or on it by the person who appears to have made, entered, recorded or stored it, unless it is proved that that person did not make, enter, record or store it.

17.8.5 State liability (s 222)

The state, the Companies Commission, the Commissioner, the Companies Tribunal, the Panel, an inspector, or any state employee or similar person having duties to perform under the Act, is not liable for any loss sustained by or damage caused to any person as a result of any *bona fide* act or omission relating to the performance of any duty under the Act, unless gross negligence is proved.

CHAPTER 18

BUSINESS RESCUE AND COMPROMISES

Farouk HI Cassim

18.1	INTRODUCTION: A RESCUE CULTURE	782
18.2	THE MEANING OF BUSINESS RESCUE	783
18.3	THE COMMENCEMENT OF BUSINESS RESCUE PROCEEDINGS.	784
	18.3.1 Commencement of business rescue by voluntary board resolution	785
	(a) Objections to the business rescue resolution	787
	(b) The powers of the court in relation to the objection	789
	18.3.2 Commencement of business rescue by order of court	790
18.4	THE DURATION OF BUSINESS RESCUE PROCEEDINGS	791
	18.4.1 The date of commencement.	791
	18.4.2 The duration of business rescue and progress reports	792
	18.4.3 The termination of business rescue proceedings	792
18.5	THE LEGAL CONSEQUENCES OF A BUSINESS RESCUE ORDER	792
	18.5.1 The moratorium.	793
	(a) Moratorium on legal proceedings	794
	(b) Moratorium on property interests	795
	18.5.2 Post-commencement finance	796
	18.5.3 Effect of business rescue on employment contracts and employees.	798
	18.5.4 Effect on contracts generally	798
	18.5.5 Effect of business rescue on shareholders and directors	799
18.6	THE BUSINESS RESCUE PRACTITIONER	801
	18.6.1 Appointment	801
	18.6.2 The qualifications of the practitioner	802
	18.6.3 Removal and replacement of the practitioner	802
	18.6.4 The remuneration of the practitioner	803
	18.6.5 Powers and duties of the practitioner	804
18.7	THE BUSINESS RESCUE PLAN	807
18.8	THE RIGHTS OF AFFECTED PERSONS	809
	18.8.1 Employees	809
	18.8.2 Employees' committees	810
	18.8.3 Creditors and creditors' committees.	811
	18.8.4 The holders of the company's securities	813
18.9	THE CONSIDERATION AND ADOPTION OF THE BUSINESS RESCUE PLAN	813

	18.9.1	Consideration of the plan	813
	18.9.2	The effect of the adoption of the plan	815
	18.9.3	Failure to adopt the plan	816
	18.9.4	The termination of business rescue proceedings	817
18.10	COMPROMISE WITH CREDITORS		817
	18.10.1	General	817
	18.10.2	The proposal	818
	18.10.3	Adoption of the proposal	819

18.1 INTRODUCTION: A RESCUE CULTURE

One of the major themes of the Companies Act of 2008 is the creation of a system of '... corporate rescue appropriate to the needs of a modern South African economy'.[1] This is amplified in s 7(k) of the Companies Act 71 of 2008 (hereafter 'the Act'), which states that one of the purposes of the Act is to 'provide for the efficient rescue and recovery of financially distressed companies, in a manner that balances the rights and interests of all relevant stakeholders'.

By 'rescue' is meant simply a reorganisation of the company to restore it to a profitable entity and avoid liquidation. This is based on Chapter 11 of the US Bankruptcy Code, Bankruptcy Reform Act 1978, which focuses on reorganising companies that are in financial difficulties and combines it with an automatic moratorium. The Cork Report[2] in the United Kingdom also emphasised the importance of the preservation of viable business enterprises as an alternative to insolvency or winding-up proceedings.[3] The objective is to save companies — not put them under liquidation. The Cork Committee proposed that companies in doubtful solvency situations should be reorganised together with their management to restore their profitability or maintain employment.[4]

The effects of insolvency are not limited to the private interests of the insolvent debtor and his or her creditors. There are other groups in society that are vitally affected by the insolvency of the debtor, such as shareholders, suppliers, employees and customers. Company law should consequently provide 'a means for the preservation of ... viable commercial enterprises capable of making a useful contribution to the economic life of the country'.[5] The Cork Report also emphasised that one of the aims of modern insolvency law is to diagnose and treat an imminent insolvency at an early rather than at a late stage. The earlier a company reorganises itself, the better the chances of success and avoidance of liquidation.

As a result of the recommendations of the Cork Report, legislation was enacted in the UK to set up new procedures for the rescue of a company as a going concern. The Insolvency Act, 1986, and the Enterprise Act, 2002, introduced in

---

[1] The Department of Trade and Industry policy paper entitled 'South African Company Law for the 21st Century: Guidelines for Corporate Law Reform' GN 1183 of 23 June 2004; *GG* 26493 at para 4.6.2.

[2] Insolvency Law and Practice: Report of the Review Committee, Chairman Sir Kenneth Cork CBE (Cmnd 8558 (1982)).

[3] See *Powdrill v Watson* [1995] 2 AC 394, per Lord Browne-Wilkinson at 442.

[4] *Powdrill v Watson* (supra) at 498.

[5] The Cork Report op cit n 2 at para 198*j*.

the UK voluntary arrangement and administration procedures which other jurisdictions refer to as business or corporate rescue.

In South Africa, the Act likewise attempts to make it easier for companies in financial difficulty to be rescued, to avoid insolvency and consequent winding-up and to continue as commercially viable entities. The fundamental purpose of a business rescue or reorganisation is to prevent a debtor from going into liquidation, with an attendant loss of jobs and possible misuse of economic resources.[6]

The economy as a whole suffers when a company is shut down. But if a company is successfully rescued or turned around, creditors will get paid, jobs will not be lost and the company will be able to pay taxes. The business rescue provisions in ss 128 to 154 of Chapter 6 of the Act import many aspects of Chapter 11 of the US Bankruptcy Code that apply to companies in financial difficulties.

When a company is placed under business rescue, it gets essential breathing space while a business rescue plan is implemented by a business rescue practitioner or turnaround expert. However, not all companies are suitable for business rescue. Much depends on the cause of the company's financial distress. In some cases, a business rescue may be a prohibitively expensive process for a company to adopt. It may be that a straightforward sale of its business to an interested purchaser would be quicker, more effective and less expensive. Even a compromise with creditors in terms of s 155 of the Act (discussed in 18.10 below) would in certain circumstances be more appropriate than an attempt to rescue or rehabilitate the company.

It should also be noted that business rescue does not necessarily entail a complete recovery of the company in the sense that after the procedure, the company will have regained its solvency, its business will have been restored and its creditors repaid. While this may be the ideal outcome, it is not always attainable.

A final caution before turning to the provisions of the Act: When a company begins to experience financial difficulties, for example, it struggles to pay its debts, or finds that its assets cannot readily be converted into cash for the payment of its obligations, it is only natural for the directors to attempt to continue to trade out of the company's financial difficulties. The directors must bear in mind the harsh penalties that would apply if s 22 of the Act, and especially s 22(1)(*b*), becomes applicable. See further chapter 12: The Duties and the Liability of Directors.

18.2 THE MEANING OF BUSINESS RESCUE

Section 128(1)(*b*) of the Act defines a 'business rescue' as follows:

> [P]roceedings to facilitate the rehabilitation of a company that is financially distressed by providing for:
> (i) the temporary supervision of the company, and of the management of its affairs, business and property;

---

[6] *NLRB v Bildisco* 465 US 513 (1983) 528.

(ii) a temporary moratorium on the rights of claimants against the company or in respect of property in its possession, and

(iii) the development and implementation, if approved, of a plan to rescue the company by restructuring its affairs, business, property, debt and other liabilities, and equity in a manner that maximises the likelihood of the company continuing in existence on a solvent basis or, it if is not possible for the company to so continue in existence, results in a better return for the company's creditors or shareholders than would result from the immediate liquidation of the company.

A 'financially distressed company' is a company that appears to be reasonably unlikely to be able to pay all its debts as they become due and payable within the immediately ensuing six months, *or* a company that appears to be reasonably likely to become insolvent within the immediately ensuing six months.[7] The company is not at this stage insolvent, either in the balance sheet solvency sense (factual insolvency) or in the cash flow or liquidity sense (commercial insolvency) (see 19.3). It is on the verge of insolvency or is experiencing liquidity problems. It frequently happens that the company is illiquid rather than insolvent. In addition, ss 129(1)(*b*) and 131(4)(*a*) require that there must appear to be a reasonable prospect of rescuing the company. Thus, in broad[8] terms, the two prerequisites for business rescue proceedings are that the company must be financially distressed and there must be a reasonable prospect of rescuing the company.

The definition of a 'business rescue'[9] indicates that there are three stages in a business rescue process, namely:

- the temporary supervision of the company's affairs,
- a temporary moratorium on claims and proceedings against the company, and
- the development and the implementation of a business rescue plan.

All three stages of a business rescue regime are vital. Section 128(1)(*b*)(iii) also spells out that the object of the business rescue plan is to restructure the company's affairs, its debts and its liabilities in a manner that maximises the likelihood of the company continuing to exist on a solvent basis or, if this is not possible, then to achieve a better return for creditors or shareholders than would result from the immediate liquidation of the company.

Despite its name, the business rescue provisions of the Act do not apply to unincorporated associations or entities such as a sole trader, partnership or a business trust. Even co-operatives have been left out in the cold. Yet all these business entities are as much in need of a business rescue process. The business rescue provisions of the Act do, however, apply to close corporations.[10]

18.3 THE COMMENCEMENT OF BUSINESS RESCUE PROCEEDINGS

Business rescue proceedings are initiated in one of two ways:

---

[7] Section 128(1)(*f*).

[8] 'Broad', because the prerequisites for court-ordered rescue are slightly different.

[9] Section 128(1)(*b*) of the Act.

[10] See item 6, Schedule 3 to the Act, which states that the provisions of Chapter 6 apply to a close corporation, and that a reference in Chapter 6 to a 'company' must be regarded as a reference to a 'corporation' and a reference to a 'shareholder' of a company or the holder of securities issued by a company must be read as a reference to a member of a corporation.

- by a resolution of the board of directors of the company to voluntarily begin business rescue proceedings, if the board has reasonable grounds to believe that the company is financially distressed and there appears to be a reasonable prospect of rescuing the company;[11] or
- an affected person may apply to a court at any time for an order placing the company under supervision and commencing business rescue proceedings.[12]

These two possibilities are discussed below.

18.3.1 Commencement of business rescue by voluntary board resolution

The Act, under the influence of Chapter 11 of the US Bankruptcy Code (see 18.1 above), introduces a debtor-friendly business rescue process even though our insolvency law system is largely creditor friendly.

Section 129(1) of the Act provides that, subject to s 129(2)*(a)*, the board of directors of a company may resolve that the company voluntarily begins business rescue proceedings and is to be placed under supervision if it has reasonable grounds for believing that two essential prerequisites are satisfied, namely that:

- the company is financially distressed (as discussed in 18.2 above), and
- there *appears* [emphasis added] to be a reasonable prospect of rescuing the company. By 'rescuing' the company is meant achieving the goals of business rescue.[13]

This provision enables the board of directors by resolution (ie majority vote) to commence business rescue proceedings. This is in accord with s 66(1) of the Act, which imposes a duty on the board of directors to manage the business of the company. The shareholders of the company do not have the right to resolve that the company should be voluntarily placed under business rescue. This follows the Australian model.[14] The board of directors is under no legal duty to consult the shareholders in resolving to place the company under business rescue. A distinct advantage of authorising the board of directors to make the decision to place the company under business rescue is that it avoids unnecessary delay and costs. It is also in accord with a debtor-friendly business rescue system and the underlying objective of a flexible business rescue regime that is uncomplicated and swift to implement. But, by the same token, it is the board of directors and not individual directors that may apply for voluntary business rescue. Individual directors may not do so.

Section 129(2)*(a)* and *(b)* imposes two important restrictions on the board resolution to commence business rescue proceedings. First, no such resolution may be adopted if liquidation proceedings have been initiated by or against the company, and secondly, the board resolution to commence business rescue proceedings has no force or effect until it has been filed with the Companies and Intellectual Property Commission ('the Companies Commission'). The business

---
[11] Section 129(1)*(a)* and *(b)*.
[12] Section 131(1).
[13] As set out in s 128(1)*(b)* discussed in 18.2 above.
[14] Part 5.3A of the Corporations Act 2001, s 436A(1).

rescue proceedings formally commence on the date of the filing of the board resolution.[15] Once the board has resolved to voluntarily place the company under business rescue, the company may not then adopt a resolution to begin liquidation proceedings, unless the resolution to commence business rescue proceedings has lapsed or until the business rescue proceedings have ended.[16]

Strict time limits are imposed for the publication of a notice of the resolution to place the company under business rescue and for the appointment of a business rescue practitioner. This is done to avoid unnecessary delay and abuse of the procedure. First, within five business days of the filing of the board resolution to commence business rescue, or such longer time as the Companies Commission on application by the company may allow, the company must publish in the prescribed manner a notice of the resolution and its effective date to every 'affected person'. This must be accompanied by a sworn statement of the facts relevant to the grounds for the board resolution.[17] An 'affected person' means a shareholder or creditor of the company, a registered trade union representing employees of the company, and each of those employees not represented by a trade union or the representatives of such employees.[18] This wide definition of an 'affected person' means that a very wide range of stakeholders are given certain rights in the business rescue process (as discussed in 18.3.1*(a)* and 18.8 below), particularly since it is each individual shareholder or creditor that is given these rights and not just shareholders or creditors as a general or collective body. This approach underscores the consultative and inclusive nature of business rescue proceedings. The disadvantage is that it increases the risk of abuse of the business rescue procedure.

Secondly, within the period referred to above, the company must appoint a business rescue practitioner who is duly qualified as such and who has given his or her written acceptance of the appointment.[19] There is thus a possible five-day period in which a company under business rescue is not under the control or supervision of a business rescue practitioner. A business rescue practitioner is a person appointed, or two or more persons appointed jointly, to oversee the company during business rescue proceedings.[20] Within two business days after the appointment of the business rescue practitioner, a notice of his or her appointment must be filed, and a copy of the notice of appointment must be sent to each affected person within five business days after the notice was filed.[21]

A failure to comply with the above provisions and their prescribed time periods would result in the lapse and the consequent nullity of the board resolution to commence business rescue proceedings and to place the company under supervision.[22] For three months after the date of the adoption of the lapsed resolution the

---

[15] Section 132(1).
[16] Section 129(6).
[17] Section 129(3)*(a)*.
[18] Section 128(1)*(a)*(i) to (iii).
[19] Section 129(3)*(b)*.
[20] Section 128(1)*(d)*.
[21] Section 129(4)*(a)* and *(b)*.
[22] Section 129(5)*(a)*.

company may not file another resolution of this nature, 'unless a court, on good cause shown on an *ex parte* application, approves the company filing a further resolution'.[23] A court in this context refers generally to the High Court with jurisdiction (or the designated or assigned judge).[24]

An interesting provision is that, if the board of directors does not adopt a resolution to place the company under business rescue even though the board has reasonable grounds to believe that the company is financially distressed, the board must[25] deliver a written notice to each affected person setting out which of the two criteria for financial distress as stated in s 128(1)(*f*)[26] applies to the company and the reasons for not adopting a resolution to commence business rescue proceedings.[27] The rationale for this provision is that it enables an affected person to lodge an application to the court to commence business rescue proceedings (as discussed below in 18.3.2 below). Strangely, s 129(7) does not explicitly provide for any sanction for a failure by the board to comply with its provisions.

(a) Objections to the business rescue resolution

At any time after the adoption of the resolution of the board of directors to commence business rescue proceedings and until the adoption of a business rescue plan (in terms of s 152), an affected person may apply to a court for an order setting aside the board resolution on the grounds that:[28]

- there is no reasonable basis for believing that the company is financially distressed,
- there is no reasonable prospect for rescuing the company, or
- the company has failed to satisfy the procedural requirements set out in s 129 (as discussed above in 18.3.1).

In considering such an application, the court may set aside the resolution on any of these grounds or if it considers that it is otherwise just and equitable to do so (further discussed in 18.3.1*(b)* below).

The court may also give the business rescue practitioner sufficient time to form an opinion on whether or not the company appears to be financially distressed or whether or not there is a reasonable prospect of rescuing the company.[29] After

---

[23] Section 129(5)*(b)*.
[24] Section 128(1)*(e)*.
[25] In terms of s 129(7).
[26] The Act incorrectly refers to s 128(1)*(e)* when the reference should be to s 128(1)*(f)*. This error is to be rectified by cl 78 of the draft Companies Amendment Bill, 2010. Section 128(1)*(f)* provides as follows:
   '"financially distressed", in reference to a particular company at any particular time, means that —
   (i) it appears to be reasonably unlikely that the company will be able to pay all of its debts as they fall due and payable within the immediately ensuing six months; or
   (ii) it appears to be reasonably likely that the company will become insolvent within the immediately ensuing six months.'
[27] See further in this regard Regulation 134(3) of the Draft Regulations to the Companies Act (*GN* 1664 in *GG* 32832 of 22 December 2009) (hereafter 'the draft Companies Regulations').
[28] Section 130(1)*(a)*(i) to (iii).
[29] Section 130(5)*(b)*(i) and (ii).

receiving the practitioner's report, the court may set aside the resolution if it concludes that the company is not financially distressed or there is no reasonable prospect of rescuing the company.[30]

Objection may be lodged by an affected person, not only against the business rescue resolution, but also against the appointment of a business rescue practitioner on the grounds that the practitioner:

- does not satisfy the requirements of s 138 (ie is not properly qualified in terms of the requirements and qualifications set out in s 138(1)*(a)* to *(e)* for a business rescue practitioner), or
- is not independent of the company or its management, or
- lacks the necessary skills, given the company's circumstances.

If an affected person lodges an application to have the appointment of the business rescue practitioner set aside, the court, in making such an order, must appoint an alternative practitioner who satisfies the requirements of s 138.[31] This alternative practitioner must also be recommended by, or acceptable to, 'the holders of a majority of the independent creditors' voting interests who were represented in the hearing before the court'.[32]

By an 'independent creditor' is meant a creditor of the company, including an employee who is a creditor, who is not related to the company, or to a director or the business rescue practitioner.[33] For these purposes, an employee is not related to the company solely as a result of being a member of a trade union that holds shares of that company.[34]

An affected person may also apply to the court for an order that 'requires the practitioner to provide security in an amount and on terms and conditions that the court considers necessary to secure the interests of the company and any affected persons'.[35]

A director of the company who voted in favour of the board resolution to commence business rescue proceedings may not apply to a court (in his capacity as an affected person) to set aside the resolution,[36] or the appointment by the company of the business rescue practitioner,[37] unless he or she satisfies the court that, in supporting the resolution, he or she had acted in good faith on the basis of information that has subsequently been found to be false or misleading.

A copy of the application made by an affected person in terms of s 130(1) (ie to set aside the board resolution to commence business rescue proceedings or the appointment of the business rescue practitioner, or to require him or her to provide security) must be served on the company and the Companies Commission.[38] Each

---

[30] Section 130(5)*(b)*.
[31] Section 130(6), which refers, incorrectly, to an 'alternate' practitioner.
[32] Section 130(6)*(a)*.
[33] Section 128(1)*(g)*.
[34] Section 128(2).
[35] Section 130(1)*(c)*.
[36] Section 130(2)*(a)*.
[37] Section 130(2)*(b)*.
[38] Section 130(3)*(a)*.

affected person must also be notified in the prescribed manner of the application.[39] This is buttressed by a provision that confers on each affected person a right to participate in the hearing of the application.[40]

(b) The powers of the court in relation to the objection

The court is given wide powers under s 130 in considering the application to set aside the company's resolution to commence business rescue.

As stated above, the court may set aside the business rescue resolution on the basis of any one of the grounds on which the application was lodged, ie no reasonable basis for believing that the company is financially distressed, no reasonable prospect of rescuing the company, or failure to comply with the procedural requirements of s 129. In addition, the court may set aside the resolution simply on the ground that, having regard to all the evidence, it is just and equitable to do so.[41]

The court may also give the business rescue practitioner additional or sufficient time to form an opinion on whether or not the company appears to be financially distressed, or whether there is a reasonable prospect of rescuing the company.[42] After receiving the report on the matter from the practitioner, the court may set aside the resolution if it decides that the company is not financially distressed or there is no reasonable prospect of rescuing the company.[43]

Where a court makes an order to set aside the company's resolution, it may[44] make any further 'necessary *and* [emphasis added] appropriate order' including an order placing the company under liquidation.[45] If the decision of the court was that there were no reasonable grounds to believe that the company would be unlikely to pay all its debts as they became due and payable, ie that the company was not in financial distress, the court may make an order of costs against any director who voted in favour of the board resolution to commence business rescue to pay the costs of the application, unless the court is satisfied that the director had acted ingood faith and on the basis of information that the director was entitled to rely on in terms of s 76(4) and (5).[46]

If the court sets aside the appointment of a business rescue practitioner, it must (as pointed out above) appoint an alternative practitioner recommended by or acceptable to the holders of a majority of the voting interests of independent creditors who were represented at the hearing.[47] The alternative practitioner may then have the duty to assess whether the company appears to be financially distressed or whether there is a reasonable prospect of rescuing the company.[48]

---

[39] Section 130(3)*(b)*.
[40] Section 130(4).
[41] Section 130(5)*(a)*(ii).
[42] Section 130(5)*(b)*(i) and (ii).
[43] Section 130(5)*(b)*(ii).
[44] In terms of s 130(5)*(c)*.
[45] Section 130(5)*(c)*(i).
[46] See chapter 12: The Duties and the Liability of Directors for a discussion of s 76(4) and (5).
[47] Section 130(6)*(a)*.
[48] Section 130(6)*(b)* read with s 130(5)*(b)*.

18.3.2 Commencement of business rescue by order of court

The other method of commencing the business rescue process is that, provided the board has not passed a resolution to commence business rescue proceedings, any affected person may, in terms of s 131(1), apply to a court at any time for an order to place the company under supervision and to commence business rescue proceedings.[49] This may be done even if the company is under liquidation proceedings. This may be contrasted with s 129(2)(a) (see above at 18.3.1), which provides that the board of directors may not resolve to commence business rescue proceedings if liquidation proceedings have been initiated by or against the company. However, s 131(1) applies only if s 129 does not apply. It follows that, where the board of directors is unable to place the company under business rescue proceedings because of the commencement of liquidation proceedings, an affected person, including a shareholder, may apply to a court in terms of s 131(1) to place the company under business rescue.

The applicant must serve a copy of the application on the company and the Companies Commission and notify each affected person of the application in the prescribed manner.[50] This notification is, of course, quite different from the notification that the company must serve[51] within five days of a court order placing the company under supervision. Each affected person has a right to participate in the hearing of an application in terms of s 131.[52]

Where the application for a court order to commence business rescue proceedings is made after the commencement of liquidation proceedings, the liquidation proceedings will automatically be suspended until the court has adjudicated on the application. However, if the court makes the order to commence with the business rescue proceedings, the liquidation proceedings will be suspended until the business rescue proceedings have ended.[53] A company that has been placed under the business rescue process in terms of s 131 may not adopt a resolution to place itself in liquidation until the business rescue proceedings have ended.[54] To the extent that business rescue overrides liquidation proceedings these provisions are in accord with the underpinning policy of preserving viable commercial enterprises rather than shutting them down by liquidation.

There are three grounds on which a court may make an order to place a company under supervision and to commence business rescue proceedings. These grounds are wider than the grounds on which the board of directors may adopt a resolution to commence business rescue proceedings (as discussed above in 18.3.1).[55] In terms of s 131(4)(a), the court must be satisfied that:

- the company is financially distressed (as defined in s 128(1)(f) and discussed in 18.2 above),

---

[49] Section 131(1).
[50] Section 131(2)(a) and (b).
[51] In terms of s 131(8)(b).
[52] Section 131(3).
[53] Section 131(6)(a) and (b).
[54] Section 131(8).
[55] Section 129(1).

- the company has failed to pay over any amount in terms of an obligation under a public regulation[56] or contract in respect of employment-related matters, or
- it is otherwise just and equitable to do so for financial reasons.

In the case of each of the above grounds the court must also be satisfied that there is a reasonable prospect of rescuing the company.

Section 131(4) thus provides an alternative ground other than financial distress for placing a company under supervision, namely the failure by the company to pay an amount due in terms of any contractual obligation or an obligation arising out of a public regulation, provided that the obligation concerns employment-related matters, such as unemployment insurance or payments to a medical aid fund. The third ground, namely that it is just and equitable for financial reasons to place the company under business rescue, is new and its scope is uncertain.

If the court decides to make an order for the commencement of business rescue proceedings, it may also make a further order appointing an interim business rescue practitioner who has been nominated by the affected person who applied for a court order for the commencement of business rescue proceedings, provided that the interim practitioner satisfies the prescribed qualifications of a practitioner stated in s 138.[57] This appointment is subject to ratification by the holders of a majority of the voting interests of the independent creditors[58] at the first meeting of creditors.[59]

On the other hand, if the court dismisses the application, it may make any further necessary and appropriate order, including an order placing the company under liquidation.[60] Section 131(7) also enables the court to make an order placing the company under business rescue and/or appointing an interim practitioner at any time during the course of any liquidation proceedings or proceedings to enforce any security against the company.

A company that has been placed under supervision in terms of s 131 must notify each affected person within five business days after the date of the order of court.[61]

18.4 THE DURATION OF BUSINESS RESCUE PROCEEDINGS

18.4.1 The date of commencement

The commencement, the duration and the termination of business rescue proceedings are set out in s 132. The date of commencement is of vital importance, because the moratorium and the restrictions and consequences of business rescue come into effect when business rescue proceedings formally commence.[62]

---

[56] 'Public regulation' is defined very widely in s 1 of the Act to mean 'any national, provincial or local government legislation or subordinate legislation, or any licence, tariff, directive or similar authorisation issued by a regulatory authority or pursuant to any statutory authority'.
[57] Section 131.
[58] As explained in 18.3.1(a) above.
[59] Section 131(5).
[60] Section 131(4)(b).
[61] Section 131(8)(b). See Regulation 134(3) of the draft Companies Regulations (at n 27) as discussed in 18.3.1 above, which applies also to s 131(8)(b) regulating the mode of giving notice.
[62] Section 133(1).

As far as the commencement of business rescue proceedings is concerned, there are three possibilities. According to s 132(1) business rescue proceedings begin:
- in the case of the initiation of business rescue by a board resolution, when the company files with the Companies Commission the resolution to place itself under supervision. But in the event that a previous resolution has lapsed (due to the company's failure to comply with s 129(3) and (4), as discussed above in 18.3.1), the business rescue proceedings are deemed (in terms of s 132(1)(a)(ii)) to commence when the company applies to the court for its consent to file another resolution,[63] or
- in the case of the initiation of business rescue by court order, when an affected person applies to the court, or
- when the court, during the course of liquidation proceedings or proceedings to enforce a security interest, makes an order placing the company under supervision.

18.4.2 The duration of business rescue and progress reports

If the business rescue proceedings have not ended within three months, or such longer time as the court (on application by the business rescue practitioner) permits, the business rescue practitioner must prepare a report on the progress of the proceedings, and follow it up with updates at the end of each subsequent month until the termination of the business rescue proceedings. The report and each update must be delivered in the prescribed manner to each affected person. These documents must also be delivered to the court if the proceedings were the subject of a court order, or to the Companies Commission in any other case.[64]

18.4.3 The termination of business rescue proceedings

Business rescue proceedings terminate[65] when:
- the court sets aside the resolution or order that began those proceedings, or the court converts the business rescue proceedings to liquidation proceedings, or
- the practitioner has filed with the Companies Commission a notice of the termination of the business rescue proceedings, or
- a business rescue plan has been proposed and rejected, but no affected person has sought to extend the proceedings (as contemplated in s 153); or alternatively, a business rescue plan has been adopted and the practitioner has subsequently filed a notice of 'substantial implementation' of that plan.

18.5 THE LEGAL CONSEQUENCES OF A BUSINESS RESCUE ORDER

The business rescue process is meant to facilitate the rescue of a company that is close to insolvency. This is achieved in two primary ways: first, by an automatic moratorium and secondly, through the skill and guidance of the business rescue practitioner.

---

[63] In accordance with the provisions of s 129(5)(b); see 18.3.1 above.
[64] Section 132(3).
[65] Section 132(2)(a) to (c).

In the USA, existing management is left largely in place. This approach is referred to as the 'debtor in possession' — ie the existing management remains in control of the company during the business rescue process. In sharp contrast, in the UK the existing management is displaced. While the board of directors may remain in office, it no longer has management functions. The administrator (in the UK) is required to take control of the property and assets of the company and to manage the business and the affairs of the company. The basis of this approach is that, since the company's financial difficulties are due to the failure of management, they should not be allowed to remain in control of the company's affairs.

The 'debtor in possession' approach is intended to encourage the board of directors to resort to business rescue proceedings at an earlier stage rather than postponing it until it is too late. Continued management by the incumbent managers also has the advantage that they are more familiar with the affairs of the company than a newly appointed business rescue practitioner.

The Act provides in s 137(2)(a) that, during business rescue proceedings, each director of the company must continue to exercise the functions of a director subject to the authority of the practitioner. The directors must also exercise any 'management functions' within the company in accordance with the express instructions or the direction of the practitioner, to the extent that it is reasonable to do so.[66] (This is further discussed below in 18.5.5.) An important safeguard that applies here is that the directors remain bound by the requirements of s 75 to disclose any personal financial interests which they or a related person may have.[67] Provided that the directors do so, they are relieved from having to comply with the requirements of s 76 regarding the standards of directors' conduct and some though not all the liabilities set out in s 77, but only to the extent that they comply with their duty in terms of s 137(2), to exercise any management functions in accordance with the instructions or directions of the business rescue practitioner.[68]

18.5.1 The moratorium

The most important consequence of the commencement of business rescue proceedings is that there is an automatic and general moratorium, ie a freeze (or 'stay') on legal proceedings or executions against the company, its property and its assets and on the exercise of the rights of creditors of the company. In brief, there is a general moratorium on the enforcement of remedies against a company that is under business rescue. This suspension of legal proceedings against the company generally applies to all the company's creditors.

The moratorium is of fundamental importance to business rescue, since it provides the crucial breathing space or a period of grace during which the company is given the opportunity to reorganise and reschedule its debts and liabilities.

---

[66] Section 137(2)(b).
[67] Section 137(2)(c).
[68] Section 137(1)(d).

(a) Moratorium on legal proceedings

The company is given extensive protection against legal proceedings. Section 133(1)(a) and (b) of the Act states that:

> During business rescue proceedings, no legal proceeding, including enforcement action, against the company, or in relation to any property belonging to the company, or lawfully in its possession, may be commenced or proceeded with in any forum, except —
> (a) with the written consent of the practitioner;
> (b) with the leave of the court and in accordance with any terms the court considers suitable.

Legal proceedings are restricted as a general principle, since they may have a detrimental effect on the outcome of the business rescue process. However, criminal proceedings against the company or any of its directors or officers do not fall within the scope of s 133(1), and are not subject to the general moratorium.[69]

There are other exceptions to this general principle of a stay in legal proceedings or enforcement action against the company. Section 133(1)(c) provides that set-off rights against any claim made by the company in any legal proceedings, whether commenced before or after the business rescue proceedings began, may be exercised against the company. Apart from this exception, set-off rights in general fall within the scope of the general moratorium. A further exception is that proceedings may take place concerning any property or right over which the company exercises the powers of a trustee.[70]

Section 133(2) specifically provides that, during business rescue proceedings, a guarantee or surety given by the company in favour of any other person may not be enforced against the company unless the court so permits and on such terms as it considers in the circumstances to be just and equitable.

If any right to assert a claim or commence legal proceedings against the company is subject to a time limit, the measurement of that time is suspended during the company's business rescue proceedings.[71] This provision protects third parties, in that the period during which the company is under business rescue is not counted when calculating the time limit to which the claim against the company is subject.

It should be noted that s 133 does not as a general rule blankly prohibit the exercise of rights to commence legal proceedings or enforcement actions — it merely makes them subject to the consent of the business rescue practitioner or the court. It may be that, where legal proceedings or an enforcement action is brought without the requisite consent of the court or the practitioner, as the case may be, such proceedings are not a complete nullity. In English law it has been held that the proceedings may be adjourned while the consent or the leave of the court is obtained.[72]

---

[69] Section 133(1)(d).
[70] Section 133(1)(e).
[71] Section 133(3).
[72] *Carr v British International Helicopters Ltd* [1994] 2 BCLC 474.

It is unclear whether s 133 extends to quasi-legal proceedings such as arbitration proceedings or tribunal proceedings.[73]

(b) Moratorium on property interests

The disposal by a company of property during business rescue is dealt with in s 134 of the Act, which provides that, subject to s 134(2) and (3), during the business rescue process a company may dispose of property or agree to dispose of property only if:

- it is in the ordinary course of its business, or
- it is a *bona fide* transaction at arm's length for fair value, that has been approved in advance and in writing by the practitioner, or
- it is in a transaction that is part of an approved business rescue plan.

Thus, if the property is not disposed of in the ordinary course of the company's business, then it must be disposed of either in an arm's length *bona fide* transaction for fair value with the prior written approval of the practitioner, or it must have formed part of the implementation of an approved business rescue plan.

During the business rescue proceedings, despite any provision of an agreement to the contrary, no person may exercise any right in respect of any property in the lawful possession of the company (eg under a lease agreement) unless the practitioner consents in writing. This applies irrespective of whether the property is owned by the company or not.[74] The practitioner may not unreasonably withhold his or her consent, having regard to the purposes of business rescue under the Act, the circumstances of the company, and the nature of the property and the rights claimed in respect of it.[75]

Before a company disposes during business rescue proceedings of any property over which a third party has any security or title interest, it must obtain the prior consent of the third party, unless the proceeds of such disposal would be sufficient to fully discharge the amount of the third party's secured or protected claim or title interest.[76] Additionally, the proceeds of the disposal must be used to promptly pay to the third party the amount of the company's indebtedness to that party, or to otherwise provide security for the amount of those proceeds to the reasonable satisfaction of the third party.[77] To elaborate, the Act essentially provides that, if the company disposes of property over which a secured creditor holds security, it may dispense with the consent of the creditor, provided that the proceeds of the disposal would be sufficient to pay the creditor in full and the company promptly so pays the creditor or, alternatively, the company provides security for the amount of those proceeds to the reasonable satisfaction of the creditor.[78] The

---

[73] See in English law *Carr v British International Helicopters Ltd* (supra), where the restriction was held to apply to proceedings for the revocation of a patent held by a company in administration, and *Re Railtrack Plc* [2002] 1 WLR 3002.
[74] Section 134(1)*(c)*.
[75] Section 134(2).
[76] Section 134(3)*(a)*.
[77] Section 134(3)*(b)*.
[78] Section 134(3)*(b)*.

effect of this provision is that the practitioner may simply pay the creditor in full and discharge the underlying transaction even before its maturity.

Where a third party is lawfully in possession of property owned by the company, under an agreement made in the ordinary course of the company's business before the commencement of business rescue proceedings, the third party may continue to exercise any right in respect of that property in accordance with the agreement.[79] However, this right is subject to s 136, and more specifically to s 136(2), which confers on the practitioner a discretion to cancel or suspend the agreement.[80] In this event, the third party's remedy is confined to a claim for damages only.[81] This is further discussed in 18.5.4 below.

18.5.2 Post-commencement finance

Post-commencement finance or new financing is one of the most important aspects of the business rescue proceedings. Creditors and financiers would obviously be reluctant to finance a company that is under business rescue proceedings. Yet additional new finance after the commencement of business rescue proceedings is often critical to the survival and the turnaround of the company's business. Not many companies that are placed under supervision would have cash or assets that could easily be converted to cash to fund their business activities. In recognition of the importance of post-commencement finance, s 364 of the US Bankruptcy Code provides that any credit extended to the company during the reorganisation or rescue process enjoys priority over unsecured claims incurred before the rescue process. This super-priority applies even if the rescue process fails. This approach provides the incentive that post-commencement financiers require, since it gives them preference or super-priority for the payment of their claims and for loans and other forms of finance which they extend to the company.

The new Act, following the example of Chapter 11 of the US Bankruptcy Code, likewise creates a statutory framework for super-priority post-commencement financing.

Section 135(2) provides that, during the business rescue proceedings, the company may obtain 'financing' that is unrelated to employment which:

- may be secured to the lender by utilising any unencumbered asset of the company, and
- will be paid in the order of preference set out in s 135(3)(b).

Section 135(2) thus permits a company to use its unencumbered assets as security for 'financing' that is obtained by the company after the commencement of business rescue proceedings. 'Financing' is not defined, with the result that it is unclear how widely a court would interpret this provision. Post-commencement

---

[79] Section 134(1)(b).
[80] The draft Companies Amendment Bill, 2010 (cl 82) proposes to amend s 136 so as to require an application by the practitioner to a court in order to cancel any agreement to which the company is a party. Furthermore, if a suspended agreement relates to security granted by the company, it nevertheless continues to apply for the purposes of s 134 with respect to any proposed disposal of property by the company.
[81] Section 136(3).

finance obtained by the company will enjoy preference in the order in which it is incurred.[82] It will also enjoy priority over all unsecured claims against the company.

The ranking of claims in respect of post-commencement finance (as set out in s 135(3)*(a)* and *(b)*) is as follows:

- First, the practitioner's remuneration, expenses and other costs (in accordance with s 143) and other claims arising out of the costs of business rescue proceedings will be paid.
- Secondly, all claims for post-commencement financing obligations that are related to employment will be paid. Employment-related post-commencement financing claims rank equally with each other, but enjoy priority over any other post-commencement financing claims, even if these are secured claims. These employment-related post-commencement financing claims also have priority over all unsecured claims against the company.[83] In this regard, all employment-related payments, including any remuneration, reimbursement for expenses or other amount of money relating to employment, that become due and payable to employees by the company during the course of the business rescue proceedings, are regarded as post-commencement financing to the extent that they have not been paid (see s 135(1)). As such, they will rank for payment directly after the practitioner's remuneration and costs and other claims arising out of the costs of the business rescue proceedings. Employment-related payments or 'money relating to employment' within the scope of s 135(1) is wider than 'wages' or 'salary', with the result that even though payment of wages in lieu of notice or redundancy payments may not be 'wages' or 'salary', they would nonetheless fall within the ambit of s 135 as 'money relating to employment'. Such payments would probably be treated as post-commencement finance (in terms of s 135(1)) and would enjoy preference in accordance with s 135(3).
- Thirdly, all post-commencement finance (unrelated to employment) will be paid. These amounts will rank in the order in which they were incurred, evidently irrespective of whether the claims are secured or unsecured, and ahead of all unsecured claims against the company.
- Fourthly, all unsecured claims against the company will be paid.

It is clear[84] that post-commencement finance unrelated to employment will have preference over all unsecured claims against the company, even if the former are not secured.

The preferences conferred by s 135 would remain in force in the event that the business rescue proceedings are superseded by a liquidation order except to the extent of claims arising out of the costs of liquidation.[85] The effect is that

---

[82] Section 135(3)*(b)*.
[83] Section 135(3)*(a)*.
[84] Section 135(3)*(b)* read with s 135(2).
[85] Section 135(4).

preference is still given even in the event of liquidation to unpaid post-rescue salaries and employment-related payments, as well as other post-commencement finance.

18.5.3 Effect of business rescue on employment contracts and employees

Section 136(1)*(a)* protects employees of the company by providing that, despite any provision of an agreement to the contrary, during a company's business rescue proceedings, employees of the company immediately before the commencement of business rescue continue to be employed on the same terms and conditions. This is subject to the following exceptions:

- changes that occur in the ordinary course of attrition, or
- the employees and the company agreeing to different terms and conditions in accordance with applicable labour laws.

Any retrenchment of employees of the company contemplated in the business rescue plan is subject to s 189 and s 189A of the Labour Relations Act 66 of 1995 and other applicable employment-related legislation.[86]

Employees are given further rights under s 144(1), which are discussed below in 18.8.1.

18.5.4 Effect on contracts generally

Despite any provision of an agreement to the contrary, during business rescue proceedings s 136(2) of the Act confers on the business rescue practitioner the right to cancel or suspend, whether entirely, partially or conditionally, any provision of an agreement to which the company is a party at the commencement of the business rescue process, other than an agreement of employment. The other party to the contract may, in terms of s 136(3), claim damages only, but not specific performance.

This wide power significantly does not apply to an employment contract. It is also subject to s 35A and s 35B of the Insolvency Act 24 of 1936.

Section 136(2) could have far-reaching and unintended consequences for persons who have contracted with a company that is subsequently placed under business rescue proceedings, particularly if the word 'cancel' in s 136(2) is given its ordinary legal meaning of entirely wiping out the contract and the rights and obligations of the parties under the agreement.[87] The right to cancel an agreement in terms of s 136(2) is in addition to the moratorium provided for in s 133(1) (discussed above in 18.5.1).

The exercise by the practitioner of his or her powers under s 136(2) could have severe consequences for the other party to the agreement, particularly if the practitioner were to cancel only those terms of an agreement that are unfavourable

---

[86] Section 136(1)*(b)*.
[87] See *CIR v Collins* 1992 (3) SA 698 (A) 711, where the court stated that the word 'cancellation' in the field of the law of contract is a well-known technical term of art, which generally '... connotes the undoing of the contract in its entirety, and the extinction of all the rights and obligations of both parties as they existed in terms of the contract'.

to the company while preserving the favourable terms of the agreement. The draft Companies Amendment Bill, 2010 (cl 82) proposes to amend the extremely wide ambit of s 136(2) by removing the practitioner's power to cancel any provision of an agreement to which the company is a party. It also proposes to provide that the practitioner may:

> ... entirely, partially or conditionally suspend, for the duration of the business rescue proceedings, any obligation of the company that arises under an agreement to which the company was a party at the commencement of the business rescue proceedings and would otherwise become due during those proceedings.

The company's obligations may be suspended, but only for the duration of the business rescue proceedings. In order to cancel an agreement, the practitioner must apply urgently to court for an order to cancel the agreement (which may even be an employment contract) on terms that must be just and reasonable in the circumstances. The practitioner's power to cancel any provision of the agreement is thus to be curbed. The draft Companies Amendment Bill proposes to further provide that the practitioner may not suspend any provision of an employment contract or an agreement to which s 35A or s 35B of the Insolvency Act applies. The proposed amendments would remove much of the sting in the widespread criticisms of s 136(2). A further proposed amendment is that if the practitioner suspends a provision of an agreement relating to security granted by the company, that provision nevertheless continues to apply for the purposes of s 134, with respect to a proposed disposal of property by the company.

In those situations where a particular contract is impeding the business rescue proceedings with the result that cancellation of the contract is necessary or desirable, the practitioner would be able to obtain the consent of the court under the proposed new amended provisions of s 136(2) (assuming that they are implemented) on the ground that cancellation of the contract is just and reasonable in the circumstances. This applies particularly to contracts that have become onerous to the company. The consent of the court would provide the essential safeguard against abuse of the practitioners' powers in terms of s 136(2).

Section 136(4) provides that, if liquidation proceedings have been converted into business rescue proceedings, the liquidator is a creditor of the company. He or she may therefore have a claim for any outstanding remuneration for work performed or reimbursement for expenses incurred before the business rescue proceedings commenced.

18.5.5 Effect of business rescue on shareholders and directors

According to s 137(1), no alteration in the classification or the status of any issued securities of a company is permitted during business rescue proceedings, unless the court otherwise directs, or this is done in accordance with an approved business rescue plan. However, the transfer of securities is permitted if it is done in the ordinary course of business.

Shareholders are 'affected persons', and, as such, are entitled to receive notices of court proceedings, meetings and other relevant events concerning the business rescue proceedings. They are also entitled to participate formally in the process.[88] (This is discussed in 18.8 and 18.8.4 below.)

As regards directors, the directors of the company are not removed from office. They continue to exercise their functions as directors, but in terms of s 137(2)(*a*) they are now subject to the authority of the business rescue practitioner. Directors must exercise any management function in accordance with the express instructions or directions of the practitioner, to the extent that it is reasonable to do so.[89] More importantly, each director must attend to the practitioner's requests at all times and must provide the practitioner with any information about the company's affairs as may reasonably be required.[90] This is further regulated by s 142 (discussed in 18.6.5 below).

If a director has impeded or is impeding the practitioner in the performance of his or her functions and powers, in the management of the company, or in the development or the implementation of a business rescue plan, the director may, on the application of the practitioner, be removed from office by a court.[91] The same would apply where a director has failed to comply with a requirement of Chapter 6 of the Act.[92] This is in addition to the right of a person to apply for a court order declaring the director delinquent or under probation in terms of s 162.

Section 137(4) provides that if, during a company's business rescue proceedings the board of directors or one or more directors purport to take any action on behalf of the company that requires the approval of the practitioner, that action is void unless approved by the practitioner. Third parties dealing with the board of directors or with any one or more directors during the business rescue proceedings must exercise caution to ensure that the particular director that they are dealing with has the requisite approval or authority to act on behalf of the company. Although it is of little assistance to a *bona fide* third party, except perhaps as a deterrent, directors who knowingly act on behalf of the company without authority to do so may, in terms of s 77(3)(*a*), be liable to the company for any loss, damages or costs sustained by the company as a result thereof.

As discussed in 18.5 above, although the directors of the company are subject to the authority and the directions of the practitioner, they are not relieved from all their statutory and fiduciary duties.[93] They must still disclose their personal financial interests or those of a related person in matters in which the company has an interest. While they may be relieved of some of the duties of directors as set out in s 76, and some of the liabilities of directors as set out in s 77, to the extent that they are subject to and act in accordance with the instructions or directions of the practitioner,[94] it is important that they are not relieved from incurring liability under s 22(1), ie by knowingly acquiescing in the fraudulent or reckless conduct of

---

[88] Section 146.
[89] Section 137(2)(*b*).
[90] Section 137(3).
[91] Section 137(5)(*b*)(i) and (iii).
[92] Section 37(5)(*a*).
[93] Section 137(2).
[94] Section 137(1)(*d*).

the company's business or insolvent trading.[95] A second carve-out is that the director will also remain liable for loss sustained by the company if he or she was a party to an act or omission by the company despite knowing that it was calculated to defraud a creditor, an employee or a shareholder of the company or had another fraudulent purpose.[96] Thirdly, as discussed immediately above, the director remains liable to the company for conduct contemplated in s 77(3)(a), ie knowingly acting on behalf of the company without authority to do so.[97]

18.6 THE BUSINESS RESCUE PRACTITIONER

18.6.1 Appointment

The business rescue practitioner has the most significant and pivotal task of overseeing the business rescue process and turning the company around by developing a suitable business rescue plan. The Act confers on him or her a powerful position. He or she supervises and advises management, and has full managerial control of the company in substitution for the board of directors and pre-existing management.[98]

The practitioner may be appointed in various ways. First, he or she may be appointed by the board of directors if the business rescue proceedings are commenced by a resolution of the board. In that event, the practitioner must be appointed within five business days of the date that the resolution was filed with the Companies Commission.[99] Alternatively, in the event of an application to court (in terms of s 131(1)) for an order to place the company under supervision, the court may appoint an interim practitioner, nominated by the affected person who made the application to the court. This would be subject to ratification of the appointment by the holders of a majority of the independent creditors' voting interests, at the first meeting of creditors.[100] A third possibility is that the court must appoint an alternative practitioner when setting aside the appointment of a practitioner appointed by the company, as a result of an objection by an affected person.[101] The court would then appoint the practitioner who is recommended or acceptable to the holders of a majority of the independent creditors' voting interests, who were represented in the court hearing.[102]

Once appointed, the practitioner has extensive powers, including the power to manage the affairs of the company in substitution for the board of directors. The practitioner has the fundamentally important function of developing and implementing a business rescue plan.[103]

---

[95] Section 77(3)(b).
[96] Section 77(3)(c).
[97] See Chapter 12: The Duties and the Liability of Directors.
[98] Section 140(1)(a).
[99] Section 129(3).
[100] Section 131(5) and s 147(1).
[101] Section 130(6)(a); see 18.3.1(b) above.
[102] Section 130(6)(a).
[103] Section 140(1)(d).

18.6.2 The qualifications of the practitioner

The qualifications of a business rescue practitioner are laid down in s 138(1)*(a)* to *(e)*. In terms of this section, a person may be appointed as a business rescue practitioner of a company only if that person:

- is a member in good standing of a profession subject to regulation by a regulatory authority prescribed by the Minister (in terms of s 138(2)),
- is not subject to an order of probation,
- would not be disqualified from acting as a director,
- does not have any other relationship with the company that would lead a reasonable and informed third party to conclude that the person's integrity, impartiality or objectivity is compromised by that relationship, and
- is not related to a person who has a relationship contemplated in the previous bullet point.[104]

18.6.3 Removal and replacement of the practitioner

The Act ensures that the practitioner may be removed from office only by means of an order of court. This may be either in terms of s 130, as discussed in 18.3.1 above (ie as a result of an objection to the appointment of the practitioner pursuant to a business rescue resolution, on the grounds that he or she is not qualified in terms of s 138, is not independent, or lacks the necessary skills), or in terms of s 139(2)*(a)* to *(f)*. This latter section provides that a court may remove a practitioner on any one of six grounds, namely:

- incompetence or failure to perform the duties of a business rescue practitioner of the particular company,
- failure to exercise the proper degree of care,
- engaging in illegal acts or conduct,
- no longer satisfying the qualifications and requirements of a practitioner as set out in s 138(1),
- having a conflict of interest or a lack of independence, or

---

[104] The Companies Amendment Bill, 2010, cl 83, proposes to amend s 138 by stipulating in s 138(1)*(a)* that the business rescue practitioner must be a member in good standing of a legal, accounting or business management profession that is subject to regulation by a regulatory authority or has been licensed as such by the Companies Commission in terms of subsection (2).

Section 138(2) is proposed to be amended to provide that, for the purposes of s 138(1), the Companies Commission may license any qualified person to practise as a practitioner in terms of the Act. The Companies Commission may also suspend or withdraw any such licence in the prescribed manner. Paragraphs *(a)*–*(c)* of s 138(2) are proposed to be deleted.

Section 138(3) is proposed to be amended to provide that the Minister may make regulations prescribing standards and procedures to be followed by the Companies Commission in carrying out its licensing functions and powers (in terms of this section) and prescribing minimum qualifications for practitioners. Different minimum qualifications for the business rescue practitioner may be prescribed for different categories of companies.

The draft Companies Regulations propose in Regulations 129 to 132 to set up a Business Rescue Practice Regulatory Board to regulate the practice of persons as business rescue practitioners in terms of Chapter 6 of the Act. It proposes to set up a register of accredited business rescue practitioners and to establish standards and codes of good practice for the conduct of business rescue proceedings.

- being incapacitated and unable to perform the functions of his or her office without a likelihood of regaining that capacity within a reasonable time.

The court may remove a practitioner on these grounds either on its own motion or upon the request of an affected person.

If a practitioner dies, resigns or is removed from office, the company or the creditor who had nominated that practitioner (as the case may be) must appoint a new practitioner.[105] This is subject to the right of an affected person to bring a fresh application[106] to set aside the new appointment (ie on the grounds that the appointed person does not satisfy the requirements of a practitioner as set out in s 138, is not independent, or lacks the necessary skills).

18.6.4 The remuneration of the practitioner

The basis of the remuneration of the business rescue practitioner is of great significance. It may even have an effect on the impartiality and the independence of the practitioner. As a matter of principle, there are various ways in which the remuneration of a business rescue practitioner could be determined. For instance, the practitioner's remuneration could be determined by agreement between the practitioner and the company or a committee of creditors[107] or by a resolution passed by the creditors, or it may be determined in accordance with a tariff laid down by statute. The basis of the practitioner's remuneration may be determined in accordance with the amount of time spent on performing the task, its complexity and the nature and the value of the property or assets involved. A time-based system of remuneration attempts to calculate the remuneration in accordance with the amount of work done by the practitioner. Remuneration in principle should be commensurate with the tasks that the practitioner is required to perform.

Section 143(1) of the Act states that the practitioner is entitled to charge an amount to the company for his or her remuneration and expenses in accordance with a tariff to be prescribed by the Minister in terms of s 143(6). The draft Companies Regulations[108] states that the practitioner may charge a maximum of R2 000 per hour, to a maximum of R25 000 per day, where the company is a state-owned or public company or a company that is required to have its annual financial statements audited, and the practitioner is either:

- an attorney in commercial practice for at least ten years,
- a member in good standing of a professional body belonging to the International Federation of Accountants who has been in commercial practice for at least ten years,
- a practising liquidator or turnaround practitioner registered for ten years, or
- a person who has a recognised degree in law, commerce or business management and at least ten years' experience in conducting business rescue proceedings.

___

[105] Section 139(3).
[106] In terms of s 130(1)(b).
[107] Formed in terms of s 145(3); discussed in 18.8 and 18.8.3 below.
[108] See Regulation 135 of the draft Companies Regulations.

In the case of any other type of company, where the practitioner has at least five years' standing or experience in respect of any of the relevant qualifications, his or her maximum remuneration may not exceed R1 250 per hour, limited to a maximum of R15 625 per day. The practitioner is additionally entitled to be reimbursed for the actual cost of any disbursement made or expenses incurred necessary to carry out his or her functions.

In addition to remuneration in accordance with this tariff, s 143(2) permits the practitioner to propose an agreement with the company for the payment of an additional fee, to be calculated on the basis of a contingency. This contingency could be that the business rescue plan proposed by him or her is adopted, or that it is adopted within a particular period of time or on the basis of the attainment of a particular result or combination of results relating to the business rescue process.[109] The justification for permitting a contingency-based fee is that it provides the practitioner with an added incentive to successfully implement a business rescue plan.

As a safeguard against abuse, s 143(3) requires such an agreement to be approved by the holders of a majority of the creditors' voting interests (as determined in accordance with s 145(4) to (6)). This majority is calculated in accordance with the number of creditors present and voting at the meeting called for this purpose.[110] Additionally, approval is also required by the holders of a majority of the voting rights of shareholders entitled to a portion of the residual value of the company on winding-up, who are present and voting at the relevant meeting.[111]

A further safeguard is that,[112] even if the agreement is approved, a dissatisfied creditor or shareholder who had voted against the agreement may apply to court within ten business days after the date of voting on the proposal, for an order setting aside the agreement on the ground that the agreement is not just and equitable, or that the remuneration provided for in the agreement is egregiously unreasonable in view of the financial circumstances of the company.

It follows from the provisions of s 143 that, while the remuneration and expenses of the practitioner will be calculated in accordance with a prescribed tariff, any additional remuneration is subject to the approval of creditors and shareholders who have an interest in the residual value of the company on winding-up.

It has already been pointed out in 18.5.2 above that the practitioner's claim against the company for his or her remuneration and expenses will rank for payment in priority to all secured and unsecured creditors.[113]

18.6.5 Powers and duties of the practitioner

Business rescue practitioners are given extensive powers to manage the company's business and to deal with its assets in order to rescue the company. The Act imposes a great deal of responsibility on them.

---

[109] Section 143(2)*(a)* and *(b)*.
[110] Section 143(3)*(a)*.
[111] Section 143(3)*(b)*.
[112] In terms of s 143(4).
[113] Section 143(5).

The success of the business rescue proceedings depends to a large extent on the competency, skill and experience of the business rescue practitioner. The practitioner has a large number of duties and functions to perform. For this purpose, he or she is given a wide range of powers, including the full managerial control of the company which he or she takes over from the company's incumbent board of directors and pre-existing management.[114] The prime function of the practitioner is to develop and implement a business rescue plan.[115]

The Act permits the practitioner[116] to delegate any power or function to a person who has been a director of the company or part of its pre-existing management. By the same token, the practitioner has the power[117] to remove from office any person who has been part of the company's pre-existing management.[118]

The practitioner may also appoint persons as part of the management of the company (whether or not to fill a vacancy), or as advisers to the company or the practitioner, provided that the approval of the court is obtained to appoint such a person where that person has a relationship with the company that would lead 'a reasonable and informed third party' to conclude that the integrity, impartiality or objectivity of that person is compromised, or where that person is related to a person who has such a relationship with the company.[119]

It must be stressed that, while the practitioner takes over the full management and control of the company, the pre-existing management is not completely displaced. It would continue to function during the process but under the authority of the practitioner.

The business rescue practitioner is regarded during the company's business rescue proceedings to be an officer of the court. He or she must consequently report to the court in accordance with any applicable rules or orders of the court.[120]

Significantly, the practitioner also has imposed on him or her[121] the duties, responsibilities and liabilities of a director of a company as set out in ss 75 to 77. While the practitioner may not be liable for an act or omission in good faith in the course of the exercise of his or her powers and the performance of his or her functions, the practitioner may nevertheless be held liable for gross negligence.[122]

---

[114] Section 140(1)*(a)*.
[115] Section 140(1)*(d)*.
[116] Section 140(1)*(b)*.
[117] Under s 140(1)*(c)*.
[118] For this purpose the practitioner does not need the consent of court. Although s 140(1)*(c)* of the Act does not implicitly refer to it, removal would have to be done in accordance with the provisions of the Labour Relations Act 66 of 1995, if applicable. The alternative would be to simply suspend, but not dismiss, a person who was part of the company's pre-existing management. Section 137(5), dealing with the practitioner's removal of a director from office with the permission of a court, has been discussed in 18.5.5 above.
[119] Section 140(2)*(a)* and *(b)*.
[120] Section 140(3)*(a)*.
[121] By s 140(3)*(b)*.
[122] Section 140(3)*(c)*(i) and (ii).

An important safeguard is that, if the business rescue process concludes with an order placing the company in liquidation, the business rescue practitioner may not be appointed as a liquidator of the company.[123]

The business rescue practitioner must, as soon as practicable after having been appointed, investigate the company's affairs, its business, property and financial situation and consider whether there is any reasonable prospect of rescuing the company.[124] Investigation of the company's financial situation is undoubtedly an important function of the practitioner. In this respect s 142, which imposes on the directors of the company a duty to co-operate with and to assist the practitioner, is a most useful provision.

In terms of s 142, the directors are required to deliver to the practitioner all books and records relating to the company that they may have in their possession. They must inform the practitioner of any other books and records of the company which are not in their possession but whose whereabouts are known to them.

Within five business days of the commencement of business rescue proceedings (or such longer period as the practitioner permits), the directors must provide the practitioner with a statement of affairs containing information (at a minimum) on the list of matters specified in s 142(3)(a) to (f). Some examples on this list are:

- any material transactions involving the company or its assets that occurred within 12 months immediately before the commencement of the business rescue proceedings,
- any court, arbitration or administrative proceedings, including pending enforcement proceedings,
- the assets and liabilities of the company and its income and disbursements within the previous 12 months,
- the number of employees and any agreements relating to their rights,
- the debtors and creditors of the company and their respective obligations to the company, and
- rights or claims against the company.

No person is entitled as against the practitioner to retain possession of any books or records of the company, or to claim or enforce a lien (or a right of retention) over such books or records.[125]

The practitioner must of course continue to monitor the company's financial situation on a regular basis. If at any time during the business rescue process the practitioner decides that there is no reasonable prospect of a successful business rescue, he or she must inform the company, the court and the affected persons and apply to court to discontinue the process and instead place the company in liquidation.[126] If, on the other hand, the practitioner concludes that there are no longer reasonable grounds to believe that the company is in financial distress, he or she must (in terms of s 142(1)(b)) inform the relevant parties and apply to court

---

[123] Section 140(4).
[124] Section 141(1).
[125] Section 142(4).
[126] Section 141(2)(a).

for a termination order if the process was initiated or confirmed by an order of court, or otherwise, file a notice of termination with the Companies Commission.

More importantly, if the practitioner during his or her investigations or during the business rescue proceedings finds evidence of reckless trading, fraud or other contravention of any law relating to the company in the company's dealings before the rescue process began, he or she must forward the evidence to the appropriate authority for investigation and possible prosecution. In addition, the practitioner must direct the management to take any necessary steps to rectify the matter, including recovering any misappropriated assets. The management must also be directed to take rectification steps if there is evidence of any voidable transactions or a failure by the company or a director to perform any material obligation relating to the company.[127] The practitioner's duty to prepare reports and updates on the progress of the business rescue proceedings has been dealt with in 18.4.2 above.

18.7 THE BUSINESS RESCUE PLAN

The most important function of the business rescue practitioner is to prepare and implement a business rescue plan for the company. For these purposes, the practitioner must first consult with the creditors of the company, other affected persons and the management of the company.[128]

The business rescue plan must contain all the information reasonably required to assist affected persons to decide whether to accept or reject the business rescue plan.[129]

According to the specific requirements of s 150(2), the business rescue plan must be divided into three parts: Part A, dealing with the background; Part B, dealing with the proposals, and Part C, dealing with the assumptions and conditions. The information required in terms of s 150(2)(a) to (c) is the minimum required. It is intended to focus on only the key objectives and to avoid being excessively prescriptive.

Part A: Background
Part A must include at least:
- a complete list of all the material assets of the company, as well as an indication as to which assets were held as security by creditors when the business rescue proceedings began;
- a complete list of creditors at the time the business rescue proceedings begin, together with an indication as to which creditors would qualify as secured, statutory, preferent and concurrent creditors, and an indication of which of the creditors have proved their claims;
- an indication of the probable dividend that would be received by creditors, in their specific classes, if the company were to be placed in liquidation;
- a complete list of the holders of the company's issued securities;

---
[127] Section 141(2)(c).
[128] Section 150(1).
[129] Section 150(2).

- a copy of the written agreement concerning the remuneration of the practitioner; and
- a statement whether the business rescue plan includes any proposal made informally by a creditor of the company.

Part B: Proposals
Part B, concerning the proposed steps to be taken in order to resolve the company's difficulties, must contain at the least the following:
- the nature and duration of any moratorium for which the business rescue plan makes provision;
- the extent to which the company is to be released from the payment of its debts, and the extent to which any debt is proposed to be converted to equity in the company, or another company;
- the ongoing role of the company, and the treatment of any existing agreements;
- the property of the company that is to be available to pay creditors' claims in terms of the business rescue plan;
- the order of preference in which the proceeds of property will be applied to pay creditors if the business rescue plan is adopted;
- the benefits of adopting the business rescue plan as opposed to the benefits that would be received by creditors if the company were to be placed in liquidation; and
- the effect that the business rescue plan will have on the holders of each class of the company's issued securities.

Part C: Assumptions and conditions
Part C sets out the assumptions and conditions that must be fulfilled for the implementation of the business rescue plan. This part must contain at least:
- a statement of the conditions that must be satisfied, if any, for the rescue plan to come into operation and to be fully implemented,
- the effect of the plan on the number of employees, and their terms and conditions of employment,
- the circumstances in which the rescue plan will end, and
- a projected balance sheet for the company as well as a statement of income and expenses for the ensuing three years, prepared on the assumption that the proposed rescue plan is adopted. These must include a notice of any material assumptions on which the projections are based, and may include alternative projections based on varying assumptions and contingencies.

The proposed business rescue plan must conclude with a certificate by the practitioner stating that any actual information provided appears to be accurate, complete and up to date, and that the projections provided are estimates made in good faith on the basis of factual information and assumptions as set out in the statements.[130]

The business rescue plan must be published within 25 business days after the appointment of the business rescue practitioner, unless a longer time is allowed by

---
[130] Section 150(4).

either the court on application made by the company, or the holders of a majority of the creditors' voting interests.[131]

The consideration and adoption of a business rescue plan are discussed further in 18.9 below.

18.8 THE RIGHTS OF AFFECTED PERSONS

Three groups of affected persons in particular must be taken into consideration, namely employees, creditors and the holders of the company's securities. They are given certain specific rights, including the general rights of an affected person (as discussed in 18.3.1 above) such as the right to:

- apply for the commencement of business rescue proceedings,
- lodge objections against such proceedings or the appointment of the practitioner,
- receive notices of business rescue decisions,
- participate in the business rescue process, and
- receive updates of the progress of the process in terms of s 132(3)*(b)*.

The three main groups of affected persons are discussed below.

18.8.1 Employees

The rights of employees during the business rescue proceedings are specifically set out in s 144 of the Act. This section provides that employees of a company who are represented by a registered trade union may exercise their rights under Chapter 6 of the Act collectively through their trade union and in accordance with applicable labour law.[132] If employees are not represented by a registered trade union, they may elect to exercise any of their rights either directly or by proxy through an employee representative or organisation.[133]

It has already been pointed out in 18.5.3 above that employees are protected by s 136(1)*(a)* from loss of employment or a change in employment terms, subject to changes that may occur in the ordinary course of attrition or to the extent that employees may agree with the company on different terms and conditions in accordance with applicable labour laws. Retrenchments must be in accordance with the Labour Relations Act 66 of 1995. The post-commencement employment-related payments and unpaid remuneration and their super-priority status in terms of s 135(3) have also been discussed in 18.5.2 above.

These provisions are further buttressed by s 144(2), which provides that any remuneration, reimbursement for expenses or other amount of money relating to employment that became due and payable *before* the commencement of business rescue proceedings, but were not paid to the employee immediately before the commencement of these proceedings, would be treated as preferred unsecured claims for the purposes of Chapter 6 of the Act. The employee is thus a preferred unsecured creditor in respect of unpaid remuneration and employment-related

---
[131] Section 150(5).
[132] Section 144(1)*(a)* and *(b)*.
[133] Section 144(1)*(b)*.

payments. Such claims would consequently rank for payment before unsecured creditors, but after post-commencement finance.

In terms of s 144(3)*(a)* to *(g)* employees are also entitled to:

(a) [receive] notice of each court proceeding, decision, meeting or other relevant event concerning the business rescue proceedings . . .;[134]
(b) participate in any court proceedings arising during the business rescue proceedings;
(c) form a committee of employees' representatives;
(d) be consulted by the practitioner during the development of the business rescue plan, and [to be] afforded sufficient opportunity to review any such plan and prepare a submission contemplated in s 152(1)*(c)*;
(e) be present and make a submission to the meeting of the holders of voting interests before a vote is taken on any proposed business rescue plan, as contemplated in s 152(1)*(c)*;
(f) vote with creditors on a motion to approve a proposed business [rescue] plan, to the extent that the employee is a creditor, as contemplated in subsection (1) [this should be a reference to subsection (2)]; and
(g) if the business rescue plan is rejected, to —
   (i) propose the development of an alternative plan, in the manner contemplated in section 153; or
   (ii) present an offer to acquire the interests of one or more affected persons, in the manner contemplated in section 153.

A medical scheme or a pension scheme, including a provident scheme, for the benefit of past or present employees of the company is classified as an unsecured creditor of the company in respect of any outstanding amounts due and payable to the trustees of the scheme at the beginning of the rescue process. In the case of a defined benefit pension scheme, the scheme is an unsecured creditor to the extent of the present value at the commencement of business rescue proceedings of any unfunded liability under that scheme.[135]

These rights of employees are additional to any other rights in terms of any law, contract, collective agreement, shareholding, security or court order.[136]

Employees' representatives must also be given an opportunity to address a meeting that has been convened to consider the proposed business rescue plan,[137] and even to make an offer[138] to purchase the voting interests of those opposed to the adoption of the (rejected) business rescue plan (further discussed in 18.9.1 below).

18.8.2 Employees' committees

Quite apart from the rights conferred on employees to be notified of and to participate in the business rescue proceedings, s 148 provides that, within ten business days after his or her appointment, the business rescue practitioner must convene and preside over a first meeting of employees' representatives. At the

---

[134] The Companies Amendment Bill, 2010, cl 87 proposes to amend this provision by requiring that such notice must be given in the prescribed manner and form to employees at their workplace, and served at the head office of the relevant trade union.
[135] Section 144(4)*(a)* and *(b)*.
[136] Section 144(5).
[137] Section 152(1)*(c)*.
[138] In terms of s 153(1)*(b)*(ii).

meeting, the practitioner must inform the representatives whether he or she believes that there is a reasonable prospect of rescuing the company. The employees' representatives would also decide at the meeting whether or not to appoint an employees' committee, and, if so, may then appoint the members of such committee.[139]

In terms of s 149, the employees' committee may consult or discuss with the practitioner any matter relating to the rescue process, but without directing or instructing the practitioner. The committee may also receive and consider reports relating to the rescue process on behalf of the general body of employees. The committee must act independently of the practitioner to ensure fair and unbiased representation of the interests of employees.

Section 149 also applies to a committee of creditors that was appointed in terms of s 147 (see 18.8.3 below).

Section 149(2) stipulates that each member of a committee of creditors or employees (as the case may be) must be:

- an independent creditor or employee[140] of the company, or
- authorised in writing by an independent creditor or employee to be a member of the committee, or
- a proxy, an agent or attorney of an independent creditor or employee, acting under a general power of attorney.[141]

18.8.3 Creditors and creditors' committees

As stated above, creditors of the company are in general, apart from some exceptions, entitled to similar rights as employees of the company during the business rescue proceedings. Like the employees, creditors are entitled to:

- notice of each court proceeding, decision, meeting or other relevant event,
- participate in any court proceedings,
- formally participate in the rescue process to the extent provided for, and
- informally participate by making proposals to the practitioner for a business rescue plan.[142]

They also have a right to vote to amend, approve or reject a proposed business rescue plan; and, if the proposed plan is rejected, they have a further right to propose the development of an alternative plan, or to make an offer to acquire the interests of any or all the other dissenting creditors of the company (in accordance with the provisions of s 153).[143]

Like the employees of the company, creditors may also form a creditors' committee, which the business rescue practitioner would consult during the devel-

---

[139] Section 148(1)*(a)* and *(b)*.
[140] That is, must not be related to the company, its directors or the practitioner (s 128(1)*(g)*). An employee (who is a creditor in terms of s 144(2)) is not related solely because he or she is a member of a trade union that holds shares of that company. This is to be amended by the Companies Amendment Bill, 2010 to refer to 'securities' of a company in place of the 'shares' of a company.
[141] Section 149(2)*(a)* to *(c)*.
[142] Section 145(1)*(a)* to *(d)*.
[143] Section 145(2).

opment of the business rescue plan.[144] The provisions of s 149 (discussed in 18.8.2 above in the context of employees' committees) also apply to a creditors' committee. A creditors' committee may be appointed at the first meeting of creditors, if the creditors decide that such a committee should be appointed.[145] The first meeting of creditors must be convened and presided over by the business rescue practitioner, within ten days of his or her appointment. At that meeting the practitioner must also inform the creditors whether he or she believes that there is a reasonable prospect of rescuing the company, and the practitioner may receive proof of claims from creditors.[146]

The voting interests of creditors are determined by the value of the amount owed by the company to the creditor, and by the status of the creditor. In this respect, s 145(4)*(a)* and *(b)* provides that secured or unsecured creditors have a voting interest equal to the value of the amount owed to the creditor. Thus, in respect of any decision voted on by the creditors of the company, each creditor has a voting interest equal to the value of his or her claim against the company, irrespective of whether the creditor's claim is secured or unsecured. Section 145(4)*(b)* provides as follows:

> [A] concurrent creditor who would be subordinated in a liquidation has a voting interest, as independently and expertly appraised and valued at the request of the practitioner, equal to the amount, if any, that the creditor could reasonably expect to receive in such a liquidation of the company.

The business rescue practitioner must (in terms of s 145(5)*(b)*) request a suitably qualified person to independently and expertly appraise and value an interest held by a concurrent creditor. Notice of the valuation must be given to the creditor at least 15 business days before the meeting to consider the proposed rescue plan, and the creditor is then given five business days to apply to court to review, reappraise or revalue his or her voting interest.[147]

The business rescue practitioner of the company also determines whether a creditor is independent for the purposes of Chapter 6 of the Act (s 145(5)*(a)*), subject to s 145(6)*(a)*, which entitles a person to apply to court within five business days to review the determination made by the practitioner. An independent creditor, as discussed in 18.3.1*(a)* above, is one that is not related to the company, its directors or the practitioner.[148] An employee (who is a creditor in terms of s 144(2))[149] is not related to the company solely because he or she is a member of a trade union that holds shares of that company.[150]

At any meeting of creditors, other than the meeting contemplated in s 151 (ie a creditors' meeting to consider the business rescue plan), all that is needed for the

---

[144] Section 145(3).
[145] Section 147(1)*(b)*.
[146] Section 147(1)*(a)*.
[147] Section 145(6)*(b)*.
[148] Section 128(1)*(g)*.
[149] That is, to the extent that any amount of money relating to employment became due and payable by a company to the employee at any time before the beginning of the business rescue proceedings and had not been paid to the employee immediately before the commencement of these proceedings.
[150] Section 128(2).

decision to be valid and binding is a decision supported by the holders of a simple majority of the independent creditors' voting interests voted on a matter.[151] It must be stressed that this does not apply to a meeting that is convened for the purpose of considering a proposed business rescue plan (discussed in 18.9.1 below).

18.8.4 The holders of the company's securities

Section 146 regulates the participation by holders of any of the company's issued securities. Similarly to the creditors and employees (see 18.8.1 above) of the company, the holders of the company's securities are entitled to:

(a) notice of each court proceeding, decision, meeting or other relevant event concerning the business rescue proceedings;
(b) participate in any court proceedings arising during the business rescue proceedings;
(c) formally participate in a company's business rescue proceedings to the extent provided for in [Chapter 6];
(d) vote to approve or reject a proposed business rescue plan in the manner contemplated in section 152, if the plan would alter the rights associated with the class of securities held by that person; and
(e) if the business rescue plan is rejected, to —
   (i) propose the development of an alternative plan, in the manner contemplated in section 153; or
   (ii) present an offer to acquire the interests of any or all of the creditors or other holders of the company's securities in the manner contemplated in section 153.[152]

It should be noted that, in the context of s 146*(d)*, s 137(1) (discussed in 18.5.5 above) provides that an alteration in the status or classification of any issued securities of a company is invalid unless it is approved by the court or forms part of an approved business rescue plan. It is worthy of emphasis that holders of a company's securities may not vote on the approval or the rejection of a proposed business rescue plan unless the rights associated with that class of securities are to be altered by the rescue plan.

Section 146 specifically applies to holders of the company's 'securities'. The section is not confined to shareholders only. 'Securities' has the meaning set out in s 1 of the Securities Services Act 36 of 2004, which includes debt instruments or debentures. A holder of a debt instrument is essentially a creditor, and as such would have a greater say in the adoption of a business rescue plan than a shareholder. The issue that needs to be settled is whether such person would be confined to the rights given to holders of securities under s 146 or whether he or she may exercise the wider rights conferred on creditors of the company.

18.9 THE CONSIDERATION AND ADOPTION OF THE BUSINESS RESCUE PLAN

18.9.1 Consideration of the plan

It has already been pointed out in 18.7 above that the business rescue practitioner must, after consulting the creditors, other affected persons, and notably the management of the company, prepare a business rescue plan for consideration at a

---
[151] Section 147(3).
[152] Section 146.

meeting held in terms of s 151,[153] and that the company must publish the plan within 25 business days of the practitioner's appointment.[154]

Section 151 imposes on the practitioner a duty to convene and preside over a meeting of creditors and any other holders of a voting interest, called for the purpose of considering the proposed plan, within ten business days after the publication of the business rescue plan. At least five business days before this meeting, the practitioner must deliver a notice of the meeting to all affected persons containing the date, time and place of the meeting; its agenda; and a summary of the rights of affected persons to participate in and to vote at the meeting.[155] This meeting may be adjourned from time to time until a decision has been taken to adopt or reject the plan.[156]

At the meeting, the practitioner is required by s 152(1) to introduce the proposed business rescue plan for consideration by the creditors and, if applicable, by the shareholders. The practitioner must inform the meeting whether he or she continues to believe that there is a reasonable prospect of the company being rescued. The practitioner must also provide an opportunity for employee representatives to address the meeting. In addition, he or she must:

(d) invite discussion, and entertain and conduct a vote, on any motions to —
  (i) amend the proposed plan, in any manner moved and seconded by holders of creditors' voting interests, and satisfactory to the practitioner; or
  (ii) direct the practitioner to adjourn the meeting in order to revise the plan for further consideration; and
(e) call for a vote for preliminary approval of the proposed plan, as amended if applicable, unless the meeting has first been adjourned [to enable the practitioner to develop a new or revised rescue plan].

To be approved on a preliminary basis, the proposed business rescue plan must be supported by the holders of more than 75 per cent of the creditors' voting interests that were voted and also by at least 50 per cent of the independent creditors' voting interests, if any, that were voted.[157] By an 'independent' creditor is meant a person who:

- is a creditor of the company, including an employee who is a creditor in terms of s 144(2) (ie unpaid remuneration, reimbursement of expenses or other employment-related amount that became due and payable before the commencement of the business rescue process), and
- is not related to the company, a director or the practitioner.

An employee is not related to the company solely as a result of membership of a trade union that holds shares (or securities) of the company.[158]

If the business rescue plan is supported by the prescribed majority voting interests of creditors, the plan is regarded as having been finally approved only if

---

[153] Section 150(1).
[154] Section 150(5).
[155] Section 151(2).
[156] Section 151(3).
[157] Section 152(2).
[158] Section 128(1)*(g)* and s 128(2).

the rights of any class of shareholders or the holders of the company's securities are not altered by the rescue plan.

If the business rescue plan is not approved by the creditors on a preliminary basis, the plan is regarded as having been rejected. It may thereafter be considered further only in terms of s 153 (see 18.9.3 on the failure to adopt the plan). The alternative here is that the holders of voting interests who approve of the business rescue plan could perhaps buy out those who disapprove.

If the business rescue plan does alter the rights of the holders of any class of the company's securities, the practitioner must immediately convene a meeting of the holders of the class or classes of securities whose rights would be altered by the plan, and call for a vote by them to approve the adoption of the proposed business rescue plan. In this event, the adoption of the plan by creditors is merely preliminary. Only if the relevant holders of the company's securities approve the plan, based on a majority of the voting rights that were exercised, would the rescue plan be treated as having been finally adopted. If, however, they oppose it, the plan is regarded as having been rejected, although it may be considered further in terms of s 153.[159]

Where the vote of the holders of the company's securities is not required, because the rescue plan does not alter their rights, the preliminary approval by the creditors constitutes a final approval of the business rescue plan, subject to the satisfaction of any conditions on which that plan is contingent.[160]

18.9.2 The effect of the adoption of the plan

According to s 152(4) of the Act, a business rescue plan that has been adopted is binding on the company, on each creditor and on every holder of securities of the company, whether or not that person was present at the meeting, voted in favour of adoption of the plan or, in the case of creditors, had proven his or her claim against the company.

This, of course, is the well-known 'cram-down' which is so essential to the successful implementation of the business rescue plan: it binds dissenting creditors and others. Section 152(5) moreover requires the company, under the direction of the business rescue practitioner, to take all the necessary steps to satisfy or attempt to satisfy any conditions on which the rescue plan is contingent and to implement the plan as adopted.

To the extent necessary the practitioner may, in accordance with the plan, determine the consideration for, and issue any authorised securities of the company, despite s 38 or s 40 (issue of authorised shares and consideration for shares) (see s 152(6)*(a)*, which overrides s 38 and s 40). The practitioner is even given the power, if the plan is approved by the shareholders, to amend the company's Memorandum of Incorporation in order to authorise and determine the preferences, rights, limitations and other terms of any securities that are not otherwise

---

[159] Section 152(3)*(c)*(i) and (ii).
[160] Section 152(3)*(b)*.

authorised but which are contemplated to be issued under the business rescue plan, despite ss 16, 36 or 37.[161]

The pre-emptive rights of shareholders under s 39 do not apply to an issue of shares by the company in terms of the business rescue plan, except to the extent that an approved business rescue plan provides otherwise.[162]

It is also provided in s 154(1) of the Act, dealing with the discharge of debts and claims, that:

> [a] business rescue plan may provide that, if it is implemented in accordance with its terms and conditions, a creditor who has acceded to the discharge of the whole or part of a debt owing to that creditor will lose the right to enforce the relevant debt or part of it.

If a business rescue plan has been approved and implemented, a creditor is not entitled to enforce a debt owed by the company immediately before the commencement of the business rescue process, except to the extent provided for in the business rescue plan.[163] Section 154 could result in the discharge of suretyship undertakings if the principal debt is extinguished.

When the business rescue plan has been substantially implemented, the practitioner must file a notice of the substantial implementation of the business rescue plan with the Companies Commission.[164]

18.9.3 Failure to adopt the plan

If the rescue plan is rejected by creditors or, where relevant, by the holders of the securities of the company, the practitioner may seek a vote of approval from the relevant holders of voting interests to prepare and publish a revised plan. The alternative is for the practitioner to advise the meeting that the company will apply to the court to set aside the result of the vote by the holders of the voting interests or shareholders, as the case may be, on the grounds that it was inappropriate.[165] The resort to the court to set aside the vote on the ground that it is 'inappropriate' is strange and perhaps too wide. Since the courts exercise only a supervisory review function under Chapter 6 of the Act, this ground for setting aside the result of the vote ought to be narrowed down.[166]

If the practitioner fails to take either of these steps, any affected person present at the meeting may do so.[167] Alternatively, if the practitioner does not take either of these steps, then any affected person or combination of affected persons may make a binding offer to purchase the voting interests of any of those opposed to

---

[161] Section 152(6)(*b*).
[162] Section 152(7).
[163] Section 154(2).
[164] Section 152(8).
[165] Section 153(1)(*a*)(i) and (ii).
[166] The Companies Amendment Bill, 2010 (cl 90) proposes to amend s 153 by inserting a new s 153(7) to provide that on an application in terms of s 153(1)(*a*)(ii) or s 153(1)(*b*)(i)(*bb*) a court may order that the vote on a business rescue plan be set aside if the court is satisfied that it is reasonable and just to do so, having regard to *(a)* the interests represented by the person or persons who voted against the rescue plan; *(b)* the provision, if any, made in the proposed rescue plan with respect to the interests of that person or persons; and *(c)* a fair and reasonable estimate of the return to that person or persons if the company were to be liquidated.
[167] Section 153(1)(*b*)(i).

the adoption of the rescue plan.[168] This may enable the approval of the plan at the resumed meeting that must be held within five business days.[169] The offer must be at a value that is independently and expertly determined, at the request of the practitioner, to be a fair and reasonable estimate of the likely return that such person or persons would receive if the company were to be immediately liquidated.[170] The determination of the independent expert may be reviewed, reappraised and revalued on application to court by either a holder of a voting interest or a person acquiring an interest in terms of a binding offer.[171]

If no person takes any of the above action (contemplated in s 153(1)), the practitioner must promptly file a notice of the termination of the business rescue proceedings (s 153(5)).

If on the other hand, the practitioner has to prepare and publish a revised plan, the plan must be published within ten business days, and the procedure for publishing and considering the new plan will apply afresh (s 153(3)).

18.9.4 The termination of business rescue proceedings
The termination of business rescue proceedings has been discussed above in 18.4.3.

18.10 COMPROMISE WITH CREDITORS

18.10.1 General
Chapter 6 of the Companies Act deals also with compromises between the company and its creditors. It may be possible for a company to enter into a compromise with its creditors without going into liquidation or winding-up. A 'compromise' is an agreement between a company and its creditors or a class of creditors that terminates a dispute over the rights of the parties which are to be compromised or their enforcement. A compromise is appropriate in cases where the normal mechanisms for reaching an agreement between the company and its creditors or class of creditors are not available. It is intended to provide the machinery for overcoming the practical difficulty that a company, and particularly a company with a large number of creditors, may experience in obtaining the individual consent of every creditor of the company to the settlement of their claims. It also prevents, in appropriate circumstances, a minority from impeding a beneficial scheme or from obtaining special advantages for themselves.

Under the Companies Act 61 of 1973 (hereafter 'the 1973 Act'), the procedures and requirements for a compromise or arrangement were dealt with in ss 311 to 313 of the Act. These sections provided the machinery for compromises and arrangements between a company and the collective body of its creditors or shareholders or any class of them, and to render these compromises and arrangements binding on all the parties concerned, including dissenting parties. The compromise or arrangement required a court application to commence the proce-

---
[168] Section 153(1)(b)(ii).
[169] Section 153(4).
[170] Section 153(1)(b)(ii).
[171] Section 153(6).

dure and also had to be sanctioned by the court as a form of protection for all the parties concerned, including minority creditors or shareholders. The compromise or arrangement was not binding unless it was sanctioned by the court. Section 311 applied whether or not the company was insolvent.

Section 155 of the new Act, dealing with compromises, applies whether or not the company is financially distressed (as defined in s 128(1)(f); see 18.2 above), provided that it is not under business rescue proceedings. The implication of s 155(1) is that, during the period when the parties are still finalising the details of the compromise, it is possible for a creditor to apply to court as an affected person to put the company under business rescue proceedings or to put it into liquidation. Putting it under business rescue proceedings would bring the negotiations for a compromise to a stop. A compromise does, however, apply even if the company is in liquidation, in which event the compromise may be made binding on the liquidator. In an attempt to simplify the process, the role of the court under the Act has been reduced.

18.10.2 The proposal

Section 155(2) provides that the board of a company, or its liquidator, if it is being wound up, may propose an arrangement or a compromise of its financial obligations to all its creditors, or to all the members of any class of its creditors. Consequently only the board of directors or the liquidator of the company has *locus standi* to propose a compromise or arrangement. This is done by delivering a copy of the proposal and the notice of the meeting to consider it, to every creditor of the company or of the relevant class of creditors whose names and addresses are known to or can reasonably be obtained by the company. These documents must also be delivered to the Companies Commission.

The proposal put forward by the board of directors or the liquidator must contain all the information reasonably required to help creditors decide whether to accept or reject the proposal. The proposal must be divided into three parts, consisting of the background to the proposal, the proposals themselves and their assumptions and conditions.[172]

Part A: Background
In terms of s 155(3)(a) Part A must contain at least the following:
- a complete list of all the material assets of the company, together with an indication of which assets are held as security by creditors as on the date of the proposal,
- a complete list of the creditors of the company as on the date of the proposal and an indication of which creditors would qualify as secured, statutory preferent and concurrent creditors under the laws of insolvency (there must be an indication as to which of the creditors have proved their claims),
- the probable dividend that would be received by creditors, in their specific classes, if the company were to be placed in liquidation,
- the complete list of the holders of the securities issued by the company and the effect that the proposal would have on them, if any, and

---
[172] Section 155(3).

- whether the proposal includes a proposal made informally by a creditor of the company.

Part B: The Proposals
In terms of s 155(3)*(b)* Part B must disclose at least the following:
- the nature and the duration of any proposed debt moratorium,
- the extent to which the company is to be released from the payment of its debts, and the extent to which any debt is proposed to be converted to equity in the company, or another company,
- the treatment of contracts and the ongoing role of the company,
- the property of the company that is proposed to be available to pay the claims of creditors,
- the order of preference in which the proceeds of property of the company will be applied to pay the creditors if the proposal is adopted, and
- the benefits of adopting the proposal as opposed to the benefits that would be received by creditors if the company were to be placed in liquidation.

Part C: Assumptions and conditions
In terms of s 155(3)*(c)* Part C must include at least the following:
- a statement of the conditions that must be satisfied, if any, for the proposal both to come into operation and to be fully implemented,
- the effect, if any, that the plan contemplates having on the company's employees, and their terms and conditions of employment, and
- a projected balance sheet for the company and a projected statement of income and expenses for the ensuing three years, prepared on the assumption that the proposal is accepted.

The proposal must conclude with a certificate by an authorised director or prescribed officer stating that any factual information provided appears to be accurate, complete and up to date, and declaring that the projections provided are estimates made in good faith on the basis of factual information and assumptions as set out in the statement.[173]

18.10.3 Adoption of the proposal

To be adopted, the proposal for the compromise must be supported by a majority in number, representing at least 75 per cent in value of the creditors or relevant class of creditors concerned (as the case may be), who are present and voting, whether in person or by proxy, at a meeting called for that purpose.[174]

Upon adoption of the proposal, the company *may* [emphasis added] apply to the court for an order approving the proposal.[175] The court may sanction the compromise as set out in the adopted proposal if it is just and equitable to do so. For these purposes the court will take account of the number of creditors of any affected class of creditors who were present or represented at the meeting, and who had voted in favour of the proposal. In the case of a company that is under winding-up,

---
[173] Section 155(5).
[174] Section 155(6).
[175] Section 155(7)*(a)*. Although s 155 (7)*(a)* is drafted in terms that appear to be permissive, in effect its terms are practically mandatory.

the court will also take into account the report of the Master that is required in terms of Chapter 14 of the 1973 Act.[176]

For the compromise to be enforceable against all the parties concerned, it will have to be sanctioned by the court.

Section 155(9) provides that an arrangement or compromise contemplated in s 155 does not affect the liability of any person who is a surety of the company.

The final step in the process is that, in terms of s 155(8), the company must file a copy of the court order sanctioning a compromise with the Companies Commission within five business days. It must also be attached to each copy of the company's Memorandum of Incorporation that is kept at the company's registered office or elsewhere, as contemplated in s 25. Section 155(8)*(c)* explicitly provides that, as of the date on which it is filed, the court order sanctioning an arrangement or compromise is final and binding on all the company's creditors or on all members of the relevant class of creditors (as the case may be).

---

[176] Section 155(7)*(b)*(i) and (ii).

CHAPTER 19

WINDING-UP

Jacqueline Yeats

19.1	INTRODUCTION	821
19.2	WINDING-UP OF SOLVENT COMPANIES	822
	19.2.1 Voluntary winding-up of solvent companies	822
	19.2.2 Winding-up of solvent companies by court order	823
19.3	WINDING-UP OF INSOLVENT COMPANIES	826
19.4	THE WINDING-UP PROCESS	827
19.5	THE LIQUIDATOR	828
	19.5.1 Powers of the liquidator	829
	19.5.2 Duties of the liquidator	830
19.6	DISSOLUTION OF COMPANIES AND REMOVAL FROM REGISTER	830
19.7	DEREGISTRATION OF COMPANIES	831
19.8	EFFECT OF REMOVAL OF COMPANY FROM REGISTER	832

19.1 INTRODUCTION

The winding-up of companies is governed by two distinct and separate pieces of legislation. The winding-up of solvent companies is regulated in terms of ss 79 to 81 in Part G of Chapter 2 of the Companies Act 71 of 2008 (hereafter 'the Act'), while the winding-up of insolvent companies is regulated in terms of Chapter XIV of the Companies Act 61 of 1973 (hereafter 'the 1973 Act'). This legislative divide is created by s 79(1)(*b*) of the Act as read with item 9 of Schedule 5 to the Act (which prescribes the transitional arrangements of the Act with respect to existing legislation).

Item 9(1) of Schedule 5 provides that, despite the repeal of the 1973 Act, and until a date determined by the Minister by notice in the *Government Gazette*, Chapter XIV of the 1973 Act continues to apply with respect to the winding-up and liquidation of companies under the Act, as if the 1973 Act had not been repealed. However, certain sections of the 1973 Act do not apply to the winding-up of a solvent company except to the extent necessary to give full effect to the provisions of Part G of the Act. The excluded sections are ss 343, 344, 346 and 348 to 353. These sections deal with modes of winding-up (s 343), circumstances in which a company may be wound up by the court (s 344), the application for winding-up of a company (s 346), commencement of winding-up by the court (s 348) and voluntary winding-up generally (ss 349–353). In the event of a conflict between one of the provisions of the 1973 Act that continues to apply and a provision of Part G of the Act with respect to a solvent company, the provision in the Act will prevail.

The notice determining the date on which Chapter XIV of the 1973 Act ceases to apply may not be given until the Minister is satisfied that alternative legislation has been brought into force that adequately provides for the winding-up and liquidation of insolvent companies.[1] In addition, the Minister may, by notice in the *Gazette*, prescribe any ancillary rules necessary to provide for the efficient transition from the provisions of the repealed 1973 Act to the provisions of the new alternative insolvency legislation.

19.2 WINDING-UP OF SOLVENT COMPANIES

A solvent company may be dissolved by:

- a voluntary winding-up initiated by the company and conducted either by the company itself or by its creditors, as determined by the resolution of the company, or
- winding-up and liquidation by court order.

The procedures for the winding-up of a solvent company, whether voluntary or by court order, are governed by the provisions of Part G of Chapter 2 of the Act and, to the extent applicable, by the laws referred to in item 9 of Schedule 5 to the Act. The procedures which may apply by virtue of Item 9 of Schedule 5 are discussed in greater detail in 19.4 and 19.5 below.

If, at any time after a company has adopted a resolution contemplated in s 80, or an application has been made to a court as contemplated in s 81, it is determined that the company to be wound up is insolvent, a court may order that the company be wound up as an insolvent company. This will take place then in terms of the laws referred to or contemplated in item 9 of Schedule 5.[2]

19.2.1 Voluntary winding-up of solvent companies

A company may be wound up voluntarily if it has adopted a special resolution to do so.[3] The special resolution may provide for the winding-up to be by the company or by its creditors. The resolution must be filed[4] together with the prescribed notice[5] and the filing fee. However, prior to such a resolution being filed, the company must:

- arrange for security satisfactory to the Master[6] for payment of the company's debts within a maximum of 12 months after the commencement of the winding-up[7], or
- obtain consent from the Master to dispense with security.

---

[1] There is currently a legislative process underway that is intended to reform the law of insolvency generally and that will result in a unified Insolvency Act. The arrangements alluded to above have been drafted with this in mind.

[2] That is, in terms of the relevant provisions of Chapter XIV of the 1973 Act.

[3] See s 80(1).

[4] When a resolution has been filed, the Companies and Intellectual Property Commission ('the Companies Commission') must promptly deliver a copy thereof to the Master.

[5] A resolution by a solvent company to wind up must be filed with form CoR 47.1.

[6] The Master is the person who holds the office of that name in terms of the Supreme Court Act 59 of 1959.

[7] Section 80(6) determines that a voluntary winding-up begins when the resolution of the company has been filed in terms of s 80(2).

The Master may only dispense with security if the company has submitted the following:

- a sworn statement by a director authorised by the board of the company stating that the company has no debts, and
- a certificate by the company's auditor[8] stating that, to the best of his or her knowledge and belief, and according to the financial records of the company, the company appears to have no debts.

Any costs incurred in furnishing the requisite security may be paid by the company.[9]

A liquidator appointed in a voluntary winding-up may exercise all powers given by the Act (or a law contemplated in item 9 of Schedule 5[10]) to a liquidator in a winding-up by the court without requiring a specific order or sanction of the court, subject to any directions given by the shareholders (in the case of a winding-up by the company) or the creditors (in the case of a winding-up by the creditors).[11]

Despite any provision to the contrary contained in a company's Memorandum of Incorporation, the company remains a juristic person and retains all its powers as such while it is being wound up. However, from the beginning of the company's winding-up it must cease carrying on its business except to the extent required for the beneficial winding-up of the company. In addition, all the directors' powers cease except to the extent that they are specifically authorised to act by the liquidator or the shareholders in general meeting (in the case of a winding-up by the company) or the liquidator or creditors (in the case of a winding-up by creditors).

19.2.2 Winding-up of solvent companies by court order

The circumstances under which the court may wind up a solvent company are many and varied and are enumerated in s 81. The court has a discretion as to whether or not to grant a winding-up order or not, and is therefore not obliged to grant the order merely because the resolution has been passed or when one of the other grounds for winding-up has been established.[12] Section 81 provides that a court may order a solvent company to be wound up if:

(a) the company has —
  (i) resolved, by special resolution, that it be wound up by the court; or
  (ii) applied to the court to have its voluntary winding-up continued by the court;
(b) the practitioner of a company appointed during business rescue proceedings has applied for liquidation in terms of section 141(2)*(a)*, on the grounds that there is no reasonable prospect of the company being rescued; or
(c) one or more of the company's creditors have applied to the court for an order to wind up the company on the grounds that —
  (i) the company's business rescue proceedings have ended in the manner contem-

---

[8] In terms of s 80*(b)*(ii), if a company does not have an auditor, a person who meets the requirements for the appointment of an auditor and appointed for the purpose may furnish the certificate.

[9] See s 80(4). If the company does not have sufficient funds these costs will have to be met by its shareholders or creditors.

[10] That is Chapter XIV of the 1973 Act and, thereafter, the alternative legislation that replaces it.

[11] See s 80(5).

[12] See *LAWSA* vol 4 (3) para 110 and the cases cited there.

plated in section 132(2)*(b)* or *(c)*(i) and it appears to the court that it is just and equitable in the circumstances for the company to be wound up; or

(ii) it is otherwise just and equitable for the company to be wound up;

(d) the company, one or more directors or one or more shareholders have applied to the court for an order to wind up the company on the grounds that —

(i) the directors are deadlocked in the management of the company, and the shareholders are unable to break the deadlock, and —

(aa) irreparable injury to the company is resulting, or may result, from the deadlock; or

(bb) the company's business cannot be conducted to the advantage of shareholders generally, as a result of the deadlock;

(ii) the shareholders are deadlocked in voting power, and have failed for a period that includes at least two consecutive annual general meeting dates, to elect successors to directors whose terms have expired; or

(iii) it is otherwise just and equitable for the company to be wound up;

(e) a shareholder has applied, with leave of the court, for an order to wind up the company on the grounds that —

(i) the directors, prescribed officers or other persons in control of the company are acting in a manner that is fraudulent or otherwise illegal; or

(ii) the company's assets are being misapplied or wasted; or

(f) the Commission or Panel has applied to the court for an order to wind up the company on the grounds that —

(i) the company, its directors or prescribed officers or other persons in control of the company are acting or have acted in a manner that is fraudulent or otherwise illegal, the Commission or Panel, as the case may be, has issued a compliance notice in respect of that conduct, and the company has failed to comply with that compliance notice; and

(ii) within the previous five years, enforcement procedures in terms of this Act or the Close Corporations Act, 1984 (Act No. 69 or 1984), were taken against the company, its directors or prescribed officers, or other persons in control of the company for substantially the same conduct, resulting in an administrative fine, or conviction for an offence.

The grounds for the winding-up of a solvent company by the court under the new Act are quite different from the grounds on which a court could wind up a company under the 1973 Act.[13] However, it is submitted that, where there are similarities between the circumstances previously listed in which a company could be wound up by a court and those which now apply under the Act, or where the same words or phrases are used, the court may be guided or even bound by existing case law in this regard. To illustrate, the 1973 Act contained a section providing that the court may wind up a company if 'it appears to the court that it is 'just and equitable' that the company should be wound up'.[14] The Act, in s 81(1)*(c)* (application by creditors) and 81(1)*(d)*(iii) (application by company, directors or shareholders), also uses the 'just and equitable' ground as part of these subsections. In *Apco Africa (Pty) Ltd v Apco Worldwide Inc*[15] the Supreme Court of Appeal made, inter alia, the following points in relation to the 'just and equitable' ground as a basis for winding-up:

---

[13] See s 344 of the 1973 Act.
[14] See s 344*(h)* of the 1973 Act.
[15] 2008 (5) SA 615 (SCA).

- this type of consideration postulates not facts, but only a broad conclusion of law, justice and equity as a ground for winding-up,[16]
- it is well settled that the power given to the court to wind up on a just and equitable ground is not confined to cases where there are grounds analogous to those mentioned in other parts of the section,[17]
- no general rule can be laid down as to which circumstances have to be borne in mind in considering whether a case comes within the phrase,[18] and
- the cases show that the application of the 'just and equitable' provision is not to be limited to cases where the substratum of the company has disappeared or where there has been a complete deadlock.[19]

The final observation above flows from the fact that the courts have evolved certain principles as guidelines in specific cases for the exercise of their discretion on the 'just and equitable ground'. These principles (which do not constitute a closed list of recognised categories for winding-up on just and equitable grounds) are:

- the disappearance of the company's substratum (which makes it impossible for a company to pursue its objects),
- illegality of objects and fraudulent purpose (the company's objects are or become illegal or the company was promoted for the purpose of perpetrating a fraud),
- a deadlock in the company's administration (which renders the company incapable of carrying on its business), and
- irretrievably destruction of the relationship in a domestic company ('or quasi-partnership').[20]

Note that the Act now recognises a management or a shareholders' deadlock[21] and fraud or illegal actions on the part of the company's controllers[22] as potentially substantive grounds for winding-up by the court. Consequently the case law that has developed around these concepts as a manifestation of circumstances which make it just and equitable for a court to wind up a company (as well as, of course, case law dealing with the concept of just and equitable grounds for winding-up generally) should prove helpful and instructive in this regard.

A shareholder may not apply to court as contemplated[23] unless he or she:

(a) has been a shareholder continuously for at least six months immediately before the date of the application; or

(b) became a shareholder as a result of —
   (i) acquiring another shareholder; or

---

[16] *Moosa NO v Mavjee Bhawan (Pty) Ltd* 1967 (3) SA 131 (T) 136H.
[17] *Loch v John Blackwood* [1924] AC 783 (PC).
[18] *Davis and Co Ltd v Brunswick (Australia) Ltd* [1936] 1 All ER 299 (PC) 309.
[19] See *In re Yenidje Tobacco Co Ltd* [1916] 2 Ch 426 (CA) 430; see also *Marshall v Marshall (Pty) Ltd* 1954 (3) SA 571 (N); *Lawrence v Lawrich Motors (Pty) Ltd* 1948 (2) SA 1029 (W).
[20] For much more detail and illustrative cases in regard to all these categories, see Blackman et al *Commentary on the Companies Act* at 14–102–14–116.
[21] See s 81(1)*(d)*.
[22] See s 81(1)*(e)* and *(f)*.
[23] In s 81(1)*(d)* or *(e)*.

(ii) the distribution of the estate of a former shareholder,
and the present shareholder, and other or former shareholder, in aggregate, satisfied the requirements of paragraph *(a)*.[24]

A court may not make an order applied for in terms of s 81(1)*(e)* or *(f)*[25] if, before the conclusion of the court proceedings:

- any of the directors have resigned or have been removed in terms of s 71 and the court concludes that the remaining directors were not materially implicated in the conduct on which the application was based, or
- one or more shareholders have applied to the court for a declaration in terms of s 162 to declare delinquent the directors, if any, responsible for the alleged misconduct, and the court is satisfied that the removal of those directors would bring the misconduct to an end.[26]

Section 81(4) determines that a winding-up of a company by a court begins when an application has been made to the court in terms of sub-s (1)*(a)* or *(b)* or the court has made an order applied for in terms of sub-s (1)*(c)*, *(d)*, *(e)* or *(f)*.

19.3 WINDING-UP OF INSOLVENT COMPANIES

As pointed out previously, this area of law continues to be regulated by the provisions of the 1973 Act until such time as it has been replaced by other appropriate legislation. It is not possible to discuss the substantive and procedural requirements for winding up an insolvent company in detail in this chapter. These requirements are complex and lengthy and are informed and supported by a wealth of developed case law spanning nearly a century. However, for the sake of completeness, a brief overview of the main facets of the winding-up of an insolvent company has been included.

The term 'insolvency' describes the situation where a company is unable to pay its debts and is governed by s 345 of the 1973 Act. In terms of this section a company is deemed to be unable to pay its debts (and is therefore insolvent and liable to be liquidated) if:

- a creditor that is owed[27] at least R100 by the company has served a demand for payment[28] and the amount has not been paid within three weeks, or
- the sheriff has issued a *nulla bona* return to a warrant of execution[29], or
- it is proved to the satisfaction of the court that the company is unable to pay its debts.[30]

In *Koekemoer v Taylor & Steyn*[31] Goldstone J stated that the statutory demand and *nulla bona* deeming provisions:

---

[24] See s 81(2)*(a)* and *(b)*.
[25] The grounds for winding-up based on fraud and illegality and/or non-compliance.
[26] Section 81(3).
[27] The debt must be due and payable.
[28] As required in terms of s 345(1)*(a)* of the 1973 Act.
[29] This means that the sheriff or messenger of the court has indicated by an endorsement on his or her return of service that he or she has not found sufficient property to satisfy the judgment, decree or court order or, alternatively, that any disposable property found did not upon sale satisfy the process. See further s 345(1)*(b)* of the 1973 Act.
[30] 'Debt' in this context means an amount of money that is due and owing.
[31] 1981 (1) SA 267 (W).

... predicate situations where a company may well be able to pay its debts but is conclusively deemed not to be able to do so, ie where a company has failed to respond positively to a statutory demand for payment or where a company has caused a return of nulla bona to be made in response to a warrant of execution.

Thus a company is deemed by the court in these situations to be unable to pay its debts even if it is fully capable of paying them. In making the determination whether a company is unable to pay its debts as contemplated, the court must also take into account the contingent and prospective liabilities of the company.[32] A company is unable to pay its debts within the meaning of s 345(1)(c) when it is 'commercially insolvent,' ie when it is unable to pay its debts as they fall due in the ordinary course of business.[33] The question is therefore not whether the company is factually solvent in the sense that its assets exceed its liabilities, but whether it can meet its obligations and thereafter continue trading. This may be proved in any manner that satisfies the court.

The power of the court to grant a winding-up order is a discretionary one.[34] However, s 347 of the 1973 Act places restrictions on the discretionary power of the court in hearing the application for winding-up. In addition, certain guidelines and principles have evolved through the cases to aid the courts in exercising this rather wide discretion. For example, where the application for a winding-up amounts to an abuse of process in that the motive is not merely to place the company in liquidation in order to establish a *concursus creditorium* but is *mala fide*, the court will not grant a winding-up order.[35] Similarly, when winding-up proceedings are used in an attempt to enforce payment of a debt which is *bona fide* disputed by the company on reasonable and substantial grounds, the court will dismiss the application for winding- up.[36] The court has a discretion whether or not to wind up a company unable to pay its debts, even where the company is factually insolvent in the sense that its liabilities exceed its assets.[37] However, generally, if this is the case, the court will not refuse the order.[38]

19.4 THE WINDING-UP PROCESS

An application to court for the winding-up of a company may be made by:

- the company itself,[39] or

---

[32] Section 345(2) of the 1973 Act.
[33] *Koekemoer v Taylor & Steyn* (supra) at 271.
[34] *F & C Building Construction Co (Pty) Ltd v Macsheil Investments (Pty) Ltd* 1959 (3) SA 841 (D). This also applies to the winding-up of solvent companies. See the remarks in this regard above at paragraph 19.2.
[35] See *LAWSA* vol 4 (3) para 112.
[36] See *LAWSA* vol 4 (3) para 113.
[37] See *SAA Distributors (Pty) Ltd v Sport & Spel (Edms) Bpk* 1973 (3) SA 371 (C); *Cooper v A & G Fashions (Pty) Ltd; Ex parte Millman* 1991 (4) SA 204 (C).
[38] Even where the majority of creditors are opposed to a winding-up, unless future creditors are adequately protected. *Ex parte Lebowa Development Corporation* Ltd 1989 (3) SA 71 (T). (See, however, *Ex parte Strydom: In re Central Plumbing Works (Natal) (Pty) Ltd; Ex parte Spendiff: In re Candida Footwear Manufacturers (Pty) Ltd; Ex parte Spendiff: In re Jerseytex (Pty) Ltd* 1988 (1) SA 616 (D) 623 for a departure from this approach).
[39] See s 346(1)(a) of the 1973 Act.

- one or more of the company's creditors (contingent or prospective creditors included),[40] or
- one or more of the company's members or the executor, administrator, trustee, curator or guardian in respect of the estate of a deceased member or one whose estate has been sequestrated or who is otherwise under disability, or the liquidator of a body corporate in the course of being wound up which is a member of the company,[41] or
- jointly by any or all of the above parties.[42]

The application takes the form of a notice of motion together with an affidavit supporting the facts on which the applicant relies for relief, ie the grounds for winding-up. In *Breetveldt v Van Zyl*[43] Margo J explained that the purpose of the application is to place before the court, the company, the creditors and the shareholders, a statement of the material facts upon which the winding-up order is claimed and to provide information to the Master, the sheriff, the liquidator and other interested parties. Every application must be accompanied by a certificate by the Master to the effect that sufficient security has been given for the payment of all fees and charges and costs necessary for the prosecution of winding-up proceedings and the administration of the company in liquidation or discharge of the company from winding-up, as the case may be.[44] Unless the application is brought by the company itself, notice of the application should be served on the company except in matters of urgency.[45] Sections 346 and 346A of the 1973 Act provide for the manner in which, and the persons on whom, service must take place. A winding-up of a company by the court is deemed to commence at the time of the presentation to the court of the application for winding-up.[46] An application is 'presented' when it is lodged with the Registrar in proper form.[47] Note, however, that it is only once the winding-up order has been granted that the winding-up is deemed to have commenced at the date of presentation of the application.[48] The court may grant or dismiss an application for winding-up or adjourn the hearing thereof or make an interim order or any other order which it deems just.[49]

19.5 THE LIQUIDATOR

A liquidator appointed in a voluntary winding-up may, upon appointment,[50] exercise all the powers given by the Act or a law contemplated in item 9 of

---

[40] See s 346(1)*(b)* of the 1973 Act.
[41] See s 346 (1)*(c)* read with s 103(3) of the 1973 Act.
[42] Section 346 (1)*(d)* of the 1973 Act.
[43] 1972 (1) SA 304 (T) 314.
[44] Section 346(3) of the 1973 Act.
[45] Rule 6(2) and 6(12) of the Rules of the Supreme Court.
[46] See s 348 of the 1973 Act.
[47] *Lief v Western Credit (Africa) (Pty)* Ltd 1966 (3) SA 344 (W) 347 and see the other cases cited in *LAWSA* vol 4 (3) para 142.
[48] *Vermeulen v CC Bauermeister (Edms) Bpk* 1982 (4) SA 159 (T) 162.
[49] Section 347(1) of the 1973 Act.
[50] The Act does not prescribe how this appointment is to take place and therefore it would seem that the procedure for appointment contained in the 1973 Act must be the appropriate one.

Schedule 5[51] to a liquidator in a winding-up by a court. The exercise of his or her powers does not require the specific order or sanction of the court, but is subject to any directions given by the shareholders in general meeting (in the case of a winding-up by the company) or the creditors (in the case of a winding-up by creditors).[52]

The provisions in the 'law contemplated in item 9 of Schedule 5' which find application here are ss 367 to 385 of the 1973 Act (which deal with the appointment, removal and remuneration of the liquidator) and ss 386 to 390 (which deal with the powers of liquidators).

It is the Master who appoints the liquidator once a winding-up order has been made. The Master may appoint any suitable person as the provisional liquidator, but this person must give security to the Master for the proper performance of his or her duties until a final liquidator is appointed.[53] The person who is to be appointed is usually determined by nomination as liquidator by meetings of creditors and members or contributories of a company, but the Master may decline to appoint the nominated person(s) on a number of grounds, including on the basis that, in his opinion, the person should not be appointed as liquidator.[54] The Master also has the power to remove a liquidator from his or her office on a number of grounds, including on the basis that he or she has failed to perform their duties satisfactorily.[55] Liquidators are entitled to reasonable remuneration for their services[56] and, once they have performed all their duties and complied with the Master's requirements, they may apply to the Master for a certificate of completion of duties and a cancellation of the security initially given by them.[57]

19.5.1 Powers of the liquidator

The powers of the liquidator as described in the 1973 Act are the same for the winding-up of solvent and insolvent companies. The liquidator has wide general powers as set out in s 386 of the 1973 Act, as well as the power (granted by the court, creditors or members of the company, as the case may be)[58] to, inter alia, bring or defend legal proceedings, agree to settlements with debtors of the company, compromise or admit claims against the company, make arrangements with creditors, submit disputes to arbitration, carry on or discontinue the business of the company, sell the property of the company, and approach the court for leave to perform any act or exercise any power for which he or she is not expressly authorised.[59]

---

[51] In other words, the relevant sections on winding-up contained in the 1973 Act until such time as these are replaced by the proposed new insolvency legislation. Thus ss 367–411 of the 1973 Act (which deal with liquidators) are relevant here.
[52] See s 80(5).
[53] See ss 367 and 368 of the 1973 Act.
[54] See s 370 of the 1973 Act.
[55] See ss 379 and 381 of the 1973 Act.
[56] See s 384 of the 1973 Act.
[57] See s 385 of the 1973 Act.
[58] See s 386(3) of the 1973 Act.
[59] See s 386(4) of the 1973 Act.

19.5.2 Duties of the liquidator

The general duties of the liquidator are to recover all the assets and property of the company, sell these to satisfy the costs of the winding-up and the claims of creditors insofar as possible, and then to ultimately distribute the balance of the insolvent estate (the free residue) to those persons legally entitled to it. In the course of the performance of this general duty, the liquidator naturally has to perform a number of specific duties, which are detailed in ss 391–411 of the 1973 Act. The multifaceted liquidation and distribution process is conducted through a series of prescribed meetings of creditors and members to ascertain their wishes. The process eventually culminates in the lodging of a liquidation and distribution account or accounts by the liquidator.[60] The assets of the estate are distributed in accordance with the liquidation and distribution account once this account has been confirmed as prescribed by the 1973 Act.[61]

19.6 DISSOLUTION OF COMPANIES AND REMOVAL FROM REGISTER

When the affairs of a company have been completely wound up and a court order of final liquidation has been made, s 82 provides that the Master must promptly[62] file a certificate to that effect,[63] together with a copy of the court order, with the Companies and Intellectual Property Commission ('the Companies Commission'). The Companies Commission must then record the dissolution and remove the company's name from the companies register.[64] It is to be noted that, although the Act deals with both concepts in ss 82 and 83 and the distinction is not always entirely clear in the legislation, dissolution and deregistration are not the same. While both have the effect of terminating the legal existence of a company, their purpose and some of their consequences are different.[65] Upon the dissolution of a company the liability of its directors, officers and members ceases, whereas this is not the case with deregistration.[66] Furthermore, the effect of declaring a dissolution void is not retrospective,[67] but when the registration of a deregistered company is restored, the company's rights and obligations prior to deregistration revive and the order declaring the deregistration void operates retrospectively.[68] This was specifically spelled out in the 1973 Act,[69] but it is to be noted that a

---

[60] See ss 412–416 and 403–405 of the 1973 Act.
[61] See ss 406–411 of the 1973 Act.
[62] No time limit is specified in the Act.
[63] The Act makes no provision for the issuing of such a certificate. Presumably then it is the Master's certificate — issued in terms of s 419(1) of the 1973 Act — which serves this purpose.
[64] See s 82(2).
[65] Blackman et al op cit n 20 at 4–171.
[66] See s 83.
[67] Thus, according to Blackman et al op cit n 20 at 4–172, intermediate acts (ie those performed between the date of dissolution and the order declaring the dissolution void) are not thereby validated.
[68] See Blackman et al op cit n 20 at 4–172.
[69] Section 73(6) provided that, where a court made an order that registration was to be restored, 'thereupon the company shall be deemed to have continued in existence as if it had not been deregistered'.

similar provision has not been included in the new Act. However, it is submitted that this is still the legal position.

19.7 DEREGISTRATION OF COMPANIES

In addition to the duty to deregister a company described above, the Companies Commission may otherwise remove a company from the companies register only in the following circumstances:

- the company has transferred its registration to a foreign jurisdiction in terms of s 82(5),[70]
- the company has failed to file an annual return in terms of s 33 for two or more years in succession and the company, on demand by the Companies Commission,[71] has failed to:
    - give satisfactory reasons for the failure to file the required annual returns,[72] or
    - show satisfactory cause for the company to remain registered,[73] or
- the Companies Commission has determined that the company appears to have been inactive for at least seven years and no person has demonstrated a reasonable interest in or reason for its continued existence,[74] or
- the Companies Commission has received a request in the prescribed manner and form and has determined that the company:
    - has ceased to carry on business, and
    - has no assets or, because of the inadequacy of its assets, there is no reasonable probability of the company being liquidated.[75]

If the Companies Commission deregisters a company as contemplated in s 82(3), any interested person may apply in the prescribed manner and form to the Companies Commission to reinstate the registration of the company.[76] The court thus has the power to restore the company's registration. Under the 1973 Act the term 'interested person' was also used in this context and it has been held that the words:

> ... must be given the widest possible connotation so as to include any person who has a financial interest of any sort, whether actual or contingent, in or against a company, or relating to it, or with which interest that company might be concerned, provided that the financial interest in question is not negligible.[77]

---

[70] This provision was inserted by the draft Companies Amendment Bill, 2010.

[71] Regulation 47 sets out the procedure for delivery of the demand letter by the Companies Commission and further provides that the Companies Commission may deregister the company if it does not respond within 20 days after the demand was posted. If the company does respond to the letter, the Companies Commission may deregister it, may require additional information, may issue a compliance notice requiring the company to file an annual return for every year that it failed to do so, or must issue a compliance certificate, depending on the circumstances. See Regulation 47.

[72] See s 82(3)*(a)*(i).

[73] See s 82(3)*(a)*(ii).

[74] See s 82(3)*(b)*(i).

[75] See s 82(3)*(b)*(ii).

[76] See s 82(3)(4). An application to reinstate a deregistered company must be made on form CoR 47.4.

[77] Per Slomowitz J in *Ex parte Stubbs: In re Wit Extensions Ltd* 1982 (1) SA 526 (W) 531.

A foreign company may apply to be deregistered upon the transfer of its registration to a foreign jurisdiction if:
- shareholders have adopted a special resolution approving such application and transfer of registration, and
- the company has satisfied the requirements for doing so.[78]

19.8 EFFECT OF REMOVAL OF COMPANY FROM REGISTER

A company is dissolved as of the date on which its name is removed from the companies register.[79] Such removal does not affect the liability of any former director or shareholder of the company (or any other person) in respect of any act or omission that had taken place before the company was removed from the register.[80] To the contrary, any liability continues and can be enforced as if the company had not been removed from the register.[81] As was explained above, this is due to the fact that one is dealing with deregistration as opposed to dissolution (ie the process which takes place after a winding-up and which has a different legal effect). The property of a company becomes *bona vacantia* upon its deregistration and vests in the state.[82]

At any time after a company has been dissolved:

(a) the liquidator of the company, or other person with an interest in the company, may apply to a court for an order declaring the dissolution to have been void, or any other order that is just and equitable in the circumstances; and

(b) if the court declares the dissolution to have been void, any proceedings may be taken against the company as might have been taken if the company had not been dissolved.[83]

The court thus has the power upon application by the liquidator[84] or other interested party to set aside a dissolution in terms of a voiding order. According to Blackman et al[85] the purpose of setting aside a dissolution is usually to complete unfinished business or to rectify an oversight in relation to a winding-up, such as the distribution of one or more of the Company's assets that had been overlooked in the final process. Note that in these circumstances the institution of proceedings against the company can proceed as if the company had not been dissolved.[86] (As explained above, an order voiding a dissolution does not operate retrospectively and intermediate acts are therefore not validated by such an order). This is the only statutory provision in regard to the consequences of such an order.

---

[78] This provision was inserted by the draft Companies Amendment Bill, 2010.

[79] Unless the reason for its removal is that the company's registration has been transferred to a foreign jurisdiction as contemplated in s 82(5). This provision was inserted by the draft Companies Amendment Bill, 2010.

[80] See s 83(1).

[81] See s 83(2).

[82] *Ex parte Sprawson: In re Hebron Diamond Mining Syndicate* Ltd 1914 TPD 458.

[83] Section 83(4).

[84] Presumably after the steps set out in s 82(1) and (2) have occurred.

[85] Op cit n 20 at 4–172.

[86] See s 83(4)*(b)*.

CHAPTER 20

INSIDER TRADING AND MARKET MANIPULATION

Richard Jooste and Rehana Cassim*

20.1	INSIDER TRADING	835
	20.1.1 General	835
	20.1.2 Common law	839
	(a) Directors' fiduciary duty	839
	(b) Do directors owe fiduciary duties to shareholders?	839
	(c) Directors' liability on the basis of misrepresentation	843
	20.1.3 Legislation	844
	20.1.4 The Securities Services Act 36 of 2004	846
	(a) General	846
	(b) 'Inside information' and 'insider'	847
	(i) Specific or precise information	847
	(ii) Which has not been made public	848
	(iii) Obtained or learned as an insider	849
	(iv) If it were made public would be likely to have a material effect on the price or value of any security listed on a regulated market	853
	(c) 'Person'	854
	(d) 'Securities' and 'regulated market'	857
	(e) Defences	859
	(f) Criminal liability	862
	(i) The 'dealing' offence	862
	(ii) The offence of dealing on behalf of someone else	867
	(iii) The 'disclosure' offence	868
	(iv) The 'encouraging' or 'discouraging' offence	870
	(v) Penalty	871
	(g) Civil liability	872
	(i) The rationale for civil liability under the Securities Services Act	872
	(ii) Bases of civil liability	872
	(iii) Interest	874
	(iv) Penalty	875
	(v) Joint and several liability	875

---

* Richard Jooste authored section 20.1 and Rehanna Cassim authored section 20.2.

	(vi)	Determination of profit made or loss avoided......	876
	(vii)	Deposit of monies and recovery of costs..........	876
	(viii)	Distribution of balance.........................	877
	(ix)	Amount the claimant is entitled to	878
	(x)	Protection of common-law rights	879
	(xi)	Criminal penalty taken into account..............	879
	(xii)	Vicarious liability..............................	879
	(xiii)	Powers of directorate in civil proceedings.........	880
(h)	Procedural matters...................................		880
	(i)	Jurisdiction	880
	(ii)	Attachments and interdicts......................	880
	(iii)	Powers and duties of Financial Services Board	880
	(iv)	Composition and functions of the directorate	882
(i)	Confidentiality and sharing of information		884
(j)	Offences committed in terms of section 440F of the 1973 Companies Act and the Insider Trading Act		884

20.2 MARKET MANIPULATION 886
   20.2.1 Introduction 886
   20.2.2 Objective of market manipulation 886
   20.2.3 The rationale of regulating market manipulation............ 887
   20.2.4 The regulation of market manipulation at common law...... 888
   20.2.5 Market manipulation under the Securities Services Act...... 889

(a)	Prohibited trading practices		889
	(i)	Manipulative trading practices...................	890
	(ii)	Committing the offence on behalf of another person, directly or indirectly	890
	(iii)	Participating in a manipulative trading practice	891
	(iv)	Creation of a false or deceptive appearance of trading activity	891
	(v)	Creation of an artificial price for a security	892
	(vi)	Placing orders to buy or sell listed securities.......	892
	(vii)	Proof of market manipulation	893
	(viii)	Regulated market...............................	893
(b)	Deemed prohibited trading practices		894
	(i)	Wash sales.....................................	894
	(ii)	Matched orders.................................	895
	(iii)	Buying orders at successively higher prices and selling at successively lower prices................	895
	(iv)	Marking the close	895
	(v)	Auctioning processes or pre-opening session	896
	(vi)	Market corner..................................	896
	(vii)	Maintaining an artificial price	897
	(viii)	Manipulating devices, schemes or artifices	897
	(ix)	Engaging in any manipulative act, practice or course of business	898

Insider Trading and Market Manipulation

		(c)	False, misleading or deceptive statements, promises and forecasts.	898
			(i) Omission of material facts	899
			(ii) Directly or indirectly	899
			(iii) Materiality	899
			(iv) Past or future performance of a company	900
			(v) Time of assessment of the statement, promise or forecast	900
			(vi) Purpose or motive not relevant	900
			(vii) Fault requirement	901
			(viii) Publication	901
	20.2.6	Defences		901
		(a)	Price stabilisation	901
		(b)	Definitional defences	903
		(c)	Additional defences in other jurisdictions	903
	20.2.7	Penalties		905
		(a)	A fine or imprisonment	905
		(b)	Administrative penalty	906
		(c)	Absence of a statutory derivative civil remedy	906

20.1 INSIDER TRADING

20.1.1 General

The use of the terms 'insider trading' and 'insider dealing' is misleading these days. The terms are used to refer to the sale and purchase of a company's securities by persons associated with the company, known as 'insiders', who are in possession of 'price-sensitive' information not generally available and gained as a result of that association. The law relating to insider trading used to be an aspect of the law that governed the conduct of the directors and officers of companies. Today, however, the approach is to regulate all trading on 'inside information', not only by 'insiders', but also by persons to whom insiders have passed on insider information, known as 'secondary insiders' or 'tippees', and persons who have otherwise wrongfully gained possession of such information. It is therefore now more correct to speak, not of 'insider trading', but of 'trading on inside information'.[1] However, for the sake of brevity we will refer to 'insider trading' in this chapter.

There are various arguments in favour of outlawing insider trading.[2]

First, it is argued that insiders are in a position of trust. They should therefore not to be permitted to abuse that position to benefit themselves, especially at the cost of the beneficiaries of that trust, namely, the shareholders. It is argued that today 'commercial morality' rejects the contention that the use of such informa-

---

[1] See SM Luiz 'Prohibition against trading on insider information: the saga continues' (1990) 2 *SA Merc LJ* 328 at 330. See MS Blackman et al *Commentary on the Companies Act* vol 1 (2002) (Revision service 7, 2010) at 5–376.

[2] See Blackman et al op cit n 1.

tion for personal gain is a normal benefit of those closely associated with a company.[3]

It has been contended that underlying the concept of insider trading is the fiduciary relationship between the insider and his or her company. This relationship underpins the misappropriation theory that the insider's wrong is his or her misappropriation of the information, ie the insider's breach of the fiduciary duty he or she owes to his or her company not to use its confidential information for his or her own purposes.[4] The wrongfulness of trading by persons who have obtained inside information from insiders, ie 'tippees', can be fitted within this theory: the tippee, too, trades on misappropriated information. So, too, can the use of information misappropriated by other means, for example, espionage or theft, be brought within the prohibition. Clearly, the misappropriation theory also provides a basis for the imposition of criminal liability and, since the wrong is a wrong done to the company, for rendering the insider liable to his or her company. But, because the theory merely provides a basis for rendering the insider's conduct wrongful in regard to his or her company, it provides no basis for rendering the insider liable to those with whom he or she deals or, indeed, for rendering the insider either criminally or civilly liable where he or she is permitted by the company to trade on such information. The theory's deficiencies 'follow from the indirect way in which it attempts to protect persons trading in shares, viz by enforcing the insider's wrong to his company'.[5]

For insider trading to constitute a wrong to the persons with whom the insider trades, this must be because the insider has a duty to disclose the inside information to them.[6] Such a duty can arise from a fiduciary relationship existing between the insider and those persons. At least in certain circumstances, the directors and officers of a company owe fiduciary duties to their company's shareholders.[7] But this imposes a duty to disclose only when the insider purchases shares; the imposition of fiduciary duties owed to the purchasers of the company's shares (ie the eventual shareholders) is more problematic. Regarding tippers it has been submitted:

> A further difficulty arises in regard to tippees. To render the tippee's conduct wrongful, he must be clothed with the fiduciary duty owed by the insider to the persons with whom he deals.[8] Such fiduciary relationships do serve an important purpose in the case of closely held

---

[3] Blackman et al op cit n 1; Louis Loss 'The fiduciary concept as applied to trading by corporate insiders in the United States' (1970) 33 *MLR* 34. The Van Wyk de Vries Commission (*Commission of Enquiry into the Companies Act* Main Report (RP 45 of 1970) at para 44.57 said: 'If witnesses have differed in regard to the method to be employed, they were all agreed on one point, namely, that insider dealing is so morally reprehensible that it should be made an offence.'

[4] See Blackman et al op cit n 1 at 5–376; *US v Newman* 664 F 2d 12 (1981), affd 722 F 2d 729 (1981), cert denied 464 US 863 (1983); *US v Carpenter* 791 F 2d 1024 (1986), affd 108 S CT 316 (1987).

[5] See Blackman et al op cit n 1 at 5–376–1.

[6] Ibid.

[7] Ibid. In the USA, the existence of such a relationship, with its concomitant duty to disclose, would now seem to be the rationale for determining whether insider trading is wrongful in terms of rule 10b-5 (promulgated by the Securities and Exchange Commission under s 10(*b*) of the Securities Exchange Act of 1934): see *Chiarella v US* 445 US 222 (1980); *Dirks v SEC* 436 US 646 (1983).

[8] In *Dirks v SEC* (supra) at 659–62 it was held: '[T]he tippee's duty to disclose or abstain is derived from [the] insider's duty . . . [T]he test is whether the insider personally will benefit, directly or

companies and management buy-outs, where the confidentiality of the information should not extend so far as to prohibit its disclosure by the directors and officers of a company to the sellers and purchasers of its shares. But in the case of shares traded on the stock exchange there is usually no question of any relaxation of the duty of confidentiality owed to the company. Thus the imposition of these fiduciary duties renders the theory incoherent. The assumption is, of course, that the insider will not disclose, because that would defeat his purpose. But it is a curious duty that serves its purpose only when breached. For, if the insider were to disclose, he would be in breach of duty to his company not to disclose its confidential information, and he would make the other party to the transaction a tippee. Furthermore, the person who happens to deal with the insider becomes a privileged trader. Unlike other persons who trade in the company's shares, he will be able to resile from the contract and claim damages.[9]

A second argument against insider trading is that:

> [I]nsider trading is harmful to the company. It is an incentive to managers to manipulate prices (eg by the timing of releases or withholding of information); it diverts managers from performing their duties to the company; and it enables managers to minimise their losses at times of stress for the company and, consequently, their incentive to avoid 'flops' by the company is lessened. What is more, insider trading undermines the company's reputation of integrity, which is, among other things, essential to its ability to raise capital.[10]

A third argument is that:

> [A]lthough there are uncertainties and undoubted elements of chance inherent in the buying and selling of shares, the insider (or person with insider information) ought not to be in a position of ascendancy over the outsider, for his ascendancy is not attributable to any industry or merit that might otherwise justify it. Fairness, it is argued, requires equality of opportunity and the inherent unfairness of the practice is reason for outlawing it.[11]

A fourth argument is the argument that trading on inside information deters investors. It is, in fact, now generally accepted that the reason for prohibiting insider trading is the inherent unfairness of the practice,[12] 'with the consequent corrosive effect that it has on confidence in the market in shares'.

Insider trading is perceived by its opponents as harmful to the integrity of the securities market because it adversely affects the public's confidence in that market. The most important function of the securities market is to act as a medium for channelling capital into economic development. If it is to fulfil this function, the investor must have faith in the integrity of the market. By undermining the integrity of the market, insider trading renders it inefficient and is, therefore, harmful to the economy as a whole. Thus the perceived harm is not so much harm to particular persons, but harm to the integrity of the market itself.[13] While insider

---

indirectly, from his disclosure. Absent some personal gain, there has been no breach of duty to stockholders. Absent a breach by the insider, there is no derivative breach [by the tippee].'

[9] Blackman et al op cit n 1 at 5–377.
[10] Ibid.
[11] Blackman et al op cit n 1 at 5–378. Thus in *SEC v Texas Gulf Sulphur Co* (401 F 2d 833 (1968) 851–2), Waterman J said: '... all investors should have equal access to the rewards of participation in securities transactions ... all members of the investing public should be subject to identical market risks.'
[12] See, eg *SEC v Texas Gulf Sulphur Co* 401 F 2d 833 (1968) 851–2, cert denied 394 US 97 (1969).
[13] *SEC v Texas Gulf Sulphur Co* (supra).

trading puts information into the market, the benefit of increased efficiency is outweighed by harm caused at an even more fundamental level.

This rationale calls for all trading on inside information (ie not only trading by insiders) to be made a criminal offence. It renders it unnecessary to impose a duty to disclose on the person trading on inside information. It also renders unnecessary reliance on some connection between that person and the company whose shares he or she trades. Although the offence involves the use of information derived from within the company, it is the use of the information, and not some connection between the person who uses it and the company, that constitutes the offence. The confidentiality of the undisclosed price-sensitive information serves, not to render unlawful its use, but to identify the price-sensitive information that may not be lawfully used. Hence the change in wording from 'insider trading' to what is more appropriately referred to as 'trading on inside information'.[14]

Some have argued that insider dealing ought not to be outlawed:

> In broad terms, the proponents of insider trading argue that insider trading improves market efficiency. They argue that insider trading speeds up the accurate pricing of securities, thus enhancing the economy's allocation of capital investment and minimising the volatility of security prices. They also argue that insider trading is a justifiable and efficient way of remunerating managers for having unearthed the inside information. The contention is that allowing insider trading benefits the firm and therefore society because of the incentive it creates to be innovative.[15]

The leader in criticising the outlawing of insider trading has been Professor HG Manne.[16] In summary,[17] he argued that no one is harmed by insider trading. The long-term investor, as opposed to speculators, will not trade on possible short-term changes in the price of the company's shares. The campaign against insider trading is, he argued, a self-righteous, holy war against sin. Insider trading, he argued, is justified as compensation to the entrepreneurs of an enterprise. Restrictions on such trading deters both people from becoming managers of companies and management from investing in their own company. What is more, the insider's relationship to the seller or purchaser of shares is not in any sense akin to that of a trustee towards his or her beneficiary. No legislation can ensure equality of bargaining position between those engaged in share transactions: the risk of the other party having more knowledge is an element of every share transaction. The stock exchange is (itself) an information exchange in which a monetary value is placed on information. Insider trading therefore produces an efficient market — one which at any point in time reflects the best possible information available. Insider trading influences the price of stock in the right direction, adding to market efficiency. In other words, insider trading results in an efficient stock market — a market free of violent fluctuations in prices where there is a continuity of trans-

---

[14] *SEC v Texas Gulf Sulphur Co* (supra); see also 20.1.1.
[15] *SEC v Texas Gulf Sulphur Co* (supra).
[16] See Manne *Insider Trading on the Stock Market* (1966); and for a discussion of Manne's views, see Painter *The Federal Securities Code and Corporate Disclosure* (1979); see also French & Rider 'Should insider trading be regulated? Some initial consideration' (1978) 95 *SALJ* 79; Hetherington 'Insider trading and the logic of law' (1967) *Wis LR* 720; Schotland 'Unsafe at any price: A reply to Manne, Insider trading and the stock market' (1967) 53 *Va LR* 1425.
[17] Blackman et al op cit n 1 at 5–379.

Insider Trading and Market Manipulation

actions and in which prices are as near as possible to levels that reflect their actual value. Therefore the interests of the investor and the economy as a whole are best served by permitting insider trading.

20.1.2 Common law

(a) Directors' fiduciary duty

If directors use confidential information for their own purposes, this is a breach of their fiduciary duty[18] and makes them liable to account to their company for any profits they may have made. Thus, if a director uses confidential price-sensitive information to buy or sell his or her company's shares, the director, it appears, will be liable to the company for any profit he or she has made. This is so even though the company may not have suffered any loss.[19]

The company can also claim profits from 'tippees' of a director if the 'tippees' knew of the director's breach of duty. The director and the tippee will be jointly liable to the company.[20] It would seem, however, that the company has no action against the director for the profits made by the tippee.[21]

(b) Do directors owe fiduciary duties to shareholders?

It has been generally accepted for a long time that directors stand in a fiduciary relationship to the company alone,[22] and therefore owe no fiduciary duties to their company's shareholders individually.[23] It follows that, where a director trades on

---

[18] See chapter 12: The Duties and the Liability of Directors.

[19] Such an action was recognised in the US case of *Diamond v Oreamuno* 24 NY 2d 494 (1969).

[20] Jones says ('Unjust enrichment and the fiduciary's duty of loyalty' (1968) 84 *LQR* 499–500) that, if the tippees knew of the director's breach of loyalty, they and he will be jointly and severally liable to the company. In *Schein v Chasen* 478 F 2d 817 (2d Cir 1973), where the action was brought not by the company, but by way of a derivative action to enforce the company's rights, the Second Circuit, applying Florida law, concluded that Florida would not only accept *Diamond* (supra) but would extend its rationale to tippees of corporate insiders and, even though they had not traded, to the insiders on the ground that they had acted 'in a common enterprise to misuse confidential corporate information'. But the US Supreme Court (*Lehman Bros v Schein* 416 US 386 (1974)) set aside the decision and remanded the matter to the Florida Supreme Court, which held that 'actual damages to the corporation must be alleged ... to substantiate a stockholders' derivative action' (*Schein v Chasen* 313 So 2d 739 (1975)).

[21] *Regal (Hastings) Ltd v Gulliver* [1967] 2 AC 134, [1942] 1 All ER 378 (HL). In *Regal's* case, which concerned profits made by directors, but not from insider trading, an unsuccessful attempt was made to hold a director liable for profits made by third parties. The House of Lords held that the company's managing director, who had bought the shares as a nominee for third parties, was not liable to account to his company for their profits: for neither the shares nor the profits ever belonged to the managing director. But see Jones op cit n 20 at 498, who says that, if one of the objects of the inexorable rule as to profits is to deter fiduciaries from following the example of the unfaithful and the dishonest, it may not be unreasonable, on the particular facts of the case, to make the dishonest fiduciary liable not only for any profits he or she has made but for the profits which his or her breach has enabled others to make.

[22] *Re Wincham Shipbuilding, Boiler, and Salt Co (Poole, Jackson and Whyte's Case)* (1878) 9 ChD 322 at 328–9 (CA); *Percival v Wright* [1902] 2 Ch 421; *Kuwait Asia Bank EC v National Mutual Life Nominees Ltd* [1991] 1 AC 187 (PC) at 217–19; [1990] 3 All ER 404 at 420–1 (PC). See JSA Fourie 'Vertrouenspligte en intrakorporatiewe verhoudings' 1985 *TRW* 119 at 133–8.

[23] *Percival v Wright* (supra); *Pergamon Press Ltd v Maxwell* [1970] 2 All ER 809.

inside information to purchase shares from one of the company's shareholders without making full disclosure, the shareholder would have no action against the director on the basis of breach of fiduciary duty.

Percival v Wright[24] is almost always cited as establishing that directors do not owe a fiduciary duty to their shareholders, and so do not have to disclose any inside information they have to shareholders when dealing with them. A shareholder therefore has no action. The case involved an action to set aside a sale of shares to directors. The plaintiff shareholders approached the directors and offered to sell their shares to them. The directors accepted the offer and purchased the shares, without disclosing that they were negotiating to sell the company's undertaking to an outsider at a higher price per share. The takeover was never completed, but on ascertaining that these negotiations had taken place, the shareholders brought an action to set aside the sale on the ground that the purchasers, because they were directors, ought to have informed them of the negotiations. Swinfen Eady J held that the purchasing directors had been under no obligation to disclose to their vendor shareholders the negotiations which ultimately proved abortive. The contrary view would place directors in a most invidious position, as they could not buy or sell shares without disclosing negotiations, a premature disclosure of which might well be against the best interests of the company. He was of the opinion that directors are not in that position.

He went on to say that there was:

> [N]o question of unfair dealing since the directors had not approached the shareholders with the view to obtaining their shares — the shareholders had approached the directors, and named the price at which they were desirous of selling.

Percival v Wright has been criticised and the view has been taken that the case 'has had a remarkable career for a lower court decision', and that the decision in that case elevated 'the corporate ghost (the *persona ficta*) over the flesh and blood owners of the company' and 'is a monument to the ability of lawyers to hypnotise themselves with their own creations'.[25]

Levin suggests that, properly understood, *Percival v Wright* is no authority for the general proposition that there is no fiduciary relationship between directors and shareholders; regarding it in this light would be taking the decision much further than it in fact went.[26] Also, in *Sage Holdings Ltd v The Unisec Group Ltd*[27] Goldstone J referred, with apparent approval, to a passage in Cilliers and Benade,[28] where:

- it is pointed out that in *Percival v Wright* it was stated that persons negotiating with directors over shares must know that the directors possess special knowledge of corporate affairs,
- it is asserted that 'the dominant consideration in the judgment was that there was no unfair dealing on the part of the directors', since the directors did not

---

[24] [1902] 2 Ch 421.
[25] Louis Loss op cit n 3 at 40–1; and see for example Fourie op cit n 22 at 133–7.
[26] See RD Levin 'Insider trading' (1967) 30 *THRHR* 135 at 140.
[27] 1982 (1) SA 337 (W), aff 1983 (2) SA 485 (T).
[28] *Company Law* 3 ed 264.

approach the members (the members approached them) and the transaction was concluded at the members' price, and
- it is argued that, 'whatever the interpretation placed on this judgment in England, the judgment ought not to be interpreted so widely by a South African court as to absolve directors from all responsibility towards the buyer or seller of the shares of their company'.

As has been stated,[29] this is probably not correct. In *Percival v Wright* counsel for the shareholders accepted that the defendants would have been under no duty to disclose 'information acquired in the ordinary course of management', for example 'a large casual profit, the discovery of a new vein, or the prospect of a good dividend'. He argued, however, that at the commencement of the takeover negotiations the directors 'became trustees for sale for the benefit of the company and the shareholders, and could not purchase the interest of an ultimate beneficiary without disclosing those negotiations'. In other words, it was merely argued that the directors owed the company's shareholders a fiduciary duty in, and only in, this very specific situation. And even that proposition was rejected by the court. The better and more generally accepted view is that *Percival v Wright* did indeed decide that a director as such does not stand in a fiduciary relationship to the company's shareholders; but that the decision is taken too far when it is said to be authority for the proposition that directors never stand in a fiduciary relationship to the shareholders.

To put it differently:[30]

> *Percival v Wright* merely established that the relationship of director and shareholder does not, as such, or without more, give rise to a fiduciary relationship.[31] Hence, while *Percival v Wright* is accepted as authority for the general proposition that directors owe fiduciary duties to the company alone, from this proposition it of course 'does not follow that the office of director of a company, for that reason alone, releases a person from what would otherwise be a fiduciary duty'.[32]

It is therefore accepted that directors may place themselves in a fiduciary relation-

---

[29] Blackman et al op cit n 1 at 5–383.
[30] See Blackman et al op cit n 1 at 5–384.
[31] *Winthrop Investments Ltd v Winns Ltd* [1975] 2 NSWLR 666 at 680 CA (NSW); *Coleman v Myers* [1977] 2 NZLR 225 CA (NZ); *Re Chez Nico (Restaurants) Ltd* [1992] BCLC 192; *Glandon Pty Ltd v Strata Consolidated Pty Ltd* (1993) 11 ACSR 543 CA (NSW).
[32] *Per* Cripps JA in *Glandon Pty Ltd v Strata Consolidated Pty Ltd* (supra) at 555–6, referring to *Coleman v Myers* (supra), where Woodhouse J said: 'In my opinion it is not the law that anybody holding the office of director of a limited liability company is for that reason alone to be released from what otherwise would be regarded as a fiduciary responsibility owed to those in the position of shareholders of the same company.' In *Platt v Platt* [1999] 2 BCLC 745 at 755–6 it was said that 'the fact that the relationship between director and shareholder does not of itself give rise to a fiduciary duty does not prevent such an obligation arising when the circumstances require it'. The duties that arise from such fiduciary relationships depend on the circumstances giving rise to them. To describe someone as a fiduciary, without more, is meaningless without further analysis, for it is the nature of the fiduciary relationship that justifies the particular fiduciary obligations attaching to it: see, eg *Re Coomber, Coomber v Coomber* [1911] 1 Ch 723 at 728–9 (CA); *Hospital Products Ltd v United States Surgical Corporation* (1984) 156 CLR 41 (HC of A); *Re Goldcorp Exchange Ltd* [1994] 2 All ER 806 at 821 (PC); *Commissioner of Taxation v B & G Plant Hire Pty Ltd* (1994) 14 ACSR 283 at 291 (HC of A).

ship to the shareholders individually by acting as agents for them,[33] or by representing to the shareholders that they are acting as agents for them.[34]

Apart from agency, a fiduciary relationship between directors and shareholders may arise in the special circumstances of the case.[35] The general principle here is that, although a limited company is a legal entity with a personality in law of its own, there is room in company law for recognition of the fact that behind it or among it the members may have rights, expectations and obligations *inter se*, which are not necessarily submerged in the company structure.[36] In such a case, some of the principles applicable to the relationship between partners come into play, even though the shareholders of the company concerned are not necessarily found to have been in substance partners.[37] 'Our law thus recognises that in the relationship between shareholders in a company there may at one and the same time be a formal pecuniary nexus and also an *intuitus personae*, a special relationship of mutual personal trust.'[38] In *Coleman v Myers*[39] it was held that a fiduciary relationship had arisen between directors and shareholders because of the family character of the company, the position of the directors in the company and their families, their high degree of inside knowledge, and the way in which they went about the takeover and the persuasion of shareholders.

It is 'generally accepted that this is a developing area of the law;[40] and there is an indication that our courts may be prepared to depart from the rule in *Percival v Wright*'.[41]

---

[33] *Allen v Hyatt* (1914) 30 TLR 444 (PC); and see *Briess v Woolley* [1954] AC 333; [1954] 1 All ER 909 (HL); *Coleman v Myers* (supra); *Glandon Pty Ltd v Strata Consolidated Pty Ltd* (supra).

[34] *Allen v Hyatt* (supra).

[35] *Coleman v Myers* (supra); *Re Chez Nico (Restaurants) Ltd* (supra) at 208. In *Glandon Pty Ltd v Strata Consolidated Pty Ltd* (supra).

[36] See *Ebrahimi v Westbourne Galleries Ltd* [1973] AC 360 at 379; [1972] 2 All ER 492 at 500 (HL); *Erasmus v Pentamed Investments (Pty) Ltd* 1982 (1) SA 178 (W) 181–3; *Rentekor (Pty) Ltd v Rheeder and Berman* 1988 (4) SA 469 (T) 500; *Tjospomie Boerdery (Pty) Ltd v Drakensberg Botteliers (Pty) Ltd* 1989 (4) SA 31 (T); *Hulett v Hulett* 1992 (4) SA 291 (A) 307.

[37] *Rentekor (Pty) Ltd v Rheeder and Berman* 1988 (4) SA 469 (T) 500. 'Partnership is, of course, a contractual relationship between natural persons. However, it does not follow that a company, and in particular a family company which is intended to retain that character, cannot enter into a relationship which resembles that of a partnership in imposing a reciprocal duty of *uberrima fides* on the parties to the relationship', *per* Stegmann J in *Tjospomie Boerdery (Pty) Ltd v Drakensberg Botteliers (Pty) Ltd* (supra) at 48. See also *Hulett v Hulett* (supra).

[38] *Per* Kriegler J in *Rentekor (Pty) Ltd v Rheeder and Berman* (supra).

[39] [1977] 2 NZLR 225 CA (NZ), noted by Barry AK Rider '*Percival v Wright — per incuriam*' (1977) 40 *MLR* 470; *Brunninghausen v Glavanics* (1999) 32 ACSR 294 at 303 CA (NSW); *Re Chez Nico (Restaurants) Ltd* [1992] BCLC 192 at 208; *Glandon Pty Ltd v Strata Consolidated Pty Ltd* (1993) 11 ACSR 543 CA (NSW).

[40] Blackman et al op cit n 1 at 5–389. See *Sage Holdings Ltd v The Unisec Group Ltd* 1982 (1) SA 337 (W); *Re Chez Nico (Restaurants) Ltd* (supra); *Glandon Pty Ltd v Strata Consolidated Pty Ltd* (supra); *Peskin v Anderson* [2000] 2 BCLC 1 at 12.

[41] See *Sage Holdings Ltd v The Unisec Group Ltd* (supra) at 366, affd 1983 (2) SA 485 (T), in which Goldstone J referred with apparent approval to a passage in Cilliers & Benade op cit n 28 at 264, where it was said that, '[w]hatever the interpretation placed on this judgment in England, the judgment ought not to be interpreted so widely by a South African Court as to absolve directors from all responsibility towards the buyer or seller of the shares of their company'. In *Brunninghausen v*

In the UK, in *Peskin v Anderson*[42] it was said by the court that it was satisfied, 'both as a matter of principle and in the light of the state of the authorities, that *Percival v Wright* is good law in the sense that a director of a company has no general fiduciary duty to shareholders', but added that it was 'also satisfied that, in appropriate and specific circumstances, a director can be under a fiduciary duty to a shareholder'. However, it considered that 'as a general proposition, a director's primary fiduciary duty is to the company':

> To hold that [a director] has some sort of general fiduciary duty to shareholders *(a)* would involve placing an unfair, unrealistic and uncertain burden on a director and *(b)* would present him frequently with a position where his two conflicting duties, namely his undoubted fiduciary duty to the company and his alleged fiduciary duty to shareholders, would be in conflict.

The following further points have been noted:

> [E]ven if the courts were now to hold that directors do, as such, owe a fiduciary duty to their shareholders, this would neither *(a)* give an action to a non-shareholder who purchases shares from a director who sells on the strength of inside information, nor *(b)* would it serve to place a duty to disclose upon an outsider (a 'tippee') who buys or sells shares on the strength of insider information given to him by a director. And, finally, in transactions conducted on the stock exchange it will normally be impossible for a shareholder to link up a sale or purchase by him with a purchase or sale by a director. However, generally the listings requirements and rules of a stock exchange require disclosure of all price sensitive information (save for limited exceptions) and are given force of law under the Securities Services Act, 2004.[43]

(c) Directors' liability on the basis of misrepresentation

A director dealing personally with a seller or a buyer seems, at least in most cases, to be under a duty to disclose any inside information that he or she may possess. This is based on the principle that, although at common law there is no general duty on contracting parties to volunteer information, there is a duty to disclose where a contract is characterised by the involuntary reliance of the one party on the other for information material to his or her decision.[44] In practice, however, this can be applied effectively only to so-called 'face-to-face' transactions and, as most share transactions are not face to face, but are transacted anonymously through the stock exchange, the effectiveness of the principle is limited. It is doubtful whether such a duty ever exists in the case of dealings on a stock exchange.[45] However, generally the listings requirements and rules of a stock exchange will require disclosure by the company of price-sensitive information.

Glavanics (supra) the Court of Appeal (Handley JA) of New South Wales declined to follow *Percival v Wright*.

[42] [2000] 2 BCLC 1 at 14.

[43] Blackman et al op cit n 1 at 5–393.

[44] See *Pretorius v Natal South Sea Investment Trust Ltd* 1965 (3) SA 410 (W) 417; *Meskin v Anglo-American Corp of SA Ltd* 1968 (4) SA 793 (W); Van Wyk de Vries Commission op cit n 3 paras 44–51; MA Millner 'Fraudulent non-disclosure' (1957) 74 *SALJ* 177.

[45] Thus, Millner op cit n 44 at 189 says: 'Stock Exchange transactions ... have a pronounced speculative character well recognised by both buyer and seller and heightened by the anonymity of the principal and the complete absence of preliminary negotiations. There is a common understand-

20.1.3 Legislation

In 1952 s 70*nov* was introduced[46] into the Companies Act 46 of 1926, which provided that every company should keep a register in which the number, description and amount of shares or debentures held by each director should be registered, and changes in such holdings are recorded together with the date and price or other consideration.

The provisions of s 70*nov* proved ineffective, however, and, on the recommendation of the Van Wyk de Vries Commission,[47] new provisions were introduced in the Companies Act 61 of 1973 (hereafter 'the 1973 Companies Act'). The Van Wyk de Vries Commission,[48] finding that the witnesses before it were unanimous in their condemnation of insider trading in all its forms, explored the various techniques to inhibit the practice. The Commission was of the opinion that the company suffers no harm as a result of insider trading and therefore, if some form of control was to be introduced, it should not be done in the area of the relationship between the director and his or her company.[49] On the other hand, the sellers and the purchasers of shares might well suffer prejudice. Since it has been held that directors owe their shareholders no fiduciary duties, the insider owes the seller of shares no fiduciary duty of disclosure.[50] However, the general law of contract imposes a duty of disclosure where there is:

> ... involuntary reliance of the one party on the frank disclosure of certain facts necessarily lying within the exclusive knowledge of the other such that, in fair dealing, the former's right to have such information communicated to him would be mutually recognised by honest men in the circumstances.[51]

As to unlisted shares, the Commission trusted that the courts would develop the law along these lines.[52] However, the Commission pointed out that, in the case of listed shares, the parties to the transaction are (exceptional cases apart) anonymous and at times it is impossible to determine the identities of the seller and the purchaser in relation to a particular contract of sale of shares. Accepting then that (with rare exceptions) there is no civil remedy available for the victim of insider trading in the case of listed shares, the Commission concluded that insider dealing in respect of such shares should be made an offence carrying a substantial penalty.[53] The Commission also considered that directors should be prohibited

---

ing in such cases that each is content to trust exclusively to his own judgment about the shares dealt in, no matter how unequal the knowledge of the parties may in fact be.'

[46] By s 49 of the Companies Amendment Act 46 of 1952.
[47] Op cit n 3.
[48] Ibid.
[49] Op cit n 3 para 44.50. The Commission said that, should a director by his inside dealing cause loss to his company, other remedies would be available for compensating the company.
[50] Paragraph 44.51.
[51] Referring here to *Pretorius v Natal South Sea Investment Trust Ltd* 1965 (3) SA 410 (W) 417. The Commission (referring to *Percival v Wright* [1902] 2 Ch 421) accepted that directors owe their shareholders no fiduciary duties, and that therefore the insider owes the seller of shares no fiduciary duty of disclosure: para 44.51.
[52] Paragraph 44.60.
[53] Paragraph 44.54–60. Although the Commission recommended only that such trading be made an offence, it was nevertheless of the opinion that 'if insider dealing is made an offence, a victim who is

from dealing in options to buy or sell listed shares in their company or its associated companies.[54] The legislature adopted the Commission's recommendations, but with one important exception: s 233 of the 1973 Companies Act made insider dealing in all shares (and not merely listed shares) an offence.[55] In addition, s 230 required a public company to keep a register of the material interests of its directors, officers and persons in any shares and debentures of the company.[56] Section 224 prohibited a director (including a person in accordance with whose directions the directors of the company are accustomed to act) from dealing in options in respect of the listed shares or debentures of his or her company, his or her company's subsidiary or holding company, or a subsidiary of his or her company's holding company.

In South Africa, it was thought that the provisions originally contained in the 1973 Companies Act had proved to be ineffective. In 1989, the Securities Regulation Panel (SRP) was established and empowered not only to make rules to regulate and investigate takeovers and mergers, but also to investigate cases of suspected insider trading.[57] The provisions prohibiting insider trading[58] were repealed, together with the prohibition of dealing in options by directors. For those provisions, a new prohibition was substituted in s 440F and the penalties were increased.[59] This new prohibition, which was based on the US Rule 10b–5 adopted by the US Securities and Exchange Commission under s 10*(b)* of the Securities Exchange Act of 1934, was subjected to a good deal of criticism[60] and was never put into force. Instead, in 1990 a new s 440F was enacted.[61]

The new s 440F, as well as the effectiveness of the SRP in policing insider trading, proved to be inadequate.[62] In January 1999, new provisions regulating

---

able to establish that he was transacting with the delinquent director would be able and entitled to institute a civil action against the director': para 44.59.

[54] Paragraph 44.43.

[55] For comments on that section, see BAK Rider & HL Ffrench *The Regulation of Insider Trading* (1979) 396–9; Derek Botha 'Control of insider trading in South Africa: a comparative analysis' (1991) 3 *SA Merc LJ* 1.

[56] The information that had to be entered in the register (kept at the registered office and open for public inspection) in terms of s 230 was the following: *(a)* the description and number or amount of shares or debentures held by each director, officer or 'person'; *(b)* the nature and extent of any material interest whatever, direct or indirect, held by each, directly or indirectly, in respect of such shares or debentures; *(c)* in chronological order, any change (including any contract for a change) in the holding or in the interest of each in the shares or debentures and specifying the consideration; and *(d)* the date on which each entry is made.

[57] Companies Amendment Act 78 of 1989.

[58] Sections 229–233 of the 1973 Companies Act.

[59] Section 4*(b)* of the Companies Amendment Act 1989.

[60] See RD Jooste 'Insider dealing in South Africa — the criminal aspects' (1990) 4 (1) *De Ratione* 21.

[61] Section 3 of the Companies Second Amendment Act 69 of 1990. This Act extensively amended the provisions introduced by the 1989 Amendment Act. The original insider trading provisions provisions in s 440F (which, as we have said, had never been brought into force) were scrapped and entirely different provisions were substituted for them in s 440F of the 1973 Companies Act.

[62] See RD Jooste 'Insider dealing in South Africa' (1990) 107 *SALJ* 588; Luiz op cit n 1; Botha op cit n 55; R du Plessis 'Binnekennistransaksies: 'n evaluasie van die huidige statutêre bepalings' (1995) 7 *SA Merc LJ* 19.

insider trading were introduced by the Insider Trading Act 135 of 1998 (hereafter 'the Insider Trading Act'). Section 17 of the Insider Trading Act repealed s 440F of the 1973 Companies Act, and s 11 replaced the Securities Regulation Panel (SRP) with the Financial Services Board (FSB) as the insider trading watchdog.

The Insider Trading Act[63] was motivated by South Africa's reintegration into the international financial markets and the government's desire to create an environment conducive to foreign investment.[64] The criminal provisions of this Act relied heavily on the UK's Criminal Justice Act of 1993. The civil liability provisions of this Act seemed to reflect some reliance on US experience and regulation.

The Insider Trading Act was flawed in a number of respects[65] and was repealed by the Securities Services Act 36 of 2004 (hereafter 'the Securities Services Act'). The insider trading provisions of the Securities Services Act[66] are an attempt to improve on the Insider Trading Act, but flaws remain and new ones have been created.

20.1.4 The Securities Services Act 36 of 2004

(a) General

As stated above, trading on the strength of inside information is now governed by provisions of the Securities Services Act,[67] which represents the latest effort to curb the practice. The Securies Services Act,[68] like the Insider Trading Act, was motivated by South Africa's reintegration into the international financial markets and the government's desire to create an environment conducive to foreign investment.[69]

The provisions of the Securities Services Act, like the Insider Trading Act, considerably broaden the scope of offences related to insider trading by prohibiting three kinds of conduct: dealing, encouraging or discouraging dealing, and improper disclosure or 'tipping'. It is not necessary for the prosecution to show that the alleged offender had dealt on the basis of unpublished price-sensitive information. It need simply be proved that the offender had known that he or she was in possession of 'inside information' (as defined in s 72 of the Securities Services Act) and that he or she had dealt in the relevant securities. The provisions further make it an offence for any person who knows that he or she has inside information to encourage or cause another person to deal, or to discourage or stop

---

[63] The reasons for placing the insider trading provisions provisions in a separate statute are set out in Chapter 4 of the Final Report by the King Task Group into Insider Trading Legislation, October 1997.

[64] See King Task Group Final Report op cit n 63 at para 1.2.

[65] See RD Jooste 'The regulation of insider trading in South Africa — another attempt' (2000) 117 *SALJ* 284; SM Luiz 'Insider trading regulation — if at first you don't succeed . . .' (1999) 11 *SA Merc LJ* 136.

[66] See Chapter VIII.

[67] The insider trading provisions provisions are in Chapter VIII of the Securities Services Act; Rehana Cassim 'Some aspects of insider trading — has the Securities Services Act 36 of 2004 gone too far?' (2007) 19 *SA Merc LJ* 44.

[68] The reasons for placing the insider trading provisions provisions in a separate statute are set out in Chapter 4 of the King Task Group Final Report op cit n 63.

[69] See the King Task Group Final Report op cit n 63 at para 1.2.

a person from dealing, in securities or financial instruments to which the information relates or which are likely to be affected by it. In order to escape liability, the accused can establish one of the defences referred to below (on a balance of probabilities). It is, moreover, also an offence for any person who knows that he or she has inside information to disclose that information to another. The accused will escape this liability if he or she can establish one of the defences referred to.

A major shift from the Insider Trading Act is the fact that liability, both criminal and civil, is no longer confined to natural persons, but has been extended to juristic persons as well as partnerships and trusts.

One of the objectives of the Insider Trading Act was, and the of new insider trading legislation, is to include an effective civil remedy without prejudicing the common-law rights of a person who suffers as a result of the insider trading. Section 77 of the Securities Services Act introduces a 'derivative' civil action which may be instituted by the FSB against persons involved in a contravention of the insider trading provisions. Money awarded to the FSB as a result of such a civil action will be distributed to those individuals affected by insider trading. Generally, the FSB has been given a wide array of powers. In addition, the Directorate of Market Abuse has been established as a committee of the FSB.

(b) 'Inside information' and 'insider'

Section 72 of the Securities Services Act contains definitions of both 'inside information' and 'insider'. It provides, inter alia, that 'inside information':

> means specific or precise information which has not been made public and which—
> *(a)* is obtained or learned as an insider; and
> *(b)* if it were made public would be likely to have a material effect on the price or value of any security listed on a regulated market.

Thus, to qualify as inside information, the information in question:

- must be 'specific or precise',
- must not have been made public,
- must be 'obtained or learned as an insider', and
- if it were made public would be likely to have a material effect on the price or value of any security listed on a regulated market.

(i) Specific or precise information

To qualify as 'inside information' the information must be 'specific or precise'. It appears that information that a takeover bid is going to be made for a company would be 'specific' information. However, it might not be regarded as 'precise' if there was no knowledge of the price to be offered or the exact date on which the announcement of the bid would be made. Similarly, information that a company's profits are in excess of expectation would be specific but not precise, unless the amount of the excess is known. On this argument, it seems that precise information will always be specific.[70] Gower says of the restriction imposed by the use of the words 'specific' or 'precise' in the English Act that:

---
[70] P Davies *Gower's Principles of Modern Company Law* 6 ed (1997) 461.

... the crucial effect of this restriction is that it should relieve directors and senior managers of the company and analysts who have made a special study of the company from falling foul of the legislation simply because they have generalised informational advantages over other investors, arising from their position in the one case and the effort they have exerted on the other. Having a better sense of how well or badly the company is likely to respond to a particular publicly known development does not amount to the possession of precise or specific information.[71]

(ii) Which has not been made public

'Inside information' is information 'which has not been made public'. A deficiency in the legislation prior to the Insider Trading Act was the uncertainty as to when price-sensitive information had been made public. This was determined on the basis of an objective 'reasonable investor' test, ie would a reasonable investor have been aware of the information?[72] Despite the merit of flexibility, the test created uncertainty for the potential dealer, and left the problem to be solved by the courts on a case-by-case basis. The legislator has now attempted to introduce a measure of certainty by adopting the approach of the UK legislation.[73] Without limiting the circumstances in which information shall be regarded as having been made public, s 74(1) of the Securities Services Act stipulates four alternative situations where the information shall be regarded as having been made public. Section 74(2) lists three circumstances where information may still be treated as having been made public despite the circumstances.

Section 74(1) provides that, for the purposes of the definition of 'inside information', information is to be regarded 'as having been made public in circumstances which include, but are not limited to, the following:

(a) when the information is published in accordance with the rules of the relevant regulated market for the purpose of informing clients and their professional advisers;[74]

(b) when the information is contained in records which by virtue of any enactment are open to inspection by the public;

(c) when the information can be readily acquired by those likely to deal in any listed securities —
   (i) to which the information relates; or
   (ii) of an issuer to which the information relates; or

(d) when the information is derived from information which has been made public.[75]

Regarding 74(1)*(a)*, note that the market does not have to have responded to the information. Therefore the moment it is published, dealing is permissible. In terms of 74(1)*(a)*, price-sensitive information contained in the annual financial statements of a public company would thus be regarded as having been made public when lodged with the Registrar of Companies.[76] It appears that this alternative is

---

[71] P Davies *Gower's Principles of Modern Company Law* 6 ed (1997) 461.

[72] See the repealed s 440F(2)*(a)*(ii) and *(b)* of the 1973 Companies Act.

[73] See s 58 of the Criminal Justice Act 1993, Part V.

[74] 'Regulated market' is defined in s 72 as meaning: 'any market, whether domestic or foreign, which is regulated in terms of the laws of the country in which the market conducts business as a market for dealing in securities listed on that market.'

[75] Presumably 'made public' is to be construed in accordance with the rest of s 74 of the Securities Services Act.

[76] See ss 9(1) and 302 of the 1973 Companies Act.

not restricted to public records in South Africa and accordingly public records in other countries also qualify.

In relation to a similar provision in the English legislation, it is stated by Gower:

> ... it is clear that this provision was intended to protect analysts who derive insights into a company's prospects which are not shared by the market generally (so that the analyst is able to out-guess his or her competitors) where those insights are derived from the intensive and intelligent study of information which has been made public. An analyst in this position can deal on the basis of the insights so derived without first disclosing to the market the process of reasoning which has led to the conclusions, even where the disclosure of the reasoning would have a significant impact on the price of the securities dealt in. This seems to be the case even where the analyst intends to and does publish the recommendations after the dealing, ie there is what is called 'front running' of the research.[77]

Section 74(2) then lists three circumstances where, despite the fact that one or more of these circumstances might *prima facie* suggest that the information has not been made public, the information may still be regarded as public. Section 74(2) provides that:

> Inside information which would otherwise be regarded as having been made public must still be so regarded even though —
> *(a)* it can be acquired only by persons exercising diligence or observation, or
> *(b)* it is communicated only on payment of a fee; or
> *(c)* it is only published outside the Republic.

With regard to the permissive cases in the UK legislation similar to those in s 74(2),[78] Gower says:[79]

> [T]he situation is, presumably, that the facts described in the subsections do not prevent the court from holding the information to have been made public, but whether the court in a particular prosecution will so hold will depend on the circumstances of the case as a whole.

Although some certainty regarding publication has been created by these provisions, questions still abound. What about information published in a financial journal? Will some financial journals suffice but not others, for example, those freely available on the news-stands, but not those sold on subscription only? Is publication in any one of the official languages sufficient? What about publication on the radio or television (and what if it is late at night)?

(iii) *Obtained or learned as an insider*

The definition of 'inside information' in s 72 speaks of 'information which has not been made public and which *(a)* is obtained or learned as an insider'. Reading 'as an insider' literally, this means that the information is 'an insider' — that is, the non-public information must obtain and learn the information 'as' an insider. This is nonsense, of course. Can one then say that the legislature must have meant 'information which is obtained or learned *by* an insider'? The Afrikaans text reads: ' "binnekennis" inligting wat spesifiek of bepaal is en nie openbaar gemaak is nie

---
[77] Davies op cit n 70 at 462–3.
[78] In the Insider Trading Act there was a fourth circumstance, namely: 'it is communicated to a section of the public and not to the public at large' (s 3(2)(*b*)). This circumstance has been omitted in the present legislation.
[79] Davies op cit n 70 at 462 n 5.

wat *(a)* verkry of te wete gekom is deur 'n binnekenner . . .'. The English text is the signed text.

There is another possible meaning, however. The legislature may have meant 'which is obtained or learned by an insider, as an insider', ie knowledge which was obtained or learned by an insider in his or her capacity as (when acting as) an insider. This alternative interpretation can, however, be dismissed, because the concept of obtaining the information 'as' or 'in the capacity as' an insider is contained in the definition of 'insider'.

Section 72 provides that:

'Insider' means a person who has inside information—
(a) through —
  (i) being a director, employee or shareholder of an issuer of securities listed on a regulated market to which the inside information relates; or
  (ii) having access to such information by virtue of employment, office or profession; or
(b) where such person knows that the direct or indirect source of the information was a person contemplated in paragraph *(a)*.

Thus the definition of 'insider' does not (simply) categorise certain persons (eg directors, officers, etc) as insiders. Rather, it identifies certain persons (usually referred to as 'primary insiders'), ie directors, officers, etc, and then declares them to be 'insiders' if they:

- have inside information, and
- have the information 'through being' a director, officer, etc, or 'through having access' to the information by virtue of their employment, etc. It then adds to this list of insiders the person (usually referred to as a 'secondary insider' or 'tippee') who has acquired inside information from a primary insider.

Thus an insider is a person holding a certain specified office or position who:

- has inside information (as defined), and
- has acquired that information 'through' his or her position (primary insider), or who has acquired the information from, and knows that he or she has acquired it from, a primary insider.

These interconnected definitions of 'inside information' and 'insider' are cumbersome and counter-intuitive. Worse, they are circular. To know whether information is 'inside information' we must know who an 'insider' is; and to know who an 'insider' is, we must know what 'inside information' is. 'Inside information' is (inter alia) information 'which is obtained or learned as [by] an insider'; and an 'insider' is (inter alia) 'an individual who has inside information'. Since the provisions of the Securities Services Act that impose criminal and civil liability turn on the meaning of 'inside information', this Act is fundamentally incoherent. Perhaps something along the following lines was intended:

'inside information' means specific or precise information which has not been made public and which, if it were made public, would be likely to have a material effect on the price or value of any securities or financial instrument.

'insider' means a person who has inside information —
(a) through —

(i) being a director, employee or shareholder of an issuer of securities or financial instruments to which the information relates; or
(ii) having access to such information by virtue of his or her employment, office or profession; and
(b) where such person knows that the direct or indirect source of the information was a person contemplated in paragraph *(a)*.

But then, of course, this is not what the definitions provide. Nor, perhaps, is it what they were intended to provide. In particular (and apart from the problem of circularity), it must be borne in mind that the legislator, it would seem, intended that information should be 'inside information' only if it is not only price-sensitive and non-public, but also possessed by certain specified persons (director, officer, etc) — and that is not the case in the suggested definitions.

It should be noted that the definition of 'insider' refers to a 'person who *has* inside information'. For the purposes of the definition, then, the question whether the individual knows that the information he or she has is 'inside information' is irrelevant. It is, however, relevant (as we shall see) when determining the questions of criminal and civil liability. Then the question turns upon whether the individual *had known* that the information was inside information.

The definition of 'insider' in s 72 of the Securities Services Act is wider in ambit than the legislation prior to the Insider Trading Act, which required the inside information to have been obtained by virtue of a relationship of trust or any other contractual relationship. However, it would seem that the definition of 'insider' is also narrower in ambit, for it no longer includes information obtained through espionage, theft, bribery, fraud, misrepresentation or any other wrongful method.[80]

The definition of 'insider' includes a person who has inside information 'through . . . being a director, employee or shareholder'. The UK legislation in this regard is almost identical,[81] eliciting the following comment in Gower:[82]

> Although it is not entirely clear, it seems that the 'through being' test is simply a 'but for' test. If a junior employee happens to see inside information in the non-public part of the employer's premises, he or she would be within the category of insider, even if the duties of the employment do not involve acquisition of that information. On the other hand, coming across such information in a social context would not make the employee an insider, even though the information related to the worker's employer. In other words, there must be a causal link between the employment and the acquisition of the information, but not in the sense that the information must be acquired in the course of the employee's employment (though the latter remains a possible interpretation of the subsection).

Persons who are insiders through having access to such information by virtue of their employment, office or profession would include lawyers, bankers, auditors, public relations consultants and other professional people. It appears that the person need not have had a connection or relationship with the company when he or she came across the information.[83] A financial analyst who uncovers inside

---
[80] See the repealed s 440F(1) of the 1973 Companies Act.
[81] See s 57(2) of the Criminal Justice Act 1993.
[82] Davies op cit n 70 at 465.
[83] Ibid.

information while researching into the current and future profits of a particular company would therefore be an insider. So too would be public servants whose office gives them access to price-sensitive information.[84]

The 'by virtue' requirement of the definition of 'insider' in s 72 of the Securities Services Act generates potential difficulties.[85] For example, does the bartender at the local golf club become an insider if he or she overhears inside information being discussed by a couple of senior executives as he or she takes their order? Clearly, the prosecution does not need to establish a business or professional relationship between the person and the company, as the 'access by virtue' category of insider in the Securities Services Act makes no mention of an 'issuer of securities'. It is unclear, however, whether there must be a functional link between the person's employment, office or profession and the company or the securities to which the information relates.[86] If such a link is necessary, persons such as the bartender, the taxi driver or the worker who gains inside information from snatches of overheard conversation would not be caught as primary insiders.[87]

It is possible, however, that the circumstances in which inside information was received could place a recipient (such as the bartender) in the secondary insider (tippee) category of offender. According to s 72 of the Securities Services Act, a secondary insider (tippee) is someone who knows that his or her price-sensitive information comes directly or indirectly from an inside source. Inside sources include any director, employee or shareholder of the company, as well as those who had access to the information by virtue of their employment, office or profession. There is no need to establish that the tippee's informant was connected with the relevant company. The prosecution simply has to prove that the tippee knew he or she had received his or her information from an inside source. To return to the earlier example, the bartender who overheard price-sensitive information being discussed at the golf club would be caught as a tippee if it could be shown that he or she knew that those persons were 'insiders'.[88]

Must (as has been suggested) the tippee know the identity of the informant?[89] If so, this would confine the scope of the legislation, which seeks to catch tippees whose indirect source of information is an insider. For example, director A may pass on price-sensitive information to his or her brother, B, who later tells his friends C and D. To insist that C and D should know the identity or the exact position of their indirect source of information will in most cases remove the prospect of successfully prosecuting subtippees who have received information from an intermediate tippee. It would have been better to cast the legislation in a manner that seeks to catch tippees solely on the basis of their knowledge of the

---

[84] Davies op cit n 70 at 465. For example, officials in the Reserve Bank.
[85] Ibid.
[86] K Wotherspoon 'Insider dealing — the new law: Part V of the Criminal Justice Act 1993' (1994) 57 *The Modern LR* 419 at 426. See also A Tridimas 'Insider trading: European harmonisation and national law reform' (1991) 40 *International & Comparative Law Quarterly* 919 at 926.
[87] Wotherspoon op cit n 86 at 426.
[88] Wotherspoon op cit n 86 at 426.
[89] See *Attorney-General's Reference (No 1 of 1988)* n 15 at 993; Wotherspoon op cit n 86 at 426–7.

specific and price-sensitive quality of the information they have received, rather than on their awareness of the identity or position of their immediate or ultimate informant.[90] Where a company acquires its own shares[91] or shares in its holding company[92] there appears to be no reason why the insider trading provisions should not apply if the company acquires the shares while in possession of inside information.[93]

(iv) *If it were made public would be likely to have a material effect on the price or value of any security listed on a regulated market*

Section 56(1)*(d)* of the UK Criminal Justice Act states this requirement slightly differently: 'if it were made public would be likely to have a significant effect on the price of any securities'. Thus s 56(1)*(d)* requires that the effect be 'significant' rather than 'material', and speaks only of 'price' rather than 'price or value'. The King Task Group proposed that the impact of the information should be material rather than significant, because of the extensive case law on the meaning of 'material', particularly in relation to fraud.[94] Luiz suggests that an objective reasonable investor test could be used.[95] This approach would accord with US law. US courts, when determining the fact of materiality, use as evidence the actual market impact, the very fact of trading by the insider, or the fact that the issuer attempted to keep the information secret (thus considering it material).[96] In *Oatorian Properties (Pty) Ltd v Maroun*,[97] where the materiality of a condition in a lease agreement had to be determined, the adjective 'material' was explained as meaning 'of serious or substantial import; of much consequence' and 'being of real importance or great consequence'.

Materiality was required under the repealed s 440F(2)*(a)*(iii) of the 1973 Companies Act, according to which the information had to be unpublished information which would reasonably be expected to affect materially the price of the securities if the information was generally available. A deficiency in the previous legislation was, however, that to qualify as inside information, the information had to relate to the internal affairs of a particular company or its operations, assets, earning power or involvement in a takeover (see below). Information relating to securities or issuers of securities generally did not qualify, such as information relating to the industry in which a company did business or information that applied in an

---

[90] Wotherspoon op cit n 86 at 427.
[91] See s 85 of the 1973 Companies Act.
[92] See s 89 of the 1973 Companies Act.
[93] See FHI Cassim 'The new statutory provisions on company share repurchases: a critical analysis' 1999 *SALJ* 760 at 777; R Cassim op cit n 67 at 54–6; New Zealand Law Commission Report No 9 *Company Law Reform and Restatement* (June 1989) para 413; Australian Companies and Securities Advisory Committee Discussion Paper on Insider Trading (2001) para 2.110; HAJ Ford, RP Austin and IM Ramsay *Ford's Principles of Corporations Law* 12 ed (2005) para 24.470. The courts in the USA have taken this view (see *Shaw v Digital Equipment Corp* 82 F 3d 1194 (1st Cir, 1996) 1204 and SEC rule 10b5–1 in terms of the Securities Exchange Act 17 CRP para 240.10b5–1).
[94] King Task Group Final Report op cit n 63 at para 3.2.20.
[95] SM Luiz op cit n 65 at 142 n 131.
[96] See B Bergmans *Inside Information and Securities Trading, A Legal and Economic Analysis of the Foundations of Liability in the USA and European Community* (1991).
[97] 1973 (3) SA 779 (A) at 785D–E.

undifferentiated way to the economy in general. For example, information that the government was proposing to reopen links with a specific country, which would significantly increase the market for a particular company's product, would not have qualified. Nor would a confidential briefing by the governor of the Reserve Bank have qualified. The current legislation (ie the Securities Services Act), just as the Insider Trading Act, contains no such limitations and the information in the above examples could qualify as 'inside information'.

(c) 'Person'

Whereas previously the offences (and civil wrongs[98] could only be committed by an 'individual' they can now be committed by a 'person'.[99] The absence of any reference to 'individual' in any of the provisions and the fact that it would be very strange to include partnerships and trusts[100] but exclude body corporates leaves little doubt that 'person' includes a corporate[101] or other legal entity.[102]

The imposition of liability for insider dealing on body corporates contrasts with the King Task Group's view:

> In view of the lack of development in our law of the jurisprudence concerning the efficacy of the Chinese Wall, the Task Group decided that both the criminal offence of insider trading and the civil remedy set out in the proposed legislation should be limited to conduct by an individual.[103]

The problem alluded to by the King Task Group is the one that arises where, for example, the corporate advisory department of a company has inside information relating to the shares in another company and the investment department of the company, which does not have the inside information, deals in the shares. Has the company dealt on the strength of the inside information? Unless some 'Chinese Wall' defence is available to the company it appears that it may be liable.

Gower explains the reluctance in the UK to include corporate bodies as follows:

---

[98] See below.
[99] See the definition of 'insider' in s 72 of the Securities Services Act. The insider trading provisions in the repealed s 440F of the 1973 Companies Act (repealed with effect from 17 January 1999) extended the prohibition to any 'person'. No reason was given in the Memorandum on the Objects of the Insider Trading Bill 1998 (B134–98) for restriction of the prohibition to individuals only.
[100] See definition of 'person' in s 72 of the Securities Services Act.
[101] In this regard s 332(1) of the Criminal Procedures Act is relevant, which provides:

'(1) For the purpose of imposing upon a corporate body criminal liability for any offence, whether under any law or at common law —
(a) any act performed, with or without a particular intent, by or on instructions or with permission, express of implied, given by a director or servant of that corporate body; and
(b) the omission, with or without a particular intent, of any act which ought to have been but was not performed by or on instructions given by a director or servant of that corporate body,

in the exercise of his powers or in the performance of his duties as such director or servant or in furthering or endeavouring to further the interests of that corporate body, shall be deemed to have been performed (and with the same intent, if any) by that corporate body or, as the case may be, to have been an omission (and with the same intent, if any) on the part of that corporate body.'

[102] See definition of 'person' in s 2 of the Interpretation Act 33 of 1957. An element of uncertainty in this regard is present because of the reference to 'he or she' and 'his or her' in s 73.
[103] See King Task Group Final Report op cit n 63 at para 3.1.2. For an excellent discussion of Chinese Walls, see R Cassim op cit n 67 at 44.

Corporate bodies were excluded, not because it was thought undesirable to make them criminally liable, but because of the difficulties it was thought would be faced by merchant banks when one department of the bank had unpublished price-sensitive information about the securities of a client company and other departments had successfully been kept in ignorance of that information by a 'Chinese Wall' or otherwise. One of those other departments might deal in the shares, in which event the bank as a single corporate body would arguably have committed an offence had the Act applied to corporate bodies.[104]

A 'Chinese Wall' is essentially an information barrier.[105] It is created by putting together administrative and organisational arrangements and structures that stop information from flowing from one part of a business to another.[106] A Chinese Wall will usually involve some or all of the following organisational arrangements: the physical separation of various departments to insulate them from each other; an ongoing educational programme to emphasise the importance of preserving confidential information; strict and carefully defined procedures for dealing with the situation where it is felt that the Chinese Wall should be crossed and for maintaining proper records when it happens; monitoring of the effectiveness of the Chinese Wall by compliance officers, and disciplinary sanctions when the Chinese Wall is breached.[107]

As stated by Cranston:[108]

> Chinese walls . . . are designed to stem the flow of information between different parts of the bank. Institutionally a Chinese Wall can involve physical separation (in some cases the occupation of different buildings); separate files for the functions separated by the Chinese Wall with no access for someone on one side of the wall to a file on the other side; consequent restrictions on physical access and controls on computer access and fail-safe systems; and controlled procedures for the movement of personnel between different parts of the bank. In some financial institutions Chinese Walls are underpinned by stop lists and no-recommendation policies.

It is to be noted that Australian law, which also includes corporate entities (and partnerships) in its scope of liability,[109] expressly provides for a Chinese Wall defence[110] as necessary accompaniment to the possibility of corporate liability for insider trading.[111] Thus a body corporate (or partnership) has a defence where it:

> . . . has in place a Chinese Wall which 'could reasonably be expected to ensure that information was not communicated', provided that the information was not communicated

---

[104] P Davies *Gower's Principles of Modern Company Law* 7 ed (2003) at 761. In the UK the insider trading provisions prohibition has not been extended to any 'person'.
[105] See KK Mwenda 'Banks and the use of Chinese Walls in managing conflict of duties' [2000] 2 *Web Journal of Current Legal Issues* 14.
[106] See C Woolley 'Chinese Walls — How thick are they?' Insurance Seminar — September 2000, available at http://www.deneysreitz.co.za/news/news.asp?Thiscat=2&ThisItem=163.
[107] Ibid. In his paper Woolley deals with, inter alia, two leading cases in the UK on the erection of a Chinese Wall, namely: *Prince Jefri Bolkiah v KPMG* [1999] 1 All ER 517 (which involved an accounting firm) and *Rakusen v Ellis, Munday & Clarke* [1912] 1 Ch 831 (which involved a firm of solicitors).
[108] R Cranston *Principles of Banking Law* (1997) 31–2. See also Mwenda op cit n 105 at 14.
[109] See s 1043A of the Corporations Act 2001.
[110] See ss 1043F and 1043G of the Corporations Act 2001. For a case in which the Chinese Wall defence was used with success in Australia, see *Asic v Citigroup* (2007) 62 ACSR 427.
[111] See R Tomasic, S Bottomley and R McQueen *Corporations Law in Australia* 2 ed (2000) at 20.9.8.

to another person in the organisation or partnership who made a decision and provided that no advice was given in respect of a transaction by the person who was in possession of the information.[112]

The US[113] and European Union Market Abuse Directives[114] provide a similar defence.

According to Rider and Ashe,[115] the reactions of the UK courts and regulatory institutions to the concept of the Chinese Wall have been mixed, due to a lack of faith in the ability to contain the flow of information within the organs of a corporate institution and the concept's reliance on the integrity of the human factor.

It is apparent that the South African legislature has not applied its mind to the possibility of Chinese Wall defences and this could be seen as a major flaw in the current provisions. In the absence of statutory Chinese Wall defences the efficacy of the operation of financial institutions such as merchant banks and stock-broking firms could be detrimentally affected. To construct an effective Chinese Wall policy may, however, be difficult.

It is to be noted that the person who deals on behalf of the body corporate could also be guilty of an offence in terms of s 73(2)(a) of the Securities Services Act.[116]

The definition of 'person' in s 72 includes a partnership and a trust, which means that the offences (and civil wrongs[117]) can be committed by a partnership or a trust, neither of which has legal personality in terms of the common law.

The inclusion of trusts and partnerships, without further elaboration, is highly questionable. Numerous questions with no clear answers arise: How is a partnership or a trust to be prosecuted? By prosecuting the individual partners or trustees? When does a partnership have the necessary knowledge for the commission of the

---

[112] Sections 1043F and 1043G of the Corporations Act 2001. See Tomasic et al op cit n 111 at 20.9.8.
[113] See SEC rules 14e–3(b)(i) and (ii) referred to in the Final Report by the King Task Group (at n 63) 9. As pointed out by R Cassim op cit n 67 at 47, Chinese walls came into existence in the US as part of the settlement agreement in *In the Matter of Merrill Lynch, Pierce, Fenner & Smith Inc* 43 SEC 933 (1968). Shortly after this case an unsuccessful attempt to use a Chinese Wall as a defence was made — see *Slade v Shearson, Hammil & Co Inc* CCH Fed SEC L Rep 193 at 329 (SDNY 1974). Rule 14e–3(b) exempts juristic persons from this rule if the individual making the investment decision on behalf of such juristic person did not have knowledge of the material, non-public information, and the juristic person had 'implemented one or a combination of policies and procedures, reasonable under the circumstances, taking into consideration the nature of the person's business, to ensure that individual(s) making investment decision(s) would not violate paragraph (a) of this section, which policies and procedures may include, but are not limited to:
    (i) those which restrict any purchase, sale and causing any purchase and sale of any such security; or
    (ii) those which prevent such individual(s) from knowing such information.'
For comment on the limitations of these defences see NS Poser 'Chinese Walls or emperor's new clothes (2)' (1988) 9 *The Company Lawyer* 203.
[114] Directive 2003/6/EC of the European Parliament and of the Council of 28 January 2003 on insider dealing and market manipulation (Market Abuse para 24).
[115] B Rider and M Ashe. *Insider Crime: The New Law* (1993) 76–8.
[116] Section 332(5) of the Criminal Procedure Act, which sought to make the directors and servants guilty of the offence unless they proved their innocence, was held to be unconstitutional in *S v Coetzee* 1997 (3) SA 527 (CC).
[117] See below.

offences? In determining if the partnership has the required knowledge, is the state of mind of each partner to be attributed to the partnership? Is it possible for the state of mind of an employee or agent of the partnership to be attributed to the partnership? If partner A knows that he or she is in possession of inside information regarding a company's shares and partner B innocently deals on behalf of the partnership in the company's shares, does the partnership have the required knowledge for commission of the dealing offence? What penalties can be imposed when a partnership is successfully prosecuted? Can the individual partners be imprisoned? If so, on what basis? Can a fine imposed on the partnership be recovered from the individual partners? Does the fact that the partnership is being treated as a separate legal entity mean that a fine imposed on the partnership may be recoverable only from the partnership's assets? But a partnership does not own the assets. They are owned jointly in undivided shares by the partners. Is it possible for a partnership to be guilty of the offences other than dealing?[118]

And regarding trusts: Does a 'trust' included in the definition of 'person' include all types of trusts? Does it include a *bewindtrust*? When does a trust have the necessary knowledge for the commission of the offence? In determining if the trust has the required knowledge, is the state of mind of each trustee to be attributed to the trust? Is it possible for the state of mind of an employee or agent of the trust to be attributed to the trust? What penalties can be imposed when a trust is successfully prosecuted? Can trustees be imprisoned? If so, on what basis? Can a fine imposed on the trust be recovered from the individual trustees? Or in the case of a *bewindtrust*, can it be recovered from the beneficiaries? Does the fact that the trust is being treated as a separate legal entity mean that the fine can only be recovered from the trust assets? But the trust does not own the trust assets — they are owned by the trustees in the case of an ordinary trust and the beneficiaries in the case of a *bewindtrust*.

It is submitted that our jurisprudence does not provide ready answers to these vital issues and legislation to provide clarity is called for.

It will also be recognised that the question of Chinese Wall defences (discussed above) also arises in relation to trusts and partnerships.

(d) 'Securities' and 'regulated market'

Section 1 of the Securities Services Act defines 'securities' very widely. It provides that:

'securities'
(a) means —
    (i) shares, stocks and depository receipts in public companies and other equivalent equities, other than shares in a share block company as defined in the Share Blocks Control Act, 1980 (Act 59 of 1980);
    (ii) notes;
    (iii) derivative instruments;
    (iv) bonds;
    (v) debentures;

---

[118] This question also arises in relation to companies.

(vi) participatory interests in a collective investment scheme as defined in the Collective Investment Schemes Control Act, 2002 (Act 45 of 2002), and units or any other form of participation in a foreign collective investment scheme approved by the Registrar of Collective Investment Schemes in terms of section 65 of that Act;
(vii) units or any other form of participation in a collective investment scheme licensed or registered in a foreign country;
(viii) instruments based on an index;
(ix) the securities contemplated in subparagraphs (i) to (viii) that are listed on an external exchange; and
(x) an instrument similar to one or more of the securities contemplated in subparagraphs (i) to (ix) declared by the registrar by notice in the *Gazette* to be a security for the purposes of this Act;
(xi) rights in the securities referred to in subparagraphs (i) to (x);

(b) excludes —
(i) money market instruments except for the purposes of Chapter IV; and
(ii) any security contemplated in paragraph *(a)* specified by the registrar by notice in the *Gazette*.

For securities to qualify they must be listed on a regulated market. Section 72 of the Securities Services Act provides that ' "regulated market" means any market, whether domestic or foreign, which is regulated in terms of the laws of the country in which that market conducts business as a market for dealing in securities on that market'. Thus insider trading in regard to unlisted securities, even those of a company which is a subsidiary of a listed company, is not prohibited by the Securities Services Act. The King Task Group was of the opinion that it was unnecessary to include unlisted securities in the legislation because the common-law civil remedies are available.[119] It is submitted that even if a common-law civil remedy is available, the exclusion of criminal liability is unwarranted.

The definition of 'securities' in s 72 of the Securities Services Act makes it clear that the prohibitions embrace all securities and financial instruments listed on a regulated market in South Africa or internationally. Instruments and securities issued by public sector bodies are included. Thus the equity, derivative and bond markets are covered. Under the legislation prior to the Insider Trading Act, only dealing in securities issued by a company was regulated. Accordingly, instruments such as an index, futures or government bonds were excluded.[120]

Although only listed securities fall within the ambit of the Securities Services Act, insider trading in these securities is prohibited, whether such dealing occurs on a regulated market or OTC (over the counter). The King Task Group was loath to exclude OTC transactions because of the loophole the exclusion would create, although they conceded that it would be difficult to discover and monitor such transactions.[121]

The prohibitions extend to securities listed on a regulated foreign market. Although the King Task Group was in favour of prohibiting an insider deal executed in South Africa in respect of securities listed on a regulated foreign

---

[119] King Task Group Final Report op cit n 63 at para 3.3.3. Regarding these remedies see below.
[120] King Task Group Final Report op cit n 63 at paras 2.1.1 and 2.1.2.
[121] King Task Group Final Report op cit n 63 at para 5.3.

market,[122] it appears that the provisions of the Securities Services Act have been so widely framed as to have an unacceptable extraterritorial reach: the provisions of the Securities Services Act would apply to securities listed on a foreign market, even if there were no territorial link to South Africa. The Securities Services Act appears to require no territorial connection between any element of the offences and South Africa.[123] Bearing in mind that the aim of the provisions is the protection of the South African financial marketplace and its users, both local and foreign, the granting of such an open-ended regulatory licence appears unnecessary.[124] It appears that such width of jurisdictional scope is not found anywhere else in the world.[125] The financial resources necessary to finance such unlimited enforcement of the legislation could be enormous and probably unwarranted and a more restricted approach appears to be called for.[126]

(e) Defences

The Securities Services Act provides certain defences to the offences created, with the exception of the 'encouraging' or 'discouraging' offence, which are dealt with below.

The Insider Trading Act, both in respect of criminal and civil liability, expressly preserved any defences that might have been available other than those provided for in the Insider Trading Act itself.[127] Thus the common-law defences[128] were preserved as well as any other statutory defences that might have been applicable. The current provisions do not expressly preserve such defences. As the Insider Trading Act has been repealed, it may be argued that these other defences are no longer available. However, a counter to this may be that, in terms of our common law, other defences are always preserved unless expressly excluded by the statutory provision in question. Whatever the merits of such arguments may be, it is submitted that legislative clarification is called for.

A common element of all the offences (and civil wrongs[129]) is that the person committing the offence must 'know' that he or she has inside information.

To know that it is inside information, primary insiders must, presumably, know:

- that it is 'specific or precise information',

---

[122] King Task Group Final Report op cit n 63 at para 5.2.
[123] Cf s 62(1) of the UK Criminal Justice Act 1993, which does require a territorial connection.
[124] As has been mentioned the King Task Group was in favour of prohibiting an insider deal executed in South Africa in respect of a security or financial instrument listed on a regulated foreign market (King Task Group Final Report op cit n 63 at para 5.2).
[125] See PC Osode 'The new South African Insider Trading Act: Sound law reform or legislative overkill?' (2000) 45 *Journal of African Law* 239 at 262. As Osode points out, 'even the United States' open-ended extra-territorial application of its securities laws by the Securities and Exchange Commission (SEC) has limitations' (Ibid). Germany and the UK have provided for restricted extraterritorial reach and Canada, Japan, Hong Kong and New Zealand make no provision at all for their legislation to apply to illicit transactions that have taken place in foreign jurisdictions.
[126] Ibid.
[127] See ss 4(3), 6(1)*(c)* and 6(2).
[128] For example, ignorance of the law (*S v de Blom* 1977 (3) SA 513 (A)).
[129] See below. Of course, in civil proceedings, proof of such awareness on a balance of probabilities will suffice, whereas in criminal prosecutions it must be proved beyond reasonable doubt.

- that it has not been made public,
- that they have obtained or learned of the information 'through' their position, and
- that 'if' [the information] were made public' it 'would be likely to have a material effect on the price or value of any securities or financial instruments'.

As far as the secondary insider is concerned, he or she — in order to be a secondary insider — must in addition know that the direct or indirect source of the information had been a primary insider (only if he or she also knows this is he or she an insider and has inside information).

An obvious difficulty in establishing whether a person knows that he or she has inside information is that many of the facts to be established will be matters of judgment. For example, whether information is 'specific or precise' is a matter of judgment. Also significant will be the question whether it has been made public. First, s 74(1) of the Security Services Act merely provides for certain 'circumstances' in which 'information shall be regarded as having been made public', and expressly states that the circumstances in which information shall be regarded as having been made public are not limited to the specified circumstances. Furthermore, s 74(2) provides that inside information which would otherwise be regarded as having been made public, must still be so regarded even though *(a)* it can be acquired only by persons exercising diligence or observation, or having expertise, or *(b)* it is communicated upon payment of a fee; or it is only published outside the Republic'.

How then can an insider 'know' whether such information has or has not been made public? And, of course, experts may disagree as to whether the information was such that 'if it were made public would be likely to have a material effect on the price or value of any security listed on a regulated market'[130]

The insider must have understood the specificity and materiality of the non-public information in his or her possession at the time he or she chose to deal. In the case of the primary insider, the prosecution would have to show the same subjective appreciation in relation to the source of the information: that the offender knew he or she had the information as a result of his or her inside position. It is clear that only subjective appreciation of these facts will do. Thus, for example, if the accused thinks (no matter how unreasonably) that the information is public, he or she does not commit the offence.[131] In the case of secondary insider dealing it does not matter whether the primary insider has consciously communicated the information to the secondary insider. As long as the secondary insider dealer has obtained the information from an inside source, even indirectly, he or she would fall within the scope of the Securities Services Act. The secondary insider dealer must, however, know that the inside information came from an 'inside' source.[132] This requirement is likely to be difficult to meet, especially if the argument is that the information came indirectly from the primary insider to

---

[130] See the definition of 'inside information' in s 72 of the Securities Services Act.

[131] See E Lomnicka 'The new insider dealing provisions: Criminal Justice Act 1993, Part V' (1994) *Journal of Business Law* 173 at 181–2.

[132] Section 72 of the Securities Services Act.

the suspect via a chain of communications. Proving that a 'subtippee' or even a 'sub-subtippee' knew that the ultimate source of the information was a primary insider could be fraught with problems.

Proof that a person had the requisite knowledge 'is likely to be a major stumbling block ... especially where there is no documentary evidence to support such claims'.[133]

Unlike the legislation prior to the Insider Trading Act, the Securities Services Act does not assist the prosecution by presuming that the requisite knowledge was present once certain facts are proved.[134] The King Task Group was of the opinion that such presumptions might be unconstitutional and accordingly did not recommend their inclusion.[135]

In dealing with the 'knowledge' requirement it has been stated[136] that 'the new Act[137] does not require that the defendant be shown to have deliberately exploited the inside information in concluding the illicit transaction, in addition to proof of mere knowledge of the inside information'.[138]

If the view taken here is that no *mens rea* is required, the view may be questionable in the light of the presumption that the legislature intended *mens rea* to be an element of liability of a statutory offence.[139] Thus it has been stated by Botha JA in *S v Arenstein*:[140]

> The general rule is that *actus non facit reum nisi mens sit rea* and that in construing statutory prohibitions or injunctions, the [l]egislature is presumed, in the absence of clear and convincing indications to the contrary not to have intended innocent violations thereof to be punishable.

In order for this presumption to be rebutted there must be considerations indicating that the legislature intended the offence to be one of strict liability.[141] Such considerations are:[142]

> ... [t]he language or the context of the prohibition or injunction, the scope and object of the statute, the nature and extent of the penalty, and the ease with which the prohibition or injunction could be evaded if reliance could be placed on the absence of *mens rea*.

It has been suggested[143] that proof of deliberate exploitation of the inside information may create serious evidentiary problems for the prosecution. If so, this may be a factor pointing to strict liability. On the other hand, whether the *mens rea*

---

[133] Tomasic et al op cit n 111 at 20.9.6.
[134] See the rebuttable presumptions in the repealed s 440F(3) of the 1973 Companies Act.
[135] Final Report op cit n 63 at paras 2.1.6 and 3.6.2.
[136] See Osode op cit n 125 at 248.
[137] Osode is referring to the Insider Trading Act but the 'knowledge' requirement is the same in the new provisions of the Securities Services Act.
[138] Osode points out that 'deliberate exploitation' is required in US and German law but no longer in Canada. See Osode op cit n 125 at 248. Osode states that 'deliberate exploitation' was a mandatory requirement in Ontario until its repeal in 1980 in response to calls by regulators and academics who persuasively argued that the repeal was indispensable to the creation of an effective insider trading provisions prohibition.
[139] See J Burchell *Principles of Criminal Law* 3 ed (2005) 500.
[140] 1964 (1) SA 361 (A).
[141] Burchell op cit n 139.
[142] See *S v Arenstein* 1964 (1) SA 361 (A).
[143] See Osode op cit n 125 at 248.

requirement would make it easier to evade the prohibition is perhaps arguable; if the accused has inside information, knows it is inside information and deals,[144] has not a *prima facie* case for *mens rea* been presented resulting in the evidentiary burden swinging to the accused? If so, the *mens rea* requirement poses no evidentiary problem for the prosecution. Perhaps there is sufficient lack of certainty in this regard to call for clarification by the legislature.

(f) Criminal liability

The Securities Services Act prohibits, as did the Insider Trading Act, four types of conduct on the part of an 'insider' who has 'inside information': dealing on one's own account, dealing on behalf of someone else, improper disclosure or 'tipping' and encouraging or discouraging dealing.

(i) The 'dealing' offence

Section 73(1)(*a*) of the Securities Services Act describes the offence that is committed when an insider deals for his or her own account on the strength of inside information. It provides:

> An insider who knows that he or she has inside information and who deals directly or indirectly or through an agent for his or her own account in the securities listed on a regulated market to which the inside information relates or which are likely to be affected by it commits an offence.

The offence is, however, not committed in the circumstances envisaged in s 73(1)(*b*), namely,

> [I]f such insider proves on a balance of probabilities that he or she —
> (i) was acting in pursuit of the completion of an affected transaction as defined in section 440A of the Companies Act [61 of 1973];
> (ii) only became an insider after he or she had given the instruction to deal to an authorised user and the instruction was not changed in any manner after he or she became an insider.

• *'to which the inside information relates or which are likely to be affected by it'*
What is meant by 'this phrase' in 73(1)(*a*) of the Securities Services Act? Surely the information never relates to the securities? Surely it relates to the business of the company, or to some matter that will increase or decrease the value of the business: it never relates to the securities themselves. Nor are securities actually 'affected' by the information — they remain as they were. The information affects the value or price of the securities, not the securities themselves. As has been seen, 'inside information' must be such that 'if it were made public it would be likely to have an material effect on the *price or value* of any security listed on a regulated market'.[145]

Subsections (1) and (2) of s 52 (the offences of dealing and encouraging, respectively) of the UK Criminal Justice Act 1993 refer to 'securities that are price-affected securities in relation to the information'. And s 56(2) provides that:

> [S]ecurities are 'price-affected securities' in relation to inside information, and inside infor-

---

[144] Or 'discloses' or 'encourages' or 'discourages' or 'stops', as the case may be.
[145] See the definition of 'inside information' in s 72 of the Securities Services Act.

mation is 'price-sensitive information' in relation to securities, if and only if the information would, if made public, be likely to have a significant effect on the price of the securities.

In terms of the provisions of the Securities Services Act it is not a requirement of the offence that the accused made a profit or avoided a loss.[146] This is really rather odd. Say, for example, an insider sells his or her shares for R100 (the current market price) when he or she has inside information which, if known, would cause the price to rise (and when known did cause the price to rise) to R200. Surely, that ought not to be an offence?

- *Dealing directly or indirectly or through an agent*

There is no exhaustive definition of 'dealing' in the Securities Services Act. Section 72 provides that 'deal' 'includes conveying or giving an instruction to deal'. It appears that 'dealing' means buying or selling or a transaction akin thereto such as bartering, but just how far the meaning goes is unclear.

It is not clear, nor was it clear in the Insider Trading Act, whether 'dealing' includes 'subscribing' for shares. Clarification that it is included is called for as there appears to be no basis for its exclusion. For example, Mr X, an employee of Company Y, knows he has inside information which, when made public, will cause the price of Company Y's shares to rise, and he subscribes for shares in Company Y. Company Y does not have the inside information. Surely this is as unacceptable as purchasing shares in Company Y?

It is submitted that where a company acquires its own shares, it is 'dealing' even though it is not able to 'deal' with them thereafter.[147]

Section 55 of the UK Criminal Justice Act 1993 does define 'dealing'. Section 55(1) provides that:

> For the purposes of this Part, a person deals in securities if —
> (a) he acquires or disposes of the securities (whether as principal or agent); or
> (b) he procures, directly or indirectly, an acquisition or disposal of the securities by any other persons.

Section 55(4) defines 'procures' as follows:

> [A] person procures an acquisition or disposal of a security if the security is acquired or disposed of by a person who is —
> (a) his agent,
> (b) his nominee,
> (c) a person who is acting at his direction, in relation to the acquisition or disposal.

Section 55(5) provides that sub-s (4) is not exhaustive as to the circumstances in which one person may be regarded as procuring an acquisition or disposal of securities by another. Section 55(2) defines 'acquire' in relation to a security to include—

> (a) agreeing to acquire the security; and
> (b) entering into a contract which creates the security.

Section 55(3) provides that 'dispose' in relation to a security includes —

> (a) agreeing to dispose of the security; and

---

[146] Cf the civil liability position. See below.
[147] In terms of s 85(8) of the Securities Services Act the shares must be cancelled.

(b) bringing to an end a contract which creates a security.[148]

It is not clear whether 'dealing' in the Securities Services Act extends:

> ... to a mere agreement to acquire or to dispose of securities, or whether dealing is to be limited to the actual acquisition or the disposal of securities and the conveying or the giving of an instruction to acquire or dispose of securities.[149]

Abstaining from dealing is not an offence and does not give rise to any criminal or civil liability. Thus it is not an offence if a person retains securities he or she would otherwise have sold because he or she has acquired inside information that they will increase in value. This exclusion is no doubt based on the severe evidential problems that a prosecution would face in such a case. *Gower* says[150] regarding the same position in the UK: 'In principle, it is difficult to defend this exclusion since the loss of public confidence in the market will be as strong as in a case of dealing, if news of the non-dealing emerges.'[151]

The Securities Services Act expressly renders insiders liable — both criminally and civilly — if they deal 'directly or indirectly or through an agent'.[152] The provisions of the Insider Trading Act[153] did not expressly refer to dealing through an agent. It only used the words 'directly or indirectly' and it appears that the legislature did not regard dealing through an agent as being implied in the word 'indirectly'. It is not clear what purpose is then served by the word 'indirectly', bearing in mind that our courts are reluctant to treat words in a statute as superfluous.[154]

It is of note that s 73(2)(a) of the Securities Services Act, which creates the

---

[148] See R Cassim op cit n 67 at 58: 'From the definition of "dealing" and, more specifically, the definition of "acquire" and "disposal" in the CJA [Cassim is here referring to the Criminal Justice Act in the UK], it seems that an individual could conceivably commit the offence of dealing if he simply *agrees* to acquire a security or *agrees* to dispose of the security. The offence would be committed at the time that the individual agrees to acquire or dispose of the security and it is irrelevant that the relevant contract is never executed. If, therefore, an individual, after agreeing to acquire or dispose of the security, subsequently changes his mind and does not acquire or dispose of the security, he will nevertheless have committed the act of dealing. This seems somewhat curious in light of the fact that abstention from dealing does not constitute an offence under the CJA.' Cassim refers to Lord Millet, A Alcock, AJ Boyle, LS Sealy and DA Bennett *Gore-Browne on Companies* 45 ed vol 2 (1986) (Supplement 53, August 2005) at 42.25.

[149] R Cassim op cit n 67.

[150] Davies op cit n 104 at 770.

[151] See R Cassim op cit n 67 at 57: 'However, it is submitted that while this may be true, it should not result in an abstention from dealing not being punishable in those instances where a prosecution would be able to produce sufficient evidence of the abstention from dealing ... It moreover seems paradoxical that discouraging another person to deal, which is not an offence under the CJA [Criminal Justice Act in the UK], does constitute an offence under the [SA] Securities Services Act. Thus, if a person is encouraged to abstain from dealing, the person encouraging the abstention from dealing commits an offence, yet abstaining from dealing in itself is not punishable.'

[152] See s 73(1)(a).

[153] Section 2(1).

[154] See eg *S v Weinberg* 1979 (3) SA 89 (A) 98. In *Couve v Reddot International (Pty) Ltd* 2004 (6) SA 425 (W) 432A–B Jajbhay AJ said the words 'directly or indirectly' have received little judicial consideration and referred to Smalberger JA's statement in *Belfry Marine Ltd v Palm Base Maritime SDN BHD* 1999 (3) SA 1083 (SCA) 1107E–F: 'By using the words "directly or indirectly" the Legislature clearly intended to extend and not restrict the expression ...'.

offence of dealing on someone else's account, does not cover dealing through an agent. It is of course possible to deal on someone else's account through an agent and the exclusion of such a possibility is incongruous. Where a person deals through a company or a close corporation, presumably the court can, where appropriate, pierce the corporate veil and treat the transaction as a case of dealing on the person's own account.

- *Knowledge*

As has been seen above, the 'dealing' offence requires knowledge on the part of the insider that he or she has inside information, although there is no need to establish that possession of inside information prompted the decision to deal.[155]

- *Defences*

Where a person is accused of insider dealing on his or her own account, criminal (and civil) liability will be avoided if he or she can prove on a balance of probabilities one of the two defences set out in s 73(1)*(b)* of the Securities Services Act.

The first defence is that the accused 'was acting in pursuit of the completion of an affected transaction as defined in s 440A of the Companies Act [61 of 1973]'.[156] This defence was provided for in the previous legislation and its rationale is difficult to understand. Is the idea here that, in the case of a takeover, the acquisition of shares of the target company by the acquirer is exempt from the prohibition? Typically, in a takeover situation, the inside information is information about a likely takeover. But that, of course, is a matter of history when the acquirer actually acquires the shares of the target. Of course, it is possible that a person may acquire control without making a takeover bid. Control can be acquired by individual purchases, or on the stock exchange. Then, under the takeover code, a mandatory offer must be made to the remaining shareholders. Does this exception, then, permit the acquirer to make such individual acquisitions or stock exchange purchases without disclosing its intentions, and hence purchase on the basis of inside information? But surely such an acquirer is not an insider, and therefore does not fall within the ambit of the prohibition in the first place? More likely, the legislator had the seller in mind. Is the legislator's intention that if X sells a controlling block of shares (the transaction is an affected transaction) he or she would not be guilty of insider trading, even if he or she had inside information relating to the value of his or her shares? But why not? Perhaps the idea was simply that, since at the time takeovers were regulated under the Securities Services Act and the Securities Regulation Code on Take-overs and Mergers, they ought not to be further regulated by the Insider Trading Act, which has since been repealed. But that would not be a very satisfactory explanation.

---

[155] The accused may of course have one of the defences provided by s 73(1)*(b)* of the Securities Services Act.

[156] Section 73(1)*(b)*(i). The defence presupposes lawful conduct on the part of an accused in the pursuit of the completion or the implementation of an affected transaction. This was held in *S v Western Areas Ltd* (2006) 2 All SA 653 (W) 666–7. As stated in 2004 *Annual Survey* 522: 'Regrettably it was not necessary for the Court to decide whether s 4(1) of the Act was unconstitutional.' This would have had a bearing on s 73(1)*(b)*(i) of the Securities Services Act.

The second defence available to the accused is that he or she 'only became an insider after he or she had given the instruction to deal to an authorised user[157] and the instruction was not changed in any manner after he or she became an insider'.[158] The rationale for this defence is clear. If a person instructs his or her broker to deal in a security and subsequent to the giving of the instruction he or she acquires inside information in relation thereto, he or she should not be guilty of an offence as long as the instruction is not changed before the dealing takes place. This is so because the inside information did not prompt him or her to deal — he or she would have dealt in the same way even in the absence of the inside information. In the repealed Insider Trading Act there was no defence formulated in this way. However, in the Insider Trading Act it was a defence that he or she 'would have acted in the same manner even without the inside information'.[159]

It is submitted that the old defence in the repealed Insider Trading Act would have covered the circumstances covered by the new defence in the Securities Services Act, but the old one is undoubtedly wider than the new one. For example, an individual who had price-sensitive information in relation to certain securities and sold them to meet pressing financial obligations, or who bought them in order to fulfil a pre-existing obligation to transfer them to another person, would have been protected by the old defence. The new defence would, however, not protect the dealer in these circumstances. It may be, however, that in these examples the offence has not been committed in the first place because the requisite *mens rea* is not present.[160]

It will be recognised that, if the old defence had been retained, it may have gone some way towards alleviating the concern expressed earlier regarding the inclusion of body corporates (see 20.1.4*(c)* above) within the ambit of the insider dealing provisions. The example was given of the corporate advisory division of a company having inside information regarding another company's shares and the investment department of the company dealing in those shares in ignorance of that information. As matters stand at present, it would appear that the knowledge of the corporate advisory division could be imputed to the company with the result that, if the other requirements for liability are present, the company could be criminally liable. If the old defence was still available, the company would escape liability on the basis that it 'would have acted in the same manner even without the inside information'.

In the UK[161] there is a defence that protects an individual who had reasonable grounds for believing that the information in his or her possession was disclosed widely enough to ensure that none of the counterparties to the transactions would be prejudiced by not having the information. There is no such defence in South

---

[157] An 'authorised user' is defined in s 1 of the Securities Services Act as meaning 'a person authorised by an exchange in terms of the exchange rules to perform such securities services as the exchange rules may permit'.
[158] Section 73(1)*(b)*(ii) of the Securities Services Act.
[159] Section 4(1)*(b)* of the Insider Trading Act 135 of 1998.
[160] See earlier (20.1.4*(e)* above) where it is suggested that it is unclear whether *mens rea* is a requirement for liability and that legislative intervention is perhaps called for.
[161] See s 53(1) of the Criminal Justice Act 1993.

Africa, nor was there in the repealed Insider Trading Act. But it would seem that, if the accused can establish this, he or she will establish that they did not know that they had inside information.

(ii) The offence of dealing on behalf of someone else

Section 73(2)*(a)* of the Securities Services Act makes it an offence to deal on the basis of inside information on behalf of someone else. It provides:

> An insider who knows that he or she has inside information and who deals, directly or indirectly, for any other person in the securities listed on a regulated market to which the inside information relates or which are likely to be affected by it commits an offence.

The offence is not committed, however, if such insider proves on a balance of probabilities that he or she:

(i) is an authorised user and was acting on specific instructions from a client, save where the inside information was disclosed to him or her by that client;
(ii) was acting on behalf of a public sector body[162] in pursuit of monetary policy, policies in respect of exchange rates, the management of public debt or external exchange reserves;
(iii) was acting in pursuit of the completion of an affected transaction as defined in section 440A of the Companies Act [61 of 1973]; or
(iv) only became an insider after he or she had given the instruction to deal to an authorised user and the instruction was not changed in any manner after he or she became an insider.[163]

The comments made regarding the two defences under the last heading are equally applicable to the defences in s 73(2)*(b)*(iii) and (iv). The defence in s 73(2)*(b)*(i) is the same as the defence in s 4(1)*(a)* of the repealed Insider Trading Act, with the difference that only authorised users can rely on the defence. This raises a problem similar to the one that arises in relation to the defence in s 73(2)*(b)*(iv) (see below), in that someone other than an authorised dealer cannot rely on the defence in s 73(2)*(b)*(i). Clients do not necessarily instruct authorised users only to act on their behalf.

With regard to the defence in s 73(1)*(b)*(ii), it was noted that the Insider Trading Act provided a wider defence. It protected an insider 'who would have acted in the same manner even without the inside information'.[164] For example, under the repealed Insider Trading Act, the insolvency practitioner who had to liquidate all the assets of an insolvent company could safely deal if they also had price-sensitive information about the securities they were about to sell. It appears that there is no longer a defence in these circumstances. The previous defence effectively avoided, in the case of certain individuals, a conflict of interest between

---

[162] In terms of s 72 of the Securities Services Act, a 'public sector body' means:
   '(a) all spheres of the government of the Republic or of any other country or territory;
   (b) the South African Reserve Bank; or
   (c) the central bank of any country or territory outside the Republic, but does not include the Public Investment Commissioners established by section 2 of the Public Investment Commissioners Act, 1984 (Act 45 of 1984).'
[163] Section 73(2)*(b)* of the Securities Services Act.
[164] Section 4(1)*(b)* of the Insider Trading Act.

their contractual or fiduciary obligations and the fact that they had personal knowledge of inside information at the time.

The defence in s 73(2)*(b)*(ii) is identical to one available under the repealed Insider Trading Act[165] with the minor difference that the term 'foreign' and not 'external' was used in the Insider Trading Act. It is doubtful whether anything turns on this difference. The precise ambit of this defence is not clear. In what circumstances would a 'public sector body' deal in securities 'in pursuit of monetary policy, policies in respect of exchange rates, the management of public debt or external exchange reserves'? The breadth and vagueness of this defence is disconcerting, because it may enable public officials, without warrant, to escape liability.[166]

The defence in s 73(2)*(b)*(iv) is similar but not identical to the defence in the Insider Trading Act. The difference between the two is that, whereas the defence in terms of the Insider Trading Act was available to any 'individual' accused of the offence in question, the new defence is only available to a person who is an 'authorised user'. An 'authorised user' is 'a person authorised by an exchange in terms of the exchange rules to perform such securities services as the exchange rules may permit'.[167] It appears that the current defence is more limited in its application than the previous one. For example, a person instructs his or her accountant to buy a certain number of shares in a company at a certain price on his or her behalf and the accountant has inside information in relation to the shares in question. He or she or she has obtained this information from another source and has not disclosed it to the client. The accountant instructs a broker ('an authorised user') to buy the shares. It appears that the accountant would be protected under the previous defence but not under the new one, because the accountant is not an 'authorised user'. It is submitted that the accountant should not be guilty of the offence as he or she would have acted in the same manner even without the inside information. What makes the situation more peculiar is that, if the accountant only became an insider after giving the instruction to the broker, the accountant would be able to use the defence in s 73(2)*(b)*(iv). Why should it make such a difference when the accountant became an insider? There is no logic to such distinction.

(iii) *The 'disclosure' offence*

The 'disclosure' or 'tipping' offence is to be found in s 73(3)*(a)*, which provides:

> An insider who knows that he or she has inside information and who discloses the inside information to another person commits an offence.

The offence is not committed, however:

> [I]f such insider proves on a balance of probabilities that he or she disclosed the inside information because it was necessary to do so for the purpose of the proper performance of the functions of his or her employment, office or profession in circumstances unrelated to dealing in any security listed on a regulated market and that he or she at the same time disclosed that the information was inside information.[168]

---

[165] See s 4(1)*(c)* of the Insider Trading Act.
[166] See, in this regard, Millet et al op cit n 148 at 42.14.
[167] Section 1 of the Securities Services Act.
[168] Section 73(3)*(b)* of the Securities Services Act.

The defence was provided for in the previous legislation,[169] although the wording 'in circumstances unrelated to dealing in any security listed on a regulated market' is new. The new wording has presumably been inserted to prevent reliance on the exception by, for example, investment advisors whose 'employment, office or profession' would no doubt relate to 'dealing in any security listed on a regulated market'. If this is the case, the new provision closes a gaping hole that existed in the previous legislation.[170]

The previous legislation provided a further defence to a person accused of the 'disclosure' offence. This has been removed from the Securities Services Act. The accused was not guilty of the offence if he or she 'believed, on reasonable grounds, that no person would deal in the securities or financial instruments as a result of such disclosure'.[171] This defence appears to have involved a subjective–objective test — was the accused's actual belief that 'no person would deal' reasonable? It is not clear why this defence was removed. Should such 'innocence' be punished? Perhaps the removal of the defence is indicative of a harder line being taken by the legislature — insiders must be deterred from divulging inside information and the only circumstances in which it will be excused will be in those provided by the exception that has been retained in s 73(3)*(b)*. The subjectivity of the defence may also have motivated its removal — enquiries into the state of mind of an accused can be problematic and this, together with the vagueness of the defence, may have led to the demise of this provision.[172]

It is a requirement, as for the other offences, that the offender understood the quality and the source of the information at the time of disclosure.[173] It does not have to be shown that the offender intended to bring about a particular result as a consequence of his or her disclosure. It does not have to be shown, for example, that he or she intended or ought to have realised that the recipient would use the information to advise others to deal in the affected securities or financial instruments.[174]

What has been stated under this heading is equally applicable in the context of civil liability for the disclosure of inside information.

Liability for the disclosure offence is not contingent on the insider being remunerated in some way for the disclosure. No doubt the severity of the penalty

---

[169] See s 4(2)*(b)* of the Insider Trading Act.
[170] The tightening of the defence may, however, have unforeseen adverse implications where insider information is disclosed to the potential acquirer of shares in a company in the course of a due-diligence investigation into the affairs of the company carried out by the acquirer. As the circumstances are related to dealing in the shares of the company, the defence would not be available to the person disclosing the information. See in this regard R Cassim op cit n 67 at 62–4.
[171] See s 4(2)*(a)* of the Insider Trading Act.
[172] Difficulty in proving the communication of inside information is evident from the Australian Capital Territory decision in *Myers v Claudianos* (1990) 2 ACSR 73 at 79. See Tomasic et al op cit n 111 at 20.9.7. See also *Hooker Investments Pty Ltd v Baring Bros Halkerston & Partners Securities Ltd* (1986) 4 ACLC 243 at 245 where this issue was considered.
[173] In other words, he or she knew he or she was an insider and that he or she had inside information. See the definitions of 'inside information' and 'insider' in s 72 of the Securities Services Act.
[174] See Wotherspoon op cit n 86 at 429.

imposed will be influenced by whether a benefit was derived or not.[175] Remuneration is not a requirement for civil liability either.[176]

(iv) *The 'encouraging' or 'discouraging' offence*

In terms of s 73(4) of the Securities Services Act a person is guilty of the 'encouraging' or 'discouraging'[177] offence if he or she:

- knowing that he or she has inside information,
- encourages or causes another person to deal or discourages or stops another person from dealing,
- in the securities listed on a regulated market to which such information relates or which are likely to be affected by it.

The essential *actus reus* of the offence is the imparting of advice to deal or not to deal in specified securities or financial instruments as opposed to substantive disclosure of the information that has led the person to give that advice. If the recipient did in fact receive inside information when encouraged or discouraged, the individual divulging that information may also have committed the disclosure offence under s 73(3)*(a)*. It is not necessary that the 'encouraging' or 'discouraging' be successful, nor is it relevant whether the advice was offered gratuitously or for personal gain.

It is to be noted that, if a person is encouraged to deal without receiving any inside information, he or she is not guilty of the offence of insider dealing if he or she deals. The dealing offence requires possession of inside information on the part of the dealer. So if Mr X says to Mr Y: 'I have inside information about Company A. I will not disclose the information but I strongly advise you to buy its shares', and Mr Y deals, he is not guilty of insider dealing.[178] It is unclear why Mr Y should escape liability. Why should liability only arise if the inside information is passed on to Mr Y? This anomaly represents a serious flaw in the legislature's attempt to combat insider trading.

The offender must 'know' that he or she has 'inside information', as defined.[179] However, the offence is committed without the recipient having known that the offender had the benefit of price-sensitive information when he or she was encouraged or discouraged to trade or not to trade. Nor does it have to be shown that the recipient actually heeded the advice given.

The existence of this offence is likely to curb overzealousness on the part of company representatives when making presentations to meetings of large shareholders or analysts.

---

[175] It is to be noted that, as far as civil liability is concerned, the insider will be liable to pay 'the commission or consideration' received (see s 77(3)*(b)*(iv) and (4)*(d)*).

[176] Any 'commission or consideration' received is, however, claimable from the insider. See below.

[177] The terms 'encourage' and 'discourage' are not defined, which was also the case with these words in the Insider Trading Act. 'Presumably encouraging or discouraging another person from dealing could take place by words or by conduct. The more subtle the encouragement or discouragement, the more difficult it would be to prove.' (R Cassim op cit n 67 at 65, who refers to S Luiz 'Insider dealing in the United Kingdom: Some comments and some comparisons' (1995) 7 *SA Merc LJ* 204 at 208.)

[178] Mr X could, however, be civilly liable (s 77(4)). See below.

[179] See the definition of 'insider' in s 72 of the Securities Services Act.

Liability is not contingent on the insider being remunerated in some way for the encouragement or discouragement. No doubt the severity of the penalty imposed will be influenced by whether a benefit was derived or not.[180] Remuneration is not a requirement for civil liability either.[181]

There are no defences for the 'encouraging' or 'discouraging' offence in the Securities Services Act. In terms of the Insider Trading Act it was a defence if the accused 'would have acted in the same manner even without the inside information'.[182] The removal of this defence from the Securities Services Act seems harsh, because there could be genuine instances where the insider would have provided the encouragement even without the inside information and the onus of proof would then be on the accused. The removal is an indication of the harder line taken in the new provisions.[183]

(v) Penalty

The maximum penalty for committing any of the offences created by the Securities Services Act is far heavier than that prescribed under the Insider Trading Act. The maximum penalty now is a fine of R50 million or imprisonment of ten years, or both such fine and imprisonment.[184] Previously, the figures were R2 million and ten years.

The increase in the fine and the period of imprisonment appears to be aimed at conveying a signal to traders that insider dealing and the related offences will not be tolerated. However, it is considered that the increases are largely 'symbolic'[185] given the extreme difficulty in securing successful prosecutions for these offences.

In the assessment of any penalty, the Court must take into account any civil liability award made in terms of the Securities Services Act that arises from the same cause.[186]

---

[180] It is to be noted that, as far as civil liability is concerned, the insider will be liable to pay 'the commission or consideration received' (see s 77(3)*(b)*(iv) of the Securities Services Act and s (4)*(d)* of the Insider Trading Act). See below.

[181] Any 'commission or consideration' received is, however, claimable from the insider. See below.

[182] See s 2 read with s 4(1)*(b)* of the Insider Trading Act. Although s 4 provided that all four the defences were available in respect of the 'encouraging' offence, those set out in s 4(1)*(a)*, s 4(1)*(c)* and s 4(1)*(d)* were, by their nature, inapplicable. It was a defence where the accused: 'was acting on specific instructions from a client, save where the inside information was disclosed to him or her by that client' (s 4(1)*(a)*); 'was acting on behalf of a public sector body in pursuit of monetary policy, policies in respect of exchange rates, the management of public debt or foreign exchange reserves' (s 4(1)*(c)*); and 'was acting in pursuit of the completion or implementation of an affected transaction as defined in section 440A of the Companies Act, 1973 (Act 61 of 1973)' (s 4(1)*(d)*).

[183] The lack of a defence could have harsh consequences. See R Cassim op cit n 67 at 65–6.

[184] See s 115*(a)* of the Securities Services Act.

[185] This is how the increase in the penalty in Australia has been described by Tomasic et al op cit n 111 at 20.9.9.

[186] Section 80(1).

(g) Civil liability

(i) The rationale for civil liability under the Securities Services Act

The rationale for the civil liability provisions is explained by the King Task Group in the following terms:[187]

> The sanction presently provided in the Companies Act against insider trading is a criminal one. Despite the fact that a person who deals with the benefit of unpublished price-sensitive information will be financially advantaged and that other parties who contra-deal in the same instrument without that information will be financially disadvantaged, our common law remedies have not developed, whether in contract or in delict, to protect the victims. Accordingly, at one level persons who have *de facto* suffered are rendered remediless because of the anonymity of the market and the possible problems of causation although harm is foreseen. At another level the advantages of a legislated derivative-type civil remedy, as demonstrated in the United States of America, include a more effective form of discouragement and of redress.
>
> The golden thread which runs throughout our criminal law is that a person is deemed to be innocent until proven guilty. The onus to prove that guilt must be discharged by the State beyond a reasonable doubt. Consequently, in South Africa and other jurisdictions, one of the problems that lie in the way of successfully combating insider trading, is that there is no legislated derivative-type civil remedy. If one adds to this the fact the offices of the Attorneys General and the police are short-staffed, then the problem is exacerbated.

In attempting to follow the King Task Group's recommendations, the Securities Services Act, like the Insider Trading Act, seeks to provide for a civil action to be brought by the Directorate of Market Abuse[188] (a committee of the FSB) against insider dealers, 'encouragers' and 'disclosers'. The action is for the recovery of the profit made or loss avoided by the insider dealer, plus a penalty. The amount recovered is to be paid into a fund to be distributed among persons who dealt in the securities in question at a certain time in relation to the insider dealing. The FSB can recover its costs plus a fee before any distribution is made.

(ii) Bases of civil liability

Except for 'discouraging', the same acts that can give rise to criminal liability can also give rise to civil liability. These have been dealt with under *(f) Criminal liability* above and are not repeated here.

The King Task Group regards the exclusion of 'discouragement' or 'stopping' from the ambit of civil liability as unacceptable.[189] 'Discouragement' or 'stopping' can be as harmful as 'encouraging' or 'disclosing' and, therefore, should have the same consequences.

- *Dealing on one's own account*

Section 77(1) of the Securities Services Act provides:

> **77.** (1) An insider who knows that he or she has inside information and who —
> *(a)* deals directly or indirectly or through an agent, for his or her own account in the securities listed on a regulated market to which the inside information relates or which are likely to be affected by it;

---

[187] King Task Group Draft Report at para 2.1.7 n 19.
[188] Previously called the Insider Trading Directorate. The establishment, composition and powers of the Directorate are dealt with in s 83 of the Securities Services Act.
[189] See King Task Group Final Report op cit n 63 at 5–7.

(b) makes a profit or would have made a profit if he or she had sold the securities at any stage, or avoids a loss, through such dealing; and
(c) fails to prove, on a balance of probabilities, any one of the defences set out in section 73(1)(b),

is liable, at the suit of the board in any court of competent jurisdiction, to pay to the board —
   (i) the equivalent of the profit or loss referred to in paragraph (b);
   (ii) a penalty, for compensatory and punitive purposes, in a sum determined in the discretion of the court but not exceeding three times the amount referred to in paragraph (i);
   (iii) interest; and
   (iv) costs of suit on such scale as may be determined by the court.

The defences available to the defendant, as set out in s 73(1)(b), are the same as those available to a person accused of the offence of insider dealing (see 20.1.4(f)(i) above).[190]

Under the Insider Trading Act[191] civil liability for insider dealing only arose if the defendant made a profit or avoided a loss. This has been changed in the Securities Services Act to include the situation where a profit has not been made but would have been made had the defendant sold the securities at any stage.[192] The effect of the change is that an insider who purchased securities as a result of insider information but has not sold them can nevertheless be liable. The change is no doubt to counter the argument that no profit is made if the securities are not sold.

- *Dealing on behalf of someone else*

Section 77(2) of the Securities Services Act provides:

(2) An insider who knows that he or she has inside information and who —
(a) deals, directly or indirectly, for any other person in the securities listed on a regulated market to which the inside information relates or which are likely to be affected by it;
(b) makes a profit for that other person or would have made a profit if the securities had been sold at any stage, or avoids a loss, through such dealing; and
(c) fails to prove any one of the defences set out in section 73(2)(b) on a balance of probabilities,

is, subject to subsection (5), liable, at the suit of the board in any court of competent jurisdiction, to pay to the board —
   (i) the equivalent of the profit or loss referred to in paragraph (b);
   (ii) a penalty, for compensatory and punitive purposes, in a sum determined in the discretion of the court but not exceeding three times the amount referred to in paragraph (i);
   (iii) interest;
   (iv) the commission or consideration received for such dealing; and
   (v) cost of suit on such scale as may be determined by the court.

The defences available to the defendant, as set out in s 73(2)(b), are the same as those available to a person accused of the offence of dealing on someone else's behalf and are set out in the outline of the criminal provisions (see 20.1.4(f)(ii) above).

- *Disclosure*

Section 77(3) of the Securities Services Act provides:

---

[190] See above.
[191] See s 6(1)(b).
[192] See s 77(1)(b) and (2)(b) of the Securities Services Act.

(3) An insider who knows that he or she has inside information and who —
(a) discloses the inside information to any other person; and
(b) fails to prove on a balance of probabilities the defence set out in section 73(3)*(b)*,
is, subject to subsection (5), liable, at the suit of the board in any court of competent jurisdiction, to pay to the board —
 (i) if the other person dealt in the securities listed on a regulated market to which the inside information relates or which are likely to be affected by it, the equivalent of the profit which the person made or would have made if the securities had been sold at any stage, or the equivalent of the loss avoided, as a result of such dealing;
 (ii) a penalty, for compensatory and punitive purposes, in a sum determined in the discretion of the court but not exceeding three times the amount referred to in paragraph (i);
 (iii) interest;
 (iv) the commission or consideration received for such disclosure; and
 (v) cost of suit on such scale as may be determined by the court.

The defence available to the defendant, as set out in s 73(3)*(b)*, is the same as the defence available to a person accused of the offence of disclosure of inside information and is set out in the outline of the criminal provisions (see 20.1.4*(f)*(iii) above).

- *Encouraging or causing another person to deal*

Section 77(4) of the Securities Services Act provides:

(4) An insider who knows that he or she has inside information and who encourages or causes any other person to deal in the securities listed on a regulated market to which the inside information relates or which are likely to be affected by it is, subject to subsection (5), liable, at the suit of the board in any court of competent jurisdiction, to pay to the board —
(a) if the other person dealt in such securities, the equivalent of the profit which the person made or would have made if the securities had been sold at any stage, or the equivalent of the loss avoided, as a result of such dealing;
(b) a penalty, for compensatory and punitive purposes, in a sum determined in the discretion of the court but not exceeding three times the amount referred to in paragraph *(a)*;
(c) interest;
(d) the commission or consideration received for such encouragement; and
(e) cost of suit on such scale as may be determined by the court.

As is the case regarding criminal liability, there are no statutory defences (see 20.1.4*(f)*(iv) above).

It is clear that encouraging or causing someone to deal can give rise to criminal liability whether the 'tippee' deals or not.[193] The position regarding civil liability is, however, different. It is clear from a reading of s 77(4) that it is only if the 'tippee' deals that the amounts referred to in s 77(4) become payable.[194]

(iii) *Interest*

The civil liability provisions in s 77 of the Securities Services Act provide for liability for, *inter alia,* 'interest'. As under the Insider Trading Act, it is not clear on what capital amount the interest is calculated, nor is it clear what period is to be used in the calculation.

---

[193] See above.
[194] See the words 'if the other person dealt' in s 77(4)*(a)* of the Securities Services Act.

(iv) *Penalty*

The civil liability provisions (s 77) provide for a penalty to be payable by the insider. Serious judicial doubts have been expressed concerning, and considerable academic criticism has been levelled against, the award of punitive damages in delictual claims.[195] In *Fose v Minister of Safety and Security*[196] Ackermann J quoted with approval the following dictum of Lord Devlin in the House of Lords:[197]

> I do not care for the idea that in matters criminal an aggrieved party should be given an option to inflict for his own benefit punishment by a method which denies to the offender the protection of the criminal law.

Ackermann J said in relation to this dictum:[198]

> In my view it becomes even more unacceptable in a country which has become a constitutional state, which has enacted an interim Constitution which is the supreme law of the land and in which extensive criminal procedural rights are entrenched.

It may well be that the Constitutional Court might adopt Ackermann J's view and find that the punitive damages provisions are unconstitutional.[199]

(v) *Joint and several liability*

Section 77(5) provides as follows:

> (5) If the other person referred to in subsections (2), (3) and (4) is liable as an insider in terms of subsection (1), the insider referred to in subsections (2), (3) and (4) is jointly and severally liable together with that other person to pay the amounts set out in subsection (2)(i), (iii) and (v), (3)(i), (iii) and (v), or (4)*(a)*, *(c)* and *(d)*, as the case may be.

The effect of s 77(5) appears to be that if Mr X, an insider who knows he has inside information, (A) deals on behalf of Mr Y or (B) discloses the inside information to Mr Y, or (C) encourages or causes Mr Y to deal in the securities in question, then if Mr Y *is liable as an insider* for dealing, Mr Y would be jointly and severally liable together with Mr X to pay the amounts for which Mr X is liable. Section 77(5), by referring to the amounts set out in sub-ss (2)(i), (iii) and (v), (3)(i), (ii) and (v), or (4)*(a)*, *(c)* and *(d)* (the amounts for which the insider, Mr X, is liable) and not the amounts set out in sub-s (1) (the amounts for which Mr Y is liable) makes it clear that the joint and several liability of Mr X and Mr Y relates to the amounts for which Mr X is liable and not the amounts for which Mr Y is liable.

The position, therefore, reading s 77 as a whole, appears to be as follows: If, for example, Mr X discloses inside information to Mr Y and Mr Y deals and makes a

---

[195] See *Innes v Visser* 1936 WLD 44 at 45, *Lynch v Agnew* 1929 TPD 974 at 978; *Esselen v Argus Printing & Publishing Co Ltd* 1992 (3) SA 764 (T) 771; *Fose v Minister of Safety and Security* 1997 (3) SA 786 (CC) 822–5; McKerron *The Law of Delict* 7 ed (1971) at 207 n 89; J Neethling *Persoonlikheidsreg* (1991) at 60, 61 n 167, 168 n 355; JC van der Walt *Delict: Principles & Cases* (1979) at 5–7; JM Burchell: *The Law of Defamation in South Africa* (1985) at 290–4 and *Principles of Delict* (1993) at 187.
[196] 1997 (3) SA 786 (CC) 827.
[197] See *Rookes v Barnard* [1964] AC 1129 (HL) 1230.
[198] *Fose v Minister of Safety and Security* 1997 (3) SA 786 (CC) 827.
[199] See Jooste op cit n 62.

profit of R1 million and Mr X is liable in terms of s 77(3) and Mr Y is liable in terms of s 77(1), the FSB can claim the R1 million twice, once from Mr X and again from Mr Y, with Mr Y jointly and severally liable with Mr X for Mr X's R1 million. Recovery of the profit twice is distinctly odd, especially considering that Mr X and Mr Y are each already liable to pay a penalty not exceeding three times the amount of the profit.[200] It is also puzzling why Mr Y should be jointly and severally liable for Mr X's payment and not *vice versa*. Possibly the legislature's intention was to give the FSB a single claim for the R1 million profit with Mr X and Mr Y jointly and severally liable therefor, but that is not what s 77 provides. A possible pointer to such intention is the fact that s 77(2), (3) and (4) is made 'subject to subsection (5)' (see s 77(4)) of s 77.

Apart from the above, a flaw in s 77(5) relates to scenario (C) above, namely, where Mr X encourages or causes Mr Y to deal. Section 77(5) provides that, if Mr Y is liable as an insider for dealing, then the joint and several liability referred to in the last paragraph arises. The problem is that Mr Y has not received the inside information. He has only been encouraged or caused to deal. Therefore he cannot be liable as an insider for dealing.

A further anomaly is that in scenario (C), there is no joint and several liability for 'costs of suit' whereas there is in scenarios (A) and (B). Also, in scenario (C) there is joint and several liability for 'the commission or consideration' received, but not in scenarios (A) and (B). There does not appear to be any rational explanation for drawing these distinctions.

(vi) *Determination of profit made or loss avoided*

Section 77(6) determines how the 'profit made, or the profit that would have been made if the listed securities had been sold at any stage, or the loss avoided' is to be determined. It provides that it is determined:

> ... in the discretion of the court which must have regard to factors such as the consideration for the dealing referred to in subsections (2), (3) and (4), the time between the relevant dealing and the publication of the inside information and any other relevant factors.

The reference in s 77(6) to 'the consideration for the *dealing* [emphasis added] referred to in subsections (2), (3) and (4)' is confusing. There is no 'consideration' for 'dealing' referred to in sub-ss (3) or (4). Subsection (2) refers to consideration for dealing on another person's account, sub-s (3) to consideration for 'disclosure' and sub-s (4) to consideration for 'encouraging' or 'causing'.

(vii) *Deposit of monies and recovery of costs*

Any amount recovered by the FSB as a result of the proceedings contemplated in s 77[201] must be deposited by the FSB directly into a specially designated trust account.[202] As a first charge against this trust account, the FSB is entitled to be reimbursed for all expenses that it has reasonably incurred in bringing such

---

[200] See s 77(1)(*a*)(ii) and (3)(ii).
[201] Section 77(6) of the Securities Services Bill 11 of 2001 provided: 'Any amount recovered by the board as a result of the proceedings contemplated in this section *or as a result of an agreement of settlement* must be deposited by the board directly into a specially designated trust account ....'
[202] Section 77(7) of the Securities Services Act.

proceedings and in administering the distributions made to claimants. In addition, it is entitled to a sum equal to 10 per cent of the gross amount recovered less any amount of costs actually recovered from the other party prior to the finalisation of the distribution account.[203]

(viii) *Distribution of balance*

The balance of the amount referred to under the last heading 'must be distributed to all claimants' who —

> (a) submit claims to the directorate within 90 days from the date of publication of a notice in two national newspapers inviting persons who are affected by the dealings referred to in subsections (1) to (4) to submit their claims; and
> (b) prove to the reasonable satisfaction of the claims officer that —
>> (i) they were affected by the dealings referred to in subsections (1) to (4); and
>> (ii) in the case where the inside information was made public within five trading days from the time the insider referred to in subsections (1) and (2), or the other person referred to in subsections (3) and (4) dealt, they dealt in the same securities at the same time or any time after the insider or other person so dealt and before the inside information was made public; or
>> (iii) in every other case, they dealt in the same securities at the same time or any time thereafter on the same day, as the insider or other person referred to in subparagraph (ii).[204]

The period of five days is arbitrary, but an element of arbitrariness is inevitable once one moves away from requiring a direct causal link between the insider dealing and the claimant's loss. The chosen approach is to disregard causation and to compensate claimants who dealt around the same time as the insider dealer.

The arbitrary approach, which was also adopted in the Insider Trading Act,[205] has been borrowed from the USA[206] and signifies a move away from the debate about the need to establish privity between insider and outsider. The insider, it is said, is effectively deemed to owe a duty of disclosure to contemporaneous traders for any transactions undertaken on the basis of inside information in the relevant financial instruments or securities.[207] By trading on the inside information, the insider is effectively deemed to have breached that duty. The theory presupposes that, since the information on which the insider trades is material, these investors would have relied on it and would have altered their conduct accordingly had the information been disclosed.[208] The causal link between the insider and the loss sustained is presumed and the loss is deemed to be sufficiently proximate; the need for privity is thus abolished.[209] The difficulty of draconian liability arising because

---

[203] Section 77(7)(*a*)of the Securities Services Act.
[204] Section 77(8) of the Securities Services Act.
[205] See s 6(6)(*a*) of the Insider Trading Act. Section 6(6)(*a*) used a period of a 'week' and not 'five trading days'.
[206] See s 20A of the Securities Exchange Act of 1934, inserted by the Insider Trading and Securities Fraud Enforcement Act of 1988.
[207] See H McVea 'Fashioning a system of civil penalties for insider dealing: Sections 61 and 62 of the Financial Services Act 1986' 1996 *Journal of Business Law* 344 at 352.
[208] McVea op cit n 207. See also P Anisman *Insider Trading Legislation in Australia: An Outline of the Issues and Alternatives* (1986) 111.
[209] H McVea op cit n 207.

of a duty owed to all contemporaneous traders is averted by limiting the damages.[210] The approach is artificial and leads to fortuitous plaintiffs and windfall recoveries which are not, as a general rule, to be encouraged. However, it is thought to be justifiable where the primary purpose is not compensation, but to further the socially beneficial goal of deterring insider dealing.[211]

The arbitrary approach can thus be defended.

But, what then of the fact that claimants must prove that they have been 'affected' by the dealing?[212] Does that not require an element of causality — whatever that element may be? And how can one speak of 'compensation'[213] where there is not, and cannot be, any causal connection — or loss? It is unclear what is meant by 'affected by the dealings referred to in subsections (1) to (4)' in s 77(8)(b)(i). It would seem certain that this is meant to be a separate and distinct requirement. But when is a person 'affected' by such dealing? Presumably, what is meant is not merely 'affected' but *harmfully* affected. But, in any event, in the case of dealings of listed shares, no one dealing is affected (either harmfully or beneficially) by insider dealing. Persons are 'affected' by the fact that the information has not been disclosed, and this holds true regardless of whether or not there is any insider dealing. If the undisclosed information will, when disclosed, cause the price of the shares to rise, all those who sell before disclosure will be detrimentally affected by the fact that the information has not been disclosed; and all those buying will benefit. And where the information when disclosed will cause the price of the shares to fall, all those who sell before disclosure will benefit from the fact that the information has not been disclosed, and all those who purchase will be harmed. The only possible effect of insider dealing on the market will be to cause the price of the company's shares to move in the right direction, ie to make the market more efficient.

(ix) *Amount the claimant is entitled to*

A claimant is entitled to an amount —

(a) equal to the difference between the price at which the claimant dealt and the price, determined by the court or a settlement, that the claimant would have dealt at if the inside information had been published at the time of dealing; or

(b) equal to the pro rata portion of the balance referred to in subsection (7)(b), calculated according to the relationship which the amount contemplated in paragraph *(a)* bears to all amounts proved in terms of subsection (8) by claimants, whichever is the lesser, unless the claims officer in his or her discretion determines that the claimant should receive a lesser or no amount.[214]

This provision does not repeat the illogical provision in the Insider Trading Act,[215] which provided that a sole claimant was entitled to an amount 'equal to the

---

[210] H McVea op cit n 207.
[211] See DM Branson 'Insider dealing — Part III' (1982) *Journal of Business Law* 536 at 538–9; McVea op cit n 207 at 353.
[212] See s 77(8)(b)(i) of the Securities Services Act.
[213] See the use of the word 'compensatory' in s 77(1)(i), (2)(ii) and (3)(ii) of the Securities Services Act and s (4)(b) of the Insider Trading Act.
[214] Section 77(9) of the Services Security Act.
[215] See s 6(7)(a) of the Insider Trading Act and criticism thereof in Jooste op cit n 63 at 302.

difference between the price at which the claimant dealt and the profit gained or loss avoided'.[216] An amount awarded to a claimant must be reduced by any amount recovered under the common law.[217]

(x) Protection of common-law rights

A claimant's common-law rights to claim any amount from the defendant are preserved save to the extent that any portion of such amount has been recovered under the Securities Services Act.[218] An amount awarded in proceedings under the Securities Services Act must be reduced by any amount recovered under the common law.[219]

(xi) Criminal penalty taken into account

In the assessment of any award under s 77 of the Securities Services Act, the court must take into account any criminal penalty which arises from the same cause and that has been previously imposed.[220]

(xii) Vicarious liability

As in the Insider Trading Act,[221] the common-law principles of vicarious liability are preserved. Section 77(11) provides that '[t]he common-law principles of vicarious liability apply to the civil liability established by this section'. What exactly is meant by this is far from clear. How can the common-law principles of vicarious liability apply to civil liability established by s 77?

Furthermore, it is unclear to what extent employers are exposed to vicarious liability in the context of insider dealing. In terms of the general principles that govern vicarious liability, the employer can escape such liability if the employee has *(a)* subjectively viewed, promoted only his or her own interests, and *(b)* objectively viewed, entirely disengaged him- or herself from his or her contractual duties.[222] In *Minister of Police v Rabie* Jansen JA said:

> It seems clear that an act done by a servant solely for his own interests and purposes, although occasioned by his employment, may fall outside the course or scope of his employment, and that in deciding whether an act by the servant does so fall, some reference is to be made to the servant's intention . . . The test is in this regard subjective. On the other hand, if there is nevertheless a sufficiently close link between the servant's acts for his own interests and purposes and the business of his master, the master may yet be liable. This is an objective test. . . .[223]

---

[216] Under the Insider Trading Act if, for example, the claimant sold 100 shares for R100 at a time when the price would have been R300 if the inside information had been public; the claimant could only claim R100 (ie the profit made by the insider, namely R200 less the price at which the claimant dealt, namely R100). If the price would have been R200 if the inside information had been public, the claimant would have received nothing.
[217] See s 77(10).
[218] Section 85.
[219] Section 77(10).
[220] Section 80(2).
[221] Section 6(11) of the Insider Trading Act.
[222] See, for example, *Minister of Police v Rabie* 1986 (1) SA 117 (A); *Ess Kay Electronics PTE Ltd v First National Bank of Southern Africa Ltd* 1998 (4) SA 1102 (W).
[223] 1986 (1) SA 117 (A) 134.

(xiii) Powers of directorate in civil proceedings

The directorate may withdraw, abandon or compromise any civil proceedings instituted in terms of s 77 of the Securities Services Act, but any agreement of compromise must be made an order of court and the amount of any payment made in terms of such compromise must be made public.[224]

Where civil proceedings have not been instituted, the FSB may apply to the court, after due notice to the other party or parties, for any agreement of compromise to be made an order of court. The parties to the agreement and the amount of any payment made in terms of this agreement must then be made public.[225]

(h) Procedural matters

(i) Jurisdiction

Only a High Court or a regional court has jurisdiction to try any of the offences referred to in ss 73, 75 and 76 of the Securities Services Act and to impose a penalty up to the maximum. In terms of s 115(a) this would be a fine not exceeding R50 million or imprisonment for a period not exceeding ten years, or both a fine and imprisonment.[226]

A court of competent jurisdiction includes the court within whose jurisdiction the regulated market has its principal place of business or head office or in which any element of the dealing or offence occurred. It is not necessary to make any attachment to found or confirm jurisdiction.[227]

(ii) Attachments and interdicts

On application by the FSB, a court may order the attachment of assets or evidence to prevent their concealment, removal, dissipation or destruction.[228]

The FSB may institute any interdict or interlocutory proceedings against a person who made a profit or avoided a loss, or who the FSB reasonably believes may have made a profit or avoided a loss as contemplated in s 77.[229]

Such proceedings may include proceedings to obtain an interdict to prevent the disposal of assets or of evidence.[230]

(iii) Powers and duties of Financial Services Board

The FSB is responsible for supervising compliance with the insider trading provisions of the Securities Services Act[231] and must exercise its powers in terms of the Financial Services Board Act 97 of 1999. The FSB may also, subject to s 83:[232]

---

[224] Section 78(1).
[225] Section 78(2) of the Securities Services Act.
[226] Section 79(1).
[227] Section 79(2) of the Securities Services Act.
[228] Section 81(1) of the Securities Services Act.
[229] Section 81(2) of the Securities Services Act.
[230] Section 81(3) of the Securities Services Act.
[231] Section 82(1).
[232] See below in 20.1.4(h)(iv).

- investigate any matter relating to an offence referred to in ss 73, 75 and 76 of the Securities Services Act, including insider trading in terms of section 440F of the 1973 Companies Act and the Insider Trading Act that was committed before the repeal of that section and that Act.[233] In relation to a matter so investigated, it may, on the authority of a warrant, at any time without prior notice:
  (i) enter any premises and require the production of any document;
  (ii) enter and search any premises for any document;
  (iii) open any strongroom, safe or other container which it suspects contains any document;
  (iv) examine, make extracts from and copy any document or, against the issue of a receipt, remove such document temporarily for that purpose;
  (v) against the issue of a receipt, seize any document;
  (vi) retain any seized document for as long as it may be required for criminal or other proceedings,
  but the board may proceed without a warrant, if the person in control of any premises consents to the actions;[234]
- institute such proceedings as are contemplated in the insider trading provisions of the Securities Services Act;[235]
- administer the proof of claims and distribution of payments;[236]
- summon any person who is believed to be able to furnish any information on the subject of any investigation or to have in that person's possession or under his or her control any document that has bearing upon that subject, to lodge that document with the FSB, or to appear at a time and place specified in the summons, to be interrogated or to produce that document;[237] and
- interrogate any such person under oath or affirmation that has been duly administered, and examine or retain for examination any document of this nature. Any person from whom any document has been taken and retained under s 82(2)*(e)* must, while that document is in possession of the FSB, be allowed to make copies of the document at that person's request and expense, or to take extracts from the document at any reasonable time and under the supervision of the person in charge of the investigation.[238]

A warrant may be issued, on application by the FSB, by a judge or magistrate who has jurisdiction in the area where the premises in question are located.[239] Such a warrant may only be issued if it appears from information under oath that there is reason to believe that a document relating to the matter being investigated is kept at the premises in question.[240] Any person from whom a document has been seized, or such person's authorised representative, may examine that document

---

[233] See s 82(2)*(a)* of the Securities Services Act.
[234] Section 82(2)*(f)*.
[235] See s 82(2)*(b)*.
[236] See s 82(2)*(c)*.
[237] See s 82(2)*(d)*.
[238] See s 82(2)*(e)*.
[239] Section 82(3)*(a)*.
[240] Section 82(3)*(b)*.

and make extracts from it under the supervision of the FSB during normal office hours.[241]

Any person who has been duly summoned and who, without sufficient cause:

(i) fails to appear at the time and place specified in the summons;
(ii) fails to remain in attendance until excused by the board from further attendance;
(iii) refuses to take an oath or to make an affirmation as contemplated in subsection (2)*(e)*;
(iv) fails to answer fully and satisfactorily any question lawfully put to him or her under subsection (2)*(e)*; or
(v) fails to furnish information or to produce a document in terms of subsection (2)*(d)*,

commits an offence and is liable on conviction to a fine or to imprisonment for a period not exceeding two years or to both a fine and such imprisonment.[242]

The FSB may, subject to the conditions it may determine, delegate the power to investigate any alleged contravention of the insider trading provisions in the Securities Services Act to any fit person, and that person has the powers of summons, interrogation and search and seizure, as set out in sub-s (2)*(d)*, *(e)* and *(f)*.[243]

If the Director of Public Prosecutions declines to prosecute for an alleged offence, the FSB may prosecute in respect of such offence in any court competent to try that offence. However, s 8(2) and (3) of the Criminal Procedure Act 51 of 1977 will not apply to such a prosecution.[244] The FSB must, at the request of the directorate, investigate any matter and summon and interrogate any person in respect of the matter.[245]

(iv) *Composition and functions of the directorate*

The Insider Trading Directorate established by the Insider Trading Act continues to exist, despite the repeal of that Act.[246] The Insider Trading Directorate is now known as the Directorate of Market Abuse and a reference to the Insider Trading Directorate in any law must, unless clearly inappropriate, be construed as a reference to the Directorate of Market Abuse.[247]

The directorate exercises the powers of the FSB to institute any civil proceedings and to investigate any matter relating to an offence.[248] The directorate is not intended to act as an administrative body when exercising these powers.[249]

The directorate must:

• report quarterly to the FSB and the Minister on its activities relating to the insider trading provisions, and

---

[241] See s 82(3)*(c)*.
[242] Section 82(3)*(d)*.
[243] See s 82(4).
[244] Section 82(9).
[245] Section 82(10).
[246] Section 83(1)*(a)*.
[247] Section 83(1)*(b)*.
[248] Section 83(1)*(c)*.
[249] Section 83(1)*(d)*.

- furnish the FSB and the Minister, at their request, with copies of such documents and records of proceedings of the directorate, as the board or the Minister may direct.[250]

The directorate consists of the chairperson and members and alternate members appointed by the Minister.[251] A member and alternate member hold office for the period that the Minister may determine at the time of his or her appointment. This period may not exceed three years. The member is eligible for reappointment upon the expiry of his or her term of office. If, when the member's term of office expires, he or she is not reappointed or a new member is not appointed, the former member must remain in office for a further period of not more than six months.[252]

Section 83(2)(c) states the following:

> The Minister may remove the chairperson from his or her office or terminate the membership of any other member on good cause shown and after having given the chairperson or member, as the case may be, sufficient opportunity to show why he or she should not be removed or why his or her membership should not be terminated.

The Minister must appoint as members of the directorate:[253]

(a) the executive officer of the board or his or her deputy, or both;
(b) one person and an alternate from each of the regulated markets in the Republic;
(c) one commercial lawyer of appropriate experience and an alternate;
(d) one accountant of appropriate experience and an alternate;
(e) one person of appropriate experience and an alternate from the insurance industry;
(f) one person of appropriate experience and an alternate from the banking industry;
(g) one person of appropriate experience and an alternate from the fund management industry;
(h) one person of appropriate experience and an alternate nominated by the Share Holders' Association of South Africa or any other similar organisation chosen by the Minister;
(i) one person of appropriate experience and an alternate nominated by the SA Reserve Bank; and
(j) two other persons of appropriate experience and alternates.

These persons are nominated by reason of their availability and knowledge of financial markets and may not be practising authorised users.[254]

The following provisions are contained in s 83(5) to (11) of the Securities Services Act:

> (5) The directorate must designate from its members a deputy chairperson who performs the functions of the chairperson when the office of chairperson is vacant or when the chairperson is unable to perform his or her functions.
>
> (6) The members of the directorate may co-opt one or more persons as additional members of the directorate.
>
> (7) All members of the directorate, other than the additional members, have one vote in respect of matters considered by the directorate, but an alternate member only has a vote in the absence from a meeting of the member whom the alternate is representing.
>
> (8) The meetings of the directorate are held at such times and places as the chairperson may determine, but four members of the directorate may, by notice in writing to the

---

[250] Section 83(1)(d).
[251] Section 83(2)(a).
[252] See s 83(2)(b).
[253] Section 83(3).
[254] Section 83(4).

chairperson of the directorate demand that a meeting of the directorate be held within seven business days of such notice.

(9) The chairperson must determine the procedure of a meeting of the directorate.

(10) The decision of a majority of the members of the directorate constitutes the decision of the directorate.

(11) No proceedings of the directorate are invalid by reason only of the fact that a vacancy existed on the directorate or that any member was not present during such proceedings or any part thereof.

(i) Confidentiality and sharing of information

In terms of s 86(1) of the Securities Services Act, no person may disclose to any other person any information acquired in the performance of functions in terms of the insider trading provisions. Any person who does so commits an offence and is liable on conviction to a fine or imprisonment for a period not exceeding two years, or to both a fine and imprisonment.[255]

Disclosure of the information does not constitute a contravention of that s 86(1) if made by:

- a person for the purpose of performing functions in terms of the insider trading provisions in Chapter VIII of the Securities Services Act,
- a person for the purpose of any legal proceedings in terms of the insider trading provisions in Chapter VIII of that Act,
- a person when required to do so by a court or any other law,
- the directorate or the FSB, if it is necessary to achieve one or more of the objects of s 2 of the Securities Services Act,
- the directorate, if it is in the public interest, or
- the directorate by publishing the status and outcome of investigations under the insider trading provisions in Chapter VIII.[256]

The directorate may share information concerning any matter dealt with in terms of the insider trading provisions in Chapter VIII with the institutions that have nominated persons to the directorate, the Securities Regulation Panel constituted in terms of s 440B of the 1973 Companies Act, the South African Reserve Bank, the Public Accountants' and Auditors' Board constituted in terms of the Public Accountants' and Auditors' Act, all self-regulatory organisations, the Financial Intelligence Centre established by the Financial Intelligence Centre Act 38 of 2001, the National Treasury, the Minister and with the persons, whether inside South Africa or elsewhere, responsible for regulating, investigating or prosecuting insider trading.[257]

(j) Offences committed in terms of section 440F of the 1973 Companies Act and the Insider Trading Act

Despite the repeal of s 440F of the Companies Act 61 of 1973 and the Insider Trading Act, the FSB is responsible for investigating alleged offences in terms of

---

[255] Section 86(2).
[256] Section 86(1).
[257] See s 84(4).

that section and the Insider Trading Act that were committed before the repeal, and for that purpose it has the powers and duties referred to in s 82.[258]

Section 440F provided as follows:

Prohibition of insider trading

(1) Any person who, whether directly or indirectly, knowingly deals in a security on the basis of unpublished price-sensitive information in respect of that security, shall be guilty of an offence if such person knows that such information has been obtained —
- *(a)* by virtue of a relationship of trust or any other contractual relationship, whether or not the person concerned is a party to that relationship; or
- *(b)* through espionage, theft, bribery, fraud, misrepresentation or any other wrongful method, irrespective of the nature thereof.

(2) For the purposes of this section —
- *(a)* 'unpublished price-sensitive information', in respect of a security, means information which —
  - (i) relates to matters in respect of the internal affairs of a company or its operations, assets, earning power or involvement as offeror or offeree company in an affected transaction or proposed affected transaction;
  - (ii) is not generally available to the reasonable investor in the relevant markets for that security; and
  - (iii) would reasonably be expected to affect materially the price of such security if it were generally available; 'generally available' means available in the sense that such steps have been taken, and such time has elapsed, that it can reasonably be expected that such information as referred to in paragraph *(a)* is or should be known to such investor as referred to in subparagraph (ii) of paragraph *(a)*.

(3) If at criminal proceedings at which an accused is charged with an offence under subsection (1), it is proved that —
- *(a)* the accused was in possession of unpublished price-sensitive information in respect of the security in question at the time of the alleged commission of the offence; or
- *(b)* unpublished price-sensitive information was obtained in the manner contemplated in subsection (1)*(a)* or *(b)*,

he or it shall be deemed, unless the contrary is proved, in the case of —
  - (i) paragraph *(a)*, to have knowingly dealt in that security on the basis of such information;
  - (ii) paragraph *(b)*, to have known that such information was so obtained.

(4) *(a)* Any person who contravenes subsection (1) shall be liable to any other person for any loss or damage suffered by that person as a result of such contravention.

(b) In the case of dealings in a security on a stock exchange or a financial market as defined in section 1 of the Financial Markets Control Act, 1989 (Act 55 of 1989), the plaintiff shall not need to prove intention or negligence towards him or it in an action contemplated in paragraph *(a)*.

(5) The provisions of this section shall not apply to dealings in members' interest in a close corporation.

(6) Subject to subsection (5), the Minister may, on the advice of the panel, by notice in the *Gazette* exempt any class of persons from the provisions of this section on such conditions and to such extent as he may deem fit, and may at any time in like manner revoke or amend any such exemption.

The Securities Regulation Panel constituted in terms of s 440B of the 1973 Companies Act must disclose to the FSB all information in its possession relating

---

[258] Section 87(1).

to an alleged offence.[259] In turn, the FSB may disclose such information to any of the institutions or persons referred to in s 86(3).[260]

20.2 MARKET MANIPULATION*

20.2.1 Introduction

Market manipulation refers to the attempt to interfere with the operation of the stock market. Stock markets operate on the principle of a free market, according to which supply and demand regulate the price of securities so that the price of a security reflects its true value.[261] Any interference with this process of price determination amounts to market manipulation. Market manipulation may result in investors being misled into buying worthless shares or selling their otherwise valuable investments below their true market price. Market manipulation thus creates an artificial picture that obscures the true value of the securities being manipulated.

The prohibition of market manipulation is not an entirely new concept in our law. It is prohibited by the common law and was prohibited by the now repealed Stock Exchanges Control Act 1 of 1985 ('SECA') and the Financial Markets Control Act 55 of 1989 ('FMCA').[262] The Securities Services Act goes much further than these Acts in prohibiting market manipulation, even to the extent that certain acts are deemed to constitute a manipulative practice. 'Market abuse' is described in the Securities Services Act as constituting three offences:

- insider trading,
- engaging in a prohibited trading practice, and
- the making or publishing of false, misleading or deceptive statements, promises and forecasts.

The latter two offences constitute market manipulation and are the focus of this section. Insider trading was discussed at length in 20.1.

20.2.2 Objective of market manipulation

The objective of manipulating the market is to make money dishonestly, either directly through transactions or by other means. A number of factors may cause a person to manipulate the market. For example, market manipulators would attempt to influence the price of a security so that they could buy the securities at a lower price, sell them at a profit, combat competitive transactions, or influence

---

[259] Section 87(2).
[260] See s 87(3). Presumably the reference to 'section 86(3)' should be to 'section 86(4)'.
* This section on market manipulation, written by Rehana Cassim, relies on the following two articles: Rehana Cassim 'An analysis of market manipulation under the Securities Services Act 36 of 2004 (Part 1)' (2008) 20(1) *SA Merc LJ* 33, and Rehana Cassim 'An analysis of market manipulation under the Securities Services Act 36 of 2004 (Part 2)' (2008) 20(2) *SA Merc LJ* 177.
[261] JJ Henning and S du Toit 'High-pressure selling of securities: From rigging the market to false trading, market manipulation and insider dealing' (2000) 21 *The Company Lawyer* 257 at 257.
[262] SECA prohibited the manipulation of 'securities', which included stocks, shares and debentures (s 1 of SECA), while the FMCA prohibited the manipulation of 'financial instruments' which included futures contracts, option contracts and loan stock on a financial market (s 1 of FMCA).

takeover bids or other large transactions.[263] In a hostile takeover the directors of the target company would generally want to secure a market price for their company's securities that is higher than the bid price, so as to induce the shareholders to reject the takeover bid. The bidder, on the other hand, would have an interest in seeing the price of those securities declining on the market. Even in the absence of a takeover offer, the management of a public company would be concerned that any fall in the market price of the company's securities would make the company vulnerable to a takeover bid which, if successful, would result in the directors being removed from office.

Those in a position to manipulate the market include issuers of securities, participants in the securities market, market intermediaries and a combination of these persons acting in co-operation or in concert with each other.[264]

20.2.3 The rationale of regulating market manipulation

One rationale of regulating market manipulation is to maintain an open and free market where the natural forces of supply and demand determine a security's price. Other reasons why market manipulation is regulated are to achieve investor confidence in the integrity of the financial markets and to protect investors from market manipulation.

If investors have confidence in the fairness of the markets, it would enhance the liquidity and the efficiency of the markets.[265] Inevitably, if investors are wary of the markets due to suspect market practices, they would be inclined to move their cash into investments that are regarded as safe or to invest in credible markets elsewhere. In Australia, where market manipulation is prohibited by the Australian Corporations Act 50 of 2001,[266] the Australian High Court in *North v Marra Developments Limited*[267] stated that it is in the interest of the community as a whole that the market is free from manipulation.

Most critics of market manipulation practices are of the view that the practice ought to be statutorily prohibited and regulated. But not all critics agree. They fear, among other things, that excessive regulation of market behaviour would inhibit legitimate market activity.[268] Another fear is that, if the legislation that prohibits market manipulation is drafted too widely, it could prohibit conduct that may otherwise be efficient.[269] It is submitted that these fears are well grounded

---

[263] Technical Committee of the International Organization of Securities Commissions Public Document No 103 *Investigating and Prosecuting Market Manipulation* (May 2000) at 6, available at http://www.iosco.org/library/pubdocs/pdf/IOSCOPD103.pdf.
[264] Technical Committee of the International Organization of Securities Commissions op cit n 263 at 7.
[265] Technical Committee of the International Organization of Securities Commissions op cit n 263 at 2.
[266] Chapter 7, Part 7.10, Division 2.
[267] (1981) 148 CLR 42 (HC Aus) 59.
[268] Shazeeda Ali 'Market abuse: It's not just a Wall Street thing' (2006) 27 *The Company Lawyer* 222 at 224.
[269] Ministry of Economic Development (New Zealand) *Reform of Securities Trading Law: Volume Two: Market Manipulation Law Discussion Document* (2002) para 63, available at http://www.med.govt.nz/templates/MultipageDocumentPage____6861.aspx.

and that overregulation of market manipulation must be guarded against so as not inadvertently to inhibit legitimate market activity.[270]

20.2.4 The regulation of market manipulation at common law

Market manipulation is prohibited in South Africa at common law, where it is known as the crime of 'rigging the market'. This common-law crime of rigging the market is predominantly based on English law. A 'rig' is essentially a fictitious operation. In the earliest reported South African case on rigging the market, *R v McLachlan and Bernstein*,[271] De Waal JP laid down the essential elements of the crime of rigging the market:

- the rigger must hold shares (generally a large parcel of shares) that he or she wishes to offload to the ignorant public, and which the rigger cannot offload other than by the creation of a fictitious market for those shares,
- the shares must be practically valueless, or have a value that is far below that at which the rigger wishes to offload them, and
- as a result of a successful rig the unsuspecting public must be left with worthless shares, at which stage the rigger withdraws his or her support by ceasing to operate, and the shares inevitably recede to the value at which they stood before the rig had commenced.

In *S v Marks*,[272] Hill J ruled, with reference to the second and third requirements for rigging the market laid down in *R v McLachlan and Bernstein*, that it was not a necessary element of rigging the market that the shares should be valueless or that members of the public should be left with worthless shares.[273] The learned Justice also modified the first requirement by stating that it is not a prerequisite for the perpetration of a rig that the rigger must hold a parcel of shares that he or she wants to offload on the public — it is only at the time when the rigger wishes to benefit from the result of his or her rigging operations that he or she must have had a parcel of shares available to offload on the buying public at a profit.[274] For instance, the rigger may manipulate market dealings by placing buying and selling orders without becoming the holder of any shares but with the aim of acquiring, at some stage during the rigging operation, a quantity of shares for offloading on the public at a later stage when the prices have risen to the desired level.[275] Alternatively, the rigger may acquire an option to buy shares, which he or she would then exercise when they are able to make a profit as a result of their manipulation.[276]

---

[270] Two critics who are strongly of the view that market manipulation ought not to be statutorily prohibited are Fischel and Ross (see Daniel R Fischel and David J Ross 'Should the law prohibit "manipulation" in financial markets?' (1991) 105 *Harvard LR* 503). See also Steve Thel '$850 000 in six minutes — the mechanics of securities manipulation' (1994) 79 *Cornell Law Review* 219, who challenges some of the arguments put forward by Fischel and Ross for not imposing statutory prohibitions against market manipulation.
[271] 1929 WLD 149 at 155, 156.
[272] 1965 (3) SA 834 (W).
[273] *S v Marks* (supra) at 846.
[274] At 846–7.
[275] At 847.
[276] At 847.

At common law a contract that involves an attempt to deceive other traders in the market is void for illegality, even where the transaction involved an actual sale or purchase of securities. In *Scott v Brown, Doering, McNab & Co, Slaughter & May v Brown, Doering, McNab & Co*[277] the plaintiff had deliberately instructed stockbrokers to purchase shares on the market at a premium to the issue price, with the sole object of inducing the public into believing that there was a *bona fide* market for the shares and that the shares were trading at a genuine premium. An action instituted by the plaintiff under its contract with the stockbrokers failed on the ground that the contract was void for illegality. On appeal, Lindley J, in ruling that the contract was illegal, stated that:

> The plaintiff's purchase was an actual purchase, not a sham purchase; that is true, but it is also true that the sole object of the purchase was to cheat and mislead the public ... his illegal contract confers no rights on him.[278]

Significantly, the statutory prohibition against market manipulation applies only to listed securities,[279] whereas the common-law offence of rigging the market applies to both listed and unlisted securities. It is important to note that the Securities Services Act does not repeal the common-law crime of rigging the market. Consequently, if an act falls outside the scope of the statutory prohibition of market manipulation in the Securities Services Act, the common-law crime of rigging the market (or other common-law remedies) could still apply.

It has repeatedly been emphasised by the courts that it is difficult to prove the crime of rigging the market because the manipulative manoeuvres are complex and are generally secretly executed and skillfully disguised by the rigger.[280] The schemes are often well planned to an extent that makes it difficult to distinguish real market fluctuations from artificial price inflations.[281]

20.2.5 Market manipulation under the Securities Services Act

(a) Prohibited trading practices

Section 75(1) of the Securities Services Act prohibits trade-based market manipulation. Trade-based market manipulation involves techniques designed to distort the market and entails conduct that interferes with the normal market mechanisms

---

[277] [1892] 2 QB 724 (CA).
[278] *Scott v Brown, Doering, McNab & Co, Slaughter & May v Brown, Doering, McNab & Co* (supra) at 729. This general principle was approved by the High Court of Australia in *North v Marra Developments Limited* (1981) 148 CLR 42 (HC Aus) 60.
[279] The definition of 'securities' is set out in s 1 of the Securities Services Act. Money market instruments have been expressly excluded from the definition (except for the purposes of Chapter IV of the Securities Services Act, which deals with the custody and administration of securities). Listed securities are defined in s 1 of the Securities Services Act as meaning 'securities included in the list of securities kept by an exchange in terms of section 12'. An 'exchange' is defined in s 1 of the Securities Services Act as meaning 'a person who constitutes, maintains and provides an infrastructure —
  (a) for bringing together buyers and sellers of securities;
  (b) for matching the orders for securities of multiple buyers and sellers; and
  (c) whereby a matched order for securities constitutes a transaction.'
[280] See for example *S v Marks* 1965 (3) SA 834 (W) 848.
[281] Henning & Du Toit op cit n 261 at 258.

of supply and demand for securities.[282] Trade-based manipulative practices typically comprise the buying or selling of a security by a person that misleads or deceives others about the trading volume or the price of that security. Section 75(1) provides as follows:

Prohibited trading practices

75. (1) No person may —
(a) either for such person's own account or on behalf of another person, directly or indirectly use or knowingly participate in the use of any manipulative, improper, false or deceptive practice of trading in a security listed on a regulated market, which practice creates or might create —
   (i) a false or deceptive appearance of the trading activity in connection with; or
   (ii) an artificial price for,
   that security;
(b) place an order to buy or sell listed securities which, to his or her knowledge will, if executed, have the effect contemplated in paragraph *(a)*.

Broadly speaking, there are two types of trade-based market manipulation practices that are prohibited:

(i) creating a false or deceptive appearance of the trading activity in connection with a listed security; and
(ii) creating an artificial price for a listed security.

In addition, s 75(1)*(b)* of the Securities Services Act prohibits the placing of an order to buy or sell listed securities which, if executed, would create a false or deceptive appearance of the trading activity in connection with that security, or an artificial price for that security.

Some noteworthy points about trade-based market manipulation are as follows:

(i) *Manipulative trading practices*

To come within the scope of s 75(1)*(a)* of the Securities Services Act, the trading practice must be 'manipulative, improper, false or deceptive'. The Securities Services Act does not define these terms. The term 'manipulative' was defined by the US Supreme Court in *Ernst & Ernst v Hochfelder*[283] as follows:

Use of the word 'manipulative' is especially significant. It is and was virtually a term of art when used in connection with securities markets. It connotes intentional or wilful conduct designed to deceive or defraud investors by controlling or artificially affecting the price of securities.[284]

(ii) *Committing the offence on behalf of another person, directly or indirectly*

Section 75(1)*(a)* of the Securities Services Act prohibits a person from using or knowingly participating in a prohibited trading practice for that person's own account or on behalf of another person, whether directly or indirectly. The word 'indirectly' implies that, if a person engages in a manipulative trading practice

---

[282] Ministry of Economic Development (New Zealand) *Reform of Securities Trading Law: Volume Two: Market Manipulation Law Discussion Document* (2002) para 64 available at http://www.med.govt.nz/templates/MultipageDocumentPage____6861.aspx.
[283] 425 US 185 (US SC, 1976).
[284] *Ernst & Ernst v Hochfelder* (supra) at 199.

through an intermediary, that person would still contravene s 75(1)(a) of the Securities Services Act. Thus the word 'indirectly' in s 75(1)(a) prevents a person from circumventing the prohibition of market manipulation by employing another person to engage in it.

Would the intermediary also be guilty of market manipulation? It follows from the words 'on behalf of another person' in s 75(1)(a) that the intermediary would indeed also be guilty of infringing the section, provided the necessary element of *mens rea* is satisfied. If an intermediary merely carries out a customer's order and honestly does not know that the instruction would result in market manipulation, he or she would clearly not be guilty of 'knowingly' participating in the manipulative trading practice.

This raises the question whether intermediaries are under a duty to satisfy themselves that their customers' transactions would not give rise to behaviour that amounts to market manipulation. In the UK the Financial Services Authority has expressed the view that an intermediary would indeed be expected to make an assessment of the behaviour of his or her customer and of the nature of the transaction in question to determine whether or not this would constitute market manipulation.[285]

(iii) *Participating in a manipulative trading practice*

As already mentioned, s 75(1)(a) of the Securities Services Act prohibits a person from *participating* in a manipulative trading practice. The word 'participate' appears to indicate that a secondary actor who gives some degree of assistance to a market manipulator would be guilty of contravening the section, provided he or she had the necessary *mens rea* at the time of such assistance. A secondary actor could for instance be an investment banker, an accountant, a lawyer or an underwriter who gives assistance to market manipulators that enables a manipulative trading practice. Examples of these practices include advising a client on a business transaction or drafting documents related to a business structure that has questionable business or accounting practices.

But what degree of participation is required by the secondary actor before he or she will have committed the offence of market manipulation? Would it suffice if the participation were minimal or would substantial participation be required? If a secondary actor were to incur liability under s 75(1)(a) of the Securities Services Act for minimal participation in the offence, it would introduce potentially far-reaching duties and uncertainties for secondary actors engaged in the day-to-day business transactions of their clients.[286] Perhaps a secondary actor ought to incur liability only if he or she substantially participates in the practice in question. This is a question of degree dependent on the facts and the circumstances of each case.

(iv) *Creation of a false or deceptive appearance of trading activity*

Creating a false or deceptive appearance of a trading activity in connection with a security means the trading practice must give a false or deceptive impression

---

[285] See Financial Services Authority Consultation Paper 59 'Market abuse: A draft Code of Market Conduct' (July 2000) at para 6.87.
[286] See *In re Charter Communications Inc. Securities Litigation v Scientific-Atlanta, Inc.; Motorola, Inc.* 443 F 3d 987 (8th Cir 2006) 992–3.

regarding the supply of or demand for that security. The words 'might create' in s 75(1)*(a)* indicate that the offence would be committed even if a false or deceptive appearance of the trading activity in connection with a security or an artificial price for that security were not in fact created — it is sufficient if the trading practice merely had the potential to create the false or deceptive impression or the artificial price.

(v) *Creation of an artificial price for a security*

Various factors could be used to determine whether or not a person's behaviour amounts to creating an artificial price for a security. These factors include the extent to which price, rate or option volatility movements for the security in question are outside their normal daily, weekly or monthly range, and whether a person has successively and consistently increased or decreased his or her bid, offer or the price he or she has paid for a security.

(vi) *Placing orders to buy or sell listed securities*

Section 75(1)*(b)* of the Securities Services Act makes it an offence for a person to place an order to buy or sell listed securities which, to his or her knowledge, if executed, would create, or might create, a false or deceptive appearance of the trading activity in connection with that security, or an artificial price for that security.

Unlike s 75(1)*(a)*, s 75(1)*(b)* does not make it an offence to place an order to buy or sell securities 'directly or indirectly'. Would one then infringe s 75(1)*(b)* if an intermediary were instructed to place an order to buy or sell securities which would have the effect contemplated in s 75(1)*(a)* of the Securities Services Act? The provision may well be contravened, because one's instructions to the intermediary could arguably constitute placing an order to buy or sell securities. Thus, even though the word 'indirectly' is not explicitly used in s 75(1)*(b)*, the offence in that section may be committed when the intermediary is instructed to place the relevant order on one's behalf.

Notably, it is not an offence under s 75(1)*(b)* for a person to place an order 'on behalf of another person', as is the case with s 75(1)*(a)* of the Securities Services Act. This could be the result of an oversight on the part of the legislature. The question thus arises whether an intermediary who was instructed to place an order to buy or sell listed securities on behalf of another person would escape liability under s 75(1)*(b)* of the Securities Services Act. The answer would probably depend on the knowledge of the intermediary, namely, whether the intermediary knew that the placing of the order would have the effect contemplated in s 75(1)*(a)*. Clearly, where a person colludes with his or her intermediary, the intermediary would, by placing the order on that person's behalf, infringe s 75(1)*(b)*.[287]

Again, the question must arise whether intermediaries have a duty to satisfy themselves that the placing of their customers' orders would not give rise to behaviour that amounts to market manipulation. It is submitted that, in principle,

---

[287] Financial Services Authority Consultation Paper 59 op cit n 285.

intermediaries ought to be required to make an assessment of the behaviour of their customers and of the nature of the transaction in question to determine whether or not this would constitute market manipulation.

(vii) *Proof of market manipulation*

It may be difficult to obtain direct evidence in the form of documents or testimony that a person has used or has knowingly participated in a prohibited trading practice. It is more likely that proof of market manipulation would be based on circumstantial or indirect evidence and on inferences based on such evidence.[288] In *Herman & MacLean v Huddleston*[289] the US Supreme Court noted that proof of intention in the context of market manipulation is often a matter of inference based on circumstantial evidence and stated that, in this context, circumstantial evidence is permissible. For instance, such inferences could be based on patterns of conduct or the fact that the offender has a pecuniary interest in a security, or by analysing the trading patterns and any irregularities which may emerge from the trading data.[290]

(viii) *Regulated market*

The prohibition in s 75(1)(*a*) of the Securities Services Act against engaging in a prohibited trading practice relates to securities 'listed on a regulated market'. Section 72 of the Securities Services Act defines a 'regulated market' as meaning 'any market, whether domestic or foreign, which is regulated in terms of the laws of the country in which the market conducts business as a market for dealing in securities listed on that market.' This means the market manipulation provisions of the Securities Services Act would apply to securities listed on a foreign market, even if there were no territorial link to South Africa, just as it does in the case of insider trading.[291] The Securities Services Act is thus particularly far-reaching in not requiring a territorial link with South Africa for a market manipulation offence to be committed under this Act.

In sharp contrast, other jurisdictions, such as the UK and the European Union, require a territorial nexus before the relevant authorities may take any action in respect of market manipulation offences.[292] It is strange that the Securities Services Act should not require any territorial link with South Africa for a market

---

[288] *Herman & MacLean v Huddleston* 459 US 375 (1983) 391; Technical Committee of the International Organization of Securities Commissions op cit n 263 at 21.

[289] 459 US 375 (1983) 391, approved in *In re Software Toolworks, Inc. Securities Litigation* 50 F 3d 615 (9th Cir 1994) 627.

[290] Technical Committee of the International Organization of Securities Commissions op cit n 263 at 21.

[291] See Osode op cit n 125 at 260 and R Cassim op cit n 67 at 66–7.

[292] See s 118(5) of the Financial Services and Markets Act 2008 and art 10 of Directive 2003/6/EC of the European Parliament and of the Council of 28 January 2003 on insider dealing and market manipulation (market abuse) (Official Journal L 96 of 12.4.2003) (the 'EU Market Abuse Directive'). Due to concerns that the European financial markets had become distorted, the European Parliament and the Council of the EU recently adopted a directive on insider dealing and market manipulation. The EU Market Abuse Directive repeals and replaces the Insider Dealing Directive (No 89/592/EEC) (Official Journal L 334 of 18.11.1989), which applied only to insider dealing and not to market manipulation (Article 20 of the EU Market Abuse Directive).

manipulation offence to be committed under the Act. It is submitted that, if manipulative behaviour occurs outside South Africa but affects a South African financial market, the FSB is rightly granted jurisdiction to investigate and pursue such conduct. But it is not clear how the South African financial markets would benefit from a prosecution of a non-resident who manipulates a foreign market where this has no effect on a South African financial market. In any event, the cost of pursuing such a prosecution on a global scale would be prohibitive.[293]

(b) Deemed prohibited trading practices

Section 75(3) of the Securities Services Act deems certain trading practices to be manipulative, improper, false or deceptive. If an activity meets the requirements of a deemed manipulative trading practice, that activity will be deemed to have contravened s 75(1) of the Securities Services Act.

The words 'without limiting the generality of subsection (1)' in s 75(3) make it clear that, if an activity does not meet the requirements of a deemed manipulative trading practice, it may still be prohibited if it infringes the general prohibition contained in s 75(1) of the Securities Services Act.

As mentioned before, two trading practices are prohibited by s 75(1) — creating a false or deceptive appearance of the trading activity in connection with a security, and creating an artificial price for a security. Some of the deemed prohibited trading practices do the former while others do the latter. These trading practices are discussed below.

(i) Wash sales

This practice involves approving or entering on a regulated market an order to buy or sell a listed security which involves no change in the beneficial ownership of that security.[294] This is known as a 'wash sale'[295] and involves a person (either directly or indirectly) being both the purchaser and the seller of securities in the same transaction. This results in the purchaser incurring no real financial obligation to the seller and there is in effect no change in the beneficial ownership of the security.[296]

A wash sale creates a false or deceptive appearance of trading activity in connection with a security. The manipulator undertaking a wash sale usually undertakes frequent trades in the security in the hope that other investors would be attracted by the increased turnover of the security.[297] The object of this practice is to gain financially by creating a small price differential between the buy and sell rates of the security in question.[298] In *United States v Brown*[299] the US Court of Appeals commented that wash sales are in the nature of deceit as they 'broadcast

---

[293] Osode op cit n 125 at 260.
[294] Section 75(3)(a) of the Securities Services Act.
[295] *Ernst & Ernst v Hochfelder* 425 US 185 (US SC, 1976) 205 n 25.
[296] Ministry of Economic Development (New Zealand) op cit n 282 at para 73.
[297] Ibid.
[298] Ibid.
[299] 79 F 2d 321 (2d Cir 1935).

the fact that a buyer and a seller have agreed to exchange the shares at a published price, when they have not done so'.[300]

(ii) Matched orders

This practice entails approving or entering on a regulated market an order to buy or sell a listed security knowing that an opposite order or orders of substantially the same size, at substantially the same time, and at substantially the same price, have been or will be entered by or for the same or different persons, with the intention of creating a false or deceptive appearance of active public trading in connection with that security or an artificial market price for that security.[301] This practice is known as a 'matched order'.[302]

The main objective of this practice is to create an appearance of renewed interest in the security in question in order to induce others to purchase the security. This is done in the hope that, if a sufficient number of new investors are attracted by the apparent increase in trading activity, the price of the security would rise.[303] Should this occur, the manipulator would thereafter sell the security at a profit.[304]

(iii) Buying orders at successively higher prices and selling at successively lower prices

This practice involves approving or entering on the market orders to buy a listed security at successively higher prices or orders to sell a listed security at successively lower prices for the purpose of improperly influencing the market price of that security. This practice has the effect of creating the misleading impression that there is a demand for or supply of the security in question at that price.[305]

(iv) Marking the close

This practice entails approving or entering on a regulated market an order at or near the close of the market, the primary purpose of which is to change or maintain the closing price of a listed security.[306] This practice is known as 'marking the close' and it is a time-specific trade-based activity. The aim of buying or selling the securities at the close of the market is to alter the closing price of the securities and thereby to mislead persons acting on the basis of the closing prices. This might be done to support a flagging price or to artificially affect the valuation of a portfolio (known as 'window dressing').[307] Since the market price is pushed to a distorted level, this practice creates a false impression regarding the demand for and the price of the securities.

---

[300] *United States v Brown* (supra) at 325.
[301] Section 75(3)(*b*) of the Securities Services Act.
[302] *Ernst & Ernst v Hochfelder* 425 US 185 (US SC, 1976) 205 n 25.
[303] Ministry of Economic Development (New Zealand) op cit n 282 at para 71.
[304] A 'pool' is essentially a similar kind of practice as a matched order but with the difference that it involves a group of persons combining their resources to buy shares and then to sell them successively from one member of the group to another in order to boost the turnover in the shares.
[305] Section 75(3)(*c*).
[306] Section 75(3)(*d*).
[307] Ministry of Economic Development (New Zealand) op cit n 282 at para 77.

Note that s 75(3)(*d*) of the Securities Services Act does not as such deem the mere entering of an order on a regulated market at or near the close of the market to be a manipulative trading practice — it is only when the *primary* purpose in doing so is to change or maintain the closing price of the security that the practice becomes manipulative. One may therefore legitimately enter an order to buy or sell securities at or near the close of the market, provided that one's primary purpose in doing so is not to change or maintain the closing price of that security.

In June 2010 the FSB found a South African derivatives trader guilty of manipulating the share prices of Beige Holdings Limited and the Cape Empowerment Trust Limited between the period 20 January 2009 and 10 February 2009.[308] Twenty-one counts of market manipulation were filed against the trader. During the period 20 January 2009 and 10 February 2009 he had placed orders in the last few minutes of the day's trade. It was alleged that, in most instances, the primary purpose of these transactions was to increase the closing price of the shares and in other instances the primary purpose was to maintain the closing price of the shares. These transactions had a clear effect on the value of the stake of these companies. For example, if the share price of the shares of Beige Holdings Limited had closed at 11 cents, the stake would have had a notional value of R75 million, but when it closed at 12 cents the notional value of the stake amounted to R82 million. It was found that the trader had created a false or deceptive appearance of the trading activity, or artificial prices, for the shares of Beige Holdings Limited and the Cape Empowerment Trust Limited. He admitted the allegations against him and the Enforcement Committee fined him R2 million for knowingly using a manipulative, improper, false and deceptive trading practice.

(v) *Auctioning processes or pre-opening session*

In terms of s 75(3)(*e*) of the Securities Services Act this practice involves approving or entering on a regulated market an order to buy a listed security during any auctioning process or pre-opening session and cancelling the order immediately prior to the market opening, for the purpose of creating or inducing a false or deceptive appearance of demand for or supply of that security. In an auction market, the placing of bids, even if they are never met by sellers, may as effectively influence the price of a security as a completed sale. This is because the placing of bids causes other bidders to raise their bids.[309]

(vi) *Market corner*

Section 75(3)(*f*) of the Securities Services Act deems the effecting of or assisting in effecting a market corner a manipulative, improper, false or deceptive trading practice. A market corner is defined in s 72 as:

---

[308] See the decision of the Enforcement Committee in the matter of the *Financial Services Board and The Directorate of Market Abuse v Timotheus Pretorius*, case 13 of 2009, available at http://www.fsb.co.za.

[309] Nancy Toross 'Double-click on this: Keeping pace with on-line market manipulation' (1999) 32 *Loyola of Los Angeles Law Review* 1399 at 1413, available at http://llr.lls.edu/volumes/v32-issue4/toross.pdf.

[A]ny arrangement, agreement, commitment or understanding involving the purchasing, selling or issuing of listed securities on a regulated market —
(a) by which a person, or a group of persons acting in concert, acquires direct or indirect beneficial ownership of, or exercises control over, or is able to influence the price of, securities listed on a regulated market; and
(b) where the effect of the arrangement, agreement, commitment or understanding is or is likely to be that the trading price of the securities listed on a regulated market, as reflected through the facilities of a regulated market, is or is likely to be abnormally influenced or arbitrarily dictated by such person or group of persons in that the said trading price deviates or is likely to deviate materially from the trading price which would otherwise likely have been reflected through the facilities of the regulated market on which the particular securities are traded.

Simply put, a market corner arises where a person, or group of persons acting in concert, buys up a substantial volume of a security, knowing that other market participants would be forced to buy from him or her at a higher price.[310]

A similar practice is known as an 'abusive squeeze', which arises where a person has a dominant position in the market and then seeks to use his or her control or influence to cause a shortage and thereby to create artificial prices.[311] Having a substantial influence over supply and extracting elevated profits thereby is not of itself abusive — the abuse lies in cornering the market and then using it to distort the market.[312]

(vii) *Maintaining an artificial price*

Section 75(3)*(g)* of the Securities Services Act deems it a manipulative, improper, false or deceptive trading practice to maintain the price for dealing in listed securities at an artificial level.

This is a general prohibition on a practice that has the effect of creating an artificial price for a security. It appears to be a repetition of s 75(1)*(a)*(ii) of the Securities Services Act, which prohibits a person from using or knowingly participating in a manipulative, improper, false or deceptive trading practice that creates an artificial price for a security, but it is in fact wider than s 75(1)*(a)*(ii) since all that needs to be proved for s 75(3)*(g)* to be contravened is that a person maintained the price of a listed security at an artificial level. It is not necessary to prove that the person intended to do so, as is the position under s 75(1)*(a)*(ii) of the Securities Services Act. Furthermore, s 75(1)*(a)*(ii) of the Securities Services Act prohibits the creation of an artificial price, whereas s 75(3)*(g)* of the Securities Services Act prohibits the maintaining of an artificial price for dealing in a listed security.

(viii) *Manipulating devices, schemes or artifices*

In terms of s 75(3)*(h)* employing any device, scheme or artifice to defraud any other person as a result of a transaction effected through the facilities of a

---

[310] Ministry of Economic Development (New Zealand) op cit n 282 at para 75.
[311] Kern Alexander 'Insider dealing and market abuse: The Financial Services and Markets Act 2000' (2001) ESRC Centre for Business Research, University of Cambridge, Working Paper No 222, available at http://www.cbr.cam.ac.uk/pdf/WP222.pdf.
[312] Alistair Alcock 'Market abuse' (2002) 23 *The Company Lawyer* 142 at 145.

regulated market is deemed to be a manipulative, improper, false or deceptive trading practice. This provision may be seen to be a catch-all provision in terms of which new devices, schemes or artifices may be regulated.

(ix) *Engaging in any manipulative act, practice or course of business*

Engaging in any act, practice or course of business in respect of dealings in securities listed on a regulated market which is deceptive or which is likely to have such effect is deemed by s 75(3)*(i)* to be a manipulative, improper, false or deceptive trading practice. This is a widely worded provision which prohibits any act, practice or course of business in respect of dealings in securities that is deceptive, or is likely to be deceptive.

(c) *False, misleading or deceptive statements, promises and forecasts*

Section 76(1) of the Securities Services Act prohibits disclosure-based market manipulation, which entails the dissemination of inaccurate information relating to the demand, supply, price or value of a security. Spreading false rumours has been said to be one of the most common manipulative devices in this regard.[313] Section 76(1) provides as follows:

> **76.** (1) No person may, directly or indirectly, make or publish in respect of listed securities, or in respect of the past or future performance of a public company —
> *(a)* any statement, promise or forecast which is, at the time and in the light of the circumstances in which it is made, false or misleading or deceptive in respect of any material fact and which the person knows, or ought reasonably to know, is false, misleading or deceptive; or
> *(b)* any statement, promise or forecast which is, by reason of the omission of a material fact, rendered false, misleading or deceptive and which the person knows, or ought reasonably to know, is rendered false, misleading or deceptive by reason of the omission of that fact.

A common scheme involving disclosure-based manipulation is known as the 'hype and dump' or 'pump and dump' scheme. This involves the touting of a company's shares through deceptive statements, with the object of inducing unwary investors to buy shares in the company to drive the price of the shares higher. After the price is 'pumped up' by all the hype, a buying frenzy is created and as the demand for the shares increases, its price inevitably rises. After pumping up the shares, the manipulators then 'dump' their shares on the market, making a handsome profit for themselves. Once they have done this, they immediately stop pumping the shares, the price falls in consequence and the deceived investors lose their money.[314]

The difference between disclosure-based market manipulation and insider trading is that insider trading entails a person dealing in securities on the basis of price-sensitive confidential information which, if publicly known, would affect the price of the securities in question, while disclosure-based market manipulation

---

[313] *Cargill v Hardin* 452 F 2d 1154 (8th Cir 1971) 1163.
[314] Ministry of Economic Development (New Zealand) op cit n 282 at para 66; Ali op cit n 268 at 222.

entails a person making or publishing false or misleading information to the market which materially affects the price of securities.[315] The difference lies in whether the information concerned is accurate or misleading and in how that information is used.[316]

Some noteworthy points about this offence are as follows:

(i) Omission of material facts

Section 76(1) of the Securities Services Act prohibits not only the making of false, misleading or deceptive statements, promises or forecasts, but also the omission (or concealment) of a material fact that renders a statement, promise or forecast false, misleading or deceptive.

(ii) Directly or indirectly

Like s 75(1)*(a)* of the Securities Services Act, s 76(1) of the Securities Services Act prohibits directly or indirectly, the making or publishing of false, misleading or deceptive statements, promises or forecasts.

(iii) Materiality

In order for s 76(1)*(a)* of the Securities Services Act to apply, the statement in question must be false, misleading or deceptive in respect of a *material* fact, or must be rendered false, misleading or deceptive by reason of the omission of a *material* fact. The role of a materiality requirement is to filter out essentially useless information that a reasonable investor would not consider significant.[317]

What should the test for materiality be? In *TSC Industries, Inc. v Northway, Inc.*[318] Marshall J rejected a formulation of the test of materiality used by the lower courts in the US that material facts include 'all facts which a reasonable shareholder *might* consider important' on the ground that it sets too low a threshold for the imposition of liability.[319] The court emphasised that, if too low a standard of materiality were set, it could result in a company and its management being subjected to liability for insignificant omissions or misstatements, and management's fear of exposing itself to substantial liability would cause it 'simply to bury the shareholders in an avalanche of trivial information — a result that is hardly conducive to informed decision making'.[320] In respect of an omitted fact the test was formulated as follows: 'An omitted fact is material if there is a substantial likelihood that a reasonable shareholder would consider it important in deciding how to vote.'[321]

According to this test, materiality depends on the significance that a reasonable investor would place on the misrepresented or withheld information.[322] It does not require proof of a substantial likelihood that disclosure of the omitted fact would

---

[315] Ministry of Economic Development (New Zealand) op cit n 282 at para 13.
[316] Ministry of Economic Development (New Zealand) op cit n 282 at para 66.
[317] *Basic Inc v Levinson* 485 US 224 (US SC, 1988) 234.
[318] 426 US 438 (1976).
[319] *TSC Industries, Inc. v Northway, Inc.* (supra) at 449.
[320] At 448–9.
[321] At 449.
[322] *Basic Inc v Levinson* 485 US 224 (US SC, 1988) 240.

have caused a reasonable shareholder to change his or her decision, but contemplates a showing of a substantial likelihood that under all the circumstances the omitted fact would have assumed actual significance in the decision of the shareholder.[323] This shows that materiality is an objective question and that it is a mixed question of fact and law.[324] In line with the test in *TSC Industries, Inc. v Northway, Inc.* perhaps the threshold under the Securities Services Act for a statement, promise or forecast being material ought not to be set too low.

(iv) *Past or future performance of a company*

A distinguishing feature of s 76(1) of the Securities Services Act, compared to the equivalent sections in foreign legislation, is that it prohibits not only the making or publishing of false statements in respect of listed securities, but also the making of false statements in respect of the past or future performance of a public company.

This is commendable, since it is quite conceivable that a misleading statement made about the past or future performance of a public company, be it a positive or a negative one, could have the effect of increasing, maintaining or reducing the price of the securities of that company.

(v) *Time of assessment of the statement, promise or forecast*

According to s 76(1) of the Securities Services Act the statement, promise or forecast is assessed at 'the time and in the light of the circumstances in which it is made'. There may well be cases where, with the benefit of hindsight, a statement, promise or forecast that was previously acceptable could subsequently be regarded as constituting market manipulation. If the statement, promise or forecast was acceptable at the time it was made, then the accused person will not be regarded as having engaged in market manipulation at that time, but the same behaviour at a later stage may well be regarded as constituting market manipulation.[325]

(vi) *Purpose or motive not relevant*

The motive for making the false, misleading or deceptive statement is not relevant. Also, for an offence to be committed under s 76 of the Securities Services Act, it is not a prerequisite that the false, misleading or deceptive statement, promise or forecast should have induced a third party to buy or sell listed securities — the mere making of the false, misleading or deceptive statement, promise or forecast constitutes an offence.

Whether a statement, promise or forecast is likely to induce the sale or purchase of securities is an objective question, and depends on its likely effect on the market for the securities.[326] If proof of motive is required to prove manipulative conduct, it becomes much more difficult to prove the offence, because it is usually very

---

[323] *TSC Industries, Inc. v Northway, Inc. TSC Industries, Inc. v Northway, Inc.* 426 US 438 (1976) 449.
[324] *TSC Industries, Inc. v Northway, Inc. TSC Industries, Inc. v Northway, Inc.* (supra) 445 and 450.
[325] Alexander op cit n 311.
[326] Ashley Black 'Regulating market manipulation: Sections 997–9 of the Corporations Law' (1996) 70 *Australian Law Journal* 987 at 1002.

difficult to ascertain with certainty what motivates a particular statement. Notably, the requirement to prove the purpose or motive of the statement, promise or forecast continues to apply to some foreign legislation.[327]

(vii) *Fault requirement*

The offence is committed where the fault element is either intention or negligence. Thus a person may be guilty of committing an offence under s 76 of the Securities Services Act not only if he or she knows that a statement is false, misleading or deceptive, but also if he or she ought reasonably to know that a statement is false, misleading or deceptive.

(viii) *Publication*

Developments in technology, most notably, the internet, have considerably increased the potential for disclosure-based market manipulation as they have changed the ways in which information is disseminated. The internet provides market manipulators with ready access to on-line newsletters, bulletin boards, chat rooms and e-mail, all of which provide a much greater scope for market manipulation. For example, an impostor can alter or falsify e-mails (known as 'spoofing') and in this way is able to manipulate the price of securities. Statements posted on the internet may range from mere opinions to subjective predictions and other unsubstantiated rumours, which could even be purported to have been confirmed by the company, to deliberately fabricated lies. The most common practice involves posting several messages on the internet in rapid succession, which all repeat the same 'prediction'. The price of a security may be influenced within minutes of posting information on the internet. Of greater concern is the fact that the internet has the effect of increasing cross-border activities.

For these reasons it is imperative that the publication and the dissemination of false information on the internet be stringently regulated in South Africa. While s 76(1) of the Securities Services Act does not specifically prohibit the dissemination of information on the internet, it is arguable that the word 'publish' in s 76(1) would include publication on the internet. Article 1(2)(c) of the EU Market Abuse Directive explicitly prohibits the dissemination of information on the internet, which is the preferable approach in view of the enormity of the problem.

20.2.6 Defences

(a) Price stabilisation

The deeming provisions in s 75(3) of the Securities Services Act are subject to the proviso that the use of price-stabilising mechanisms regulated in terms of the rules or listing requirements of an exchange would not constitute a prohibited trading practice.

Price stabilisation involves trading in a security at the time of an offer of

---

[327] See, for instance, para 9 of the Securities Exchange Act of 1934 48 Stat 881 (1934), codified at 15 USC para 78*a et seq* and ss 1041E and 1041F of the Australian Corporations Act 50 of 2001 which prohibit disclosure-based market manipulation.

securities to prevent or slow down a decline in the market price of the security.[328] It usually involves trading by issuers, underwriters or those participating in the offer of securities to prevent the offer from failing.[329] The stabilisation is only allowed to be used to prevent or slow down a decline in the price of securities, but not to raise the price. Price stabilisation is sometimes necessary because an offer of securities may lead to a fall in the price of the securities due to the sudden increase in supply or to imperfections in the pricing and allocation process.[330] To counteract the effect of this artificially low price, the underwriter of an offer may for instance try to stabilise the price of the securities by purchasing the securities, or offering to purchase them, for a limited period after their issue or sale.

The main purpose of price stabilising mechanisms is thus to establish an orderly secondary market for securities following an offer of securities.[331] These mechanisms are legitimate, because they help to promote investor confidence in the market for a new issue of shares, and the general opinion is that this enhanced confidence is of benefit to the market.[332] Price-stabilisation mechanisms would also assist corporate fundraising, since companies would be more inclined to raise funds in this way if they have the assurance of knowing that there would be some kind of initial support for the price of the securities.[333]

Chapter 5 of the JSE Listings Requirements sets out the requirements that must be complied with before embarking on price stabilisation. The most important requirement is that adequate disclosure must have been made in all communications issued by the issuer or the stabilising manager[334] to prospective investors in the securities that stabilisation may take place in relation to the relevant offer.[335] While stabilisation creates the impression that there is a demand for the securities at a particular price and while it may artificially affect the share price or create a false or misleading appearance with respect to trading in the offered shares, it would not be manipulative if it were disclosed to the public, since investors would have been forewarned that stabilisation may occur.[336] A further important require-

---

[328] Ministry of Economic Development (New Zealand) op cit n 282 at para 76.
[329] Ibid.
[330] Ministry of Economic Development (New Zealand) *Securities Legislation Bill Regulations: Discussion Document* (2006) para 141, available at http://www.med.govt.nz/templates/MultipageDocumentPage_18258.aspx.
[331] Rule 5.99 of the JSE Listings Requirements.
[332] Ministry of Economic Development (New Zealand) op cit n 282 at para 143.
[333] Ibid.
[334] The stabilising manager is the entity responsible for the stabilising action. In terms of rule 5.118 of the JSE Listings Requirements the stabilising manager must be a member of the JSE, Life Offices' Association of South Africa, Council of South African Banks, Merchant Bankers' Association, Bond Exchange of South Africa or any other person in South Africa or elsewhere (whether natural or juristic) in good standing and acceptable to the JSE. The stabilising manager must also satisfy the JSE that it has net tangible assets of not less than R2 billion in jurisdictions acceptable to the JSE, and must undertake that throughout the stabilisation period it will maintain at least R2 billion of its assets in these jurisdictions (rule 5.118(d) of the JSE Listings Requirements).
[335] Rules 5.104(a) and 5.110 of the JSE Listings Requirements.
[336] ASIC Policy Proposal on Market Stabilisation (Mar 2005) at 22, available at http://www.asic.gov/au/asic/pdflib.nsf/LookupByFileName/PPP_market_stabilisation.pdf/$file/PPP_market_stabilisation.pdf.

ment is that the stabilisation may take place only during the stabilisation period, which is limited to a maximum of 30 calendar days.[337]

(b) Definitional defences

Apart from the price-stabilisation defence, s 75 of the Securities Services Act does not make provision for any other defence to market manipulation and s 76 does not make provision for any defence at all. It is submitted that it is possible for a definitional defence to be raised under ss 75 and 76. A definitional defence is one that goes to the question of whether there was market manipulation in the first place.

For instance, a person accused of knowingly participating in a manipulative trading practice under s 75(1)(a) of the Securities Services Act may raise a defence that he or she did not knowingly participate in the trading practice, that is, that he or she lacked the intention to participate in the trading practice. Alternatively, a person accused of market manipulation under s 76(1) of the Securities Services Act may raise the defence that he or she did not know or could not reasonably have known that the statement published was misleading in respect of a material fact. These are merely examples of definitional defences which, it is submitted, may be raised to a charge of market manipulation under ss 75 and 76 of the Securities Services Act.

(c) Additional defences in other jurisdictions

In contrast, leading foreign jurisdictions make specific provision for a number of defences to market manipulation, in addition to a price-stabilisation defence. For instance, in the US and the EU, if a company buys back its own shares in compliance with certain requirements, the share buy-back would not constitute market manipulation.[338] The possibility of market manipulation is commonly regarded as a serious consequence of the recognition of a right of a company to buy back its own shares.[339] Directors of a company who undertake a share

---

[337] Rules 5.104 and 5.105 of the JSE Listings Requirements.

[338] See rule 10b–18 of the Securities Exchange Act of 1934, 17 CFR para 240.10b–18 (Purchases of certain Equity Securities by the Issuer and Others) and art 8 of the EU Market Abuse Directive. These requirements relate to the manner of the share buy-back, the timing, the price and volume of the shares repurchased.

[339] Blackman et al op cit n 1 at 5–56. See also UK Consultative Document 'The Purchase by a Company of its Own Shares' (Cmnd 7844) (1980) (popularly known as Gower's consultative Green Paper) para 11 at 9–10, where Gower points out that allowing companies to buy their own shares may lead to market-rigging. A similar objection is made by Adolf A Berle and Gardiner C Means *The Modern Corporation and Private Property* rev ed (1967) at 159–60. The possibility of insider trading is also commonly regarded as a serious consequence of recognising the right of a company to buy back its own shares. In this regard FHI Cassim has argued that all companies, whether or not their shares are listed on the stock exchange, ought to be declared 'insiders' for the purposes of the prohibition against insider trading so as to compensate a seller of shares who suffers loss by selling his or her shares to the company as a result of the company's use of confidential information which is not publicly known (see FHI Cassim 'The new statutory provisions on company share repurchases: A critical anaylsis' (1999) 116 *SALJ* 760 at 777). This would not apply to unlisted securities as these do not fall within the scope of the Securities Services Act, but it could be of relevance to the common-law liability of insider trading (see R Cassim op cit n 67 at 55).

buy-back with the intention of affecting the market price of the shares would be guilty of market manipulation. The share buy-back defence has been permitted for economic reasons; for instance, it could be used to strengthen the equity capital of issuers, which would clearly be in the interests of investors.[340]

Another defence that may be raised, under art 1(2)(a) of the EU Market Abuse Directive, is the defence that one's reasons for entering into a transaction or order to trade were legitimate and conformed to accepted market practices on the relevant regulated market. Section 123(2) of the UK Financial Services and Markets Act 2008 provides that the Financial Services Authority in the UK may not impose a penalty on a person who has engaged in market manipulation if, after considering representations made by that person in response to a warning notice[341] it finds, on reasonable grounds, that that person believed, on reasonable grounds, that his or her behaviour had not amounted to market manipulation or that that person had taken all reasonable precautions and had exercised all due diligence to avoid such behaviour. This defence is known as the 'reasonable belief and reasonable care' defence.[342] Similarly, according to s 1317S(2) of the Australian Corporations Act 50 of 2001 a person accused of market manipulation may apply to court for relief on the ground that he or she had acted honestly and, having regard to all the circumstances of the case ought fairly to be excused for the contravention.

A further defence is that of a Chinese Wall (see also the discussion in 20.1.4(c) above). A Chinese Wall is a physical and an operational segregation of functions within a multi-functioning organisation. This arrangement is set up to prevent information flowing from one group of persons or department in an organisation to another group of persons or department in the same organisation. The rationale behind a Chinese Wall is to protect juristic persons from incurring liability for insider trading or market manipulation as a result of the knowledge of their employees being attributed to them in law.[343] Even though the prohibition of market manipulation in the Securities Services Act applies to juristic persons,[344] a Chinese Wall defence has surprisingly not explicitly been provided in the Securi-

---

[340] See Recital 33 to the EU Market Abuse Directive.

[341] In terms of s 126(1) of the Financial Services and Markets Act 2008, if the Financial Services Authority proposes to take action against a person under s 123 it must first give him or her a warning notice. If the Financial Services Authority then decides to take action against such a person it must give him or her a decision notice (s 127(1) of the Financial Services and Markets Act 2008).

[342] Paul L Davies *Gower and Davies' Principles of Modern Company Law* 8 ed (2008) at 783.

[343] See *Harrods Ltd v Lemon* [1931] 2 KB (CA) 157, and Richard Jooste 'Insider dealing in South Africa' (1990) 107 *SALJ* 588 at 597. For a further discussion of Chinese Walls, see R Cassim op cit n 67 at 46–54.

[344] 'Person' is defined in s 72 of the Securities Services Act to *include* a partnership and a trust. Section 2 of the Interpretation Act 33 of 1957 defines 'person' as including:
  '(a) any divisional council, municipal council, village management board, or like authority;
  (b) any company incorporated or registered as such under any law;
  (c) any body of persons corporate or unincorporate.'
Thus it seems that a reference to 'person' in the Securities Services Act is to both natural and juristic persons and that therefore the prohibition of market manipulation in the Securities Services Act applies not only to natural persons but also to juristic persons as well as to partnerships and trusts.

ties Services Act. In contrast, in the UK explicit provision has been made for a Chinese Wall defence.[345]

Perhaps ss 75 and 76 of the Securities Services Act may be said to be excessively stringent compared to foreign legislation, because the only possible defence to market manipulation provided for is that of price stabilisation, and possibly a definitional defence. In certain instances it may be difficult to distinguish non-manipulative trading that leads to an increase in market activity or an alteration in the market price for securities, from manipulative trading that has the same effect but is undertaken for an impermissible purpose. For instance, trading at the end of the day is common because market participants monitor developments during the day before taking a position before the close of trading.[346] As legitimate trading is concentrated at the end of the day, it would be erroneous to regard all trading at the end of the day as evidence of manipulation.[347] A person accused of market manipulation under the Securities Services Act would not be able to raise a defence that his or her reasons for entering the transactions or orders to trade were legitimate and that he or she had conformed with accepted market practices on the relevant regulated market, or that he or she had exercised due diligence, such as seeking expert advice before acting. Moreover, even if a juristic person has established a Chinese Wall, this would not necessarily be a defence under the Securities Services Act. This could result in unjust convictions and could have the undesirable effect of inhibiting legitimate trading. As discussed earlier in 20.2.3, the fear of inhibiting legitimate market activity has always been a reason propounded by the critics of market manipulation for opposing the statutory regulation of market manipulation.

20.2.7 Penalties

The penalties for market manipulation provided for in the Securities Services Act are a fine or imprisonment, and administrative penalties.

(a) A fine or imprisonment

Section 115*(a)* of the Securities Services Act provides that a person who contravenes ss 75 or 76 of the Securities Services Act is liable on conviction to a fine not exceeding R50 million or to imprisonment for a period not exceeding ten years, or to both such fine and imprisonment.

In order for a sanction for market abuse to be effective, the sanction must be sufficiently dissuasive and proportionate to the gravity of the offence and to the gains realised, and it must be consistently applied. While the maximum amount of R50 million may be strongly dissuasive, it may not necessarily be proportionate to the gains realised, especially in instances where companies simply regard it as just

---

[345] See the Code of Market Conduct MAR 1.8.5E. The Financial Services Authority in the UK has issued a code containing useful guidance on whether or not behaviour amounts to market abuse, referred to as the 'Code of Market Conduct'.
[346] Fischel & Ross op cit n 270 at 520.
[347] Op cit n 270 at 520–1. Fischel and Ross give further examples where manipulative trades may be indistinguishable from non-manipulative trades, such as short sales and making successive bids at higher prices.

another cost of doing business, particularly where the profits realised significantly exceed the penalty imposed.[348] One way of ensuring that the fine imposed is proportionate, is to make provision for a separate maximum penalty for individuals and for companies, with a higher maximum penalty prescribed for companies. In contrast, there is no limit to the amount of the penalty that may be imposed by the Financial Services Authority in the UK, which is empowered to impose a penalty of such amount as it considers appropriate.[349]

(b) Administrative penalty

The Securities Services Act establishes an enforcement committee, which is empowered to impose an administrative penalty on a person who has contravened the Securities Services Act or who has failed to comply with that Act.[350] This administrative penalty must be paid to the FSB. An administrative penalty may be imposed both on persons who engage in insider trading and on those who engage in market manipulation. However, this compensatory amount is payable to the FSB only in respect of insider trading, for distribution to victims who were affected by the insider dealing.[351] Regrettably, no such similar provision is made in the Securities Services Act in respect of market manipulation. It is conceded that, in certain instances of market manipulation, it may be difficult to calculate accurately the amount of the loss incurred by victims, but in those instances where the incurred losses are calculable, the administrative penalty that is payable by the market manipulator to the FSB ought to be distributed to victims of the market manipulation, as is the case with insider trading.

(c) Absence of a statutory derivative civil remedy

The Securities Services Act renders market manipulation a criminal but not a civil offence.[352] While provision has been made in s 77 of the Securities Services Act for statutory civil liability resulting from the offence of insider trading prohibited in s 73 of that Act, no such provision has been made in respect of market manipulation. Consequently, persons who suffer loss as a result of the actions of a market manipulator are left to seek their own civil remedy.

The absence of a statutory derivative civil remedy seems to indicate that the South African legislature perceives market manipulation as a wrong against the market, rather than as a wrong against those individuals who are directly affected. In other words, the provisions of the Securities Services Act on market manipulation appear to be aimed at the public good, but not necessarily at individual protection, when both underlying objects could easily be attained. Perhaps the

---

[348] See Carlos Conceicao 'The FSA's Approach to Taking Action Against Market Abuse' (2007) 28 *The Company Lawyer* 43 at 45.

[349] See s 123(1) of the Financial Services and Markets Act 2008.

[350] The Enforcement Committee is a committee established by the FSB (see s 97 of the Securities Services Act). The Registrar or Deputy Registrar of Securities Services or the Directorate of Market Abuse are empowered to refer market abuse matters for consideration to the Enforcement Committee, which is empowered to impose an administrative penalty on a person accused of market abuse (see ss 94*(e)* and 102–5 of the Securities Services Act).

[351] See ss 77 and 105 of the Securities Services Act.

[352] See s 115.

Securities Services Act ought to move away from a statutory criminal remedy for market manipulation only and introduce a statutory civil remedy. A criminal remedy alone may have the effect of only few successful actions being brought for market manipulation since the criminal standard of proof beyond a reasonable doubt is much more difficult to meet than the relatively lighter civil standard of proof on a balance of probabilities. This may have the effect of not effectively deterring persons from engaging in market manipulation. Also, the absence of a statutory civil remedy may result in a victim being denied the opportunity to recover the losses he or she incurred as a result of the market manipulation.

CHAPTER 21

TRANSITIONAL ARRANGEMENTS

Farouk HI Cassim and Maleka Femida Cassim

21.1	INTRODUCTION	909
21.2	CONTINUATION OF PRE-EXISTING COMPANIES	909
21.3	EXERCISE OF FUNCTIONS OR POWERS BY THE COMPANIES COMMISSION	910
21.4	PENDING FILINGS	910
21.5	MEMORANDUM OF INCORPORATION AND RULES	911
	21.5.1 Types of companies and names	911
	21.5.2 Memorandum of Incorporation	912
	21.5.3 Rules	913
	21.5.4 Shareholder agreements	913
21.6	PRE-INCORPORATION CONTRACTS	914
21.7	PAR VALUE OF SHARES, TREASURY SHARES, CAPITAL ACCOUNTS AND SHARE CERTIFICATES	914
	21.7.1 Par value shares	914
	21.7.2 Share certificates	916
21.8	COMPANY FINANCE AND GOVERNANCE	916
	21.8.1 Office of director, company secretary, auditor and prescribed officer	917
	21.8.2 Right to seek remedy	917
	21.8.3 Company records	917
	21.8.4 Prohibitions and restrictions on the amendment of provisions of the Memorandum of Incorporation	918
21.9	COMPANY NAMES AND NAME RESERVATIONS	918
	21.9.1 Name reservations	918
	21.9.2 Defensive names	919
	21.9.3 Translation or shortened form of name	919
21.10	CONTINUED APPLICATION OF THE 1973 ACT TO WINDING-UP AND LIQUIDATION	919
21.11	COURT PROCEEDINGS AND ORDERS: PRESERVATION AND CONTINUATION	920
21.12	GENERAL PRESERVATION OF REGULATIONS, RIGHTS, DUTIES, NOTICES AND OTHER INSTRUMENTS	920
21.13	TRANSITION OF REGULATORY AGENCIES	920
21.14	CONTINUED INVESTIGATION AND ENFORCEMENT OF THE 1973 ACT	921
21.15	REGULATIONS	922

21.1 INTRODUCTION

The Companies Act 71 of 2008 (hereafter 'the Act') was signed into law on 8 April 2009. It was subject to a waiting period of one year during which it could not come into operation.[1] The Act comes into operation on a date fixed by the President by proclamation in the *Government Gazette* in terms of s 225. The Transitional Arrangements, contained in Schedule 5 to the Act, deal with the arrangements for the transition of pre-existing companies, as at the date on which the new Act comes into operation.

'Pre-existing companies' continue to exist as companies in terms of the new Act. 'Pre-existing companies' are juristic persons that, immediately before the effective date:[2]

- were registered in terms of the Companies Act 61 of 1973 (hereafter 'the 1973 Act') (other than as external companies),
- were in existence and recognised as 'existing companies' under the 1973 Act,
- were deregistered in terms of the 1973 Act and subsequently re-registered under the new Act, or
- were registered in terms of the Close Corporations Act 69 of 1984[3] and subsequently converted to a company (in terms of Schedule 2 of the Act).

As a general principle, the new Act applies equally to pre-existing companies as to companies incorporated in terms of the Act (see in this regard the definition of a 'company' in s 1 of the Act, which includes pre-existing companies).

It is notable that many (but not all) of the transitional provisions apply as of the 'general effective date', which is defined as the date on which s 1 of the Act comes into operation.[4] The 'general effective date' must not be confused with the 'effective date'. The 'effective date' of any particular provision of the Act means the date on which that particular provision of the Act comes into operation.[5]

21.2 CONTINUATION OF PRE-EXISTING COMPANIES

The continued existence of pre-existing companies is catered for in the Transitional Arrangements. This states that every pre-existing company that, immediately before the general effective date of the Act, was incorporated or recognised as an existing company under the 1973 Act,[6] continues to exist as a company as if it had been incorporated and registered in terms of the new Act. It also bears the same name and the same registration number that had been previously assigned to it (subject to item 4, which is discussed in 21.5 below).[7]

---

[1] Section 225 of the Act.
[2] See the definitions of 'pre-existing company' and 'company' in s 1 of the Act. See also Schedule 5 item 3(3).
[3] Hereafter 'the Close Corporations Act'.
[4] Schedule 5 item 1(1)(*a*).
[5] In terms of s 225 (see s 1). It could well be that, in respect of a number of provisions of the Act, the 'effective date' may coincide with the 'general effective date'.
[6] This includes the handful of unlimited companies formed under the Companies Act 46 of 1926, that survived the repeal of the 1926 Act by the Companies Act of 1973.
[7] Schedule 5 item 2. The draft Companies Amendment Bill, 2010 (cl 115(2)(*b*)) proposes to insert four new provisions in item 2. The first of these is a provision regarding translated names of

21.3 EXERCISE OF FUNCTIONS OR POWERS BY THE COMPANIES COMMISSION

Item 1(3) of Schedule 5 provides for a transitional period for the transfer of power to the Companies and Intellectual Property Commission ('the Companies Commission'). Despite any other provision of the Act, the Minister,[8] by notice in the *Government Gazette*, may determine a date on which the Companies Commission may assume the exercise of any particular function or power assigned to it in terms of the Act. Until that date, the Companies Commission may not perform that function or exercise that power. It is the Minister who, until that date, has the authority to and bears the responsibility of performing the functions or exercising the powers assigned to the Companies Commission in terms of the Act.

21.4 PENDING FILINGS

Any matter that was filed with the Registrar in terms of the 1973 Act, before the effective date, and that was not fully addressed at that time, must be concluded by the Registrar in terms of the 1973 Act, despite its repeal.[9] In other words, pending filings must be completed under the 1973 Act. Where a pending filing involves the incorporation and registration of a company, the company is regarded to have been registered in terms of the 1973 Act, and to be a 'pre-existing company' for all purposes of the new Act.[10]

---

pre-existing companies, and in particular, the concluding expressions of company names. A pre-existing company (whose name satisfied s 49 of the 1973 Act, dealing with formal requirements as to names of companies, concluding expressions and subjoined statements) is not required to change the concluding expression of its name as appropriate for the relevant category of company (in terms of s 11(3)*(c)* of the Act) *solely* on the ground that any part of its name was in an official language other than English. The company may moreover continue to use a translated name that, immediately before the effective date, was registered and otherwise met the requirements of s 50(2) of the 1973 Act, dealing with the use by a company of a translated name or translated words in a name.

Secondly, the draft Amendment Bill also proposes that the formal requirements for company names under s 49(5)–(7) of the 1973 Act will continue to apply to a pre-existing company that, immediately before the effective date, was engaged in winding-up by a court, voluntary winding-up, judicial management, conversion of the type of company or any other circumstance contemplated in those provisions.

The third new item that is proposed to be inserted by the draft Amendment Bill deals with the retention by a pre-existing company of all the powers set out in the 1973 Act in respect of its issued and outstanding shares, to the extent necessary to give full effect to s 35(6) and item 6(2) of Schedule 5, dealing with issued par value shares of pre-existing companies (see further below at 21.7).

Fourthly, the draft Amendment Bill proposes that if, as a consequence of the coming into effect of the new Act and the repeal of the 1973 Act, a conflict, dispute or doubt arises within two years after the effective date concerning the particular manner or form in which, or time by which, a pre-existing company is required to: *(a)* prepare its annual financial statements, convene an annual general meeting, provide to its shareholders copies of its annual financial statements, any notice or any other document; or *(b)* file any particular document with the Companies Commission; or *(c)* take any other particular action required in terms of the Act or the company's Memorandum of Incorporation, the company may apply to the Companies Tribunal for directions, and a member of the Tribunal may make an administrative order that is appropriate and reasonable in the circumstances.

[8] The 'Minister' means the member of the Cabinet responsible for companies. This is the Minister of Trade and Industry.
[9] Schedule 5 item 3(1).
[10] Schedule 5 item 3(3).

No company may convert to a close corporation after the new Act comes into force.[11] However, pending conversions that were already filed by then must be concluded in terms of the Close Corporations Act. In this regard, the Transitional Arrangements provide that any conversion of a company to a close corporation in terms of s 27 of the Close Corporations Act, that was filed with the Registrar before the effective date and that had not been fully addressed at that time, must be concluded by the Registrar in terms of the Close Corporations Act, despite the repeal of s 27.[12]

21.5 MEMORANDUM OF INCORPORATION AND RULES

21.5.1 Types of companies and names

Pre-existing companies are generally *deemed* to have changed their names, insofar as this may be required, in order to comply with the provisions of the new Act regarding the concluding expressions in company names, as appropriate for the relevant category of company (eg Inc., NPC), as well as the other requirements of s 11(3).[13]

In this regard, pre-existing section 21 companies (that were incorporated under s 21 of the 1973 Act) are recognised as non-profit companies under the new Act. Such companies are deemed to have amended their Memorandums of Incorporation as at the general effective date to state that they are non-profit companies, and to have changed the concluding expressions of their company names to 'NPC'. Pre-existing companies do not have a Memorandum of Incorporation; they have instead a memorandum of association and articles of association. The reference to 'Memorandum of Incorporation' in this context must therefore be understood to refer to the memorandum of association of the pre-existing company, as explained below in 21.5.2.

Similarly, every pre-existing section 53*(b)* company (that is, a company that was incorporated under the 1973 Act with a constitution that imposed personal liability jointly and severally on the directors and past directors in terms of s 53*(b)* of that Act) is deemed to have amended its Memorandum of Incorporation as at the general effective date of the new Act to expressly state that it is a personal liability company, and to have changed the concluding expression of its name to 'Inc.' or 'Incorporated'.

Pre-existing companies that were registered under the 1973 Act, and yet fall within the definition of a state-owned company under the new Act, are deemed to have amended their Memorandums of Incorporation as at the general effective date, and to have changed the concluding expressions of their names to 'SOC'.

---

[11] Schedule 3 item 2(3), which repeals s 27 of the Close Corporations Act 69 of 1984; see further chapter 3: Types of Companies.

[12] Schedule 5 item 3(2).

[13] Item 4(1)*(a)*–*(d)* of Schedule 5 read with cl 115(3)*(a)* of the draft Companies Amendment Bill, 2010 (which proposes to substitute the erroneous references to s 11(3)*(b)* in items 4(1)*(a)*–*(d)* with a general reference to s 11(3); and to substitute the incorrect reference in item 4(1)*(b)* to s 53*(c)* of the 1973 Act with a reference to s 53*(b)* of that Act). See further chapter 4: Formation of Companies and the Company Constitution.

The company limited by guarantee, as classified by the 1973 Act, has no counterpart under the new Act.[14] An entity that was incorporated under the 1973 Act as a company limited by guarantee may choose to become a profit company under the new Act, whether a public or a private company. It does so by filing a notice to that effect and changing the concluding expression of its name to correctly reflect the type of company that it will be. The notice must be filed within 20 business days after the general effective date of the new Act. If a company limited by guarantee fails to file such a notice, it is deemed to have amended its Memorandum of Incorporation to expressly state that it is a non-profit company, and to have changed its name as appropriate, with effect from the general effective date.

A matter that is left vague and ambiguous in the draft Companies Amendment Bill, 2010, relates to the expression '(RF)' in the names of pre-existing companies with constitutions containing restrictions or prohibitions on the amendment of certain provisions of the constitution (in terms of s 15(2)(b) and (c) of the Act). The effect of the draft Amendment Bill in its present form apparently is that certain types of companies are *deemed* to have changed their names to include '(RF)' where required, whereas other types of companies are not deemed to have done so and may consequently be required to file a notice of name change together with a copy of the requisite special resolution. In this regard, pre-existing Section 21 companies, Section 53(b) companies, state-owned companies and companies limited by guarantee are *deemed* to have included '(RF)' where required[15] — but, oddly, the same does not apply to pre-existing public and private companies with constitutions containing restrictions or prohibitions on the amendment of certain provisions.

21.5.2 Memorandum of Incorporation

Pre-existing companies are given two years in which to amend their constitutions, without any charge or fee, to align their provisions with the requirements of the new Act. This would result in a very useful savings in costs. The relevant amendment to the Memorandum of Incorporation may be filed without charge, at any time within two years of the general effective date of the Act. The reference to the 'Memorandum of Incorporation' of a pre-existing company in this context means the memorandum of association and articles of association of a pre-existing company. The basis of this apporach is the definition of the 'Memorandum of Incorporation' in s 1 of the Act, which defines the Memorandum of Incorporation of a pre-existing company as the document that sets out rights, duties and responsibilities of shareholders, directors and others within and in relation to a company, and other matters by which a pre-existing company was structured and governed

---

[14] Except for the section 21 company, which in terms of the 1973 Act was classified as a public company limited by guarantee. Under the new Act it would no longer be a company limited by guarantee.

[15] See item 4(1)(a)–(d) of Schedule 5 read with cl 115(3)(a) of the draft Companies Amendment Bill, 2010, which proposes to replace the reference to s 11(3)(b) in these subitems with a general reference to s 11(3).

before the effective date. This wide definition would include both the memorandum of association and the articles of association of a pre-existing company.

A pre-existing company may similarly alter its name insofar as necessary to meet the requirements of the new Act, by filing a notice of name change together with a copy of the relevant special resolution (contemplated in s 16), without any charge or fee, within the two-year period after the general effective date.[16]

During this two-year transitional period, if there is a conflict between a provision of the Act and a provision of a pre-existing company's Memorandum of Incorporation, the latter provision would prevail (except to the extent that Schedule 5 provides otherwise),[17] and notably, a compliance notice may not be issued to the company in respect of the inconsistency. To elaborate, until such time as a pre-existing company has filed an amendment to its Memorandum of Incorporation to align it with the new Act, neither the Companies Commission nor the Takeover Regulation Panel ('the Panel') may issue a compliance notice to the company in respect of conduct that is inconsistent with the new Act but consistent with the company's Memorandum of Incorporation.[18] This is only logical, because it is specifically provided (as stated above) that the pre-existing company's Memorandum of Incorporation prevails over a conflicting provision of the Act during this time.[19]

21.5.3 Rules

The Transitional Arrangements preserve any binding provisions that are comparable in purpose and in effect to the rules of a company (as contemplated in s 15(3)),[20] regardless of the style or the title of those provisions, that were adopted by a pre-existing company before the general effective date of the new Act. Such provisions continue to have the same force and effect for a period of two years as of the general effective date, or until changed by the company. After the two-year period, these provisions will have force and effect only to the extent that they are consistent with the Act.[21]

21.5.4 Shareholder agreements

The binding force and effect of shareholder agreements of pre-existing companies is dealt with in the draft Companies Amendment Bill, 2010 (cl 115(3)*(c)* and *(d)*). This proposes to insert a new item in the Transitional Arrangements[22] to the effect that a pre-existing shareholder agreement (or, to be more precise, any agreement

---

[16] Schedule 5 item 4(2).
[17] Schedule 5 item 4(4)*(a)*.
[18] Schedule 5 item 4(4)*(b)*.
[19] Item 4(4) is proposed to apply also in the event of: (i) a conflict between the Act and a binding provision comparable to a company rule (in terms of s 15(3) of the Act) of a pre-existing company, in which case the binding provision will prevail; and (ii) a conflict between the Act, or the company's Memorandum of Incorporation, and a provision of an agreement comparable to a shareholder agreement (in terms of s 15(7) of the Act) of a pre-existing company, in which case the agreement will prevail, except to the extent that the agreement or the Memorandum of Incorporation provides otherwise (see the draft Companies Amendment Bill, 2010, cl 115(3)*(d)* read with *(c)*).
[20] See chapter 4: Formation of Companies and the Company Constitution.
[21] Schedule 5 item 4(3)*(a)* and *(b)*.
[22] As item 4(3A); see also the proposed amendment of item 4(4) above.

that the shareholders of a pre-existing company had adopted between or among themselves, under whatever style or title, comparable in purpose and effect to an agreement contemplated in s 15(7) of the Act) of a pre-existing company will continue to have the same force and effect for two years as of the general effective date of the Act, or until amended by the shareholders who are party to the agreement.

The shareholder agreement will prevail in the event of a conflict with the new Act or the company's Memorandum of Incorporation, except to the extent that the agreement or the Memorandum of Incorporation provides otherwise. A compliance notice may not be issued to the company in respect of conduct that is inconsistent with the Act but consistent with the agreement. There is thus a two-year transitional period for the validity of shareholder agreements even if they conflict with the Act or the company's constitution.

After the two-year period, the shareholder agreement will have force and effect only to the extent that it is consistent with the new Act and the company's Memorandum of Incorporation.

21.6 PRE-INCORPORATION CONTRACTS

Section 21 of the Act, on pre-incorporation contracts, does not apply to pre-existing companies.[23] This is because companies that are already incorporated would manifestly not enter into a pre-incorporation contract.

Section 21 is also not applicable to companies whose incorporation and registration are pending. This is because pending company registrations, that were already filed under the 1973 Act by the time that the new Act comes into effect, must be concluded under the 1973 Act (as discussed above in 21.4). Such companies are therefore regarded as 'pre-existing companies'[24] with the effect that s 21 will not be applicable to them.

21.7 PAR VALUE OF SHARES, TREASURY SHARES,[25] CAPITAL ACCOUNTS AND SHARE CERTIFICATES

21.7.1 Par value shares

Section 35(2) of the Act is an important provision, which states that shares do not have a nominal or par value under the Act, subject to the Transitional Arrangements. While under the 1973 Act the share capital of a company could be divided into shares having a par value or no par value, the new Act finally jettisons the concept of par value shares for new companies formed under the Act.

Despite the repeal of the 1973 Act shares, including par value shares, issued by a pre-existing company and held by a shareholder immediately before the new Act comes into effect would generally continue to have all the rights associated with the shares (see s 35(6)). As a transitional measure, par value shares issued by a

---

[23] Schedule 5 item 5; see chapter 4: Formation of Companies and the Company Constitution.
[24] Schedule 5 item 3(1) and (3).
[25] The reference to treasury shares, which are not defined in the Act, was an oversight in the first place. The draft Companies Amendment Bill, 2010 (cl 115(4)) proposes the deletion of the reference to treasury shares from this item.

pre-existing company will continue in existence, subject to regulations made by the Minister for their transitional status and their conversion into no par value shares.

In this regard, the Transitional Arrangements provide that despite s 35(2), any shares of a pre-existing company that have been *issued* with a nominal or par value and that are held by a shareholder immediately before the effective date continue to have the nominal or par value assigned to them when they were issued.[26] The continued existence of par value shares is subject to regulations made in terms of item 6(3) of Schedule 5 to the Act, which requires the Minister, in consultation with the member of Cabinet responsible for national financial matters, to make regulations providing for the transitional status and conversion of any nominal or par value shares and capital accounts of pre-existing companies. These regulations are to take effect as of the general effective date of the Act. Provision must be made by the regulations for the preservation of the rights of the shareholders associated with such shares to the extent that doing so is compatible with the purposes of item 6 or, where this is not possible, for compensation to be paid to the shareholders for the loss of any such rights.[27]

The draft Companies Regulations[28] provide that a pre-existing company may not, after the new Act has come into effect, authorise any new par value shares. If, before the new Act has come into effect, a company has any authorised class of par value shares from which it has issued any shares before the effective date, the company may issue further shares of that class at any time *after* the effective date, and may do so until it has converted its par value shares into no par value shares. If, on the other hand, the company has not issued any shares of the authorised class of par value shares before the effective date, then the company must not issue any shares of that class after the effective date, unless it has first converted that class of authorised shares into no par value shares by way of a board resolution.

Every existing par value share of a pre-existing company must be converted into a no par value share within five years of the effective date. Failure to comply would result in a compliance notice being served on the pre-existing company, which, if ignored, could have far-reaching consequences for the company. An amendment to a pre-existing company's Memorandum of Incorporation to effect a conversion of par value shares must be approved by a special resolution of the shareholders of the company.[29]

---

[26] Schedule 5 item 6(2).

[27] As discussed above, the draft Companies Amendment Bill, 2010 (cl 115(2)*(b)*) also proposes to insert a new provision (as item 2(4) of Schedule 5) dealing with the retention by a pre-existing company of all the powers set out in the 1973 Act in respect of its par value or nominal value shares that were issued and outstanding as at the effective date, to the extent necessary to give full effect to s 35(6) and item 6(2) of Schedule 5. The reference to 'outstanding' shares is strange. 'Outstanding shares' is terminology used in the USA to refer to issued shares of a corporation that are held by its shareholders. Shares issued to shareholders are said to be 'outstanding shares' until they are reacquired, redeemed or cancelled. In the context of cl 115(2)*(b)*, since there are no treasury shares, it is redundant.

[28] Regulation 35 of the draft Companies Regulations Pursuant to the Companies Act, 2008 (Act 71 of 2008), GN 1664 *GG* 32832 of 22 December 2009.

[29] Ibid.

The draft Companies Amendment Bill, 2010[30] proposes to insert a further useful provision to the effect that the appraisal rights of dissenting shareholders do not apply to the conversion by a pre-existing company of its par value shares into no par value shares in terms of the Transitional Arrangements and the proposed regulations.

Banks (as defined in the Banks Act 94 of 1990) are exempt from s 35(2) and the abolition of par value shares until a date to be declared by the Minister, after consulting with the member of Cabinet responsible for national financial matters.[31]

21.7.2 Share certificates

Where a share certificate issued by a pre-existing company fails to satisfy the requirements of s 51(1) to (4) of the new Act, dealing with the registration of certificated securities, it will neither constitute a contravention of s 51 nor invalidate the share certificate.[32]

21.8 COMPANY FINANCE AND GOVERNANCE

Notwithstanding anything to the contrary in a company's Memorandum of Incorporation, the provisions of the new Act relating to the following matters apply with immediate effect to all pre-existing companies as from the effective date:[33]

- the duties, conduct and liability of directors,
- the rights of shareholders to receive any notice or to have access to any information,
- meetings of shareholders or directors, and adoption of resolutions, and
- Chapter 5 of the Act, which regulates fundamental transactions, takeovers and offers, except to the extent that they are exempted by that Chapter.

It must be borne in mind that, in respect of a non-profit company that has voting members, a reference in the Act or in the Schedules to a 'shareholder' is a reference to the voting members of a non-profit company.[34]

Despite anything to the contrary in a company's Memorandum of Incorporation, the approval of any distribution, financial assistance, insider share issues or options, is subject to the Act, even if any such action had been approved by a company's shareholders before the effective date.[35] It is notable that this applies despite anything to the contrary in a company's Memorandum of Incorporation.

---

[30] Clause 115(4).
[31] Schedule 5 item 6(1).
[32] Schedule 5 item 6(4).
[33] Schedule 5 item 7(5).
[34] Section 10(4).
[35] Schedule 5 item 7(6).

21.8.1 Office of director, company secretary, auditor and prescribed officer

The Transitional Arrangements provide for the continuity of the office of directors, prescribed officers, company secretaries and auditors of pre-existing companies. In this regard, a person holding office as a director, a prescribed officer, a company secretary or an auditor of a pre-existing company immediately before the effective date continues to hold that office as from the effective date, subject to the company's Memorandum of Incorporation and the Act.[36]

However, any person who, in terms of the new Act, is ineligible to be or is disqualified from being a director, an alternate director, a prescribed officer, a company secretary or an auditor, is regarded as having resigned that office as from the effective date.[37] Where a pre-existing company has fewer than the minimum number of directors as required by the new Act, it is deemed (as from the general effective date) to have a number of vacancies on the board equal to the difference between the requisite minimum number of directors and its actual number of directors.[38]

A vacancy in the office of director, company secretary or auditor of a pre-existing company as from the effective date is to be filled in accordance with the new Act. This applies irrespective of whether the vacancy arises by either of the above two provisions or otherwise.[39]

21.8.2 Right to seek remedy

Regarding remedies, any person has a right to seek a remedy in terms of the new Act, even with respect to conduct pertaining to a pre-existing company and occurring *before* the effective date. However, this does not apply where the aggrieved party had already commenced proceedings in a court of law in respect of the same conduct before the effective date.[40]

21.8.3 Company records

Where a pre-existing company fails to maintain any company record for the duration of the period prescribed by s 24(1) of the new Act (namely for a period of seven years or any longer period specified by any other applicable public regulation), it will not be in contravention of the Act if it had disposed of that record before the effective date, and at a time at which it was not required by any public regulation to continue to maintain that record.[41]

---

[36] Subject to item 7(2) of Schedule 5 (Schedule 5 item 7(1)).
[37] Schedule 5 item 7(2) read with the draft Companies Amendment Bill, 2010 (cl 115(5)).
[38] Schedule 5 item 7(3). Item 7(3) comes into effect as from the general effective date; item 7(2) takes effect on the effective date.
[39] Schedule 5 item 7(4).
[40] Schedule 5 item 7(7).
[41] Schedule 5 item 7(8)*(a)*. 'Public regulation' means any national, provincial or local government legislation or subordinate legislation, or any licence, tariff, directive or similar authorisation issued by a regulatory authority or pursuant to any statutory authority (s 1).

21.8.4 Prohibitions and restrictions on the amendment of provisions of the Memorandum of Incorporation

Any prohibitions on the amendment, and any restrictive or procedural requirements impeding the amendment of any provision of a pre-existing company's Memorandum of Incorporation, will continue to have the same validity as they had under the 1973 Act, despite a failure by the company to have drawn attention to the provision in a Notice of Incorporation as required by the new Act[42] (and, evidently, despite a failure to include the expression '(RF)' as part of its name).

It will also not be a contravention of the Act for a pre-existing company to have failed to include in its Notice of Incorporation in terms of the 1973 Act a prominent statement, comparable to that required by s 13(3) of the new Act, that draws attention to any prohibition on the amendment or any restrictive or procedural requirement impeding the amendment of any provision of the Memorandum of Incorporation and its location.[43] This provision is only logical, as the 1973 Act did not require such a statement.

The doctrine of constructive notice will apply when the company files a notice of the relevant prohibition or restriction on amendment. In this regard, from the time that a pre-existing company files a notice of the relevant provision, s 19(4) of the new Act will apply to that provision,[44] with the result that persons will be regarded as having received notice and knowledge of the prohibition or restriction on the amendment of certain provisions of the company's Memorandum of Incorporation. (The reference to s 19(4) in this item should instead have been a reference to s 19(5).)

21.9 COMPANY NAMES AND NAME RESERVATIONS

The Transitional Arrangements generally enable names reserved or registered as defensive names under the 1973 Act to continue to be so reserved or registered under the new Act.

21.9.1 Name reservations

A reservation of a company name in terms of (s 42 of) the 1973 Act, that was in effect before the effective date, is regarded as a reservation in terms of (s 12 of) the new Act as from the effective date.[45] Such a reserved name must, however, satisfy the criteria for company names as set out in s 11 of the new Act.[46]

If the Companies Commission believes that a name does not satisfy these criteria, it must notify the person for whose use the name was reserved and invite the person to reserve a substitute name. In this event such person may file, at no charge, a request for the reservation of a substitute name that does satisfy the

---

[42] Schedule 5 item 7(9).
[43] Schedule 5 item 7(8)(*b*); see also ss 13(3) and 15(2) read with cl 11 of the draft Companies Amendment Bill, 2010, and chapter 4: Formation of Companies and the Company Constitution.
[44] Schedule 5 item 7(10).
[45] Schedule 5 item 8(1).
[46] See chapter 4: Formation of Companies and the Company Constitution.

requirements of the new Act, at any time within 120 business days after the date of the Companies Commission's notice.[47]

21.9.2 Defensive names

Moreover, a registration of a defensive name that was granted in terms of (s 43 of) the 1973 Act, and was in effect immediately before the effective date, must be regarded as if it had been registered in terms of (s 12 of) the new Act (as from the effective date).[48] The draft Companies Amendment Bill, 2010, proposes to include not only registrations of defensive names, but also renewals of the registration of defensive names within the scope of this provision.

Although the Transitional Arrangements presently provide for the expiry of any such registration of a defensive name on the earlier of the date the name is used by a company or the second anniversary of the general effective date, the draft Companies Amendment Bill, 2010 (cl 115(6)), proposes to repeal these expiry provisions. It simultaneously proposes that such defensive names will be regarded as if they had been registered as from the actual date on which the registration was granted, as opposed to the effective date. This will, of course, affect on the calculation of the period of registration of a defensive name which may, in terms of s 12(9) of the Act, be registered for a period of two years and renewed for a further period of two years.

21.9.3 Translation or shortened form of name

Where a translation of a name or a shortened form of a name was registered in terms of s 43 of the 1973 Act, and was in effect immediately before the effective date, it is deemed to be a registration of that name as if it had been registered as a name of the relevant company in terms of the new Act.[49]

21.10 CONTINUED APPLICATION OF THE 1973 ACT TO WINDING-UP AND LIQUIDATION

Despite the general repeal of the 1973 Act, Chapter XIV of that Act continues to apply with respect to the winding-up and liquidation of companies under the new company law regime.[50]

However, an exception is created in respect of solvent companies. Sections 343, 344, 346, and 348 to 352 of Chapter XIV of the 1973 Act do not apply to the winding-up of a solvent company, except to the extent necessary to give effect to the provisions of Part G of Chapter 2 of the new Act, which deals with the winding-up of solvent companies and deregistration. Where there is a conflict, in respect of a solvent company, between a provision of Chapter XIV of the 1973 Act and a provision of Part G of Chapter 2 of the new Act, the provision of the new Act prevails.[51]

---

[47] Schedule 5 item 8(2).
[48] Schedule 5 item 8(3)(*b*).
[49] Schedule 5 item 8(3)(*a*).
[50] Schedule 5 item 9(1).
[51] Schedule 5 item 9(2) and (3).

Chapter XIV of the 1973 Act will apply to the winding-up and liquidation of companies until a date determined by the Minister, by notice in the *Government Gazette*. The Minister may not give such notice until he or she is satisfied that alternative legislation has been brought into force, which adequately provides for the winding-up and liquidation of insolvent companies. The Minister may also, by way of notice in the *Gazette*, prescribe ancillary rules as may be necessary to provide for the efficient transition from the provisions of the 1973 Act to the provisions of the alternative legislation.[52]

21.11 COURT PROCEEDINGS AND ORDERS: PRESERVATION AND CONTINUATION

The Transitional Arrangements provide for the preservation and continuation of court proceedings and court orders in terms of the 1973 Act. In this regard, when the new Act comes into effect, any proceedings in any court in terms of the 1973 Act, immediately before the effective date, are continued in terms of the 1973 Act as if it had not been repealed. Furthermore, any court order in terms of the 1973 Act, and in force immediately before the effective date, continues to have the same force and effect as if the 1973 Act had not been repealed, subject to any further order of the court.[53]

21.12 GENERAL PRESERVATION OF REGULATIONS, RIGHTS, DUTIES, NOTICES AND OTHER INSTRUMENTS

The Transitional Arrangements also make provision for the general preservation of regulations,[54] rights and duties, notices and other instruments.

In this regard, any right, entitlement or obligation in terms of the 1973 Act remains valid, as from the date that the right, entitlement or obligation first arose, subject to the provisions of the new Act.[55] A notice given or a document served (or filed)[56] in terms of the 1973 Act is considered as a notice given in terms of a comparable provision of the new Act, as from the date that it was actually given, or as a document satisfactorily served (or filed) for a comparable purpose of the new Act,[57] as the case may be. Where an order was given by an inspector in terms of the 1973 Act and was in effect immediately before the effective date, it continues in effect, subject to the provisions of the new Act.[58]

21.13 TRANSITION OF REGULATORY AGENCIES

The registers of companies, external companies, reserved names and delinquent directors, respectively, as maintained by the Companies and Intellectual Property Registration Office (CIPRO) in terms of the 1973 Act, are each continued as the

---

[52] Schedule 5 item 9(4) read with (1).
[53] Schedule 5 item 10(1) and (2).
[54] Although the heading of Schedule 5, item 11 refers to 'regulations', 'regulations' are not explicitly referred to in the body of item 11.
[55] Schedule 5 item 11(1).
[56] See the draft Companies Amendment Bill, 2010 (cl 115(7)).
[57] Schedule 5 item 11(2) and (3).
[58] Schedule 5 item 11(4).

relevant registers of companies, external companies, reserved names and directors required to be established by the Companies Commission in terms of the new Act.[59] The registers thus continue to be valid.

The Commissioner is the person who occupied the post of chief executive officer of CIPRO immediately before the general effective date of the Act. He or she is regarded as having been appointed on the general effective date as the Commissioner (in terms of s 189), for a term to be determined by the Minister.

Employees of CIPRO or the Office of Companies and Intellectual Property Enforcement in the Department of Trade and Industry become employees of the Companies Commission on the effective date.[60] Provision is also made for the transfer of departmental employees in accordance with relevant labour law and collective agreements, their pension fund membership, pension and retirement benefits, and the continuity of any decisions, proceedings, rulings and directions applicable to them.[61] All the records, contractual rights and liabilities of CIPRO, as well as all the movable assets used by it and the Office of Company and Intellectual Property Enforcement, are generally transferred to the Companies Commission as at the general effective date of the Act.[62]

As at the general effective date, the assets and liabilities of the Securities Regulation Panel (established by s 440B of the 1973 Act) are transferred to the Takeover Regulation Panel.[63] Persons holding office (immediately before the general effective date) as member, chairperson, deputy chairperson or Executive Director of the Securities Regulation Panel are regarded to have been appointed to similar offices in respect of the Takeover Regulation Panel as at the general effective date. Similarly, employees of the Securities Regulation Panel become employees of the Takeover Regulation Panel. The terms and conditions of office or employment of all such persons are identical to those before the general effective date, and they retain their rights to participate in, as well as their vested rights to, any pension scheme or medical scheme, subject to any further determination by the Takeover Regulation Panel in the exercise of its authority (set out in ss 200(1), 200(2)*(b)* and 210(3)).[64]

21.14 CONTINUED INVESTIGATION AND ENFORCEMENT OF THE 1973 ACT

Provision is made for the continued investigation and enforcement of the 1973 Act.

Despite the repeal of the 1973 Act, any investigation by the Minister or the Registrar in terms of that Act, and pending immediately before the effective date,

---

[59] Schedule 5 item 12(9).
[60] Schedule 5 item 12(1) and (2).
[61] Schedule 5 item 12(3)–(5).
[62] Schedule 5 item 12(6).
[63] Ibid.
[64] Schedule 5 item 12(7). However, if, after the general effective date, a person referred to in item 12(7)*(c)* or *(d)* resigns from an office in or terminates his or her employment by the Panel, and is subsequently appointed to an office within or re-employed by the Panel, ss 22(1), 200(2)*(b)* and 210(3) apply with respect to that person as if he or she were being so appointed or employed by the Panel for the first time (item 12(8)).

may be continued by the Companies Commission; while any investigation or other matter being considered by the Securities Regulation Panel may be continued by the Takeover Regulation Panel.[65]

When the new Act comes into effect, for a period of three years after the effective date, the Companies Commission may exercise any power of the Registrar,[66] while the Takeover Regulation Panel may exercise any power of the Securities Regulation Panel in terms of the 1973 Act, to investigate and prosecute any breach of that Act. This applies to contraventions of the 1973 Act that occurred during the period of three years before the effective date. A court is furthermore empowered in these circumstances to make any order that could have been made by a court in terms of the 1973 Act. In exercising this authority, the Companies Commission or the Takeover Regulation Panel must, significantly, conduct the investigation or other matter in accordance with the 1973 Act.[67]

21.15 REGULATIONS

For a period of 60 business days from the effective date, the Minister may make any regulation contemplated in the Act without satisfying the procedural requirements set out in s 223 or elsewhere in the Act, provided that the Minister has published the proposed regulations in the *Government Gazette* for comment for at least 30 business days.[68]

---

[65] Schedule 5 item 13(1)*(a)* and *(b)*.
[66] Or the Minister, in terms of the draft Companies Amendment Bill, 2010 (cl 115(9)).
[67] Schedule 5 item 13(1)*(c)* and (2).
[68] Schedule 5 item 14.

INDEX

A

ACCESS TO RECORDS see COMPANY RECORDS, ACCESS TO ACCOUNTABILITY AND TRANSPARENCY REQUIREMENTS
- Non-profit companies 85
- Personal liability companies 78
- Profit companies 68, 77
- Public companies 75, 77
- State-owned companies 82

ACCOUNTING RECORDS see also FINANCIAL STATEMENTS 544–550
- Electronic format 545
- Non-profit company 545
- Offences relating to 544
- What must be included 544–545

ACTION
- Meaning 161

ACTUAL AUTHORITY 174
- Express 174
- Implied 174

ADVERTISEMENTS
- Public offerings of company securities 601

AFFECTED TRANSACTION
- Definition 665

AGENCY
- By estoppel **see** Ostensible authority
- Director acting on behalf of company 173–174
- Pre-incorporation contracts and 141–142
- Relationship between holding company and subsidiaries 52–54
  - Factors determining existence 53
- Statutory
  - Application of section 21 134
  - Definition of pre-incorporation contracts and 143
  - Effect of 143
  - Method of contracting on behalf of company to be formed 142

AGENCY/ALTER EGO DOCTRINE
- Exception to principles of separate legal personality 39, 48–50
- Factors emphasised in applying 49
- Liability of shareholders and directors 49
- When company agent of directors and shareholders 48–49

AGENTS
- Directors as 384

AGREEMENT
- Definition of 143–144

ALLOTMENT see PUBLIC OFFERINGS OF SECURITIES, Allotments and acceptance of subscriptions

ALTERABLE CONDITIONS see MEMORANDUM OF INCORPORATION, Alterable conditions

ALTERNATE DIRECTOR 377
- Definition 377
- Fiduciary duties of 464

ALTERNATIVE DISPUTE RESOLUTION see also COMPANIES TRIBUNAL, Adjudicating proceedings 23, 772–773

923

ALTERNATIVE DISPUTE RESOLUTION (cont.)
   Stakeholder relationships and 454–457
      Appropriate process 455–456
      Business relationships 456
      Companies Tribunal 456
      Confidentiality 456
      Decision relating to must be in writing stipulating reasons 457
      Expert recommendation 456
      King III 454–457
      Mediation 455
      Principle and precedent 456
      Processes to be adopted for internal and external 455
      Rights and interests 456
      Time available to resolve 455–456
AMALGAMATIONS see MERGERS
ANNUAL FINANCIAL STATEMENTS see FINANCIAL STATEMENTS, Annual ANNUAL
   GENERAL MEETING (AGM)
   Matters raised by shareholders 344
   Minimum business to be conducted at 343–344
   Public company 77
   Shareholders' meeting 347
      Distinction between 343–344
   Transparency and accountability 344
ANNUAL RETURN 550
ANTI-AVOIDANCE PROVISION 7
   Elements 7
APPARENT AUTHORITY see OSTENSIBLE AUTHORITY
APPRAISAL RIGHTS OF DISSENTING SHAREHOLDERS 22–23, 636–637, 719–739
   Acquisition of shares, not constituting 729
   Alteration of class rights 732–739
      Class right, what is 734
      Dilution of voting rights 736
      Inconsistency between sections 164(2)(*a*) and 37(8) 732–733
      Leapfrogging 736–736
      Materially adverse (or material and adverse) to rights or interests 737–739
         Effect of including 'interests' 737–739
         'Material and adverse' and 'materially adverse', difference between 733
      Memorandum of Incorporation
         Changes reducing value of shares 734–735
         To be amended 735–737
      Prerequisites for 735
      Variation of class rights at common law 736–737
      Where only one class of shares 733–734
   Application to particular classes of shares 724–725
   Appraisal procedure 720, 722–729
      Acceptance of offer 726–727
      Court application to determine value 720–721, 727–729
         Cost orders 728–729
         Interest from action approved by resolution to payment 728
         Minimisation of involvement 727
         Order varying company obligations 729
         Orders made by court 728–729
         Shareholders not accepting offer joined as parties 727
         When 727
      Demand by dissenting shareholder 720, 723–726

Index 925

APPRAISAL RIGHTS OF DISSENTING SHAREHOLDERS — Appraisal procedure —
 Demand by dissenting shareholder (cont.)
  Demand notice 725
  Requirements to be satisfied 723–724
 Notice of adoption of resolution 723
 Notice of objection by dissenting shareholder 720, 722–723
  Exceptions 723
  Prior to vote 723
 Offer by company 720–721, 726
 Statement of appraisal rights 722
 Check on business judgments 720
 Conflicting values 719–720
 Disposal of all or part of assets or undertaking 656–657
 Distribution, not constituting 729
 Exit mechanism for shareholders 22, 719
 Fair value, determination of 731–732
  Appointment of appraisers 732
  Delaware courts and other jurisdictions 732
  Method not stipulated by legislation 731
  Time for valuation 731
 Flaws and limitations of 729–731
  Complex and rigid steps 729
  Costly for dissenting shareholders 731
  Delay experienced by dissenting shareholders 730–731
  Failure to comply with procedure
   Company suffers no adverse consequences 730
   Shareholders can lose right 729–730
 Fundamental transactions and 616
 Mergers and fundamental transactions 619, 636–637
 Partial dissents 724
 Remedy, distinction from court approval for mergers 635–636
 Resolution to be adopted 720
 Revocation of special resolution 725
 Rights to shares relinquished
  Only right to be paid fair value 725
  Reinstatement, circumstances 725
 Scheme of arrangement 663–664
 Shareholders remedies 22, 637
 Triggered in certain circumstances 719
 Triggers for **see also** APPRAISAL RIGHTS OF DISSENTING SHAREHOLDERS, Alteration of class rights 721–722
 What is 636–637, 719
 When entitled to be paid fair value of shares 720
 When exercised 22
 Which shareholders entitled to use 724
ARTIFICIAL PRICE, MAINTENANCE OF
 Prohibited trading practices 897
ASSETS AND PROPERTY **see** PROPERTY AND ASSETS
AUCTIONING PROCESSES OR PRE-OPENING SESSIONS
 Prohibited trading practices 896–897
AUDIT AND INDEPENDENT REVIEW 550–553
 Companies required for 550–551
 Independent review
  Forms of 551–552
 Private companies, when exempted 552–553

AUDIT AND INDEPENDENT REVIEW (cont.)
  Review engagement 551
  Who may review 552
AUDIT COMMITTEE 419–420, 441, 445–446, 560–561, 564
  Accountable to board of directors 420
  Advantages 564
  Appointment of 560
  Duties of 560–561
  Expenses 561
  Functions of 446
  Independence 445
    Of auditor 561
  Internal audits 422
  King III Report and Code 441, 445–446, 564
  Members of 420, 445
    Fiduciary duties of 464–465
    Memorandum of Incorporation and company rules
      Enforcement of and effect on 138–141
        Failure to comply with rules or Memorandum of Incorporation 141
        In exercise of functions 139
    Number of 560
    Requirements for 560
  Nomination of auditor 561
  Private company 70, 77
  Public company 75, 77, 419, 441, 560
  Requirements in terms of King III 564
  Standard of conduct 420
  State-owned company 82, 419, 441, 560
  When elected 420
AUDITORS 391–392, 553–556
  Annual financial statements 392
  Appointment of 553–554
    Firm as 554, 555
    Procedure before 555
    Requirements for 553–554
    Retired 554
  Contract, breach of 570–571
    Apportionment of damages 570–571
    Negligence 571
    When liable 570
  Damages for liability
    Apportionment 573
    Measure of 572–573
  Delict
    Liability
      Breach of statutory duty 571–572
      Common law action 571–572
      What must be proved 572
  Duties of registered 558–560
    Appropriate qualifications 558
    Conflict of interest 569
    Criteria for audit 558
    Entity or firm to decide on person responsible 558–559
    Responsibility for keeping books to be indicated 559–560

Index

AUDITORS (cont.)
   Economic loss, pure
      Liability for 572
   Independence 561
   Independent from company 392
   Legislation governing profession 556–560
      Limitation of liability 577–578
   Liability of 566–589
      Civil 568–583, 588
         To clients 568–573
            Breach of contract 570–571
            Delict 571–572
            Duties to 568
            Grounds for liability to client 570–572
            Measure of damages 572–573
            Pure economic loss 572
            Reasonable care and skill 568–569
         To third parties 573–583
            Common law 573–577
            Current position 578–583
            Legislative intervention 577–578
            Limitation by Auditing Profession Act 577–578
            Negligent misrepresentation causing financial loss 573–577
            Representation of correctness of financial statements 581–583
            Requirements for in terms of current position 578–583
            Type of liability incurring 573
            When unaware of incorrectness 582–583
      Criminal 566–568, 588
      Disciplinary 589
         Sanctions imposed by disciplinary committee 589
      Reportable irregularities 584–588
         Actions after sending report to IRBA 584–585
         Criminal and civil liability 588
         Definition of 584
         Failure to 584, 588
         IRBA guide 585–588
         Submission to IRBA 584–585
   Negligent misrepresentation causing financial loss
      Auditors' liability 573–577
         Case law 576–577
         Particular circumstances 574
         Policy considerations 574–575
         Reasonable foreseeability of reliance by third party 574–575
         What must be established in terms of common law 575
   Nominated by audit committee 561
   Public companies 75, 77, 392
   Reasonable care and skill 566–568
      Contractual term 568
      Legal advice to be obtained when necessary 569–570
      Standard of care must meet changing circumstances 568–569
      Supervision and review of work of employees 569
      When suspecting dishonesty 569
   Registration 556–558
      Firms 557–558
      Individuals that may be registered 556–557

AUDITORS — Registration (cont.)
    Individuals that may not be registered 557
    Person not registered as an auditor
        Functions that such person may perform 558
        Functions that such person may not perform 558
    Registered auditor
        Consent of IRBA to employ certain persons 558
        What not allowed 558
  Resignation or removal 554
  Right of access 392, 555
    Court order to enforce 556
  Rights and restricted functions 555–556
  Rotation 555
  State-owned company 82, 392
  Transitional arrangements 917
  Vacancies 554–555
  Who may be appointed 391–392
AUTHORISED SHARES 198
AUTHORITY
  Actual 174
  Authority and capacity as prerequisites for binding contract 154
  Express 174
  Implied 174
  Meaning 154
  Ostensible 174–176
    Breach of fiduciary duty 176
    Requirements for 175–176
  Ratification 178
  Usual 176–178

B

BENEFICIAL INTEREST **see also** SECURITIES, Certificated, beneficial interest in
  Definition 227, 332
BILL OF RIGHTS
  Application of to companies 29
BOARD COMMITTEES 418–422, 441–442
  Appointment of 418–419
  Audit committee 70, 75, 77, 82, 138–141, 419–420, 441, 445–446, 560–561, 564
  Compulsory committees 419–422
  Consultants 419, 442
  Electronic communications 426
  Fiduciary duties of 464–465
  King III 441–442
  Legal responsibility of board for conduct of committees 418–419
  Members of 419
  Nomination committee 422, 440–441
  Non-director members 419, 442
    Standards of conduct and liability 419
  Recommended committees 422
  Remuneration committee 422, 441, 443
  Risk committees 422, 441–442, 446
  Social and ethics committee 19, 68, 70, 75, 82, 420–422, 474–475
BOARD MEETINGS 422–426, 441
  Calling a meeting 422–423
  Decisions without convening a meeting 426–427

Index

BOARD MEETINGS (cont.)
    King III 441
    Minutes 425–426
    Notice of 423–424
        Exception 423
        Exclusion of certain members 424
        Fair and reasonable 423
        Period for 423–424
        Quorum 424
        Voting 424–425
            Casting vote of chairperson 425
            Loaded votes 424
            Prevention from 425
            Voting agreements 425
    Resolutions 425–426
    'Round robin' 426–427
        When may be taken by means for 427
BOARD MEMBERS
    Memorandum of Incorporation and company rules
        Enforcement of and effect on 138–141
            Failure to comply with rules or Memorandum of Incorporation 141
            In exercise of functions 139
BUSINESS JUDGMENT RULE
    Derivative actions 712–713
    Directors' duties of care, skill and diligence 513–515
        Application 515
        Effect of 513
        Informed and reasonable decisions protected 513–514
        Rationality 513–514
        Requirements for 513–514
        Scope 514–515
        When applicable courts will not impose own judgment 514
BUSINESS NAMES **see also** COMPANY NAMES
    Registered names and 117
BUSINESS RESCUE **see also** BUSINESS RESCUE PLAN; BUSINESS RESCUE
    PRACTITIONERS 15–17, 781–817
    Affected persons, rights of 809–813
        Creditors and creditors' committees 811–813
            Consultation with business rescue practitioner 812
            Independence of 812
            Valuation of interests 812
            Voting interests of, how determined 812
            Voting rights to amend, approve or reject business rescue plans 811
            What entitled to 811
        Employees 798, 809–810
            Preferred unsecured creditor 809
            Representatives of to make proposals for business rescue plans 810
            What entitled to 810
        Employees' committees 810–811
            Criteria for 811
            Meeting with business rescue practitioner 810–811
        Groups of 809–813
        Holders of company's securities 813
            What entitled to 813
        Rights given 809

BUSINESS RESCUE (cont.)
- Application for 15
- Commencement of proceedings 784–791
  - By order of court 790–791
    - Business rescue practitioner, appointment of 791
    - Dismissal of application 792
    - Grounds for 790–791
    - Liquidation proceedings and 790
    - Procedure 790
  - By voluntary board resolution 785–789
    - Application to be filed 788
    - Business rescue practitioner, appointment of 786
      - Objections to 788
    - Failure to comply 786–787
    - Grounds for setting aside of 787
    - Notice of resolution to every 'affected person' 786
    - Objections to 787–789
      - Powers of court 789
    - Prerequisites for 785
    - Restrictions on 785–786
    - Setting aside of 788
    - When not adopting 787
- Definition of 783–784
- Duration of 791–792
  - Date of commencement 791–792
  - Duration 792
  - Progress reports 792
  - Termination 792
- Effect of 16, 798–801
  - On contracts 798–799
    - Right to cancel or suspend 798–799
  - On employment contracts and employees 798
  - On shareholders and director 799–801
- Employees 16–17
- Entities not applying to 784
- Financially distressed companies 15, 784
- Insolvency, avoidance of 782–783
- International background 782–783
- Legal consequences of order 792–801
  - Debtor in possession 793
  - Exercise of duties under authority of business rescue practitioners 793
  - Moratorium 16–17, 793–796
    - On legal proceedings 794–795
      - Claims subject to time limit 794
      - Criminal proceedings not subject to 794
      - Exceptions 794
      - Subject to consent of business rescue practitioner 794
    - On property interests 795–796
      - Subject to consent of business rescue practitioner 795
      - Third party in possession of property 796
      - When may dispose of or agree to dispose 795
  - Post-commencement finance 796–798
    - Ranking of claims 797
    - Statutory framework for 796
    - Unencumbered assets as security for 796–797

Index

BUSINESS RESCUE (cont.)
  Liquidation proceedings converted in 788
  Meaning of 783–784
  Moratorium on legal proceedings 16–17
  Notice to creditors during merger procedure 632–633
  Rescue, meaning of 782
  Stages of 783
  Termination order 807, 817
  Trade unions 16–17
  Voluntary by resolution of board of directors 16
  Winding-up, distinction from 16
BUSINESS RESCUE PLAN see also BUSINESS RESCUE; BUSINESS RESCUE
    PRACTITIONERS 16, 17, 807–809
  Alteration of rights of holders of securities 815
  Assumptions and conditions 808
  Background 807–808
  Certificate stating accuracy, currency and that estimates made in good faith 808
  Consideration of 813–815
    Criteria for approval 814
    Indication that business rescue possible 814
    Meeting of creditors and holders of voting rights 813–814
  Effect of adoption 815–816
  Failure to adopt 815, 816–817
  Proposals 808
  Publication 808–809
  When vote of holders of company's securities not required 815
BUSINESS RESCUE PRACTITIONER see also BUSINESS RESCUE; BUSINESS RES-
    CUE PLAN 16–17, 786, 801–807
  Access to records 806
  Additional appointments 805
  Appointment of 786, 791, 801
    Objections against 788
    Ways of 801
    When set aside 788
  Liquidator, may not be appointed as 806
  Officer of court 805
  Powers and duties of 17, 804–807
    Business rescue plan 807–809
    Investigation of company affairs 806
    Main function 805
    Monitoring of financial situation 806
    Same duties, responsibilities and liabilities as director 805
  Pre-existing management 805
  Profession of 17
  Qualification of 802
  Removal and replacement 802–803
  Remuneration of 803–804
    Additional fee subject to approval by creditors and shareholders 804
    Prescribed tariff 803, 804
    Safeguards against abuse 804
  Statement of affairs to be submitted within 5 days of appointment 806

C

CAPACITY
  Authority and capacity as prerequisites for binding contract 154

CAPACITY (cont.)
    Meaning 154
CAPACITY OF A COMPANY see LEGAL CAPACITY OF A COMPANY
CAPITAL MAINTENANCE CONCEPT 10
CAPITAL PROFITS
    Dividends out of 265
CASH MERGER 644
CAUTIONARY ANNOUNCEMENTS 675
CENTRAL SECURITIES DEPOSITORY (CSD) 233
    Registration of uncertificated securities 233–235
    Transfer of uncertificated securities 237
CERTIFICATE TO COMMENCE BUSINESS
    Requirements for formation of company 9
CERTIFICATED SECURITIES see SECURITIES, Certificated
CESSION
    In *securitatem debiti*
        Not a disposal of all or part of assets or undertaking 650
        Transfer of securities
            Certificated 226–227
            Uncertificated 237
    Of rights
        Transfer of securities 223
CHAIRPERSON OF BOARD OF DIRECTORS 388–389, 444
    Casting vote 389
    Fiduciary duty to act objectively 389
    King III 444
    Usual authority 177
CHIEF EXECUTIVE OFFICER 444
    King III 444
CHINESE WALL
    Insider trading 854–857
    Market manipulation 904–905
CIVIL ACTIONS 779
CIVIL LIABILITY see AUDITORS, Liability of, Civil; INSIDER TRADING, Liability, Civil
CLASS ACTION 749
CLOSE CORPORATIONS 9–10, 64
    Co-existence of previous legislation alongside new legislation 96
    Control of and holding/subsidiary relationship 195–196
    Conversion from company to not allowed 96
    Conversion to companies 96–98
        Accompanying documents 97
        Effect of 97–98
        Procedure 97
    Gross abuse of juristic personality of
        Examples of 57–59
    Holding company, as 190
    New approach 95
    Policy on 64
COMMON LAW
    Auditors' liability
        Civil, to third parties 573–577
        Delictual 571–572
    Directors
        Disclosure of personal financial interests 516

Index

COMMON LAW (cont.)
    Doctrine of constructive notice 168
    Insider trading
        Fiduciary duties 839–843
        Misrepresentation 843
    Market manipulation 888–889
    Personal action
        Shareholders remedies 743–744
    Piercing the veil and 44–47, 54
    Pre-incorporation contracts 141–142
    Relationship between company and shareholder 135–136
COMMON LAW DERIVATIVE ACTION 12, 20
COMMUNAL OR GROUP INTERESTS
    Non-profit companies 83–84
COMPANIES **see also** COMPANY NAMES; COMPANY RECORDS; COMPANY RULES;
    TYPES OF COMPANIES 96–98
    Accompanying documents 97
        Effect of 97–98
        Procedure 97
    Control of and holding/subsidiary relationship 194–195
    Conversion of 98–99
        Company name, end of 98
        Memorandum of Incorporation to be amended 98
        Personal liability company 98–99
    Contracting with shareholders 37–38
    Debts and liabilities 35–36
    Definition of 27–28
    Groups of **see also** Holding/Subsidiary relationship
        Agency relationship between holding companies and subsidiaries 52–54
        Exceptions to principle of separate legal personality 50–54
    Legal concept 26–61
    Legal personality 28–38
    Legal proceedings, institution of by or against 36–37
    Limited liability 31–32
    Management of business of 36
    Organs of 329
    Perpetual succession 32
    Profits 34–35
    Property and assets 33–34
    Relationship between bodies constituting 329
    Separate legal personality 28–38
        Exceptions 38–61
    Transactions, entering into on behalf of 36
    Types of **see** TYPES OF COMPANIES
    When 'deemed not to be a juristic person' 59
COMPANIES AND INTELLECTUAL PROPERTY COMMISSION **see** COMPANIES
    COMMISSION
COMPANIES COMMISSION 755–759
    Alternative dispute resolution 23
    Commissioner 759
    Compliance certificate 769
    Compliance notice 768–771
        Administrative fine for failure to comply 770–771
        Challenge before Competition Tribunal 769
        Failure to comply 769–770

COMPANIES COMMISSION — Compliance notice (cont.)
    Format and contents of..768–769
    Issuing of...768–769
    Objection to...769
    To whom issue...768
    What are required of person issued to................................768
    When requirements satisfied.......................................769
  Complaints to..763–772
    Compliance notice...768–771
    Initiating a complaint...763–764
    Investigations and inspections by.................................766–768
    Prescription...763–764
    Response to..764–765
  Confidential information..761–762
  Consent order..771–772
  Fraudulent or reckless and insolvent trading
    Power to determine whether company engaging in.......................541
  Functions of..757–758
  Jurisdiction...755
  Investigations and inspections by....................................764–768
    Entry and search...766–767
        Offences relating to...767
    Inspector..764–765
    Investigator...764–765
    Outcome of..767–768
    Powers to support...765–767
    Questioning..765
    Response to...764–765
    Warrant to enter and search.......................................765–766
  Legislation to be enforced...756
  Locus standi..749
  Minister..759
  Monitoring compliance...24
  Objectives of..756
  Referral or non-referral to court..772
  Reporting, research and public information...............................758
  Transitional arrangements..762, 910, 920–921
  Winding-up of company..771
COMPANIES TRIBUNAL..759–762
  Adjudicating proceedings..773–775
    Conducted expeditiously and in accordance with principles of natural justice.........774
    Powers...774
    Witnesses..774
    Who may participate..774
  Alternative dispute resolution.......................................23, 456
  Company name disputes..113
  Confidential information..761–762
  Decisions binding on Companies Commission............................761
  Exemptions regarding unalterable provisions in Memorandum of Incorporation.........121
  Functions of..759–761
  Matters referred to single member or panel................................761
  Members of..761
  Order may be filed in court...761
  Shareholders' meeting
    Power to authorise on failure of company to convene.......................348

Index 935

COMPANIES TRIBUNAL (cont.)
    Transitional arrangements 762, 920–921
COMPANY FORMATION 8–9
    Incorporation
        Memorandum of 8–9
        Notice of 8
    Requirements for 8
COMPANY NAMES 108–117
    Change of 113–114
        Criteria for names 114
        Different category of profit company 114
        Effect of 114
        Procedure 113
    Criteria 108–111
        Concluding words or name ending 109
        Delict of 'passing off' 110
        Expression '(RF)' 109
        Hateful names or names falling outside freedom of expression protection 110, 111
        Misleading names falsely implying non-existent association 110, 111
        Registration number as 109
        Restrictions 109–111, 112–113
        Similar names 109, 110
        Symbols 108
        Words in any language 108
    Defensive names 115–116
        'Direct and material interest' relating to name 115–116
        Period of registration 115–116
        Purpose of 116
        Renewable 116
        Transitional arrangements 919
    Ending indicating type of company 111
        Conversion of companies 98
        Non-profit company 84, 109
        Personal liability company 78, 109
        Private company 69, 76, 109
        Public company 75, 76, 109
        Restrictive or procedural requirements stipulated in Memorandum of Incorporation 122
        State-owned company 83, 109
    Registration 111–112
        Amendments 112
            Failure to 112
        Compliance notice 112
        Disputes 112–113
            Referral to Companies Tribunal 113
            Referral to South African Human Rights Commission 113
        Duplicated names 112
        Interim names 112
        Name ending indicating type of company 111
        Restricted names 112–113
        Unsuitable names 105, 111
    Reservation of 108, 114–115
        Abuse of reservation system 115
        Compliance with criteria for names 114–115
        Period of 115
        Purpose of 114

COMPANY NAMES — Reservation of (cont.)
    Transferral of 115
    Transitional arrangements 918–919
  Translation or shortened form
    Transitional arrangements 919
  Transitional arrangements 911–912, 918–919
  Use of 116–117
    Authorisation to use 117
    Business names 117
    Failure to properly describe name 116, 117
    Non-compliance with requirements 116–117
    Notices and official publications 116
    Outside place of business, not necessary 116
    Trading names 116
COMPANY OFFICERS, INDEMNIFICATION **see** DIRECTORS, Indemnification
COMPANY RECORDS **see also** ACCOUNTING RECORDS; FINANCIAL STATEMENTS;
  RETENTION OF RECORDS 365–371
  Access to 367–370
    Accounting records 368
    By business rescue practitioner 806
    Exercising right to access information 369–370
      During business hours 369
      Members of company 370
    Failure to accommodate request for access 370
    Financial statements 549
    Memorandum of Incorporation and information rights 367
    Other legislation 367–368
    Records that may be inspected or copied by persons with beneficial interest 367
    Shareholders' interests and 368–369
  Board meeting
    Minutes 425–426
    Resolutions 425–426
  Derivative actions 714
  Location of 371
  Records for tax purposes 365
  Records to be kept indefinitely 365
  Securities register 366
  Social and ethics committee 421–422
  Transitional arrangements 917
  What must be maintained and retention period 366
COMPANY RULES 129–131, 399
  Amendment 130
  Binding 129, 130
  Enforcement of and effect of on relationships 135–141
    Between company and director 138–141
      Alteration of Memorandum of Incorporation and rules 140
      Contract of service 140
      Failure to comply with rules or Memorandum of Incorporation 141
      Implications 139–140
      In exercise of functions as directors 139
      Removal from office 140–141
    Between company and prescribed officer, member of audit committee or board
      committee 138–141
      Failure to comply with rules or Memorandum of Incorporation 141
      In exercise of functions 139

Index

COMPANY RULES — Enforcement of and effect of on relationships (cont.)
 Between or among shareholders *inter se* 137–138
 By shareholders against company 137
 Whether shareholders bound only in capacity as shareholders 135–136
Made by 129
Memorandum of Incorporation and 129
Ratification 130
Regulation of 129
Status of 133–141
 Meaning of provisions, uncertainty 134
 Relationships created by 135–141
  Between and among shareholders *inter se* 137–138
   Enforcement of Memorandum of Incorporation and rules 137–138
  Between company and shareholder 135–137
   Enforcement of rights by shareholder against company 137
   Whether shareholders bound only in capacity as shareholders 135–136
 Statutory contract 134
 Unilateral alteration 134
Transitional arrangements 131, 913
When effective 120
COMPANY SECRETARY 389–390, 444, 562–563, 564–565
 Appointment of 562
 Duties 390, 562–563, 565
 Juristic person or partnership as 562
 King III 444, 564–565
 Private companies 70, 77, 389
 Public companies 75, 77, 389
 Register 562
 Registration of 563
 Requirements 390
 Resignation or removal 563
 Role of 389
 Transitional arrangements 917
 Usual authority 176, 177
 When appointed 389, 562
COMPARABLE OFFERS 671–672, 675
COMPLIANCE RISK 448
COMPLIANCE WITH LEGISLATION, RULES, STANDARDS, CODES 439, 448
 Compliance risk 448
 King III 448
 Working understanding of, directors to have 448
COMPROMISE WITH CREDITORS 817–820
 1973 legislation 817–818
 Court order to be enforceable 819–820
 Filing 820
 Intention of 817
 Proposal 818–820
  Adoption 819–820
  Board of Directors or liquidators *locus standi* to 818
  Certificate stating accuracy, currency and that estimates made in good faith 819
  Divided into 818–819
   Assumptions and conditions 819
   Background 818–819
   Proposals 818
 What is 817

COMPROMISE WITH CREDITORS (cont.)
   When appropriate 817
COMPULSORY ACQUISITIONS AND SQUEEZE-OUT 670–671
CONFIDENTIAL CORPORATE INFORMATION
   Duty of avoiding conflict of interest
      Corporate opportunity rule
         Common law 490–492
         Statutory law 502
   Duty to communicate to company 504
CONFIDENTIALITY
   Breach of
      As offence 775–776
   Insider trading
      Sharing of information 884
   Regulatory agencies 761–762
   Takeovers and offers 675
CONFLICT BETWEEN OLD AND NEW RULES 2–3
CONFLICT OF INTEREST
   Auditors 560
   Duty of directors **see** DUTIES OF DIRECTORS, Fiduciary, Avoiding conflict of interest
CONSENT ORDER
   Following Companies Commission investigation 771–772
CONSIDERATION
   Meaning of 208
CONSTITUTION OF COMPANY see MEMORANDUM OF INCORPORATION
CONSTITUTIONAL RIGHTS
   Shareholders to decide fate of takeover bid 478
CONSTRUCTIVE NOTICE DOCTRINE see DOCTRINE OF CONSTRUCTIVE NOTICE
CONTRACTS
   Breach of by auditor
      Liability to client 570–571
   Effect of business rescue on 798–799
   Shareholder can not bind company with 35
CONTRACTUAL DUTIES
   Evasion of
      Abuse of separate legal personality 40–42
CONTRAVENTION OF COMPANIES ACT
   Personal liability of directors 61
CONVERTIBLE SECURITIES 278–279
CORPORATE CITIZENSHIP
   King III Report and Code 436–437
      Impact of company operations on society and environment 436–437
   Social and ethics committee 474–475
CORPORATE FINANCE 241–326
   Acquisitions by company of shares in its holding company (indirect re-purchases) 282–287
   Distributions **see also** Distributions 241–268
   Financial assistance for acquisition of securities **see also** FINANCIAL ASSISTANCE,
      For acquisition of securities 287–310
   Financial assistance to directors **see also** FINANCIAL ASSISTANCE,
      To directors, prescribed officers, related and interrelated companies 310–326
   Repurchases (buy-backs) **see also** REPURCHASES (BUY-BACKS) 268–282
CORPORATE GOVERNANCE 432–458
   Audit committees 445–446, 564
   Boards and directors 437–444
   Company secretary **see also** COMPANY SECRETARY 564–565

Index 939

CORPORATE GOVERNANCE (cont.)
   Compliance with laws, rules, codes and standards 448
   Corporate citizenship 436–437
   Function of 433
   History 563
   Information technology, governance of 448
   Integrated reporting and disclosure 457, 565–566
   Integrity as principle of 433
   Internal audit 448–449
   King III Code of Corporate Governance Principles **see** King III Report and Code
   King III Report on Corporate Governance in Southern Africa **see** King III Report and Code
   Leadership, ethical 435–437
   Risk governance 446–447
   Stakeholder relationships, governance of 449–457
   Values of 436
   What is 432–433
CORPORATE OPPORTUNITY RULE 489–497
   Application of by courts 491–497
   Breach of, how to determine 490
   Corporate opportunity includes property, assets and confidential information 490–491
   Legislation 501–502
   Line of business test (United States) 489–490
   No-profit rule, distinction between 491–497
   What is 489
CORPORATE REPORTING 13–14
CORPORATE VEIL see also PIERCING THE VEIL OF CORPORATE PERSONALITY
   Distinction between lifting and piercing 42–43
COSTS
   Appraisal rights 728–729
   Derivative actions 715–716
COURTS
   Appraisal rights of dissenting shareholders 720–721
   Business rescue proceedings
      Commencement of by order of court 790
      Powers of 789
   Companies Commission referrals 772
   Corporate opportunity rule 491–497
   Derivative actions **see** DERIVATIVE ACTIONS, Court involvement
   Directors
      Duties of care, skill and diligence
         When will not impose own judgment 514
      Relief by court against 526–528
         Application to proceedings instituted by party other than company 428
         Case law 527–528
         Discretion of court 527
         Grounds for 527
         Must have acted honestly and reasonably 527–528
   Disposal of all or part of assets or undertaking 656
   Mergers **see** MERGERS, Court approval
   Order of for
      Right of access to records for auditor 556
   Power to convene shareholders' meetings 348–349
      General policy not to interfere with internal domestic affairs 348–349
      When possible 348
   Scheme of arrangement 663

COURTS (cont.)
  Transitional arrangements... 920
CREDITORS
  Business rescue
    Meeting with regarding business rescue plan 813–814
    Rights of
      Consultation with business rescue practitioner............................. 812
      Independence of 812
      Valuation of interests... 812
      Voting interests of, how determined 812
      Voting rights to amend, approve or reject business rescue plans 811
      What entitled to... 811
  Compromise with **see** COMPROMISE WITH CREDITORS
  Debenture holders... 214
    Trustees as... 215
  Independent
    Meaning of 814
  Mergers
    Notice to and objection by.. 632–633
    Objecting.. 632
    Protective measures for... 639
CRIMINAL LIABILITY **see** AUDITORS, Liability of, Criminal; INSIDER TRADING, Liability, Criminal; PUBLIC OFFERINGS OF COMPANY SECURITIES, Liability, Criminal
CRIMINAL PENALTIES 24, 775
CUMULATIVE PREFERENCE SHARES 201

D

DAMAGES
  Apportionment
    Auditors' liability 573
      For breach of contract 570–571
      Measure of 573
  Directors' liability 530–531
  Shareholders
    Claim for 163–164
      Restraining company from contravening Act 742–743
    Whistle-blowers.. 752–753
DE FACTO DIRECTOR 380–381
  Shadow director, distinction between 382–383
DE JURE DIRECTOR 378
DEBENTURE STOCK CERTIFICATES... 214
  Mortgage bond, difference between 214
  Repayment of loans and interest... 215
DEBENTURES
  Debenture stock certificates... 214, 215
  Holder a particular kind of creditor.. 214
  Issuing of.. 210
  Terms of issue.. 214
  Trust deed to represent debenture holders 215
    Debenture holders beneficiaries 215
    Reasons for.. 215
    Repayment of loans and interest.. 215
    Trustees are creditors of company 215
  What is.. 212–214

Index 941

DEBENTURES (cont.)
    What is not 214
DEBT INSTRUMENTS **see also** DEBENTURES 212–217
    Conversion from shares to 244–245
    Debentures as 212–215
    Issuing of 212
    Legislation governing 212
    Meaning of 212
    Qualification of issuing of 212
    Trust deed to represent debenture holders 215–216
    Trustees 216
        Invalidation of releases 216–217
        Requirements for 216
    Special privileges 216
    Voting rights attaching and holding/subsidiary relationship 189
DEBTS
    Of company belong to company 35–36
DECLARATORY ORDER
    Shareholders remedies 22
DECRIMINALISATION 23–24
DEFENCES
    Insider trading 859–871
DEFERRED SHARES 204
DELICT
    Auditors' liability for
        Breach of statutory duty 571–572
        Common law action 571–572
        What must be proved 572
DELINQUENT DIRECTORS 404–407
    Grounds for delinquency 405
    Locus standi of persons bringing applications 404
    Order to declare as 21
    Setting aside or suspension of order 407
    Shareholder remedies 21
    Terms of order and conditions 407
DERIVATIVE ACTION 11, 20–21, 698–718
    Access to information 714
    Accessibility 700
    By whom brought 698
    Commencement or continuation of legal proceedings 704–705
    Common law 698–699
        Abolition of 701–702
    Company engaging in legal proceedings to protect itself 707
    Costs 715–716
        Interim cost order 716
    Court involvement 700, 705
        Application for leave and discretion of court 706–708
        Criteria guiding court 707, 708–714
            Best interest of company 710–714
                Business judgment rule 712–713
                Controlling persons 711–712
                Directors and rebuttable presumption 712
                Rebuttable presumption that not in 710–722
                    Related persons 711
                    Third parties 711

DERIVATIVE ACTION — Court involvement — Criteria guiding court (cont.)
    Good faith 708–709
      Serious question of material consequence to company 709–710
    Exceptional circumstances if court application before demand 707
  Demand served on company 703, 705
    Application to set aside 705
    Company's response 706
    Compliance with 707
    Investigation of 705–706
    Report by investigator 705–706
  Discontinuation, compromise or settlement proceedings, permission to 718
  Fiduciary duty of best interest of company 469
  Foss v Harbottle Rule 698–699, 701
  Judicial discretion to grant leave to 700
  Locus standi to institute action for 702–703
  Meaning 698
  Protection of legal interests of company 703–705
  Ratifiability principle 700, 701
  Ratification or approval by shareholders 717–718
  Related steps to protect legal interests of company 703–705
  Remuneration and expenses 714–715
    Liability for 715
  Security for costs 716
  Shareholder remedy 20–21
  Statutory 698–700
  Substitution of person to whom leave for was granted 716–717
  Who may apply for leave for 702–703
    Categories of applicants 703
    Directors 702–703
    Prescribed officers 702–703
    Related companies 703
    Shareholders, registered and those entitled to be registered 702
    Substitution of person granted to 716–717
'DIRECT AND MATERIAL INTEREST'
  Meaning 116
DIRECTORATE OF MARKET ABUSE **see** INSIDER TRADING, Directorate of Market
  Abuse
DIRECTORS 17–18
  Appointment of 393–395
    By board of directors or other stakeholders or outsiders 394–395
    By persons named in Memorandum of Incorporation 393
    By shareholders 394
    Consent to be a 395
    Terms of 395–396
      Memorandum of Incorporation or service contract 395
  Authority and representation **see** AUTHORITY, ACTUAL AUTHORITY, OSTENSIBLE
    AUTHORITY; USUAL AUTHORITY
  Authority to issue shares
    Board of directors and 205
    Directors' liability for non-compliance with s 41 206
  Board of **see also** BOARD COMMITTEES; BOARD MEETINGS
    Appointment
      King III 440–441
    Business rescue proceedings
      Commencement of by voluntary resolution 785–789

Index

DIRECTORS — Board of (cont.)
- Chairperson 444
  - King III 444
- Compliance with legislation, rules, standards, codes 439, 448
- Composition
  - Balance of power and authority 440
  - King III. 439–440
  - Supervisory 439–440
  - Two-tier. 439
  - Unitary 439, 440
- Corporate citizenship 436–437
- Directors
  - Appointment 394–395
  - Removal by 410
- Ethical leadership. 435–436
  - King III. 435–436
- Information technology governance 446
- Integrated reporting and disclosure 457
- Internal audit 448–449
- Legal duty and responsibility to manage 375
- Number of directors on 440
- Performance assessment 443
  - King III. 443
- Responsibilities
  - Balance between stakeholder groupings 439
  - Compliance with legislation, rules, standards, codes 439, 448
  - King III. 438–439
- Risks, governance of 446–447
- Rotation of directors 440
- Stakeholder relationships, governing of 449–457
- Vacancies on. 408–409
  - Filling of. 408–409
  - When arises 408
- Business rescue, effect on 799–801
- Consent to be a 395
- Contract of service 140
- Definition of 375–378, 463–464
  - As contemplated in section 66 376–378
  - 'By whatever name designated' 376
  - Fiduciary duties and 463–464
  - 'Includes' 375–376
  - 'Occupying the position of a director' 376
- Delinquent 404–407
  - Grounds for delinquency 405
  - *Locus standi* of persons bringing applications 404
  - Order to declare as 21
  - Setting aside or suspension of order 407
  - Terms of order and conditions 407
- Derivative actions **see also** DERIVATIVE ACTIONS
  - *Locus standi* to institute action 702–703
- Disclosure of personal financial interests 515–521
  - Common law principles 516
  - Declaration of interest in existing contracts 519–520
  - Direct interest 516
  - Disclose and recuse 519

DIRECTORS — Disclosure of personal financial interests (cont.)
    'Interest', meaning of 517
    Failure to declare 521
    Material interest 516–517
        Meaning of 'material' 517
    Non-compliance and court application 517
    Notice in advance 520
    'Personal financial interest', meaning of 516
    Proposed transactions 516–517
    To be approved by board 517
    To whom 520
    What must be disclosed 517–519
        Director to be aware of or know of 518
    When not necessary 520–521
  Dismissal of as employee 395
  Disqualification of 399, 400–404
    Application of section 69 399
    Consequences of 402
    Duration of 404
    Exemptions from 402–403
        Exercise of court's discretion 402–403
            Unrehabilitated insolvent 402
        Statutory 403
    Grounds for 400–401
    Ineligibility, distinction from 400
    Memorandum of Incorporation 401
    Offences 400
    Public register 404
  Distributions, authorisation of 246
  Duties of **see** DUTIES OF DIRECTORS
  Financial assistance to **see** FINANCIAL ASSISTANCE, To directors, prescribed officers,
    related and unrelated companies
  Fraudulent or reckless trading **see** FRAUDULENT OR RECKLESS TRADING
  Indemnification and insurance 521–526
    Advances and indemnities to defend legal proceedings 524–525
        Derivative actions instituted against 524
        Repayment 525
        Shareholder approval not necessary 525
    Exemption from duty or liability 523
    Liability insurance 525–526
    Limitation of personal liability 521–522
    Payment of fines and penalties 525
    Prohibition of any exemptions or indemnities 522
    Restitution 526
    When indemnity permissible 523
    When indemnity prohibited 523
  Induction 443
    King III 443
  Ineligibility 399–400
    Application of section 69 399
    Consequences of 402
    Disqualification, distinction from 400
    Grounds for 400
  Insolvent trading **see** INSOLVENT TRADING
  Legal position of 383–386

Index

DIRECTORS — Insolvent trading (cont.)
    As agents 384
    As managing partners 385–386
    As trustees 384–385
    Sui generis 386
  Liability 530–534
    Agency/alter ego doctrine 49–50
    Application of legislation 530
    Breach of duty of care, skill, diligence 531–532
    Breach of fiduciary duty 531
      Disgorgement of profits not covered 531
      Loss, damages and costs 531
      Ultra vires doctrine (old regime) 156, 158, 164
    Claims for loss, damages or costs 530–531
    Decisions contravening Act 533–534
    Financial assistance **see** FINANCIAL ASSISTANCE, For acquisition of securities, Liability of directors; FINANCIAL ASSISTANCE, To directors, prescribed officers, related and unrelated companies
    Gross negligence 530
    Indirect repurchases 284–285
    Issuing of shares and non-compliance with section 41 207
    Joint and several 530
    Misrepresentation and insider trading 843
    Personal liability companies 79–80
    Prescription period 530–531
    Ratification by shareholders of breach **see** DUTIES OF DIRECTORS, Ratification by shareholders of breach
    Relief by court **see** DUTIES OF DIRECTORS, Relief by court
    Repurchases 280
    Under section 77(3) 532–534
    Unlawful distributions **see** DISTRIBUTIONS, Directors liability for unlawful
    When liable 532–533
  Manager, distinction from 387–388
  Managing director 388
  Meaning 259
  Memorandum of Incorporation and company rules
    Enforcement of and effect of on relationships with company 135–141
      Alteration 140
      Contract of service 140
      Failure to comply with rules or Memorandum of Incorporation 141
      Implications 139–140
      In exercise of functions as directors 139
      Removal from office 140–141
  Non-profit companies 89
  Number of 392–393
    Failure to have required 393
    Minimum 392
    Non-profit companies 89
    One director company 392–393
    Personal liability companies 77, 392
    Private companies 69–70, 76–77, 392
    Public companies 75, 76–77
  Office of
    Transitional arrangements 917
  Oppression remedy **see also** OPPRESSION REMEDY 21–22

DIRECTORS — Oppression remedy (cont.)
    Application relating to exercise of powers 690
Oppressive of prejudicial conduct **see also** OPPRESSION REMEDY
Performance assessment 443
    King III 443
Personal liability of **see** PERSONAL LIABILITY OF DIRECTORS
Probation 404–407
    Grounds for 406
    Locus standi of persons bringing applications 404
    Setting aside or suspension of order 407
    Shareholder remedies 21
    Terms of order and conditions 407
Qualification of 399–400
Ratification of unauthorised or *ultra vires* act by special resolution 162–163
Record of 396–399
    Failure to accommodate request for access 399
    Information to be contained 396–399
    Inspection of 397–399
        Direct request for or through attorney 398
        Members 397–398
        Non-members 398
        Request to exercise right to access 398
    Location of 397
    Retention of 397
Relief by court against 526–528
    Application to proceedings instituted by party other than company 428
    Case law 527–528
    Discretion of court 527
    Grounds for 527
    Must have acted honestly and reasonably 527–528
Removal from office 140–141, 409–415
    Breach of contract, if constituting 414–415
    By board of directors 410
        Court application to review 414
    By shareholders 409–410
        Section 71 overrides provisions in Memorandum of Incorporation or agreement ... 409–410
        When not within scope of section 71 409–410
    Damages, claims for 414–415
    Loaded voting rights 412–413
        Memorandum of Incorporation 413
        Section 71 provisions 413
        Shares hold by director 412
    Ordinary resolution 411–412
        Best interest of company 411–412
        Not be passed informally 411
        Requirements for approval 412
    Notice to 410–411
    Presentation by 411
Remuneration 416–418, 443–444
    Disclosure in annual financial statements 418
    King III 443–444
    No automatic right to 416–417
    Not contingent on company earning sufficient profits 418
    Prohibition by Memorandum of Incorporation 417
    Special resolution required 417

Index

DIRECTORS — Remuneration — Special resolution required (cont.)
    Not retrospectively effective 417
  Resignation 415–416
    Contract for fixed period 416
    Not fiduciary power 416
    Of entire board 416
    Post-resignation duties 497–500, 501
    Puppet directors 416
    Unilateral act 415, 498
  Retirement from office 415
  Statutory statement of duties 17–18
  Terms of office 396
  Training 443
    King III 443
  Types of 376–383, 437–439
    Alternate 377
    Appointed in terms of Memorandum of Incorporation 376
    De facto director 380–381
    De jure 378
    Elected by shareholders 377–378
    Ex officio 376–377
    Executive 437
    Independent non-executive 437–438
    King III 437–438
    Nominee 378–379
    Non-executive 437–438
    Puppet director 379
    Shadow director 381–383
    Temporary 378
  Ultra vires act or and legal capacity of company 162–163
  Who are 375–383
DISCIPLINARY LIABILITY **see** AUDITORS, Liability of, Disciplinary
DISCLOSURE **see also** REPORTING, INTEGRATED 13, 457, 565–566
  King III 457
  Ratification of breach of directors' duties by shareholders 528–529
  Takeovers and offers 669–670
DISCLOSURE-BASED MANIPULATION **see** MARKET MANIPULATION, Disclosure-based manipulation
DISPOSAL OF ALL OR GREATER PART OF ASSETS OR UNDERTAKING 649–658
  Approval and requirements 652–654
    Appraisal rights of dissenting shareholders 656–657
    Court approval 656
    Exemptions 657–658
    Shareholder approval required 652
    Special resolution of shareholders of disposing company 654–655
      Meeting requirements 655
      Notice to shareholders 654–655
      Ratifies specific transaction 654
      Voting rights controlled by acquiring party or party acting in concert disqualified 655
    Special resolution of holding company 655–656
    Takeover Regulation Panel 656
    Third party may apply to court for transfer 652
    Turquand Rule 653
    Whether agreement binding without shareholder approval 653
  Court approval **see also** MERGERS, Court approval 656

DISPOSAL OF ALL OR GREATER PART OF ASSETS OR UNDERTAKING (cont.)
  Dispose, meaning of 649–651
  'Greater part', meaning of 651–652
    Method of calculation 652
    More than 50% of assets or undertaking 651–652
    Value to be calculated at fair market value 651
  Requisite approvals of (section 115) **see** MERGERS, Requisite approvals of (section 115)
  What is not a disposal 650–651
    Granting of pre-emption rights not part of 650
    Passing of mortgage bond over assets 650–651
    Pledge or cession in *securitatem debiti* 650
DISPOSE
  Meaning of 649–651
DISPUTE RESOLUTION **see** ALTERNATIVE DISPUTE RESOLUTION
DISSOLUTION
  Non-profit companies 87
DISTRIBUTIONS 241–268
  Acquisition of own shares and 241–242, 243
  Acquisition of shares in holding companies 241–242, 243
  Authorisation of 246
    By board of directors 246
    Memorandum of Incorporation, provisions of 246
    Shareholders not permitted to 246
    Unalterable provision 246
  Cash payments in lieu of share capitalisation 244
  Conversion of shares into debt instruments 244–245
  Definition of 242–246
    Liquidation distributions excluded 243
  Direct or indirect transfers 243, 245–246
  Directors' liability for unlawful 259–268, 533–534
    Court order setting aside section 46 decision 261, 533
    Director, meaning of 259
    Legislation 259
    Limit on amount of damages, loss and costs 262–263
    Limitations 261
    Knowledge of unlawful distribution 260, 533
    Partial implementation of distribution 261
    Participation in board resolution required 260
    Participation in resolution acknowledging solvency and liquidity test 260, 533
    Prescription 261–262
    Relief from liability 261
    Repurchases and 280
    When liable 259–260
  Enforcement of 259
    Acknowledgement of liquidity and solvency test 259
  Incurring of a debt or obligation in favour of own or holding company's shareholder 245
  Indirect repurchases 284
  Maintenance of capital principle 241
  Making of demand, tendering of shares in terms of appraisal remedy .. 245
  Non-monetary obligations 245
  Own shareholders and shareholders of group 245
  Redemption of own shares 244
  Repurchases and 276
  Restoration of any part of consideration paid for shares to shareholder 244
  Solvency and liquidity requirement 246–259

Index

DISTRIBUTIONS — Solvency and liquidity requirement (cont.)
    Accounting principles 252
    Auditor's opinion 251
    Balance sheet test 252
    Claims in respect of previous authorised distributions 254
    Contingent assets 253–254
    Contingent liabilities 252, 253–254
        Vinculum juris between claimant and company 254
    Differences between sections 44 and 45 250
    Directors entitled to rely on information, opinions, reports and statements by others 251
    Directors' liability 260
    Distribution proceed after acknowledgment by directors 247
    Excess of liabilities over assets 256
    Groups of companies 258
    How enquiry should be made 250–251
    Justifications 247–248
    Legislation 248–249
        Australia 254–255
        New Zealand 253
        United Kingdom 253
    Periodic testing 247
    Predictions not actual solvency and liquidity 250
    Preference shareholders, rights of 256–257
        Fixed preferential returns on shares 257
    Reconsidered if distribution not completed 247
    Resolution to be adopted acknowledging application 247
    Schemes aiming to set aside 258–259
    Solvency and liquidity test 246
    Solvency aspect of test, when satisfied 249
    Subjective or objective 249–250
    Unlawful distributions **see also** DISTRIBUTIONS, Directors' liability for unlawful
        Recovery of 263
    Valuation of all material assets 253
    When must be met 247, 257–258
    When met 249
    Whether able to pay debts as they become due and payable 254–256
  Types of 243
DIVIDENDS 243
  Distributions 243
  Out of profits 263–268
    Capital profits 265
    Memorandum of Incorporation 263
    Pre-incorporation profits 263
    Profit from disposal of fixed assets 266
    Realised and unrealised profits 266–267
    Retained profits 264
    Revenue profits 264
        What is 267–268
    Rules devised by courts 263–268
    Subsidiary profits 263–264
    Unrealised increase in value of company's fixed assets 266–267
DOCTRINE OF CONSTRUCTIVE NOTICE 168
  Abolishment, effect on Turquand Rule 173
  Capacity of company 19
  Common law 168

DOCTRINE OF CONSTRUCTIVE NOTICE (cont.)
   Exception 79
   Personal liability company 168
   Restrictions and prohibitions on amendment of Memorandum of Incorporation 122–123
   Special conditions in Notice of Incorporation 168
DOCTRINE OF UNANIMOUS ASSENT **see also** UNANIMOUS ASSENT AT COMMON
   LAW 336–338
DOMESTIC COMPANIES 95
   Exception to principles of separate legal personality 47–48
DOUBLE JEOPARDY 779
DUTIES OF DIRECTORS 17–18, 459–528
   Care, skill and diligence 461, 504–515
      Common law prior to Act 504–508
         Based on delictual or Aquilian liability for negligence 505
         Bias in favour of inexperienced director 506
         Case law 506
         Continuous attention to company affairs not necessary 507
         Delegation 510–511
         Depends on type of company or director, skills, knowledge, position and
           responsibilities 505
         Knowledge and experience 505–506
         Lenient attitude by courts 505
         Official not director to perform duties honestly and properly 507
         Special qualifications not necessary 507
         Subjective test 505
      Liability for breach of 530–531
      Statutory requirements 508–510
         Banks Amendment Act 19 of 2003 508
         Business judgment rule 513–515
           Application 515
           Effect of 513
           Informed and reasonable decisions protected 513–514
           Rationality 513–514
           Requirements for 513–514
           Scope 514–515
           When applicable courts will not impose own judgment 514
         Delegation (sections 76(4) and (5) 511–513
           Compliance with 512–513
           Directors allowed to rely on persons authority delegated to 511–512
           Knowledge that makes reliance unwarranted or unreasonable 512
           Reasonable belief in reliability 512
           Reliance on information, opinions, recommendations, statements and reports 512
           Whom may rely on 511–512
         Diligence, meaning of 510
         Fair and equitable standard of care 509
         Nature of company, decision in question, position of director and responsibilities 510
         Objective standards
           Flexible and reasonable 509–510
           Prescribed as minimum standard 509
         Section 76(3)(c) requirements 508–510
         Subjective standard at common law remains part of 508
           When taken into account 508
         United States and Canadian legislation 507–508
   Codification of, partial 461–463
      Advantages and disadvantages 462

Index 951

DUTIES OF DIRECTORS — Codification of, partial (cont.)
    Common-law jurisdictions 462
    Existing defects and conflicts 462
    Object of 462
  Common law duties 461
  Fiduciary 17–18, 463–475
    Acting within powers 483–485
      Common law 483
      Disregard for constitutional limitations 484
      Distinction between lack of authority and abuse of authority 484
      Liability for lost, damages or costs 484
      Shareholders' right to claim damages 484–485
      Statutory 483–484
    Avoiding conflict of interest 485–504
      Common law 485–500
        Accountability for profits received in breach 485–486
        Conflict between personal and company interests 485–486
        Conflicting duty 486
        Corporate opportunity rule **see also** CORPORATE OPPORTUNITY RULE 489–497
        No-conflict rule **see also** NO-CONFLICT RULE 486–487
        No-profit rule **see also** NO-PROFIT RULE 486, 487–489
        'Possibly may conflict' **see also** DUTIES OF DIRECTORS, Post-resignation 486
        Post-resignation duties 497–500
        Trust law influence 485
      Statutory law 500–504
        Corporate information 502
        Corporate opportunity rule 501–502
        Insider information 502
        Intention of benefiting company 503
        Knowingly causing harm 502–503
        May not use information for personal advantage 500–501
        May not use information to cause harm 501
        Non-profit rule 501
        Post-resignation duties 502
        Restrictions while acting as director 500
        Section 76(2)(*a*) requirements 500–503
        Section 76(2)(*b*) requirements 503–504
    Best interest of the company, duty to act in 467–469, 475–477
      Act fairly between shareholders 468
      Derivate actions 468
      Independent judgment, exercise of and 480
      Meaning of 'company' 467–469
      Only company can claim from errant director 469
      Subjective test 476
      Subsidiaries, directors of 469
    Breach of
      Liability for
        Ultra vires doctrine 156, 158, 164
        Ostensible authority and 176
        Ratification by special resolution 162–163
    Communicating information to company 503–504
      Confidential information 504
      Information required to be communicated 504
      Legislation 503
    English law, influence of 463

DUTIES OF DIRECTORS — Fiduciary (cont.)
    Evasion of 193
        Abuse of separate legal personality and 40
    Good faith 461, 466, 475–477
        Test for 476
    Holding/Subsidiary relationship 442–443
        Group boards 442–443
        Holding company 192
        No duties to group only to respective companies 190–191
        Nominee directors 192
        Subsidiary companies and independence of board 192–193
        Whether transactions are for the benefit of their companies 191–192
    Honesty 461, 476
    Independent judgement, duty to exercise. 480–483
        As part of duty to act in interest of company 480
        Contractual obligations 481
        Future voting 480–481
        Nominee directors 481–483
            Australia and New Zealand 482
            Conflict of interests 481–482
            May not be a 'dummy' or 'puppet' 483
        Voting agreement and 480
    Insider trading 839
        Whether duty to shareholders 839–843
    Liability for breach of 529–530
    Loyalty 305, 461, 466
    Pluralist or stakeholder approach 470–471
        Company performing social service and profit making function 471
        Diversity of stakeholder and economic interests in large public companies 471
        Ignoring shareholder interest in favour of stakeholder interest 470
        Jurisdiction following 472
        Promote stakeholder interest 472
    Proper purpose, exercise of powers for 477–480
        Constitutional right of shareholders to decide fate of takeover bid 478
        Four step test (*Extrasure Travel Insurances Ltd v Scattergood*) 478
        Improper use of power to issue shares 478–480
        Issuing of shares (section 38) and 479–480
        Objective test 478
        Statutory and common-law obligation 477–478
    Relationship
        Elements of 466
    Shareholder value approach 471–473
        Jurisdictions whom adopted 472
        King III 473
        Stakeholder interest subordinate to profit maximisation 471–472
    Shareholder and stakeholder interest, difference between .469–473
    Social and ethics committee 474–475
    To whom owed 467
    Whether company integral part of society 470
    Who is a fiduciary 465–467
    Who owes 463–465
        All types of directors 463–464
        Director, definition of 463–464
        Members of audit or board committees 465
        Prescribed officers 465

Index

DUTIES OF DIRECTORS — Fiduciary — Who owes (cont.)
    Senior employees or managers 464–465
  Financial assistance
    Duty of loyalty 305
  Post-resignation duties
    Duty to avoid conflict of interest 497–500
      Application by courts 498–499
      Balance between freedom of individuals and fiduciary duty of loyalty and good faith 498
      Can not by resigning avoid 497–498
      Guiding principles 499–500
  Ratification by shareholders of breach 528–530
    Breach of statutory duty 529–530
    Breaches ratifiable 529
    Disclosure by ordinary resolution 529
    Majority consent 529
    Release, difference between 529
  Relief by court 526–528
    Application to proceedings instituted by party other than company 528, 530
    Case law 527–528
    Discretion of court 527
    Grounds for 527
    Must have acted honestly and reasonably 527–528
  Sources of 475

E

ECONOMIC LOSS, PURE
  Auditors' liability for 572
ELECTRONIC COMMUNICATION
  Board meetings 426
  Shareholders
    Meetings 352–353
    Written resolutions 364
ELECTRONIC LODGEMENT AND FILING 9
ELECTRONIC SETTLEMENT SYSTEM (STRATE) 232–233
EMPLOYEE SHARE SCHEMES
  Financial assistance pursuant to
    For acquisition of securities 302–303
    To directors, prescribed officers, related and interrelated companies ... 319–320
  Public offering of company securities 599–600
EMPLOYEES
  Business rescue and **see also** BUSINESS RESCUE, Employees 16–17, 798, 809–810
  Directors, dismissal as 395
  Shareholders as 37–38
EMPLOYMENT CONTRACT
  Business rescue and 798
ENFORCEMENT 23–24
  Companies Commission 24
  Criminal liability 24
  Criminal penalties 24
  Decriminalisation 23–24
  Monitoring of compliance 24
ESTOPPEL
  Agency by **see** Ostensible authority
  Statutory
    New company law regime 160

ESTOPPEL — Agency by (cont.)
    Ultra vires doctrine (previous company law regime) 158
EX OFFICIO DIRECTOR 376–377
    Fiduciary duties of 464
EXECUTIVE DIRECTORS 437
    Fiduciary duties of 463, 464
EXTERNAL COMPANIES 9, 90–95
    Application of legislation to 93–95, 106–107
        Applicable sections 93–94
    Definition 90–92
    Foreign companies
        Distinction from 90–91
        When conducting business of non-profit activities 91
    Place of business 92
    Policy approach to 94
    Protection of third parties 92
    Registration 92–93, 105–107
        Advantages of 94
        Failure to 95
        Register of prescribed information maintained by Companies Commission 106
        Time period for registration 105, 106
    Securities offered to public in South Africa 93
    Types of 92–93

F

FALSE OR MISLEADING STATEMENTS
    Offence of 776
    Personal liability of directors 61
FIDUCIARY
    Who is 465–467
FIDUCIARY DUTIES OF DIRECTORS **see** DUTIES OF DIRECTORS, Fiduciary
FINANCIAL ASSISTANCE
    For acquisition of securities 287–310
        Authority for provision of financial assistance 301
        Contravention of section 44, consequences 306–310
            Criminal consequences 308
            Liability of directors 308–310
                1973 legislation 308–310
                How to avoid 310
                Shareholders' claims for damages 310
            Statute of limitations and prescription 309
            Subjective knowledge 309
            Voidness of transaction 309
        Statutory Turquand Rule 306–308
            Effect of 397
            Voidness 306
        Extension to 'related or interrelated' company 306
        Fair and reasonable terms for 302, 303–306
            Best interest principle 304
            Directors' duty of loyalty 305
            New Zealand 304–305
            Reasonable *quid pro* 303
        'For the purpose of or in connection with' 297–299
            Distinction between 'purpose' and the motive or reason why purpose formed 297–298
        Historical background 287–288

Index

FINANCIAL ASSISTANCE — Personal liability of directors (cont.)
　Impoverishment test 294–296, 297
　Legislation 288–289
　Meaning of 'financial assistance' 289–297
　　Assistance, what is 289
　　　Prohibitions 295–296
　　What is financial assistance 296–297
　　What is not financial assistance
　　　Bond over immovable property 289–290
　　　Continuation of loan 291
　　　Direct object of securing, or raising money to pay of or reduce loan 292
　　　Distribution of dividend 291
　　　Payment of debt 291
　Memorandum of Incorporation, compliance with 302
　Purchase of or subscription for securities 299–301
　　Exchange of shares 300
　　Options 301
　　Prohibition 301
　Pursuant to employee share scheme or special resolution 302–303
　Sections 44(3) and (4) requirements 302–306
　Solvency and liquidity test 302
　Special resolution as requirement for 302–303
Meaning of 'financial assistance' 289–297, 428
To directors, prescribed officers, related and interrelated companies 310–326
　Abuse, legislation to prevent 310–311
　Ambit of 'financial assistance' not clear 314
　Comparison between old and new provisions 315
　Contravention of section 45, consequences of 321–325, 430–431
　　Criminal consequences 321
　　Liability of directors 322–324, 431
　　　Court order setting aside decisions contrary to section 45 322–323
　　　For loss, damages or costs 322, 431
　　　How to avoid 323
　　　Indemnification and relief 323
　　　Knowledge of directors at relevant time 322, 431
　　　Liability to any persons 324
　　　Liability to shareholders 323–324
　　　Prescription of claims 323
　　Void resolution or agreement 322, 430–431
　Direct or indirect 429
　Disclosure in annual financial statements 325–326, 431
　　1973 legislation 325
　　2008 legislation 325
　　Not all financial assistance to be disclosed 325–326
　　Remuneration, what is included 325
　　Value of interest 325–326, 431
　Employee share scheme, financial assistance pursuant to 319–320
　Exceptions 428
　Legislation (section 45) 311–312, 427–428
　Loan of something other than money 313–314
　Loans from one company to another
　　Relationships of directors 318
　Notice of 319, 321, 430
　Prescribed officers 316
　Related and interrelated persons 316–317

FINANCIAL ASSISTANCE — To directors, prescribed officers, related and interrelated companies (cont.)
  Requirements or conditions for authorisation 318–321, 429–430
    Memorandum of incorporation conditions or restrictions 429
    Pursuant to employee share scheme or special resolution 319, 320–321, 429
    Solvency and liquidity test 319, 429
    Written notices to shareholders and representative trade unions 319, 321
  Solvency and liquidity test 319, 429
  Special resolution prior to 319, 320–321, 429–430
    When void 322
  Transactions covered 312–314
  Transactions excluded 313–315, 428
    Accountable advances to cover legal expenses 315, 428
    Amount to defray person's expenses for removal at company's request 313, 428
    Anticipated expenses to be incurred by person on behalf of company 315
    Lending money by company whose primary business is lending of money 315, 428
  Trusts, loans to 317
  Void transactions
    Impact on related transactions 324–325
    Third parties 324
  Who may not be assisted 316, 428
  Who must be assisted 316–318
  Written notices to shareholders and representative trade unions 319, 321, 430
    Time period 430
FINANCIAL RECORDS see ACCOUNTING RECORDS; ANNUAL RETURN; AUDIT AND INDEPENDENT REVIEW, FINANCIAL STATEMENTS
FINANCIAL REPORTING STANDARDS
  Financial statements and 545–547
    Prescribed 546–547
    Reasons for compliance with 546
FINANCIAL REPORTING STANDARDS COUNCIL 14, 549
FINANCIAL SERVICES BOARD
  Insider trading
    Delegation of power to investigate 882
    Powers and duties 880–882
FINANCIAL STATEMENTS see also ACCOUNTING RECORDS 545–547
  Access to 549
  Annual 548–549
    Remuneration of executive directors 549
    What must be disclosed 548–549
    What must be included 548
    When prepared 548
  Directors' remuneration 418
  Disclosure of financial assistance to directors et al 325–326, 431
  Financial reporting standards and 545–547
    Prescribed 546–547
    Reasons for compliance with 546
  Meaning 547
  Non-profit companies 85
  Offences relating to 546
  Private or non-public companies 13, 70, 77
  Public companies 13–14, 75, 77
  Requirements for 545–546
  Responsibility for 549–550
  Summary of 547

FINANCIAL YEAR 547–548
FINANCIALLY DISTRESSED COMPANIES
    Meaning 15
FOREIGN COMPANIES 9
    Deregistration upon transfer of registration to foreign country 832
    External companies, distinction from 90–91
    When conducting business of non-profit activities 91
FORMATION OF COMPANIES **see also** INCORPORATION OF COMPANIES; PRE-INCORPORATION CONTRACTS; REGISTRATION; SHAREHOLDER AGREEMENTS 100–152
    Philosophy and principles 101–102
    Right not a privilege 101
    Simplicity and flexibility 101–102
FOSS V HARBOTTLE RULE 11, 20
    Derivative actions and 698, 701
FOUNDERS **see** INCORPORATORS
FRAMEWORK OF LEGISLATION 5
FRAUD
    Personal liability of directors 60–61
FRAUDULENT OR RECKLESS TRADING 534–538
    Companies Commission
        Power to determine whether company engaging in 541
    Contravention of legislation 534–535
    Criminal sanctions 534
    Factual insolvency distinguished from commercial insolvency 537–538
    Knowledge of 536
    Legislation 534
        1973 legislation 534
        Object of 535
    Liability for loss, damages, costs 534
    Party to 536–537
    Personal liability of directors 60
    Recklessly 537–538
    Requirements for liability 535–536
    Single isolated act of dishonesty 537
    Single person defrauded 537
FREEZE-OUT MERGER 644–647
    Cash-out 645
    Purpose of 644–645
    Share-holder voting and structure 645–647
    Triangular merger 646–647
    Two-party merger 645–646
    Two-step 647
FUNDAMENTAL RIGHTS
    Companies and 28–29
FUNDAMENTAL TRANSACTIONS **see also** DISPOSAL OF ALL OR PART OF ASSETS AND UNDERTAKINGS; MERGERS; SCHEME OF ARRANGEMENT; TAKE-OVERS AND OFFERS 616–617
    Appraisal rights 616
    Court approval if significant minority opposed to 617
    Regulatory arbitrage 617
    Statutory merger 616

G

GOOD FAITH
    Derivative actions

GOOD FAITH — Derivative actions (cont.)
  Criteria to guide discretion of courts in granting leave 708–709
GROSS ABUSE
  Of juristic personality of close corporations
    Examples of 57–59
GROUP BOARDS 442–443
  King III 442–443
    Best interest of subsidiary   442
    Fiduciary duties of subsidiary directors   442
GROUPS OF COMPANIES **see also** HOLDING/SUBSIDIARY RELATIONSHIP 179–196
  Common law not sufficiently developed to deal with problems related to   181
  Holding/subsidiary relationship 183–190
  Legal intervention to prevent camouflaging of economic reality and abuse 179–181
  Nature of group   178
  Separate legal persona of individual companies 181–183

H

HOLDINGS
  Definition   183
HOLDING/SUBSIDIARY RELATIONSHIP 183–190
  Control at board meeting level   184
    Chairperson's vote   185
    Right to appoint or remove directors holding majority of voting rights   185
    Voting rights   185
  Control at general meeting level 184–185
  Definitions
    Holding   183
    Subsidiary   183
  Directors' fiduciary duties and 190–193
    Holding company   192
    No duties to group only to respective companies 190–191
    Nominee directors 192
    Subsidiary companies and independence of board 192–193
    Whether transactions for the benefit of their companies 191–192
  Holding company
    Close corporation can be   190
    Directors' fiduciary duties 192
    Juristic persons, only   189
  Interrelated relationship   196
  Legislation 183–184
  Possibilities to be present to establish   184
  Related relationship 193–196
    Between
      Individual and juristic person   194
      Two individuals   194
      Two juristic persons   194
    Control of 194–196
      Close corporation 195–196
      Company 194–195
        When controlling 194–195
      Trust 196
  Shares, number of not determining factor in determining 185–186
  Subsidiary
    Directors' fiduciary duties and independence of board 192–193
    Trust cannot be 190

HOLDING/SUBSIDIARY RELATIONSHIP — Subsidiary (cont.)
    Undertaking controlled by company cannot be 190
    Voting rights..185–189
        Attaching debt instruments 189
        Determining factor...185–186
        Held by person in fiduciary capacity................................. 188
        Instructions or with consent or concurrence of another person 188–189
        Nominees 188
        Shareholder agreements 189
        Shares held by moneylenders as security for money lent........................ 189
        Trusts... 188
        When exercisable in certain circumstances 186–188
    Wholly owned subsidiary, when.. 185

I

IMMOVABLE PROPERTY
    Mergers
IMPOVERISHMENT TEST 294–296
INCORPORATION OF COMPANIES 101–103
    Memorandum of..102–103
    Notice of...8, 103
        Rejection by Companies Commission 104–105
            Discretionary... 105
            Mandatory..104–105
    Procedure for 102–103
    Right not privilege 101–102
INCORPORATORS 102
    Number required... 102
    Responsibilities.. 102
INDEMNIFICATION AND INSURANCE **see** DIRECTORS, Indemnification and insurance
INDEPENDENT JUDGMENT, DUTY TO EXERCISE **see also** DUTIES OF DIRECTORS,
    Fiduciary 480–483
INDEPENDENT NON-EXECUTIVE DIRECTORS 437–438
    Evaluation of independence 438
    King III 438
    Review after term of nine years 438
INDIRECT REPURCHASES 282–287
    Convertible shares.. 284
    Directors' liability 284–285
    Distributions 284
    Limitation..283–284
    Non-applicability of sections 48(4) and (5) 285
    Post 1999... 282
    Prior to 1999.. 282
    Rationale for acquisition 285–287
    Requirements of
        Section 46..282–283
        Section 48(3)... 284
    Shares held by subsidiaries 284
    Voting rights 285
INDOOR MANAGEMENT RULE **see** TURQUAND RULE
INDUCTION
    Of directors and King III.. 443
INFORMATION TECHNOLOGY, GOVERNANCE OF 447
    Charter and policies 447
    King III 447

INITIAL PUBLIC OFFERING **see** PUBLIC OFFERINGS OF SECURITIES, Initial public offering
INSIDER **see** INSIDER TRADING, Insider
INSIDER INFORMATION **see** INSIDER TRADING, Insider information
INSIDER TRADING 835–886
   Arguments in favour of outlawing 835–839
      Abuse of position of trust 835–836
      Ascendancy over outsider 837
      Criticism against 838
      Deters investors 837
      Disclosure of inside information 836–837
      Harmful to company 837
      Harmful to integrity of securities market 837
      Misappropriation theory 836
      Tippees 836–837
      'Trading on inside information' 838
   Attachment of evidence or assets 880
   Civil liability 847, 872–886
      Amount claimant entitled to 878–879
      Bases of 872–874
         Dealing on behalf of someone else 873
         Dealing on one's own account 872–873
         Disclosure 873–874
         Encouraging or causing another person to deal 874
      Cost recovery 876–877
      Criminal penalty taken into account 879
      Deposit of monies 876
      Distribution of balance 877–878
         Arbitrary approach 877–878
         Claimants distributed to 877
      Interest 874
      Joint and several liability 875–876
      Penalties 875
      Powers of directorate during civil proceedings 880
      Profit made or loss, determination of 876
      Protection of common law rights 879
      Rationale under Securities Services Act 872
      Vicarious liability 879
   Chinese wall 854–857
   Confidentiality and sharing of information 884
   Common law 839–843
      Director's fiduciary duty 839
         Misrepresentation 843
         To shareholders? 839–843
            Case law indicating that not owing duty 840–842, 843
            Duty arising because of special circumstances 842, 843
   Corporate bodies **also** INSIDER TRADING, Persons
   Criminal liability
      Offences
         Dealing offence **see also** INSIDER TRADING, Dealing offence 859–871
            Acting in pursuit of completion of affected transaction 865
            Body corporates 865
            Only became insider after give instruction to deal to authorised user 866
            Wide disclosure of information not prejudicing counterparts (United Kingdom) 866

Index

INSIDER TRADING — Criminal liability — Offences (cont.)
    Dealing on behalf of someone else 867–868
        Authorised user 868
        Comparison with defences in Insider Trading Act 867–868
        Legislation 867
        When not committed 867
    Disclosure offence 868–870
        Belief that person would not deal as result of disclosure 870
        Legislation 868
        Quality and source of information disclosed 870
        Remuneration 870
        When not committed 868
    'Encouraging' or discouraging' offence 870–871
        Actus reus of 870
        Knowledge of inside information 870
        Legislation 870
        No defences in Securities Services Act 870
        Remuneration 870
        Requires possession of inside information by dealer 870
    Penalties for 871
Dealing offence 862–867
    Criminal liability
        Abstaining from dealing 864
        Circumstances when not committed 862
        Deal and dealing, meaning of 863–864
        Defences **see also** INSIDER TRADING, Defences 865–867
        Description of 862
        Direct or indirect dealing through agent 863
        Knowledge 865
        To which inside information relates or which are likely to be affected by it 862–863
        United Kingdom legislation 863–864
Defences **see also** INSIDER TRADING, Criminal liability, Offences 859–871
    Knowledge of inside information as common element for all 859–861
        Matter of judgment 860
        Proof of knowledge 861
        Understanding of specificity and materiality of public information 860
    Mens rea 860–861, 866
    Secondary insiders must know that source primary insider 860
Directorate of Market Abuse 882–884
    Composition of 882–884
    Functions of 882–883
    Powers of during civil proceedings 880
Disclosure-based manipulation
    Insider trading, difference between 898–899
Financial Services Board
    Delegation of power to investigate 882
    Powers and duties 880–882
Historical development 844–846
Inside information 847–854, 859
    Definition 847
    Duty to avoid conflict of interest 502
    Material effect on price or value of listed security if public 853–854, 860
    Obtained or learned as an insider 849–853, 860
        Interpretation 849–850
    Qualifications for 847–854

INSIDER TRADING — Inside information (cont.)
   Specific or precise information 847–848, 859
   Which has not been made public 848–849, 860
      Price-sensitive information 848
      When information been made public 848
      When not public although circumstances suggest that has been made public 849
   Insider
      By virtue of employment 851–852
      Definition 850–851
         Information excluded from 851
      Secondary (tippee) 852–853
      Whether person know that in possession of insider information 851
      Who is 850
   Interdicts 880
   Jurisdiction 880
   Legislation 844–886
   Offences **see also** INSIDER TRADING, Criminal liability, offences
      Committed in terms of repealed legislation 884–886
   Penalties
      Civil liability 875
      Criminal liability offences 871
   Persons
      Offences and civil wrongs committed by 854–857
         Chinese wall 854–857
         Corporate bodies
            Australia 855–856
            United Kingdom 854–855
         King Task Group's view 854
      Persons acting on behalf of body corporate 856
      Trusts and partnerships 856–857
   Securities and regulated market 857–859
      Only listed 858
      Regulated market, definition of 858
      Securities, definition of 857–858
      Securities listed on foreign regulated market 858–859
   Securities Services Act 36 of 2004 846–884
INSIDER TRADING DIRECTORATE **see** INSIDER TRADING, Directorate of Market Abuse
INSOLVENCY **see also** WINDING-UP
   Business rescue as alternative 782–783
   Factual distinguished from commercial 537–538
INSOLVENT TRADING 534–535, 538–542
   Companies Commission
      Power to determine whether company engaging in 541
   Contravention of legislation 534–535
   Criminal sanctions 534
   Duty to cease trading 539–541
   Factual insolvency distinguished from commercial insolvency 537–538
   Identification and recognition of insolvency stage 541
   Legislation 534
      1973 legislation 534
      Purpose of 539
      Section 22(1)(*b*) 539–541
   Liability for loss, damages, costs 534

INSOLVENT TRADING (cont.)
    Solvency and liquidity test 540–541
    What are insolvent circumstances 540
INSOLVENT, UNREHABILITATED
    As director 402
INSURANCE AND INDEMNIFICATION see DIRECTORS, Indemnification and insurance
INTENTION OF LEGISLATION 2
INTERESTED PERSON
    Application by to deem company not to be juristic person 55
    Meaning 55
INTERNAL AUDIT 448–449
    Charter for 449
    King III 448–449
    Written assessment of company's effectiveness 449
INTERPRETATION OF LEGISLATION 6–7
    Anti-avoidance provision 7
    Inconsistency between 6
    Substantial compliance 7
INTERRELATED PERSONS 14
INTERRELATED RELATIONSHIP
    Holding/subsidiary relations 196
INVESTIGATIONS AND INSPECTIONS see COMPANIES COMMISSION, Investigations and inspections by
ISSUED SHARES 198

J

JURISTIC PERSONS
    Holding companies must be 189–190

K

KING III REPORT AND CODE 433–434, 563–566
    Application of 434
    Audit committees 445–446, 564
    Compliance with laws, rules, codes and standards 448
    Board of directors
        Appointment of 440–441
        Chairperson 444
        Committees 441–442
        Composition of 439–440
        Group boards 442–443
        Meetings 441
        Responsibilities 438–439
    Chief Executive Officers 444, 564–565
    Company secretary 444
    Corporate citizenship 436–437
    Directors
        Induction and training 443
        Performance assessment 443
        Remuneration 443–444
        Types of 437–438
    History 563
    Information technology, governance of 448
    Integrated reporting and disclosure 457, 565–566
    Leadership, ethical 435–436
    Philosophy of 'apply or explain' 434–435

KING III REPORT AND CODE (cont.)
  Principles and recommendations 435–457
  Risk governance. 446–447
  Stakeholder relationships, governance of 449–457
'KNOWING', 'KNOWINGLY' OR KNOWS
  Definition 260, 502–503, 518, 536

L

LEADERSHIP, ETHICAL
  King II Report and Code 435–436
    Assessment, monitoring and reporting on company's ethical foundation   436
    Sustainability   436
    Values underpinning corporate governance   436
LEAPFROGGING 736–736
LEGAL CAPACITY OF COMPANY 19–20, 154, 167
  Capacity and authority as prerequisites for binding contract   154
    Meaning of
      Authority   154
      Capacity   154
    Directors and   162
      Breach of fiduciary duty. 156, 158, 160
        Double special resolution to absolve from (United Kingdom)   163
        Ratification of   162
      Lack of authority resulting from lack of capacity   160
  Doctrine of constructive notice   20
  Estoppel, statutory
    New regime   160
    Previous regime   158
  Exceeding, when
    Determined by objects clause in memorandum of association, previous regime   154
  Historical development 154–155
  How to determine
    Objects clause of memorandum of association   154
    Previous company law regime   154
  Memorandum of association (previous regime)
    Objects clause   154
  Memorandum of Incorporation (new regime)
    Objects clause   159
  Powers and rights of an individual or natural person (new regime) 158–159
    Common-law jurisdictions   159
  Prescribed officers and   162
    Ratification of unauthorised acts not possible   161
  Ratification of *ultra vires* transactions or unauthorised acts by company or directors 162–163
  Restrictions under new legislation 159–161
    Effect of   161
    Memorandum of Incorporation may impose on optional basis 159, 161
  Shareholders'   162
    Claim for damages 163–164
    Right to restrain
      Executed or executory contracts   165
      Performance of contract 156, 158, 160, 165
      Unauthorised act 164–165
  Third party's right to damages 165–166
    Right to damages
      Insiders not excluded   166

Index

LEGAL CAPACITY OF COMPANY — Third party's right to damages — Right to damages (cont.)
        Knowledge and good faith 165–167
            Burden of proof 167
            Knowledge of limitation in Memorandum of Incorporation 167
            Separate requirements 167
            When not protected 166
    Turquand Rule 20
    Ultra vires doctrine **see also** *Ultra vires* doctrine 19–20
        Confined to null and void transactions 155
        Consequences of (new regime) 161–162
        Failure of 156–157
        Historical development 154–155
        Legal consequences of 155–156
        New regime 160–161
        Object of 155
        Reform of 157–158
LEGAL CONCEPT OF A COMPANY **see** COMPANY, LEGAL CONCEPT
LEGAL PERSON
    Difference from human person 28
LEGAL PERSONALITY **see** SEPARATE LEGAL PERSONALITY
LEGAL PROCEEDINGS
    Institution of by or against company 36–37
LIABILITIES **see also** AUDITORS, Liability of; DIRECTORS, Liability; PERSONAL LIABILITY OF DIRECTORS
    Of company belong to company 35–36
LIABILITY INSURANCE FOR DIRECTORS AND OFFICERS 525–526
LIMITED BY GUARANTEE, COMPANY 66
LIMITED INTEREST COMPANIES 67
LIMITED LIABILITY 31–32
    Meaning 31
    Shareholders 32
LIQUIDATION PROCEEDINGS **see also** WINDING-UP
    1973 Act, continuing application of 919–920
    Business rescue proceedings and 790
        Conversion to liquidation proceedings 788
LIQUIDATOR 828–830
    Duties of 830
    Powers 829
    Voluntary winding-up 828–829
    Winding-up order and appointment by Master 829
LIQUIDITY AND SOLVENCY TESTS **see also** DISTRIBUTIONS, SOLVENCY AND LIQUIDITY REQUIREMENT 10
    Cash payment in lieu of capitalisation shares 210
    Financial assistance
        For acquisition of shares 302, 303
        To directors, prescribed officers, related and unrelated companies 319, 429
    Insolvent trading 540–541
    Mergers 627
    Preference shares 203
    Repurchases 277
LOANS **see** FINANCIAL ASSISTANCE

M

MAINTENANCE OF CAPITAL PRINCIPLE 241

MANAGEMENT OF COMPANY
  Shareholder no right to manage business 36
MANAGER 387–388
  Director, distinction from 387–388
MANAGING DIRECTOR 387–388
  Usual director 176–177
MANAGING PARTNERS
  Directors as 385–386
MANDATORY OFFERS 670, 675
MANIPULATING DEVICES, SCHEMES OR ARTIFICES
  Prohibited trading practices 897–898
MANIPULATIVE ACT, PRACTICE OR COURSE OF BUSINESS
  Prohibited trading practices 898
MARKET ABUSES
  Offences relating to 886
MARKET CORNER
  Prohibited trading practices 896–897
MARKET MANIPULATION 886–907
  Deemed prohibited trading practices 894–898
    Artificial price, maintenance of 897
    Auctioning processes or pre-opening sessions 896–897
    Buying at successively higher prices and selling at successively lower prices 895
    Manipulating devices, schemes or artifices 897–898
    Manipulative act, practice or course of business 898
    Market corner 896–897
    Marking the close 895–896
    Matched orders 895
    Wash sales 894–895
  Defences 901–905
    Definitional 903
    Other jurisdictions 903–905
      Chinese wall 904–905
      Reasonable belief and reasonable care 904
      Share-buybacks 903–904
    Price stabilisation 901–903
      Purpose of 902
      Requirements for 902–903
      What is 901–902
  Disclosure-based manipulation 898–901
    Directly or indirectly 899
    Fault requirement 901
    'Hype and dump' 898
    Insider trading, difference between 898–899
    Legislation 898
    Materiality 899–900
    Omission of material facts 899
    Past or future performance of company 900
    Publication 901
    'Pump and dump' 898
    Purpose or motive not relevant 900–901
    Time of assessment of statement, promise or forecast 900
  False, misleading or deceptive statements, promises, forecasts **see** MARKET MANIPU-
    LATION, Disclosure-based manipulation
  Objective of 886–887
  Penalties 905–907

MARKET MANIPULATION — Penalties (cont.)
    Absence of statutory derivative civil remedy 906–907
    Administrative penalty 906
    Fine or imprisonment... 905–906
  Proof of.. 83
  Prohibited trading practices **see also** MARKET MANIPULATION, Deemed prohibited
    practices... 889–894
    Artificial price for security 892
    False or deceptive appearance of trading activity 891–892
    Legislation 890
    Manipulative trading practices 890
      Participation in 891
    Offence committed on behalf of person, directly or indirectly 890–891
    Placing orders to buy or sell listed securities................................ 892–893
      Intermediaries 892–893
    Regulated market... 893–894
    Types of... 890
  Regulation of
    Common law 888–889
      Application to both listed and unlisted securities 889
      'Rigging the market' 888–889
    Rationale of 887–888
    Securities Services Act.. 889–901
      Deemed prohibited trading practices 894–898
      Prohibited trading practices 889–894
    What is 886
MARKING THE CLOSE
  Prohibited trading practices 895–896
MATCHED ORDERS
  Prohibited trading practices 895
MATERIAL
  Definition 116, 517
MEETINGS **see** BOARD MEETINGS; SHAREHOLDERS' MEETINGS
MEMBERS
  Non-profit companies.. 85, 88–89, 331
    Membership costs 89
    Membership register 88
    Rights and obligations... 89
    Voting and non-voting... 88
MEMORANDUM OF ASSOCIATION (PREVIOUS REGIME)
  Objects clause
    Failure of *ultra vires* doctrine because of drafting of.......................... 156–157
    Legal capacity of company determined by 154–155
    Subjective 17
MEMORANDUM OF INCORPORATION 117–128
  Access to records and information rights 367
  Allocation of powers between organs of company............................. 119
  Alterable conditions.. 118, 119
    Changes to.. 120
    Meaning 120
  Amendment of 118, 124–128
    By court order... 126
    By means of sections 36(3) and (4) 127
    By whom proposed.. 123
    Form of 125

MEMORANDUM OF INCORPORATION — Amendment of (cont.)
    How to amend 124–125
    Methods of 126–127
    Notice of Alteration. 127
    Notice of Amendment 126
    Procedure after amendment 126
    Restrictions and prohibitions on 103, 121–124, 125
    Special resolutions 124–125
    Unilateral alteration 134
    When amended 124
    When contested by shareholder 126
    When taking effect 126
Anti-avoidance provisions of legislation 120
Authenticity of versions 128
Authorisation for 204–205
Class rights, alteration and appraisal rights 734–735, 735–737
Company rules and 129
Consistency with legislation 120
Consolidations of 128
Contents of 119–121
Contractual claims 415
Correction of patent errors 127–128
    Notice of alteration 127
    Potential abuse 127–128
Default rules **see** Memorandum of Incorporation, Alterable conditions
Directors
    Appointed in terms of 376, 393
    Disqualification 401
    Removal from office 409, 413
    Remuneration of 417
Distributions, authorisation of 246
Dividends out of profits 263
Doctrine of constructive notice 122–124
    Abolition subject to exceptions 123
    Implications of on restrictions and prohibitions on amendment 123–124
Enforcement of and effect of on relationships 135–141
    Between company and director 138–141
        Alteration of Memorandum of Incorporation and rules 140
        Contract of service 140
        Failure to comply with rules or Memorandum of Incorporation 141
        Implications 139–140
        In exercise of functions as directors 139
        Removal from office 140–141
    Between company and prescribed officer, member of audit committee or board
        committee 138–141
        Failure to comply with rules or Memorandum of Incorporation 141
        In exercise of functions 139
    Between or among shareholders *inter se* 137–138
    By shareholders against company 137
    Whether shareholders bound only in capacity as shareholders 135–136
Financial assistance to directors 429
Flexible content 118
Matters not addressed by legislation 120–121
Objects clause
    Not mandatory 159

Index

MEMORANDUM OF INCORPORATION (cont.)
- Personal liability company 78
- Philosophy 117–119
- Prescribed form 121
- Procedure relating to incorporation 102–103
- Prohibitions on amendment 103, 121–124, 125
- Relationships created by 135–141
  - Between company and shareholder 135
    - Whether shareholders bound only in capacity as shareholders 135–136
- Repurchases, conflict with 275–276
- Restrictions on company capacity 159–161
  - Consequences of *ultra vires* acts 161–162
  - Effect of 161
  - Ratification by special resolution 162–163
  - Shareholders' claim for damages 163–164
  - Shareholders' right to restrain unauthorised acts 164–165
  - Third party's right to damages
    - Insiders not excluded 166
    - Knowledge and good faith 165–167
      - Burden of proof 167
      - Knowledge of limitation in Memorandum of Incorporation 167
      - Separate requirements 167
      - When not protected 166
- Restrictive, procedural requirements regarding amendment 103, 121–124, 125
  - Transitional arrangements 918
- Ring-fenced (RF)
  - Expression in company name 122
- Shareholders
  - Special resolutions 362
- Shareholders' agreements and 131
- Shareholders' meetings 345, 347
  - Convening of meetings by authorised persons 348
  - Period of notice 349
  - Quorum 357
- Status of 133–141
  - Meaning of provisions, uncertainty 134
  - Relationships created by 135–141
    - Between and among shareholders *inter se* 137–138
      - Enforcement of Memorandum of Incorporation and rules 137–138
    - Between company and shareholder 135–137
      - Enforcement of rights by against company 137
    - Whether shareholders abound only in capacity as shareholders 135–136
  - Statutory contract 134
  - Unilateral alteration 134
- Transitional arrangements 119, 912–913, 918
- Translations of 128
- Two-document constitution abandoned 117–118
- Unalterable conditions 118, 119, 246
  - Exemption form 121
  - Meaning 119–120, 275
- United States approach 118–119
- What is 117

MENS REA
- Insider trading and defences 861–862, 866

MERGERS 14–15
   Agreement 624–627
      Cash consideration 626–627
      Matters dealing with   625
      Merger consideration 625–626
      'Pooling type' transactions   626
      Securities of merger company held by another merger company   625
   Amalgamating or merging company, meaning of   619
   Amalgamation, difference between 619–621
   Appraisal rights of dissenting shareholders 619, 636–637
      Principal protective measure   637
      What is 636–637
   Balance of interest of all shareholders 618–619
   Business rescue proceedings
      Company under 632–633
   Concept of 619–621
   Court approval 631–632, 634–636
      Appraisal remedy, distinction between 635–636
      Can only rely on when voted against resolution   635
      Exceptional circumstances   634
      When required 634–635
      When set aside   635
   Creditors
      Notice to 632–633
      Objecting   632
      Protection of . . . . '.   639
   Definition   619
   Fundamental transactions 616–617
   Judicial nature and effect of 621–623
      Assets and liabilities 621, 623
      Automatic liability of acquiring company for obligations and liabilities   622
      Contractual rights and obligations of disappearing company 622–623
      Disappearing company not winded-up but only deregistered   622
      Existing liabilities and pending proceedings against or by merging company   623
      Immovable property   622
   Implementation of 633–634
      Deregistration of disappearing company   633
      Filing of notice of merger   633
      Registration certificate for new companies   633
      Taking effect according to agreement   633
      Transfer of assets or undertaking 633–634
   Notice to creditors 632–633
   Objecting creditors   632
   Reasons for   15
   Requirements   15
   Requisite approvals of (section 115) 628–632
      Approval by special resolution called for this purpose 628–631
         75% of voting rights   629
         Companies Bill 2007   629
         Disqualification of voting rights controlled by acquiring party   630
         Minority shareholder protection 629–630
         Object of legislation   630
      Court approval restricted to certain circumstances 631–632
      Disposal of all or greater parts of assets
         Special resolution by holding company 631

Index 971

MERGERS — Requisite approvals of (section 115) (cont.)
    Exception 628
    Shareholders' objections 15
    Shareholders, protection of 638–639
        Appraisal right 638
        Court approval 638
        Role of board of directors 638–639
        Shareholder approval 638
    Solvency and liquidity test 627–628
        Legislation 627
        Submitted at shareholders' meeting 627
    Statutory 618
        Procedure 624–634
            Implementation of 633–634
            Merger agreement 624–627
            Notice to creditors 632–633
            Requisite approvals of 628–632
            Solvency and liquidity test 627–628
            Type of companies applicable to 624
    Types of structures 619–620, 639–648
        Cash merger 644
        Existing companies dissolve and new company created ... 619, 620
        Freeze-out merger 644–647
            Cash-out 645
            Purpose of 644–645
            Share-holder voting and structure 645–647
            Triangular merger 646–647
            Two-party merger 645–646
            Two-step 647
        Interested or controlled merger 644
        One company fuses into other and latter company survive ... 620
        'Pooling' type 626, 640
        Short form 647–648
            Benefits 648
        Triangular 640–644
            Companies involved do not need to disappear 642
            Liabilities in separate legal entity 641
            Merger consideration 642–643
            Purpose and advantages 641–642
            Reverse 643–644
            Separate wholly owned subsidiary 641
            Shareholders of would-be acquirer not any voting and appraisal rights in merger 642
            Structure 640–641
    Underpinning policy 617–619
    What is 618
MINORITY PROTECTION see SHAREHOLDERS, Remedies
MISREPRESENTATION
    Insider trading
        Common law 839
MORATORIUM
    Business rescue 16–17, 793–796
        On legal proceedings 794–795
            Claims subject to time limit 794
            Criminal proceedings not subject to 794
            Exceptions 794

MORATORIUM — What is — On legal proceedings (cont.)
    Subject to consent of business rescue practitioner 794
  On property interests 795–796
    Subject to consent of business rescue practitioner 795
    Third party in possession of property 796
    When may dispose of or agree to dispose 795

MORTGAGE BOND
  Debenture stock certificate, difference between 214
  Over assets
    Not a disposal of all or part of assets or undertaking 650

MOVABLE PROPERTY
  Shares as 199

N

NAMES OF COMPANIES **see** COMPANY NAMES
NEGLIGENT MISREPRESENTATION CAUSING FINANCIAL LOSS **see** AUDITORS, Negligent
misrepresentation causing financial loss

NEW COMPANY LAW REGIME
  Main themes of 4
  Purposes of 4
  Reasons for 3–4

NO-CONFLICT RULE 486–487
  Application of 488

NO-PROFIT RULE 486, 487–489
  Application of 487
    Other case law 488–489
    Regal (Hastings) Ltd v Gulliver 487–488
  Corporate opportunity rule, distinction between 491–497
  Meaning of profit 487
  What is 487

'NO REFLECTIVE LOSS' PRINCIPLE 743, 744–745
  Overlap between share-holder and corporate actions 744–745
  When applicable 744

NOMINATION COMMITTEE 422, 440–441

NOMINEE DIRECTOR 378–379
  Advantages 378
  Conflict of interest 378–379
  Duty to exercise independent judgment and 481–483
    Australia and New Zealand 482
    Conflict of interests 481–482
    May not be a 'dummy' or 'puppet' 483
  What is 378

NOMINEES **see also** SECURITIES, Certificated, Beneficial interest in; SHAREHOLDERS, Beneficial and registered shareholders
  Beneficial interest in certificated securities 227
    Disclosure of 227–232

NON-EXECUTIVE DIRECTORS 437–438
  Duties 437
    Fiduciary 463, 464
  Independent 437–438
    Evaluation of independence 438
    King III 438
    Review after term of nine years 438
  Part-time 437

Index

NON-PROFIT COMPANIES 9, 65–66, 83–90
    Assets and income. 86
    Audit and independent review 550–551
    Characteristics of 84–86
    'Communal or group interests' 83–84
    Conversion to profit company prohibited 89
    Definition. 83–84
    Directors of 89
        Appointment or election 89
        Number of 89
        Prohibition against loans, securing debts of obligations, giving financial assistance 89
    Disclosure, transparency and audit requirements 85
    Disposal of all or part of assets or undertaking to non-profit company 90
    Financial benefit or gain. 86–87
    Financial statements 85
    Formation by three or more persons as incorporators. 84
    Fundamental transactions. 89–90
    Incorporators of 84, 88
    Members of 85, 88–89
        Shareholders, difference between 331
    Merger with another non-profit company 90
    Merger with public company not allowed 90
    Name, ending of 84
    Objects and policies. 86–87
    Objects under 1973 Act 83–84
    Oppression remedy 682
    Pre-existing section 21 companies 90
    Profit companies, distinction from 66
    Purpose of 65
    Regime for 85
    Requirements for. 83
    Rules of 86
    Statutory provisions not applicable to 85
    Taxation. 87
    Voting rights 88–89
    Winding-up or dissolution 87
NON-VOTING SHARES 11

O

OBJECT OF COMPANY **see** LEGAL CAPACITY OF A COMPANY
OBJECTS CLAUSE **see** MEMORANDUM OF ASSOCIATION (PREVIOUS REGIME),
    Objects clause; MEMORANDUM OF INCORPORATION, Objects clause
OFFER
    Meaning 665–666
'OFFER TO PUBLIC'
    Definition of 596
OFFENCES 775–778
    Accounting records. 544
    Breach of confidence 775–776
    Criminal sanctions 775
    False statements 776
    Hindering administration of Act 778
    Insider trading **see** INSIDER TRADING, Civil liability; INSIDER TRADING, Criminal
        liability, Offences; INSIDER TRADING, Offences
    Non-compliance with compliance notice issued in terms of Act 777

OFFENCES (cont.)
  Penalties **see** PENALTIES
  Reckless conduct... 777
  Search and entry by Companies Commission................................... 767
OFFERS **see** TAKEOVERS AND OFFERS
OFFICE BEARERS **see** AUDITOR; CHAIRPERSON OF BOARD OF DIRECTORS; COMPANY SECRETARY; MANAGER; MANAGING DIRECTOR
OPPRESSION REMEDY..21–22, 680–698
  Available relief..695–698
    Applicant must indicate relief sought....................................... 697
    Order to purchase shares of shareholder omitted............................. 697
    Section 163(2) remedies..695–696
  Conduct of business (section 163(1)(*b*)......................................688–689
    Affairs of company..688–689
    Business of company..688–689
    Omission of conduct.. 689
    Ongoing or past conduct.. 689
  Exercise of powers of director or prescribed officers............................ 690
    Past and ongoing conduct... 690
    Prescribed officers, functions relating to.................................... 690
  Grounds for relief..680–681, 686–687
  Legislation..680–681
  Oppressive, unfairly prejudicial or unfairly disregards interests...................692–695
    Allegation, may not be based on.. 695
    Interests, interpretation of... 693
    Motive underlying conduct... 695
    Unfair, interpretation of...693–695
    Unfairness, interpretation of... 694
  Purpose of..680–681
  Related person, conduct of..690–691
  Relevant 'conduct'..680, 687
  Result of act or omission of company (section 163(1)(*a*)).......................687–688
    Acts or omissions referred to..687–688
  Who may apply for relief...681–686
    Capacity of shareholder or director.......................................684–686
      English law.. 686
      Interests and rights of applicant.......................................684–685
    Directors.. 683
    Members of non-profit companies.. 682
    Quasi-partnerships..685–686
    Related persons... 682
    Shareholders... 682
      Majority and minority.. 683
      Registered... 682
OPPRESSIVE OR PREJUDICIAL CONDUCT **see** OPPRESSION REMEDY
ORDINARY SHARES.. 204
OSTENSIBLE AUTHORITY...174–175
  Breach of fiduciary duty... 176
  Requirements for...175–176
  What is.. 174
  When arising... 175
OWNER-MANAGED COMPANIES... 68

P

PAR VALUE SHARES... 11
  Transitional arrangements..914–916

Index

PARTIAL OFFERS 671–672, 675
PARTICIPATING PREFERENCE SHARES 200–201
PARTNERSHIPS **see also** QUASI-PARTNERSHIPS 64–65
    Insider trading
        Offences and civil wrongs by 856–857
        Unlimited number of partners 65
PASSING OFF, DELICT OF
    Company names, criteria for 110
PENALTIES **see also** OFFENCES 778
    Criminal liability offences 24, 775, 871
    Directors, indemnification and insurance
        Payment of fines and penalties 525
    Insider trading 871
    Market manipulation 905–907
PERPETUAL SUCCESSION 32
PERSONAL ACTION
    Shareholders remedies 743–744
PERSONAL FINANCIAL INTEREST
    Meaning 516
PERSONAL LIABILITY COMPANIES 36, 67, 77–80
    Accountability and transparency requirements 68, 75, 78
    By whom used 78
    Characteristics 77–78
    Definition 77–79
    Directors
        Liability of 79–80
            Co-debtors 79
            Directors and company *singuli et in solidum* liable 79
            Extend of 79–80
            Removal of personal liability provision from constitution 80
        Number of 78
    Doctrine of constructive notice 168
    Memorandum of Incorporation 78
    Names, ending of 78
    Pre-existing section 53(*b*) companies 78–79
PERSONAL LIABILITY OF DIRECTORS **see also** DIRECTORS, Indemnification and
    insurance 60–61
    Acting without authority 60
    Causing company to act contrary to Companies Act of Memorandum of Incorporation 61
    Contravention of Companies Act 61
    False or misleading statements 61
    Fraud 60–61
    Reckless trading 60
    Unlawful distributions 61
PERSONALITY RIGHTS
    Companies and 29
PIERCING THE VEIL OF CORPORATE PERSONALITY 38–39
    Abuse of separate legal personality and 39–42
        Evasion of directors' fiduciary duties 40
        Evasion of contractual duties 40–42
    Common law approach 44–47, 54
        General principles 45–46
        Group of companies 50–54

PIERCING THE VEIL OF CORPORATE PERSONALITY (cont.)
   Lifting the veil, distinction from 42–44
   Shareholder remedies 23
   Statutory provisions 54–59
      Advantage of 55
      Application or proceedings 55
      Company declared not to be juristic person 59
      Interested person 55
      Orders 59
      Rights, obligations and liabilities 59
      Unconscionable abuse 56–59
PLAIN-LANGUAGE APPROACH 2
PLEDGE
   In securitatem debiti
      Not disposal of all or part of assets or undertaking 650
PLURALIST APPROACH 449–450
   Fiduciary duties of directors 469–474
'POOLING' TYPE MERGERS 626, 640
PRE–EMPTIVE RIGHTS
   Granting of
      Not a disposal of all or part of assets or undertaking 650
   Private companies
      Distinction between sections 8(2)(*b*) and s 39 74
      Transferability of securities, private companies 71, 77
   Public companies 77
   Right of transfer of securities, when subject to 224–225
PRE-EXISTING COMPANIES 65
   Transitional arrangements 65, 149, 909
PRE-INCORPORATION CONTRACTS 141–152
   Abuse, potential of 148
   Agency principles 141–142
   'Agreement', definition of 143, 144
   Cession of option 152
   Common law hurdles 141–142
   Definition of 143
   Determining type of contract involved 152
   Formalities for 144
   Liability of promoter 146–149
      Abuse, potential 148
      Balance of conflicting rights and liabilities 147
      Claims against company 148
      Exception 147
      Judicial discretion to balance liability of promoter and company 149
      Personal liability against third party 148–149
      Rejection of contract 147
      When company not subsequently incorporated 147
      Whether can contract out of liability 148
      With whom jointly and severally liable 147–148
   Lodgement and filing at Companies Commission no longer necessary 144
   Methods of contracting on behalf of company to be formed 142–143
      'Shelf' companies 142–143
      Stipulatio alteri 142
      Statutory agency 142
   Notarial certification not necessary 144
   Offer made to promoter 152

PRE-INCORPORATION CONTRACTS (cont.)
    Promoter 'purports to act for entity and not 'profess' or declare 144
    Ratification of 143–144, 145–146
        Failure to ratify or rejection of contract 145–146
        Liability of agent 146
        Period to ratify 145
    Retrospectively 146
    Rights of parties between execution of contract and ratification thereof 149
    Significance of 141
    Statutory agency 142–149
        Application of section 21 143
        Definition of pre-incorporation contracts and 143
        Effect of 143
    Stipulatio alteri 142, 145, 150–152
        Disadvantages of 151
        Election to accept or adopt benefit of contract after incorporation 150–151
        Parties to contract prior to election 151
        Personal liability of promoter 151
        Promoter or trustee acting as principal 150
        What is 150
    Transitional arrangements 914
    Written agreement 143–144
PRE-INCORPORATION PROFITS
    Dividends out of 263
PREFERENCE DIVIDENDS 201
PREFERENCE SHARES 200–204
    Arrear dividends 201
    Construction of 200
    Cumulative 201
    Liquidity and solvency test 202, 256–257
    Participating 200–201
    Preferred rights 200
        Surplus profits 200–201
        To be exhaustive 200
    Preference dividends 201
    Preferential right to dividend 200, 202
    Winding-up 201–202
        Surplus assets 202
    Value of and preference to return of capital 202–203
PREJUDICIAL CONDUCT, RELIEF FROM OPPRESSIVE OR **see** OPPRESSION REMEDY
PRESCRIBED OFFICERS 386–387
    Definition 386
    Derivative actions
        Locus standi to institute action 702–703
    Fiduciary duties of 464–465
    Financial assistance to **see** FINANCIAL ASSISTANCE, To directors, prescribed officers, related and unrelated companies
    Memorandum of Incorporation and company rules
        Enforcement of and effect on 138–141
            Failure to comply with rules or Memorandum of Incorporation 141
            In exercise of functions 139
    Liability of 530–534
        Application of legislation 530
        Breach of

PRESCRIBED OFFICERS — Liability of — Breach of (cont.)
    Duty of care, skills and diligence 531–532
    Fiduciary duty 531
        Disgorgement of profits not covered 531
        Loss, damages and costs 531
    Decision contravening Act 533–534
    Gross negligence 530
    Joint and severally 530–531
    Prescription period 530–531
    Relief by court 530
    Under section 77(3) 532–534
    When liable 532–533
    Wrongful distributions 533
  Not a director 386
  Oppression remedy
    Application relating to exercise of powers 690
  Persons designated 386–387
  Transitional arrangements 917
  Ultra vires acts and legal capacity of company 162
PRESCRIPTION
  Claims for loss, damages or costs resulting from breach of duty 530–531
  Complaints to Companies Commission 763–764, 779
  Directors' liability for unlawful distributions 261–262
  Prescribed officers, liability of 530–531
PRICE STABILISATION 901–903
  Market manipulation and
    Purpose of 902
      Requirements for 902–903
      What is 901–902
PRIMARY OFFERING **see** PUBLIC OFFERINGS OF SECURITIES, Primary offering
PRIVATE OR NON-PUBLIC COMPANIES 66, 69–74
  Audit and independent review 550–551
    When exempted 552–553
  Audit committee 79
  Characteristics of 69–70, 76
  Company secretary 70, 77
  Corporate reporting 13
  Definition 69
  Directors, number of 69–70, 76–77
  Financial statements 70
  Names, ending of 69, 76
  Pre-emptive rights 74, 77
  Public company, distinction from 69, 76–77
  Requirements for 69
  Securities
    Not offered to public 69
    Transferability restricted 69, 71–74
      Effect of 72–73
      Manner of form of restriction 71–72
      Pre-emptive rights distinction between s 8(2)(*b*) and s39 74
  Social and ethics committee 70, 77
PROFIT COMPANIES 9, 65–68
  Accountability and transparency requirements 68
  Characteristics 67–68
  Exceptions 68

Index

PROFIT COMPANIES (cont.)
- Non-profit, distinction between 66
- Owner-managed companies 68
- Purpose of 66
- Shares owned by 'related persons' 68
- Single director companies 68
- Single shareholder companies 68
- Types of 66–68
  - Personal liability company 67, 77–80
  - Private company 66, 69–74
  - Public company 66, 74–77
  - State-owned company 67, 81–83

PROFITS
- Of company belongs to company 34–35
- Shareholders and 34–35

PROHIBITED TRADING PRACTICES **see** MARKET MANIPULATION, Prohibited trading practices

PROMOTER
- Liability of and pre-incorporation contracts 146–149
  - Abuse, potential 148
  - Balance of conflicting rights and liabilities 147
  - Claims against company 148
  - Exception 147
  - Judicial discretion to balance liability of promoter and company 149
  - Personal liability against third party 148–149
  - Rejection of contract 147
  - When company not subsequently incorporated 147
  - Whether contracting out possible 149
  - With whom jointly and severally liable 147–148
- Personal liability and *stipulatio alteri* 151

PROOF OF FACTS 780

PROPERTY AND ASSETS
- Of company belong to company 33–34
- Shareholders 33–34
  - Insurable interest 34
  - Legal interest 34

PROPERTY RIGHTS
- Shares 199

PROSPECTUS **see** PUBLIC OFFERINGS OF SECURITIES, Prospectus requirements

PROXIES **see** SHAREHOLDERS, Proxies

PUBLIC COMPANIES 66, 74–77
- Accountability and transparency requirements 68, 75, 77
- Annual general meeting 77
- Audit committee 75, 77, 419, 560
- Auditor 75, 77
- Characteristics of 75–76
- Company secretary 75, 77
- Corporate reporting 13
- Definition 74–75
- Directors, number of 75, 76–77
- Financial statements 75
- Name, ending of 75, 76
- Pre-emptive rights 77
- Private company, distinction from 69, 76–77
- Securities

PUBLIC COMPANIES — Securities (cont.)
    Freely offered to public 75
    Listing of 76
  Shareholders, number of 76
  Social and ethics committee 68, 77, 420

PUBLIC OFFERINGS OF SECURITIES 591–613
  Advertisements relating to 601
  Allotments and acceptance of subscriptions 611–613
    Conditional allotment if listed securities 613
    Minimum interval before allotment or acceptance 612–613
    Restrictions 612
    Time limits 611
    Voidable allotments 612
  Dealers in securities 598
  Employee share schemes
    Standards for qualifying 599–600
      Compliance officers 600
    Whether offer to public 599–600
  Exemptions 597–599
  Initial public offering 592
  Legislation 591
  Liability 606–611
    Criminal 610–611
    Of experts and others 609
    Untrue statements in prospectus 607–609
      Defences for 607–608
      Responsibility for 609–610
      When regarded to be included 607
      Without consent 608
      Who is liable 608
  'Offer to public', definition of 596
  Primary offering 592
  Prospectus 601–611
    Consent to use name 604
    Contents of 603–604
    Legislation 601–603
    Untrue statements in, liability for 607–609
      Ambit of 607
    Variation of agreement mentioned in 604
  Restriction on 593–594
  Secondary offerings 592–593, 604–605
    Prospectus or written statement 604–605
    Written statement, requirements for 605
  Similar offers or offer in a series of offers 599
  Single one-off offers to maximum of 50 persons 599
  Types of offers 591–593
  What constitutes 594–597
    Case law 595–596
    Whether offer to limited group offer to public 596–597
    Whether share exchange qualify as offer for subscription of shares ... 595–596
  What not constituting 597–599

PUBLIC REGISTER
  Of disqualified directors 404

PUPPET DIRECTORS 379
  Resignation of directors 416

Index 981

Q

QUASI-PARTNERSHIPS
    Exception to principles of separate legal personality 47–48
    Oppression remedy 685–686

R

RATIFIABILITY PRINCIPLE 700, 701
REASONS FOR IMPLEMENTATION OF NEW LEGISLATION 3–4
RECKLESS CONDUCT
    Offence of 777
RECKLESS TRADING see FRAUDULENT OR RECKLESS TRADING
REDEEMABLE SHARES 203–204, 244
    Indirect repurchases 284
    Repurchases 275, 278
REDEMPTIONS
    Repurchases 272
REGISTERED OFFICE 107–108
    Companies with more than one office 107
    Documents to be kept at 107–108
    Purpose of 107
REGISTRATION CERTIFICATE 104
    Business commencement 104
    Date 104
    Evidence of registration and registration 104
REGISTRATION OF COMPANIES 103–108
    Certificate of registration 104
    External companies 105–107
        Register of prescribed information maintained by Companies Commission 106
        Time period for registration 105, 106
    Name, when unsuitable 105
    Procedure 103–104
    Registered office 107–108
    Rejection of Notice of Incorporation by Companies Commission 104–105
        Grounds for
            Discretionary 105
            Mandatory 104–105
REGULATED MARKET
    Definition 858
REGULATORY AGENCIES see COMPANIES COMMISSION; COMPANIES TRIBUNAL
RELATED PARTIES
    Derivative actions
        Locus standi to institute actions 703
        Rebuttable presumption 711–712
    Financial assistance to **see** FINANCIAL ASSISTANCE, To directors, prescribed officers,
        related
        and unrelated companies
    Meaning 14
    Oppression remedy 684
    Shares owned by 68
RELATED RELATIONSHIP
    Holding/subsidiary relationship 193–196
    Between
        Individual and juristic person 194
        Two individuals 194
        Two juristic persons 194

RELATED RELATIONSHIP — Holding/subsidiary relationship (cont.)
    Control of 194–196
        Close corporation 195–196
        Company 194–195
            When controlling 194–195
    Trust 196
RELIEF FROM OPPRESSIVE OR PREJUDICIAL CONDUCT **see** OPPRESSION REMEDY
REMEDIES **see also** SHAREHOLDERS, Remedies 748–755
    Alternative procedures for complaints or securing rights 750
    Locus standi, extension of 748–750
        By whom can applications be made 749
        Class action 749
        Companies Commission 749
        Take-over Regulation Panel 749
    Purpose of Act must be promoted 750–751
    Restraining company from contravening Act and damages 753–754
        Shareholders only may apply for damages 754
        Who may 753–754
    Transitional arrangements 754–755
    Whistle-blowers, protection of 751–753
REMUNERATION **see also** DIRECTORS, Remuneration
    Derivative actions 714–715
    Insider trading
        Disclosure offence 870
        'Encouraging or discouraging' offence 870
    What is included 325
REMUNERATION COMMITTEE 422, 441, 443
REPORTABLE IRREGULARITIES
    Auditor's liability for 584–588
        Actions after sending report to IRBA 584–585
        Criminal and civil liability 588
        Failure to 584, 588
        IRBA guide 585–588
        Submission to IRBA 584–585
    Definition 584
REPORTING, INTEGRATED 565–566
    Credibility 566
    Financial reports 457, 565–566
    Independent assurance 566
    King III 457, 565–566
    Sustainability 457
    Transparency 457
    What should be included 565–566
REPRESENTATION **see** AUTHORITY
REPURCHASES (BUY-BACKS) **see also** INDIRECT REPURCHASES 11, 268–282
    Acquisition of own shares 274
        By gift or inheritance 274–275
        Redeemable shares 275
    Acquisition of shares in holding company **see** INDIRECT REPURCHASES
    Compliance with section 46 274
        Section 48 compliance 272–273
    Conflict with Memorandum of Incorporation 275–276
    Directors' liability 280
    Distributions 276

Index

REPURCHASES (BUY-BACKS) (cont.)
   Enforceability of agreement to acquire shares 279–280
      When not 279
   Historical development 268–270
   Justifications for 270–271
   Market manipulation
      As defence (United States and European Union) 903
   Prior to 1999 268
   Reasons for 269–270
   Redemptions 272
   Regulations 272–279
   Requirements for 276–279
      Acquisition of more than 5% of issued shares 277
      Board proposal and resolution 277
      Difference between sections 48 and 114 277–278
      Directors or prescribed offers, repurchases from 277
      Series of transactions 278
      Shareholders
         Authorisation 276
         Being one or more of subsidiaries 278
         Informing 276–277
      Shares left being redeemable or convertible 278
      Solvency and liquidity test 277
      Treasury shares 280–282
RESOLUTIONS see SHAREHOLDERS, Resolutions
RESTRAINT OF TRADE
   Abuse of separate legal personality and 40–42
RETAINED PROFITS
   Dividends out of 264
RETENTION OF RECORDS see also COMPANY RECORDS 365–366
   Board meeting minutes and resolutions 425–426
   Records relating to directors 397
   Register of securities 220, 366
REVENUE PROFITS
   Dividends out of profits 264
      What is 267–268
RIGGING THE MARKET 888–889
RIGHTS OF SECURITIES HOLDERS
   Application to protect 739–742
      Common-law principles on enforcement of Memorandum of Incorporation 740–741
      Direct recourse by shareholder against director 740
      Procedure 739–740
      Rights, meaning of 741–742
      Scope of 740
RING-FENCED (RF)
   Company name, ending of 104, 122
RISK, GOVERNANCE OF 446–447
   Board of directors responsible for 446
   Disclosure of 447
   Expressed in board charter 446
   King III 446–447
RISK MANAGEMENT COMMITTEE 422, 441–442, 446
   King III 441–442
'ROUND ROBIN' RESOLUTION 426–427

S

SARBANES-OXLEY ACT 2002 (USA) 434
SCHEMES OF ARRANGEMENT 658–664
   1973 Legislation. 659–661
   Appraisal rights of dissenting shareholders 663–664
   Approval and other requirements 661–664
      Special resolution by shareholders 661–662
   Court approval restricted to certain circumstances 659, 663
   Independent expert 662
      Report by 662–664
   Proposal for 658–659
      Reorganisation of share capital
         Ways of 658–659
      When may not 658
   Takeover Regulation Panel 663
SCOPE OF LEGISLATION 5–6
SECONDARY OFFERING **see** PUBLIC OFFERINGS OF SECURITIES, Secondary offering
SECTION 21 COMPANIES 90
SECURITIES
   Acquisition is contract of subscription or allocation 221
   Acquisition of
      Financial assistance **see** FINANCIAL ASSISTANCE, For acquisition of securities
   Certificated 218–239
      Beneficial interest in 227–232
         Disclosure by nominees 227–232
            1973 legislation 228
            Circumstances person regarded to have in public company 230–231
            Company subject to Takeover Regulations 229
            Nomine officii 230
            Notice in writing to disclose 229
            Requirements in draft Companies Regulations 229–230
            What must be disclosed 228–229
            When must information be disclosed 228, 231–232
            When no disclosure required 230–231
         Meaning of 227
         Nominee holdings 227
      Issue and allotment 221–222
         Allotment or acceptance of offer 221–222
         Governed by legislation and common-law rules of contract 221
         Issue of 222
         Offer 221
      Register of 218–220, 366
         Disclosure of beneficial interest 219–220
         Distinguished by numbering system 220, 221
         Electronic format 220
         Manner to be kept in 220
         Requirements 218–220
         Restriction of transfer 220
         Retention of records 220
         Shareholders' information 329–330
         Trust, kept in 220
      Security certificates 220–221
         Contents of 220–221
         Failure of requirements for 221

Index

SECURITIES — Certificated — Security certificates (cont.)
- Numbering system 221
- Signatures 221
- Transfer of securities 222–223
- Transfer 222–227
  - Cession of rights 223
  - Legislation 222
  - Purchaser as shareholder 223
  - Reasons for 224
  - Restrictions 223–226
    - Cession of shareholders' rights 225
    - Directors' discretion to refuse registration 226
    - Ineffective if transfer takes place 224
    - Restrictive interpretation of 224
    - Right of transfer subject to right of pre-emption 224–226
    - To non-shareholders 224
  - Security by cession *in securitatem debiti* 226–227
  - Security certificates 222–223
- Convertible 278–279
- Definition 212, 218, 299, 857–858
- Equal status of 218
- Holders, rights of **see** RIGHTS OF SECURITIES HOLDERS
- Listing of, public companies 76
  - Advantages of 76
- Meaning 71–72
- Options **see** SECURITIES, Subscription, Options for
- Private company
  - Not offered to public 69
  - Transferability restricted 69, 71–72
    - Compliance in terms of company's constitution 72–73
    - Effect of 72–73
    - Manner of form of restriction 71–72
    - Pre-emptive rights 71, 73
    - Pre-emptive rights distinction between sections 8(2)(*b*) and 39 ... 74
    - Transfer by approval of board 71
    - Transfer, meaning of 72–73
- Public offerings of **see** PUBLIC OFFERINGS OF SECURITIES
- Registration and transfer of 218–239
  - Certificated securities 218–232
  - Equal status of securities 218
  - Uncertificated securities 218, 232–239
- Shares and 199
- Subscription
  - Options for 217
    - Authority to issue 217
    - No restriction on authority of board of directors 217
    - Option holder as contingent creditor 217
- Uncertificated securities 218, 232–239
  - Beneficial interest in 239
    - Challenges 239
    - Registration options 239
    - Regulated companies 239
  - Central Securities Depository (CSD) 233, 233–235
  - Definition 218
  - Electronic settlement system (STRATE) 232–233

SECURITIES — Uncertificated securities (cont.)
    Legislation 232
    Liability relating to 238–239
        Indemnity 238
        Transfer instruction giver must warrant legality and correctness 238
        Unlawful actions 238
    Registration of 233–235
        Central Securities Depository (CSD) 233–235
        Holdings and transfer model 234–235
        Register 233–234
        Request for inspection 235
        Statement at prescribed intervals 235
    Security by cession in *securitatem debiti* 237
    Substitution 237–238
    Transfer of 235–237
        By whom 235
        Fraud, illegality or insolvency 236
        How effected 235–236
        How transfer will take place 236
        Insolvency 236
        Power of participant or Central Security Depository 237
        Protection of good faith transferee 236–237
SECURITIES REGISTER **see** SECURITIES, Certificated, Register of
SECURITIES REGULATION PANEL 845–846
SECURITY FOR COSTS
    Derivative actions 716
SENIOR MANAGERS OR EMPLOYEES
    Fiduciary duties of 464–465
SEPARATE LEGAL PERSONALITY 28–38
    Abuse of 39–42
        Evasion of director's fiduciary duty 40
        Overcoming contractual duty 40–42
    Bill of Rights and 29
    Concept of 28–30
    Exceptions 38–61
        Agency/alter ego doctrine 39, 48–50
        Company groups 50–54
        Domestic companies 47–48
        Piercing the corporate veil
            Common law approach to 44–47
            Distinction between lifting and piercing 42–43
        Quasi-partnerships 47–48
        Underlying partnership intentions 39, 47–48
    Fundamental rights 28–29
    Groups of companies 181–183
    Legal consequences 31–38
        Can sue or be sued in own name 36–37
        Debts and liabilities of company belong to company 35–36
        Limited liability 31–32
        May contract with shareholders 37–38
        Perpetual succession 32
        Profits of company belong to company 34–35
        Property and assets of company belong to company 33–34
        Shareholder no right to manage company's business or enter into transaction on its
            behalf 36

SEPARATE LEGAL PERSONALITY (cont.)
    Personality rights 29
    Salomon v Salomon & Co Ltd 30–31
SERIOUS QUESTIONS TO BE TRIED, TEST FOR
    Derivative actions 709–710
SERVING DOCUMENTS 779–780
SHADOW DIRECTOR 381–383
    Common law recognition 382
    De facto director, distinction between 382–383
    Other jurisdictions 382
    Parent for subsidiaries 382
    Reasons for 381
    What is 381–382
SHARE BUYBACKS **see** REPURCHASES (BUY-BACKS)
SHARE CAPITAL 198
    Requirement for formation of companies 9
SHARE CAPITALISATION **see** SHARES, Capitalisation
SHARE CERTIFICATES
    Transitional arrangements 916
SHARE PREMIUM 198
SHAREHOLDER ACTIVISM 451, 454
SHAREHOLDER AGREEMENTS 131–133
    Advantages 131
    Alterable provisions of legislation 132
    Anti-avoidance provisions of legislation 132
    'Any matter relating to the company' 131
    Disadvantages 131
    Memorandum of Incorporation and 131
    Minority shareholders, protection of 132
    Transitional arrangements 913–914
    Voting agreements 133
    Voting rights through and holding/subsidiary relationship 189
SHAREHOLDER APATHY 451–454
SHAREHOLDER REMEDIES **see** SHAREHOLDERS, Remedies
SHAREHOLDER VALUE APPROACH 18–19, 471–473
    Jurisdictions whom adopted 472
    Stakeholder interest subordinate to profit maximisation 471–472
SHAREHOLDERS 329–335
    Access to company records 368–369
    Agent, not 36
    Amendment of Memorandum of Incorporation 126
    Apathy 451–454
    Appraisal rights **see** APPRAISAL RIGHTS OF DISSENTING SHAREHOLDERS
    Authority to issue shares
        When shareholder approval
            Not required 206
            Possibility of change of control in company 206–207
            Required 206
    Beneficial and registered 331–335
        Beneficial interest 331–333
            Definition 332
            Identity of beneficial owner of shares 331–332
            Reasons for 332
        Disclosure of 333–334
            Early warning device for potential takeovers 333

SHAREHOLDERS — Beneficial and registered — Disclosure of (cont.)
    How should disclosure take place 333–334
        Promotes market transparency 333
        Register of.. 334
        When should be disclosed.. 333
        When to be made 333–334
    Nominee or beneficial shareholder 331
        Meaning.. 331–332
    Notices of meetings.. 335
    Proxy appointments 335
    Register of disclosures 334
    Voting by 334–335
Business rescue, effect on 799–801
Capitalisation of shares... 211
Claims for damages
    Director's duty to act within powers not fulfilled 484
    Financial assistance
        For acquisition of securities 310
        To directors et al 324
Constitutional right to decide fate of takeover bid 478
Contracts with company 37–38
Damages, claimed for 163–164
Debts and liabilities of company 35–36
Definition... 330, 682
Directors
    Elected by.. 377–378, 394
    Fiduciary duties for breach by
        Only company can claim damages 469
    Removal of by 409–410
Derivative actions **see also** DERIVATIVE ACTIONS
    Locus standi to institute action... 702–703
    Ratification or approval of wrong 717–718
Disposal of part or all assets or undertakings
    Approval by.. 652–654
Distributions, authorisation of not permitted 246
Employment of by company 37–38
Enforcement of rights by against company....................................... 137
Financial assistance to directors
    Written notice to.. 319, 321, 430
Interests of versus interest of stakeholders....................... 18–19, 449–450, 469–473
Liability
    Agency/alter ego doctrine 49–50
    Limited 32
Meetings... 343–344
    Adjournment of 357–359
        Deemed quorum 358
        Notice of 358
        Period of 359
        Voluntary 358–359
    Annual general meeting
        Difference between 343–344
    Attendance and participation 352
    Chairpersons at 354
    Conduct of 352–353
    Convening of 344–349

SHAREHOLDERS — Meetings — Convening of (cont.)

- Company with one shareholder 348
- Definition of 343
- Demand by shareholders to meet 346–347
  - Court order to set aside 347
  - Purpose of to be described 347
  - Withdrawal of 347
- Electronic communication 352
  - Notice to inform of 352
  - Reasonably accessible for electronic participation 353
- Failure to convene 348–349
  - Authorisation by persons mentioned in Memorandum of Incorporation 348
  - Companies Tribunal 348
  - Courts 348–349
- Location of 352
- Mergers 627
- Notice of 349–352
  - Content of 349–352
    - Financial statements, summary of for annual general meeting 350
    - Sufficient information to come to intelligent conclusion 350
  - Failure to give and defects in 351–352
    - Material defect 351
  - Period of 349
- Postponement of 357–358
  - Deemed quorum 358
  - Notice of 358
  - When quorum not present 358
  - Where quorum present 357–358
- Quorum 355–357
  - Deemed 358
  - For matter at meeting to be considered 356
  - For meeting to commence 356
  - Once meeting has commenced 356–357
    - At time business conducted 356–357
    - Memorandum of Incorporation requirements 357
    - Shareholders leaving during meeting 356
  - What is 355
  - When more than two shareholders 357
- Voting at 353–355
  - Exercised in own interests 354, 355
  - Poll 354
    - Advantage 354
    - How and when may be demanded 354
    - Procedure 354
    - Value count 354
  - Right to vote, limitations 355
  - Show of hands 353–354
    - Advantage 353
    - Disadvantages 353–354
    - Head count not value count 353
  - Voting agreements 354–355
- When must be held 345–347
  - Filling of vacancy in terms of section 70(3) 346
  - Memorandum of Incorporation requirements 347
  - Referral to shareholders in terms of Act or Memorandum of Incorporation 345

SHAREHOLDERS — Meetings — When must be hold — Voting agreements (cont.)
    When AGM of shareholders required (public company) 347
    Written and signed demands for delivered to company 346–347
  Who may 344–345
Members and 331
Memorandum of Incorporation and rules
  Enforcement of Memorandum of Incorporation and rules 137–138
Mergers
  see MERGERS, Shareholders, protection of
Minority, protection of **see also** SHAREHOLDERS, Remedies
  Shareholders agreement 132
No right to
  Enter into transactions on behalf of company 36
  Manage company's business 36
Nominee **see** SHAREHOLDERS, Beneficial and registered shareholders
Number of
  Public companies 75
Personal liability
  Debts 36
Profits of company 34–35
Property and assets of company 33–34
  Insurable interest 34
  Legal interest 34
Proxies 339–343
  Company sponsored invitation to appoint 342–343
    Invitation, format 342
    Reasons for 343
    Shareholder not bound to appoint persons named by company 342
  Delivery of notices to proxy 340
  Procedure to appoint 339–340
  Revocation of appointment 340–341
    Complete and final cancellation of authority to act on behalf 340
    Suspension if 340–341
  Time period for delivery of appointment to company 340
  Validity of appointment 340
  Voting 340–341
    Against shareholder's instructions 341
    On poll 341
    Three way or two way 341
  Who may be appointed as 339
Record date to determine shareholder rights 335–336
  Publication of 336
  Requirements 335–336
Relationship between company and 135–137
  Between and among shareholders *inter se* 137–138
  Enforcement of rights by against company 137
  Whether bound only in capacity as shareholders 135–136
Remedies 20–23
  Application to protect rights of securities holders **see** RIGHTS OF SECURITIES HOLDERS,
    Application to protect
  Appraisal rights **see** APPRAISAL RIGHTS OF DISSENTING SHAREHOLDERS
  Common-law personal action 743–744
  Declaratory order 22
  Delinquent director, order to declare 21

Index

SHAREHOLDERS — Remedies (cont.)
    Derivative actions **see** DERIVATIVE ACTIONS
    Oppressive or unfairly prejudicial conduct, relief from **see** OPPRESSION REMEDY
    Oppression remedy **see** OPPRESSION REMEDY
    'No-reflective loss' principle 743, 744–745
        Overlap between shareholder and corporate actions 744–745
        When applicable 744
    Piercing the veil of corporate personality 22
    Probation, order to place director under 21
    Restraining company from contravening Act 742–743, 753–754
        Claim for damages 742–743, 754
        'No reflective loss' principle 743
        Remedy for damages against person causing company to act inconsistently 743
  Repurchases 278–279
  Resolutions 359–362
    Ordinary 360
        Ratification of breach by director of fiduciary duties 528–529
        Removal of directors 411–412
    Proposing 359–360
        Amendment of 360
        Clarity and specificity 360
    Special 360–362
        Approval requirements 360
        Disposal of all or greater part of assets, disposing company 631, 654–655
            Meeting requirements 655
            Notice to shareholders 654–655
            Ratifies specific transaction 654
            Voting rights controlled by acquiring party or party acting in concert disqualified .. 655
        Disposal of all or greater part of assets, holding company 631, 655–656
        Financial assistance to directors 429–430
        Lower percentage of voting rights to approve 360
        Matters for 361–362
        Memorandum of Incorporation requirements 362
        Mergers 628–632
            75% of voting rights 629
            Companies Bill 2007 629
            Disqualification of voting rights controlled by acquiring party 630
            Minority shareholder protection 629–630
            Object of legislation 630
        Remuneration of directors 417
        Requirements for 362
        Schemes of arrangement 661–662
        Special by holding company 631
    Written 362–365
        Consent required 362–363
        Electronic communication 364
        Informing shareholders of 365
        Restrictions 364–365
        Support required 363–364
            Difference between voting on written resolution and voting at meeting 363–364
            United Kingdom 363
        Time within which consent must be obtained 364
        When adopted 363
  Right to restrain performance of contract
    Executed or executory contracts 165

SHAREHOLDERS — Right to restrain performance of contract (cont.)
    New company law regime 165
    Ultra vires doctrine 156, 158, 160
  Securities register... 329–330
  Securities, transfer of 223
  Ultra vires act and legal capacity of company 162
  Unanimous assent at common law... 336–338
    Authority to litigate 337–338
    Permits informal methods of shareholder consent 336
    When can not be used 337
    When used.. 337
    Where special resolution required 338
  When compliance with formalities not required 336–338
    Companies in which every shareholder is also a director..................... 338
      Difference in decisions taken as director and shareholder 338
      Requirements 338
    Companies with one shareholder 338
    Unanimous assent at common law... 336–337
  Whether bound to company only in capacity as shareholders..................... 135–136
    Common law... 135
SHAREHOLDERS' MEETINGS see SHAREHOLDERS, Meetings
SHARES
  Authorised... 198
  Authorisation for 204–205
    Must be set out by Memorandum of Incorporation 204–205
  Authority to issue... 205–207
    Board of directors and... 205
    Directors' liability for non-compliance with section 41 207
    Possibility of change of control in company 206–207
    When resolution not adopted to retroactively authorise issuing of shares 206
    When shareholder approval
      Not required 206
      Required 206
    Within classes 205
  Buybacks... 11
  Capitalisation 210–211, 243, 244
    Alternative to distributing profits as cash dividends......................... 210
    Cash payment in stead of 210
      Solvency and liquidity test 210
    Contractual relationship between shareholders and company 211
    Effect of.. 211
    Issuing on *pro rata* basis.. 210
    Issuing void when 211
    May be issued from different classes 210
    What is 211
    What may be capitalised.. 211
  Classes of 199–204
    Based on different rights 199–200
    Capitalisation 210
    Equal rights... 199
    Preference shares 200
  Consideration for 207–210
    'Consideration', meaning of 208
    Safeguards 208–209
    Trust agreement 209–210

SHARES — Consideration for (cont.)
    When may be issued 207
    Deferred 204
    Definition 198
    Financial assistance to company for purchasing of 11
    Holding/subsidiary relationship 185–186
    Issued 198
    Label of value 199
    Movable property 199
    Nature of 198–199
    Non-voting 11
    Ordinary shares 204
    Owned by related persons 68
    Par value 11, 914–916
    Property rights 199
    Redeemable shares 203–204, 244
    Securities, wider term than 199
    Transactions, disclosure of
        Takeovers and offers 669–670
    Trust agreement 209–210
    Voting rights attaching and holding/subsidiary relationship 189
    When may be issued **see also** SHARES, Authority to issue; SHARES, Consideration for 207–208
'SHELF' COMPANIES 142–143
    Method of contracting on behalf of company to be formed 142–143
SHORT FORM MERGERS 648
SOCIAL AND ETHICS COMMITTEE 19, 420–422, 474–475
    Access to information 421–422
    Application of legislation 474
    Corporate citizenship, monitoring of 474–475
    Exemption from requirement 420
    Functions 421–422, 474–475
    Not direct duty to stakeholders 475
    Private companies 70, 474
    Public companies 68, 75, 420, 474
    State-owned companies 68, 82, 421, 474
    Structure 420, 474
SOLVENCY AND LIQUIDITY TEST **see also** DISTRIBUTIONS, Solvency and liquidity
      requirement 10
    Cash payment in lieu of capitalisation shares 210
    Financial assistance
        For acquisition of shares 302, 303
        To directors, prescribed officers, related and unrelated companies 319, 429
    Insolvent trading 540–541
    Mergers 627
    Preference shares 203
    Repurchases 277
SOUTH AFRICAN HUMAN RIGHTS COMMISSION
    Company name disputes 113
SPECIAL RESOLUTIONS **see** SHAREHOLDERS, Resolutions
SQUEEZE-OUT AND COMPULSORY ACQUISITIONS 670–671
STAKEHOLDER RELATIONSHIPS, GOVERNING 449–457
    Dispute resolution 454–457
        Appropriate process 455–456
        Business relationships 456
        Companies Tribunal 456

STAKEHOLDER RELATIONSHIPS, GOVERNING — Dispute resolution (cont.)
    Confidentiality 456
    Decision relating to must be in writing stipulating reasons 457
    Expert recommendation 456
    King III... 454–457
    Mediation 455
    Principle and precedent... 456
    Processes to be adopted for internal and external 455
    Rights and interests.. 456
    Time available to resolve.. 455–456
  Enlightened shareholder value approach 449
  Institutional investors 453
  Interests of stakeholders and shareholders......................... 18–19, 449–450, 469–473
    King III... 473
  Mediation 455
  Pluralist approach.. 449–450
  Shareholder activism... 451–454
    Absence of undermines managerial compliance................................ 452
    How to encourage 451–452, 454
  Shareholder apathy... 451–454
    Reasons for... 452–453
      Costs 453
      Lack of knowledge of rights and powers................................ 452–453
  Stakeholder-inclusive approach.. 449–451
    Balance between stakeholder groupings.. 450
    Constructive engagement 451
    Corporate reputation and... 451
    King III... 449–451
    Transparent and effective communication 451
STAKEHOLDERS
  Interests of
    Promotion of.. 19
    Shareholders interests, difference between 18–19
STATE LIABILITY 780
STATE-OWNED COMPANIES 67, 81–83
  Accountability and transparency requirements 68, 82–83
  Audit and independent review... 550–551
  Audit committee and auditor 82, 419, 560
  Characteristics 81–82
  Company secretary... 82
  Definition 81
  Exemptions... 82
  Name, ending of 83
  Pre-existing.. 8
  Social and ethics committee... 68, 83, 420
STATUTORY AGENCY
  Method of contracting on behalf of company to be formed 142
STATUTORY ESTOPPEL see ESTOPPEL, STATUTORY
STATUTORY MERGER see MERGERS
STIPULATIO ALTERI
  Disadvantages of... 151
  Election to accept or adopt benefit of contract after incorporation 150–151
  Method of contracting on behalf of company to be formed 142
  Parties to contract prior to election... 151
  Personal liability of promoter.. 151

Index 995

STIPULATIO ALTERI (cont.)
    Pre-incorporation contracts 145
    Promoter or trustee acting as principal 150
    What is 150
SUBSIDIARIES **see also** HOLDING/SUBSIDIARY RELATIONSHIP
    Definition 183
    Directors' duty to avoid conflict of interest 501
    Group boards 442–443
    Profits
        Dividends out of 263–264
    Repurchases and shareholders of 278
SUBSTANTIAL COMPLIANCE 7
SUCCESSION **see** PERPETUAL SUCCESSION
SUI GENERIS
    Directors, types of 386
SUSTAINABILITY
    Ethical leadership and 436

T

TAKEOVER REGULATION PANEL
    Alternative dispute resolution 23
    Complaints to **see** COMPANIES COMMISSION, Complaints to
    Disposal of all or part of assets or undertaking 656
    Locus standi 749
    Scheme of arrangements 663
    Takeovers and offers 667–669
TAKEOVER REGULATIONS 674–677
    Company subject to
        Disclosure of nominees in certificated securities 229
    Takeovers and offers 666–667
TAKEOVERS AND OFFERS 664–677
    Affected transactions 665, 675
    Applicable legislation 664–665
    Application of Act and Takeover Regulations 666–667
    Cautionary announcements 675
    Comparable and partial offers 671–672, 675
    Compulsory acquisitions and squeeze-out 670–671
    Confidentiality 675
    Definitions
        Affected transactions 665
        Offer 665–666
    Disclosure in share transactions 669–670
        Application of requirements 669
        Disclosure notices 669
        Number of issued securities 669–670
    Exemption by Panel 668
    Mandatory offers 670, 675
        Threshold 670
        When legislation applicable 670
    Prohibited dealings before and during offer 673–674
    Regulation by legislation 668–669
    Regulation of by Takeover Regulation Panel 667–669
        Compliance notice 668
        Object of 667
        What must be ensured 667–668

TAKEOVERS AND OFFERS (cont.)
   Restrictions on frustrating action 672–673
   Takeover Regulations 674–677
TAXATION
   Non-profit companies 87
TEMPORARY DIRECTOR 378
THIRD PARTIES
   Auditors' civil liability to **see** AUDITORS, Civil liability, To third parties
   Contract for benefit of **see** *Stipulatio alteri*
   Derivative actions 711
   Financial assistance to directors et al
     Void transactions and impact on 324
   Right to damages
     Insiders not excluded 166
     Knowledge and good faith 165–167
       Burden of proof 167
       Knowledge of limitation in Memorandum of Incorporation 167
       Separate requirements 167
       When not protected 166
   Turquand Rule
     Put on inquiry 170, 172
     Relying on forged documents 170
     Whether independent rule 171
       Put on inquiry 172
     With knowledge of or suspecting irregularities 170
TRADE UNIONS
   Business rescue and 16–17
   Financial assistance to directors, notice to 319, 321, 430
TRADING CERTIFICATE
   Requirements for formation of company 9
TRADING NAMES **see also** Company names
   Registered names and 117
TRAINING
   Of directors and King III 443
TRANSITIONAL ARRANGEMENTS 2, 909–922
   Companies Commission 762, 910, 920–921
   Companies Tribunal 920–921
   Company finance and governance 916–918
     Office of director, company secretary, auditor and prescribed officers 917
     Right to seek remedy 917
   Company names 918–919
     Defensive names 919
     Name reservations 918–919
     Translation or shortened form 919
   Company records 917
   Company rules 131, 913
   Continued investigation and enforcement of 1973 Act 921–922
   Court proceedings and orders 920
   Memorandum of Incorporation 119, 912–913
     Prohibitions and restrictions on amendment 918
   Par value shares 914–916
   Pending filings 910–911
   Pre-existing companies 65, 149, 909
   Pre-incorporation contracts 914
   Preservation of regulations, rights, duties, notices and other instruments 20

TRANSITIONAL ARRANGEMENTS (cont.)
- Regulations 922
- Regulatory agencies 762
  - Transition of 920–921
- Remedies 754–755
- Share certificates 916
- Shareholder agreements 913–914
- Types of companies and names 911–912
- Winding-up and liquidation 919–920

TRANSPARENCY 13

TREASURY SHARES
- Nature of 280–282
- Other jurisdictions 281–282

TRIANGULAR MERGER 640–644
- Companies involved don't need to disappear 642
- Liabilities in separate legal entity 641
- Merger consideration 642–643
- Purpose and advantages 641–642
- Reverse 643–644
- Separate wholly owned subsidiary 641
- Shareholders of would-be acquirer not any voting and appraisal rights in merger 642
- Structure 640–641

TRUST AGREEMENT
- Consideration for shares and 209–210

TRUST DEED
- To represent debenture holders 215
  - Debenture holders beneficiaries 215
  - Reasons for 215
  - Repayment of loans and interest 215
  - Trustees are creditors of company 215

TRUSTEES
- Debt instruments 216
  - Invalidation of releases 216–217
  - Requirements for 216
- Directors as 384–385

TRUSTS
- Certificated securities
  - Register of 220
- Control of and holding/subsidiary relationship 196
- Debt instruments and 215–216
- Financial assistance to 317
- Insider trading
  - Person that commit offences and civil wrongs 856–857
- Subsidiary, cannot be 190

TURQUAND RULE 169–173
- 2008 company legislation 171–173
- Capacity of company 20
- Common law 169–171
  - Application of rule 170
  - Effect of 169
  - Intended for outsiders 171
  - Internal formalities and company compliance 169
  - Protection of *bona fide* third parties against internal company irregularities 169
  - Third parties
    - Put on inquiry 170

TURQUAND RULE — Common law — Third parties (cont.)
    Relying on forged documents 170
    With knowledge of or suspecting irregularities 170
    Whether independent rule 171
  Disposal of all or part of assets or undertakings 653
  Doctrine of constructive notice
    Effect of abolishment on 173
  Financial assistance for acquisition of shares and 306–308
  Statutory formulation of 171–172
    Alignment with common law rule 172
    Intended for outsiders 172
    Third parties
      Put on inquiry 172
      Reasonably ought to know of non-compliance with internal formalities 172
TYPES OF COMPANIES 9, 62–98
  Close corporations 9–10, 64, 95–98
  External 9, 90–95
  Foreign 9
  Limited by guarantee 66
  Non-profit 9, 65–66, 83–90
  Partnerships 64–65
  Personal liability company 77–80
  Policy 63
  Pre-existing companies 65
  Private 69–74
  Profit 9, 65–83
  Public 74–77
  Purposes 63–64
  State-owned company 81–83
  Transitional arrangements 911–912

U

ULTRA VIRES DOCTRINE **see also** LEGAL CAPACITY OF A COMPANY, *Ultra vires* doctrine
  Definition 155
  Director's liability for breach of fiduciary duties 156, 158, 160, 164
  Legal capacity of company 19–20
    Confined to null and void transactions 155
    Failure of 156–157
    Historical development 154–155
    Internal control mechanism (new regime) 161
    Legal consequences of 155–156
      External 155–156
      Internal 155–156
    New regime 160–161
    Null and void transactions 155
    Object of 155
    Ratification of *ultra vires* action by special resolution 162–163
    Reform of 1973 legislation 157–158
      Abolishment of external consequences 157
      Director's liability for breach of fiduciary duty 158
      Not void by reason only of lack of capacity or authority 158
      Preservation of internal consequences 157–158
      Shareholder's lost right to restrain performance of contract 158
      Statutory estoppel 158

Index

ULTRA VIRES DOCTRINE — Legal capacity of company (cont.)
    Shareholders
        Entitlement to restrain company from performing contract............156, 158, 160, 165
UNALTERABLE CONDITIONS see MEMORANDUM OF INCORPORATION, Unalterable conditions
UNANIMOUS ASSENT see DOCTRINE OF UNANIMOUS ASSENT
UNCERTIFICATED SECURITIES see Securities, Uncertificated
UNCONSCIONABLE ABUSE
    Close corporations legislation...56–57
    Gross abuse of juristic personality of close corporations
        Examples of..57–59
    Statutory provisions...56–59
    When occurring.. 56
UNLAWFUL DISTRIBUTIONS
    Personal liability of directors.. 61
UNRELATED PARTIES
    Financial assistance to see FINANCIAL ASSISTANCE, To directors, prescribed officers, related
    and unrelated companies
USER–FRIENDLINESS.. 2
USUAL AUTHORITY...176–177
    Chairperson of the board of directors... 17
    Chief executive director... 177
    Company secretary.. 177
    Implied usual... 176
    Managing director..176–166
    Restricted usual... 176

V

VICARIOUS LIABILITY... 879
VINCULUM JURIS... 254
VOLUNTARY RESOLUTION OF DISPUTES see ALTERNATIVE DISPUTE RESOLUTION
VOTING AGREEMENTS.. 133
    Board meetings.. 425
    Duty to exercise independent judgment....................................... 480
    Shareholders' meetings..354–355
VOTING RIGHTS
    Appraisal rights of dissenting shareholders
        Dilution of voting rights by alteration of class rights........................... 736
    Business rescue plans...813–814
        Creditors.. 811
    Directors
        Removal of and loaded.. 413
    Disposal of all or greater part of assets or undertaking
        Controlled by acquiring party or party acting in concert disqualified................ 655
    Holding/subsidiary relationship..185–189
        Attaching debt instruments... 189
        Determining factor..185–186
        Held by person in fiduciary capacity..................................... 188
        Instructions with consent or concurrence of another person...................188–189
        Nominees... 188
        Shareholder agreements... 189
        Shares held by moneylenders as security................................. 189
        Trusts.. 188

VOTING RIGHTS — Holding/subsidiary relationship (cont.)
    When exercisable 186–188
    Indirect repurchases 285
    Mergers
        Requisite approvals of (section 115) 629
            Disqualification controlled by acquiring party 630
        Non-profit companies 88–89
    Triangle
        Shareholders of would-be acquirer not any 642
    Shareholders meetings
    Special resolutions
        Lower percentage to approve 360

W

WAITING PERIOD 2
WASH SALES
    Prohibited trading practices 894–895
WHISTLE-BLOWER PROTECTION 751–753
    Compensation for damages 752–753
    Employee and Protected Disclosures Act 753
    Persons protected by 752
    Protections granted 752
    System to receive disclosures 752
    When protective measures applicable 752
WIDELY HELD COMPANIES 67
WINDING-UP 821–832
    1973 Act, continuing application of 919–920
    Application for
        By Companies Commission 771
        By whom 827–828
        Form of notice of motion and accompanying documents 828
    Deregistration 831–832
        Circumstances for 831
        Dissolution 830–831
        Foreign company upon transfer of registration to foreign country ... 832
        Reinstatement 831
    Dissolution of companies 830
        Setting aside of 832
    Insolvent companies 826–827
        Discretionary power of court 827
        When insolvent 826–827
    Legislation governing 821–822
    Liquidator **see** LIQUIDATOR
    Non-profit companies 87
    Preference shares 201–202
    Process of 827–828
    Removal from register, effect of 832
    Solvent companies 822–826
        By court order 822, 823–826
            Criteria for conclusion 826
            Grounds for 823–824
            Just and equitable ground 824–825
            When can shareholder apply for 825–826

Index

    Voluntary winding-up 822–823
        Grounds for 822
WINDING-UP — Solvent companies — By court order (cont.)
        Security, when can Master dispense with 822
    Surplus assets 202
    Value of and preference to return of capital 202–203
WRITTEN RESOLUTIONS see SHAREHOLDERS, Resolutions